THE CLARENDON EDITION OF THE WORKS OF JOHN LOCKE

THE CORRESPONDENCE

THE CORRESPONDENCE OF
John Locke

EDITED BY E. S. DE BEER

IN EIGHT VOLUMES

Volume Six

LETTERS NOS. 2199–2664

OXFORD
AT THE CLARENDON PRESS
1981

Oxford University Press, Walton Street, Oxford OX2 6DP
OXFORD LONDON GLASGOW
NEW YORK TORONTO MELBOURNE WELLINGTON
KUALA LUMPUR SINGAPORE HONG KONG TOKYO
DELHI BOMBAY CALCUTTA MADRAS KARACHI
NAIROBI DAR ES SALAAM CAPE TOWN

Published in the United States by
Oxford University Press, New York

British Library Cataloguing in Publication Data
Locke, John
The correspondence of John Locke
Vol. 6: Letters nos. 2199–2664
1. Locke, John
2. Philosophers – England – Correspondence
I. Title II. De Beer. Esmond Samuel
192 B1296 80–41053
ISBN 0 19 824563 7

Printed in Great Britain
at the University Press, Oxford
by Eric Buckley
Printer to the University

CONTENTS

LOCKE'S LIFE: PRINCIPAL DATES FOR THIS VOLUME

THIS table is planned to provide dates that should be serviceable to readers of the correspondence. It is not a chronological framework for Locke's life.

The principal difficulty in its compilation is that for many incidents in his life precise dates do not exist. Thus, if the mention is accurate, Locke was acquainted with Robert Boyle on 20 May 1660; there is nothing to show how much earlier the acquaintance was made. Unsatisfactory as many of them are, the dates are the best available.

In the dates *a.* (for *ante*) is to be taken to imply shortly before. In the dates for books when a precise date accompanies the word 'published' it is to be taken as the date of the earliest notice that the book had been, was, or was about to be, published, and not necessarily as the day of publication.

1697 *a.* 17 March. *A Letter* (to Bishop Stillingfleet) published. *A Second Vindication of the Reasonableness of Christianity* published.

21 June–26 November. Locke attends almost all Board of Trade meetings.

Early September. *Mr. Locke's Reply* to Stillingfleet's *Answer to his Letter* published.

1698 23 January. William III offers Locke employment.

5 July. The New East India Company established.

11 July–20 October. Locke attends almost all Board of Trade meetings.

11 October. William Molyneux dies.

c. November. *Mr. Locke's Reply* to Stillingfleet's *Answer to his Second Letter* published. The fourth edition of *Some Thoughts concerning Education* published.

1699 6 June–22 November. Locke attends almost all Board of Trade meetings.

11 December. The fourth edition of the *Essay* advertised.

LOCKE'S LIFE:
PRINCIPAL DATES FOR THIS VOLUME

2199. CHRISTOPHER TILSON to LOCKE, 19 February 1697 (*2045*, *2212*)

B.L., MS. Locke c. 20, ff. 186–7. Locke was in London this day and at Oates on the 22nd: Journal; no. 2202. He perhaps travelled by the coach to Bishop's Stortford on Saturday the 20th.

Sir

It is desired that you will please to meet the rest of the Commissioners for Appeales in the Dutchy Court to morrow at ten of the clock in the forenoon to consider of matters now lying before them. I am

Sir

Your most faithfull humble Servant

CHRIS TILSON

19th. February 1696

Mr Locke

Address: To John Locke Esqr These

Endorsed by Locke: C: Tilson 19 Feb 9$\frac{6}{7}$

2200. BENJAMIN FURLY to LOCKE, 19 February/1 March 1697 (*2127*, *2287*)

B.L., MS. Locke c. 9, ff. 140–1. There are extracts from letters from Furly relating to G. H. van Rettwich in D'Aranda's letters to Locke about this time: no. *2192*, etc.; no. *2248* belongs with them.

Rotterdam primo March 1697[a]

Dear Sir

I doubt not but Mr. D'Aranda has given you some Account of a new way of cure lately discovered, or at lest practis'd, in these Provinces, by application of something to the urine onely, at a distance from the Patient: one of which Practitioners is in this Towne, and has helpt divers persons of great Accidents, and distempers, without any the lest application outward or inward to the Patients themselvs. The Doctors have oppos'd him all they can; But the Peremptory testimony of the Patients that they are cured,

[a] *This line is perhaps written by an amanuensis.*

sound and well, has left them no other offensive weapons, than those prophetick ones, that they will find themselvs deceived, that they are not cured, but wilbe worse than ever, after a while. In the meane while he gets a great deale of mony, and spoyles, for that while, the Doctors Trade. He cures the poore for nothing. The Rich he makes pay him sufficiently, so much as they can agree when they are cured.

This has made me search my Library to see if I can find any writers that speak of such kind of cures—but find none but Dr. Flud who, in his Philosophia Mosaica, mentions an Earl in England who, and his daughters, did assure him that they cured many people of the yellow Jaundice, sometimes at 100 miles distance from the Patients.[1]

I am now to acquaint you, that there is a German in Amsterdam, a man whom Dr. Kohlhans has known many years, an expert chymist, and honest man, nothing less than a cheat. Who presses him hard, to enquire of me, if I can not give some address by which he might make appear to the K. or Parliament of England, that he has an art to make the English spirits of Molasses, or Cyder, every way as good, and pure as the french spirits: to the great advantage of the Nation, and disadvantage of the french.

I told the Doctor That I could give his friend an Address to yourself, a member of that Honourable Committee to whom the cognisance of affaires of that nature, are, ni fallor,[2] by Act of Parliament committed.[3] With this assurance, that if his Art be found advantageous to England, he should meet with suitable incouragement.

This day he receivs answer, that he is glad that I am able to help him to rights, and that his art is so fix, and of so great advantage, that it is unconceivable till it be demonstrated. But by reason of his present gowtyness he is in no state to come over into England. But would gladly hav me authorised to see the proofe made here in a small quantity. And that in order to it a Gallon of all the sorts of English spirits made of molasses, and cydar might be sent to me by the packet boat, not to lose time, and I shall not repent my being concerned in the Affaire.

[1] Robert Fludd or Flud, M.D. (*D.N.B.*), *Philosophia Moysaica*, Gouda, 1638; English translation as *Mosaicall Philosophy*, 1659. For the precise reference see p. 12 below.

[2] 'Unless I'm mistaken.'

[3] The Board of Trade was established by royal commission and not by act of parliament.

I thought I could not do amisse, nor wel avoyd to give you notice of this affair, who knows what may be in it. But as for my being authorised to see the proofe made, it being a thing I have no Judgment of; I know not what to say to it. Tho I can have the opinion of the most knowing french and Dutch brokers, that throughly understand it.

I should be glad if we could see you here with the Plenipotentiaries,[1] and that you might be concerned in that glorious Peacemaking, which we all with outstretched necks are expecting—

I have not else to ad save my and my wives kind respects to your self Sir Fr. and my Lady Masham, mr. Popple and his lady, when you see them, remayning

Deare Sir
your humble servant
BENJAMIN FURLY

Address (written by an amanuensis): To John Locke Esquire One of his Majesties Commissioners etc—etc— In London

Postmark: FE 22

Endorsed by Locke: B. Furly 1 Mar 97 Answered Mar. 1.

2201. MARTHA LOCKHART to LOCKE [20? February 1697] (*2159, 2246*)

B.L., MS. Locke c. 15, ff. 66–7. Month and year from Locke's endorsement. The letter was written apparently on the morning of the day on which Locke left London. He left probably on 20 February: p. 1 n.

You have been Extreamly ill nature'd to use any body so much in Your power ill and by a barbarous way of proceeding not let me se you before You Went. I Came home almost as much out of breath as your self, left Company and dinner to se You, and met with the ill news You were just gon I sent after your chair but could not overtake it. but all these reproaches signifie nothing for I'me almost persuaded Ev'ry body will Consider themselves too much to think much of their frends being Well or ill pleas'd. I Could notwithstanding all this not help telling you I wish you a good journey and good success from the Countrey air to your health I doe suppose I shall not need to trouble You with many Excuses for not Coming

[1] No. *2166*, etc.

for I fancy you'le hardly mis me nor will I trouble you with my Complement's to my Lady since in rage to you for using me like a dog I've sent them by Sir Fr: with the patternes you desired. did not my inclination to You overcome my present wrath I should resolve not to se Oats 'till You Came to town, but when I Consider this may happen only to punish my self I shall Come as soon as I Can. in the mean time if you would not have me rail at you send Word as soon as you can how you recover your health and what was the reason You would not put it in my power to take leave of you before you went who after all must Ever be

Your affect: servant
M LOCKHART

Address: For Mr Lock going post to the Countrey
Endorsed by Locke: M. Lockhart Feb.[a] $9\frac{6}{7}$

2202. LOCKE to WILLIAM MOLYNEUX, 22 February 1697 (*2189*, *2221*)

Some Familiar Letters, pp. 173–82. I have filled in the names Sherlock and Leibnitz where the editor printed 'Dr. *S*—' and 'Mons. *L*—'. Answers nos. *2131*, *2170*, and *2189*; answered by no. *2221*.

Oates, 22. Febr. $169\frac{6}{7}$.

Sir,

I fear you will be of an opinion that I take my picture for my self, and think you ought to look no farther, since that is coming to you, or is already with you. Indeed we are shadows much alike, and there is not much difference in our strength and usefulness. But yet I cannot but remember, that I cannot expect my picture should answer your letters to me, pay the acknowledgments I owe you, and excuse a silence as great as if I were nothing but a piece of cloath overlay'd with colours. I could lay a great deal of the blame on business, and a great deal on want of health. Between these two I have had little leisure since I writ to you last. But all that will bear no excuse to my self for being three letters in arrear to a person whom I the willinglyest hear from of any man in the world, and with whom I had rather entertain my self, and pass my hours in conversation, than with any one that I know. I should take it amiss if you were not angry with me for not writing to you all this

[a] *Locke first wrote* Nov

while; for I should suspect you loved me not so well as I love you, if you could patiently bear my silence. I hope it is your civility makes you not chide me. I promise you, I should have grumbled cruelly at you, if you had been half so guilty as I have been. But if you are angry a little, pray be not so very much, for if you should provoke me any way, I know the first sight of a letter from you would allay all my choler immediately; and the joy of hearing you were well, and that you continued your kindness to me, would fill my mind, and leave me no other passion. For, I tell you truly, that since the receipt of your letter in September last, there has scarce a day pass'd, I am sure not a post, wherein I have not thought of my obligation and debt to you, and resolved to acknowledge it to you, though something or other has still come between to hinder me. For you would have pityed me to see how much of my time was forced from me this winter in the country (where my illness confin'd me within doors,) by crowds of letters which were therefore indispensibly to be answer'd, because they were from people whom either I knew not, or cared not for, or was not willing to make bold with; and so you, and another friend I have in Holland, have been delay'd, and put last, because you are my friends beyond ceremony and formality. And I reserv'd my self for you when I was at leisure, in the ease of thoughts to enjoy. For that you may not think you have been passed over by a peculiar neglect, I mention to you another very good friend of mine, of whom I have now by me a letter, of an ancienter date than the first of your three, yet unanswer'd.[1]

However, you are pleased out of kindness to me, to rejoyce in yours of September 26. that my notions have had the good luck to be vented from the pulpit, and particularly by Mr. Bentley, yet that matter goes not so clear as you imagine. For a man of no small name, as you know Dr. Sherlock[2] is, has been pleased to declare against my doctrine of no innate ideas, from the pulpit in the Temple, and, as I have been told, charged it with little less than atheism. Though the Doctor be a great man, yet that would not much fright me, because I am told, that he is not always obstinate against opinions which he has condemned more publickly, than in

[1] The friend in Holland appears to be identical with the 'very good friend' and is identifiable as Furly, whose letters of 28 August/7 September and 5/15 September (nos. *2122*, *2127*) bear no notes of answers. Locke had not yet received no. *2200*.

[2] Dr. William Sherlock: no. *1325*. He printed the substance of this attack in 1704: no. *3558*.

an harangue to a sundays auditory. But that 'tis possible he may be firm here, because 'tis also said, he never quits his aversion to any tenent he has once declared against, 'till change of times bringing change of interest, and fashionable opinions open his eyes and his heart, and then he kindly embraces what before deserved his aversion and censure. My book crept into the world about six or seven years ago, without any opposition, and has since passed amongst some for useful, and, the least favourable, for innocent. But, as it seems to me, it is agreed by some men that it should no longer do so. Something, I know not what, is at last spyed out in it, that is like to be troublesome, and therefore it must be an ill book, and be treated accordingly. 'Tis not that I know any thing in particular, but some things that have hapned at the same time together, seem to me to suggest this: what it will produce, time will shew.[1] But, as you say in that kind letter, *magna est veritas et prevalebit*; that keeps me at perfect ease in this, and whatever I write; for as soon as I shall discover it not to be truth, my hand shall be the forwardest to throw it in the fire.

You desire to know what the opinion of the ingenious is, concerning Mr. Whiston's book. I have not heard any one of my acquaintance speak of it, but with great commendation, as I think it deserves. And truly, I think he is more to be admired, that he has lay'd down an hypothesis, whereby he has explain'd so many wonderful, and, before, unexplicable things in the great changes of this globe, than that some of them should not go easily down with some men, when the whole was entirely new to all. He is one of those sort of writers that I always fancy should be most esteem'd and encourag'd. I am always for the builders who bring some addition to our knowledge, or, at least, some new thing to our thoughts. The finders of faults, the confuters and pullers down, do but only erect a barren and useless triumph upon human ignorance, but advance us nothing in the acquisition of truth. Of all the motto's I ever met with, this, writ over a water-work at Cleve, best pleased me, *Natura omnes fecit judices paucos artifices*.[2]

[1] Samuel Bold (p. 65 n.) also noticed the outbreak: p. 271. As Socinianism and Unitarianism gained ground views put forward in the *Essay* that were considered favourable to them became subject to attack; in addition the use made by Toland in *Christianity not Mysterious*, 1696, of Locke's epistemological doctrines directed attention to their bearing on religious knowledge: Yolton, pp. 8–11, 118. Locke amplifies his statement in no. 2340.

[2] 'Nature made all men critics but few craftsmen.' Varied from 'Omnes natura judices, non artifices fecit', the inscription on the base of the column bearing the

I thank you for the account you gave me of your linen manufacture. Private knavery, I perceive, does there as well as here destroy all publick good works, and forbid the hope of any advantages by them, where nature plentifully offers what industry would improve, were it but rightly directed, and duly cherished. The corruption of the age gives me so ill a prospect of any success in designs of this kind, never so well laid, that I am not sorry my ill health gives me so just a reason to desire to be eased of the employment I am in.

Yours of the 5th. of January, which brought with it that curious and exact description of that non-descript animal, found me here under the confinement of my ill lungs; but knowing business of several kinds would make it necessary for me to go to London as soon as possible, I thought it better to carry it thither my self, than send it at random to the royal society. Accordingly when I went up to town, about a fortnight since,[1] I shew'd it Dr. Sloane, and put it into his hands to be communicated to the royal society; which he willingly undertook; and, I promise my self it will be published in their next transactions. Dr. Sloane is a very ingenious man, and a very good friend of mine; and, upon my telling him that your correspondence with the secretary of the society had been of late interrupted, he readily told me, that, if you pleased, he would take it up, and be very glad if you would allow him the honour of a constant correspondence with you.

You shew your charitable and generous temper, in what you say concerning a friend of mine in Holland, who is truly all that you think of him.[2] He is marryed there, and has some kind of settlement; but I could be glad if you in Ireland, or I here (tho' of the latter say nothing to others) could get him a prebendary of 100 or 200*l.* per annum to bring him over into our church, and to give him ease, and a sure retreat to write in, where, I think, he might be of great use to the christian world. If you could do this, you would offer him a temptation would settle him amongst us; if you think you cannot, I am never the less obliged to you, for offering to one, whom you take to be a friend of mine, what you are able. If he should miss the effect, yet I have still the obligation to you.

Iron Man (Mars) that faced the fountains in the 'Amphitheater' in the New Park (Tiergarten) to the west of Cleves; the column was erected in 1653: Gorissen, *Conspectus Cliviæ*, pp. 45, 47, and pls. 164, 166.

[1] Locke was at Oates on 9 February, and went to London a day or two later: no. *2195* n.

[2] Le Clerc.

When yours of the 3d. instant met me in London, when I was there lately,[1] I was rejoyced at my journey, though I was uneasie in town, because I thought my being there might give me an opportunity to do you some little service, or at least shew you my willingness to do it. To that purpose I went twice or thrice to wait upon Mr. Methwin, though he be a person in whose company I remember not that I was ever but once in my life. I missed him, by good luck, both times, and my distemper encreased so fast upon me, that though I went to London with an intention to make some stay there, yet I was forced away in eight days, and had not an opportunity to see Mr. Methwin at all. You will, perhaps, wonder to hear me call my missing of him *good luck*, but so I must always call that which any way favours my design of serving you, as this did. For hereupon I applyed my self to a friend of mine who has an interest in him,[2] and one to whom your worth and friendship to me is not unknown, who readily undertook all I desired on your behalf. And I promise my self, from thence, that you will find Mr. Methwin will be as desirous of your acquaintance as you are of his.

You will, in a little time, see that I have obey'd, or rather anticipated a command of yours, towards the latter end of your last letter.[3] What sentiments I have of the usage I have received from the person you there mention, I shall shortly more at large acquaint you. What he says, is, as you observe, not of that moment much to need an answer; but the slye design of it I think necessary to oppose; for I cannot allow any one's great name a right to use me ill. All fair contenders for the opinions they have, I like mightily; but there are so few that have opinions, or at least seem, by their way of defending them, to be really persuaded of the opinions they profess, that I am apt to think there is in the world a great deal more scepticism, or at least want of concern for truth, than is imagin'd. When I was in town I had the happiness to see Mr. Burridge; he is, he says, speedily returning to you, where I hope his book,[4] which is received with great applause, will procure him something more solid than the name it has got him here; which I look upon as a good fore-runner of greater things to come. He spoke something of his intention to set about my book, but that I must leave to you and him. There is lately fallen into my hand a paper of

[1] It bears the London postmark for 12 February.
[2] Apparently Freke: pp. 79–80.
[3] Locke alludes to his *Letter* to Stillingfleet: no. *2178* n., etc.
[4] The Latin history of the Revolution: nos. *1945*, *2041* n.

Mons. Leibnitz, writ to a gentleman here in England, concerning several things in my Essay.[1] I was told, when I was in London, that he had lately ordered his correspondent to communicate them to me, and something else he has since writ hither. He treats me all along with great civility, and more complement than I can deserve. And being, as he is, a very great man, 'tis not for me to say there appears to me no great weight in the exceptions he makes to some passages in my book, but his great name and knowledge in all parts of learning, ought to make me think, that a man of his parts says nothing but what has great weight in it; only I suspect he has, in some places, a little mistaken my sense, which is easie for a stranger, who has (as I think) learn'd English out of England. The servant I have now[2] cannot copy french, or else you should see what he says: When I have all his papers you shall hear farther from me. I repine as often as I think of the distance between this and Dublin.

I read that passage of your letter to my lady Masham which concerned her sight; she bid me tell you, That she hopes to see you here this summer. You will, possibly, wonder at the miracle, but that you must find in Mr. Norris's book. She has, 'tis true, but weak eyes, which Mr. Norris, for reasons he knew best, was resolv'd to make blind ones. And having fitted his epistle to that supposition, could not be hinder'd from publishing it so; though my lady, to prevent it, writ him word that she was not blind, and hoped she never should be. 'Tis a strange power, you see, we authors take to our selves; but there is nothing more ordinary, than for us to make whomsoever we will blind, and give them out to the world for such as boldly as Bayard[3] himself. But 'tis time to spare you and your eyes. I am, with the utmost respect and sincerity,

Sir,

Your most humble, and most affectionate servant,

JOHN LOCKE.

[1] Gottfried Wilhelm Leibniz, 1646–1716, the philosopher and mathematician (Locke probably wrote Leibnitz). For the piece see no. 2243; it was transmitted to Locke by Thomas Burnett of Kemney: p. 60. Leibniz commented on Locke's remarks about it here and in nos. 2243 and 2254 in letters to N. Remond, 14 March 1714, and to Caroline of Ansbach (the Princess of Wales), 10 May 1715: *Phil. Schriften*, ed. Gerhardt, iii. 612; Kemble, *State Papers*, pp. 530–1.

[2] Timothy Kiplin.

[3] Generally 'as bold as blind Bayard'. The saying goes back at least to the fourteenth century, Bayard being a horse: *Oxford Dict. English Proverbs*; *O.E.D.*, s.v. Bayard.

2203. MRS. ELIZABETH STRATTON to LOCKE, 23 February 1697 (2177, *2247*)

B.L., MS. Locke c. 18, ff. 226–7. Answers no. 2177.

Bristoll feb 23th ($169\frac{7}{6}$)

Deare Cosin

yours of Jan 15th I had answer'd before now if I could puruse my deare Husbands accounts with as ⟨little⟩[a] trouble as you can, but the great weakness of my deare mother, and the frequent violent pain I have in my head and eyes with the heavieness of my heart makes me very unfit for business, I have at length Carefully Lookt Over your account as fare as I can understand it, if Barns's rent have not bin accounted for, then, I think Vealls is forgot likewise, which you make no mention of neither did I think that either of them did belong to this account, but when I find you doe charge me with 28l: and take no notice of Vealls rent I suppose you doe forget the thirty pounds my Husband paid to Mr Clarke (in Aprill (95) in part of that years rent) and by his letter he acknowledgeth he did recive it, you see by my former account I began with Gullock supposeing Barns and Veall had bine accounted for and one great reason made me think so was, when freinds askt my Husband what he owe Mr Lock he answer'd about 14l: and I found what I had drawn up came neare the sum mentioned I was sattisfied with it and should have lookt no more after it if you had not found it nessecary, but if wee add John Vealls and Joseph Barns account to the former I think I am Debitor[b] to you: 13l–19s–10d; beside the 30l already paid I hope this will give you full sattisfaction, if not, my Son Peter Stratton designs to see London in June and if you desire it I will send you, by him my Husbands booke, I did hope I should have seen you hear last summer and then you would have done this business with much less trouble you know I did offer you that whoever did undertake your business might have the sight of my Husbands booke or papers if Mr Lyde would have bine so kind as to have seen me but once in this sad yeare and half it would have eas'd both you and me I dout by this time you may be almost as weary of reading as I of writing and therfore will conclude and turn over to the account when I have given you the humble service of my deare mother brother and Sister Chapman with my son and daughters.

Deare Cousin I am Your faithfull freind and Humble servant

ELIZABETH STRATTON

[a] *MS.* sittle [b] *MS.* Dr

I intreat you if you can give me sum advise for the pain of my head and eyes

[On reverse of f. 226: Mrs. Stratton's statement of her account with Locke in respect of rents payable by John Veall and Joseph Barnes, with notes by her about remittances to Locke, etc., and numerical references by him apparently to an account-book.]

Address: To Mr John Lock to be left for Edward Clarke Esq at Richards Coffe hoase neare temple bar London

Postmark: FE 26

Endorsed by Locke: E: Stratton 23. Feb $9\frac{6}{7}$ Answered Mar. 3

2204. PAUL D'ARANDA to LOCKE, 24 February 1697 (*2197*, *2238*) with extract from BENJAMIN FURLY to D'ARANDA, [9/19 February 1697]

B.L., MS. Locke c. 3, ff. 42–3. For the date of Furly's letter see p. 76.

Bath the 24th: Febr: $169\frac{6}{7}$.

Sir

So desirous I am of fancying my self doing you some service, that for want of better occasions I lay hold of such trifles as this of letting you know that by a letter I last week received from Mr Benjamin Furly, he, in that part of it which answers mine to him concerning their German curer of Maladys, says. 'As to our new Doctor I assure you he causes himself to be well pay'd by those who have money; the one half so soon as the patient finds any relief, by which they may be assured that he has the secret he pretends to, and the rest when they themselves acknowledge that they are cured.

'I had this day a stupendious account from one whose son of twelve years old he has had in hand now 6 weeks, who had been in hands of several Doctors and Surgeons in this Town without any successe twelve months. The child had a caries or bone-eater in diverse parts of his Body; his arm cut open almost the length from the shoulder to the elbow; and his one Thigh laid open to the bone; his teeth falling out of his mouth; his body swelled as big as two; his hunger voracious; several who stood by attesting that they saw the child in this condition. And now, it eats as another child, is fresh and sound, the body in a good temper, and all it's wounds healed, saving one hole which he keeps open, and out of which he produces matter, which they every day wipe off with fresh linnen, and lay nothing to it but fresh linnen. And the lad is so well that if his Parents would permit him he would be riding upon his scates.

'And whereas our Reasoners say the sweat is nothing but the effect of imagination. He averred to me that the lad knew nothing of any design to make him sweat; but told his mother he found himself sickish, and such stirring in his body as if he should vomit, and purge, and the sweat dropped from his fingers, so that, quoth he, it could not be the effect of imagination.

'I asked him if he knew any body that he had cured of the stone? he said yes a Neighbour of his, a Dyer, and wished me to speak to the man, to have the relation of the cure from himself.

'It's to be fear'd that this German being not brought up to the study of Phisick but Theology, he, wanting due skill in Bodies and Distempers, may possibly think all things are cureable by one method, and may fail in many things that he undertakes for want of skill.

'It is, as you say, pitty the Knowledge of such a thing should fall into ill hands, they might make a bad use of it.

'Since my last I find Dr Flud, in his mosaic Philosophy, gives an account of such operations practised by a noble Earl[1] in England, who cured people of the yellow Jaundice, sometimes at an hundred miles distance from the Patient, and mentions the very method of the cure, suppressing oncly the name of the Tree whose ashes were mixt with the Urine into a paste. It's to be found in his 3 Book, Sect. 2. Ch: 7, p: 287.

'A certain french Author Monsr. de Vallemont intituled la Phisique Occulte ou Traitté de la Baguette divinatoire,[2] assures us that it is the Ashe Tree. Perhaps the Doctor has expressed it in his Latine treatise, which I have lent to some body that has not restored it to me etc———.' This is what Mr Furly writes, to which I have nothing to add, but promise to give you copy of all he may write me farther of the same matter, and assurance that I am

Sir

Your most humble servant

PAUL D'ARANDA

[1] Fludd has 'a Noble-man of no mean rank'.

[2] Abbé Pierre Le Lorrain de Vallemont, *La Physique Occulte*, etc., Paris, 1693; new ed., Amsterdam, 1696; later editions.

Are there any hopes that the Bill for a General Naturalization, now before the House of Commons, may passe?[1]

Address: To John Locke Esqre at Mr Pawlings, over against the Plough-Inn in Little-Lincolns-Inn-fields at London

Postmark: FE 26

Endorsed by Locke: P: DAranda 24° Feb $9\frac{6}{7}$

2205. CORNELIUS LYDE to LOCKE, 24 February 1697 (2176, 2208)

B.L., MS. Locke c. 15, ff. 151–2. Answers no. 2176; answered by no. 2208.

Stanton weeke the 24th February $9\frac{6}{7}$

Sir

Yours I Received of the 15th January According to your order I gave mary doleman twenty shillings which was verry sesonable and doe returne you many thanks for your Remembering of her francis Carpenter doe desire some thing of the agreement may be under hand if you give me orders I will make him a short grant in your name and to your use or for what time or how you shall thinke fitt he doe not Intend to dwell in the house this yeare but the next but will make use of ⟨himself⟩.[a] the repareing the house and bounds will be 3 li or 4 li a yeare safed to you and more if it shold be as it have beene these two yeares barns had it, I have not Received Hannyes rent but he promised that I shall be sure of it before our Ladie day and hope will not faile with all due Respects Sir I am

Your assured friend and ser:

COR: LYDE

Address: For Doct: Locke at mr Pawlings over against the plough in Little Lincolns feilds London

Postmark: FE 26

Endorsed by Locke: C: Lyde 24 Feb. $9\frac{6}{7}$ Answered 3 Mar.

[a] *MS.* hims?

[1] The bill was read for the first time on 22 February; it was rejected on the second reading on 2 March. See further no. *2206*.

2206. ANONYMOUS to LOCKE, [late February 1697]

B.L., MS. Locke c. 23, ff. 186–7. The date is shortly after the first reading of the General Naturalization Bill on 22 February; the writer looks forward to the second reading on Tuesday, 2 March, when it was defeated. I cannot identify him.

Sir

What hath been done allready by you to serve your Country, hath not only testified your honourable love to it and mankinde; but by the good success of your servicces it plainly appeare's, none was soe capeable. But since the sinews of warr and strength of a Kingdome is not only money; but people; perfect therefore your noble designements for good and by your successfull pen encourage the multiplication of the latter, as you have preserved the former, by makeing the way reasonable to an Act of generall naturalization. And since there may be as many mistaken Objections about this as the coyne, I have reason to believe they will be as easily reconciled as soon as you have given your judgment to your Country in this affaire. There are three sorts of Opponents, the one for fear it should make England to powerfull and happy, which you have mett with before; the common obstructers of all good to this nation, whose principalls when unmasked will make their Arguments of noe force. One other who for fear of Schism in a greater Multitude, will rest themselves contented with what are allready converted, nay unconverted, instead of walking about doeing good and preaching and converting all nations; for these their owne arguments will answere their objections and cover them with shame. But then for the third sorte, their objections may seem more sensible and moveing, I mean the Merchant, tradeing, handicraft and labouring people of this Kingdome, who will say that this Act will lett in such of other nations, who will outtrade underworke underlive and eat the bread (not menconing their delicacies) out of their mouthes to their utter ruine; to these it may be truly said that the Lawes of England allready without any other naturalization lett in All Alien friends who may by merchandize trade or other lawfull wayes acquire and get any treasure or goods personall whatsoever and may maintaine any action for the same[a] as our natives; which is the only ill consequence, if any, in a generall naturalization, but indeed this is an evill only for want of a naturalization; for such strangers

[a] *Perhaps followed by a stop.*

comeing here, Leech like, suck our vitall riches till they are full, and then must drop of into their owne Countries to lay their treasure out, being uncapeable of purchaseing or layeing it out here (a great loss to this Kingdome). In short wee have all the effects of a Naturalization allready that are complained of by some, tho without reason or consideration, for the interest of England, as well as trade, is consumption of our product and what a vast Item in that account is made when each stranger one with the other spend[a] of our product 10l. per annum by computation; which is repaid from abroad when such person is exercised in some trade or exportable comodity which being sent abroad brings in to support that expence with an overplus and consequently makes his trade and labour parte of our treasure. What advantage hath accrewed to this nation allready by the many profitable arts and foreigne wayes of trade taught us by such strangers, may bee seen in many instances in fact true. About 30. or 40. yeares since an Eminent Clothier in the West of England sent for severall Dutch people to worke with him, by whome he learn't the best and cheapest way of spinning and makeing fine woollen Cloth, which hath propagated that sort of manufacture to the greatest perfection in the world and even to this day hath preserved and advanced that trade with us. Wee have of later times by the many strangers comeing here gotten the perfect manufactory knowledge and insight into the arts and trade of Holland, Spane and France etca, before unknown to us, the particulars whereof are to universall to be here ⟨inserted⟩;[b] for which formerly wee exported vast treasure, which is now (in respect of that) not only kept at home; but by the exportation of such manufactures wee have great returnes from abroad which bring the ballance of trade on our side. Wee have many foreigne farmers in Lincolnshire and other Countyes and traders in London and elsewhere who make the best tenants and payments of rents, but our lawes preventing leases to be granted to such deprieve our native Landlords of such advantages. but then as to the rich foregners, they and their treasure are locked out, they can't purchase here, tho our owners want money and our lands new masters. A thousand pounds layed out in land etca. by a foreigner is soe much clear gaines to the English nation for our Subjects money that might be layed out on the same purchase will not be exported but layed out in profitable trade manufacture and new improvements; was our Country as Holland

[a] *MS.* spend: *apparently.* [b] *MS.* inferted

open to the reception of such, the pulse of our government would be enlivened by new accessions of vitall treasure insted of being exhausted. Who would live in a continent continually exposed to warr and the insults of an Ambitious neighbouring prince and the more unjust arbitrary power of their owne, when he may be secure in his liberty and estate in a free country defended from such cares by that sea which convey the treasure of the world to it. the most happy scituation for universall trade and commerce; by this the inhabitants of our Isle att their owne election may be neighbours to or farther removed from the rest of the world as the occation of trade or warr require. The deer Leaps and avenues of a well contrived Parke for the benefit of its Master for multiplication and preservation of the heard, are made inviteing and easey to let in but difficult to let out, and such is the case of that Kingdome truly in its owne interest, and when its otherwise the motion is retrograde and unnaturall, such as are the polities of tyrants by banishments to compleat their arbitrary power; which could not be soe easily effected with the multitude. And for the Objection that numbers of Enemys may be sent over to subvert our Government, like the bowells of the Trojan horse; This is but of one single example and of as single force, for its hoped the Nation will not be soe intoxicated, but will have such qualifications in the naturalization by such Oath registry etca. as for that purpose shall be thought meet to prevent such new guests from haveing any hand in the government till wee are assured they are good members thereof, and certainly wee must have a greater proportion of friends then enemys come over being in amity with all most all the world, except one Kingdome, whereof good parte of the natives are in our interest by the bonds of gratitude, being socoured from the tyranny of their prince. farthermore such foreigners soe transplanted here in 10 or 20 yeares would become good Englishmen and lovers of their protection in this Country perhaps more then many of our owne natives, and better enured to their duty of Obedience, by their property secured and their enlargement from a more severe subjection. What evill hath Holland and other states and free Countries received by its multitude of strangers? What strength what benefit and what treasure? What poverty and weakness hath ensued to Kingdomes and Empires by severe lawes and arbitrary power dispeopling them, whereby they have been exposed to the insults of a much less well peopled state made equall in their strength by their multitude to vast dominions History both auntient and moderne will evince. Nay our owne seas could not secure us was it not for our Navall force supplying the defect of people to garde our Coasts which would be more sensibly defitient were wee in a Continent secured only by the common boundaries and barriers of Kingdomes. But to conclude this tedious letter, was England in proportion as well peopled as Holland it would be invincible and its treasure inexhaustible, it would be the mart of the world and the ballance of peace and warr would be then intirely ours. Sir, The good intention of this letter to my King and Countrie will I hope excuse the faults and tediousness of it. and since few things in soe large a field are mentioned to the encouragement of the thing designed, its hoped your penn will fully and speedily enlarge on this subject to perfect soe glorious a designe soe worthy of yourselfe and the good will you allsoe bear to your King and Countrie the prosperity whereof and the gratefull acknowledgments of your past services to it is the designe of this paper and of

your most humble servant
a true Englishman

consider the necessity of expedition in this affaire since the Bill is to be read the second time next tuesday.

Address: These For Dr Lock present
Endorsed by Locke: Anonymus Feb. $9\frac{6}{7}$

2207. [JAMES JOHNSTOUN?] to [LOCKE?], 27 February 1697 (*2101*, *2225*)

B.L., MS. Locke b. 4, ff. 86–7; enclosures ff. 92–7. In the Locke MSS. the letter is accompanied by the following pieces (ff. 88–108), all relating to the trial of Thomas Aikenhead: I. Indictment of Aikenhead, clerical copy with corrections by Locke; II. Aikenhead's petition to the Lord Justice General; III. Depositions of the witnesses against Aikenhead; IV. Aikenhead's petition to the Lord Chancellor (of Scotland) (nos. II–IV were enclosed with the letter); V. Lord Anstruther to Robert Cuningham, 26 January 1697, the original letter; VI. Aikenhead's paper, and a copy of his letter to his friends, 8 January 1697, clerical copies corrected by Locke; VII. Duplicates of no. VI; the passages there corrected by Locke are here given correctly; VIII. Anonymous letter from Edinburgh to a Mr. W(?) in London, in part about Aikenhead and vindicating the Scots government's proceedings against some witches in Renfrewshire. All these pieces except no. VII are marked by Locke. Nos. II–IV, VII, and VIII, are written by the same hand as the letter. The letter and the eight pieces are printed from the present manuscripts, together with other pieces, in *A Complete Collection of State Trials*, ed. W. Cobbett, T. B. Howell, et al., vol. xiii, 1812, cols. 917–40. The letter alone is printed here.

The editor of *State Trials* suggested that the letter was written by Locke to Sir Francis Masham. That is unlikely as Locke was probably at Oates on 27 February. The reasons for attributing the letter to Johnstoun, although it is not in his hand, are that the extracts from the Scottish laws against blasphemy suggest that the writer was a Scot; that he was an associate of Lady Masham; that his final 'Farewell' occurs also in Johnstoun's letter no. *1616*; and that his use of the word respects ('My respects to Lady Masham') occurs also there and in Johnstoun's letters nos. *2225* and *3379*. Johnstoun perhaps alludes to this letter in the opening sentences of no. *2225*.

Thomas Aikenhead, who was about 18 years old, was tried in Edinburgh on 23 December for blasphemy, and was sentenced to be hanged on 8 January and to be buried under the gallows: *D.N.B.*; Macaulay. There are notices of the proceedings in the *Post Boy*, 19 January, and the *Flying Post*, 28 January, and a series in the *Protestant Mercury*, 18 November 1696 (which states that 'the crime against him was for being a priest'), 1, 8, and 13 January 1696/7.

London 27th feb: $169\frac{6}{7}$

Sir

You have enclosed (to satisfie your curiosity) the evidence against Aikenhead and two of his Petitions. If the process come you shall have it or it shall be left where you shall order. The flying post bore that he had not retracted till the day of Execution which you see is false.

The first act of parliament in Scotland against Blasphemy is act 21 parl: 1 sess: 1 Ch: 2d. anno 1661.[1] which has two articles, By the first *railling upon or cursing God, or any of the persons of the Trinity is punishable with death*, these are the words, and here retracting availeth nothing. The next article is, that *denying God, or any of the persons of the Trinity and obstinatly continueing therein is punishable with death*.

The next act is the 11th. of Tweeddal's Session of Parliament two years agoe,[2] and was obtained by trick and surprise. It ratifies the former act and adds, that *whether by writing or discourse To deny, impugne, querrell, argue, or reason against the being of God or any of the persons of the Trinity, or the authority of the Scriptures, or a providence is for the first fault punishable with imprisonment till they retract in sackcloth*

[1] Act no. 216 of 1661 in the modern enumeration; assented to on 16 May: *The Acts of the Parliaments of Scotland*, 1814–44, vii. 202–3.

[2] Act no. 14 of 1695, assented to on 28 June: ibid. ix. 386–7. John Hay, second earl and first marquis of Tweeddale (Scotland), lord high commissioner to the parliament in 1695: *D.N.B.*

in the Church. For the second with imprisonment and a years Rent till as in the first case. and for the third, they are to die as obstinat blasphemers; so that retracting after the third fault signifys nothing.

It's plain Aikenhead must have died by the first act, since it was his first fault as he himself pleads in his petition, and that he did retract which delivers him from the second article of the first act. Now the words of the first article being *railing* and *cursing*, no evidence except that of Mr Mungo Craigs[1] (in which he is said to have called Christ an imposture) seems to answer the meaning of those words, and as to this Craig Aikenhead in his speech in which he owns other things, denies his evidence and no doubt he is the decoy who gave him the books and made him speak as he did, and whose name is not put in the copy of the petition to the Justiciary sent to you, because the writer would spare Craig.

The age of the witnesses is observable and that none of them pretend, nor is it laid in the Indictment that Aikenhead made it his bussines to seduce any man. Laws long in dessuetude should be gently put in Execution and the first example made of one in circumstances that deserve no compassion, whereas here ther is youth, Levity, docility, and no designe upon others.

farewell

My respects to Lady Masham

Endorsed by Locke: Aikenhead $9\frac{6}{7}$ The Acts against Blasphemie.

2208. LOCKE to CORNELIUS LYDE, 3 March 1697 (*2205*, *2226*)

The Pierpont Morgan Library, New York. Transcribed from Xerox print Answers no. *2205*; answered by no. *2226*.

Oates 3 Mar $169\frac{6}{7}$

Sir

I thanke you for paying the 20s I desired you to my Cosin Mary Doleman. If you please to send me a little short draught of such a writeing as you will advise between Francis Carpenter and me it will I thinke be best to execute it my self. I thinke it need be noe more than what may be writ on the Backside of a letter

I the last post received a letter from my Cosin Stratton[2] where in She sends me some particulars of her husbands account which she

[1] A man of this name was author of *A Satyr against Atheistical Deism*, Edinburgh, *1696*.

[2] No. *2203*.

never mentioned before whereby I finde I was lead into the same mistake about John Veale as I was about Jos: Barnes for where as I charge him in the Note I sent you with being in debt to me 25° Mar 1695. for a years rent—£22–0–0 I finde now he had paid it to my Cosin Stratton and therefor it ought to stand in the paper I sent you thus

1695. Sept. 29 John Veale Dr for half a years rent £11–0–0

And whereas I there say Mr Popham never allowd but 4s for the taxes of 4s per pound for the Lords rent I finde he allowd my Cosin Stratton for two half years 8s. Both which I must beg you to rectifie. now that my cosin acknowledges the receit of these sums

Mr Clarke informs me that you are put in one of the Commissioners for the raiseing the cappitation tax.[1] He desires you would not neglect to act in it since thereby you may be soe usefull to the Government and your country and neighbourhood. I am of his minde and thinke you will doe ill to decline it. I hope Hanny will be prevailed with to pay you the money within the time he has promised. I am

Sir

your most faithfull servant

JOHN LOCKE

Address: For Cornelius Lyde Esquire at Stanton weeke To be left at Mr Codringtons in High Street Bristoll

2209. LOCKE to PHILIPPUS VAN LIMBORCH, 4 March 1697 (2126, *2222*)

Amsterdam University Library, MS. R.K., Ba 257 o. Printed in *Some Familiar Letters*, pp. 391–3; postscript and address in Ollion, p. 211. Answered by no. *2256*.

Oates 4° Mar 169$\frac{6}{7}$

Vir Amplissime

Inter negotia publica et privatam valetudinem tam parum mihi

Oates 4 Mar 169$\frac{6}{7}$

Excellent Sir,

As between public affairs and private infirmity so little leisure for study

[1] Lyde was appointed one of the commissioners for Somerset in the Land Tax act of 1695, 6 and 7 W. and M., c. 3; these commissioners were also to assess the tax on Marriages, Burials, etc., imposed for five years by 6 and 7 W. and M., c. 6, also enacted in 1695.

conceditur otii literarii, ut sperem diuturnum meum silentium, non ex imminutâ ⟨omnino⟩[a] in te voluntate aut amicitiâ ortum, tibi, quæ tua est in amicos lenitas, excusatum fore. An tu mihi ego ve tibi novissimè literas dederim quærere nolo. Satis egomet mihi culpandus videor quod tam diu careo fructu suavissimæ tuæ Consuetudinis: et magnus mihi dolendusque in curriculo vitæ meæ hiatus apparet qui destitutus literarum inter nos commercio, vacuus ea voluptate fuit, quæ maxima cum sit, ex benevolentia solùm, mutuisque amicorum sermonibus percipitur. Præteritam hiemem cura infirmæ sanitatis rure totam absumpsit. Nisi quod negotia nonnulla importuna subinde irrepentia, totum id quicquid erat temporis quod amicis destinaveram invito abriperent. Adeo ut non in tuo solum sed et multorum mihi amicissimorum ære alieno quo modo me redimam nescio si taciturnas mea nomine negligentiæ suspecta sit: Tu scio humanior es quam ut eo me condemnare velis crimine. Quanquam enim tardior aliquando mihi in respondendo calamus, animus tamen nunquam deficit, et si quando hac utor ⟨libertate⟩[b], erga eos solum utor ⟨quibuscum⟩[c] non solummodo vitam civilem sed intimam solidamque amicitiam mihi colendam propono; Quibus multum me scio debere et quibus insuper cupio

[a] *MS.* omnio [b] *MS.* liberate [c] *MS.* quibscum *altered from* quibcum

---

has been granted me that I hope that you, such is your lenity towards your friends, will excuse my prolonged silence, which has by no means arisen from any lessening of my goodwill or friendship towards you. I do not want to inquire whether you wrote last to me, or I to you. I myself seem sufficiently to blame for doing so long without the profit of your very delightful company; and I am aware of a great and regrettable gap in the course of my life, a gap which, there being no correspondence between us, was devoid of that pleasure which at its greatest is obtainable only from the kindness and reciprocal utterances of friends. Care of poor health here in the country consumed all last winter, except that some importunate affairs, now and then stealing in, against my wishes tore from me all that time, whatever there was of it, that I had designed for friends. So that, if my taciturnity is suspected of being due to negligence, I do not know how I shall free myself from debt not only to you but to many of my dearest friends; I know that you are too kind to condemn me for that crime. For although my pen is sometimes too slow in answering, still my intention is never wanting, and if I ever take this liberty, I take it only with those with whom I intend to maintain not only courteous relations but a close and solid friendship; I know that I owe them much and

me plurimum debere.[1] Ego nuper Londinum profectus post octidui ⟨incommodam⟩[a] et anhelosam moram præpropero reditu huc me recipere coactus sum. Hac pulmonum imbecilitas me brevi spero restituet pristino otio. Valetudinario seni quid restat præter vota pro patria. Naturæ et imbecillitati cedendum est. Hoc mihi si concedatur, libri et literæ, amicorumque interrupta vel impedita commercia optima illa senectutis oblectamenta redibunt. Quid enim in republica literaria agatur, civili implicato vix scire vacat. Apud nos sane disceptationibus et rixis maximam partem impenditur scripturientium ⟨atramentum⟩[b]. Si disputantium fervor solo veritatis amore accenderetur laudanda esset litigantium industria et contentio sed non ita semper tractantur argumenta ut ea ad veritatem stabiliendam elucidandamve quæsita credere possis. In mea de intellectu humano dissertatione jam tandem aliquid repertum est non ita sanum, idque a viris haud infimi subsellii reprehensum.[2] Siquid ego eorum argumentis edoctus reprehensione dignum reperirem, gratus agnoscerem et haud invitus corrigerem. Id cum non fit, rationem mihi reddendam censeo cur non mutaverim sententiam cum nihil

[a] *MS.* incommadam [b] *MS.* artrimentum

I wish to owe them very much more.[1] Having gone to London recently, after a week's uneasy and gasping stay I was compelled to return precipitately to this place. This weakness of the lungs will, I hope, shortly restore me to my former leisure. What is there left for an infirm old man except prayers for his country? One must submit to nature and weakness. If leisure is granted me, books and learning and intercourse with friends, at present interrupted or obstructed, those best pleasures of old age, will return. For there is scarcely time for one who is engaged in the service of the realm to know what is going on in the commonwealth of learning. With us, indeed, the ink of those who want to write is, most of it, expended on disputes and quarrels. If the ardour of the disputants were kindled solely by the love of truth their diligence and exertion would be praiseworthy, but the arguments are not always so handled that you can believe that they are devised for establishing and elucidating the truth. Something not particularly sound has now at length been found in my dissertation concerning Human Understanding, and found fault with by men not of the lowest rank.[2] If, instructed by their arguments, I should find anything that deserves censure I would gratefully acknowledge it and not unwillingly correct it. As that is not the case I consider that I ought to give my reason for not having

---

[1] Varied from Cicero: no. 6 n.
[2] 'Scis tu med esse imi subsellii virum?': Plautus, *Stichus* 489 (Lambinus; later texts read *imi subselli* and *unisubselli*). See pp. 5–6 above.

reperiam in eâ a veritate alienum. Hæc mea defensio[1] aliquam partem præteritæ hiemis, prout tulit valetudo, occupatam habuit. Sed quid ego Te moror nostris nugis? Quid tu illic, vosque alii studiis utilioribus intenti agatis aveo scire. Næ ego iniquus officiorum exactor si a te festinatas postulem literas in scribendo ipse tantus cessator. verum tu scio id facies ne nimis serio mihi irasci videaris. Vale Vir Optime et ut facis me ama tui studiosissimum

J LOCKE

Dilectissimam fæminam tuam liberosque reliquosque amicos nostros Amstelodamenses Veneos Guenelonosque quæso meo nomine salutes

Domina Cudworthia tibi plurimam dicit salutem.

Historiam quam tibi mitto de rebus nostris Latino idiomate scriptam[2] tibi haud ingratum fore confido

Address: Mÿn Here Mÿn Here Limborch bÿ de Remonstranse Kerck op de Kaisars Graft t'Amsterdam

Noted by van Limborch on cover: Redditæ mihi sunt per D. Barker 13 Maji 1697. rescripsi eadem die.

---

changed my opinion since I find nothing inconsistent with truth in it. This defence of mine[1] took up some part of last winter, according as my health permitted. But why do I detain you with our trifles? I want to know what you, and others besides you, are doing there, intent on more useful studies. Assuredly I, who am myself so dilatory in writing, would be making an unfair demand on your services if I requested a speedy letter from you, but I know that you will send one lest you should seem to be too angry with me. Good-bye, best of men, and continue to love me your most devoted

J Locke

Please give my greetings to your dear wife and children and the rest of our Amsterdam friends, the Veens and the Guenellons.

Mrs. Cudworth sends you her best regards.

I trust that the history of events in this country, written in Latin,[2] that I am sending you will not be unwelcome.

---

[1] Locke probably refers to his *Letter* to Stillingfleet: no. *2178* n., etc. It was published perhaps already, and in any case not later than 17 March: Journal.

[2] Burridge's history of the Revolution: no. *1945*, etc.

2210. JOHN CONYERS to LOCKE, 4 March 1697 (*2581*)

B.L., MS. Locke c. 7, ff. 61–2. John Conyers, *c.* 1650–1725, a second cousin of Sir Francis Masham; matriculated at Oxford 1666; barrister, Middle Temple, 1672; M.P. for East Grinstead, etc., 1695–1725: Foster; Morant, *Essex*, i. 49. His brother Sir Gerard Conyers was Lord Mayor of London in 1722–3.

Sir

I shall be ready to serve you in any thing and there fore if you would have me putt in the specification of your 1000l in my name or Sir Francis Masham's, or both, I leave it to your choice, and if you please to putt it in your own name I heare send you the like specification as is done for Mrs Barrington[1] vizt.

Mr John Locke: 1000 secured on a Moiety of the Mannor of Bennefield[2] in Northamptonshire by Mortgage Dated 3. July. 1694.

Witnesses. Geo: Ayres
Tho: Brome
Oliver Marton.[3]

I do not intend to give in my specification till after the Parliament is up[4] so that it will be time enough to give me your commands; if you do not intend to mention your own name: and if you do it in your name there will be no need of my giving in any specification of it in respect of the Trust.—I cannot yet receive the Interest but am promised some mony, which I do expect every day, and assoon as I can gett it you shall be sure to have it: My service to my Lady Masham who am

Sir
Your very humble servant
JO: CONYERS

Mar: 4. 1696.

Address: For John Locke Esqre att Oates in Essex.

Endorsed by Locke: J. Conyers 4° Mar $9\frac{6}{7}$

[1] Mary Barrington, d. 1727, daughter of Thomas Barrington and sister of Sir Charles (no. *1438*), and perhaps her sister Anne (p. 555, n. 4; she married probably about 1698): Noble, ii. 49. Through his maternal grandfather Conyers was a second cousin of Thomas Barrington. The mortgage appears to have been an investment made by Locke on his own behalf: pp. 127, 555.

[2] Benefield, near Oundle. The manor may have belonged to William Henry van Nassau van Zuylestein, earl of Rochford (*D.N.B.*): *V.C.H.*, *Northants*. iii. 79, 92.

[3] He was Conyers's clerk: no. 3242.

[4] It was prorogued on 16 April.

2211. LOCKE to EDWARD CLARKE, 5 March 1697 (2193, 2213)

B.M., Add. MS. 4290, f. 84. Printed in Ollion, pp. 242–3; Rand, pp. 502–3.

Oates 5 Mar 9$\frac{6}{7}$

Dear Sir

Though the inclosed were all ready to be sealed up under your cover, yet I staid from doeing of it till our letters came in expectation that I might hear from and have a word to say to you. Your letter which came just now is fuller than I expected or could wish, for I could be glad if Mrs Clarkes better health gave her and you lesse occasion of writeing on that subject. The messenger is soe near goeing that I shall not have time to consider and answer her letter now and therefor must defer it to the next post. As to your two questions in hast I say 1st That the beginings of a dropsie are not to be neglected and I fear hers will increase and prevaile upon her if by suitable remedies a stop be not put to it and the sooner the better. 2° The recommending the use of a remedie that one does not know is very warily to be done, and can have noe other reasonable foundation but the Truth, Memory, and Judgment of him that vouches the experience of it. and therefor you are a better Judg than I how far Mr Phillips is to be relyd on in the case. Cannot the receit be got? trie that, for I would be very glad Mrs Clarke had speedily some easy safe and effectual remedie which possibly this may be. By the next post I shall write to you farther. I am

Dear Sir

Your most affectionate humble servant

J LOCKE

My service to the Batchelor

I beg your pardon for the trouble of the inclosed and thank you for the last

Endorsed by Clarke: Mr. Lock of Mrs Clarks Case with respect to a Dropsie etc: Received the 8th. March 1696. Answered the 9th.

2212. CHRISTOPHER TILSON to LOCKE, 5 March 1697 (*2199, 2272*)

B.L., MS. Locke c. 20, ff. 188–9.

Sir

It is desired that you will please to meet the rest of the Commissioners of Appeales at the Dutchy Court on Monday next[1] between four and five of the Clock in the Afternoon without faile. I am

Sir

Your most faithfull humble servant

CHRIS TILSON

5th. March 1696

Mr Locke

Address: For John Locke Esqr These

Endorsed by Locke: C: Tilson 5 Mar $9\frac{6}{7}$

2213. LOCKE to EDWARD CLARKE, 8 March 1697 (i) (2211, 2215)

B.L., MS. Locke b. 8, no. 93. Copy, made apparently by an amanuensis of Clarke or Mrs. Clarke who copied also nos. 2214 and 2291. The original sent by Locke with the original of no. 2214 and with no. 2215. Printed, apparently from the original letter, in Rand, pp. 504–6. Words omitted by the copyist and some other readings are here supplied from Rand.

Oates 8 Mar $9\frac{6}{7}$

Dear Sir

your Letter with Mrs.[a] Clarke's Inclos'd I could only acknowledge the receit of by[b] the last Post, but had not time before the messenger went to weigh her case, which upon consideration I take to be this.

Her last great desease[2] soe weakned her Bloud that it has never since recover'd its former strength. And hence it has come to passe that her nourishment has never been turn'd into good and perfect bloud but a great part of it has remain'd indigested and crude, and soe has been apt (as happens in such cases) to get out of the

[a] *MS.* M.[is]　　[b] *Rand omits* by

[1] 8 March.　　[2] In the winter 1695–6: no. 1962, etc.

sanguinary Vessels into the habit[1] espetially into the Legs and this is the cause of their swelling.

This Load of crude and watery humors stagnateing in the Legs and not circulateing as it should in the veins and arteries, grows cold there and thereby increases the weaknesse of the bloud, when it is reassum'd as it is every night all or a good part of it into the bloud again and thereby augments the disease.

The way to cure this as I imagine, is to get out this watery humor and to[a] prevent the generateing of more.

I know in these cases purgatives are usually made use of in the first place to cary off the watery humors, which I should by no meanes advise in her case, because though purgatives doe carry of the present load of water or phlegmatick humors, yet they doe at the same time carry of also the strength of the bloud and soe usually the present benefit receiv'd by them is soon overballanc'd by a greater increase of the mischief, espetially in weak and broken constitutions; For the bloud being thereby lesse able than before to make good bloud the indigested humors are increased by the future food not sufficiently master'd.

I thinke then the main of the Cure turns upon ⟨the⟩[b] strengthening of the bloud first by a very nourishing and spare Diet; 2° By drinking very little and that only of liquors that strengthen the bloud. 3° By as much exercise in the open air as the patient can bear. 4°: By warming and restorative medicines. 5°. By avoiding such things as check or oppresse the naturall heat, as pensivenesse, want of exercise, intemperate eating or drinking and particularly chilling the bloud with this ⟨extra . . .⟩[c] humor, which is done by siting up late, for the humor falling most into the Legs in the evening it there grows cold and the longer it stays there the more soe, and then in the night when the Legs are laid almost even with the rest of the Body, returning into the veins fils them with this crude humor and helps to put out and as it were drown the natural heat and therefore I should thinke it of great moment in this case to goe to bed very early and to lie there long and almost constantly and not to rise and sit up any longer then just for exercise, For then the whole Body being kept warm the legs as well as the rest and

[a] *Rand omits* to [b] *Supplied from Rand; presumably omitted by the copyist.*
[c] *Supplied from Rand; the copyist here leaves a space to indicate an omission.*

[1] The bodily 'system': *O.E.D.*, s.v. Habit, *sb.*, 5b.

they not hanging down, the water not ⟨sinkeing⟩[a] into them, nor[b] swelling them, the crude humor constantly circulateing with the bloud is more and more digested and part of it made good bloud, and that part which remains watery is separated out of the masse by the kidneys and the bladder. whereas it looses the benefit when it stagnates in the legs and grows cold there to the prejudice of the bloud when it returns into it. And I doubt not but the superfluous water would[c–] quickly by the urinary passages be separated[–c] out of the bloud if ⟨more⟩[d] credulitys[e] were not continually generated by the supplys of new meate and drinke ill digested and therefore I looke upon the cheife part of the cure to lye in restoring strength to the bloud. but if it be thought that cannot be done unlesse the load of crude humors be removed, I thinke that may be effected by diuriticks mixed with warming and strengthening Medicines with a great[f] deale lesse damage or danger to the patient then by purging, which will signifie very little in small quantity, and large purgations[g] will very much weaken her if she can (which I conclude she cannot) bear them. And to her legs themselves both to strengthen the ⟨tone⟩[h] of the parts that they may not receive these humors, and to discusse[1] what may remain in them fomentations may be used.

This Sir is the sum of ⟨what I think of⟩[i] Mrs:[j] Clarkes case and cure without inlargeing into particular remedies which a Physitian upon the place will[k–] be alwayes best[–k] judg of to suit them to present circumstances, and[l] alter them as he sees occasion. That which addes to my hopes of Mrs:[j] Clarkes speedy Recovery is the time of the year which brings with it strength and vigour to all sorts of people, espetially to weake and low tempers. I earnestly wish an easy and quick recovery to Mrs: Clarke and am

Dear Sir

your[m–] affectionate humble servant[–m]

JOHN LOCKE

Address: ⟨For Edward Clarke, Esq., Member of Parliament, at Richards Coffee House, within Temple Bar, London. Frank.⟩[n]

[a] *MS.* snikeing [b] *Rand reads* not [c–c] *Rand reads* would be quickly . . . passages, separated [d] *Supplied from Rand; the copyist here leaves a space to indicate an omission.* [e] *Rand reads* crudity [f] *Rand reads* good [g] *Rand reads* purgatives [h] *Supplied from Rand; the copyist here leaves a space to indicate an omission.* [i] *Supplied from Rand; presumably omitted by the copyist.* [j] *MS.* M[js]: [k–k] *Rand reads* will always be best [l] *Rand reads* or [m–m] *Rand reads* your [most affectionate humble servant] [n] *From Rand. There is neither address nor endorsement on the copy.*

[1] In the obsolete medical sense, to dissipate, dispel, or disperse: *O.E.D.*

2214. Locke to Mrs. Mary Clarke, 8 March 1697 (2135, 2258)

B.L., MS. Locke b. 8, no. 92. Copy; for the copyist see no. 2213 n. Printed from this copy in Rand, pp. 507–8. Sent with the original of no. 2213 and with no. 2215.

Oates the 8° Mar $9\frac{6}{7}$

Deare Madam

If your kind Letter of the 27 Feb: had brought me as good an account of your health as it did of your Children, I should have been perfectly Rejoyced. But though some remains of your late great desease continue still to trouble you yet I hope a little care and a few remedies used now at this advantageous time of the Year will put an end to the swelling of your Legs and then will restore you again to a perfect state of health. To this purpose the first thing you should have a care of is your Diet; Whereby I mean the whole course of your way of liveing. First then I would have you goe to bed constantly very early and lye pretty long in the morning, the first of these will prevent the uneasy swelling of your legs which alwayes comes on and increases most at night, the other will help to dissipate and carry of the superfluous humors in your body by warmth and perspiration: In the next place you should eat two or three times a day, always good nourishment and of easy digestion and never make a quite full meale but leave of with some kind of appetite, by this meanes your meate will digest the better and be all turn'd into strong and good nourishment, and cruditys will be avoided which increase the cold and indigested humors which fall into your Legs, and there is nothing better for food in your case then to eat good store of well baked light bread with your meate or alone, and one little glass of good warm wine at your dinner will not be amisse. And takeing the air every day when it is fair on horseback or in your Coach will doe you good. To warm and strengthen your blood Greenginger or preserv'd or candid Elecampane[1] roots taken ⟨n⟩ow[a] and then a little in the morning and afternoon ⟨I⟩[a] think you will find benefit by, though in your case I know nothing soe good if you will take it as Garlike, Cut a Clove of Garlike in 2 or 3 or more pieces and wraping it up in butter or any other thing that you like swallow it every morning, and soe

[a] *Covered by blot.*

[1] Horseheal.

likewise in the afternoon will be very effectual I doubt not. I beleive you are not thirsty because you doe not complain of it. But for your drinke make such a sort of smale Ale as you will find on the other side, and let that be your ordinary drink, only if you find the tast of the ingredients to strong, you may mix with it some of your ordinary small ale or Bear when you Drink it. but drinke none of your other drinke without a good proportion of this diet drink mixed with it. Pray send me word in your next how your water is colour'd and what quantitys you make of it, and what alteration you find in your self upon the use of these things; I wish you a quick recovery of your former strength and health in all the parts of it; and am

Deare Madam

Your most affectionate humble servant

JOHN LOCKE

My Lady and Mrs Masham give you their humble service and are concern'd for your health.

My ⟨wife⟩[a] I see has quite forgot me but pray tell her I remember her.

Take Century
Wormwood
Broom tops
Hartstongue
Sage.
Liver wort.
Agrimony
Worm wood sage of each 2 handfulls
Horse radish roots scraped
⟨Dwarf⟩[b] Elder root sliced of each 4 Ounces
Daucus or wild carret seeds bruised 3 Ounces
The Yellow pill of half a dozen Sevil Oranges

Put these Ingredients into 2 Gallons of small ale, wort instead hops and let it work with them in it

Turn it up and when it is fine drink it.

If any of these Ingredients cannot be got make it with the Remainder of them.

Endorsed by Clarke: Copy of Mr. Lock's Letters to Mrs Clarke and to mee touching her Health, Received from Him the 10th. and sent to Her the 11th. March 1696.

[a] *MS.* wike [b] *MS.* Dwar

2215. Locke to Edward Clarke, 8 March 1697 (ii) (2213, 2231)

B.L., MS. Locke b. 8, no. 94. Printed in Rand, pp. 503–4. Apparently sent with the originals of nos. 2213 and 2214.

Oates 8° Mar $9\frac{6}{7}$

Dear Sir

You will see by the two annexed letters what I thinke is to be done in Mrs Clarkes case. To her I have given some particular directions suited to the method proposed in my letter to you. But how they will suit her humor or stomach or other circumstances tis impossible at this distance to know and therefor as to the particular medicines I have set them down rather to please her, than that I think that the safest way of proceeding, only *the garlick* I should expect much from if she be inclined to use it. But for her diet exercise and goeing very early to bed and lyeing abed most of her time I thinke I cannot be mistaken in. The diet drinke I have prescribed for her ordinary drink will doe her good if she keep to it alone. For if she takes it it will doe her good, if she dislikes the tast and drinks but little of it, the drinking but little is one of the best remedies for her. *But if you will have my opinion her life is not to be venturd upon directions at this distance, and therefor I thinke it necessary to consult some Physitian upon the place, who may adapt his method and medicines to all the whole collection of Symptoms he shall observe in her.* I have writ my opinion to you as I have done, that if you thinke it may be of any use to her you may send it to any physitian in those parts which she and you shall think fit to make use of, or make what other use of it you please. If there be any thing else I can doe for her or you in the case, you are but to let me know it and I shall doe it the best I can. As to your Sherborne apothecarys medicine recommended by Mr Phillips I can say noething to it unlesse I know it. I thinke people not used to the practise of physick soe apt to mistake and confound cases. and I think soe little of the art of medicine lyes in secret remedies and receits, that I should noe more use an unknown medicine upon unskilfull peoples recommendation than venture to let any one bloud in the darke. If the case were desperate and noe thing else would doe tis reasonable to trye any thing. But that god be thanked is not Mrs Clarkes case. *It may grow to a dropsie if not looked after and prevented, but I hope there is noe difficulty in it to make any one doubt of its cure.* And I beleive I can direct you to one in London who will fully convince you in that point. It is old Mr Papillions wife[1] who I have been told had such swellings in her legs from an hydropical humor that they were of an excessive bignesse and large quantitys of water run from them, and yet notwith standing she was since perfectly recoverd. Of the truth of this you can easily informe your self and possibly learne what was done to her. I am

Dear Sir

your most affectionate humble servant

JOHN LOCKE

My humble service to the Batchelor from whom I shall be obleiged by a word or two when his leisure will permit

My Lady gives you her humble service

Endorsed by Clarke: Mr. Lock about Mrs. Clarkes sicknesse etc: Received the 10th. March 1696. Answered fully the 11th. and sent Betty's Letter to Him Enclosed etc:

2216. ALEXANDER BERESFORD to LOCKE, 10 and 11 March 1697 (*2195*)

B.L., MS. Locke c. 3, ff. 181–2.

Machin-barns[2] 10 March 169$\frac{6}{7}$:

Honoured Sir

Being near, and having a convenient way of sending to you, I lay hold of it to return my humble thanks for your letter to Mr Johnson. At my second waiting on him, (which was, as the first, by my Lady Clinton's direction) he told me, since I had named you for a man I was known to, he much wish't to receive my character from you, before he spoke to the Bishop of Sarum,[3] that he might do it with more assurance: which made me likewise diferr another's application for me to the Bishop; that my first attempt might be made with my whole force at once, though later. Mr Johnson had your letter on monday seavennight;[4] on the wednesday following the Bishop introduce'd me at his own house to Mr Methwyn, and

[1] Thomas Papillon: no. *904*. His wife Jane, daughter of Thomas Broadnax, died in 1698: *D.N.B.*

[2] Matching Barns, about 2 miles NE. of Oates, was a manor in Hatfield Broadoak; it may have belonged to a member of the Barrington family: Morant, *Essex*, ii. 508.

[3] Burnet and Johnstoun were first cousins.

[4] 1 March.

requested his favour to me. Mr Methwyn said he had only two considerable places under him, the pursebearer and secretary, and for those had two persons allready in his eye, and could think of nothing in his present disposal agreeable for me. Finding that he thought of giving me a good place or none, I repeated to him with some earnestness that my circumstances were such as would make me glad of a very mean place, with the hope of his farther favour if he found me fit for it. Hereupon he appointed me to wait on him at his lodging towards the end of this week, which accordingly I design next friday morning. What the issue will be as yet I cannot guess, but whether good or not, your Favour is the same, Sir, and is acknowledged with as much thankfullness as any you have ever bestow'd; I may say farther (and said to a wise good man it is my advantage, though to others it would not be so) it is employd in releif of as sharp a necessity as any favour you have ever bestowd. And Sir that you may be the less dissatisfied in having appeard for one no better known, 'tis proper I should tell you, that, (besides my Lady Clintons interest with Mr. Johnson) another, who, having known me many years, recommended me to the Bishop (with as good a character as I could wish, or a much worthier person deserve) is in such esteem with him, that the Bishop in my hearing told Mr Methwyn he was a very excellent person, and his character to be relied on.—I wrote the greatest part of this at Machin-barns, but dar'ed not stay to finish it, having a considerable charge of Lady Franklyn's[1] money about me. However having still an opportunity by goodman Perry, I'm glad to send it, beleiving the account it self of what has past, as well as my thanks, to be seasonable. Let me Sir present my most humble service to my Lady Masham, and add that I am,

Sir,

Your most obliged most faithfull humble servant

ALEX: BERESFORD

Pynest[2] 11 March $9\frac{6}{7}$:

Address: To the honoured John Locke Esqr at Oates present this

Endorsed by Locke: A: Beresford 10 Mar $9\frac{6}{7}$.

[1] Probably Anne, daughter of Robert Rich, third earl of Warwick (G.E.C.), and niece of Charles Rich, the fourth earl (no. *199*); married, first, Thomas Barrington, son of the second and father of the third and fourth baronets; secondly, Sir Richard Franklyn, bart., of Moore Park, Rickmansworth, Herts., who died in 1695: G.E.C., *Baronetage*, i. 28; iii. 126.

[2] Pyenest was a manor in Waltham Holy Cross: *V.C.H.*, *Essex*, v. 161.

2217. Sir William Honywood and other Commissioners of Appeals to Locke, 13 March 1697 (2095, 2218)

B.L., MS. Locke c. 11, ff. 227–8. Answered by no. 2218.

Sir

We met this day in order to take a measure about our proceeding to heare the causes of Appeales now lying before Us, And this matter being of moment We thinke it best for all of Us to meet and consider thereof, And to that end have appointed to sit at the Dutchy Court next Fryday being the 19th: instant about ten in the morning, and hope you will not faile to be there at that time. Wee are

Sir

Your humble servants

Wm Honywood

Ri. Beke

Geo: Dodington

Edm: Chaloner

Dutchy Court 13th: March 1696

Mr Locke

Address: To John Locke Esquire [at Oates, by Joslyn, Bishops Stortford] Frank Wm Honywood

Postmarks: MR 13; BL (?)

Endorsed by Locke: Sir Wm Honywood etc: 13 Mar $9\frac{6}{7}$ Answered 15

2218. Locke to Sir William Honywood and other Commissioners of Appeals, 15 March 1697 (*2217*)

B.L., MS. Locke c. 11, f. 228. Draft or copy, probably written by an amanuensis. Written on a blank page of no. *2217*, which it answers.

Oates 15 March $9\frac{6}{7}$

Gentlemen

I just now received the honour of Yours of the 13 Instant and am sorry my health is not yet so well confirmed as to permit me to waite upon you at the Dutchy Court on Fryday morning next. The rule that was made in Michaelmas terme last makes me hope there will be noe need of any new measures to be taken concerning the Appeales and soe noe great need of me on Fryday morning next upon that account. I was lately in Town and went thither with a designe to stay. But my ilness grew soe fast upon me that in less than a week my life was in danger and I was forced to get out of town again. I hope now for warme weather in a little time that I may venture to Town with less danger and be able to stay there as well as I did all the last Summer. And then if God please to allow me health I shall constantly attend, and be glad of the occasion of waiteing upon you as often as there shall be any causes to be heard. I am

Gentlemen,
Your most humble servant
JOHN LOCKE

2219. LOCKE to DR. (later Sir) HANS SLOANE, 15 March 1697 (*2160*, *2224*)

B.M., Sloane MS. 4036, ff. 290–1. Answers no. *2160*; answered by no. *2224*.

Oates 15 Mar 9$\frac{6}{7}$

Sir

You will not wonder if I am concerned to make soe trivial a thing as those peices of horny substance you were pleased to accept from me when I was in town, of as much worth to you as I can, give me leave therefor here inclosed to give you a copy of what I learnt and remarked upon the place concerning this odd case, which I have at last found out amongst my papers. you have it just as I set it down for my owne memory and therefor must excuse the way it is expressed in[1]

There was lately in our neighbourhood a Japonese. I heard not of him till he was gon or else would have sought an oportunity to have spoke with him, for I am told he speaks English a little. We have soe little commerce with Japan and there are soe few of that country come into ours, that I thought it would not be unacceptable to you to know where he is to be found. The direction sent me was as followeth

Enquire for Mr Bango at the Stationers
over against the East India house in
Leadenhall street[2]

[1] Locke refers to the young man whom he saw at the Charité in Paris in 1678: nos. 397, 478. His account was published in *Philosophical Transactions*, xix (1697), 594–6.

[2] Sloane calls him a Chinese: p. 56.

I shall not say any thing to you concerning the heads to be talkd on with him, you know soe well better than I what questions are fit to be asked concerning that country. I would only be resolvd in this one whether the Importation of gold and silver be prohibited there

You see what poor returns I make to your large present of pamphlets, for which I desire you to accept my thanks. I am

Sir your most humble servant

JOHN LOCKE

Address: For Dr Sloane at his house in South hampton Square[1] at the Corner of South hampton street in Bloomsbery London.

2220. JOHN BONVILLE to LOCKE, 16 March 1697 (*2144, 2235*)

B.L., MS. Locke c. 4, ff. 76–7.

London March the 16: 169$\frac{6}{7}$

Honoured Cousin

Sir yours of the 25th february I Received It doe Rejoyce my heart of your Cumfortable Journy and the benifitt of the Ayer I pray god Long to Continue your health If it be his Blesed will, To Answar your Request consirning what our Asersers[2] There Is nothing don to purpose yet, but This day one of our Comon Counsell men came to me and Tould me to morow or A friday next the Comistioners[3] will meet Att guildhall, and he valentarily promised me to goe with me to compleat our matters. and when soe don I will give you the particulers.

your of the 9th presant Instant I Received, Accordingly my son went to his french Masters house, and he give This Answar, Tis very posable but that he may heare of such A one As may be for your purpose and when he have Knowledg of it he will Aquaint me with it. but this he say the french are poore and are not Able to com soe far backward and foreward, Thefore he would desire the Gentleman to send word, upon what Conditions or Terms when he Com,[4]

[1] An alternative name about this time for Bloomsbury Square.

[2] Assessors.

[3] I cannot identify them.

[4] The inquiry was probably for a tutor for Francis Cudworth Masham: pp. 77, 147–8, etc.

Another Thing I must Aquaint you with According To Knowledge, of A young man, A marchant, newly out of his Time, And Late ly Com to England, he was sent by his master to franc, he Is As capable to Learn french As any that was born and brought up in franc. And from franc he was sent to Egipt to A place caled Grand Cairo. There he Larnt both the Arabick And Turkish Tongue, writes and read the Arabick tongue very well, he Knowes the maners and Customes of That Cuntry. he Lived to my Knowledg In Egipt About six yeares. And he purpose to Returne thether Againe, only waiteing and hopeing for A peace. This young man I Thought good to Aquaint you with becaues I have A parfect Knowledg of him, His owne Mother have been and Is still A Lodger In my House 14 yeares. I bles God we are All In Health Att presant, I doe Earnestly desire and will bagg of God This marcy may be Long Continued To you, which Is The prayer

of your Obliged Kinsman and Humble Sarvant

JNO: BONVILLE:

Address: For Mr Locke [at Oates, by Joslyn, Bishops Stortford]
Postmark: MR —
Endorsed by Locke: Bonville 16° Mar $9\frac{6}{7}$

2221. WILLIAM MOLYNEUX to LOCKE, 16 March 1697 (2202, *2240*)

The Carl H. Pforzheimer Library, New York. Transcribed from photostat. Printed, omitting the postscripts, in *Some Familiar Letters*, pp. 183–9. Answers no. 2202; answered by no. 2243.

Dublin. March. 16. $169\frac{6}{7}$

I must confes (Dear Sir) I have not lately (if ever in my life) been under a greater concern than at your long Silence. Sometimes I was angry with my self; but I could not well tell why: and then I was apt to blame you, but I could les tell why. as your Silence continued, my Distraction Increased; till at last I was happily releived by yours of the 22th of Febr. which came not to my hands till the 10th Inst. I then perceived I was to charge some part of my troubled Time to the Conveyance of your Letter, which was almost three weeks on its way hither. And that which added to my Concern was the want of even your shadow before me, for to this Moment I have not received that, which will be apt on its Appearance to make me an Idolater. Mr Howard writes me word, he has sent it from London above five weeks ago, but I hear nothing off it from Our Correspondent to whom tis Consigned in Chester. However, seing I know the substance to be in safety and wel, I can bear the Hazard of the Shadow with some Patience, and doubt not but my Expectation will be satisfyed in due time.

Both Whiston and Bentley are positive against the Idea of God being Innate.[1] and I had rather reley on them (if I would reley on any Man) than on Dr Sherlock;[a] Tis true the Latter has a great name; but that, I am sure, weighs not with You or Me. besides, you rightly observe, the Doctor is no Obstinate Heretick, but may veer about when an other Opinion comes in Fashion, for some men alter their Notions as they do their Cloaths in Complyance to the Mode. I have heard of a Master of the Temple who during the siege of Limerick writ over hither to a certain Prelate to be sure to let him know by the first Oppertunity when ever it came to be surrendred. which was done accordingly, and Immediately the Good Doctors Eyes were opened and he plainly saw the Oaths to King Wil, and Q. Mary were not only expedient but Lawful and Our Duty.[2] A Good Roaring Train of Artillery is not only the Ratio Ultima Regum,[3] but of other men besides.

I fancy, I pretty wel gues what it is that some men find Mischeivous in your Essay. Tis opening the Eyes of the Ignorant, and rectifying the Methods of Reasoning, which perhaps may undermine some received Errors, and so abridge the Empire of Darknes, wherein tho the Subjects wander deplorably yet the Rulers have their Profit and Advantage. But tis ridiculous in any man to say in general your book is Dangerous; Let any fair Contender for Truth

[a] *Underlined in MS. and then altered to* Dr S— *presumably by the editor of* Some Familiar Letters.

---

[1] According to Whiston 'we collect our Idea's of the Divine Attributes, by considering what is good, great, ... and venerable among Men, and ascribing every such thing to the Divine Nature; ... By accumulating all things that appear Perfections in Men, ... and removing all Imperfections necessarily adhering to them, we arrive at the Notion of an Infinitely Perfect Being; which is but another name for God, ...': *A New Theory of the Earth*, p. 44. Bentley argues that knowledge of the existence of God can be obtained by the sole use of reason and that an innate idea of it is not asserted by religion: *A Confutation of Atheism*, third lecture, 1692.

[2] Sherlock was Master of the Temple from 1684 until his suspension in 1689; he was reinstated in 1690 and continued as Master until 1705. His change of heart was immediately associated by contemporaries with the Battle of the Boyne.

[3] The phrase is associated with Richelieu: Evelyn, *Diary*, ed. de Beer, ii. 125 n.

sit down and shew wherein tis Erroneous. Dangerous is a Word of an uncertain signification; every one Uses it in his Own Sense. A Papist shall say tis Dangerous at Rome because perhaps it agrees not so wel with Transubstantiation; and a Lutheran, because his Consubstantiation is in hazard; but neither consider whether Transubst. or Consubst. be True or False. but taking it for Granted that they are true or at least gainfull, whatever hitts not with it, or is against it, must be Dangerous.

I am extreamly obleidged to you, for your introducing a Correspondence between Dr Sloan and Me. and it would be the Greatest Satisfaction imaginable to me, could I but promise my self Materials in this place fitt to support it. However I shall soon begin it by sending him an Account of the largest Quadruped that Moves on the Earth, except the Elephant, with which this Country has antiently been plentifully stockd; but are now quite perishd from amongst us. and is not to be found, for ought as I can learn, any where at present but about New England, Virginia. etc.[1]

And now I come to that part of your Letter relating to Monsieur Le Clerk which greives me every time I think on't. there are so many Difficultys in what you propose concerning him, that I know not how they will be surmounted. The Clergy here have given that Learned Pious and Candid Man a Name that will frighten any Bishop from serving him, tho otherwise inclinable enough in his own Breast.[2] I know but two or Three that are in any Post in the Church capable to Help him, on whom I could relye to do it; but at the same time I know them to be such Cautious, Wary Men, and so fearful of the Censure of the rest of the Tribe, that they would hardly be brought to it. I take Monsieur Le Clerk to be One of the Greatest Scholars in Europe, I look on him as One of the most Judicious, Pious, and Sincere Christians that has appeard publickly; and it would be an Infinite honour to us to have him amongst us. but I fear an Eclesiastical preferment will be very Difficult to be Obtaind for him. and Indeed when I troubled you to give me some account of him, it was in Prospect of bringing him into my own family, could his Circumstances have allowd it; for I took him to be a Single Man, and One of the Refugees in Holland, and wholy

[1] The Irish elk. An account by Dr. Thomas Molyneux was published this year in *Philosophical Transactions*, xix. 489–512.

[2] The existing distrust of Le Clerc's views may have increased as Toland became more prominent. In the introduction to his translation of Le Clerc's *De l'incredulité* (no. *2170*) he implied that Le Clerc was a friend: Barnes, *Le Clerc*, pp. 182–3.

unprovided for. On his own Account I am hartily glad he has any Settlement there, but for my own sake I could wish he were in other Circumstances. But notwithstanding these Difficultys, I have venturd to break this Matter to A Clergyman here in a Considerable Post Dr.[a]– Edw. Smyth, Dean of Our Cathedral in this Citty,–[a] a Gentleman who is happy in your Acquaintance, and is a person of an Extensive Charity, and great Candour.[1] He relishd the thing extreamly; but moved the forementiond difficultys, and raised some farther scruples concerning Monsieur Le Cl. Ordination, for Ordaind he must necessarily be to capacitate him for an Ecles. Preferment. and he questiond whether He would submit to those Oathes, and subscription of Assent and Consent, that are requisite thereto. But he Promised me, that when he Attends the K. this summer into Holland as his Chaplain, He will wait on Monsieur Le Cl. at Amsterdam, and discourse with him farther about this matter. This Gentleman is the likeliest Eclesiastick in Ireland to Effect this busines, for He is a rising man in the Church, and tho he be very zealous in his own Principles, yet tis with the greatest Charity and Deference to others, which I think is the true Spirit of Christianity. I have not mentiond you in the least to my Coz. Smyth in all this Matter.

I am extreamly Obleidged to you for the Good Offices you have done me to Mr Methwin our Lord Chancellour. I promise my self a great deal of satisfaction in the Honour of his Lordships Acquaintance. And I could wish, if it were consistent with your Convenience, that you would Let me know the Person you desired to mention my Name to his Lordship.

I am hartily glad to understand that you have taken notice of what the Bishop of Worcester says relating to your Book. I have been in Discourse here with an Ingenious Man upon what the Bishop alledges, and the Gentleman observed that the Bishop does not so Directly object against your Notions as Erroneous, but as misused by Others, and Particularly by the Author of Christianity not Mysterious. but I think this no very just Observation; the Bishop directly Opposes your Doctrine, tho, tis true, he does it on the Occasion of the foresaid Book. I am told the Author of that

[a–a] *Deleted in MS., apart from* Dr ....Dean of ...., *presumably by the editor of* Some Familiar Letters. *For the words* my Coz. Smyth *below the editor substituted* him *but did not mark the MS.*

[1] Edward Smyth was dean of St. Patrick's from 1696 to 1699.

Discourse is of this Country, and that his Name is Toland, but he is a stranger in these parts, I beleive if he belongs to this Kingdom, he has been a good while out of it, for I have not heard of any such remarkable Man amongst us.[1]

I should be very glad to see Monsieur Leibnitz's[a] Paper concerning your Essay. He is certainly an Extraordinary Person, especially in Mathematicks; but really to speak freely of him in relation to what he may have to say to you, I do not expect any great matters from him; for My thinks (with all Deference to his great Name) he has given the world no Extrordinary Samples of his Thoughts this way; as appears by two discourses he has printed, both in the Acta Erudit. Lipsiæ, The first Anno. 1694. pag. 110. De Primæ Philosophiæ Emendatione. etc. the other Anno 1695. pag. 145. Specimen Dynamicum. which truly to me is in many place⟨s⟩[b] unintelligible. But that may be my Defect, and not His.

I beg you would excuse me to My Lady Masham for the Error I committed relating to her Ladiship. I ever lookd on Mr Norris as an Obscure[2] Enthusiastical Man, but I could not think he would[c] impose on the World so notorious a falsity in matter of Fact. I wish Authors would take more Pains to open than to shut mens Eyes, and then we should have more succes in the Discovery of Truth . . . . . . But I have almost outrun my Paper.

I am

Ever Honourd Sir

Your most Affectionate and most obleidged Humble servant

W: MOLYNEUX

My Brother gives you his most Humble service.

My Son shall rectify his stile to young Mr Masham, twas a sin of Ignorance, for wee took him to be Sir Francis's Only Son. I ⟨hop⟩e[d] it will be excused.

Address: To John Locke Esquire at Mr Pawlings overagainst the Plow Inn in Little Lincolns Inn Fields London.

Postmark: MR 29

Endorsed by Locke: W: Molyneux 16 Mar 9$\frac{6}{7}$ Answered 10 Apr.[e]

[a] *Altered to* L...'s *in MS., presumably by the editor of* Some Familiar Letters. [b] *Edge of page.* [c] *Here* knowingly *is interlined, probably by the editor of* Some Familiar Letters. [d] *Covered by seal.* [e] *The date is smudged.*

[1] If he had not gone already, Toland was now about to go to Ireland: p. 82, etc.

[2] Perhaps in the obsolete sense, intellectually dark, unenlightened, rather than in the current figurative sense, hard to understand, lacking in perspicuity: *O.E.D.*

2222. PHILIPPUS VAN LIMBORCH to LOCKE, 16/26 March 1697 (2209, *2256*)

B.L., MS. Locke c. 14, ff. 103–4. Copy by van Limborch in Amsterdam University Library, MS. R.K., III D 16, ff. 182–4. Printed from the copy in *Some Familiar Letters*, pp. 380–91. Answers no. 2126.

Vir Amplissime

Citius tuis, decimo quinto demum Octobris diē mihi redditis, respondissem: verum quoniam judicium meum de tractatu Anglicano in linguam Gallicam verso[1] petiisti, tempus a reliquis curis vacuum quæsivi, ut tractatum illum elegantissimum uno tenore perlegere, omniaque illo contenta considerare et expendere possem. Maxime mihi opportunum videbatur tempus hoc hybernum, quo ab exercitiis academicis feriari solemus: sed et illud frigore suo acutissimo non leviter impetum scribendi remoratum est. Legi totum tractatum a capite ad calcem, nec unica lectione contentus, eum relegi. Interim huc perlatus est Actorum Lipsiensium mensis October, quo tractatus illius compendium pro Doctorum illorum more nobis exhibetur.[2] Primo ajunt, autoris illius Pockii nomen esse dici (credo eos incerto rumori temere fidem adhibuisse, et in nomine una aberrasse literâ:) tum in compendio quod confecere, omnia quibus aliquam autori invidiam conflari posse putant sedulo enumerant, ut systematum

---

Excellent Sir,

I should have replied sooner to your letter, which was not delivered to me until the 15th of October, but since you asked for my opinion of the English treatise that has been translated into French[1] I sought a time free from other charges, so that I could read through that very choice treatise uninterruptedly, and consider and ponder everything contained in it. This winter season, when we are accustomed to have a holiday from academic courses, seemed to me an especially suitable time; but that impulse to write has been not a little held back by the very keen cold. I have read the whole treatise from beginning to end, and, not content with a single reading, have re-read it. Meanwhile the Leipzig *Acta* for the month of October has been brought here. In it we are presented with an abridgement of that treatise in the manner of those doctors.[2] First they assert that its author's name is said to be Pockius (I suppose that they have rashly given credit to some uncertain report and have gone astray in one letter in the name); then in the abridgement that they have composed they industriously specify everything by which, they think, some ill will against the author can be

---

[1] Coste's translation of *The Reasonableness of Christianity*.

[2] pp. 463–9. This is followed by a second article, pp. 469–74, on Locke's *Vindication* and Edwards's *Socinianism Unmask'd* (no. *2063*).

Theologicorum contemtum ulcisci velle videantur. Extollunt magnifice Joannem Eduardi, quod præclare[1–] hactenus in Anglia contra Socinianam hæresin variis scriptis militaverit, librumque ediderit Meditationum quarundam de causis et occasione Atheismi, ⟨hodierni⟩[a] præsertim sæculi; in quo passim autoris hujus anonymi sententias, ut periculosas et a Socinianismo ac Atheismo non alienas, perstrinxit.[–1] Subjungunt hisce compendium duorum scriptorum, quorum alterum brevis pro tractatu illo est apologia; alterum, Joannis Eduardi, titulo, Socinianism unmask'd. Tu illos tractatus rectius me nosti. Videntur dolere, quod Meditationes Eduardi ipsis ad manum non fuerint; alias et illarum compendium habuissemus. Systema Theologiæ me scripsisse nosti: Non tamen eo in pretio apud me Systemata sunt, ut non hunc exiguum tractatum multis Systematibus præferam: imo plus veræ Theologiæ ex illo, quam ex operosis multorum Systematibus hausisse me ingenue profiteor. Sed vero Theologiam autor ille tradit nimis facilem, nimis laxam, quæ salutem angustis humanorum decretorum vinculis alligatam minime cupit; nec orthodoxiam ex sectarum Confessionibus, sed solo verbo divino arcessit. Hoc crimen est, quod Socinianismi et

[a] *MS.* hodieri

---

produced, so that they seem to want to take vengeance on his contempt for theological systems. They praise John Edwards very highly because he has hitherto[1–] fought gloriously in England against the Socinian heresy in various writings and has published a book of *Some thoughts concerning the causes and occasion of atheism, especially in the present age*, in which he has everywhere found fault with the opinions of this anonymous author, as dangerous and as no different from Socinianism and atheism.[–1] To this they append an abridgement of two books, one of them a short defence of that treatise, the other, by John Edwards, entitled *Socinianism unmask'd.* You know those treatises better than I do. They seem to regret that Edwards's *Thoughts* was not at hand for them; otherwise we should have had an abridgement of it also. You know that I have written a system of theology; systems are, however, not in so great esteem with me that I do not prefer this small treatise to many of them; on the contrary I frankly own that I have drawn more true theology from it than from the laborious systems of many [other writers]. But indeed that author teaches a theology that is too easy, too loose, one that is strongly averse to a salvation held fast in the strait fetters of human decrees and that derives orthodoxy not from the confessions of sects but from the word of God alone. This is a crime that

---

[1–1] Quoted, with slight adjustment, from the end of the first article in the *Acta*. For Edwards's *Some Thoughts* see no. *1954*.

Atheismi infami convitio a Doctoribus systematicis traduci meretur: non aliter ac si, qui humana placita religiose adorare recusant, eo ipso omnem religionem ejurare censendi essent. Ego autoris in hoc tractatu scopum summopere laudo; scopum suum feliciter esse assecutum, solideque ipsum quod intendit probasse judico. Imprimis placent mihi duo: Methodus accurata historiæ Euangelicæ, quam cap. IX.[1] tradit, et per quam varia loca in Euangeliis, in speciem obscura, feliciter admodum interpretatur: Et perspicua illa deductio argumentorum, quibus ostendit cur D. Jesus Christus in terris degens, non expressis verbis docuerit, se esse Messiam.[2] Hæc autori huic peculiaria sunt, ipsiusque judicium ingeniique perspicaciam clare demonstrant. In iis autem plurima sunt, quibus præcipuum libri sui argumentum, quod est, fidem quod Jesus sit Christus eam esse per quam justificamur, luculenter confirmat. Habes hic judicium meum de tractatu hoc, quem tertio relegere statui. Petis autem, ut si quædam in illius lectione observaverim, tibi scriberem. Ego in tractatu adeo eximio vix quicquam, quod tibi proponi meretur, observavi: ita sibi penitus me habet assentientem, ut exigua sint quæ observaverim, quæque principali ipsius scopo nihil officiunt, et quæ forsan a me plene intellecta non sunt.

---

deserves to be traduced by the systematic doctors under the infamous reproach of Socinianism and atheism; just as if those who refuse to pay religious reverence to human decrees were for that to be deemed to renounce all religion. I commend highly the author's object in this treatise; I consider that he has happily achieved it, and has solidly proved what he intended to prove. Two things especially please me: the exact ordering of the Gospel history which he narrates in chap. ix,[1] and whereby he very happily explains various passages in the Gospels that are obscure in appearance; and that perspicuous sequence of arguments whereby he shows why the Lord Jesus Christ while dwelling on earth did not teach in express words that he was the Messiah.[2] These things are peculiar to this author and clearly indicate his judgement and the penetration of his mind. Moreover there are many things among them by which he excellently confirms the principal matter discussed in his book, which is that the faith that Jesus is the Christ is that faith by which we are justified. You have here my opinion about this treatise, which I have decided to read again for the third time. You ask me further to write to you if I have taken notice of anything in reading it. I have taken notice of scarcely anything worth putting before you in so excellent a treatise; it commands my assent so thoroughly that those things of which I have taken notice are inconsiderable and not at all detrimental to its main object, and perhaps I have not fully understood them. But since you ask for my

---

[1] In the first English edition (1695) pp. 76–161.
[2] In the French translation ch. viii; in the English 1695 pp. 61–76.

Quia vero judicium meum requiris, ego hæc qualiacunque tibi expendenda propono; non quia alicujus pretii sunt, sed ut morem geram tuæ voluntati. Statim in initio autor dicit, super lapsu Adami fundatam esse doctrinam de redemtione. Equidem certum est, Adami lapsum a doctrina de redemtione non excludi: attamen et propria cujusque nostrum peccata ab ea secludenda non sunt. Plurimorum Doctorum sententia est, Dominum Jesum nos liberasse e miseria, in quam per Adami peccatum incidimus, et in eundem fœlicitatis statum, quem in Adamo amisimus, restituisse. Ego puto illos exiliter nimium de immenso Christi beneficio sentire; ipsumque ex multis peccatis, ut Apostolus Rom. V. loquitur, nos liberasse, et ad statum multo fœliciorem, vitam nimirum æternam in cœlis, perduxisse. Huic addo: quod ibidem dicatur, Adamum per peccatum amisisse immortalitatem, et factum esse mortalem. Si immortalitas autori huic significet, quod Adamus, si non peccasset, moriturus non fuisset; et mortalitas, quod per peccatum moriendi necessitatem contraxerit, verissimam ejus sententiam judico. Si vero immortalitas, ut vox illa proprie sonat, illi significet moriendi impossibilitatem, non recte dici puto, Adamum fuisse creatum immortalem. Ego sententiam meam plenius explicui in Theologia mea Christiana lib. II. cap. XXIV. Verum hæc immortalitas, hoc est, immunitas a morte, alterius plane est generis quam immortalitas Dei; sicut et

---

opinion I put these [notes] before you, such as they are, for you to ponder; not because they are of any value, but in order to comply with your wish. Right at the beginning the author says that the doctrine of redemption is based on the fall of Adam. It is indeed certain that Adam's fall is not excluded from the doctrine of redemption; nevertheless the particular sins of each one of us are not to be separated from it. The opinion of most teachers is that the Lord Jesus has freed us from the misery into which we fell through Adam's sin and has restored us to the same state of happiness as we lost in Adam. I think that they have far too mean an opinion of the immense benefit of Christ, and that he has freed us from many sins, as the Apostle says in Romans 5, and has led us to a far happier state: to life eternal in Heaven. To this I add: it is said in the same place that Adam lost immortality through sin and was made mortal. If immortality means for this author that Adam, if he had not sinned, would not have had to die; and mortality, that Adam by sin brought upon himself the necessity of dying: I consider that his opinion is altogether true. But if immortality means for him the impossibility of dying, as is the proper meaning of the word, then I think that the statement that Adam had been created immortal is not correct. I have set forth my opinion more fully in my *Theologia Christiana*, book II, chapter xxiv. But this immortality, that is, immunity from death, is clearly

mortalitas, seu moriendi potentia, multum differt a morte, seu moriendi necessitate. Quare etiam minus commode mihi dictum videtur pag. 230.[1] quod Adami immortalitas sit imago Dei ad quam conditus est: et licet concederetur, alibi immortalitatem vocari imaginem Dei; non tamen exinde sequeretur, quando Adamus ad imaginem Dei conditus dicitur, illam imaginem esse immortalitatem: non enim necesse est, omnia quæ alibi Scriptura imagine Dei designat, eâ comprehensa esse, quando hominem ad imaginem Dei conditum esse dicit: Sufficit eximiam quandam in homine esse qualitatem, respectu cujus imaginem Dei referre dici possit. Inter alia loca video pag. 232.[2] citari ad Rom. VIII. 29. ubi dicimur a Deo præcogniti et prædestinati ut simus conformes imagini Filii ejus, ut ipse sit primogenitus inter multos fratres. Putat autor, illa imagine, cui conformes esse debemus, designari immortalitatem et vitam æternam. Ego autem non tam vitam æternam, quam modum ad vitam æternam perveniendi, quo fideles Christo similes esse debent, hic significari credo, nimirum per crucem et afflictiones; quam imaginem Dominus discipulis indicat Luc. XXIV. 26. Nonne oportuit Christum ista pati, atque intrare in gloriam suam. Hanc

---

of another kind than the immortality of God; just as mortality or the possibility of dying also differs greatly from death or the necessity of dying. For this reason it also seems to me that it is not well said on page 230[1] that Adam's immortality is the image of God in which he was made; and although it might be allowed that immortality is called the image of God elsewhere, nevertheless it would not then follow that, when Adam is said to have been made in the image of God, that image is immortality; for it is not necessary that everything which Scripture elsewhere designates as the image of God should be included in it when Scripture says that man was made in the image of God; it suffices that there is in man some extraordinary quality, in respect of which he can be said to represent the image of God. I see that on p. 232[2] there is cited among other passages Romans 8: 29, where we are said to have been foreknown and predestined by God to be conformed to the image of His son, so that he may be the first-born among many brothers. The author thinks that immortality and eternal life are designated by that image to which we should be conformed. I on the other hand believe that here is meant not so much eternal life as the way of attaining eternal life, by which the faithful are to be like Christ: that is, through the cross and afflictions; this is the image which the Lord points out to the disciples in Luke 24: 26: 'Ought not Christ to have suffered these things and to enter

---

[1] In 1695 p. 199.
[2] In 1695 p. 201.

explicationem totius capitis series evincit. Jam enim vers. 17.[1] dixerat; hæredes sumus Dei, cohæredes autem Christi, siquidem cum ipso patimur, ut unà cum ipso glorificemur: Eaque occasione multus est, ut fideles hortetur ad crucem et afflictiones Euangelii causa sustinendas; inter alia argumento a voluntate divina petito, quod per crucem nos ad salutem velit perducere; et ne id ipsis absonum videatur, ⟨Deum⟩[a] iis quos diligit tot dura in hoc mundo immittere, exemplum illis Christi proponit, cujus imagini ut sint conformes Deus eos prædestinavit, et consequenter ad crucem ferendam vocavit: et in sequentibus porro ostendit, illas afflictiones non posse ipsos separare ab amore Dei, quo ipsos in Christo complectitur. Hinc et Scriptura passim aliis in locis inculcat, nos gloriæ Christi fore consortes, si et cum ipso crucem sustinuerimus, 2. Tim. II. 11, 12. et præsertim, Hebr. II. 10. decebat ut ipse propter quem sunt omnia, et per quem sunt omnia, multos filios in gloriam adducendo, principem salutis ipsorum per afflictiones consecraret. Et hoc potissimum argumento fideles ad constantem persecutionum tolerantiam hortatur, 1. Pet. IV. 12, 13. Hebr. XII. 1, 2, 3. Hanc credo esse imaginem Christi, cui ut conformes simus Deum nos

[a] *MS.* Deus; *in van Limborch's copy* Deum

into his glory?' The course of the whole chapter confirms this explanation. For he [*sc.* St. Paul] had already said in verse 17:[1] 'We are heirs of God, and coheirs with Christ, if so be that we suffer with him in order that we may be glorified together with him'; and taking this opportunity he at some length exhorts the faithful to endure the cross and afflictions for the Gospel's sake; among others by an argument drawn from the will of God, that He wants to lead us through the cross to salvation; and lest it should seem incongruous to them that God should send so many hardships in this world on those whom He loves, he puts before them the example of Christ, to whose image God had predestined them to be conformed, and consequently had called them to bear the cross; and he shows further in what follows that those afflictions cannot separate them from the love of God, with which he embraces them in Christ. Hence also Scripture impresses on us in many other places that we shall be sharers in Christ's glory if we have also endured the cross with him, 2 Timothy 2: 11, 12, and especially Hebrews 2: 10: 'It was fitting that He for Whom are all things and by Whom are all things, by bringing many sons to glory, should consecrate the prince of their salvation through afflictions.' And especially by this argument he exhorts the faithful to the steadfast endurance of persecutions, 1 Peter 4: 12, 13, Hebrews 12: 1, 2, 3. I believe this to be the image of Christ to which the Apostle says that

[1] Of Romans 8.

prædestinasse ait Apostolus Rom. VIII. 29. consentaneë iis quæ leguntur Act. XIV. 22. et 2. Timoth. III. 12.

Pag. 246.[1] ait Autor, sibi non occurrere, quod D. Jesus ipse sibi tribuat titulum Sacerdotis, aut mentionem faciat ullius rei quæ ad sacerdotium refertur. Munus Christi sacerdotale in Apostolorum Epistolis, et præcipue in Epist. ad Hebræos nobis plenius esse descriptum, manifestum est; nec negari potest,[a–] D. Jesum[–a] nusquam in Euangeliis sibi Sacerdotis titulum tribuere: Attamen negandum non videtur, quod sibi alicubi actionem sacerdotalem tribuat: diserte enim ait, se animam suam λύτρον ἀντὶ πολλῶν daturum, Matth. XX. 28. Sanguinem suum vocat sanguinem Novi Fœderis, qui pro multis effunditur in remissionem peccatorum, Matth. XXVI. 27.[2] Negare non possumus hunc esse actum qui ad sacerdotium respectum habet. Quare fortasse præstitisset hoc præteriisse, neque hominibus calumniæ occasionem quærentibus quippiam suppeditasse, quod cum aliqua specie carpere posse videntur.

Præter hæc in tractatu hoc quædam occurrere mihi videntur, quæ vix inter se conciliari possunt; nisi forte autor mentem suam plenius explicet. Pag. 13.[3] ait; Cum Adam pulsus sit è paradizo

[a–a] *MS.* potest. D. Jesum

God has predestined us to be conformed, Romans 8: 29, agreeably to what is to be read in Acts 14: 22 and 2 Timothy 3: 12.

The author says on p. 246[1] that he does not remember that the Lord Jesus himself bestows on himself the title of priest, or makes mention of anything relating to [his] priesthood. Christ's priestly office is manifestly more fully described for us in the Epistles of the Apostles, and especially in the Epistle to the Hebrews; nor can it be denied that the Lord Jesus nowhere in the Gospels bestows on himself the title of priest; but it does not seem deniable that he somewhere attributes priestly action to himself; for he expressly says that he will give his life a ransom for many, Matthew 20: 28. He calls his blood the blood of the New Covenant, which is shed for many for the remission of sins, Matthew 26: 27.[2] We cannot deny that this is an act that relates to priesthood. Perhaps therefore it would have been better to have omitted this and not to have provided men who seek opportunities for misrepresentation with something that they seem to be able to carp at with some show [of reason].

Besides these there seem to me to occur in this treatise some things that can scarcely be reconciled with one another, unless perhaps the author will set out more fully what he has in mind. On p. 13[3] he says that since Adam

---

[1] In 1695 p. 214. [2] A slip for verse 28. [3] In 1695 p. 10.

terrestri, omnisque ejus posteritas ea propter nascatur extra hunc deliciarum locum; inde naturaliter sequi debet, omnes homines morituros, et in æternum sub potentia mortis mansuros, atque ita penitus fore perditos: ex eo autem statu per Christum liberatos docet, et quidem per legem fidei, quam postea fuse ostendit Euangelio contineri. Haec meo judicio vere dicuntur. Verum non satis capio, quomodo cum his bene concilientur, quæ leguntur pag. 250. et 266.[1] quod qui justi sunt non indigent gratia, sed jus habent ad arborem vitæ. Illi enim, quatenus Adami posteri, etiam sub potentia mortis æternum manere debe⟨n⟩t:[a] quomodo ergo per suam justitiam jus possent acquirere ad arborem vitæ, ita ut nulla gratia indigeant? cu⟨m an⟩tea[a] docuerat, omnes ex illo statu necessariæ mortis liberatos, et quidem per legem fidei: Unde sequi videtur, liberationem illam non posse fieri nisi per legem fidei. Ergo non per perfectam legis operum obedientiam. Nam ex miseria liberare gratiæ est, quam lex operum excludit. Tum nec cum principio isto commode satis conciliare possum, quod autor dicit, qua ratione illi, qui de Christo nihil quicquam inaudiverunt, salvari possint.[2] Si enim per Adamum necessariæ morti ac æternæ sunt

[a] *Page rubbed.*

---

was expelled from the earthly paradise, and that on that account all his posterity is born outside that place of delights; it should naturally follow from that that all men should die and should remain for ever under the power of death, and so be utterly lost; but, he declares, they were freed from that state by Christ, and indeed by the law of faith, which, as he afterwards shows copiously, is contained in the Gospel. In my opinion these statements are true. But I do not grasp satisfactorily how what is to be read on pages 250 and 266[1] is to be properly reconciled with them, that the righteous have no need of grace, but have a right to the tree of life. For they, inasmuch as they are Adam's posterity, must also remain for ever under the power of death; how then could they through their own righteousness acquire a right to the tree of life, so as to have no need of grace? Since he had declared previously that all men are freed from that state of necessary death, and indeed by the law of faith: whence it seems to follow that that deliverance cannot come about except by the law of faith. Therefore not by perfect obedience to the law of works. For deliverance from misery belongs to grace, which the law of works excludes. Again I cannot well enough reconcile with that principle what the author says of the grounds on which those who have heard nothing whatsoever of Christ can be saved.[2] For if by Adam they are

---

[1] In 1695 pp. 217, 232.   [2] In 1695 pp. 251–3.

obnoxii, e quâ per solam legem fidei beneficio Christi liberentur, non videtur illis sufficere posse, quod lumine naturæ aliquas fidei illius, quod Deus sit misericors, scintillas habeant; sed per illam fidei legem, quam Deus salutis obtinendæ conditionem statuit, servari debere videntur. Video Doctores Systematicos hic multum offendi; atque ideo neque acquiescere quinque illis fructibus, quos D. Jesum adventu suo in mundum hominibus contulisse docet autor.[1] Ego in Doctorum Systematicorum gratiam nihil in veritatis præjudicium docendum judico; et si quid illi præter rationem carpant, indignationem eorum spernendam censeo. Sed considerandum, an non majus quid dici possit et oporteat, quod ipsis licet non satisfaciat, minus tamen forsan offendet, et meo judicio plenius rei veritatem exhibet. Video fructus quidem indicari Prophetici ac Regii muneris Christi, nullos vero Sacerdotalis. Quid si ergo addatur hic muneris Sacerdotalis fructus, quod mundus Deo sit reconciliatus, adeo ut nunc per Christum omnibus omnino hominibus remedium paratum sit e miseria sua, in quam occasione peccati Adami, propriisque peccatis inciderunt, emergendi, et salutem æternam consequendi. Hoc posito, puto explicari posse, qua ratione,

---

subject to necessary and eternal death, from which they are freed only through the law of faith by the benefit of Christ, it does not seem possible for it to suffice for them that by the light of nature they should have some sparks of that belief that God is merciful, but it seems that they must be saved by that law of faith which God has ordained as the condition for obtaining salvation. I see that the systematic doctors are greatly offended at this, and therefore are also not satisfied with those five advantages which, the author declares, the Lord Jesus conferred on men by his coming into the world.[1] I consider that nothing to the prejudice of truth should be declared to gratify the systematic doctors; and if they carp at anything beyond reason I think that their indignation may be contemned. But it is to be considered whether something greater cannot and ought not to be said, which, although it may not satisfy them, may perhaps offend them less and which in my opinion exhibits the truth of the matter more fully. I see that the advantages conferred by the prophetic and kingly offices of Christ are pointed out, but none conferred by his priestly office. How then would it be if there were therefore added here the advantage conferred by the priestly office, that the world has been reconciled to God, so that there has now been prepared by Christ for all men whatsoever a remedy by which they may emerge from their misery into which they have fallen by occasion of Adam's and their own sins, and by which they may attain eternal salvation? If this

---

[1] In 1695 pp. 256–90.

salvis principiis ante positis, ii qui de Christo nihil ne fando quidem audiverunt, per Christum salvari possint: Nempe quod Deus illis, qui (ut autor hic ait pag. 292)[1] instinctu luminis naturæ ad gratiam ac misericordiam ejus confugiunt, delictorumque resipiscentiam agunt, eorumque veniam supplices petunt, gratiam per Christum impetratam applicet, ipsisque propter Christum remissionem peccatorum et justitiam imputet: Atque ita beneficium, quod ubi Christus prædicatus est non nisi per directam in Christum fidem obtineri potest, illi sine directa in Christum, ipsis non prædicatum, fide consequantur per gratiosam imputationem divinam; qui favores et beneficia sua latius extendere potest quam promissorum Verba ferunt. Ut ita omnium salus in sacrificio Christi propitiatorio fundetur. Puto hæc non multum a sententia autoris hujus differre, et iis quæ Euangelio continentur consentanea esse. Ultimum caput[2] per omnia amplector: Omnia credenda et observanda ut salutem consequamur Euangeliis et Actis contineri credo; nullumque novum articulum in Epistolis Apostolicis superaddi: quæ alii novos fidei articulos urgent, non novi articuli sunt, sed aut magis dilucidæ articulorum jam antea traditorum explanationes; aut doctrinæ

---

is stated I think that it can be explained on what ground, the principles stated above being preserved intact, those who have heard nothing of Christ, not even by hearsay, can be saved by Christ: [it is] surely because God attaches the grace obtained by Christ to those who (as this author says on p. 292)[1] by the instinct of the light of nature fly for succour to his grace and mercy, and repent of [their] misdeeds, and humbly ask pardon for them; and grants them for Christ's sake the remission of sins, and imputes righteousness to them; and so through the gracious imputation of God, Who can spread His favours and benefits more widely than the words of the promises prescribe, those without direct belief in Christ, who has not been preached to them, may attain the benefit which, where Christ has been preached, cannot be obtained except through direct belief in him. So that the salvation of all men is thus founded on the propitiatory sacrifice of Christ. I think that this does not differ greatly from this writer's opinion and is agreeable to what is contained in the Gospel. I value highly the last chapter[2] throughout: I believe that all things that are to be believed and observed in order to our attaining salvation are contained in the Gospels and the Acts; and that no new article [of belief] is added [to them] in the Apostolic Epistles; what others urge as new articles of belief are not new articles but either clearer explanations of articles already delivered or vindications of previously delivered teaching from objections, especially those of

---

[1] In 1695 pp. 252–3. [2] In 1695 pp. 290–304.

antea traditæ ab objectionibus præcipue Judæorum vindicationes: cujus illustre nobis documentum præbet Epistola ad Romanos.

Hæc sunt paucula illa quæ mihi inter legendum occurrerunt, quæque tibi expendenda propono. Fortasse autoris mentem per omnia non plene assecutus sum. Verum exigua hæc sunt, et extra principalem autoris scopum, quem argumentis omni exceptione majoribus eum probasse judico, adeo ut me sibi habeat penitus assentientem. Imprimis laudo, quod tam candide et ingenue, nec minus solide, resipiscentiæ et bonorum operum necessitatem demonstret, et per legem fidei non penitus esse abolitam legem operum, sed mitigatam. Ego illorum hominum Theologiam non capio, qui fidem, qua nobis merita Christi applicamus, etiam ante ullum resipiscentiæ actum, nos coram Deo justificare docent. Hac enim persuasione imbuti facile mediis in sceleribus homines incauti sibi justitiam ac salutem adscribunt, modo in se fiduciam minime vacillantem deprehendant. Et Doctores improvidi hanc temerariam confidentiam alunt, dum hominibus impiis et sceleratis, modo circa vitæ finem fiduciam in Christi meritis firmam profiteantur, salutem sine ulla hæsitatione addicere non verentur. Hujus generis exemplum in nostra civitate recens, quod oblivione obliterari non debet, commemorabo. Præterita æstate ancilla quædam, ut heri sui ædes

---

the Jews; the Epistle to the Romans provides us with a notable example of this.

These are those very few things which have occurred to me in the course of reading and which I put before you for you to ponder. Perhaps I have not fully understood the author's meaning throughout. But these are inconsiderable and outside the author's main object, which I consider he has made out by entirely unexceptionable arguments; so much so that he has my complete assent. I praise him especially for showing so candidly and frankly, and not less solidly, the necessity of repentance and good works, and that the law of works is not entirely abolished by the law of faith, but is mitigated by it. I do not understand the theology of those men who declare that the faith by which we attach the merits of Christ to ourselves justifies us in the sight of God, even before any act of repentance. For heedless men who are still in their sins, being imbued with this persuasion, readily ascribe righteousness and salvation to themselves if only they perceive in themselves an unwavering trust. And unforeseeing teachers nourish this rash confidence as long as they are not afraid, with no hesitation whatsoever, to adjudge salvation to impious and wicked men, if only towards the end of their lives they profess a firm trust in the merits of Christ. I shall mention a recent example of this kind in our city that ought not to be blotted out in oblivion. Last summer a certain maidservant set fire at night to her master's house

spoliare possit, noctu eas incendit. Mortis damnata fidem suam in Christi meritis verbis emphaticis coram ministro verbi divini, qui moriturae adfuit, prolixe professa est: Ille sceleratae non tantum indubiam salutis spem fecit, sed et postridie pro concione illius fidem prolixe populo commendavit, adeo quidem, ut dicere non veritus sit, se, sola ignominia excepta, talem sibi vitae exitum optare; multis applaudentibus, aliis vero (non Remonstrantibus modo sed et Contraremonstrantibus) non sine indignatione talem encomiasten cum suo encomio reprehendentibus. Verum tandem manum de tabula. Tu pro solita tua benevolentia prolixitati meae ignosces. Vale Vir Amplissime mihique semper Venerande. Salutem a me plurimam dices Dominae Masham. Salutat te uxor, filia ac filius, qui suas hisce adjunxit, quas ut sereno respicias vultu rogo.

Tui Amantissimus
PHILIPPUS A LIMBORCH

Amstelodami 26 Martii

Address: For Sir John Locke at Mr. Pawlings over against the plough in Little Lincolns Inne feilds London

Postmark: AP 3

Endorsed by Locke: P: Limborch 26 Mar 97

---

so that she could rob it. Condemned to death, she professed at length and in emphatic language her faith in the merits of Christ in the presence of the minister of God's word who was with her when she was about to die. He not only gave the wicked woman sure hope of salvation but also next day in place of a sermon praised her faith to the people at length; indeed so much so that he was not afraid to say that he desired for himself such a departure from life, save only the disgrace. Many applauded but others (not only Remonstrants but Contraremonstrants also) indignantly condemned such an encomiast together with his encomium. But it is time for me to end. With your usual kindness you will pardon my longwindedness. Good-bye, my excellent and ever revered Sir. Please give my best regards to Lady Masham. My wife sends you greetings, as do my daughter and son. He has added to this letter one from himself; please look at it with an unruffled face.

Your most affectionate
PHILIPPUS VAN LIMBORCH

Amsterdam
26 March 1697

2223. Frans van Limborch to Locke, 16/26 March 1697 (*2419*)

B.L., MS. Locke c. 13, ff. 178–9. Frans van Limborch, later Francis Limborch, was born on 23 July 1676, N.S. Later letters record his attempts to establish himself as a merchant in England and his first marriage to Sara Waller (no. *3316*), who died in 1710; he married secondly Elizabeth Tully in Dublin and died near Athlone in 1738: Barnouw, *Philippus van Limborch*, p. 27.

Frans frequently writes vocalic y as y or ij; I have ignored this throughout. His j for 'I' should perhaps be rendered as i.

Amsterdam 26 March 1697

Much Esteemed and Honoured Sir.

I should long since have embolded my self to take the liberty of troubleing your worth, with these few lines of mine, had nott on the one side my rudenesse in the English language, and on the other the true Respect to your worth and singular erudition detained me hitherto, as knowing my self inable to produce anything worthy to be showne you. Butt Sir my father writing att present to your goodself, and j, assicuring my self thatt your dis [a] will succour the defects, deared nott differ any longer to ⟨offer⟩[a] your Worth with these few (tho vicious) lines my most humble respects and servise, and to testify you by them my sincere inclination, and greatt desires to be so happy, as to be in any manner acquainted with such an eminent person, the more because j flatter my self with the hopes, thatt (if it pleases the Mercifull God to spare your good self, and me some yeare longer in this l⟨ife⟩[a] which by his divin mercy and grace j wish with all my heart) I shall have the honour to kisse your hands in England.

I bestowed almost four years in the servise of a merchand, whose principall trade is for England; and when the resting years of my servise shall be due, j hope to see England, and to offer my servise to some merchands there, by whatt occasion my greatest wishes are, to be so happy, and to have the honour to offer you my most humble servise, as knowing and being fully persuaded, j shall finde no body in all England, that is to assist me in all my occurrences, with a greater faithfullnes, prudence, and a more sincere inclination then your worth.

In the mean while, Honoured Sir, whilst j flatter my self with the hopes, j offer you with these few lines my very humble service and shall always esteeme my self very happy, if j can meet interim with

[a] *Page torn.*

Any the least occasion, whereby j can testify you really, how sincearily j am, and shall alwayes without any reservation continue to be, who[a] after the tender of my most sincere respects, and most humble servise subscribes himself.

Honoured Sir

Your most humble, faithfull and obedient servant

F: V: LIMBORCH.

Address: For Sir John Locke, Present In London under Covert.

Endorsed by Locke: F. V: Limborch 26 Mar 97 Answered 25 May

2224. DR. (later Sir) HANS SLOANE to LOCKE, 18 March 1697 (2219, 2227)

B.L., MS. Locke c. 18, ff. 120–1. Answers no. 2219; answered by no. 2227.

London March 18. 1696.

Sir

I most humbly thank you for Your last letter and the inclosed account of the monstrous nailes, I had befor shown the Royall Society the nailes and promised to return you their thanks for them and to begg what you have now sent about them, they thinking it a matter of great curiosity and ordering the nailes to be kept in their musæum. Wee have very little new only Postellus's manuscript works[1] were exposed here to sale and no body would give above ten pounds for them; they consisted of severall pieces he had gather'd att Constantinople and were curious for those who lov'd the Rabbinicall learning but he being halfe a madd man and having vented some odd notions here as well as in print they were contemn'd now, though heretofor the Sorbonne had offered largely for them with a design as was thought to burn such works he being one of their number. One at Rome has publish'd Bibliotheca Hispana vetus[2] and Paulinus who writes on some naturall subject every Francfort Mart[3] has now printed a book de asino.[4] You once did me the favour to promise me the loan of a book called Beautes de la Perse,[5] if you have an opportunity I shall be glad to see it and speed-

[a] *Interlined.*

---

[1] Guillaume Postel, 1510–81, scholar and mystic: *Encyclopaedia Judaica*, where some of his surviving MSS. are mentioned.

[2] By Nicolás Antonio; 2 vols., 1696.

[3] See no. *1034*.

[4] C. F. Paullini (*A.D.B.*), *De Asino Liber Historico-physico-medicus*, Frankfurt, 1695.

[5] By A. Daulier-Deslandes; Paris, 1673. L.L. no. 2261.

ily return it safely. I will take care to have some discourse with the Chinese you mention, he came from Emoy,[1] I talk'd with him once but the Language made us have little conversation, I saw him on board the ship when she first arrived when I went to inquire after a brother in law of mine[2] who was supracargo of her and left behind and was the occasion of this man's coming. I hope you'le give us leave to print the strange story of the nailes and I intend they shall be graved if you consent. I shall send you doun Dr Molyneux's letter printed very soon[3] and remain

Your most obedient and most humble servant

HANS SLOANE.

Address: To John Locke Esqr. at Oates near Bishopstafford Essex.

Postmarks: MR 18; LA

Endorsed by Locke: Dr Sloane 18 Mar $9\frac{6}{7}$ Answered 22

2225. JAMES JOHNSTOUN to LOCKE, 20 March 1697 (*2101, 2207?, 2387*)

B.L., MS. Locke c. 12, ff. 31–2.

Lond. 20 March 97.

Sir

I had in some sense answered yours before I received it, which I hope you got. You will readily pardon me for using then another hand since it saved you the trouble of reading mine tho that was not my reason. I and the bishop of Salisbury have done Mr Berrisfurd[a][4] what service we can. I know not if it will succeed. I give you many thancks for your letter to the bishop of worcester.[5] I thinck you use him verry decently but I doubt much that he will be of my mind and the truth is strict reasoning can hardly appear to him against whom it is, a verry mannerly thing. I was much his servant once and will alwyse have for him the respect that is due to his caractere

[a] *Spelling doubtful; perhaps* Berrisfield

[1] Presumably Amoy.

[2] I have failed to identify the brother-in-law. A supracargo (more frequently supercargo) was an officer on board a merchant ship whose business it was to superintend the cargo and the commercial transactions of the voyage: *O.E.D.* For the supercargoes on the East India Companies' ships trading in China see H. B. Morse, *The Chronicles of the East India Company trading to China 1635–1834*, 1926–9, i. 66–77; see also no. *3046* n.

[3] No. *2170* n.

[4] Alexander Beresford: pp. 32–3, etc.

[5] Locke's *Letter* to Stillingfleet. Johnstoun is included in the distribution list for it.

and knowledge, but after the usage I met with from him upon a certain occasion,[1] I shall not willingly have any variance with him. My humble respects to My Lady Masham and many thancks to her and you for your Invitation but the trees doe not bud yet. when I can get that tryall[2] you shall have it. Our opinions about the peace ebbe and flow at present we are pretty confident of it. Its plain the Emperor would have the King of Spain dye before the peace.[3] he nou asks that the confederats will be guarantés of that succession which is odde on many accounts, tho one is sufficient against it that Spain has not yet determined the succession. Its thought Madam Maintenon is so zealous for a peace because she hopes to be declared Queen.[4] She is noe doubt maried to him long agoe. I know our late Queen[5] in her own house gives her alwyse the right hand when they are alone. you see a casheered secretary cannot writ a letter without news in it.

I am
Sir
your faithfull humble servant
J. JOHNSTOUN

Endorsed by Locke: J: Johnstown 20 Mar $9\frac{6}{7}$ Answered 26

2226. CORNELIUS LYDE to LOCKE, [*c.* 20 March 1697] (2208, 2230)

B.L., MS. Locke c. 15, ff. 153–4. The draft indenture, here summarized, forms part of the letter; it has additions and corrections by Locke and Clarke, and there is a further draft correction by Locke on f. 155. Date reckoned from postmark and Locke's endorsement. Answers no 2208; answered by no. 2230.

Sir

Yours I Rec: of the 3d Instant when you see mr Clarke our good friend you Lett him know that there have beene no thing wanting in me to serve this Government in this tax, but have taken a great

[1] It is possible that Stillingfleet informed Johnstoun in 1688 about Burnet's danger from emissaries of James II: Clarke and Foxcroft, *Burnet*, p. 236.

[2] Perhaps that of Aikenhead. No report of the proceedings against him was published.

[3] Leopold I; Charles II.

[4] 'Madam Maintenon is our friend and will keep the Peace, if possible, as she made it, not out of any kindness she has to us, but from a notion that the King's [Louis XIV] engaging in business impairs his health': Matthew Prior, Paris, 10 April 1698, N.S., in H.M.C., *Bath MSS.* iii. 204–5.

[5] Mary of Modena.

deale of paynes and maney Jorneys to supplie the place of a Comisioner. I have for hannys rent the Last yeare a good Tanner Engaged to pay it but not presently, and hanny have promised me that when Ladie day Coms I shall have this yeares rent your tenant Jo: veale is behinde a yeares rent at our Ladie day but I hope will pay then or in a short time after I have of yours about 7 li of Silver money which I Rec: of barns miclemus rent good brode money but will not hold at 5s–2d per ounce if you please I wold pay in your yeares Tax for buck hill and beluton which may be some advantag if you Thinke fitt,[1] I have sent you a short draught you may alter as you please, the tearme you may Lett it be for 7 yeares or for your Life or as you thinke fitt Sir with my herty service to you and to mr Clarke I am your Humble ser:

COR LYDE

[Indenture made 23 March 1696 [i.e. 1696/7] between John Locke of High Laver, Essex, esquire, and Francis Carpenter of the parish of Publow, butcher. Locke lets to Carpenter that part of the tenement called Buckhill lying in the parish of Publow now occupied by Joseph Barnes and John Hanny, and forming part of the estate which Locke holds by lease from Alexander Popham deceased, from 25 March next ensuing for ninety-nine years at the annual rent of £30 of lawful money of England payable in two equal instalments at Michaelmas and Lady Day, 'and soe in proportion for soe much of the last half year as shall be expired at the death of him the said' Locke. If payments or parts of payments are twenty days in arrears Locke or his assigns can re-enter the premises. Carpenter and his executors, etc., are to perform 'the offices of Overseere of the Poore, Constable, Tythingman and all other Personall-Offices belonging to the said Tenement' and to repair when necessary 'the dwelling house outhouses gates stiles hedges and ditches takeing on the Premises what is nessesary for the same'. Locke will 'pay all Rates taxes and Impositions whatsoever which shall be taxed on the premises tythes Tenths Adjustments and minister dues only Excepted'.]

I will if you send it downe sealed I will get a Counter part and bond for performance. I thinke it ought to be in stampd paper

COR: LYDE

Address: For Doct: Locke At mr: Pawlings over against the Plough in Little Lincolns feilds London

Postmark: MR 22

Endorsed by Locke: C Lyde Mar 9$\frac{6}{7}$ Answered 26 Mar 97

[1] By 8 and 9 Wm. III, c. 2 (no. *2154* n.) hammered silver coins were to pass after 1 December 1696 only by weight at *5s. 2d.* per ounce troy in all payments except taxes and loans to the crown, when they were to be received for a time at *5s. 4d.* and in some cases at *5s. 8d.* per ounce.

2227. LOCKE to DR. (later Sir) HANS SLOANE, 22 March 1697 (*2224*, 2296)

B.M., Sloane MS. 4036, ff. 294–5. Answers no. *2224*.

Oates 22 Mar $9\frac{6}{7}$

Sir

You have done too great an honour to those odde nails I sent you to lodg them in the Royal Societies Musæum. And if you thinke the history of them worth the publishing to the world with a cut of them you know you may command me in greater matters than that, only I thinke what I writ for my owne private memory ought to be revised and corrected a little before it appear in the world. To which possibly I may finde something to adde, for if I misremember not I visited this yonge man a second time, and tooke some farther notes, these I will looke out amongst my papers and bring to town with me and then you shall dispose of the whole as you think fit. In the meane time you may have a draught made of those peices I gave you and have them graved too if you think fit, but in a plate that may be laid a side till I have the allowance of my health and the weather to wait upon you. But that as you thinke fit.

I sent you this morning Les Beautez de la Perse But had not time to write by the same hand. I hope it will be with you before this, you may be pleased to keep it till I come to town

When Dr Molineux's letter is printed you may be pleased to leave one for me at my Lodging sealed up and directed to be kept there till I come to town because I shall bring up with me the last volume of Transactions to be bound in which that must have a place. I thinke it will be convenient to send a couple of them to Dublin, one to the Author Dr Molyneux and the other to his brother Mr Wm: Molyneux, from whom I received it. If you have noe better way to convey them. Mr Churchill will doe it if they be put into his hands. I am

Sir

Your most humble servant

JOHN LOCKE

Address: For Dr Sloane at his house in Southampton street in Bloomsbery London.

Postmark: MR 24

2228. THOMAS BURNETT of Kemney to LOCKE, 24 March 1697 (*2565*)

B.L., MS. Locke c. 4, ff. 197–8. Thomas Burnett of Kemney (the modern form is Kemnay; it is in Aberdeenshire), 1656–1729, a first cousin of Dr. Gilbert Burnet; married, 1713, Elizabeth, daughter of Richard Brickenden, of Inkpen, Berks. Early in 1695 he went to Hanover, where he won the regard of the Electress Sophia and of Leibniz; he corresponded with Leibniz from 1695 to 1713, and kept him in touch with English thought. He also made the acquaintance of Catharine Trotter, later Mrs. Cockburn (no. *3153*), and correspondence between them from 1701 to 1705 is extant: George Burnett, *The Family of Burnett of Leys*, ed. J. Allardyce, New Spalding Club, 1901, pp. 119–25, etc.; Leibniz, *Die philosophischen Schriften*, ed. C. J. Gerhardt, vol. iii, 1887, pp. 161–329 (pp. 151–60 are introductory to this correspondence); *Correspondance de Leibniz avec l'électrice Sophie*, ed. O. Klopp, vol. ii, 1873, pp. 262–6; Mrs. Catharine Cockburn, *Works*, ed. T. Birch, 1751, ii. 153–207.

Sir

I send you the inclosed paper from your great and just admirer my worthie freind Mr Leibnitz att Hanover.[1] I can make no other Apologie for transmitting the same to yow so late; Bot the regret I have That I could not recover it sooner out of the hands of those that were more curious to see then willing to restore it. My oun coppie was so much used to peices that I have sent yow a trew double of it; And have transcrybed out of a late letre of Mr Leibnitz two or three passages which relate to your self and your excellent Essay upon humane understanding, which I have subjoyned to the foot of the paper of Remarques.[2] Yow may see Sir / Whow much

[1] The composition is 'Quelques remarques sur le livre de Mons. Locke intitulé Essay of Understanding'. The date of composition is unknown; it is perhaps 1695. On 7/17 March 1696 Leibniz, who was at Hanover, sent Burnett a copy; he had already had a copy made formerly ('que j'avois déjà fait copier autres fois'; for the form *autres-fois* see Cotgrave). On 17/27 July he wrote to Burnett, permitting him to show the copy to anyone and expressing a wish that Locke should see it. On receiving this permission Burnett sent the copy to Alexander Cunningham, who showed it to Locke: Leibniz, *Phil. Schriften*, ed. Gerhardt, iii. 180; p. 86 below.

There are three copies of the 'Remarques' in the Lovelace Collection, MS. Locke c. 13. Locke obtained a copy shortly before 22 February of this year: above, pp. 8–9; it is perhaps ff. 158^{c}–161. The present copy is probably ff. 158^{a-b}; it was written for Burnett and bears, written by him, the excerpt which he transcribed from Leibniz's letter; it is apparently the original of the version sent by Locke to Molyneux and printed as part of no. 2243 (Locke made some corrections on these two copies from one another). The third copy, ff. 162–5, was sent by Le Clerc to Locke: p. 73; it was corrected by Leibniz and is the most important version. For the texts and their history see Leibniz, *S.S.* VI. vi, introd., pp. xvii–xix, and p. 3 (this volume is devoted to Leibniz's criticism of Locke). The Le Clerc text is printed there, pp. 4–9, and as Appendix I of this volume.

[2] A passage from Leibniz's letter of 1/11 February 1697: Leibniz, *S.S.* VI. vi. 9 n.; p. 93 below.

he desyreth even to be instructed from Yow; And (if I be not much mistaken efter I have knouen him so long) will even be glad to be overcome by yow; provyding knowledge be the more advanced. As he is of the most universal learning, and fyne spirit of any (I think) beyond seas, so He is of such ane excellent temper That if Treuth cary away the pryze he is rejoysed On what ever syde the victory be: Bot it is most lyklie yow will aggree in the same sentiments in most things. I am to wryte back to him againe within 10 or 12 dayes.[1] Iff yow have any word to him, or any Commands for me I shall be glad of ane opportunity to serve you both. Your conjunct labours after trew Ideas of knouledge will certainly stryke out a light which most be both bright and spreading. I shall be glad to know when I may have the happinesse of seeing your heir in toun, For it is not possible to expresse in a letter the great caracter Monseur Leibnitz heth of yow as he heth so amplie and often declared Himself to

Sir

your most humble and devoted servant

THOMAS BURNETT

of Kemney

London=Westminst:

24 Martij –97

I shall be glad to have the account of your recept of the inclosed, with the pleasure of your commands which yow may direct for mr Thomas Burnet of Kemney Scots gentleman in the house of Mistris Barham in Park-street[2] Westminster, over against the bishop of Wosters lodgings there, This Adresse will be most sure.

Sir as the desyre to serve you heth given me the boldnesse to wryt to yow with the inclosed, so from the same reason I take the libertie to acquaint your Curiositie with the advyces I have in Mr Leibnitz last letter. That Mr Spanheim att Berlin his second Volume upon Julians works is actually printed now with the best and most notes upon S Cyrillus his answer the former volume containing only the text of julians work ittself.[3] There is a great

[1] Burnett wrote to Leibniz on 3 May: Leibniz, *Phil. Schriften*, ed. Gerhardt, iii. 197–9.

[2] The southern part of what is now Queen Anne's Gate. Stillingfleet died there in 1699.

[3] See no. *1802*. Burnett is repeating information sent to him by Leibniz on 1/11 February: *Phil. Schriften*, ed. Gerhardt, iii. 189. The book has a single title-page, dated 1696 (dedication 12 April), but is in two volumes. Notice in *Acta Eruditorum*, November 1696 (pp 489–500).

eloge of dr Bentley upon the occasion of the explicatione of a passage off Philostratus. The Epithete he gives him is *Insulis Britannis Oriens Sidus* or some such lyk words.[1] Mr Cuninghame came to me yesterday, And tels me he had received your letter to the bishop of Woster for Mr Leibnitz.[2] I am to send him a parcel of good english books with the parting of the plenipotentiaries;[3] Bot I am perswaded your peice (Especiallie in a present) will be more acceptable then the whole bundle. I take the freedom also to lett yow know That being with Dr Bentley the day efter your letter to the bishop came out, he had read it all over the night before; And was mightelie well pleased (as he said) with the elegant maner of wryting in it, finding it nervous, and yet not one hard word against the bishop in it.[4] Such wryting will never creat any more then a civile dispute. He sent your book the same day to Woster. Mr Leibnitz desyres earnestly in his last the best peices writt of late about the restoring of the coin, and of trade. I have sent him what I had by my self of Mr Launds[5] and what is attribut to yow on that subject.[6] As there is non can inform me better what are worth the buying of these peices; So I wold gladlie have a list of the best, That I might send him the titles at leist first. I remember To have seen once a peice with a catalouge of what was then come out upon coin and trade printed at the end of it: Bot I could nather see nor hear of it againe

Address: For John Lock Esq;

Endorsed by Locke: T: Burnet 24 Mar $9\frac{6}{7}$ Answered 29

2229. Dr. Robert South to Locke, 25 March 1697 (*2314*)

B.L., MS. Locke c. 18, ff. 167–8. For the writer see no. *102* n., etc. He and Locke knew one another at Christ Church if not already at Westminster.

Sir

I have received and perused your Learned Answer to Bishop Stillingfleet; and that with Equall Satisfaction and Instruction: and I cannot tell whether it delighted me more, as the Noble

[1] 'Novum idemque iam lucidum litteratæ Britanniæ sidus': 'Observationes', p. 19. This statement is not from Leibniz's letter.

[2] See Burnett to Leibniz, 3 May, as above.

[3] Pembroke set out with the king on 24 April: *London Gazette*, 26 April.

[4] Bentley had been Stillingfleet's chaplain and was now a prebendary of Worcester.

[5] Lowndes.

[6] Locke sent Burnett for Leibniz a copy of *Several Papers relating to Money, Interest and Trade etc.*, *1696*: Burnett to Leibniz, 3 May, as above; Locke's distribution list.

Product of your Philosophy, or as a Testimony of your Kindnesse and Respect to your Old Acquaintance.

It is not for me either in point of Discretion or good manners to interpose in the Controversy between you; But every Judicious Reader must oun you to be much Waryer, and more exact, and Distinct in your Answers, than your Adversary has bin in his Arguments, or perhaps is Capable of Being: for all that this man Writes, seemes (to me at least) to have bin written Apace and, (as I shrewdly suspect) will be forgotten so too.

If I should except against any Thing in your Book it would be, that you have given too much Honour to One who desires it too much, to deserve it; I have Known the man of old, and for that Reason, cannot but thin⟨k⟩[a] of him as I doe.[1]

But still I ought by no meanes to question, but that Such a man as You Know very well what you doe, whether I understand the Reason of it or no.

The Onely Concerne, I have upon me Now, is to acknowledge (which I doe most gratefully) the favour of the Worthy Present you made me, and the Honour you have thereby passed upon

Worthy Sir

Your very humble and much obliged servant

ROBERT SOUTH

25 March 97

Address: For the Worthy esteemed mr John Lock etc. These.

Endorsed by Locke: R: South 25 Mar 97 Answered 5 Apr:

2230. LOCKE to CORNELIUS LYDE, 26 March 1697 (*2226*, 2290)

The Pierpont Morgan Library, New York. Transcribed from Xerox print. Answers no. *2226*.

Oates 26 Mar 97

Sir

I am very sure Mr Clarke will be glad to know that you have soe carefully given your assistance for the raiseing of the tax which I

[a] *Page torn.*

[1] I have failed to trace a particular clash.

assured my self you would doe and that you would not neglect such an oportunity of serveing your country by[a] doeing equall justice to every body. noething makeing the taxes come with more unwillingnesse and discontent from the people than when they see others doe not bear an equall share in the burthen with them.

I thank you for your care about Hannys rent. I thinke you propose well to pay away the hammerd money you have of mine for my taxes at the rate of 5s–8d per ounce as the act allows,[1] and therefor I desire you will with that money pay soe many months of my taxes for those two estates of mine in Publoe and Belton as that money will be sufficient to satisfie, and the collectors I thinke must give receits for soe many months taxe received that it may not be demanded again, and my tenants must be acquainted with how much you have paid or rather have copys of the collectors receits put into their hands that they may not pay it again. I hope the ill state of our money will now quickly be at a full end and you will have noe more trouble of this kinde. I am sorry it occasions you any now, but as I doe not this to make any gain of the money at 5s–8d per ounce soe I would not willingly loose any more by it, haveing lost enough already in the Guineas.

The businesse of the lease to Francis Carpenter I must defer till I goe to London because I doe not use to set my hand and seale till I have advised with those who are better skild in those matters than I, by which means I have all my life avoided suits and controversies. I am

Sir

your most humble servant

JOHN LOCKE

Address: For Cornelius Lyde Esquire at Stanton Weeke To be left with Mr Codrington in Highstreet Bristoll

Postmarks: MR 30; GC (?)

[a] *Doubtful reading; page torn?*

[1] 8 and 9 Wm. III, c. 2, § 2: p. 58 n. 1.

2231. Locke to Edward Clarke, 26 [March] 1697 (2215, *2234*)

B.L., MS. Locke b. 8, no. 119. Printed in Rand, p. 516. The correct month from Clarke's endorsement and from his answer, no. *2234*, which is evidently dated correctly.

Oates 26 May 97

Dear Sir

I writ to Mr Cor: Lyde as you desired me about acting in raiseing the tax. He writes me word in a letter I received this post that he hath done soe, and by what he says I guesse he hath been very active. He desires me to give you his service

If I were not soe before yet I am now perfectly of the minde that it is best the money Sir St: Evans promises should be paid to Mr Churchill. But I fear the difficulty is not soe great where to pay it as how to get it

My Lady returnes you her very many thanks for the trouble and pains you have been at in the businesse depending and is very sensible how much she is obleiged to you for the hopes you give her that it will now quickly be brought to a conclusion

That[a] which you tell me in the postscript of your last heartily vexes me, as I beleive it will you when I come to speake with you, there is noe help now, it must now take its course. I am

Dear Sir

your most humble servant

J Locke

My service to the Batchelor. Pray let the inclosed goe with yours to the post house

Endorsed by Clarke: Mr. Lock to Place the money in mr. Churchills handes that Sir St: Evans payes etc: Received the 29th. March 1697. Answered the 30th.

2232. Samuel Bold to [Locke], 26 March 1697 (*2312*)

B.L., MS. Locke c. 4, ff. 19–20. The letter is addressed to the author of *The Reasonableness of Christianity*; whatever Bold may have guessed or heard or read, he had no certain knowledge of the authorship. He sent the letter to the Churchills for forwarding: p. 69.

Samuel Bold, 1649–1737, was vicar of Shapwick, Dorset, from 1674 to 1682; rector of Steeple in the Isle of Purbeck from 1682 until his death (the

[a] *Preceded by a symbol*, q *for quære, apparently not written by Clarke or Locke.*

rectory of Tyneham was joined to that of Steeple in 1722): *D.N.B.*; Dorset Nat. Hist. and Archæol. Soc., *Proc.* lxxiii (1951), 160; lxxiv (1952), 60, 77. His earliest publication is a sermon, 1675: *T.C.* i. 210. In 1682 his sermon against persecution was published by Richard Janeway. Awnsham Churchill published for him first in 1683; from 1697 onwards the Churchills published five tracts by him in vindication of *The Reasonableness of Christianity* and the *Essay* (they were reissued with a collective title-page in 1706). Locke also befriended him, and it was to him that Locke dictated 'Some Thoughts concerning Reading and Study for a Gentleman' (the original manuscript, which is among Desmaizeaux's papers in the British Museum (Sloane MS. 4290, ff. 11–14) is in Bold's hand). At the time when he wrote the present letter Bold was already involved in the controversy about the *Reasonableness*. In a course of sermons on Philippians he preached one on ch. 3, v. 8. He did not intend to print it, but finding 'the *Proposition* laid down in that Sermon, most unmercifully traduced by Mr. *Edwards*, in his Books writ against *The Reasonableness of Christianity*, etc.', he published it with an answer to Edwards as *A Short Discourse of the True Knowledge of Christ Jesus. To which are Added, Some Passages in the* Reasonableness of Christianity, *etc. and its* Vindication. *With some* Animadversions *on Mr.* Edwards's Reflections *on the* Reasonableness of Christianity, *and on his Book, Entituled,* Socinianism Unmask'd: for this see Bold's *Reply*, preface. Edwards attacked this piece in *A Brief Vindication of the Fundamental Articles of the Christian Faith . . . with some Animadversions on two other late Pamphlets, viz. Mr.* Bold . . .: *T.C.* iii. 21. Bold answered this in *A Reply to Mr.* Edwards's *Brief Reflections on A Short Discourse*, etc., which he mentions in no. *2233*.

Locke owned copies of eleven pieces (1680–99) by Bold, including the *Short Discourse* and the *Reply*: L.L., nos. 374–84; eight pieces (1695–9) by Edwards: L.L., nos. 1024–30[a]; and *Animadversions on . . . the Reasonableness . . .*, Oxford, 1697: L.L., no. 702.

Honoured Sir

I have now read your very Rational, exact, and ful Answer to mr Edwards's books.[1] which very much confirms me in my perswasion of your pious Design, and most Judicious procedure in your most excellent Treatise The Reasonableness of Christianity etc. You have pinn'd matters so closely on mr Edwards, and set forth the Truths you before published in such a clear light, and given such a perfect Demonstration of them, if mr Edwards[a] do not publickly acknowledge his faults, and set his seal to what you have so fully prooved, I shal be hard put to it, to maintain the Charitable opinion of Him, I have hitherto striven to entertain. We are certified of a very eminent Prophet, that He had such passions as other men had.[2] But I cannot but bewail the Clergy, that they so

[a] *MS.* Edws, *cramped at end of line.*

[1] The *Second Vindication*: see below and p. 69.

[2] Elijah: James 5: 17.

ordinarily suffer (if not provoke) their passions to transport and carry them to greater Indecencies, than the rest of mankind commonly do. As if it were their priviledge to set no bounds to themselves, but were to exceed the generality in their faults and Intemperancies to as great a degree, as they conceit their Office doth raise them above the vulgar. How deplorable is our case, when those who are peculiarly engaged to study the Christian Religion, do make it their busyness, rather to give the world proofs of the Raging Furious Spirit of a Party, than of the meek and charitable spirit of that Holy and Good Religion they are obliged to instruct people in? You have bin treated very Injuriously, and with detestable Disingenuity. I am glad to finde you resent It so calmly, and with a temper so becoming a sincere Disciple and follower of your Meek and patient Lord, And that you have made so good a use of your Adversaries base, and unworthy Conduct, as to take occasion from It, to contribute the most, that I think any man hath done to set the world right, and bring people to be Judicious and good Christians. I heartily pray, that you may abundantly see the desired success of your Labours, and may stil go on in such ways as you conceive most proper, to heal our Divisions, and reduce us all to a true Christian Frame. Let not men's Ingratitude discourage you. Be not weary in wel doing, in due time you shal reap. How ill so ever you are treated here, you serve a good and Faithful Master, who wil not forget your work and Labour of Love which you have shewed towards his Name. your Reward is with your Lord. You have given a more satisfactory account of the Covenant of Grace,[1] than I ever mett with in any books on that Subject. You have directed us all, to the true and right way of pressing people to read and study the Holy Scriptures.[2] I am entirely beholden to you, for helping me to observe and improve the Divine wisdom in our Saviours Conduct, to the resolving of several doubts, which must have retained much strength, without the Light you have given for the removing of them. You have fixed (I think) on the only proper and effectual method to convince and bring the Deists to espouse Christianity.[3] They are generally (as far as I can guess) persons of good parts, and

[1] The reference is probably general rather than to the passages dealing specifically with the Covenant: *Reasonableness*, 1695, pp. 193–9, 298–9.

[2] This apparently refers to the opening passage of the *Reasonableness*; the rest of the book exemplifies the principles stated there.

[3] Locke said that this was the principal object of the *Reasonableness*: no. *2002* n.

if they wil but approve themselves Honest, I apprehend you have done them, as wel as Christianity it self, the greatest and best service it is possible for man to do them. Sir, I thank you most heartily for your charitable and kind Acceptance of my mean papers, and for the great Honour you have done me, in condescending to take notice of me, in your publishing your further thoughts upon the subject treated of, And that you have bin pleased to acquaint the publick, as wel as me with the True History of the birth of your Reasonableness of Christianity as delivered in the Scriptures, and your design in publishing It, by so particular and obliging an Address to me.[1] I wish your expressing so great Respect to me, who have lain under an Ill eye, ever since I appeared against Persecution,[2] may not prove some prejudice to your most excellent Book. Had I known you would have stooped so low as to vindicate my sermon and Animadversions against mr Edwards's Postscript[3] (for which singular favour I return you my most solemn thanks) I would not have troubled the publick with my Insignificant Reply to Him, which was writ in haste, and hath some things not so clearly expressed, as they might have bin, had I taken a little more time, before I had sent them to the press; but as it happens, A hasty writer, is answered in his own way. but all my defects are fully made up by that compleat answer you have bin pleased to give to His Reflections on what I had writ. Sir I have a very tender and Affectionate sense of the mighty obligations I am under to you, in that you have not only defended the cause, but me too, who am

Sir,

Your Most Humble and obliged servant

SA: BOLD

March. 26th 1697.

Steeple. near Wareham Dorsetshire

Address: To the author of the R. of C: etc. present

Endorsed by Locke: S. Bold 26° Mar 97

[1] It is printed in the form of a letter to Bold in the preface of the *Second Vindication*.

[2] On 26 March 1682, when the brief for the persecuted Huguenots was read at Shapwick, Bold preached a sermon which he published as *A Sermon against Persecution*; it went through four editions in the year. L.L., no. 378 (an edition dated 1683). It was presented by the grand jury of Dorset, whereupon Bold published *A Plea for Moderation towards Dissenters*, 1682. L.L., no. 379 (the issue of 1683). He was then prosecuted in the episcopal and civil courts and was imprisoned and fined: *D.N.B.* (The 1683 issue of *A Plea*, which, like that of 1682, was published by R. Janeway, has on its last page an advertisement by Awnsham Churchill.)

[3] The animadversions appended to his *Brief Vindication*.

2233. SAMUEL BOLD to AWNSHAM [and JOHN?] CHURCHILL, 26 March 1697 (*2257*)

B.L., MS. Locke c. 4, f. 14.

Steeple March 26th. 1697.

Worthy Sirs

I received the last week yours with the second vindication of the Reasonableness of christianity etc (the most Rational and Compleat Answer I ever saw to any book) and mr Locks Answer to the Bishop of worcester, which is excellently wel done, and I am very glad He hath answered that Chapter so far as concerns his Essay, For some weeks agoe some of the Clergy giving me a visit (which they seldom do) they were pleased to ask me what I thought of my Incomparable Author Mr Lock (or to that effect) now that great man the Bishop of worcester had shewn the weakness and the dangerousness of his chief principles in that Book I so admired, his Essay on Humane Understanding? whilst I paused a little, one seemed to express his apprehension that I had not read the Bishops book. I then answered I had, and did wonder so great a man should write so little to the purpose, and in that manner He had done in that chapter with respect to mr Lock, for, said I, the Bishop doth not quote right, He misrepresents mr Locks sense, and his own Arguments are not concluding. This occasioned a little heat, but I fetched down both books, and made out what I said so clear in several instances they could not reply a word. But at last concluded, the mistake must be in me, for they could not believe a man of such prodigious learning and Reason should be out. upon which I desired we might entertain our selves with other subjects, for I did not think it worth the while to contend with persons when they did manifest they laid more stress on a person's name, than on sensible evidence and strict reasoning. I hope people will now be satisfied. for Mr lock book is a most delicate, neat, and clear answer. I received 12 of my Replies.[1] but the other two books mistook their way, and I suppose have lost themselves. I thank you for all; I have inclosed a letter which I desire you to superscribe to the Author of the Reasonableness, and to send It to him as soon as you can. I am

your obliged friend and servant

SA: BOLDE.

[1] *A Reply to Mr.* Edwards's *Brief Reflections*: p. 66 n.

Address: To Mr Awnsham Churchill Bookseller at the Black Swan in Pater-Noster-Row London post paid 6d

Postmark: MR 29

Endorsed by Locke: S: Bold 26 Mar. 97

2234. EDWARD CLARKE to LOCKE, 30 March 1697 (2231, *2239*)

B.L., MS. Locke c. 6, f. 119. Printed in Rand, p. 509. Answers no. 2231; answered by no. 2242.

London March the 30th. 1697.

Deare Sir,

Your Letter, with the inclosed for Mr. Lyde came safe, and I have putt it into the Post-House with my own hand etc:

Sir[a]– St: Evans hath paid fifty pounds to Mr. Churchill for your use, and hath one of the Notes you left with mee Delivered up to Him–[a]

Pray give my humble service to my Lady, And acquaint her Ladyship That the Bishop[1] assures mee, That Doctor Cornwall's security[b]– is Renewed for–[b] the money in Baines his Handes according to my desire, soe That there will bee noe need of my Lady's Writeing to the Bishop at all about it etc:

The Bishop will convey the securityes, that are Renewed, to my Lady the next time Sir Francis Returns to Oates, And I will use my utmost endeavours to gett every thing else settled before the Bishop leaves the Town; I desire my Lady's Excuse for not Writeing to Her, indeed I have not time, But I am, Her Ladyships And

your most Affectionate Faithfull servant

EDW: CLARKE

The College are Intirely yours etc:

I am concern'd that any thing in my last Letter should vex you, But I thought it was necessary for mee to acquaint you with what I did at that time, since which I have taken effectuall Care, That it shall not come out 'till the next Terme, and before that time, I presume what ever is Design'd to bee added will bee conveyed to mee etc.[2]

a–a *Marked by Locke for attention.* b–b *MS.* security is Renewed is Renewed for

1 Dr. Edward Fowler.

2 This may refer to the third edition of *Two Treatises of Government*. It did not appear until 1698. The alterations from the second edition are slight.

2235. *J. Bonville, 30 March 1697*

Address: These, For John Locke Esqr. [at Oates, by Joslyn, Bishops Stortford]
Frank: Edw: Clarke:
Postmarks: MR 30; GC
Endorsed by Locke: E: Clarke 30 Mar 97 Answered Apr. 9.

2235. JOHN BONVILLE to LOCKE, 30 March 1697 (*2220*, *2368*)

B.L., MS. Locke c. 4, ff. 78–9.

London march the 30th: 97

Honoured Cousin

Sir I hope you have Received mine sent Last week. I have got nothing don yet Consirning our Matters. our Coman counsell man went with me to the Comistiners and they Tould us it was to soone yett. I have been with severall Coman counsell men In severall wards who are my Aquaintanc, and are Asersers, to understand what method they take. And I doe finde as for stocks it is much as it was Last yeare, and I Apprehend as for bonds and bills upon Interest, will fall very short what it was Exspected, I find All of This minde, what need I be at soe much charg, when I Know my mony Is in Honist hands, and I have noe occation to call it in, An honist man will not tak Any Advantage, tho ther Is such and act, but If I find my mony dubyus: I can but goe and In form against my self, and it is but to pay double, and this will be well Enough. This I find to be the Language of All people and of sum, that this Is their case,

Last night I was going Throw Aldgate and mett Sir Frances going towards white chapple, he Tould me that in the morning he heard that you was prety well, which with my heart I was glad to heare, I bless god we are prety well Att presant, No more at presant, I Am

Deare Cousin
your Obliged Kinsman and faithfull Sarvant
J: BONVILLE

Address: For Mr Locke [at Oates, by Joslyn, Bishops Stortford]
Postmark: MR 30
Endorsed by Locke: J: Bonville 30 May 97

2236. JEAN LE CLERC to LOCKE, 30 March/9 April 1697 (*2174*, *2285*)

B.L., MS. Locke c. 13, ff. 113–14. Printed in Bonno, *Le Clerc*, pp. 98–9.

A Amsterdam le 9 d'Avril 1697.

En remettant, Monsieur, de vous répondre d'un ordinaire à un autre, il est arrivé que je vous suis devenu plus redevable qu'auparavant, en recevant le Thucydide, que vous m'avez fait la grace de m'envoier.[1] Je vous en suis bien obligé, et je tâcherai de vous en marquer ma reconnoissance; car quoi que j'eusse déja l'édition de *Portus*,[2] qui étoit la meilleure, j'ai été ravi d'avoir celle d'Angleterre, étant amoureux, comme je le suis, de cette espece de livres. Je voudrois que mon *Hammond* fût déja achevé pour vous rendre un volume de la même taille. Cependant l'histoire de la Médecine, composée par mon frere, et trois volumes de ma façon, dont deux sont l'*Ars Critica* et l'autre un petit livre sur les Loteries, composé et publié il y a près d'un an, mais sans nom, tiendront la place d'un plus grand volume. J'ai lû avec plaisir les défenses de la *Reasonnableness.* C'est un terrible homme, que Mr. Edward, et qui sent le Jurieu, dans la foiblesse et dans la violence des raisonnemens. Il seroit bien facile de l'étriller. Je voudrois bien savoir si Mr. Burnet, l'Auteur des *Archæologiæ*, a offert de se retracter, comme il le dit.[3] Une autre chose, que j'ai oublié plus d'une fois de vous demander, c'est ce que Mr. *Bury* est devenu. Mr. Jurieu a débité dans son *Latitudinaire*, qu'il avoit été honteusement déposé, et même *convaincu d'adultere*. Je serois fâché que cela fût vrai, et s'il ne l'est pas, je m'étonne que Mr. *Bury* le laisse passer, s'il est vivant, car M. Jurieu dit le tenir de l'Evêque d'Excester sa partie.[4] Il ne paroit rien de nouveau ici qui vaille la peine. Mr. Coste travaille à vostre Ouvrage, mais un peu lentement. Il me disoit dernierement que s'il trouvoit occasion d'entrer dans une maison de condition, en qualité de précepteur, il seroit ravi d'en profiter. C'est un fort

[1] The edition by Dr. John Hudson (no. *3248*), Oxford, 1696: pp. 167–8.

[2] Æmilius Portus, a scholar of Italo-Cretan origin: *A.D.B.*; published at Frankfurt, 1594. For his work in the edition see p. 167, n. 7.

[3] This is Thomas Burnet, Master of the Charterhouse. It was not he but John Woodward who, according to Edwards, was willing to retract some of his opinions: *Some Thoughts concerning the Several Causes . . . of Atheism* (no. *1954* n.), pp. 83–4.

[4] Jurieu's book is *La Religion du Latitudinaire*, 1696; I have not seen a copy. Bury appended a vindication of himself to his *Latitudinarius Orthodoxus*, 1697. The bishop of Exeter is Sir Jonathan Trelawney (bishop 1689–1707; *D.N.B.*); he was *ex officio* visitor of Exeter College.

honête homme, et qui seroit bien capable de s'acquiter de cet emploi. Il ne sait l'Anglois que par les[a] livres, c'est à dire, qu'il l'entend lors qu'il le lit, mais qu'il ne le sauroit parler, non plus que moi, faute d'habitude. Si quelcun de vos amis avoit besoin de précepteur, et qu'il lui donnât de quoi s'entretenir, il ne sauroit trouver d'homme plus sage et plus reglé, outre qu'il sait beaucoup de choses utiles pour un emploi comme celui-là, les belles lettres, l'histoire, etc. Vous mobligerez, Monsieur, si vous voulez bien vous en informer, et de m'en avertir, si vous trouviez quelque chose de semblable. Vôtre livre de L'éducation a été traduit en Flammand, sur la derniere édition.[1] Si vous souhaitiez de le donner à Mr. de Limborch en cette Langue, qu'il entend sans doute mieux que la Françoise, vous n'avez qu'à me le marquer. Je suis fâché d'avoir si peu d'occasions d'envoier des paquets en Angleterre, il y auroit déja longtemps que vous auriez les livres, dont je vous ai parlé. On attend avec impatience la flotte de Rotterdam, parce qu'on ne peut rien envoier, que par le retour du convoi. Cependant mon paquet sera prêt pour la premiere occasion. Je suis, Monsieur, de tout mon coeur Vôtre très-humble et très-obeïssant serviteur

J LE CLERC.

Mr. Leibnits Mathematicien de Hanovre aiant ouï dire, qu'on traduisoit vôtre ouvrage, et qu'on l'alloit imprimer, a envoié ici à un de mes amis ce jugement qu'il en fait, comme pour le mettre à la tete.[2] Cependant il a été bien aise qu'on vous le communicât, et il m'a été remis entre les mains, pour cela. On m'a dit mille biens de ce Mathematicien; il y a longtemps que *magna et præclara minatur*,[3] sans rien produire, que quelques demonstrations détachées. Je croi néanmoins qu'il ne vous entend pas, et je doute qu'il s'entende bien lui-même, ce qui soit dit entre nous. J'attendrai que Mylord

[a] *Or* le; *badly written.*

---

[1] It was published at Rotterdam; the engraved title-page is dated 1697, the printed, 1698. It appeared probably about November: p. 261.

[2] See p. 60. Leibniz mentioned the piece in a letter to Henri Basnage de Beauval (*D.B.F.*) about August 1696. Basnage asked for it, suggesting that it might be prefixed to the translation now being made at Amsterdam (Coste's translation). On 3/13 February Leibniz sent it to Basnage, but was averse to its being added to the book without Locke's permission: Leibniz, *Phil. Schriften*, ed. Gerhardt, iii. 127–8, 130, 134. Basnage and Le Clerc were friends. This text of 'Quelques remarques' is printed as Appendix I to this volume.

[3] 'He threatens us with great and fine things.' Varied from Horace, *Satires* II. iii. 9 ('multa et praeclara minantis'), of delayed literary production.

Privy-seal[1] soit ici, pour lui présenter moi même ma Critique,[2] parce que ce sera une occasion plus commode pour le remercier.

Address: A Monsieur Monsieur Locke, in little Lincoln's inne fields. at Mr. Pawlings, over against the plough London.
Postmark: AP 10
Endorsed by Locke: J: le Clerc 19 Apr 97 Answered May. 8

2237. FRANCIS NICHOLSON to LOCKE, 30 March 1697 (*2446*)

B.L., MS. Locke c. 16, ff. 157–8. Francis Nicholson, 1655–1728; lieutenant-governor of Virginia 1690–2; governor of Maryland 1694–8; of Virginia 1698–1705; etc.: *D.N.B.*; *Dict. American Biog.*

Maryland Port Annapolis March 30. 97.

Right Honourable

I hope you will be pleased to excuse this presumption: But I should be very much wanting in my Duty, if I did not own how much I am obliged to your Honour for being my Friend, and having a good opinion of me, which Edward Randolph Esquire[3] writ me an account of. Though I have not the happiness of being personally acquainted with the most ingenious and learned Authour of *Human Understanding*; yet if he is pleased to continue his favourable opinion of me, I shall endeavour (God willing) not to doe any thing which may give You cause to withdraw your Honours Protection of me.

The Reverend Mr. James Blair[4] president of the Royal College of William and Mary[5] in Virginy, is desired by us the Trustees of the said College to go for England, in order to sollicite some Affairs of the said College. This is designed (God willing) by him. And if your Honour pleaseth he will give You a full account of all the Virginy Affairs, especially concerning the College. And to inrich the Library of it, we are humble Intercessours for all your Honours Works.

[1] Lord Pembroke. [2] The *Ars Critica.*

[3] 1632–1703; at this time surveyor-general of Customs in America and deputy-auditor of Maryland: *D.N.B.*; *Dict. American Biog.*

[4] p. 302 n.

[5] The college was founded in 1693 by royal charter; its establishment was due to Blair, who was supported by Nicholson.

An account of this his Majestys Province, is sent by me to your Lordships of the Council of Trade and foreign plantations,[1] so will not trouble your Honour with a repetition of it. I dare answer that tis an honest and true one, though it is but a weak one, which must be owned by him, who craves leave to assure You that I shall look upon my self as very fortunate whenever I shall have the honour of serving You. For upon Notice, it shall cordially be complyed with by Him who desires leave to subscribe him self

Your Honours obliged and obedient humble servant

FR: NICHOLSON

Endorsed by Locke: F: Nicholson 30 Mar 97 Answered 7 Sept.

2238. PAUL D'ARANDA to LOCKE, 4 April 1697 (*2204*, *2260*) with extracts from BENJAMIN FURLY to D'ARANDA, 9/19 February and 2/12 March 1697

B.L., MS. Locke c. 3, ff. 44–5.

London the 4th. of April 1697

Sir

If you thought it a fault to defer answer to mine the small time between receiving it and writing yours of primo March, how much more reason have you to blame my not sooner paying due returne to that, as I should have done had I not been unable to say any thing to the purpose, concerning the gloves sent to Dr. Guenelon, till I could speak to Mr Teut about it, as I have now done; and he tells me that, which I did not before know, the bundle of Gloves was by him ship'd, with other things addressed to his Father, on the same day he received it from me, and on a vessel intending to depart with the convoy then ready to sail, but that, by I know not what accidental hindrance, that ship was left behind then and so has been forced to remain here for want of convoy all the winter, till now that she is sail'd, and now lying at Harwich waiting onely a good wind to put over with the rest of the richly laden fleet under good convoy thence for Holland. he assures me that as soon as the ship arives there the pacquet will be deliver'd by his Father to the Doctor, to whom I will write how it is sent and what is in it, as yours directs; there is not I think any Danger of its being lost if the ship

[1] *Cal.S.P.*, *Col.*, vol. xv, no. 862, dated 27 March 1697; received 21 June; read in Council 7 July. It was accompanied by a collection of documents, no. 864.

arive safe. Young Mr Teut, who pays you his humble service, does not speak of returning to Holland yet, tho he believes his Father will order him home this summer. He has spent this winter in learning the Mathematicks and Italian, on his own desire almost against his fathers will, whose purse being made of a Toad's skin[1] hinders that youths making a fourth part of the improvement he is capable of and inclined to, as if the treasures such parsimony may amasse for him to inherit could be in any measure so valuable to him as the bettering his knowledge and improving the right use of his understanding would be in the enjoyment of the small matter lesse which such attainments might cost now.

I am glad to see my reason for not complying with Mr Furlys order[2] confirm'd by your better judgement.[a] Since[a] I came home being once in company with Mr Charleton, one of the secretarys to the Royal Society,[3] I first told and a few hours after read to him all Mr Furly wrote me of the Germans Cures which you have seen and what he since wrote me on the same subject vizt:

'19th: febr: 1697. S: N:

[D'Aranda repeats, with slight verbal differences, and the omission of the first paragraph, the extract from Furly's letter which he had copied in his letter of 24 February to Locke. He continues with an extract from another letter from Furly:]

'The 12th. March 1697. S: N:

'—Our Sympathetick Gentleman goes on curing: He has lately undertaken three of my next neighbours, one miserably afflicted with the Gout, of which I shall after a while be able to give you a particular account how he succeeds.

'He begins to take upon him, stirs not out of doors now without a Coach and servant, and values himself high, talking of a thousand guldens to cure some great men of our Gouvernment, and makes ordinary merchants that can pay it give him 1, 2 or 300 Ducatons, as they are under more or lesse distempers or pains.'

This last note seems to me as great a proof of his working the great cures pretended to, as can well be desired, it being very improbable

[a] *MS.* Judgement. On Since

[1] Said of covetous persons: *Oxford Dict. English Proverbs.* [2] No. *2197.*
[3] William Charleton (Courten) was never a fellow of the Society; Walter Charleton, M.D. (*D.N.B.*), ceased to be a fellow about 1668. The present secretaries were Sloane and Richard Waller, with Edmond Halley as assistant secretary.

any would give such rates as pay without good assurance that they are not like to be cheated of it. When Mr Furly writes me the promised particulars concerning this mans successe on his gouty neighbour, you shall if you please have copy of what he says.

I have since my coming to Town as well, as by letter to Mr Souverain[1] before, made inquiry for such a french Tutour as you desire for the young gentleman in your house,[2] but do not yet hear of any I should dare recommend to you, who can be had at anything like a moderate rate. We have, as you well observe, tought that people to over value themselves very much; And its difficult finding among them one who is really knowing, of good morals and manners, free from that volage vain humour which renders too many of that country insupportable in the familys where they come, and when one does rarely meet with such a one he can scarce aske a rate more extravagant than he, (especially if ⟨he⟩[a] have any friends acquainted with men of Estates and quality to recomend him) in a little time finds one or other willing to give. I shall continue my inquiry for one to serve you and as soon as I hear of one I think duely qualifyed shall let you know it, mean while it may be necessary that you please to hint to me about what salary he may expect, not to trouble you with advice of such as may happen to think themselves above accepting it. After I had two years since seen many I could not like so well, I was glad to take one who had serv'd Mr Franklin (Post Master General)[3] four years for £15:– per annum to teach my son[4] for £20:– though he knew nothing more than bare Lattin and his native language, because I was assured of his sobriety and modest behaviour, a year since he removing from me by Mr Franklin's giving him a place in the Post-office I took Mr Souverain, a truely valuable man in almost every respect, without making any agreement with him, but believe I must allow him more, because he knows himself not inferior to one La Roche to whom I had in vain offer'd £30:– and he refused on better grounds than I had thought, having since placed himself where he has £50:– per annum while he stays in

[a] *Word supplied;* have *is interlined.*

---

[1] Perhaps the man mentioned in no. 1442.
[2] Francis Cudworth Masham.
[3] Thomas Frankland; second baronet July/August of this year: no. *1366*.
[4] D'Aranda had two sons, Paul, 1685–1732, and William Henry, 1688–1713: *Notes and Queries*, cl (1926), 105, 139.

England and £80:– a year when he shall travel abroad. which I mention onely as proof of what you said and that twill not be easy having one who may be deserving your esteem without giving somewhat more than perhaps your friend had suposed he might be well serv'd for. If you take a clergyman and he have hopes of in time being presented to some benifice it will incline him to be content with much the lower sallary.

My wife owns her obligation to you for the visit was intended her, and is with me much griev'd that your old distemper renders you lesse able to bear the City air than formerly. It's your friends and the publick who will loose by your retirement, and not you, who know how to enjoy your self better out of the worlds noise than others who delight most in't can do in the midst of it. May you receive all the free breathing and farther benefit good contrey air can give, and not wa⟨nt⟩[a] any of those truest comforts which ease of Body, a contented mind, good Books, conver⟨se⟩[a] of a few well chosen friends, and distance from courts can yield. And if there be any thing of your service here in Town which you shall have occasion to employ others more in than if you came oftener hither your self, which you think me capable of any part of, I beg you'l please to dispose allways as freely of me as you would of your own hands; I mean while I am in Town, for I must own that after having long hoped to recover such a measure of health as might enable me to settle to buisinesse here, in order to the better raising my sons in it, under my own eye, now beginning to despair of ever attaining it, and finding the Town does not so well agree with me as cleerer air, I am neer resolving on also retiring to the Country as soon as I can fix on a pleasant wholesomely scituated small habitation, not too far distant from London. While I was at Bath my stomack seem'd perfectly cured by drinking the water, tho my body was kept low and weak by it's, this time, dayly purging me neer as much as those of Epsom[1] would have done, and ever since my coming thence the indisposition in my stomack, returning, has continued on[b] me[b] with some such severe accesses as have brought me very low, tho I still keep a fresh collour, which makes most out of my house think

[a] *Page cut away for seal.* [b] *MS.* onme

[1] A spring of water charged with sulphate of magnesia (Epsom salts). The salt was extracted first by Dr. Nehemiah Grew (no. *363*), who published an account of it in 1695: A. C. Wootton, *Chronicles of Pharmacy*, 1910, i. 340–6; Partington, *Hist. of Chemistry*, ii. 696–7.

me more troubled with melancholy (that I know my self free from) than pain. I have thoughts of going to Bath once more about a month hence, if the Holland pacquet boats having (as it's expected they will) free passage do not tempt me to try the water of Aix la Chapelle which if I should resolve on shall be advised you that if I may be serviceable to you in Holland I may receive your commands to

Sir

Your most humble servant

PAUL D'ARANDA

The tedious length of this the more needs your excuse for my having I doubt given you a second time copy of a letter of Mr Furlys already sent you by a letter I now see I wrote from Bath the 24 february

Address: To John Locke Esqre. [at Oates, by Joslyn, Bishops Stortford]
Endorsed by Locke: P: D'Aranda 4 Apr. 97

2239. JOHN FREKE and EDWARD CLARKE to LOCKE, 6 April 1697 (*2234*, 2242)

B.L., MS. Locke c. 8, f. 227. Written by Freke, apart from Clarke's initials and the address. Answered by no. 2242.

Aprill the 6th 1697

Dear Sir

Yours of the 2d I look on as a direct challenge which I am bound to answer or forfeit my honour what ever reasons might otherwise have to continue safe in silence, but to own the truth to you I had prepared my goose quill to have attaqued you this Post though I had not been provoked to it by your Letter

You say you provoke me to write because I have more leisure than the Grave. I confess I have soe but what if I had nothing to write worth your notice? may not I be as well excused for want of matter as he for want of time? and I assure you till yesterday I neither knew any thing of Publick matters or which concernd you in particular that was worth the postage of a Letter to inform you of

Tis a great while since that mr Popple undertook to tell you that I had spoken to mr Methwin about mr Molyneux and that he received your recomendation very civilly and answered he should always have a great regard for any body you thought worthy of your esteem and you gave soe advantageous a charracter of mr Molyneux he should covet his acquaintance and therefore he must desire the favour of you to recomend him to mr Molyneux and because I had sent you this message by mr Popple I thought it needless to give you any other answer to what you writ to the Grave on that subject about a week after mr Popples Letter was sent to you. But what would you say if after all mr Methwin should not goe into Ireland? I believe twould be a disappointment to others as well as mr Toland, who is gone thither[1] and left I know not how many debts behind him in England notwithstanding to my knowledge he has received the vallue of near 80li since Christmas and above 60li of it by the means of a friend of yours[2]

I have not been at the Great House a good while the Inhabitant[3] is always too busie for me to speak with him or else he is out of Town and tis but fit (as my Lord Shaftesbury said) that when he is at leisure he should be at leisure.[4] When I saw him last he had nearly read your Letter to the B of W[5] with which he declared himself extremly pleased and on Sunday last my Lord Ch Justice Holt held forth in its comendation and a clergieman then presant said he had not read it but heard a man of eminence in the Church say that there was not a word amiss in it and here that you may not be too vain by thinking your self the onely Author of an Answer that is allowd to be excellent give me leave to tell you that the Author of the Reasonableness of Christianity has gaind great fame by his second vindication which is said to be the fullest and perfectest answer that was ever written to any book since Chilingworth[6] and that in this Book he has unanswerably made good what he asserted in his Reasonableness of Christianity. I have endeavourd to inform my self what the universitys say of those answers but cant yet receive any satisfaction therein though I had great hopes to have heard the sentiments of Oxford from one Mr Wynne who is

[1] See p. 82, etc.

[2] Identifiable as Freke; in 1694 Toland regarded Mr. Freke as 'the primum mobile of my happiness': Toland, *Collection of Several Pieces*, ii. 294.

[3] Somers. He was appointed Lord Chancellor on 22 April.

[4] I have not found the remark elsewhere. Although no positive evidence is extant, Freke is likely to have been in contact with Shaftesbury in 1676 and later, and in any case as a friend of Clarke and Locke had access to personal knowledge of him.

[5] The bishop of Worcester; Locke's *Letter* to Stillingfleet.

[6] *The Religion of Protestants*, first published in 1638: no. 849. It was written in answer to books by a Jesuit controversialist.

come thence lately to attend the Lord Pembroke into Holland but I can learn nothing yet from him though I have set a friend on him to chatechize him about it and I hope he will be able to doe it before his departure for the Hague now that his Lordship has putt off his Journey (which was appointed for Thursday next) till Moonday next and if he goe then (as some doubt) he cannot have his Colleague with him for Sir Joseph Williamson though he has got out of his bed for some few days yet is not able to stir out of his chamber[1]

The Earl of Monmouth is it seems recoverd of his health and quitted his lodging in the Tower[2] for a Gentleman told me he saw him this day at the Lord Sunderlands, where Court continues to be made as much or more than ever and tis buzed about that he is bringing the Lord Rochester Malborough and Godolphin into play if soe I fancy my Lord Monmouth[a] and he Cant piss in a Quill[3]

We talk mightily of the haste the King is in to be gone but that is but what is usuall every year about this seazon when the Conclusion of the Session is desired[4]

Saterday last the votes (which you say you see) will tell you the Bill for laying a Duty of 12li–12s a Ton on wine to be paid by the Retailer (which was to have raised Six hundred thousand pounds) was thrown out after it had been read twice and past through the Comittee which put our Ministry into great disorder and made them rage terribly and endeavour to make his Majesty resent it to the utmost and particularly against Sir W Y and Mr Cl[5] the latter of which had all along opposed the Duty and shewn the house unanswerably that it would be noe supply and yet endanger the ruin of our Woollen manufacture but our managers without attempting to answer his reasons would try their strength and found their weakness by the Question

But this day the Court is put at ease again for the Comittee of the Whole House has voted to lay aside the Duty on Woolen manufactures also and that as an equivalent for that and wine one shilling in the pounds more shall be raised on Land and the Dutys

[a] *MS.* Monm̄

[1] Pembroke left London with the king on 24 April; Williamson left on 12 May: Luttrell, iv. 215, 223, 225.

[2] On 30 March the house of lords ordered him to be discharged: *L.J.*

[3] Agree in all things: *O.E.D.*, s.v. Piss, *v.*; see also Quill, *sb*².

[4] Parliament was prorogued on 16 April.

[5] Sir Walter Yonge and Edward Clarke; on 3 April. For the king's and Shrewsbury's views on their conduct see *Shrewsbury Corr.*, pp. 478–9.

of Tonnage and poundage on goods imported onely doubled for 2 years and 3 quarters, which will be a more effectuall supply and the Act or Acts for it may be passed in less time than the Acts for the other Dutys could have been finished soe that probably the parliament will be up by this day fortnight. I shall be glad to see that day

And now I come to the business I should have written to you about this night if I had not received yours yesterday. I have got half a hundred of Chocalat Nutts for you which I think good and cheap and I want your orders to whom to send them. they are now at the College[1] and I must tell you your Sallery may now be received as soon as the Holydays[2] are over of which I shall also inform Mr Churchill

The Grave joins with me in the tender of service to my Lady and her son etc:

We are
Yours
JF E: C:

Address: These, For John Locke Esqr. [at Oates, by Joslyn, Bishops Stortford]
Frank: Edw: Clarke:
Endorsed by Locke: J: Freke 6. Apr 97 Answered 9

2240. William Molyneux to Locke, 6 April 1697 (*2221*, 2243)

The Carl H. Pforzheimer Library, NewYork. Transcribed from photostat. Printed in *Some Familiar Letters*, pp. 190–1. Answered by no. 2254.

Dublin. Apr. 6. 1697.

Honour'd Sir

In my last to you, of March. 16th, there was a Passage relating to the Author of *Christianity not Mysterious*. I did not then think, that he was so near me, as within the Bounds of this Citty. But I find since, that he is come over hither, and have had the Favour of a Visit from him. I now understand (as I intimated to you) that he was born in this Country; but that he has been a great while abroad; and his Education was for some time under the Great Le Clerk.[3]

[1] Probably the cacao-nuts (or beans; no. *1839* n.) taken by Syl to Mrs. Smithsby's lodgings: p. 100. I cannot identify the College.
[2] Easter day this year fell on 4 April. [3] This is untrue: no. *1653*; pp. *661–2*.

But that for which I can never Honour him too much is his Acquaintance and Friendship to you, and the Respects which on all Occasions he expresses for you. I propose a great Deal of Satisfaction in his Conversation; I take him to be a Candid Free Thinker, and a Good Scholar. But there is a Violent sort of spirit that Reignes here, which begins already to shew it self against him; and I beleive will Increase Dayly, for I find the Clergy alarmd to a mighty Degree against him: And last Sunday he had his Welcom to this Citty by hearing himself Harangued against out of the Pulpit by a Prelate of this Country.[1]

I have at last received My most Esteemd Friends Picture; I must now make my gratefull Acknowledgements to you for the Many Idle Hours you spent in Sitting for it to gratify my Desire. I never look upon it but with the Greatest Veneration. But tho the Artist has shewn extrordinary Skill at his Pencil; Yet now I have obtaind Some Part of My Desire, the Greatest remains unsatisfyd; and seing He could not make it Speak and Converse with me, I am still at a Loss. But I find you are resolved, in some Measure to supply even that too, by the Kind Presents you send me of your Thoughts, both in your Letters, and in Your Books as you Publish them. Mr Churchil tels me I am obleidged to you for One or two of this Kind, that you have been pleased to Favour me with. They are not yet come to Hand, but I return you my Hartiest thanks for them. I long indeed to see your Answer to the Bishop of Worcester. But for Edwards, I think him such a Poor Wretch, he Deserves no Notice. I am

Most Worthy Sir
Your Affectionate Humble servant
W: MOLYNEUX

Address: To John Locke Esquire at Mr Pawlings overagainst the Plow-Inn in Little Lincolns Inn Fields London.

Postmark: AP 23

Endorsed by Locke: W: Molyneux 6° Apr 97 Answered May 3

[1] Toland gave an account of his visit to Ireland in *An Apology for Mr. Toland*, 1697. His statements agree with Molyneux's.

2241. [THOMAS FIRMIN?] to [LOCKE?], [8 or 9 April 1697?] (*1954, 2329*)

B.L., MS. Locke c. 6, f. 37. Upper part of a small leaf; the rest torn away. The writer is identifiable by the contents, and more generally by the spelling and handwriting. The letter was probably addressed to Locke, who, as a commissioner for Trade and Plantations, was concerned with the employment of the poor. The date is fixed by the passing of the Royal Lustring Company's bill by the lords. It passed with some amendments on 7 or 8 April: Luttrell, iv. 207 (the lords' *Journals* give no proceedings on these days).

Deare Sir

I Received yours and had answered it soner but that I was willing at the same time to give you an account of the fate of our bill in parliament for the lutestring company[1] which yesterday passed the house of Lords with som small amendments at the desire of the smuglers that appeared in great numbers against it and they good men ought to be incoraged. We Expect this bill will be greatly to the Advantag of the company which of late have suffered so much by bringing in french goods and makeing other in Spitle feilds that for 8 months past we have sold little or nothing, a little time will show the effect . . .[a]

. . . booth linen and woolen. but I have seen one of each sort to goe with boath hands which if people could be brot to is the finest way of spining in the world.[2] I would not advise you to put your country people upon Spining flax they will earne much more in spining wool, my poor people spin 800 yards of yarn for 1d and they are but few that can earne 6d a day tho they work 16 howers. I have made 700 peces of cloth in about 18 months time at 5l a pece one with a nother, and 4 parts in 5 have been paid to the poor have been forward to draw ⟨jo⟩ynt stock. to ⟨who⟩ hath . . .[b]

[a] *Lower part of leaf torn away.* [b] *The rest is missing.*

[1] No. *1926*.

[2] This refers to the use of the double wheel, which is associated with Firmin: p. 236; Fox Bourne, ii. 366 (in the report on trade between England and Ireland, 31 August 1697: ii. 363–72).

2242. LOCKE to EDWARD CLARKE, 9 [April] 1697 (*2239*, *2249*)

Rand, pp. 518–19, as 9 August 1697. Part of word in square brackets supplied by Rand. The month is improbable as Locke was in London about 9 August, and Clarke in Somerset. Dr. Fowler's failure to deliver the securities, and the cacao-nuts, link the letter with nos. *2234* and *2239*, both of which, according to his endorsements, Locke answered on 9 April.

Oates, 9th August, 1697.

Dear Sir,

The Bachelor writ me word that he has got ½ hundred cacao nuts for me. He remembers his friends I see when he does not tell them so. Pray pay him what they cost again, and for your pains I promise you a dish of chocolate when they are made up. Pray give him also my thanks for his very kind letter which I received from him to-day.

Sir Francis was here since your last, but he brought not the securities as you thought he would. The Bishop talked of [deli]vering them to him, but did not. Who can help dreaming?

My Lady has writ again to Cambridge and Chelmsford about Whitehead's bond. I am in some doubt about it. When she has got all the light she can about it, it shall be sent to town.

That which in my last I writ to you should take its course must do so now, and therefore you need not do anything to stop or delay it. I shall satisfy you about it when I see you, and it will be all for the better.

I hope you have none but good news from Chipley and that Mrs. Clarke mends, since I hear nothing more from thence. I shall be heartily glad of it. There being nobody more concerned for you and yours than,

Dear Sir,

your most affectionate humble servant,

J. LOCKE.

My Lady is yours and the College's humble servant.

I cannot but admire the pranky tricks that are in the world. But to me it is strange they should not be se . . . ore.

Endorsed: Mr. Locke to pay for ½ hundred of cacao nuts, etc. Received the 12th August, 1697. Answered in part per Mr. Freke the 13th. And fully the 13th per Sir Francis Masham, etc.

2243. Locke to William Molyneux, 10 April 1697 (*2240*, 2254)

Some Familiar Letters, pp. 192–205. I have filled in the names Popple, Leibnitz, and Smyth, where the editor printed 'Mr. *P*—', etc. Answers no. *2221*; answered by no. *2262*.

Oates, 10 April. 1697.

Dear Sir,

Though I do not suspect that you will think me careless or cold in that small business you desired of me, and so left it in negligent hands, give me leave to send you a transcript of a passage in my friend's letter,[1] which I received last post.

"'Tis a great while since that Mr. Popple undertook to tell you that I had spoken to Mr. Methwin about Mr. Molyneux, and that he received your recommendation very civilly, and answer'd, He should always have a great regard for any body you thought worthy of your esteem; and you gave so advantageous a character of Mr. Molyneux, that he should covet his acquaintance, and therefore he must desire the favour of you to recommend him to Mr. Molyneux."

Thus, my friend, whose words, though in them there be something of complement to my self, I repeat to you just as they are in his letter, that you may see he had the same success I promised you in my last.

In obedience to your commands, I herewith send you a copy of Mr. Leibnitz's paper. The last paragraph, which you will find writ in my hand, is a transcript of part of a letter, writ lately to his correspondent here, one Mr. Burnet, who sent it me lately, with a copy of Mr. Leibnitz's paper. Mr. Burnet has had it this year or two, but never communicated it to me till about a fortnight agone. Indeed Mr. Cunningham procured me a sight of it last summer, and he and I read it paragraph by paragraph over together, and he confessed to me, that some parts of it he did not understand; and I shew'd him in others, that Mr. Leibnitz's opinion would not hold, who was perfectly of my mind. I mention Mr. Cunningham to you, in the case, because I think him an extraordinary man of parts and learning, and he is one that is known to Mr. Leibnitz. To answer your freedom with the like, I must confess to you, that Mr. Leibnitz's great name had raised in me an expectation which the sight of his

[1] Freke's: no. *2239*.

paper did not answer, nor that discourse of his in the acta eruditorum, which he quotes, and I have since read, and had just the same thoughts of it, when I read it, as I find you have. From whence I only draw this inference, That even great parts will not master any subject without great thinking, and even the largest minds have but narrow swallows. Upon this occasion I cannot but again regret the loss of your company and assistance, by this great distance.

I have lately got a little leisure to think of some additions to my book, against the next edition, and within these few days have fallen upon a subject that I know not how far it will lead me. I have written several pages on it, but the matter, the farther I go, opens the more upon me, and I cannot yet get sight of any end of it. The title of the chapter will be Of the Conduct of the Understanding, which, if I shall pursue, as far as I imagine it will reach, and as it deserves, will, I conclude, make the largest chapter of my Essay.[a1] 'Tis well for you you are not near me, I should be always pestering you with my notions, and papers, and reveries. It would be a great happiness to have a man of thought to lay them before, and a friend that would deal candidly and freely.

I hope, e'er this, you and your brother have received printed copies of what the Doctor communicated to the royal society.[2] I presume it is publish'd before this time, though I have not seen it, for Dr. Sloan writ me word, some time since, that it would be speedily, and told me he would send it to you. And, if Mr. Churchill has taken that care he promised me, I hope you have also received my letter to the Bp. of Worcester, and that I shall soon receive your thoughts of it.

The business you proposed to Dr. Smyth is generously designed, and well managed, and I very much wish it success. But will not Dr. Smyth be persuaded to communicate to the world the observations he made in Turky? The discourse I had with him satisfies me they well deserve not to be lost, as all papers laid up in a study are. Methinks you should prevail with him to oblige his country.[3]

[a] *Printed* Fssay

---

[1] The piece was never completed or incorporated in the *Essay*; it was eventually printed as an independent piece in Locke's *Posthumous Works*, 1706. See no. 3647.

[2] This relates to the piece on the Scolopendra: nos. *2170*, *2224*.

[3] Edward Smyth had already contributed to the *Philosophical Transactions* two papers on his observations when at Smyrna: xix. 228–30, 288–90; an extract from the minutes of the Oxford Philosophical Society containing information from him is printed ibid. xx. 295.

Though my paper be done, yet I cannot close my letter till I have made some acknowledgments to you for the many great marks you give me of a sincere affection, and an esteem extremely above what I can deserve, in yours of the 16th. of March. Such a friend, procured me by my Essay, makes me more than amends for the many adversaries it has raised me. But, I think, no body will be able to find any thing mischievous in it, but what you say, which I suspect, troubles some men; and I am not sorry for it, nor like my book the worse. He that follows truth impartially seldom pleases any set of men; and I know not how a great many of those who pretend to be spreaders of light, and teachers of truth, would yet have men depend upon them for it, and take it rather upon their words than their own knowledge, just cook'd and season'd as they think fit. But 'tis time to release you, after so long a trouble. I am perfectly,

Dear Sir,

Your most humble, and most faithful servant,

JOHN LOCKE.

[Enclosure:]

Réflexions de Mr. Leibnitz sur *l'Essay de l'Entendement Humain* de Monsieur Locke.[1]

Je trouve tant de marques d'une penetration peu ordinaire dans ce que Mons. Locke nous a donné sur l'entendement de l'homme, et sur l'education, et je juge la matiere si importante que j'ay cru ne pas mal employer le temps que je donnerois à une lecture si profitable; d'autant que j'ay fort medité moi même sur ce qui regarde les fondemens de nos connoissances. C'est ce qui ma fait mettre sur cette feuille quelques unes des remarques qui me sont venues en lisant son *Essay de l'Entendement*. De toutes les recherches il n'y a point de plus importante, puis que c'est la clef de toutes les autres.

Le premier livre regarde principalement les principes qu'on dit estre nés avec nous. Mons. Locke ne les admet pas, non plus que les idées innées. Il a eu sans doute de grandes raisons de s'opposer en cela aux prejugés ordinaires, car on abuse extremément du nom d'*idees*, et de *principes*. Les philosophes vulgaires se font des principes à leur phantasie, et les Cartesiens, qui font profession de plus d'exactitude, ne laissent pas de faire leur retrenchement des idees preten-

[1] For versions see p. 60, n. 1. In *Some Familiar Letters* this piece is printed in italic, with proper names and special words and phrases in roman. Here it is printed in roman, with the special words and phrases in italic, but the proper names in roman.

dües, de l'etendüe, de la matiere, et de l'ame; voulant s'exempter par là de la necessité de prouver ce qu'ils avancent; sous pretexte que ceux qui mediteront les idées, y trouverent la meme chose qu'eux, c'est a dire, que ceux qui s'accoutumeront à leur jargon et à leur maniere de penser, auront les memes preventions, ce qui est très veritable. Mon opinion est donc qu'on ne doit rien prendre pour principe primitif, si non les experiences et l'axiome de l'identicité ou (ce qui est la même chose) de la contradiction, qui est primitif, puis qu'autrement il n'y auroit point de difference entre la verité et la fausseté; et toutes les recherches cesseroient d'abord, s'il estoit indifferent de dire oüi ou non. On ne sçauroit donc s'empecher de supposer ce principe, dès qu'on veut raisonner. Toutes les autres verités sont prouvables, et j'estime extremement la methode d'Euclide qui sans s'arreter a ce qu'on croiroit estre assez prouvé par les pretendües idées a demontré (par exemple) que dans une triangle un côté est tousjours moindre que les deux autres ensemble. Cependant Euclide a eu raison de prendre quelques axiomes pour accordés, non pas comme s'ils estoient veritablement primitifs et indemonstrables, mais par ce qu'il se seroit trop arretté, s'il n'avoit voulu venir aux conclusions qu'après une discussion exacte des principes: Ainsi il a jugé à propos de se contenter d'avoir poussé les préuves jusqu'à ce petit nombre de propositions, en sorte qu'on peut dire que si elles sont vraies, tout ce qu'il dit l'est aussi. Il a laissé à d'autres le soin de demontrer ces principes memes qui d'ailleurs sont deja justifiés par les experiences. Mais c'est dequoy on ne se contente point en ces matieres: c'est pourquoi Appollonius, Proclus, et autres, ont pris la peine de demontrer quelques uns des axiomes d'Euclide. Cette maniere doit étre imitée des philosophes, pour venir enfin à quelques establissemens, quand ils ne seroient que provisionels; de la maniere que je viens de dire. Quant aux idées j'en ay donné quelque eclaircissement dans un petit Ecrit imprimé dans les *Actes des Sçavans* de Leipzig au mois de novembre, 1684. pag. 537. qui est intitulé *Meditationes de cognitione, veritate, et ideis*, et j'aurois souhaité que Mr. Locke l'êut veu et examiné, car je suis des plus dociles, et rien n'est plus propre à avancer nos pensées que les considerations et les remarques des personnes de merite, lors qu'elles sont faites avec attention et avec sincerité. Je diray seulement ici, que les *idées vrayes* ou *reelles* sont celles dont on est asseuré que l'execution est possible, les autres sont douteuses ou (en cas de preuve de l'impossibilité) chimeriques. Or la possibilité des idées se prouve tant *à priori* par des demonstrations, en se servant de la possibilité d'autres idées plus simples, qu'à *posteriori* par les experiences, car ce qui est ne sçauroit manque d'estre possiblé. Mais les idées primitives sont celle dont la possibilité est indemonstrable, et qui en effet ne sont autre chose que les attributs de dieu. Pour ce qui est de la question, *s'il y a des idées et des verités crées avec nous*, Je ne trouve point absolument necessaire pour les commencemens, ni pour la pratique de l'art de penser, de la decider: soit qu'elles nous viennent toutes de dehors, ou qu'elles viennent de nous, on raisonnera juste pourveu qu'on garde ce que j'ay dit cy dessus et qu'on procede avec ordre et sans prevention. La question de *l'origine de nos idées et de nos maximes* n'est pas préliminaire en philosophie, et il faut avoir fait de grands progrés pour la bien resoudre. Je crois cependant pouvoir dire que nos idées (meme celles de choses sensibles) viennent de nôtre propre fonds, dont on pourra mieux juger par ce que j'ay publié touchant la nature et la communication des substances et ce qu'on appelle *l'union de l'ame avec le corps*. Car j'ay trouvé que ces choses n'avoient pas esté bien prises. Je ne suis nullement pour la *tabula rasa* d'Aristote, et il y a quelque chose de solide dans ce que Platon appelloit *la reminiscence*. Il y a meme quelque chose de plus, car nous n'avons pas seulement une *reminiscence* de toutes nos pensées passées, mais encore un *pressentiment* de toutes nos pensées futures. Il est vray que c'est confusement et sans les distinguer, à peu prés comme lorsque j'entends le bruit de la mer; j'entends celuy de toutes les vagues en particulier qui composent le bruit total; quoique ce soit sans discerner une vague de l'autre: Et il est vray dans un certain sens que j'ay expliqué, que non seulement nos idées, mais encore nos sentimens naissent de nostre propre fonds et que l'ame est plus independante qu'on ne pense, quoi qu'il soit toujours vrai que rien ne se passe en elle qui ne soit determiné.

Dans *le livre ii.* qui vient au detail des idées, j'avoue que les raisons de Mons. Locke pour prouver que *l'ame est quelquefois sans penser à rien*, ne me paroissent pas convainquantes; si ce n'est qu'il donne le nom de *penseés* aux seules perceptions assés notables pour estre distinguées et retenues. Je tiens que l'ame et meme le corps n'est jamais sans action, et que l'ame n'est jamais sans quelque perception. Même en dormant on a quelque sentimens confus et sombre du lieu où l'on est et d'autres choses. Mais quand l'experience ne le confirmeroit pas je crois qu'il y en a demonstration. C'est à peu prés comme on ne sçauroit prouver absolument par les experiences s'il n'y a point de vuide dans l'espace et s'il n'y a point de repos dans la matiere. Et cependant ces sortes de questions me paroissent decidées demonstrativement, aussi bien qu'à Mr. Locke. Je demeure d'accord de la difference qu'il met avec beaucoup de raison entre la *matiere* et *l'espace*. Mais pour ce qui est du *vuide* plusieurs personnes habiles l'ont crû. Monsieur Locke est de ce nombre, j'en étois presque persuadé moy même, mais j'en suis revenu depuis long temps. Et l'incomparable Monsieur Huygens qui étoit aussi pour le vuide, et pour les atomes, commenca à faire reflexion sur mes raisons, comme ses lettres le peuvent temoigner. La preuve du vuide prise du mouvement, dont Mr. Locke se sert, suppose que le corps est originairement *dur*, et qu'il est composé d'un certain nombre de parties inflexibles. Car en ce cas il seroit vray, quelque nombre fini d'atomes, qu'on pouroit prendre, que le mouvement ne sauroit avoir lieu sans vuide; mais toutes les parties de la matiere sont divisibles et pliables. Il y a encore quelques autres choses dans ce second livre qui m'arretent, par exemple lors qu'il est dit chap. 17. que *l'infinité ne se doit attribuer qu'à l'espace, au tems, et aux nombres*. Je crois avec Mr. Locke qu'à proprement parler on peut dire qu'il n'y a point d'espace, de temps, ni de nombre, qui soit infini, mais qu'il est seulement vrai que pour grand que soit un espace, ou temps, ou bien un nombre, il y a toûjours un autre plus grand que luy sans fin, et qu'ainsi le veritable *infini* ne se trouve point dans un tout composé de parties. Cependant il ne laisse pas de se trouver ailleurs, sçavoir dans *l'absolu*, qui est sans parties et qui a influence sur les choses composées, parce qu'elles resultent de la limitation de l'absolu. Donc *l'infini positif* n'étant autre chose que l'absolu, on peut dire qu'il y a en ce sens un idée positive de l'infini et qu'elle est anterieure à celle du fini. Au reste en rejettant un infini composé on ne nie point ce que les Geometres demonstrent de *seriebus infinitis*, et particulierement l'excellent Mr. Newton. Quant à ce qui est dit chap. 30. *de ideis adæquatis* il est permis de donner aux termes la signification qu'on trouve à propos. Cependant sans blamer le sens de Mr. Locke je mets un degrê dans les idées selon lequel j'appelle *adequate* celle où il n'y a plus rien à expliquer. Or toutes les idées des qualités sensibles, comme de la lumiere, couleur, chaleur, n'estant point de cette nature, je ne les compte point parmis les *adequates*, aussi n'est ce point par elles memes, ni *a priori*, mais par l'experience que nous en sçavons la realité, ou la possibilité.

Il y a encore bien de bonnes choses dans le *livre iii.* où il est traité des mots ou termes. Il est très vray qu'on ne sçauroit tout definir, et que les qualités sensibles n'ont point de *definition nominale*, et on les peut appeller primitives en ce sens là. Mais elles ne laissent pas de pouvoir recevoir une *definition réelle*. J'ay montré la difference de ces deux sortes de definitions dans la Meditation citée cy dessus. La *definition nominale* explique le nom par les marques de la choses; mais la *definition reelle* fait connoitre *à priori* la possibilité du defini. Au reste j'applaudis fort à la doctrine de Mons. Locke touchant la demonstrabilité des verités morales.

Le iv. ou dernier livre, où il s'agit de la connoissance de la verité, montre l'usage de ce qui vient d'estre dit. J'y trouve (aussi bien que dans les livres precedens) une infinite de belles reflexions. De faire là dessus les remarques convenables, ce seroit faire un livre aussi grand que l'ouvrage même. Il me semble que les axiomes y sont un peu moins considerés qu'ils ne meritent de l'estre. C'est apparement parce qu'excepté ceux des Mathematiciens on n'en trouve guere ordinairement, qui soient importans et solides: j'ay tache de remédier à ce defaut. Je ne méprise pas les propositions identiques, et j'ay trouvé qu'elles ont un grand usage même dans l'analyse. Il est très vray, que nous connoissons nôtre existence par une intuition immediate et celle de Dieu par demonstration, et qu'une masse de matiere, dont les parties sont sans perception, ne sçauroit faire un tout qui pense. Je ne meprise point l'argument inventé, il y a quelques siecles, par Anselme, qui prouve que l'étre parfait doit exister; quoique je trouve qu'il manque quelque chose à cet argument, parce qu'il suppose que l'estre parfait est possible. Car si ce seul point se démonstre encore, la démonstration toute entiere sera entierement achevie. Quant à la connoissance des autres choses il est fort bien dit, que la seule experience ne suffit pas pour avancer assez en physique. Un esprit penetrant tirera plus de consequences de quelques experiences assez ordinaires qu'un autre ne sçauroit tirer des plus choisies, outre qu'il y a un art d'experimenter et d'interroger, pour ainsi dire, la nature. Cependant il est toujours vray qu'on ne sçauroit avancer dans le detail de la phisique qu'à mesure qu'on a des experiences. Mons. Locke est de l'opinion de plusieurs habiles hommes, qui tiennent que la forme des Logiciens est de peu d'usage. Je serois quasi d'un autre sentiment; et j'ay trouvé souvent que les paralogismes meme dans les mathematiques sont des manquemens de la forme. M. Huygens a fait la même remarque. Il y auroit bien à dire là dessus; et plusieurs choses excellentes sont meprisées parce qu'on n'en fait pas l'usage dont elles sont capables. Nous sommes portés à mespriser ce que nous avons appris dans les écoles. Il est vray que nous y apprenons bien des inutilités mais il est bon de faire la fonction *della crusca*, c'est à dire de separer le bon du mauvais. Mr. Locke le peut faire autant que qui que ce soit; et de plus il nous donne des pensées considerables de son propre crû. Il n'est pas seulement *Essayeur*, mais il est encore *Transmutateur* par l'augmentation, qu'il donne du bon metail. S'il continuoit d'en faire present au public, nous luy en serions fort redevables.

[Note added by Burnett:]

Je voudrois que Mons. Locke eut dit son sentiment a Mons. Cunningham sur mes Remarques, ou que Mons. Cunningham voulut nous le dire librement. Car je ne suis pas de ceux qui sont entestés, et la raison peut tout sur moy. Mais les affaires de negoce detournent Mons. Locke de ces pensées, car cette matiere de negoce est de très grande entendue et meme fort subtile et demi-mathematique, etc.[1]

2244. SYLVESTER BROUNOWER to LOCKE, 10 April 1697 (*2147, 2250*)

B.L., MS. Locke c. 4, ff. 181–2.

Sir

I delivered your letters to Mr: Pawling and Dr: South as soon as I came to Town, and that to mr: Barker[2] the day after; Mr. Pawling I did not see then nor since. Doctor South presents his humble service to you, and thanks you for your Letter, and enquird very kindly after your health, as did Mr: Pollexfen and Mr: Hill[3] the day following; they both present their Service to you. Dr: Cyprianus is in Town and lodges next Door to the Black posts in Germain street. This day I sent per James Lanham 1 Bottle of Orange flower water, and 2 bottles of Hungary water,

[1] For the source of this passage see p. 60. [2] No. *1191*, etc.
[3] Abraham Hill: *D.N.B.* Like John Pollexfen he was a commissioner for Trade and Plantations.

directed to My Lady, tyed, and seal'd, I did not put them in a basket because James Lanham said he could carry them safer without it; I received seven shillings and six pence for them, being so much they cost. I went also with Mr: Churchill to Newgate Market, to look for the yellow time,[1] but there was none in the Market, nor is there any brought, unless when bespoke, which Mr: Churchill did against next Saturday morning, to be put up and sent as you directed. My Country man most humbly thanks My Lady for the kinde Entertainment he received there he is here yet, but expects every day to be called upon to be gone. Since I came to Towne there have been Letters sent from the Board to Biddeford,[a] Barnstaple etc to let them know that the squadron designed for New-found-land is now actually at Spithead, and Colonel Gibson went down to Portsmouth the 8th Instant, to Embark himself and his Forces;[2] Else I know nothing, but that the Instructions for My Lord Bellomont are a patching up in great haste.[3] I humbly thanke My Lady and You for the kindness I received when last at Oates and am

Sir

Your most humble most obedient and most Faithful servant

S BROUNOWER

Whitehall

Aprill the 10th: 1697.

JL

Address: For Sir Francis Masham Bart: Member of Parliament [at Oates, by Joslyn, Bishops Stortford]

Frank

Postmark: AP 10

Endorsed by Locke: S: Brownover 10 Apr. 97 Answered 14

[a] *Or* Biddleford

---

[1] This is listed by Dr. John Beal among the kinds of thyme: *Philosophical Transactions*, xi (1676), 587.

[2] John Gibson, 1637?–1717; knighted 1705: *D.N.B.* The letters were ordered to be sent on 8 April: Board of Trade Journal.

[3] Bellomont was appointed governor of New York, Massachusetts Bay, and New Hampshire, and captain-general during the war of the forces there, on 16 March: *Cal.S.P., Dom.*, 1697, pp. 59–60. His commissions and instructions were under discussion at this time; the draft instructions were approved by the king on 15 April: *Cal.S.P., Col.*, vol. xv, nos. 895, 904, 940. He proved an energetic and honest administrator, if rather too much a Whig partisan: ibid., vols. xvi–xviii, prefaces.

2245. JOHN DERBIE to LOCKE, 10 April 1697 (*2196*)

B.L., MS. Locke c. 7, f. 205.

Sherborne Aprill 10: 1697

Honoured Sir

I was latly at London to waight on you but had not the Hapyness to see you, being out of Towne. Our kinsman John Keene have lernt soe far as the Conntery scoles can teach him, and being desirous for Oxon I am willing to Contrubute to the utmost of my abillity to advance him, but of late mitting with gret lossess cannot doe as I would, if I am at 16 or 20ll year charge its the most I am capapable of doing at present, therfore my Humble request, is to beg your advice and asistence if you think A place may be obtained for him under a good master, I am loath should lose his time, and hoping to have a Lyne from you, shall be very thankfull and remaine

your most Humb servant
JOHN DERBIE

my wife presents her service to you;

Address: To mr John Lock Humbley present

Endorsed by Locke: J. Derbie 10 Apr 97 Answered 21

2246. MARTHA LOCKHART to LOCKE, 15 April [1697] (*2201, 2253*)

B.L., MS. Locke c. 15, ff. 68–9. Year from Locke's endorsement.

London. Apr. 15th

You left me so heartily angery when you went out of town that after the letter I writ to you, that morning without any return, I took a resolution nether by letter, or message you should hear from me: but good nature that still overcomes the poor women and that is so little known that it is allmost not believed by the men, has changed my resolution; and given you this new trouble from me. tho to excuse this eseyness of temper to my self, I have the pretence of some business with you.

I am asham'd it has been so long out of my power, to pay my enttrest money, which indeed was your frend and my untrusty steward, mr Pauling's fault. I have the years inttrest now in my hand, and desire you'le send an order to some body to receive it, and delever me your's, and Mr Bondvill's recipts, and now I must againe renew my complaints to you of Pauling, who I have very folishly forbore he has yet nether seen me, nor given any satisfaction for the 30ll. which I told you he made use of. nor pay'd to the man the debtt he preteend'd of 20 ll pound. so had (or shall he) dy before this matter is adjusted I lose Fifty pound for my folly of trusting a man that before had deceiv'd me he takes I find great advantage of my good nature, on the one hand, and lazyness or unskillfullness on the other. if it be not to Much trouble I will desier you to writ to him, for if he dos provoke me much longer, I will resolve to put it out of my own hand, and I am sure it will not be for his reputation to have this storry known in which a man can invent noe excuse, to Cover an open Breach of trust: what I desire is a discharge of a debtt of 20 ll, he pretend'd for severall monthes to have pay'd (but has not) and now that; this is discover'd, pretends that his haveing answer'd for my debtt, tho with out order, Makes him of right use my money, this 6 months: and that he has noe time to make up an acount he says is due to him for writing over my Cornish leashes[1] for the remaining ten pound. I own to you tho I have in my life gone throw very ill hand's, yet I have not meett with any thing more provoking then this.

My humble service to my lady, tell her I doe extreemly long to wait upon her: that I have had unavoidable hinderances as yet; and at present, I have such a spirit of Matrimony runing throw my small family, that I've not one of your old aquantance left, and have great difficulty to find anew set of servants, to my mind; when this is over I shall make my long inteended vissit to you. in the mean time, doe me the favour to make my excuse to my Cosen Masham, that her Comission's have been delayd, tell her 2 wedings in my family must beg pardon for me; Small was mary'd on sunday. for a week before, and a week affter, ther is nothing to be done. I must still increase this trouble by beging on favour more if you would advise a frend that has Tallies of pro,[2] on the Herditory excise payable in about 20 monthe's to put 'em in to the Bank; on the new proposall,[3] or to keep them till they become due. haveing

[1] No. *1694*, etc.

[2] A tally of pro 'operated as a modern cheque on a banker, being given forth in payment from the Exchequer, as a charge upon some public accountant, for him to pay the sum expressed thereon, out of the revenues in his hands': *O.E.D.* It was made out *pro*, for or in favour of someone. See also Clapham, i. 11 n.

[3] That for the ingrafting of tallies: no. *2154*. The subscription opened on 26 April: Acres, i. 81.

800 ll in tallies, whither it would not be best, to venture on half with a Bank Bill:[1] that way[a] to this I beg your answer. My Sister Forffor[2] gives you her most humble service, and comes abeging to you for advice, her son being still troubld with worms she has been mightyly recomend'd to Rabells drop's,[3] but dares not venture without your advice to give him them, the Child is very much troubled with shiverings, turning on a sudain pale, and often a gresey past rises in his mouth, at first wakening complain's of pain in his Belly: but none of this are constant. tho I have noe apoligie to make for my sillance, yet I doe for this tedious epistle shall Conclude in telling you I am to much obligd to you by any qurell to leave being

Your most Faithfull Servant ML

C:C:[4] is so to you all.

Endorsed by Locke: M: Lockhart 15 Apr. 97 Answered 19

2247. MRS. ELIZABETH STRATTON to LOCKE, 18 April 1697 (*2203*, *2265*)

B.L., MS. Locke c. 18, f. 228.

Bristoll April 18th ⟨1697⟩

Deare Cousen

I recivd yours in March and shoul⟨d⟩[b] have answer'd it much sooner had not sickness prevented me, in two days after the receit of your letter I was taken violently ill which I thought would have ended all my accounts in this world, but I have now preety well recover'd it only I have by fits a very violent Cough, I have heartily desir'd to se you and would gladly be advised by you I give you many thanks for the kind advise you gave me in your last and will indevou'r to follow it, for it's very unpleasant to be a useless person, yet I doubt the heavines of my heart adds very much[c–] to the[–c] distemper of my body tho[d] I doe not find it in my powr[e–] to prevent[–e] it, this is the first I have writ tho I have long desir'd to set that small account to rits between you and I, as to the eight shillings rec: of Mr Palmer[5] I beleeve 4s: of it belongs to

[a] *Doubtful reading.* [b] *Edge of page.* [c–c] *MS.* much to to the [d] *This word may be deleted.* [e–e] *MS.* powr to / to prevent

[1] Apparently a sealed bill: no. *1891*. [2] Lady Forfar.
[3] A preparation of vitriol: Journal, 25 July 1679, 17 Oct. 1698.
[4] Cousin (Joanna) Cutts. [5] Popham's bailiff: no. *2167*.

Peter Stratton his Lords rent being 1l–2s a year and yours being but one pound nineteen shillings I know nothing under a pound have any alowence that its[a] only the 4s: can belong to you on that account, you will find on my Husban⟨ds⟩[b] account and mine 19s: and 6d: paid to Mr Palmer 20th Nov (1694) and 19s–6d: paid him may 9th 1695) but you allow but one 19s–6d. to me in your last account so that alowing this I think the ballence of the account is 14l–3s–10¾d. I hope this will give you full sattisfaction tho I think Mr Loyd[1] might with a little trouble have spard you and me a great deale, but it is the course of the world when a man looses his estate his Wid: looses his freinds. but our good God is very kind to me in giveing me content with my portion, I hope I shall more and more experience his kindness to me and mine. my Deare mother lyes in great weakness, my brother and Sister Chapman give you their humble service, and so doe my son Peter Stratton, and my two daughters, and none more cordially then deare Cousin

Your most affectionate Cousin and Humble Servant

ELIZABETH STRATTON

pray if you have any convenience let my cousin Grigg[2] know we long to hear from him, I have receiv'd from a freind a very pleasing and Honourable account of him.

Address: For Mr John Locke to be left for Edward Clark Esq at Richards Coffee house neare Temple Bar London

Postmark: AP 21 (?)

Endorsed by Locke: E: Stratton 18° Apr 97 Answered 30

2248. BENJAMIN FURLY to ——, 20/30 April 1697

B.L., MS. Locke c. 9, f. 144. Excerpt from a letter. I have failed to identify the copyist.

Mr. Furly says in his letter dated the 30 Aprill 1697 about the Doctor in Holland[3] that he can assure me from the Patients themselves, whom he hath spoken with, that he hath cured old Aches, wounds, blindness in children, that have been severall years blind by accident, produces strange effects in bodies afflicted with the gout, Stone in the bladder and kidney, falling sickness, etc, of

[a] *Doubtful reading.* [b] *Edge of page.*

[1] Cornelius Lyde. [2] Her nephew William Grigg: no. 2020.

[3] G. H. van Rettwich: no. *2192* n., etc.

which he has many underhand, that have shewed me what effect it has had on them which gives them hopes of a full cure. I have seen them sweat as in a bath, of both sexes, and understood that he purges them and makes them vomit, tels them the next day where they have had pain and upon what part he works. He says further. I am well acquainted with him and do constantly as any new occasion emerges give account to Dr. Lock and mr. Popple, of the advance he makes. Mean while our Doctors say 't is impossible according to their dead spiritless corpuscular Philosophy,[1] that he should effect any thing by working upon the urine at a distance, and that people sweat so is only the effect of their own imagination, and that it will weaken and ruin them in the end, tho they testify that hitherto they grow strong, have better stomachs etc—

A Child at Delft that was blind and now sees as well as I, who has other distempers, he causes to sweat at Delft, as much as here only by practising upon his water. I have not time to inlarge etc—

2249. EDWARD CLARKE to LOCKE, 22 April 1697 (*2242, 2251*)

B.L., MS. Locke c. 6, f. 120. Printed in Rand, pp. 509–10.

London April the 22th. 1697.

Deare Sir,

I write now cheifely to Desire a Particular Favour of you, Which is to Lend mee two hundred pounds, for which, togather with the money I now owe you upon Account, you shall have any security from mee that you can Desire for the Repayment thereof at six moneths End, with Interest at 6. per Cent, And I hope if you have, or can Command soe much, you will obleige mee with it, In regard I have a Particular occasion for it at this time etc:

I tooke up the inclosed[2] at the Coffee House last night, and take this first opportunity to convey it to you; and I wish you would teach your Freind that writes it, to Direct his Letters soe for the future, that They may come Franke as I presume Hee intends they

[1] The Corpuscularian, here the same as the Atomic philosophy, is that taught by Epicurus and revived and modified by Gassendi, Boyle, and their followers. Locke cites 'the corpuscularian Hypothesis' in *Essay*, IV. iii. 16. Coste translates this as 'l'hypothese des Philosophes *Materialistes*' and adds a note which clarifies Furly's use of 'spiritless': 'Qui expliquent les effets de la nature par la seule consideration de la grosseur, de la figure, & du mouvement des parties de la Matiere.'

[2] Probably no. *2247*.

should doe, which must be by Incloseing them in a Case Directed to mee, and not as Hee now Directs Them etc:

Pray give my humble service to Sir Francis and my Lady, and bee assured that I am,

Your most Affectionate and obleiged Freind and Servant,

EDW: CLARKE:

I have with a greate deale of Difficulty gott in Mr. Barnard againe according to my Ladyes and your Desire etc:

Address: These, For John Lock Esqr. [at Oates, by Joslyn, Bishops Stortford]
Frank: Edw: Clarke:

Postmark: AP 22 (twice)

Endorsed by Locke: E: Clarke 22 Apr 97 Answered 26

2250. SYLVESTER BROUNOWER to LOCKE, 24 April 1697 (*2244, 2434*)

B.L., MS. Locke c. 4, ff. 183–4.

Whitehall April the 24th: 97

Sir

Your Letter of the 16th: I received, together with Mrs: Masham's, The Palsy water you pleas'd to write for, I endeavour'd to get, to have sent it per Mr: Slater, but could not, For Peter, Mrs: Lockharts man, who used to get it for his Mistriss, had left her, and is gon out of Town, they directed me to Man's,[1] or any other Coffe house, to enquire for it by the name of Mrs: Bennets Cephalick water, accordingly I went to several Coffee houses, but they neither had it, nor knew it by either name, Mrs: Smithsby has sent you some, which she got of a friend and thinkes it is the right, but if it should prove otherwise, if you please to let me know it and I'le make further inquiry; Mrs: Lockhart and Mrs: Cutts still talk of goeing to Oates the latter end of the next week, but I am almost of Mrs: Small's (who yesterday left her Mistriss for good and all) minde, that the changeing of all her Servant will hinder her. I have not seen Mr: Clarke, but Mr: Freke presents his service to you, I caried the Cacaonutts to Mrs: Smithsby's Lodgings and left your direction concerning them with her, she presents her service to you and would be glad to see you in Town again, as some in our Office

[1] It was at Charing Cross and near Scotland Yard: Lillywhite, no. 778.

do, she hath been serv'd just as we are, for her Petition and the King's reference upon it;[1] and Our Establishment with the King's reference upon it, are both accidentally, on purpose, lost in the Treasury. By Mr: Slater I sent a Note of the particulars what the things I sent about a fortnight ago cost viz 2 bottles of Hungary Water each 2s: 6d:, One quart of Orange flower water 2s:, The bottle 4d, A Letter 2d which makes the 7s: 6d: I received of James Lanham for it. The things I sent to day are as follows viz a litle bundle directed to your self wherein is the Palsey water for which Mrs: Smithby paid, 1 bottle of Hungary water 2s: 6d: A quart of Orange flower water, 2s:–d: A pint of Orange flower water 1s: –d: The quart bottle 4d: The pint bottle 3d: Two Quarts of Oyl 5s: –d The bottle –s: 8d: A basket, Paper and packthread 6d: a Letter 2d: Porterage for the Cocaonuts 8d: which amounts to 13s: 1d: I received of James Lanham, Mr: Churchill told me this morning that he cannot get the Yellow time. I am

Sir

Your most humble most Faithfull and Obedient Servant

SBROUNOWER

JL

Address: For Sir Francis Masham Bart Member of Parliament [at Oates, by Joslyn, Bishops Stortford]

Frank

Postmarks: AP 27; WR

Endorsed by Locke: S: Brownover 24 Apr 97

2251. EDWARD CLARKE to LOCKE, 29 April 1697 (*2249*, *2259*)

B.L., MS. Locke c. 6, f. 121. Printed in Rand, pp. 510–11.

London Aprill the 29th. 1697.

Deare Sir

I heartily thanke you for your verie Kind and obleigeing Letter by the last post, and particularly for your greate readinesse to supply mee with 200l. as I desired, In order to which I shall use my utmost Endeavours to gett in the severall summes mentioned in your Letter to bee due to you, But I cannot yett meete with my

[1] She petitioned for compensation for twelve years' arrears of a pension of £1,000 per annum granted to her father William Smithsby in 1637. The petition was referred to the Surveyor-General of Crown Lands in July 1696: *Cal. Treasury Papers, 1556/7–1696*, p. 532; *Cal. Treasury Books*, xi. 193.

Lord Ashley, or Sir Stephen Evans, tho I am in hopes to speake with them both in a Day or two, and I hope to better purpose then my Application with your Letter to Mr. Conyers was this morning; Hee tells mee playnely thre is not one penny of that money due to you for Interest now to bee gott, neither could I gett Him to Assigne any certaine time when it should bee payd mee for you, I will apply to Him againe as occasion offerrs, and gett in that, and the money oweing from my Lord Ashley and Sir Stephen Evans to you, if it bee possible, And you may bee assured that I will not presse Mr. Churchill too hard in this matter, but shall carefully pursue all the Directions in your Letter, and give you a further Account thereof as I Proceed, And shall Ever Remaine

Your most truly Affectionate and obleiged servant,

EDW: CLARKE

The College are yours and my Lady's hearty servants etc:

The Grafting on the Bank the last session has not as yet either Worsted or Betterr'd theire Actions, They Remaining much as they were, what Effects it may have, Wiser men then I cannot guesse, But the Parliament Alterr'd nothing of theire former tenure but what they Consented to etc.[1]

Address: These, For John Lock Esqr. [at Oates, by Joslyn, Bishops Stortford]
Frank: Edw Clarke:

Postmark: AP 29

Endorsed by Locke: E: Clarke 29 Apr 97

2252. ANTHONY ASHLEY COOPER, styled Lord Ashley, later third earl of Shaftesbury, to LOCKE, 30 April [1697] (*1922*, *2415*)

B.L., MS. Locke c. 7, ff. 118–19. Year from Locke's endorsement.

London. Ap. the 30th:

Mr Lock

Had your occasions wayted ever so little longer I am in hopes I should have prevented your letter, as to that part which relates to

[1] The price of Bank stock about 1 April was £54 in cash or £68 in notes (presumably the Bank's Sealed Bills or other instruments: no. *1891* n.; Clapham, i. 290–1); about 20 April it was £56 or £69; this price continued until the end of May: table of prices in Thorold Rogers. For the ingraftment of tallies see no. *2154*. The new Bank act (ibid., n.) enlarged the Bank's powers without interfering unduly with its administration.

the 50l. for I had just sent Wheelock into the Country to receive some money that hee might have paid You the first thing hee did. Hee will bee in Town again the end of next week. and I doubt not but to pay the money, as You have order'd it, immediatly after.

I have every week expected my Mother's coming to Town, and am forc'd to wayt still here in that expectation: otherwise I should upon the rising of the Parlement[1] have wayted on my Lady Masham att Oates, and[a] propos'd to my self the happiness of meeting You there. I Beg You would present my most humble service to my Lady; and that You Your self would beleive mee, what You very justly may,

Your Sincere Humble Servant

A: ASHLEY.

Address: For Mr Lock [at Oates, by Joslyn, Bishops Stortford]
Free A. Ashley
Postmark: MY 1
Endorsed by Locke: L: Ashley 30 Apr 97

2253. MARTHA LOCKHART to LOCKE, 1 May [1697] (*2246, 2362*)

B.L., MS. Locke c. 15, ff. 70–1. Year from Locke's endorsement.

London May 1

Your answer to my last was the first word of your writing I ever saw since you left this place tho I find by you that you have writ how it has miscary'd I cant imagin. Your reproaches are all so kind that I must take them. tho some of 'em I think are unjust to me t'would mortifie me if I did not feell as firm and honest an intention in whithall as You Contrey foulk are so very brag of. I have this day pay'd 25 pound to Mr Churchill an taken his recipt for so much as yours did directt me. I am still under the power of the priz office, from home I expect a dispatch every day but your old acquantance Robin Muray who is now made a Knight takes state upon him[2] and I am affraid will expect more solicitation then I am willing to give. I give you many thankes for your advice to my sister for her son

[a] *Smudged; perhaps deleted.*

[1] On 16 April.
[2] Robert Murray, a commissioner of Prizes, knighted on 23 April: Le Neve, *Pedigrees*, p. 458. I have found no connection between him and Locke.

which to make Your Compliement perfect to her I cut out of my letter and sent to her as you writ it. I have noe great hope of meetting with your frend Mr Cleark it is long since I have been a Bedchamber Women that he has I sopose long agoe I ever was one[1] and you kno' I am Aukert at makeing my Court to great men except to yourself. upon this new Chang of a lord Chamberland[2] I have got an opertunity of disposing I hope to My advantage my jewells for Mr Bandley who is in Mr Coolings place[3] is to make the Kings presents to some of the Publick ministers that are returning and has promis't to me the shall be dispos'd of at the same advantage as the Jeweler's would have. I must beg of you to contrive some way for me to Come at those in Your hand and in stead of that pledg you shall have what security you can aske·that I can give. My land is a good hunder'd and 60ll a year[4] but if you dont think that a suficent I will lodg Tallies for five hunderd pound in few monthes due or give my obligation to return money or the dimonds in any time you shall name. but I am very loth to lose this occasion that seem's to git me fairly Rid of 'em to my advantage. pray let me have Your answer as to this. My humble service to My lady My Husband Sir Fr: and all the rest with you. the King has had an admirable pasage in 22 hours and this day 7 of his 9 representitves open'd shop.[5] I wish they may sell us good penyworths. befor I goe to HamtenCourt[6] I resolve notwithstanding all my reproaches of inconstancy to wait on My lady Masham and hear all your saturs against Court ladyes as you are pleas'd to call us. My Co Cutts I am afraid wont come with me her Brother and she are in some term's of settling her affarr's which god knows want much more then I fear he is able if he was willing to doe he has sold his Rright to Mr Caroll's estat to his Brother for 6000ll.[7] I long

[1] Clarke as Queen Mary's Auditor-General was presumably responsible for the payment of her household.

[2] Sunderland was appointed on 19 April in place of Charles Sackville, sixth earl of Dorset (*D.N.B.*).

[3] Richard Cooling (no. 620), who died about 19 June of this year, appears to have been secretary to the successive Lords Chamberlain. Bandley is an error; Cooling was replaced about 24 April by John Stanley, the commissioner for Stamp Duties (nos. *1036*, etc.): Luttrell, iv. 216, 347.

[4] Probably her property in Cornwall.

[5] The Lords Justices. Shrewsbury and Pembroke were absent.

[6] As a former Bedchamber Woman Mrs. Lockhart presumably kept her lodgings there.

[7] In 1696 Lord Cutts was granted the property, worth £2,000 per annum, of John Caryll (titular Baron Caryll 1701; *D.N.B.*) who had been attainted. Cutts sold it this year to Caryll's brother Richard: *Cal. Treasury Books*, xi. 177–80; Luttrell, iv. 303; M. de Trenqualéon, *West-Grinstead*, etc., [1893], ii. 85–90.

extreemly to chang my tea an Chat as you call it hear for a little with you in the Countrey. I am

Your obligd and humble servant

ML

My lord Cutts has done Sam's besness[1] and makes a mighty merit of the return's of ungratitud he meetts of a family he has so much and offten serv'd

Endorsed by Locke: M. Lockhart 1° May 97 Answered 7

2254. LOCKE to WILLIAM MOLYNEUX, 3 May 1697 (2243, *2262*)

Some Familiar Letters, pp. 206–11. I have filled in the names Coste and Leibnitz where the editor printed 'Mr. *C*—' and 'Mr. *L*—'. Answers no. *2240*; answered by no. *2269*.

Oates, 3. May. 1697.

Dear Sir,

Though the honour you do me in the value you put upon my shadow be a fresh mark of that friendship which is so great an happiness to me, yet I shall never consider my picture in the same house with you, without great regret at my so far distance from you my self. But I will not continue to importune you with my complaints of that kind; 'tis an advantage greater than I could have hoped, to have the conversation of such a friend, though with the sea between; and the remaining little scantling of my life would be too happy if I had you in my neighbourhood.

I am glad to hear that the gentleman you mention in yours of the 6th. of the last month,[2] does me the favour to speak well of me on that side the water, I never deserved other of him, but that he should always have done so on this. If his exceeding great value of himself do not deprive the world of that usefulness, that his parts, if rightly conducted, might be of, I shall be very glad. He went from London, as I heard afterwards, soon after I left it the last time. But he did me not the favour to give me a visit whilst I was there, nor to let me know of his intended journey to you; if he had, 'tis possible I might have writ by him to you, which I am now not sorry I did not. I always value men of parts and learning, and think I cannot

[1] Samuel Masham was commissioned as an ensign in Cutts's regiment, the Coldstream Guards, on 23 April: Dalton, *English Army Lists*, iv. 173.
[2] Toland.

do too much in procuring them friends and assistance. But there may happen occasions that may make one stop ones hand. And 'tis the hopes of what use young men give, that they will make of their parts, which is to me the encouragement of being concerned for them. But, if vanity increases with age, I always fear whither it will lead a man. I say this to you because you are my friend for whom I have no reserves, and think I ought to talk freely where you enquire, and possibly may be concerned; but I say it to you alone, and desire it may go no farther. For the man I wish very well, and could give you, if it needed, proofs that I do so. And therefore I desire you to be kind to him; but I must leave it to your prudence, in what way, and how far. If his carriage with you gives you the promises of a steady useful man, I know you will be forward enough of your self, and I shall be very glad of it. For it will be his fault alone, if he prove not a very valuable man, and have not you for his friend.

But I have something to say to you of another man. Mons. Le Clerc, in a letter I lately received from him,[1] writes thus:

Mons. Coste me disoit dernierement que s'il trouvoit occasion d'entrer dans une maison de condition en qualité de precepteur il seroit ravi d'en profiter. C'est un fort honête homme, et qui seroit bien capable de s'acquiter de cet emploi. Il ne sait l'Anglois que par les livres, c'est à dire, qu'il l'entend lors qu'il le lit, mais qu'il ne le sçauroit parler non plus que moi, faute d'habitude. Si quelque un de vos amis auroit besoin de precepteur, et qu'il lui donnât de quoi s'entretenir, il ne sauroit trouver d'homme plus sage et plus reglé, outre qu'il sait beaucoup de choses utiles pour un emploi comme celui là, les belles lettres, l'histoire, etc.

This Mr. Coste is he that translated my book of Education, upon which occasion I came to have some acquaintance with him by letters, and he seems a very ingenious man; and Mr. Le Clerc has often, before any thing of this, spoke of him to me with commendation and esteem. He has since translated The Lady's Religion,[2] and The Reasonableness of Christianity into French. You may easily guess why I put this into my letter to you, after what you said concerning Mr. Le Clerc in your last letter but one.

[1] No. *2236*.

[2] *A Lady's Religion*, an anonymous book, first published this year; Coste gives the author's name as Stephens, meaning perhaps the Revd. William Stephens (*D.N.B.*); the preface was attributed to Toland, who disclaimed it: Carabelli, *Tolandiana*, p. 32. Coste's translation was published at Amsterdam in 1698. L.L., nos. 1652–3. See further nos. *3155*, *3468*.

You are willing, I see, to make my little presents to you more and greater than they are. Amongst the books that Mr. Churchill sent you, you are beholden to me (since you will call it so) but for one; and to that the Bp. of Worcester, I hear, has an answer in the press, which will be out this week.[1] So that I perceive this controversie is a matter of serious moment beyond what I could have thought. This benefit I shall be sure to get by it, either to be confirmed in my opinion, or be convinced of some errors, which I shall presently reform, in my Essay, and so make it the better for it. For I have no opinions that I am fond of. Truth, I hope, I always shall be fond of, and so ready to embrace, and with so much joy, that I shall own it to the world, and thank him that does me the favour. So that I am never afraid of any thing writ against me, unless it be the wasting of my time, when it is not writ closely in pursuit of truth, and truth only.

In my last to you I sent you a copy of Mr. Leibnitz's paper, I have this writ me out of Holland concerning it:[2]

Mr. Leibnitz Mathematicien de Hannover aiant oui dire, qu'on traduisoit votre ouvrage, et qu'on l'alloit imprimer, a envoié ici à un de mes amis ce jugement qu'il en fait, comme pour la mettre à la tete. Cependant il a été bien aise qu'on vous le communicât. Il m'a été remis entre les mains pour cela. On m'a dit mille biens de ce Mathematicien. Il y a long temps que *magna et præclara minatur*, sans rien produire que quelques demonstrations detachées. Je croi neanmoins qu'il ne vous entend pas, et je doute qu'il s'entende bien lui même.

I see you and I, and this gentleman, agree pretty well concerning the man; and this sort of fidling makes me hardly avoid thinking that he is not that very great man as has been talked of him. His paper was in England a year, or more, before it was communicated to me, and I imagin you will think he need not make such a great stir with it.

My Essay, you see, is translating into French, and it is by the same Mr. Coste above-mention'd. But this need not hinder Mr. Burridge in what he designed, for Mr. Coste goes on exceeding slowly, as I am told.

[1] *The Bishop of Worcester's Answer to Mr. Locke's Letter, concerning some Passages relating to his Essay of Humane Understanding* . . . Stillingfleet dates it from Worcester, 27 March 1697; a postscript is dated 26 April. The book is advertised in *Flying Post*, 11 May; *London Gazette*, 13 May. L.L., no. 2789.

[2] This also is quoted from no. *2236*.

You see how forward I am to importune you with all my little concerns. But this would be nothing to what I should do if I were nearer you. I should then be talking to you *de quolibet ente*,[1] and consulting you about a thousand whimsies that come sometimes into my thoughts. But with all this I unfeignedly am,

Dear Sir,

Your most faithful humble servant,

JOHN LOCKE.

The poem that was sent you by Mr. Churchill, amongst the other books, I believe will please you, there are some noble parts in it.[2]

2255. DR. PIETER GUENELLON to LOCKE, 3/13 May 1697 (*2191*, *2292*)

B.L., MS. Locke c. 11, ff. 76–7. Perhaps transmitted by W. Barker: see p. 140.

Monsieur

Je vien de recevoir l'honneur de la visite de Monsieur baker,[3] dont je vous suis fort obligé. il ma donné de vostre part vostre lettre escrite a l'Evesque de Worchester. je vous en remercie, et je conte pour excellent tout ce qui sort de vos mains. Monsieur baker nous a trouvé dans l'embaras du deuil, que nous venons de prendre sur la mort de nostre belle mere,[4] qui est morte martyre, de plusieurs maux extremes et invincibles. un rein ulceré, l'autre petrifié dans son parenchyme. la vessie ulcerée, la matrice schyrrheuse et carcinomateuse, ayant peu avant la mort erodé le sphincter de la vessie, de sorte quelle ne pouvoit retenir son urine, qui decouloit a goutte comme une eau forte meslée d'une matiere purulente et tres fætide. de sorte que Dieu luy a fait une tres grande grace de l'avoir retirée de se monde. ces circonstances ont rendu sa mort plus souffrable a mon beau Pere, qui l'aimoit passionement. il se porte graces a Dieu assez bien, et le reste de la famille. je me suis enquis de cet allemand qui pretend de guerir les maladies par l'application des remedes aux urines.[5] laudatur ab his, culpatur ab

[1] 'About anything in the world'.

[2] The poem is named on p. 134; it is *King Arthur*, 1697, by Sir Richard Blackmore. L.L., no. 341.

[3] W. Barker here and below.

[4] The third Mevr. Veen.

[5] G. H. van Rettwich: no. *2192* n., etc.

illis.[1] c'est un empyrique. un homme sans estude, qui cepandant s'enrichit au depans de la vaine superstition des hommes, qui donnent facilement dans l'extraordinaire et le merveilleux. pour moy je ne scaurois croire qu'un excrement qui n'a plus aucun commerce avec le corps, et estant de plus distant de plusieurs lieux, puisse agir sur ce corps. j'attribue ses succes a la folle imagination de quelque gens, et quelque incident heureux quon attribue a faux a ce pretendu Medecin. Monsieur Daranda ma fait l'honneur de mescrire depuis peu deux lettres. je ne manqueray pas de luy respondre au plustost des que nos funerailles sont achevées, en attendant j'espere de recevoir le pacquet quil nous envoye de vostre part, et quon dit estre arrivé au tessel, et le livre. Guidotii thermæ britannicæ[2] quil à la bonté de m'envoyer par la voye de Rotterdam.

jay conjuré Monsieur Baker de penser a quoy je pourois luy estre utile icy. je m'en vay le trouver dans son logement. il repard ce soir pour la Haye, mais j'espere de le revoir plus a son loisir pour luy marquer combien j'estime tout ce qui me vient de vostre part, estant d'un tres profond respect,

Monsieur,

Vostre tres humble et tres obeissant serviteur

P. GUENELLON

d'Amsterdam ce 13 Mey 1697.

Ma femme qui se trouve tousjours vostre obligée vous presente avec ses enfans ses treshumbles respects.

Address: For Mr. John Locke London

Endorsed by Locke: Dr Guenellon 13 May 97

2256. PHILIPPUS VAN LIMBORCH to LOCKE, 3/13 May 1697 (*2222*, *2318*)

B.L., MS. Locke c. 14, ff. 105–6. Perhaps transmitted by W. Barker: see p. 140. Answers no. 2209.

Vir Amplissime ac multis mihi nominibus colende

Hodie gratissimas tuas mihi tradidit D. Baker,[3] qui cum Illustris-

---

Excellent Sir, and for many reasons to be honoured by me,

Mr. Baker,[3] who says that he came here with the most illustrious earl

---

[1] 'He is praised by some and blamed by others': Horace, *Satires*, I. ii. 11.

[2] Thomas Guidott, M.B. (*D.N.B.*), *De Thermis Britannicis*, 1691.

[3] W. Barker: no. 2209, endorsement.

simo Comite Pembrokiensi se huc appulisse ait: Addidit et donum tuum, historiam nempe de rebus Anglicis,[1] quam ego mox perlegere statui. Conspectis tuis literis, mirabar nullam in iis mearum quas 26 Martii satis prolixas ad te dedi mentionem fieri: Verum cum animadverterem tuas jam 4 Martii scriptas, mirari desii. Meas, quibus filius meus suas linguâ Anglicanâ adjunxit, fideliter jam tibi traditas esse, nullus dubito. In illis quædam, quæ in lectione libri de Rationabilitate Religionis Christianæ observaveram, tuo rogatu, annotavi, tibique judicanda proposui. Ego ex tarditate literarum nullum in amicitia tua frigus collegi, neque ideo in scribendo tardior fui. Frigus tamen aliquod me in scribendo aliquanto tardiorem fecit: frigus nempe intensum diuturnæ hyemis: Volui morem gerere voluntati tuæ; ideoque primo librum illum legere et relegere, et quæcunque aut obscurius dicta, aut aliqua pleniore explicatione indigere videbantur, tibi proponere, prout in epistola mea jam procul dubio vidisti. De te semper credidi, negotia quibus implicaris in causa esse, quod minus crebras ad me scribas epistolas. Nullum in amicitia nostra frigus suboriri posse persuasissimus sum: inconcusso ac immobili illa nititur fundamento. Otium, quod desideras, ego tibi opto, ac valetudinem, quantam ætas senilis fert.

---

of Pembroke, delivered your most welcome letter to me to-day; he also added your present, the history of English affairs,[1] which I have decided to read forthwith. On looking at your letter I was surprised that no mention is made in it of my lengthy enough letter that I sent you on 26 March; but when I noticed that yours was written already on 4 March I ceased to be surprised. I have no doubt that mine, to which my son added one by himself in English, has now been duly delivered to you. At your request I set down in it some observations that I had made in the course of reading the book about the Reasonableness of the Christian religion, and put them before you for you to judge. I did not infer from the slowness of your letter any coldness in your friendship, nor was I rather slow in reply for that reason. Some coldness however made me somewhat slower in writing; that is, the intense cold of this long-lasting winter. I wanted to comply with your wish; and for that reason first to read and re-read that book and [then] to put before you whatever seemed either somewhat obscurely expressed or to need some fuller exposition, as doubtless you have by now seen in my letter. As to yourself, I have always believed that the affairs in which you are engaged are responsible for your writing letters to me less frequently. I am fully convinced that no coldness can arise in our friendship; it rests upon an unshaken and immovable foundation. I wish for you the leisure that you desire, and health as much as old age permits. Meanwhile I have also learnt

---

[1] Burridge's *Historia*.

Interim et labores tuos rei literariæ impendi summa cum voluptate ex tuis intellexi. Spero me Tractatum tuum de Intellectu humano, et quæ nunc pro illius defensione scripsisti, aliquando Latine lecturum, ut eius lectione in multis magis confirmer, multa etiam mihi hactenus incognita addiscam.[1] Optime fecisti, quod eorum, quæ sine causa ab aliis reprehensa sunt, defensionem scripseris, eorumque veritatem ab objectionibus vindicaveris. Nuper ostensus mihi fuit libellus Anglicus, hoc titulo: The exceptions of Mr. Edwards in his Causes of Atheism, against the Reasonableness of Christianity, as deliver'd in the Scriptures, examin'd; and found unreasonable, unscriptural, and injurioux.[2] Vidi in illo et tuum et meum nomen occurrere; et quidem pag.38. mentionem fieri disputationis meæ non tantum cum Don Balthasare, sed et colloquii mei cum lectissima illa Virgine:[3] Verum est, colloquium hoc ita commemorari quasi cum viro celebri habitum esset: sed omnes, quibuscunque historia illa aliquatenus innotuit, satis norunt, non virum, sed puellam fuisse. Ego, quanquam autor ille meam qualemcunque operam longe supra merita deprædicet, maluissem tamen nullam illius mentionem factam, totumque hoc negotium, quan-

---

from your letter with very great pleasure that your labours are employed on learning. I hope sometime to read in Latin your treatise on the Human Understanding and what you have now written in its defence, so that by its perusal I may be more assured about many things and may also learn many hitherto unknown to me.[1] You have done very well to write a defence of those things that have been found fault with by others without occasion, and to vindicate their truth from objections. There was recently shown to me an English pamphlet with this title: 'The exceptions of Mr. Edwards in his Causes of Atheism, against the Reasonableness of Christianity, as deliver'd in the Scriptures, examin'd, and found unreasonable, unscriptural, and injurious.'[2] I saw that your name and mine occur in it; and indeed on p. 38 mention is made not only of my disputation with Don Balthasar but also of my conversation with that very notable young woman.[3] It is true that this conversation is mentioned as if it had been held with a well known man; but everyone to whom that story has become at all known knows well enough that it was not a man but a girl. Although the author praises my achievement, such as it was, far above its merits, I should nevertheless have preferred that no mention had been made of it, and that this whole affair,

---

[1] Burridge's translation was not published until 1701. It does not contain any excerpts from Locke's controversy with Stillingfleet.

[2] No. *1954* n.

[3] '*Mr. Limborch* . . . in his most famous and weighty Disputations against the Jews . . . one of which we have in his *Amica Collatio cum erudito Judæo*.' There is no mention of a young woman.

quam mihi non inglorium, æternæ si fieri posset oblivioni tradi, propter puellam omni honore dignissimam, cujus famæ maligni obtrectatores detrahere non desinunt: Ipsa vero animo constanti ac infracto contra luctatur, et sibi probe conscia, insanæ plebis maledicta contemnit. Venii nostri uxor, post diuturnos languores, et gravissimos calculi cruciatus, ante sex dies diem suum obiit, et ante biduum sepulta est. Uxor mea, liberique plurimam tibi precantur salutem. Salutem a me quam officiosissime dices Dominæ Masham. Vale.

Tui Amantissimus
PHILIPPUS A LIMBORCH

Amstelodami 13 Maji

12
16 X 97
18

Address: For Sir John Locke London
Endorsed by Locke: P: Limborch 13 May 97

---

though not inglorious to me, should if possible be consigned to eternal oblivion; this on account of a girl who is most worthy of all honour and of whom spiteful detractors are not ceasing to speak ill. She herself, however, contends against this with steadfast and unbroken spirit, and, knowing herself thoroughly, disregards the abusive words of the senseless vulgar. Our friend Veen's wife, after prolonged weakness and very severe torments from the stone, died six days ago and was buried the day before yesterday. My wife and children send you their best wishes. Please give my best respects to Lady Masham. Good-bye.

Your most affectionate
PHILIPPUS VAN LIMBORCH

Amsterdam 13 May
1697.

2257. SAMUEL BOLD to [AWNSHAM and JOHN CHURCHILL?] 5 May 1697 (*2233*, *2278*)

B.L., MS. Locke c. 4, f. 15. Fragment; lower part cut away; no address. The salutation, the general style, and the preservation of the letter among Locke's papers, indicate that it was addressed to the Churchills.

Steeple May 5th. 1697.

Worthy Sirs

I thank you for the Animadversions on the Reasonableness of

Christianity etc.[1] I have now read them over, they are writ with Temper, But the Author lamentably mistook and misrepresents the Reasonableness of Chistianity. There is hardly any thing in them relating to the Reasonableness etc but what may be fully answered from what the Author of the Reasonableness hath already published. But if the Author of the Reasonableness etc wil be pleased to answer these Animadversions, I believe He wil take occasion to furnish the publick with very profitable Instructions. I shal be glad to hear that the Author of the Reasonableness is at Leisure, and wil Answer this Author. I have writ observations on the Animadversions all along as I read over what He hath writ about the Epistles, And what we are to believe concerning christ. that is, his first, and last parts. If the Author of the Reasonableness be not at present at leasure to Answer this new Author, if my Observations may be of any use, you shal have them, if you require them, as soon as I can get time to transcribe them.[2]

I am

your affectionate friend and servant

SA: BOLDE

Endorsed by Locke: S. Bold 5° May 97

2258. LOCKE to MRS. MARY CLARKE, 7 May 1697 (2214, 2291)

Rand, pp. 511–12. Words in square brackets are supplied by Rand. The date is questionable. On 8 May Clarke forwarded to Locke a letter dated 1 May which appears to have been from Mrs. Clarke: p. 115. If it was the letter from her mentioned in the present letter, then the date of this letter is wrong.

Oates, 7th May, 1697.

Madam,

I am very sorry to find by yours of May 1st that the diet drink I directed failed to do you that good which you thought for some time you found in the use of. I should have been very glad that that without any other prescriptions would have recovered you. But since you find it does not do, and you think a severe course must be taken in the case, I know not how wholly to dissent from you, that something more effectual should be done, but the question is what?

[1] *Animadversions on a Late Book entituled the Reasonableness of Christianity as delivered in the Scriptures*, Oxford, 1697. L.L., no. 702.

[2] See further pp. 145–6, 270.

You seem in your letter to Mr. Clarke to think purging would be useful. I do not know but it may. But this I know, that at this distance to tell in what manner, how much and how often, is impossible in a constitution and case like yours, and that which I cannot venture upon. You commend particularly Dr. Musgrave's purges. I cannot but thereupon ask you whether you have talked to him about them. For methinks that as well as other considerations should have been an encouragement to you to consult him in your present case. For this I think absolutely necessary, that you should have the advice of some able physician, not by letter and at a distance, but of one who, by being upon the place and talking with you, might by discourse, and sight, and everything, inform himself of all those many particulars, which are necessary to be known and considered to give all the light and certainty is to be had in such a case. Besides that I know not what farther to advise. And the more I am concerned for your health and recovery, the more unfit and unreasonable I find it for me to tamper in the dark, especially to venture on those which you call severer remedies, which are in danger to do as much harm when misapplied, as there is good to be expected from them where they are proper and fit. Give me leave, therefore, to press you again to have recourse to some able physician, who may see and talk with you, and be at hand to observe the effects of his prescriptions, and to change them quick upon any occasion. And when you are in such hands, if anything I can say or do may be of any service to you, there shall be nothing I shall more willingly do than whenever I can any way imagine [would] be for the recovery of an health which I am so much concerned for, and which I so earnestly [desire]. I am,

Dear Madam,

your most humble and faithful servant,

J. LOCKE.

Pray give my service to my dear wife, and tell her that by her civil but very cold letter to me, I begin to suspect her thoughts begin to look a little after another husband.

My Lady Masham and all this family present their service to you, and are concerned for your health.

Address: These present. To Mrs. Mary Clarke at Chipley.

2259. EDWARD CLARKE to LOCKE, 8 May 1697 (*2251, 2261*)

B.L., MS. Locke c. 6, ff. 122–3. Printed in Rand, pp. 512–13.

London May the 8th. 1697.

Deare Sir,

The inclosed,[1] by what misfortune I Know not, tho dated the 1rst., came not to my handes untill this morning, or else you had been sooner troubled with my Desires for your Thoughts upon it, Which I earnestly begg of you etc: I have againe Press'd Mrs. Clarke's comeing to Town, as the Best meanes that can bee taken to Restore Her former Health, Which I desire you to Forward all you can, and Direct that in the meane time which you thinke most safe and Proper for Her, Which will bee the greatest Obligaon you can Lay upon

Your most Affectionate Faithfull servant
EDW: CLARKE:

I[a]– have gott your twenty five pounds out of Sir Stephens handes etc:–[a]

The College are yours and my Lady's humble servants

Address: These, For John Locke Esqr. [at Oates, by Joslyn, Bishops Stortford]
Frank: Edward Clarke:

Postmark: MA 8

Endorsed by Locke: E: Clarke 8° May 97 Answered 10

2260. PAUL D'ARANDA to LOCKE, 8 May 1697 (*2238, 2342*) enclosing BENJAMIN FURLY to [D'ARANDA?], 2/12 April 1697, and JOHN SPADEMAN to [D'ARANDA?], 21 April/1 May 1697

B.L., MSS. Locke c. 3, f. 46 (the letter), and c. 9, ff. 142–3 (the enclosures). The enclosures are copies made by D'Aranda.

London the 8th: May 1697

Sir

Please to excuse my being much from home for the benefit of the Country air's having hindred my sooner sending the by my last

a–a *Marked by Locke for attention.*

[1] See p. 113 n.

promised copy of a letter from Mr Furly which this serves to cover. Under it I have copy'd a few lines on the same subject out of a letter of Mr Spademan,[1] one of the English ministers at Rotterdam. Two letters since received from Mr Furly say not any thing more of sympathetick Cures, when he writes me ought farther of it you shall have copy sent you. I pay you thanks Sir for the advice brought me by yours of 14 April, which came in good time for Mr. Wagensel, who I think went hence for Holland at same time with the King. More thanks than a letter can pay are also due to you for your kind care and good wishes for my health, which is in a little better state than when I last wrote you and I would hope may yet mend more when I come to Bath whither I intend to go in eight days. That it may please God to grant you continuance of usual advantage by the good air you breath is most heartily wish'd by

Sir

Your most humble servant

PAUL D'ARANDA

Address: To John Lock Esqre: [at Oates, by Joslyn, Bishops Stortford]
Postmark: MA 8
Endorsed by Locke: P: DAranda 8° May 97

[Enclosure:]

Rotterdam the 12th. April 1697

I have been the longer ere I answer'd your letter that I might be able to give you some certain account of the German that has the name of the Sympathetick Doctor.

I have spoken with divers that have received great advantage by him, and do find it absolutely true, beyond all reasonable occasion of Doubt, tho our Philosophers do still continue to argue the impossibility of it, That he does really cause people to sweat, purge, and vomit, without the least application of any thing immediately to the Patients outwardly or inwardly, yea, which is wonderfull, that he sometimes causes particular parts of the body to sweat, while other parts remain untouch'd; as one child that is blind, he causes to sweat onely at the Eyes that it drops from the Eyes as Tears: But this I have onely by report and from his own mouth, the child dwelling out of Town, but I purpose to go thither and see and

[1] No. *1348*, etc.

examine it. I have also been inform'd that he has perfectly cured one child in Delft, that was blind, to the great joy of the Parents.

I have spoken with a Gentlewoman in this Town who has been, for these twenty two years in such a condition, lame of hands and feet, that she has not been able to dresse or undresse her self, but has been lay'd to bed and taken up as a child; which she got with a fright when she was about 20 years old: at present she walks about the House as nimbly as most woemen; and tho formerly she could not have taken up her scizzers from the ground, she now can, and has in a great measure the use of her hands and fingers.

My next Neighbour, save one, his wife having been dropsical, and, for some years, gone with her legs swaddeled, and was so weak that she could bear no cold, but if she went out in cold weather was seized with a violent loosenesse, is so far restored, by sweating and purging, that she leaves off her swathe-bands, and has been abroad in bitter weather without any inconvenience by it, and recovered her stomach.

Another Gentlewoman, an acquaintance of my wife's, who has been eighteen years lame, her ham strings shrunk, her kneepan dislocated, a callous substance grown in her knee, which was as great as her head, and afflicted with the Stone; he has, by sweating and vomiting, brought a Stone from her, strech'd her sinews so that both her legs are of an equal length, abated the swelling in her knee, which she shewed us, and is no bigger than it should be, so that she walks, tho but weakly, without crutch or staff, which in eighteen years before she could not do, and is in great hopes of perfect recovery. I, with my wife and four other men and women sat by her bed-side two hours to see her sweat. She saith she now distinctly feels his operation under her knee-pan tho she sweat her whole body through.

The forementioned Gentlewoman that has been lame twenty two years, saith that sometimes she feels pain onely on one side and sometimes all her Body through as if she lay upon a rack, which he sayth he cannot help, being necessitated to give her a great deal more payn at some times than at others.

Another neer Neighbour a Batchellor of fifty years old, that has many years had the Gout, is, by sweating, so far advanced, that whereas when he began he could neither open nor shut his hand, his fingers being crooked and stiff, he can now open and shut them as swift and as easily as I can, which I saw him do, and his distemper is driven down to his Ancles, and the Operator tells him he will drive it out at his Toes.

He has now under his hands a young daughter of Mr. Thomas Augustines, who has from her birth been in a miserable state (supposed to have come by a fright of the mother when with child) not able to use her hands or legs, having no strength in either, her knees bowing in so that one must use force to draw them asunder and if one puts one's fingers between them it pinches hard. This child my wife and I went to see, that we may be able to witnesse what effect his operations may have upon it. This is certain, he makes the child sweat, not onely in bed but sitting in it's chair. The child is under all this pleasant, and not without understanding, but cannot well speak. But it happens that he many times fails in his attempts to make this child sweat, and therefore he dares not promise himself much successe.

There is a person of quality in this Town whom he has twenty times attempted to make sweat, but cannot move him.

The Child that I formerly mention'd to you, that was so dropsical, ravenous in eating, and had such Cankers in his bones, he continues yet to bring pieces of bones from: But his dropsy begins to return, and that with a feaver; which makes the Doctors clap their hands and say, so it will go with all his Patients, but the Father saith— If my child should dy, whom I know he cannot make immortal, I shall always speak well of the man and his art.

Yet this I find generally, that they all say that they seem not to advance now in proportion to what they did in the beginning.

Van der Slaart has publish'd in the *Boek-saal* of *Rabus*, a Notarial Atestation of his distemper and cure, as also has another, and yet Dr. *Lufner* of this Town, has in the same *Boek-saal* of the months January and February 1697: publish'd a letter to prove the impossibility of his working upon Bodyes at a distance by working on their Urine:[1] And among other wise reasons why the people do sweat (for that is too evident to be denyed and would be a bold giving the lye to many persons of known probity, who cannot have any interest in it, unlesse any man can find interest: in suffering extraordinary pain, giving money and lying to boot) that it is not by any thing that he does that they do sweat: But onely by their own immaginations lying close covered in their Beds. alledging that

[1] No. *2192*. Lufner should be Lufneu. Pieter Rabus (1660–1702; *N.N.B.W.*) edited *De Boekzaal van Europa* from 1692 to 1701.

van Helmont (as he has been informed from a man of good repute, in whose house he resided two years) was wont to cure people by raising in them a strong immagination that he could cure them.[1] But to this I think that example, above mention'd, of mr. Augustines childs sweating in it's chair, is sufficient refutation, for that child could not be prepossessed with any such immagination nor was it in bed closely covered. Not to mention what the other; the gouty Batchellor, told me, to confute that fancy, that he sweated the first time unexpectedly on the Sunday, whereas, he had expected that he would not go to work on him till monday: and that now many times he knows not when he will work upon him, but while he sits in Company, with a glasse of wine in his hand (for he does not order his Patients any manner of abstinence from any thing they have a mind to) he feels a glowing in his breast and thereupon retires to his bed.

Thus much for what he does. Now for the Man, from that Small conversation I have had with him, having been once in his company accidentally, where he came to one of his Patients; and once a quarter of an hour at his House, he being then in haste to go out; and last Sunday half an hour in my House where he came to see my youngest Son, who I told him was restlesse to find his Art.

I find him, pretty shallow, rambling in his discourse, and as raw in his Education as a squabling freshman, that studys the art of wrangling, calls it Divinity, and values himself upon it.

I think it is a want of judgement in him that he does not advise his Patients to take more care of themselves; For we know how much rest and warmth and a good dyet conduce to health, and I am sure if that alone, without medicine contributes so much to the relief of nature, it cannot be hurtfull to add that to all the relief he is able to give.

I find therefore many that are convinced that he works upon the Patients, who yet doubt whether he has the art of curing any throughly; and these make their remarks upon such as dye under his hands.

They say also, that besides his ignorance in the structure of the Body, the discerning distempers, and the way of cure, which, they think would add much to his art, and give more hopes of successe,— He takes more in hand, out of greedinesse of gain, than he can in good conscience manage.

[1] Perhaps J. B. van Helmont rather than his son the Baron.

And hence comes a report that he throws many Patients urines into a pot together, and so sweats them all alike: it being, they say, impossible that he should boyl in distinct vessels so many urines as are brought to him dayly.

I fear I shall have wearyed you with these relations, yet as any thing else remarkable comes to my knowledge I shall impart it to you—etc

B: F:

P:S: Since writing the above I have been to visit my Neighbour with my Wife and youngest Son, and have sat by his bed half an hour, in a dropping sweat, He tells us that he voyds much gravel in his urine. He hath been miserably afflicted with the gout these eleven years, abandon'd by all Doctors, and has seldom been free even in the hottest of the summer. He tells me, that since I saw him last, his hands began to swell and pain him anew, in so much that he began to despair, and had gotten elder water and Brandy on his hands to asswage the pain, which the Doctor finding, and seeing the reason of it, told him that what to him seem'd a sign of despair, was to him an infallible one of cure, which he should see and be able to walk in May. He says that his feet now burn as fire, and he feels it driving downwards, so that he has not any pain in his hands and is again full of Courage.—

Rotterdam 1 May 1697.

As to your postscript about our Sympathetick Doctor I need not be large because my Neighbour Mr. B: F: has given a particular account of it: All that I need to say is, that this method has been successefull in curing such Ulcers and external accidents as no other medicines could heal; As to internal distempers 'tis not found so proper. The cures of my Neighbour Mr. van der Slaart and some others, are as real and firm as any ever were, and there is not the least ill symtom remains, tho our Phisicians had prognosticated a dangerous relaps as to which they are thankfully disappointed. As to the manner of curing, though very mysterious, yet in my opinion, it's very lawfull and nothing akin to any magical operations etc—

J: S:

Endorsed by Locke: B. Furley 12 Apr 97 and J: Spademan. May 97

2261. EDWARD CLARKE to LOCKE, 13 May 1697 (*2259*, 2264)

B.L., MS. Locke c. 6, f. 124. Printed in Rand, p. 513. Answered by no. 2264.

London May the 13th. 1697.

Deare Sir,

Your verie Kind and obleigeing Letter by the last Post came safe to mee, for Which, and all other Instances, of your Reall Freindshipp towards mee and mine, I Return you my hearty Thankes.

I have Written to my Wife in the best manner I can contrive to induce Her comeing to Town with all the speed Possible, And I hope it will Prevayle with Her, That there may bee noe meanes wanting to Preserve Her, whose Life is of soe much moment to mee and mine:

I[a]– have gott your five and twenty pounds from Sir Stephen Evans,–[a] But Mr. Conyers hath been soe much taken up with the Businesse of the Term, that Hee has not yett done any thing further for getting in of the Interest-money due to you, I shall continue to Presse Him as often as I have any opportunity, and will gett the money payd if it bee possible etc:

Pray give the Batchelors and my humble service to my Lady and accept the like your selfe from,

Your most Affectionate Faithfull and obleiged servant

EDW: CLARKE:

The Parliament was this day Prorogued to the 17th. of June next

Address: These, For John Locke Esqr. [at Oates, by Joslyn, Bishops Stortford] Frank: Edw: Clarke:

Postmarks: MA 13; GC

Endorsed by Locke: E: Clarke 13 May 97 Answered 17

2262. WILLIAM MOLYNEUX to LOCKE, 15 May 1697 (2254, *2269*)

The Carl H. Pforzheimer Library, New York. Transcribed from photostat. Printed in *Some Familiar Letters*, pp. 211–15. Answers no. 2243; answered by no. 2277.

Dublin. May. 15th. 1697.

My Most Honourd Friend.

Nothing could excuse my keeping your Kind Letter of Apr. 10.

a–a *Marked by Locke for attention.*

so long by me unanswerd, but an unexpected and Melancholy Accident that has lately befallen a Dear Sister of Mine who on the 24th of Last Month lost her Husband the Lord Bishop of Meath a Learned and Worthy Prelate.[1] Our Whole Family has so deeply partaken in this trouble, that we have been all under a great Concern; but more particularly my self, who am intrusted by the Good Bishop with the Disposal of some of his Affairs. This has of late so taken me up that I had not time to take the satisfaction of writing to you; But the Hurry of that busines being somewhat abated, I resume the Pleasure of Kissing your Hands, and of Assuring you with what a Deep sense of Gratitude I receive the Kindnes you have done me with My Lord Chancellor Methwin. I hope we shall see his Lordship soon here, for we understand He parts from Lond. the 18th Inst.[2]

I am extreamly obleidged to you for the trouble you have been at in Communicating to Me Monsieur Leibnitz Paper, and I am now sorry I ever put the task on you: for to speak freely to you, as I formerly did, I find nothing in this Paper to make me alter the Opinion I had of Monsieur Leibnitz Performances this way. He is either very unhappy in Expressing, or I am very dull in apprehending his thoughts. I do not know, but some of the Doubts he raises concerning your Essay, may proceed from his unacquaintance with Our Language; And this makes me yet more earnest to Procure the Translation of your Essay; But Mr Burridge since he last arrived here has been wholy Imployd in overtaking his Busines in the Country, to which he is run much in Arrear. He is Chaplain to my Lord Chancellor Methwin, and on that account I hope he will keep much in town, and I shall then ply him hard.

I will give you a thousand Thanks for the Present of your Letter to the Bishop of Worcester, but I need not give you my Opinion of it, otherwise than as you find it in the Following Paragraph of a Letter which I received concerning it from a Reverend Prelate of this Kingdom (the Present Bishop of Cloyn[3] between our selves) 'I read Mr Lockes Letter to the Bishop of Worcester with great satisfaction, and am wholy of your Opinion, that he has fairly laid the Great Bishop on his Back; But tis with so much gentlenes, as if he were afraid not only of hurting him, but even of Spoiling or

[1] Anthony Dopping, born in 1643; D.D. 1672; bishop of Kildare 1679; of Meath 1682; died 25 April: *D.N.B.*

[2] So *Post Boy*, 18 May. He left London on the 21st: *London Gazette*, 24 May.

[3] St. George Ashe. He was translated to Clogher on 25 June of this year.

tumbling his Cloths. indeed I cannot tell which I most admire, the great Civility and good Manners in his Book, or the force and clearnes of his Reasonings. And I fancy the Bishop will thank him privately, and trouble the world no more with this Dispute.'

You see thereby My Friends, and my Own Opinion of your Book; and I can tell you farther, that all those whom I have yet conversed with in this Place concerning it, agree in the same Judgement: and another (Bishop too) told me, that tho your *Words were as Smooth as Oyl, yet cutt they like a two-edged sword.*

At the same time that Mr Churchil sent me your Letter to the Bishop, he sent me likewise the Second Vindication of the Reasonablenes of Christianity. If you know the Author thereof, (as I am apt to surmise, you may) be pleased to let him know, that I think he has done Edwards too much Honour in thinking him worth his Notice, for so vile a Poor Wretch certainly never appeard in Print. But at the same time tell him, that as this Vindication contains a farther Illustration of the Divine Truths in the Reasonablenes of Christianity, he has the thanks of Me and of all fair Candid Men that I converse with about it.

In giving you the Opinion we have here off your Letter to the Bishop of Worcester, I have rather chosen to let you know particularly that of Some of Our Bishops with whom I converse; for this Rank, if any, might seem inclinable to Favour their Brother, could they do it with any shew of Justice. And yet after all I am told from London that the Bishop is hammering out an Answer to you.[1] Certainly some men think, or Hope the World will think, that Truth always goes with the last Word.

You never write to me, that you do not raise new expectations in my longing Mind of partaking your Thoughts on those Noble Subjects you are upon. Your Chapter concerning the *Conduct of the Understanding* must needs be very Sublime and Spacious. Oh Sir! never more mention to me Our Distance as your Losse. Tis my Disadvantage; tis my Unhappines. I never before had such reason to deplore my Hard Fate in being Condemned to this Prison of an Iland.; but one day or other I will get loose, in Spite of all the Fetters and Clogs[a-] that incumber[-a] me at present. but if you did but know in what a Wood of Busines I am ingaged (by the greatest

a–a *MS.* Clogs that / that incumber

[1] p. 107; Molyneux had evidently not received no. 2254 as yet.

part whereof I reap no other advantage than the satisfaction of being serviceable to my Friends) you would pitty me. But I hope soon to rid my hands of a great Part of this Trouble, and then I shall be at more Liberty; till which happy time and for ever I remain

Your Most Faithfull Friend and Most Humble Servant

W: MOLYNEUX

Address: To John Locke Esquire at Mr Pawlings overagainst the Plough Inn in Little Lincolns Inn Feilds London

Postmark: MA 29

Endorsed by Locke: W: Molyneux 15° May 97 Answered 15 Jun.

2263. J. V. [or J. N.?] to LOCKE [May 1697]

B.L., MS. Locke c. 23, ff. 188–9. Date from Locke's endorsement. The initials are almost certainly J. V. I cannot identify the writer.

Honoured Sir

I have read over your book of the reasonableness of Christianity, and with much satisfaction as to many of the matters contained in it: But I must confesse my self to be unable to remove those difficulties which seem to attend one of your notions about which if you please farther to explain your self You will not only gratifie mine, but the expectation of many others. I have found it to be wonder'd at by several ingenious persons that Mr Edward's should confine his dispute to your doctrine of one Article,[1] and never touch upon what is by some thought more material to be objected viz: concerning the Future State of Unbelievers, or unrighteous men. If I and others do not mistake; It is your sentiment that there is no future punishment after this life, but death; which you make to be the same with annihilation or ceasing to be. For this, I conceive to be your notion that unrighteous persons will never live again after they die, or if they rise again at the Day of Judgement they will be sentenc'd to death again, to everlasting death i.e. to be annihilated: For I think there is not one place in your whole book that speaks of any other punishment but death, and you could not have avoided mentioning of it since you have had occasion to speak so very often of the reward of the righteous if you thought there were any other punishment.[2]

[1] In *Socinianism Unmask'd*.

[2] Locke does not state his views clearly in *The Reasonableness of Christianity*. He apparently distinguished between the unbelievers (especially the involuntary unbelievers) and the workers of iniquity; the former, if they live righteously, have 'a claim of Right to Eternal Life'; 'an Exclusion from Paradise, and loss of Immortality,

Now I beg leave to represent to you that this Opinion militates against the immortality of the Soul, and against the Doctrine of the Torments of Hell. Against the Immortality of the Soul, which hath been accounted to be a celebrated, and renowned Doctrine of the Ethnick Philosophers, and confirmed by Divine Revelation. For Solomon tells us that when A man dies the Body goes to the Dust; and the Spirit to God that gave it.[1] And our Saviour gives this Counsel to his disciples in the 10th of St Mat. v. 28 Fear not them which Kill the body but are not able to kill the Soul: but rather fear him who is able to destroy both Soul, and body in Hell. By Soul here cannot be meant the life as by Soul, You say, that is understood in St Mark 8 ch. 38 v.[2] For it will not be good sense, Fear not them which Kill the body but are not able to Kill the Life. I further observe that by destroying, Killing is not here signified but a different sort of punishment as appears by comparing this place with the 12th of St Luke 5 v. But I will forewarn you whom you shall fear, Fear him who after he hath killed hath power to cast into Hell; which intimates that after a Man is killed; He is capable of suffering other punishment (probably by reason of the immortal Soul) He may be cast into Hell; And now that I am speaking of Hell I shall take occasion in the second place to repræsent to you that your doctrine seems to set aside its Torments and wholly to extinguish all its Fire. For 'tis impossible that one who ceases to be should be sensible of any pain. Nothing feels Nothing. And yet there are many Texts of Scripture which threaten pain, and Misery, and some of them an Eternity of it against the Disobedient. In the description of Christs comming to Judgement we find the sentence against unrighteous Men to be, Depart from me ye cursed into everlasting fire prepared for the Devil, and his Angels,[3] and in the conclusion; These shall go away into everlasting punishment but the righteous into life eternal,[4] where by punishment

is the Portion of Sinners': pp. 11, 13. John Milner (*D.N.B.*) thought that Locke believed in the annihilation of the wicked: *An Account of Mr. Locke's Religion*, 1700, pp. 151–2 (the citation there of *The Reasonableness* corresponds to p. 208 in the first edition). There is little about hell in the book. In a manuscript, 'Resurrectio et quæ sequuntur', Locke regards it as 'evident that the wicked shall die and be extinguished at last', but they will suffer long and severe torment before their extinction: King, 1830, ii. 139–51 (B.L., MS. Locke c. 27, ff. 162 ff.; dated by Mr. Long *c.* 1699). On the subject generally see D. P. Walker, *The Decline of Hell*, 1964; for Locke's views, pp. 94–5.

[1] Ecclesiastes 12: 7.

[2] The writer's slip for Mark 8: 35–8: *Reasonableness*, p. 15.

[3] Matthew 25: 41.

[4] Ibid., 46.

cannot be understood (I conceive); one that is not felt by them, as Death is not. The Parable of the Field seed, and Tares is to the same purpose St Mat 13 ch. where its said that as the Tares are gathered, and burnt in the fire, so shall it be in the end of this World: The Son of man shall send forth his A⟨ngels⟩[a] and they shall gather out of his Kingdom all things that offend, and th⟨ey wh⟩ich[a] do iniquity, and shall cast them into a Furnace of Fire; There s⟨hall be⟩[a] wailing, and gnashing of Teeth. In the same chapter is contained ⟨the par⟩able[a] of the Nets being cast into the sea much to the same effect; The sam⟨e p⟩unishment[a] being threatened. The Parable of the rich Man, and Lazarus is a further illustration of this. And though there be a rule in Divinity that there must be no arguing from Parables yet it is to be interpreted with a limitation (as indeed Parables themselves are). For so far as Parables are instructive, and we keep close to the main scope, and design of them without expatiating to far into the consideration of circumstances we may venture safely to reason from them. For else they would be insignificant. Now such Parables as threaten pain cannot reasonably be supposed to threaten a ceasing to be. Again we read of the worm which never dieth[1] by which a Mans conscience is commonly understood which gnaws, and torments him; We read also of the Wrath to come;[2] And in St John 3 ch. 36 v of the Wrath of Gods abiding on him who believeth not the Son. I could mention several other places of Scripture out of the Revelations, and other books to the same purpose: But I shall content my self to offer this only to your consideration, that whereas you conceive that life in Misery cannot be understood by the word Death pag. 5, There are 2 things which seem to inferr that it may. One, that sensible punishments or pains are in several of those Texts which I have cited set in direct opposition to life Eternal in the very same verse. And so also in the 2d ch to the Romans where we read that God will give Eternal life to those who continue in Well-doing; but will render to those who obey unrighteousnesse; Indignation, and Wrath, Tribulation, and Anguish. The second thing is that Misery, or Torments is expressly described by Death in the Revelations 21 ch. 8 v. But the fearful, and the unbelieving, and abominable etc. shall have their part in the Lake which burneth with Fire and

[a] *Page torn.*

[1] Mark 9: 44, 46, 48. [2] Matthew 3: 7; Luke 3: 7; 1 Thessalonians 1: 10.

Brimstone; which is the Second Death. If you please to publish your thoughts more largely on this subject it may satisfie those who are prejudiced against your book chiefly upon this account that it seems to disarme the Terrors of Hell, and so weakens the bands of Religion.

I am your Humble Servant

J. V.

Address: For The Author of the Reasonablenesse of Christianity These

Endorsed by Locke: Anonymus May 97

2264. LOCKE to EDWARD CLARKE, 17 May 1697 (*2261*, *2266*)

B.L., MS. Locke b. 8, no. 117. Discoloured and torn. Printed in Rand, p. 514. Answers no. *2261*; answered by no. *2266*.

Oates 17 May 97

Dear Sir

I have just time before the messenger goes to acknowledg the favour of yours of the 15th. I ⟨a⟩m[a] sorry the Interest I expected from Mr Connyers does not come to supply your occasions and therefor what is wanting to make up Sir Stephens and my Lord Ashleys I ⟨mu⟩st[a] refer you to mr Churchill for. Those interessed with me in the Mortgage are Sir Charles Barringtons two sisters[1] who have as I remember £4000 upon it. If they are paid their interest and[b]– not I mine–[b] I have reason to be not soe well satisfied. Pray did Mr Connyers say any thing on that point? If not I leave it to you whether it may not be convenient to aske him the first oportunity you can meet with. I thanke you for what you have done with him upon this matter already and am glad you thinke my money safe. By yours of the 13th I finde you have pressed Mrs Clarke to come up. I hope even the journey it self may doe her good. My humble service to the Batchelor. I writ to him the last post and am

Dear Sir

your most affectionate humble servant

J L

Sir Francis and my Lady salute the Colledg

[a] *Page torn.* [b–b] *MS.* and I not I mine*; the second* I *is interlined, the first left standing.*

[1] p. 24.

Address: For Edward Clarke Esquire member of Parliament at Richards Coffee house within Temple Bar London
Frank

Endorsed by Clarke: Mr. Lock about his Businesse with Mr Conyers etc: Received the 21th. May 1697. Answered the 22th in parte.

2265. Mrs. Elizabeth Stratton to Locke, 20 May 1697 (*2247, 2283*)

B.L., MS. Locke c. 18, f. 229.

bristoll May 20th (1697)

Deare Cosin

I recivd yours of Aprill 30th two days after the death of my deare Mother. since which I have never bine well but have a continuall pain in my head, it's better this day then it is most times. I am not fit for trouble but I meet with many since my dear Husbands dea⟨th⟩,[a] I have never seen Mr Lyde since, if he would have favourd me so far I should willingly have shown him all the concern, I have this day compar'd the account but doe not find that either the two last payments to Mr Palmer of 19s-6d. per payment have bine accounted for. I know Lords rent was not allways paid as soon as it's dew but at the first convenience but if you think it otherwise I leave it wholly to you, and shall be sattisfied with your account. I should be glad to see you this summer and hope it may consist with your convenience, My Son Peter Stratton designs to wait on you about a month hence when I think his time is out, He thinks by the perswation of friends he will not set up yet, but will stay with his master who is a very Honest man and have bine, and I beleve will be, a very Kind friend to him if not a Father. haveing always had a kindness for our whole family. if you desire it I will procure him to draw out the last years account and bring it up with him but I think there's no need of it, he gives you his humble service and so doe my brother and Sister Chapman, and my two daughters, and none more heartily then deare Cousin

your most affectionate Cousin and Humble Servant

Elizabeth Stratton

I think if I could speake you I should by your direction have some ease in my head

[a] *Edge of page.*

Address: For Mr John Locke to be left at Mr Pawlings Overagainst the plough in Little Lincolns Inne feidls in London.

Postmark: MA 24

Endorsed by Locke: E. Stratton 20 May 97 Answered 13 Jun.

2266. EDWARD CLARKE to LOCKE, 22 May 1697 (2264, 2267)

B.L., MS. Locke c. 6, ff. 125–6. Printed in Rand, pp. 514–15. Answers no. 2264; answered by no. 2267.

London May the 22th. 1697.

Deare Sir,

Your obleigeing Letter of the 17th. came not to hand untill last night, And I went early this morning to Mr. Conyers Chamber to have spoken with Him upon the subject matter of your Letter to mee, But could not meete with Him, and have been since Informed That Hee is gone out of Town for the Holy-dayes,[1] soe that I shall not bee able to doe any thing with Him in that Businesse untill his Return againe, When I will not fayle to waite on Him concerning it, and give you a further Account thereof; I[a]– have Received your fifty pounds of my Lord Ashley, and delivered Him your Receipt,–[a] and will Execute, and Leave security in Mr. Churchills handes for that, and the other moneys I am in your Debt, and shall ever Remaine,

Your most Affectionate and obleiged humble servant

EDW: CLARKE:

My humble service to my Lady etc:

Address: These, For John Locke Esqr. [at Oates, by Joslyn, Bishops Stortford]
Frank: Edw: Clarke:

Postmark: MA 22

Endorsed by Locke: E: Clarke 22 May 97 Answered 24

a–a *Marked by Locke for attention.*

1 Whit Sunday fell on 23 May this year.

2267. LOCKE to EDWARD CLARKE, 24 May 1697 (*2266*, *2274*)

B.L., MS. Locke b. 8, no. 118. Printed in Rand, pp. 515–16. Answers no. *2266*.

Oates 24 May 97

Dear Sir

This is only with my thanks to acknowledg the receit of yours of the 22th: where in you expresse soe much care concerning the businesse with Mr Conyers. I know not whether it will be best to make it a businesse to him on purpose or whether when you can luckily meet with him again it will not be better to enquire again whether he hath any news yet or hopes of money for the Interest because you know the presseing occasion I have for it, and then upon his answer to aske whether the others concerned in the Mortgage are as far behind as I am. But I need not ins⟨tr⟩uct[a] you how to finde out the state of that matter

I writ to the Batchelor about a fortnight a gon under your Cover. In it I sent him a copy of all that I had received from Rotterdam concerning the Cures of the Sympathetick Doctor. And I also inclosed a letter for Monsieur le Clerc.[1] Not haveing received a word from him since: And you not mentioning in any of yours anything about it I am in some pain about that letter. My humble service to him. I am

Dear Sir

your most affectionate humble servant

J LOCKE

My Lady returns her service to the Colledg

Address: For Edward Clarke Esquire Member of Parliament at Richards Coffee house within Temple Bar London Frank

Postmark: MA 26 (?)

Endorsed by Clarke: Mr Lock about his Businesse with Mr Conyers etc: Received the 26th. May 1697. Answered the 27th per Mr. Freke:

On the cover there is also a money sum by Locke:

2	9	4
	1	7
2	10	11

[a] *Page torn.*

[1] Locke's answer to no. *2236*; it was dated 8 May.

2268. RICHARD COOTE, first earl of Bellomont, to LOCKE, [25?] May 1697 (*2270*)

B.L., MS. Locke c. 7, ff. 128–9. Locke's date in the endorsement is probably that of the writing of the letter; if it is a date of receipt the letter should be dated a day or two earlier. For the writer see no. 1128; for his appointment as governor of New York, etc., see p. 94, n. 3.

London 2⟨5th.⟩[a] May 97.

Sir

I was in hopes to have seen you in town by this time, and that your health would have allow'd of it. I have I Confesse some Interest in wishing you here, because I go up-hill in all the steps I make towards my departure for America, and your Influence on our great men would I am Confident dispose them to use more dispatch in sending me away, and also send me in a better Capacity of serving the King and the Countries where I am to go, than I find I am like to be sent. To be short I meet with great delays in the several offices, and not with that regard from some of the great men, that I expected: whereby I mean their sending me naked of every thing that those Countries desire and stand in need of for their defence and security against the French, and therefore not in Circumstances of recommending my selfe to the good liking of the people there.[1]

I beg the favour of you to recommend me a good sort of French man to be Governour to my sons,[2] I would have him Civill good humour'd and Learned both in Latin and greek, in both which my eldest is a pretty good proficient, as his Master Monsieur Cappel[3] assures me. Another qualification I Covet in a Governour is the Speaking a pure French. I Intend god willing to send my eldest son the Latter end of Summer to Utrecht, where I will have him to read the greek and Latin Authors Critically with Monsieur Grevius,[4] and then a Course of Philosophy there, or with Monsieur Le Clerc at Amsterdam. I ask pardon for the Liberty I take in this Letter in

[a] *Page torn.*

---

[1] About 14 May Bellomont sent the Lords Justices a memorial on his military equirements: *Cal.S.P.*, *Col.*, vol. xv, no. 1022.

[2] Nanfan Coote, *c.* 1681–1708; second earl of Bellomont 1701; and Richard Coote, . 1683–1766; third earl 1708: G.E.C. For their governor see p. 157 n.

[3] Jacques-Louis Cappel.

[4] Græevius.

troubling you with things that only relate to my selfe. I heartily wish you health and Conclude

Sir

Your most faithfull humble servant

Bellomont

Address: For John Locke Esqr. One of the Right honourable Lords of the Councell of Trade and Plantations

Endorsed by Locke: E: Bellomont 25 May 97 Answered 28

2269. William Molyneux to Locke, 27 May 1697 (*2262*, 2277)

The Carl H. Pforzheimer Library, New York. Transcribed from photostat. Printed in *Some Familiar Letters*, pp. 215–19. Answers no. 2254; answered by no. 2277.

Dublin. May. 27. 1697.

Honour'd Dear Sir

The Hints you are pleased so friendly to communicate to me in yours of the 3d Inst. concerning Mr T.[1] are fresh marks of your Kindnes, and Confidence in me; and they perfectly agree with the Apprehensions I had conceived of that Gentleman. Truly to be free, and without Reserve to you, I do not think His management since he came into this Citty has been so prudent; He has raised against him the Clamours of all Partys; and this not so much by his Difference in Opinion, as by his Unseasonable Way of Discoursing, propagating, and Maintaining it. Coffee-houses and Publick Tables are not proper Places for serious Discourses relating to the Most Important Truths. But when also a Tincture of Vanity appears in the Whole Course of a Mans Conversation, it disgusts many that may otherwise have a due Value for his Parts and Learning. I have known a Gentleman in this town that was a Most strict Socinian and thought as much out of the Common road as any man, and was also known so to do; but then his Behaviour and Discourse was attended with so much Modesty, Goodnes, and Prudence, that I never heard him publickly Censur'd or Clamourd against, neither was any man in Danger of Censure by receiving his Visits or keeping him Company. I am very loath to tell you how far tis otherwise with

[1] Toland. He claimed that while he was in Dublin he kept his opinions to himself: *Apology*, p. 6.

Mr T. in[a–] this place;[–a] but I am perswaded it may be for his advantage that you know it, and that you friendly Admonish him of it, for his conduct hereafter. I do not think that any man can be Dispensed with to Dissemble the Truth, and full perswasion of his Mind in Religious Truths, when duly called to it, and upon fitting Occasions. but I think prudence may guide us in the Choise of proper Oppertunitys, that we may not run our selves against rocks to no purpose, and inflame Men against us unnecessarily. Mr T. also takes here a great Liberty on all occasions to vouch your Patronage and Friendship, which makes many that rail at him, rail also at You. I beleive you will not approve of this, as far as I am able to Judge by your shaking him off in your Letter to the Bishop of Worcester.[1] But after all this, I look upon Mr T. as a very ingenious Man, and I should be very Glad of any Oppertunity of Doing him service, to which I think my self indispensibly bound by your recommendation. One thing more I had almost forgott to intimate to you; that all here are mightily at a Losse in Guessing what might be the Occasion of Mr T. coming at this time into Ireland. He is known to be of no Fortune or Imploy, and yet is observed to have a subsistance; but from whence it comes no one Can tell certainly. These things joynd with his great forwardnes in appearing Publick makes people surmise a thousand Fancys. If you could give me light into these matters, as far as it may help me in my own Conduct, I should be much obleidged to you.

By the Books which Monsieur Coste has translated I perceive his Inclinations would be extreamly agreable to mine. and I should be very happy could I give him at present any incouragement to come into my Poor Family. But I have a Gentleman with me in the House whose Dependence is wholy upon me: and I cannot find fault with my Little Boys Progres under him. When I formerly made enquiry from you about Monsieur Le Clerk I was in some Prospect of providing for this Gentl. whom I now have by the Favour of a Good Friend who is since Dead, so that at present

a–a *MS.* in this / this place

---

1 In *Christianity not Mysterious* Toland used Locke's 'epistemological doctrines as the basis from which to explain his own radical religious beliefs', but had 'gone beyond the bounds of Locke's principles' in the stress that he laid 'upon clarity and distinctness as the criteria of certainty': Yolton, *John Locke and the Way of Ideas*, pp. 118, 125. In *A Discourse in Vindication of the Doctrine of the Trinity* (no. 2189) Stillingfleet implied, if he did not state, that Locke shared Toland's views; Locke objected to this in his *Letter*, pp. 58–62, 90–1, 223–6.

Having no oppertunity of disposing of him to his Advantage I cannot conveniently part with him. However I do not know how soon it may be otherwise; and therefore be pleased in the mean time to let me know something farther off Monsieur Coste: as whether he be a Compleat Master of the Latin Tongue, or other Language, whether a Mathematician, or given to Experimental Philosophy, what his Age, and where Educated. as to the Belles Lettres, L'Histoire: etc. Monsieur Le Clerk has mentiond them already in his Character.

I am mightily pleased to find that some others have the same thoughts of Monsieur Leibnitz as you and I. His performances in Mathematicks has made the World mistaken in him. But certainly in other Attempts I am of your opinion, He no more understands himself, than others understand him.

Mr Churchil Favourd me with the Present of Sir R. Blackmores K. Arthur. I had Pr. Arthur before,[1] and read it with Admiration, which is not at all Lessend by this second Peice. All Our English Poets (except Milton) have been meer Ballad-makers in Comparison to him. upon the Publication of his first Poem I intimated to him, through mr Churchils hands, how excellently I thought he might Perform a Philosophic⟨k⟩[a] Poem[2] from many touches he gave in his Pr. Arth. particularly from Mopas's Song.[3] And I perceive by his preface to K. Arth. he has had the like Intimation⟨s⟩[a] from others, but rejects them as being an Enemy to all Philosophick Hypotheses.[4] Were I acquainted with Sir R. Blackmore I could assure him (and if you be so I beseech you to tell him) that I am as little an Admirer of Hypotheses as any Man, and never proposed that thought to him with a Designe that a Philosophick Poem should run on such a strain. A Natural History of the Great and Admirable Phænomena of the Universe is a subject, I think, may afford sublime Thoughts in a Poem. and so far, and no farther, would I desire a Poem to Extend.

You see I am carried beyond my designed Bounds by the Mark on tother side this Leaf.[b] But as I am never weary of reading Letters

[a] *Edge of page.* [b] *Molyneux had reserved a blank space for the seal.*

---

[1] *Prince Arthur*, 1695. [2] Molyneux elaborates this in no. *2288*

[3] Book iv, pp. 95–7. Johnson reprinted it in his account of Blackmore in the *Lives of the Poets*.

[4] pp. viii–xi; but what the 'others' wanted of Blackmore was treatises on medical or scientific subjects rather than more poems.

from you; so I think I am never tired of Writing to you. Howeve⟨r⟩[a] tis time I releive you by subscribing my self intire⟨ly⟩[a]

Your Most Affectionate and Devoted Servant
W: MOLYNEUX

Endorsed by Locke: W: Molyneux 27° May 97 Answered Jun. 15

2270. RICHARD COOTE, first earl of Bellomont, to LOCKE, 29 May 1697 (*2268*, *2587*)

B.L., MS. Locke c. 7, ff. 130–1.

London 29th. May 97.

Sir

I am very thankfull for the favour of your Letter, and your kind expressions towards me. my eldest son being a pretty good proficient in the greek and Latin, I would willingly have a Governour that were well skill'd in both, and such an one as we Call a very good Scholar. I shall not send my youngest son with his brother, because having not a genius for Latin (though otherwise Ingenious enough and very Lively) I was not willing to put any force on him, and therefore have had him taught to design, Learn French, and arithmetick, and the usuall exercises as dancing and fencing. The Governours businesse therefore will be only to assist my eldest son in his Studies here so long as he Continues with Monsieur Cappel, and afterwards at Utrecht; for I expect he shall Learn as much from his Governour as from his Schoolmaster or Tutor. but Indeed the Chief end of my taking a Governour is to keep my son from falling into ill Courses, such as a great part of our youth run into. I am with all my heart

Sir
Your most faithfull humble servant
BELLOMONT

Address: For John Locke Esqr. One of the Right honourable Lords Commissioners of the Counsell of Trade [at Oates, by Joslyn, Bishops Stortford]

Postmarks: MA 29; TL (?)

Endorsed by Locke: L: Bellamont 29° May. 97

[a] *Edge of page.*

2271. WALTER CROSS to LOCKE, 1 June [1697]

B.L., MS. Locke c. 7, f. 187. The year from Locke's endorsement. The writer is identifiable as the minister in charge of the Independent congregation in Ropemakers' Alley from 1675 to 1701; probably about 1685 at Utrecht, where he is said to have assisted John Howe (no. *873*): Walter Wilson, *Hist. . . . of the Dissenting Churches and Meeting-houses in London* . . . [etc.], 1808–14, ii. 535–6; see also J. Erskine of Carnock, *Journal*, p. 178, etc.

Cross was now at work on his book *The Taghmical Art: or the art of expounding Scripture by the points, usually called accents, but are really tactical*, which appeared in 1698, 'printed for the Author'. L.L., no. 892.

June 1

Honord Sir

I have digested that bussines over and over about the hebr: points. two things move to publish itt one is because (tho hinted at by some as Reinb:[1] says our translators were Coasters they knew not the Compass nor needle viz the points R. Jehu Musc:[2] says the heaps of Comments arise from the ignorance of the accents which wee have Lost) I am in the opinion none hes made itt their bussines as I have and for any thing I know itt may dy with mee without publishing and my bleeding renders my Life Very Uncertain. A Second is the greatnes of the use for the accents 34 in number serve for a Syntaxe, Rhetoric and Logic to the bible; excepting Some different Significations of words itt entirely determins the sense of the o: T: and Leavs no roome for Volums of Critics

My intentions about itt are thus first to print the rules in 5 or 6 sheets and exempls useful without offence in 5 or 6 more. iff the Learnd world be Convinced by itt they may incourage mee or whom they wil to point a translation intirely for tho it hes Coast mee 11 or 12 years pains a boy after ruls given may Learn itt in a weeke

That which I would intreat your favor in is to endeavor to engadge some noble soul or other to incourage mee in the matter My sicknes makes me need itt and 50 or 100 lib would I am sure be weel spent money for public good. Many hes 1000 per annum for Less service. I wil give but this instance, gen 1. 2 v in the beginning god created: he Created the heavens and the earth. and as to the earth; itt was without forme and Void. two things the points informe me off 1 that the heavens or heights and earth contain the whole of the creation : 2 that the earth is the sole subject Moses undertakes to discourse of itt is not the Nominative to was but the

[1] Andreas Reinbeck, *Doctrina de Accentibus Hebræorum*, Brunswick, 1692.

[2] Perhaps Rabbi Judah ben Joseph Moscato, *c.* 1530–*c.* 1593, author and preacher: *Encyc. Judaica*.

proposd subject parted from the greater part which solvs abundance of quæstions in the following discourse. excuse one more gen 10 21 judg 1 13 no Critic can inform me why Japhet should be the elder and Caleb not the younger or that itt is soe butt by these points

Pardon this trouble I mak my application to yow for few or no Clergymen wil incourage me N [a] Con

WA CROS⟨S⟩[a]

Ropemakers alley
Moare feilds

Address: For His Honord freind Mr Locke att Sir Francis Massams to be Left with Mr Joselin Shopkeeper in Bishops Startford Essex

Postmark: IV 1

Endorsed by Locke: W. Crosse 1 Jun. 97

2272. CHRISTOPHER TILSON to LOCKE, 5 June 1697 (2212, 2325)

B.L., MS. Locke c. 20, ff. 190–1.

Sir

The Court of Kings bench having at length given their opinion that the Depositions taken by the Commissioners of Excize ought not to be taken in Evidence before the Commissioners of Appeales but that the Witnesses be againe Examined vivá voce,[1] And the Commissioners of Appeales having received the directions of the Lords of the Treasury to proceed according to the Rule and Judgment of the said Court, They have appointed Fryday next[2] at 3 of the Clock in the Afternoon for hearing and determining the matter on Mr Breedons Appeale, and purpose to proceed on the rest with all Expedition. This I signifye to You by their command and Remaine

Honoured Sir
Your most faithfull and obedient servant
CHRIS: TILSON

5th: June 1697

Address: To John Locke Esqr [at Oates, by Joslyn, Bishops Stortford]

Postmarks: IV 5; LV

Endorsed by Locke: C: Tilson 5 Jun. 97

[a] *Letters lost owing to seal.*

[1] This question was raised in 1696: nos. 2094–5.

[2] 11 June.

2273. Mrs. Elizabeth Berkeley, later Burnet, to Locke, 8 June 1697 (*2198*, *2315*)

B.L., MS. Locke c. 3, ff. 207–8.

Sir

I can honestly excuse my no sooner paying my thanks for the favour of being remembered, by my absence from Town and not knowing my obligation; but I don't so well know how to make a good excuse for my troubleing you at all with my thanks; which are too worthless to atoon for the interuption they give you; as my ignorance made me guilty of the first fault, if I am still in the wrong I intreet it may be imputed to the same cause; but tho you are pleased to suppose me capable of such a present,[1] I own the subject is much too nice for me, not from any obscurity in the expressing your thoughts, but unacquantedness with the matters you treat of; my litle reading and knowledg renders me uncapable to Judg of what depends on speculation, yet I am allways pleased with that sencerity and good temper of mind that is visable in all your writtings: tho I confess I could have sometimes wished a litle less sharpness in your last,[2] but perhaps 'tis only the respect I have for both partyes makes every thing of that nature so sensebly affect me; I could not hope escapeing the severest sencure, did I not beleeve you could forgive every thing that was accompened with a good meaning, tho otherwise as inexcusable as is this Freedom in

Sir

Your Obliged Humble servent

E. Berkeley

June: 8: 97:

Address: For Mr Locke [at Oates, by Joslyn, Bishops Stortford]

Postmark: IV 10 (?)

Endorsed by Locke: E: Berkeley 8° Jun. 97

[1] Probably the *Letter* to Stillingfleet. Mrs. Berkeley is named in the distribution list for it.

[2] Mrs. Berkeley perhaps alludes to the postscript to Locke's *Letter* to Stillingfleet.

2274. Edward Clarke to Locke, 10 June 1697 (*2267, 2299*)

B.L., MS. Locke c. 6, f. 127. Printed in Rand, p. 517.

London June the 10th. 1697.

Deare Sir,

Yesterday I mett with Mr. Conyers as Luckily as you could have Wish'd, And Discoursed Him in the manner you Proposed in your last Letter to mee, And playnly found That the other Partyes Concern'd in the Mortgage had Received part of theire money, but could not Discover how much, nor the time when They Received it; Hee sayes there will bee some money for you likewise before the End of this Term,[1] but pretends Hee does not yett Know how much, And this was all that I could possibly draw out of Him, though I tryed all the Wayes I could thinke of etc:

The[a]– constant Hurry of Businesse hath made mee hitherto forgett to acquaint you, That in the Begining of May last I Received the 25l. that was due from Sir Stephen Evans to you, And about a Weeke after I Received 25l. from Mr. Churchill by your Order and gave Him a Receipt, on the 20th. of May I Received of my Lord Ashley 50l. and gave Him the Receipt you sent mee up for that purpose, And the same Day Executed a Bond to you of 400l. Penalty, for payment of 200l. with Lawfull Interest for the same on the 21th. of August next to you, the other hundred pound included in that Bond being for one yeares Annuity due to you on the 25th. of March last:–[a2] The Batchelor joynes with mee in his hearty service to you and my Lady, And wee hope to see you speedily, which will be a greate Comfort and satisfaction to

your most Affectionate Faithfull servant

Edw: Clarke:

Address: These, For John Lock Esqr. [at Oates, by Joslyn, Bishops Stortford] Frank: Edw: Clarke:

Postmarks: IV 10; RS (?)

Endorsed by Locke: E: Clarke 10 Jun 97 Answered 14

a–a *Marked by Locke for attention.*

1 Trinity term, this year 4–23 June.

2 The bond is B.L., MS. Locke b. 8, no. 172, an engraved form completed in manuscript. Clarke's signature is witnessed by Awnsham and John Churchill. He added a memorandum dated 8 July 1701: 'I payd Mr. Churchill by Mr. Locks Order 212l. for Principall and Interest due, And the Bond was then delivered up to be cancell'd etc:'

2275. W. Barker to Locke, 11/21 June 1697 (*1191, 2304*)

B.L., MS. Locke c. 3, ff. 147–8.

Sir

The Obedience I shall allways pay to your Commands ever put's in mind of my Duty, which I had performed sooner had I been in any wise settled, As soon as I arrived at Rotterdam Delivered your Book to Mr Furley,[1] since that have been at Amsterdam, and there delivered to Mr Limborch Mr Burridge's Book which I received by your Order from Mr Churchill, as also your Letters to the Bishop of Worcester, one to Dr Guenellon, two to Monsr: Le Clerc,[2] which they took as a favour. I have also made enquiry after Gravius's Roman Antiquities[3] whereof there is now six Tomes finished, but the whole sett will be twelve when compleat, the price of those already done, in Quires amount to 86 Gulders,[a] according to this account here inclosed which I find to be the Cheapest I could gett.

We have but little News here but what you will have in the Gazette. I can only say that the Peace begins to move a little and Yesterday the three Imperiall Ministers Met My Lord Villers and Sir Joseph at my Lords, where they had a long Conference this day they met againe and had a Conference with the Pensionarius, the matter thereof is as yett kept very private.[4]

These 2 inclosed were left for me at Amsterdam and happend to ly so long[5] the which I hope you will pardon and in the meantime I shall take it as a very great favour if you will be pleased to employ me in any thing that may be serviceable to you, and at all times freely Command me who shall ever acknowledge myself with all respect to be

Sir

Your most obedient and most humble servant

W. Barker

Hague June the $\frac{11}{21}$ 1697

[a] *MS.* Gul^ds^:

---

[1] Locke's *Letter* to Stillingfleet: p. 158.

[2] One copy was for Coste: p. 154.

[3] *Thesaurus Antiquitatum Romanarum*, altogether 12 vols., folio, Utrecht, 1694–9.

[4] The principal Imperial minister was Dominikus Andreas, Count Kaunitz. Villiers; Sir Joseph Williamson; Lord Pembroke's. The Pensionary is Anthonie Heinsius (*N.N.B.W.*)

[5] Presumably nos. *2255–6*.

Be pleased to direct for me in French at his Excellencys at the Hague or give them to Mr Brounover what hath my address

Endorsed by Locke: W: Barker 21 Jun. 97

2276. WILLIAM WARREN to LOCKE, 12 June 1697

B.L., MS. Locke c. 23, ff. 63–4. I have failed to trace the writer elsewhere. Edward Warren (nos. *1812A*, *2679*) was perhaps a kinsman.

Worthy Sir

About :13: years agoe I saw aletter: which you sent to my Cossen Mr. William Lock of Cearne. in the countey of Dorset[1] which. Leatter he shewed to me. since which time I could. never heare from you. not maney: yeares since I was in Companey with Doctor Manders.[2] who was our Minister but is now master of Baliel: Colledge in oxford. The Docter: told me that he: knew you but did not know whether you: were alive or. Dead. now. my verey. good Frind Mr Edward Wake[3] of Christ Church In oxford he assured me that you were alive. and that he knew you so did Doctor Pitt[4] licke wise Doctor Manders was in our Parish most part of the last winter. and he advised me for. to write unto you. Being so neare Related: your father and my father were brother and Sisters children. Sir: I am the man that. your father did: Commonly call by the name of Cossen Dorset: Sir: I have bin severall times at Pensford at your Fathers house. the last time I was their: youre Father and you and my selfe Road to: Cainsom[5] to Mr Cudringtuns house. another day we were in Vited to your Unckel: Mr: Peter Locks house. and the last jurney iwent with you and your Brother Thomas was to bristow. where I dranke to much of bristow milke.[6] for which Crime your father the next day. layd afine upon me in the Inn which Cost me: 4d: Sir. I have had a great longing for to see you or to heare from you: I had Directions from St: Gilles by my Lord of

[1] William Locke of Cerne Abbas wrote to Locke on 7 June 1682; Locke replied on 22 July (lost), and William wrote again on 2 October: nos. *713*, *735*. There are no traces of further correspondence.

[2] Roger Mander, *c.* 1649–1704; D.D. 1688; rector of Spettisbury, with Charlton Marshall, 1684–1704; Master of Balliol 1687–1704: Foster.

[3] Edward Wake, 1664–1732; matriculated from Christ Church 1679; B.A. 1682; M.A. 1685; D.D., Lambeth, 1724; rector of Broadwell, Gloucestershire, 1697–9; etc.; canon of Canterbury 1721–32: ibid.

[4] Probably Dr. Robert Pitt: no. *2987*.

[5] Probably Keynsham.

[6] Sherry: *O.E.D.*

Shaftons Stuerd Mr: Dallicoatt[1] to writ this superscripshion on my Leater. no more at present: I rest your

Humbell Servant
WM WARREN

Charleton Marshell neere Blandford In the Countey of Dorset

Jun: the: 12: 1697

Address: For the Worshipfull John Locke. esqr In Dorsett Court in Channell Row near Westminster London

Postmark IV 14

Endorsed by Locke: W: Warren 12 Jun 97

2277. LOCKE to WILLIAM MOLYNEUX, 15 June 1697 (*2269*, *2288*)

Some Familiar Letters, pp. 220–5. Answers nos. *2262* and *2269*; answered by no. *2288*.

Oates, 15. June 1697.

Dear Sir,

I have the honour of your two obliging letters of the 15th. and 27th. of May, wherein I find the same mind, the same affection, and the same friendship, which you have so frankly, and so long, made me happy in. And, if I may guess, by the paragraph which you transcribed out of your friend's letter into yours of the 15th. of May, I shall have reason to think your kindness to me is grown infectious, and that by it you fascinate your friends understandings, and corrupt their judgments in my favour. 'Tis enough for me, in so unequal a match, if mighty truth can keep me from a shameful overthrow. If I can maintain my ground, 'tis enough, against so redoubtable an adversary, but victory I must not think of. I doubt not but you are convinced of that by this time, and you will see how silly a thing it is for an unskill'd pigmy to enter the lists with a man at arms, versed in the use of his weapons.

My health, and businesses that I like as little as you do those you complain of, make me know what it is to want time. I often resolve not to trouble you any more with my complaints of the distance between us, and as often impertinently break that resolution. I never have any thoughts working in my head, or any new project

[1] See no. 747.

start in my mind, but my wishes carry me immediately to you, and I desire to lay them before you. You may justly think this carries a pretty severe reflection on my country, or my self, that in it I have not a friend to communicate my thoughts with. I cannot much complain of want of friends to other purposes. But a man with whom one can freely seek truth, without any regard to old or new, fashionable or not fashionable, but truth merely for truth's sake, is what is scarce to be found in an age, and such an one I take you to be. Do but think then what a pleasure, what an advantage it would be to me to have you by me, who have so much thought, so much clearness, so much penetration, all directed to the same aim which I propose to my self in all the ramblings of my mind. I, on this occasion, mention only the wants that I daily feel, which makes me not so often speak of the other advantages I should receive from the communication of your own notions, as well as from the correction of mine. But, with this repining, I trouble you too much, and, for the favours I receive from you, thank you too little, and rejoyce not enough in having such a friend, tho' at a distance.

As to the gentleman, to whom you think my friendly admonishments may be of advantage for his conduct hereafter,[1] I must tell you, that he is a man to whom I never writ in my life, and, I think, I shall not now begin. And, as to his conduct, 'tis what I never so much as spoke to him of. That is a liberty to be only taken with friends and intimates, for whose conduct one is mightily concerned, and in whose affairs one interesses himself. I cannot but wish well to all men of parts and learning, and be ready to afford them all the civilities, and good offices in my power. But there must be other qualities to bring me to a friendship, and unite me in those stricter tyes of concern. For I put a great deal of difference between those whom I thus receive into my heart and affection, and those whom I receive into my chamber, and do not treat there with a perfect strangeness. I perceive you think your self under some obligation of peculiar respect to that person upon the account of my recommendation to you; but certainly this comes from nothing but your over-great tenderness to oblige me. For, if I did recommend him, you will find it was only as a man of parts and learning for his age, but without any intention that that should be of any other consequence, or lead you any farther, than the other qualities you should find in him, should recommend him to you. And therefore, whatsoever you

[1] Toland.

shall, or shall not do for him, I shall no way interest my self in. I know, of your own self, you are a[a]– good friend–[a] to those who deserve it of you; and for those that do not, I shall never blame your neglect of them. The occasion of his coming into Ireland now, I guess to be the hopes of some employment, now upon this change of hands there.[1] I tell you, *I guess*, for he himself never told me any thing of it, nor so much as acquainted me with his intentions of going to Ireland, how much soever *he vouches my patronage and friendship*, as you are pleased to phrase it. And as to his subsistence, from whence that comes, I cannot tell. I should not have wasted so much of my conversation, with you, on this subject, had you not told me it would oblige you to give you light in these matters, which I have done, as a friend to a friend, with a greater freedom than I should allow my self to talk to another.

I shall, when I see Sir R. Blackmore, discourse him as you desire. There is, I with pleasure find, a strange harmony throughout, between your thoughts and mine. I have always thought, that laying down, and building upon hypotheses, has been one of the great hindrances of natural knowledge;[2] and I see your notions agree with mine in it. And, though I have a great value for Sir R. Blackmore, on several accounts, yet there is nothing has given me a greater esteem of him, than what he says about hypotheses in medicine, in his preface to K. Arthur,[3] which is an argument to me that he understands the right method of practising physick; and it gives me great hopes he will improve it, since he keeps in the only way it is capable to be improved in; and has so publickly declared against the more easie, fashionable, and pleasing way of an hypothesis, which, I think, has done more to hinder the true art of physick, which is the curing of diseases, than all other things put together; by making it learned, specious, and talkative, but ineffective to its great end, the health of mankind; as was visible in the practice of physick, in the hands of the illiterate Americans; and the learned physicians, that went thither out of Europe, stored with their hypotheses, borrowed from natural philosophy, which made them indeed great men, and admir'd in the schools, but, in curing

a–a *Printed* good a friend

[1] New Lords Justices were appointed on 14 May and sworn in on 31 May. But Toland arrived in March and Locke perhaps refers to Methuen.

[2] *Essay*, II. i. 10; IV. xii. 12–13.

[3] p. x. The passage may have been based on the *Essay*.

diseases, the poor Americans, who had scaped those splendid clogs, clearly out-went them. You cannot imagin how far a little observation, carefully made, by a man not tyed up to the four humours; or sal, sulphur and mercury; or to acid and alcali, which has of late prevailed, will carry a man in the curing of diseases, though very stubborn and dangerous, and that with very little and common things, and almost no medicines at all.[1] Of this I could, from my own experience, convince you, were we together but a little while. But my letter is too long already. When I am writing to you, the pleasure of talking to you makes me forget you are a man of business and have your hands full. I beg your pardon for it. 'Tis time to dismiss you. I am,

Dear Sir,
Your most affectionate, and
most faithful humble servant,
JOHN LOCKE.

2278. SAMUEL BOLD to AWNSHAM CHURCHILL, 25 June 1697 (*2257, 2359*)

B.L., MS. Locke c. 4, f. 16. Fragment.

Steeple, June. 25. 1697.

Worthy Sir
I sent six sheets of my Observations on the Animadversions on the Reasonableness of christianity etc to your father[2] saturday last, desiring Him to send them to you as soon as He could get an opportunity. He sent me word the same day, It was done, so that I hope you have them by this time. Those sheets contain all I have to say to the 2 first parts of the Animadversions, except about half a page in the next sheet, if you shal require me to send up the remainder of my observations, which are upon the third part of the Animadversions. If you think fit to have my Observations printed, I must desire you to give me timely notice, that I may transcribe What is behind, which I think wil be about three sheets, or 3 and a half more. I was so weary with transcribing those already sent, I have proceeded no further than the end of the second part of the Animadversions, nor shal I begin to transcribe any more, til

[1] There is a similar passage in Locke's letter of 20 January 1693 to Dr. Thomas Molyneux: no. 1593.
[2] Probably William Churchill of Dorchester: no. *1913*.

I know your determination concerning them. I would be glad if the Author of the Reasonableness would look those sheets over, and see whether I have done Him, and the subject any Right, and that you would have his Judgment whether they may be fit for the publick or not, and accordingly either to have them printed, or to send them back to me. I read this week the Bishop of Worcesters Answer as He cals It to mr Locks letter.[1] It doth not satisfy me at all. I hope Mr Lock wil find time to make matters thoroughly plain. Tho I read the Bishop's book in haste, I thought several things did occur to me, that might justify my thinking the Bishop's book not a ful Answer.

Endorsed by Locke: S: Bold to A Churchill 25 Jun 97

2279. FRANCIS GASTRELL, later bishop of Chester, to LOCKE, 1 July [1697] (*2515*)

B.L., MS. Locke c. 9, ff. 207–8. Year from Locke's endorsement. Francis Gastrell, 1662–1725; a nephew of Edward Bagshaw (no. *115* n.); student of Christ Church 1680; B.D. 1694; preacher at Lincoln's Inn 1694–1714; D.D. 1700; bishop of Chester 1714: *D.N.B.*

Christchurch Jul: 1

Sir

The letter you was pleased to honour me with gave me such large and obliging assurances of your extraordinary civility to me and esteem for my late performance,[2] that I should appear very insensible or very ungratefull if I did not immediately return you my most humble acknowledgments. I am very well satisfied that your great candour and readinesse to incourage every thing that tends to the service of Religion and Truth has disposed you to overrate what I have done, but I am too well pleased with your good opinion of me to say any thing to lessen it, whatever faults or defects I may be conscious of. If I have really succeeded in any thing I have writ I must own to you what I am sure the world will take notice of, that I am very much beholding to your reflexions upon Humane Understanding, and I shall be very glad if I should be soe happy as to convince others that your notions will most effectually

[1] p. 107, n. 1.

[2] Gastrell was this year's Boyle Lecturer and published his sermons as *The Certainty and Necessity of Religion in general*. L.L., no. 1213. The book was advertised in *London Gazette*, 17 May.

serve the purposes of Religion for which they were principally intended. When I return to town, which will be at the beginning of September, I hope to enjoy the happinesse of that conversation which the rigour of the winter-season denied me. I should be surer I believe of meeting you in town if I came sooner but some businesse that calls me from this place will occasion my stay from town as long as my lecture will give me leave.

I am Sir

Your most obliged Humble Servant

FRANCIS GASTRELL

Address: To Mr. Locke to be left at Mr Churchills a bookseller in Pater-noster-row London

Postmark: IY 2

Endorsed by Locke: F: Gastrell 1 Jul. 97

2280. LOCKE to LADY MASHAM, 3 July 1697 (1322)

B.L., MS. Locke c. 24, ff. 193–4. Folded and sealed; apparently the letter sent to Lady Masham.

London 3 Jul *97*

Madam

I have soe little time to throw away, that though my letters are of noe great value, yet I cannot but be vexed that any of them should miscary because some of my time was laid out upon them, and that which addes to my vexation is that you were thereby disappointed of your expectation and soe kept in pain. I can only answer for my self that I writ on Tuesday night last[1] and I hope before this time you have it. If neither that nor one that I sent by Bishop Startford Coach this morning have already told you, to rid you of that doubt I acknowledgh here again the receit of your two letters of 28th, your two of 29th, and one of the 30th Jun, to which I must now adde yours of 2d instant which I received this afternoon.

As to the cheif matter of all those of June, I shall repeat here again in short what I writ you by this days coach. viz That upon the receit of your letters I proceeded with Mr de l. T[2] just as you directed and he caried himself just as you could have wished. For after I had bargaind with him upon his termes and your way of payment which he without scruple accepted I then mentiond my

[1] 29 June. [2] La Treille: p. 152 n.

Lord B:[1] to him and told him you set him at liberty again and he might treat with my Lord if he pleased. He seemd mightily pleasd and obleiged by your generous way of proceeding, but replyd he preferd your Ladyship and soe immediately confirmd our bargain again and will be at Oates the next weeke or the following. In the proposeing of it I told him, that the reason that moved you to come up to his rate, was his soe frankly offering to come and be with the child till you could be provided. This last cariage of his has extremly pleased me and I like the man better than ⟨ever⟩[a] I did before. for he seemd to doe it with pleasure and both Mr Popple and he seemd very glad he was to come to Oates

Mrs Lockhart was in town Wednesday but went back to Hampton Court[2] the same night, when I see her next I shall remember Mrs Smals[3] account, and ten to one vex her about it

As to Mr Clarke of Hollingburys proposition[4] I say this That since you have engaged your self, if you have but £50 of your owne to lend I will adde my £50 to make it up or more if you want it provided it be your own private money and not the Trustees, for I will not mix any money of mine with theirs, not that it will be lesse safe, but it will confound the account. And therefor I would advise you by noe means to mix any other money with that nor to make any such proposition to the Trustees for I think it will not looke well. Another thing I would advise you never again to looke out a securitie till you have the money ready in your hands or ⟨are⟩[b] sure to have it at a certain day, or else you will be perplexed as now you are under an uncertainty of Mr Wottons. I beleive you may depend upon Mr Churchill him and Mr Clarke I shall I guesse see tomorrow and shall aske your questions. When I shall see the Bishop of Glocester I know not for he comes to town Saturdays and goes out Mondays and is in the Country all the weeke. but I will endeavour it as soon as I can. But that I may not be thought to have said it Transiently I here desire you again to consider whether it will not be better to loose a little interest than to perplex the account, which I guesse will be enough soe at best. If you have a minde[c] to sell the plate, you must looke in the will[5] whose consent you must have. the Executors or Trustees. I thinke it is yet in th

[a] *MS.* every [b] *MS.* a [c] *MS.* aminde

[1] Identifiable as Bellomont: p. 157, n. 1. [2] p. 104. [3] pp. 96, 10
[4] Perhaps Great or Little Hallingbury, between Oates and Bishop's Stortford rather than Hollingbury Hill near Brighton in Sussex. [5] Mrs. Cudworth'

Executors possession and then you may aske his consent and soe you account to him for it, and he to us when he delivers over to us the whole estate and discharges himself of it. and then in the mean time you may dispose of it as your owne money till that time. If Mr Wotton pay in that £50 that is now in the Trustees names and we shall noe doubt consent to place it out upon such security as you shall approve of and soe, that you may be[a] sure[a] if you receive it Mr Clarke of Hollingburys freind may have it. and if the personall security proposed be good they may give one bond to the Trustees for that and an other bond to me for mine, But to conclude and put you at Ease If the security be good, what you want I will make up of the £100 soe that Mr Clarke may depend on the money. I am

Madam

Your Ladyships most humble servant

J Locke

My humble service to Sir Francis Mrs Masham Mr Tikell Mrs Smith and Jack. I love Totty more than you can thinke and pray remember me kindly to him. You will now I thinke in a few days be at ease in that tender part.

Endorsed by Locke: JL to L: Masham 3 Jul 97

2281. Anonymous to John Churchill, [3? July 1697]

B.L., MS. Locke c. 23, ff. 200–1. Date: The postmark gives the day of posting as Saturday. Edwards's *Brief Vindication* is advertised in *The Flying Post*, Thursday, 1 July–Saturday, 3 July. It is unlikely to have been published before 1 July. The letter appears to have been written very soon after the publication of the book. Hence the date here assigned to it.

Sir

I am not now in a condition to come abroad else I would give you an account by word of mouth what I now design by letter. This morning I received Mr Edwards's brief vindication etc[1] being a further abuse of a man who no ways deserves it and even upon an

[a] *MS.* besure

[1] *A Brief Vindication of the Fundamental Articles of the Christian Faith, as also, of the Clergy, universities, and publick schools, from Mr. Lock's reflections upon them in his Book of Education,* [etc.] *With some animadversions on two other late pamphlets, viz. of Mr. Bold, and a nameless Socinian writer,* 1697. L.L., no. 1028.

account that merits the highest commendation if he is the worthy author of the Reasonableness of Christ etc. this late book of Mr Ed's contains likewise some remarks on Mr Locks Education etc. all which he dedicates to the two Universities and gives us in a letter the imprimatur of the Vice chancellour etc[1] which I am sure by what I heard from Cambridge came very unwillingly the Vice-chancellour making this reflection on Mr Edw's book that no one was fit to be the author of it but a prevaricator.[2] this goes currently about as the judgment of the ViceChanc. at Cambridge, together with this passage from Mr Ed's book which I find is omitted in print that Mr Lock was Governour of the Seraglio at Oats with others of the like nature. Pardon this crude Scribble. I am under a present indisposition. this I hope will be of some service therefore you may communicate it to the persons concerned in order to their enquiry about the truth of what I have said

Yours etc

Address: To Mr John Churchill at the black swan in Pater noster Row. London

Postmark: London Penny Post: T SAT; P A– 4

Endorsed by Locke: Anonymus to J: Churchill Jul. 97

2282. FRANCIS CUDWORTH MASHAM to LOCKE, 5 July 1697 (*1750, 2613*)

B.L., MS. Locke c. 16, ff. 14–15.

Oates July 5 1697

Honoured Sir

You have done me so great a favour to trouble your self concerning a Tutor for me that I cannot acknowledge it so much as I would but I hope I shall deserve your kindness and that of all my Freinds for I will indeavor it as much as possibly I can. I long to see you in my Garden for I love you more then you can think. Pray Sir doe me the

[1] The imprimatur was signed by Henry James, D.D.; President of Queens' College 1675–1717; vice-chancellor 1683–4, 1696–9; regius professor of divinity 1699–1717 (Venn); Covel; John Balderston, D.D.; Master of Emmanuel 1680–1719; vice-chancellor 1687–8, 1706–7 (ibid.); and Joseph Beaumont, D.D.; Master of Peterhouse 1663–99; regius professor of divinity 1674–99 (*D.N.B.*). Covel was vice-chancellor in 1688–9 and 1708–9.

An imprimatur at this time (except perhaps for some academic books) was commendation and not a licence to print.

[2] The Prevaricator at Cambridge corresponded to the *Terræ Filius* at Oxford, making a satirical speech at the Commencement.

favour to present my humble service to Mr. de la Treille and to tell him that I am extreamly glad to heare I shall have the happiness to have him my Tutor and that I will study to please him in all things. My Father Mother and Sister present theire humble services to you.

I am Sir

Your most humble and Obedient Servant

FRA: CUDW: MASHAM

Pray Sir doe me the favour to present my service to Mr Pawling and Mrs Pawling and to all theire family.

Address: For Mr Locke These Present

Endorsed by Locke: F: C: Masham 5° Jul 97

2283. MRS. ELIZABETH STRATTON to LOCKE, 5 July 1697 (*2265, 2316*)

B.L., MS. Locke c. 18, ff. 230–1.

bristoll July 5th 1697

Deare Cosin

I thought my son Peter Stratton would have seen you before this. but I find his Master think's it not fit for him to take a Jorney to London till their business makes it nessecary which I percive will not be till neare September, unless you desire to see him sooner, he is a very sober man, and I doubt not but will doe very well in his trade, his Master is a very Honest man and have a good estate and great kindness for Peter, and I am glad he is so wise as to be governd by him, I am sorry you think you shall not come down to bristoll this summer, I did hope to have eas'd my mind to you and have advis'd with you, for I doe beleeve did you know my curcumstancys you would not desire me to pay you 10l. especially since my deare Husband spent so much time and money in your business without chargeing any thing to you, but my children have the less for all expences, my deare made his will some time before he dye'd (but had severall great Loss'es after the makeing it) he gave my two daughters 200l a peece but with all my care I can never yet make up 300l for both, and have since uppon Ocation contracted severall smaller debts, the liveing that was settle'd on me[1] there is so much

[1] No. *2132*.

goes out of it for payments and repair that it brings in but little, yoe[a] see[a] at present I am not in a cappacity to pay you.

I give you many thanks for your kind advise and will labour to follow it, I have in persuit of it, bine let blood and cut of my hair by further advise and by the blessing of God have receiv'd good by it, for tho I have still a weake head it is not so constantly painfull and thro mercy my mind is somwhat easier then it had bine. I endevour to be wholly resignd to the will and wisdome of our good God.

as to your business with Mr Palmer, I find the last rent paid to him was dew 25 March 95,[b] which[b] payment of 19s - 6d and the same sum paid once before is not accounted with you uppon your last account, I hope you nor I shall have noe further trouble in it, tho if Mr Lyde would have spent but a little time in Looking one the book it might have save'd all this labour, my brother and Sister Chapman give you their humble service and so doe my two daughters, my son Peter Stratton is in the country with his Sister Hasell, who would be all glad to see you and none more then deare Cousin,

your most affectionat Cosin and Humble Servant
ELIZABETH STRATTON

Address: For Mr John Locke to be left at Mr Pawlings Overagainst the plough in Little Lincolns Inne feilds in London

Postmark: IY 7

Endorsed by Locke: E: Stratton 5° Jul. 97

2284. R. DE LA TREILLE to LOCKE [*c.* 8? July 1697] (*2286*)

B.L., MS. Locke c. 13, ff. 18–19. The writer is probably either the man mentioned in no. *1470*, etc., or a kinsman. Date: Locke and la Treille met apparently after 29 June and probably not until Friday, 2 July. According to Locke la Treille engaged himself at that meeting to enter Lady Masham's service: pp. 147–8. La Treille writes in the present letter that he expects to see Locke on the following day (*demain*), and it might be regarded as anticipating that meeting. But it appears to have been written after la Treille had engaged himself. If Locke's date in the endorsement is a correct date of

[a] *Doubtful reading.* [b] *MS.* 95) which

receipt, he must have received the letter late on 3 July; but the first sentence of the letter is scarcely compatible with a meeting on the preceding day, and a business meeting on a Sunday is unlikely. In view of la Treille's request to be allowed until Tuesday to make up his mind a date 7 or 8 July seems the likeliest, Tuesday being the 13th.

Monsieur

Depuis la derniere fois que j'ai eu l'honneur de vous voir j'ai communiqué à quelques uns de mes amis ce qui s'étoit passé entre nous, sans pourtant vous nommer ni Mylady M. Ils m'ont generalement tous blâmé, et memes avec aigreur, d'avoir negligé l'ocasion de voiager lors qu'elle se presentoit à moi si favorablement sans avoir fait aucune démarche pour cela. Ils m'ont representé comment tous les eforts qu'ils avoient fait jusques ici pour me procurer quelque place avantageuse avoient été inutiles par cette seule raison que je n'avois point encore voiagé; ils m'ont dit que je me trouverois encore dans le méme état au sortir de la maison où j'avois si grande envie d'entrer, qu'on se lassoit enfin d'agir toujours sans fruit pour la méme personne, et que je meritois d'etre abandonné si je rejettois moimeme les ocasions qui se presentoient de m'avancer. Je vous avouë que ces reproches m'ont fait beaucoup de peine, et je me suis trouvé tellement balancé entre la peur de déplaire à mes amis, et l'inclination que j'ai d'aller aupres de Mr. M: que je ne sai presque de quel côté me tourner. Qu'on est malheureux lors qu'on se trouve en de telles circonstances où quelque parti qu'on prenne on ne peut se dispenser d'encourir la disgrace des personnes qu'on a le plus de raison d'aimer et d'estimer. Je vous conjure, Monsieur, de ne me vouloir point de mal du suspens ou je parois étre, ce ne sont pas mes mouvemens, ce sont ceux de mes amis que je suis. J'estime et je respecte au dernier point Sir Fr. et Mylady. je me trouverois trop heureux d'avoir le soin de l'education d'un enfant qui promet autant que leur fils, et vous ne pouvés douter que je ne regardasse comme un bonheur extréme pour moi l'avantage de demeurer avec vous, pour qui j'ai une estime et une veneration au delà de toute expression. Mais enfin, Monsieur, je ne suis pas en état de suivre mes inclinations, je doi preferer l'utile à l'agréable et sur tout n'eloigner pas de moi des amis à qui je suis redevable de mille soins et de mille services. J'aurai l'honneur de vous voir demain et de vous entretenir plus au long sur ce sujet. Je ne demanderois de retardement que jusqu'a Mardy, apres quoi je vous promets de n'user plus de delais à quoi que cela puisse m'exposer de la part de mes amis. Je suis avec tout le respect que je doi

Monsieur

Vôtre tres-humble et tres-obeïssant serviteur

R. DE LA TREILLE

Endorsed by Locke: R: de la Treille 30 Jul 97

2285. PIERRE COSTE to LOCKE, 6/16 July 1697, and JEAN LE CLERC to LOCKE, 9/19 July 1697 (*2107*, *2480*; *2236*, *2289*)

B.L., MS. Locke c. 7, ff. 144–5. Coste's letter is printed by G. Bonno in *Revue de Littérature comparée*, xxxiii (1959), 168–70; Le Clerc's, in Bonno, *Le Clerc*, p. 100.

[Coste:]

A Amsterdam ce 16. Juillet.

Monsieur,

Il y a long-temps que je souhaite pouvoir vous remercier de l'honneur que vous m'avez fait de m'envoyer vôtre dernier Ouvrage.[1] Lors que Mr. leClerc me le donna, j'étois au lict accablé d'une violente fluxion qui est une suite d'un mal encore plus fâcheux, dont j'ai été tourmenté par intervalle, depuis près de deux ans. Après avoir essayé plusieurs remedes qui tous m'ont soulagé sans me guerir entierement, je me suis déterminé, par avis d'un Medecin, à prendre des bains chauds, qui me font extremement suer, et qui ont par ce moyen dissipé une partie de cette fluxion, qui me causoit des douleurs presque continuelles à la tête, et aux dents tantôt d'un côté, tantôt de l'autre. Je souffre de ce mal depuis plus de deux mois sans presque aucun relache. On a remarqué durant tout le cours de ce mal, que lors qu'il se dissipoit il revenoit precisément à cinq heures après midi, et duroit bien avant dans la nuit, et s'il venoit à cesser pour quelque temps, il revenoit encore à la pointe du jour. Ces retours periodiques étoient toûjours accompagnez de fiévre; c'est pourquoy on m'a fait prendre le kinkina pendant deux ou trois jours; mais comme il me gâtoit l'estomac, j'ai été obligé de le quitter. Je n'ai presque point d'appetit, et je ne dors qu'à la faveur du laudanum dont on me donne quelques grains tous les soirs. Je ne sçai si les bains qui semblent

[1] The *Letter* to Stillingfleet: p. 140.

me soulager, comme je viens de dire, me gueriront entierement. Quoy qu'il en soit, je suis en meilleur état que je n'ai encore été. Je profite de ce temps de relache pour vous remercier de vôtre beau présent. J'ai été fort surpris de vous voir attaqué si violemment sur d'aussi foibles prétextes. Cela feroit croire qu'on a eu plûtôt en veuë de vous chagriner que de vous remettre dans le bon chemin. Le bruit a couru ici que vôtre Adversaire revenoit à la charge. Il n'y a pas grande apparence à cela. Et si cela étoit, ce seroit un nouveau sujet de triomphe pour vous.

Après vous avoir remercié, Monsieur, de vôtre présent, j'ai de nouvelles graces à vous rendre pour le soin que vous prenez depuis si long-temps, pour me procurer un établissement en Angleterre. Je souhaiterois pouvoir vous en témoigner ma reconnoissance autrement que par des paroles, mais si un desir sincere de reconnoître une obligation doit être compté pour quelque chose, lors qu'on ne peut passer jusqu'aux effets, je vous prie de me tenir compte de ma reconnoissance.

Du reste, vous voulez sçavoir ce que je puis demander pour les appointemens, si je prens le parti que vous me proposez. Voici en deux mots ce que j'ai à dire sur cet article. Deux jours après avoir appris que vous aviez trouvé jour à me placer en Angleterre, je reçus une Lettre d'un de mes Amis qui est à Vesel,[1] dans laquelle il me proposoit d'entrer chez un Colonel François, pour y élever deux Enfans de 12 à 13 ans à condition qu'on me donneroit outre la Table et le Logement, cent écus par an. J'ai écrit à cet Ami que je ne pouvois luy répondre positivement sur cela, avant que d'avoir reçu des nouvelles d'Angleterre où l'on me proposoit une pareille place sans m'en dire les conditions. Plusieurs raisons m'obligent à préferer le parti que vous me proposez. Je me feray un grand honneur d'être auprès de vous, et je tacherai de profiter de cette proximité. D'ailleurs je suis bien aise d'apprendre l'Anglois. Je suis assez jeune pour cela; mais si j'attendois davantage, je n'y serois plus à temps. J'embrasserai donc avec plaisir la place que vous avez eû la bonté de me procurer; et pour les appointemens, *cæteris positis*[2] je croy qu'ils doivent être de 25 piéces par an pour le moins. Comme je ne puis tirer aucun secours d'ailleurs pour m'entretenir, je ne pourrois m'engager sans cela. Si vous voulez m'apprendre la qualité de la personne chez qui vous voulez m'introduire, vous me ferez plaisir. J'espére qu'il sera satisfait de moy: du moins je ne

[1] Wesel, on the Rhine. [2] 'The rest being settled'.

negligerai rien pour cela.[1] Si le Traité[2] se conclut, je partirai d'ici lors que le Roy retournera en Angleterre. Il me faut, à peu près, ce temps pour mettre ordre à mes affaires.

Je travaille, Monsieur, à la traduction de vôtre Ouvrage de *l'Entendement*; mais mon peu de santé ne m'a pas permis de l'avancer beaucoup. Le Libraire[3] souhaite avec passion de l'imprimer, et je ne le desire pas avec moins d'ardeur. Si j'étois en Angleterre, j'y pourrois travailler plus facilement et plus rapidement qu'ici, où plusieurs autres soins, dont je ne puis me dispenser, me detournent de temps en temps de cette occupation. J'ai traduit, à la priere de M. Buys[4] Pensionnaire d'Amsterdam le Ch.X. du IV. Liv. où vous traitez de *l'existence de Dieu*. Vos raisonnemens luy ont paru fort justes aussi bien qu'à Mr. Hudde[5] Bourgmestre de cette ville, à qui il a communiqué mon Cayer.[6] Ils ne se sont point apperçus ni l'un ni l'autre de ce que vôtre Censeur y a trouvé à redire,[7] parce qu'ils n'ont songé à y voir que ce qui y est veritablement. Je suis, avec un profond respect,

Monsieur,

Vôtre très-humble et très-obeïssant serviteur

COSTE

[Le Clerc:]

Voici, Monsieur, une Lettre de Mr. Coste qu'il m'a envoiée pour vous l'adresser. J'avois dessein d'y en joindre une pour répondre à la vôtre et pour vous remercier de vôtre Ouvrage contre l'Evêque de Worcester, mais je suis si empêché qu'il m'est impossible de le faire à présent. Cependant je n'ai pas voulu retarder d'envoier à la poste cette Lettre, qui est écrite depuis l'Ordinaire passé. Mr. Coste met ce qu'il demande au plus juste, afin qu'il ne faille pas écrire davantage pour cela. Je suis scandalisé du

[1] Locke could scarcely as yet have offered Coste a place at Oates; he perhaps did so on 20 July in his answer to this letter, after la Treille had withdrawn: pp. 157–8. He perhaps wrote to Coste while he believed that Molyneux wanted a tutor: pp. 106, 133–4.

[2] At Ryswick.

[3] Presumably Anthony Schelte; the translation was published in 1700 by his half-brother and successor Hendrik Schelte.

[4] Willem Buys, 1661–1749; pensionary of Amsterdam 1693–6; diplomatist: van der Aa.

[5] No. 1213, etc.; pp. 206, 257, etc.

[6] 'A quire of written paper', etc.: Cotgrave, who gives *cahier* as a variant. Boyer also treats *cahier* as a variant.

[7] Stillingfleet criticizes *Essay* IV. x in his *Discourse in Vindication of the Doctrine of the Trinity* (no. 2189), pp. 246–52.

procedé de Mr. Stillingfleet, et surpris qu'il soit si neuf en Philosophie. Si l'on vouloit traiter aussi à la rigueur son chapitre Contre *Courcelles*,[1] qu'il fait ses Antagonistes, on le mettroit en poudre. Il n'entend rien dans la matiere, et il n'a point examiné les passages qu'il cite. Il appelle *gross mistake* ce que *Courcelles* dit d'un passage de S. Hilaire,[2] et il n'y a rien de plus assuré que Courcelles a raison. Je pourrai vous en dire davantage une autre fois. Cependant je vous suis très-obligé. Comme je voi que vous n'avez pas vû la Critique, je vous prie d'envoier ce billet à Mr. *Huguetan*[3] qui ne manquera pas d'en faire donner un exemplaire. J'ai perdu l'occasion d'envoier à Londres, parce qu'un homme, qui y négotie, m'avoit promis de m'avertir quand il y envoieroit, et qu'il ne la pas fait. Il en faudra chercher une autre. Je suis vôtre très-humble et très obeïssant serviteur

LE CLERC.

A Amsterdam le 19 de Juillet 1697.

Address (written by Le Clerc): A Monsieur Monsieur Locke at Mr. Pawlings in little Lincolns inne fields, over against the plough London.

Postmark: IY 15

Endorsed by Locke: Coste and Le Clerc 16 Jul. 97 Answered 20 and 23

2286. R. DE LA TREILLE to LOCKE, [*c.* 17 July 1697] (*2284*)

B.L., MS. Locke c. 13, f. 20. Date from Locke's endorsement. La Treille entered Lord Bellomont's service as governor to his sons; they were granted passes on 27 August to go to Holland: *Cal.S.P.*, *Dom.*, 1697, p. 334.

Monsieur

Puis que je ne puis pas avoir l'honneur de vous parler je me croi obligé de vous écrire pour vous faire savoir qu'il m'est impossible de demeurer plus long tems dans le suspens où vous me tenés. J'ai tâché de prendre les voies les plus honnêtes qu'il m'a été possible pour obtenir de vous ou de My lady M: mon degagement, mais j'ai eu le chagrin de voir que tout ce que j'ai fait a eu le malheur de vous deplaire, et les choses sont venuës à un tel point que je ne

[1] *Discourse*, pp. 76–100. For Courcelles see no. *1178*.

[2] '. . . his gross mistake . . .', p. 77.

[3] Probably Marc Huguetan, the most interested of the brothers in bookselling; he was in England in 1695: nos. *1855*, *1933*.

doi plus penser à entrer chés Mylady Masham. Ainsi je croi que vous ne devés pas trouver mauvais si je cherche les ocasions de disposer de moi d'une autre maniere, puis que je ne suis pas en état de vivre sans emploi. Cela n'empêchera pas que je ne conserve toujours pour vous tout le respect que je vous doi et que je ne sois tres sincerement

Monsieur

Votre tres-humble et tres-obeïssant serviteur

R. DE LA TREILLE

Address: To John Locke Esqr

Endorsed by Locke: de la Treille 17 Jul. 97

2287. BENJAMIN FURLY to LOCKE, 17/27 July 1697 (*2200*, 2424)

B.L., MS. Locke c. 9, ff. 145–6.

Rotterdam 27 July 1697

Deare Friend

I received yours and understanding that the Professor Grævius was in Town, I went to his quarters but found that morning departed. But having been with my wife, her son, and your little friend[1] 8 days at Maarsen with that Gentleman that wrote that Treatise of the Attributes of God, publisht in English by the Baron van Helmont,[2] I went to utrecht express to enquire of the Professor if he had received the Euripides I sent him 2 years agoe from yourself;[3] and I find he had it, and saith he has writ you 3 severall letters by certain students that went for England, and was wondring that he got no answer from you, as he had expected, having wrote you something concerning Monsieur Toinard, which would please you,[4] and desired me to tender his service to you, and tell you he would now write to you—

I am now to thank you, tho' late, for the present sent me by mr. Barker, of your Letter to the Bishop of Worcester, which I read with extraordinary delight and pleasure, how it will please his Lordship to be so Genteelly exposed, or how he will be able to

[1] Arent Furly.

[2] Maarsen is probably Maarssen, 4 miles NW. of Utrecht; Dr. Paulus Buchius (no. *1364*, etc.) lived there: p. 720. His book is *The Divine Being*: no. *1702*, etc.

[3] Nos. *1786*, 1920.

[4] No letters from Toinard to Grævius that belong certainly to 1695–7 are extant. The most recent extant letters between Grævius and Locke date from May and July 1695: nos. *1897*, 1920. There is no trace of a further letter from Grævius to Locke until May 1698: no. *2436*.

discharge his duty, without chargeing you positively with those things so insinuated by him, that all that read him must conclude he intended should pass for your sentiments or discharge you of them, I see not. And certainly his Lordship can never think, that he can with any Justice decline one of the two, by silence.

I have now to inform you, that our silly Sympathetick Coxcomb, being slain by prosperity, keeping his Coach, making costly array, falling to drinking, and eaten up by Jades, is at last run away, having neglected his patients to their generall discontent some time, before his marching off. So that now it must pass for a most certain truth, that he never wrought upon any one body, how many so ever there have been, that have sweat, as if in a bath, both in, and out of their beds, some to no effect, some to good effect, and some to ill[1]—To no effect is a considerable example of a Bedchamberman to the Elector of Bronswick Hannover, who, upon my letter to the Baron van Helmont, and his information to the Princess, came hither, and was three weeks here, but found no advantage by his sweating and so returnd.[2] One woman or mayden in Town complains that he so terribly oversweat her, that she is utterly ruined in her health by it, being so weakned, that she fals into continual sweats as Dr. Kolhans informs me—

I must now let you know that the Baron V.H. after having honoured us with a visit of Eight days returnd for Amsterdam, and yesterday morning set forward from thence towards Bohemia i.e. I beleev, Sultzbach[3]. putting off his voyage for England till he returns thence—

In Amsterdam he has publisht by Wetstein a new Translation of the 4 first chapters of Genesis, with the explication thereof and notes upon it: which when he talks of it he calls his discourses—He favoured me with 2 Copies whereof I send, with this, to Joseph Wright for you one. How capable he is to do so regular, and orderly a thing, you know. The true author I beleeve to be Knorr, with whose Plumes the good old man decks himself:[4] But how he wil cover himself, if (he being a Netherlander) the Reader shall see, p. 41 that a German was the Author, as these words Nostri dicunt

[1] Furly apparently still believed in van Rettwich in April: pp. 98–9, 116–20.

[2] The elector is Ernst August; the princess, the Electress Sophia. Van Helmont was in Hanover in March 1696 and probably remained there until early in 1697: Sophia, *Briefe . . . an die Raugräfinnen*, etc., ed. E. Bodemann, 1888, pp. 135, 155–6.

[3] No. *1764*.

[4] *Quædam præmeditatæ et consideratæ cogitationes super quatuor priora capita . . . Genesis*, 1697. L.L., no. 1416. An English translation was published in 1701: *T.C.* iii. 227.

Wimmlen; Galli Grouïller[1] to move, squirm, or frisk as fishes in the waters: and a little further, Pisces hic separatim non nominantur, sed sub reptili vel motatili Wimlenden,[2] i.e. the moving, squirming frisking creature: for these two words the verb, *Wimmlen*, and the participle *Wimlenden*, are not low Dutch but high Dutch words. And there is one that has already observd it, and threatens to expose the poore Gentleman, but perhaps will stay till the larger treatise, which he promises, and to which he saith this small Treatise is but a forerunner: least the world should lose that part of that worthy Gentlemans labours.[3] For this Journey to S., seems to be onely to get that treatise and then we shall have no more of his Verbal discourses, as, I feare, he calls that Gentlemans works. However, if we cannot get them, but that way, I had rather have them so than want them—

He brought me 6 sheets of Monsieur Knorrs Historia Evangelica, secundum 4 Evangelistas,[4] printed in Sultzbach, in form of a Dialogue betwixt a Cabbalista Catechumenus and Christianus—in which he explains all the Cabbalistical terms in the N.T. I askt why it went not forward, but could get no answer, but that Printers were od folk that he had paid for 500 Copies. That it was about 25 sheets I prest for a copy of the manuscript, and said we would get it done here, if could have the 6 sheets from Sultzbach, he said they made him now pay toll every where for all that he had, and he would not be at the charge and trouble. But said the Duke of Wolfenbuttel (with whom Knors son dwells)[5] will print it. And would fain have had me sell to that Prince (who has the best library in Europe)[6] the original MS. of the Inquisition.[7] But I have no mind to part with it

[1] 'Our people say Wimmlen; the French, Grouïller' (sc. for Hebrew *sheretz*).

[2] 'Fishes are not mentioned separately here, but under creeping and moving Wimlenden.'

[3] This appears not to have been published.

[4] Leibniz, who was a friend of Knorr, mentions a *Harmonia Evangelica* that was printed at Frankfurt: *Otium Hanoverianum*, ed. J. F. Feller, 1718 (Ravier, no. 337), p. 224; I have not traced a copy. He mentions also a manuscript, 'Messias puer', a history of the early life of Christ illustrated from Kabbalist writings; van Helmont tried unsuccessfully to get it published in Amsterdam: Leibniz, *S.S.* I. v. 55, 109, 235.

[5] Anton Ulrich, 1633–1714, duke of Brunswick-Wolfenbüttel; ruling the principality from 1685 while his elder brother, Duke Rudolf August, lived in retirement; succeeded as duke 1704: *A.D.B.*; for the younger Knorr's connection with him: Elizabeth Charlotte, duchess of Orleans, *Aus den Briefen . . . an die Kurfürstin Sophie*, ed. Bodemann, ii. 40.

[6] In 1661 it was said to possess 116,351 books in 28,415 volumes, 2,003 of them being manuscripts: O. von Heinemann, *Die Herzogliche Bibliothek zu Wolfenbüttel*, 1894, pp. 71–2.

[7] The Toulouse 'Liber Sententiarum'.

Two things I cannot omit to note, that whereas I find this Author to build very much upon a distinction he makes between Aretz, Adamah, and Sadeh, p. 45. 46. 57. etc seqq. and betwixt Elohim, and Jehovah Elohim. upon a search into the hebrew Concordance[1] where I find Aretz used by moses and the other writers above 2000 times and Adamah above 200 times I find no difference betwixt Adamah and Eretz—and Sadeh I find above 300 times and many times for a land or countrey, as the land of Moab etc—as wel as Eretz and Adamah. Yea in the same verse sometimes I meet, Aretz and Adamah, as Gen. 1. 24. 25. where its said let Aretz bring forth nephesh chajah, behemah varemes. And v. 25. And Elohim made Chajah haaretz—veeth Col vemes ha adamah—And the same thing is Gen. 1. 11. 12. ascribed to Elohim (without the addition of Jehovah) which Gen. 2. 9. is ascribed to Jehovah Elohim. So that what to make of these mysteries I know not.[2]

But I will not trouble you longer with my observations, on this Treatise, desireing rather to see yours, when you have read them.

I could heartily wish to see the so long desired peace, that we might be so happy as to come and see you there, seing we have no hopes of seing you here. But I feare the confusions in Poland betwixt the two elected Kings,[3] will retard the work at Ryswyck; for till that be determined, Its like things will go but slowly forward. However we seem (without any proclamation of an Armistitium) to enjoy a Cessation of Arms, the Generals having frequent conferences, and passes to and fro being graunted very readily to all that seek them—

I have nothing else worth your notice, so with tender of due respects and humble service from my dearest, and self to your self Sir F. and my Lady I rest

Sir

your affectionate friend and humble servant

BENJAMIN FURLY

Your little Friend tenders his small service to you, and thanks you for his presents, he pursues his studies hard in hopes to overtake,

1 Probably Noldius, *Concordantiæ* (no. 562). *Bibliotheca Furleiana*, p. 37, no. 377.

2 I have not tried to check Furly's transliteration.

3 John Sobieski having died on 7/17 June 1696, Augustus the Strong, elector of Saxony, and François-Louis de Bourbon, prince of Conti (*D.B.F.*), were rival candidates for election as his successor. Augustus was successful, and was crowned as Augustus II on 5/15 September of this year.

my wives son that has learnd almost 7 years—I am vext that John[1] has never seen you since his being in England and chide him for it—

P.S. our Sympathetick I heare has been returnd some days, he was by a servant of his frighted away with a story of the Gentleman of Hannovers being dead, and the Electors threatning to hang him, if he could catch him, a Gentleman of the Elector of Brandenburghs[2] have said so, in the Inn on the great market of another man. Having thus frighted the goose away, his man and mayd servant ran away with linnen, woollen, plate and all they could find. And himself lyes in bed having broke his thigh they say—

2288. WILLIAM MOLYNEUX to LOCKE, 20 July 1697 (2277, 2310)

The Carl H. Pforzheimer Library, New York. Transcribed from photostat. Printed in *Some Familiar Letters*, pp. 225–31. Answers no. 2277; answered by no. 2310.

Dublin. July. 20. 1697.

The latest Favour I received from my ever Honourd Friend was of the 15th of June, and I have it before me to acknowledge with all due Gratitude. I was mightily surprised to see the Bishop of Worcesters Answer to your Letter; I thought he would have let that Matter fall, and have privately thanked you, and have said no more; this was the Least I expected from him, for I think indeed he might have gone farther, and made his Publick acknowledgements to you. This had been like a Man of Ingenuity and Candor; and by this he had been more valuable in the Opinion of all I converse with here than by the shiftings, windings, and turnings he uses in his last peice. You wel observe the Bishop has shewn himself a Man at his Weapon; but I think him *Andabatarum more Pugnare*;[3] He winks as he fights. However, in the Postscript he shews a sample of the Old Leven, and must not let you go without coupling his Observations on a Socinian Book[4] with his Confutation of yours, as if there were something so agreable between them, that they cannot be wel

[1] John Furly. [2] Frederick III, elector 1688; king in Prussia 1701.

[3] 'That he fights in the manner of the blindfold gladiators': the phrase comes from St. Jerome: Erasmus, *Adagia*, II. iii. 33. The word 'wink' is used here in the obsolete sense, to close one's eyes: *O.E.D.*

[4] Stillingfleet does not name it; it is *The Agreement of the Unitarians with the Catholick Church*, 1697; it is attributed to Stephen Nye. See Carabelli, *Tolandiana*, p. 39.

seperated. This is such an indirect Practise, and seems such an invidious Insinuation, that I cannot but give it the name of Malice.

I am obleidged to you for the Confidence you put in me by communicating your Thoughts concerning Mr T.[1] more freely than you would do to every One. He has had his Opposers here; as you will find by a Book, which I have[a–] sent to[–a] you by a Gentlemans Servant to be left for you at your Lodging. wherein you will meet a Passage relating to your self; which tho with decency, yet I fear will not redound much to the Authors Advantage; for with very great Assurance (a usual companion of Ignorance) he undertakes to *demonstrate* the Immateriality of the Soul, and to shew the falsity of your Argumentation wherein you assert that we have no proof; but that God may communicate a Power of Thinking to a Certain system of Matter. But this is all but Assertion and Promise; we are so unhappy as yet to want this *Demonstration* from this Author; and I fear we shall ever want it from him and I beleive you will be of my Opinion when you read his Book.[2] The Author is my Acquaintance, but two things I shall never forgive in his Book; The One is the Foul Language and Opprobrious Names he Gives Mr Toland;[b] The other is, upon several Occasions calling in the Aid of the Civil Magistrate, and delivering Mr Toland[b] up to secular Punishment.[3] This indeed is a killing Argument, but some will be apt to say, that where the strength of his Reason faild him, there he flys to the strength of the Sword. And this minds me of a Busines that was very surprising to many, even several Prelates, in this Place, The Presentment of some Pernicious Books and their Authors by the Grand Jury of Middlesex.[4] this is lookd upon as a Matter of Dangerous Consequence, to make Our Civil Courts judges of Religious Doctrines; and no one knows upon a Change of affairs, whose turn it may be

a–a *MS.* have sent / sent to b *MS.* Td

[1] Toland.

[2] Peter Browne (bishop of Cork 1710; *D.N.B.*), *A Letter in Answer to a Book Entituled,* Christianity not Mysterious, *as also to all those who set up for Reason and Evidence in Opposition to Revelation and Mysteries*, Dublin, 1697. L.L. no. 500. There was also a London edition this year.

[3] Toland quotes some passages in his *Apology*, pp. 8–16.

[4] This was on 17 May; *The Reasonableness of Christianity*, *A Lady's Religion* (p. 106), and *A Letter to a Convocation-Man* (by Francis Atterbury) were presented at the same time: Luttrell, iv. 226–7; J. Gailhard, *The Epistle and Preface to the Book against the Blasphemous Socinian Heresie Vindicated*, 1698, pp. 82–3.

next to be Condemned. But the Example has been followd in[a–] our County[–a] and Mr ⟨Toland⟩[b], And his book have been presented here, by a Grand Jury, Not one of Which (I am perswaded) ever read One Leaf in Christianity not Mysterious.[1] Let the Sorbone for ever now be silent, a Learned Grand Jury directed by as Learned a Judge does the busines much better. the Dissenters here were the cheif Promoters of this Matter; but when I asked one of them, What if a Violent Church of England Jury should present Mr Baxters Books as pernicious and condemn them to the flames by the Common EXECUTIONER;[2] He was sensible of the Error, and said he wishd it had never been done.

I must not forget to thank you for the Countenance I have received from Lord Chancellor Methuen since his coming into Ireland. I know 'tis all owing to your and your Friends indeavours. My Lord is a Person from whom the Kingdom expects very well, for hitherto his Management has been very Promising. Mr Burridge is his Chaplain, and expects very soon to be setled in a Parish here in Dublin,[3] and then he promises me to prosecute the Essay with Vigour.

My Brother gives you his most humble service, He is told by Mr Burridge, that you had sent him a Book in Medicine,[4] but by what Hand, he could not inform him. He has such a Value for every thing that comes from you, that he desired me to let you know that no such Book came to his hands, or else he had not all this while deferd his Acknowledgements.

I perceive you are so happy as to be acquainted with Sir Richard Blackmore, he is an extrordinary Person, and I admire his two Prefaces as much as I do any Parts of his Books; the first wherein he exposes the Licensiousnes and Immorality of our Late Poetry is incomparable; and the second wherein he prosecutes the same subject, and Delivers his thoughts concerning Hypotheses is no less Judicious. and I am wholy of his opinion relating to the Latter however the History and Phænomena of Nature we may venture at and this is what I propose to be the subject of a Philosophick Poem

[a–a] *MS.* in our / our County [b] *MS.* Tolands

[1] I have not found a copy of this presentment. The MS. reading 'County' is altered silently to 'country' in *Some Familiar Letters*.

[2] Richard Baxter, the Presbyterian divine.

[3] I have not found him as a holder of a living in Dublin.

[4] Boulton, *A Treatise of . . . Muscular Motion*: no. *2191*. For the identification see p. 190.

Sir R. Blackmore has exquisite touches of this kind dispersed in many places of his Books (to pas over Mopas Song) I'll instance one particular in the most profound speculations of Mr Newtons Philosophy thus curiously touch'd in King Arthur, Book 9th, pag. 243.

The Constellations shine at his Command,
He form'd their radiant Orbs, and with his hand
He Weigh'd, and put them of with such a force
As might preserve an Everlasting Course.

I doubt not but Sir R. Blacmore in these lines had a regard to the proportionment of the Projective Motion to the Vis Centripeta that keeps the Planets in their Continued Courses.

I have by me some Observations made by a Judicious friend of Mine on both Sir R. Blackmores Poems; if they may be anywise acceptable to Sir R. I shall send them to you; they are in the Compas of a sheet of Paper. And[a-] were it[-a] proper, I should humbly desire you to procure for me from Sir R. the Key to the Persons Names in both his Poems;[1] Most of the first I have already; and a great Many in the second; but Many I also want which I should be very glad to understand. But if herein I desire any thing disagreable, I beg Sir Richards pardon, and desist.

Ever since you first mentiond to me that Monsieur Le Clerk might be inticed into Ireland by a Moderate Incouragement, it has sat greivous on my Spirit that it lay not in my Power to procure for him what might be worth his Acceptance. I should reckon it (next to your Friendship) one of the Greatest Glorys of My Life, that I could be able anywise to contribute to transplanting him hither. 'Tother day I ventur'd to mention it to a Great Prelate here, the Bishop of Clogher, lately translated to that rich Bishoprick.[2] He was pleased to favour the proposal Immediately, and gave me Directions, that I should enquire, whether Monsieur Le Clerk would be willing to take Orders in Our Church, and to submitt to the Oaths and Injunctions thereof; and How far he is Master of the English Language. He told me he doubted not but he might procure for him 150 or 200 lbs pr An. in some place of Ease and retirement.

a–a *MS.* And were / were it

1 Molyneux probably means such names as Bothan (Henry Booth, Lord Delamere), Canvallo (William Cavendish, earl of Devonshire), Sakil (Charles Sackville, earl of Dorset), and Laurus (Dryden): *Prince Arthur*, pp. 164–7.

2 St. George Ashe, translated from Cloyne on 25 June: p. 122, n. 3.

Be pleased therefore, Dear Sir, to let me be informd in these particulars, and in whatever else you think requisite in managing this affair.

I have protracted this Letter as if I had a designe to kill you by tyring you to Death. I beg your Excuse for it. I am

Dear Sir

Your most Affectionate Humble servant

W: MOLYNEUX

Address: To John Locke Esquire at Mr Pawlings overagainst the Plow-Inn in Little Lincolns-Inn-Feilds London

Postmark: IY 31

Endorsed by Locke: W: Molineux 20 Jul 97 Answered Sept. 11

2289. JEAN LE CLERC to LOCKE, 27 July/6 August 1697 (*2285, 2300*)

B.L., MS. Locke c. 13, ff. 115–16. Printed in Bonno, *Le Clerc*, pp. 100–2.

A Amsterdam le 6 d'Août 1697

Je viens, Monsieur, tout à l'heure de voir Mr. Coste, que j'ai trouvé en beaucoup meilleur état, qu'il n'a été depuis qu'il vous a écrit, car il avoit été assez mal. Mr. Guenelon l'a vû, outre son Medecin ordinaire, et ils ont jugé que quelques remedes antiscorbutiques lui pourroient faire du bien, ce qui a en effet réüssi. Il meurt d'envie de se mieux porter, pour se mettre en chemin; mais il est impossible qu'il l'entreprenne dans l'état, où il est. Il seroit ravi de profiter à l'instant d'une condition aussi agréable, que celle qui s'offre; mais une maladie n'est pas une chose, dont on soit le maître. S'il continue à se porter mieux, il pourra envoier ses Livres avant lui, ou en tout cas, on les envoiera après. Il en a plus qu'un voiageur ne peut mener avec lui. C'est un jeune homme d'un naturel fort doux, fort patient, et tout à fait éloigné de la débauche. Il a d'ailleurs assez d'aquis soit pour les belles Lettres, soit pour la Philosophie; et comme il est judicieux et posé, il peut encore beaucoup plus aquerir. Il sait non seulement le François comme sa Langue Maternelle, mais encore comme une Langue qu'il a étudiée, et dont il sait les regles par méthode. Il est trop interessé dans sa santé, et il n'oubliera rien pour la recouvrer au plûtôt, de sorte que vous pouvez compter de l'avoir le plûtôt qu'il lui sera possible. Cependant s'il lui arrivoit quelque chose, qui ⟨retardât⟩[a] son rétablissement, je ne manqueroi pas de vous en avertir, afin que Mr. le Chevalier Mascham se pourvoie d'un autre, si Mr. Coste ne peut pas quitter la Hollande assez tôt.

Vous m'aviez demandé, Monsieur, le prix des Antiquitez Romaines,[1] et leur usage. Il y en a six volumes qui paroissent, qui coûtent déja à ceux qui ont souscrit 90 francs[2] ou environ. Il y a de bons traitez, mais il y en a plusieurs de communs, et le tout est assez mal disposé. Il y a quantité de belles figures, mais en partie inutiles et qui augmentent le prix de l'Ouvrage considerablement. Les Libraires parlent encore de six autres volumes, qui comprendront des livres assez communs, comme la *Notice de l'Empire*[3] et divers Traitez de *Lipse*,[4] et qui ne couteront guere moins, que les autres; mais je doute beaucoup qu'ils achevent cet ouvrage, le prix dégoutant tout le monde. Il est d'ailleurs fort difficile de se servir de ce Recueuil, les pieces étant mêlées, et y aiant plusieurs indices. Il seroit à souhaiter que quelcun fît un Dictionaire de tout cela, et qu'il y ajoûtât ce qui y manque, car après tout ce ne sera pas un ouvrage, qui donne une idée complette des antiquitez Romaines, et dans lequel on puisse trouver l'éclaircissement de ses difficultez. *Mr. Gronovius* a entrepris un *Thesaurus Antiquitatum Græcarum* en 5. volumes,[5] dont trois seront composez des images des Dieux et des personnages illustres, et deux de traitez concernant les antiquitez Greques. Le premier paroit, et tout le monde en est dégouté; le choix des personnages et des figures étant très-mauvais, et l'explication encore pire; *Mr. Gronovius* n'aiant ni jugement, ni stile. Je vous suis obligé, Monsieur, du Thucydide,[6] mais je ne laisserai pas de dire que le texte de l'edition de Henry Etienne,[7] ou de Portus est plus correct que celui d'Oxford. Pour bien imprimer des livres de cette nature, il faut une peine infinie. Il y a de bonnes choses dans les notes de

[a] *MS.* retordât

[1] Grævius's compilation: p. 140.
[2] Gulden, as in no. *2174*.
[3] The *Notitia Dignitatum Imperii Romani*.
[4] Justus Lipsius, 1547–1606: *Biog. nationale de Belgique*.
[5] Jacobus Gronovius: no. *1541*; his *Thesaurus*, 12 vols. in 13, folio, was publishing from 1697 to 1702.
[6] p. 72.
[7] Henri Estienne II (1528–98; *N.B.G.*) published in 1564 an edition of Thucydides with the Latin translation of Lorenzo Valla (ibid.). Estienne revised the text and the translation; the latter was further revised later by Æmilius Portus (p. 72, n. 2).

Mr. Hudson, et qui peuvent servir à éclaircir plusieurs endroits du texte; mais elles devroient être dessous et la version à côté, ce qui est beaucoup plus commode. Je ne dis pas cela, pour diminuer le prix de vôtre présent, que j'estime beaucoup, et plus encore la maniere dont vous me l'avez fait. Je voudrois que ma *Critique* pût vous divertir, je croirois vous avoir témoigné par là une partie de ma reconnoissance. Elle se débite si bien deça la mer, qu'il faudra revenir à une autre edition, qui sera plus correcte, dans peu de mois.[1] Cependant on rimprimera toute ma Philosophie, en meilleurs caracteres, et corrigée avec exactitude.[2] J'espere que vous en serez plus content, que de la premiere édition; Car j'y change beaucoup, sur tout pour le style, qui sera plus Latin et plus net. Cela seroit déja fait, sans *Hammond*, qui m'occupe tout entier. Nous en sommes à la 1. Ep. à Timothée. On sera surpris des fautes, et des fausses citations de cet habile homme. Je prie Dieu, Monsieur, qu'il vous conserve en parfaite santé, et je suis de tout mon coeur entierement à vous

J LE CLERC.

Ma femme vous baise les mains.

Address: A Monsieur Monsieur Locke at Mr. Pawlings in litle Lincolns inne fieds, over against the plough London

Postmark: — 30

Endorsed by Locke: le Clerc 6 Aug 97 Answered 6

2290. LOCKE to CORNELIUS LYDE, 3 August 1697 (2230, 2293)

Staatsbibliothek Preussischer Kulturbesitz, Berlin. Transcribed from photograph.

London 3 Aug 97

Sir

The indisposition of my health that kept me soe long in the country, has been the occasion also of my soe long silence. The lease for F: Carpenter I have put into Mr Clarkes hands, who will be at Sutton Court on Saturday morning next.[3] His stay will be soe very short there, that I trouble you with this note beforehand to

[1] A corrected edition was published in London in 1698; a new edition, at Amsterdam in 1700.

[2] The first collected edition was published in 1698: pp. 178, 422.

[3] 7 August.

let you know that he will be then there and I would desire you to speake there with him that morning. I shall write more at large by him, and am

Sir

your most humble servant

J LOCKE

It would be convenient too, if you could give notice to Fr: Carpenter to be there when you speake with Mr Clarke, that his businesse may be then setled.

Address: For Cornelius Lyde Esquire at Stanton weeke To be left with Mr Codrington in Highstreet Bristoll.

Postmarks: AV 3 (?); GC

2291. LOCKE to MRS. MARY CLARKE, 3 August 1697 (2258, 2569)

B.L., MS. Locke b. 8, no. 120. There is also a copy (no. 121), made by the writer who copied nos. 2213 and 2214. Printed in Rand, pp. 517–18.

London 3. Aug. 97

Dear Madam

Though we have had as good successe in the use of the remedies I prescribed as I could expect, and am mightily rejoyced at the advances of your recovery, yet I think it convenient for you now a little to vary them. I have ordered you two bottles of a stomachical cordiall which you will receive by Mr Clarke. whereof I would have you take five spoonfuls every morning at least two or three hours before dinner, but as much earlier as you can conveniently goe abroad in your coach, for the earlier the better, because upon takeing of it, it is requisite you should take the air in your coach for at least two hours. The like quantity you are to take again in the afternoon three or four hours after dinner with the like aireing after it. After the first weeke you should instead of five take seven spoonfuls, and as you finde it agree with you increase it to nine and there stop. You may for all this continue to drinke of your diet drinke as often as you please, for these two doe not at all interfere one with an other. But the Garlick I would have you at least for some time leave off, and instead of it take this which I thinke a more agreeable remedie. I hope I shall hear of the good effects of it; and that you are perfectly recovered to your former strength and state of health. I am sure I wish for it with a very particular concerne and am

Dear Madam

Your most affectionate humble servant

J LOCKE

Pray give my hearty love and service to my wife

Her father I hope will make my apologie for my not writeing to her.

Address: These present To Mrs Mary Clarke at Chipley[a]

2292. DR. PIETER GUENELLON to LOCKE, 3/13 August 1697 (*2255*, *2326*)

B.L., MS. Locke c. 11, ff. 78–9.

Monsieur,

Je me serviray de l'occasion presente que m'offre Monsieur Cost pour vous renouveller nos respects. Ma femme a recu enfin le Pacquet de Gangs[1] dont vous l'honorez. elle ne peut qu'estre confuse se voyant si fort vostre debitrice, et hors d'estat de se revanger. il vous est si naturel d'obliger tout le monde, qu'on peut conter comme un tresor, l'honneur de vostre amitié, je vous assure Monsieur quelle nous est tres chere, et que nous voudrions la mieux meriter, que nous ne faisons. je suis tres ayse que Monsieur Cost, dont je cognois le merite, aye trouvé un si bon employ par vostre moyen, et quil aura le bonheur d'estre aupres de vous, pour qui il a une si profonde estime: je vous assure que cela le fera partir plustost quil n'auroit fait, estant a peine en estat de le faire, ayant souffert depuis longtemps un rheumatisme opiniastre, pour lequel je luy ay conseillé de se servir d'antiscorbutique et de se mouvoir plus quil n'a fait. Mon fils pierre est de retour de leyden, mon Neveu[2] qui avoit soin de luy, estant allé demeurer a la haye, pour s'appliquer aux playdoyers. nous avons icy depuis quelque temps le fils du fameux tanaquillus faber,[3] qui s'establit icy pour enseigner les humanitez, et principalement les mathematiques, ayant la reputation de la scavoir a fond. il me presse de permettre quil enseigne l'algebre a mon fils, le croyant capable de cela. il est vray

[a] *There is no endorsement. The copy is endorsed by Clarke* Copy of Mr Locks Letter to Mrs. Clarke Dated the 3d. of August 1697

[1] *Gants*: p. 75; for the transmission see p. 109.

[2] No. *2028*

[3] Tanneguy Le Fèvre; the father and the son had the same name: no. *606*.

quil y a l'esprit fort porté et quil ne fait rien avec plus d'attachement. outre quil a une facilité merveilleuse a les comprendre. il nous fait tous les jours par repetition trois ou quatre demonstrations d'Euclide sans hesiter: et na eu besoin que d'un jour pour connoistre tous les points et cercles du globe terrestre, et leur usages, en sorte que formant (proprio Marte)[1] une dissertation sur ce subject, il s'hazarda le lendemain de demonstrer le globe en presence de plusieurs personnes. je l'occupe aussy presentement au græc, a l'histoire universelle, et aux antiquitez, et l'attache encore (avant que de passer outre aux historiens particuliers) a Phedre, Terence, et Plaute pour la pureté du langage simple.

ayant le bonheur d'avoir de l'excellent thee imperial,[2] ma femme prend la liberté de vous en envoyer. si Monsieur Cost n'oseroit s'en charger, nous vous l'envoyerons par la voye de Monsieur Cowls, qui de courtier[3] quil estoit icy s'en va s'establir Courtier juré a Londres et comme il a beaucoup de choses a transporter et quil est de mes amis je ne doubte pas quil n⟨e⟩[a] s'en veuille charger.

Pardonnez Monsieur qu'on ause vous presenter si peu de chose. ma femme et toute la famille vous fait une profonde reverence, et je suis comme je le doibs,

Monsieur,

Vostre tres humble et tres obeissant serviteur

P. GUENELLON

d'Amst. ce 13 aoust 1697.

Address: A Monsieur Monsieur J. Locke chevalier etc. etc. Londres

Endorsed by Locke: P: Guenellon 13. Aug. 97 Answered 7.

2293. LOCKE to CORNELIUS LYDE, 4 August 1697 (2290, *2295*)

The Pierpont Morgan Library, New York. Transcribed from Xerox print. Answered by no. *2295*.

London 4° Aug 97

Sir

I have herewith sent you the draught of the lease sent me for Francis Carpenter which I have not executed according to that

[a] *Page torn.*

[1] 'On his own initiative' or 'by his own exertions'. As 'nostro Marte' in Erasmus, *Adagia*, I. vi. 19.

[2] Apparently a special kind of tea: *O.E.D.*, s.v. Imperial A 8.

[3] Broker or agent.

forme because several things were to be altered in it as you will see. Besides the terme is not agreed nor is it expressed that he should doe the personal services as Constable or Tytheing man etc which I looke on it he is to bear and I only pay the taxes. But if of them he will pay those to church and pore I will consent then to make him a lease for my life, otherwise I shall not be willing to make the lease for above a[a] yeare.[a] We are now god be thanked like to have peace again and then trade will again flourish, and with the flourishing of trade rents will rise again. But since I cannot be there my self I have referd the whole matter to Mr Clarke by whom you will receive this and what he and you shall agree to be reasonable I shall consent to.

What money you have of mine in your hands that you can pay to Mr Clarke in gold I have desired him to take, silver will be to heavy to trouble him with, and that therefor I must desire you to advise with him about a forme of a bill to be returnd by, that I may be sure to receive it in milled Silver money or Guineas, and not in any paper payment. I hope you have by this time received all my Lady days rents. But that I shall see by the accounts between us which I would desire the favour of you to send me when your leisure will permitt for then I shall be able to see what stands out in arear and what order to take about it. I never write to you but I am very sensible of the trouble I give you and of the obligation I have to you which I shall always acknowledg and am

Sir

your most humble servant

JOHN LOCKE

Address: For Cornelius Lyde Esquire at Stanton Weeke

2294. EDWARD FOWLER, bishop of Gloucester, to LOCKE, 11 August 1697 (2112, *2814*)

B.L., MS. Locke c. 8, ff. 143–4. Written probably at Tunbridge Wells or Epsom.

Sir

I thank you for your kind Enquiry after my health. I thank God I perceiv a manifest change for the better in my son;[1] but I can yet

[a] *Altered from* six (?) years *to* this *and then to* a yeare

[1] Richard Fowler, born *c.* 1671; B.A. Oxford, 1692; LL.B., Cambridge, 1710: Venn.

make no great brags of myself. My waters make a shift to pass in 24 hours. I am by every body told, that my bringing him and myself will signify nothing without staying a Considerable time. I am therefore like to stay a moneth longer, and therefore to make London but a little more than my Roade to Gloster. But, Sir, I will do what I can (if you stay so long) not to leav it till I have waited on you. I hope Mr Addison has brought you Crosses and Woottons Bonds before now; I ordered him so to do at my going hence. I have sent my Lady word of it, and that I have at last received the full of Sir T Abnys debt.[1] I suppose you know that upon my going to the Lord Chancellours, the last Controversy was decided by him. Tho I stayd not long enough to get my discharge from John Cudworth. But Addison promised I should have it at my return. I should have been thankfull to you, Sir, had you given me some information about your own state of health; but I hope you'ld not have stayed so long in London, if you had not your health there: which is wished by no man in the world more than by

Sir

Your Humble Servant,

E G

Aug. 11

My kind respects to mr Pawlin et.

Address: To John Lock Esqr, at mr Paulin's, on the back side of Lincolns Inn new Square; over against Boswell Court,[2] London
E Glocest. frank

Postmark: AV 12

Endorsed by Locke: Bp: Glocester 11 Aug 97 Trust Answered 30

2295. CORNELIUS LYDE to LOCKE, 12 August 1697 (2293, 2302)

B.L., MS. Locke c. 15, ff. 156–7. Probably enclosed in no. *2299*. Answers no. 2293; answered by no. 2302.

August 12th 97

Worthy Sir

According to your order I have paid mr ⟨Clarke⟩[a] the ballance of your Acount and also what is behinde I will Indevore to Receive

[a] *MS.* Carke

[1] Sir Thomas Abney, 1640–1722; Lord Mayor of London 1700–1: *D.N.B.* He was a younger brother of Sir Edward Abney, the husband of Lady Masham's half-sister.

[2] Boswell's Court opened south from Hooker's Court, which by 1707 was called New Boswell Court; the latter ran south from Carey Street, a little to the east of Plough Alley: Strype's Stow, iv. 119 and map; Hatton, *New View*.

as soone as I Can for money have beene scarse among them of late. I Cant gett Jos: Hannys Last yeares rent but have had many faire promises but faile in performanc it, wee have agreed the matter with fra: Carpenter where I hope you will have your rent well paide and your disbursments not so Large. Sir my son in Holland I understand is to take his degree aboute this time and in 3 months[a] desine to Come for England where I shall beg the favor of you if you finde him deserving to direct him in his seting out in the world. I Am glad to here that you are recovered of your illnes. Sir with my hearty Respects to you I am your obligd friend and Ser:

COR: LYDE

Address: For Doct: Locke at mr Pawlings overagainst the plough in Little Lincolns feilds London

Endorsed by Locke: C Lyde 12 Aug. 97 Answered 28

2296. LOCKE to DR. (later Sir) HANS SLOANE, 14 August [1697?] (2227, 2496)

B.M., Sloane MS. 4059, ff. 284–5. The only years between 1689 and 1704 in which 14 August fell on a Saturday are 1697 and 1703. Locke was evidently in London when he wrote the letter. He was there throughout August 1697 and is extremely unlikely to have been there at any time in 1703.

Sir

Saturday morning
14 Aug

Mr Connyers since I saw you last told me that you and he had agreed on to morrow as a day for your goeing to Waltham-stow[1] if I consented. I am always willing to consent to enjoy my friends, and noe occasion of mine forbids it to morrow, soe that if your resolution hold I beg the favour of you to send me word some time to day, that I may be ready against the hour that you shall appoint to doe me the favour to call on me here. I am

Sir

Your most humble servant

J LOCKE

Address: For Dr Sloane at his house in Southampton stree in Bloomsbery

[a] *MS.* mõn:

[1] Conyers had property there: Morant, *Essex*, i. 49; *V.C.H.*, *Essex*, vi. 286.

2297. CHARLES MORDAUNT, third earl of Peterborough, formerly second Viscount Mordaunt and, later, earl of Monmouth, to LOCKE, [*c.* 14 August 1697] (*1977*, *2306*)

B.L., MS. Locke c. 16, ff. 121–2. Printed in King, pp. 238–9. The *London Gazette* of Thursday, 12 August contains a dispatch from Paris, 12 August, N.S., about an engagement between the fleets of J.-B.-L. Desjean, baron de Pointis (*N.B.G.*), and Vice-Admiral John Nevell (*D.N.B.*) on 27–31 May, and notices of the contest in Poland (p. 161). Peterborough wrote presumably on receipt of this issue; his letter would reach London in time for Locke to reply on 17 August.

Mr Lock

you know the impatience Countrey Gentlemen have for News we are here as Found of a Gazette as the Sparks are of their mistresses with you, we lay waggers of ponty and nevill and Conti and Saxe to passe away the Time, and instead of playing att pickett,[1] pray give us a letter now and then to decide who has wonn. this request is made you not only by my self, but some other of your humble servants.

PETERBOROW

direct yours for me to be left att the post house in Chippenham.[2] Wiltshire

Address: For Mr Lock to be left att the office of the Commissioners of Trade Whitehall

Endorsed by Locke: E: Peterborow Aug. 97 Answered 17

2298. LEONARD ADDISON to LOCKE, 14 August 1697 (*2145*)

B.L., MS. Locke c. 16, f. 36.

Sir

I am engaged this morninge to goe out of towne and shall not returne till about Thursday or Fryday next. I was yesterday severall tymes to find out Mr Edwards about passinge the last order Cudworth v Bishopp Gloucester, but could not meet with him, he very seldom comeing to the office, I mett with Mr Peachills Agent, who

[1] Piquet.

[2] Peterborough's seat at Dauntsey (no. *1411*) was about 7 miles NE. of Chippenham, which was on the main road from London to Bath and Bristol.

tells me he cannot consent that the Bonds be delivered till the assignment be executed by the Bishopp; but I am in hopes Mr Edwards will passe the order otherwise however if you have occasion to see either of the Bonds that are in the Masters hands my Clerke shall gett you Coppyes of them from the Master. I am

Sir

your humble Servant

LEONARD ADDISON

14° August 1697

Address: To John Locke Esqr These present

Endorsed by Locke: Trust Addison 14 Aug 97

2299. EDWARD CLARKE to LOCKE, 14 August 1697 (*2274*, 2305)

B.L., MS. Locke c. 6, f. 128. Printed in Rand, pp. 519–20. For the lost answer see p. 183.

Wells August the 14th. 1697.

Deare Sir,

I was soe taken up at Sutton, That I could not gett any opportunity of writeing to you from thence, But I can now informe you, That I spent a greate deale of time with your new tenant Francis Carpenter, and had greate Difficulty to gett Him under Covenants to doe the Offices of Overseer of the Poore, Constable, Tythingman, Surveyor of the High-Wayes, and other Personall offices, which, by reason of That Tenement hee now is, or shall hereafter bee Lyable to, and the rather for that Hee is this verie yeare made Overseer of the Poore, Which, if you had payd for, would have cost the better part of five pounds; The Church and Poore Rates Hee positively refused to pay, or allow any part towards it, I did all I could to have brought Him up to Discharge those Payments, But I could not prevayle, Indeed His obstinacy was such in that poynt, That by my insisting soe much on it, I had like to have lost your Tenant quite; Upon the whole matter, Being satisfied, there is a much greater Advance made by Him, in the Rent, and by the Covenants for Repayres of the House, out-houses, Gates, Barrs, and Fences, And by doeing the Personall-Offices belonging to the Tenement at his own Costs and Charges, then would have been Consented by any other Person whatsoever, I concluded with Him and Hee has Sealed a Counterpart with a Bond for performance of Covenants which are Left in Mr. Lydes handes untill you have Executed the Lease, and sent it down to Him, But because Hee desires I should bee a Witt-nesse to your signing the Lease, as well as his Executeing the Counterpart, I doe not now trouble you with it, But will bring it up with mee at my Return; I have Received from Mr. Lyde for your use, the summe of thirty nine pounds, eight shillings and six pence, And his Account, The money I will Return to you with the first opportunity that I can doe it, soe as you may bee sure to Receive it in Mill'd-money or Ginneas, And the Account Mr. Lyde has given mee for you, I will bring up with mee, if you doe not in the meane time order mee to send it to you by the Post; The Inclosed Hee gave mee to bee Conveyed to you:[1] For Assise-News I have none worth mentioning to you, there haveing nothing happened here but what is usuall, and ordinary; I am just now ready to take horse for Chipley where I hope to bee this Evening,[2] and to find all well there, as I hope this will find you, Which is the hearty Prayer of,

Your most Affectionate Faithfull servant,

EDW: CLARKE:

My sonn Presents you his humble service etc:

Endorsed by Locke: E: Clarke 14 Aug: 97 Answered 17

2300. JEAN LE CLERC to LOCKE, 15/25 August 1697 (*2289, 2348*)

B.L., MS. Locke c. 13, ff. 117–18. Printed in Bonno, *Le Clerc*, pp. 102–3.

A Amsterdam le 25. d'Août 1697.

Il y a quelques jours, Monsieur, que je me donnai l'honneur de vous écrire, pour répondre à quelques unes de vos Lettres, aus-quelles je n'avois pas encore répondu, et pour vous dire des nou-velles de la santé de Mr. Coste. Lui même vous rendra celle-ci et vous pourra témoigner de bouche avec quelle estime nous parlons ici de vous. Nous avons bû à vôtre santé plus d'une fois chez lui, chez Mr. Teute[3] et chez moi, avant qu'il partît d'ici; et plût à Dieu que nos souhaits pussent vous rendre vigoureux et robuste

[1] Probably no. *2295*.
[2] From Wells by Glastonbury to Taunton was about 32 miles; Chipley was about 5 miles further.
[3] Probably the father.

pour longues années! Vous n'en manqueriez pas assurément. J'espere que Mr. le Chevalier Masham et vous serez content de Mr. Coste, qui est non seulement de très-bon sens, mais d'une humeur douce et complaisante, outre qu'il a autant de lumieres qu'il en faut pour ce qu'il entreprend et qu'il est en état d'en aquerir tous les jours. Comme nous nous voyions assez souvent, je pers par son absence, car je suis *perpaucorum hominum*,[1] sur tout en cette ville où tout est Marchand. Mais il lui étoit desavantageux d'y demeurer plus long-temps, et je dois avoir plus de plaisir de le savoir dans un lieu, où il sera mieux, que de chagrin de l'avoir perdu. On va rimprimer mes Ouvrages Philosophiques, beaucoup retouchez, et en meilleur caractere. Comme Mr. *Boyle* n'a pas pû voir ma Dédicace, je l'ôterai et j'y en mettrai une nouvelle à la place. Ce sera la Dédicace de l'Ontologie, que je changerai un peu, et qui servira pour la Logique, l'Ontologie, et la Pneumatologie.[2] On y joindra aussi la Philosophie des Orientaux, revüe et augmentée.[3] Le tout aura quatre volumes in 8. dont la Physique en fera deux. Je mettrai après la Logique ma Dissert. *de Odio theologico ab invidia ducto*,[4] où je ferai voir avec quel art on rend la verité odieuse, par des exemples anciens et modernes. J'y fronderai comme il faut bien des mal-honêtes gens, sans les nommer, ni les désigner. J'ai sous la presse un abregé d'Histoire Universelle,[5] qui sera achevé dans quinze jours. C'est un Ouvrage composé depuis plus de douze ans, et que j'ai seulement un peu revû. Je chercherai ensuite une occasion de vous l'envoier au plûtôt. Les *Patres Apostolici* paroîtroient déja, si l'Indice étoit fait.[6] Ils sont dédiez à Mr. l'Archevêque de Cantorbery au nom de Mrs. Huguetan. C'est moi qui lui en ai demandé la permission, et qui ai fait la Dédicace. J'ai eu aussi soin de cet Ouvrage, quoi que je n'y aie pas pû faire grand'chose, et les Libraires ont voulu, que mon nom y parût, malgré moi, car cela n'en valoit

[1] 'Very particular in the choice of friends': Terence, *Eunuchus*, 409.

[2] The original edition of the *Logica* arrived too late for Boyle: no. *1446* n. The collective edition has a single dedication to Locke.

[3] Le Clerc's translation of Thomas Stanley's *History of the Chaldaick Philosophy*: nos. *1325*, *1329*.

[4] No. *1486* (as 'De argumento theologico', etc.). The dissertation was not published separately.

[5] *Compendium Historiæ Universalis ab Initio Mundi ad Tempora Caroli Magni*, published in 1698: p. 422. L.L., no. 771.

[6] A new edition of *SS. Patrum qui Temporibus Apostolicis floruerunt, Barnabæ, Hermæ . . . Opera*, originally edited by J.-B. Cotelier (no. *1224*) and published in 1672; Le Clerc's edition appeared in 1698.

pas la peine. Vous voiez, Monsieur, que je m'occupe plus que cinq ou six Beneficiers, qui n'ont des rente, que pour dormir, manger, boire, et chanter. C'est là peutêtre un de ces *rongemens d'esprit* dont parle Salomon,[1] mais je ne saurois qu'y faire. Cependant je me porte bien par la grace de Dieu, et je suis, Monsieur, de tout mon coeur tout à vous.

J LE CLERC.

Mr. Coste vous rendra deux livres de ma part, dont celui de Medecine est de mon Frere[2] et l'autre de moi.

Address: A Monsieur Monsieur Locke A Oates.

Endorsed by Locke: le Clerc 25 Aug. 97

Miscellaneous notes by Locke on cover:
America Bry[a] pars 3a Franc. 1592 p. 297
Virginia English[3]

2301. LOCKE to ESTHER MASHAM, 24 August 1697 (2124, 2327)

Newberry Library, Chicago: copy of the original letter by Esther Masham in her letter-book, pp. 23–4. Transcribed from microfilm. Printed in Fox Bourne, ii. 456; by Professor Maurice Cranston in *Newberry Library Bulletin*, 2nd ser., no. 4, July 1950, pp. 130–1. The explanatory notes were written by Esther.

London 24 August 1697

Deare Dab.

There was nothing wanting to compleat the Satisfaction your obligeing Letter of the 20th brought me, but the motive from your self of writeing. Had inclination procured me the favour and not the commands of another you had made me perfectly happy. However the good and kind things you say in it make a great amends for that defect, and I Should be very unreasonable if so many good words you have put into your Letter should not hinder me from complaining. They are more and better than I deserve and you may beleeve they have no ordinary charms in them since they go a great way towards reconciling me to my old and great enemie Winter. At least you wish for him with so peculiar a way of

[a] *Interlined.*

[1] Ecclesiastes 1: 14, etc.
[2] Perhaps Daniel Le Clerc's *Histoire de la Medecine*: no. *2121*.
[3] Both books are by Theodor de Bry; the *Virginia* was published at Frankfurt in English in 1588 and in Latin in 1590. L.L., nos. 507–9.

kindnesse to me that I cannot be Angry with you for doeing it. For since you think I cannot have your Company without his, I should be better pleas'd with his comeing than the Czars,[1] and like him better, crownd as he is with Turnips and Carrots,[2] than the great Duke with all his Rubies and Diamonds. This may convince you that whatever keeps me in Town it is not my Inclination. And your reproach of not comeing to you whilst I can live here is a little besides the matter. Did I stay here no longer than I lived here I should quickly be at your [a]Town without houses, for in this where there are so many too many, I do not live. To live is to be where and with whom one likes. Do not therefore Deare Dab any more reproach your Joannes on this point, as you will answer it an other day. You huddled up the end of your Letter to get to the man in [b]black and the Mellon, which you relishd best, either the Discourse of the one or the taste of the other I shall know when I see you. For if you have no sweet sayings laid up by you of that days collection I know what I know, I long to be examining of you because I am

Deare Dab.

Your most humble and most obedient servant

JOANNES

Pray present my humble service to Sir Francis my Lady and Deare Totty.

2302. LOCKE to CORNELIUS LYDE, 28 August [1697] (*2295, 2307*)

The Pierpont Morgan Library, New York. Transcribed from Xerox print. Correct year from contents. Answers no. *2295*; answered by no. *2313*.

London 28 Aug. 79[c]

Sir

I have an account from Mr Clarke of his receit of the money which you mention to have paid him in yours of the 12th instant

[a] Mr Locke use to laugh at Mr Low the Minister of our Parish for calling his Parish, his Town, when there is not two houses together in it [b] The man in black was Mr Low [c] *Locke wrote first apparently 97; having blotted the 9 he added a fresh 9 after the 7*

[1] Peter the Great, who was now in the United Provinces. Prior to Peter the sovereign of Russia was commonly styled in England the Great Duke of Muscovy.

[2] So nos. 809, 1083.

I am sorry Hannys backwardnesse gives you any trouble and would not presse you to an increase of it did I not apprehend that unlesse you be quick with him the money may be lost for such debts the older ⟨they⟩[a] grow the harder they are to be got in. I shall be very glad to welcome your son to England when ever he comes, and you may assure your self of all the directions and other assistance I can give him in his seting out or any thing else I can be serviceable to him in in the practise of physick. This or any other oportunity to acknowledg the favour you doe me in lookeing after my little affairs in your neighbourhood will be always acceptable to me. I am

Sir

your most humble servant

JOHN LOCKE

Address: For Cornelius Lyde Esquire at Stanton Weeke. To be left with Mr Codrington in Highstreet Bristoll

Postmarks: AV 28; GC

2303. JOHN WYNNE, later bishop of Bath and Wells, to LOCKE, 31 August/10 September 1697 (*2190*, *2330*)

B.L., MS. Locke c. 23, ff. 127–8.

Honoured Sir

I received your letter, and am very glad that you have put an opportunity into my hands of letting you know how ready I am to serve you. I had it in my thoughts before to go to the Auction att Leyden, but since you have been pleas'd to honour me with your commands, I shall not fail to go thither, If my Lord[1] will be pleas'd to dispence with my absence so long. I shall take care to observe your directions very punctually both att Leyden and Amsterdam. If Mr Barker or my self should not go to Amsterdam again (for we have been once there since our arriveal in Holland) I shall employ another Gentleman of my acquaintance, well known to Mr Wetstein to do your busines with him. I have been told the Polyglott Bible[2] sells commonly much dearer here than in England, and that it seldom goes at an auction for less than a 100 guilders, which is

[a] *MS.* the

[1] Pembroke.

[2] Apparently Walton's Polyglot, 1655–7. It is not known when Locke acquired his copy. L.L., no. 324.

almost double to what I have known it sold for sometimes in England; for there it is commonly bought in Auctions and sales for 5l.–10s. or 6l.

My Lord enjoyes his health perfectly well, and is in hopes his stay here will not be very long. It is generally thought the Peace will be sign'd by the 20th of September, which is the Time the French have lately Sett for the Confederates to accept of their Termes. The Germains have all along oppos'd the conclusion of the Peace with all their might: And tis not known whether they may not engage the Confederates to take some new resolutions by the offers of greater succours to carry on the war on their side. Tis certain the last French Paper deliverd in att Reyswick wherein the French assume a more arrogant and imperious air than they had done before, and revoke some of their former concessions, has rais'd the indignation of some of the Confederates to a very high pitch.[1] But notwithstanding this their just resentment of such an indignity, It is generally supposed that some other necessary considerations will oblige them att this time to accept of A peace att any rate.

My Lord orderd me to return you his service. If there be any thing else wherein I may be capeable of serving you here, you cannot oblige me more than by laying your commands upon

Honoured Sir

your most oblig'd humble servant

JOHN WYNNE

Hague Aug. 31 S.V 97.

Address: To The Honoured John Locke Esqre

Endorsed by Locke: J. Wynne 31 Aug 97 Answered Oct 1.

2304. W. BARKER to LOCKE, 31 August/10 September 1697 (*2275, 2392*)

B.L., MS. Locke c. 3, ff. 149–50.

Sir

I can not but gratefully acknowledg the favours you have so often conferred on me, and as far as I am able make my uttermost

[1] On 1 September, N.S., the French ambassadors at Ryswick delivered to the ambassador mediator a memorial in which Louis XIV declared that he would keep Strasbourg and required acceptance of his proposals by 20 September, N.S.: *The Acts and Negotiations . . . of the General Peace concluded at Ryswick*, 1698, pp. 102–4.

endeavours to improve all opportunity's that may in any wise conduce to your service, Therefore humbly take leave to acquaint you that I have received the Honour of yours of the 22d past wherein were two Letters which I delivered according to Order and in further obedience to your Commands presented your most humble service to His Excellency,[1] who hath commanded me to give you his Service and is glad to hear of your good health, for which my wishes shall be as long as I live, hoping you will (when ever you think any thing is in my power) continue me in the Honour of your Commands, that my hearty obedience and ready Complyance thereto shall shew that I will omitt no occasion to prove with all respect that I am

Sir

your most humble and most obedient servant

W. BARKER

Hague September the 10th NS: 1697

Address: To the Honble: John Locke Esqr at the Office of Trade and Plantations In Whitehall

Endorsed by Locke: W: Barker 10 Sept 97 Answered 1° Oct

2305. LOCKE to EDWARD CLARKE, 2 September 1697 (*2299*, *2308*)

B.L., MS. Locke b. 8, no. 122. Printed in Rand, pp. 520–2. Answered by no. *2308*.

London 2° Sept. 97

Dear Sir

I suspected before yours of the 30° Aug: came that you had not received mine of the 17th which I writ to thank you for yours of the 14th and for the care you had taken about my businesse whilst you were at Sutton. What my not hearing from you sooner made me apprehend I am now perfectly confirmed in by your letter which I know would have mentioned that letter of mine if it had come to your hands. It haveing little more in it but my thanks for your setleing of the businesse with Carpenter and giveing your self the trouble of receiveing my money, the losse is not great, though the miscariage I like not,

[1] Pembroke.

As to Mrs Clarke whose health makes the businesse of your letter, I am glad to hear that there remains noe other symptoms of her ilnesse than the swelling and piting[a] of her legs. It is I confesse what is by noe means to be neglected, but tis what I have great confidence will be masterd if she will continue to follow rules, as by the good successe she has found of it I beleive she has done hitherto. As to the continueing her bitter drinke, since as you say she has found noe very sensible amendment in the use of it, more than what she might have expected from her former course, I thinke it would be convenient, she should returne to the use of her Garlick again whilst you are there, that you haveing seen the effects both of the one and the other, which I desire you and her to observe as nicely as you can and to discourse of one with an other, by this means when you come to town I may be able to judg which method of the two is best for her or whether any thing else may be orderd for her advantage better, than I can by any thing can be said in a letter. I desire you to give her my humble service and to tell her that since she eats drinks sleeps and looks well I have noe doubt at all but we shall wholy master the swelling of her legs by the blesseing of god, if she will take care not to make too much hast and be well to soon. My Love to my wife, whom I easilie beleife the finest yong woman in your country. not by vertue of the top knots[1] you speak of, but of those good qualities and accomplishments which are her more visible ornaments. My service to your son, and to Mrs Burges if she be with you. your son John[2] was lately well. Mr Pawling saw and spake with his landlady, and I have deliverd your message to Mr Malpus, who is very well satisfied and has promised me if the child should need his care in your absence he will not be wanting, and has promised me to let me know it if any thing should aile him. Mr Freke has been in town this weeke and is very well, and has writ to you since he came. Father Wallop[3] is dead. I wish you and your familie all manner of happynesse and am

Dear Sir

Your most humble and most affectionate servant

J Locke

My humble service to your son.

[a] *Or* piling

[1] Probably knots of ribbon worn on the head: *O.E.D.* Boyer translates the word as *fontange*.

[2] A son Jack is mentioned in 1695: no. 1863.

[3] Richard Wallop, born in 1616; Cursitor Baron of the Exchequer 1696; died on 22 August: *D.N.B.*

All that I desired you in my letter that was lost to adde to your former favour was only that when you returned the money you received for me of Mr Lyde you would doe it soe as I might be sure of it in mild money or Guineas, but I am not in hast for it but leave it to oportunity and your leisure

Address: For Edward Clarke Esquire member of Parliament at Chipley near Taunton Frank.

Postmark: SE 2

Endorsed by Clarke: Mr. Locke for Mrs. Clarke to Return to the Garlick etc: Received the 5th. September 1697, Answered the 6th. And sent Him a Byll on Mr. Churchill for 39: 08: 06d. being the money I Received of Mr Lyde for his use etc:

2306. CHARLES MORDAUNT, third earl of Peterborough, to LOCKE, 4 September 1697 (*2297*, *3230*)

B.L., MS. Locke c. 16, ff. 123–4. Printed in King, p. 239.

Sir

we all return you thanks for your charitable Correspondance, but the Lady is a little out of humour since your last, having long agoe settled the peace with the restitution of Strasbourgh, Luxembourgh and Lorraine, and sunk and destroyed all, or most of Ponti squadron, not considering the generous Knight Errantry of our Admiralls, who scorn to beat their Ennemies with odds, nine to Five being shamefull Advantage,[1] the next letter you are pleasd to writt this way addresse it to the lady who stayes here some time longer, i hope in fower or five days after you have received this to see you in London, for I take itt for Granted the Essex Lady[2] is not to attract, while the sun has so much influence

Sir

your most affectionate servant,

PETERBOROW.

Sept 4th 97

Address: For Mr Lock att the office of the Commissioners of Trade att Whitehall. London.

Postmark: SE 6

Endorsed by Locke: E: Peterborow 4 Sept 97

[1] In the engagement in May Nevell was reported to have had 22 men of war, and Pointis, 10: Luttrell, iv. 262. The Lady is Lady Peterborough. [2] Lady Masham.

2307. CORNELIUS LYDE to LOCKE, 4 September 1697 (2302, *2313*)

B.L., MS. Locke c. 15, ff. 158–9.

Sept: the 4th 97

Sir

I Received A Letter from my son in Holland by which I understand he is to take the degree of a Doct: in a short time and doe desire your Letter of recomendation to some practistioners in Amsterdam that he might see some of the practis of that place, which he thinks will be a greate advantage to him as you was pleased formerly to Intimate you may direct to him, to Samuell Lyde to be Leaft at mr John Rikfords An English ordinary in Leydon. I have not Received any of your rent that is behinde since I sa mr Clark but according to his advise I will Take bond of Jos: Hanny for his as being a better way to recover it of him and get the rest as soone as possible with all due Respects Sir I Am your obligd friend and Ser:

COR: LYDE

Address: These For Doct: Locke at mr Pawlings overagainst the plough in Little Lincolns feilds London

Postmark: SE 4

Endorsed by Locke: C: Lyde 4 Sept 97

2308. EDWARD CLARKE to LOCKE, 6 September 1697 (2305, 2309)

B.L., MS. Locke c. 6, ff. 130–1, with an enclosure, f. 129. Printed in Rand, p. 523. Answers no. 2305; answered by no. 2309.

Chipley September the 6th. 1697.

Deare Sir,

The money that I Received of Mr. Lyde for your use, I have Returned, with a greater summe of my own money to Mr. Churchill, Who I hope will in a few dayes have Actually Received the same; And to the end you may not want when your occasions Require it, I have by the Inclosed Desired Mr. Churchill to pay it you in Mill'd-money or Ginneas on Demand, But pray ask it not of Him, untill the latter End of this, or the Begining of the next Weeke, for by that time Hee will have Received the money due on the Bylls I have desiered Him to Receive for mee; The money I Received of Mr. Lyde was at two payments, viz: on the 7th. o

August 35l:12s:, And on the 12th. following 03l:16s:06d: In All thirty nine pounds eight shillings and six pence, for which summe I have drawn the Inclosed Byll on Mr. Churchill, But cannot imagine what should occasion the Miscarryage of your Letter of the 17th. of August that you Writt to mee etc:

Mrs. Clarke joynes with mee in Her Particular Thankes to you for your greate Care and Concern for Her, And intends to morrow, shee haveing taken the last of the Bitter-Infusion this day, to Return to the Garlick Course agen, the Effects of which I will observe as nicely as I can, and give you the most Exact Account I am capable of at my Return to Town, Since the Writeing of my last to you, Shee has complayned of an unusuall fullnesse in Her Body, which creates an uneasinesse to Her for an hower or two after Her first sleepe, but goes off againe in the morning before shee Rises, I Know not what the consequence of it may bee, and therefore trouble you with the mentioning of it, Which, with Mrs. Clarke's, your Wife's, my sonn's, and my humble service and Thankes for all your Favours concludes this from,

Your most Affectionate and obleiged humble servant,

EDW: CLARKE:

My humble service to Mr. Freke when you see Him, and to Mr. Pawling and all his Family etc:

Address: These, For John Locke Esqr. at Mr. Pawlins-House over against the Plow, In Little-Lincolns-Inn-Feilds, London:
Frank: Edw: Clarke:
Postmark: SE 8
Endorsed by Locke: E: Clarke 6 Sept. 97 Answered 9

[Enclosure:]

Chipley September the 6th. 1697.

Sirs

I Desire you on sight hereof to pay to John Locke Esqr. or Order the summe of thirty nine pounds, eight shillings, and six pence, in Mill'd-money or Ginneas, And place it to the Account of, £ s. d 39:08:6:

Your Reall Freind and Servant,

EDW: CLARKE:

For Mr. Awnsham and John Churchill
Bookesellers in Pater-Noster-Row London
These:

Signed by Locke: John Locke

2309. LOCKE to EDWARD CLARKE, 9 September 1697 (*2308*, 2351)

B.M., Add. MS. 4290, ff. 85–6. Printed in Ollion, pp. 243–4; Rand, pp. 524–5. Answers no. *2308*.

London 9 Sept 97

Dear Sir

I returne you my thanks for yours of the 6th which came safe yesterday with the bill inclosed which I shall make use of according to your direction. I am glad the change of medecines falls out whilst you are at home, that the several effects of the different courses may be observed. The fulnesse you mention Mrs Clarke has of late felt after her first sleep, I hope upon the change she was goeing to make when you writ will goe quite off and she will here noe more of. I looke upon it to be of noe consequence and soe shee need not trouble her thoughts about it

I came just now from your son John at Little Chelsy.[1] I desired Mr Malpus if any thing should happen to him to acquaint me with it. A day or two since the Mistris had sent to him to let him know the child had a cough and she feard a consumption,[2] upon which Mr Malpus went thither and reported to me the symptoms. I went thither my self to day and was glad to finde the Mistris's care had represented it to her m⟨ore⟩[a] dangerous than I found it. He was abroad in the feilds when I came, he looks well, eats well and sleeps well and coughed not once all the time I was there, nor had not as he told me coughed above once or twice since dinner, this was between five and six a clock. I thinke there is noe manner of danger in it. However I have orderd him some things and hope the next news I shall hear of him is that his cough is quite gon. They have promised to send me word the begining of the weeke, And if there be any occasion (as I beleive there will not) I will visit him again. I am

Dear Sir

Your most affectionate humble servant

J LOCKE

Pray give my service to your wife and my wife and to your son

[a] *Blotted.*

[1] A hamlet in Chelsea and Kensington, about where the modern Beaufort Street joins the Fulham Road: T. Faulkner, (*Chelsea*), 1829, i. 138–47; (*Kensington*), 1820, pp. 607–8.

[2] A wasting disease, not necessarily tubercular: *O.E.D.*

Mr Freke was well this morning and remembers you and Mr Pawling is your humble servant

Address: For Edward Clarke Esquire member of Parliament at Chipley near Taunton
Frank

Postmarks: SE 9; GC

Endorsed by Clarke: Mr. Lock of my sonn John's Indisposition etc: Received the 12th. September 1697. Answered the 13th.

2310. LOCKE to WILLIAM MOLYNEUX, 11 September 1697 (*2288*, *2311*)

Some Familiar Letters, pp. 232–5. Answers no. *2288*; answered by no. *2324*.

London, 11 Sept. 1697.

Dear Sir,

If you have received my reply to the Bishop[1] before this comes to your hand, I shall need say no more to the first paragraph of your obliging letter of the 20th. of July. Mr. Churchill tells me, he has taken care you should have it with speed. I have order'd another to Mr. Burridge, who has, by his undertaking, some concernment now in my Essay. I am not delighted at all in controversie, and think I could spend my time to greater advantage to my self, But, being attack'd, as I am, and in a way that sufficiently justifies your remarks on it, I think every body will judge I had reason to defend my self; whether I have or no, so far as I have gone, the world must judge.

I think, with you, the dissenters were best consider, That what is sauce for a goose is sauce for a gander. But they are a sort of men that will always be the same.

You thank me for what is owing to your own worth. Every one who knows you, will think (if he judges right) that he receives as much advantage as he gives by the countenance he shews you. However, I am obliged by your thanks to me, for, if I do not procure you as much good as you are capable of receiving from any one that comes to you from hence, 'tis my want of ability, and not want of will. My heart and inclination, wherein the friendship

[1] *Mr. Locke's Reply to the Right Reverend the Lord Bishop of Worcester's Answer to his Letter*, etc., 1697. It is dated from London, 29 June. Locke appended to it an answer to Thomas Burnet (of the Charterhouse), *Remarks upon an Essay concerning Humane Understanding*, 1697. L.L., no. 1797.

lies, will always be such, as I can presume, will not displease you, in a man whom I am very sensible you love.

Here was, the last year, a book in physick published by a young lad not twenty, who had never seen the university.[1] It was about the motion of the muscles, with as good an explication of it as any I have yet seen. I believe I might have spoke to Mr. Churchill to send your brother one of them, for the sake of the author; (for, as to the subject it self, I fear I shall never see it explained to my satisfaction) whether he did it or no I have not yet asked; but the book it self is not worth your brother's enquiry or acknowledgement; though being written by such an author, made it a kind of curiosity. I should be very glad if I could do him here any service of greater importance. But I having now wholly laid by the study of physick, I know not what comes out new, or worth the reading, in that faculty. Pray give my humble service to your brother, and let me know whether he hath any children, for then I shall think my self obliged to send him one of the next edition of my book of Education,[2] which, my bookseller tells me, is out of print; and I had much rather be at leisure to make some additions to that, and my Essay of Humane Understanding, than be employed to defend my self against the groundless, and, as others think, trifling quarrel of the Bishop. But his Lordship is pleased to have it otherwise, and I must answer for my self as well as I can, till I have the good luck to be convinced.

I was not a little pleas'd to find what thoughts you had concerning hypotheses in physick. Though Sir R. B's vein in poetry[3] be what every body must allow him to have an extraordinary talent in, and though with you I exceedingly valued his first preface, yet I must own to you, there was nothing that I so much admired him for, as for what he says of hypotheses in his last. It seems to me so right, and is yet so much out of the way of the ordinary writers, and practitioners in that faculty, that it shews as great a strength and penetration of judgment, as his poetry has shew'd flights of fancy, and therefore I was very glad to find in you the same thoughts of it. And when he comes luckily in my way, I shall not forget your wishes, and shall acquaint him with the observations you mention. And the key you desire I shall

[1] No. *2191*; p. 164. Boulton was said to be aged twenty when he matriculated rom Brasenose College, Oxford, on 29 November of this year.

[2] The third edition appeared in 1695; the fourth, which appeared in 1699, contains substantial additions to §§ 7, 94, and especially 167.

[3] Sir Richard Blackmore.

send you, if it be fit to be asked of him, which I am at present in some doubt of.

Tho' I coul'd my self answer many of your questions concerning Mons. Le Clerc, yet I have sent them to him himself, with the reason of them. I have not yet received his answer, the expectation whereof has delay'd my writing to you for some time. In the mean time, till I hear from him, I thank you in his name and my own.

I shall be very glad to hear from you how the linen manufacture goes on, on that side the water, and what assistance the parliament there is like to give to it,[1] for I wish prosperity to your country, and, very particularly, all manner of happiness to you. I am unfeignedly,

Sir,

Your most affectionate, humble servant,

JOHN LOCKE.

What I told you formerly of a storm coming against my book, proves no fiction. Besides what you will see I have taken notice of in my reply, Mr Serjeant, a popish priest, whom you must needs have heard of, has bestow'd a thick octavo upon my Essay,[2] and Mr. Norris, as I hear, is writing hard against it.[3] Shall I not be quite slain, think you, amongst so many notable combatants, and the Lord knows how many more to come?

2311. WILLIAM MOLYNEUX to LOCKE, 11 September 1697 (2310, *2324*)

The Carl H. Pforzheimer Library, New York. Transcribed from photostat. Printed in *Some Familiar Letters*, pp. 236–8. Answered by no. 2376.

Dublin. Sept. 11th. 1697

Honoured Sir

My last to you was of July 20th. since which time I have not had the Happines of a Line from you. But I am satisfyd you are

[1] Nos. 2129, *2131*. The subject had recently been examined by the Board of Trade. The Board sent a report to the Lords Justices on 31 August; woollen manufactures in Ireland were to be restricted, and the manufacture of linen was to be encouraged. The report is printed in Fox Bourne, ii. 363–72.

[2] Father John Sergeant (no. *2085*), *Solid Philosophy Asserted*, 1697. L.L., no. 2626.

[3] This probably refers to *An Essay towards the Theory of the Ideal or Intelligible World*, which was published in 1701–4.

better imployd; and indeed when I see dayly what swarms of Angry Wasps do arise against you (besides many which reach not our View in this Place) I wonder not that you should be so far ingaged as to have little time to throw away on Me. tother Day I met with the last Effort of Mr Edwards Malice;[1] I do now hartily pitty the Poor Wretch; He is certainly Mad, and no More to be taken notice of hereafter than the Railings of Olivers Porter in Bethlem.[2] I have seen also a Philosophical Writer against you of an other strain, one J.S. that writes against all Ideists;[3] this Gentleman, tho Civil, yet to me is absolutely unintelligible, so unfortunate I am. Who he is I know not, but should be glad to learn from you; and what you think in general of his Book.

Mr. T.[4] is at last driven out of our Kingdom. the Poor Gentleman by his imprudent Management had raised such an universal outcry, that twas even Dangerous for a Man to have been known once to Converse with him. This Made all Wary Men of Reputation Decline seing him, insomuch that at last he wanted a Meals-Meat[5] (as I am told) and none would admit him to their Tables. The little[a]– Stock of–[a] Mony which he brought into this Country being exhausted, he fell to borrowing from any One that would Lend him ½ a Crown; and Run in det for his Wigs, Cloaths, and Lodging (as I am informed) and last of all to Compleat his Hardships, the Parliament fel on his Book, Voted it to be Burnt by the Common Hangman, And Orderd the Author to be taken into Custody of the Serjeant at Arms, and to be Prosecuted by the Attorny General at Law.[6] Hereupon he is fled out of this Kingdom; and none here knows where he has directed his Course. I did beleive you might be a great while to come a stranger to these proceedings unles I had intimated them to you; and that is one of My Designes in writing this to you.

I am here very Happy in the Friendship of an Honourable Person, Mr Molesworth, who is an Harty Admirer and Acquaintance

a–a *MS.* little Stock / Stock of

[1] See p. 149.
[2] He was a favourite of the wits: see Prior's Dialogue between him and Cromwel in *Literary Works*, ed. Wright and Spears, 1959, pp. 655–63 and the note, which gives other occurrences; see also *Tatler*, no. 51.
[3] Father John Sergeant. [4] Toland.
[5] A meal, a repast: *O.E.D.*
[6] This was voted on 9 September. The book was to be burnt twice on Saturday the 11th: at 12 noon on College Green before the Parliament House; at 1 p.m. before the Tholsel of Dublin: *Journal of the House of Commons ... Ireland*, ii. 903–4.

of yours;[1] We never Meet, but we remember you; He sometimes comes into my House, and tells me, tis not to pay a Visit to me, but to pay his Devotion to your Image that is in My Dining Room.

I should be glad to hear farther from you concerning Monsieur Le Clerk and Monsieur Coste in relation to what I formerly writt to you concerning those Gentlemen.

I am
Sir
Your Most obleidged Humble servant
W: MOLYNEUX

Address: To John Locke Esquire at Mr Pawlings overagainst the Plow-Inn in Little Lincolns Inn Fields London

Postmark: SE 20

Endorsed by Locke: W: Molyneux 11 Sept. 97 Answered 10. Jan

2312. SAMUEL BOLD to LOCKE, 17 September 1697 (*2232, 2486*)

B.L., MS. Locke c. 4, ff. 21–2.

Honored Sir

I lately received from mr A. Churchil your Admirable Reply to the Bishop of Worcester's Answer to your Letter etc.[2] The Bishop was never so genteely treated by any man, as you treat Him, nor any writer so effectually Answered, and vanquished as He is as to those points you have made the subjects of your Reply. The Learned and men of sense wil certainly wait with great Impatience to have the like satisfaction from your other part.[3] I heartily wish your Health and Leisure may be such, It may not be very long before they are gratified. Mr Churchil sent me your Reply as presented from your self to me.[4] The Honour Sir, you have done me therein, and my sense of It so great, I hope you wil pardon

[1] Robert Molesworth, 1656–1725; created Viscount Molesworth of Swords (Ireland), etc., 1716; author of *An Account of Denmark, as it was in the year 1692*, 1694 (L.L., no. 950): *D.N.B.*

[2] pp. 189, 196.

[3] In his *Reply* Locke answered only those passages in Stillingfleet's *Answer* that relate to the Unitarian controversy, but promised to answer other passages not bearing directly on the Doctrine of the Trinity: pp. 166–7.

[4] Bold is named in the distribution list for the *Reply*.

my want of words wherby fitly to express It. I esteem your vouchsafing to do me so great an Honour, much more than if any Bishop in the Kingdom had conferred the best preferment in His Diocess on me. There is not any point you have taken notice of in your Reply, that I can imagin you have left His Lordship room to say anything of, but that He is perfectly Answered and overcome, except one; where He or those of His party may perhaps pretend they have some scope.[1] I crave leave to mention that place, And to make a little alteration in my Lord's words, whereby you wil perceive what I apprehend may be alledged by them as my Lords sense. The place in His Lordship's vindication of the Doct: of the Trinity, is p. 252. the words I place thus, Sometimes Nature is taken for the thing It self in which those properties are. And so Aristotle took nature for a corporeal substance etc. (that is, thus Aristotle understood the Term Nature, when speaking of corporeal Beings, He called It, i.e. Nature, A corporeal substance. Corporeal Substance, and corporeal Nature was the same with Him) But not withstanding Aristotle gave such an Account of nature as reaches only corporeal beings, yet Nature and Substance are of an equal extent. And so (or thus) that which is the subject of powers etc is the nature (of the thing discoursed of) whether we speak of bodily or spiritual things. (The Bishop seem's to take nature, and substance for different terms which stand for one and the same Idea, viz that confused Idea we have of the unknown something, which must support Accidents, powers, and properties, whether this something be Body or Spirit. So that by Nature, He means Body, or Spirit. All spiritual beings are of the same nature, because they are all spirits. All corporeal beings are of the same nature, because they are Bodies. Thus a Horse, and a stone, etc are of the same nature, because they are Bodies, and not spirits. Bodily, and spiritual things, are distinguished by their natures one from Another, taking nature in this sense, for the substances or unknown supports of powers etc. But spiritual beings are not distinguished one from Another, nor Bodily one from Another by their Natures, taking nature in this sense, but by their natures, as Nature signifies powers and properties). The nature of things properly belong to our Reason etc. (This is very obscure, but I conceive some thing to this purpose may be said; By the exercise of our Rational faculty about the Ideas we have got, we come to be

[1] In what follows Bold comments on Locke's *Reply*, pp. 117–22.

satisfied there is something which supports powers etc, and we have ground to form that uncertain obscure Idea of something or substance. And to form some maxims concerning substance, as that all substance is either Spirit or Body. And we by arguing from these maxims which are also called Reason, come to know the nature of things, that is, whether they are Body, or Spirit. I think much may be said against this Account, and that the Bishop doth mistake on many accounts as to these matters. I forbear to say any more, for I am sure you see a great deal further than I do. pardon I beseech you this Trouble and Accept the Heartiest thanks imaginable for your excellent Book, from

Your most Humble and obliged servant

SA: BOLD

Steeple Sept: 17. 1697.

Address: To the Honoured Mr Locke
Endorsed by Locke: S: Bold 17 Sept. 97

2313. CORNELIUS LYDE to LOCKE, 21 September 1697 (*2307*, 2332)

B.L., MS. Locke c. 15, ff. 160–1. Apparently a second answer to no. 2302; answered by no. 2332.

Sept. the 21st 97

Sir

Yours I Received of the 28th: of August and since I have taken A bond of Jos: Hanny for 4li-10s due to you for I Thought, if he shold have an action brought against him it wold be much Easier by a bond, for the penalty will beare the charge, the bond will be due at miclemus next, he drives a good trade as formerly, but verry backward to pay, soe if you please to order me to sue him I will or what you please. Sir I heartily Thanke you for the greate Kindnes you was pleasd to mention in your Last to my Son. I hope you will finde him deserving. if it may be for his advantage I wold meete him in London where I hope he may be in November with all Respects I Am your

obligd friend and ser

COR: LYDE

if mr Clarke is Come to towne my Kind service to him by whome

I sent up your account which is Large at buck hill but it was what his agreement was with mr Stratton as he say

here is greate Joy of the good news of Peace[1]

Address: These For Doct: Locke at mr Pawlings over against the Plough in Little Lincolns feilds London

Postmark: SE 24

Endorsed by Locke: C: Lyde 21 Sept 97 Answered Oct. 19

2314. DR. ROBERT SOUTH to LOCKE, 22 September 1697 (*2229, 2597*)

B.L., MS. Locke c. 18, ff. 169–70. South is included in the distribution list for Locke's *Reply* to Stillingfleet.

Sir

I begg your Pardon that I have bin so Slow in my Returnes for the late Present you made me of Your Second Excellent Discourse in answer to Bishop Stillingfleet: In which with great Strength you follow your own Blow and with Equall Dexterity ward off, or rather repell, His; So that for my own part I cannot see[a] how he will be able to encounter you for the future, unlesse possibly with *Injunctions*, which he calls *Silenceing men by Authority*,[2] and which he is much better at, than at Silenceing them by Argument.

All that doe you Justice, must Own you a great master of Philosophicall Learning, acquired by Long and Deep thought, as well as felicity of Apprehension: and may much more deservedly place you in the first Rank of the Professors of it, than your Antagonist can claim the Place you allott him in your 53 page:[3] Though it must be confessed that after so *much favour* done him in those Superlative Commendations, you doe him *Right* also in your Answers; and wheresoever you doe so, I dare undertake that He will not look upon it as a Panegyrick. He shewes what a Philosopher he is, by talking of *a Common Nature* (in Created Beings)

[a] *Interlined, apparently by Locke.*

[1] The treaties between France and England, the United Provinces, and Spain were signed at Ryswick on 20 September, N.S. There are notices in the *London Gazette*, 16 September, and in the other papers.

[2] Not found; perhaps a loose allusion to *Discourse in Vindication*, preface, pp. xxv–xxvi.

[3] 'Your Lordship has been so long in the first Rank of the Men of Letters, and by common consent, setled at the top of this learned Age, that . . .'

really existing in the Severall Individualls denominated from it;[1] Whereas there is no such Really Existent Being, as a Common Humanity; but it is onely a Notion formed and drawn off by the mind from the Agreement it observes in Severall Particulars or Individualls, and so becomes Applicable to, and predicable of all, and Every One of them. And it is manifest, that Aristotle never intended more, but broke with his master Plato, upon this very Point.

As for your generally, as well, as justly Admired and Learned *Essay of Human Understanding* (which through Spight, and Envy, (as I verily think) more than any Thing else, has bin made the Occasion of most of the Opposition you have found), I heartily wish, it were translated into Latine, that so the World might reap the benefitt of so Comprehensive a Subject in a Comprehensive Language, there being no Reason that a Work of so great a Value and so peculiar a Character should be Kept within the Narrow Compasse of our Native Tongue.

Sir I heartily wish you Health and long life to perfect whatsoever else you may have under your Hand. And when I Come to Westminster[2] I shall make it my Businesse to inform my Self where your Abode is and not fail to wait upon You there with my Gratefull Acknowledgments for all your Civillities to

Worthy Sir

Your old freind and very humble and much obliged servant

ROBERT SOUTH

Cavesham.[3] 22 September 97.

Address: For his worthy and much esteemed freind mr John Lock These.

Endorsed by Locke: Dr South 22 Sept 97 Answered Oct. 2

2315. MRS. ELIZABETH BERKELEY, later Burnet, to LOCKE, 22 September 1697 (*2273*, 2321)

B.L., MS. Locke c. 3, ff. 209–11; ff. 210–11 are identifiable as the enclosure by the mentions of it in f. 209, the letter. Answered by no. 2321.

22: Sep: 97:

Sir

I know I ought not to send you so ill write a letter that must

[1] *Discourse in Vindication*, p. 253; quoted in *Reply*, p. 126.
[2] South was a prebendary of Westminster from 1663 until his death.
[3] Caversham, near Reading, where South had an estate.

give you trouble in the reading were the sense allowable, but transcribing is a task I want patiance for, at least very unwillingly undergo; but it will be more to my advantage in preserving those favourable thoughts you have too hastely intertained of me, if you will take my advise and not read the inclosed at all but burn or return it me again, I having hardly had time to read, I'm sure not to consider it as I ought before I troubled you with it; however I have observed your request in takeing a fredom that is not pardonable but as a proof of sincerity. 'tis not hard to express esteem where wee really find wee have it, and 'tis much easyer making excuses for my own deffects of which I'm so aboundantly sinsable; by sending a letter so faulty in sense English etc: I know I expose my ignorance, but I would be so humble to be content to be thought on as I am; I am sure a complement tho never so justly turned, could be of no service, and if the inclosed is as useless It is because I cant tell how to make any letter from me any otherwise. my intention has ben good and you must excuse the performance. I am not quite of your mind as to the necesity of your vindication, you owe it perhaps to your self and in that respect it is reasonable and fitt, but all things considered could you be content to dispence with your own right I think it would be most charitable and best to be silant; their being not a great many able and fewer willing to make a good and right use of this dispute.[1] I hear my Lord has some thoughts of writing, but hope he will not, not having heard him speak of doing it, or of your Book, which I was glad of 'till I had sent this, that I might be the less biased, had I had opertunity to hear proper Judges discours of your Book my letter might have had fewer of such week inquieries, but you love to convers with childeren and see the naturall productions of the mind, unasisted by art, and unposest by others notions, mine is too much so, which will I hope be an apoligie for the deffects as well as pl⟨ain⟩[a] dealing of

Sir

Your Faithfull servent

E. B.

[a] *Page torn.*

---

[1] Locke included Mrs. Berkeley in the distribution list for his *Reply* to Stillingfleet. She comments on the *Reply* in the enclosure; her page-references, so far as I have tested them, appear to be accurate, except that p. 37 should be p. 36, and p. 18 should be p. 108.

2315. *Mrs. E. Berkeley, 22 September 1697*

Address: For Mr Locke to be left at Mr Castle's[1] Bookseller, next Scotland-yard by White Hall

Postmark: SE 24

Endorsed by Locke: E: Berkeley 22 Sept. 97 Answered Oct.

[Enclosure:]

Sir

Being on a journy when your Book came first out I neither gott the favour of that you were pleased to send me nor time to read any other, indid I took one in sheets as I went throw Oxford and read great part of it but twas with so many inturuptions, that I was willing to give it a second reading which has defered my thanks longer then my obligations would otherwise have allowed; you have indid put the tryall of my Frindship on a pretty hard service not only in respect of my ignorance which is not my fault but misfortune, but in respect of the persons consarned in the dispute, and I can't tell how I could be impartiall did not the esteem I have for both make me so, but to satisfy you 'tis not lasyness or unwillingness to obey you I have sett down some reflections I made in my second reading your Book, which is the best way to convince you how incapable I am of being any more so tasked. being in a Frinds House I have not so much command of my time, or if I had should perhaps want skill to shorten this letter by useing any other method then taking the Book as I read it and refering you to the pages by which I hope you'll gess my meaning tho am sorry to give you so much trouble to so litle purpose; but being your own fault I ought to be excused at least forgiven. In severall places of your Book I thought you were a litle too Criticall in observeing small faults in the exactness of writing that did not imediatly relate to your self or matter of your complaint, to correct such errors in a Frind is kind and allowable, or to expose a vain pretender to knowledg, but my Lords reputation for larning is so justly established and of so publick a benefit, that all needless reflections ought to be avoided, sinse 'tis of less ill consequence to have it thought you mistook my L— then that my L— mistook the truth; and had you more willingly used your art to clear what was I owne too obscure in my Lords books then to make that

[1] Edward Castle, a minor publisher from 1696 to 1709 or later. He joined with A. and J. Churchill in the publication of Locke's three answers to Stillingfleet, of his *Second Vindication of the Reasonableness of Christianity*, and of Wynne's *Abridgment*, 1696.

obscurity more observable, you might I fancy have found less disagreement in your Ideas, and don what well became the generosity and disinterestness of Mr Locke tho it was more then the laws of a just defence obliged you to; and would both sides but take the same pains to find wherin they mean alike as they do to show wherin they defer or mistake truth in their maner of defending it, I can't but beleeve the oposistion would be reduced to a few perticulers; and the rest found only a dispute of words that seem to clash when both intend the same thing.—41: why *the Author* if you will beleeve me I have and do still hear my Lord speak of you with great esteem, but suppose the occation of atacking your book (which I confes I am very sorry for but is now past recal) was the considering it as the originall and foundation of what is called the new way of reasoning, and from whence they fecthed thier best Materialls, and having a generall dislike from some foreseen ill consequences he thought might folow this way of proving by Ideas, especially requiring such degrees of evidence as necesary to certenty, he thought him self obliged to write against it, which he might indid have well enough don without naming your Book, but that perhaps my Lord thought would have made you a party farther then he designed, for your book being very well known to most who are fitt to read my Lord Vind:[1] had they found *certenty* by *Ideas* etc: opposed they would very naturally have beleeved my Lord had your Book in his thoughts, so that only argueing against it as he supposes it an unsartin way to certenty, but discharging it of all the bad purposes to which my Lord thinks it used contrary to its Authors intention, he thought I am perswaded he had taken the least offencive way; and what he ment by saying they were *used* to *other purposes* etc: methinks is plain, you designed your Book as a rule and help to the ataining knowledg etc: and they have as my Lord aprehends built such proposistions on your *foundation* as ⟨overturns⟩[a] and weekens faith, my Lord disliking *that* oposed it as the shortest and surest way, since if the foundation is wrong the superstructure falls of it self, and you know 'tis a comon thing in answering Books to take in more then is objected that so answering it in its greatest strenth the dispute may be the sooner ended; this is only to

[a] *MS.* overtuns *or* overturs

[1] *A Discourse in Vindication of the Doctrine of the Trinity.*

convince you of a truth I would fain have you beleeve, and had I art or rethorick would use it to perswade you to: that my Lord had no will to reflect or show any further dislike of your Book then at that time he thought necesary for the safegard of the truth he defended, and if a litle sharpness sometimes mix'd his Ink, he then forgot Mr Locke and ment only the abusers of his Notions;—37: why should you think that a willfull, might it not be an inosent mistake, at least for want of reading your Book carefully;—44: this taking a too severe advantage you must suppose *them* was ment your way of certenty by Ideas,—46: *its due place*, I would fain see this dispute agreed it would be an aditionall to the joy for the peace;—50: tis not only certenty in clear and distinct Ideas but in the agreement and disagreement of them too that my Lord desents from; sure my Lord mistakes you in applying the word certenty, you require it ⟨in⟩[a] order to knowledg, and my Lord aprehends you do the same in matters of faith or that others make that use of it, tho faith and certenty as I remember you observe are deferent acts of the mind;—52: 53: after so much gentleness some other parts read a litle harsh, as if you were willing to expose your adversarys erors as well as larn your own, especially as I remember the dialouge semes too resenting;—62: dos not my Lord aprehend the word *Idea* too liable to be mistaking for sensible objects only, so that at lenth all faith will be discared or left very loose and precarious and people only beleeve what is so evident that they cant but beleeve it;—72: no harm in Ideas but in the certenty of proving by them; or perhaps my Lord dislikes the way of coming to all our knowledg by them, and dos not think the soul such an empty Cabinet as you suppose; 75—I think they may sometimes seem new when they are borrowed from others, observeing not long since that I fell upon some thoughts which apperd new to me, not knowing I had read or heard them before, till a litle after reading an answer to a Book I had read two years before, I found my own thoughts and allmost my own words, which made me think some impressions were surely left in my memorie and that those borrowed thoughts were only awakend by some accidentall hint, tho I knew it not; but that one may light into an others thoughts and expresions I don't at all doubt, having some times don it where I am pretty sure I had no leader only from a mind too apt to object, and a restless desiere to find

[a] *Word omitted by the writer.*

satisfaction which I would not allways do in Books probably for want of Judgment to see the force of their arguements—78: methinks thise two places agrees all the dispute about Ideas and their use, and so stated you are both of the same mind, indid I think both your times too valueable to be so imployed, for if your way of proving and knowing is found a clear and easy method it will be aproved and used when time has smothed the prejudices and stilled the fears of its oposers, and if it is not so and only shows the promisd land of knowledg but brings not to it, it will like former skeems fall into disuse of it self; for my own part I have this objection against your Book that it seems to make the ways of speculation so plain and easy as tempts into those mases where the unskillfull lose themselves, so that perhaps the placeing needless barocadoes at the enterence of knowledg is no more then necesary to afright all unarmed and week persons from presuing to aproach;—82: is not that paragraph a needless reflection;—83: if the agreement of the Idea of 3: yet: 1: cant be made out, and yet no certainty or rationall beleif can be without it, don't that distroy the Article my Lord defended, tho I confess if you say this relates to the certainty of knowledg, not the rule of faith which depends on revelation I am answerd;—89: I rather think what my Lord condemns is making certainty necesary in those things were it is not to be had, and leveing all lose and doubtfull where it is not—96: but dos not those my Lord writes against make it unreasonable to beleeve what can't be redust to this certainty of knowledg and is not that the ill purpose that is made of your Ideas contrary to what you designed them for;—98: this was indid an inconsideration that my Lord uses not to be guilty of, and I am sorry you made it more visable by repeating;[a] for my Lords reason,[a] least others take the advantage and use it to other purposes then either of you intend by writting;—18: pray do not think any would be willing to have you of the *Heretical side* it is thought no small misfortune by a great many only to have you suspected as a favourer of them —110: my Lord refered not to the sign or word Nature and per sone but the reality of what was signifyed by them in the sense in which he took them;—125: may not my Lords words be thus understood, he supposes those defering propertis of things of which he has clear Ideas flow from some deference in the unknown substance or nature of that being they subsist in, of which we

[a] *The punctuation is doubtful.*

can have no clear Idea, only the necesety of such a support maks us conclud their is such an one, which I presume therefore is called by my Lord an allowed princeple of reason, because all our Ideas falls without it, yet wee can have no distinct Idea of it;—130: dos not spirituall and Corporeal substance take in all Nature, perhaps Aristole thought all substance Corporeal, and so Nature and body were of equall extent to him, but I beg pardon for I know not his system nor any other of Philosephy;—135: but a like *perticuler Nature* is in other men;—144: are both sides willing to make each others sense intelligible, and not to put a Foraign sence when a more agreeing might be found—this consideration of Nature I presume is ment not of universall Nature but the Nature of man; —145: that which deferences humane Nature from all other beings, and never varies being allways found in humane Nature, therefore I gess my Lord calls it an intire *Notion* of *it self* but their are perticulers in the Nature of Peter that differences him from John etc: that can't be so considered as an intire or constant Idea of humane Nature;—148: I find now I only fancy I understand at all this nice dispute, but 'tis only the shadow or vision of knowledg, for by second thoughts I conclude if 'tis inteligible to others it is not so to me, who am too litle verst in speculation to find where the true strenth of this dispute rests; for by what my Lord sayed of the comon Nature of man I thought he had placed it in the likeness or sameness of that internall frame, or unknow substance which was peculiar to that order of Beings, but in this defenition of person, methinks he makes that internall fram to deffer in every individual, and theirin to place personality; for if I suppose no externall difference, then the difference must be internall or none at all; except by this *peculiar maner* of *subsistance* is ment not a different internall substance, but distance of place, seperat existance and self consiousness, tho methinks the two first are external differences; I am by this convinct I neither understand the terms or what is ment by them, and hope you will forget so soon as read all the impertinances of this long letter; tho now I have gon thus farr I will at least show I have not laid by your book before I came to the end of it;—154: and is not that *Idea* and *generall name* founded on a reality of Being;—155: is this sharpness necesary to truth;—158: put but *its own* Nature here instead of *those* of *its one kind* and then tell me what your Frend ment by kind and that is if I mistake not what my Lord means by the Comon Nature of man and what he calls *incommunicable* to all *those* of *its one kind* or Nature, will I think make what my Lord means by personality—162: 'tis not the same to err in the maner of proving, and lay down propositions which are feard as ment to weaken the docterine my Lord thinks a truth devinely revelled;—169: I hope that *due light* will not be so strong to hurt week eyes, I confess my self one of those Cowards who am in pain, and fear with many more the ill use and consequences of this dispute, I mean that week or ill affected persons may make of it; and therefore hartely wish that the glory of a private victory might be sacrificed to a Publik benefet, but who will offer so beloved a sacrifice I cant tell it being more then the law of Justice exacts;

2316. Mrs. Elizabeth Stratton to Locke, 25 September 1697 (*2283, 2625*)

B.L., MS. Locke c. 18, f. 232.

Bristoll Sept 25th (1697)

Deare Cousin

Since my last to you I thought my son would have seen you before now but his Masters busine's would not permit it, tho now I think it will not be long before he will be in London in his Masters business, for tho his time of aprentisship be Over yet he still continues with him and I hope yet will be much for his advantage, I should be very Glad to have seen you here to have advisd with you about my son Peters settelment, his Master Mr Baily and Mrs and her Mother who lives with them, are all exceeding kind to him, and are willing he should have their daughter, and I have good reason to beleeve her father will make her worth a 1000l, and will take him in partner in his trade he is a very Honest and good man, and I think did you know him as we doe you would mightily approve it, but the young Gentilewoman doe not so readily embrace it as her freinds, and we, did think she would, but as far as I can find she thinks Peters fortune doe not answer hers tho I hope she will be perswaded to it, for indeed as far as I can dissern nothing in the city can be so advantageous to him tho he is very well belovd here and very well fitted for his trade but I think to begin with so sollid and substantiall a trade's man as Mr Baily is would doe him a great kindness both for soul and body; I think I did hint somthing of Mr Baily kindness before supposeing my son would have seen you before now I know he will gladly advise with you and I beleeve will be governd by you, I bless God I have at present preety good health but it adds to my trouble that I am noe way able to assist my son, but I must submit to the wise providence of God, I shall be Glad to heare of your wellfare humbly beging your excuse, and will take leave when I have given you the Humble service of my brother and sister Chapman and my two daughters, my daughter Ann Hasell lyes in with a daughter and is preety well but she nor Peter knows not of my writing. Deare Cousin

Your most affectionate Cousin, and humble servant

ELIZABETH STRATTON

Address: For Mr John Lock to be left at Mr Pawlings Over against the plough in little Lincolns Inne Feilds in London

Postmark: SE 27

Endorsed by Locke: E: Stratton 25 Sept. 97

2317. ELIZABETH CLARKE to LOCKE, 26 September 1697 (*2949*)

B.L., MS. Locke c. 6, ff. 155–6. Printed in Rand, p. 522.

Ivey Church[1] Sep: the 26 ⟨1697⟩

Sir

I could not omitt so good an opertunity of returning you my thankes for your last fine present, but that which I thought the greatest favour, was, considering the abundance of business you have, that you should yet find a time to thinke on me, I also do assure you that I am extreamly glad to hear of your health, and that you may long injoy it, is the wish of

Sir

Your most obliged humble Servant

ELIZ: CLARKE

Address: These To John Locke Esqr present

Endorsed by Locke: El. Clarke 26 Sept 97

[1] The home of Thomas and Mrs. Stringer.

2318. PHILIPPUS VAN LIMBORCH to LOCKE, 28 September/8 October 1697 (*2256*, 2340)

B.L., MS. Locke c. 14, ff. 107–8. Copy by van Limborch in Amsterdam University Library, MS. R.K., III D 16, f. 185. Printed from the copy in *Some Familiar Letters*, pp. 394–7. Answered by no. 2340.

This letter introduces an inquiry into proofs of the Unity of God other than those provided by revelation: that is, that there is one god only, the creator and ruler of the universe, and not a plurality of gods, as in heathen belief. The doctrine of the Trinity (Trinitarianism as against Socinianism or Unitarianism) is not concerned.

Vir Amplissime

Mense Martio scripsi tibi epistolam satis prolixam.[1] Hac æstate cum viris aliquot primariis sermonem de variis habui; inter alia sermo incidit de tractatu, de quo in superioribus meis judicium meum scripsi.[2] Omnes eum summopere laudabant. Unus[3] vero titulum sibi non satis placere affirmabat, tanquam nimis exilem pro dignitate materiæ quæ toto opere tractatur. Autoris hujus longe diversum ajebat fuisse institutum a plerorumque scriptorum consuetudine, qui exigui pretii libris titulos magnificos præfigere solent; hunc autem libro magnifico exilem præfixisse titulum: oportuisse titulum aliquatenus respondisse dignitati operis, ut et ille lectores allicere posset. Alius vir (idem qui tibi antehac Sladum nostrum commendatum esse voluit, quod tibi soli dictum velim, nomen enim suum ob rationes quasdam celatum voluit)[4] se bis

---

Excellent Sir,

I wrote you a lengthy enough letter in March.[1] This summer I had a discussion with some leading men about various subjects; among other things there occurred a discussion of the treatise about which I wrote you my opinion in my former letter.[2] They all praised it exceedingly. One[3] indeed declared that the title did not fully satisfy him as being too meagre for the dignity of the subject treated in the whole work. This author's practice, he said, was very different from the custom of most writers, who are wont to prefix magnificent titles to books of small value; he on the other hand had prefixed a meagre title to a magnificent book; the title ought to have corresponded to some extent to the dignity of the work, so that it also could attract readers. Another man (the same who formerly wanted our friend Sladus to be recommended to your care; I wish this to be told to you alone, for he wanted his name to be concealed for certain reasons)[4] said that he

---

[1] No. *2222.*

[2] *The Reasonableness of Christianity*, read by van Limborch in Coste's translation.

[3] Apparently M. de Hertogh or A. van den Ende: p. 259.

[4] Johannes Hudde; for the identification see further p. 257.

tractatum illum perlegisse ajebat: laudabat illum summopere, autoremque fidei Christianæ objectum, quod præcipuum totius libri argumentum est, solidissime probasse affirmabat. Unum autem desiderabat: nimirum, quod autor jam statim ab initio vulgarem de peccato originis sententiam rejecerit ac refutaverit: potuisse autorem, intactâ illâ sententiâ, nihilominus præcipuum tractatus sui argumentum adstruere: nunc multos, quorum mentibus alte sententia illa insedit, lecto libri initio, antequam ad principale ejus argumentum accedant, offendi, atque ita præjudicium contra autorem concipere, ut sequentia non ea animi serenitate quæ requiritur legant, sicque alieniores reddi; cum potius ipsorum benevolentia captanda fuisset, ut judicio integro expendant sententiam, veram quidem, sed communi Theologorum appetitui minus consentaneam; qui fere omnes fidei Christianæ aliquid de suo admixtum cupiunt, quasi ea suo cœtui peculiaris sit, et alii ab illa excludantur. Qui error ut eorum animis eruatur, alliciendi potius sunt, quam dogmatis alicujus minus sibi probati assertione alienandi. Candide tibi scribo, quid viri hi desideraverint. Hac occasione, ut fieri solet, sermo ad alia deflexit, et quidem, quibus argumentis solidissime Dei unitas

---

had twice read through that treatise; he praised it exceedingly and declared that the author had very solidly demonstrated the object of the Christian faith, which is the principal subject of the whole book. But he found one thing amiss: namely that from the very beginning the author had rejected and refuted the common opinion regarding original sin; the author, leaving that opinion untouched, could nonetheless have established the principal argument of his treatise; as it is, many in whose minds that opinion is deeply rooted are offended on reading the beginning of the book before they come to its main argument, and accordingly conceive a prejudice against the author, so that they do not read what follows with the requisite serenity of mind and are thus rendered the more averse, when rather their goodwill should have been courted, so that they might ponder with impartial judgement an opinion that indeed is true but that agrees little with the common craving of theologians, who almost all want something of their own to be admixed with the Christian faith, as if that faith were peculiar to their own religious body [*coetus*] and others were excluded from that faith. In order that this error may be eradicated from their minds they are to be enticed rather than to be alienated by the assertion of some dogma of which they do not approve. I write to you candidly what these men found amiss. On this occasion, as usually happens, the discussion digressed to other subjects, and in fact to the arguments with which the unity of God is most solidly proved.

probetur. Idem ille vir primarius affirmabat, se argumenta quædam irrefragabilia requirere, quibus probetur, ens æternum, seu per se existens, seu undiquaque perfectum, esse tantum unum. Desiderabat quædam in argumentis Hugonis Grotii, libro primo de Veritate Religionis Christianæ:[1] Addebat, audivisse se, tractatum tuum de Intellectu humano in linguam Gallicam verti:[2] multum se tribuere judicio tuo, ac summopere versionem illam desiderare. Quæsivit ex me, num in illo tractatu etiam unitatem entis a se existentis adstruxisses? Ego me ignorare respondi, qui tractatum, utpote lingua mihi ignota conscriptum, nunquam legerim. Voluit itaque serio tibi per me commendari, ut, si in tractatu tuo quæstionem hanc intactam reliqueris, illius adstructione tractatum augere velis, unitatemque entis independentis solide adstruere. Manifestum videtur, ens independens quod omnem in se complectitur perfectionem, unicum tantum esse: Ille tamen hoc ita probari cupiebat, ut argumentum nulla parte laboraret. Ante triduum mihi aurem vellicari jussit, et a me quæri, an jam ad te scripsissem, et aliquod a te responsum accepissem. Non credideram ipsum id

---

That same leading man declared that he was seeking for some irrefragable arguments by which it may be proved that an eternal being, whether existing of itself or in every respect perfect, is only one [*i.e.* that there is only one being of the kind]. He found some things wanting in Hugo Grotius's arguments in the first book of his *De Veritate Religionis Christianae*.[1] He added that he had heard that your treatise concerning the Human Understanding is being translated into French;[2] that he values your judgement highly and exceedingly desires that translation. He asked me whether in that treatise you had also established the unity [*sc.* uniqueness or oneness] of a being existing of itself. I replied that I did not know, having never read that treatise, since it is written in a language that I do not know. He therefore wanted me seriously to recommend it to you that, if you have left this question untouched in your treatise, you will willingly enlarge your treatise by establishing it and will solidly establish the unity of an independent being. It seems clear that an independent being that embraces all perfection in itself is one only [*i.e.* unique]; he desired, however, that this should be proved in such a way that the argument should nowhere be laboured. Three days ago he ordered me to be reminded and to be asked whether I had yet written to you and had received any answer from you. I had not believed that he wanted it so earnestly, but since I see that he has this matter at

---

[1] No. *1823*, etc. [2] See p. 156.

tam enixe voluisse; sed quia video rem hanc ipsi cordi esse, scriptionem meam ulterius differendam minime statui. Rogo, si id negotia tua permittant, ut mihi responsum scribas, quod ipsi prælegere possim; ita tamen temperata tua scriptione, ut minime subolere ipsi possit, me tibi ipsum aliquatenus indicasse; quod ipsi minus gratum foret. Posses ita respondere, quasi ego tibi scripserim, viros quosdam eruditos de hac materia disserentes, ex ipsis aliquem qui te magni æstimat, de ea tuum voluisse audire judicium, et ut quæstionem hanc in tuo de Intellectu humano tractatu expenderes desiderasse. Vides quam aperte tecum agam, et quid ab amicitia tua exspectare ausim. Hagam Comitis nuper excurri; salutavi Illustrissimum Comitem Pembrokiensem, et per integram horam varios cum ipso, etiam de rebus Theologicis, sermones habui. Virum in tam excelsâ dignitate constitutum tantum in rebus sacris studium posuisse summopere miror. Ita sermonibus ejus afficiebar, ut vix per semihoram ipsi adfuisse mihi visus sim, cum tamen ab eo digressus integram horam esse elapsam deprehenderim. Ego Viro illi Excellentissimo longævam vitam precor, ut regni Anglicani negotia ipsius auspiciis fœliciter administrentur: Tibi vero valetudinem prosperam, ut cogitata tua orbi erudito communicare possis. Vale Amplissime Vir.

---

heart I have decided that I could not put off writing any longer. If your affairs permit please send me an answer that I can read to him; but let what you write be so managed that he cannot suspect that I have to some extent revealed his identity to you, because that would displease him. You could reply as if I had written to you that, when some scholarly men were discussing this matter, one of them, who esteems you highly, wanted to hear your opinion about it and desired that you would consider this question in your treatise concerning Human Understanding. You see how openly I deal with you and what I venture to expect from your friendship. I visited The Hague recently; I paid my respects to the most illustrious earl of Pembroke and talked with him for a whole hour about various subjects, even theological. I am exceedingly surprised that a man appointed to such high office has bestowed so much study on sacred matters. I was so affected by what he said that it seemed to me that I was with him for scarcely half an hour, whereas after leaving him I discovered that a whole hour had gone by. I pray that this most excellent man may have a long life so that the affairs of the English realm may be happily administered under his auspices; but for you that you may have good health, so that you may be able to impart

Salveat plurimum Domina Masham. Salutat te uxor mea et filia, nec non filius, qui summas tibi pro amicissimis literis gratias agit.

Tui Amantissimus
PHILIPPUS A LIMBORCH

Amstelodami 8 Octobris

20
16 X 97
5

Address: To John Locke Esqr. att the honorable office of trade and plantations att Whitehall London

Postmark: OC 2

Endorsed by Locke: P: Limborch 8 Oct. 97 Answered 29

---

your thoughts to the scholarly world. Good-bye, excellent Sir. My best regards to Lady Masham. My wife and daughter send you greetings, as does my son, who thanks you heartily for your most friendly letter.

Your most affectionate
PHILIPPUS VAN LIMBORCH

Amsterdam 8 October
1697

2319. LOCKE to DR. JOHN COVEL, 29 September 1697 (*676*, *2322*)

B.M., Add. MS. 22910, f. 463. Draft in B.L., MS. Locke c. 24, f. 32. The text of the letter sent agrees closely (apart from punctuation) with the final version of the draft; the only substantive passage cancelled in the draft is printed below. On the blank spaces of the letter Covel wrote drafts of nos. *2322* and *2481*. Printed in Fox Bourne, ii. 413. Answered by no. *2322*. The letter relates to Edwards's *Brief Vindication* (p. 149).

London 29 Sept 97

Reverend Sir

I am told the Booksellers in Cambridg have made bolder than they should with the booke you will herewith receive, by pasting a paper over the Authors Epistle to the Bookseller. Tis pitty soe excellent a treatise as this is should loose the authority and recommendation your name gives to it. I therefor send you one with all its ornaments displaid, as our shops here afford them: And you will doe well to Keep it safe, that posterity may know, as well as this present age, who lent his helping hand to usher into the world soe cleanly a peice of divinity, and such a just model of manageing of controversie in Religion, to be a pattern for the youth in his own Colledg, and in the rest of the Universitie to imitate. This is all at present, till I have a fitter oportunity to talke with you about what the dull stationer here made bold to strike out notwithstanding it had the warrant of your *Imprimatur*.[a] Tis not that I pretend to be interessed in the Controversie wherein Mr Edwards is a party: but hearing he had named me in the title of his booke I thought my self concerned to read it: And haveing perused it I think it will not misbecome our old acquaintance to doe you this right. I lay all those titles, you have thought me worthy of, at your feet, and am

Reverend Sir
your humble servant
J LOCKE

Address: For the reverend Dr John Covell Master of Christ Colledg in Cambridg

Endorsed by Covell: Mr Lock my Answer Mr Lock

2320. LOCKE to CARY MORDAUNT, countess of Peterborough, [September/October 1697?] (*1488*, 3475)

B.L., MS. Locke c. 24, ff. 196–7. Draft. Some passages printed in King, pp. 5–6; the whole in Locke, *Educational Writings*, ed. J. L. Axtell, 1968, pp. 393–6. The endorsement indicates a date after 19 June 1697, when Monmouth succeeded as third earl of Peterborough. The draft is closely related to F. Marx's letter of 4/14 November (no. *2344*). There was no need for Peterborough to wait until the treaty was signed before sending Lord Mordaunt to the Netherlands; Lord Bellomont obtained passes for his sons in August: p. 157 n. The draft is unlikely to have been written about the second half of August as Peterborough makes no reference to its subject in the letters which he wrote to Locke in that period (nos. *2297*, *2306*). The date of Lord Mordaunt's birth is unknown; it was probably in 1679 or 1680.

[a] *Originally, apart from current alterations, the draft continued:*
If you will doe the like honour to some thing I may chance to write relateing to some transactions at the Hague I will promise you that you shall not receive the like affront, nor shall a word of it be kept from the world.[1] I lay all those titles you have thought me worthy of the honour of at your feet and am

[1] Covel was appointed chaplain to Princess Mary in 1680. If he did not act as a spy on the Prince's household he joined in malicious gossip with some of Mary's English ladies. A letter written by him on 5/15 October 1685 to the English envoy Bevil Skelton (no. *745*) fell into William's hands and Covel was sent home immediately. How much Locke knew about the incident cannot be ascertained; he had perhaps

Madam

In obedience to your Ladyships commands I take the libertie to present you in writeing with some part of what you had the patience to hear me discourse in your presence the last time I had the honour to wait upon you. I have always thought that to direct a yonge gentlemans studys right it is absolutely necessary to know what course of life either by the distinction of his quality or fortune or by the choise and determination of his parents he is designed to.[1] The want of a due regard to this is often the cause that a great part of his time is painfully thrown away in studys and exercises wholy besides his purpose whilst others of absolute use and necessity are wholy overseen and neglected

My Lord Mordants[a] birth without any more adoe tells every one what he is to be in the world and directs us to consider what may conduce to make him an accomplished and great man in his[b] country.[b] But your Ladyships enquiry being now barely in reference to the choise and conduct of his studys twill be besides the present businesse to medle with anything but bookes and learning

My Lord is goeing now to a place where he may have masters and Tutors of all kindes and in all the arts and sciences.[2] The first thing therefor to be considerd when and how far a man should use a Tutor and to that I thinke the same answer should be given as to one that askes how long a child should be guided by leading strings and to that every one will readily say till he can goe alone. When a man knows the termes sees the method and has got an entrance into any of the sciences, twill be time then to depend upon himself relye upon his own understanding and exercise his own faculties which is the only way to improvement and mastery.[3] Only where the studys are in themselves knotty and hard there the Tutors help is longer usefull and to be left of by degrees reserveing that assistance only for difficult cases

[a] *Substituted for* your sons [b] *Substituted for* the world

heard that Covel and two of Mary's ladies had tried to alienate her from William with a view to her eventual marriage with a French prince: Droste, *Overblyfsels va Geheugchenis*, ll. 5314–29 and Fruin's note, pp. 460–6.

[1] Education for social rank is implied or stated in *Some Thoughts concerning Education*: e.g. A§§ 183, 202; C§§ 195, 217; and in 'Some Thoughts concerning Reading and Study for a Gentleman'.

[2] Utrecht: no. *2344*.

[3] There is a related passage in *Some Thoughts*, C § 94 (pp. 159–60).

History[1] is esteemd one of the most necessary studys for a gentleman and in it self one of the most entertaining and most easy, And soe it is and therefor should be begun with. But to profit by it a yonge gentleman will at first seting out have need of a guide. If not to explain some difficulties in the language, yet to make him remarke the particular Beautys and excellencys of the Author he reads and teach him to observe the most important things in it Relateing to a mans private conduct in common life, or to the turns of state in publick affairs

To this purpose I think it would be most advisable for my Lord M   to begin with Livys history which is the great repositary of the Roman Antiquities, as well as the best history of that state.[2] In the reading of this author I thinke it would be usefull to him that somebody should explain all the Roman Customs as any expressions in the course of the history give occasion to take notice of them. Other critical expositions where with men versed in that sort of learning use to abound I thinke my Lord   neither needs nor ought to be troubled with. Yonge persons of quality should have none of their time wasted in studys which will be of noe use to them when men. They must have time allowd them for diversion and recreation, these are as necessary as study,[3] and what can be spared from health and diversion should be all imploid only in necessary and to them usefull parts of knowledg. To the explication therefor of the customs and manners of the Romans as they occur in Livie it would be well to joyn the Turns of State and the causes upon which they depended. This is fit to Remarke to a yonge Nobleman and make him take notice of in his Reading

The great end of such[a] historys[a] as Livy is to give an account of the Actions of men as embodied in societie and soe is the true foundation of politicks.[4] But the flourishing or decays of commonwealths depending not barely on the present time, or what is don within themselves, but most commonly on remote and precedent

[a] *Altered from* well writ history

---

[1] Ibid., A §§ 172(i and ii), 173; C §§ 182–4.

[2] In *Some Thoughts* Locke recommends that boys should begin with 'easier' historians, 'such perhaps as *Justin*, *Eutropius*, *Quintus Curtius*, etc.'; he does not mention Livy in this connection: A § 173; C § 184.

[3] Ibid., A § 185; C §§ 108 (not in A), 197.

[4] 'The Art of Government . . . is best to be learn'd by Experience and History, especially that of a man's own country'; 'Some Thoughts concerning Reading', etc., in *A Collection of Several Pieces*, p. 237.

constitutions and events and a train of concurrent actions amongst their neighbours as well as themselves. The order of time is absolutely necessary to a due knowledg and improvement of history,[1] as the order of sentences in an author is necessary to be kept to, to make any sense out of what he says.

To Chronoligie Geographie too should be added for the right use and understanding of history. The scene of the action contributes always to the memory of it, and is very often soe necessary to a clear conception of the fact, that it cannot distinctly be comprehended without it

Though Chronologie and Geographie be both of them usefull[a] to History, yet a very nice and criticall knowledg of either of them is not at all necessary noe not soe much as convenient for a yonge Gentleman. The knowing the figure of the earth, The meridian, Æquator Tropicks Polar Circles and Poles and thereby longitude and latitude by the figures placed on the sides of particular maps is enough to begin with[2] and a little of this every day just before he begins to read Livy will quickly lead him to the knowledg and use of Maps and then he has as much Geographie as need be taught him. If he has aminde to be more exact in this knowledg being thus far enterd he will be able to goe on well enough of himself, and whether for thus much he will need any printed systeme or noe I know not but leave it to his Tutor

When he is perfect in the use of Maps which he should always have before him when he reads history it will be time enough to enter upon Chronologie and there without troubleing him with the several accounts of years and months that have been used in the world I thinke it is enough to make him conceive the Julian Period, and then setle in his minde[b] the several great Epochs that are most remarkeable in History. as Particularly the Creation of the world, The[c] Olympiads, The building of Rome, the birth of our Saviour, and the Hegira. and to make him remember in what year of the Julian period each of these Epochs began. For this the explication of some small part of Strauchii Breviarium Temporum and Helvicus's Chronologie will be enough.[3] and every time he

[a] *Substituted for* necessary [b] *Substituted for* memory [c] *Followed by* first *del.*

[1] *Some Thoughts*, A § 172(i); C § 182. [2] Ibid., A §§ 170–1; C §§ 180–1.
[3] Ibid., A § 172 (ii); C § 183. For Strauch see nos. *778*, *943*. Helvicus is C. Helwich. *Theatrum Historicum sive Chronologiæ systema novum*, 1609. It went through several

comes to a lecture in a Latin Historion to aske him in what year of the Julian Period Rome was built. in a Greeke historion, in what year of the Julian period the The first Olympiad was and soe of the rest. For the only way to setle the memory of any number in any ones head is often to repeat it.

With the reading of History I thinke the study of Morality should be joynd, I mean not the Ethicks of the Schools fitted to dispute,[1] but such as Tully in his Offices. Puffendorf De officio hominis et Civis et de Jure Naturali et Gentium[2] and Aristotle and above all the New Testament teaches, wherein a man may learne how to live. which is the businesse of Ethicks, and not how to difine distinguish and dispute about the names of virtues and vices.

True politicks I looke on as a Part of Moral Philosophie which is noething but the art of conducting men right in societie and supporting a communitie amongst its neighbours. Wherein Aristotle may be best to begin with, and then afterwards if he pleases he may discend to more moderne writers of Government either as to the foundations and forms of politick societies, or the art of ruleing them.

With these he may after some little time joyn a course of Natural philosophie Chymistry or which I should rather choose to begin with Anatomie because that consists only in seeing the figure texture and situation of the parts and some little matter about their use. For I thinke in all the sciences the easiest should always be began with, which are those that lye nearest the senses. and from thence by degrees to proceed to those that are more ⟨abstract⟩[a] and lie wholy in thought.

This Madam I thinke is enough to begin with. Farther directions I thinke may be best deferd till we see what my Lord best relishes in these, and how these rules happen to be followed or deviated from and with what successe that farther advice may be given as best suits the occasion. For possibly he may fall into hands where

[a] *MS.* abstact

editions, including two at Oxford, 1651 and 1662: Madan, nos. 2170, 2599. English translations 1677 (?), 1687. Locke owned copies of the Marburg 1629 and Oxford 1662 editions: L.L., nos. 1418–19.

[1] Locke expresses his disapproval of disputations in *Some Thoughts*, A§ 177, C§ 189.

[2] Ibid., A § 175; C § 186. For the *De Jure Naturæ et Gentium* see no. 844. The *De Officio* was published in 1673. L.L., no. 2403.

he is goeing which may put him into a better method than what is here proposed.

Endorsed by Locke: Education[a] 97 To the Countesse of Peterborow

2321. Locke to Mrs. Elizabeth Berkeley, later Burnet, [early October 1697] (*2315*, *2328*)

B.L., MS. Locke c. 24, ff. 24–5. Draft. Written by an amanuensis, with a correction by Locke. Answers no. *2315*; answered by no. *2328*.

Sir

I am extreamly sensible of the favour you have done me in peruseing my Book and makeing those observations you have done, and you have answered the expectations I had from the Friendship you honoured me with in being at the pains to remark to me, what you judge faulty in my management in this Controversie. I am soe much concerned for your good opinion that my first thoughts were to give you a perticular account of all those places you refer to. But considering how little time I have for soe long a Letter as that would be, and how much I should trespass upon your time in it, I thought it better to reserve it till I have the honour to wait upon you in Town. When I discourse with you on those points I shall see how far you allow of my reasons: And where I finde you continue to think me in an error I shall know what use to make of it another time. But it would be to presume too much on your leisure[b] to expect those answers from you in writeing, which I may hope from a personall conversation with you: And it would ill become me to put you to such a penance for my advantage. Onely one thing give me leave here to take notice of, the words I mean are these *Pray doe not think any would be willing to have you of the Hereticall side: It is thought noe small misfortune by a great many onely to have you suspected as a favourer of them.* That misfortune whatever it be I know noe body it is soe much owing too as my Lord. What share soever my private concern has in it in particular, I perhaps, who am very careless of what Gossiping or Ill will says of me, might have taken noe notice of what reflected personally on me, had not his Lordship in what he published endeavoured to have brought the way of Truth and knowledge

[a] *Beneath this are written* L.M. *deleted and* $\frac{97}{A}$; *the* A *possibly not by Locke.* [b] *Substituted by Locke for* goodness

(as it appears to me to be) in that suspition. But I shall not trouble you with any more on this or any other particular of your Letter at present. I shall with some impatience hope for an oppertunity to debate those matters an easier way to you in Town wherein I promise my self the advantage and satisfaction of justifying or mending my self

Endorsed in Locke's hand: J L to E B Oct. 97

2322. Dr. John Covel to Locke, 4 October 1697 (i) (2319, *2459*)

B.L., MS. Locke c. 7, ff. 161–2. Draft in B.M., Add. MS. 22910, f. 463, on blank space in Locke's letter, no. 2319. Extracts from the draft are printed in Fox Bourne, ii. 414. Enclosed in no. *2323* for forwarding. Answers no. 2319.

Christ College. Cambridge. Oct. 4. 1697.

Worthy Sir

I received your severe letter and your Present (as I suppose you intended them To an Old Acquaintance,) very kindly. For I must ever so interpret the meaning of my Freinds, when they are so free as to tell me of what they think in me to be a Fault, and thereby do give me an opportunity of removing Prejudices, if there happen to be any misrepresentations or Mistakes. But now I hope you will rather count this a meer Misfortune, when I tell you the plain truth of the matter. The Author was of my own Year, and I knew him formerly, better it seems than I know him now. He meeting me one day told me that he had a new Book for the Presse, which Mr Professor and the Vicechancellor had perused and they had given their *Imprimatur* to it; and he askt my leave to adde my Name also. I told him, if it was what They had read and approved of, I should not deny him that, (which indeed I then thought a) small favour. You tell me that you have read over the Book, which I solemnly protest is more then ever I yet did; and till it was printed I assure you I never so much as saw it or knew the least syllable of its Contents, much lesse of your Name; and the Author to the Bookseller in a manner ownes this to be the whole Truth. Now I do confesse my self indeed extreamly guilty of too much Credulity and Easinesse herein, but not in the least of any known or design'd disrespect to you, or any Party whatever. You have taught me hereafter not to be over apt too hastily either to

Believe the Reports, or to Trust the Judgements of other men. Mr Vicechancellor himself (after some high words, as I hear, with the Author,) commanded that Page to be covered; so that he seemes thereby to disown some part of your charge, as well as I must the whole.

Now my old Freind (for I will yet lay claim to your Freindship as well as your Acquaintance) if you dare trust my Narrative, let not this *cleanly* Brat or *Peice of Divinity* (as you Name it) ly at my door. I thought J.L. had known J.C. so well, as at least to have a little expostulated such a matter as this with him before he had charg'd him so warmly and so home. I hope this may something recover me in Your Good Opinion; if not, however till I see you, I shall own *no other Titles* then,

Worthy Sir,

Your Affectionate Freind and humble servant

JOH: COVEL.

Address: These For my worthy freind Mr John Lock

Endorsed by Locke: J. Covel 4 Oct 97

2323. DR. JOHN COVEL to LADY MASHAM, 4 Octobe 1697 (*2347*)

B.L., MS. Locke c. 7, f. 176. Copy written by Lady Masham.

Chr: Coll: Cambr. Oct. 4th 1697

We have now Deare Madam ended all our matters with M Whitehead and givn him our full discharge so that you may dispos of the Bond as your Ladyship shall think fiting.

I must beg the favour of transmiting this letter to Mr Lock I received one last post from him in Lond: but know not where t direct this. I percive he took it very heinously that my name is in pretended *Imprimatur* to a book of Mr Edwards, and truly till h shall understand the Truth of the story he might well count me Vain and Pittifull fellow instead of an Old Freind. Edwards b chance met with me and told me the Old Professor and Vic Chancellor had perus'd and Licens'd a book of his for the Pres and ask'd my leave to add my name also. He was of my Year an Old Acquaintance and I told him if they had read it and approv' of it I was content he should do it: I never then saw the book c knew one jot what or whom it concern'd; but it proves a Vile peice of railing and unmannerly treating of Mr Locke. The Vice-Chancellor hath call'd him to account for saying many things which it seemes he charg'd him to leave out, but for my self beleive me Madam I knew no more of the matter then you did. I confess I was to blame to give leave for my name to be put to what I knew nothing of, but a Wiser Man then I may be so traduc'd; and beleeve me it shall make me a greater Infidel in such matters for the future. should I see Mr Locke or your Ladyship to tell you every Circumstance he and you may really count me a Fool and a Coxcomb but not guiltie of any Wilfull disrespect to him whom I Honour and esteeme most sincerely. I should be glad to heare if he can harbour more kind and generous thoughts of me,

Madam

Your Most Obedient and Most Humble Servant.

Endorsed by Locke: J: Covel 4 Oct 97 to L: Masham

DR. JOHN COVEL to LOCKE, 4 October 1697 (ii)

B.L., MS. Locke c. 7, f. 163. This is an antedated letter, sent by Covel to Locke on 2 August 1698: pp. 457–9, where it is printed.

2324. WILLIAM MOLYNEUX to LOCKE, 4 October 1697 (*2311, 2331*)

The Carl H. Pforzheimer Library, New York. Transcribed from photostat. Printed in *Some Familiar Letters*, pp. 238–42. Answers no. 2310; answered by no. 2376.

Dublin. Oct. 4th. 1697.

Honourd Sir

I perceive we were each of us mindfull of t'other on the 11th of last Month; for off that date was your Last to me, as you will find mine likewise to you bore the same.

You have already Answerd some of my impertinent inquirys in that Letter. you tell me therein, who J.S. is that writes against You. I do not now wonder at the Confusednes of his Notions, or that they should be unintelligible to me. I should have much more admired had they been otherwise. I expect nothing from Mr Serjeant but what is abstruse in the highest degree.

I look for nothing else from Mr Norris; I thought that Gentleman had enough ont, in his first Attempt on your Essay. but he's so overun with Father Malbranch and Plato, that tis in vain to indeavour to sett him right. and I give him up as an inconvincible Enemy.

But above all these I should wonder at the Bishop of Worcesters Obstinacy, did I not think that I partly know the Reason thereof. He has been an Old Souldier in Controversys and has hitherto had the Good Luck of Victory. But now in the Latter end of his Wars to be laid on his Back (as he thinks the World would certainly say, unles he has the last Word) would wither all his former Laurels, and Loose his Glory. Your Reply to him is not yet come to hand; but I can wait with the More Patience, because I am pretty wel satisfyd in the Matter already.

I am very glad to understand that we are to expect an other Edition of your Education with Additions. I never thought you writ too Much on any subject whatever.

I have formerly written to you to know farther concerning Monsieur Coste, who translated some of your Books into French. I fancy by that Gentlemans Inclinations to your Works, He and I should agree very well. Pray let me know, whether to his Belles Lettres he has any skill in Mathematicks, Natural History, etc. as also what his Circumstances are as to his Education, Parentage. etc. for According to these I may judge whether I can give him any incouragement to come hither.

You had been troubled with this Letter sooner, but that I waited for the Inclosed to satisfy your Enquiry concerning our Linin Manufacture.[1] You will find thereby that we have framed a Bill to be Enacted for the Incouragement thereof. This Bill is now before the Council of England pursuant to our Constitution of Parliament. What Alterations, Additions, and Amendments it may receive there we know not, but I am apt to think you will have the Consideration and Modelling thereof at your Committee of Trade.[2] We are very sensible, that the Act we have drawn up (whereof the Inclosed are the Heads) is not so perfect and Compleat as it may be. but this we thought a fair beginning to so great an Attempt, and that time must be given for a farther Progres

[1] B.L., MS. Locke c. 30, ff. 67–8, and perhaps f. 69.

[2] On 28 October the English Privy Council referred the bill to the Board of Trade: Journal, 29 October (p. 329).

and carrying it higher by Additional Laws as Occasion may require. The Wollen Manufacture of England was not establishd at that high Pitch (to which now tis raisd) by any One Law, or any one Generation. it must be so with us in relation to our Linen; but this we hope may be a fair step towards it; est aliquid prodire tenus. etc.[1]

James Hamilton of Tullymore Esquire[2] is an[a–] Indefatigable Promotor[–a] of this Designe, and I may say indeed the whole Scheme is owing to his Contrivance. He is an harty admirer of Yours, and communicated to me the Inclosed Abstract purposely for your satisfaction; desiring me, with it to give you his Most Humble Service, and to request of you your thoughts concerning this Matter by the first Leasure you can spare.

Whilst Our House of Commons were framing this Bill; Our Lords Justices communicated to us some papers which they had Received from the Lords Justices of England laid before them by your Board. But these Papers coming in a little too late, when we had just closed the Bill, and a very little time before our last Adjournment for three weeks; All we did with them was to remitt them again to our Lords Justices and Council, with the Houses desire, that if their Lordships should think fitt to excerp any thing out of those Papers and add it to our Act, whilst they had it before them in order to be transmitted into England, their Lordships might do therein as they pleased, and the House would agree to any such additions, when the Act came before us transmitted in due form under the Seal of England. Whether the Lords Justices wil make any such additions out of those papers I cannot yet tell; but I am sure there were many things in those papers that highly deserved to be put in Execution.[3]

My Brother gives you his most Humble service, and should be very Proud of the Present of your Education. for tho he has yet only two Daughters,[4] yet he is in Hopes of Many Sons; and the

[a–a] *MS.* an indefatigable / Indefatigable Promotor

[1] 'One can get to a certain point (if no further).' An ungrammatical variation of Horace, *Epistles* I. i. 32: 'est quadam prodire tenus, si non datur ultra'.

[2] He is called Col. Hamilton. Member of the Irish Parliament in 1692–3, 1695–9, and 1703–5. He presented a linen bill to the Irish house of commons on 26 August: *C.J., Ireland*.

[3] For the papers see *Cal. S.P., Dom.*, 1697, pp. 345, 364. The Irish parliament was adjourned on 25 September.

[4] Catherine and Margaret, born in 1695 and 1696: Sir C. Molyneux, *Account of the Family* of Molyneux, p. 42.

Girls Minds require as much Framing, as the Boys, and by the same Rules. And that I take to be the Cheif Part of Education. I am

Yours most sincerely
W: MOLYNEUX

Address: To John Locke Esquire at Mr Robert Pawlings overagainst the Plow-Inn in Little-Lincolns Inn-Fields London
Postmark: OC 11
Endorsed by Locke: W: Molyneux 4 Oct. 97 Answered 10 Jan

2325. CHRISTOPHER TILSON to LOCKE, 9 October 1697 (*2272, 2333*)

B.L., MS. Locke c. 20, ff. 192–3.

Sir

None of the Commissioners besides Your self and Mr Dodington being at present in Town, The meeting which was to have been on Monday next is put of till a further opportunity, Which is signifyed to You by

Sir
Your most faithfull humble Servant
CHRIS TILSON

9th October 1697
Address: To John Locke Esqr.
Endorsed by Locke: C: Tilson 9 Oct. 97

2326. DR. PIETER GUENELLON to LOCKE, 9/19 October 1697 (*2292, 2345*)

B.L., MS. Locke c. 11, ff. 80–1.

Monsieur,

Je ne scaurois vous assez marquer combien je suis sensible de la part que vous prenez a l'Education de mon fils. je profiteray de vos bons conseils, et sur cela jay fait reduire ses exercices mathematique a deux lecons la sepmaine. Monsieur le Clerq a la bonté de passe ses estudes en reveüe une fois la sepmaine. et je puis vous dire san exageration quil suffit de luy dire vostre sentiment sur la conduitte quil doibt tenir, pour ly faire acquiescer. Monsieur Daranda qui s charge de cette lettre a passé icy comme un esclair,[1] on n'a presque pu le voir, n'arrestoit presque jamais chez luy, et nous aurions extremement souhaitté de lavoir a quelque respas chez nous, pour nous entretenir de vous plus a loisir. a l'occasion que tout nouvellement la carte de Monsieur Witsen est reimprimée avec des additions et des corrections notables, et qu'une petite carte nouvelle d'Asie est enrichie de ces decouvertes, jay cru de mon devoir de vous les envoyer[2] et je me serviray de l'occasion des livres que Monsieur la Motte[3] envoye a Monsieur Coste. cett aimable Monsieur Coste, comment se porte t'il. j'espere que sa santé est plus affermie qu'a son despart d'icy. et je crois que le bonheur d'estre aupres de vous l'anime comme d'une vie nouvelle, sachant combien il vous estime et revere, on ne scauroit comprendre combien peu les gens se remuent et se rejouissent icy de la paix tant la deffiance pour la france est grande. j'espere pourtant quelle sera heureuse et solide, et que Dieu conservera longtemps vostre bon roy, qui est comme le premier Mobile de touts les confederés.

jay fait vos Compliments a Monsieur Limborgh. Mon beau pere et toute la famille vous ⟨p⟩resente[a] ses respects. et bien particulierement ma femme et mes enfans. et je suis avec toute la soumission que je vous doibts,

Monsieur

Vostre tres humble et tres obeissant serviteur

P. GUENELLON.

d'Amsterd. ce 19 Oct. 1697.

Address: For Sir John Locke. London.

Endorsed by Locke: Dr. Guenellon 19 Oct: 97 Answered Feb. 5

[a] *Covered by seal.*

---

[1] The journey is mentioned on p. 247.

[2] For Witsen's large map of Siberia (1687) see no. *2028*; Cahen, as cited there, notes a copy with a manuscript date 1698: p. 57. Witsen published also 'Carte nouvelle de la Grande Tartarie', no date, 0·95 × 0·52 m, a reduction of his large map: Cahen, pp. 87–9. Either it or C. Allard, 'Exactissima Asiæ delineatio . . . extracta ex authenticis tabulis D. N. Witsen', etc., 0·58 × 0·50 m, no date (1696?; ibid., pp. 86–7) is likely to be the present small map.

[3] Lagier de la Motte, apparently a journalist and bookseller's hack, who is known mainly by his unpublished correspondence with Desmaizeaux: Labrousse, *Bayle*, 2 n., etc.; *Inventaire critique*, pp. 13–15, etc.; Haase, *Einführung*, p. 410, etc. He was a friend of Coste, who dedicated to him the third edition (1721) of his translation of *Some Thoughts concerning Education.*

2327. LOCKE to ESTHER MASHAM, 13 October 1697 (2301, 2426)

Newberry Library, Chicago: copy of the original letter by Esther Masham in her letter-book, pp. 26–7. Transcribed from microfilm. Printed in Fox Bourne, ii. 457; by Professor Maurice Cranston in *Newberry Library Bulletin* 2nd ser., no. 4, July 1950, pp. 131–2. The explanatory note was written by Esther.

London 13 October 1697

Beauty and Honour are two tempting things, but a heart Deare Dab that you are possess'd of is proof against all of that kind. If therefore you have any more Jealousie, but just so much as shows your concern for me, you are unjust to your self and your Joannes too. The wishes I made to be with you remain the same I brought to Town with me: and if you can but defend me against your own fears I promise you to defend you against all the [a]Dutchesses and Beautys in Christendom. I beleeve you as innocent and sincere as the Country can produce and I think I may presume I shall hold out longer against the false fashons, than the ill air of the Town for my heart I am sure is better than my Lungs so that your part is safe. I do not much rejoyce in the *Plump* you make such show of in your Letter. If you were so much concernd as you talk of you would pine away a little in my absence. But with all the Love you brag of there is not that Sympathie should be. If there were Separation would always abate something of your good mean, as it always you know, does of mine, and as thin as I am when I part from you I always return thinner. But what I am abated in bulk I always return increas'd in affection. If this does not satisfie you I will make up the rest of the account when I see you at Oates where I long to tell you how much and how sincerely I am

Deare Dab

Your most humble and most affectionate servant

JOANNES.

[a] I pretended to be Jealous upon his visiting the Dutchess of Grafton.[1]

---

[1] Isabella, daughter of Henry Bennet, earl of Arlington; widow of Henry Fitz-Roy, first duke of Grafton; married secondly, 1698, Sir Thomas Hanmer: G.E.C.

2328. Mrs. Elizabeth Berkeley, later Burnet, to Locke, 13 October 1697 (2321, *2491*)

B.L., MS. Locke c. 3, ff. 212–13. Answers no. 2321.

Sir

Tho the excellent use you put your time to, and the benefet so many receive by your studys makes me allmost as unwilling to rob you of any of your retired moments as you can be, to be so injured; yet I hope so short a viset as to pay my thanks for your excuseing as well ment my last too long interuption, will be forgiven. I am since senseble by talking with my L— that I mistooke his sense in severall places, about Nature and persone, but 'tis not strang I should do it, who am alltogether unaquainted with scolastick terms, and his L— not designing his book for such readers, twas the less necesary his explaining of them, aprehending they were more universally understood and agreed in then it seems they are; when I reflect I am ashamed of what I ventur'd to your perusall, and at my first reading your answer I had some pain, by your supposing I *Judged* as *faulty* what I *remarked*: indid I did not but sent my first thoughts, for you to determine, if they were right or not; and for my own part I am so fully perswaded of the integrety of your intentions (and shall not easyly chang my mind) that there needs no care or thought to Justify your self to me, or if there did was it worth your time; therefore am glad you answerd not more largly my last; a trouble I neither intended you, or expected you should give your self, when I writt; it was more then enough to read it; my consarn for your being not misunderstood is for others not my self; I conclude your aim is to make people better and wiser, and hope you will remember the world is mostly made up of Childeren in the worst sense, who must be flatered to their duty by seeming to beleeve they do it, who are froward, and fond of present goods, and must be humer'd and condesended to, to perswade them to their reall tho absent intrest. Another part of your letter that made me condemn my self was, *that when I sayed it was a misfortuen to have you only suspected to favour eror*, I feared I had so exprest it as if my L— had so insenewated; but truely I had no such design, for in conversation I have oft heard him declar the contrary; nor did I mean more then that many deprived them selves of the benefet they might reap by your books by carelessly taking in prejudices and caractures without examination; and if you will permit me to give my opinion, I beleeve mistakes of this kind are chefly owing, and propegated, by such who endevour to support their erors by giving out there being aproved and allowed of by persons of known vertue and good sense; nor can I gett it out of my mind that my too inconsiderat and I fear unfortunate, mentioning a passage of a letter from this place,[1] increast your consarn in vindicating your self; tho except I misrepresented that passage, or allterd its sense by my maner of reading it, their was no cause for it; you will I hope excuse this so farr looking back, but every fresh occation of regreet, makes me angre with my self, since 'tis a great agrevation to what is of it self matter of grife, to aprehend it was in some measure of our own procureing; I am with great respect

Sir

Your Obliged Humble servent

E BERKELEY

13: Oct: 97:
at Mr Wylds in Worcester;

I send not this direction to ingage you in a useless corespondance but that if you think it at any time necesary you may be at no trouble in knowing where to direct to me, for I doubt I shall hardly be in Town before you leve it, so must defer my hopes of seeing you to next spring, if it please God I live so long.

Endorsed by Locke: E: Berkeley 13 Oct 97

2329. THOMAS FIRMIN to LOCKE, 15 October 1697 (*2241*)

B.L., MS. Locke c. 8, ff. 112–13.

Deare Sir

I should be glad to see you if you came this way if you doe not I will weight upon you, I have met with a yorksheire man that is willinge to take of my poor peopls yarne[2] and to give me Huckerbucks for it such as I have sent you a pece of to look upon, I am necessitated to turne of a great number of my poor people because I cannot sell there commodity being a little dearer then other lyning tho much better.

[1] See no. *2198*. [2] See p. 84 and *D.N.B.*

I intend for to viset Mrs Tillotson[1] next Tuesday it being her birth day if you will goe with me I will either borow or hier a coach to weight upon you. this is all at present from

dear sir your humble servant
THO FIRMIN

October 15th, 1697

26 yards huckerback being for }
2 doss of Napkins at 18d a yard } 1 - 19 -

I have broad for table linen.

Address: For John Lock Esquire at Mr Pawlins in little Lyncolns Infeilds over against the plow.

Endorsed by Locke: T: Firmin 15 Oct 97

2330. JOHN WYNNE, later bishop of Bath and Wells, to LOCKE, 15/25 October 1697 (*2303*, *2366*), enclosing HENDRIK WETSTEIN to WYNNE, 14/24 October 1697

B.L., MS. Locke c. 23, ff. 83, 129–30. Wetstein's letter is in the hand of the writer who wrote no. *917*, etc., apart from the note of books at the end, which is in another hand.

Honoured Sir

I should have sent you an account sooner of the discharge of my commissions att Leyden, If the greatest part of my time since had not been taken up in Visits and journeys of Curiosity, which came the most thick upon me, because I then apprehended that our stay here would not be so long, as it has since prov'd to be. The Books that you had given Commission for were generally very fair and well condition'd: but in my judgment there were but few good pennyworths. Many of them went to the shop price, and very few much under: so that of all I bid for, I carried but two, and they are Plutarch[2] and Tacitus,[3] the former for 30 g., the latter for 22 g. When I was at Amsterdam Mr Wetstein's Brother[4] (for he himself was not att home) told me that the Acta Eruditorum etc had been sent two moneths before to England: so that I did not doubt but you had received them. soon after I receiv'd your last,

[1] Elizabeth French, a niece of Cromwell; married Tillotson 1664; died in 1702: *D.N.B.*, art. Tillotson.
[2] Perhaps for Lord Ashley: p. 369.
[3] Identifiable from p. 280 and Locke's Journal, 22 January 1698, as the edition 'in usum Delphini', Paris, 1682–7. L.L., no. 2827.
[4] (Johan) Lucas Wetstein: no. *1178*.

I writt to Mr Wetstein for them, and he sent me the enclos'd answer. If the books are not to be had at Mr Mortier's,[1] be pleas'd to let me know, and I'le send to Mr Wetstein again. I shall take care to bring Mr Bayle's Dictionary[2] and the rest of your Books along with me. We expect to come for England in a little time after the Germans have brought their matters to an End, which they are like to do some time next week.[3] The King is expected here in a little time, and we suppose we shall come along with him. The French Ambassadors made some exceptions to the Great Seal of England, because the King is there stil'd King of France, and it was some daies after the arriveal of it here, before they could be perswaded to admitt of it.[4] My Lord[5] accepted of your service and respects very kindly, and order'd me to return you his. My Lord is pleas'd to allow me the honour and happines of his conversation very frequently; And there is none he mentions with more distinguishing marks of respect than your self. His Lordship's respect and esteem for you is of infinitely more weight and consideration: but I take the liberty to assure you that none can be more real and sincere than what I profess for you, who am

Honoured Sir

your most humble and oblig'd servant

JOHN WYNNE

Hague oct. 25 N.S. 97.

Address: To The Honoured John Locke Esquire att the Council of Trade office in White-Hall.

Endorsed by Locke: J Wynne 25 Oct. 97

[Enclosure:]

Monsieur

J'ai bien reçû votre agréable[a] par laquelle me dites, que Mr. Loke Vous avoit mandé qu'il avoit demandé à Mon Correspondant à Londres les Acta Lips: de Anno 94. etc. que je Lui avois envoye il y a quatre mois: et que mon correspondent avoit dit n'avoi

[a] *Doubtful reading; abbreviated in MS.*

[1] David Mortier, 1673–*c.* 1722, a member of the Amsterdam bookselling family operating in London from *c.* 1696 to *c.* 1711: van Eeghen, i. 107; iii. 253–6.

[2] The *Dictionaire historique et critique*, the first edition, 1697. L.L., no. 237.

[3] The treaty between Louis XIV and the Emperor, the Catholic, and some Protestant princes of the Empire, was signed on 30 October, N.S.

[4] The Great Seal was affixed to the ratification of the treaty, which was complete on 12 October, N.S.; for it and the French objection to it see H.M.C., *Bath MS.* iii. 167–80.

[5] Pembrok

rien reçû. Surquoi je dois Vous dire Monsieur, que je n'ai pas envoyé lesdits Acta à mon Correspondant ordinaire. Mais que je les ai rendu ici à Mr. Mortier, Libraire françois à Londres dans un pacquet avec l'adresse à Messieurs Churchil Libraires à Londres pour le rendre à Mr Loke. Je Vous prie de mander distinctement cela audit Mr. Loke, avec qu'il fasse que Messieurs Churchill s'informent dudit Mortier pour avoir le pacquet. Je Vous ai envoyé aujourdhui par la barque ordinaire les livres que me demandez; et le reste des Acta pour Mr. Loke.[1] Je n'ai pas pris de payement pour le pacquet que j'ai envoyé par Mr Mortier, puis que je veux auparavant savoir si Mr Loke l'a reçu. Je suis,

Monsieur,

Votre très humble Serviteur

H. WETSTEIN

Amsterdam 24 octobre 1697

ci-joint

1[a] Acta maij. Junij et supl: II tomes: 3vs[2]	—: 15–
1 œuvres posthumes de Moliere ce[b3]	—: 15–
	f. 11: 10:–

Endorsed by Locke: H Wetstein 24 Oct. 97

2331. WILLIAM MOLYNEUX to LOCKE, 16 October 1697 (*2324*, *2339*) with JAMES HAMILTON to MOLYNEUX, 13 October 1697

The Carl H. Pforzheimer Library, New York. Transcribed from photostat. Hamilton's letter is a copy made by an amanuensis; it is written on the same sheet as Molyneux's letter; the explanatory notes to it are written by Molyneux. For Hamilton see p. 221. Answered by no. 2376.

[Hamilton:]

Tollymore October the 13°. 1697

Dear Sir

I finde by a Letter from Dublin that Sir Francis Brewster[4]

[a] *Preceded by* 1 Hornij Geographia fol— f 10:– *deleted.* [b] *Doubtful reading.*

[1] On 26 November Locke received the issues of the *Acta* from January 1696 to April 1697, with parts 11 and 12 of the second supplement and part 1 of the third: Journal.

[2] Locke received these on 22 January 1698 with the Plutarch, the Tacitus, and the Molière: Journal. [3] Amsterdam, 1689. L.L., no. 2008.

[4] He was a Dublin alderman, a member of the Irish parliament, and a writer on

Continues to Object against the Linnen Bill, he was not in Town when I came thence, but I hear he is either gon or going for England, and I suppose will carry his Objections with him, I Desired him, when wee first attended the Committee of the Councill to Putt what Objections he had in Writing which he has not, that I know off, don, and in that Case I had Offered my Answers to them as I did to Mr. Knox's[1] (which were in Writing) to the Committee; the Committee seem'd Satisfyd with what I Answered. I intreat you to give Mr. Lock some hint of this Matter, and in Case Sir Francis Object against the incorporating part of the Bill, that he[a] may be put in minde that the first thing in the Shcheme Offered[b] to my Lord Capell in 1695 and Layd before the House of Commons,[2] is, that the Undertakers may be incorporated in which Case there is to be but one Corporation in the whole Kingdome, to Consist of Persons that Shou'd Advance the Stock for Carrying on of the Manufacture, and wholy framed for manageing the Trade of the Linnen and Hempen Manufactures through the whole Kingdome, Now if the Corporations to be Errected by the present Bill are Capable of ingroseing or Cramping thereof (as Sir Francis and Mr. Knox pretend) sure the Scheme they two as well as my selfe proposed,[c] and which they still Praise and commend as the most Effectual Means for making the Manufactures Nationall, is in three Main particulars much more Subject to Objections.[d] for supposing there were in England Thirty two East-India Companys with the like Priviledges (excepting that of Confirming the sole Trade to one of the Companys) that the present Company Enjoys, I suppose there wou'd be noe Complaint of Monopolizing the Trade. next the Persons incorporated by the Bill are the Gentry of the Country, whose Interest it is that there be no ingrosing of the Trade to the prejudice of the Inhabitants of the Kingdome, and in the third place the Corporations of the several Countys are chiefly Errected to put the Laws concerning the Manufactures in Execution, and need not deale in the Merchandize part thereof unless

[a] Mr Locke [b] by Sir Fr. Brewster [c] in Lord Capels Time [d] than what Mr Hamilton now proposes

economic questions: *D.N.B.*; Horsefield. For his present journey to England see H.M.C., *Buccleuch MSS. at Montagu House*, ii. 561–70.

[1] See Molyneux's letter below.

[2] On 22 November: *C.J., Ireland*; the committee for the improvement of trade, including the linen manufacture, was appointed on 4 October. The bill was dropped when the parliament was adjourned on 14 December.

they Please, Whereas by the Scheme in 1695[a] the Corporation was chiefly Employd in the Merchandizing part, and I suppose wou'd only concern themselves in the other part as Subservient to theire own Interest in Carrying on theire Trade and making thereof Proffitable to themselves. I begg your Pardon for this long Letter, which (could[b] I have Expressd my selfe in Fewer Words) Should have been Shorter.

I am your most Humble Servant
JAMES HAMILTON

[Molyneux:]

Dubl: Oct. 16. 1697.

My ever honourd Friend.

The foregoing is a Letter which I lately received from Mr Hamilton whom I mentiond to you at large in my last of the 4th Inst. The Letter it self will expres the Reason of My sending it to you, and the few Notes in the Margin will make it yet Plainer, than to need any further explication. In my last I sent you a full Account of what Our Parliament had done about the Linen-Manufacture. This is still in Relation to the same subject; and therefore you will not count me impertinent in sending it so hastily on the Heels of tother. After our Parliament had drawn up the Heads (as we call them) of the Linen Manufacture Bill, and sent it to our Privy Councill to be transmitted in form into England, it seems Sir Fr. Brewster and Mr Knox (a Merchant of Belfast) objected violently against it at the Council Board: and Mr Hamilton was heard to what[c] they Objected, and he satisfyd the Board. But now Mr Hamilton is apprehensive that Sir Francis may make a stir in England about the same thing; and ⟨ther⟩efore[d] he Desires me to write to you about it; for we judge, this whole matter will come under the Consideration of your Council of trade.

I have a thought in my Mind to propose to you as one of that Council, which is indeed of a Mixt Nature, both Mathematick and Mercantile. and as it respects the Latter it may lye in your Way to promote it by your Authority. Tis, that All our Companys and Factorys abroad, in the East and West Indies, Northern or Southern parts of the World should be obleidged to keep an Astronomer in their Respective Places accurately to take the Longitudes and

[a] Lord Capels time [b] *Substituted by Molyneux for the amanuensis's* woud?
[c] *MS.* wt. [d] *Page torn.*

Latitudes thereof. this in various and Distant parts of the World would soon rectify our Geography; and tend much to advance Navigation and consequently Trade. I am

Your Most Affectionate Humble servant

W: MOLYNEUX

Address: To John Locke Esquire at Mr Pawlings overagainst the Plow-Inn in Little Lincolns Inn Feilds London

Postmark: OC 25

Endorsed by Locke: W Molyneux 13 Oct 97 Answered 10 Jan

2332. LOCKE to CORNELIUS LYDE, 19 October 1697 (*2313*, 2372)

The Pierpont Morgan Library, New York. Transcribed from Xerox print. Answers no. *2313*.

London 19 Oct 97

Sir

I received by mr Clarke the money you paid him for me and the copy of the accounts you sent me by him. I have cast my eye upon the account and presume I shall finde it very right when I have time to looke into it. But that will not be whilst I am in town. both because of the business I have here, and because of my other papers relateing to such matters, which are all in the country. But as soon as I get thither I shall write more particularly to you about them.

I thinke you have done well to take a bond from Hanny but as soon as it is due upon the bond it must be looked after or else I feare it will be hard to be gott. Therefor pray presse him for it, that it may if possible be got in without a suit, but if he will not pay it otherwise he must be sued.

I have by my Cosin Peter Stratton sent you Fr: Carpenters lease to which as you desired Mr Clarke is witnesse. My Cosin intends to come to Sutton himself and has promised me to deliver it to your own hands. and I desire you would deliver to him Fr: Carpenters counterpart and his bond for performing of conditions, with whom I shall take order to have them conveyd to me by some safe hand

You say you will meet your son in town at his comeing over if it may be for his advantage. I take[a] a father advice and assistance to be always of advantage to his son espetialy at his first seting out into the world what service I can doe your son you need not doubt of. I shall be glad to see you in town and wish I may be here when you come. I am

Sir

Your very humble servant

JOHN LOCKE

The peace was proclaimed here to day

Address: For Cornelius Lyde Esquire at his house at Stanton weeke

2333. CHRISTOPHER TILSON to LOCKE, 19 October 1697 (*2325, 2334*)

B.L., MS. Locke c. 20, ff. 194–5.

Sir

The Commissioners for Appeals have appointed to meet in order to proceed in the business of Appeals on Wednesday being the 20th instant at four of the Clock in the Afternoon in the Dutchy Court, and desire You will please to be there at that time

I am

Sir

Your most faithfull humble Servant

CHRIS TILSON

19 October 1697

Address: To John Locke Esqr These

Endorsed by Locke: C: Tilson 19 Oct 97

2334. CHRISTOPHER TILSON to LOCKE, 22 October 1697 (*2333, 2357*)

B.L., MS. Locke c. 20, ff. 196–7.

Sir

Mr Dodington and Mr Chaloner will meet You at the Treasury Chambers on Monday next at 4 of the Clock in the Afternoon

[a] *Followed by* his *deleted.*

according to your desire Which is signifyed to You by their command from

Sir

Your most faithfull humble Servant

CHRIS. TILSON

22d. October 1697

Address: To John Locke Esqr These

Endorsed by Locke: C: Tilson 22 Oct. 97

2335. SIR STEPHEN EVANCE to LOCKE, 22 October 1697 (*1189*, *2341*)

B.L., MS. Locke c. 8, ff. 75–6.

October the 22 97

Sir

This day mr Clarke showes mee, a bill of 50l of mine that is payable to you, itt spesefeyes interst, but hope you will nott take interst considering itt was in such money that i have bine a grate loser, the 50l is redey For you, i am

Sir your most Humble servant

STE: EVANCE

Address: For Doctor Lock These

Endorsed by Locke: Sir St: Evance 22 Oct 97

2336. DR. (later Sir) THOMAS MOLYNEUX to LOCKE, 25 October 1697 (*1670*, 2500)

The Carl H. Pforzheimer Library, New York. Transcribed from photostat Printed in *Some Familiar Letters*, p. 289.

Sir

I should oftner make acknowledgments to You for Your Favors, and express the great esteem I bear You, but that this Barren Place affords little else to say, and this I cant think reason enough to trouble One so busy and usefully engaged as You allways are. yet I would not omitt thanking You by this worthy Gentle Man Mr Berrisford[1] Your Acquaintance, for a Present of a Book I understand by my brother You designed for me,[2] tho I was so unlucky as to miss of it; and allso communicate to You the inclosed Letter

[1] Probably Alexander Beresford, who desired employment in Ireland: pp. 32–3.

[2] Boulton's *Treatise of Muscular Motion*: pp. 164, 190.

which the Bishop of Clogher[1] was pleased, (perhaps out of his to partial Friendship) to tell me deserved to be made publick, and desired me accordingly to transmitt it to Dr. Slone:[2] but this I would not do, unless it have Your Approbation allso, so that tis wholy at Your Disposal to do with it as You please as is likewise

Sir

Your very Affectionate Friend and humble servant

THO: MOLYNEUX

Dublin. Oct: 25th 1697.

Address: To John Lock Esquire These

Endorsed by Locke: T: Molyneux 25 Oct 97

2337. LOCKE to NICOLAS TOINARD, 26 October 1697 (*1828*, *2355*)

The Historical Society of Pennsylvania, Philadelphia. Transcribed from photostat. Answered by no. *2355*.

London. 26 Oct 97.

Si J'ai oubliè d ecrir en Francois faut d'exercise Je n'ai pas pourtant oubliè de vous aimer. La paix est sans doubte agreable a tout le monde, et un chaque un espere y trouver son compte. Pour moy J'y trouverai tout ce que me manque pour me rendre heureux si cette lettre vous trouve en bonne santè et me fait apporter de vos nouvelles. Je l'envoy expres.

Si vales, et omnia commodè tecum, (scio enim te nostri esse memorem) rescribas ocyus et grandi epistolâ. Post tam diuturnum silentium nihil mihi acceptius, nihil jucundius esse potest, quam legere et quæ tu scripseris, et de te.[3]

J'envoy ceci a tout hazard par la premiere occasion, quand je scaurois votre addresse Je ecriray plus au longe J'ay plusieurs chose à vous dire et à vous demander en attendant Je suis de tout mon cœur

Monsieur

Votre tres humble tres fidele et tres oblige serviteur

JOHN LOCKE

[1] St. George Ashe.

[2] The paper, on swarms of insects in Ireland, was published in *Philosophical Transactions*, xix (1697), 741–56.

[3] 'If you are well and if all goes well with you (for I know you remember me) please reply quickly and in a big letter. After so lengthy a silence nothing can be more welcome and pleasing to me than to read both what you have written and about yourself.'

Comme il n'y a point de post encore etabli J'ai envoyè cellecy par un Gentilhomme de ma connoissance qui m'a promis de vous trouver.[1] Quand vous me faits l'honeur de m'ecrire servi vous s'il vous plait de cette addresse

For mr John Locke
at mr Pawlings overagainst
the plough in Little Lincolns Inne feilds
London

Address: A Monsieur Monsieur Toinard chez Monsieur des Noyers devant l'Espée royale dans la rüe Mazarin á Paris

Endorsed by Toinard: 20. Octre 97. m. Nelson.

2338. SIR JOHN SOMERS, later Baron Somers, to LOCKE, [26? October 1697] (2186, 2384)

B.L., MS. Locke c. 18, ff. 165–6. Date: Brewster left Dublin on or shortly after 8 October; he was at Eyford in Gloucestershire on or shortly before 20 October, on his way to London: H.M.C., *Buccleugh MSS. at Montagu House*, ii. 561–72 *passim*; no. *2331*. The possible Tuesdays are 19 and 26 October; the latter seems preferable.

Tuesd.

Sir

I desire you would please to deliver Sir Francis Brewsters Paper[2] to the Bearer, because he will deferr no longer his speaking to mee upon it. He has said so often that the proposal sent from England about the linnen manufacture was impracticable in some parts of it that I wish you thought it fit to speak with him upon that subject. You will laugh at mee for suggesting to you that it would please better if the double Wheel had another name then Mr Firmins.[3] I am

Your most humble servant
J. SOMMERS.

Address: To Mr Locke

Endorsed by Locke: Sir[a] J: Sommers Octob.[b] 97

[a] *Altered from* L. [b] *Substituted for* Nov *or* Nov 1

[1] John Nelson: p. 263. [2] Perhaps a copy of MS. Locke c. 30, ff. 65–6
[4] p. 84.

2339. WILLIAM MOLYNEUX to LOCKE, 28 October 1697 (*2331, 2360*) enclosing copies of WILLIAM KING, bishop of Londonderry (later archbishop of Dublin) to MOLYNEUX, 26 October 1697, and MOLYNEUX's reply, 27 October

The Carl H. Pforzheimer Library, New York. Transcribed from photostat. The bishop's letter and Molyneux's reply are copies made by an amanuensis. Printed in *Some Familiar Letters*, pp. 242–52. Answered by no. 2376. For King see nos. *1530, 1544,* 1583.

Dublin. Oct. 28th. 1697.

My most Honourd Friend

If Men could destroy by a Quil, as they say Porcupines Do,[1] I should think your Death not very far off. But whatever Venom they Mixt with their Ink against you, I hope it is not Mortal; I am sure in my Opinion tis not the least Harmfull or Dangerous. Your Reply to the Bishop of Worcester shews how vainly the mightyest Champion spends his Darts at you, and with what Force and strength of Reason you return them on their own Heads. But notwithstanding this, I verily Beleive he will offer again at his weak Efforts; for he that was so fully possesd of his own Sufficiency, as to think he could deal with your first Letter to him will certainly never lay down the Cudgels till his Blood be about his Ears. and if he thought himself obleidged in honour to justify his first Blunders, much more will he think himself so now, when he is thrown over head and ears in the Mire. To pas by all the rest of your Reply (wherein you have given him many a severe Wound) I think he is no where so clearly and disgracefully foild, as by the conversation between you and your Friend concerning his Notions of *Nature* and *Person*.[2] But above all, the Consequence you draw from thence of his being obleidged to write against his own Vindication of the Trinity, must needs wound him to the Hart; and indeed I do not see how tis possible for him to avoid the Force of that Blow by all his Art and Cunning. Yet write he will, I am sure on't, and power forth an abundance of Words; But so he may forever; I envy not the place of his Amanuensis.

But all this while I have forgot to return you my Acknowledgements for the Favour of your Book; I am extreamly obleidged to

[1] The belief that the porcupine could shoot its quills at its enemies goes back to Classical Antiquity; it appears not to have been contradicted until the eighteenth century: Buffon, *Histoire naturelle*, ed. C. S. Sonnini, 1798–1808, xxxi. 249–52.

[2] pp. 117–61.

you for remembring m⟨e⟩[a] amongst your other Friends whenever you are pleas⟨d⟩[a] to obleidge the Learned World with any of your Happy Thoughts. I had no sooner perused them, but they were snatchd out of My Hands by My Lord Chancelor[1] (so covetious are all Men of whatever comes from you) and he has them yet.

Amongst the other Small Craft, that appears against you I meet with One J. H's State of England in relation to Coyn and trade.[2] I hear the Authors name is Hodges. He is much of a Class in this particular as Mr Serjeant in relation to your Essay, that is, both to me Unintelligible.

The Inclosed is a sample of What this Place produces against you; I wish you may not say, that it resembles our Mountains and Bogs in being Barren and Useles. I have ventur'd to send you my short answer thereto; for a Longer I think it did not deserve. I have not seen the Bishop[b] since this has pasd between[c] us.[c] But we are so good Friends, that this Busines will cause no Anger between us.

I am

Your Most obleidged Humble servant

W: MOLYNEUX

My[d-] Son gives his service to young Mr Masham and desires he would excuse his Long Silence. Tis truly my Fault, for I generally write on such a sudden and in such hast to you, that I afford not time to his slow Pen and Invention.[-d]

[Enclosure:]

Johnstown October 26th. 1697

Sir

I have mett with Mr. Locks Reply to the Bishop of Worcester and have had Leisure to Look it over here. I medle not with the Controversy between them. but Confess I am a litle Surprizd at what I finde p. 95. and 96 where wee have these Words *To talk of the* Certainty of faith, *seems all one To me*, *as to talk of the Knowledge of beleiving*, and *when it is brought to* Certainty, faith *is Destroyd.* and *bring it to* certainty, *and it Ceases to be* faith. and he in Terms owns

[a] *Page torn.* [b] *Abbreviated in MS.; underlined, presumably by the editor of* Some Familiar Letters *for expansion.* [c] *Deleted in MS., presumably by the editor of* Some Familiar Letters. [d–d] *Deleted in MS., presumably by the editor of* Some Familiar Letters.

[1] Methuen.

[2] No. *2194*. Hodges published a *Supplement* this year also: Horsefield, no. 423. L.L., no. 1467.

p. 93 *with*[a–] *me to know and to be certain, is the same thing what I know, that I am certain of; and what I am certain of, that I know.* and p. 92[–a] *knowledge I finde in my Selfe; and I Conceive in others, consists in the perception of the Agreement or Disagreement of the imediate Objects of the minde in thinking, which I Call ideas, and p. 83 certainty Consists in the perception of the Agreement or Disagreement of Two Ideas.* Now to me it seems that according to Mr Lock I cannot be said to know any thing Except there be two ideas in my minde, and all the Knowledge I have must be concerning the Relation these two ideas have to one another and that I Can be certain of nothing else, which in my Opinion Excludes all Certainty of Sense and of single ideas, all Certainty of Consciousness such as willing beleiving knowing etc and as he Confesses all Certainty of faith, and lastly all Certainty of Remembrance, of which I have formerly Demonstrated, as soon as I have forgott or do not actually think of the Demonstration, for I suppose you are well aware that in Demonstrating Mathematicall Propositions Tis not always from Actuall ⟨perception⟩[b] of the Agreement of Ideas that wee assume other Propositions formerly Demonstrated to inferr the Conclusion but from Memory: and yet wee do not think our selves less certain on that Account.[1] If this be the Importance[2] of Mr. L: Words as it seems to me to be, then wee are not Certain of what wee See, hear or feel, wee are not Certain of the Acts of our own Mind, wee are not Certain of any thing that Remains in our minds meerly by the Strength of our Memory. and lastly wee are not Certain of any Proposition. tho God and Man Wittness the truth of it to us. and then Judge how litle certainty is left in the world, and how near this last comes to Mr. Tolands Proposition that Authority or Testimony is only *a means of information, not a ground of Perswasion*[3] for I must own that I think I am only perswaded of the truth of a thing, in proportion to the Certainty I have of it. and if Knowledge and Certainty be Reciprocally the same and Consist in the perception of the Agreement or Disagreement of two ideas, where I do not perceive these, tho God and man, nay the whole World Should testify to me that they do Agree or Disagree, I cannot be certain of it. I must Profess my Selfe of another Opinion, and I think I am as certain there was

a–a *Enclosed in square brackets; in the margin the word* out *written apparently by the amanuensis.* b *MS.* preception

1 This passage may have led to the alteration of *Essay* IV. i. 9 in the fourth edition.
2 In the obsolete sense, import: *O.E.D.*
3 *Christianity not Mysterious*, sections i, §§ 8–9; ii, § 11 (ed. 1696, pp. 13–15, 37–8).

such a Man as Mr. L: from the Testimony of you and other Circumstances, tho I perceive no Agreement or Disagreement in this Case between the Two Ideas to Convince me of his being, as that the 3 Angles of a Straight lined Triangle are equall to two right Angles, where I actualy perceive the Agreement or rather Equality, or, that the area of a Cyclois[1] is equall to triple the Generating Circle. of which I am Certain by Memory tho I do not at present perceive the Demonstration, or any Agreement between the ideas of three Circles and a Cyclois. only remember that I once perceived it.

Lett me further add that *Agreement* and *Disagreement* are Metaphoricall Terms when Applyed to ideas for *Agreement* properly I thinke either Signifys first a Compact between two Persons, or secondly Two things fitting one Another as the two parts of a Tally or thirdly the likeness of Two things as of a pair of Coach-horses or fourthly the Aptitude of Two things to Support or preserve one another. so severall Meats Agree with the Stomack, but I do not finde that in a Proposition the ideas have an Agreement in any of these Senses, and I rather think the old Way of Expressing this Matter ought to be retaind; I Learnd in Smiglecius[2] that when the Species intelligiblis of the predicate was the same with the Species of the Subject, the one might be Affirmd of the other, and when the Medius terminus was the same with the one Extreme Terme in one of the Premisses and the other Extreme the same with it in the other of the Premisses the one might be Affirmd of the other in the Conclusion because of the old Axiom quæ sunt idem uni tertio sunt idem inter se,[3] you may use the Metaphoricall Term of Agreement here instead of identity but Mr. L: has told us p. 153. that *Metaphoricall Expressions (which seldom terminate in truth) Shou'd be as much as possible avoided, when men undertake to Deliver* Clear and Distinct Apprehensions, *and Exact Notions of things*;

I Do finde that Mens thoughts do not differ so much as there words, and that most Men are of one Mind when they come to

[1] The cycloid is usually the curve traced by a point on the radius of a circle within, on, or without, its circumference, as the circle rolls along a straight line; but in *Glossographia Anglicana Nova*, 1707, this curve is called the cycloidal curve, 'and the Space which is comprehended between the Curve and the Right Line, is what we call the *Cycloid*'.

[2] Martinus Smiglecius (Śmiglecki), S.J., *Logica*, first published at Ingolstadt in 1618; Oxford editions 1634, 1638, 1658: Madan, no. 2413, etc.

[3] 'Things which are the same as a third thing are the same as one another.' There is a variant in no. *579*.

understand one another, and have the same views. and hence many Controversys are only verball, I doubt not but my difference from Mr. L: in this Matter may be of the same Nature, and perhaps if I had Carefully read his Book of *Humane Understanding* I might perceive it but I have neither Opportunity Leisure or Inclination to do so, and beleive a great part of the world to be in the same Circumstances with me and I verily beleive that the Expressions I have noted in his Reply will seem Unwary to them as well as to me.

I Do finde he claims a Liberty that will not be allowd him by all, p. 92 *to please himself in his Terms* so they be used Constantly *in the same and a known sense.* I remember others have Claimed the same liberty under the Notion of making theire own Dictionary, but I reckon the Changeing a term tho I Declare my Sense and forewarn the Reader of it, to be a very great injury to the World, and to introduce a new one, where there is one Altogether to Signify the same thing, equally injurious; and that a Man has only this Liberty, where he introduces a new thing, that has yet no name. and I beleive you see my reasons for being of this Opinion, and therefore shall not Mention them. let me only Observe that the Want of this Caution seems to me to have brought most of Mr. L.'s troble on him: words were indeed Arbitrary Signs of things in those, that first imposed them, but they are not to us.[a] when wee use the best Caution wee can we are Apt to Transgress in Changing them, and when wee do so out of Weakness, wee must ask Pardon, but must not Claim it as Liberty, it being really a fault. a few Minutes lying on my hands has given you this troble, and I know your kindness to Mr. L: will not make it ungratefull to you, whilst it Assures that I am

Your most Affectionate humble Servant

William[b] Derry[b]

I could never Comprehend any Necessity for a criterion of certainty to the understanding, any more than of one to the eye, to teach it when it Sees; let the eye be rightly Disposed and Apply an Object to it, if duly Applyd, it will force it to see, and so Apply an Object to an understanding duly qualifyd, and if the Arguments or Object be as they ought to be, they will force the understanding to Assent and remove all Doubts; and I can no more tell, what is in the Object, or Arguments, tha⟨t⟩[c] ascertains my understanding;

[a] *Interlined;* to *is perhaps altered from* so

[b] *This name is deleted in MS.,* [pr]*esumably by the editor of* Some Familiar Letters.

[c] *Edge of page.*

than I Can tell what it is in light, that makes me see; I must say that the same God that Ordered light to make me see, Ordered truth or rather certain Objects to ascertain my Understanding and I beleive Mr. L: can hardly give any other reason why his Agreement etc. of Ideas shou'd Cause Certainty.

THE ANSWER.

Dublin October 27°. 1697

My Lord

I am Extreamly Obliedged to your Lordship that having a few Minutes lying on your hands in your Retirement from this Town, you are pleased to Bestow them on my friend and me; I should have acknowledged the favour more Early, had your servant staid for an Answer when he Delivered yours to me, but he was gon out of my Reach before I was aware of it.

And now my Lord all the Answer I shall troble your Lordship with at present is this, That your Lordship is much in the right on't, that had you read Mr Locks Essay of Humane unders.[a] more carefully and throughout; you had never made the Objections you raise against him in your Letter to me; for your Lordship would have found his fourth Book abundantly Satisfactory in the Difficultys you propose; and particularly the second and eighteenth Chapters of the fourth Book are a full Answer to your Lordships Letter.

But your Lordship says, you have neither *opportunity*, *Leisure*, or *Inclination* to read the Essay. my Lord, I would not then have *Leisure* or *Inclination* to Animadvert on a Book, that I had not,[b] if[b] not *Inclination*, at least *Leisure* to read; this with Submission I cannot but say is great Partiality. if your Lordship says, your Letter relates to his Reply to the Bishop of Worcester; neither will this do in my humble Opinion; seeing your Lordship seems to Surmise (as indeed you guesse rightly) that the Essay might have Sett you right in this Matter.

I am
my Lord your Lordships most humble Servant
W: MOLYNEUX

Address: To John Locke Esquire at Mr Pawlings overagainst the Plow Inn in Little Lincolns Inn Fields London

Endorsed by Locke: (i) W: Molyneux 28 Oct 97 Answered 10 Jan: (ii) Wm Molyneux 28 Oct. 97

[a] *Edge of page; a letter may be lost.* [b] *MS.* not (if

2340. Locke to Philippus van Limborch, 29 October 1697 (*2318*, *2352*)

Amsterdam University Library, MS. R.K., Ba 257 p and q. Printed in *Some Familiar Letters*, pp. 398–401; address printed in Ollion, p. 211. The part in French was written by Pierre Coste; a draft for it is printed in Appendix II; it contains an important passage that was omitted from the letter. The part in Latin, which is on a separate scrap of paper, was written by Locke. Answers no. *2318*; answered by no. *2352*.

[Written by Coste:]

Monsieur

Si mon nom est venu à la connoissance de ces habiles gens avec qui vous vous entretenez quelquefois, et s'ils daignent parler des mes Escrits dans les conversations que vous avez avec eux, C'est une faveur dont je vous suis entierement redevable. La bonne Opinion que vous avez d'une personne que vous voulez bien honorer de vôtre amitié les a prévenus en ma faveur. Je souhaiterois que mon Essai concernant l'Entendement fut écrit dans une Langue que ces excellens hommes pussent entendre, car par le jugement exact et sincere qu'ils porteroient de mon Ouvrage je pourrois compter surement sur ce qu'il y a de vray ou de faux et sur ce qu'il peut y avoir de tolerable. Il y a sept ans que ce Livre a été publié. La premiere, et la seconde édition ont eû le bonheur d'être generalement bien reçuës: mais la derniére n'a pas eû le même avantage. Apres un silence de cinq ou six années on commence d'y decouvrir je ne sçai quelles fautes dont on ne s'etoit point apperçú auparavant; Et ce qu'il y a de singulier, on prétend trouver matiere à des controverses de Religion dans cet Ouvrage où je n'ai eû dessein de traiter que des questions de pure speculation Philosophique.[1] J'avois resolu de faire quelques additions, dont j'ai déja composé quelques unes qui sont assez amples, et qui auroient pû ⟨paroitre⟩[a] en leur place dans la quatriéme Edition que le Libraire se dispose à faire,[2] Et j'aurois voluntiers satisfait a votre desir ou au desir d'aucun de vos amys en y ⟨inserant⟩[b] les preuves de l'unité de Dieu qui se presentent à mon Esprit. Car je[c] suis[c] enclin à croire que l'Unité de Dieu peut etre aussi evidemment demonstre que son existance; et qu'elle peut etre établie sur de preuves qui ne laisseront aucun suject d'en douter. Mais j'aime la Paix, et il y a

[a] *MS.* poroitre [b] *MS.* insera-; *page rubbed.* [c] *My transcript reads* Je ne suis, *probably in error.*

[1] This amplifies a similar statement on p. 6. [2] It appeared in 1700.

des gens dans le monde qui aiment si fort les criailleries et les vaines contestations, que je doute, si je dois leur fournir de nouveaux sujets de dispute.

Les remarques que vous me dites que d'habiles gens ont faites sur le *Reasonableness of Christianity* etc sont sans doute fort justes, et il est vray que plusieur Lecteurs ont êtés choquez de certaines pensées qu'on voit au commencement de ce Livre, lesquelles ne s'accordent pas tout-a-fait avec des Doctrines communément reçuës. Mais sur cela je suis obligé de renvoyer ces Messieurs aux deux defenses que l'Auteur a faites de son Ouvrage. Car ayant publié ce petit Livre, comme il le dit luy-même, principalement afin de convaincre ceux qui doutent de la Religion Chretienne, il semble qu'il a esté conduit à traiter ces matieres malgré luy, car pour rendre son Livre utiles aux Deistes, il ne pouvoit point se taire entierement sur ces articles, auxquels ils ⟨s'aheurtent⟩[a] dès qu'il veulent entrer dans l'examen de la Religion Chretienne. Je suis

Monsieur

Votre tres humble et tres obeissant serviteur

JOHN LOCKE

Londres 29 Oct 1697[b]

[Written by Locke:]

Vir Amplissime

Ne mireris quod linguâ Gallicâ responsum a me sit acceptissimis tuis Latinis 8° hujus mensis mihi scriptis, liceat mihi me tibi excusare et negotiorum multitudine quæ otium negat; et Linguæ Latinæ dissuetudine quæ expedite scribere prohibet. Hanc meam epistolam aliis vel prælegendam, vel monstrandam ex tuis colligo: virorum præcellentium censuræ stili negligentiâ me objicere minime decorum judicavi. Quicquid enim tua vel humanitas vel amicitia

---

Excellent Sir,

Lest you should be surprised at my replying in French to your very welcome Latin letter written on the 8th of this month may I be permitted to excuse myself to you on account of both the multitude of affairs that denies me leisure, and a want of practice with Latin that prevents my writing it readily? I gather from your letter that this of mine is to be either read or shown to others; I judged that it would be most improper by carelessness of style to expose myself to the censure of distinguished men; for whatever your kindness or friendship is wont to excuse in me can cause nausea in

---

[a] *MS.* s'aheurtant [b] *The signature and date written by Locke.*

in me excusare solet, aliis vel nauseam vel certe non condonandam molestiam creare potest. Scripsi igitur quod dicendum habui linguâ vernaculâ et festinatim, Galloque in suam linguam vertendam tradidi. Ex quo exorta est inter Episcopum Wigorniensem (qui me quæsitâ causâ aggressus est) et me disputatio: gens theologorum togata in librum meum mire excitatur, laudataque hactenus dissertatio illa, tota jam scatet erroribus, vel saltem continet latentia errorum vel scepseos fundamenta, piâ doctorum virorum curâ nunc demum detegendis. Ad unitatem dei quod attinet, Grotii fateor in loco a te citato argumenta non abunde satisfaciunt. Putasne tamen quempiam, qui deum agnoscit posse dubitare numen illud esse unicum. ego sane nunquam dubitavi, etiamsi fateor mihi ex hac occasione cogitanti videtur altius aliquanto elevandam esse mentem, et a communi philosophandi ratione segregandam siquis id philosophice vel si ita dicam physice[1] ⟨probare⟩[a] velit, sed hoc tibi soli dictum sit. Uxorem tuam dilectissimam, liberosque officiocissime saluto.

[a] *MS.* propare

---

others or certainly unpardonable distress. I therefore wrote in my own language and hastily what I had to say, and delivered it to a Frenchman to be translated into his. Since a debate has arisen between the bishop of Worcester, who has attacked me on a far-fetched pretext, and myself, the cassocked tribe of theologians has been wonderfully excited against my book, and that dissertation that had hitherto been commended now teems throughout with errors or at least contains the latent foundations of errors or scepticism, which must now at last be laid bare by the pious diligence of learned men. As to what concerns the unity of God, I grant that Grotius's arguments in the passage cited by you are not fully satisfactory. But do you think that anyone who acknowledges [the existence of] God can doubt that that deity is unique? I certainly have never doubted it, although I confess that it seems to me, as I take this opportunity to think about it, that the mind must be raised to a somewhat higher level and separated from the ordinary manner of philosophizing if anyone wants to prove it philosophically or, if I may speak thus, physically;[1] but let this be to you alone. I send my best respects to your dear wife and children.

---

[1] 'The Knowledge of Things, as they are in their own proper Beings, their Constitutions, Properties, and Operations, whereby I mean not only Matter, and Body, but Spirits also. . . . This in a little more enlarged Sense of the Word, I call *φυσική, or natural Philosophy*': *Essay*, IV. xxi. 2.

Address (written by Locke): Mÿn Heer Mÿn Heer Limborch bÿ de Remon stranse Kerck op de Kaisars Gracht t'Amsterdam

Noted by van Limborch: (i: beneath date of letter): Recepta 16 Novembris. (ii: at head of Latin part): 29 Octob. 1697.

2341. SIR STEPHEN EVANCE to LOCKE, [late? October 1697] (*2335, 2346*)

B.L., MS. Locke c. 8, ff. 73–4. The letter appears to be the antecedent of no. 2346, which implies a date near the end of October.

Sir

I have Axamined the Accompt and Finde not sow much by 22l due to you, but i have bine gratley ronged by mr[a] Hayter, but i will pay you the money if you please to abate the interest or will pay you in Exchecher notes,[1] which i take for money, which is what ofers From

Sir

your most Humble servant

STE: EVANCE

Address: For Doctr Jno Lock These

Endorsed by Locke: Sir S: Evance Oct 97

2342. PAUL D'ARANDA to LOCKE, [November 1697] (*2260, 2623*)

B.L., MS. Locke c. 3, f. 47. Date from Locke's endorsement.

Sir

Please to pardon me that being under a kind of necessity of attending a buisinesse in the City I cannot wait on you this morning as I had intended, and must therefore send you this to let you know that by the best information I can have the malt Tickets[2] of your number will scarce yield more than about £7: 5s: -d

[a] *Doubtful reading.*

---

[1] Correctly Exchequer Bills; issued first in 1696; issued from 1697 onwards under a new statute and bearing interest at the rate of 5*d.* per cent a day (7·6 per cent per annum): Dickson, *Financial Revolution*, pp. 365–73. Despite Locke's protest (p. 251) Evance paid him in these bills: list in Journal, 14 November.

[2] Tickets for the lottery loan ('Adventure') of £1,400,000 established by 8 and 9 Wm. III, c. 22 (royal assent 16 April 1697) and secured on excise duties on malt,

each ticket—And that my Wife remembers well that your servant came not to my House till on the evening of the Tuesday that I went from home towards Holland, that she offer'd to send the two letters he brought inclosed in hers to me that evening, but that he took them both back with him saying his order was to deliver them at the Post-office if I were gone;[1] and I can hardly doubt but she remembers right in it, because it agrees with what she wrote me the same evening: I hope the letters I deliverd you[2] or others you may receive may be answers to them, and may prove that they went safe tho by post. and so that their not coming time enough to be carryed by me caus'd no other prejudice than the charge of their postage. I am

Sir

Your most obedient servant

P: D'ARANDA

Endorsed by Locke: P: Daranda Nov. 97

2343. PETER STRATTON to LOCKE, 1 November 1697 (*2187*, *2354*)

B.L., MS. Locke c. 18, ff. 241–2.

Bristoll the 1st: November 1697.

Honoured Sir

According to your order I have delivered your Letter to mr Lyde with the Lease and have Received from him the Counterpart and Bond to performe Conditions which shall send you when you give orders; likewise I did speake with mr. Sanders about Veale and he teleth that he did cut down a pretty many oaken shrouds[3] of which he had the barke but it was such which was a shade to the ground on which they stood; he sayth he doe not Know of any that the Bodys is cut down; soe cannot heare that there is any

mum, etc.; drawing was to begin on 10 August. A ticket was in effect an investment at a low rate of interest. Most of the tickets for this loan failed to sell, and the government used the unsold tickets as a form of currency. Locke may have received the present tickets in payment or part-payment of his salary as a Commissioner for Trade and Plantations: Ewen, *Lotteries*, pp. 132–3; Dickson, *Financial Revolution*, p. 49; Steele, *Politics of Colonial Policy*, p. 43; B.L., MS. Locke c. 17, ff. 227–8 (memorandum by Popple, 5 August 1697).

[1] These were perhaps Locke's letters, now lost, to Le Clerc and Guenellon of 6 and 7 August: nos. *2289*, *2292*, endorsements.

[2] One was probably no. *2326* from Guenellon.

[3] Loppings or branches: *O.E.D.*, Shroud, *sb.*[3]

damage don; which is all but my Humble service to your selfe. I subscribe my selfe Sir

your Dutifull and Obedient Kindsman
PETER STRATTON

my Mother Bro: and Sisters Presents their service to you

Address: To John Locke Esqr at mr. Pawlings over Against the Plow in Little Lincoln In Feilds In London

Postmark: NO 3

Endorsed by Locke: P: Stratton 1 Nov 97

2344. FRIDERIC MARX to [LOCKE?] 4/14 November 1697

B.L., MS. Locke c. 15, ff. 226–7. I have not traced Marx elsewhere. The letter is closely related to no. 2320.

Honoured Sir

The many obligations and favors which I have received from you since I had the Honor to be Known to you, and Especially, In bringing me, a stranger, into such a Noble family, where I have hitherto lived so happily, and for the good advices, which I from time to time received, and still receive, Induce and oblige me to have allways a great veneration and respect for you; And although I am not in a condition to express my grateful mind to you, I shall allways pray, that God may reward you, for all, what you have been pleasd to Doe for me. I have received your letter, and return you my Humble thanks for the Honor you doe me, and the good advice you have given me; According to your request, I shall give you an account concerning My Lord Mordaunt healt, studys, and what way, they are layd before him; His Lordship is very well In his health, and the air agrees extremly with him. I endeavord to follow the Method, which you have been pleasd to prescribe us; My Lord has every day a Hour with Professor Grævius, In which Hour his Lordship is taught the antient Geographie, comparing it with the new one, and to understand the Maps, for it is impossible to read Historie, without Knowing them, and the places, which occurre In it; for which purpose My Lord reads Pomponius Mela, which My Lord will finisch In a months time, and being perfect In the Maps, then he is to begin the Roman and Universall Historie, where Professor Grævius will explain to him all the Customs and manners of the Romans, the Turns of state, and upon what they depended, and all things belonging to such a colledge;[1] In begining, this, My Lord will also begin Chronologie which will come very easy to him, if he ones understands the several Epochs; The second My Lord has begun Is In Natural Philosophie, where My Lord does not trouble himself with Logic and other unecessarys,[2] but only Monsieur Girant, who has been recommended by P: Grævius, gives him a touchd[a] of Philosophie and In six months time, My Lord will be gone thourow most part of Philosphie; At whome his Lordship exercises himself In Morality, and where he finds any difficulty In Tullys offices or Puffendorf, he advises with P: Grævius; he also studys Greek att whome, and In the Latin style he composes every day some Epistle or some other Exercise to show Professor Grævius. My Lord rises every morning very early, and Imploys his time very well, and Professor Grævius takes delight In teaching him, and I hope My Lord will make such use of this place, and his Masters, that In time he will answer My Lords and Ladys Peterborows, and your exspectation. I was sorry that I could not have the happiness to have paid my duty to you, before we went out of England, the sudden departure would not leat me have time to wait upon you; I am highly obliged for the good advices you have given me in your letter, I shall allways follow them, and doe such things, what becomes a Honest men, and a person In my condition; I shall be carefull and diligend In the place where I am; And because I never had the Honor to be in such a post before, and perhaps I should commit any thing, which thorow Experience I did not know, I hope My Lord and Lady Peterborow, and you Sir will advise and correct me, and I shall be willing to mend, and take care hereafter not to committ the same again; I have sent My Lord Peterborow a particular account of all my receits and disburtments, and I shall doe so every month If My Lord and Lady pleases, to whom If you please and you tink convenient to present

[a] *Doubtful reading.*

---

[1] In the Dutch sense, a course of lectures, as in no. *1179*, etc.

[2] Marx expresses himself badly. Logic is not associated with natural philosophy: *Essay*, IV. xxi. 2, 4. Locke gives the scope of a course in 'Elements of Natural Philosophy': *Collection of Several Pieces*, pp. 179–230; and discusses the subject more generally in *Some Thoughts concerning Education*, A §§ (178)–82; C §§ 190–4.

my humble Duty when you see them; Recommending me to your farther favor, I remain

Sir

Your most Humble, obedient servant

FRIDERIC MARX.

My Lord Mordaunt presents his Humble service to you.

Utrecht Novemb: 14. 1697.

Endorsed by Locke: F. Marx 14° Nov: 97

2345. DR. PIETER GUENELLON to LOCKE, 5/15 November 1697 (*2326*, *2401*)

B.L., MS. Locke c. 11, ff. 82–3. Le Fèvre probably did not deliver the letter until some time in March 1698: p. 342.

Monsieur,

Celle cy vous sera rendue par Monsieur le Fevre dont je vous ay parlé dans mes precedentes.[1] j'esperois quil s'arresteroit icy, et il est certain que nous perdons beaucoup a son despart, puisque nous avons personne icy aussi capable d'enseigner les Mathematiques. Nos theologiens (dont la persecution est tousjours terrible) l'ont chagriné d'une maniere indigne, il a inseré le factum dans la preface a sa dissertation *de futilitate Poetices*.[2] vous trouverez, (s'il a l'honneur de vous converser)[a] quil a beaucoup de probité et de scavoir et quil est du nombre des theologiens sinceres. il s'estoit rendu ici amis et familier avec Monsieur le Clerq, et je croy quil a appuyé son dessein de passer en Engleterre. il est pas necessaire Monsieur que je vous prie de luy donner entrée dans vostre amitié, vous qui donné un accueil favorable a tout le Monde, et particulierement a des personnes doctes et eclairees. Jay receu hier vostre replique a l'Evéque de Worchester, dont je vous suis infiniment obligé. il est entré dans un champ avec vous, dont il ne sortira jamais vainqueur. la fine philosophie le passe, et on voit facilement quil ne s'entend pas luy mesme bien des fois. toute la famille vous presente ses

[a] *Edge of page; closing bracket supplied.*

[1] p. 170. The younger Tanneguy Le Fèvre.
[2] Published in Amsterdam this year.

treshumbles respects. Ma femme, nos enfans et moy bien particulierement, qui suis,

Monsieur,

Vostre tres humble et tres Obeissant serviteur

P. GUENELLON.

d'Amsterd. ce 15 Nov. 1697.

Address: For Sir Johan Locke at Mr. Powling in little incolns inne fields London

Endorsed by Locke: Dr. Guenellon 15 Nov. 97 Answered Mar. 21

2346. LOCKE to SIR STEPHEN EVANCE, 6 November 1697 (*2341*)

B.L., MS. Locke c. 24, f. 41. Draft. Answers no. *2341*.

London 6 Nov 97

Sir

There is due to me upon your two notes £268–1–9 principal: And for interest £29–12.8.[a] Soe that the whole is £297–14–5.[b] This is what is due to me. And why you should make[c] difficultie to pay it me in current money when you received it in current money which you paid away for such I doe not see. However haveing present occasion for my money I shall consent to receive it, as you offer in your letter to pay it, in exchequer bills, if I may presently have them to supply my occasions, upon receit whereof Mr Clarke will deliver you up your two notes.[1] I am

Sir

your most humble servant

J L

£268– 1–9
29–12–8
297–14–5

Endorsed by Locke: JL to Sir S: Evance 6 Nov. 97

a *Altered from* above £28–15–0 b *Altered from* above £296–16–9 c *A blot here may cover a short word* (a *or* any).

1 Locke states his account with Evance in no. 2356.

2347. DR. JOHN COVEL to LADY MASHAM, 6 November [1697] (*2323*)

B.L., MS. Locke c. 7, ff. 177–8. Copy written by Lady Masham. Year from Locke's endorsement.

Nov 6th

I had answer'd, Deare Madame, your very obliging Letter sooner had I not beene till Monday last in the Countrey with my Neice, and in a Hurry of business ever since. I am as heartilie sorry and assham'd for haveing my Name to Mr Edwards's rude book, as you can wish me or imagine me But since I told mr Locke, that I was perfectly trepan'd into it, and never saw it, Nor knew one Syllable of its Contents, Nor ever heard or Dream'd that Mr Locke was Concern'd in it, I hope I may deserve both your and his Compassion and Pitty rather then displeasure. I never set my hand to it, but he meeting me in the street told me he had a booke going to the Press, which the Proffessor and Vicechancellor had Perus'd and Licens'd, and he ask'd my leave to joyne my name to them; I told him if they had past it, he might put my Name if he pleas'd; but by all that is Truth, I never ask'd one word more about it. I owne my fault (and it proves a great one) to be so foolishly Credulous; But I think I know both your Ladyship and Mr Lock to be Persons of that Justice, as not to Count that Wilfulness in me, or base Designe, which upon my Solemne Word, was a meere misfortune, and Could I publish it to the World I would, if this satisfie not, I must bewayl my unhappy weakeness and beare the blame. I do heartilie thank Your Ladyship for giveing me your free thoughts, and really I Condemne myself of a very high Inadvertencie; Could you tell me how I may recover my owne reputation here in, I should count my self both happy and highly oblig'd to you; those that know me not, may very well take me for one of the same *Gangræna* Spirit;[1] but You and they that do know me I hope will beleeve it was as far from my temper as I assure you it was from my knowledge.

Good Madame, preserve me still in your good Opinion; and if you shall adde, to your many obligations, yet this mighty one to recover me also in Mr Lockes favour and former Friendship

[1] Edwards was a son of Thomas Edwards (1599–1647; *D.N.B.*), author of *Gangræna: or a Catalogue and Discovery of Many of the Errours, Heresies, Blasphemies and Pernicious Practices of the Sectaries of this Time*, 1646 (three parts, published separately).

Your Justice will be as great as your kindness to him who ever was and must be,

Madame,

Your Ladyships Most faithfull and most humble servant

Endorsed by Locke: J Covell to Lady Masham 6. Nov. 97

2348. JEAN LE CLERC to LOCKE, 7/17 November 1697 (2300, 2403)

B.L., MS. Locke c. 13, ff. 119–20. Printed in Bonno, *Le Clerc*, pp. 104–6. The letter was not delivered until about March 1698: p. 342.

A Amsterdam le 17. de Novembre 1697

Je ne puis pas, Monsieur, vous écrire de Lettre, pour peu que je retarde, sans être obligé de vous remercier, tant vos bienfaits sont fréquens. Mr. Furly m'a remis cette semaine vôtre Seconde Lettre à Mylord de Worcester,[1] avec le livre de Mr. Whiston,[2] dont je vous suis extrémement obligé. J'ai lû la Lettre à Mr. Stillingfleet, pour voir si cet habile homme avoit quelque difficulté à faire plus considerable, que ce qu'il avoit proposé; mais j'ai été surpris de n'y trouver rien, qui soit d'aucune consequence. *Invidiam movere novit, philosophiæ planè est imperitus. Quòd si ejus scripta ad Theologiam et Historiam Ecclesiasticam pertinentia expenderentur, quot et quanta invenirentur, ex quibus intelligere liceret famam perfacilè acquiri, inter Druidas? Expertus loquor.*[3] Mr. Whiston a beaucoup d'esprit et de genie, mais il tort[4] beaucoup Moïse, et il suppose bien des choses touchant sa tradition parmi les Payens, qui n'ont pas le fondement qu'il croit. *Mr. Burnet* les avoit déja étalées,[5] mais il ne m'avoit nullement persuadé. Ces Messieurs prennent des conjectures des Philosophes ou de pures fictions Poëtiques, pour des traditions anciennes, comme il seroit aisé de le faire voir. Cependant j'aime les gens de ce génie, parce qu'il y paroît de la liberté et

[1] Locke's first *Reply* to Stillingfleet.

[2] The *New Theory of the Earth*: no. *1684* n., etc.

[3] 'He knows how to stir up ill will, but he is quite unskilled in philosophy. For that matter, if his writings in regard to theology and Church history were carefully considered, how much strong evidence would they afford that a reputation is very easily acquired among the Druids? I speak from experience.'

[4] This form occurs in a proverb in Cotgrave, s.v. Tordre: 'Il ne se tort pas qui va plain chemin. . . . *He that goes on plaine ground spraines not his foot.*'

[5] Le Clerc perhaps alludes to *Archæologiæ Philosophicæ*, pp. 190–9, where Burnet argues that the ancients, including the Greek philosophers, derived their traditions about the end of the world not from Moses, but from descendants of Noah prior to his time. See also *Theory of the Earth*, ii. 19–21.

de l'amour de la verité, que l'on ne voit gueres dans les écrits des Théologiens. Pour l'affaire d'Irlande dont vous me parliez,[1] je vous dirai que nôtre ami est tout à fait résolu de n'aller jamais en païs d'Inquisition, à moins qu'il ne fût appellé publiquement, et tel qu'il est, en sorte qu'il fût à couvert de toutes questions, et de toute chicane. Ni la prudence, ni la conscience ne lui permettent pas d'en user autrement. Il se livreroit pieds et poings liez aux Druides de ce païs-là, qui le traiteroient à discretion, s'il y vouloit demeurer. D'ailleurs il n'entend l'Anglois, que pour lire, mais il ne sauroit soûtenir aucune conversation; de sorte qu'il seroit bien éloigné d'être en état de se charger d'une Cure, et il ne croit pas qu'il soit permis d'emploier un Vicaire. Il n'y a qu'une Université, où il pût être de quelque usage, pour les Langues, la Philosophie, ou l'Histoire. Je croi qu'il fera mieux de renoncer à tout cela, et de servir Dieu dans le poste où il est, que de s'exposer à devenir l'esclave des quelques Druïdes bourrus. Il m'a néantmoins chargé de vous remercier très-humblement, de vôtre souvenir, et de vous assûrer qu'il en a toute la reconnoissance possible. Je suis toûjours après mon *Hammond*, qui ne paroîtra qu'au commencement de l'année prochaine. Quoi que je lui fasse quartier sur une infinité de choses, j'y ai trouvé plus à reprendre que je ne croiois. J'aurois néanmoins déja fait, si une troisiéme édition de *Morery*[2] n'étoit venue à la traverse. Cela m'a fait beaucoup perdre de temps, mais l'Ouvrage va être fait. Jamais méchant livre ne s'est si bien vendu, que celui-là, et c'est dommage qu'on n'en ait un bon; car pour celui-là, quelque changement qu'on y fasse, il ne sauroit le devenir, étant essentiellement mauvais. Je suis obligé de perdre mon temps à ces sottises, parce que quelque chose de meilleur ne seroit pas mieux recompensé. C'est là le mal de la Hollande. Mais qu'y faire? Il faut prendre patience, et s'aquiter gayement de son devoir. Celui qui porte cette Lettre en Angleterre est un fort honête homme, qui est fils du celebre Mr. le Fevre de Saumur, dont j'ai parlé plusieurs fois dans ma Critique.[3] Il est bon humaniste et de plus Mathematicien et Philosophe. Mr. Bothwel,[4] secretaire d'Etat, l'emmene en Angleterre. Il m'a témoigné de l'envie d'avoir l'honneur de vous connoître, et si vous êtes à Londres, il ne manquera

[1] Nos. *2170*, 2202, *2288*, 2310, *2311*. 'Nôtre ami' is Le Clerc.

[2] See above, no. *1653*. The edition in preparation appeared in 1698.

[3] The *Ars Critica*; see the *Index Scriptorum* appended to the second edition.

[4] Apparently William Blathwayt, the secretary at war: no. *1981*. He attended William III on campaign.

pas de vous y chercher; sinon il remettra cette Lettre à vôtre adresse. Il ne paroit rien de nouveau ici qu'un *Callimaque* fort bien imprimé en deux volumes in 8°. avec des notes accablantes de Mr. *Spanheim*, qui y fait tout entrer, et qui y met les bonnes choses sous des monceaux d'inutiles.[1] Il y en a quelques unes de Mr. *Bentley*, qui sont de bon goût. Je vois qu'il a entrepris de recueuillir les fragmens des Poëtes Grecs. J'ai fait un semblable dessein, sur ceux de deux Poëtes Comiques, *Menandre* et *Philemon*,[2] et j'en ai un beaucoup plus grand nombre de fragmens qu'il n'y en a dans *Stobée* et dans le Recueuil de *Grotius*,[3] et même en meilleur état. J'ai dessein de les traduire en prose Latine et d'y joindre des Notes; mais si je savois que Mr. *Bentley* dût les publier bientôt, j'attendrois, pour ne pas prendre une peine inutile. Si vous pouviez, Monsieur, vous en informer par quelqu'un de vos amis, sans me nommer, je vous serois bien obligé. Ces fragmens sont si fort à mon goût, que je les copie avec le plus grand plaisir du monde, et que je ne puis me lasser de les lire. Mr. *Bentley* a envoié à Utrecht les fragmens de *Callimaque* qu'il avoit recueüllis. Je n'oserois lui demander la même chose, et je ne sai s'il auroit prêts ceux de *Menandre* et de *Philemon*; mais je lui pourrois faire honneur de ce qu'il auroit de particulier, en cas qu'il en voulût user de même. Ce qui me reste à faire ne demande pas beaucoup de temps, et je l'acheverai dans les intervalles que j'aurai dans mon travail sur la Bible, que je reprendrai bien tôt. Voila, Monsieur, à quoi je m'amuse. Je vous souhaite une aussi bonne santé qu'à moi, et je prie Dieu qu'il vous conserve encore longues années, malgré les envieux. Je suis, Monsieur, entierement à vous

J LE CLERC.

Endorsed by Locke: J Le Clerc 17 Nov. 97 Answered 22 Apr:
Q Menander Dr. Bently
Dr Bently promises the fragments

[1] The edition for which Theodorus Grævius prepared the text: no. *1802*.

[2] Le Clerc's edition appeared in 1709, and was criticized fiercely by Bentley: Barnes, *Le Clerc*, pp. 214–24. See further p. 423.

[3] Joannes called Stobæus collected excerpts from the older Greek writers in the fifth century. Grotius published editions (*Dicta Poetarum*, etc.) in 1623 and 1625.

2349. JOSEPH CRAMPHORNE to LOCKE, 8 November 1697 (*2353*)

B.L., MS. Locke c. 7, f. 183. Cramphorne writes later from Sawbridgeworth in Hertfordshire, 2 miles north of Harlow. The endorsement shows that his business was with the Masham Trust.

November the 8th. 1697.

Sir

I did designe to have beene with you att London this day (to have given satisfaction in the Tytle of an Estate in order for a Mortgage thereupon, about which supose Mr. Clarke[1] has given you Notice) but being prevented by unexpected businiss thought fitt to acquaint you that I canot be with you 'till Saterday or Munday next. att which time I will not fayle rest Sir

Your Sarvent att Command
Jo^p: CRAMPHORNE

Address: To Mr. Lock att Mr. Pawlings over against the plough in Little Lincolns Inn Fields Lond.

Postmark: NO 10

Endorsed by Locke: J Cramporne 8 Nov 97 Trust

2350. JEREMY THOMAS to LOCKE, 11 November 1697

B.L., MS. Locke c. 20, f. 127. See nos. 2346, 2351, and 2356.

Sir

By the order of Sir Stephen Evance I waited on mr Clarke at the Excise office to pay him according to your letter to Sir Stephen only craveing the allowance of two notes each for £11 under his hand for your use, but he said you must be acquainted therewith before he could cleer with me so I waited this evening to have acquainted you with the same but not finding you at home shall call to morrow morning and shew you the nots who am Sir

Your most humble servant
JEREMY THOMAS

November 11th 1697

Address: For Dr John Locke These

Endorsed by Locke: J: Thomas 11° Nov. 97

1 Perhaps 'Mr Clarke of Hollingbury' (p. 148) rather than Edward Clarke.

2351. Locke to Edward Clarke, 12 [November 1697?] (2309, 2356)

Rand, p. 530. Rand supplies the date as January 1698. The date assigned to the letter here is based on its connection with no. *2350*.

12th ⟨November 1697⟩

Sir,

Mr. Thomas the . . . has been here with me about the money, and has promised to pay both the notes with the interest, only abating £22. Which leaving one of Mr. Hayter's notes in your hand with that remain due upon it, and keeping your two notes for the £22 till I can consult my accounts in the country to see how it stands, this I agree to, and am,

Sir,
your most humble servant,
J. Locke.

Address: For Edward Clarke, Esq.

Endorsed by Clarke: Sir Stephen Evans. Mr. Locke.

2352. Philippus van Limborch to Locke, 18/28 November 1697 (2340, 2395)

B.L., MS. Locke c. 14, ff. 109–10. Copy by van Limborch in Amsterdam University Library, MS. R.K., III D 16, f. 200. Printed from the copy in *Some Familiar Letters*, pp. 402–5, without the date and with omissions or alterations to conceal Hudde's participation; the second sentence ('Ut aperte . . . Consul D. Hudde') is printed from the copy with wrong date in Ollion, p. 214 n. Answers no. 2340; answered by no. 2395.

Amplissime Vir

Gratissimas tuas 29 Octobris scriptas recte accepi, Viroque magnifico,[1] cujus potissimum rogatu ad te scripsi, prælegi. Ut aperte tecum agam; qui argumenta tua de quæstione proposita videre desiderat, est honoratissimus civitatis nostræ Consul D. Hudde.

Excellent Sir,

I have duly received your most welcome letter written on 29 October and have read it to the Magnifico,[1] at whose request it mainly was that I wrote to you. To be open with you: the man who wants to see your arguments about the question put before you is the highly honoured burgomaster of our city, Mr. Hudde. It does not seem possible that the particular matter

[1] In later letters, from no. *2432* onwards, van Limborch and Locke generally use this designation for Hudde, probably as a guard should their letters go astray. It is not in any way satirical or derogatory.

Res ipsa de qua quæritur a nemine sano in dubium vocari posse videtur: ipsa enim Deitatis notio unitatem involvit, nec permittit ut illa pluribus communis credi possit. Quare, me judice, nemo qui attente secum considerat quid voce Dei intelligamus, pluralitatem Deorum asserere potest. Quia tamen eam ab Ethnicis asseri videmus, et contra eos Scripturæ autoritate pugnari non potest, rationibus è natura petitis convincendi sunt. Quare ejusmodi requirit argumenta D. Consul, quibus solide demonstretur, ens independens et perfectum esse tantum posse unicum. Ex solide adstructa essentiæ divinæ unitate porro facili negotio omnia attributa divina, nostrumque tam erga Deum quam proximum officium, deduci posse certissimus est. Cartesium dicit unitatem illam non probasse, sed præsupposuisse. Ipse sibi demonstrationem scripsit, sed eam ajebat subtiliorem esse: Et quia multum tuo tribuit judicio, tua argumenta avidissime videre desiderat. Prælegi illi epistolam tuam: gaudebat quod in ea affirmes, te id præstare posse: tanto enixius jam tua argumenta desiderat. Dolebat tibi litem temere motam: quoniam autem, ne fortasse novis litibus et suspicionibus præter tuam intentionem vel minimam præbeas ansam, publico scripto argumenta tua proferre gravaris, rogat ut ea privatim ad me

---

that is being inquired into can be called in question by any sane person: for the very notion of deity involves unity, nor does it permit that deity can be believed to be common to several. Wherefore in my opinion no one who carefully considers with himself what we understand by the word God can assert a plurality of gods. Since, however, we see that plurality is asserted by the heathen, and as the authority of Scripture cannot be used in contending against them, they are to be convinced by reasons drawn from nature. This is why the Burgomaster requires arguments of such a kind that it may be solidly demonstrated by them that an independent and perfect being [*ens*] can be one only [*unicus*]. He is altogether certain that all the divine attributes and our duty, as well towards God as towards our neighbour, can furthermore be readily deduced from the unity of the divine essence [*essentia*] when that has been solidly established. He says that Descartes has not proved that unity but has presupposed it. He has composed a demonstration for himself, but said that it is too subtle; and as he values your judgement highly he very keenly desires to see your arguments. I read your letter to him; he was glad that you can perform what you affirm in it: he now all the more eagerly desires your arguments. He was sorry about the dispute that has been inconsiderately started with you; but since you are unwilling to disclose your arguments in a public writing, lest by chance you should unintentionally offer even the slightest occasion for new disputes and suspicions, he asks you to write them privately to me under promise o

scribas, sub promisso silentii. Ille hæc evulgare minime intendit, sed ad propriam suam instructionem et in veritate confirmationem requirit. Duobus præter illum viris intima mihi amicitia conjunctis, qui priori nostræ conversationi interfuerunt, D. de Hertoghe[a] Fisci Hollandici Advocato,[1] et D. Advocato van den Ende,[2] et præter illos nulli omnino mortalium, ea communicabuntur: nisi forte et D. Clerico ea prælegi permittas, quod tui arbitrii est; ipso enim ignaro hæc omnia ad te scribo. Rem facturus es D. Consuli maximopere gratam: et quod fidis solummodo amicis, et quidem paucis adeo, concreditur, cujusque nullum a me ⟨cuiquam⟩[b] apographum dabitur, id dispalescere non potest. Quin imo, ut tanto honestius apographum denegare queam, suaserim ut id in epistola tua enixe a me stipuleris. Nolim ego te genti togatæ, tanquam scepseos fundamenta jacientem, magis suspectum fieri: plerosque illorum alieno judicio, tanquam nervis alienis mobile lignum,[3] præcipites in laudem ac vituperium immerentium rapi certus sum. Cum tuas legerem, lepida mihi Thomæ Mori in sua Utopia fabella incidit. Refert is, cum Raphael Hythlodæus coram Cardinale

[a] *In* Some Familiar Letters*:* Hartoge [b] *Supplied from van Limborch's copy.*

---

silence. He does not in the least intend to divulge them but wants them for his own instruction and confirmation in the truth. Besides to him they will be communicated to two men, both intimate friends of mine, who were present at our former conversation, Mr. de Hertoghe, Advocate to the Treasury of Holland,[1] and the advocate Mr. van den Ende,[2] and besides them to no mortal whatsoever; unless perhaps you allow them to be read to Mr. Le Clerc, which is a matter for your decision; for he knows nothing of all this that I am writing to you. You will do the Burgomaster a very great favour; and since it will be entrusted only to faithful friends, and indeed to very few, and since no copy of it will be given by me to anyone, it cannot get abroad. Indeed, so that I may the more decently refuse a copy, I would advise you to stipulate that earnestly on my part in your letter. I should not like you to become more suspected by the cassocked tribe as if you were laying the foundations of scepticism; I am sure that most of them are carried away headlong by the judgement of others 'like puppets that dance when others pull the strings'[3] into praise or blame of those who do not deserve it. When I read your letter a pleasant story of Thomas More's in his *Utopia* occurred to me. He relates that, when Raphael Hythloday had discoursed

---

[1] Mattheus de Hertog or Hartogh; the audit office of the county of Holland: Huygens, *Journaal*, volume of notes on the index.
[2] No. *1456*.
[3] 'Ut nervis alienis mobile lignum': Horace, *Satires*, II. vii. 82.

Archiepiscopo Cantuariensi doctissime de Republica disseruisset, legis quendam peritum commoto capite et labiis distortis quicquid dixerat improbasse, ac statim omnes qui aderant pedibus in Jurisperiti illius ivisse sententiam: Cum vero Cardinalis Hythlodæi sententiam probabat, mox quæ ipso narrante contemserant omnes, eadem neminem non certatim laudibus esse prosequutum. Simile quid tractatui tuo evenit: qui antea integro sexennio communi applausu exceptus fuit, nunc insurgente contra te magni nominis Episcopo totus erroribus scatet, et latentia continet scepseos fundamenta. Ita solet Theologorum vulgus non ex suo sed alieno sapere cerebro. Verum talium judicio epistola tua nequaquam exponetur. Quod vero linguæ Latinæ desuetudinem prætexis, quæ expedite scribere prohibet, plane me in ruborem dedit. Quale itaque tuum de me judicium esse censebo, cujus stylus cum tuo comparatus plane sordet? Epistolæ tuæ omnes, etiam veloci calamo scriptæ, sunt non tantum puræ et tersæ, sed et vividæ ac elegantes; quæ si tibi displiceant, quid de meis judices non difficile mihi est colligere. Nihilominus amicitia tua fretus confidenter quicquid in calamum venit tibi scribo, de benignitate tua, quæ defectus meos boni consulere novit, plane securus. Imposterum

---

most learnedly about the common weal in the presence of the Cardinal Archbishop of Canterbury, a certain lawyer with shaking of his head and twisted lips had condemned all that he had said, and immediately all who were present had fallen in with the lawyer's opinion; but when the Cardinal commended Hythloday's opinion they were soon vying with one another in praising what they had all contemned while he was speaking. The like has happened to your treatise; what was formerly for a whole six years received with general applause now, when a bishop of great name rises up against you, teems throughout with errors and contains the latent foundations of scepticism. The common run of theologians are wont in this way to draw wisdom not from their own but from others' brains. But your letter shall in no wise be exposed to the judgement of such fellows. As for your pretext of want of practice with Latin, which prevents your writing it readily: it quite puts me to shame. What sort of opinion, then, shall I suppose you have of me, whose style is thoroughly mean in comparison with yours? All your letters, even those written in haste, are not only pure and polished but also lively and elegant; if they displease you it is not difficult for me to gather what you think of mine. Nevertheless, trusting in your friendship I boldly write to you whatever comes to my pen, thoroughly assured of your kindness, which knows how to take my defects in good part. But if hereafter you continue to use that excuse you will make me more fearful of writing. And so you readily see that this excuse can by no means be admitted. But if

vero si ea excusatione uti pergas timidiorem me in scribendo facies. Excusationem itaque hanc minime admitti posse facile vides. Si vero negotia tua tardius nobis concedant responsum, nolim nimia festinatione graviora negligas, sed tempus ad scribendum eligas minus occupatum. Quicquid et quandocunque scripseris, gratissimum erit: interim si cito des bis te dedisse[1] gratus agnoscam. Dedit mihi hebdomade proxime elapsa D. Clericus tuum de liberorum educatione tractatum in linguam Belgicam versum,[2] pro quo dono magnifico summas tibi ago gratias: uxor et filia eum attente legunt: ego, ubi illæ satiatæ fuerint, integrum, quod et ipsis commendavi, a capite ad calcem perlegam. Vale Amplissime Vir. Salutari te quam officiosissime jussit D. Consul. Salveat plurimum Domina Masham. Salutant te uxor mea ac liberi.

Tui Amantissimus
PHILIPPUS A LIMBORCH.

Amstelodami 28 Novembris

9
16 97
12

Address: To John Locq Esqr. att the honourable office of trade and plantations att Withehall London

Postmark: NO 22

Endorsed by Locke: P. Limborch 28° Nov 97 Answered 21 Feb

---

your affairs allow a reply [only] rather tardily I should wish you not to neglect more serious matters through too great haste, but to choose some less busy time for writing. Whatever and whensoever you write, it will be most welcome; meanwhile if you give quickly I shall gratefully acknowledge that you have given twice.[1] Last week Mr. Le Clerc gave me your treatise on the education of children translated into Dutch,[2] for which splendid present I thank you heartily. My wife and daughter are reading it attentively; when they have had their fill I shall read through the whole of it from beginning to end, as I recommended to them also. Good-bye, excellent Sir. The Burgomaster bade me give you his best respects. My best regards to Lady Masham. My wife and children send you greetings.

Your most affectionate
PHILIPPUS VAN LIMBORCH.

Amsterdam 28 November
1697

---

[1] 'Bis dat qui cito dat': Erasmus, *Adagia*, I. viii. 91.

[2] p. 73.

2353. JOSEPH CRAMPHORNE to LOCKE, 20 November 1697 (*2349*, *2769*)

B.L., MS. Locke c. 7, f. 184.

London. November the 20th. 97

Sir

I have mett sev'rall disapoyntments, e'ls had seen you before this time, but this onley to desire you woud not be from home for I designe to waite on you this day about one of the clock. No more att present but rest

Yours to serve

JO[P]: CRAMPHORNE

Address: To Mr. Lock att Mr. Pawlings over against the Plough in Little Lincolns Inn fields

Endorsed by Locke: J: Cramphorne 20° Nov. 97 Trust

2354. PETER STRATTON to LOCKE, 24 November 1697 (*2343*, *2530*)

B.L., MS. Locke c. 18, ff. 243–4.

Bristoll the 24th: November 1697.

Honoured Sir

I did the 1st: of this Instant give you an account that I had the lease and Bond from Mr. Lyde and not heareing from you makes me afraid the letter did miscarry which is the reason I Trouble you with this; which with my Humble Service to your selfe is all from him that is Sir your Dutifull Kindsman

and obedient Servant

PETER STRATTON.

Address: For John Locke Esqr at mr. Pawlings over Against the Plow in Little Lincoln In Feilds In London

Postmark: NO 26

Endorsed by Locke: P: Stratton 24° Nov 97

2355. Nicolas Toinard to Locke, 26 November/ 6 December 1697 (*2337*, *2373*)

B.L., MS. Locke c. 21, ff. 187–9. Answers no. 2337; answered by no. 2412.

+

6. Decembre 97.

Je vous ecriray, Monsieur, cete fois-cy en style laconique, et je le feray plus amplement dez que je le pouray à droiture apres la retablissement du Paquebot,[1] ou par autre voie que cellecy dont je me sers precairement.

Vous m'avez rendu justice par la continuation que vous me marquez de l'honneur de votre bienveillance, puisqu'il n'y a personne qui s'interesse plus que moy à tout cequi vous regarde.

Le Gentilhomme qui m'a donnè des nouveles de votre bonne santé,[2] m'a aussi apris le bon etat auquel sont vos afaires, et l'emploi que vous avez: dont j'ay autant de joie pour vous qu'en doit avoir pour lui même l'etat que vous servez. Pour cequi est de la situation où je suis, elle consiste en deux mots. J'ay pour le moins autant de santé que vous m'en avez vu, et j'ay quelques facultéz de plus par le deceds d'une mere et d'une sœur. Avec cela neanmoins la-facheuse conjoncture du tems peut me permetre de dire cequ'un de vos anciens amis a autrefois dit: *Possessiunculæ meæ offendiculo mihi sunt*,[3] mais Dieu garde de mal tous ceux qui ont plus de sujet de s'en plaindre.

m. Nelson a eté fort surpris quand il a vu qu'il ne m'etoit pas inconnu. cela vient de ceque j'ay toujours aimé le canada, et tout cequi y a relation. Par la je savois le mauvais traitement qu'il a receu, quoiqu'il l'Anglois à qui les François de Canada avoient le plus d'obligation.

Il m'a bien apris de belles choses. entr'autres qu'un m. Watson en premiere instance chirurgien de Couventry a fait de grandes decouvertes dans les Mathematiques, et qu'il avoit pensé de faire des horloges avec de petites boules de verre.[4] J'en ay fait part

[1] The regular service between Calais and Dover.

[2] He is named below: John Nelson, 1654–1734, New England statesman: *D.N.B.*; *Dict. American Biog.*; *Dict. Canadian Biog.*

[3] 'My little bits of property are a source of annoyance to me.' Varied from Cicero, *Ad Atticum* XIII. xxiii. 3, which Toinard quoted in no. *1293*; 'offendiculo' is perhaps remembered from Pliny, *Epistles* IX. xi. 1, where it occurs in a different context.

[4] Toinard's report is probably incorrect: p. 359. He perhaps refers to Samuel Watson, a Coventry blacksmith who sold a clock to Charles II: Evelyn, *Diary*, ed. de Beer, iii. 112 n.

à m. Hartsouker,[1] qui m'est venu voir arivant d'Holande. c'est un maitre-faiseur de *lentes*[2] pour les Microscopes, et il m'a dit qu'il aprouvoit assez cela, et qu'il m'enseigneroit le moien d'en faire un grand nombre à la fois, et tres rondes, mais qu'il y avoit a craindre qu'eles ne s'usassent par le frotement. Je luy ay dit que j'en avois autrefois fait d'etain avec une dizième de cuivre, cequi les rend dures. Il les estime pour cela plus que celes de verre. Je faisois à ces sortes d'horloges un petit trou proche du diafragme, par lequel passoit un tuyau en pié de chevre par les deux bouts, pour donner issuë à l'air d'embas que chassent les boules qui tombent. l'incommodité de ces horloges est qu'eles doivent être de grand volume à l'usage que l'on en veut faire pour les Longitudes.

l'un des Triumvirs est venu ici depuis quelque tems à cause de la pourpre de son patron.[3] nous avons fort parlé de vous. Je vais le regaler en lui aprenant de vos nouveles.

Si M. Nelson qui m'a dit devoir s'en aler dans trois semaines, veut se charger de quelques livres, je vous en enverray plusieurs qui ont eté faits sur la Pâque à l'ocasion de cequ'en a ecrit le P. Lami, l'un *ex Aratoribus in vitulâ meâ*.[4]

Tout le texte que vous savez est entierement imprimé en 136. pages.[5] Quelque soin que l'on y ait aporté, il est echapé des fautes, mais en general la composition de l'ouvrage est belle, et les caractérismes en tête des pages ont leur agreement. Vous en avez deja des feuïlles que m. Leers a du vous faire tenir. La principale est cele de la Pâque, et vous verrez au retour de m. Nelson comment elle est executée avec les Notes dont elle est chargèe. Vous aurez aussi tout ceque j'ay fait graver de medailles apelées abuzivement *Samaritaines*, et celles des *Herodiades* avec leur cronologie.[6] Je n'en ay pas encore donné les livres au Public, non plus que quelques autres, où je me suis apliqué par divertissement.

[1] Nicolaas Hartsoeker, 1656–1725, microscopist: *N.N.B.W.* He was a son of Christiaan Hartsoeker, the Remonstrant minister (no. *1163*).

[2] Probably the Latin word. The word lens was coming into use in English about this time: *O.E.D.* The French word is *lentille*.

[3] Formentin; Coislin (no. *672*), who was created a cardinal on 22 June, N.S., of this year.

[4] '(One) of the ploughers with my heifer' (alluding to Judges, 14: 18; quoted already in nos. *1087*, *1523*). This is Father Bernard Lamy, author of *Harmonia sive Concordia Quatuor Evangelistarum*, 1689: no. *1119*. Here and in later letters Toinard probably alludes to Lamy's *Traité historique de l'ancienne Pâque des Juifs*, 1693 (L.L., no. 1664). Toinard sent Locke copies of the *Harmonia* and five or six other works by or relating to Lamy in January by Nelson: p. 289; Journal, 1 March 1698; L.L., nos. 292, 1661–2, 1665, 1667, 1669?, 2921.

[5] Toinard's Harmonia: nos. *1777*, etc.

[6] See p. 491.

On m'a voulu engager dans une compagnie pour le commerce d'une Riviere d'ou on tireroit des biens immenses si elle etoit en de bonnes mains come seroient celles des Anglois qui surpassent tous les Europeans en fait de colonie. C'est la Riviere du Senegal en Afrique.[1] Il y a sur la gauche et au bas de cete Riviere trois nations de Negres que l'on trouve en[a] la montant selon l'ordre qui suit. *Jalofes*, *Foûles*, *Mandingues*.[2] on n'en connoit point encore au dela. ces nations ont chacune leurs langues tres diferentes. Les Jalofes et les Foûles ne content continuement que jusques à *cinq*, et puis ils disent: *cing et un*, *cing et deux*, *cing et trois*, *cing et quatre*. Ils ont un mot pour *dix* come nous, et apres ils recommencent: *dix et un*, et c. Je nescay si je vous ay fait voir un Dictionaire Espagnol et *Guarani* que j'ay trouvé par hazard en Portugal.[3] cete langue est en usage depuis la R. de la Plate jusques à cele des Amazones, et l'on n'y conte que jusques à *quatre*; et pour *cing* on dit *une main*. Avez vous remarquè que les Grecs ont deux mots pour dire *dix*. c'est à savoir δέκα et κόντα. car ils disent τριάκοντα, τεσσαράκοντα, et c. et je nescay d'où est venu εἴκοσι pour *vint*, qui devroit etre, δυόκοντα. Il y a la même chose chez les Latins pour *dix*, qui est *decem*, et *ginta*. qui se trouve dans *triginta*, *quadraginta*, et c. Le viginti est come *biginta*, en quoi il n'y a pas une si grande irregularité que dans l'εἴκοσι des Grecs. on veut que je fasse une petite Dissertation la dessus. Les Mandingues qui est la troizieme nation au dessus de l'embouchûre du Senegal vont trafiquer avec les Anglois au bas de Gambie, partie par terre et partie par eau.

Comme[b] je n'avois pas intention de faire une si longue letre, j'avois sur la 4. page reserve de l'espace pour l'adresse, ainsi que vous le reconnêtrez par la situation des lignes que j'y ay ecrites avec des renvois.[c] me restant du blanc sur cete page, cela sera cause que je commenceray dez à present à vous être importun,

[a] *Here the fourth page of the letter starts. Toinard originally left space for the address, but eventually covered the whole page.* [b] *Here the fifth page of the letter starts, on a fresh leaf. Locke has inserted the date* 6 Dec. 97 [c] *The marks on pp. 3 and 4 to show the sequence of the text.*

---

[1] The Compagnie du Sénégal, which was reconstituted in 1696: P. Cultru, *Histoire du Sénégal*, 1910, pp. 63–5.

[2] I have not traced the source of Toinard's statement. For the three nations see J. Barbot in A. and J. Churchill, *Collection of Voyages*, vol. v, 1732, pp. 25–6, etc. The modern names are generally Wolof or Oulof, Fula (Peul), and Mandingo.

[3] Antonio Ruiz de Montoya, S.J., *Tesoro de la lengua Guaranni*, Madrid, 1639; *Arte, y Vocabulario de la lengua Guarani*, 1640; *Catecismo de la lengua Guarani*, 1640; all parts of the one work.

en vous priant de me mander pourquoi on ne met pas en usage le moien *Pro dulcorandâ aquâ salsâ*, dont il y a un livret in 12. Londini 1684.[1] M. Nelson dit que plus de cent personnes ont la machine necessaire pour cela, et je ne comprens pas comment on neglige une chose de cete importante.

L'autre est que dans quelques unes de vos letres de 1680. vous me parliez d'une machine pratiqueé à Londres pour aler contre le courant des rivieres. Vous m'en prometiez alors un dessin.[2] n'a ton point tenté de nouveau le vaisseau double du chevalier Petti?[3] Je suis parfaitement,

monsieur, Votre

Je loge au même endroit.

Address: For Mr John Locke at Mr Pawlings overagainst the plough in Little Lincolns Inne feilds London
Postmark: DE 6
Endorsed by Locke: Toinard 6 Dec. 97 Answered 25 Mar

2356. Locke to Edward Clarke, 6 December 1697 (2351, 2361)

B.L., MS. Locke b. 8, nos. 124, 123. Discoloured and torn. Printed in Rand, pp. 525–6.

Oates 6 Dec. 97

Dear Sir

I got hither safe the day I parted from you.[4] And did in a very short time finde the benefit of the air here. which has in a great measure taken off that horrible oppression which I had constantly upon my lungs in town. I now breath pretty easy whilst I sit still. And my nights passe without that panting for breath. which soe often tormented me in town, and made my life there not worth the keeping. Upon coughing or stiring I find the shortnesse of my breath. But I must not hope to be cured all at once and at this time of the year after I have foolishly lett it grow soe far upon me. After what I have sufferd in town tis heaven to be at soe much ease

[1] 'For sweetening salt-water.' For the book see no. *1087*.
[2] No. *594*, etc.
[3] See no. *470*. No fresh experiments are known after 1665.
[4] Locke was in town on 29 November and at Oates on 4 December. He did no attend the meetings of the Board of Trade on 29 November, 1 and 3 December.

as I thank god I am. And I could wish our Master[1] would trie what country air by the fires side with some few other little things would doe against ill lungs.

My Lady Masham would have writt to you by Sir Francis to thank you for your kindenesse in her businesse, but I hinderd her, to save your time telling her so and that you would beleive me in the case without the trouble of her writeing or your reading a letter

I here inclosed send you the true state of the account between me and Sir Steven Evance. Soe that there needs noe more now but his paying you the ballance and delivering up to you your two notes for the two eleven pounds and then you may deliver up Hayters note for the £50 which is in your hands, only I beg you that before you deliver it up, you cutt off all that is writ under it by Thomas,[2] ⟨For⟩[a] if he has Hayters note up he need h⟨av⟩e[a] noe more. I have noe thing to demand of him. Nor would be exposd to any claim or wrangle, from him. For I am well satisfied of the honesty of the man. And desire to be quite clear of him.

One thing I am in doubt about and would beg you to satisfie your self in before you setle this businesse and that is, whether upon those of the Exchequer notes, which were received into the Exchequer upon loan the interest was not allowed from their date to the time they were paid into the Exchequer. If soe, then it is over counted to me by Sir Steven. For the Exchequer will not pay it to me again and therefor Sir Steven must not count it to me as soe much interest due from the exchequer. And if interest be now due upon those bills from their date, and not from their receit into or issue again out of the exchequer, I doe not see to what purpose their receit into the Exchequer was indorsed, and the days from their date to that time counted. But this can better be resolvd by those versed in these matters than by any reasoning of mine.[3] I am

Dear Sir

Your most affectionate humble servant

J LOCKE

[a] *Page torn.*

[1] Probably William III, although his health at this time was not worse than usual. When Locke waited on the king on 23 January 1698 what he told Lady Masham about the interview was that the king wanted to discuss his own health: Institute of Historical Research (University of London), *Bulletin*, xl (1967), 215. It may have been the subject of the letter to Somers mentioned below: see p. 302.

[2] Probably Jeremy Thomas: p. 256.

[3] As interest did not accrue on Exchequer Bills while they were held by revenue collectors or by the Exchequer they were endorsed to show when they were acquired or paid by them: Dickson, p. 369.

My Lady gives her service to the Batchelor and I mine

I here inclosed send a letter to my Lord Chancellor.[1] Not that you need deliver it to him with your own hands. It is enough if you will doe me the favour to leave it with his porter if noe other businesse cary you to my Lord himself. I make bold to give you this trouble because I would be sure to have this letter come safe to him. Because what is in it must goe farther, and may possibly be expected

Address: For Edward Clarke Esquire member of Parliament at Westminster

Endorsed by Clarke: Mr. Lock with Sir Step: Evans his Account. And Directions thereupon, with a Letter inclosed to my Lord Chancellor, etc: Received per Sir F: M: the 7th. December 1697. Answered in parte the same day. Answered in further parte the 16th.

[Enclosure:]

1697	Sir Steven Evance Dr	
12 Nov 97	To a bill bearing date 6th of Aug: 95	£218–1–9
	To interest due upon the same bill at 5 per Cent being two years one quarter and 6 days	24–13–5
	To a bill bearing date 14 Oct 95	50–0–0
	To interest due upon the same for 2 years and 29 days at 5 per Cent	05–3–11
		297–19–1

1697	Sir Stephen Evance Cr	
12 Nov	By Exchequer Bills[2] deliverd to Mr Clarke and interest due upon them	271–19–8
	Remains due to me	25–19–5
		297–19–1
	If the two bills under Mr Clarkes hands which Sir Stephen Evance hath for £22 paid me be due to him then there will due to me only	£3–19–5

2357. CHRISTOPHER TILSON to LOCKE, 7 December 1697 (*2334*, *2720*)

B.L., MS. Locke c. 20, f. 198.

Sir

Mr Dodington and Mr Chaloner having signed the Order of Affirmation in the Cause of William Hucks with Sixteen Pounds

[1] Somers. He was created 'Baron Sommers of Evesham' on 2 December.
[2] p. 246.

Costs I have sent You the same enclos'd, and desire You to return it me again signed by the first opportunity, and am

Sir

Your most faithfull humble servant

CHRIS: TILSON

December 7th 1697

Address: These For John Locke Esqr at Sir Robert Masham's at Oates near Bishop's Stortford in Essex

Postmarks: DE 7; LV

Endorsed by Locke: C. Tilson 7 Dec. 97 The order sent back signed and inclosed to my Cosin King 10

2358. SIR WALTER YONGE to LOCKE, 9 December 1697 (*1401, 2383*)

B.L., MS. Locke c. 23, ff. 166–7.

London Dec. 9th. 1697.

Sir

Yesterday I received the favor of your kind letter from Sir Francis Masham, and this morning I deliver'd to our secretary[1] the bill of Lading for your friends books, which were before taken care of, the ship is now at the Key, and as soon as the books can be come at they shall be discharged with as little cost as may be, and deliver'd to Mr Bonville as you order.

I have been with Mr Popple about the Tutor you mention'd for Sir Richard Carew,[2] he saies he thinks 'tis Mr Skinner you mean who is a person he can answer for, if he be not too old to undertake such a charge, being upwards of three score, I beg the favor to know from you whether this is the Gentleman you meant, and if I can be any other way serviceable to you, your commands will alwaies oblige

Sir

Your most affectionate friend and humble servant

WALTER YONGE

My Wife returns you her humble service and thanks you for your

[1] Probably John Sanson, secretary to the Commissioners of the Customs *c.* 1692–1705: Chamberlayne; Luttrell, v. 545. Yonge was one of the Commissioners. The books were probably Coste's: Locke, Journal, 1 February.

[2] 1683–1703 (or 1704); fourth baronet 1692; of Antony, Cornwall: G.E.C., *Baronetage*, ii. 126.

kind remembrance; I bless God she is pretty well though she has now and then some little remains of her Chollick.

Address: For John Locke Esqr [at Oates, by Joslyn, Bishops Stortford] Frank Walter Yonge

Postmark: (London receiving office, defective)

Endorsed by Locke: Sir W. Yonge 9° Dec 97 Answered 3 Jan

2359. SAMUEL BOLD to AWNSHAM [and JOHN?] CHURCHILL, 15 December 1697 (*2278, 2568*)

B.L., MS. Locke c. 4, f. 17.

Steeple Decemb: 15th. 1697.

Worthy Sirs

I received the last week 12 of my Observations on the Animadversions etc.[1] There are some Errata's, but I suppose it is too late now to send an account of them. I pray you send one of them to Mr Ollife[2] if you can, or let one be delivered when He shal order It to be called for. and another for mr Webb, when He shal order It to be called for. I have run over the Bishop of Worcesters late Answer as it is called to mr Lock's second letter.[3] But if I can make a Judgement conc⟨er⟩ning[a] It, and upon such a hasty perusal, I think he does not unde⟨r⟩stand[a] mr Locks Essay, That what He hath writ is little other than downright sophistry, especially where He pretends to make the way of Idea's Inconsistent with It self. And I fancy his own Maxims, may be managed to his disadvantage, and wil reach to what He hath no mind they should. But how any man shal be rationally satisfied of the truth of His maxims but by observing the agreement or disagreement of those Ideas whereof they consist, or how any man shal be satisfied of the proof of anything by these maxims, any other way than by observing the agreement etc of these Ideas with what is to be proved, is not very clear to me, unless the Maxims must be taken up gratis, and

[a] *Page torn.*

---

[1] *Observations on the Animadversions (lately printed at Oxford) on . . . The Reasonableness of Christianity*, 1698. L.L., no. 376. For the *Animadversions* see pp. 112–13; for the manuscript of the *Observations*, pp. 145–6.

[2] Probably John Ollyffe, 1647–1717, who was rector of Almer, a dozen miles north of Steeple, from 1673 to 1694: *D.N.B.*

[3] *The Bishop of Worcester's Answer to Mr. Locke's Second Letter . . .*, 1698. Stillingfleet dates it from Worcester, 22 September 1697. L.L., no. 2790.

upon Authority, and deductions must be made from them afterwards without the help of Idea's, which I think will be a very peculiar way of Reasoning, and of coming to certainty. His Historical part I take to be the best, It affords some entertainment, but the greatest discovery It has yet made to me, is, that the several sorts of Philosophers, were at a loss, and did not really understand in what certainty of knowledg did consist. And what ever those (He speaks of) who talk'd of a Criterion, did make that to consist in, I suspect they could not place It in anything surer than the agreement or disagreement of Ideas is. which makes me a little wonder at his complaining for want of a Criterion, in mr Locks Essay. And his opposing other mens Ideas of things, to mr Lockes. And speaking of both parts of a Contradiction being true, when the Ideas are not the same. And several such things. but to help myself out, and get a better understanding of the Bishops meaning, I must when I have leisure, read his book over again, and bestow as much time upon his little book, as would have bin needful, if He had made it a great deal bigger, provided He had bin at the pains to have made his own thoughts in several places clearer, and had inserted fewer quotations, or have taken care that his quotations were really to his purpose, for I suspect some of these are not. Seeing his Lordship is so willing the controversy should End, It seem's something strange to me He should start new points. I am apt to think the Author of the Remarks on mr Locks Essay etc is He who writes the occasional letter, but who He is I do not know.[1] I am a little surprized, to find men of parts making such a stir, and scattering Jealousies, and putting such kind of questions, when I cannot perceive the least ground for their suspicions, and mythinks they might easily learn from the Essay to answer their own questions. What it is, that makes a Cluster of writers appear as it were just at the same time (and so many years after the publication of the Essay) against the Essay, I do not know.[2] But sure there is something at the bottom, which they do not yet speak out. Pardon this tryal and exercise of your patience, and I wil promise you not to trouble you to this degree for a while. give my

[1] The author of the *Remarks* is Thomas Burnet of the Charterhouse: p. 189, n. 1. He continued with *Second Remarks*, 1697, and *Third Remarks*, 1699. L.L., nos. 1795, 1799. The other piece may be *An Occasional Letter concerning Some Thoughts about a National Reformation*, 1698, of unknown authorship; alternatively Bold may mean *The Occasional Paper*, which is attributed to Richard Willis (*D.N.B.*); ten instalments were published in 1697–8. L.L., no. 2118 (nos. 1–6).

[2] Locke noticed this in February: p. 6; see also p. 243.

humble service to Mr Lock, and to the Author of the Reasonableness etc. I cannot but resent the treatment they have mett with for their most worthy labours with some Indignation. I am

your humble servant. S. B.

Address: To Mr Awnsham Churchill

Endorsed by Locke: S: Bold 15 Dec. 97

2360. WILLIAM MOLYNEUX to LOCKE, 18 December 1697 (*2339*, 2376)

The Carl H. Pforzheimer Library, New York. Transcribed from photostat. Printed in *Some Familiar Letters*, pp. 252–3. Answered by no. 2376.

Dublin. Dec. 18. 1697.

Dear Sir

Tis now above three Months since I heard from you, your last being of Sept. 11. You will therefore excuse my Impatience if I can forbear no longer, and send this meerly to Know, how you do. Tis an Anguishing thought to me, that you should be subject to the Common frailtys and Fate of Mankind; But it would be some alleviation to my trouble, that, if you are ill, I should know the Worst of it. This has so wholy taken up my Mind at present, that I have no Inclination to write One word More to you in this; but again to repeat my request to you, that you would let me know how you are, for till I know this, I am Dissatisfyd, I am extreamly uneasy; But for ever shall be

Your Most Affectionate Admirer and Devoted Servant

W: MOLYNEUX

Address: To John Locke Esquire at Mr Pawlings overagainst the Plough Inn in Little Lincolns Inn Fields London

Postmark: DE 29

Endorsed by Locke: W. Molyneux 18 Dec 97 Answered 10 Jan

2361. LOCKE to EDWARD CLARKE, 20 December 1697 (2356, 2367)

B.L., MS. Locke b. 8, no. 125. Printed in Rand, pp. 526–7.

Oates 20 Dec. 97

Dear Sir

I returne you my hearty thanks for your two letters of 16th and 18th which came just now to my hands. Tis an extraordinary kindenesse in your want of time, and your care of setleing the account with Sir Steephen is soe too. But I would not have it intrench too much upon your affairs a leisure hour in the holydays will doe it time enough

I read soe much of your two letters to my Lady as concerned her she is extremly sensible of your kindenesse in it and hopes now by your assistance to see an end of that vexatious businesse

I returne my thanks to Madam for the favour of hers, but have not time before this messenger goes to answer it. Pray give my service to her and my love to my wife

My service also and thanks to the Batchelor for his kinde letter. and pray let him know that haveing now an oportunity by a private hand, there come to him the half dozen dried apples he desired. I sent noe more to him because he desired noe more. But my Lady haveing given me her whole stock which is nine more, they are all at his service if he pleases. and I shall keep them for him, till he refuses them and till I hear the[a] 6 I now send are arived well conditioned and unsquobd.[1] I am

Dear Sir

Your most affectionate and most humble servant

J Locke

Address: For Edward Clarke Esquire these

Endorsed by Clarke: Mr. Lock touching his Affayre with Sir Stephen Evans etc. Received the 20th. December 1697. Answered the 23th.

2362. Martha Lockhart to Locke, [20 or 21 December 1697] (2253, 2365)

B.L., MS. Locke c. 15, ff. 72–3. Locke's date is probably a date of receipt; in that case the date is likely to be 20 December, when the Civil List was in committee. Alternatively the date would be 21 December, when the Civil List was voted by the commons. Answered by no. 2365.

Sir

Ime very glad to hear the country air has had its usial success in restoring you to your health which I doe heartily wish to you the continuence of. I delay'd writing to you till now having undertood by my cosin Cutts (who I now find was [b] intended me

[a] *Or* these; *page torn.* [b] *Page torn and faded.*

[1] To squab is to squash or squeeze flat: *O.E.D.*

the favour to let [a] from you [a] of the tally: which soon after you went came safe to my hands. had you thought it convenient for you I can foresee no danger could have hap'ned in trusting my diamonds with some frend of your's here who in your absence might have receiv'd the tally from me and dilliver⟨d⟩[a] them to me. tho I don't pretend to have a nice understanding in bussiness Yet I think I'me pretty sure there could ⟨be no⟩[a] hazard to you in receiving a tally ⟨imm⟩ediatly[a] worth 200 ll. for a debt of ⟨t⟩hat[a] sumn accounting it as a pawn or payment which you pleas. and that if you would not have let it been transferd to your use in your absence, the delay Could have been of no consequence. as indied my not being Mistress of my diamonds is to me, for the reasons I have formerly told you. but I shan't trouble you ⟨further⟩[a] with this only desire you'le let ⟨me⟩[a] kno when and in [a] you'le receive my debt. the 200 ll I owe You. whither or no you'le take the tally I've now ready and I think can't but be for your service or if you'de rather have it in mony when and where It must be paid in. I desire I may kno what intrest ⟨is⟩[a] due both on this and the 300 ll since ⟨t⟩he[a] mony I last paid to Mr Churchill ⟨and⟩[a] what you set off for the mony I laid ⟨ou⟩t[a] for my Lady and Cosen Masham, and I shall take care to pay it. I'me sorry to be force't to trouble you so long with these trifles. for news the parliament has been so kind to the civell list to day that I hope twill raise the credit of us Courtiers with the country gentlemen 'tis hoped now that the court will be able to give weighty argument's to Convince the stiffest of them when they happen to differ. the King of france has writ a very kind letter (writ and directed with his own hand) to his Brother of great Britain on his Grandson's marriage;[1] the Duke of St Alban's[2] go's imediatly with the Kings compliment. I wish you a very merry Xmas and am Sir

Your very humble servant

M L

many services to my Lady and all her familly. from me and my Cosen Cutts.

by way of postscript Mrs Pasmore is in great mortification he

[a] *Page torn and faded.*

---

[1] Louis, duke of Burgundy, married Mary Adelaide of Savoy on 7 December N.S.; William received Louis XIV's letter on 19 December: Luttrell.

[2] Charles Beauclerk, Charles II's elder son by Nell Gwynne: *D.N.B.*

Mr Waters having been to wait on Mr Popple he discourages him to hope for any thing that office she gives her humble duty to you and hopes you will not forget him.

I hope you hold me releas'd of my promis to you concerning Mr Pauling who has never been here

Endorsed by Locke: M Lockhart 21 Dec. 97 Answered 24

2363. THOMAS TENISON, archbishop of Canterbury, to LOCKE, 21 December 1697 (2031, 2378)

B.L., MS. Locke c. 19, ff. 184–5. Answered by no. 2378. The letter relates to Edwards's *Brief Vindication*: pp. 149–50.

Dec. 21. 97.

Sir

Dr. James the ViceChancellor of Cambridge came to me together with the Bishop of Ely[1] in order to the giving you satisfaction about the Imprimatur: but, upon inquiry, I found you had bin gone, about a fortnight, into the Country.

Dr. James assur'd me that, before he gave the Imprimatur, he had order'd the blotting out of divers passages, and particularly that about Oats-Hall: That Mr Edwards had written to him that He had smooth'd many things; and that He himself perus'd the book with the less care, because the doctor had acquainted him with the Approbation of dr. Beaumont, tho his hand was not then to the Imprimatur; But, it seems, the Professors sonn[2] had said some such thing to Dr. Edwards.

D. Edwards was forbidden to print the Imprimatur at London;[3] but, notwithstanding, did it; displeasing, thereby, the Licencers, and the Chancellor himself the duke of Sommersett[4] who is, by no means satisfyd, with that practice.

Whitehall (they say) was never mention'd, nor the Horrid word you told me of:[5] but there was mention of the Seraglio at

[1] Dr. Simon Patrick: no. *1912*.

[2] Probably Charles Beaumont, vicar of Stapleford, Cambridgeshire, 1686: Venn.

[3] While the Vice-Chancellor's imprimatur might be recognized at the universities as no more than a commendation, in London it might be regarded as an attempt to infringe the liberty of the press.

[4] Charles Seymour, sixth duke, chancellor of the university from 1689 to 1748.

[5] According to Locke both the passage and the word were in Edwards's text at some stage: p. 300.

Oats, which gave great offence and was orderd to be struck out. This is the summ of what was said by d. James.

God give you Health. I am

Sir

Your Assured Fr:

THO: CANTUAR:

Address: For Mr. Lock [at Oates, by Joslyn, Bishops Stortford]

Postmark: DE 21

Endorsed by Locke: A.Bp: Tenison 21 Dec. 97 Answered 15 Jan

2364. NATHANIEL HODGES to LOCKE, 21 December 1697 (*1932*)

B.L., MS. Locke c. 11, f. 216.

Dear Sir

According to the Genius of the age I have been at least twelve moneths in the wise projection, and promising prospect of a journey to London, in order to save me the trouble of writing a Letter. And having now safely reached, as I thought, to the end of my design, I find my politiques too short, and am forced to doe that at last, which might have been done so long agoe with so much more safety to my credit, as well as satisfaction to my mind. A great part of the businesse of both, was to bring an old man, though in a very different way of addresse, to visit an ancient freind. Though I would not have chosen the present method, yet it will serve in the best sense to bring the old man, the old freind to you, the more unweildy part of the composition onely being left behind. Yet so it is, I know not how, the dead weight me thinks, would fain come along; and although almost in the grave, seem's unwilling at any rate to learn the way of separation from a beloved companion it hath long drudged on with in a dirty road. And me thinks upon this present perception I am ready to conclude that though sure the freindship of virtuous minds can never die, yet, that a resurrection alone can be of force to reunite freinds together after their long last taking leave. You must not wonder at this odd reflexion so much out of the way, I was gotten so near to you in my thoughts that I had almost forgotten I was writing, and as our freind Sancho saith, where I thought of my Dapple, could not forbear to speak of him.[1] If I had been talking with you, you would have forgiven the impertinence, and it may be have set me right in a notion I have a great mind should be true, viz That the reunion of whole freinds, as well as the whole man, will be a part of happinesse else where, as here it is. Since you are not near enough to doe the one, I doubt not but you will be so kind, as to doe the other. I have met with a learned man who would rifle me of this pleasing imagination, and like one fallen into the hands of theeves, cry'd out upon a suddain without thinking where I was, or whether it were to any purpose. When I began, my meaning was to have told you of the pleasing conversation I have held with you when you thought not of it, in those mastering thoughts of things in which you have so much obliged your old freinds, and made you so many new, and how many euge's[2] I have met with quod amicum haberem etc.[3] I have been told of one who hath read the reasonablenesse of Christianity three score times over.

If I had had the good fortune to have met you here, I had a great deal of this sort of chatte to have entertained you with, which having not the same sound in a Letter as it would have had from word of mouth, I will content my self to keep close to the businesse in hand, of letting you know that as I have been ever your true, so that I am now in more than one sense your old freind, and

faithfull humble servant

N. HODGES

London December: 21. 1697.

Address: For John Locke Esquire

Endorsed by Locke: N Hodges 21 Dec. 97 Answered 1 Jan 9$\frac{8}{9}$

Further endorsed by Locke: N: Hodges

2365. LOCKE to MARTHA LOCKHART, 24 December 1697 (*2362*, *2517*)

B.L., MS. Locke c. 24, ff. 185–6. Draft. Answers no. *2362*.

Oates 24 Dec 97

Madam

I returne you my thanks for the concerne you expresse for my health, which had brought me soe low before I came out of town that it left me little heart to thinke of writeing to any body,

[1] See no. 1900.

[2] Commendations; for the use of the word in English see *O.E.D.*

[3] 'On having a friend' (of such distinction).

much lesse to promise to write about a businesse that I had then noe prospect would come to any thing in my days at least it seemd in vain to talke any more about it till I heard the tally was in your power and that you could dispose of it. These circumstances made me little thinke of writeing however Mrs Cuts[a] might mistake me. I neglected not for all that to take care to be informed what might be done in the case in my absence whenever you got the Tally again in your hand. You seem to me full of complaint in your letter of how much I have neglected to doe what I might have done for you that you force me against my temper to a justification of my self to a person whom I thought I had never been neglectfull towards in any thing wherein I had been capable to serve her. As to the present matter to shew my ready compliance with any desire of yours give me leave to say that the things you tell me I might have left in to⟨wne⟩[b] in some freinds hands etc: have been formerly at your instance brought to town and that with out[c] hazard two or three times, and when I have had it in town and seen you almost every day for above a quarter of a year togeather, noe use at all has been made of it nor soe much as a word spoke of it all that time and soe it was brought to town only to be caried back again with the same hazard. This seemd a little strange to me but you know I never complaind of it. When I was last in town you proposed to me the Tally. I informed my self of the nature of it as soon as I could and then told you I would take it and orderd my affairs accordingly and expected it. But it was delaid and delaid till at last I produceing the forme of the assigenment for your hand I was told you had made an other use of this particular Tally of your three and it was not then in your power: but you should have it this day and an other day and a third day: all which I patiently waited not without great inconvenience to my health which[d] I sufferd very much in all that time and at last came out of town without it: For I must tell you that I had come away a great deale sooner had I not staid on purpose to put an end to this businesse. Of all this I complained not though it was very prejudicial to my affairs and made me ridiculous to some whom I had concerned in it. But still you tell me that I might have left such order that it might have been done in my absence. But haveing

[a] *Or* Mr Cuts [b] *Blotted.* [c] *Doubtful reading. Locke wrote first* some *or* noe; *then apparently deleted this word and wrote* small; *then deleted* small *and the preceding word if he had not already done so, and substituted the present word.* [d] *Followed by* made me *deleted.*

consulted as knowing men in the case as any I know in England, they assured me that It cannot be done in my absence unlesse I can get some body to sweare what they doe not know (and such acquaintance I have not that I can aske that of) for unlesse it be sworne within ten days after the transfer that it is bought at noe higher a discount than six per Cent: the Tally is forfeited.[1] You aske me whether I will take the Tally for my money: I tell you yes and that I have for that purpose orderd my affairs accordingly, and that it is not my fault that it is not already done. If you please I will hence forth looke upon the Tally as mine and will come to London as soon as I can to make it mine in the formes. If this will not satisfie you pray send me word what will, for I am willing to doe whatever is possible to content you.

You demand of me what interest is due since the money paid to Mr Churchill. I answer as much as from our Lady day last which is now three quarters of a year. The money I was to pay you for my Lady and Mrs Esther Masham is £5–18–0 which I allow as soe much received of you. The remainder that is due to me and my Cosin Bonville you may if you please let alone till I come to town as well as you did when I was there last, but you reserved it to be done when you transferd the Tally and soe make one worke of all Togeather and I thought you had reason. If you have the money ready by you designed for this purpose as you seeme by your letter, you may please to lay it by for me if you had rather pay it out of your hands I will endeavour to finde a way to content you in that too.

I returne you my humble thanks for the news you did me the favour to send me, I cannot pay you in that kinde from hence But wish you a very merry Christmas and am glad the parliament has done soe much to make it soe.[2]

My Lady Masham and her family returne their service and thanks for your remembrance of them. My Lady upon my giveing her your service said she should be very glad to see you here. but it lookes like a jest to say anything more of it. I am

Madam

Your most humble and most obedient servant

JOHN LOCKE

Endorsed by Locke: J L to Mr Lockhart 24 Dec. 97

[1] This was enacted by 8 and 9 Wm. III, c. 20 (royal assent 1 April 1697), §§ 57–8: Dickson, *Financial Revolution*, pp. 353–6.

[2] By the vote on the Civil List on 21 December: p. 273 n.

2366. JOHN WYNNE, later bishop of Bath and Wells, to LOCKE, 27 December 1697 (*2330, 2386*)

B.L., MS. Locke c. 23, ff. 131–2.

London dec. 27. 97

Honoured Sir

My Lord[1] arrived here last Sunday was sevennight, having had a very good passage, though he was forc'd to stay long, first for wind and then for water: for we were frozen up att Rotterdam for about a fortnight. I expected to have heard farther from you in reference to the Acta Eruditorum etc which I had sent for to Mr Wetstein; whose answer to me I sent enclos'd in a letter to you, And having heard nothing from you since, I did not know what I could do more without farther direction. The Books that I bought for you I have deliverd into Mr Churchill's hands, of which I shall subjoin a catalogue with the prices.[2] I promis'd my self the satisfaction of seeing you upon our return into England, and am very sorry to ⟨fin⟩d[a] my self disappointed: But I hope to find some other oppor⟨tun⟩ity[a] of paying you the just respects and acknowledgments which I owe you. I have mett with all the satisfaction that I could have desir'd in my Lord's service, and have receiv'd allready many obligeing marks of his Lordship's favour, with the kind promises of more when opportunity shall serve, of all which I am very sensible how great a share I owe to you. soon after the holidaies I intend to take my leave of my Lord, and to return to Oxon: where I shall be very forward to lay hold of any occasion of letting you know with what respect and service I am

Honoured Sir

your most oblig'd humble servant

JOHN WYNNE.

	guilders	st	
Plutarch 2. Vol.	—30. –	00	
Tacitus 4. Vol.	22:	00	I had 11. guilders
Bails Diction.	30:	00	for a pound
Acta Eruditorum etc	00:	15	English.
Moliere ———	00:	15	
	83.	10	

[a] *Page torn.*

[1] Pembroke.

[2] For the various books see pp. 227–9.

2367. *Edward Clarke, 28 December 1697*

Address: To The Honoured John Locke Esqre att Sir Francis Massam's att Oates in Essex.

Postmark: DE 28

Endorsed by Locke: J: Wynne 27 Dec. 97 Answered Jan. 3

Noted by Locke on the blank sheet facing the body of the letter:

$$\frac{11}{7} \quad \frac{83}{.77} \qquad \frac{11}{7} \quad \frac{83}{.6} \quad 10$$

$$.6$$

£7:12–0

2367. Locke to Edward Clarke, 28 December 1697 (2361, 2369)

B.L., MS. Locke b. 8, no. 126. Discoloured. Printed in Rand, pp. 527–8.

Oates 28 Dec. 97

Dear Sir

The holydays[a] put our messenger[1] and consequently the course of our letters out of Order which is the cause I returne my Ladys and my thanks to you for our respective concernes in your two letters of the 23 and 25th, not by the post but by the Carrier

I am obleiged to you for being at this new trouble with Sir Stephen. The £1–13–0 for the use of the £22 must be allowed him, for it was omitted in my calculation of the interest. But he must deliver up your two notes for the two eleven pounds to you. And pray let noething remain on Hayters note for the £50. but let it be torne off, and the endorsement (, if that be necessary too,) blotted out before you deliver it up, that there may be noe more matter of dispute with this Gent. But you receiveing the remaining £2–6–5 there may be a full end. I have not sent back the two accounts you sent me inclosed because I see noe need there will be of them now that I allow the £1–13–0 which is the difference between them: and am not very sure of the safe conveyance by the Carrier, Though I take this first oportunity to send you my answer to your question, that it may come to your hand and the businesse be ended whilst your holydays last. Our fires side give their

[a] *Or* holy days

[1] Presumably between Oates and Bishops Stortford.

services to yours. I write this in hast and am Mrs Clarkes, my Wives, the Batchelors, and your

most humble servant

J LOCKE

Pray as soon as this businesse is ended with Sir Stephen Let Mr Churchill have such of my Exchequer[a] notes[a] as will serve best to pay my tax which in his last he writes me word is now demanded of him

Address: For Edward Clarke Esquire these.

Endorsed by Clarke: Mr. Lock to Receive the 2l: 6s. 5d. Ballance of Sir Stephen Evans, And give Exchequer Notes to Mr. Churchill to pay his Tax etc: Received the 29th December 1697. Answered the 30th. in parte.

2368. JOHN BONVILLE to LOCKE, 29 December 1697 (*2235, 2374*)

B.L., MS. Locke c. 4, f. 82b.

London Dec the 29th: 1697

Honoured Cousin

Sir This day I have Got home Too boxes which came From Holland, Sir walter young ordered Mr Savig, I sopose he Is Their secretary, To send om to my house,[1] They have not yet given me The Account of The Charges, only I paid The Carman 2s, I beleeve the boxes wayes betweene 3 or 4 cwt, my wife have Inquired for orenges, There Is non good Tell next week, If Then they are good And at your price I will send you som, I have Allsoe paid Mrs Slade Twenty shillings. I heare mr Firmin Is ded,[2] But not Leaveing soe good A Carecter as was Imagened by most, he was, as I understand, A man much confided In, by A great many of Charitable Gentlemen and others, for the Reliffe of the poore but Inricht him self There by, If This be true or noe I know not, but This I doe Know An Am Asured of it, He that Is faithfull To the death, shal

[a] *Substituted for* bank bills ?

[1] See p. 269. Probably Richard Savage, at this time Plantation Clerk in the Customs House; secretary in succession to Sanson 1705–10: Chamberlayne; Luttrell v. 545; vi. 540. [2] He died of a fever on 20 December

receive A Crowne of Life, My Wife with my son Gives Their Hearty Sarvis to you

I Am

Deare Cousin your Faithfull Kinsman And Humble Sarvant

JNO: BONVILLE:

Address: For Mr Locke [at Oates, by Joslyn, Bishops Stortford]

Postmark: DE 30

Endorsed by Locke: J:Bonville 29 Dec 97 Answered Jan. 10

2369. LOCKE to EDWARD CLARKE, 30 December 1697 (2367, *2371*)

B.L., MS. Locke b. 8, no. 127. Discoloured. Printed in Rand, pp. 528–9. Answered by no. *2371*.

Oates 30 Dec 97

Dear Sir

To send you my answer as soon as I could (our ordinary messenger faileing last post) I ventured it by the Carrier but not knowing whether that might come safe to your hands I repeat it here again. Viz That the £1–13–0 for interest for the £22– must be allowed to Sir Steph: Evance For in the casting up the interest due to me I tooke in the whole sum for the whole time not considering that that £22– was paid almost a year and an half before, I say almost 18 months because he has made it full 18 Months but tis not soe much short as need any new calculation for it. Soe that you must receive of him as the Ballance due to me £2–6–5 and then the notes on both sides being deliverd up (care being first taken that noe thing writ under or indorsed on Hayters for the £50– to me be left there untorne off or unefaced, which may cause me any trouble) I hope I have forever done with that Gent:

I hear there is a bill goeing on in your house about the hammerd money[1] cannot there be a clause put into it to obleige by some penalty the Tellers of the exchequer to receive and pay by weight as well as by tale and to obleige them and all the receivers of the severall branches of his Majesties revenue to cut all false peices of milled money that are counterfeit coin or clipd. If these two things be not some way or other provided for this session I fear

[1] It had its first reading on 21 December It received the royal assent on 14 January (9 Wm. III, c. 2).

you will be over run again very quickly with false and clipd coin which you will not get out of again a second time, for I finde that that sort of ware is made a pace and spread every where. What doe you thinke of makeing the penalty on the Teller or his underofficer that does it, to pay double the sum he shall take a receit for before he has weighd it or if weighing it it be not that full weight which the law shall require

I shall take care of the grafts when the season comes

Pray give the inclosed with my service to Mrs Clarke. I wish her and you and your whole fires side a happy new year. I am

Dear Sir

Your most affectionate humble servant

J Locke

My Lady gives her service and wishes a happy new year to you and yours.

Endorsed by Clarke: Mr. Lock to Receive 02l: 06s: 05d: Ballance of Sir Step: Evans his Account etc: Received New-yeares day 1697. Answered Ditto:

2370. Mrs. Frances St. John to Locke, 30 December [1697] (*1806, 2524*)

B.L., MS. Locke c. 18, ff. 50–1. Year from Locke's endorsement.

December the 30

It was a very great addition to my Joy, that from your own kinde hand, I should reseive the account of your having in any degree, recovered that ill staite of health you was under at your going out of town, for which I could not but be extreemly troubled

It being a generall misfortune that your streingth will not permitt, without so great Injury to your self, a longer stay in that plaice wherin you are capable of doing so great servis to the Publick, tho' in what soever Corner, of the earth, faite disposes of Good Mr Lock, he will ever be that person, by whome others may benifitt, as I have expeirenced tho' not with such an improv'ment as might be expected under so great an Advantidg in your good Conversation, the reflection of which gives me a pleasant satisfaction, and had great reason to Lament my misfortuan of missin you both hear and at your own Lodgings those few opertunity

I could get for attempting it, but wish I could make you a vissitt att your chimney Corner were I might Laugh with you, for I promiss I would have no design upon you for runing a race tho' I wish you were able for your own sake:

I am not able to answer those many kinde things My D Father has said to me in his letter, and a seccond part of which I reseived from Cosen Masham, but will reffer my self to your own goodness to beleive how much oblidged I think my self to you for retaining so kinde a rememberence of me whilst self Interist must ingaig me to Love and Value so kinde a Friend as your self, for I must acknowlidg a pride, in that Title by which I desire to Conclud my self your adopted Daughter,

and your most oblidged Humble Servant

FRA ST JOHN

I beg my servis to Lady Masham to whome I shall ever acknowlidg my self obliged very much

Mr St John[1] and all hear are your servants, we are not yet without fears of good Sir Walter[2] who is often ill

Address: For John Lock Esq'r [at Oates, by Joslyn, Bishops Stortford]
Postmark: DE 30
Endorsed by Locke: F: St John 30 Dec. 97

2371. EDWARD CLARKE to LOCKE, 1 January 1698 (2369, 2379)

B.L., MS. Locke c. 6, f. 132. Printed in Rand, pp. 529–30. Answers no. 2369; answered by no. 2379.

New-yeares-day 169$\frac{7}{8}$

Deare Sir,

I have only time to Return you Mrs. Clarke's, The Batchelor's, and my hearty Thanks for your obleigeing Letter by Sir Francis, Which, I Received from Him this morning at the Coffee-house, and the Inclosed were imediately Delivered as Directed

I[a-] yesterday settled your Affayre with Sir Stephen in every particular according to your Directions, and Received the l:06s:05d. Ballance due to you:[-a]

[a-a] *Marked by Locke for attention.*

[1] The writer's husband.

[2] Her father-in-law. He survived until 1708.

I will Doe All I can to make such a Provision as you suggest for the Cutting and Distroying of all Base, Counterfeite, and unlawfully Diminish'd-money, And for obleigeing the Tellers in the Exchequer, and All other Receivers of the Kings Revenues and Taxes to Receive and Pay by Weight as well as by Tale, And doe hope for better successe then in the severall Attempts I have formerly made to the same purpose:

May your health and strength bee Renewed with the New-yeare, And may all other Blessings Attend you that this World can afford, Mrs Clarke, and all mine joyne with mee herein, And in the like good wishes to my Lady; I am Hers and

Your most Affectionate Faithfull servant

EDW: CLARKE:

Address: These, For John Locke Esqr. [at Oates, by Joslyn, Bishops Stortford]
Frank: Edw: Clarke:

Postmarks: IA 1; GC
Endorsed by Locke: E: Clarke 1 Jan $9\frac{7}{8}$ Answered 16

2372. LOCKE to CORNELIUS LYDE, 5 January 1698 (2332, *2382*)

The Pierpont Morgan Library, New York. Written by an amanuensis apart from the date, the subscription, and two corrections, which are all written by Locke. Transcribed from Xerox print. Draft in B.L., MS. Locke c. 26, ff. 81–2. There are several deletions in the draft. It is accompanied also in Locke's hand and on the same sheet, by statements of his accounts with various tenants. These are not printed here. Answered by no. *2382*.

Oates 5 Jan 169

Sir

Whilst I was in town want of time and health hinderd me from peruseing your account But haveing got a little more leisure since I came into the Country I have at last done it and have here again sent it you drawn into a plain and easy Method wherein any error will presently be made appear. There is onely one thing wanting which is the several dates or days of the Month and Year[a]– where you–[a] received or paid any thing, which are absolutely necessary to the keeping of an account clear and should never be omitted

[a–a] *MS.* Year wherein / wherein you

but I could not adde them because you had not set them down in your papers, onely the times when you paid the two sums for me to Mr. Clarke I have set down in the forme they should be, because I could finde them, in his account with me. Upon the Ballance of the whole account as I have drawn it up I finde you received 4s more than you have paid besides the 3s. that is due from Jos: Barnes, which I have made him Debtor for and not you: for you ought not to charge your self, nor to be charged with any Money before you have receiv'd it. Soe that the whole difference between our two accounts is £0–7s.–od But tis possible the mistake may be in the Charge of the sums you have received from my tennants made by me espetially those from Veale and Barnes. for you haveing not set down in your account either the time when, or the Sum which you at any time received from them, but seting down their full years Rent as paid either in money or bills, I was fain to see what was the overpluss of their rents above their Disbursments and that I have charged on you as received by you in Money, and soe possibly have made some mistake that way, though I have taken all the Care I could to avoid any error. If there be any error you by your book will be able easily to finde it, and shew me where it is. I hope you will have noe difficulty in understanding the method I have here put the account in, because it is that which is found easiest and therefore generally made use of in all accounts. But if you finde any difficulty in it I leave you to your own way, onely I beg the favour of you that without troubleing your self to set down what the Rent is, you will onely for the future set down what you receive for me in money, and what you pay, and the time when, as alsoe a Copy of the Bills which you receive of my tenants that you allow, and the time they deliver them to you and if there be in them the payments of a runing Charge, that the time be specified how far they have paid for example where it is said by 3 quarters tax paid to the King if the Tennant added *ending such a time* there could then be noe mistake in his accounts afterwards concerning that matter.

You will finde that Tho: Sommers is charged in my account here sent, as Debtor to me 25° Aprill 1695. £1..2s..7d. for arrears unpaid. This if I did not mention in the Rent roll which I at first sent you I ought to have mentioned it, as severall others which were then in arrear to me, which I must beg the favour of you to speak to them for, though it was due before the time that you began to doe me this favour. Those arıears were as followeth, as you may see in the account

Tho: Summers	£1.. 2s..7d	
William Gullocke	£2.. 5..3	
El: Hopkins ...	—..11..6	
David Harol.	—.. 1..—	

The $\frac{1}{12}$ of Tho: Sommers's due for the payments of the year ending 25.° Mar: 96. he has made to be but 12s..6d. which by my account is three shillings short of what it should be. What was paid that Year, of which he is to pay one penny in a shilling, was as followeth.

The Ks. tax	£4.. 1s..2d
Poor	3.. 6..8
Lords Rent	1..19..—
	9.. 6..10

Now $\frac{1}{12}$ of £9..6.– is by my account £–..15s..6. and soe I have charged him in my account and consequently William Gullock who is to pay $\frac{1}{6}$ which is double. I have charged £1..11..–. But I fear Sir I have tired you too much, but it is to make every thing the easier hereafter for when once it is setled in a method every thing will lye plain[a] to be seen at first view as you may observe by the included account in which there can be noe mistake, but what will presently shew it self, if the Sums paid and received be right set down with their respective times. One thing more the perusall of your account puts me in minde to mention to you: I doe not finde that you have paid any thing to[b] Pope for the little slip in the common mead that I used to rent of him. I must desire you to pay him ⟨to⟩[c] our Lady day last and to let him know I rent it of him noe longer than till that time. I beg your pardon for the severall troubles I give you and am

Sir

Your most humble servant

JOHN LOCKE

[a] *Doubtful reading.* [b] *Followed by* the *apparently expunged.* [c] *An indecipherable symbol; word supplied from the draft.*

2373. NICOLAS TOINARD to LOCKE, 6/16 January 1698 (*2355, 2375*)

B.L., MS. Locke, c. 21, f. 190. The letter and the books sent with it were carried by John Nelson, who forwarded them to Locke on 23 February: pp. 326–7, 357–8. Answered by no. 2412.

+

A Paris Ce 16. Jan. 98.

Je vous ay deja marqué, monsieur, par voie d'Holande l'obligation que je vous avois non seulement de l'honneur de votre souvenir mais encore de ceque vous m'aviez procuré la connoissance de M. Nelson. Ses belles qualitéz et les bons ofices qu'il a rendus aux Canadiens François etoient venus il y a longtems jusques à moy, parceque j'ay toujours etes curieux de tout cequi a relation aux colonies. ainsi ce ne m'a pas eté un petit plaisir de jouïr de l'entretien d'un aussi galant homme qu'est m. Nelson, qui m'a apris des choses dont j'ay une extrême satisfaction parcequ'elles vous regardent: et comme je scay que je ne vous suis pas tout à fait indiferent, je vous reitere ici que le texte de l'ouvrage pour lequel vous avez marqué tant d'estime, est entierement achevé en 136. pages. Les Preface, Notes et Tables iront leur train.[1]

Plusieurs gens ont ecrit sur la principale question qui a donné ocasion à ceque vous en avez vu, et comme l'Auteur qui aravit in vitula meâ[2] a trouvé diferens contradicteurs contre lesquels il sest defendu par six reponses je vous envoie tout cequ'il a fait en ce genre la avec quelques ecris qui ont éte faits sur ce sujet la, dont les autres ne valent pas la peine d'etre lus.

J'ay ajouté une Relation d'un voiage François fait au Detroit de Magellan, dont l'Auteur est un jeune homme de ma connoissance.[3] Mons. D'Iberville, Gentilhomme François Canadien de Monreal, en pouroit bien faire de belles de la Baye de Hudson où il a eté quatre fois par mer, et trois fois par les terres et rivieres. Je l'exhorte à cela. Il est ⟨tres⟩[a] particulier de m. Nelson, qu'il a connu en Canada, et c'est lui qui prit l'eté dernier le port de ce nom.[4] Ils se rencontrèrent avant hier à me rendre visite.

[a] *MS.* dres?

[1] The Harmonia.

[2] Father Bernard Lamy: p. 264.

[3] François Froger (1676–1715; *N.B.G.*), *Relation d'un voyage fait en 1695, 1696 et 1697 aux côtes d'Afrique, détroit de Magellan . . . par M. de Gennes*, Paris, 1698. The identification from Locke's Journal, 1 March 1698. L.L., no. 1190. There were several later editions.

[4] Pierre Lemoyne, sieur d'Iberville, 1661–1706: *Dict. Canadian Biog.* He captured Port Nelson, alternatively Fort York, in what is now the province of Manitoba, on 13 September 1697, N.S.

Je vous recommande deux instructions, l'une touchant l'Aqua salsa dulcorata qu'aucun Prince ny etat ne devroit negliger, et l'autre touchant la machine qui aloit sur la Tamise contre la marée. Vous m'en aviez promis autrefois une Description faite par Mr Hook.[1] Je souhaite que vous soiez encor plus longtems à vous aquiter de votre parole qu'il n'y en a que vous me l'aviez fait esperer, et que je sois en etat en ce tems la de vous en faire souvenir une seconde fois. En atendant je demeure parfaitement et tres sincerement, Monsieur, Votre tres humble—

Monsieur de Tilmont Auteur de quatre volumes in 4. de l'*Histoire des Empereurs*, et de quatre autres vols. aussi in 4. intituléz *Memoires pour servir à l'Histoire Ecclesiastique*, mourut ici le 10. de ce mois apres une maladie de peu de jours.[2] Il m'avoit fait present de ces exemplaires et je lui dis au dernier: *Semper ego acceptor tantùm, nunquam-ne reponam*,[3] et je me prometois[a] de lui donner dans quelque tems Du Grec et du Latin pour le François dont il m'avoit regalé, mais Dieu en a disposé autrement. Il etoit bien plus jeune que moy, tres homme de bien et personne d'une condition tres distinguée. Il laisse mons. son Pere agé de quatre vint dix ans et d'une trempe d'esprit admirable.

Il parêtra bientost une belle Edition Gr-L. de St Athanase par les PP. Benedictins.[4] Le Principal Auteur est fort de mes amis, et qui a fait une grande recherche des Exaples d'Origene, qu'il peut presque donner entiers sur les Pseaumes, Je lui donnerai ceque j'en ay ramassé.[5] Drusius n'a pu tout voir.[6]

Noted by Locke: Toinard 16 Jan $9\frac{7}{8}$ Answered Mar. 25

[a] *Altered from* promets

---

[1] No. 656.

[2] L. S. Le Nain de Tillemont, born in 1637, son of Jean Le Nain, who died on 9 February, N.S., of this year, aged 85: *N.B.G.* The *Histoire* as far as Jovian was published at Paris in 1690–7. The *Mémoires*, also originally published at Paris in quarto, started publishing in 1693.

[3] 'Am I always to be a receiver only and never to retaliate?' Varied from Juvenal i. 1, which has *auditor* for *acceptor*, referring to the endless recitations of their compositions by aspiring authors to circles of friends invited for the auditions.

[4] The edition published this year by the Congregation of St. Maur.

[5] Bernard de Montfaucon: *N.B.G.* He published his edition of the *Hexapla* of Origen in 1713.

[6] This probably refers to *In Psalmos Davidis Veterum Interpretum quæ exstant Fragmenta* . . ., which Drusius published in 1581.

2374. JOHN BONVILLE to LOCKE, 8 January 1698 (*2368, 2391*)

B.L., MS. Locke c. 4, f. 80.

London January the 8th $9\frac{7}{8}$

Honoured Cousin

Sir sinc my Last in which I gave you Account of the Arivall of 2 Cases of books: The palace of Whitehall Is Laid In Ashes.[1] It was to Late before we hard of it, otherwise I and my son Would been there to help mrs Lockhart, This day I have sent by Lenham $\frac{1}{2}$ cwt of orenges I hope they will pleas you. They cost with the basket: 5s: 3d. I have This day paid the Custom house Charges for the 2 Cases, Twenty Eight shillings and six penc, I Bless God we Are all well at presant, God Grant The same blessing Ever To you, of which I shall be very Glad to heare, I Am

Deare Cousin your Faith Kinsman And Humble Sarvant

JNO: BONVILLE

Address: For Mr Locke [at Oates, by Joslyn, Bishops Stortford]

Postmark: IA 8

Endorsed by Locke: J: Bonville 8 Jan $9\frac{7}{8}$ Answered 10 and 19

2375. NICOLAS TOINARD to LOCKE, 9/19 January 1698 (*2373, 2393*)

B.L., MS. Locke c. 21, f. 191. Answered by no. 2412.

+

ce 19. 98.

Depuis cele dont monsieur Nelson a bien voulu se charger j'ay lu un livre intitulé L'Amerique Angloise composé par m. Richard Blome et traduit de l'Anglois.[2]

Il est imprimé à Amstredam 1688. et comm'il y est parlé d'un plan de Philadelphie capitale de Pensylvanie comme sil etoit ce me semble gravé,[3] vous me feriez bien plaisir de me l'envoier par les ocasions qui vont se presenter, et d'y joindre des cartes de ces

[1] The fire that began on 4 January and destroyed the principal buildings between the Banqueting House and the river.

[2] Richard Blome (*D.N.B.*), *The Present State of His Majesties Isles and Territories in America*, 1687. The French translation was published in Amsterdam in 1688 (perhaps an earlier issue in 1687).

[3] Probably T. Holme, *A Portraiture of the City of Philadelphia*, published *c.* 1683.

païs la en cas qu'eles soient publiques, car j'aime extremement tout cequi a relation aux colonies en quoi les Anglois surpassent toutes les autres nations. Au reste ce ne m'a pas eté une petite joie de voir dans la Caroline des[a] lieux qui portent un nom qui me sera toujours en veneration.[1]

Je vois citer une Traduction du Rosch-haschana faite par Boutingius.[2] cela est-il de votre connoissance? Je ne scai ou la prendre ny la mander. Il y a bien plus de trente ans que j'ay traduit ce codex avec celui de Pesachim tout entier et plusieurs autres fragmens de la mischna et Genara[3] qui pouront parêtre en leur tems apres le texte Grec que vous savez. J'ay quelque idée qu'il y a encore de nouveaux codices Mischnici traduis en Angleterre,[4] outre le meme Rosch-haschana à Copenhage que je n'ay pu avoir d'Holande.[5]

Quand le Paquet-boot sera retabli je vous ecriray frequemment si vous voulez m'honorer de votre correspondance. Cependant permetez moi de me dire, monsieur, votre tres—

J'ay en ma disposition une admirable carte mss. de tout le Canada faite par un habile ingenieur qui a eté 22. ans sur les lieux.

Noted by Locke: Toinard 19 Jan 9$\frac{7}{8}$ Answered Mar. 25

2376. LOCKE to WILLIAM MOLYNEUX, 10 January 1698 (*2360*, *2407*)

Some Familiar Letters, pp. 253–61. Answers nos. *2311*, *2324*, *2331*, *2339*, and *2360*; answered by no. *2407*.

Oates, 10 Jan. 169$\frac{7}{8}$.

Dear Sir,

Your gentle and kind reproof of my silence[6] has greater marks of true friendship in it, than can be express'd in the most elaborate professions, or be sufficiently acknowledg'd by a man who has not

[a] *Doubtful reading; altered from* deux?

[1] See no. 287.

[2] Apparently a slip for Hendrik Houting, who published a translation of this tractate at Amsterdam in 1695: Bischoff, *Talmud-Übersetzungen*, p. 40.

[3] See pp. 613–14.

[4] See p. 362.

[5] Poul Vinding (1658–1712; *Dansk biog. Lexikon*) made a translation of the treatise; it was published in Copenhagen without date; the dedication is dated from Oxford, 18 December 1678.

[6] No. *2360*.

the opportunity nor ability to make those returns he would. Tho' I have had less health and more business since I writ to you last than ever I had for so long together in my life, yet neither the one nor the other had kept me so long a truant, had not the concurrence of other causes drill'd me on[1] from day to day in a neglect of what I frequently purposed, and always thought my self obliged to do. Perhaps the listlesness my indisposition constantly kept me in, made me too easily hearken to such excuses; but the expectation of hearing every day from Mons. Le Clerc, that I might send you his answer,[2] and the thoughts that I should be able to send your brother an account that his curious treatise concerning the Chafers in Ireland[3] was printed, were at least the pretences that serv'd to humour my laziness. Business kept me in town longer than was convenient for my health: all the day from my rising was commonly spent in that, and when I came home at night my shortness of breath and panting for want of it made me ordinarily so uneasy, that I had no heart to do any thing; so that the usual diversion of my vacant hours forsook me, and reading it self was a burden to me. In this estate I linger'd along in town to December, till I betook my self to my wonted refuge in the more favourable air and retirement of this place. That gave me presently relief, against the constant oppression of my lungs, whilst I sit still: But I find such a weakness of them still remain, that if I stir ever so little I am immediately out of breath, and the very dressing or undressing me is a labour that I am fain to rest after to recover my breath; and I have not been once out of the house since I came last hither. I wish nevertheless that you were here with me to see how well I am: For you would find, that, sitting by the fire's side, I could bear my part in discoursing, laughing, and being merry with you, as well as ever I could in my life. If you were here (and if wishes of more than one could bring you, you would be here to day) you would find three or four in the parlour after dinner, whom you would say pass'd their afternoons as agreeably and as jocundly as any people you have this good while met with. Do not therefore figure to your self that I am languishing away my last hours under an unsociable despondency and the weight of my infirmity. 'Tis

[1] Led me on: see no. *282*.

[2] Molyneux inquired about Le Clerc in his letter of 11 September; Le Clerc wrote to Locke on 7/17 November, refusing to go to Ireland, but his letter did not reach Locke until about March of this year: pp. 193, 254.

[3] See pp. 234–5.

true I do not count upon years of life to come, but I thank God I have not many uneasy hours here in the four and twenty; and if I can have the wit to keep my self out of the stifling air of London, I see no reason but by the grace of God I may get over this winter, and that terrible enemy of mine may use me no worse than the last did, which as severe and as long as it was let me yet see another summer.

What you say to me in yours of the 4th Oct.[1] concerning the B. of W. you will I believe be confirm'd in, if his Answer to my second Letter, of which I shall say nothing to you yet, be got to you.

Mr. Coste is now in the house with me here, and is tutor to my lady Masham's son. I need not I think now answer your questions about his skill in mathematicks and natural history: I think it is not much; but he is an ingenious man, and we like him very well for our purpose; and I have a particular obligation to you for the reason why you enquir'd concerning him.

I come now to yours of 28th Oct.[2] wherein you have found by this time that you prophesied right concerning the B. of W. and if you can remember what you said therein concerning abundance of words, you will not, I suppose, forbear smiling, when you read the first leaf of his last Answer.

If there be not an evidence of sense and truth, which is apt and fitted to prevail on every human understanding, as far as it is open and unprejudiced; there is at least a harmony of understandings in some men, to whom sense and nonsense, truth and falshood, appears equally in the respective discourses they meet with. This I find perfectly so between you and me, and it serves me to no small purpose to keep me in countenance. When I see a man, disinteressed as you are, a lover of truth as I know you to be, and one that has clearness and coherence enough of thought to make long mathematical, i.e. sure deductions, pronounce of J. H. and J. S.'s books that they are unintelligible to you;[3] I do not presently condemn my self of pride, prejudice, or a perfect want of understanding, for laying aside those Authors, because I can find neither sense or coherence in them. If I could think that discourses and arguments to the understanding were like the several sorts of cates to different palates and stomachs, some nauseous and destructive to one, which are pleasant and restorative to another; I should

[1] No. *2324*. The bishop of Worcester. [2] No. *2339*.
[3] James Hodges and Father John Sergeant.

no more think of books and study, and should think my time better imploy'd at push-pin than in reading or writing. But I am convinced of the contrary: I know there is truth opposite to falshood, that it may be found if people will, and is worth the seeking, and is not only the most valuable, but the pleasantest thing in the world. And therefore I am no more troubled and disturb'd with all the dust that is raised against it, than I should be to see from the top of an high steeple, where I had clear air and sunshine, a company of great boys or little boys (for 'tis all one) throw up dust in the air, which reach'd not me, but fell down in their own eyes.

Your answer to your friend the bishop[1] was certainly a very fit and full one to what he had said, and I am obliged to you for it: But he nevertheless thought his objections so good, that I imagine he communicated them to my antagonist; for you will find the very same in his answer, and almost in the same words. But they will receive an answer at large in due time.[2]

It will not be at all necessary to say any thing to you concerning the linen bill, which made so great a part of your letter of Oct. 4th, and was the whole business of that of Oct. 16th.[3] You know (I believe) as well as I what became of that bill. Pray return my humble thanks to Mr. Hamilton for his kind expressions concerning me, and for the favour he did me in thinking me any ways able to serve his country in that matter. I am so concern'd for it, and zealous in it, that I desire you to assure him, and to believe your self, that I will neglect no pains or interest of mine to promote it as far as I am able; and I think it a shame, that whilst Ireland is so capable to produce flax and hemp, and able to nourish the poor at so cheap a rate, and consequently to have their labour upon so easy terms, that so much mony should go yearly out of the king's dominions, to enrich foreigners, for those materials and the manufactures made out of them, when his people of Ireland, by the advantage of their soil, situation, and plenty, might have every penny of it, if that business were but once put into a right way. I perceive by one of your letters, that you have seen the proposals for an act sent from hence.[4] I would be very glad that you and Mr. Hamilton, or any other man, whom you knew able, and a disinteressed well-wisher of his country, would consider them

[1] Dr. William King.

[2] Locke refers to *Mr. Locke's Reply to the Right Reverend the Lord Bishop of Worcester's Answer to his Second Letter*, 1699; Locke dates it 4 May 1698.

[3] Nos. 2324 and 2331.

[4] See p. 221.

together, and tell me whether you think that project will do, or wherein it is either impracticable or will fail, and what may be added or alter'd in it to make it effectual to that end. I know, to a man a stranger to your country, as I am, many things may be overseen, which by reason of the circumstances of the place, or state of the people, may in practice have real difficulties. If there be any such in regard of that project, you will do me a favour to inform me of them. The short is, I mightily have it upon my heart to get the linen manufacture established in a flourishing way in your country. I am sufficiently sensible of the advantages it will be to you, and shall be doubly rejoyced in the success of it, if I should be so happy that you and I could be instrumental in it, and have the chief hand in forming any thing that might conduce to it. Imploy your thoughts therefore I beseech you about it, and be assured, what help I can give to it here shall be as readily and as carefully imploy'd, as if you and I alone were to reap all the profit of it.

I have not yet heard a word from Mons. Le Clerc in answer to my enquiries, and the questions you ask'd, or else you had heard sooner from me.[1] I must beg you to return my acknowledgments to Mr. Molesworth in the civilest language you can find, for the great complement you sent me from him. If he could see my confusion as often as I read that part of your letter, that would express my sense of it better than any words I am master of. I can only say that I am his most humble servant, and I have been not a little troubled, that I could not meet with the opportunities I sought to improve the advantages I propos'd to my self, in an acquaintance with so ingenious and extraordinary a man as he is.

I read your brother's treatise,[2] which he did me the honour to put into my hands, with great pleasure, and thought it so unreasonable to rob the publick of so grateful a present by any delay of mine, that I forthwith put it into Dr. Sloane's hand to be published, and I expected to have seen it in print long e'er this time. What has retarded it I have not yet heard from Dr. Sloane, who has not writ to me since I came into the country: But I make no doubt but he takes care of so curious a piece, and the world will have it speedily. I must depend on you, not only for excusing my silence to your self, but I must be obliged to you to excuse me to your brother for

[1] See p. 293, n. 2; Locke has returned to no. *2311*.
[2] See p. 293.

not having written to him my self to thank him for the favour he did me. I hope e'er long to find an opportunity to testify my respects to him more in form, which he would find I have in reality for him, if any occasion of that kind should come in my way. In the mean time I believe, if he saw the length of this letter, he would think it enough for one of a family to be persecuted by so voluminous a scribler, and would be glad that I spared him. I am both his and,

Dear Sir,

Your most affectionate and most humble servant,

JOHN LOCKE.

2377. DR. PHILIPPE GUIDE to LOCKE, 11 January 1698 (3075)

B.L., MS. Locke c. 11, ff. 124–5. The writer is said to have been M.D. of Montpellier. He published medical books in Paris in 1674 and 1676. He was admitted a licentiate of the Royal College of Physicians on 2 April 1683, and continued to practise in London until his death in 1718. He published some further books in London: Haag; Munk, i. 429; L.L., nos. 1359–60[a].

Monsieur

Sir Francis Masson[1] m'ayant dit que vous ne desapprouviés pas la resolution que nous avons de deffendre nostre bon droit, contre les pretentions du Dr. Lincaster,[2] j'ay creu que vous ne trouveriés pas mauvais que je vous informe plus au long de ce qui se passe, comme c'est une affairre qui peut avoir quelque suite et qui peut estre de consequence. Le parti de quantité d'honestes gens que l'on appelle dissenters, lesquels se trouveront a la fin envelopés dans le cas des refugiés, vous cognoissant Monsieur aussi bien intentioné pour le bien public que vous l'estes, vous ne manquerés pas d'estre sensible a ce qui peut alterer la paix et le repos commun; J'espere qu'avec toute vostre penetration singuliere dans les sciences et dans la polytique vous n'aurés pas moins de charité a nous fournir quelque expedient qui puisse deffendre de pauvres estrangers que l'on attaque les premiers comme un parti foible et peu en estat de se deffendre, voici le cas comme il a

[1] Masham.

[2] William Lancaster, D.D.; vicar of St. Martin in the Fields 1692–March 1694, October 1694–1717; provost of Queen's College, Oxford, 1704–17: *D.N.B.* He claimed baptismal fees for himself and his clerk in respect of a child baptized in the French church in the Savoy; the case was heard by Sir John Holt, who disallowed the claim: R. Burn, *The Ecclesiastical Law*, 9th ed., 1842, i. 116.

esté plaidé au docteurs communs; Je trouve l'affairre d'autant plus delicate que his Grace the Archebishop of Canterbery a qui j'ay eu l'honneur d'en parler aujourdhuy, quoy qu'il soit convenu avec nous qu'il n'est rien deu pour le sacrement, veut pourtant que nous en venions a un Compromis avec le Dr. Lancaster.[1] dans ce compromis, il faudra sans doute que nous convenions de donner un certum quid, un pris fixe ce qui est assez contraire au principe que les sacrements et les dons spirituels ne peuvent pas estre appreciés, d'ailleurs nous aurons a essuyer les réproches de Messieurs les dissenters qui pourront se plaindre de nostre facilité a ployer. Sir Francis me sera tesmoin que je luy ay donné l'ambarras d'en parler a ses amis de la Chambre, on s'estonne ou se recrie contre le procedé du Dr. Lincaster, mais on ne nous offre n'y avis n'y credit n'y argent pour nous deffendre. Pardonnés moy Monsieur la liberté que je prens de vous desrober des moments si precieux et que vous employés si dignement a developer les matieres les plus espineuses. J'aprens avec douleur que vostre retraite a la Campagne ne vous a pas esté si avantageuse pour le restablissement de vostre santé que les autres fois, vous aves senti de la difficulté de respirer, c'est un symptome qui peut avoir des causes si differentes qu'il n'est pas estonnant que les Medecins se trouvent souvent bien ambarassés a les démesler et a y apporter les remedes, si on osoit Monsieur en parler devant un maitre habile comme vous on diroit que la cause la plus ordinaire vient d'un gonflement de cette membrane tres delicate qui tapisse les dedans des bronches, qui ne peut se grossir sans rendre ce petits tuyaux plus estroits, et ainsi moins capables de recevoir la quantité ordinaire d'air necessaire a la respiration.[a] L'infirmité de cette membrane est de mesme nature que celle de la membrane de l'oeil que nous appellons conjonctive, qui dans les yeux tendres et subjects aux fluxions se trouve en desordre a la moindre occasion de froid ou de chaud etc. Apres le secours des remedes generaux propres a l'un et a l'autre de ces maladies, Elles sympatisent enco dans les specifiques le Camphre usité dans les Collyres et propr a resoudre les tumeurs se trouve souvent estre assez utile dan les difficultés de respirer. J'en ay fait usage en lozange dont j'e fais prendre la grosseur d'une lentille que l'on tient dans la bouch

[a] *End of line; abbreviated as* respi^{n}?

[1] Tenison and Lancaster, who was a protégé of Compton's, may have been o bad terms.

pendant qu'avec une pipe ordinaire et vuide on attire l'air a travers son tuyau. cet air forcé de cette maniere penetre plus profondement dans les lieux les plus estroits et estant plein de la subtilité du camphre de la petite astriction de terra Japonica[1] qui y est jointe, on soppose[2] au relachement de ces parties, j'en ay veu de bons effects, je vous en envoye un petit eschantillon par Curiosité.

Si j'estois assez heureux Monsieur de pouvoir vous estre utile en quelque chose j'en aurois une extreme joye Personne asseurement ne vous honore plus que je fais. je suis

Monsieur

Vostre tres humble et tres obeissan serviteur

P. GUIDE.

Sir Francis ma fait la grace de me donner des nouvelles de My Lady son Epouse et du progrés que fait Monsieur son fils je suis ravi qu'il soit tombé en d'aussi bonne mains et qu'a la fin on ait trouvé un digne maitre[3] d'un disciple aussi rare. Si j'osois profiter de ce petit reste de papier j'asseurerois icy My Lady de mes tres humbles respects mille pardon Monsieur a la liberté que je me donne

Endorsed by Locke: Dr Guide 11 Jan $9\frac{7}{8}$ Answered 15

2378. LOCKE to THOMAS TENISON, archbishop of Canterbury, 15 January 1698 (*2363*)

B.L., MS. Locke c. 24, ff. 270–1. Draft; many alterations, some in ink other than that of the original composition. Answers no. *2363*.

15 Jan. $9\frac{7}{8}$[a]

May it please your Grace

I beg leave to owne to your Grace the great sense I have of the honour you did me in giveing your self the trouble of writeing me the letter which I received from your grace the later end of the last month And I should sooner have returnd my acknowledgments due for such a favour had I not thought it more becomeing the Respect due from me to your Grace to stay a little in a matter that seemd not to require hast for the convenience of this Bearer, Mr King,[4] a Gentleman of the Innes of Court, to wait upon your

[a] *Probably in the later ink.*

[1] Catechu: *O.E.D.*

[2] Perhaps a slip for 's'oppose' or 'suppose', the latter with the literal meaning, to set under: Cotgrave.

[3] Coste.

[4] Peter King, Locke's cousin.

Grace with my letter[a] than to use the common post, which has formerly failed me to your Grace. It is not the only misfortune I owe to my ill lungs that I was out of town when my Lord Bishop of Ely[1] did me the favour to give himself upon my account the trouble your Grace mentions. and I shall not faile to take the first oportunity to acknowledg it to him. By what Dr James says I finde he gave his imprimatur to the booke upon confidence that Mr Edwards had obeyed his order of blotting out divers passages in it and was satisfied with Mr Edwards's writeing him word *that he had smoothd many things*. How Mr Edwards had smoothd it would have been very evident to the world if the booksellers who printed his booke in London, for the printer in Cambridg would not defile his presse with it, had not smoothd it over again and blotted out many things. Soe much care[b] had the booksellers of the reputation of their presses that they would not give it their imprimatur till those passages which the modestie of these Trades men could not bear were blotted out and till they saw it was done, not trusting to Mr E ds's smoothing But how smooth a peice it is, how worthy to be recommended to the youth of the university for their immitation by those reverend names that stand before it to vouch by the imprimatur they are set to that there is noething in the booke against religion or good manners appears sufficiently in what is left in as it is now. Though the publique talke at[b] Whitehall and that other word which your Grace as becomes you thinks too horrid to name were in it will appear not to be groundlesse when the matter shall come to be looked into.

But Dr James says that *Mr Ed 's was forbidden to print the Imprimatur*[c] *at London, though he did it, displeaseing thereby the Licencers. And the Chancellor himself the Duke of Somerset*. Supposeing this all soe as he says. I appeale to your Grace and my Lord Bishop of Ely whether this story of Dr James told to your Grace can be satisfaction to me or any body. The booke is gon and goes abroad into the world with those Reverend licencers names to the imprimatur. The vice Chancellor the professor of divinity[2] and other eminent Doctors of divinity and heads of houses in the University of Cambridg are publishd by Mr Edwards as ⟨approvers⟩[d] of his booke. Tis alledgd that they and others are displeased with him

[a] *Interlined above* service, *which is not deleted.* [b] *Doubtful reading; blurred* [c] *Ending doubtful.* [d] *MS.* apprvers

[1] Simon Patrick. [2] Dr. James; Dr. Joseph Beaumont

for it But the world sees not any ⟨marke⟩[a] of the least displeasure. And the booke carrys up and down with it the appearance of being the favorite of the University and is not with standing what has been said to your Grace by Dr James like to doe soe to posterity. How ⟨mu⟩ch[b] to the Credit of that university I must leave to your Grace and my Lord Bishop of Ely to judg. as for my private concerne in it I shall not neglect to take care of that in its due time. For as for that maske of white paper pasted of late over the imprimatur[c] on those of the books that are sold in Cambridg, all that hear of it laugh at it as a pretty invention. This plaister they say confesses there is a soar though it be too narrow to cure or cover it

I beg your Graces pardon for deteining you soe long upon the occasion the concerne I know your Grace has for the University and that which your grace has been soe favourably pleased to expresse for me has emboldend me thus farr and raised in me the confidence to trouble your Grace with soe long a letter. I am

Endorsed by Locke: J L to A: Bishop Tenison 15 Jan. 9⅞

2379. Locke to Edward Clarke, 16 January 1698 (*2371*, 2398)

B.L., MS. Locke b. 8, no. 112. Printed in Rand, pp. 530–1. Answers no. *2371*.

Oates 16 Jan. 9⅞

Deare Sir

Though I am lazyer than ever you knew me or than ever I knew my self, yet the delay or shortnesse of my letters has always some consideration of you and your time in it

I thank you again for your pains in puting an end to my affair with Sir Stephen

I finde by the votes you have not been unmindefull of the provision you promised to doe all you could to make. I hope now it will be sufficient and effectuall. tis noe more than needs I assure you.

I am assured that here are Gentlemen who have lately but already declared to stand for Parliament men the next election. And there has been great feasting lately not far from hence as it is understood to that purpose. Can you tell any Reason for it or meaning of it?[1] This bearer can tell you the names

[a] *MS.* make [b] *Page torn.* [c] *Ending doubtful.*

[1] The present parliament met first on 22 November 1695. The Triennial Act (1694) limited its continuance to three years.

The good and hearty wishes you sent me from your self Madam and family on New years day I returne you for you and yours for ages to come. But to make my hopes accompany my wishes for my freinds and self you must setle the floating Island.[1]

My service to the Batchelor when he returns. I hear[a] he is at present out of town. I am

Dear Sir

Your most affecti⟨ona⟩te[b] humble servant

J LOCKE

My service to your fires side.[c]

Did my Lord Chancellor never say any thing to you upon occasion of my letter to him. and what the Gentleman whose health was concerned in it said upon it.[2] Pray when you see my Lord and have time enquire as far as you see fit

Address: For Edward Clarke Esquire at Richards Coffee house within Temple Bar London

Endorsed by Clarke: Mr Lock Received by Mr. King the 17th January 1697. Answered the 18th.

2380. COMMISSARY JAMES BLAIR to LOCKE, 20 January 1698 (*2545*)

B.L., MS. Locke c. 4, ff. 8–9. James Blair, 1655–1743; divine; the bishop of London's commissary in Virginia 1689–1743; originator and first president of William and Mary College: *D.N.B.*; *Dict. American Biog.*; p. 74.

Blair came to England about July 1697, ostensibly on behalf of the college, but also to seek the recall of the governor of Virginia, Sir Edmund Andros (p. 560). Examined by the Board of Trade on 25 August, he wrote, perhaps with Locke's help, a report on the condition of Virginia. In October, at the Board's request, he and two other men presented a report on 'the Publick State' of Virginia: M. G. Kammen in *Virginia Magazine of history and biography* lxxiv (1966), 141–69 (where the first report is printed); P. Laslett in *John Locke: Problems and Perspectives*, ed. J. W. Yolton, 1969, pp. 160–3.

Jan. 20. 169$\frac{7}{8}$

London at the Surgeons Armes in St Martins Street

Sir

I hope your goodnes will pardon the abruptnes of this Address

[a] *Or* fear [b] *Blotted.* [c] *Locke adds the words* turn over

[1] Probably a current phrase; Richard Head (*D.N.B.*) published a facetious pamphlet, *The Floating Island*, 1673.

[2] This is perhaps the letter mentioned on p. 268. The gentleman may be the king

which makes bold to intrude upon yow in your Retirement. The extraordinary countenance and Assistance wherewith you favoured me, while you was in the City, encourages me to enquire, with a most particular concern, after your health in the Countrey. I have not offered, since you went, to stirre in any business at the Councill of Trade and plantations; fearing lest in your absence I should have marred and mismenaged it, by an untimely forcing it into other hands, and other methods than you had contrived. But I can not but flatter my self with the hopes, that God, who made you such an eminent instrument of detecting the Constitution and Government of Virginia, will likewise furnish you with health and opportunities to redress the Errours and abuses of it. It is expected that the business of the Plantations will shortly be taken into consideration; and my Lord of Canterbury a feu days ago expressed himself with abundance of concern for your being out of the way. He told me he had wrote to you, but had no answer; which made him apprehend the bad state of your health: Perhaps his letter might not be right addressed. I promised his Grace to write to you, and to acquaint him with what I should learn of your health or resolutions to come to London: which I think my self obliged to acquaint you with, as a further Apology for my giving you this trouble, and for the request I must conclude with, that by your Amanuensis yow'l let me know, what to say to his Grace on this occasion. I pray God to restore yow to your health, and am

Sir

Your most obliged, humble servant.

JAMES BLAIR

Endorsed by Locke: J: Blair 20 Jan $9\frac{7}{8}$

2381. ANDREW FLETCHER of Saltoun to LOCKE, 25 January 1698 (*1851*, *2389*)

B.L., MS. Locke c. 8, ff. 135–6. MS. Locke c. 8, f. 122, Henry (?) Fletcher about his health, was probably enclosed with the letter.

London Jan: 25th 1698:

Sir

I heard of your being gone out of toun a very little afte⟨r⟩[a]

[a] *End of line.*

it was told me that you wer come to it.[1] And was very sorry that I did meet with you; having many things to say to you which I can not well do by a letter. However most of these being things that concerned my self and my owen privat satisfaction I shal wave them till mitting. And beg your pardon to trouble you with what concernes my brother. A fourthnight after he came home he had a collick in his belly, afterwards a flux, which ended in ane other collick. Now of late he has had a most violent fit of collick, still in his belly which has lasted 3 days; thos collicks he was never subject to befor. Since his returne he has been lickways much troubled with belching up of wind which he was not befor. He is still troubled with fits of vapours tho not so much as befor, and is more sensible in the time of them than he was. He eats and slips well; but is still much troubled with the sturring in his nerves in time of slipe. His wife persuaded him to take some of the Ens Veneris, but it had no operation upon him. She desirs to know whither any phisical diet; or woman milk will be good for him. He has drunck nothing but wine and water since he came home except since this rigorous weather, and because of the pain in his belly he has left of the drinking water. I have writ you the account with all the circumstances it was writ to me, because I know it was necessary to do so. You may returne me ane answer at your owen leasur; for I hope their is nothing dangerous or that requirs hast. My hunble service my good Lady; you may tell her that notwithstanding all the endevour of honest men amongst whom Sir F. did signalize himself as much as any, I am affrayed the libertys of this are at an end.[2] All the favour I beg of you, for my self is that henceforth when you come to London you would send a porter to let me know you are come. I am

Sir

Your most obliged servant

A FLETCHER

Endorsed by Locke: J: Fletcher 25 Jan $9\frac{7}{8}$ Answered 31

[1] This probably refers to Locke's visit to London from 21 to 24 January: no. 2384.

[2] Fletcher probably alludes to the commons' vote on 18 January to grant half-pay to the disbanded commissioned officers of the army until they should be otherwise provided for. See further p. 312.

2382. CORNELIUS LYDE to LOCKE, 26 January 1698 (2372, 2390)

B.L., MS Locke c. 15, ff. 162–3. Answers no. 2372; answered by no. 2390.

Jan: the 26th $9\frac{7}{8}$

Sir

Yours I Received with the account which I must Confes was not made in that order which is Common with merchants to doe but as to the truthe of it I hope not Inferior to them, which I have not beene much aquanted[a] with but I Like your method well as to the mistake of 4s you will finde to be none as here mentioned the 3 due from barnes I have Received but not Els of the areares mentioned. Jos: Hanny have promised many times but faile and I Am Loffe[1] to areast him for feare it will be his rueing but doe hope to gett the Tanner that paide the Last to pay it in sometime the sums due from Sumers Gullock Hopkins Haroll you did not mention in the rent Roll but I shall Endevor to Received of them wishing you all helth and happines I Am your obliegd friend and ser

COR: LYDE[b]

the mistake is in Rec: of the Lords[c] baylie which was 8s and the charge but 4s in the account

Sir I Heartily thank you for your Kind Letter to my son: in Holland of which I had an account of him, also that he have taken his degree[2] and hope in some time to see him and that he himselfe may acknowledg your Kindnes to him. Sir I Am

Your Humble ser COR: LYDE

Address: For Doct: Locke at mr: Pawlings overagainst the plough in Little Lincolns feilds London

Postmark: IA 28

Endorsed by Locke: C: Lyde 26 Jan $9\frac{7}{8}$ Answered Feb. 5

[a] *MS.* aquãnt; *end of line.* [b] *There is here a marginal note, apparently written by Edward Clarke:*

rec: by me 79 li–14: 6d
paid . . . . . 79 –18–6
as in the account sent

[c] *MS.* L^{ds} *or* L^{ts}

[1] Loath; a mis-spelling.
[2] He graduated M.D. at Leyden on 20 December, N.S.: R. W. Innes Smith *English speaking students of medicine at Leyden.*

2383. SIR WALTER YONGE to LOCKE, 27 January 1698 (*2358, 2388*)

B.L., MS. Locke c. 23, ff. 168–9.

London Jan. 27th. 1697.

Dear Sir

I endeavour'd to wait on you during the short time you lately spent in Town, but was not so fortunate to find you at home, and the next morning I understood to my great trouble and surprize, that your indisposition forced you to return so soon into the Country.[1] I hope by that time this reaches you the fresh Air will have so far recruited you that it may be excuseable in me, to give you the trouble of perusing the enclosed, by which you will see how generously the Archbishop encourages Mr Cross[2] in his undertaking. I have since received another letter from him wherein he presses to know what you and I will doe for him, and saies the charge of printing it amounts to 45 lb. I am ready to doe my part, but being not acquainted amongst the men of letters can promise little from others, but presume you may have spoken to severall. If you please at your leisure to write two lines to Mr Cross or my selfe to acquaint him what encouragement you can give him, I shall gladly impart it to him, and promote his work as farr as I can. I heartily wish you health and am

Sir

Your most faithfull friend and humble servant

WALTER YONGE

You have the services of all here.

Upon second thoughts I shall enclose both letters.

Address: For John Locke Esqr. [at Oates, by Joslyn, Bishops Stortford] Frank Walter Yonge

Postmark: IA 27

Endorsed by Locke: Sir W. Yonge 27 Jan 9⅞. Answered 31

2384. LOCKE to SIR JOHN SOMERS, Baron Somers, 28 January 1698 (*2338*)

B.L., MS. Locke c. 24, ff. 228–9. Draft; many alterations; only select variants are given below, and they are in part reconstructed. Printed in King, pp. 247–8; with omissions, in Cranston, pp. 434–5.

[1] See no. 2384. [2] Walter Cross of *The Taghmical Art*: p. 136.

Fox Bourne and Cranston suggest that the place offered to Locke was that of secretary to Portland, who was going as ambassador to Paris, or of secretary to the embassy in Paris. That is unlikely as Matthew Prior already held the place. It was perhaps that of secretary of state in succession to Shrewsbury, who wanted to retire at this time: Institute of Historical Research (University of London), *Bulletin*, xl (1967), 213–19; see also Luttrell, iv. 332.

Locke came to town on Friday 21 January: Journal.

May it please your Lordship

Sunday in the evening after waiting[a-] on the King[-a] I was to wait upon your Lordship, it being as I understood him his Majesties pleasure that I should doe soe before I returnd hither. my misfortune in missing your Lordship then I hoped to repaire by an early diligence the next morning. But the night that came between destroid that purpose and me almost with it. For[b-] when I was laid in my bed my breath faild me.[-b] I was fain to sit up right in my bed where I continued in this posture a good part of the night with hopes that my shortnesse of breath would abate and my lungs grow soe good naturd, as to let me lie down to get a little sleep wherof I had great need. But[c-] my breath constantly faileing me as often as I laid upon my pillow at three I got up[-c] and soe sat by the fire till morning.[d] My ⟨case⟩[e] being brought to this extremitie There was noe roome for any other thought but to get out of town immediately. For after the two precedent nights without any rest I concluded the agonies I labourd under soe long in the second of them would hardly faile to be sure death the third If I staid in town. As bad weather therefor as it was I was forced early on Monday morning to seeke for a passage and by good luck found an empty Cambridg coach just seting out which brought me hither.[1]

His Majestie was soe favourable as to propose the imployment your Lordship mentiond. But the true knowledg of my owne weake

a–a *Substituted for* I had been at Kinsington b–b *Substituted for* I went to bed at my usuall hour but when I was there could not lie down for want of breath which faild me as soon as my head was upon the pillow. This obleged me cold as it was to sit c–c *Substituted for* But all in vain. Haveing endured the cold and uneasinesse [*variants* a continual agonie *and* an unexpressible uneasinesse] I was in till three in the morning I rose d *Followed by* when leaning against my man who placed himself by me I got a short nap. e *Or* life; *both words are struck out.*

1 On this day (Monday, the 24th) 'a great frost broke, which had continued about 3 weeks, with great snowes; the river Thames frozen over with it, so that in some places several persons went acrosse it': Luttrell.

state of health made me beg his Majestie to bethinke of some fitter person and one more able to serve him in that important post, to which I added my want of experience for such a businesse. That[a]– your Lordship may not thinke this an expression barely of modestie I crave leave to explaine it to your Lordship and though there in I discover my weakenesse. My temper, always shie of a crowd and strangers, has made my acquaintance few and my conversation too narrow and particular to get the skill of dealeing with men in their various humours and drawing out their secrets.–[a] Whether this was a fault or noe in a man that designed noe bustle in the world I know not this I am sure it will let your Lordship see that I am too much a novice in the world for the imployment proposed

Though we are soe odly placed here that we have noe ordinary conveyance for our letters from Monday till Friday[1] yet this delay has not fallen out much amisse. The King was graciously pleased to order me to goe into the Country to take care of my health. These 4 or 5 days here have given me a proof to what a low state my lungs are now brought and how little they can beare the least shock. I can lie down again indeed in my bed and take my rest, but bateing that I finde the impression of these two days in London soe heavie upon me still, that the least motion puts me out of breath and I am under a constant uneasienesse even when I sit still. which extends farther then the painfulnesse of breathing and makes me listlesse to every thing soe that methinks the writeing this letter has been a great performance.

My Lord I should not trouble you with an account of the

a–a *Substituted for* That you may not thinke it an expression barely of modestie, I crave leave to explain to your Lordship. If I have had the good luck to produce any thing which has found approbation and procurd me your Lordships good opinion, it has been (if your Lordship please to reflect on it) the consideration of things. The search of truth I confesse has been the employment of my thoughts. But for man that Animal incertum varium multiplex as Tully cals him[2] I have as much avoided as I could, reduceing my conversation to a few of the best I could finde and soe am ignorant of the practise how to deale with the diversity of humors and makes and the arts of diveing into their thoughts. They who know my way of liveing can assure your Lordship that this is soe for which I shall give your Lordship this demonstrative instance that when I am in town I doe not goe once in three months to a Coffee house and never to seek company but to finde some one with whom I have particular businesse.

---

[1] That is, by the postal service.

[2] 'That uncertain, inconstant and complex animal'. Conflated from 'animal hoc providum, sagax, multiplex . . . quem vocamus hominem' and 'si ne in uno quidem . . . unus animus erit idemque semper, sed varius, commutabilis, multiplex': *De Legibus*, I. vii. 22; *De Amicitia*, XXV, § 92.

prevailing decays of an old pair of lungs were it not my duty to take care his Majestie should be disappointed and therefor that he lay any expectation on that which to my great misfortune every way I finde would certainly faile him, and I must beg your Lordship for the interest of the publick to prevaile with his Majestie to thinke on somebody else, since I doe not only fear but am sure my broken health will never permit me to accept the great honour his Majestie meant me.[a]

Endorsed by Locke: J L to L. Chancellor 28 Jan 9$\frac{7}{8}$

2385. Hilary Reneu to Locke, 28 January 1698

B.L., MS. Locke c. 18, ff. 15–16. The writer, who is sometimes called Ranue, was later governor of the Lustring Company: Scott, *Joint-stock Companies*, iii. 84, 86.

Lustringhous[1] London 28 January 169$\frac{7}{8}$

Sir

I Received your obliging Letter of the 15th: Instant the 20 Ditto. I am glad to heare that you aprove of my Endeavours to keep in England, the manufactur of Alamodes and Lustrings[2] Which is difficult divers ways. One among others is that Those that Can Serve in that are Overwhelmed with Businesse, I Leave to your kindnesse for the Lustring Company and your zeal for the publik good to Act for this publick affaire[b] which Concerns Poor and Rich, and the Memorial sent you is yours. I may be without it, But as thursday[3] next our Company is to Proceed Upon a New Election of directors if you please to send me your Proxy I shall Votte for you if you Empower Me In writing to the Company

[a] *A deleted passage follows:* As it would be unpardonable to betray the Kings businesse by undertakeing what I should be unable to goe through, soe it would be the greatest madnesse [to my self *interlined*] to put my self out of the reach of my freinds dureing the small time I am to linger on in this world only to die a little more rich or a little more advanced [*variant for* honourable]. He must have an heart strangely touchd with wealth or honour who at my age labouring for breath can finde any great relish in either of them [b] *Doubtful reading; word altered.*

[1] In Austin Friars: Strype's Stow, ii. 132.

[2] Alamode is a thin light glossy silk fabric; lustring or lutestring, a glossy silk fabric: *O.E.D.* Boyer gives as equivalents *sorte de Taffetas* and *Taffetas lustré* or *Taffetas double*.

[3] 3 February.

As here Under But Either by the Post or penny Post I should have your Answer Ready against that time. I Remain

Sir

Your Most humble Servant

H RENEU[a]

1697

Gentlemen

In my absence I have sent my Proxy to etc. to Votte for me att the generall Court

I am —

To the governour deputy governor and assistants of the Lustring Company.

Address: To John Locke Esqr: In Oates

Endorsed by Locke: E: Reneu 28 Jan $9\frac{7}{8}$ Answered 31

2386. JOHN WYNNE, later bishop of Bath and Wells, to LOCKE, 29 January 1698 (*2366*, 2472)

B.L., MS. Locke c. 23, f. 133. Locke wrote on a blank space a draft of his later letter to Wynne, no. 2472.

Honoured Sir

My stay att London after I had receiv'd your letter[1] was so short, that I had not time to make you any return from thence: And since that I have been in so unsettled and moving a posture that I have not found leisure to reflect on that which lies deepest in my mind; and that is the sense I have of my obligations to you. These I must alwaies own are so many and so great, that the highest acknowledgments I can make must fall very much short of them. And I account it no small accession to all your favours that you are pleas'd to entertain so favourable an opinion of me, as those kind expressions of respect and esteem you bestow upon me in your last assure me you do. I shall alwaies be very forward to lay hold of any occasion of letting you and others know how just a value I have for you: and endeavour to make the most gratefull returns I can for all your favours, which I shall constantly

[a] *The initials are written as a monogram; hence Locke's error in the endorsement.*

[1] Written on 3 January: no. *2366* endorsement.

acknowledge in expressions of the highest honour and respect, If I may not be able to do it in more real services. I left your Bill in a freind's hand to receive the money from Mr Churchill because I had not time to receive it my self. I received your Book which was left for me att my Lord's,[1] but did not then know whether I ow'd it to you or Mr Churchill; but now that I do, I return you my most humble thanks. I had the honour to present your service to My Lord before I left his Lordship, which his Lordship received with such expressions of respect as he usually dos what comes from you. My Lords kind invitations, together with the satisfaction I propose in your conversation, are such powerfull Inducements to bring me up to London sometime this year, that I know of nothing that can divert me from it. I am with the greatest service and respect

Sir

your most oblig'd humble servant

JOHN WYNNE

Oxon Jan 29. $9\frac{7}{8}$

Address: To The Honoured John Locke Esquire att Sir Francis Massam's att Oates in Essex.

Postmark: FE 3

Endorsed by Locke: J. Wynne 29 Jan. $9\frac{7}{8}$

2387. JAMES JOHNSTOUN to LOCKE, 2 February 1698 (*2225, 2431*)

B.L., MS. Locke c. 12, ff. 33–4.

Golden Square 2 Fer. $9\frac{8}{7}$.

Sir

I thought that you only used the Gown ill which was worse than if you had used me so, for at present the gown is more capable (tho not more willing) to serve you, then I am.[2] I am glad you have got your litle life (which will be great when its done) to its shelter again. I shall rather chuse to loose the satisfaction of seeing you here then to doe it upon such termes. That you should hazard

[1] Probably Locke's first *Reply* to Stillingfleet; Pembroke.

[2] Gowns were worn as the insignia of the legal and clerical professions: *O.E.D.*, svv. Gown and Gownsman. Here Johnstoun perhaps alludes to physicians, who also wore them.

your litle for any great good is verry commendable but its more probable that you will loose your litle then doe the other. However if you are sanguine enough to hope to doe any great good at this tyme I am glad of it for it shews a gayety in your blood that makes me hope it will circulate yet a while. I would rather you lived uneasy under disappointments then dyed satisfied that it signifyes nothing to live; which I apprehend is your case. what can a man expect to see who has seen the restauration and Revolution prove disseases instead of remedies![1] Every thing seems a lincke in the Chain. Pajon[2] has put the Machine so in my head that I thincke I shall never get it out of it tho I doe what I can. sure a man is to be rewarded hereafter barely for his endeavours, and not for the effects of them, which (succeed or not) are to be imputed to something else. You and many other honest men in this and the last age have made it your work to bring men by knowledge to reason and man no doubt is not capable of a greater and better work. You have succeeded in a great measure, but after all where are we now? for Instance in matters of religion (which will needs govern all the other parts of knowledge) Bigottry its true is a declining principle but its evidently a growing Interest almost all over Europe and will be so here too when church recovers which will recover unlesse others prove as bad as they. Nou bigottry growing the stronger must grow the principle too in tyme. what a prospect is this? but to give you a better one and comfort you a young Courtier, bottle beer is laid aside and severall other reformations are on the wheell, and the next summar if you come to Twittenham[3] you may see the King at London or windsor when you will for I verily beleeve you may help to mend not the body of the state but the King's body. My Lady Masham will for-

[1] The disappointment of some Whigs with the achievements of the Revolution emerged about this time, notably in the Standing Army controversy and in the publication of republican books, such as Milton's prose works, Ludlow's *Memoirs*, and Algernon Sidney's *Discourses*. They might fear an alliance between a Protestant king commanding a standing army, and the adherents of Divine Right. The merits of their cause are obscured by their failure to appreciate the danger from Louis XIV and the fact that in England the king depended on parliament for the maintenance and discipline of the army. For the controversy see Lois G. Schwoerer, '*No Standing Armies!*', 1974, pp. 155–87.

[2] Apparently Claude Pajon, 1626–85, the French Protestant divine who opposed the doctrine of absolute predestination: Haag. He held more or less that after the creation the machine of the world functioned without further divine intervention: Labrousse, *Bayle*, i. 154 n.

[3] Twickenham, where Johnstoun occupied a house with a notable garden in 1702 and earlier: D. Lysons, *Environs of London*, 2nd ed., 1811, II. ii. 773–4.

give this, for Twittenham in the place of London is the same thing to her. Mrs Johnson and I wish her all happiness. I really thincke if the ways were once good I shall see you.

I am with all sincerity,
Your true friend and humble servant
J JOHNSTOUN

Endorsed by Locke: J: Johnstoun 2 Feb. 9$\frac{7}{8}$ Answered 25

2388. SIR WALTER YONGE to LOCKE, 3 February 1698 (*2383, 2409*)

B.L., MS. Locke c. 23, ff. 170–1.

London Feb. 3d. 169$\frac{7}{8}$.

Dear Sir

I have the favor of yours of Jan. 31th. by which I am glad to find you are in some measure releived from the ill effects of your late being in Town, I hope a little more time will perfectly restore you; Since my last I received the enclosed from Mr Cross, which at his request I transmitt to you; All I can add is that since I received yours I gott Mr Churchill to goe to Mr Cross, and he tells me he thinks he has convinced him that his book may be printed for much less then he imagins, but the copy is at present with the Archbishop. My Wife I bless God continue to have her health pretty well, only has at times some remainder of her cough, which has never perfectly left her; she gives you her humble service, and I am

Dear Sir
Your most faithfull friend and servant
WALTER YONGE.

Address: For John Locke Esqr. [at Oates, by Joslyn, Bishops Stortford]
Frank Walter Yonge.

Postmark: FE 3

Endorsed by Locke: Sir W. Yonge 3 Feb 9$\frac{7}{8}$. Answered 14

2389. ANDREW FLETCHER of Saltoun to LOCKE, 3 February 1698 (*2381, 3018*)

B.L., MS. Locke c. 8, ff. 137–8.

Sir

I did not receve this seven years a letter has troubled me so much as your last; both upon account of what you writ to me of your self, and of my brother: but I hope that the spring which is near at hand will recover you: his distemper I take to be more dangerous; tho I can assure you it proceeds from no secret discontent, but indeed I belive from to much thoughtfulness. My mother[1] writs to me that she begins to be troubled agen with pains in her stomach, tho nothing near so bad as formerly; yit for fear they should grow worse she desirs I would send heir some of that medicine I brought her when I went last home. I am informed their is one sels it heir by your allowance; I beg only that your man would writ me his direction, and how I shal call for it, for I do not know the name of the medecine. My humble service to my Lady Masham. It will be very hard if we are to be left in this evill world without our old friends; who I thinck are the only confort we have. I am

Sir

Your most obliged servant

A FLETCHER

London the 3d of Feb: 1698.

Address: For John Locke Esquire [at Oates, by Joslyn, Bishops Stortford]

Postmarks: FE 3 (?); TN

Endorsed by Locke: J: Fletcher 3 Feb 9$\frac{7}{8}$ Answered 18

2390. LOCKE to CORNELIUS LYDE, 5 February 169[8] (*2382, 2449*)

The Pierpont Morgan Library, New York. Transcribed from Xerox prin[t]. Answers no. *2382*.

Oates 5 Feb 9[…]

Sir

I drew the account you did me the favour to send me into t[h]… method I sent it you in, not that I made any doubt of any thi[n]…

[1] Catherine, daughter of Sir Henry Bruce of Clackmannan: W. C. Mackenz[ie], *Andrew Fletcher of Saltoun*, 1935, p. 1.

in your account but as a forme to be used between us hereafter if you liked it as being the clearest and that which best discovers any mistakes if any should happen as I perceive ther[a] did that of the 4s difference. which I shall rectifie when I understand whether you mean that he receivd 8s of you or you 8s of him: For you say the mistake is in the Receit of the Lords Baylie which was 8s and the charge but 4s in the account. But since you say you have not been much acquainted with that method of account and perhaps it may be too troublesome to you I have on the backside of this letter sent you a draught of a much simpler method which is only to set downe your receits and disbursments for me just in the order of time as each of them happens with the date prefixed to each of them. This writ only in two columns without any more adoe will serve the turne and is the shortest and plainest method can be used. Pardon me that I give you this trouble about soe slight a matter But it is to shorten your pains for the future.

As to Hanny I leave you to your discretion to deale with him as you thinke most convenient. I would not deale hardly with any body But if I lose my money by neglect I deale hardly by my self and that noe body ought to expect of me

Your Son when he comes to England, next to your self will not be welcomer to any body than to me and I shall be glad if it may Lye any way in my power to doe him any service or you or any of your family. I am

Sir

Your very much obleiged and humble servant

J LOCKE

Pray give my humble service to Mrs Strachy and her son and daughter[1] and to my Cosin Lyde[2] their neighbour when you see them.

I crave leave to minde you here again of what I said concerning Pope in the close of my last letter Because I finde not any mention of it in your answer and soe fear you may possibly have forgotten it.

Address: For Cornelius Lyde Esquire at Stanton weeke To be left with Mr Codrington at his house in Highstreet Bristoll

Postmarks: FE 8; GC

[a] *Altered from* it?

---

[1] No. *38* n.; but perhaps her daughter-in-law.

[2] No. *966*, etc.

1697	Received				
Apr 3	Of Nath: Sumers		..	15	..
May 16	Of John Veale in money . .		.5	.7	6
	In bills as followeth				
	Paid Mar 28 for a quarters tax for the King ending 25 Mar	£3–3–4			
	By 10 pays to the poor paid Apr 2	1–2–3			
	For a Mason and Tender one day Apr 16 .	0–2–6			
	Paid to the Trainers May 9	0–0–7			
		4–8–8			
May 23	Of Eliz Hopkins		..	.2	.
Jun 26	Of Dav: Harol		..	.2	6
Jul 4	Of the Lords Baylife allowance for a years tax		..	.4	.

1697	Payd			
Aug 3	To Edw: Clarke Esquire . .	23	.5	4
Sept 14	For bread for the poor of Pensford	.1	..	.
169 7/8				
Jan 8	To Mr Rich: Codrington of Bristol for his bill on John Richards of London, payable & sent to you	20	..	.

2391. JOHN BONVILLE to LOCKE, 8 February 1698 (*2374, 2417*)

B.L., MS. Locke c. 4, f. 81.

London February the 8th $9\frac{7}{8}$

Honoured Cousin

Sir pray Give me Leave to Aquaint you, The occation of my write-ing: at this time, my Cousin Garrington haveing, Imployd my son In sum busines for him, And finding him very prignant, e have A great desire That my son may be his Asistant at the ffic, which Is Cald, An Asistant to the Corrispondant with mr Garrington.[1] And he tell me that he may doe it with out Any indranc of the Lirning of his Trade, the place Is 40 l par anum, But I promise nothing tell I Advise with you, for I Am not willing o doe Any Thing in these matters with out your Aprobation nd direction, To which I Humbly desir your speedy Answar, am glad to heare that you have Received All the things which sent, My wife And son give Their Humble sarvis To you, The Lord Continue his blesed presanc with you,

I Am Deare Cousin your faith full Kinsman and Humble Sarvant

JNO: BONVILLE

ddress: For Mr Locke [at Oates, by Joslyn, Bishops Stortford]

ostmark: FE 8

ndorsed by Locke: J: Bonville 8 Jan $9\frac{7}{8}$ Answered 11

392. W. BARKER to LOCKE, 10 February 1698 (*2304*)

L., MS. Locke c. 3, ff. 151–2.

r

I have received the honour you were pleased to do me on the h Instant, and esteem myself infinitely obliged for the favour, ou so kindly are pleased to express, I must acknowledge my Duty ade me so troublesome, Therefore crave your Pardon for being impertinent, hoping you will except of my Mite, The Book ing at that time the best Collection of What pass'd at Risewyck,[2]

[1] A man named Abraham Garington was 'assistant to the correspondent of Excise Salt Duty' about 1694: *Cal. Treasury Books*, 1693–6, p. 1267.

[2] Probably *Relation de ce qui s'est passé devant & dans la negotiation de la Paix à Rysvic*, ols., The Hague, 1697.

The Treacle was sent me from Venice by my Lord Manchesters Secretary;[1] the Wooden Box containing a little Spanish Chocolate the which I humble desire you would be pleased to accept, I must also make a great acknowlegement, for your kind welcomeing me home, and a more larger one, for the continuall Course of all your kindnesses to one who so little deserves it, Forgive me if I am troublesom in the acquainting you, that the Last Week my Old Adversary would have renewed my trouble, but I fortunately escaped their Malice by a safe retirement to the Stamp Office, where I shall (by the kindness of Mr Popple) remaine till fixed again with in the Verge of the Court.[2]

I have obey'd your Commands. The Gloves which are ready shall be directed according to Order, and be sent down in the Box mentioned, which will be by Saturday next. I humbly intreat you to excuse this rudeness, and beleive I shall ever acknowledge myself to be

Sir

Your most obedient and most humble servant

W: Barker

Stamp Office Feb: the 10th $9\frac{7}{8}$

Address: To John Lock: Esqre [at Oates, by Joslyn, Bishops Stortford]

Postmark: FE 10

Endorsed by Locke: W: Barker 10 Feb. $9\frac{7}{8}$[a]

[a] *Locke has written, in blank space, tenses of* venio *and their English equivalents.*

---

[1] Charles Montagu, fourth earl and first duke of Manchester (*D.N.B.*), was ambassador to Venice from December 1697 to April 1698; his secretary was Abraham Stanyan, diplomatist and author: ibid. For Venice treacle see no. *618*, etc.

[2] The Stamp Office had as its controller Pawling; Popple was secretary to the Board of Trade. The Verge of the Court was the area within the jurisdiction of the Lord High Steward and consequently a sanctuary from arrest for debt; by this time it commonly denoted the precincts of the palace of Whitehall: *O.E.D.* The Board of Trade's rooms appear to have been in the eastern part of the palace until the fire on 4 January of this year; it was then allotted rooms in the Cockpit, occupying them from 2 March: p. 370. If the identification of Barker as its clerk in 1707–10 is correct he was presumably in its service already, and given leave of absence by Popple to enable him to find security from arrest until it returned to Whitehall.

2393. Nicolas Toinard to Locke, 11/21 February 1698 (*2375*, *2411*)

B.L., MS. Locke c. 21, f. 192. For its possible transmission see p. 396, n. 3.

+

Ce 21. Fevr. 98.

Je croi, monsieur, que vous aurez à present receu ceque je vous ay envoié par M. Nelson. Je vous ay deja remersié par voie d'Holande de m'avoir procuré la connoissance de ce Gentilhomme avec qui j'ay eu des conversations egalement instructives et agreables.

Un jeune homme de mes amis[1] doit dans quelque tems passer en Angleterre. Je vous adressai autrefois son oncle, qui ne demeura pas assez de tems à Londres pour avoir l'honneur de vous y salüer. Je vous prie de faire en faveur du neveu ceque vous vouliez faire pour l'oncle, en cas qu'il se fust trouvé ocasion de lui rendre service, ainsi que vous me le marquâtes alors.

Je vous recommande toujours de me faire reponse sur ceque je vous ay prié de me mander *De dulcorata Aqua salsa.* on trouva pour cela une machine à Gambie, lorsque nous prîmes ce poste.[2] On l'a aportée ici, et j'aprens tout nouvelement que l'on veut y faire l'experience sur l'eau de mer. Je souhaite passionnement que cela reüssisse, estimant que ce seroit une des plus importantes decouvertes de nos jours, et que l'on ne devroit pas avoir negligée comme l'on a fait jusques à present.

Plusieurs gens de ma connoissance ont imaginé ici diferentes machines pour remonter les rivieres sans tirer de dessus le ferme; c'est pourquoi je vous prie de me mander qu'est devenüe celle dont vous m'avez otrefois mandé qu'on se servoit sur la Tamise, et qui refouloit la marée. Par une de vos letres vous m'en promîtes un dessin qu'avoit fait M. Hoock.

Quand le Paquebot sera retabli, je me feray un extrême plaisir de renoüer notre ancien commerce.

Tout le texte de l'ouvrage qui est *tua cura*,[3] est entierement achevé, et l'on ne le sait pas. J'ay des raisons pour ne le pas dire.

Je suis parfaitement, Monsieur,

[1] Aleaume: p. 356, etc. For his uncle and his family see no. *539* n.

[2] The French captured Fort James, near the mouth of the Gambia, in 1695: Froger, *Relation d'un voyage*, ed. 1700, pp. 20–32.

[3] 'The thing you are concerned for': so 'tua cura palumbes', 'tua cura Lycoris': Virgil, *Eclogues*, i. 58; x. 22. The Harmony.

2394. DR. JOHN WOODWARD to LOCKE, 14 February 1698 (*1994*)

B.L., MS. Locke c. 23, ff. 107–8.

Lond. 14. Febr. 97.

Sir

On Saturday Night I received your Letter, and gave immediate direction for the præparing some of the Assa fœtida in Tincture. You may please to begin with one Spoonfull at first, encreasing the Dose to two, three, or four Spoonfulls, as you find it agree with your Stomach. Take it only in the morning, and your usual Breakfast about an hour after it. We have had none of this Medicine for a long time from the East Indies: nor is there one grain of it that is good to be got about this Town. This I procured privately (for its Importation is prohibited) from Holland: and tho' much better than any to be got here, yet 'tis not so very good as I could wish. When 'tis so, it is a very generous and efficacious Medicine: tho I am ready to inform you, when ever you shall please to command me, of several others not less efficacious in your Case, and that are more easy to be procured and very good too. If this answer your Expectations, which I hope it will, you may send for more as soon as you please; for I shall be very forward in embraceing that or any other Opportunity of being serviceable to a Person of your Character and Worth. I am

Sir Your most humble servant

J WOODWARD

Address: To The Honoured Mr John Locke with a small Vial.

Endorsed by Locke: Dr Woodward 14 Feb $9\frac{7}{8}$

2395. LOCKE to PHILIPPUS VAN LIMBORCH, 21 February 1698 (*2352, 2400*)

Amsterdam University Library, MS. R.K., Ba. 258 a and b. The part of the letter in French was written by Coste; an English draft for it is printed in Appendix II, where there is a note about a French draft. On 4 April Locke sent van Limborch an altered copy; a passage is omitted and there are some minor variations: no. 2413. The altered copy is printed in *Some Familiar Letters*, pp. 410–16. The passage omitted in the copy of the French part is printed in Ollion, pp. 211–12; the part of the letter in Latin, ibid., p. 21[illegible] Answers no. *2352*; answered by nos. *2406* and *2410*.

2395. *P. van Limborch, 21 February 1698*

[Written by Coste:]

Oates 21 Feb $9\frac{7}{8}$[a]

Monsieur

La question que vous m'avez proposée, vient de la part d'une personne d'un genie si vaste et d'une si profonde capacité, que je suis confus de l'honneur, qu'il me fait de déferer si fort à mon jugement dans une occasion où il luy seroit plus avantageux et plus sûr de s'en rapporter à luy même. Je ne sai quelle opinion vous avez pû luy donner de moy, seduit par l'amitié que vous me portez; mais une chose dont je suis fort assûré, c'est que, si je ne consultois que ma propre reputation, j'eviterois d'exposer mes foibles pensées devant une personne d'un si grand jugement, et que je ne me hazarderois pas à regarder cet Article comme une Question à prouver, bien des gens étant peut-étre d'avis qu'il vaut mieux le recevoir en qualité de Maxime, parce que selon eux, il est mieux établi sur les fondemens ordinaires que si l'on tachoit de l'expliquer par des spéculations et des raisonnemens un peu éloignez de ceux qu'on a accoûtumé de faire en cette rencontre. Mais je sai que la Personne par qui je croy que cette Question vous a été proposée, a l'esprit autrement tourné. Sa candeur et sa probité égalent sa science et ses autres grandes quallitez. S'il ne trouve pas mes raisons assez claires ou assez convainquantes, il ne sera pas pour cela porté à condamner aussitôt mon intention, ni à mal juger de moy sous prétexte que mes preuves ne sont pas aussi bonnes qu'il l'auroit souhaité. Enfin, moins il trouvera de satisfaction dans mes raisonnemens, plus il sera obligé de me pardonner, parce que, quelque convaincu que je soi de ma foiblesse, je n'ai pas laissé d'obeir á ses ordres. J'écris donc simplement parce que vous le voulez l'un et l'autre, et je veux bien, Monsieur, que vous fassiez voir, s'il vous plait, ma Lettre à cet excellent homme et aux autres personnes qui se trouverent dans vôtre Conference. Mais c'est aux conditions suivantes: la prémiere que ces Messieurs me promettront de m'apprendre librement et sincerement leurs pensées sur ce que je dis: la seconde, que vous ne donnerez aucune copie de ce que je vous écris à qui que ce soit, mais que vous me promettez de jetter cette Lettre au feu, quand je vous prierai de le faire. A quoy je serois bien aise que vous eussiez la bonté d'ajouter une troisiéme condition, C'est que ces Messieurs me feront

[a] *Date inserted by Locke.*

l'honneur de me communiquer les raisons sur lesquelles ils établissent eux mêmes l'unité de Dieu.

> La question dont vous me[a] parlez,[a] se reduit à ceci, *Comment l'Unité de Dieu peut étre prouvée?* ou en d'autres termes, *Comment on peut prouver qu'il n'y a qu'un Dieu?*

Pour résoudre cette question, il est nécessaire de savoir avant de venir aux preuves de l'Unité de Dieu, ce qu'on entend par le mot de Dieu.

L'idée ordinaire, et à ce que je croy, la veritable idée qu'ont de Dieu ceux qui reconnoissent son existence, c'est Qu'il est un Etre infini, éternel, incorporel, et tout parfait. Or cette idée une fois reconnüe, il me semble fort aisé d'en deduire l'Unité de Dieu. En effect un Etre qui est tout parfait, ou pour ainsi dire, parfaitement Parfait, ne peut être qu'unique; parce qu'un Etre tout parfait ne scauroit manquer d'aucun des attributs, perfections ou dégrez de perfections qu'il luy importe plus de posseder que d'en être privé; car autrement il s'en faudroit d'autant qu'il ne fut entierement parfait, Par exemple, avoir du pouvoir est une plus grande perfection que de n'en avoir point; avoir plus de pouvoir est une plus grande perfection que d'en avoir moins, et avoir tout pouvoir (ce qui est etre tout puissant) C'est une plus grande perfection que de ne l'avoir pas tout. Cela posé, deux etres Tout-puissans sont incompatibles; parce qu'on est obligé de supposer que l'un doit vouloir necessairement ce que l'autre veut, et en ce cas là l'un des Deux dont la volonté est necessairement déterminée par la volonté de l'autre, n'est pas libre, et n'a pas par conséquent cette perfection-là, car il est mieux d'étre libre que d'étre soumis à la détermination de la volonté d'un autre. Que s'ils ne sont pas tous deux reduits à la necessité de vouloir toûjours la même chose, alors l'un peut vouloir faire ce que l'autre ne voudroit pas qui fut fait; auquel cas la volonté de l'un prévaudra sur la volonté de l'autre, et ainsi celui des deux dont la puissance ne sauroit seconder la volonté, n'est pas Tout-puissant, car il ne peut pas faire autant que l'autre. Donc l'un des Deux n'est pas tout puissant, donc il n'y a ni ne sauroit y avoir deux Tout-puissans, ni par conséquent deux Dieux.

Par la même idée de perfection nous venons à connoître que dieu est *Omniscient*; or dans la supposition de deux Etres distincts qui

[a] *MS.* me, parlez

ont un pouvoir et une volonté distincte, c'est une imperfection de ne pouvoir pas cacher ses pensées. Mais si l'un des deux cache ses pensées á l'autre, cet autre n'est pas Omniscient, car non seulement il ne connoit pas tout ce qui peut etre connu, mais il ne connoit pas même ce qu'un autre connoit.

On peut dire la même chose de la Toute-présence de Dieu: il vaut mieux qu'il soit par tout dans l'etenduë infinie de l'espace que d'etre exclu de quelque partie de cet espace, car s'il est exclu de quelque endroit, il ne peut pas y operer, ni savoir ce qu'on y fait, et par conséquent il n'est ni Tout-puissant ni *Omniscient*.

Que si pour aneantir les raisonnemens que je viens de faire, on dit que les deux Dieux qu'on suppose, ou les deux cent mille (car par la même ⟨raison⟩[a] qu'il peut y en avoir deux, il y en peut avoir deux millions parce qu'on n'a plus aucun moyen d'en limiter le nombre) Si l'on oppose, dis-je, que plusieurs Dieux ont une parfaite toute-puissance qui soit exactement la même, qu'ils ont Aussi la même connoissance, la même volonté, et qu'ils existent également dans le même point[b–] individuel, c'est seulement multiplier le même[–b] Etre, mais dans le fonds et dans la verité de la chose on ne fait que reduire une pluralité supposeé à une veritable unité. Car de supposer deux Etres intelligens, qui connoissent, veulent et font incessamment la même chose, et qui n'ont pas une existence separée, c'est supposer, en paroles, une pluralité, mais poser effectivement une simple unité. Car être inseparablement uni par l'entendement, par la volonté, par l'action et par le lieu, c'est être autant uni qu'un Etre intelligent peut être uni à luy-même; et par conséquent, supposer que là où il y a une telle union il peut y avoir deux Etres, c'est supposer une division sans division, et une chose divisée d'avec elle même.

Considerons un peu plus à fonds la Toute-présence de Dieu. Il faut de toute nécessité que Dieu soit Tout-présent, à l'infini; à moins qu'il ne soit renfermé dans quelque petit coin de l'Espace, sans que nous sachions, ni pourquoy, ni comment, ni par qui, ni en quel lieu: je dis un petit coin parce qu'une certaine partie déterminée de l'Espace, de quelque étendüe qu'on la suppose, est fort peu de chose si elle est comparée à l'Espace infini. Or si Dieu a une Tout-puissance infinie, c'est je croi, un preuve approchant de la démonstration, qu'il ne peut y avoir qu'un Dieu. Quelle

[a] *MS.* mison? [b–b] *Interlined.*

que soit la nature, l'être ou la substance de Dieu, là où Dieu est, il y a certainement quelque chose de réel et qui est plus réel, que tous les autres Etres. Supposons donc que cet Etre réel existe dans tel point Physique de l'Espace qu'on voudra supposer, je dis qu'il s'ensuit demonstrativement de là qu'un autre Etre réel de la même espéce, ne sauroit être dans le même point individuel de l'Espace; car en ce cas-là, il n'y auroit qu'un seul Etre dans ce point, parce que là où il n'y a aucune différence ni à l'égard de l'espéce, ni à l'égard du lieu, il ne peut y avoir qu'un seul Etre. Et qu'on ne s'imagine pas que ce raisonnement ne peut être bon qu'à l'égard du Corps et des parties de la Matiére; car on peut, je pense, l'appliquer fort bien à ce qu'on appelle *l'Espace pur*, qui est ce qu'il y a de plus éloigné de la Matiére. Car deux points physiques d'Espace ne peuvent pas plûtôt être reduits en un seul, que deux Atomes physiques de Matiére etre reduits à un seul Atome. La raison de cette impossibilité est fondée sur ce que, si deux points d'espace pouvoient être reduits en un, tout l'Espace pourroit être reduit en un seul point physique; ce qui est aussi impossible, qu'il est impossible que toute la Matiére pût etre reduite à un seul Atome.

Pour moy qui ne connois pas ce que c'est la Substance de la Matiére, je connois encore moins ce que c'est que la Substance de Dieu; mais je sçai pourtant que cette Substance est quelque chose, et qu'elle doit exclurre d'où elle est toutes les autres Substances de la même espéce, (s'il pouvoit y en avoir de telles,). Si donc Dieu est immense et présent par tout, c'est pour moy une démonstration qu'il n'y a qu'un Dieu, et qu'il n'y en peut avoir qu'un seul.

Je me suis hazardé à vous écrire mes réflexions sur ce sujet, comme elles se sont présentées à mon esprit, sans les ranger dans un certain ordre qui pourroit servir peut-être à les mettre dans un plus grand jour si on leur donnoit un peu plus ⟨d'étenduë⟩.[a] Mais ceci ⟨doit⟩[b] paroître devant des personnes d'une si grande pénétration, que ce seroit les amuser inutilement que de développer davantage mes pensées. Telles qu'elles sont, je vous prie de m'en écrire votre opinion et celle de ces Messieurs, afin que, selon le jugement que vous en ferez, je puisse, pour ma propre satisfaction les examiner de nouveau et leur donner plus de force, (ce que ma mauvaise santé et le peu de loisir qui me reste, ne me permettent pas

[a] *MS.* d'éttendüe, *altered from* d'attendüe   [b] *MS.* doir

de faire présentement) ou bien les abandonner tout-à-fait comme ne pouvant etre d'aucun usage. Je suis[a]–

Monsieur

Vôtre tres humble et tres obeïssant serviteur

JOHN LOCKE.–[a]

[Written by Locke:]

En tibi Vir Amplissime, quia voluntati tuæ et aliorum expectationi obtemperare par est, epistolam de re non exili, mole certè non exiguam, an argumentorum pondere non levem penes me non est statuere. Tuum istud esto judicium, et si libet Domini Clerici (quem officiosissime saluto). vos prælectam inter vos, et serio examinatam, vel igni mandate, vel viro eximio aliisque, quorum causâ scripta est, ostendite, prout vobis visum fuerit. Cavete vero ne vestra erga me amicitia mentem vestram benevolentiâ abductam avertat a justo rigore. Siquid enim in ⟨ea⟩[b] vel parum solidè vel parum cautè dictum reperiatis, mallem totam tenebris sepeliri, quam futili aliqua ratiocinatione in causâ tam seriâ ineptire vel me ipsum censuræ exponere tantorum virorum. Apographum cave ne cuiquam des

Nuper a filio tuo gratissimas accepi literas quibus certiorem me facit se brevi ad nos transmigraturum. Incommodè accidit

[a–a] *In Locke's hand.* [b] *MS.* eo

There, excellent Sir, since it is proper to comply with your wish and the expectation of others, is a letter on no meagre subject, certainly not small in bulk, whether not light in the weight of the arguments it is not for me to decide. That must be for your judgement and, if you will, for Mr. Le Clerc's, to whom I send my most respectful greetings. When you have read it over between you, and examined it seriously, either consign it to the flames or show it to the excellent man and the others for whose sake it was written, as you see fit. But take care lest your friendship for me diverts your minds, led astray by goodwill, from their just rigour. For if you should find in my letter anything not solidly or not cautiously enough expressed I should prefer the whole to be buried in darkness rather than to trifle with some worthless reasoning in so serious a matter or to expose myself to the censure of men of such standing. Take care not to give a copy to anyone.

I recently received a very welcome letter from your son in which he informs me that he will shortly cross to this country. It unfortunately happens that I, being driven out of London by the difficulty of breathing the city air and the weakness of my lungs, shall be absent when the new

me gravi aeris urbani halitu, pulmonumque imbecillitate Londino expulsum abesse cum appulerit novus hospes, qua tempestate (sicubi alias) novo advenæ et rerum nostrarum imperito opportunè adessem. sed spero ad me huc pertendere non gravabitur. Domina Masham materfamilias illum enixe invitat, et gestit in filio paternam utriusque agnoscere et colere amicitiam. Hospes meus Londinensis *Pawling* illum docebit iter et proficiscendi tempora et commoda. Brevis est transitus nec incommodus. Ad eundem *Pawling* etiam scripsi ut si qua alia in re filio tuo vel consilio vel operâ utilis esse possit, ut pro viribus ⟨adjuvet⟩.[a] Vir probus est et cui filius tuus tuto fidere potest, et spondeo facturum. Fæminam tuam optimam et filiam inprimisque filium nomine ⟨meo⟩[b] salutes. Ad Guenellonem nostrum sub initio hujus mensis scripsi. illum familiamque ejus Veneumque cæterosque nostros meo nomine salutes rogo

Noted by van Limborch: (i: beneath date at head of letter): Recepi 21 Mart. 98. (ii: at head of part in Latin): 21 Febr. 169$\frac{7}{8}$

[a] *MS.* adjuvit [b] *MS.* me

---

visitor arrives, at a time of all others when I might seasonably have assisted a newcomer and one inexperienced in things here. But I hope that he will not grudge pushing on to me here. Lady Masham, the mistress of the house, earnestly invites him and is longing to recognize and cultivate in the son the friendship that existed between their fathers. My London host, Pawling, will tell him about the journey and the times and opportunities for setting out. It is of short duration and not troublesome. I have also written to the same Pawling to do his utmost to help your son if he can be useful to him in any other matter by giving him advice or practical assistance. He is an honest man and one whom your son can safely trust, and I promise that he will do [what is asked of him]. Please give my greetings to your excellent wife and daughter, and especially to your son. I wrote to our friend Guenellon at the beginning of this month. Please give my greetings to him and his family, and to Veen and our other friends.

2396. JOHN NELSON to LOCKE, 23 February 1698

B.L., MS. Locke c. 16, ff. 131–2. For the writer and for the letter and books carried by him see pp. 263, 264, 289.

Sir

Though I have been some time since arived at London yet through indispostion and your absence, your leter and books from mr Toinard have not been sent forward, in our passage from Calais we mett with such weather as allmost fild us with water wherein we had lik't to have perished, soe that my trunck and things were all wetted, in your books you have likewise suffered, of which you must take care to preserve them by driing of them, I am troubled for the misadventure on your sake, but since it could not be avoided, I hope you will rather receive satisfaction from our Escape which was great, then be concern'd at your Damage, I hope that the season of the year will shortly admitt your returne unto towne, before my goeing to America, soe that I may have the Advantage and honor of takeing my leave of you, as being one, for whom, I have a very profound respect and am

Sir your most humble and Obedient Servant
JOHN NELSON

London Feb: 23: 1698

Address: For The Honourable John Lock Esqr etc These

Endorsed by Locke: J: Nelson 23 Feb 9$\frac{7}{8}$

2397. GEORGE WALLS to LOCKE, 24 February 1698 (1761)

B.L., MS. Locke c. 23, ff. 56–7.

Gray's Inne Feb: 24th—9$\frac{7}{8}$

Honour'd Sir

As I formerly tooke the libertie to lay before you some part of the hard usage I had met with in relation to my smal living in Worcester shire;[1] I now take the boldnes humbly to entrete your assistance in order to my deliverance from it; which a letter of yours to my Lord Chancellor in my behalfe would (I conceive) be the most probable meanes of effecting. The Rectory of Toplow near Windsor is verie likely to be soone vacant by the death of Mr Lovet the incumbent, whose life is now despair'd of.[2] Tis in the guift of the seals; and the valu of it about 120l per annum; and if you shal plese to dispose his Lordship to think me worthy of it; twould lay me under all the obligation to you that one made easie

[1] Walls was rector of Holt, Worcestershire, from 1695 until his death in 1727.

[2] Thomas Lovet, M.A.; rector of Taplow, Bucks., from 1681 until his death early in 1699; prebendary of Ely 1692–9: Venn.

for the remainder of his life ought to acknowledg. most earnestly desiring your health and preservation. I remaine

Honour'd Sir

your most affectionat and oblig'd humble servant

G WALLS

Address: For John Lock Esqr [at Oates, by Joslyn, Bishops Stortford]
Postmark: FE 24
Endorsed by Locke: Dr Walls 24 Feb. 9$\frac{7}{8}$ Answered 28

2398. LOCKE to EDWARD CLARKE, 25 February 1698 (2379, *2399*)

Rand, pp. 532–3. 'The address is discoloured and the paper dropping to pieces.' Words in square brackets are supplied by Rand. Answered by no. *2399*.

Oates, 25th February, 1697–8.

Dear Sir,

I return my thanks to the College and my friends at the Pine Apples[1] for the concern for my health which they express in your obliging letter of the . . . instant. As for a speedy recovery which you wish me, the little progress I make in the recovering of my breath, since the great relief I found in the first night I was here, gives me no expectation of it. And for a perfect recovery, as you also [wish] me, my lungs are too much decayed and my life too far spent to permit the hopes of [it]. The cruel, sharp weather which this winter continues still upon us here is [not] at all favourable to either. What warmer weather will do when the approach [of the] sun shall be able to prevail, we shall see when the season comes. In the meantime I am as careful of myself by the fireside as you can desire. My time is all divided between my bed and the chimney-corner, for not being able to walk for want of breath upon the least stirring, I am a prisoner not only to the house, but almost to my chair, so that never did anybody so truly lead a sedentary life as I do.

I beg you to give my humble service to Mrs. Clarke. I am sorry I hear nothing of making what use is to be had in town for

[1] Mrs. Clarke and some of the children appear to have stayed in London from about December 1697 until the summer of 1699, with perhaps an interval in the summer of 1698: nos. 2361–2611 *passim*. The Pine Apples was evidently the sign or name of their London lodging: p. 329.

her perfect recovery. If it comes itself I am better pleased, but if it does not, and she sits still and does nothing to g[ain it], I am not at all pleased. My service to the rest of your fireside, especially to my wife and to the Bachelor.

I writ some time since to Mr. Popple to give you a copy of my project about the better relief and employment of the poor[1] since our Board thought not fit to make use of it, that now the House was upon that consideration you might make use of it, [if] it should suggest to you anything that you might think useful in the case. It is a matter that requires every Englishman's best thoughts; for there is not any one thing that I know upon the right regulation whereof the prosperity of his country more depends. And whilst I have any breath left I shall always be an Englishman.

I wish you a little more ease and a great deal of happiness. And am . . .

Endorsed: Mr. Locke of the present state of his health, etc. Received the 28th February, 1697. Answered the 1st March.

2399. EDWARD CLARKE to LOCKE, 1 March 1698 (2398, 2408)

B.L., MS. Locke c. 6, f. 133. Printed in Rand, pp. 533–4. Answers no. 2398; answered by no. 2408.

London March the 1st. 169$\frac{7}{8}$

Deare Sir,

I am heartily Concern'd you improve noe faster in your Health, But I hope now the Warm-Weather will perfectly sett you up againe, which I most heartily wish and Pray for etc:

Mr. Popple hath obleiged mee with a Coppy of your Paper touching the Poore, And shall make the Best use I can of it, When ever I can find Ingenuity, Honesty, and Industry enough to make a proper Law for the Putting it in Execution; The Batchelor is with mee and Mrs. Clarke, your Wife, and All the younge Fry at the Pyne-Apples, yours and my Lady's humble servants to whome Wee all desire our service may bee presented;

[1] The document is printed in Fox Bourne, ii. 377–91.

Your Letter for Holland that came Inclosed in your last to mee, I have delivered into the Post-House with my own hand and am,

your most Affectionate and obleiged humble servant

EDW: CLARKE:

The Duke of Shrewsbury is expected in Town this Weeke, And 'tis said will bee Chamberlaine etc:[1]

The Weather hath been such hitherto, untill now, That Mrs. Clarke has not yett taken any thing for Her Distemper, But is notwithstanding, I thanke God, indifferently well, And I hope will now bee Advised etc:

Address: These, For John Locke Esqr. [at Oates, by Joslyn, Bishops Stortford]
Frank: Edw: Clarke:

Postmark: (G.P.O., indecipherable)

Endorsed by Locke: E. Clarke 1 Mar $9\frac{7}{8}$ Answered 19

2400. PHILIPPUS VAN LIMBORCH to LOCKE, 1/11 March 1698 (2395, *2406*)

B.L., MS. Locke c. 14, ff. 111–12. Copy by van Limborch in Amsterdam University Library, MS. R.K., III D 16, f. 201. The last two paragraphs, with alterations to conceal Hudde's identity, are printed from the copy in *Some Familiar Letters*, pp. 406–8. Answered by no. 2413.

Amplissime Vir

Quod semper in votis habui, ut, postquam omnis tui denuo videndi spes decollasset, filius meus in Angliam abiens optatissimo tuo conspectu non tantum, sed et prudentissimo consilio ac sapientissima directione fruatur, ejus mihi nunc potiundi spem proximam affulgere, est quod mihi summopere gratuler: Omnes enim sinceri ac prudentis amici partes Te erga ipsum impleturum certus sum. Quare eum multis Tibi non sum commendaturus: sufficit amico

---

Excellent Sir,

A ray of hope of my soon obtaining what I have long desired, [namely] that, after all [my] hope of seeing you anew had failed, my son, going hence to England, might enjoy not only the wished-for sight of you but also your prudent advice and wise direction, is a matter on which I may most heartily congratulate myself; for I am sure that you will perform towards him all the offices of a sincere and prudent friend. For that reason I shall not recom-

---

[1] Shrewsbury, who had been ill at his seat in Gloucestershire, came to Windsor about 9 March; he again fell ill and did not come to London until November. He did not become Lord Chamberlain until 25 October 1699.

candidissimo unum hoc dixisse, meum esse filium, et quicquid illi officii præstiteris, id mihi præstari, meque per id Tibi reddi obligatissimum. Destinaveram illum ego in prima adolescentia studiis humanioribus: Verum illi præ Musis Mercurius, et negotiosa mercatorum commercia placent. Ego animo ejus non obluctandum censui, certus nihil invita Minerva eximium præstari posse. Quare mutato vitæ instituto, iis, quibus mercatura constat, imbuendum curavi: in quibus se sedulum, vigilantem et attentum ostendit. Postea, ut negotiandi peritiam acquireret, mercatori eum tradidi, cui ex lege nostri contractus octo annis ministrare debuit; ita tamen, ut sex prioribus annis solummodo hero suo (liceat mihi hac voce uti) esset obligatus, duo vero posteriores arbitrio meo essent relicti. Verum nondum expleto quinquennio ego filium meum gravissima de causa domum revocavi; quam paucis Tibi exponam. Quæsivi ego hominem negotiandi peritissimum, et sedulum. Talem reperi quidem, sed præterea præsumtuosum, morosum, et, quod pessimum, plumbeas iras gerentem;[1] qui toto illo tempore, et præsertim posterioribus annis, cum filium meum in negotiationis ipsius arcana penitius penetrare suspicabatur, eum non tantum duriter, sed et contumeliose tractavit, et a negotiis

---

mend him to you with many words; it is enough to say only this to a most candid friend, that he is my son, and that whatever service you do for him is done for me, and that I am thereby rendered extremely obliged to you. I had intended him in his earliest youth for polite studies. But Mercury and the merchants' busy traffic please him more than the Muses. Being sure that nothing excellent can be done against the grain, I thought that his inclination ought not to be opposed. As his course in life had been changed I saw to his being instructed in the practice of commerce; in this he showed himself diligent, vigilant, and attentive. After that, in order that he should acquire business experience, I entrusted him to a merchant whom by the terms of our contract he was obliged to serve for eight years; the terms were such, however, that he was bound to his master (if I may use that word) for the first six years only, but the last two were left to my decision. But before five years were ended I recalled my son home for a very serious reason which I shall show you in a few words. I sought a man much experienced in business, and diligent. I found such a man, but in addition he was presumptuous and morose and, worst of all, his anger was 'heavy as lead'.[1] During all this time, and especially in the later years when he suspected my son of penetrating too far into his business secrets, he treated him not only harshly but also abusively, and calling him away from more important, put him to meaner employments; and in order to do that with

---

[1] Adapted from Plautus, *Poenulus*, III. vi. 18.

gravioribus avocatum vilioribus applicuit: utque id prætextu aliquo faceret, filium meum quasi omnium ignarum, et qui nihil fere toto illo quinquennii spatio addidicerat, coram me criminatus est. Cum distinctius inquirerem, quid in filio meo desideravit; potissimum causatus est, illius caracteres non esse bonos. Ego semper hominem blande compellavi. Sed nuper eò delapsus est, ut diceret, filium meum non satis ingenio valere ut mercaturam addiscat, esse ipsum sibi oneri magis quam usui: itaque mihi se considerandum dare, an non alteri vitæ generi illum applicandum censeam. Ego re cum uxore et amicis quibusdam maturo consilio deliberata, filium domum revocare statui. Videbam quidem, obstare filio posse, quod ministerii sui annos non explesset; et facilius credi hero quam ministro, si qua controversia oboriatur: sed ad altera parte prævidebam, filium multo indignius ab ipso in posterum habitum iri, neque ullam mihi cum ipso in posterum expostulandi reliquam fore occasionem; semper enim objicere potuissel, me monitum nihilominus filium vitæ generi, cui idoneus non esset, applicatum velle: præterea ex aliis, quibus cum ipso nenotium fuit, audiebam, inter mercatores indolem ejus truculentam esse notissimam; quorum quidam mihi affirmabant, non mirari es, quod filius integrum sexennium non impleret, sed se non sine

---

some pretext complained of my son in my presence, as if he was totally ignorant and had learnt almost nothing in that whole period of five years. When I inquired more precisely as to what he found wanting in my son, he alleged principally that his handwriting was not good. I always spoke the man fair. But recently he sank so far as to say that my son does not possess sufficient ability to learn commerce and that he is a burden for him rather than a help; and so he invited me to consider whether I did not think that he should be put to some other kind of life. Having considered the matter maturely with my wife and some friends I decided to recall my son home. I saw indeed that it could stand in his way that he had not completed the years of his service, and that if any dispute arose the master would be believed more readily than the servant; but on the other hand I foresaw that my son would be much more unworthily treated by him in the future, nor would any opportunity of remonstrating with him in future remain for me; for he could always have objected that I had been warned and had nevertheless determined to put my son to a kind of life for which he is not fit; moreover I had heard from others who had dealings with him that his truculent nature was well known among the merchants, some of whom assured me that they were not surprised that my son had not completed his full six years, but had heard not without wonder that he had been able to hold out for more than four in the service of so morose and so truculent a man. Therefore, deeming that of two evils the least was to be chosen and

admiratione audivisse, quod ultra quadriennium in famulatu hominis adeo morosi ac truculenti perdurare potuerit. Quare ex duobus malis minimum eligendum, et occasionem hanc minime mihi negligendam ratus, post paucos dies ad ipsum redii, dixique, nolle me filium ipsi esse oneri, neque eum vitæ generi cui aptus non sit applicare; itaque reliquum, quod adhuc restabat ministrandi tempus illi remittere: meque filii capacitatem exploraturum, ut cui vitæ instituto aptus sit cognoscam. Ille hoc inopinato meo sermone perculsus, cum honeste revocare dicta sua non posset, acquievit: sed rogavit, ne filium statim domum abducerem, sed diebus aliquot ipsi concederem, ut negotia, quæ tum satis spissa erant, facilius expedire posset. Ego, ut honori filii consulerem, facile consensi; quia hac petitione ipso facto priores suos sermones satis aperte revocare videbatur. Verum post duas elapsas hebdomadas filium domum revocavi, et statim profectus sui specimina domi meæ conficere jussi. Ostendi ego illa peritis mercatoribus, qui ea approbant, et post varios cum filio meo sermones habitos eum scientia ad negotiationem necessaria abunde instructum affirmant, mihique autores sunt, ut ipsum, antequam totum se negotiationi applicet, quamprimum in Angliam mittam, ut mercatores Anglos, quorum commercia desiderat, ipse adeat. Nunc eum

---

that this opportunity was by no means to be neglected by me, I returned to him a few days later and said that I did not want my son to be a burden to him or to put my son to a kind of life for which he was not suited; and so would release him from the remaining period of my son's service; and I would investigate my son's capacity so as to learn for what course in life he was suited. Being upset by this unexpected language from me, since he could not decently retract what he had said he agreed; but he requested me not to take my son away home at once but to grant him to him for some days, so that he [the merchant] could more readily dispatch some business affairs, which were sufficiently numerous at that time. In order to provide for my son's repute I readily consented, for by the very fact of his making this request he appeared to be retracting openly enough what he had said earlier. But after two weeks had gone by I recalled my son home and immediately bade him compose there some examples that would show his progress. I have shown them to experienced merchants, who commend them and, after having had various talks with my son, assure me that he is amply equipped with the knowledge necessary for commerce and advise me, before he altogether applies himself to it, to send him to England as soon as possible so that he may meet the English merchants with whom he wishes to have dealings. I now commit him to your protection; and if any exertion of yours, whether in advising him or in recommending him to honourable merchants,

tuæ commendo fidei; et si qua tua opera, sive consulendo, sive eum honestis mercatoribus commendando, illi in honesto hoc proposito utilis esse potest, rogo per amicitiæ nostræ jura, ut eam illi impertiri velis. Scio paternum de filio testimonium posse esse suspectum. Tu nosti quis et qualis ego sim. Hoc unum tantum affirmabo, ipsi omnem herilem pecuniam fuisse concreditam, ipsumque illam integro triennio administrasse; in qua administratione se maxime fidelem ostendit, cum tamen multa millia, imo aliquot centena florenorum millia acceperit et expenderit, et quandoque triginta florenorum millia auri, et amplius, simul in potestate sua habuerit; quæ magna sunt irritamenta homini adolescenti, et duriter ac contumeliose tractato. Cum aliquoties hero ostenderem sollicitudinem meam, qui novemdecim aut viginti annorum adolescenti tantam pecuniæ summam crederet; respondit, ipsum esse honestis moribus, non dilapidatorem; tales non indigere pecunia; ac proinde tuto eam illi committi: se in ejus fide plane esse securum. Vix ea cum tanta filii mei vituperatione conciliari possunt. Sed ego semper credidi, et etiamnum credo, ipsum sperasse se per querelas de exiguis filii mei profectibus a me impetraturum, ut eum non ante expletum octennium ad me revocarem. In qua opinione me sermones ejus cum amicis, quibus se nequaquam

---

can be serviceable to him in this honourable design, I ask you by the rights of our friendship willingly to bestow it on him. I know that a father's testimony concerning his son can be suspect. You know who and what I am. I shall tell you only this one thing, that all his master's money was entrusted to him and he managed it for a whole three years; he showed himself eminently trustworthy in managing it when, nevertheless, he received and paid out many thousands, indeed some hundreds of thousands of gulden, and sometimes had thirty thousand and more gulden in cash at once in his control; which are great incitements for a young man, and one harshly and abusively treated. When at various times I expressed to the master my anxiety on account of his entrusting to a youth of nineteen or twenty so large a sum of money he answered that my son was virtuous and no spendthrift; such young men do not need money and accordingly it was safely entrusted to him; he was completely free from care in reliance on him. These statements can scarcely be reconciled with so much censure of my son. But I have always believed, and still believe, that he hoped by complaints of my son's poor progress to obtain from me [a promise] not to recall him to me before the eight years were ended. His conversations with his friends, to whom he says that he by no means expected such a decision by me to recall my son, confirm me in this opinion. I wanted to pour all this into your, my dearest friend's, bosom, so that you should be fully informed about my

tale meum de revocando filio decretum exspectasse ait, confirmant. Hæc in tuum amici mei sincerissimi sinum effundere volui, ut plene de filii mei statu instructus sis. Ipse tibi, si necesse sit, multa particularia, quæ chartæ committere prolixum nimis foret, narrare poterit. Velim autem hæc Tibi soli dicta; hæc enim nihil ad alios. Filius Tibi ostendet heri sui apocham, qua ipsius rationes accepti et expensi approbat; quæ unica sufficiens fidelitatis filii documentum est.

Hac occasione mitto tibi quædam ex Paulo Servita excerpta,[1] quæ Historiæ Inquisitionis inseri possunt. Ego autores, quos nunc evolvo, majore cum applicatione ad materiam Inquisitionis lego, quam antehac, et si quid, quod ad majorem illius illustrationem facere possit, occurrat, illud excerpere soleo, et historiam meam locupletiorem reddere. Tu, si velis, aliis a me antehac ad te missis et hæc adjungere poteris. Quæ mihi ante triennium ex Itinerario du Mont suppeditasti,[2] ea quanto magis considero, tantò magis historiæ meæ inserenda judico. Licet enim leges Pontificiæ secretum confessionis revelari vetent, multa tamen in favorem fidei fiunt legibus prohibita, quas sancivisse videntur eum tantum in finem, ut simpliciores iis irretiti facilius caperentur. Itaque non tantum

---

son's position. If need be he will be able to recount to you many particulars which it would be too tedious to commit to paper. But I wish these things to be told to you alone, for they are no concern of others. My son will show you his master's acquittance by which he confirms his accounts of receipts and payments as correct, which by itself is a sufficient proof of my son's trustworthiness.

I take this opportunity to send you some extracts from Paul the Servite[1] which can be inserted in my *Historia Inquisitionis*. I am reading the authors whom I now study with greater attention than formerly to the subject of the Inquisition, and if anything occurs that can throw greater light on it I usually extract it and render my *Historia* the richer. If you wish you will be able to add these also to others that I have formerly sent you. The more I consider what you sent me three years ago from du Mont's itinerary,[2] so much the more do I think that it ought to be inserted in my *Historia*. For although the Pontifical laws forbid the disclosure of secrets uttered in confession, yet many things are done on behalf of the faith that are forbidden by laws which they seem to have enacted with the sole object of entangling the more simple-minded in them and so catching them more easily. I think therefore that not just the laws of the Inquisition should be considered, but chiefly its deeds and proceedings, which are very often in direct conflict

---

[1] Fra Paolo Sarpi, the historian of the Council of Trent: *N.B.G.*
[2] No. 1804.

Inquisitionis leges, sed præcipue gesta et acta illius, quæ cum legibus sæpissime adversa fronte pugnant, consideranda censeo. Unum hoc expendi meretur, quod du Mont ait, Confessarios Melitenses obligatos esse Inquisitoribus revelare, quicquid ipsis in secreta confessione negotium fidei spectans confitentur homines. Secretas illas confessiones Inquisitoribus revelari, nullus dubito: Legem de ea revelanda exstare credere vix possum: fortasse confessariis hoc mandatur viva voce, licet nulla ejusmodi lex exstat. Quibus accedit, quod sit homo Reformatus, et peregrinus, qui inter peregrinandum hoc ex quorundam incolarum sermonibus hausit, quorumque relationes quandoque valde esse incertas, imo falsas, ex itinerariis quibus Belgium describitur sæpius ipse deprehendi. Quare considerandum, quomodo ejusmodi cavillationes Pontificiorum solide retundi possint. Quicquid vero hujus sit, digna mihi hæc narratio visa[a] est,[a] quæ historiæ meæ inseratur.[b] Si quæ talia Tibi inter legendum plura occurrunt, rogo ut et mihi ea impertiri velis.

Scripsi ante duos aut tres menses, D.Consulem Hudde argumenta tua de unitate divina videndi desiderio teneri. Ego aperte et rotunde tecum agere volui, et quod mihi in mandatis datum erat celare

[a] *Van Limborch's copy reads* videtur [b] *Here the copy adds a clause* si scriptoris alicujus pontificiis non suspecti autoritate confirmari posset.

with the laws. This one thing that du Mont says deserves to be pondered, that the Maltese confessors are bound to disclose to the Inquisitors anything pertaining to matters of faith that men confess to them in secret confession. I have no doubt that those secret confessions are disclosed to the Inquisitors; I can scarcely believe that there exists a law to disclose them; perhaps this is ordered to confessors orally although no law of that sort exists. To which is to be added that the man is a Protestant and a foreigner who while travelling drew this from the remarks of some of the inhabitants; such people's reports, as I myself have more than once found out from itineraries in which the Low Countries are described, are sometimes very doubtful or even false. It is therefore to be considered how the Pontificians' chicaneries of that kind can be solidly refuted. But however this may be, this narration has seemed to me worthy of insertion in my *Historia*. If more such things meet you when you are reading, please impart them to me.

I wrote [to you] two or three months ago that the Burgomaster Mr. Hudde is possessed by a desire to see your arguments concerning the unity of God. I wanted to deal openly and roundly with you, and could not conceal what I was charged to do. I was unwilling to interrupt your more serious affairs or to cause you any trouble. I know that, if you can obtain it from your mind and your affairs, your arguments will be most welcome to the Burgomaster, for he values both your penetration and your judgement very highly

non potui. Nolui ego graviora tua negotia interturbare, aut aliquid Tibi molestiæ creare. Scio, si ab animo ac negotiis tuis impetrare possis, argumenta tua D.Consuli fore gratissima; maximi enim et acumen et judicium tuum facit. Si vero negotia tua tempus attentæ ejusmodi meditationi et diffusiori scriptioni requisitum tibi non concedant, aut aliquam forte inde tibi creandam molestiam verearis (de quo tamen Te securum esse jubeo) ego a Te monitus Consuli prout potero Te excusatum reddam. Velim tamen eo in casu excusationis rationes a Te mihi suppeditari: Malim autem, ut, si sine incommodo, aut incommodi metu, possis, Te Consuli gratiam hanc facere, ut materiam hanc, quam jam diu animo volvit, tua opera explanatiorem habeat. Vale Vir Amplissime: salutat Te uxor mea ac filia. Salutem plurimam meo nomine Dominæ Masham dices.

Tui Amantissimus
PHILIPPUS A LIMBORCH

Amstelodami 11 Martii

14
16 98
20

Endorsed by Locke: P: Limborch 11 Mar $9\frac{7}{8}$ Answered 2 Apr

---

But if your affairs do not allow you the time requisite for such careful consideration and for writing at any length, or if perchance you fear that it may cause you some disquiet (though I bid you to have no fear about that), when I am informed by you I shall make your excuse to the Burgomaster as best I can. But in that case please supply me with reasons for your being excused, although I should prefer, if you can do it without inconvenience or fear of inconvenience, that you should do the Burgomaster this favour, so that by your means he may have a clearer exposition of this matter, which he has been turning over in his mind this long time. Good-bye, excellent Sir; my wife and daughter send you greetings. Please give my best regards to Lady Masham.

Your most affectionate
PHILIPPUS VAN LIMBORCH

Amsterdam 11 March
1698.

2401. Dr. Pieter Guenellon to Locke, 4/14 March 1698 (*2345*, *2520*)

B.L., MS. Locke c. 11, ff. 84–5.

d'amsterdam ce 14 Mars 1698.

Monsieur

nous recusmes avanthier celle quil vous a plu nous escrire du 5 fevrier. elle nous apprend le triste estat ou vous vous este trouvé depuis peu. Dieu soit loué de vostre recouvrement et ce seroit pour nous une affliction tres sensible si Dieu venoit a vous retirer, puisque cela nous raviroit un veritable amis, que nous estimons le plus cher thresor que nous possedions.[a] toutes les fois que nous recevons de vos lettres, tousjours remplies des marques de vostre bienveuillance, nostre respect se rallume, et nous ne cessons de souhaitter de vous revoir encore une fois. cette ardeur va jusqu'a la, qu'assurement si nous n'estions retenu par l'extreme caducité de mon pere qui allite depuis deux ans, agé de nonante six,[1] l'esté prochain ne se passeroit pas, sans que nous allassions vous embrasser, ma femme en parle tous les jours, et mon fils qui vous regarde comme son grand protecteur, et qui n'estime rien audessus de vos conseils et de vos bonnes graces, aspire avec impatience a ce moment heureu de vous voir et de profiter de plus pres de vos grandes lumieres. ne craignez pas je vous prie que la trop grande application luy gaste l'esprit, car quoy quil ne soit pas revesche ny desobeissant, il ayme tellement le jeu et les divertissements, que s'il n'estoit captivé aux heures de ses maistres il avanceroit trop peu. ses maistres, qui le louent, disent tous, quil apprend en badinant. il a la conception heureuse, l'esprit vif ⟨et⟩[b] enjoüé, le corps robuste et grand pour son age. il n'est tout au plus occupé que six heures le jour, et souvent moins, entre ses sept Maistres il y en a trois qui ne le voyent que deux fois la sepmaine, pour le crayon, l'escriture et la flute, Monsieur le Clerc va commencer un college[2] de logique, et il me conseille d'y joindre mon fils. je ne scaurois Monsieur vous marquer assez le ressentiment que jay de la tendresse que vous avez pour cet enfant, mais je puis vous dire en verité que sa plus grande passion est celle par la quelle il revere vostre merite et sou-

[a] *Or* possedrons [b] *MS.* en

[1] An error, perhaps for 86: no. *1973* n.
[2] A course of lectures, as on p. 249, etc.

haitte que vous puissiez vivre jusqu'ace quil soit en estat de vous aller faire la reverence.

Mais pour venir a ce que vous me demandez pour prevenir les mesprises qui pouroient survenir sur ce que j'ay en garde pour vous, je suis bien ayse que l'attestation notariale et authentique que je vous envoye, renouvelle la verité du fait, et serve d'appuy aux lettres que vous avez de moy sur ce subject. il est vray, que mon pere, mon beau pere et ma femme, le scavoient desja parfait-tement. que mon livre de compte en fait mention, et que de plus j'en ay une notice particuliere. et afin quil ny manque rien de part et d'autre pour nous mettre reciproquement en repos, je vous prierois dans la premiere lettre que vous me ferez l'honneur de m'escrire, de marquer que je n'ay rien de vous que le contenu de l'attestation sy jointe. il pouroit se rencontrer quelque lettre parmis vos papiers, qui fit mention de l'ancien despost que je vous ay entierement rendu, et cela pouroit embarasser (en cas de mort) vos heritiers et leur donner quelque faux soubcons comme si jeusse plus a leur rendre. le Notaire qui a fait cette acte, est neveu de mon frere de Wilde. il est fort discret et tres employé.

Vous me demandez si le livre de monsieur Witsen de la tartarie ne paroistra pas bientost.[1] je croy vous avoir desja mandé autrefois quil est achevé d'imprimer il y a quatre ans, c'est un gros in folio en flamend, les exemplaires demeurent supprimez parce quil pretend retrancher et changer quelques feuilles et en adjouster des nouvelles. Jay un exemplaire en blanc par sa faveur, dans mon cabinet, que jay lu tout entier. il ne met pas permis de le communi-quer sans son ordre. le gros du livre contient des recueils de dif-ferents memoires pour verifier sa carte, mais il s'estend souvent audela de sa carte jusquaux indes, la perse, la mer noire, et la crimée. je crain que quelque laron de francois se prevaudra de son retardement, comme a desja fait le pere D'Avril dans son voyage de la tartarie.[2] Monsieur Witsen donne a connoistre son larcin dans sa preface, et dit quil avoit donné pour ce pere des Memoires a Monsieur d'Ablancourt.[3] le pere le Conte fait aussy mention dans ses memoires de la chine[4] de plusieurs decouvertes que ceux de sa

[1] No. *2028*. [2] Ibid.

[3] J.-J. de Frémont d'Ablancourt, who died probably at The Hague in 1693: no. *462*.

[4] Louis-Daniel le Comte, S.J., *Nouveaux memoires sur l'état present de la Chine*, 2 vols., Paris, 1696, etc.; Amsterdam, 1697, etc.; English translation 1697, etc. Locke obtained a copy of one of the Paris editions in 1699: pp. 568–9, 631. L.L., no. 827.

societé ont fait dans la tartarie septentrionale, et fait esperer quil nous en donneront[a] des cartes. je crain que ce sera en partie au despans de Monsieur Witsen. car son livre n'est pas si reservé quil n'en puisse eschaper quelque exemplaire pour ces Messieurs. je croy mesme quil seroit de la prudence de Monsieur Witsen de faire traduire son livre en francois, en attendant quil perfectionne son ouvrage pour prevenir les surprises de ces Messieurs, qui se prevalent de tout, et regardent les autres nations comme leur vassaux. pour appuyer les bons sentiments que vous avez de la religion du Czar je vous diray que la veille de son depart, estant chez mon frere de Wilde il entra en discour avec Monsieur Brand, Ministre Arminien, qui avoit eu une conference avec son prestre touchant l'Euchariste.[1] il luy dit ces propres paroles. *Vous autres Messieurs aymez trop la dispute et a philosopher. faut il tant de raffinements pour connoistre que Jesus Christ est nostre Messie et d'obeir a sa Morale? cela ne suffit il pas pour nostre salut? et si Dieu c'est enoncé avec moins d'Evidence en quelques endroits, pourquoy se donner cariere pour en faire des explications, puisque cela est subject a des esgarements?* c'est dans cette pensée que les Moscovites ne permettent que tres rarement les sermons, et qui s'abstiennent en tel cas d'expliquer des passages obscurs. je scay de sa bouche quil abhorre les persecutions, et quil ne trouve rien de plus tyrannique que de forcer la Conscience. Mais Monsieur j'abuse de vostre temps, ma lettre passe les bornes. je finis avec la priere et les souhaits de toute la famille, que Dieu veuille prolonger vos jours, vous donner des nouvelles forces, et une santé, je ne diray pas parfaitte, a vostre age mais au moins supportable. jay parle a Monsieur le clerc qui vous salué. il s'est chargé de dire aujourdhuy a Monsieur Limborgh la cause du retardement de vostre responce. Ma femme, monsieur veen, de Wilde, et mes fils joignent leur treshumbles respects au miens, qui suis veritablement

Monsieur,

Vostre tres humble et tres obeissant serviteur

P GUENELLON.

Endorsed by Locke: Dr Guenellon 14 Mar 98 Answered 21

[a] *Or* donneroit?

[1] While in Amsterdam Peter visited Jakob de Wilde frequently, inspected his collection of antiquities, and signed his name in his visitors' book: Uffenbach *Merkwürdige Reisen*, iii. 637–8. Peter arrived in London on 10 or 11 January, O.S. *London Gazette*, 13 January, etc. Johannes Brandt, 1660–1708; brother of Caspar Brandt (no. *1919*); officiating in Amsterdam from 1684: *N.N.B.W.*

2402. Dr. Egbertus Veen to Locke, 5/15 March 1698 (*1454*)

B.L., MS. Locke c. 23, ff. 9–10.

Doctissime Vir

Nolui ut hæc opportuna occasio elabatur sine literis nostris, quas diu non dedimus. Contenti per Guenellon aliquoties valetudinem tuam intellexisse, afflixit tamen nos posterior nuncius de sanitate tua aliquomodo vacillante, quam ex mora diuturniore Londini contraxeras. Speramus noxam hanc a te superatam fore mutatione loci et aeris: Nos quod attinet valemus per Dei gratiam prospere in hac nostra solutudine et orbanitate uxoris dilectissimæ, si tamen daretur aliquando occasio te revidendi, non parum delectaremus gratissima tua consuetudine, cujus identidem memoriam sæpius cum gaudio mente renovamus. Degit nunc in patria vestra natu major filius nostri de Wilde, cui improvisa et vix sperabilis occasio favit una cum Celsissimo Imperatore Moscoviæ in Angliam ⟨proficisci⟩,[a] faxit Deus ut vanus sit metus noster, qui anxios ⟨nos⟩[b] habet, ne hoc vivendi genus cum tam longe a nobis dissitis hominum moribus ipsum a studiis et moribus nostris distrahat nimis: etiam et hoc nos sollicitos tenet, quid consilii capiendum, si forte instet Majestas sua illum comitem in moscoviam velle ad filium suum quem ibidem octennium et unigenitum obtinet, et quem

[a] *MS.* proficissi [b] *MS.* non

Learned Sir,

I did not want this seasonable opportunity to slip away without a letter from me, not having written for a long time. I was satisfied at various times to learn through Guenellon of your good health, but was distressed by later news of your somewhat uncertain condition, which you had brought on by a rather long stay in London. I hope that with change of place and air you will have overcome this trouble. As concerns myself, by the grace of God I am in good health, alone as I am and bereaved of a most beloved wife; if, however, an opportunity of seeing you again were some day given me I should not a little rejoice in your most agreeable company, the remembrance of which I frequently and joyfully renew in my mind.

The elder son of our de Wilde is now spending some time in your country; an opportunity, unforeseen and scarcely to be hoped for, of journeying to England with the most exalted Emperor of Muscovy favoured him. May God grant that our fear, which keeps us anxious, may be groundless: that this kind of life with men whose customs are so very distant from ours may draw him too far from our pursuits and customs; we are also worried by the question of what we ought to decide if His Majesty should perhaps earnestly wish him to accompany him to Muscovy, to instruct his only son

Animus patri est aliquando huc mittendi bonis literis moribusque imbuendum. forte inanis et nimis ⟨immaturus⟩[a] hic noster metus est: tamen non potui non hanc nostram curam tibi viro nobis addictissimo et faventi revelare certi te nobis nec re nec consilio defuturum: vale et me, ut ante, amare persevera, qui est

Dominationis Vestræ cultor integerrimus

EGB VEEN

15 Martii 1698 Amstelod:

Address: Spectatissimo Doctissimo Viro Domino Johanni Lock

Endorsed by Locke: E: Veen 15 Mar 98 Answered 20 Apr:

[a] *MS.* immaturis

in good learning and conduct, a boy eight years old whom he has there and whom he intends at some time to send to this country. This fear of ours is perhaps groundless and too premature; nevertheless I could not but disclose this anxiety of ours to a man most devoted and well disposed to us, being assured that you will not fail us in deed or advice. Good-bye, and, as before, continue to love me,

Your most sincere servant

EGB VEEN

15 March 1698, Amsterdam.

2403. JEAN LE CLERC to LOCKE, 5/15 March 1698 (*2348, 2453*)

B.L., MS. Locke c. 13, ff. 121–2. Printed in Bonno, *Le Clerc*, pp. 106–7.

A Amsterdam le 15 de Mars 1698

Je croiois, Monsieur, que vous auriez reçu une Lettre, que je vous écrivis l'année passée par Mr. le Fevre, fils du fameux le Fevre de Saumur. Mais je vois, par une Lettre qu'il a écrite à Mr. Guenelon nôtre ami, qu'il ne vous a point rendu celles qu'on lui avoit remises pour vous. Je lui écrirai pour l'obliger de vous les envoier. Vous verrez que je vous remerciois pour ce que vous aviez écrit en faveur de nôtre ami, qui n'est pas d'humeur d'aller jamais en païs d'Inquisition, après en être sorti une fois en sa vie. Je crois qu'il a raison et qu'il fera bien de ne se mettre jamais à la discretion des Druides. Nous sommes ici scandalizez de la querelle que Mr Stillingfleet vous a faite, et je ne comprens pas ce que cet homme prétend faire, si ce n'est *facere invidiam.*[1] C'est là un secret Theologique, non pour sauver les ames, mais pour les faire perir, s'il leur étoit possible. J'ai ajouté à ma Logique la Dissertation *de Odi*

[1] 'To stir up ill will.'

Theologico ex invidia ducto, que vous y verrez; car tout est à présent imprimé et l'on en envoiera incessamment en Angleterre. Je suis près de la fin de mon Hammond, qui verra le jour au commencement du mois prochain, comme je l'espere.[1] Je serai déchargé d'un grand fardeau, et quoi que je ne sois pas résolu de me reposer, je jouirai d'une espece de repos, en travaillant à un ouvrage de mon crû. Je suis si pressé des épreuves, que je corrige, que je n'ai pas le temps de vous entretenir plus au long. Je le ferai à la premiere occasion, n'aiant écrit ces mots, que pour ne pas laisser partir le fils de Mr. Limbourg, sans me donner l'honneur de vous écrire. Je suis, Monsieur, de tout mon coeur entierement à vous.

J LE CLERC.

Address: A Monsieur Monsieur Locke A Londres

Endorsed by Locke: J: Le Clerc 15° Mar 98 Answered 22 Apr

2404. LOCKE to PETER KING, later first Baron King, 7 March 1698 (*2149*, 2405)

B.L., MS. Locke c. 40, ff. 1–2.

Oates 7° Mar $9\frac{7}{8}$

Dear Cosin

I had yours of the 17th Feb: before me to answer it just as yours of the 5th instant was brought me. And must own myself to have been more tardy in returning my Ladys thanks by you to Mr Freke for his opinion, and to you for your care in getting and sending it than she would be pleased with. You must forgive your share in this my neglect and make it up to Mr Freke by your care in representing my Lady to Mr Freke as sensible of the favour she has received from him and as gratefull for it as tis possible for anyone to be in the like case

I have because you desire it here sent you a prescription for a purge. When it is brought you home from the Apothecarys I would have you pour from it about one third part and throw it away, the two remaining third parts I would have you swollow. If this works not above five times with you, increase the dose the next time. and soe the third time till you take the whole potion prescribed in the bill unlesse you finde that a lesse quantity will give you nine or ten stools

[1] See p. 422.

You are in hast to have it sent you this weeke before you goe to your new lodgings. But this is to be noe consideration with you. For first you are by noe means to take it whilst the winde remains either North or East unlesse you have a minde this physick should doe you not any good but very much harme. In the next place you must take it three times at least with an intervall of three or four days betwixt each taking. And every day you doe take it you must keep in the whole day warme by the fires side and not stir out without the dore and be sure not to take any the least cold in the days of intervall upon all which accounts I thinke it necessary for you wholy to forbear takeing any thing till the weather be setled much warmer. I thank you for your concerne for my health. My service to Mr Clarke and Mr Freke. I am

Dear Cosin

your most affectionate Cosin and servant

J LOCKE

℞ Tamarindi ℥s
sennæ
rhabarb ana ℥is
coq: in: S.q.Aq. commun
Colaturæ ℥iij dissolv:
Mannæ
Syr ros solut: ana ℥i
m: f. potio purgans
cap. mane cum regimine

Address: For Mr Peter King at Mr Fursmans in Bolt Court in Fleet street London

Postmark: MR 9

2405. LOCKE to PETER KING, later first Baron King, 8 March 1698 (2404, 2437)

B.L., MS. Locke c. 40, ff. 3–4.

Oates 8° Mar 9$\frac{7}{8}$

Dear Cosin

I writ to you yesterday but in such hast and hurry that I did not read over my letter and præscription. I therefor send you here again a prescription for a potion for you writ at more leisure which is that which (if it differs at all from the other) I would have you follow. You must not take it till this cold weather is gon and this North East winde comes about to the South or West. I would have you take it three or four times leaveing three or four days every time between. The first time you take it I would have you take but two thirds of the potion here prescribed which you may measure by spoonfulls throwing away every third spoonfull, the next time increase your dose two or three spoonfulls and soe every time you take it, till you take the whole unlesse the former dose gave you nine or ten stools for then I would not have you augment the dose for I would not have it worke beyond that. The day that you take it you must neither stir out nor read, and the days of interval you must be sure to keep your self warme and not take cold, which is one reason why you should stay for warmer weather before you take it, though you change your lodging first. I wish you your health and am

Dear Cosin

Your most affectionate cosin and humble servant

J. LOCKE

My Lady thanks you for your complement to her in your last letter to me and gives you her service and thanks for your care of her businesse and begs you not to forget her service and thanks to Mr Freke for the opinion he did her the favour to give in it and desires you also to give her service to Mr Clarke.

℞ Tamarind ℥s
sennae ʒij
Rhabarb ʒjs
coq: in S.q. aq: com:
Colaturæ ℥iij dissolv:
Mannæ
Syr Ros solut ana ℥j
M: f: potio purgans quam cap: mane cum custodiâ

Pray doe me the kindenesse to send me the gazett in which is the proclamation against Atheisme Blasphemie and prophanesse[1]

Address: For Mr Peter King at Mr Fursmans in Bolt court in Fleet Street London

Postmark: MR 9

[1] A proclamation for 'Preventing and Punishing Immorality and Prophaneness' was issued on 24 February: Steele, no. 4246. It was not reprinted in the *London Gazette*.

2406. Philippus van Limborch to Locke, 11/21 March 1698 (*2400*, *2410*)

B.L., MS. Locke c. 14, f. 113. Answers no. 2395; answered by no. 2413.

Amplissime Vir

Gratissimas tuas, 21 Februarii scriptas, postquam jam filius meus in Angliam abierat hodie demum accepi. Perlegi illas, et cum D. Clerico attentius perlegam, quia id ita jubes. Nihil autem in iis invenio, quod ipsa calumnia ad carpendum detorquere possit. Prius tuum argumentum semper mihi unitatem divinam persuasit. De altero non cogitaveram; eoque impensius eo delector, quod novum mihi argumentum suppeditaveris: Verum dubito an hoc ad gustum Cartesianorum sit futurum.[1] Ego hodie D. Clericum conveniam, et tuas illi legendas dabo. Guenellonus proxime elapsa hebdomade, cum jam filius itineri esset accinctus, mihi a te salutem dixit, teque cum acutissimo morbo non sine vitæ discrimine conflictatum narravit. Deo gratias ago maximas pro restituta tibi valetudine, quam tibi vegetam ac diuturnam precor, tum communi Ecclesiæ ac Republicæ, tum et privatim mea causa. Filius meus die solis[2] Amstelodamo discessit, die Mercurii cum navigio profecturus in Angliam, ubi illum jam appulisse nullus dubito. Fasciculum literarum a variis amicis ad te deferet:[3] Imprimis illi

---

Excellent Sir,

I received your most welcome letter, written on 21 February, only today after my son had already left for England. I have read it through, and shall read it through more attentively with Mr. Le Clerc, as you bid me to do so. But I find nothing in it that calumny itself can twist in order to carp at it. Your first argument has always persuaded me of the unity of God. I had not thought about the second, and am so much the more delighted with it because you have supplied me with a new argument; but I question whether it will be to the taste of the Cartesians.[1] I shall meet Mr. Le Clerc today and shall give him your letter to read. Last week, when my son was just ready for his journey, Guenellon gave me your greetings and told me that you had been afflicted by a very severe illness, not without danger to your life. I thank God heartily for the restoration of your health and pray that it may be vigorous and long lasting both for the sake of the Church and of the state in general, and for my own sake as an individual. My son left Amsterdam on Sunday,[2] intending to set out for England with the vessel on Wednesday. I have no doubt that he has already arrived there. He will bring you a packet of letters from various friends.[3] I charged him first of all to inquire for you

---

[1] This is amplified in no. *2410*. [2] *6/16* March.
[3] Nos. *2401–3* and a lost letter from Furly: p. 379.

in mandatis dedi, ut apud D. Pawling te quærat. Multis nominibus ego Dominæ Masham sum obligatus. Ego filio in mandatis dedi, ut si te Londini non inveniat, ruri te quærat, et tuam de omnibus suis negotiis requirat sententiam. Tam amicam Dominæ Masham invitationem filius meus gratissimo accipiet animo, et a sua parte paternam utriusque amicitiam colere et agnoscere pro viribus conabitur. Interim novis me illi beneficiis obligatum gratus agnoscam: Illa opere implebit, quod ego voto tantum præstare possum. Sed dum paria referre non licet, ipsa animum gratum, et ad omnia obsequia paratissimum acceptabit, donec occasio se offerat opere ipso præstandi, quod nunc voto solummodo possum. Scio paria semper amicitiæ officia esse non posse, et tam ea constare, beneficia grate accipiendo, quam liberaliter dando. Nunquam mihi animum ad referendum deësse patiar. Dum has scribo, literæ a filio Brielâ ad me deferuntur, quibus, quia navigium ad trajectionem deërat, se Brielæ subsistere coactum ait. Quia autem tuæ jam ad me delatæ sunt, inde navigium jam appulisse, ipsumque discessisse colligo. Filia mea non satis firma est valetudine. Ante quadriennium graviter decubuit; ex illo morbo convaluit quidem, sed vigorem illum pristinum neutiquam recuperavit: sæpius infestatur febricula, anhelitus quandoque est angustior, accedit

---

at Mr. Pawling's. I am indebted to Lady Masham on many accounts. I have charged my son, if he does not find you in London, to seek you in the country and to ask for your opinion about all his affairs. He will most gratefully accept Lady Masham's friendly invitation and on his side will do his utmost to cultivate and recognize the friendship that existed between their fathers. Meanwhile I shall gratefully recognize that I am indebted to her for fresh acts of kindness. She will fulfil in deed what I can perform only in wish. But so long as I cannot make an equal return she will accept a grateful spirit and one most ready to do her any service; until an opportunity presents itself of my performing in very deed what at present I can perform only in wish. I know that the duties of friendship cannot always be equal and that they consist as much in gratefully accepting kindnesses as in liberally bestowing them. I shall never suffer myself to lack the will to repay her. While I have been writing this letter one from my son at Brielle has been delivered to me; he says in it that he was compelled to stay there as the vessel for the crossing was not there. But since your letter has been delivered to me I gather thence that the vessel has now put in and that my son has departed. My daughter's health is not steady enough. Four years ago she was seriously ill; she indeed recovered from that illness, but has by no means regained her former strength; she is often troubled by a slight fever, her breathing is sometimes rather constricted, and there come a lassitude

membrorum lassitudo, aliaque incommoda his connexa: proxima tamen æstate melius se habuit. Hyems hæc sæva ac diuturna multum illi obfuit; attamen nunc minus afflictam vidimus, quam hyeme præcedente: unde et mihi spes affulget, proximam æstatem majus quid ad sanitatem ejus collaturam. Hac hyeme aliquatenus vixit; sed præcedente penitus languit, ut jam de hectica metuere inceperim. Alias prolixæ admodum est staturæ, qua fratrem suum ferme æquat. Vale Vir Amplissime ac feliciter age. Commendo tibi filium meum. Salutem quam officiosissimam a me dices Dominæ Masham, cui omnia prospera voveo. Salutat Te, Dominamque Masham uxor ac filia.

Tui Amantissimus
PHILIPPUS A LIMBORCH

Amstelodamii 21 Martii

16
16 X 98
5

Address: Amplissimo Doctissimo Consultissimo Viro D. Joanni Locke
Endorsed by Locke: P. Limborch 21 Mar 9$\frac{7}{8}$ Answered 2 Apr

of the limbs and other troubles connected with these; last summer, however, she was in better health. This cruel and prolonged winter has been very prejudicial to her; nevertheless we saw that she was less afflicted then than in the preceding winter; whence there is a ray of hope for me that next summer will bring some greater [improvement] to her health. This winter she had some life in her; but in the preceding winter she was completely listless, so that I had begun to fear a hectic fever. For the rest she is rather tall in stature, in which she almost equals her brother. Good-bye, excellent Sir, and may you be happy. I commend my son to you. Please give my best respects to Lady Masham, to whom I wish all prosperity. My wife and daughter send greetings to you and Lady Masham.

Your most affectionate
PHILIPPUS VAN LIMBORCH

Amsterdam 21 March
1698

2407. WILLIAM MOLYNEUX to LOCKE, 15 March 1698 (2376, 2414)

The Carl H. Pforzheimer Library, New York. Transcribed from photostat. Printed, omitting the last paragraph and the postscript, in *Some Familiar Letters*, pp. 262–4. Answers no. 2376; answered by no. 2414.

Dublin. Mar. 15. 169$\frac{7}{8}$

Dear Sir

In the midst of my Trouble for your Long Silence, soon after

I had writ to two or three Friends to Inquire after your Health; I was happily Releived by yours of Last January the 10. from Oates. I am hartily concernd that you past over the last Winter with so much Indisposition; but I rejoyce with you that you have scaped it, and Hope you will yet Passe over many more. I could make to you great Complaints likewise of my Own late Ilnes; but they are all Drown'd in this One, That I am Hindred for a while in seeking a Remedy for them. I fully Purposed to be at the Bath this Spring early, but I am Disappointed at present, and cannot stir from hence till Lord Chancellour Methuen return to this Kingdom.[1] it has pleased the Young Lord Woodstock[2] by Directions from his Majesty to Chose My Lord Chan. Methuen, Mr Van-Homrigh present Lord Mayor of this Citty,[3] and My self, to be his Guardians, and Managers of his Affairs in this Kingdom. Nothing can be done without two of us, so I am ty'd by the Leg. Were it only in my Health that I am disappointed, I could the easier bear it. But I am Delayd from embrasing My Dear Friend, which is most Greivous of all. Yet I hope it will be so but for a Time; for if My Lord Chan. comes over in any Convenient season I will certainly get loose. But this I cannot Hope for till the Parliament in England Rises.[4] I should be glad to know from you, when that is expected: for indeed they bear very hard upon us in Ireland; How justly they can bind us without our *Consent* and *Representatives*, I leave the *Author* of the *Two Treatises of Government*[5] to Consider. But of this I shall trouble you farther an other Time, for you will hear more hereafter.

I have seen Bishop of Worcesters Answer to your second Letter. 'Tis of a Peice with the Rest, and you know my thoughts of them already. I begin to be almost of Old Hobbs opinion, that were it Mens Interest they would Question the Truth of Euclides Elements,[6] as now they Contest almost as full Evidences.

[1] He came to England in December 1697 and did not return to Ireland until August.

[2] Henry Bentinck, 1682–1726; styled Viscount Woodstock 1689–1709; succeeded as second earl of Portland 1709; created duke of Portland 1716: G.E.C., where there is an account of the grant (1697) of land in Ireland to him.

[3] Bartholomew Vanhomrigh, the father of Vanessa: Swift, *Journal to Stella*, ed. Sir Harold Williams, 1948, i. 64 n.

[4] Methuen was member for Devizes.

[5] Locke had not acknowledged his authorship to Molyneux. For the particular constitutional question arising between England and Ireland at this time see *Cal. S.P., Dom.*, 1699–1700, preface, pp. xlviii–lviii. But Molyneux was concerned with the larger issue, '*How far the Parliament of* England *may think it Reasonable to intermeddle with the Affairs of* Ireland, *and Bind us up by Laws made in their House*': Molyneux, *The Case of Ireland's being bound* (p. 376), p. 4. See Clark, *Later Stuarts*, pp. 319–21.

[6] A very free reminiscence from *Leviathan*, pt. i, ch. xi.

I am very Glad Monsieur Coste is so wel setled as you tell me; I designed fully to Invite him over hither. and if you know any other Ingenious French Man of that sort, or any such hereafter comes to your knowledge; I should be very glad, you would give me Intimation thereof.

I had certainly answerd that part of your Letter Relating to the Linen Manufacture, but that I dayly expected to do it more effectually by Mr Hamilton himself, who gave me Hopes of his going into England, and was resolved personally to wait on you about it. He is Master of the whole Mistery (and that I cannot pretend to be) and would have discoursed you most satisfactorily concerning it. I promised him a Letter to you when ever he goes over. which will now be very speedily, and then I doubt not but you will Concert Matters together much for the Good of this Poor Kingdom.

My Brother gives you his Most Humble Service and thanks you for the Care you took about his Discourse concerning Chaffers We hear from Dr Sloan that it is printed.

My[a-] Son has inclosed here a Little Complement to young Mr Masham, which he desires you to present.[-a]

I am

Your Most Humble servant

W: MOLYNEUX

Mr Burridge gives you his service, and Orders me to Assure you that he goes on dayly with the Essay. I hope to bring with me or send over to Mr Churchil a good parcel of it very Speedily for the Pres, and this will be an Ingagement on him to go on with the Translation with all Diligence. Pray let Mr Churchil know this and that will serve for an answer to a late Letter he writ to me about it.

Address: To John Locke Esquire at Mr Robert Pawlings overagainst the Plough Inn in Little Lincolns Inn Fields London

Postmark: MR 23

Endorsed by Locke: W: Molyneux 15 Mar $9\frac{7}{8}$ Answered Apr. 6

a–a *Deleted in MS., probably by the editor of* Some Familiar Letters.

2408. LOCKE to EDWARD CLARKE, 19 March 1698 (*2399*, 2420)

B.L., MS. Locke b. 8, no. 116. Printed in Rand, pp. 534–5. Answers no. *2399*.

Oates 19 Mar 9$\frac{7}{8}$

Dear Sir

I should sooner have returned you my thanks for the concerne you expresse for my health in your last to me did I not know that you are soe well satisfied of my sense of your kindenesse there in that I may presume your multitude of businesse will excuse me if I am not importunately punctuall in returning you my thanks the very next post. The weather I thank god is now become warmer and has a little released me from My close confinement to the chimny corner. But though I have been a little in the open air which I finde refreshing to my lungs yet I can enjoy it noe other wise than by siting in it For I have not breath enough yet to walke and therefor have been without the moat but twice since I came hither and that only to crawl to a seat we have in the Tarras walke where I can at my ease lazily enjoy the sun and breath the fresh air. I am pleased also with the returne of moderater weather upon an other account for I hope I shall now hear that Mrs Clarke has made use of the conveniency of the Season for the perfecting the recovery of her health. I shall take my share in it and shall be exceeding glad to be assured that there is not the least remain of her late distemper. Pray give her and my wife and the rest of your fires side my most humble service. I am

Dear Sir

Your most affectionate humble servant

J LOCKE

My Lady gives her humble service to you and Mrs Clarke and the yonge folke of her acquaintance. and Desires you would very particularly in her Name acknowledg to Mr Freke the favour he has lately done her in his opinion on the clause of her fathers will of which she is extremly sensible.

Pray give my humble service to the Batchelor and thanks for the booke he sent me which I received not till yesterday

I thank you for the care you tooke of my last inclosed, and beg leave to trouble you now again with an other

Endorsed by Clarke: Mr. Lock of the Present State of his Health etc: Received the 21th. March 1697. Answered the 9th.

2409. SIR WALTER YONGE to LOCKE, 22 March 1698 (*2388*, *2681*)

B.L., MS. Locke c. 23, ff. 172–3.

London March 22th. 169$\frac{7}{8}$

Dear Sir

Having received several of the specimens of Mr Crosses intended book, one of which I have already delivered to my Lord Chancellor, as I doe herein at his desire enclose another for you; I think my selfe obliged to acquaint you, that I did not impart to him what you wrote me in your former letter concerning that matter, because Mr Churchill told me it was very uncertain when his work would be printed; so that you are perfectly at liberty to consider what encouragement you shall think fitt to give him, and may be informed from Mr Churchill when the book it selfe is like to be published, which I am wholly ignorant of having not lately seen either of them.

Mr Clarke desires me to tell you that he received your letter by the last post and put the enclosed with his own hand into the Generall Post Office. Your friends at the College and in Bedford row[1] are all Well and I am

Dear Sir

Yours most affectionately

WALTER YONGE.

Address: For John Locke Esqr. [at Oates, by Joslyn, Bishops Stortford] Frank Walter Yonge.

Postmark: MR 22

Endorsed by Locke: Sir W. Yonge 22 Mar 9$\frac{7}{8}$

2410. PHILIPPUS VAN LIMBORCH to LOCKE, 22 March/1 April 1698 (*2406*, 2413)

B.L., MS. Locke c. 14, f. 114. Copy by van Limborch in Amsterdam University Library, MS. R.K., III D 16, f. 202. Excerpts, with some alterations to conceal Hudde's participation, etc., are printed from the copy in *Some Familiar Letters*, pp. 408–10; the passage 'D. Consul impense addictus est . . . aut aliquid æquipollens', in Ollion, p. 214 n. Answers no. 2395; answered by no. 2413.

[1] The existing street, running south from Theobalds Road, to the west of Gray's Inn. The friends are probably Mrs. Clarke and the children.

Vir Amplissime

Doctissimas tuas literas 21 Februarii datas, Martii 21 die recte accepi. Paucis id eadem die literis per filium meum tibi tradendis significavi. Attente tuas cum D. Clerico relegi. Ita judicamus, argumentis invictis te unitatem essentiæ divinæ adstruxisse, nihilque in argumentatione tua desiderari. Verum nondum D. Consuli eas ostendendas censuimus, nisi sententia tua propius explorata. D. Consul impense addictus est Philosophiæ Cartesianæ: itaque dubitamus, an argumentum ab omnipræsentia divina desumtum illius applausum impetraturum sit. Scimus spiritum Cartesianis esse cogitationem; cogitationem autem nullum ad spatium habere respectum; ac proinde nec essentiam divinam esse in spatio; sed omnipræsentiam illi attribui relative, cum respectu ad operationes suas: prout hanc sententiam clare exprimit Burmannus *Synops. Theol. lib. I. cap. XXVI. § XII. Est ergo omnipræsentia Dei nihil aliud, quam denominatio extrinseca, nata ex operatione Dei, qua in omnibus rebus corporeis operatur, et propter illam operationem iis præsens esse dicitur.* Et prolixius § præced. XI.[1] Tu autem ipsam essentiam divinam ubique præsentem asseris: quod nos tecum agnoscimus; sed dubitamus, an id Cartesii placitis addictus approbaturus sit. Quare

---

Excellent Sir,

On 21 March I duly received your learned letter dated 21 February. I told you so on the same day, in a few words in a letter to be delivered to you by my son. I have re-read yours attentively with Mr. Le Clerc. It is our opinion that you have established the unity of the divine essence [*essentia*] by invincible arguments and that nothing is wanting in your reasoning. We thought, however, that the letter ought not to be shown to the Burgomaster without a closer investigation of your opinion. The Burgomaster is exceedingly devoted to the Cartesian philosophy; we therefore question whether an argument drawn from the omnipresence of God will obtain his approval. We know that for the Cartesians spirit is thought; but thought has no relation to space, and accordingly the divine essence is not in space; but omnipresence is attributed to it relatively, with respect to its operations; just as Burman clearly expresses this opinion, *Synops. Theol.*, book I, ch. xxvi, § xii: 'The omnipresence of God is therefore nothing other than an extrinsic denomination, derived from God's operativeness, by which He operates in all bodily things, and by reason of that operativeness is said to be present in them'; and at greater length in the preceding § xi.[1] You however assert that the divine essence itself is present everywhere; which we recognize with you; But we doubt whether a man devoted to Descartes's opinions

---

[1] Frans Burman (1628–79; *N.N.B.W.*), *Synopsis Theologiæ*, first published in 1671. Van Limborch discusses God's omnipresence in *Theologia Christiana*, II. vi. 6–8.

expendendum tibi proponimus, an non argumentum hoc a scripto tuo abesse possit, cum et sine eo divinæ essentiæ unitas abunde probata sit: Aut si retinendum censeas, an non, ut Philosophis illis magis arrideat, addi possit, duo distincta entia non posse operationem suam perficere in eodem spatii puncto. Verum tum aliqualem cum argumentatione præcedente affinitatem habere videtur. Similiter in initio, quando quæstionis statum proponis, describis Deum, quod sit Ens infinitum, æternum, incorporeum, etc. Notum est, Cartesianos abhorrere a voce incorporeus, tanquam negativa, quæ nihil positivum affirmet; ipsos autem substituisse vocem cogitans, quam omnem corporis ideam excludere, et vocem esse affirmativam ac positivam gloriantur. An non ergo in illorum gratiam, ne argumentum alias solidum minori in pretio habeant, addi possit, incorporeum, sive cogitans, aut aliud æquipollens. Ignosces, Vir Amplissime, nostræ libertati. Nihil nos in argumentatione tua desideramus; sed vellemus, ut pauculis mutatis (si fieri possit) ea perinde Viro illi honorato, in cujus gratiam eam conscripsisti, placeat. Verum est aliud, quod mihi imputandum credo, qui D. Consulis mentem non plene tibi aperuerim. Quantum ex ipsius sermonibus percepi, agnoscit ille quidem, evidens satis esse, unum tantum hujus universi esse rectorem: Sed argumentum

---

will approve of it. Hence we put it before you for you to ponder, whether this argument cannot be left out of what you have written, since even without it the unity of the divine essence is amply proved; or, if you think that it should be retained, whether, in order that it may be more pleasing to those philosophers, it cannot be added that two separate beings cannot perform their operations in the same point of space. Then indeed it seems to have some affinity with the reasoning that precedes it. Likewise at the beginning, when you set out the question at issue, you describe God as a being infinite, eternal, incorporeal, etc. It is well known that the Cartesians dislike the word 'incorporeal' as negative and affirming nothing positive; they on the other hand have substituted [for it] the word 'thinking', and glory in its excluding any idea of body and being an affirmative and positive word. [We ask], therefore, whether to please them, lest they undervalue an otherwise solid argument, 'incorporeal or thinking', or something equivalent, cannot be added. Excellent Sir, please forgive our freedom. We find nothing wanting in your reasoning; but we should wish that with a few small changes, if they can be made, it should equally satisfy that honoured man, to please whom you have composed it. But there is another matter for which I think that I am to blame: that I have not fully disclosed to you what the Burgomaster has in mind. As far as I have gathered from his remarks he indeed recognizes that it is sufficiently evident that there is only one ruler of this universe; but he desires an argument by which it may be proved that a

desiderat, quo probetur Ens, cujus existentia est necessaria, tantum posse esse unum, et quidem ut id argumentum a necessitate existentiæ desumatur, et a priori (ut in Scholis loqui amant) non a posteriori concludat: hoc est, ex natura necessariæ existentiæ probetur, eam pluribus non posse esse communem: Narrabat enim, se cum aliis de materia hac disserentem, dixisse, ⟨quod⟩[a] si tale ens existat, præter Deum unicum a quo nos dependemus, illud ens minime nos spectare, quia ab eo non dependemus: Atque hoc nobis sufficere, ut Deum unum toto corde amemus et colamus. Sed tum disquirendum, an tale ens necessario existens possit esse præter Deum necessario existentem a quo nos dependemus. Si quid itaque, ut D. Consulis curiositati plene satisfiat, addendum putes, illud exspectabo: interim literas tuas sollicite asservabo ac nulli ostendam. Die Saturni in ædibus D. van den Ende adfui D. Consuli, qui me conspicatus statim quæsivit, an literas a te accepissem? Ego, non ausus fateri me accepisse, nec affirmavi, nec negavi, sed aliud ac rogabar respondi; D. Guenellonem a te accepisse literas, quibus te hac hyeme cum gravissimo morbo conflictatum, et ubi convalueris ad me scripturum significas. Ergo, inquiebat, aliquantisper adhuc exspectandum est. Vale, Vir Amplissime, et si quid in toto

[a] *MS.* quid

being whose existence is necessary can be only one [*i.e.* unique], and indeed that that argument should be taken from the necessity of the existence and should infer *a priori*, as they are accustomed to say in the schools, and not *a posteriori*, that is, that it may be proved from the nature of necessary existence that that existence cannot be common to several; for he related that when he was discussing this subject with some other persons he had said that, if such a being exists, other than the unique God on whom we are dependent, that being does not concern us in any way, since we are not dependent on it; and that this suffices for us, that we should love and worship the one God with our whole hearts. But then it must be asked whether there can be such a necessarily existing being other than the necessarily existing God on whom we are dependent. If, then, you think that anything should be added to satisfy fully the Burgomaster's curiosity I shall await it; meanwhile I shall keep your letter carefully and show it to nobody. I met the Burgomaster on Saturday at Mr. van den Ende's house; immediately on seeing me he asked whether I had received a letter from you. Not venturing to own that I had received one, I said neither yes nor no, but answered [a question] other than I was asked; that Mr. Guenellon had received a letter in which you intimate that you had been troubled by a very serious illness this winter and that you would write to me when you had recovered. 'Then we must wait a while longer', he said. Good-bye, excellent Sir, and if anything in his whole affair has been done amiss by me through imprudence

hoc negotio a me per imprudentiam forte peccatum sit, benignus ignosces. Salveat quam officiosissime Domina Masham. Salutat te uxor ac filia, omnesque amici.

Tui Amantissimus
PHILIPPUS A LIMBORCH.

Amstelodami ipsis cal. Aprilis

16 $\overset{9}{\underset{3}{\times}}$ 98

Address: Amplissimo Consultissimo Viro D. Joanni Locke
Endorsed by Locke: P Limborch 1 Apr 98 Answered 2.

---

please kindly pardon it. My best respects to Lady Masham. My wife and daughter and all our friends send you greetings.

Your most affectionate
PHILIPPUS VAN LIMBORCH.

Amsterdam 1 April
1698

2411. NICOLAS TOINARD to LOCKE, 24 March/3 April 1698 (*2393*, 2412)

B.L., MS. Locke c. 21, ff. 193–4. Answered by no. 2442.

+

A Paris ce 3. Avril 1698.

Depuis que vous m'avez fait l'honneur de m'adresser monsieur Nelson, je vous ay, monsieur, ecrit plusieurs fois et par diferentes voies pour vous remercier de m'avoir procuré la connoissance de ce galant homme dont j'avois bien oui parler par nos Canadiens François. Il a bien voulu se charger de quelques nouveaux livres que je vous ay envoiéz dans la pensée qu'ils seroient de votre goust cependant comme il y a longtems que vous les devriez avoir receus votre silence, monsieur, me donne beaucoup d'inquietude. Monsieur Aleaume,[1] qui vous presente celleci m'en tirera pendant le sejour qu'il fera à Londre par le soin qu'il voudra bien prendre de me donner des nouveles d'une santé aussi chere que m'est la votre c'est un parfaitement honête homme et de mes particuliers amis et vous m'obligerez sensiblement de lui marquer dans les occasions

[1] p. 319.

qui pouront se presenter combien vous m'honorez de vôtre bien veillance. Je vous adressay autrefois un de ses oncles, mais il ne fut pas assez de tems en Angleterre pour pouvoir vous y saluër. Je suis parfaitement, monsieur, votre tres humble et tres obeissant serviteur

TOINARD

Je vous remercie de votre excelent livre de l'*Education des enfans.*[1] Je nescai à qui j'ay l'obligation de l'avoir receu. Il en sera bientost parlé dans notre Journal des Savans.[2]

Address: For Mr Mr John Locke at Mr Pawlings overagainst the plough in Little Lincolns Inne feilds London

Endorsed by Locke (f. 194): Toinard 3. Apr. 98 Answered May 19 and Jun. 12

Noted by Locke beneath address: Aleaurie[3]

2412. LOCKE to NICOLAS TOINARD, 25 March 1698 (*2411*, 2442)

B.M., Add. MS. 28,753, ff. 30–1. Printed in Ollion, pp. 124–7. The letter did not arrive until about October: p. 492. Answers nos. *2355*, *2373*, and *2375*; answered by no. *2497*.

Oates 25 Mar 1698.

Multa sunt quæ me festinantem hactenus impedierunt quo minus voluntati ad scribendum pronæ non obtemperaverit manus. Valetudo hac hieme ad fauces orci[4] redacta: serus librorum quibus me cumulasti adventus et irrita τοῦ paquetboat expectatio. Mr Nelson rediens pene naufragus in mare: arca illius aquâ salsâ perfusa quam degustarunt libri, in ea inclusi. in terra ægrotus, ego rure absens,

---

Oates 25 Mar 1698

There are many things which, when I have been hastening [to write to you], have hitherto hindered me, so that my hand has not complied with my will when that was disposed to write. My health, brought this winter to the jaws of death;[4] the late arrival of the books with which you have overwhelmed me, and the vain waiting for the packet-boat. Mr. Nelson, when returning, almost ship-wrecked at sea; his chest drenched with salt water, which the books enclosed in it tasted. He an invalid on land, I absent

---

[1] No. *1905*.
[2] In the Amsterdam reprint, xxvi. 278–82 (21 April 1698).
[3] The wrong rendering is due to an accidental mark above the *m* of Aleaume in the text of this letter.
[4] *Æneid*, vi. 273.

unde libri quos ad me tam benigne miseras non nisi ineunte jam mense martio ad me pervenerunt humidi sane et ignis indigi.

Munus hoc tuum mihi a te gratissimum, opus ab authore ingratum.[1] dolet sane quod *in vitulâ tuâ* Hoc semper metuebam eoque animo te toties et tam enixè olim rogitavi ut ederes quod tam paratum habuisti ne plagiariorum subdolæ artes tibi hæsitanti fraudi essent. Multi appud nos quibus schedulam unam aut alteram Har: tuæ monstraverim laudantes opus formamque operis avide expectant rogantque sæpius quando tandem prodibit. Legi *Aratoris* istius tractatum primum, mallem illud argumentum a tè defensum. Itinerarium amici tui[2] cum voluptate perlegi, multa si coram adessem rogarem præcipue de insula Cayenne ubi diutissime commoratus est. v.g. si observaverint longitudinem penduli eâ in insulâ quæ liniæ ⟨æquinoctiali⟩[a] tam vicina est.[3] Si Indi in vicinio deum præter astra vel colunt vel agnoscunt, et quo cultu. Quot annos communiter vivunt. Quæ herba sit illa Pite[4] de qua ⟨loquitur⟩[b] et si altitudine Canabim æquet et si in agris sponte nascatur. Si

[a] *MS.* aquinoctiali [b] *MS.* loquiter

in the country; hence the books which you had so kindly sent me reached me only at the beginning of March, very wet and in need of a fire.

This gift of yours, as being from you, is most welcome, the work, as being by the author, is unwelcome;[1] it is sad indeed because 'with your heifer'. I always feared this and, being thus minded, implored you formerly so often and so earnestly to publish what you had in such readiness lest the crafty tricks of plagiarists should defraud you while you hesitated. Many in this country to whom I have shown one page or another of your Harmony, praising the work and its plan, eagerly await it and frequently ask when it will at last appear. I have read that ploughman's first treatise; I should prefer to see that argument defended by you. I have read through with pleasure your friend's account of his journey;[2] I would ask [him] many questions if I were present, especially about the isle of Cayenne, where he stayed a very long time, *e.g.* whether they have observed the length of the pendulum in that island, which is so near the equinoctial line.[3] Whether the Indians in the neighbourhood worship or recognize a god besides the stars, and with what kind of worship. How many years do they usually live? What sort of herb is that Pite[4] of which he speaks? and whether it reaches hemp in height and whether it grows wild in the fields. Whether the vanilla beans which are produced there are of as pleasant scent as those

[1] Father B. Lamy: p. 264, etc.

[2] Froger. He was at Cayenne from 3 to 25 September 1696: *Journal*, ed. 1700, pp. 154–72.

[3] Jean Richer had observed this in 1672–3: no. 469 n.

[4] Froger, p. 162. It is a kind of agave.

Vanillæ quæ illic producuntur æque grati sint odoris ac illæ quæ nobis ex nova Hispania[1] asportantur, et multa alia. Sed hæc hactenus, nolo enim te quæstionibus ultra fatigare.

Gaudeo tam commodum nuncium meas tibi attulisse literas,[2] aveo multum illum videre ut multa de te sciscitarem, pauca enim sitienti animo non satisfaciunt quanquam magnâ perfusus fuerim lætitiâ ex literis tuis quibus de sanitate tuâ adhuc integrâ me certiorem facis. precor deum optimum maximum ut te salvum validumque diutissime conservet

Illum Watsonum ⟨quem⟩[a] tibi nominavit non novi nec credo in mathematicis esse eximium. Forsan in horologiis construendis aliquid enixus est sed eâ ipsâ in arte Tompiono nostro æqualem esse multum dubito. De vitri usu in formandis horologiis cum Tompiono sermones olim habui, unde didici inutile esse commentum. addidit insuper vir illâ in arte peritissimus, et sagax in seligendo etiam ære ex quo fiant laminæ (quibus rotularum poli inseruntur), et ipsæ rotulæ magnam curam esse adhibendam; Aliquas enim esse illius metalli portiunculas quas si in opere horologico evitare nescias, inæqualis erit horologiorum motus, quantamlibet aliàs adhibeas in concinnandâ machinâ ἀκρίβειαν. Non

[a] *MS.* quam

which are brought to us from New Spain;[1] and many other questions. But so much for this, for I do not want to weary you with further questions.

I am glad that so agreeable a messenger brought you my letter.[2] I greatly desire to see him in order to ask him many things about you, for few do not satisfy a thirsty spirit; although I was filled with great joy by your letter in which you inform me of your still unimpaired health. I pray that Almighty God may long preserve you safe and sound.

I do not know that Watson whom he named to you, nor do I think that he is distinguished in mathematics. He has perhaps achieved something in clock construction, but I greatly doubt whether he is equal to our Tompion in that art. I had formerly some discussions with Tompion about the use of glass in clock-making, from which I learnt that it is a useless invention. He, being a man very experienced in that art, and shrewd, added further that great care is to be used in selecting the brass from which are made the plates into which the ends of the axles of the wheels are inserted, and the wheels themselves; for there are some small portions of that metal which you must avoid in clock-making; if you do not know how to do so the movement of the clocks will be uneven, however much precision you use in putting a machine together. Nevertheless I think that the art which

[1] The Spanish possessions in North and Central America.
[2] Nelson, the bearer of no. 2337. Locke now answers no. 2355.

negligendam tamen censeo, quam monstrare promisit Hartsoeker, artem formandi globulos vitreos exactè rotundos et si fieri possit quam minimos, ad microscopia utiles.

Triumvirum meo nomine rogo quam officiocissime salutes. gaudeo illum et vivere et valere.

Lætor maxime opus tandem perfectum impressumque esse paginis 136. Quando possim ego promittere amicis meis hisce in regionibus qui impatienter expectant. quanto citius tanto melius. numismata a te edita ut dicuntur Samaritana et Herodiada[1] ni fallor omnia habeo et tibi accepta refero. Ego etiam ex quo te vidi nescio quo fato aliquorum librorum auctor factus omnia ad te transmitterem nisi quod vernaculâ usus, tibi Barbarus sum. Hollandiæ cum essem vacuas aliquas horas impendi literis ad amicum in Anglia de ratione instituendi, quem tum parvulum habebat, filii. Tractatus hic Gallicè uti et Belgicè Amstelodami prodiit, rogavi ut inde at te transmitteretur Gallicæ versionis exemplar, Bibliopola promisit se facturum, et libellum spero ante hac ad manus tuas pervenisse.[2] cupio tuum de eo judicium. si probas quartam brevi habebit editionem cum auctario.[3] Ante octo annos etiam publici juris feci

---

Hartsoeker promised to demonstrate is not to be neglected, that of making small glass balls, exactly round and as minute as possible, for use in microscopes.

Please give my best respects to the Triumvir. I am glad that he is alive and well.

I greatly rejoice that the work is at least finished and printed in 136 pages. When can I promise it to my friends in these parts who are impatiently awaiting it? The sooner the better. If I am not mistaken I have all the so-called Samaritan and Herodiad coins[1] that you have published, and am indebted to you for them. Since I saw you I too, by I, know not what fate having become the author of some books, would send them all to you were it not that, having used the vernacular, I am a barbarian to you. When I was in Holland I spent some leisure hours on letters to a friend in England about the method of educating his son, who was then a child. This treatise has appeared at Amsterdam in French and also in Dutch; I asked that a copy of the French translation should be sent thence to you; the bookseller promised to do so and I hope that the little book has reached your hands by now.[2] I desire your opinion of it; if you approve it will shortly have a fourth edition with additional matter.[3] Further I published eight years ago *An Essay concerning Human Understanding*, a work in folio, which I think will appear shortly in a language better known to you than that in which it was written. I desire the more eagerly that the translation may be hastened so

---

[1] Locke is careless or at best ambiguous: see p. 264.
[2] It had now reached Toinard: p. 357.
[3] See p. 190, n. 2

Tentamen de Intellectu humano, opus in folio, quod brevi credo prodibit in linguâ tibi notiore quam quâ scriptum est. Versionem eò studiosius maturandam cupio ut si possit me vivo ad te pervenire possit quem novi æquum juxta ac perspicacem fore judicem, nec favore nec ira utramvis in partem inclinatum.

Quod dicis de Arithmetica Africanorum et Brasiliensum maxime placet. Nescio an olim te rogaverim ut mihi indicares siquos noveris populos qui numerationis nodum alicubi quam in denario locaverint.[1] siquos noveris rogo denuo ut me certiorem fias, id enim aveo scire, et jam diu quæsivi. De moribus incolarum ad flumen Senegal sitarum siquid novisti, id mihi scire pergratum esset.

De *Κόντα* Græcorum nihil ante fando audivi. *τὸ* ginta Latinorum inde venisse minime dubito. plura de his etiam et aliis non levis momenti nobis innotescerent, si non interiisset magno nostro incommodo tanta multitudo Græcorum scriptorum

Roganti quorsum methodus dulcorandi aquas non reducatur ad praxin, Respondeo, Nescio plane. De machina *νεωλκῇ* recte objurgas; semel post reditum in Angliam vidi, sed cum ejus usum neglectum crediderim, altum enim de eo silentium, non ultra inquisivi. Si Londinum iterum per valetudinem liceat reverti, de his te certiorem faciam. Ad me enim quod attinet gratularis mihi in

---

that if possible it may reach you while I am alive, you who I know will be an impartial as well as a perspicacious judge, not inclined to either side by favour or displeasure.

What you say about the Africans' and Brazilians' arithmetic is most acceptable. I do not know whether I asked you formerly to tell me whether you know any peoples who have placed the nodus of numeration elsewhere than in the number ten.[1] If you know any such I ask you anew to inform me, for I am eager to learn about it and have long since been inquiring about it. If you know anything about the customs of the people living by the Senegal river I should be extremely pleased to learn it.

I have hitherto heard nothing said about the *κόντα* of the Greeks. I have no doubt that the Latin -ginta has come from it. If so large a number of Greek writers had not perished to our great misfortune, many things about these and other matters of no small moment would be known to us.

To your question why the method of sweetening waters has never been put into practice I answer, 'I simply do not know'. You rightly upbraid me about the towing machine. I saw it once after my return to England, but when I thought that its use had been neglected, for there was profound silence about it, I inquired no further. If my health allows me to return again

[1] For Locke's interest see his Journal, 8 October 1677 and 24 April 1679; B.L., MS. Locke c. 33, f. 11, note dated 28 March 1679 (printed by Professor Lough, p. 282).

tam prospero statu res meas esse. agnosco negotium salario satis locuples mihi non quærenti oblatum, sed sero tandem cùm jam ingravescit senectus et valetudo satis incommoda, receptui aliquando canendum est, ut mihi intra limites meos reducto vacet quod reliquum est vitæ otio literario placidè impendere, id ego jam dudum fecissem nisi invitum me et secessum quærentem amici aliquot non infimi ordinis detenuissent. sed hæc inter nos.

Philadelphiæ ichnographiam si prostet, ad te mittam.[1] Rosch-hascana per Boutingium apud nos nusquam reperio. Zeraim pars prima Latine reddita per Guisium hic habetur;[2] reliqua vertere in animo habuit sed morte int⟨erceptus.⟩[a] Hanc partem ad te si libet mittam. Si quem habes Caleti vel Dieppæ cui res tibi destinatas mittere possem, facilius esset librorum commercium, Londino enim plurimùm absum, et hujusmodi res aliorum diligentiæ commissæ negligentius plerumque curantur. Sed te nimium fatigo. Vale Vir optime et me uti facis ama

Tui amantissimum

JL

[a] *Part of word covered by sealing-wax.*

to London I shall inform you about these things. As to what relates to myself you congratulate me on my affairs being in such a prosperous state. I acknowledge that an employment, rich enough in salary, has been offered to me without my seeking it, but late in the day, when age and infirmity are growing burdensome; I must sound a retreat some time, so that when I am withdrawn within my bounds what remains of life may be free for me to spend quietly in learned leisure; I would have done so long since if friends not of the lowest rank had not held me back against my will when I was seeking retirement. But this between ourselves.

I shall send you the ground-plan of Philadelphia if it is on sale.[1] I find Bouting's Rosch-haschana nowhere here. We have here the first part of Zeraim translated into Latin by Guise;[2] he intended to translate the rest but was prevented by death. I shall send you this part if you wish. If you have anyone at Calais or Dover to whom I could send things designed for you the traffic in books would be easier, for I am generally away from London, and matters of this kind when entrusted to others are for the most part attended to rather negligently. But I am overtiring you. Good-bye, best of men, and continue to love me

Your most affectionate

JL

The direction on your letter of 6 December is correct. The same should always be kept to, wherever I shall be.

[1] Locke now leaves no. *2355* for no. *2375*.

[2] *Misnæ Pars: Ordinis primi Zeraim tituli septem*, translated and edited by William Guise (*D.N.B.*), and published at Oxford in 1690 by Edward Bernard.

Inscriptio literarum 6° Dec: datarum recte se habet. eadem semper servanda ubicunque fuero.

Address: A Monsieur Monsieur Toinard chez Monsieur des Noyers devant l'Épèe royale dans la rüe mazarin à Paris

Endorsed by Toinard: Mars 25. 98.

2413. Locke to Philippus van Limborch, 2 and 4 April 1698 (*2410*, *2432*)

Amsterdam University Library, MS. R.K., Ba 258 d and e. The part of the letter in French, dated 2 April, was written by Coste on a large sheet of paper, one side of which forms the cover and bears the address; the alteration of the draft of no. 2395 in preparation for this part is noted in Appendix II. The part in Latin, dated 4 April, is written on a small piece of paper; it clearly refers to the French part, and the figure 4 in the date appears to have been altered, perhaps from 2. The French part is printed in *Some Familiar Letters*, pp. 410–16; the address and the Latin part, in Ollion, pp. 214–16. The letter answers nos. *2400*, *2406*, and *2410*; and is answered by no. *2432*.

The French part is a repetition of the French part of no. 2395, but omitting a passage to comply with van Limborch's recommendation in nos. *2406* and *2410*, and with some small variations. The omitted passage extends from 'Considerons un peu plus à fonds' to the end of the succeeding paragraph, 'qu'il n'y en peut avoir qu'un seul'. The variants affecting words are: First paragraph: for 'des spéculations et des raisonnemens un peu éloignez de ceux qu'on a accoûtumé de faire en cette rencontre' read 'des speculations et des raisonnemens au quelles tout le monde n'est pas accoutumè'.

'il ne sera pas pour cela porté': omit 'pas' (which is interlined in the letter of 21 February).

Paragraph beginning 'Par la même idée': after 'ne pouvoir pas cacher ses pensées' add 'à l'autre' (in the later letter the opening of the following sentence, 'Mais si l'un des deux cache ses pensées à l'autre', was omitted by Coste and is interlined by Locke; the added 'à l'autre' appears to have originated in Coste's omission, and to have been deliberately retained by Locke).

Paragraph beginning 'Que si pour aneantir': for 'dans le même point individuel' read 'dans le même lieu'.

Last paragraph: 'que de développer': omit 'de'.

The subscription and date are written by Locke:

Je suis
Monsieur
Votre tres humble et tres obeissant serviteur
John Locke

Oates 2 Aprill 1698.

[Written by Locke:]

Oates 4 Apr 98

Vir Amplissime

Gratissimas tuas 11°. 21° Martii et Calendis Aprilis datas per filium tuum accepi, Qui ab urbe absentem me hic rure invisit, præsentiâque suâ dominam Masham meque sibi devinxit. Ad illum quod attinet, tibi pro certo sit, me omni curâ studio, gratiâ et consilio quantum in me est statuisse ipsi inservire et tui et sui ipsius causâ; ita re ⟨quantum⟩[a] potero, verbis plura amicus amico[1] non addam

Probo consilium tuum de addendis quæ inter legendum occurrunt ad historiam Inquisitionis pertinentibus, gratias ago pro excerptis ex P: Servita quæ mihi misisti, quæ locis suis inserrere non negligam. Quod olim ex *Du.Mont* indicavi dubito an inserendum sit, non quod illa quam excripsi observatio non pertineat optime ad libri tui argumentum sed quod aliquis mihi dubium fecit an auctor ille unquam ea inviserit quæ describit loca. Habitat, uti mihi dictum est, Hagæ comitis, de viro igitur illiusque fide certior factus quid statuendum demum de illo ipse rectius judicabis.[2]

[a] *MS.* quntum

Oates 4 Apr 98

Excellent Sir,

I have received your most welcome letters of 11 and 21 March and 1 April through your son who, as I am away from the city, is visiting me here in the country, and now that he is here has endeared himself to Lady Masham and me. As to what relates to him, you may be sure that both for your sake and his I have determined as much as is in me to be of service to him in every way with care, attention, friendship, and advice; as much as I can in deed; as a friend to a friend[1] I shall add nothing more in words.

I commend your intention of adding to the *Historia Inquisitionis* relevant passages that occur when you are reading. Thank you for the extracts from Paul the Servite that you have sent me; I shall not neglect inserting them in their proper places. I doubt whether what I formerly pointed out to you from du Mont should be inserted, not because that notice that I copied is not eminently relevant to the subject of your book, but because someone has made me doubt whether that author ever visited the places that he describes. He lives, as I was told, at The Hague; being informed therefore about the man and his trustworthiness you will yourself judge better what is to be finally decided about him.[2]

Since Mr. H is so thoroughly devoted to the Cartesian philosophy Mr. Le Clerc and you were certainly right in warning me. If the Cartesians are

[1] No. 1751.

[2] There appears to be no adequate ground for doubting Dumont's good faith.

Recte sane Dominus Clericus et Tu monuistis quandoquidem[a] Dominus H ita penetus addictus sit Philosophiæ Cartesianæ. Si Cartesiani ita intelligendi sint de Spiritu quod sit Cogitatio et non substantia cogitans verbis sane deum ponunt re tollunt. Cogitatio enim actio est quæ per se non subsistit sed alicujus substantiæ actio est. Sed tecum hæc lis mihi non est. cum Domino H certe non erit: igitur quod suasisti, jam omisi illud ex omnipræsentiâ argumentum, quod unicum credo a priore argumentum est quo demonstrari possit Unitas Divini Numinis. Non miror igitur quod istis principiis penitus imbutus quærit quod semper frustra quæsiturus est argumentum quod tam male instituta Philosophia nunquam præbebit nec præbere potest. Optime igitur fecistis quod me in disputationes argutiasque Cartesianas me incidere non permisistis.

Alterum quod monuisti de termino *incorporeus* id non mutavi 1° Quia cum Cartesiano mihi rem esse me suspicari non opus est. 2° Quia si agnoscerem Dominum H esse Cartesianum ideo terminus *Incorporeus* vel *immaterialis* non esset ex definitione dei omittendus Quoniam quicunque de deo recte cogitare velit debet ab ipso amovere materiam omnem sive Corporietatem. Quod sane *cogitatio* non facit quicquid in contrarium sentiant viri Cartesii placitis

[a] *Substituted for* si?, *which is not properly deleted.*

---

to be understood concerning Spirit, that it is Thought [*Cogitatio*] and not a thinking substance, they certainly assert God in words [and] annul Him in deed. For Thought is an action that does not exist of itself but is an action of some substance. But this dispute is not between you and me, and will certainly not be between Mr. H and me; therefore, as you have advised, I have now omitted that argument from omnipresence which I believe is the only *a priori* argument by which the unity of the Godhead can be demonstrated. I do not wonder therefore that one so thoroughly imbued with those principles is seeking what he will always seek in vain, an argument that so ill-founded a philosophy never will or can provide. You have therefore done very well in not allowing me to become involved in Cartesian disputations and subtleties.

As to your other warning, that about the term 'incorporeal': I have not altered it: first, because there is no need for me to suspect that I have to do with a Cartesian; secondly, because, if I recognized that Mr. H is a Cartesian, the term 'incorporeal' or 'immaterial' would not on that account have to be omitted from the definition of God since whoever wants to think rightly about God ought to remove all matter or corporeity from Him. 'Thought' certainly does not do this, whatever the men devoted to Descartes's opinions suppose to the contrary. But enough of this; I do not want to detain you

addicti. Sed Hæc hactenus. Nolo te Speculationibus philosophicis melius occupatum detinere. Te Uxorem tuam filiamque, Veeneos, Guenelones, Clericosque nostros summo affectu saluto, Eorumque gratissimis literis per filium tuum ad me datis brevi respondebo. Vale et ut facis me ama tui Amantissimum

J L

Dicas rogo Domino Guenellon literis illius 14° Martis datis me 21° Martis respondisse

Filius tuus promiserat mihi plurium dierum moram sed expediendi negotii sui cura citius illum hinc abripuit quam aliàs permisissem. verum quum illum meo consilio credidisti nollui rebus suis providè intentum a recto tramite deflectere

Address (written by Locke): Mÿn Heer Mÿn Heer Philip van Limborch bÿ de Remonstranse Kerck op de Kaÿsers Gracht t'Amsterdam

---

with philosophical speculations when you are better employed. I send my most affectionate greetings to you, your wife and daughter, and to our friends the Veens, Guenellons, and Le Clercs; I shall shortly answer their very welcome letters that were given to me by your son. Good-bye and continue to love me your most affectionate

JL

Please tell Mr. Guenellon that I answered his letter of 14 March on the 21st.

Your son promised me that he would stay some days longer, but his concern to dispatch his business has torn him hence sooner than I would otherwise have permitted. But since you had entrusted him to me as an adviser I did not want to turn him from the right path when he was wisely intent on his affairs.

2414. Locke to William Molyneux, 6 April 1698 (*2407*, *2422*)

Some Familiar Letters, pp. 265–8. The original letter contained a passage relating to the younger Tanneguy Le Fèvre, the antecedent of a passage in no. *2422* which was also omitted in the printing. Answers no. *2407*; answered by no. *2422*.

Oates, 6 April. 1698

Dear Sir,

There is none of the letters that ever I receiv'd from you gave me so much trouble as your last of March 15th. I was told that you resolv'd to come into England early in the spring, and lived in the hopes of it more than you can imagine. I do not mean that I had greater hopes of it than you can imagine; but it enliven'd me, and contributed to the support of my spirits more than you can think. But your letter has quite dejected me again. The thing I above all things long for is to see, and embrace, and have some discourse with you before I go out of this world. I meet with so few capable of truth, or worthy of a free conversation, such as becomes lovers of truth, that you cannot think it strange if I wish for some time with you for the exposing, sifting, and rectifying of my thoughts. If they have gone any thing farther in the discovery of truth than what I have already published, it must be by your encouragement that I must go on to finish some things that I have already begun, and with you I hop'd to discourse my other yet crude and imperfect thoughts, in which if there were anything useful to mankind, if they were open'd and deposited with you, I know them safe lodg'd for the advantage of truth some time or other. For I am in doubt whether it be fit for me to trouble the press with any new matter; or if I did, I look on my life as so near worn out, that it would be folly to hope to finish any thing of moment in the small remainder of it. I hoped therefore, as I said, to have seen you, and unravel'd to you that which lying in the lump unexplicated in my mind, I scarce yet know what it is my self; for I have often had experience, that a man cannot well judge of his own notions, till either by setting them down in paper, or in discoursing them to a friend, he has drawn them out, and as it were spread them fairly before himself. As for writing, my ill health gives me little heart or opportunity for it; and of seeing you I begin now to despair: And that which very much adds to my affliction in the case is, that you neglect your own health on considerations, I am sure, that are not worth your health; for nothing, if expectations were certainties, can be worth it. I see no likelihood of the Parliament's rising yet this good while; and when they are up, who knows whether the man, you expect to relieve you,[1] will come to you presently, or at all. You must therefore lay by that business for a while which detains you, or get some other body into it, if you will take that care of your health this summer which you design'd, and it seems to require: and if you defer it till the next, who knows but your care of it may then come too late. There is nothing that we are such

[1] Methuen.

spendthrifts of as of health; we spare every thing sooner than that, tho' whatever we sacrifice it to is worth nothing without it. Pardon me the liberty I take with you: You have given me an interest in you; and it is a thing of too much value to me to look coldly on whilst you are running into any inconvenience or danger, and say nothing. If that could be any spur to you to hasten your journy hither, I would tell you I have an answer ready for the press,[1] which I should be glad you should see first. It is too long: The plenty of matter, of all sorts, which the Gentleman affords me, is the cause of its too great length, tho' I have pass'd by many things worthy of remarks: But what may be spared, of what there is, I would be glad should be blotted out by your hand. But this between us.

Amongst other things I would be glad to talk with you about before I die, is that which you suggest at the bottom of the first page of your letter.[2] I am mightily concern'd for the place meant in the question you say you will ask the author of the treatise you mention, and wish extremely well to it; and would be very glad to be inform'd by you what would be best for it, and debate with you the ways to compose it. But this cannot be done by letters, the subject is of too great extent, the views too large, and the particulars too many to be so manag'd. Come therefore your self, and come as well prepar'd in that matter as you can. But if you talk with others on that point there, mention not me to any body on that subject; only let you and I try what good we can do for those whom we wish well to. Great things have sometimes been brought about from small beginnings well laid together.

Pray present my most humble service to your Brother; I should be glad of an opportunity to do him some service. That which he thanks me for in my care about his discourse concerning the Chaffers, was a service to the publick, and he owes me no thanks for it. I am, Dear Sir,

Your faithful, and most humble servant,

JOHN LOCKE.

[1] Locke's second *Reply* to Stillingfleet: p. 295.

[2] 'How justly they can bind us without our *Consent* and *Representatives*, I leave the *Author* of the *Two Treatises of Government* to Consider.'

2415. ANTHONY ASHLEY COOPER, styled Lord Ashley, later third earl of Shaftesbury, to LOCKE, 9 April [1698] (*2252, 2427*)

B.L., MS. Locke c. 7, ff. 120–1. Printed in Rand, *Shaftesbury*, pp. 306–7. Year from Locke's endorsement.

London. Ap. the 9th:

You have been extreamly kind in the trouble you have put yourself to, on my account, for a Plutarch;[1] which I have not yet receiv'd, but expect from Mr Pauling, who has promis'd me to send it. I wish I could say I have had great need of it; and that I had been of late more Conversant with the Antients, and less with the People of the Age. I am sure it had been better for my self: And, for any thing that I, or any meer Honest Man is able to do in publick affaires in such a generation as this, I think it would have been altogather as well for my Country and Mankind, if I had don nothing: So, fruitless have my Endeavours been, and so little profitt arisen from those Years I have entirely given from my self to the Publick;[2] whilst in the mean, I my self grow good for nothing: but rather grow liker and liker to that sort whome I act with, and convers amongst. Neither is it without cause that a Man may fear such an Alteration in himself, when one sees such shipwracks around one, and that many an Honesty that has held out former Times, and endur'd Storms, has been cast away in these happy Times when wee expected Vertue and Honesty should have succeeded better then ever. However, this is not by way of excuse for my self, or as preparing you for some new Turn. for I hope I am still Honest and shall keep so; which it may be I should not; if I had follow'd even the very best examples, and the Advices of the very best Friends. But if I have any Honesty left I owe to your Good Friend and mine, Old Horace: and when I have heard of the wonderfull things to be done for the Publick by coming into the Court (as they call it) His words have sounded in my Ear

—quia me vestigia terrent
Omnia te adversum spectantia, nulla retrorsum.[3]

[1] pp. 227, 280.

[2] Ashley had been a member of parliament since 21 May 1695.

[3] 'Because the foot-prints frighten me, all pointing towards you and none coming back': Horace, *Epistles* I. i. 74–5; said by the Fox on his visit of condolence to the sick Lion.

But no more of this. I hope the time is not long ere I shall Chang the unprofitable and ungratefull studdy of these Moderns of ours, for a hearty Application to the Antients: and then you shall as You desire hear enough from me concerning those.

My servant Wheelock went into the Country for a Fortnight and left not Money in Town or had it not. But I write to him this post to dispatch it and send me returns. I am Glad to hear my Lady Masham is in Town that I may have the happiness to wayt on her. and I am glad to find you keep where you are, though I loose your Company yet a while.

I am your sincere Humble servant

A: ASHLEY.

Address: For Mr Lock [at Oates, by Joslyn, Bishops Stortford]
Free A: Ashley

Postmark: AP 9

Endorsed by Locke: L: Ashley 9 Apr. 98

2416. OLIVER CHENEY to LOCKE, 9 April 1698 (*3191*)

B.L., MS. Locke c. 5, ff. 82–3. For the writer see no. 407. A child named Oliver Cheny was baptized at St. Catherine's, Dublin, in July 1697, and other persons with this surname appear in the register of the parish: *Registers of S. Catherine, Dublin* (Parish Register Soc. of Dublin, 1908), p. 106, etc.

London April 9th. 98.

Having had the honour, Sir, of your favour and countenance (many years agoe) at Montpellier, obliges me, as often as I come hether, to pay you my most humble acknowlegements thereof. to whch end, I went to the Cock-pit.[1] being told that I should there finde means of performing the same. where I found (my old friend) Mr Popple. who gave me the Superscription of this letter. by which I presume to beg your acceptance of my most humble service And I doe so much the rather presume to give you the trouble of this scrawl becaus I doe sometimes see your picture in the hous of one of my neighbours at Dublin. the Worthy and Learned Mr Molyneux. to whom, if you have any commands I shal be proud

[1] The part of the Palace of Whitehall to the west of King Street and south of the Holbein Gate. After the fire of 4 January in the eastern part of the palace (p. 291) some government offices, etc., were housed in it; rooms were allotted to the Board of Trade about the end of the month. The Board met generally at Popple's house in Essex Street until 28 February, and met here regularly from 2 March: L.C.C. *Surrey of London*, vol. xiv, 1931, pp. 29, 74–5, etc.; the Board's Journal.

of being the messenger thereof. I shal part hence towards Ireland on thirsday next and if your commands be only by letter. you may be pleased to direct the same to be left with Mr Barker Apothecary over against Sommerset hous in the strand. But if I can serve you in any thing farther than by letter. I'l waite of you upon the least notice. which, will not incommode me. having horses here in town. I shal be glad also to receive your commands to Exeter or any where thereabout. For (to the end that I may spend 8 or 10 days time amongst my wives relations) I design to imbark at Beddyford[1] for Waterford. and so to Dublin. where my wife and sonn impatiently expect me

Your most obedient servant
OL. CHENEY

My wife and sonn are your humble servants. the latter has maryed a very pretty woman of a good familie and had 1000 li with her. he has also a sonn

Address: To John Lock Esqr [at Oates, by Joslyn, Bishops Stortford]
Postmark: AP 9
Endorsed by Locke: O: Cheney 9° Apr 98 Answered 11

2417. JOHN BONVILLE to LOCKE, 9 April 1698 (*2391, 2423*)

B.L., MS. Locke c. 4, f. 82a.

London Aprill the 9th 1698

Honoured Cousin

Sir This Inclosed Is our Account[a] I hope you will find it right, I have mentioned my Ladyes name for what I have Laid out for her, as for mrs Slade, what I have paid her, it is Knowne To be for my Lady. I have seekt up An downe but cannot get such A table, but If she pleas I will gett her A new one, for About 7s which shall be very good, Sir In your next If you pleas to Let me know where mrs Lockhart dwell, I think it may be conveniant to wait on her, because shee was Telling of me, of A relation, that was going to be

[a] *This account is missing: see pp. 378, 383.*

[1] Bideford in north Devon.

maried, and she did hope to help me to her custum, Deare Cousin I shall be Heartely glad to see you in Towne, The Lord be with you I Am Deare Cousin your faith full Kinsman and Humble Sarvant

JNO: BONVILLE

my wife and Son Give Theyar Humble Sarvis To you,

Address: For Mr Locke [at Oates, by Joslyn, Bishops Stortford]
Postmark: AP 9
Endorsed by Locke: J: Bonville 9 Apr 98 Answered 15

2418. SAMUEL BENSON to LOCKE, 11 April 1698 (*632*)

B.L., MS. Locke c. 3, ff. 171–2.

Sellake[1] Ap: 11–98

Sir

Were this my Addresse to any One but Mr Lock, I should beleive that my very name must bee forgotten, but your caracter is still to owne those that once had the honour of beeing ackquainted with you; it has bin my misfortune to have bin but once at London this twenty years, and therefore could not have the happinesse of seeing the man, that I alwaies had as great a regard for as for any one living, that I did not see you when in towne, I can give noe account for but this, that falling under the Late Kings displeasure and beeing summoned by him to come up, I thought it prudence to haste to my Country retierment as soone as possible; as an obscure beeing is most proper for sutch an One as I am, that never could or desiered to make a figure, soe I thanke God I am fitted with one. I rejoice in the advancement of others, and looke upon it as one of the happiest Omens of this Reigne that you are in an emmient station in it. I am desierous as long as I live in this world to doe some service to my Freinds, and since my meane circumstances will not give me an opportunity to doe it my selfe I use that little interest I have in solliciting others; this makes mee now your Petitioner, for a Son of Mrs Lawrences, I suppose his Mother is not perfectly a strainger to you, both the young mans Parents are very industrious and honest; their having last yeare failed of an advantage Mr Speaker[2] promised them, makes them

[1] Near Ross, Herefordshire. Benson was vicar from 1684 until his deprivation as a nonjuror in 1690.
[2] Paul Foley, Speaker since 1695.

very sollicitous of getting some employment for him that may helpe him to live in the world, they having a large Familey. It is myne and my Wife's request, that you will afford your interest, to put him into som Clerks place, if sutch may be had, or at least to give your advice, what is best to doe with him, he is a very honest and sober youth; if you thinke fitt to comply with our desiers, every thing shall bee done to qualifie him for your favour and Patronage. by your answering our requests you will doe an act of charity, and infinitely obleige

Your Freind and Servant
SAM: BENSON

My Wife sends her service and respects to you.

Address: For John Locke Esqr This

Endorsed by Locke: S. Benson 11 Apr 98

2419. FRANS VAN LIMBORCH to LOCKE, 12 April 1698 (*2223, 2606*)

B.L., MS. Locke c. 13, f. 180.

London 12 April 1698.

Honoured Sir

This is onely to cover the inclosed from Mr Samuel Lock,[1] which he had promised to deliver me in the fore going week, but having been hindred by severall impediments, he delivred itt me yester night; Sir I know not what to say, or how to render my most humble respects to you, for your very greatt favours to me, by which j receive heere so many favours from Mr Lock, that he, to show his readinesse in favouring a person, recommanded to him by your worth, he bought allready some sugars in order to loade them in a vessel of him which goes for holland this week, and consigne them to me; and he is ready to give recommandations to some other merchands, of which I shall gratefully accept.

Now Sir j further take the liberty to acquaint your worth by this, that j finde my staying heere by the above sayde reason, being but to be very short, j intend to come downe againe to Oates in the mid of next week, to give your worth there my humble and hearty thanks, for all of your favours, being in hopes j shall once have occasion to show in any manner my gratitude; in the mean

[1] For him see p. 645; the letter is lost.

while Honoured Sir j pray god he'll give you a good health and take your worthy person in his divin protection and subscribe my self with all my heart

Honoured Sir

Your most oblidged and devoted servant

F: V: LIMBORCH

Pray give my humble respects to Mr Masham and Mr Coast.

I received last Saturday one from my father, who with my mother and si⟨ster⟩[a] give their humble servise to your worth.—and are all (grace to god) very well.

Address: To John Locke Esqr.

Endorsed by Locke: F: Limborch 12 Apr. 98

2420. LOCKE to EDWARD CLARKE, 15 April 1698 (2408, 2425)

B.L., MS. Locke b. 8, no. 131. Printed in Rand, pp. 535–6.

Oates. 15 Apr 98

Dear Sir

Though listlesness from indisposition be almost as potent a clog ⟨as⟩[b] hurry from businesse to make one slow in writeing, yet my letters would be both frequenter and longer to you did I not consider how much you are taken up with indispensible occasions, and that you have scarce time at liberty to read long ones. I take a word from you when you have leisure for it very kindely and thank you for a short letter without grumbling that it is not more. I am glad to hear Mrs Clarke is in soe good hands.[1] I hope his skill and directions and her compliance will in concurrence quickly set her perfectly to rights soe that she will injoy many years of health to come. My humble service to her and your fires side and to the Batchelor. I am

Dear Sir

Your most affectionate humble servant

J LOCKE

Address: For Edward Clarke Esquire member of Parliament. To be left at Richards Coffee house within Timple Bar London

[a] *Page torn.* [b] *Word omitted by Locke; the three succeeding words are interlined.*

[1] Dr. Robert Pitt's: p. 381.

2421. RICHARD BOULTON to LOCKE, 19 April [1698] (*2430*)

B.L., MS. Locke c. 4, f. 146. Year from Locke's endorsement. For the writer see *D.N.B.* His two treatises (nos. *2191*, 2310, and below) were published by A. and J. Churchill.

London April 19

Sir

Though Gratitude is the least Return, that can be made for Favours received from One of Your Character; who have with ⟨Universal⟩[a] Applause appeared in a Controversy, where the Name of Your Adversary, was enough to raise the Common Cry of some Men in Opposition to Truth; Yet the Thoughts of the Person to whom I am bound to make my acknowledgements made me hitherto Guilty of a Fault, I would now Excuse by a Trifle which perhaps may rather make an Addition to it: but the Best of it is, This small Book[1] cannot have more Mistakes in it, than what will be easily passed by and forgiven, not at all deserveing Your Notice.

Since I was Obliged to You for Your Last Favours, I have got a little Interest in the Universitye, which I am now to loose, because it is too Chargeable to keep, and I have only the Misfortune to see, of what advantage such freinds might be were I able to stay amongst them; and the only encouragement I now have is, That it lyes in the Power of One, that is not only an Improver of Real Knowledge, but delights to encourage those that seek after it, to enable me to Conquer such difficultyes; and I am bolder to beg such a favour since Your Letter may assure me of it; for I am tould by my Tutor that there is an Exhibition given to Brazen-Nose College by My Lord Mordant, and the Worthy Dr. Goodall to whom I am very much Oblig'd for his Favour and Encouragement, tells me You are so intimately acquianted with him, that would you be pleased to Write a Letter to him in Favour of Me I need not Question but he'll give it me.[2]

And Sir if I must be obliged to You for what advantages may fall to me by such a Favour, You know best whether it will be most

[a] *MS.* Uiversal

[1] Probably Boulton's *A Treatise concerning the Heat of the Blood: and also of the Use of the Lungs*, 1698. L.L., no. 406.

[2] Boulton matriculated from Brasenose College, Oxford, on 29 November 1697. The scholarship which he sought was established in 1571 by the will of John Mordaunt, second Baron Mordaunt of Turvey: *Brasenose Quatercentenary Monographs*, iv. 8–19 (Oxford Hist. Soc., vol. lii, 1909). It is questionable whether Peterborough could influence the award, more especially as the barony had devolved on his cousin Lady Mary Mordaunt, who was duchess of Norfolk at this time.

proper I should carry the Letter to his Lordship or not. All I have more to ask is that You would be pleased to pardon this Boldness, since Your former Favours encourage

Worthy Sir

Your most obliged obedient and Most Humble Servant

RICHARD. BOULTON.

Endorsed by Locke: R: Boulton 19 Apr 98

2422. WILLIAM MOLYNEUX to LOCKE, 19 April 1698 (2414, 2471)

The Carl H. Pforzheimer Library, New York. Transcribed from photostat. Printed, with an omission, in *Some Familiar Letters*, pp. 269–71. Answers no. 2414.

Dublin. Apr. 19. 1698.

Most Honourd, Dear Sir

I have formerly had thoughts of coming into England, as I have told you, on Occasion of My Health. But since the receipt of yours of Apr. 6. which came to my Hands but this Morning, That Consideration weighs but little with me; The Desire of seing and Conversing with you has drownd all other Expectations from my Journy, and now I am resolved to accomplish it, let what will come on't. Your Perswasions and Arguments I think have something in them of Incantation; I am sure their Charms are so powerfull on me on all Occasions I can never resist them. I shall therefore imbrace you, God Willing, as soon as ever the Parliament of England Rises. I fix this Period now, not so much in Expectation of our Chancelors Arrival,[1] as on an other Account. My Dear Friend, Must therefore know, that the Consideration of what I mentiond in my last from the Incomparable Author of the Treatise etc. has moved me to put pen to paper, and Commit some thoughts of mine on that Subject to the Pres in a small octavo Intitled *The Case of Irelands being Bound by Acts of Parliament in England Stated.*[2] This you'll say is a Nice subject, but I think I have treated it with that Caution and Submission, that It cannot justly give any offence insomuch that I scruple not to put my Name to it, and, by Advice

[1] Methuen.

[2] There are two issues or editions dated 1698: '*Dublin*, Printed by *Joseph Ray*, and are to be Sold at his Shop in *Skinner-Row*' and 'Dublin, by and for J.R. and are to be sold by R. Clavel and A. and J. Churchill'. Locke's copy probably belongs to the first issue: L.L., no. 2012. Wing lists an edition by W. Boreham as dating also from this year. The text contains about 30,000 words.

of some good Friends here, have presumed to dedicate it to his Majesty. I have Orderd some of them to[a–] Mr. Churchil[–a] to be presented to you, and some of your Friends. and they are now upon the Road towards you. I have been very free in giving you my Thoughts on your Peices, I should be extreamly obleidged to you for the like freedom on your side upon mine. I cannot pretend this to be an Accomplisd Performance, it was done in hast, and intended to overtake the Proceedings at Westminster, but it comes too late for that, What effect it may possibly have in time to come, God and the Wise Council of England only knows. but were it again under my Hands I could considerably amend, and add to it. But till I either see how the Parliament at Westminster is pleasd to take it, or till I see them Risen, I do not think it adviseable for me to go on tother side the Water. Tho I am not apprehensive of any Mischeif from them, Yet God only knows what Resentments Captious Men may take on such Occasions.[1]

The[b–] Character you give me of Monsieur Le Fivre is very agreable to my Desires in all things, save his being Married; How that may sute with his coming to live in my Family I cannot wel tell. However I will defer the farther Consideration hereof, till I come into England, at which time I hope to have some personal Conversation with the Gentleman Himself, which will better enable me to come to a resolution in this Matter, than any farther[c] Account by Letter. As to the other Part of his Character of being Careles in his outward Garb, I should easily pas it over; tho I must Confes tis an excellent Quality in a Tutor to be a Person of a genteel Dres, Good Mein, and Gracefull Addres.[–b][2]

My Brother gives you his most Respectfull service. He has now ready a Discourse On our Giants Causway, which indeed is a

[a–a] *MS.* to Mr / Mr Churchil [b–b] *Deleted in MS. presumably by the editor of* Some Familiar Letters. [c] *Or* further

[1] On 21 May the English house of commons, on a complaint by Methuen and urged by Clarke, appointed a committee to examine the book, to inquire into its authorship, and to report on 'what Proceedings have been in *Ireland*, that might occasion' it; the king was to be asked to punish the author. The committee's report was read on 22 June, and on the 27th the house resolved that the book was 'of dangerous Consequence to the Crown and People of *England*' as denying the dependence of Ireland on 'the Imperial Crown of this Realm'; but the house seems to have been concerned with the Irish parliament's proceedings rather than with the book, and in addressing the king for the 'punishing and discountenancing those that have been guilty' of what had occurred did not name Molyneux: *C.J.*; James Vernon, *Letters*, ed. G. P. R. James, 1841, ii. 83–4, 93–4.

[2] This apparently responds to a passage in no. 2414 that was omitted by the 1708 editor. The younger Tanneguy Le Fèvre.

stupendious Natural Rarity; he has addresd it to Dr Lister, but you will soon see it in the Transactions.[1]

Mr Burridge goes on now with some speed, I had lately an Occasion of Writing to Mr Churchil, and I gave him an Account of His Progres. I hope the whole will be finishd soon after Midsummer. and indeed in my Opinion he performs it incomperably.

I am
Dear Sir
Your Most Affectionate Humble servant
W: MOLYNEUX

Address: To John Locke Esquire at Mr Pawlings overagainst the Plow Inn in Little Lincolns Inn Fields London
Postmark: AP 25
Endorsed by Locke: W: Molineux 19 Apr 98

2423. JOHN BONVILLE to LOCKE, 23 April 1698 (*2417, 2428*)

B.L., MS. Locke c. 4, f. 83.

London Aprill the 23d: 98

Honoured Cousin

Sir Be plesed to Axcept ½ cwt of Orenges which my Wife present to you, with her Harty sarvis, I have given them into the hands of Lenham, he promiseth faithfully to bring them safe to you, I Am sory that sum Erers is made in our Accounts, which I would rectifie If you pleas to send them Againe, with your marks where the Erer Lies, I waited on my Lady. I purpose to send her A nue Table This day sevennight. I Tould her that there Is but Little diferanc between and ould one and A nue one, when Every thing considered, Deare Cousin I shall be much rejoyced to heare of your wellfarr, for I feare The Long continuanc of This sharp wether Is not Axeptable to you, nor to Any The Lord continue health to you, and presarve you mutch Longer Amongst us If it be his blesed will, which Is and Ever shall be the prayer of your Faithfull

Kinsman and Humble Sarvant
JNO: BONVILLE

Address: For Mr Locke [at Oates, by Joslyn, Bishops Stortford]
Postmark: AP 23
Endorsed by Locke: J Bonville 23 Apr 98 Answered 25

[1] *Philosophical Transactions*, xx (1698), 209–23; there is an earlier paper by Dr Molyneux, ibid. xviii (1694), 175–82, and a plate with explanation in vol. xix no. 235. Dr. Lister is Martin Lister, *c.* 1638–1712; F.R.S. 1671; M.D. 1684: *D.N.B.*

2424. Locke to Benjamin Furly, 28 April 1698 (*2287, 2572*)

B.L., MS. Eng. letters, c. 200, f. 15. Printed in T. I. M. Forster, *Epistolarium*, 1845, pp. 12–14; *Original Letters*, 2nd ed., 1847, pp. 63–5.

Oates 28 Apr 98

Dear Freind

I received with great joy the account you writ me by Mr Limborch[1] of your and your wives health and the promiseing estate of all your children. I count it the greatest comfort of a father, which I am very glad you have in all your sons to a degree not common in any age and very rare in this. may you live long in prosperity to enjoy it with the greatest satisfaction. My little freind[2] I finde deceives not my expectation. I pretend not you know to prophesie. But ever since I first knew that child I could not for bear thinkeing that he would goe a great way in any thing he should be set to, and would not make a mean figure in the world. Pray remember me very kindely to him, and tell him that I am very glad to hear soe well of him for I love him exceedingly

I am vexed at the dishonesty of your brother in law[3] for your sake because it is like to be troublesome to you, and for my owne sake because it is like to hinder me from seeing of you this sommer, and what may be come of me next winter I know not. I was forced to goe to town in December last:[4] but in two days stay there I was almost dead and the third I was forced to flye for it in one of the bitterest days I have known, for I veryly beleive one nights stay longer had made an end of me. I have been here ever since in the chimny[a] corner and write this by the fires side, for we have here yet noe warmth from the sun though the days are almost at their full length[5] and twas but yesterday morning that it snowd very hard for near two hours togeather. This great indisposition of my health which is not yet recoverd to any great degree keeps me here out of the air of London and the bustle of affairs. I am little furnished with news, and want it lesse. I have lived long enough to see that a mans endeavours are ill laid out upon any thing but him

[a] *MS.* chiñy

[1] Frans van Limborch.
[2] Arent Furly.
[3] Probably Cornelis Huys, brother of Furly's second wife: Thijssen-Schoute, *Uit de Republiek der Letteren*, pp. 170–2; for his dispute with his sisters see pp. 740–4.
[4] A slip for January: pp. 307–9, etc.
[5] The longest day was 10 June.

self, and his expectations very uncertain when placed upon what others pretend or promise to doe. I say not this with any respect to my private concernes (which I owne give me noe cause of complaint since my desires are confined in a narrow compasse) but in answer to what you say with publick views. Now there is peace I wish it may last my days. If not I wish I and my freinds may scape the disorders of warr. But after all every one must take his lot according to the fate of the age he lives in. You must pardon this Hum Drum from a man who is very much remote from the commerce of the world, and yet when he has the pen in his hand cannot forbear saying some thing to an old and valued friend such as you are. I am almost quite alone here now. Sir Francis My Lady, and Mrs Masham are all now at London and have been for some weekes. If a wish could bring you hither you and I in a day or two would have a good deale of talke togeather. I know not what we may doe when we are spirits, but this earthy cottage[1] is not I perceive soe easily removed. I live in hopes yet of seeing you this sommer: for a composition is better than law and I know you love not wrangleing. My service to your Lady and your sons. I am not well satisfied that I saw not your Son John all the time he was in England,[2] though I know not whom to be angry with for it. I am

Dear Friend

Your most affectionate friend and servant

J LOCKE

2425. LOCKE to EDWARD CLARKE, 29 April 1698 (2420, *2429*)

The Pierpont Morgan Library, New York. Transcribed from Xerox print. Answered by no. *2429*.

Oates 29 Apr 98

Dear Sir

Upon the death of his mother[3] Sir Francis Masham has desired me to supply him with £100 which he has present need of upon this occasion. I writ to my Lord Ashley lately for £50 which he owes me but haveing noe positive answer when it will be paid I desire you would let me know whether you can conveniently let me have an hundred pounds upon this occasion, that soe much as you shall send me word will consist with your convenience to pay I may

[1] See no. 70. [2] p. 162. [3] No. 1983.

draw a bill on you for. I have not sent you the state of the account between us because I thinke you will have more leisure for it after the parliament is up. I desire you would not mention Sir Francis's borrowing of this money, to any body

I hope Mrs Clarke has received benefit by Dr Pitts[1] prescriptions. I should be very glad to hear she is perfectly recoverd. My humble service to her to my wife to your fires side and to the Batchelor. I am

Dear Sir

Your most humble and most affectionate servant

J Locke

Address: For Edward Clarke Esquire member of Parliament. To be left at Richards Coffee house within Temple Bar London Frank

Endorsed by Clarke: ⟨Mr.⟩[a] Lock to Know what money I can supply Him with etc: Received the 2d. of May 1698. Answered the 3d.

2426. Locke to Esther Masham, 29 April 1698 (2327, 2603)

Newberry Library, Chicago: copy of the original letter by Esther Masham in her letter-book, pp. 42–3. Transcribed from microfilm. Printed in Fox Bourne, ii. 461–2; by Professor Maurice Cranston in *Newberry Library Bulletin*, 2nd ser., no. 4, July 1950, p. 132. The explanatory note was written by Esther.

Oates 29 Apr. 1698

It is better to be taken up with businesse at London than to freeze in the Country. I can scarce be warm enough to write this by the fires side: you should therefore be so *Gratieuse* to come and comfort your poor solitary Berger who suffers here under the deep winter of Frost and Snow. I do not hyperbolize in the case, the day Mr Coste came home it snow'd very hard a good part of the morning. My affection for your Service haveing thaw'd me a little I proceed to your businesse. Matters being as you State them I see nothing at present you have more to do but to presse for the sending your Legacies, since you judge it best to have them in your own hands as soon as you can. To the paying your Grandfathers presently there is no manner of exception. If they make any Difficulty

[a] *MS.* r

[1] Dr. Robert Pitt: no. *2987*.

in remitting your Grandmothers, we shall know what is to be said when we see their objections or what they demand. When I see you here I shall have a better oportunitie to discourse you at large by word of mouth how you may offer them such satisfaction about the *remplassement* as in Reason they cannot refuse.[1] My thanks to my Daughter[2] for the favour of her remembrance. My Service to her and all the rest of my friends in Town especialy Sir Francis and my Lady. I am of all the Shepherds of Forest

Gentile Bergere

your most humble and most Faithfull Servant

[a]CELADON THE SOLITARY

2427. ANTHONY ASHLEY COOPER, styled Lord Ashley, later third earl of Shaftesbury, to LOCKE, [*c.* 30 April 1698] (*2415*, 2608)

B.L., MS. Locke c. 7, ff. 122–3. Date from postmark and Locke's endorsement

I forgot when I writ last in answer to yours, to desire to know from you to whome I should pay the 50l which I have now ready for you I sent to enquire of Mr Popple to know if he had receiv'd any order from you as to that particular: and I should now send to M Pauling: but that is it late at night and I send this to you by thi post that I may know the sooner from you in case I hear nothing from Mr Pauling.

I am Your sincere Friend and Humble servant

A: ASHLEY.

Address: For Mr Lock [at Oates, by Joslyn, Bishops Stortford]
Free A: Ashley

Postmark: AP 30

Endorsed by Locke: L: Ashley May 98 Answered 6

[a] Mr Locke subscribd himself *Celadon* alluding to the Romance of Astrea[3] I us to read him after Suppers.

[1] Esther's maternal grandparents Sir William Scott de la Mezangère and his wi Catherine died in France in 1681 and 1684. He left Esther 1,000 *livres*; her gran mother, 2,500 *livres*, but owing to the terms of her will Esther could not obta payment at present. Henry Masham went to Rouen in June to receive these ar other legacies and sums owing; for the time being Esther received 3,250 *livres*, wor £205 7*s.* 7*d.*: Letter-book, pp. 47–8, 50.

[2] Mrs. Frances St. John.

[3] Honore d'Urfé, *Astrée*, first published in 1607–27; English translation 1657–

2428. JOHN BONVILLE to LOCKE, 30 April 1698 (*2423, 2464*)

B.L., MS. Locke c. 4, f. 84. The lower half of the sheet, bearing the address on the verso, has been cut off.

London Aprill the 30th 1698

Honoured Cousin,

Sir I have Rec our Account Againe and have drawne it out Againe I hope it is to your satisfaction,[a] as for the 100 l I should not knowne Any thing of but by your mark, I have This day sent my Lady A Table I hope it will pleas her, I paid 7s for it, which I have Included in This Acc, Lenham promised to take care of it, I hope you have rec the orenges According to your Expitation, I hope they are good, Deare Cousin I Think The time Long Tell I see you, I doe Heartley wish That I Could be Any wayes Sarvesable to you, for your good, whether heare In Towne, or Any where Elc, The Lord be your soport, The Lord strengthen you In your outward man and In your Inward man, The Lord Keepe you by his Allmighty power Through faith To Salvation, which shall be The prayer of your faithfull Kinsman and Humble Sarvant

JNO: BONVILLE

my wife and son Give their Humble Sarvis to you

Address: [the lower half of 'Startford' survives.]

Endorsed by Locke: J: Bonville 30 Apr 98 Answered May 6

2429. EDWARD CLARKE to LOCKE, 3 May 1698 (2425, 2433)

B.L., MS. Locke c. 6, ff. 134–5. Printed in Rand, p. 536. Answers no. 2425; answered by no. 2433.

London May the 3d. 1698.

Deare Sir,

Yours of the 29th. of the last moneth came to my handes yesterday, for which I thanke you, And shall readily Pay upon Demand any Byll you shall draw on mee for fowerscore pounds, But a greater summe then That, I cannot conveniently Answere at present, my Wife, and Family being in Town, which occasions a

[a] *This account is missing.*

more then ordinary Expence to mee, at this time; Mrs Clarke joynes with mee in Her true Love and Service to you, I hope shee mends upon Doctor Pitts Prescriptions, of which you shall have a Particular Account, as soon as I can gett time to Write to you; I am

Your most Affectionate Faithfull servant

EDW: CLARKE

The Batchelor is your servant etc: And the Greate-House[1] desires to bee Kindly Remembred to you etc:

Address: These, For John Lock Esqr. [at Oates, by Joslyn, Bishops Stortford
Frank: Edw: Clarke:

Postmarks: MY 3; LV(?)

Endorsed by Locke: E: Clarke 3 May 98 Answered 7

2430. RICHARD BOULTON to LOCKE, 3 May [1698] (*2421*)

B.L., MS. Locke c. 4, f. 147. Year from Locke's endorsement.

London May 3d

Sir

I have wrote down to Oxford to be acquianted with what yo thought necessary about the Scholarship, and My Tutor deferrin his Answer at the last hath told me, that I am too late, it being i the mean time disposed of, and possess'd by another. I am equall obliged to You as if I had got it, and can easily be content with such disappointment in my hopes, it being my constant fortune hithert to meet with nothing else. There are some other Questior which Mr. Churchil tells me are in Your Letter, which I hav Reason to be glad to answer, to one that hath so much Interes and may, if I could expect such Favours, make interest for me whe something else falls which My Lord Mordant hath the disposein of, but I fear those will be too late for me, and longer than I ca wait for them.[2] I have been in Brazen-Nose about 9 months, ar was encouraged to come there by him who is My Tutor, who

[1] Somers.

[2] For the Mordaunt scholarship see p. 375. On 25 May Boulton was granted Frankland scholarship. His name remained on the college books until 15 Novemb 1700: *Brasenose Quatercentenary Monographs*, iv. 20–1; *Register, 1509–1909* (Oxfo Hist. Soc., vols. lii, lv, 1909).

Tuterage I have for Nothing, I am enter'd a Battler there, and it will, if I stay, cost me about 25 Pound a Year, hitherto I made shift to stay there hopeing for Encouragement, but in that College there is none that properly belongs to Physick, so that cou'd I get it, I could not keep it long. I Beg your Pardon for being so Bold, and in haste, subscribe.

Sir
Your oliged and Most Humble Servant
R. BOULTON

Endorsed by Locke: R: Boulton 3 May 98

2431. JAMES JOHNSTOUN to LOCKE, 4 May 1698 (*2387*, *2745*)

B.L., MS. Locke c. 12, ff. 35–6.

Lond. 4 May. 98

Sir

I writ only to let you know that I thinck of going to the Bath about ten days hence so that if you resolve on going with us you will be in toun next week. we will goe in 4 days in the chariot and I shall have riding horses with me so that you may use sometymes the one and sometymes the other. Mrs Johnson hopes you will come and renew the lease of your lyfe there in your own countrey. pray give her compliments and mine to My Lady Masham. I was sorry I could not wait on her when she left this place as I intended. I was keept busy day and night to save a poor french gentleman who was trepanned by knaves into an experiment upon Guinnys. he is condemned to die but the Judges have told the King that it were hard to take his lyfe.[1] pray remember me to young Master.[2]

I am
Sir
Your most faithful humble servant
J. JOHNSTOUN.

Endorsed by Locke: J: Johnstown 4° May 98 Answered 18

[1] Peter Fermont (Fremont?) of Lyons, who was convicted, probably on this day at the Old Bailey, of sweating guineas; his petition for a reprieve was referred to Lord Chief Justice Sir John Holt, who reported on 24 May. He was hanged on the 25th: *Cal.S.P., Dom.*, 1698, pp. 243, 266–8; Luttrell, iv. 378–9; J.-B. Du Bos to Toinard, 10 June, N.S. (B.N., MS. N. Acq. fr. 560, ff. 249–50); Vernon, *Letters*, ii. 78.

[2] Francis Cudworth Masham.

2432. PHILIPPUS VAN LIMBORCH to LOCKE, 6/16 May 1698 (2413, 2443)

B.L., MS. Locke c. 14, ff. 115–16. Copy by van Limborch in Amsterdam University Library, MS. R.K., III D 16, f. 203. Printed, with slight omissions, from the copy in *Some Familiar Letters*, pp. 416–21. Answers no. 2413; answered by no. 2443.

Vir Amplissime

Literas tuas postremas recte mihi fuisse traditas, jam ex filio cui id significavi intellexeris. Statim eas Viro Magnifico prælegi: Verum quia tunc occupatior erat, aliud designavit tempus magis oportunum prolixiori colloquio, quod materiæ gravitas mereri videtur. Paucis itaque ab hinc diebus me denuo ad se vocavit, iterumque epistolam tuam legimus. Probat argumenta tua, supposita illa quam adhibes Dei definitione: Ens enim undiquaque perfectum, seu, quod eodem redit, omnes in se complectens perfectiones, non nisi unum esse posse, manifestum est. Verum ille quærit argumentum, non ex definitione Dei desumtum, sed ex ipsa ratione naturali, et per quod in definitionem Dei deducamur. Hac nempe methodo instituit demonstrationem suam. I. Datur ens æternum, independens, necessitate naturæ suæ existens, et sibi ipsi sufficiens. II. Ens tale est tantum unum, et plura istiusmodi entia esse nequeunt. III. Illud Ens, quia est unicum, omnes in se complectitur perfectiones: atque hoc Ens est Deus. Primam propositionem Vir Magnificus ait te in tractatu tuo de Intellectu humano egregie adstruxisse,

---

Excellent Sir,

You will by now have learnt from my son that, as I told him, your las letter was duly delivered to me. I immediately read it to the Magnifico but as he was then rather busy he appointed another time, more convenien for a longer conversation, which the importance of the subject seems to deserve. Accordingly a few days ago he again summoned me to himself, anc we read your letter a second time. He approves of your arguments, tha definition of God that you use being assumed; for it is manifest that a bein perfect in every respect, or, which comes to the same thing, embracing al perfections in itself, cannot but be one. But he is seeking an argument taken not from the definition of God, but from natural reason itself, and by whic we may be led to the definition of God. Indeed he has established his own demonstration in this way: I. There is given an eternal being, independent existing by the necessity of its own nature, and sufficient to itself. II. Such a being is only one, and there cannot be more than one being of the same sort III. That being, because it is unique, embraces all perfections in itself; anc this being is God. The Magnifico says that you have excellently establishe the first proposition in your treatise concerning the Human Understandin

iisdem plane argumentis, quibus ipse in sua demonstratione usus est, adeo ut suas cogitationes in argumentatione tua expressas viderit.[1] Tanto enixius secundam propositionem a te probatam videre desiderat; qua solide probatâ, tertia nullo negotio ex duabus prioribus deduci potest. Secundam, ait, omnes Theologos ac Philosophos, quin et ipsum Cartesium, præsupponere, non probare. Non dubito, quin mihi omnem suam argumentationem communicaturus sit: credo autem non id facturum, antequam tua argumenta viderit; ut tuas cogitationes, quas ipse es meditatus, cum suis conferre possit. Verum hic ambigere quis posset,[2] an non pro. positionum harum ordo mutari, et quæ nunc secunda est tertia, et quæ nunc tertia est secunda esse debeat: hoc est, an non, quando probatum est, dari ens æternum, independens, sibi ipsi sufficiens, exinde porro possit probari, illud in se omnes complecti perfectiones; quia fieri nequit, ut enti æterno, independenti, sibique sufficienti, ulla perfectio desit: atque ita probato, ens illud omnes in se complecti perfectiones, porro inferatur, illud ens tantum esse unum. Verum huic methodo hæc objicitur difficultas,[3] quod deprehendamus esse duas naturas tota essentia diversas (loquor terminis eorum qui hanc movent difficultatem) Cogitationem et Exten-

---

by just the same arguments as he has used in his demonstration, so much so that he saw his own thoughts expressed in the course of your reasoning.[1] This makes him desire so much the more earnestly to see the second proposition proved by you; it being solidly proved, the third can easily be deduced from the two preceding. He says that all theologians and philosophers, indeed even Descartes himself, presuppose, do not prove, the second. I have no doubt that he will impart to me the whole of his reasoning; but I think that he will not do so before he has seen your arguments, so that he can compare your thoughts, the outcome of your reflections, with his own. Here, however, someone could be in doubt[2] whether the order of these propositions ought not to be changed, and whether that which is now the second ought not to be the third, and that which is now the third ought not to be the second, that is, when it has been proved that there is given an eternal being, independent, sufficient to itself, whether it cannot then be proved that it embraces all perfections in itself; because it is impossible for any perfection to be wanting in an eternal being, independent, and sufficient to itself; and, it being thus proved that that being embraces all perfections in itself, whether it may then be inferred that that being is only one. But this difficulty[3] is put forward against this way [of arranging the propositions]

---

[1] This appears to refer to *Essay*, IV. x. 3–6; the passage appears in the *Abregé*: pp. 82–4. [2] Van Limborch's interjection: see p. 434.
[3] Apparently Hudde's rejoinder.

sionem: supposito dari cogitationem æternam et independentem, a qua ego dependeo, statuere quis posset, etiam esse extensionem seu materiam æternam, sibi ipsi sufficientem, et a cogitatione æterna minime dependentem: sic statuerentur duo entia æterna; et tamen ex positione materiæ æternæ et independentis minime sequeretur, eam in se complecti omnes perfectiones. Quare primo probandum videtur, ens æternum et independens esse tantum unum, antequam omnes in se complecti perfectiones probari possit.

Quod si secunda propositio, ens independens tantum esse unum, non possit probari, nihil religioni, seu necessitati ens illud unice colendi, decedere videtur: Quia ego totus ab illo uno ente, quod me produxit, dependeo; illi ergo soli sum obligatus, illud ex toto corde, tota anima diligere, illiusque præceptis per omnia obedire debeo. Si præter illud ens aliud forte existat, quia ab eo non dependeo, illud neutiquam me spectat,[a] neque id ullam in me operationem exserere potest. Imo neutrum horum entium de altero ullam notitiam habere, aut ullam in alterum operationem exserere posset: Quoniam enim sibi ipsi est sufficiens, ergo nec per alterius positionem aut remotionem ullam acquirere potest majorem perfectionem, aut de

[a] *Van Limborch's copy reads here* . . . spectat, neque ego ad id relationem habeo, neque id ullam in me . . .

---

that we may find out that there are two substances [*naturae*] differing completely in essence (I speak in the terms of those who raise this difficulty), Thought and Extension; supposing that there is given eternal and independent thought on which I am dependent, someone could conclude that there is also eternal extension or matter, sufficient to itself, and not at all dependent on eternal thought; thus two eternal beings would be set up; and yet it would in no wise follow from the positing of eternal and independent matter that it embraces all perfections in itself. Wherefore it seems that it must first be proved that an eternal and independent being is only one before it can be proved that it embraces all perfections in itself.

And yet, if the second proposition, that an independent being is only one, cannot be proved, it seems to take nothing away from religion or the necessity of worshipping that being alone; since I am wholly dependent on that one being that produced me; I am therefore under obligation to it alone and ought to love it with my whole heart and whole soul, and to obey its precepts in all things. If besides that being another should perchance exist, since I am not dependent on it it in no respect concerns me, nor can it exert any operative power upon me. Indeed neither of these beings could have any knowledge of the other or exert any operative power upon the other; for since each is sufficient to itself it follows that it can neither acquire greater perfection nor lose anything of its perfection through the positing or putting

sua perfectione quicquam amittere; alias sibi non esset sufficiens. Licet itaque Veritatis scrutatori summopere gratum sit, evidenter demonstrare posse, ens independens esse tantum unum; si tamen forte contingat, illud evidenter demonstrari non posse, nihil tamen religionis necessitati et perfectioni propterea decessurum videtur, quoniam ens, a quo ego dependeo, est tantum unum. Hæc fuit sermonum Viri Magnifici summa, quantum ego mentem ejus percepi.

Ego argumentationis tuæ filum in tractatu tuo de Intellectu humano non legi. Probasse te, ens aliquod esse a quo dependes, illudque ens esse æternum et sibi ipsi sufficiens, nullus dubito: argumentum quo id probatur evidens est et clarum. Verum an ibidem probaveris, te ab uno tantum ente dependere, neque fieri posse ut a pluribus dependeas, ignoro. Argumentatio Viri Magnifici infert quidem, me ab ente æterno dependere, sed nondum vidi ab ipso probatum, ab uno tantum ente me dependere: Quod tamen spectat primam propositionem: Nam in secunda ponitur, præter illud ens æternum a quo ego dependeo aliud nullum esse ens æternum. Itaque similiter hic præsupponi videtur, me ab uno tantum ente dependere: saltem id nondum distincte probatum audivi; quod tamen primo probandum videtur, antequam ad probationem propositionis secundæ procedatur. Tum et dispiciendum, an quidem

---

aside of the other; otherwise it would not be sufficient to itself. Although, then, it would be extremely gratifying to the searcher after truth to be able to demonstrate clearly that an independent being is only one, yet if perchance it turns out that that cannot be clearly demonstrated, yet nothing, it seems, will on that account be taken away from the necessity and perfection of religion, since the being on which I am dependent is only one. This was the sum total of the Magnifico's remarks, so far as I understood his meaning.

I have not read the thread of your reasoning in your treatise concerning the Human Understanding. I have no doubt that you have proved that there is some being on which you are dependent and that that being is eternal and sufficient to itself; the argument by which this is proved is plain and clear. But I do not know whether you have proved in the same place that you are dependent on one being only and that it is impossible for you to be dependent on more than one. The Magnifico's reasoning indeed implies that I am dependent on an eternal being, but I have not yet seen it proved by him that I am dependent on one being only. But that relates to the first proposition; for it is posited in the second that there is no other eternal being besides that eternal being on which I am dependent. And so it seems to be presupposed in the same way here that I am dependent on one being only; at least I have not yet heard it precisely proved; yet it seems that this should first be proved before one proceeds to the proof of the second proposition.

ratio permittat, supponi materiam æternam ac sibi sufficientem: Si enim ens sibi sufficiens et æternum sit necessario omni modo perfectum; sequitur, materiam, quæ est substantia iners omni motu ac vita destituta, non posse concipi æternam sibique sufficientem.

Voluit Vir Magnificus, ut tibi distinctius qualem desideret probationem perscriberem: Verbis suis te quam officiosissime salutari jussit; pro suscepto in sui gratiam labore gratias agit: Dolet valetudinem tuam afflictam: et si ea minus permittat subtilioribus indulgere cogitationibus, minime cupit ut te fatiges meditationibus, tibi ob valetudinem afflictiorem molestis, aut valetudini noxiis. Precatur interim tibi valetudinem firmam ac vegetam; et si ea permittat, ut de propositione secunda, prout nunc a me ex mente illius proposita est, judicium tuum scribas, rem facies ipsi gratissimam. Interim ego multis me nominibus tibi obstrictum profiteor, non tantum quod hoc tuo responso mihi gratificari volueris; sed et potissimum pro multis ac magnis, quibus filium meum prosecutus es officiis et beneficiis, quæ per epistolam mihi significavit, prolixius ea, ubi ad nos redierit, prædicaturus, et singillatim enarraturus: tunc, si potero, meritas tibi habiturus sum gratias: sed quantæcunque illæ sint, nunquam tamen beneficiis tuis pares esse poterunt. Exspectassem quidem filii mei

---

Then also it is to be considered whether reason indeed permits the supposition of matter eternal and sufficient to itself: for if a being sufficient to itself and eternal is necessarily perfect in every way, it follows that matter, which is an inert substance, destitute of all motion and life, cannot be conceived as eternal and sufficient to itself.

The Magnifico wanted me to write to you more precisely the kind of proof that he desires. He bade me give you his best respects; he thanks you for the labour that you have undertaken for his sake; he is sorry about your ill health; and if it allows you less indulgence in rather subtle [trains of] thought he desires you on no account to tire yourself with reflections troublesome because of your ill health, or harmful to it. Meanwhile he wishes you sound and vigorous health, and if it permits you to write your opinion about the second proposition as it has now been put by me in accordance with what he has in mind you will do him a very great favour. Meanwhile I acknowledge that I am obliged to you on many accounts, not only because you have been ready to favour me with this your reply, but chiefly for the many and great services and favours that you have bestowed on my son. He has told me of them by letter, and when he returns to us he will recount them at greater length and tell us everything in detail. Then, if I can, I shall thank you as you deserve; but, however great my thanks, they will never be able to equal your favours. I should indeed have awaited my son's

reditum: sed non ingratum tibi fore credidi, quamprimum Viri Magnifici judicium de tua epistola cognoscere. Tu ipse judicabis de illius methodo, et quid rescribendum sit. Hoc unum addo, ipsum lectâ tuâ epistolâ nullum illius apographum petiisse, sed conditionibus quas stipularis acquievisse; et si petiisset, ego modeste recusassem: Verum ea est humanitate, ut hoc a me flagitare noluerit. Verum tandem tempus est manum de tabula tollere. Vale Vir Amplissime. Uxor, filia, omnesque amici te salutant, omniaque fausta tibi precantur.

Tui Amantissimus
PHILIPPUS A LIMBORCH

Amstelodami 16 Maji

9
16 98
19

Address: To John Locke Esqr. at Mr Pawlings overagainst the plough in Little Lincolns Inne fields London

Postmark: MY 9

Endorsed by Locke: P: Limborch 16° May 98

---

return; but I thought that it will not be disagreeable to you to learn as soon as possible the Magnifico's opinion of your letter. You will judge his way [of proof] for yourself and how you should reply. I add only this, that after your letter was read he did not ask for a copy, but acquiesced in the conditions that you stipulate; and if he had asked for one I should have discreetly refused. But such is his courtesy that he would not have pressed me for this. But it is time at last for me to finish. Good-bye, excellent Sir. My wife, my daughter, and all our friends send you greetings and all good wishes.

Your most affectionate
PHILIPPUS VAN LIMBORCH

Amsterdam 16 May
1698

2433. LOCKE to EDWARD CLARKE, 7 May 1698 (*2429*, *2435*)

B.M., Add MS. 4290, f. 87. Part printed in Forster, p. 62; the whole, in Rand, pp. 536–7. Answers no. *2429*.

Oates 7° May 98

Dear Sir

Finding by yours of the 3d that your convenience at this time suits not I have been unwilling to strain it as far as you say you could make it reach and therefor have drawn a bill on you only for £55 payable to Sir Francis. the remainder I have made up else where. I desire it may be paid him on sight, when he comes, though I presume you will not hear of him in two or three days.

My Lady Masham has said some thing to me concerning my wife. Since she has been here she has been very reservd. if it be her usual temper tis well. If it be present thoughtfulnesse tis worth your consideration. How I shall carry my self to her you must instruct me for I love her and you know I am at your disposal to serve you[1]

She tels me she thinks Mrs Clarke mends. I am very glad to hear it, and am the apter to beleive it because she says she is very observant of the Doctors rules.[2] My service to her your fires side and the Batchelor. I am

Sir

your most affectionate friend and faithfull servant

J Locke

Address: For Edward Clarke Esquire member of Parliament. To be left at Richards Coffee house within Temple Bar London
Frank

Endorsed by Clarke: Mr. Lock to Pay £55 to Sir Francis Masham etc: And of Betty's being verie Reserved etc: Received the 10th. May 1698 Answered fully to all partes the same day etc:

2434. Sylvester Brounower to Locke, 7 May 1698 (*2250*, *2439*)

B.L., MS. Locke c. 4, ff. 185–6.

London May the 7th: 1698

Honoured Sir

I send per James Lanham a box of Colours and Oyl directed to the Lady Masham at Oates, vizt:

1lb: of spanish brown mixt with red Led	–:–:5
2d: priming 4lb: of white Led with ½ a ball of whiting	–:1:8
3d: priming 4lb: of clean white Led	–:2:–
1½ pint of Lindseed Oyl	–:–:10

[1] Betty was suspected of having engaged in a secret correspondence with a man p. 398, etc. Rand suggested that he might be the younger (Thomas?) Stringer (no. *631*): pp. 59–60 and n.

[2] Dr. Robert Pitt.

½lb: of Turpetine Oyl	–:–:6
1 great brush	–:–:6
2 small brushes	–:–:5
a Deal Box	–:–:6
	–:6:10½

Sir I have enquir'd of several Housepainters concerning the painting of the Seat, and the most rational account (as it seem'd to me) I could get concerning it, I shall here set down. vizt It is agreed that the Seat has been painted with Size, and that is the reason why the colour comes off; 'Tis much more difficult now to paint the Seat, and to make the Colours stick to the Wood, than if it had never been painted; Therefore the old Colours are to be got off as clean as maybe either with Scraping, washing etc; If the Seat should be prim'd over but once the colour must be laid on so thick that the Oyl will never pierce the Wood and therefore in a short time in warme weather will scale off again.

Therefore for the preservation of the Wood, as well as for the Colours to stick fast it is necessary to be primd 3 times.

First with the red Colour which is Spanish Brown and red Led mixt, prepared with Lindseed and Drying Oyl.

The bladder markd 2 upon the paper which is white Led and whiting is for the second priming and prepar'd as the former.

The bladder mark'd 3 is pure white Led for the third and last priming and prepared with Lindseed and Turpetine Oyl. If the Weather is any thing like each of those Colours will dry in a Days time.

Now to use it, 'twill be necessary to have 2 or 3 New pepkins that never had any grease in them, otherwise it will for ever keep the Colours from drying. A hole must be made in the bladder and the Colour Squeez'd into the pepkin, and part of the Lindseed Oyl put into a bottom of a broken glass bottle, and in working or laying on the first priming to deep now and then the pencil in the Oyl for the more easier running of the Colour, no matter how often, nor whether all the Wood be coverd equally with the colour so it is but wetted well with Oyl that it may soacke into the Wood, when that is Dry, we come to the second priming which bladder is markd 2 and may in the same manner be squeez'd into the first pepkin Provided it be first made very clean with Crum of bread that none of the former Colour remain, or else into a new one must be us'd and laid on with clean Lindseed Oyl as the first but somewhat thicker though no matter if the red is seen through it. Now we come to the third priming which is pure white Led and must be usd as the former two, but only with Turpetine Oyl and no other, and must cover the whole worke that no patches be seen.

The great pencil is for to Cover, and the less to go into the Corners, the great pencil is tyed about with Pack thread because it should not spatter the Colours nor make the worke all in stroakes which new pencils are apt to do, And every time they are us'd must be made very clean with soap and milk warm water, for if once the colours Dry in it they will become perfectly useless, The other small pencill I suppose will serve for paste, as you designe it.

Sir I tooke Colours but for 9 yards or 81 foot supposing the sealing to have no great occasion to be new done and the posts if it be necessary may always be done when ever you please if there should not be colours enough, but I am perswaded they rather impos'd more Colours upon me than necessary.

I hope My Lady and Company got well home and found you in good health which I heartily wish and pray for, And besides the many Obligations I am bound to you for I humbly thanke for your kindness and Civility to me when last at Oates, and hope if any thing comes within distance of my being serviceable to you offers, You will be pleased to imploy

Sir

Your most humble, most Obedient and most Dutifull Servant

S BROUNOWER

There has nothing yet been done at the Treasury about our Pay, but Mr: Glanville, and Mr: Taylor ascribe it to the slackness of our Lords in solliciting the Lords of the Treasury.[1]

Address: To the Honoured John Locke Esqre: at Oates. These with a box Directed to the Lady Masham

Endorsed by Locke: S: Brownover 7 May 98 Directions for Glot painting

[1] William Glanville and John Taylor were two of the four First Clerks of the Treasury at this time: Chamberlayne. The former was probably the son of William Glanville of the Alienation Office (no. *210*, etc.); for him see Evelyn, *Diary*, ed. de Beer, iii. 84 n.

2435. LOCKE to EDWARD CLARKE, 9 May [1698] (2433, 2438)

B.L., MS. Locke b. 8, no. 29. Printed in Rand, p. 294. Correct year from Clarke's endorsement and contents.

Oates 9° May 89

Dear Sir

I am very glad to see my wife here though not pleasd with the occasion that brought her hither. I shall doe all I can to serve you in this matter and my Lady and I have consider about it more than once since she came something whereof you will perceive in my letter of Saturday.[1] Pray give my service to Madam and thanks for the letter she sent me inclosed in yours. Pray tell her I hope she is better and has received more advantage by the Doctors[2] prescriptions than she thinks. Tell her that I shall have my eyes as open for her service as I can and am her humble servant and yours

J Locke

Endorsed by Clarke: Mr Lock's Letter Received the 11th May 1698. Answered the 12th.

2436. JOANNES GEORGIUS GRÆVIUS to LOCKE, 11/21 May 1698 (1920, *2555*)

B.L., MS. Locke c. 10, ff. 44–5.

Honoratissimo et Clarissimo Viro Joanni Locke S.D. J. G. Graevius. Vivisne et vales praestantissime Vir? Diu nihil de te audio. Litterae quoque nostrae mutuae diu siluerunt; non tamen meus in te amor refrixit, qui tam alte meis medullis est infixus, ut inde nunquam effluere possit. Aveo scire quid nunc rerum geras, et num tua sit valetudo confirmatior. Ego in hac grandiore aetate satis recte

---

To the highly honoured and distinguished John Locke J. G. Graevius sends greeting.

Are you alive and well, eminent Sir? I have heard nothing about you for a long time. Our reciprocal letters also have long since ceased; nevertheless my love of you has not grown cold; it is so deeply infixed in my heart that it can never pass away from it. I am eager to know what you are doing now and whether your health is more firmly established. I myself am well enough at this advanced age, nor have my labours or my lucubrations as yet been

---

[1] No. 2433.

[2] Dr. Robert Pitt.

valeo, nec labores, nec lucubrationes mihi adhuc graves fuerunt. Te in rerum gravissimarum assiduis meditationibus versari duo libri a te editi et in linguam Belgicam versi de cultu divino[1] me docuerunt, quos ego legi cupidissime et cum fructu magno: ego in tenui, ut semper labore. ⟨Exercent⟩[a] me etiamnunc Tulliani libri.[2] Grevius noster communis amicus gravissima valetudine menses ante aliquot conflictatus est, sed nunc ⟨confirmatus⟩[b] plane valet et te salutat. A Toinardo hic habes litteras, quas mihi attulit cum involucro ad me adolescens Gallus, sed qui diu illas circumtulit, antequam mihi eas tradiderit, ut aeque sero ad me venerint, quas mihi Toinardus scripserat, quam hae ad Te.[3] Vale vir amicissime, ut diutissime valeas sine ulla noxa et molestia Deum precor Trajecti D. XXI Maii *CIↃ IↃC LXXXXVIII.*

Qui has tibi tradet Olearius, gente Saxo, est juvenis optimus et vitae probatissimae, optimarumque doctrinarum percupidus summi[c] in Theologia Doctoris et Professoris in Saxonia filius, qui sibi summo honori ducit te videre et coram venerari.[4]

[a] *MS.* Exercens [b] *MS.* confirmatur [c] *Doubtful reading.*

---

burdensome to me. Two books on the worship of God, published by you and translated into Dutch,[1] have informed me that you are engaged in constant reflection on the most important matters; I have read them most avidly and with great profit; whereas I am engaged, as always, in inconsiderable labour. Cicero's works still keep me busy.[2] Our common friend de Grev was seriously ill some months ago, but has now recovered; he is quite well and sends you his greetings. Here is a letter from Toinard which a young Frenchman brought to me in a wrapper addressed to me, but he had carried it about for such a long time before he delivered it to me that a letter that Toinard had written to me came as late to me as this will come to you. Good-bye, best of friends. I pray God that you may keep well for a long time without any harm or disquiet. Utrecht, 21 May 1698.

Olearius, a Saxon by race, who will deliver this letter to you, is an excellent young man, of most estimable conduct, and very desirous of the best kind of learning; he is a son of a leading doctor and professor of theology in Saxony, and considers that it will be a high honour for himself to see you and to pay his respects in person.[4]

---

[1] *The Reasonableness of Christianity*; the Dutch translation is mentioned by Le Clerc in *Bibliotheque choisie*, vi. 388.

[2] The *Speeches*; the last volume appeared in 1699: no. *1637*, etc.

[3] Two extant letters from Toinard to Grævius probably belong to this period, one dated 23(?) February 1698, N.S., the other 10 March, N.S., no year: Royal Library, Copenhagen, Böll. Brevs. U. 4°, nos. 978–9. The letter from Toinard to Locke now forwarded may be no. *2393* of 11/21 February.

[4] The father is Johannes Olearius, 1639–1713, professor of theology at Leipzig

Address: For Mr John Locke at Mr Pawlings overagainst the plough in Little Lincoth Inne feilds London

Endorsed by Locke: Grævius 21 May 98

2437. Locke to Peter King, later first Baron King, 12 May 1698 (2405, 2448)

B.L., MS. Locke c. 40, ff. 5–6.

Oates 12 May 98

Dear Cosin

I under stand by Sir Francis that the Act for the two millions is like to be quickly dispathed in their house.[1] I desire you therefor by the next post to send me word what incouragements or discouragements you finde from Mr Fr:[2] or others for or against subscriptions. For tis possible as I hear from you I may give you commission for a larger subscription than what I formerly orderd. But that pray take care to subscribe unlesse I send you orders to the contrary. Direct the letters you shall write to me on this occasion to be left for me at Mr Harrisons at the Crown in Harlow[3]

from 1677: *A.D.B.* His son Gottfried Olearius (no. *1745*) spent a year at Oxford about 1694; this appears to be another son.

[1] On 4 May Charles Montagu, the Chancellor of the Exchequer, in response to a proposal by the East India Company to lend the king £700,000 at 6 per cent interest, provided that parliament would confirm the Company's charter for thirty-one years, announced to the house of commons sitting in committee on ways and means that there were prospective subscribers who would lend £2,000,000 to the king, provided that they might have the sole right of trading to India: *Cal.S.P., Dom.*, 1698, p. 226. In spite of the Company's protests the house adopted Montagu's proposals, and a new company was established by an act, 9 Wm. III, c. 44, 'for raising a Sum not exceeding Two Millions upon a Fund for Payment of Annuities after the Rate of Eight Pounds per Centum per Annum and for settling the Trade to the East Indies', which received the royal assent on 5 July.

The principal works for the history of the English East Indies trade at this time are John Bruce, *Annals of the Honourable East-India Company* . . . (*1600–1708*), 1810; Scott, *Joint-stock Companies*, ii. 128–89; and Morse (cited p. 56, n. 2).

The two companies, correctly styled 'The Company of Merchants of London trading into the East Indies' and 'The English Company trading to the East Indies', are distinguished in later notes, in accordance with the common usage of the time, as the Old and New Companies.

[2] King had cousins Thomas and John Freke. John, whom Locke designates in his ledger (B.L., MS. Locke c.1, p. 74) 'Mr. John Freke of Bread Street Milliner', was a stock-jobber (the current name at this time for a stock-broker). He edited *The Course of the Exchange* (no. *2758*) for a time. In his letters to King Locke usually calls him 'your cousin' or 'your cousin Freke'; unless there is an indication to the contrary 'Mr. Freke' without qualification, as here, is to be taken to be Locke's friend the bachelor. Thomas was probably the Presbyterian divine who was minister at the chapel in Bartholomew Close from 1706 until his death in 1716: Wilson, *Dissenting Churches*, iii. 377–8. Locke possessed a copy of his sermon on the storm of 1703: no. 3514. Letters from both brothers below.

[3] No. 1433.

You never sent me word whether you deliverd my Letter to my Lord Chancellor and what effect it had.[1] How does the bar gown sit on your shoulders?[2] I am

Dear Cosin

Your most affectionate Cosin and humble servant

J Locke

What would be best of all would be for you to come hither on Tuesday[3] and spend this week here as I desired you in my last. My Lady bids me presse you earnestly which I doe

Address: For Mr Peter King at his chamber or at Mr Potmans in the Middle Temple London

Endorsed by King: Mr Locke May 12. 1698

2438. Locke to Edward Clarke, 13 May 1698 (2435, 2441)

B.L., MS. Locke b. 8, no. 132. Discoloured and torn. Printed in Rand, pp. 537–8.

Oates 13 May 98

Dear Sir

I received your two of May the 10th just now and have had time just to read them over and in hast to answer what relates to my wife. My Lady and I have as strict an eye as possible over that affair, but there is yet not the least appearance of a letter goeing or comeing But we doe not thinke your fears or our care discharged by that: if there shall be any such we presume they will not escape that care which is taken to discover them. If there were any amour begun. which your letter makes me suspect, yet the breakeing o the correspondence soe early in an age like hers may at this distance probably make it die. This I say is probable but not to be presumed on. There is never soe much cunning and opiniatrity as in these cases where the affection is once engaged and therefor cannot blame your caution nor bethinke my care and attention i I can doe you any service in it. For I should for her ⟨s⟩ake[a] as wel as yours be very much troubled if any such irremediable misfortune should befall her

[a] *Page torn.*

[1] The letter is lost.

[2] King was to be called to the bar shortly.

[3] 17 May.

Madams health I shall discourse frank⟨l⟩y[a] to you of when I have had time to consider the prescriptions and what you tell me have been the effects of them, only in generall upon reading over the bills I think they are al⟨l⟩[a] directed to those in⟨t⟩entions[a] which ought to be proposed and pursued in her cure. I wish her health my service to her and your fires side for by my fires side I write this. I am

Dear Sir

your most affectionate and most humble servant

J LOCKE

My Lady gives you and mrs Clarke her humble service

Endorsed by Clarke: Mr. Locks letter touching my daughter Betty, And Doctor Pitts Prescriptions etc: Received the 16th. May 1698. Answered[b-] the 17th. That I had paid Sir Francis the 55l. as desired etc:[-b]

2439. SYLVESTER BROUNOWER to LOCKE, 14 May 1698 (*2434, 2505*)

B.L., MS. Locke c. 4, ff. 187–8.

London May the 14th: 1698

Honoured Sir

I received Your Letter of the 9th: Instant (with the inclosed to Mr: Alexander Cunningham) last Wednesday. I had much ado to finde his Lodgings which was not till to day, and is at one Mr: Lisburne's in Doverstreet in Albemarle buildings[1] at the upper end of St: Jame's street, I deliver'd the Letter to his Man, and told him I would come again to wait on his Master, but in the mean time gave him Direction of my Lodgings and Office in case he had any thing that requires haste for you

Sir I hope the Colours and Oyls are come safe to Oates with the Direction, which is the best I could get and do not doubt will answer the Ends design'd for. My Wife[2] humbly thanks you for your kinde remembrance of her both when I was in the Country,

[a] *Page torn.* [b–b] *Doubtful readings.*

[1] The general name for the new houses in Dover Street, Albemarle Street, and the south part of Bond Street: Strype's Stow, vi. 78.

[2] She may formerly have been a servant at Oates: letters and notices below.

as in your Letter, and presents her most humble Duty to you as doth

Sir

Your most humble and Faithfull Servant

S BROUNOWER.

Sir pray give me leave to insert, in answer to a Letter I received from Mrs: Masham that my Wife, hath been looking for the Plodd[1] she sent a Pattern of, and enquird not only at the Shop she was directed but all over Round Court[2] and Covent Garden but could not match it, it being a new thing and Sells well, But the Shopkeeper she is directed to hath one of them Plodds in the Loom which will be ready next weeke, and then she will be sure to looke after it and follow further Direction[a]

Address: To the Honrd: John Locke Esqr at Sir Francis Masham's at Oates

Endorsed by Locke: S Brownover 14 May 98 Answered Jun. 20

2440. LOCKE to [SIR GEORGE TREBY], 17 May 1698

Derbyshire Record Office, Matlock: Fitzherbert MSS. Damaged down central fold; hence the supplied words and letters. Transcribed from Xerox print. Summarized in H.M.C., *Rep.* xiii, App., pt. vi, p. 47. Most of the Fitzherbert MSS. derive from Treby; this and the contents of the letter show that it was addressed to him.

Sir George Treby, *c.* 1644–1700, was Lord Chief Justice of the Common Pleas from 1692 until his death: *D.N.B.*

Oates 17 May 1698

My Lord

The obligations I receive from your Lordship always prevent my requests: And your favours to me have this peculiar increase of value that they cost me not soe much as the asking. I had a designe when you passed through our neighbourhood the last Assizes[3] not only to have kept up the priviledg you allow me of stoping you on the high way; But also to have made a petition to you on the behalf of my Cosin King a student of the Middle Temple. But my

[a] *Locke adds a note:* At Mr Kendals a Bit maker at the Golden Stirrop overagainst the Ks arms in st Martins lane

[1] A variant of plaid, a woollen cloth probably with a tartan pattern: *O.E.D.*

[2] See above, no. *878*. Round Court adjoining the Strand was noted for mercers' shops, etc.: Strype's Stow, vi. 75.

[3] The assize opened at Chelmsford on 16 March: *London Gazette*, 14 February 1697/8.

health that confined me then within dores, robd me of that oportunity, as well as hinderd me from the honour of waiting on you when I was last in town. The time now appro⟨ac⟩hing for a call to the Bar I intended to be a sollicitor to you for a favou⟨ra⟩ble recommendation of him to the Benchers: But I find My Lord I am again prevented. My Cosin sends me word of the great favours he has al⟨re⟩dy received from you on this occasion beyond what he could expect or des⟨erve.⟩ Though the testimonys he has given of himself make me hope you will ⟨not⟩ have cause to repent this extraordinary marke of honour to him or think it w⟨as m⟩isplaced on a worthlesse subject: Yet my Lord give me leave to put ⟨in for⟩ a share in the obligation; and to enjoy the pleasure of acknowl⟨edging⟩ this new favour, which the nearest Kinsman I have in the world re⟨ceiving⟩ the benefit of, I cannot but think my self to have a title to thank you for. The multiplying of bonds to those to whose worth one is tied by esteem and inclination is I think a pardonable ambition. I must therefor beg your Lordship to looke on me noe lesse obleiged by what you have done for my Cosin than he himself is: And I beg leave to wait upon your Lordship when I come to towne, to testifie more fully the sense I have of it and the g⟨r⟩atitude wherewith I am

My Lord

⟨Your⟩ Lordships most humble and most obedient servant

JOHN LOCKE

Endorsed: J: Locke May 17. 98

2441. LOCKE to EDWARD CLARKE, 20 May [1698] (2438, 2445)

B.L., MS. Locke b. 8, no. 133. Year from Clarke's endorsement. Printed in Rand, pp. 538–9.

Oates May 20

Dear Sir

Thinke not of your Children too confidently for fear of negligence of them to their ruin; Nor too suspitiously for fear of your owne needlesse trouble. The first part of this belongs to my Lady and me on whom you have now transferd that care, and we have and doe carefully put on your eyes but have hitherto seen noe thing of what you suspected and we have been soe watchfull that if any letter had passed one way or the other I thinke it could not have scaped us, and therefor the later part of my first sentence I recommend now to you. I thank you for answering my bill. We are all here very well and present you and Mrs Clarke our services. I have had company with me here ever since the begining of the weeke which has hitherto hinderd me from considering at leisur the bills you sent me. the first time I get shall be imploid in it. I am

Dear Sir

Your most affectionate humble servant

J LOCKE

My humble service to the Batchelor.

Address: For Edward Clarke Esquire member of parliament at Richards Coffee house within Temple Bar London
Frank

Postmark: MY 23

Endorsed by Clarke: Mr. Lock of His and my Ladys being verie watchfull over Betty etc: Received the 23th. May 1698. Answered the 26th.

2442. LOCKE to NICOLAS TOINARD, 20 May 1698 (2412, *2444*)

B.M., Add. MS. 28,728, ff. 32–3. Printed in Ollion, pp. 127–8. For transmission see p. 429. Answers no. *2411*; answered by no. *2450*.

Oates 20 May 98

Præterito mense Martii ad te literas dedi, quibus literas librosque mihi per Nelsonem a te missas ad manus meas pervenisse, uti par erat gratus agnoscebam.[1] An illæ ad te pervenerint hæve perventuræ sint in hac tabellariorum difficultate vel defectu nescio: hoc certò scio te mihi chariorem esse neminem nec quenquam esse a quo aut acceptiora sunt amicitiæ indicia aut cui libentius agnosco. Incommodè mihi accidit quod Monsieur Al . . u . . ier[a2] Londinum

[a] *Word altered; some letters illegible.*

Oates 20 May 98

I sent you a letter last March in which, as was proper, I gratefully acknowledged that the letter and books that you sent me by Nelson had reached my hands.[1] In this scarcity or, rather, lack of posts I do not know whether that letter has reached you or whether this one will do so; this I know for certain, that no one is dearer to me than you, nor is there anyone from whom tokens of friendship are more welcome or to whom I more gladly acknowledge them. It happened unseasonably for me that Monsieur Al . . u . . ier[2] visited London in my absence. I duly received here in the

[1] No. 2412; it did not reach Toinard until about October: p. 492.
[2] Aleaume; the letter is no. *2411*.

me absente invisit. litteras tuas 3° Apr: datas ad me illius manu Londinum allatas recte hic rure valetudine detentus recepi. sed hac mea rusticatione intercepta occasio illum et visendi et salutandi. cui optabam quibus poteram officiis testari quanti te faciam, quâque essem voluntate erga advenam a te mihi commendatum. Tardus nimis hiemis discessus me hic detinuit frigoribus suis oppressum diutius quam destinaveram. Spero me brevi jam adolescentis anni teporibus refocillatum posse urbem revisere; Gestioque illic complecti amicum illum tuum eoque nomine mihi colendissimum, ut sciat quicquid ego aut sum aut possum, id totum tuum esse. Tractatulum de liberorum educatione de quo nimis magnificè et ipse loqueris et alii tuo instinctu nimis magnificè, uti audio, locuti sunt curavi ego ut tibi ex Hollandia transmitteretur. Quartam hic jam bibliopola meditatur editionem. beneficium mihi præstabis magnum, et amicitiâ nostrâ dignum, si mihi indicare velis quid tu in illo reprehendas vel quovis modo immutandum censeas ut ⟨hæc⟩[a] nova editio emendatior te consulente exeat. Scio vulgò huic meæ institutioni objici hanc methodum speculatione quidem luculentam et concinnam, in ipso opere et praxi evanescere uti plurima otiosorum hominum et in recessu meditantium non incongrua

[a] *MS.* hac

---

country, where I have been detained by ill health, your letter to me of 3 April, which he had brought to London. But by this my rustication I have been deprived of an opportunity of seeing and greeting one to whom I wished to prove by what services I could, how much I value you and [how great] is my goodwill towards a stranger recommended by you to me. The too slow departure of winter has kept me here overcome by its cold longer than I had intended. I hope shortly, refreshed by the warmth of the growing year, to be able to revisit the city; and I long to embrace there that friend of yours, and on account of that friendship a person to be highly esteemed by me, so that he may know that whatever I am or whatever I can do is entirely yours. I have arranged to have sent to you from Holland the small treatise about the education of children of which you speak too highly and of which others at your instigation, as I hear, have spoken too highly. The bookseller here is now considering a fourth edition. You will do me a great favour, and one befitting our friendship, if you will please point out to me what you find fault with in it or in what way you think that it should be altered, so that this next edition, thanks to your advice, may go forth more correct. I know that it is commonly objected to my [plan of] education [*institutio*] that, while this way is indeed clear and well-fashioned in theory, it comes to nothing in actual work and practice, like many not incoherent contrivances [*figmenta*] made by leisured men studying in retreat from the world; if, however, you want to put them into use, the too hard and obstinate

figmenta, quibus tamen si in usum redigere velis, non respondet dura nimis et obstinata rerum tractandarum natura. Quibus liceat mihi hâc in causâ reponere. Desinant aliquando de infantum indole tam male ominari. culpa docentum discipulorum ingenio non raro imputatur: Sed videns sciensque dico hac leni et libero homine dignâ disciplinâ aliquos jam apud nos elevari. Sed de harmonicis quid tandem? Vides quod olim prædixeram tibi hæsitanti et tam diu parata supprimenti obrepserunt alii et laudem tibi uni debitam occuparunt. et alii itidem occupabunt. Quin prodeat ergo opus perfectum utile et ab omnibus jam dudum expectatum. De republicâ literareâ siquid novi expectas nihil apud nos habetur quod tibi offerre possum. Pauca Latine Scripta apud nos prodeunt, Gallice nulla, Anglica tibi barbara sunt. Quæ commentatus sum *de intellectu humano* brevi spero prodibunt in linguâ tibi non ignotâ, hoc eò impatientius expecto ut tuum de lucubrationibus meis judicium sciam. Vale Vir Optime et ut facis me ama tui amantissimum

J Locke

Triumvirum nostrum rogo ut meo nomine quam officiosissime salutes.

Address: A Monsieur Monsieur Toinard Chez Monsieur des Noyers devant l Espèe royale dans la rüe Mazarin à Paris

Endorsed by Toinard: 98. 20. May.

---

nature of the things to be handled will not respond. May I be allowed to answer those [who speak thus about this matter]: Let them cease hereafter from predicting so much evil from the disposition of young children. The fault of the teachers is not seldom imputed to the character of the pupils. But I say from experience and knowledge that some in this country are now being brought up with this gentle discipline, one befitting a free man. But what now of the harmonics? You see what I had foretold long ago: while you were hesitating, and holding back what had so long since been made ready, others have stolen upon you and have taken possession of the praise that is due to you alone; and others in like manner will take possession of it. Then why not let appear an excellent, useful work, and long awaited by everyone? Should you expect anything new from the commonwealth of learning, there is nothing in this country that I can offer you. Few works in Latin appear here, none in French, and those in English are barbarous for you. What I have written about the Human Understanding will appear I hope shortly in a language not unknown to you; I await this the more impatiently in order to know your opinion of my lucubrations. Good-bye, best of men, and continue to love me your most loving

J Locke

Please give my best respects to our friend the Triumvir.

2443. Locke to Philippus van Limborch, 21 May 1698 (*2432*, *2460*)

Amsterdam University Library, MS. R.K., Ba 258 f. An English draft is printed in Appendix II, where there is a note on a French draft. Written by Coste; some corrections by Locke, and the subscription and postscript written by him. Some words rubbed. Printed in *Some Familiar Letters*, pp. 421–4; postscript and address, in Ollion, p. 216. Answers no. *2432*; answered by no. *2460*.

Oates 21 May. 1698.

Monsieur.

Si ma santé ne me permettoit pas de satisfaire commodément l'envie, que j'ai d'executer les ordres de ce grand homme qui reçoit si favorablement mes reflections, toutes mediocres qu'elles sont, il est pourtant vrai que je ne saurois la sacrifier pour une meilleure occasion que celle qui me porte à examiner le sujet où il m'a engagé, et qui me fournit le moyen de luy faire voir combien je suis prêt à luy obeïr. Mais je ne prétens pas qu'en cette recontre il me soit obligé d'un tell sacrifice, car si je ne hazarde point ma reputation auprés de luy, je suis fort assuré que ma santé ne sera point interessée par ce que je vais écrire. Ayant à faire à un homme qui raissonne si nettement, et qui a si bien approfondi cette matiere, je n'aurai pas besoin de parler beaucoup pour me faire entandre. Son extreme penetration l'y fera sentir d'abord le fondement de la preuve que je vais proposer, de sorte que sans qu'il soit necessaire que je m'engage dans ⟨de⟩[a] longues deductions, il pourra juger si elle est bien ou mal fondée.

Je ne puis m'empecher de remarquer l'exactitude de son jugement par rapport à l'ordre qu'il a donné à ses Propositions et il est vray comme il l'a fort bien remarqué qu'en mettant la troisieme à la place de la seconde les Theologiens, les Philosophes, et Descartes luy-même supposent l'unité de Dieu sans la prouver.

Si par la Question qui me fut d'abord proposée, j'eusse compris comme je fais presentement, quel etoit le but de cet habile homme, je n'aurois envoyé la Réponse que je vous ai envoyée, mais une ⟨beaucoup⟩[b] plus courte, et plus conforme à l'ordre de la nature et de la raison, où chaque chose paroit dans son meilleur jour.

Je croy que quiconque reflechira sur soy-même, connoitra evidement sans en pouvoir douter le moins du monde, qu'il y ⟨a⟩[c] eû de tout éternité un Etre intelligent. Je croy encore qu'il est év⟨ident⟩[c] à toute homme qui pense qu'il y'a aussi un Etre infini.

[a] *Page rubbed.* [b] *MS.* beuacoup [c] *Page rubbed and torn.*

Or je dis qu'il ne peut y avoir qu'un Etre infini, et que cet Etre infini doit être aussi l'Etre éternel, parce que, ce qui est infini, doit avoir eté infini de toute éternité, car aucunes additions faites dans le temps, ne sauroient rendre une chose infinie, si elle ne l'est pas en elle même, et par elle même, de toute éternité. Telle étant la nature de l'infini qu'on n'en peut rien ôter, et qu'on n'y peut rien ajouter, D'où il s'ensuit que l'infini ne sauroit être separè en plus d'un, ni être qu'un.

C'est lá, selon moy, une preuve *à priori* que l'Etre eternel independant n'est qu'un; et si nous y joignons l'idée de toutes les perfections possibles, nous avons alors l'idée d'un Dieu eternel, infini, omniscient, et tout-puissant etc.

Si ce raisonnement s'accorde avec les Notions de l'excellent homme qui doit le voir, j'en serai extremement satisfait. Et s'il ne s'en accommode pas, je regarderai comme une grand faveur s'il veut bien me communiquer sa preuve que je tiendra secrette ou que je communiquerai comme venant de sa part, selon qu'il le jugera à propos. Je vous prie de l'assûrer de mes tres humbles respects. Je suis

Monsieur

Vôtre tres humble et tres obeïssant serviteur

J Locke

Spero filium tuum jamdudum ad vos sanum[a] salvumque rediisse illum quæso uxoremque tuam dilectissimam reliquosque nostros amicos communes officiosissime nomine meo salutes[1]

Address (written by Locke): Mÿn Heer Myn Heer Limborch bÿ de Remonstranse Kerck op de Kaisars Gracht t'Amsterdam

2444. Nicolas Toinard to Locke, 21/31 May 1698 (2442, *2450*)

B.L., MS. Locke c. 21, f. 195.

+

ce dernier may, 98.

Votre long silence, monsieur, me donne une extrême inquietude, d'autant plus que monsieur Aleaume à qui j'avois donnè une letre

[a] *Or* sannum; *altered from* sansum?

[1] 'I hope your son has long since returned to you safe and sound; please give my best respects to him and to your dear wife and to the rest of our common friends.'

pour qu'il eust l'honneur de vous salüer, m'a mandé que vous etiez à la campagne, et que monsieur Lister m'a dit ici que si vous aviez eu de la santé vous oriez fait le voiage de France.[1] Je souhaite que mons. Du bosc[2] qui vous doit presenter celeci, vous trouve retabli et en ville. c'est un de mes meilleurs amis, et je n'ajoûteray rien pour vous prier de lui rendre service, etant persuadé du plaisir que vous vous faites d'avoir de semblables ocasions. Je suis parfaitement, monsieur, votre tres humble et tres obeissant serviteur

TOINARD

Faites moi la grace de me mander, si votre santé vous le permet, quel est votre sentiment touchant les livres dont monsieur Nelson a bien voulu se charger pour vous.

Endorsed by Locke: Toinard 31 May 98

2445. LOCKE to EDWARD CLARKE, 23 May 1698 (2441, 2447)

B.L., MS. Locke b. 8, no. 134. Printed in Rand, p. 539.

Oates 23 May 98

Dear Sir

I cannot neglect this oportunity by Sir Francis to assure you that we are here all well and for ought I can say to the contrary just such as you would have us. There has not one letter passed one way or 'tother which we have not with all care imaginable

[1] Dr. Martin Lister (p. 377) went to Paris in December with d'Alonne (p. 413) and other men, to prepare for the reception of Portland, who was going there as ambassador: Luttrell, iv. 320–1. He stayed there for some months and published his observations as *A Journey to Paris*, 1699. L.L., no. 1765.

[2] Jean-Baptiste Du Bos, 1670–1742, miscellaneous author. He was the son of a Beauvais merchant. He graduated B.A. at the Sorbonne in 1691. As a reward for his services in minor diplomatic posts he was made commendatory abbot of Notre-Dame de Ressons in 1723. His principal publication, *Réflexions critiques sur la poésie et sur la peinture*, 1719, led to his election to the Académie française in 1720; two years later he became its permanent secretary. The book was highly praised by Voltaire. He wrote several historical works, notably *Histoire critique de l'établissement de la monarchie française dans les Gaules*, 1734, which Montesquieu criticized adversely. He was a friend of Bayle as well as of Toinard: *N.B.G.*; *D.B.F.*; A. Lombard, *L'Abbé Du Bos*, 1913; R. Shackleton, *Montesquieu*, 1961. Sixty-three letters from Du Bos to Toinard are preserved in the Bibliothèque Nationale, MSS. N.Acq. fr., vol. 560; they are cited here by their numbers in A. Lombard, *La Correspondance de l'Abbé Du Bos*, 1913, where some extracts are printed.

Du Bos arrived in London on Sunday, 29 May/8 June: letter to Toinard, 10 June, N.S. (Lombard, no. 51).

observed, and there has not that we can find been the least intention or endeavour to write or send any one secretly and what ever have passed one way or other there has still care been taken that they should first come to my Ladys hands or mine. You will doe well to observe to at your end (if the people are soe near) as well as you can.

I hear of a subscription goeing about now for the raiseing of two millions for which the Parliament will raise a fund to pay 8 per Cent pray tell me whether you thinke it a good way to dispose of ones money, and whether you would advise me to subscribe For I know you perfectly understand it.[1] Pray let me know your opinion of it in your next. My humble service to your fires side. I write this by mine and thinke I shall not this year be warme without a fire. I am

Sir

Your most humble and most affectionate servant

J Locke

My Lady gives her service to You and Mrs Clarke and the Batchelor. I am the Batchelors most humble servant

Address: For Edward Clarke Esquire member of Parliament at Richards Coffee house within Temple Bar London

Endorsed by Clarke: Mr. Lock to bee Informed of the Nature of the Subscription etc: Received the 24th May 1698 Answered the 26th.

2446. Francis Nicholson to [Locke?], 26 May 1698 (*2237, 2543*)

B.L., MS. Locke c. 16, ff. 159–60. Comparison with Nicholson's other letters in the Lovelace Collection indicates that this one was addressed to Locke individually, and not to the Board of Trade.

Maryland May 26. 98

Right Honourable

Gratitude obligeth me to pay you the best of my acknowledgment for your having been pleased not only to speake favorably o

[1] p. 397. According to Luttrell about £700,000 was subscribed to the projected new company on 6 and 7 May; the books were closed for the time being on 1 May, when £1,200,000 had been subscribed. These were only promises or applications to subscribe; the effective subscription was made on 14, 15, and 16 July following the royal assent on 5 July to the act establishing the company.

me; but to recommend me to some of his most sacred majestys great ministers of state; which the reverend Mr Blayer[1] gives me an account of. And I hope in God so to behave my self in the station wherin I am, that mauger all my enimies, both secret and open, to be able to clear myself of their calumnys and accusations: or else shal not presume to desire your Friend ship.

I endeavour to give your Lordships a full and just Account of this his majestys province by the Honourable Sir Tho. Laurence Baronet his majestys Secretary thereof; which I hope will be to your Lordships satisfaction.[2] Which to find, and allso that I am continued in your favour, will be very acceptable to him who is

Your most obliged and obedient humble servant

FR: NICHOLSON

Endorsed by Locke: F. Nicolson 26. May. 98 Answered Aug. 25

WILLIAM THOMAS to LOCKE, [28? May 1698]

The letter is lost. A memorial that accompanied it is printed here with no. *2452*, which relates to it.

2447. LOCKE to EDWARD CLARKE, 30 May 1698 (2445, 2458A)

Rand, pp. 540–1.

Oates, 30th May, 1698.

Dear Sir,

I have acquainted my Lady with the acknowledgments you make to her on occasion of your daughter, to which she replied that she is extremely glad of her company, and she hopes she shall enjoy it as long as you and her mother can spare her, and she takes it for a favour that you would use that freedom with her. These were her own words. This I dare assure you from what my Lady has said to me, that she is very glad of her company, and that you need not upon this account be in any haste to change your lodging, for my Lady is very glad if she can in this or any other occasion do you or yours any manner of service in acknowledgment of those many obligations she has to you.

[1] Commissary James Blair.

[2] Sir Thomas Lawrence, third baronet, d. 1714: G.E.C., *Baronetage*, ii. 61. He was secretary of Maryland from 1691 or 1692 to 1698 and from 1701 to 1714. The papers carried by him are *Cal.S.P.*, *Col.*, vol. xvi, nos. 517–19.

My wife tells me that her mother writes her word that she is worse than she was. If this be anything more than an apprehension pray send me word, that I may again revise the prescriptions have been given her, which upon reading of them I thought very suitable to her case. But if the swelling of her legs increase, I doubt not but what Dr. Pitt, who is a careful as well as a knowing physician, will take it into his consideration.

I thank you for the care you promise me to take that I receive no inconvenience by the indiscretion of a man which mightily surprised me.[1] But as there is no fence against other people's folly, so I think nobody is to answer for other people's follies but they themselves.

I was thus far in my letter when I received yours of the 28th with the votes enclosed, for which I return you my thanks, as also for what you say upon that subject.

The best time of gathering and drying any plant to be kept for use is before it have any appearance of beginning to blow; and this rule my friend John Barber may observe not only in wormwood-sage but all other herbs. The best way of drying is in the shade.

Pray if you see Mr. Thomas[2] give him my service and thanks for his letter and the enclosed paper; and tell him that I received his with other letters to-day, so little a while before our messenger returns to Bishop's Stortford with our letters that I have not time to give him my answer about so weighty a business before the post goes. But that he need not give himself the trouble to come hither about it, for that I hope the weather in a little while will be so warm that I shall be able to venture to town, for I conclude it will not be winter all the year.

The last Friday the letters came not till after my wife had writ and sealed hers to you. Upon the opening and reading that which was directed to her by you the blood came suddenly into her face and she was in great disorder, and with a kind of rage broke open again the letter she had writ to you. This I have learnt since from one who saw and observed it. I name you the day that you may recollect what was in that letter to her, or in hers to you or her mother, and by either of these consider whether you can gather anything. If there were in the letter which she at that time

[1] This may allude to the commons' proceedings about *The Case of Ireland*: p. 377 n. 1. The committee quoted about 25 passages from it in its report, but no part of pp. 22–7, which derive from *Two Treatises of Government* and in which Locke is named as the reputed author of the second treatise. [2] William Thomas: see p. 418

received anything said to her about your removing your lodgings, or the like, you may possibly from thence have some further light into the matter you suspect. I am,

Dear Sir,

your most faithful and most humble servant,

J. LOCKE.

My humble service to Mrs. Clarke, the Bachelor, and your son.

My Lady Masham gives her humble service to Mrs. Clarke, yourself and the Bachelor.

Address: For Edward Clarke, Esq., Member of Parliament, at Richard's Coffee House, within Temple Bar, London.

Frank.

Endorsed: Mr. Locke, touching Mrs. Clarke's health. The best method of drying of herbs, and about Betty. Received the 1st June, 1698. Answered the 2nd.

2448. LOCKE to PETER KING, later first Baron King, 30 May 1698 (2437, 2455)

B.L., MS. Locke c. 40, ff. 7–8.

Oates 30° May 98

Dear Cosin

I hope by this time you are actualy a Barister or very near being one. I shall be very glad to hear it is soe as soon as it is done.

By Thursday lasts votes[1] I finde the house of Commons has voted That his Majesty be impowered to name Commissioners to receive subscriptions for advanceing of two millions etc. I desire you that you would subscribe five hundred pounds for me, but in your owne name. unlesse you finde by Mr Clarke or Mr Freke[2] that they have reasons against your subscribeing For I would have you consult with them and advise with them as if it were for your self for I would not have it known to any body that it is for me. You will also know by them when is the time to subscribe, for I would have you be one of the first and by noe means let slip the occasion of subscribeing and as soon as the act is passed I would desire you to send me by some Coach that passes through Harlow the Act it self, or an abstract of it, and a copy of the Commission for takeing

[1] 26 May. [2] Probably the Bachelor.

subscriptions Directed to be left with Mr Harison at the Crown in Harlow for me. I am

Dear Cosin

Your most affectionate Cosin and humble servant

J LOCKE

Address: For Mr Peter King of the Middle Temple To be left at Mr Potman in the Middle Temple London

Postmark: IV 1

Endorsed by King: Mr Locke. May. 30. 1698.

2449. CORNELIUS LYDE to LOCKE, 31 May 1698 (2390, 2456)

B.L., MS. Locke c. 15, ff. 164–5. Answered by no. 2456.

May the 31th 98

Honoured Sir

The many Kindneses you have shewne to me and not only to me but to my son[1] which I doe most heartely acknowledg and return you most hearty thanks that you was plesed to take such notice of my son and to assure him of your friendship which I finde he have greate esteeme of and doe depend more upon it then any thing. he is young and I doe Conceve it must be time before he may be fit to practis I desire to be guided wholy by you in the managing of him and if it might be Conveniant to put him into some buisness that might aford him A maintenance and also to minde his studies wold be a greate Kindnes to me haveing many sons to take Care of which I will Leave to your thought untill I have the happines to see you here In your native Country which I doe here you have some thoughts of in a Little time if you Come downe pray take my house for your home where you shall be as welcom as any friend in the world. I have Received the greatest part of your rents due for the Last yeare and hope to have the remainder in some short time hannys I have not yeat he failes in all his promises I have spoke to An Attorny to sue him and shall doe it speedely if you doe not for bid it with all due Respects Sir

I Am your obliegd friend and ser:

COR: LYDE

[1] Samuel Lyde, the doctor from Holland; as 'the Doct:' in the postscript.

my Kind servic to mr. Clarke and his Familie. the Doct: present is service to you.

ddress: These For Doct: Locke at mr. Pawlings overagainst the Plough in ittle Lincolns feilds London

ostmark: IV 3

ndorsed by Locke: Cor: Lyde 31 May 98 Answered Jun. 11

450. NICOLAS TOINARD to LOCKE, 2/12 June [1698] (2444, 2454)

.L., MS. Locke c. 21, f. 196. Year from contents. Answers no. 2442.

+

ce 12. Juin

Ce mot, monsieur, n'est que pour vous marquer de combien 'inquietudes j'ay eté soulagé en recevant l'honneur des vôtres u 20. de may. cele du mois de mars ne m'a point eté rendüe, et je 'avois aucune connoissance que vous ussiez encore les livres dont . Nelson avoit bien voulu se charger.

Puisque je suis delivré d'une grande peine du coté de votre santé, ermetez moi de me plaindre de ceque vous ne m'avez pas prouré la connoissance de mons. Dalone[1] que je n'ay u ici que par azard et que depuis peu de tems qui a eté une tres grande perte our moi. m. son Pere etoit de notre ville, et m. son oncle paternel oit l'un de mes meilleurs amis. J'ay eté persuadé que ce Gentilomme vous connoissoit parfetement par l'estime toute particuliere i'il a pour vous; et qui n'en a point pour peu qu'il vous connoisse? m'a bien afligé en m'aprenant que si votre santé vous l'avoit ermis, j'aurois eté assez heureux pour vous embrasser ici à ocasion de l'Ambassade. A present que la saison vous sera plus mmode, je voudrois qu'il vous prist envie de venir evider ici

[1] Abel Tassin d'Alonne, c. 1646–1723. He was reputed to be a son of William II Orange. He was born out of wedlock. After the death, c. 1656, of his mother's sband, –Tassin d'Alonne, a French officer in the Dutch service, he was acknowged by the latter's brother, –Tassin, a Parisian advocate, as his nephew. He was ncess Mary's secretary from when she came to Holland and on 3 April 1689 became r principal secretary and master of requests. In December 1697 he was sent with . Martin Lister and others to Paris to prepare for Portland's reception, and reined there until Portland's return. About November William III appointed him retary for Dutch affairs. After William's death he returned to The Hague, where perhaps acted as an agent for Portland: Droste, *Overblyfsels van geheugchenis*, 427–9, 442–3 (notes); *Corr. van Willem III en van Portland*; *London Gazette*, 4 April 9; Luttrell; H.M.C., *Bath MSS.*, vol. iii (Prior papers). He is probably 'Dalone' the distribution list for the first edition of Locke's *Essay*; see also nos. 1128 n., 5, *1568*.

pour un peu de tems la consomption. Je puis vous assurer que l'air de Paris est aussi bon qu'il ait jamais eté, et tous les honestes gens reconêtront que le sejour en sera plus agreable des que vous y serez.

Je vous ecriray une otre fois ἁρμονικῶς. Votre livre de l'*Education des Enfans*, a eté ici estimè de tout le monde. On a mis dans la Preface une chose touchant les enfans de Siam,[1] et je crois vous en avoir dit une aussi belle touchant ceux de canada. En tout cas je vous l'ecriray une otre fois. Le tems me presse aujourdhui.

J'ay doné à m. Du bos une letre pour vous. c'est un jeune homme qui sait deja beaucoup. Il est Auteur de la Dissertation des 4 Gordiens. Il a repondu en Latin à m. Cuper, qui n'est pas de son opinion, mais sa reponse n'est pas encore imprimée.[2]

J'ay eté depuis quelque tems tres occupé a faire des Extraits et Traductions de quelques mss. castillans et Portugais que j'ay, pour donner des positions de lieux à une personne fort entendüe qui travaille à de nouveles cartes de Geografie.[3] cela m'a eté recommandé par un de mes amis.—Je suis parfaitement, Monsieur—

2451. John Tatam to Locke, 3 June 1698

B.L., MS. Locke c. 19, ff. 178–9. The writer matriculated at Cambridge in 1682, and graduated B.A. in 1686 and M.A. in 1689. In 1689 he succeeded his father as vicar of Sutton-on-the-Hill, and retained the benefice until his death in 1733: Venn.

Darbyshire. Sutton on the Hill. June 3. 1698

Sir

Your known abilities to advice, as well as opportunities and Interest to promote and procure redress of publick Grieveances and that noble and generous spirit which shines in all those your writings that I have had the Advantage and happiness to peruse and hath engaged you (if am not very much misinformed) to do very extraordinary Kindnesses for some of your Antagonists encourage me, an utter stranger to your person, so far to presume

[1] A short extract from S. de la Loubère, *Du Royaume de Siam*, 1691 (p. 537); the translator's (Coste's) preface.

[2] Du Bos published in 1695 his *Histoire des quatre Gordiens, prouvée et illustrée par médailles*. Gijsbert Cuper (1644–1716; classical scholar: *N.N.B.W.*) controverted his view in *Historia Trium Gordianorum*, 1697. Du Bos published his answer to his critics in 1700: no. *2748*.

[3] Identifiable as Guillaume Delisle, 1675–1726; member of the Académie des Sciences 1702: *D.B.F.*; *N.B.G.*.; *Journal des Sçavans*, 8 March 1700 (pp. 187–95).

upon your Candour and Generosity as to entreat you to use your best Interest for an Act of Parliament to prevent those frequent vexatious Lawsuits as well as private Quarrels about the manner of setting out the tenth or tith of hay and corn; for notwithstanding the statutes of the 27. of Hen: 8. and the 32d of Hen: 8. and the 2. of Ed. 6. do oblige all persons to set out their tiths after such way and manner as hath been usual and Customary in the Parishes and Places where the tiths arise, yet it is so difficult to prove what is the Custom of a Place (most antient records of such customs having been lost in the unhappy Civil wars) that those Statutes tho plain and full enough to an honest mind, are far otherwise to Lawyers and troublesome persons: Who tho it hath been the usual Custom of a Parish for the tith of hay to have been set out time beyond memory when it is fully made and cured (and the oldest persons living not able to give above 10 or 20 instances and it may be only of the tith of 2 or 3 acres that hath been set out in grass so soon as cut and made into handcocks)[1] yet some Lawyers will have those few peevish instances to destroy the Custom, whilst others are of another opinion; and there are not wanting too many troublesom persons (having indeed an aversion from paying any tiths at all and loving according to the proverb, to pinch on the Parsons side)[2] who take advantage from these different Judgements and the uncertain Determination of the Law, and set out the tith, which ought to be of hay, in grass so soon as cut and made into small cocks, and when they have so set out the tith, do spread about their own nine parts after such a manner that the owner of the tith's cannot possibly so much as come to and much less spread about and cure his said tyth grass (for tis no other, tho I meet with no law but what is for tith hay which is grass made and cured) till the owner of the nine parts hath fully made and cured them, by which peevish doings the tith is made little worth nay frequently so spoiled that it is not worth carrying away, which yet it must be, least the owner of the ground bring his Action for the injurie it does his Aftergrass. Thus also tho it hath been the usual custom of a Parish to set out the tith of corn in shocks, yet some cross people will throw out the said tith of corn in sheaves unbound to the great trouble of the owner of the said tith and no less prejudice to the tith it self; That

[1] I have not found the word elsewhere.

[2] This was applied to curtailing alms-giving as well as tithes: *Oxford Dict. English Proverbs*.

it is difficult to prove what is the customary way of tithing in any Parish is plain because the records of those customs are generally lost, and I conceive it is utterly unfit that those who pay tiths should be witnesses about the manner of paying them because they are parties; and I am well informed that an Impropriator in a late tryal about the Custom of setting out the tith of corn brought several witnesses, some of them 60 or 70 or more years old, who swore it had been the Custom of that place ever since they could remember to set out the tith of corn in shocks, and on the other hand the person who disputed the Custom with the Impropriator produced as many or more witnesses who swore quite contrary viz: that it was the Custom ever since they could remember till about 6 or 7 years ago for the tith of corn to be thrown out into the furrows in sheaves unbound; Now that there were persons perjured in this cause is manifest, and whether it is ended yet or ever will be I cannot say: I could give several other instances of the like Nature, but these I beleive will satisfie you that it is highly requisite for the way and manner of setting out the tith of hay and corn to be positively ascertained by a plain Act of Parliament which I humbly and earnestly entreat you to procure and perhaps a short act to the following purpose might do the business viz: 'That all persons whatever shall so order and manage, make and cure the tenth part of their Corn and hay for the respective Impropriators, Rectors, Vicars, Curates or any other persons to whom the said tiths do belong, as they do order and manage, make and cure their own nine parts.

'That all persons whatever shall give notice to the Impropriato etc to whom the tiths of Corn and hay so orderd and managed made and cured ought to be paid or to his Agent, that he or hi Deputie or servant may go and see the said tiths to be set forth an severed from the nine parts; And in case the owner of the said tith (Due notice being given) shall neglect to go in due time, that the the occupier or owner of the Lands where the said tiths are, sha call two substantiall honest neighbours to himself and by thei Assistance and Direction truly and justly without fraud or guile se out the said tiths.

'That all persons neglecting to observe this Act shall forfei treble the value of the said tiths which are unduly managed or mad or unjustly set forth, to be recovered with full costs and charges b the owner of the said tiths.

'That every person to whom tiths of hay and Corn ought to be paid shall freely pass with such Carts teams or other Carriages as he shall judge meet and convenient to carry away his said tiths, either by the common way or by any other such way as the owner or occupier of the land carries away his nine parts; And that no owner of tiths or his Deputies or Agents shall be liable to any Action for any grass or corn that his horses oxen etc shall against the Will of their driver snatch and eat in their passage for, or during the loading of the said tiths or in their return with them.'

I add these last to prevent also frequent vexatious suits;

Pray Sir Pardon this trouble and presumption from a person that is an utter stranger to your person; And let me humbly entreat you to Improve this proposal which is made and would be I beleive for the Advantage, ease and Quiet of all persons whether payers or Receivers of tiths, and also prevent much perjury, many private angry disputes and Quarrels as well as tedious and costly Lawsuits, nor can any objection be fairly made against it; So that I hope it may pass pretty easily if it be with your Cultivation and by your Interest brought into the house before the Parliament rises; I only once more beg pardon and the favour of a line or two what your thoughts are of my proposal and whether I may hope to have you engage in its behalf, your so engaging I am sure (if I much mistake not) will be a farther benefit to the publick from your generous Endeavours, and if you pleas to espouse it, it will no doubt pass into a Law, so deservedly great is your Interest.

I subscribe as I am Sir

Your very much obliged (tho unknown) servant

JOHN TATAM.

Sir

if you please to honour me so far as to let me have a line or two from you how I may best direct to you, with your permission I shall trouble with some other matters which want redress and may I hope receive it from your Endeavours; if you please to interest yourself about them; you may please to direct your letter to be left at Mr. Bots a mercer in Darby for

your servant JOHN TATAM.

pray as I am stranger to you so be pleased to keep my name a stranger to others (for I blush at my boldness in this attempt to disturb your thoughts which are no doubt employd for the advancement and Interest of your countrey in one respect or other) and if you wholly disapprove my proposal, pray only let me know so much and burn this letter. and so let it be forgotten.

Address: These To Mr. John Lock present To be left at Mr. Churchill's at the Black-Swan in Pater-Noster-Row (to be sent as above directed with all due care) London

Postmark: IV–

Endorsed by Locke: J: Tatam 3. Jun. 98

2452. WILLIAM THOMAS to LOCKE, 4 June 1698 (*1937, 2457*)

B.L., MS. Locke c. 20, ff. 157–8. The project mentioned in the letter is identifiable as B.L., MS. Locke c. 30, ff. 127–8, written by Thomas and initialled by him; it is printed below.

London 4th June 1698

Sir

This day day sevenight I troubled you with a letter and an enclosed project to which I beg'd the favour of your answer, but have not as yet heard any thing of it which makes me apprehend it miscarried. It was superscribd by Mr Clarke for greater security, and if lost will much concern me. If it came to your hands I beg the favour of you to give me your opinion tho never so short of it for I shall not adventure to proceed on it without your approbation. I can assure you Sir that I have writ much beneath the true commendation of that place by Mr Dampier[1] and others whom I have talked withall on that subject tho without discovering the least part of my intentions. Your answer by the first post will be a very great favour to Sir your most Obliged and humble

Servant W THOMAS.

My Mother is not well but your humble Servant.

Address: This for John Locke Esqr [at Oates, by Joslyn, Bishops Stortford]

Postmarks: IV 4; GC

Endorsed by Locke: W. Thomas 4° Jun 98 Answered 7

[1] Probably William Dampier, 1652–1715, the circumnavigator: *D.N.B.* His first book, *A New Voyage round the World*, was published first in 1697. L.L., no. 910 (2nd ed., also 1697).

2452. *W. Thomas, 4 June 1698*

A Memoriall concerning the setling a Colony on the Istmus of Darien in America.[1]

The sending Colonys abroad has in all Ages been so verry advantagious to all Nations, that it's needless to repeat the Arguments for it, or urge any thing for the proof and confirmation of a matter of whose truth the whole World is notoriously satisfyed. Thus Rome and Athens flourishd of Old, and England in this last Age, and particularly in the late Warr, where the profits drawn from her own Colonys kept the Ballance of Trade on her side, which otherwise had unavoidably to her infinite damage been against her. It is a difficult thing to determine nicely the great advantages we daily receive from the possessing of Barbados, the Leeward Islands and Jamaica, not to mention what we have on the Main or other small Islands, and what an Inlett we have by them into the richest part of America, if we would but lay hold on and improve the advantages we are already Masters of and seem disposd to point us the way to greater acquisitions. The Scituation and Soil are the two great advantages to be lookd for in any new Settlement, and where they meet in an eminent degree, the Success will in all reason be proportionate to the undertaking. It is manifest to all that the possession of our Islands has brought us to rivall that mighty Kingdom Spain in the verry Center of its power and wealth, and that we draw from the labour and industry of our own People Advantages superior to those they reap from their rich mines of Potosi etc. It is also not to be denyd that since our Colonys have hitherto provd so advantagious and so far encreasd our Power and wealth in those parts as well as at home, that if we could plant a fresh one more commodiously and with greater advantages by Nature than are in any we yet possess, the publick wealth and power of England would be proportionably encreas'd. For the effecting of this no place seems by scituation and all other circumstances so proper as the Istmus of Darien. It is that verry neck of Land that joins the two mighty continents of America. It is inhabited by Indians under their own

[1] Some of the statements about the Isthmus come from Dampier's *New Voyage*; the rest are from word of mouth, in part gathered perhaps when Thomas was in the West Indies in 1693: no. *1629*.

The Scottish East India Company's project for a settlement in Darien was the subject of an inquiry by the Board of Trade in the summer of 1697; on 10 September the Board recommended that Golden Island (p. 633) and a port on the adjacent coast should be occupied for the crown of England: the Board's Journal; Wafer (no. *290* n.), introd., p. li. The first Scottish expedition sailed in July of this year.

Governors and never was subject to the Spaniards who possess vas tracts of Land to the N. and S. of them, and so seems reservd by Providence for us her favourite Nation. It separates the N. and S. Seas by a small tract of Land not exceeding 30 or 40 leagues. It has many considerable Rivers but especially 3 running into the S. Sea. The names of the Rivers are that of Santa Maria, Chepo and Congo, the first of which has high swelling tides of 17 or 18 feet, of sufficiently known advantage in Careening Ships, and runs into the Gulph of St Michael not farr from the famous City of Panama. This Country has also some less Rivers with good Bays for Shipping to the N. Sea. The Nation of the Indians are gallant Enemys to the Spaniards, and ever friendly to the English who by frequent marches through their Country have setled a fair Correspondence with them. It abounds with fresh water and the Valleys produce Sugar Canes, with the grain and fruits of those Countrys in wonderfull plenty. The Steepness of the Hills and almost perpendicular depth of the Gullys make it the most defensible Country in the World, and places may be found where Nature has left nothing almost for Art to do to render them impregnable. It lyes near to the Gold Mines whose dust ⟨is⟩[a] brought down to the late fort of Santa Maria and the more distant one of Pocamora.[1] And now I am speaking of the Gold mines I can adventure to demonstrate that neither Spaniards nor Indians have ever opened them and that what they find in the Rivers are nothing more than the Abortions or Spewings out of that mettal from the veins of the Mines in the mountains, and then washd down by the violence of the Torrents in the season of Rain, and it is principally after that time that the Spaniards and Indians search for it among the Sand. It need not be said what a diligent Search might do on this occasion if due encouragement were given. This Country lyes in the verry Center of America, and might in no long time be capable of giving Lawes to a great part of the trade on the N. and S. Seas. It affords sufficient materialls for Shipping, especially great quantitys of Whitewood[2] of experienc'd virtue against being eaten by the worms. It lyes verry properly for making considerable discoverys of the Spice Islands and other parts of India, and tis not improbable but the

[a] *MS.* in

[1] This name is unknown to Dampier and Wafer.
[2] See *O.E.D.* Wafer mentions it, but not its value for ship-building: p. 60.

N.W. passage it self may be attempted with greater success than from hence. Neither is it impossible but a method may be contrivd to shorten the Carriage especially of the less bulky goods from India, by unloading on the S. Coast and carrying over land about 20 or 30 leagues and putting them on board again on the N. verry indifferent Ships serving well enough for either of those voiages and thereby saving a tedious and hazardous sailing round the Cape. There is room enough for a mighty Settlement of our Nation without offending the Indians or possessing any parcell of grounds the Spaniards can lay claim to. The setling this place will not meet with so many difficultys as some of our Plantations have, by reason our People are more accoustumed to leave their Native Country and try their fortunes abroad, and that there is all imaginable reason to hope that many Familys of the Northern and other Plantations will readily change their Seats on so fair a prospect of making themselves more easy and thriving on the Istmus. For its healthiness it is at least equall to Jamaica and the other great American Islands, subject to no more inconveniencys, than they and to be improvd by a Settlement as they have been already. It lyes in about 9 degrees of N Latitude And by having its waters always running its hills high and little or no boggy ground in the Valleys with a Constant breese of the Trade wind, not subject to infectious mists and damps. Upon the whole matter I cannot see why a good Settlement on this Istmus might not be the most advantagious of all we possess in America to this Nation, as also as prejudiciall to us should the French our Rivall Neighbour, or any other Nation possess themselves of it: In all probability they will not fail to make use of those advantages which we have in our hands but think not worth our notice. If the Circumstances of the Affairs of Europe favour us, and the wisdom of this Nation think fitt, at any time vast Acquisitions may be made to the N. and S. and even over all that rich and mighty Continent.—It may not be amiss for the reasons alledgd and many more to be added if need were, that if his Majesty think fitt a freindly Correspondence with the Indians be maintaind and Possession of the Istmus or at least of part of it be taken in his Majestys name, to be kept by a Fort to be built on some advantagious peice of ground mannd with such a force and provided with such stores as his Majesty may judge reasonable, till such time a more particular discovery may be made and a Sufficient number of People arrive from all parts to begin and finish a Settlement which may prove the terror of our Enemys, and glory of England.

WT.

Endorsed by Locke: Darien

2453. JEAN LE CLERC to LOCKE, 7/17 June 1698 (*2403, 2531*)

B.L., MS. Locke c. 13, ff. 123–4. Printed in Bonno, *Le Clerc*, pp. 107–8.

A Amsterdam le 17. de Juin 1698.

Il y a long-temps, Monsieur, que j'aurois dû me donner l'honneur de vous écrire, mais j'ai été obligé de retarder, en attendant que Mrs. Huguetan me dissent qu'ils avoient des exemplaires de Hammond[1] en Angleterre. Vous trouverez donc un billet ci-joint, dans lequel je prie Mr. Huguetan, qui est là,[2] de donner à celui qui le lui presentera un exemplaire de Hammond, et quatre de ma Philosophie. Le Hammond, et l'un de ces quatre exemplaires seront, s'il vous plait, pour vous. Vous verrez que la Dédicace, qui vous regardoit, a été mise à la tête, car n'aiant jamais eu de nouvelle de Mr. Boyle, ni d'aucun des siens, je n'ai pas crû devoir laisser celle qui s'adressoit à lui.[3] J'ai mis à la fin de la préface ce que j'ai fait à cette seconde Edition, qui est infiniment plus belle et meilleure que l'autre. Je vous supplie de disposer ainsi des trois autres exemplaires; d'en envoier un à Mr. l'Evêque de Salisburi, à qui une partie du 2. Tome est dédiée; et de donner les deux autres chez vous, l'un à Mr. Coste, l'autre au fils de Madame Masham, qui m'a fait une honêteté, à quoi je ne m'attendois pas. Je lui avois envoié le petit livre concernant l'Histoire Universelle,[4] plûtôt pour faire plaisir à Mr. Coste, que pour m'en faire de fête auprès d'elle. L'édition de Pindare[5] est fort belle, mais je n'ai pas encore eu le temps de l'examiner avec un peu de soin. Je vois, par l'autre livre, que Mr. le Docteur Bentley s'est attiré un redoutable adversaire sur les bras. Quoi qu'il ait raison de croire les Lettres de Phalaris supposées, il y a bien des incidens dans ce procès et personnels et autres où il semble avoir tort; mais il faut attendre sa

[1] *Novum Testamentum Domini Nostri Jesu Christi ex Versione Vulgata, cum Paraphrasi et Annotationibus H. Hammondi.* Translated from English into Latin and edited by Le Clerc, 2 vols., folio, 1698. L.L., no. 1382.

[2] Probably Marc Huguetan rather than either of his brothers: see p. 157, n. 3.

[3] See pp. 168, 178.

[4] The *Compendium Historiæ Universalis*: p. 178.

[5] The edition by R. West and R. Welsted published at Oxford in 1697.

réponse. Cependant j'ai peur que ⟨cette⟩[a] querelle ne dégenere en personalitez.[1] J'ai eu occasion de faire demander à Mr. Bentley, s'il étoit toûjours dans le dessein de faire imprimer les fragmens des Poëtes Grecs; par le moien de Mr. Wotton, qui m'a envoié la 2. Edition de son livre, mais je n'ai reçu aucune réponse, parceque Mr. Wotton est à la campagne, et Mr. Bentley à Londres. Quoi qu'il réponde, je croi que je ne me tiendrai pas de publier mes fragmens de *Menandre* et de *Philemon*, dès que j'en aurai le loisir.[2] Dès que j'ai eu achevé Hammond j'ai travaillé, sans discontinuation, à une harmonie des Evangiles, que j'ai achevée en Grec, et en suite en Latin.[3] Le commencement est entre les mains de l'Imprimeur. Comme on ne parle à Paris, depuis quelque temps, que d'Harmonies, la pensée m'en est venue, et je me persuade que la mienne sera aussi bien executée que les autres. J'ai vû quelques essais, que Mr. Toinard envoia ici, il y a trente ans, à Elzevier,[4] ou il me semble qu'il y a bien des défauts. Je ne sai s'il les aura corrigez. Le Clergé de France lui offrit, il y a quelques années, une gratification, pour la publier, mais il la refusa.[5] Le bruit court qu'il travaille à l'imprimer, quoi qu'il ait dit que non, dans une Lettre à Wetstein. Quoi qu'il en soit, la mienne étant autrement disposée, et sa Chronologie étant de plus très-fausse, quoi qu'il affecte de savoir l'impossible dans des choses de cette nature, je n'ai pas peur de la sienne, qui viendra quand elle pourra. Je joindrai une Paraphrase à la mienne, avec quelques notes, où je n'ai point peur de me rencontrer avec lui. Il est trop bon Catholique, pour entendre l'Ecriture comme moi.

[a] *MS.* celle

[1] William Wotton (D.D. 1707; the scholar: *D.N.B.*) included in the second edition of his *Reflections upon Ancient and Modern Learning*, 1697, a dissertation by Bentley showing that the letters attributed to Phalaris are supposititious; Bentley also exposed the alleged letters of Themistocles, Sophocles, Euripides, and others, and Æsop's fables. In reply Charles Boyle (later fourth earl of Orrery; *D.N.B.*), the editor of Phalaris, published about March *Dr. Bentley's Dissertations on the Epistles of Phalaris and the Fables of Æsop examin'd* (L.L., no. 412). This is the book mentioned by Le Clerc. Bentley published his second *Dissertation* in 1699: p. 576.

[2] See p. 255.

[3] *Harmonia Evangelica, cui subjecta est Historia Christi ex quatuor Evangeliis concinnata*, published in 1699. L.L., no. 776. See Barnes, *Le Clerc*, p. 141.

[4] Daniel Elsevier took some sheets of Toinard's 1678 Harmony with him when he returned from Paris to the United Provinces in 1679 or 1680: no. *594*. He died in October 1680; Le Clerc did not settle in Amsterdam until 1683; the sheets were probably available through Hendrik Wetstein at that time: no. *778*. Toinard is unlikely to have sent specimens, manuscript or printed, to Elsevier at an earlier time.

[5] According to Cuissard this was in 1690: Soc. archéol. et hist. de l'Orléanais *Mém.* xxviii (1902), 41.

Un Druide a écrit à Mr. Limb. nôtre ami, le contenu de l'Acte contre les blasphemateurs, qui l'a fort scandalisé;[1] et il ne manquera pas de lui en dire son sentiment avec sa moderation et sa candeur ordinaire. Il ne faut point faire de livres contre les gens que l'on veut punir, ni punir ceux contre qui l'on fait des livres. Je suis, Monsieur, de tout mon coeur tout à vous

J LE CLERC.

Address: A Monsieur Monsieur Locke at Mr. Pawlings in little Lincolns inne fields over against the plough. London[a]

Postmark: IV 13

Endorsed by Locke: J: le Clerc 17 Jun 98 Answered Jul. 14 and[b]– Nov. 17–[b]

2454. NICOLAS TOINARD to LOCKE, 8/18 June 1698 (*2450*, 2458)

B.L., MS. Locke c. 21, f. 197. Text perhaps incomplete. Perhaps answered by no. 2504.

+

ce 18. Juin. 98.

Je vous ecrivis, monsieur, la semaine derniere pour vous marquer la joie que j'avois d'avoir apris par vous même de vos nouveles, é que cele que vous m'avez fait l'honneur de m'ecrire le mois de mars dernier ne ma pas eté rendüe. S'il y avoit quelque chose qu'il m'importast de savoir, je vous prie de me le mander.

M. Du bos qui sera je croix assez heureux pour vous trouver à Londres, poura vous indiquer quelques petis endrois où il faut coriger le François dans votre livre. Je les luy ay fait remarquer lorsque je luy ay donné cet ouvrage à lire, et je tiens à grand honneur le present que vous m'en avez fait. On a mis dans la Preface que *les Siamois n'enmaillote point leurs enfans.* Je crois vous avoir dit que les canadiens metent leurs enfans dans une maniere de petites bieres d'ecorce d'arbre, où il y a de la mousse é de la pouriture d'arbre, sur quoi reposent les enfans. Ils metent sur cete

[a] *The address is repeated on verso of cover.* [b–b] *Added later to the original endorsement.*

[1] A bill against blasphemy. It had passed both houses by 1 June and received the royal assent on 5 July, becoming 9 Wm. III, c. 35. Burnet wrote to van Limborch about it on 27 May, setting out its provisions; van Limborch's answer is lost. Burnet wrote later, explaining its limited object: Clarke and Foxcroft, *Burnet*, pp. 346–8; p. 460 below.

biere une peau qui couvre l'enfant, é ils le sanglent par dessus afin qu'il ne tombe pas. Ils dressent contre les parois de leur cabanes cete biere un peu inclinée, en sorte que l'enfant y dort en partie debout è en partie couché. Ils metent sous sa petite nature un tuyau d'ecorce qui porte l'eau de l'enfant hors de son berceau. Feu m. Gendron estimoit beaucoup cete maniere de ne point enmailloter les enfans, é confirme parfaitement ceque vous dites page 15. et 16. de l'edition de 95.[1]

Il est bon d'ajoûter que les enfans sont de cete façon la netoiéz fort prontement, car la mere prend avec la main l'endroit de la mousse qui est sale é la jete, é en substitüe d'autre, en remuant é aprochant le reste.

J'ay connu trop tard ici mr Dalonne. Je n'ay pas laissé de bien profiter des deux conversations que j'ay euës avec lui, où entre otres choses nous avons parlé *De dulcorata aqua salsa*. Je nescai comment on ne suit pas une chose aussi importante qu'est cele la. m. Leyster[2] n'y croit pas.

M. Perrot[3] maître de notre vererie qui a fourni tous les vitraux de notre catedrale[4] qui sont d'une beauté charmante en bleu rouge et vert m'a prié de savoir si à Londres l'Eglise de st Pol[5] n'oroit pas besoin de pareils vitraux. Il en fourniroit par Nante ou Roüen cequ'il faudroit, à juste prix.

2455. LOCKE to PETER KING, later first Baron King, 9 June 1698 (2448, 2462)

B.L., MS. Locke c. 40, ff. 9–10.

Oates 9 Jun 98

Dear Cosin

Had not Sir Francis gon from hence on Monday last[6] much earlier than he uses to doe you had received this my congratulation of being called to the bar, and my thanks for your care in my businesse a weeke sooner than now you are like to doe. Our messenger failed the last post, which has made the delay soe long

If the bill for the two millions passe I desire you to send me down the breviat of it, and the bill it self as soon as either of them can be

[1] The French translation of *Some Thoughts*. [2] Dr. Lister. [3] No. 390.
[4] Ste. Croix in Orléans. [5] St. Paul's.
[6] 6 June. King was called to the bar on 3 June: *Middle Temple Records: Minutes of Parliament*, ed. C. T. Martin, 1904–5, p. 1458.

had, But to subscribe however according to my former direction as soon as there is an oportunity, unlesse I send you contrary orders, only you will obleige me by consulting Mr Freke[1] or others knowing in such affairs to informe yourself the best you can, what is said for or against it and to informe me of it

The terme is now at an end.[2] and can not you come down now hither for a few days. You know you will be very welcome to every body here and to me in particular who should be very glad to have some talke with you. My Lady gives you her service. I am

Dear Cosin

Your most affectionate Cosin and servant

J Locke

Sir Francis signed the paper, you had prepared, here, which I returnd not to you because I may have use of it here. In my opinion it seemd best to refer to the mortgage. But you haveing thought otherwise it was signed just as you drew it.

Address: For Mr Peter King of the Middle Temple To be left at Mr Potmans in the Middle Temple London

Postmark: IV 13

Endorsed by King: Mr Locke 9 June. 98

2456. Locke to Cornelius Lyde, 11 June 1698 (*2449*, *2463*)

The Robert H. Taylor Collection, Princeton, New Jersey. Transcribed from photostat. Answers no. *2449*; answered by no. *2463*.

Oates 11° Jun 98

Sir

I shall always be glad of any oportunity wherein I may doe you or any of yours any service. Particularly your son the Doctor who you haveing designed for Physick and he haveing taken his degree in that facultie it would I thinke be an injury to him and to you to divert his thoughts now to any other imployment. I should not think it necessary to say this to you did not yours of the 31 May seem to looke that way as if you were willing to get some other imployment for him till he were of age to practise Physick. To

[1] Probably the Bachelor: p. 397, n. 2. [2] It ended on 6 June.

which give me leave ⟨to⟩[a] say that he will be of age to practise as soon as he has knowledg and skill enough to doe it and the sooner he has that the better. But the study of Physick is soe large that it will take up a mans whole time and thoughts if he should live the age of one of the Patriarchs and after all there would be a great deale for him to learne. The consequence which I draw from this is that if you intend your son should practise physick, that you should think of noe thing but his applying himself wholy and entirely to that study. But where he should begin to practise first and when; and where in the meane time he should apply him self to his improvement in that science can be determined by noe body but you according to such allowance as your circumstances and the consideration of your other children will permit you to make him. in which it is not fit for me to medle.

I thanke you for your care of my little concernes in your neighbour hood. I leave Hanny wholy to your discretion who are a better judg what is fit to be done with him than I can be at this distance. I hope you have acquainted Goodman Pope, that the little slip in the common mead which I formerly rented of him I have had noething to doe with since our Lady day last was twelve month. Pray give my humble service to Mrs Strachy and all that good family and to my Cosin Lyde and to your son the Doctor. I am Sir

Your most humble servant

LOCKE

Address: For Cornelius Lyde Esquire at Stanton weeke To be left at Mr Codringtons in High Street Bristoll

Postmarks: IV 14; GS (?)

2457. WILLIAM THOMAS to LOCKE, 11 June 1698 (*2452, 2547*)

B.L., MS. Locke c. 20, f. 159.

London 11th June 1698.

Sir

You judge verry right in thinking I might have some concern in the project I sent you, for it is wholy my own. As to the doubt you raise of my getting nothing by it, I can only say that tho my fortune is verry narrow yet I have a soul as much above the thoughts

[a] *Word omitted by Locke.*

of making a private advantage, as any Man whose circumstances are ever so much superior to mine. The only thing that I request of you is to give me your opinion as to the project itself and whether if put in execution it might not be advantagious to the publick, for if it be so I may easily propose to find such a profit for my self as may answer my desires which I assure you are very moderate. As for my own part I have weighd it with all the little judgement I have, and can as yet find nothing to contradict my thoughts of its being usefull; however I am by no means so fond of the creature of my own imagination as to think my own judgement sufficient, but shall ever own it as a particular happiness that I can submit it to the censure of so worthy and discerning a Person as your Self. I goe for Salisbury next week and sometime within a fortnight at your leisure beg your answer directed thither. In the mean time with all imaginable acknoledgement[a-] of your favours[-a] I am

Sir

your most Obliged most humble and most Obedient Servant

W THOMAS

Address: This for John Locke Esqr [at Oates, by Joslyn, Bishops Stortford]
Postmarks: IV 11; GC
Endorsed by Locke: W: Thomas 11 Jun. 98 Answered. 30

[a-a] *MS.* acknoledgement of your / of your favours

2458. LOCKE to NICOLAS TOINARD, 12 June 1698 (*2454, 2470*)

B.M., Add. MS. 28,753, ff. 32–3. Printed in Ollion, pp. 129–30. Answered by no. *2470*.

Oates 12 Jun 98

Defectus τῶν *Pacquet boats* magnum incommodum amicis post ingrata longi silentii intervalla redeuntibus in antiquum literarum commercium. Scripsi ad te Dilectissime Toinarde circa finem mensis Martii in quibus literis et epistolas[a] cum libris per Nelsonem mih

[a] *Altered from* epistolam

Oates 12 Jun 1698

The lack of the packet-boats is a great inconvenience to friends who are returning to their former correspondence after unwelcome intervals of prolonged silence. I wrote to you, most dearly beloved Toinard, about the end of March; in that letter, as was proper, I gratefully acknowledged, with what haste I could, your letters together with the books that you sent me b

a te missas[a] qua potui festinatione gratus ut par erat agnovi. Sero enim ad me pervenerunt ista tua diu ante illi reddita, munera, veteris et non imminutæ amicitiæ tuæ documenta. Circa medium mensis Maii ad tuas 3 Aprilis datas itidem respondi Epistolamque meam amici cujusdam curæ commisi, qui spondebat se provisurum ut recte ad te perveniret, et insuper ut aperiret nobis tutum et facile literarum commercium. Quorsum hæc tam minutim? Nempe ut intelligas me nullam scribendi prætermisisse occasionem, et magnopere cupere consuetudinem nostram literarum posse in integrum restitui. Hactenus solum, mea saltem ex parte, primæ salutationes Veteris amici post longam absentiam restituti, nec dum scio an eousque processerim: Incertus enim sum an literarum mearum quæpiam præter primam ad te pervenerit. nimis gravis sanè, nisi tibi probe notus essem, vel oblivionis vel negligentiæ significatio, quarum nomine nullo modo tibi suspectus esse vellem. Multa habeo tibi dicenda si munitam ad te viam reperire possem. Interim de opere musico quid? et quando tandem prodibit?[b] Rogo, urgeo, efflagito, ut meus est mos,[1] ut festinetur ut appareat, ne detur locus ampliùs aliis prævertendi, et quod tibi debetur laudis in eo argumento præripiendi. Hoc monitum toties a me et tantopere

[a] *Altered from* missam [b] *Question mark supplied at end of line.*

Nelson. For those gifts of yours, proofs of your old and undiminished friendship, that you had handed over to him long before, were late in reaching me. About the middle of the month of May I also answered yours of 3 April and committed my letter to the care of a certain friend who promised to see to it that it duly reached you, and further that it would open for us a safe and easy [channel for our] correspondence. Why all this so minutely? Simply so that you may know that I have neglected no opportunity of writing and very greatly wish that our intercourse by letter can be completely restored. So far these, at least from my side, are only the first greetings of an old friend restored after long absence; nor do I yet know whether I have succeeded to that extent, for I am uncertain whether any of my letters except the first has reached you. If I were not so well known to you this would be an exceedingly grievous sign of forgetfulness or negligence, of which I should not wish you in any way to suspect me. I have many things to say to you if I could find a safe route to you. Meanwhile what of the musical work? and when will it at last come out? I beg, urge, demand, as is my wont,[1] that it be hastened so that it may appear, lest others be given further opportunity of anticipating it or of snatching from you the praise that is due to you on that ground. I should not again repeat here this warning that I have so often and so earnestly reiterated, were it

---

[1] Horace, *Satires* I. ix. 1; quoted in no. *23* also.

ingeminatum non hic iterum repeterem nisi audirem huic materiæ jam etiam in Hollandia operam dari.[1] Cum enim tuum prædicatum ubique, optatum avide, expectatum diu, omnibus moverit salivam et tamen nunquam appareat, vide an non aliis se huic argumento ingerendi occasionem præbueris. Hoc mihi sine conjecturâ notum quod familiares mei identidem me rogitant. Quando tandem habebimus etc

Hæc amico Rothomagum proficiscenti tradita.[2] Illic aliquamdiu commoratur. Quodsi facilior tibi non occurrat mittendi occasio Ille quicquid a te acceperit mihi cum curâ afferet si ita inscribatur

A Monsieur
Monsieur Henry Masham chez Monr: LeGendre
à Roüen
pour faire tenir à Mr Locke
à Oates

Je suis
Monsieur
Vôtre tres humble et tres obeissant serviteur
JOHN LOCKE

Address: A Monsieur Monsieur Toinard chez Monsr: des Noyers devant l'Espée royale dans la Rüe Mazarin à Paris

Endorsed by Toinard: 12. Juin 98.

---

not that I hear that attention is now being paid in Holland also to this matter.[1] For since your [work], everywhere praised, eagerly desired, [and] long awaited, has made everyone's mouth water and yet never appears, see whether you have not provided others with an opportunity of thrusting into this subject. I know this without guessing because my friends repeatedly ask me, 'When at last shall we have etc?'

This letter is entrusted to a friend who is starting for Rouen;[2] he is staying there for some time. If you meet with no more favourable opportunity of sending he will bring carefully to me whatever he receives from you if it is thus addressed:

2458A. LOCKE to EDWARD CLARKE, 20 [June?] 1698 (2447, 2469)

Owing to misdating this letter is printed as no. 2537.

[1] Locke may refer to Toinard's Harmony, but more probably to a plagiarism. Le Clerc's letter, no. *2453*, did not reach him until 13 June or later. He perhaps heard some report from Coste, who was well informed about Le Clerc: see no. *2480*.

[2] Henry Masham sailed from Rye on 19 June: p. 440.

2459. DR. JOHN COVEL to LOCKE, 20 June 1698 (*2322*, *2467*)

B.L., MS. Locke c. 7, ff. 164–5. Answered by no. 2467.

Chr. College. Cambridge. Jun. 20. 1698.

Worthy Sir

I got well home I blesse God, and returne my hearty respects to you and to my Lady and all the worthy family.

This present year 1698. is according to the present Greeks *Paschalian*[1] the year of the world. 7206.

The Jewish account you have in Abendana.[2] viz. 5458.

In the year 1693. a very ingenious man, a Saxon, (who was with me) said that year according to the *Chinese* account was of the world, 960170. or thereabouts.[3]

I have here sent you the *English Votaryes*.[4] It will make you sometimes laugh, sometimes pity the condition of those times, but often admire the Goodnesse of God who hath brought us out of that darknesse.

The passage which I told you of, about the first cap. of St John is St Augustines Confess. lib. 7. cap. 9.

If I have forgot any thing else, be pleased at your leisure to intimate your desire in that or any thing else wherein I am able to serve you; and withall remind me of that author who ⟨quotes⟩[a] Thucidides for *οὐχ ἁρπαγμον ἡγήσατο*; I have forgot it, unlesse it be *Pezelius*. etc.[5]

With all true respect I am,

Sir,

your most affectionate and most humble servant

J. Cov.

[a] *MS.* quoths

[1] Modern Greek *Πασχάλιον*, Paschal canon.

[2] No. 475, etc. *The Jewish Kalendar . . . beginning at the 28th of the moon Tebeth in the year of the Creation, 5458. and continuing to the 10. of Sebatt 5459. inclusively. . . . An Almanack for the year of Christ*, *1698*.

[3] I have not identified Covel's informant or found his figure elsewhere. Far higher figures are given by other writers. e.g. M. Martini, S.J., *Sinicæ Historiæ Decas Prima*, 1658, pp. 4, 120 (Locke derived the figure in *Essay*, II. xiv. 29, from Martini, either this or the edition of 1659: L.L., nos. 1925–6); A. Greslon, S.J., *Histoire de la Chine*, etc., 1671, p. 42.

[4] John Bale, bishop of Ossory (*D.N.B.*), *The Actes of Englysh Votaryes*, 1546; later editions 1548–51, 1550, 1551, 1560.

[5] The quotation is from Philippians 2: 6: 'thought it not robbery (to be equal)': so the Authorized Version. Christian Pezel 1539–1604: *A.D.B.* I have not traced the passage.

I had forgot the story of the Monster. it is in, *La prima parte delle lezzioni di M. Benedetto Varchi nella Accademia Fiorentina*, pag.106.b. it is in 8vo. printed, *In Fiorenza.* M.D.L.X.[1]

Address: For Mr Lock.
Endorsed by Locke: Dr Covel 20 Jun 98 Answered Jul. 1

2460. PHILIPPUS VAN LIMBORCH to LOCKE, 21 June/1 July 1698 (2443, *2482*)

B.L., MS. Locke c. 14, ff. 117–18. Copy by van Limborch in Amsterdam University Library, MS. R.K., III D 16, f. 205. The last paragraph, beginning 'Viro magnifico postremas' is printed from the Amsterdam copy in *Some Familiar Letters*, pp. 424–5. Answers no. 2443.

Vir Amplissime

Filius meus ex Anglia redux prolixe officia ac beneficia tua narravit, et affectum vere paternum, quo et consilio et opere negotia ipsius promovisti, deprædicavit. Summam etiam Domini ac Dominæ Masham, quin et totius familiæ, erga se expertum ait benevolentiam, quantam ne a proximis ⟨quidem⟩[a] consanguineis exspectare ausit: Adeo ut, dum in Anglia commoratus est, nec parentes nec consanguineos sibi defuisse glorietur, nec se condignas amicis adeo benevolis unquam posse habere gratias passim testetur. Equidem me pro tantis beneficiis tibi, nec non Domino ac Dominæ Masham, maxime obligatum profiteor, neque eorum memoriam dum spiritus

[a] *Word omitted by van Limborch.*

Excellent Sir,

My son on his return from England told us at length of all your services and acts of kindness, and proclaimed aloud the truly fatherly affection with which you forwarded his affairs by both advice and action. He says that he also experienced very great goodwill towards himself on the part of Sir Francis and Lady Masham, and indeed of the whole family, such as he would not have dared to expect even from very near relations: so much so that he brags that while he stayed in England he lacked neither parents nor relations, and declares to everybody that he can never be sufficiently grateful to such kind friends. For my part I acknowledge that I am very greatly obliged to you and also to Sir Francis and Lady Masham for such great acts of kindness,

---

[1] Covel quotes the passage in no. *2474*. Locke may have wanted it to replace the vague notice of a monstrous birth in *Essay*, III. vi. 27.

hos reget artus[1] animo meo unquam excidere patiar. Habes me, qualem diu habuisti, totum tuum, et ad omnia quæcunque de me disponere tibi placuerit promtum ac paratum. Dominæ Masham literis ad ipsam datis gratias ipse agerem, si vel Anglicæ linguæ, vel Gallicæ gnarus, alterutra scribere, et mentem meam commode exprimere possem. Nunc utriusque linguæ imperitia me patrocinium tuum implorare compellit, ut tu meo nomine quod officii mei est præstes: Oro itaque, ut meo ac uxoris, nec non filii ac filiæ nomine quam officiosissime Dominum ac Dominam Masham, et omnes honoratissimæ illius familiæ liberos salutes, proque maximis in filium nostrum collatis beneficiis humillimas agas gratias, pro quibus nos perpetuo tam honoratæ familiæ devinctos profitemur, et ad omnia obsequia obstrictos. Ego summe Reverendi D. Kudworthi amicitiam[2] in dignissima illius filia revixisse maxime mihi gratulor. Utinam hic ipsam cum lectissimo marito ac liberis excipere liceret, ac opere ipso quam me ipsi devinctum agnoscam ostendere! Filius quidem aliquam illius spem fecit, sed incertam. Optarim ego, ut inchoata illa de itinere Hollandico deliberatio in decretum ranseat.

ıor will I ever allow the remembrance of them to slip out of my mind 'while)reath of life shall rule this frame'.[1] You have me such as you have long had ne, altogether yours, and ready and prepared to be at your disposal for vhatever you please. I should myself have thanked Lady Masham in a letter ddressed to her if I were versed in English or French and were able to write n one or other language and express suitably what I have in mind. As it is, ny lack of knowledge of either language compels me to beg your advocacy nd to ask you to discharge on my behalf what is a duty of mine. I pray you herefore on behalf of myself and my wife, and also of my son and daughter, o give our most dutiful respects to Sir Francis and Lady Masham and to all he children of that most honourable family, and to express our humble hanks for the very great kindnesses they have conferred on our son, for vhich we acknowledge ourselves forever obliged to that honourable family, nd bound to their service in all things. I greatly congratulate myself on the evival of my friendship with the highly to be revered Mr. Cudworth[2] in is most worthy daughter. Would that it were permitted to me to welcome er here with her excellent husband and children, and to show in very deed ow much I recognize that I am obliged to her. My son indeed gave us some ope of that, but uncertain. I should wish that that unfinished consideration f a journey to Holland may turn into a decision to make it.

---

[1] Quoted by van Limborch in no. *1101*.

[2] Four letters from Cudworth to van Limborch, 1668–87, are extant, and nine pies of letters from van Limborch to Cudworth, 1666–89: Amsterdam University ibrary, *Catalogus der Handschriften*, vol. iv, pt. i, 1911.

Reverendissimi Episcopi Salisburiensis uxor, quæ una cum filio meo in Hollandiam venit, Roterodami subito in morbum lethalem incidit: postero die apparuere varioli aliquot, qui quarto die omnes disparuerunt; accessit, ut audio, diarrhæa cum tormine in intestinis, ac postridie, die videlicet decimo octavo Junii mane hora nona diem suum obiit.[1]

Viro Magnifico postremas tuas ostendi: ille pro labore rogatu suo a te suscepto maximas agit gratias: non tamen in tua argumentatione acquiescit. Methodus illius primo loco probat, dari Ens aliquod per se existens ac sibi sufficiens: Deinde, illud Ens esse tantum unum: Tertio, illud Ens in se complecti omnes perfectiones, ac proinde esse Deum. Tu vero in tua argumentatione præsupponis, omni homini attente meditanti evidens esse, dari Ens infinitum, cui nihil addi aut demi possit. Atqui id idem ipsi est, ac supponere, dari Ens undiquaque perfectum. Quæ est tertia ipsius thesis. Adeo ut ex præsupposita illius thesi tertia probes secundam, cum secunda prius probari debeat, antequam ex illa concludi possit tertia. Hæc fuit causa, cur ego Tibi considerandum dederim, an non ordo illius mutari debeat, et quæ illius tertia est ⟨non⟩[a] debeat esse secunda thesis. Verum ut argumentatio proce-

[a] *Supplied from van Limborch's copy.*

The Right Reverend the bishop of Salisbury's wife, who came to Holland together with my son, suddenly contracted a fatal illness in Rotterdam; on the following day there appeared some pocks, which all disappeared on the fourth day; diarrhœa, as I hear, was added with griping of the guts, and on the following day, namely 18 June, she died at nine o'clock in the morning.[1]

I have shown your last letter to the Magnifico; he is most grateful to you for the labour undertaken by you at his request; nevertheless he is not satisfied with your reasoning. His own way proves in the first place that there is given some being existing of itself and sufficient to itself; then that that being is only one [*i.e.* unique]; thirdly, that that being embraces all perfections in itself and consequently is God. You, however, presuppose in your reasoning that it is evident to every man who thinks carefully that there is given an infinite being which nothing can be added to or taken from. But that for him is the same thing as to suppose that there is given a being perfect in every respect. Which is his third proposition. So that you prove the second proposition by means of his third, which has been pre-supposed whereas the second ought first to be proved before the third can be inferred from it. This was the reason why I put it to you to consider whether his order ought not to be changed and whether what is his third proposition ought not to be the second. But in order that the reasoning should advance

---

[1] Mary, born Scott, a Dutch lady of Scottish extraction, Burnet's second wife Clarke and Foxcroft, *Burnet*, pp. 352–3.

dat, non deberet ea thesis præsupponi, sed ex prima thesi probari. Aut si illius methodus placeat, deberet prius ex eo quod sit Ens æternum ac sibi sufficiens probari illud esse unum; et hoc probato porro exinde deduci, illud esse infinitum, seu undiquaque perfectum. Argumentationem suam mihi nondum communicavit: An communicaturus sit, valde dubito. Idem ipsum qui te scrupulus retinet. Metuit iniquas Theologorum censuras, qui omnia, e schola sua non hausta, atro carbone notare, ac infami exosissimarum hæresium nomenclatura traducere solent. Tentabo tamen, an prolixiore colloquio, quod mecum instituere velle dixit, aliquatenus elicere possim, quod scripto tradere gravatur. Vale Vir Amplissime. Salutat te uxor, filius ac filia, imprimis ego

Tui Amantissimus
PHILIPPUS A LIMBORCH

Amstelodamii Cal. Julii

Address: For John Locke Esqr. at Mr. Pawlings overagainst the ploug in Little Lincolns Inne fields London

Postmark: IV 24

Endorsed by Locke: P. Limborch 1 Jul. 98

[logically] that proposition ought not to be presupposed but ought to be proved from the first proposition. Or else, if his way is approved, it ought first to be proved from the fact that there is a being eternal and sufficient to itself, that that being is one [*i.e.* is unique]; and, that being proved, it ought in turn thence to be deduced that that being is infinite or perfect in every respect. He has not yet imparted his reasoning to me; I very much doubt whether he will do so. That same uneasiness that holds you back holds him back. He fears the unjust judgements of theologians who are wont to give a black mark to everything that is not drawn from their own school and to traduce it with the infamous names of the most detestable heresies. I shall try, however, whether in a lengthier conversation, which he has said he wants to arrange with me, I can elicit to some extent what he is loath to commit to writing. Good-bye, excellent Sir. My wife, son, and daughter send you greetings, as do I,

Your most affectionate
PHILIPPUS VAN LIMBORCH

Amsterdam 1 July
1698

2461. THOMAS WATKINS to LOCKE, 23 June 1698

B.L., MS. Locke c. 23, ff. 65–6. The writer was one of the four clerks of the Privy Seal from *c.* 1682 until *c.* 1698.

Whitehall 23d June 98

Honoured Sir.

I have presum'd to give you the trouble of this letter at the Request of an honest Gentleman Collonell Staples who has for these many years been an officer in his Majesty's Horse-guards;[1] To whom his Majestie as a mark of his favour, has been pleased to give his Royall word, That his Son, a young Gentleman, now a Student in the Temple, shall have a Grant of the place of one of the Comissioners of Appeals for regulating the Excise, so soon as there shall happen any vacancy: And He, having been informed, That you are one in that Comission, and being desirous to bring his Son into somthing of Business as early as he could, He desires me to begg the favour from you, to know whither you will please to accept of a present in Consideration of your surrender of your interest in that Commission. Now Sir, if you please to favour me with your Answer to this, direct'd to me at the Signet office in Whitehall, I shall acquaint him with it so soon as possible; Sir, I begg your pardon for this freedome and if I can doe you any service in my poor Capacity, I shall be most ready to be commanded by you, being. Sir.

Your very humble servant.

THO: WATKINS

Your old friend Sir Fleetwood Sheppard[2] desird me to give you his service.

Address: This To John Locke Esqr. [at Oates, by Joslyn, Bishops Stortford]

Postmark: IV 26

Endorsed by Locke: T Watkins 23 Jun 98 Answered Jul. 1

[1] John Staples, traceable in the Guards from 1678 until 1694: Dalton, *English Army Lists*, vols. i–iii; Chamberlayne. The son may be Charles Staples; matriculated at Oxford 1692; admitted, Middle Temple, 1694: Foster.

[2] No. *1990*.

2462. Locke to Peter King, later first Baron King, 27 June 1698 (2455, 2466)

B.L., MS. Locke c. 40, ff. 11–12. Excerpt printed in John Campbell, Baron Campbell, *The Lives of the Lord Chancellors*, etc., 1845–69, iv. 570–1.

Oates 27 Jun 98

Dear Cosin

Your company here had been ten times welcomer than any the best excuses you could send. But you may now pretend to be a man of businesse and there can be noe thing said to you. I wish you good successe in it, and doubt not but you have the advice of those who are better skild than I in the matter. But yet I cannot for bear saying thus much to you, that when you first open your mouth at the bar it should be in some easie plain matter that you are perfectly master of, that you may not be out in what you have to say, nor be liable to stumble in, but can talke as easily about, as any thing you know without danger of being at a losse

I am told that the Act about the two millions will give leave to all people to subscribe that will, even after the two millions are subscribed and that then every ones subscription shall be reduced in proportion soe as to make the just summ of two millions, if the act passes and you are sure it is soe you need not make such hast to subscribe as directed in my former letters Because we may have time to consider the act. But if the books are to be shut and noe subscriptions admitted after the full sum of two millions is subscribed I would then have you take the first oportunity of subscribeing.[1] For this I would desire you to take care of that I may have £500 in that company espetialy if Mr Freke[2] and Mr Clarke incourage your subscribeing. If you finde them against it pray let me know before you subscribe. I am

Dear Cosin

Your most affectionate Cosin and humble servant

J Locke

Address: For Mr Peter King of the Middle Temple To be left at Mr Potmans in the Middle Temple London

Endorsed by King: Mr Lock June 27. 98.

[1] The subscription was opened on 14 July and closed on the 16th as soon as £2,000,000 had been subscribed: p. 408, n. 1.

[2] Probably the Bachelor.

2463. CORNELIUS LYDE to LOCKE, 27 June 1698 (*2456*, *2560*)

B.L., MS. Locke c. 15, ff. 166–7. In view of the postmark Lyde's date for the letter is probably two or three days late. Answers no. 2456.

June the 27th 98

Sir

Yours I Received of the 11 and doe heartely thank you for your advise and doe Intend my son[1] shall Come to towne in some short time and wayte upon you for he tells me he his Exceedingly obliegd to you for your greate Kindnes to him. you was plesed to wish him to be some tyme In An apothecary house[2] that he may see the towne practis if I might Know when you may be in towne I wold have my son be there for I desire haveing such a friend that he might be wholly guided by you, you was plesed in your Last to Leave Jos: Hannyes Conserns with me, I have beene not willing to arest him dubting he wold goe to Gaole and soe throw away good money after bad I feare, for he is verry Poore, what he may be able to doe in time I dont Know for Popes strap of ground the Reson it was not brought to the Last acount he being in my debt Cant Come to Rekon with him but will take Care that the new tenant shall pay Ever since he have had it with all due Respects to you I Am your obliegd friend and servant

COR: LYDE

Address: For Doct: Locke at mr. Pawlings overagainst the Plough in Little Lincolns feilds London

Postmark: IV 27

Endorsed by Locke: C: Lyde 27 Jun 98 Answered Feb 16

2464. JOHN BONVILLE to LOCKE, 28 June 1698 (*2428*, *2635*)

B.L., MS. Locke c. 4, f. 85.

London June the 28th: 98

Honoured Cousin

Sir sum time Agoe I Advised with you consirning sum busines In the Exise offic, for my son, I still being Incoraged by sum frind

[1] Dr. Samuel Lyde.

[2] In London at this time the members of the Society of Apothecaries acted as general practitioners, and the members of the Royal College of Physicians (and other graduates in medicine) mainly as consultants. See below, no. *2987* n.

now In the offic, to Aply my self to Esqr Clark,[1] which I have don severall times, which he have given me his promise, and now very shortley there Is as I Am Informed, sum nue ones to be put In, as soone as the parllement break up, which Is soposed it will be this week, Sir I Humbly Intreat that faviour of you To signifie your willingnes and desire, to Esqr Clark, for The promotion of my son, to sum busines in that offic. I should not be soe desirous in my Aplycation, If I did not Know my son to be Capable boath for capacity and Learning, And Another thing: which is more then All I do find my trade parnitious to him, Especially: In melting and when I burn charcole, but this I take no notis of to him because I would not disincorage him, I shall be glad If it may be the will of god, that such A thing may be. Sir I Know your word In this matter will be very Afectuall, and prevelant with Esqr Clark, Deare Cousin If you pleas, Let Esqr Clark heare from you speedely, And at the same Time I shall be heartly glad to heare from you, I was in great hopes to seen you in London befor this time, my wife and son give their Humble Sarvis to you, The Lord be with you,
I Am

Deare Cousin your Faithfull Kinsman and Humble Sarvant

JNO: BONVILLE:

Pray: My Humble Sarvis To My Lady Masham

Address: For Mr Locke [at Oates, by Joslyn, Bishops Stortford]
Postmark: IV 28
Endorsed by Locke: J: Bonville 28° Jun 98 Answered Jul. 1

2465. JOSEPH OFFLEY to LOCKE, 28 June 1698

B.L., MS. Locke c. 16, ff. 168–9. I cannot identify the writer.

Sir

I was taken yesterday morning with a violent fitt of the winde Collick, but it went of pretty well towards noone and soe continued all the afternoone and night, a Gentleman comeing to see me last night gave me some rubub steep't in Aniceed water telling me it was extraordnary good for my distemper, which I tooke some last night and some this morning, I was pretty well when I began

[1] Edward Clarke, who was a commissioner of Excise from 1694 to 1700. The younger John Bonville apparently obtained a post in the Excise about this time: no. *1771* n.

my Journey this morning, but a little on this side Epping I was taken ill againe, which I guess to be from takeing the Anniceed water and rubub, which has soe bound me that I could not soe much as breake winde backward all this day; I have beene att the Crowne att Harloe ever since eleven a clock, and have continued ill ever since, though I have taken a Glister[1] which ha's worck'd pretty well with me, but it ha's not att all removed the paine which is in my bowells; I begg the favour of your advice whether I had best take any thing to purge me, or what I had best doe, and if you have any medicine good for me I begg the favoure you will send me some of it by my man, for here is noething to be had here to purge unlesse some rose budds boiled, unless a man that lives in towne ha's any thing who I have sent to but he is not att home; I would not have troubled you but in a case of this necessity here being noe Physician neere; I fancy somewhat that would purge me moderately would cure me if it were safe to take it; pray Sir pardon this trouble especially considering it is from one in great paine and in a strange countrey

I am Sir your most humble servant

JOS: OFFLEY

Harlow tuesday night June the 28th: 1698.

I was told by one that came from Rye that Major Masham[2] sailed from thence for France on Sunday last was sevennight.

I desire you to send me what is best for me to drinck; for the Ale that sowers in my stomach, and any drinck that binds me makes me worse.

Address: For John Lock Esq att Sir Francis Mashams

Endorsed by Locke: J: Offley 28 Jun. 98

2466. LOCKE to PETER KING, later first Baron King 29 June 1698 (2462, 2468)

B.L., MS. Locke c. 40, ff. 13–14. Perhaps written on 28 June for dispatch on the 29th.

Oates 29° Jun 98

Dear Cosin

Yours of the 24th I received not till just now. The enquiry that I cheifly make now about the bill is whether the subscriptions be

[1] A clyster; an enema or suppository. [2] Henry Masham: pp. 382, n. 1, 430

limited precisely to two millions or whether it gives leave to all to subscribe that will beyond that summ to a certain time and that then the whole sum subscribed shall be reduced, if it exceeds two millions to just that sum by a proportionable abatement of every ones subscription. The reason why I make this enquiry you will finde in mine by Mr Churchill yesterday. viz Because if the subscription be limitted to precisely 2 millions it is desired you should take the first oportunity of subscribeing; if not but there is a liberty for exceeding that sum of 2 Millions then you need not make soe very much hast to subscribe. My Lady gives you her service. I am

Dear Cosin

Your most affectionate Cosin and humble servant

J LOCKE

Address: For Mr Peter King of the Middle Temple To be left with Mr Potman in the Middle Temple London

Postmark: IY 1

Endorsed by King: Mr Lock June 29. 98.

2467. LOCKE to DR. JOHN COVEL, 1 July 1698 (*2459, 2474*)

B.M., Add. MS. 22,910, ff. 474–5. Answers no. *2459*; answered by no. *2474*.

Oates 1° Jul 98

Reverend Sir

I received the booke you sent me safe entituled the Acts of English Votarys written by Johan Bale. I mention the title soe particularly that if I should dye before I restore it again you may demand it of my Executor for though it be but a little booke yet possibly it is not every day to be met with and tis fit you should have your own again and not loose by the favour you have done me in lending it me.

I returne you my thanks for the severall obleigeing particulars in your letter and have soe little reason to complain of your forgetting any thing that I rather wonder at your remembring soe much, some whereof I my self had forgott. And yet I am forced to beg the favour of you to let your man transcribe the discription of the monster and the womans confession out of Benedetto Varchi because it is a booke I know not where to meet with and I shall have occasion to make use of the story

The authors name you enquire after is Pezelius

My Lady gives you her humble service. I am

Reverend Sir

your most humble servant

J LOCKE

Address: For the Reverend Dr Covell Master of Christs College in Cambridg

Endorsed by Covel: Mr Lock. Pezelius.

2468. LOCKE to PETER KING, later first Baron King, 3 July 1698 (2466, 2506)

B.L., MS. Locke c. 40, ff. 15–16. Passages, with a passage from no. 2897, printed as a single letter in King, pp. 251–2.

Oates 3° Jul 98

Dear Cosin

I am glad that you are soe well enterd at the bar It is my advice to you to goe on soe gently by degrees and to speake only in things that you are perfectly master of till you have got a confidence and habit of talkeing at the bar I have many reasons for it which I shall discourse to you when I see you

I thinke your advice is right to subscribe as early as one can and therefor as soon as the Commission is out[1] to receive subscriptions I desire you to subscribe the sum I mentioned to you only in the mean time I desire you to tell me what arguments you meet with from others for or against subscribeing and to send me the act as soon as printed or a breviate of it and a copy of the Commission for takeing subscriptions as soon as it can be got. I say this not but that I hope to be soon in town to prevent it, but if ill weather should hinder me again. But this warme day (which has been the third that I have been able this year yet to passe without fire) gives me hopes that this comfortable weather which I have soe long wished for is settleing in, that I may venture to town, in a few days. For I would not take a journey thither to be driven out again presently

[1] It was preparing on 2 July: Luttrell.

Locke's accounts with King show that King subscribed for £500 stock on 14 July and bought a further £500 stock on 21 October (first and second instalments paid). King paid the tenth and final instalment on 5 January 1700. In addition Locke invested £250 in the company's trading account (p. 504), paid in five instalments 25 October 1698–20 July 1699. The investment was in King's name: B.L., MS. Locke b. 1 ff. 202–3.

as I am sure our late cold weather would have done, For my lungs are yet very weake and my breath short as you would have thought if you had been by me when I rose today. I must own to you that now at the writeing of this I finde the benefit of this warme day more than I have any thing since I have ⟨be⟩en[a] in ⟨the⟩[a] country, and I hope the triall of a few more such will put me in a case to venture to town with hopes of bearing it. I for many reasons impatiently long for it and am

Dear Cosin

Your most affectionate Cosin and servant

J LOCKE

My Lady Masham gives you her humble service

Address: For Mr Peter King of the Middle Temple To be left at Mr Potmans in the Middle Temple London

Endorsed by King: Mr Locke July. 3. 98.

2469. LOCKE to EDWARD CLARKE, 4 July 1698 (2458A, 2525)

B.L., MS. b. 8, no. 135. Printed in Rand, pp. 541–2.

Oates 4 Jul 98

Dear Sir

You have not more expected me than I have wished to be in town long before this. Yesterday was the comfortablest day I have had these six months because the warmest. I sat several hours of it in the warm air and found my self soe refreshd that I concluded a few more such would make me fit for the town and presumed soe far that I should have them now, that I concluded upon comeing to town to wards the end of the weeke. To day we have winterly weather again and I feel the want of what I hoped for, more warm baskeing in the open air. However upon the receit of yours of the 2d to day I am resolvd to come on Friday[1] if I can promise my self to make any stay there when I come. For if there should be such weather as this when I am there I doubt whether I shall be able to stay in town three days. I hope I shall finde the Batchelor in town

[a] *Page torn.*

[1] 8 July.

on Friday. I should be very sorry to Misse him. I am his and your humble servant

J LOCKE

My Lady my wife and all here are your dutifull[a] or humble etc. Pray let Madame know the same for her self

Address: For Edward Clarke Esquire member of Parliament at Richards Coffee house within Temple Bar London Frank

Postmark: IY 6

Endorsed by Clarke: Mr. Locke That Hee will bee in Town Fryday next Received the 6th. July 1698.

2470. NICOLAS TOINARD to LOCKE, 6/16 July 1698 (2458, 2473)

B.L., MS. Locke c. 21, ff. 198–9. Answers no. 2458; answered by no. 2483.

+

ce 16. Juïllet 98

Je voudrois, monsieur, que votre santé vous permist de faire un tour à Londres afin que monsieur Du bos qui est de mes particulier amis, pust avoir lhonneur et le bonheur de vous y salüer. Je luy a donné une letre pour vous qu'il vous a envoiée ne vous trouvan pas à Londres lorsqu'il y ariva.[1]

Je n'ay receu que[b] deux[b] letres de vous, outre cele du 26. Oct. 97 dont mr Nelson fut porteur que deux. L'une du 20. May et l'otr du 12. Juin. Je n'ay point receu cele du mois de mars.[2] J'ay un extrême impatience de savoir les beles choses dont vous donez[c] pa me regaler, suivant ces paroles: *Multa habeo tibi dicenda si munita ad te viam reperire possem.*[3] Quoique le Paquebot ne soit pas encor retabli, il passe continuelemant des barques de Douvre à Calais qu portent les letres. Il faut pour cela avoir une adresse à l'une ou l'otre de ces deux villes d'ou apres eles vont à droiture à Londres e a Paris.

Je vous ay envoié touchant votre livre de l'Education des enfan la maniere dont les Canadiens elevent les leurs. A propos d

[a] *MS.* dubtifull? [b] *Altered from* de [c] *Word altered from* dont?; *readi doubtful.*

---

[1] No. *2444.* [2] Nos. 2337, 2442, 2458, and the laggard no. 24
[3] 'I have many things to say to you if I could find a safe route to you': p. 42

Canada je nesai si je vous ay dit qu'aiant u la partie d'une peau de ces beufs qui sont sur la Riviere de Missisipi, j'en ay fait trier une maniere de laine ou duvet qu'ont ces animaux sous leur grand poil ainsi que les castors, et que j'en ay fait faire des bas pour l'hyver la faizant filer avec de la laine de Segovie. cela ma fort bien reüssi, mais aiant voulu faire la même tantative en chapeaux j'ay ete condanné aux depans. La partie de la peau que j'avois n'etoit que de dessous le ventre et d'un veau. outre cela ele a eté peu conservée. Que si l'on avoit de la peau de dessus le dos et des grans beufs, on auroit un poil bien plus long qui seroit encore meilleur à filer, quoique peutêtre il ne valust rien à foûler.[1]

Touchant ceque vous m'ecrivez *de opere musico*, je vous ay deja mandé que tout le texte est fait. A l'egard de la *Batavie*,[2] ils ne pouront l'executer come est le mien. De plus les caracterismes ne seroient pas les mêmes quand ils oroient un de mes anciens exemplaires où j'ay changé et rectifié une infinité de chôses. cependant je vous suis sensiblement obligé de l'interest que vous y prenez.

Je me suis exercé ces derniers jours à traduire de castillan en françois une belle relation de voiage qui n'est pas nouvele; mais quoiqu'imprimée depuis long tems, ele n'est pas connüe. cela ma mené plus loin que je ne pensois. J'ay bien des chôses touchant la Riviere du Senegal dont j'ay fait faire une grande carte.[3] si cete Riviere etoit en de bonnes mains, on en tireroit de grandes richesses. Il y ut en l'année 1675. une grande revolution en ce païs la pour cause de religion par un more tartufe mahometan: cequi causa la mort à un grand nombre de gens par des batailles et desolations de païs. J'en ay la Relation mss. faite sur les lieux par le commandant françois qui y etoit.[4]

. . .[a]

Croiez moi tous⟨jours ⟩[a] parfaitement votre

Address: For Mr John Locke at Mr Pawlings overagainst the plough in Litle Lincolns Innefeilds London

Endorsed by Locke: Toinard 16 Jul 98 Answered 15 Aug

[a] *Tear for seal; a dash or a single word may be lost in the first line.*

---

[1] Toinard later calls this animal the cibola; he continued with this project in 1700: nos. *2673*, *2693*, *2725*, etc.

[2] Holland.

[3] I have failed to identify the book or the map.

[4] A marabout who promised an age of plenty usurped the kingdom of Kayor from about 1677 to 1681: J. Barbot in A. and J. Churchill, *Collection of Voyages*, vol. v, 1732, 62.

2471. Locke to William Molyneux, 9 July 1698 (*2422, 2490*)

Some Familiar Letters, p. 271.

London, 9 July. 1698.

Dear Sir,

I am just come to London, where your former promise, and what Mr. Churchill since tells me, makes me hope to see you speedily. I long mightily to welcome you hither, and do remit to that happy time abundance that I have to say to you. For I am,

Dear Sir,

Your most affectionate humble servant,

John Locke.

2472. Locke to John Wynne, later bishop of Bath and Wells [July 1698] (*2386*)

Written on blank space of no. *2386* (B.L., MS. Locke c. 23, f. 133). Draft. Locke came to town on 8 July (pp. 443, 447); the draft was written apparently a few days later.

Sir

Methinks I am goeing to doe an insolent thing in writeing[a–] to tell you[–a] that I am come to town for it lookes as if I expected you shall take a journey of near fifty miles to come and meet me here. But what may one not be allowed to ⟨do⟩[b] to see a man one so much desires to be acquainted with and who makes soe obleigeing advances towards it. Your letter of January last and Mr Churchil's telling me you desired him to give you notice when I came to town will

2473. Locke to Nicolas Toinard, 14 July 1698 (*2470, 2476*)

Present ownership unknown. Transcribed from MS. copy, made *c.* 1871, in B.M., Add. MS. 28,836, f. 13. Printed in Ollion, pp. 130–1. Forwarded by Du Bos: p. 448; his letter to Toinard, 16/26 July (Lombard, no. 56).

London 14 Jul 9

Enfin Monsieur j'ay eu le bonheur de voir votre excellent am Monsr. du Bos et de l'assurer de mes très humbles respects et d mes services. S'il n'étoit pas de vos amis son propre merit ne mar

[a–a] *The words* writeing to you *are written above* tell you, *which is altered to* tell in yo *and left standing.* [b] *MS.* doeing; *the words* allowed to *are substituted for* excused f

queroit pas de me fair son tres humble serviteur Mais comme il est a vous je ne puis pas m'empecher de me plaindre de ce que je ne puis pas assez temoigner par mes services l'estime et la reconnoissance que j'ai pour vous. Quand j'arrivoi a Londres vendredi passè il n'etoit pas en ville depuis son retour j'ay tache tous les jours de le saluer à son logis sans l'y jamais trover et le seul fois que j'ay eu le bonneur de le voir encore a etè a mon logis où il me fit l'honeur de me venir voir. le seance de notre conscile tous les matins[1] et les affaires que j'ay eu avec plusieurs amis qui se hatent a partir pour les provinces en diligence pour l'election du prochain parliament[2] m'ont empechè de donner tout mon temps a Monsieur Du Bos comme j'aurois souhaitè, mais j'esper de trouver l'occasion de lui temoigner quel cas je fais de votre recommendation et de vos amis

Quod de sanitate mea adeo solicitus es pro tuâ facis amicitiâ. Severitatem novissimæ hiemis vix eluctatus ad urbem nuper accessi eo festinatius ne amicus tuus, cui omnem meam operam industriam officia, quantum in me esset destinaveram, mihi elaberetur.

Nudius Tertius obvius mihi factus est Dominus Dalon[3] qui multa de te et humanitate tuâ et de tuâ erga me amicitiâ prædicavit. Undique accipio benevolentiæ tuæ documenta, etiam ⟨coram⟩[a] testari ⟨liceat⟩[b] quali animo valetudinis meæ incommodis aliis id accessit quod impedivit quo minus te Parisiis salutarem et ⟨amplecterer⟩[c]. Felix ille dies si deus concessisset.

[a] *MS.* ceram; *probably an error of the transcriber's.* [b] *MS.* licet. [c] *MS.* mplectrer

---

You act in accordance with your friendship in being so solicitous about my health. Having scarcely surmounted the severity of last winter I came to town recently, the more hastily lest your friend for whom I had intended all my exertions, industry, and services, as much as there is in me, should escape me.

The day before yesterday I met Mr. Dalon[3] who was full of praise of you and your kindness and of your friendship for me. I receive proofs of your goodwill from all sides; would that I might in person bear witness with what feelings. It has been added to the other disadvantages of my ill health, that it has prevented me from greeting and embracing you in Paris. A happy day that, if God had granted it.

---

[1] The Board of Trade at this time sat generally on five mornings (Monday–Friday) in each week. With three exceptions Locke attended every sitting between 1 July and 20 October: the Board's Journal.

[2] Pursuant to the Triennial Act (6 and 7 W. and M. c. 2) parliament was dissolved by proclamation on 7 July; the new parliament was to meet on 24 August.

[3] A. Tassin d'Alonne.

Satis Ἁρμονικῶς tibi scribere non possum quia harmoniam non video. Angor sane animo quod vos non vobis.[1] Sed hæc raptim ut tradam Domino du Bos aliquid quod a me tibi transmittat.[2] Aliàs et pluribus ad te a tuo devotissimo.

JL

Metuo an intelligas quod linguâ Gallicâ in principio hujus epistolæ scripsi. Longæ dissuetudini ignoscendum est.

I cannot write to you harmoniously enough because I do not see a Harmony. I am truly vexed by your 'sic vos non vobis'.[1] But this in haste, so that I may deliver to Mr. du Bos something from me to transmit to you.[2] At another time and at greater length to you from your most devoted

JL

I am afraid that you may not understand what I have written in French at the beginning of this letter. Long disuse is to be forgiven.

2474. Dr. John Covel to Locke, 25 July 1698 (2467, 2477)

B.L., MS. Locke c. 7, ff. 166–7. Answers no. 2467.

Et cosi sarebbero forzati a rispondere i Peripatetici à quel Mostro, che nacque l'anno 1543 in Avignone; il quale nacque dopo tre dì, che era nata della medesima una bambina, la quale non visse un'hora, et era cosi fatto. Egli haveva la testa d'huomo da gl'orecchi in fuori, i quali insieme col collo, braccia, e mani erano di cane, et cosi il membro virile; le gambe et i piedi con un picciol segno di coda di dietro, e tutte le membra canine erano coperte di pelo lungo, et nero, come era il cane, col quale confessò poi esserci ghiaccuta[3] quella tal donna, che l'haveva partorito. Il restante del corpo dal collo infino alla cintura, era tutto d'huomo colle coscie et le gambe bianchissime; il quale mezzo abbajava et mezzo havrebbe voluto favellare, ma mugolava; et dicono, che egli fece delle braccia croce in atto di volersi raccomandare, il che ò non crederebbero i Peripatetici, ò direbbero, che fusse stato a caso. Visse tanto, che fu portato da Avignone a Marsilia al Christianissimo Rè Francesco il quale l'ultimo giorno di Luglio fece abbruciare la donna et il cane

[1] No. *398*.
[2] Locke took the letter on 16 July to Du Bos, who forwarded it with his letter of that date (16/26 July): Lombard, no. 56.
[3] An error for *giacciuta* (*giaciuta*).

insieme. Benedetto Varchi della generatione de' mostri. cap. 2do. stampat. in Fiorenza. 1560. 8vo.

Ulysses Aldrovandus in his book *de Monstris* (printed at Bonon. 1642. pag. 570d:) just mentions this Monster, of which Varchi speakes; but makes it two yeares after. *Non valdè dissimilem fœtum anno salutis supra sesquimillesimum quadragesimo quinto, tradit Magius in Miscellaneis natum esse Avenione partibus supernis humanis, et infernis caninis; ideoque Franciscus Galliarum rex matrem cum fœtu concremari jussit.*[1]

Christ College. jul. 25. 1698.

Worthy Sir

I have been ill this month, but could not forget your commands so soon as I could get into my study. I have sent you *Varchi*'s words, and a confirmation of the same story out of *Aldrovandus*. I heare Dr Tyson is writing something upon a *Homo sylvestris* which was brought from *Angola* and died here in England and he Anatomised it.[2] Had I lighted on this subject when we were last together, I could have told you of many things true on my own knowledge concerning it. Our Dr Moo⟨re⟩[a] and others would be puzled greivously, to tell us how the two *Plasticks* of the Dog and the woman combin'd to make *Varchi*'s monsters body, and it would be a more knotty question to ask what kind of Soul it had![3]

With due respect to you and all the Worthy family at Oates, I am,

Sir

Your very faithfull and most humble servant

JOH: COVEL.

Address: These To John Lock. Esqr. At Sir Franc. Masham's house in Oates. Essex.

Endorsed by Locke: Dr Covel 25 Jul 98

[a] *Page torn.*

[1] The book is *Monstrorum Historia*. 'Magius in his Miscellanea relates that in A.D. 1545 a not very dissimilar foetus was born at Avignon, having the upper parts human and the lower canine; Francis, king of France, accordingly ordered the mother to be burned along with the foetus.'

[2] Edward Tyson, M.D. (no. 600), *Orang-Outang, sive Homo Sylvestris, Or, The Anatomy of a Pygmie*, 1699. L.L., no. 3004.

[3] '. . . the *Frame of the Body*, of which I think most reasonable to conclude the *Soul her self* to be the more particular *Architect* . . . and that the *Plastick power* resides in her, as also in the Souls of Brute animals . . .': Dr. Henry More, 'The Immortality of the Soul', p. 101, in *A Collection of Several Philosophical Writings*, 1662.

2475. Ezekiel Burridge to Locke, 25 July 1698 (*1952, 2495*)

B.L., MS. Locke c. 4, ff. 207–8.

Honoured Sir

This day Sennight I sent away a piece of your Essay by a Citizen of this town, who has promis'd me to deliver it to Mr Churchil; it was to go with Mr Molyneux, but I wanted one day more to looke it over, after it was transcrib'd by several hands, which was occasion'd by Mr Molyneux's suddain resolution to go away. I hope tis now in the hands of my good friend Mr Churchil,[1] which it had not been, had it gone with Mr Molyneux; for I find he alter'd his resolution at Chester, goes first to the Bath, and afterwards to London.

I wou'd, Sir, have done you justice, if I cou'd; but I am very doubtful of my performances, therefore must intreat you to give your self the trouble to look it over, and to mark very freely what you find amiss: when you have done so I will use my best endeavours to amend it. it has had the approbation of some here, besides Mr Molyneux, (who I believe has much the same concern for it that you yourself have) but this will not give me ease till I have your censure.

Mr Molyneux will inform you what avocations have hinder'd its being now finish'd, or indeed long since, and will apolozise for me. I have told Mr Churchil what I propose to do, he I know will inform you. I wou'd willingly order matters so as that it might be finish'd about Michaelmas term;[2] I mean printed.

The Gentleman who is the bearer, is one of your admirers, and desir'd the favour of carrying a letter that he might have the Opportunity and happiness of seeing you. he has been bred among the dissenters, is a moderat, sober, and studious young gentleman, and is going to travell. It will be, I believe, the later end of August before Mr Molyneux go to London, none has a greater honour and respect for you than he has, and your good friends in London lately

[1] Burridge's Latin history of the Revolution (no. *1945*, etc.) was published by the Churchills in 1697.

[2] From 23 October to 28 November.

made him a hearty return, which he is throughly sensible of. I ask your pardon for this boldness, I am

Sir with all respect

Your most Humble and devoted servant

EZEKIEL BURRIDGE

Lord Chancellor's Dublin.[1]

July 25. 1698.

Address: To John Lock Esqre. at Mr Robert Pawlet's over against the Plow in Little Lincoln's Inn fields London

Endorsed by Locke: E: Burridge 25° Jul. 98

2476. NICOLAS TOINARD to LOCKE, 25 July/4 August 1698 (2473, 2483)

B.L., MS. Locke c. 21, f. 200. Answers no. 2473; answered by no. 2483.

+

ce 4. Aoust 98.

J'ay receu cele que vous m'avez envoiée par voie de Roüen[2] é aussi l'honneur ce votre derniere par m. Du bos. Il a bien perdu, monsieur, de vous avoir vu si peu; Il a neanmoins bien connu ceque vous valez. Il a emporté come un trezor tous les livres qui sont de vous, tant avouéz que non avouéz, é il ma mandé une chôze qui ne me surprend point, que vous passez pour un homme qui a sauvé l'Angleterre, à l'ocazion des monnoies. Je me fais d'avance un extreme plaizir de lire ceque vous avez imaginé pour un si grand euvre.

Je vous ay deja ecrit que vous devez dormir en repos ἁρμονικῶς. m. Dalonne m'a deja afligé par la nouvele que vous me repetéz que sans votre indisposition je vous orois embrassé ici. ce seroit la plus grande satisfaction que je pûsse ressentir. Votre grand emploi où vous etes si necessaire, ne me permet pas d'esperer ce bonheur lorsque le nouvel ambassadeur viendra.[3]

m. Du Bos m'a dit qu'il vous avoit parlé d'un voiage entrepris par ordre du Roi charles second en l'année 1669. pour la mer du sud. Le chef etoit un Aleman catolique apelé Char Henri[a] Olerke dans

[a] *This name written in margin;* Olerke *starts a new line.*

[1] John Methuen.

[2] Probably no. 2458.

[3] Edward Villiers, earl of Jersey; he arrived in Paris on 1/11 September.

le memorial qu'il en a donné le 28. Janvier 1670. au Gouverneur de Baldivia D. Pedro de montoya à qui il ala se rendre par delicatesse de consience. J'ay ce memorial en castillan, où sont les ordres qu'on lui donna en Angleterre, et je voudrois avoir s'il se pouvoit une relation de son voiage, car la fregaté é la Pinke qu'il avoit ont du revenir à Londres.[1] ce n'est que par curiozité ceque je vous en demande parceque je me suis depuis peu à traduire quelques voiages castillans des mers du sud.

Faites moi la grace de me mander s'il n'y a pas bien ôtre chôze du voiage de Drac que ceque l'on en a publié.[2] J'atens la Relation du Voiage fait nouvelement aux terres australes par les Holandois du cap de Bonne Esperance,[3] mais ils n'y oront pas mis tout. Je suis

Mr Morel l'Antiquaire[4] se porte bien.

Marked by Locke: Answered Aug. 15

2477. LOCKE to DR. JOHN COVEL, 26 July 1698 (*2474*, *2479*)

B.M., Add. MS. 22,910, ff. 476–7. Answered by no. *2481*.

London 26 July 98

Reverend Sir

I writ to you from Oates to acknowledg the favour of the book you sent me, and to desire the words of the Italian author concerning the monster. since which I have not had the honour of a letter from you. The commencement,[5] which has intervened, may be a sufficient reason for your silence in a matter that seemd noe more presseing than that. at least it has made me to forbear importuneing you again about it at soe busy a time. I here with

[1] See no. *629*. Du Bos made some inquiries about Don Carlos (Olerke, etc.) and learnt Narbrough's correct name before he met Locke; when they met Locke said that he did not remember Don Carlos: letters to Toinard of 8 and 24 July, N.S. (Lombard, nos. 52, 55). See further p. 491.

[2] Nothing new for Drake of any note had been published since 1628.

[3] The voyage of Willem de Vlamingh in 1696–7; an account of it was sent home from Batavia on 30 November 1697, N.S.: J. E. Heeres, *Het Aandeel . . . The Part borne by the Dutch in the Discovery of Australia, 1606–1765*, 1899, pp. 83–7. See also p. 479.

[4] Probably André Morell, 1646–1703, numismatist; he was a Swiss Protestant. *N.B.G.*

[5] The ceremony corresponding to the Act at Oxford. It was held on the first Tuesday in July and the preceding Monday: Chamberlayne (1694, p. 738); this year, 4 and 5 July.

now send you the booke I promised you at Oates, which I told you was then in the presse, and should be glad to have your opinion of it.[1] The discourse you then made me about the *Imprimatur* soe fully satisfied me that I was not mistaken in your freindship. that I shall not be unwilling you should put into my hands the means of vindicateing you to the world in that matter. I therefor desire you that you would now send me the letter that you offerd to write to me,[2] that I might publish concerning that affair. For though your name stands printed equaly amongst the others yet I shall be glad to have it in my power to clear you in that point, and to shew the world, that they ought not to involve you in the same opinion with the others which that memorable transaction when examind and looked into will be found to deserve. I am

Reverend Sir

your most humble servant

J LOCKE

You may be pleased to direct to me at Mr Pawlings overagainst the plough in Little Lincolns Inne feilds [a] London

Address: For the Reverend Dr Covell master of Christs Colledge in Cambridg

Endorsed by Covel: Mr Lock.

2478. J.-B. DU BOS to LOCKE, 27 July/6 August [1698] (*2489*)

B.L., MS. Locke c. 7, ff. 215–16. Printed by G. Bonno in *Revue de littérature comparée*, xxiv (1950), 484. Year from Locke's endorsement. For the writer see p. 407, n. 2.

a la haye Le 6 d Aoust

Je suis trop sensible monsieur a toutes les bonté que vous avez eues pour moy, pour attendre plus lontemps a vous en marquer ma reconoisance. vous ave fait des amitiez a bien des persones qui les meritoient mieux que moy, mais jamais vous nen fites a persone qui i fut plus sensible. Si jamais je fais un autre voyage dAngleterre, je vous prie destre persuadé que le plaisir de vous voir fera plus de la moitie du motif de mon voyage.

[a] *Page torn.*

[1] Perhaps Walter Cross, *The Taghmical Art* (pp. 136–7): pp. 564–5.
[2] The offer does not appear in the extant correspondence; the letter is the enclosure in no. *2481*.

Jarive ici Lundi[1] au soir. jestois debarqué le dimanche a neu heures du soir a Maeslandhus apres un trajet tres envieux qu m'obligea de coucher quatre nuits a bord du batiment.

Jay trouvé ici en arivant un livre nouvellement imprimé qu sapelle *observations dun voyageur en Angleterre.*[2] le livre ne merit point que vous le lisiez, car je ni ai rien apris, moy qui conois tre imparfaitement le pais.

lon a imprimé aussi ici une relation de lexpedition de Cartagen que lon donne pour estre de monsieur de Pointis.[3] jen doute beau coup, car quand je partis de Paris le relation de cet officier nestoi pas encore en estat de paroistre, et il ne devoit la faire imprime qu'au retour dun voyage quil alloit faire en Poitou. les plans qu sont dans cette relation me paroissent tres juste, autant que j puis me souvenir de ce que jay vu a Paris. je vous envoieré ce livr par la premiere comodite. je suis

Monsieur

Vostre tres humble et tres obeissant serviteur

DU BOS.

Address: To Master John Locke at mr Pavvlings over against The ploug in little lincolns Inne fields at London

Postmark: AV 4

Endorsed by Locke: du Bos 6. Aug. 98 Answered 15

2479. DR. JOHN COVEL to LOCKE, 28 July 1698 (*247 2481*)

B.L., MS. Locke c. 7, ff. 168–9.

Christ College. Cambridg. July. 28. 9

Worthy Sir

Understanding that it lyes in your way to contribute somethin to the preferring of this bearer, Mr Waterhouse,[4] I cannot bu give him this just commendation. He is a very Ingenious Yout and hath been a hard student and sober; and I will pronoun

[1] 25 July/4 August.

[2] Identifiable as H. M. de V. (Henri Misson de Valbourg), *Memoires et observati faites par un voyageur en Angleterre*, 1698. Notice in *Journal des Sçavans*, 16 Mar 1699 (pp. 204–5).

[3] Pointis (p. 175 n.), *Relation de l'expédition de Carthagène*, Amsterdam, 1698. S pp. 455–6.

[4] Benjamin Waterhouse; admitted to Christ's College 1692; matriculated 169 B.A. 1696; M.A. 1699: Venn.

him a very good schollar, of a free Education and far from Pedantry; I ever had a favour for him for his deserts which onely recommended him ever to my favour; what kindnesse you shew him, he will ever acknowledge with gratitude, and I assure you it shall ever thankfully be remembred by me. I should not be so prodigal in his prayse, or offer to promote him, or any at this time of the world, did I not know him so well, as to venture my own credit upon him.

Sir,

Your ever affectionate and humble servant

JOH: COVEL.

I sent you by the Coach the Extract out of *Varchi* and a passage out of Aldrovandus to the same story.

Address: These To the truely Worthy John Lock Esq.

Endorsed by Locke: Dr. Covel 28 July 98

2480. PIERRE COSTE to LOCKE, [July/August 1698] (*2285*, *2601*)

B.L., MS. Locke c. 7, f. 146. Printed by G. Bonno in *Revue de littérature comparée*, xxxiii (1959), 173–5. The date is fixed roughly by Locke's endorsement. The letter apparently follows a letter from Amsterdam to Coste, one written after 16/26 July (see postscript), but perhaps before no. *2478*. This gives a date about the end of July.

Coste's Amsterdam correspondent is probably Lagier de la Motte (p. 223): pp. 649, 650.

Monsieur,

Je viens de recevoir une Lettre de Mr. Marret, où il m'apprend que vous luy avez donné mes Cayers. Je vous en suis bien obligé. J'avois résolu avant cela de vous écrire, pour vous faire parte de quelques nouvelles que j'ai reçuës de Hollande. Le livre Latin de Mr. Huygens sur la pluralité des Mondes paroit en Hollande.[1] Mr. LeClerc l'a lû et le trouve fort bon. Il trouve seulement que Mr. Huygens conjecture un peu trop en voulant rechercher comment sont faits les Habitans de la Lune.

On vient d'imprimer une Relation de l'Expedition de Carthagene par Monsieur de Pointis. Elle contient six feuilles en grand *in 12*. Il y a deux Cartes, dont l'une est le plan de la Ville et Rade de

[1] Christiaan Huygens, *Κοσμοθεωρός, sive de Terris Coelestibus earumque Ornatu Conjecturæ*, 1698. L.L., no. 1537.

Carthagene et de ses Forts; l'autre est la Route que fit Pointis dans sa retraite, lors qu'il rencontra l'Escadre Angloise. Ces deux Cartes sont gravées à Paris au dépens de Mr. de Pointis, on en a envoyé les planches à Amsterdam, où cet Ouvrage a été imprimé. Mr. Pointis parle fort mal des Flibustiers qu'on vante tant dans d'autres relations.[1]

Il y a deja six feuilles imprimées de l'Harmonie de Mr. LeClerc. Elle sera de la même forme que son Pentateuque. La Paraphrase est un Discours suivi, divisé par Chapitres de la façon de Mr. LeClerc. Le P. Lamy a écrit à Mr. LeClerc qu'il faisoit aussi imprimer une Harmonie,[2] et qu'il ne croyoit pas que Mr. Toinard fit jamais imprimer la sienne pour le Public. Il parle dans cette Lettre de Mr. le Vassor.[3] Il dit qu'il étoit sorti depuis long temps de chez les Péres de l'Oratoire, qu'il avoit été autrefois fort lié avec le feu Archeveque de Paris[4] et le P. de la Chaize,[5] mais que la liaison avoit cessé depuis assez long-temps sans qu'il en sut la raison, et qu'il souhaiteroit qu'il put etre à son aise en Angleterre parce qu'ils avoient été autrefois bons amis. Voilà de l'humanité dans un Pretre pour une personne qui n'a pas les mêmes idées de religion que luy. La chose est digne de remarque pour la rareté du fait.

Mr. Guenellon attend avec impatience réponse à la Lettre qu'il vous a écrite.[6] Il a grande envie de vous envoyer son Fils. Il vous saluë aussi bien que Mademoiselle Guenellon. Le petit Enfant de Mr. LeClerc[7] est toûjours fort malade.

On dit bien du mal en Hollande de la Religion des Dames. On en soupçonne le veritable Traducteur, et on l'achete.[8]

On me mande de Hollande qu'on y a appris que Mad. le Cene[9] est arrivée en Angleterre depuis assez long temps.

Je vous prie, Monsieur, de faire tenir ce paquet à Mr. Marre[t] s'il n'est pas encore parti, ou de le faire mettre à la poste s'il es[t]

[1] p. 454.

[2] Father Bernard Lamy published his *Harmonia* in 1689: no. *1119*. He was now preparing his *Commentarius* on it. It was published in 1699. L.L., no. 1671. Lamy was a friend of Le Clerc's of long standing: Barnes, *Le Clerc*, p. 51.

[3] No. *1796*.

[4] François de Harlay-Chanvallon, archbishop of Paris 1671–95: *N.B.G.*

[5] François de la Chaise, S.J., confessor of Louis XIV from 1674 to 1709: ibid.

[6] Evidently a lost letter. Locke apparently wrote to him about August: p. 467.

[7] No. *1747*.

[8] p. 106. The translator was Coste.

[9] Presumably the wife of Charles Le Cène. She apparently brought Coste some books and a letter from a friend, with a transcript of the notice of the French translation of *Some Thoughts concerning Education* in the *Journal des Sçavans*, 21 April 1698: B.L., MS. Locke c. 7, f. 151.

parti. Je vous souhaite une bonne santé, et suis avec un profond respect,

Monsieur,

Votre très-humble et très-obeissant serviteur

COSTE

On a commencé d'imprimer la Traduction de votre Ouvrage le 26me. de Juillet.[1]

Endorsed by Locke: Coste Aug. 98

2481. DR. JOHN COVEL to LOCKE, 2 August 1698 (*2479, 2549*)

B.L., MS. Locke c. 7, ff. 170–1 and 163. Draft of the enclosure in B.M., Add. MS. 22,910, f. 463, on blank space in Locke's letter to Covel, 29 September 1697 (no. 2319). Answers no. 2477.

Christ Coll. Cambridge. Aug. 2d. 1698.

Worthy Sir

I have enclosed a letter to you, which I hope will answer fully what you desire, and do both you and my self justice. I have dated it as my first letter to you was, that if you think fit to use it, it may look as written when my first letter was, and just upon the coming out of Edw his book.

I have last week sent you the words of *Varchi* and also refer'd you to *Aldrovandus* for the same thing; if I knew what use you made of it, I might give you some other informations of like nature.

I made bold likewise to recommend to you an Ingenious Youth, Ben. Waterhouse, whome I took particular notice of in the College for a sober, studious youth, yet of a free and discerning spirit. if it lyes in your way to do him good, I pray assist him for my sake.

I sent the extract out of *Varchi* to *oates*, not knowing where else to direct; I hope it is come safe to your hands. I shall be very desirous of a frequent commerce of letters with you, as occasion offers, being

(Worthy Sir)

Your very humble servant

JOH. COVEL.

If the enclosed letter be not satisfactory, let me know wherein

[1] Coste's translation of the *Essay*.

I can farther make reparation to your or my own name and it shall be done.

I thak you for your book,[1] I shall look into it and then freely give you my opinion of it.

Address: These for John Lock Esquire at Mr Pawlings overagainst the plough in little Lincolns Inne fields London.

Endorsed by Locke: Dr Covel 2 Oct 98

[Enclosure:]

Christ College. Cambridge. Oct. 4th. 1697.

Worthy Sir

You might indeed be very justly offended at me when you saw my name to the *Imprimatur* of Mr Edwards his late book; and I must confesse that I am as much asham'd of it my self. But when I have inform'd You of the whole matter of fact, I hope you will rather pity my Misfortune, then count me guilty of the least disrespect to you. Mr Edwards is of my own year in the University, and I have known him a long time, though not so well as I know him now. He meeting me one day in the publick street, told me that he was going to the presse with a little book, which he had shew'd to the Vicechancellor and the Professor, and that they had licenc't it to be printed; and he ask't me to give him leave to adde my name also. I told him, if they had read and approved of his book, he might, if he pleased, make use of my name and so we parted. Now I do solemnly assure you that I never saw the book till long after it was printed, neither did I know the least syllable of its contents, or that you were in any manner concern'd, much lesse that you were so ill treated in it. I appeal to Mr Lock himself and every body else with whome I have been so long acquainted, whether they ever found in my Nature or Behaviour any rude or uncivil conversation, or that I ever approved of it in others; for I declare to all the world, that in all discourses (whether they be by word or pen) I do think good Manners as absolutely necessary as good Reasoning. And therefore I hope you will believe, that if I had been in the least conscious of your unhandsome usage in that Piece, I would not have so much injur'd my self or you, or so farre violated the common bonds of Freindship

[1] Perhaps Cross's *Taghmical Art*: p. 453.

betwixt us, as to have approved of it. This I must humbly offer as my Vindication to the world, and as my just Excuse to your self.

Worthy Sir,

Your most humble servant

JOH: COVEL.

Address: These To Joh: Lock. Esq. At Sir Fran. Masham's house in Oates Essex.

Endorsed by Locke: Dr Covel 4 Oct 97

2482. PHILIPPUS VAN LIMBORCH to LOCKE, 8/18 August 1698 (*2460*, *2485*)

B.L., MS. Locke c. 14, ff. 119–20. Copy by van Limborch in Amsterdam University Library, MS. R.K., III D 16, f. 206. English translation by T. Rees printed in *The Christian Reformer*, ii (1835), 28–9. Not received by Locke until March 1699; answered by no. 2557.

Vir Amplissime

Lator harum est Samuel Crellius, celebris illius Joannis Crellii nepos.[1] Abeuntem in Angliam non potui sine literis ad Te dimittere. Scio nomen multis esse exosum, ac hominem ipsum ob diversam de religione sententiam plurimis minus esse gratum. Ego vero ob dissensum in religione neminem odisse, sed quemcunque ob consensum in fundamento Christo amare didici. Te etiam Tolerantiæ Christianæ patronum novi: quare nec alloquium viri,

---

Excellent Sir,

The bearer of this is Samuel Crellius, a grandson of the celebrated Joannes Crellius.[1] As he is leaving for England I could not let him go without a letter to you. I know that the name is detested by many people and that the man himself is unacceptable to very many on account of difference of opinion in regard to religion. I assuredly have learnt to hate nobody on account of disagreement in religion but to love anyone soever on account of agreement in Christ the foundation. I know you also for an advocate of Christian toleration; so I am sure that you do not shudder at conversation with a man

---

[1] Joannes Crellius was one of the principal Socinian theologians, and was rector of the school at Raków from 1612 to 1633: *A.D.B.* His grandson Samuel Crellius, 1660–1747, studied under van Limborch and was also a notable theologian: ibid. Locke possessed a number of their books: L.L., nos. 723, 876–83a, 884, 1960. A brother of Samuel was a physician in London; he is probably Dr. Christopher Crell, a licentiate of the Royal College of Physicians (the Mr. Crell whom the third Lord Shaftesbury befriended, is not identifiable with Samuel Crellius). See further no. *2832*.

in variis licet tecum non sentientis, horrere certus sum. Vir est eruditus et pius. Quæ negotia ipsum in Angliam vocent penitus ignoro. Hoc scio, ipsum maximo tui videndi desiderio teneri. Quos ibi familiares habeat nescio. Tu pro tua prudentia facile perspicies quanta familiaritate excipiendus sit. Alias etiam Angliam vidit, et tunc Episcopo Sarisburiensi innotuit. An nunc hoc rerum statu, et recens edito contra negantes alicujus ex SS.Trinitatis personis deitatem edicto,[1] illi gratus sit futurus, valde dubito. Virum illum Reverendissimum calide satis edictum illud ursisse in postremis ipsius ad me literis non sine admiratione legi. Ego rotunde ac candide respondi, et qualis pro veritatis defensione zelus sit demonstrandus ostendi; nempe non igneus ille, qui edictorum severitate contradicentibus os obstruere molitur; sed qui argumentorum pondere de veritate convictos reddit. An παῤῥησία mea grata fuerit, incertus sum. Ego quod officii mei esse credidi scripsi. Res est maximi momenti, in qua dissimulatione uti non licet. Scio sententiam meam nullius esse in edicto aut procudendo, aut impediendo, ponderis: Attamen quoniam Episcopo suas in sinum meum querelas (uti scribit) effundere placuit, nec ab officio meo alienum duxi amico aperte quod sentio scribere. Ego

---

although he does not think like you about various things. He is a scholarly and devout man. I do not know at all what affairs call him to England; this I know, that he is possessed by a very great wish to see you. I do not know what friends he has there. You in virtue of your prudence will readily perceive with how great a degree of intimacy he is to be received. He has visited England on another occasion and he then became known to the bishop of Salisbury. I very much doubt whether he will be welcome to him in this present state of things and in view of the recently published edict against those who deny the godhead [*deitas*] of any one of the persons of the Trinity.[1] I read not without surprise in his last letter to me that that Right Reverend man urged that edict warmly enough. I replied roundly and candidly, and pointed out what kind of zeal should be shown in defence of the truth: that is, not that fiery sort that strives to stop the mouths of gainsayers by the severity of edicts; but that which convinces them of the truth by the weight of arguments. I am doubtful whether my freedom of speech was welcome. I wrote what I believed it was my duty to write. The matter is of the greatest importance; it is not permissible to dissimulate about it. I know that my opinion is of no weight in either fashioning or obstructing the edict; but since it pleased the bishop, as he writes, to pour his complaints

---

[1] The Blasphemy Act, directed against persons brought up as Christians who 'deny any one of the Persons of the Holy Trinity to be God'. For it and Burnet's letter see p. 424, n. 1.

valde metuo, ne edictum hoc novæ persecutionis initium sit futurum. A parvis initiis sensim crudelitas incrementum capit, cujus cursus, quando zelo pro divina gloria palliatur, frustra sistitur; indomitæ plebis impetu suffulta omnia perrumpit obstacula, donec ad ἀκμὴν pervenerit. Exemplorum plenæ sunt antiquiores et modernæ historiæ. Verum querelarum satis. Ego post ultimas meas Virum Magnificum non vidi: semel me ad se vocavit: Verum exiveram, et non nisi sera vespera domum redii. Quare alia occasio exspectanda fuit. Nunc aliquot hebdomadibus usus est valetudine minus secunda, quare illius compellandi, ac præsertim de materia subtiliore disserendi, nulla occasio fuit. Vale, Vir Amplissime: Salutat te uxor ac liberi mei. Salutem omnium nostrum nomine dices Domino ac Dominæ Masham, totique familiæ, cui omnia prospera ex animo vovemus.

Tui Amantissimus
PHILIPPUS A LIMBORCH

Amstelodami 18 Augusti

4
16 X 98
19

Address: Amplissimo Eximio ac Consultissimo Viro D. Joanni Locke Londini at Mr. Pawlings overagainst the plough in Little Lincolns Inne feilds.

Endorsed by Locke: P: Limborch 18 Aug 98 Answered Mar. 5

---

into my bosom I considered it not inconsistent with my duty openly to write to a friend what I think. I greatly fear that this edict may be the beginning of a new persecution. Cruelty increases little by little from small beginnings; its course, when it is cloaked with zeal for the glory of God, is checked in vain; supported by the violence of the untamed rabble, it breaks through all obstacles until it reaches the highest pitch. Older and modern histories are full of examples. But enough of complaints. I have not seen the Magnifico since my last letter; he summoned me once, but I had gone out and did not return home until late in the evening; so I have had to await another opportunity. He has now for some weeks been in poor health, so that there has been no opportunity of speaking to him and especially of discussing a rather subtle subject. Good-bye, excellent Sir; my wife and children send you their greetings. Please greet Sir Francis and Lady Masham and the whole family from all of us; we send them our heartiest wishes for their prosperity.

Your most affectionate
PHILIPPUS VAN LIMBORCH

Amsterdam 18 August
1698

2483. Locke to Nicolas Toinard, 15 August 1698 (*2476, 2497*)

The Historical Society of Pennsylvania, Philadelphia. Transcribed from photostat. Answers nos. *2470* and *2476*; answered by no. *2497*.

London 15 Aug. 98

Je vous remercie Monsieur de vos deux obligeants lettres du 16 Juillet et du 4 du courant. Ce Gentlehomme qui vous rendra cellui ci m'apporta une de ces deux, Je ne pas eux pourtant le honeur de le voir jusques à ce matin et je ne pouvois pas obtenir de lui ni son nome ni son logè, il m'a seulement marquè quil partiroit en deux jours. pardonnez moi dunc si parmi bien des affairs dont je suis à present empechè de tout costè, Je ne laisse pas de vous faire mes reconnossances dans une jargon qui vous doibt bien rebuter, si vous ne l'enterpretez pas par la connoissance que vous avez de mon cœur pulstost que par les paroles que vous lirez

Je ne doubt pas que le laine de bufs de la riviere de Missisipi put servir aussi a fair des chappeaux aussi bien que des bas Mais les ouvriers par tout, au moins chez nous, sont fort dificiles à se tourner à quelque chose de nouveau

De opere musico je suis et je serai tousjours fort impatient jusqueaceque je le voi tout a fait achevè

Je m'assure que vous ne prendrais pas la pein de traduir quelque chose qui n'est pas excellent dans son gendre c'est pourquoy j'attend avec beaucoup d'impatience cette relation que vous avez soub main.

En Monsieur du Bos vous m'avez procurè un ami semblable à vous meme qui enterpret tout en ma faveur et qui fait grand cas de mes bagatelles. c'est vous qui l'a infectè par un prevention en ma faveur En veritè Monsieur parmi tant d'obligations que je vous a, il n'y a pas une apres l'honeur de votre amitiè qui me touch tant au cœur que son amitie dont je suis redevable entirement à vous. Je vous prie de me conserver ce tresor que vous m'avez procurè avec tant de bontè

La relation du voyage du fregate de Charles Henri Olerke m'est inconue et je croi qu'elle n'a jammais parue mais je ne manquerai pas de la rechercher par tout et si je la puis deterrer vous en orez les nouvelles.

Du voiage de Drake je croy qu'il n'y a pas otre chose que ce qu'est publiè, pourtant je chercerai parmi les Curieuses

Comme vous prenez plaisir de traduir les voiages et relations Espagniols je serois bien aise que vous voudriez bien traduire Navaretti de China[1] en langue chrestienne. Je suis parfaitement

Monsieur

Votre tres humble serviteur

JOHN LOCKE

Je vous prie de fair mes tres humbles baises maines a Monsieur du Bos et au Capitain marin.

Address: A Monsieur Monsieur Toinard chez Monsieur des Noyers devant l'Espèe royale dans la rüe Mazarin à Paris

Endorsed by Toinard: 15. Aoust. 98.

2484. EDWARD CLARKE and LOCKE to SIR THOMAS WILLIS, 2 September 1698

B.L., MS. Locke c. 24, f. 286. Draft written by Locke. Sir Thomas Willis, *c.* 1614–1701; created a baronet 1641; of Fen Ditton, Cambridgeshire: G.E.C., *Baronetage*, ii. 148. The letter relates to the Masham Trust: nos. 1968, 2798, 2812.

London 2 Sept 1698

Sir

The money that you have given us bond for being in trust for the Lady Masham and consequently hers in reality, we have thought it convenient, she being of the same minde, that the interest of that mony as well as other parts of that estate which is entrusted to us should, as it becomes due, be paid into her hands. we therefor desire you, that what shall be due from you to us on this account you would hereafter pay to my Lady Masham or her order as to our receiver authorized by us to receive and discharge you for the same we rest

Sir

your most obedient servants

Endorsed by Locke: E: Clarke and JL to Sir Th: Willis 2 Sept. 98 Trust

[1] Friar Domingo Fernández de Navarrete, *Tratados historicos, politicos, ethicos, y religiosos de la monarchia de China: descripcion breve de aquel imperio* . . . [etc.], Madrid, 1676. A summary in Italian appeared in A. Anzi, pseud. (V. Zani), *Il genio vagante*, 1693, iv. 495–511. An English translation of the greater part of book vi appeared in A. and J. Churchill's *Collection of Voyages and Travels*, 1704. There is a full account of the book in Navarrete, *The Travels*, edited by J. S. Cummins from the Churchills' translation, Hakluyt Society, 2nd ser., vols. cxviii–cxix, 1962.

There is nothing to show how Locke heard of the existence of the book. It is unknown when the Churchills first considered publishing a collection of voyages. Here Locke appears to be inquiring on his own account. See further pp. 569, 603, 615, 731–2.

2485. PHILIPPUS VAN LIMBORCH to LOCKE, 2/12 September 1698 (*2482, 2494*)

B.L., MS. Locke c. 14, ff. 121–2. Copy by van Limborch in Amsterdam University Library, MS. R.K., III D 16, f. 207. Printed, with omissions and some alterations (*inter alia* Crellius becomes 'N.N.'), from the copy in *Some Familiar Letters*, pp. 426–8; the passage 'Hisce feriis . . . Epist. XXXIX. XL et XLI.', in Ollion, p. 216 n. Answered by no. 2498.

Vir Amplissime

Post ultimum meum cum Viro Magnifico colloquium nulla ipsum conveniendi occasio fuit: Aliquamdiu febricula laboravit. Verum etsi aliquoties eum conveniam, nihil ulterius ex ipso elicere spero. Hisce feriis canicularibus apud nos aliquot diebus fuit D. Volderus, in Academia Lugduno-Batava Philosophiæ Professor:[1] illi sermones meos cum Viro Magnifico narravi; addidi, me desiderare audire, quibus ille argumentis unitatem entis per se existentis sibique sufficientis adstructurus sit. Respondebat ille, se jam a pluribus annis similes cum ipso habuisse sermones; sed alia illi non esse argumenta præter illa quæ jam mihi dixit: Diu illum circa hanc quæstionem hæsisse; illum etiam eandem proposuisse Benedicto de Spinoza, qui ad eam etiam responderit, eaque responsa inter Epistolas ejus exstare, Epist.XXXIX. XL. et XLI.[2] Addebat, minime sibi probari Viri Magnifici argumentationem, qua

Excellent Sir,

Since my last conversation with the Magnifico there has been no opportunity of meeting him; he has for some time been suffering from a slight fever. But although I may meet him at various times I do not hope to elicit anything further from him. During these last August holidays Mr. de Volder, professor of philosophy in the University of Leyden,[1] was with us for some days. I told him about my talks with the Magnifico; I added that I want to hear with what arguments the Magnifico will establish the unity of a being existing of itself and sufficient to itself. Mr. de Volder replied that he had had similar talks with him during some years; but the Magnifico had no arguments other than those that he had already stated to me. The Magnifico [he said] had been long at a stand about this question; he had also proposed it to Benedict de Spinoza, who also answered it, and his replies are extant among his letters, epist. xxxix, xl, and xli.[2] Mr. de Volder added that he did not approve of the Magnifico's reasoning, by which he contends that, if we suppose that thought existing of itself is given, and further,

[1] Nos. *651*, *1511*.

[2] Spinoza's letters were published in his *Opera Posthuma*, 1677. These three are numbered 34–6 in modern editions. For Hudde as addressee see Spinoza, *Œuvres*, trans. and ed. C. Appuhn, 1907–29, iii. 382–3.

contendit, si supponamus dari cogitationem per se existentem, et præterea materiam seu extensionem, quod neutra ullam alterius possit habere cognitionem: Extensionem quidem ⟨(aiebat)⟩[a] nullam habituram cognitionem Cogitationis: fieri autem non posse, quin Cogitatio cognitionem sit habitura Extensionis: Quia cum Cogitatio per se existat, sibique sit sufficiens, etiam est infinita: ac proinde vi infinitæ suæ cogitationis necessario cognoscit Extensionem existentem. Sed cum regererem, Virum Magnificum improbare methodum, qua Enti per se existenti sibique sufficienti probantur inesse alia attributa, antequam probatum sit, illud esse tantum unicum; Respondebat: Necessario de tali ente debere affirmari, illud esse infinitum, verum in sua natura: Cogitationem quidem esse infinitæ scientiæ, materiam infinitæ extensionis, siquidem per se existat. Sed inde sequi colligebam, etiam alia attributa posse probari: probata enim infinitate, etiam probari posse alia illi inesse, sine quibus infinitas concipi nequit. Quod non negavit. Atque ita mecum sentire videbatur, unitatem ejusmodi entis tali methodo frustra quæri, sed oportere thesin secundam esse tertiam. Hæc paucis Tibi significare volui, ne alia penes Virum Magnificum esse argumenta credas, neque ea frustra exspectes.

[a] *Supplied from van Limborch's copy.*

---

matter or extension, neither can have any knowledge of the other: extension, he said, will indeed have no knowledge of thought; but it cannot be but that thought will have knowledge of extension, because since thought exists of itself and is sufficient to itself it is also infinite; and accordingly in virtue of its being infinite necessarily knows that extension exists. But when I [van Limborch] rejoined that the Magnifico rejected a way by which other attributes are proved to appertain to a being existing of itself and sufficient to itself before it is proved that that being is unique, he [de Volder] replied that it ought necessarily to be affirmed of such a being that it is infinite, infinite, that is, in its own nature; that it ought to be affirmed that thought is of infinite knowledge, matter of infinite extension, inasmuch as they exist of themselves. But I [van Limborch] inferred that it follows thence that other attributes also can be proved; for infinity having been proved other attributes, without which infinity cannot be conceived, can also be proved to appertain to that being. Which he [de Volder] did not deny. He therefore seemed to think with me that the unity of a being of that kind would be sought in vain by such a way, but that the second proposition ought to be the third. I wanted to intimate this to you in a few words lest you should think that the Magnifico has other arguments and should await them in vain. I should think that the Magnifico has prescribed for himself this way of investigating the truth, and that when he himself is unable to find

Crediderim ego, Virum Magnificum hanc sibi investigandæ veritati præscripsisse methodum, et cum ipse quæ sibi satisfaciant argumenta invenire nequeat, ea apud alios quærere. Difficile mihi videtur probatu, ens necessitate suæ naturæ existens esse tantum unum, antequam ex necessaria existentia alia, quæ eam necessario comitantur, attributa deduxeris. Si Vir Magnificus ea habeat, operæ pretium foret ea erudito orbi communicare.

Nuper Professor van der Waeijen tractatulum quendam Rittangelii edidit, illique prolixam ac virulentam contra D. Clericum præfixit præfationem, qua explicationem initii Euangelii Joannis a D. Clerico editam refutare conatur.[1] Ego æquitatem et judicium in illo scripto desidero. In fine etiam contra me insurgit, verum paucis, quia in Theologia mea Christiana scripsi Burmannum pleraque, quæ in sua Synopsi Theologiæ habet de Omnipotentia divina, descripsisse ex Spinozæ Cogitatis Metaphysicis.[2] Ille non negat, sed contendit Burmannum propterea non esse Spinozistam;

---

arguments that satisfy himself he seeks them from other persons. It seems to me difficult to prove that a being existing by the necessity of its own nature is only one before you have deduced from necessary existence other attributes which necessarily accompany it. If the Magnifico has such arguments it would be worth the effort to communicate them to the scholarly world.

Professor van der Waeyen has recently published a certain short treatise by Rittangel, and has prefixed to it a lengthy and virulent preface against Mr. Le Clerc, in which he tries to refute the explanation of the beginning of the Gospel of St. John that Mr. Le Clerc has published.[1] I find fairness and judgement wanting in what he has written. At the end he rises against me also, but in few words, because I wrote in my *Theologia Christiana* that Burman had copied the greater part of what he has about divine omnipotence in his *Synopsis Theologia* from Spinoza's *Cogitata Metaphysica*.[2] He does not deny this, but contends that Burman is not on that account a Spinozist, a thing which I have nowhere written. Neither of us will make any reply to so silly a writer. A few weeks ago I gave Samuel Crellius, a grandson of the celebrated Joannes Crellius, a letter to convey to you, but as yet he is staying in Rotter-

---

[1] Johannes van der Waeyen (Waeijen), 1639–1701; professor of theology at Franeker from 1679: *N.N.B.W.* The book is J. S. Rittangel (d. 1652; *Jewish Encyc.*), *Libra Veritatis et de Paschate Tractatus*, with prefixed van der Waeyen's *Dissertatio de Λόγῳ adversus Johannem Clericum*, Franeker, 1698. Notice in *Acta Eruditorum*, xvi (1698), 455–9.

[2] The attack is in the *Dissertatio*, pp. 177–95. According to Le Clerc it originated in a remark in his (Le Clerc's) defence made by van Limborch: *Parrhasiana* (p. 637) p. 408. For Burman and his *Synopsis* (1st ed., 1671) see p. 353. Spinoza published his 'Cogitata metaphysica' in 1663 as part of his treatise on Descartes. Van Limborch remarks on Burman's copying them in *Theologia Christiana*, II. xv. 6–9. For van Limborch's answer to van der Waeyen see pp. 487, 518–19, etc.; for a further attack on van Limborch by Burman's sons, nos. *2724*, *2742*.

quod ego nusquam scripsi. Neuter nostrum tam inepto scriptori quicquam reponet. Dedi ante paucas hebdomadas Samueli Crellio, celeberrimi Joannis Crellii nepoti, literas ad Te perferendas: Verum ille adhuc Roterodami commoratur. Vir est eruditus, et moribus probatis. Non tu ex eorum es genere, qui viri, non per omnia tecum in religione sentientis, alloquium horreas. Ille quando advenerit de statu nostro plura tibi dicere poterit. Hac hebdomade D. Guenellonus me tuis verbis salutavit, quodque postremis meis literis nondum responderis excusavit.[1] Gratissimæ mihi semper sunt literæ tuæ, et quanto crebriores tanto gratiores: sed non sum importunus adeo exactor, ut cum meliorum laborum dispendio eas a te flagitem. Scio responsi tarditatem non oblivioni mei, sed negotiis quibus obrueris adscribendam. Spem fecit Guenellonus nonnullam profectionis tuæ instante hyeme in Galliam, et reditus tui in Angliam per Hollandiam nostram. Si id confirmandæ valetudini tuæ inservire queat, opto summis votis, ut iter hoc perficias, ut tui post tam diuturnam absentiam videndi et amplectandi, ac fortasse ultimum vale dicendi, occasio detur. In civitate nostra jam ab aliquot diebus est cognatus quidam tuus, tibi cognominis, filius Samuelis Locke mercatoris Londinensis;[2] sæpius adest filio

---

dam. He is a scholarly man and of excellent character. You are not a man of the kind who shudder at conversation with a man who does not think like them about everything relating to religion. When he arrives he will be able to tell you a great deal about the state of things with us. This week Mr. Guenellon gave me your greetings and made your excuses for your not having answered my last letter.[1] Your letters are always very welcome to me, and the more frequent, so much the more welcome; but I am not so importunate an exactor as to demand them from you at the cost of better labours. I know that the slowness of the answer is to be ascribed not to forgetfulness of me but to the affairs with which you are overwhelmed. Guenellon gave us some hope of your journeying to France this coming winter and returning to England by way of our Holland. If that can serve to strengthening your health I wish with all my heart that you may make this journey, so that an opportunity may be given [us] of seeing and embracing you after so lengthy an absence, and perhaps of saying a last farewell. A certain kinsman of yours, of your surname, a son of Samuel Locke, a London merchant,[2] has been for some days now in our city; he is rather often with my son. I strongly approve of this young man's character. I am glad by services of any kind to your relation to be able in some measure to show my love and regard for you. I should like him to offer me more opportunities

---

[1] See p. 456.
[2] John Lock: p. 499 n. The father had befriended Frans van Limborch in London: 373.

meo. Juvenis illius mores mihi valde probantur. Gaudeo me qualibuscunque officiis erga consanguineum tuum aliquatenus ostendere posse amorem ac observantiam erga te meam. Velim eum plures de se bene merendi occasiones mihi præbere; ad omnia officia me paratissimum esset experturus. Vale Vir Amplissime. Salutem Tibi, ac Dominæ Masham totique familiæ, dicit uxor, filia ac filius, imprimis ego

Tui Amantissimus
PHILIPPUS A LIMBORCH

Amstelodami 12 Septembris

Inserendum Historiæ Inquisitionis pag. 109. post lin. 38. Si Inquisitores in officio negligentes aut remissiores sint,[a] pœnam suspensionis ab ingressu Ecclesiæ per quadrimestre temporis spatium eo ipso incurrere decrevit Synodus Senensis, anno Domini CIↃCCCCXXIII. celebrata; mandatque eadem Synodus, *ut in Provincialibus seu Synodalibus Conciliis pro modo culpæ seu negligentia contra tales negligentes ultra prædictam pœnam provideatur de remedic*

[a] *Van Limborch cites in the margin* Richerii Hist. Concil. lib. III. cap. I. § 1. p. 9.[1]

of deserving well of him; he would find me fully prepared for services o every kind. Good-bye, excellent Sir. My wife, daughter, and son sen greetings to you and to Lady Masham and the whole family, as I do mysel

Your most affectionate
PHILIPPUS VAN LIMBORCH

Amsterdam 12 September
1698

For insertion in my *Historia Inquisitionis*, page 109, after line 38. Th Council of Siena held in the year of our Lord 1423 decreed that, if Inquisitor are negligent or too remiss in their duty, they thereby incur the penalt of suspension from entering a church for the space of four months; and th same Council orders 'that in Provincial or Synodal Councils a suitabl remedy be provided over and above the aforesaid penalty against suc negligent persons proportionably to their offence of negligence, notwith

[1] Edmond Richer, *Historia Conciliorum Generalium*, Cologne, 1680–1. The passag is slightly modified to form the quotation. History of the council in C. J. von Hefel *Conciliengeschichte*, 1855–90, VII. ii. 389–409.

opportuno, privilegiis, ⟨exemptionibus⟩[a], *consuetudinibus et statutis contra præmissa disponentibus, non obstantibus quibuscunque.* Sed[1] paucos contra hoc decretum delinquere, et aut negligentia, aut lenitate pœnam suspensionis incurrere persuasus sum; cum omnis mansuetudo ab hoc tribunali exulet, et quicunque munere hoc Inquisitoris ornentur statim omnem, non dico misericordiam, sed humanitatem exuant.

D. Clericus, quem mox conveni, plurimum Te salvere jubet. Brevi literas ad Te dare constituit.

Address: For John Locke Esqur. at Mr. Pawlings overagainst the plough in Little Lincolns Inne feilds London

Postmark: SE 12

Endorsed by Locke: P: Limborch 12 Sept 98 Answered Oct. 18

[a] *MS. exemtionibus*

---

standing any privileges, exemptions, customs and statutes whatsoever determining to the contrary'. But[1] I feel sure that few offend against this decree and either by negligence or by lenience incur the penalty of suspension, since all clemency is banished from this tribunal and whoever is honoured with this office of Inquisitor immediately puts off all, I shall not say mercy but human nature.

Mr. Le Clerc, whom I met recently(?) bids me send you his best regards. He intended to write to you shortly.

2486. Samuel Bold to Locke, 10 September 1698 (*2312, 2493*)

B.L., MS. Locke c. 4, ff. 23–4.

Steeple. Sept: 10th. 1698.

Honoured Sir

Your Condescention, and Kindneses to me when I was in the City, and the concern you have manifested for my Health (as I understand by Mr Churchill) when you heard I was under some Indisposition, upon my returne into the Country, are so very surprizing,[2] I hope you will excuse my want of words to express my gratitude, and relate the sense I have of the obligations I am under to you. I bless God, I am now in such a state of Health, as I have usually enjoyed of late in this place. In a little time after I had recovered

[1] Van Limborch resumes.

[2] Probably in the obsolete sense, captivating: *O.E.D.*

some strength, I began to read Mr Jenkins's *Reasonableness an certainty of the Christian Religion.*[1] In reading over his preface, whicl is not very short, I found a quotation out of your Essay[2] etc whicl He pretended (as some others have done) to finde fault with, and t write two pages almost, as a confutation of what you had said This put a stop (for that time) to my reading in that Book. for was willing (if I could) to obtain a distinct knowledge of his Argu ments and Reasons, and of their ful strength, that I might the mor fully perceive wherein your oversight did lie, And that I migh give you some proof how much I esteem your condescending t honour me to so great a Degree, as to admit me to be of the num ber of those, to whom you vouchsafe the name of Friend; by repre senting to you clearly, how a person might perceive that ther was some Defect and weakness in that part of your book. For I ar perswaded, you would receive It as a greater Instance of Friendshi from anyone, to be fairly acquainted with a mistake that may trul be discovered in your writings, than to have all the Trivial objec tions answered by Him, which have bin either Invidiously, o through want of a Just Consideration, published against you Books. I did first of all read over all He said upon that point, then read every sentence distinctly by It self, and paused awhil at the end of every one of them, and thought as wel as I could o every branch, but could not for my heart bring any thing to be upon What He had quoted out of your Essay, nor indeed to hav any relation to what you had delivered. But at last, fearing m thoughts might not this way be steady enough, and that the might be stil something of moment, which I had overlook'd, c had escap'd my observation, I took pen and paper in hand, resolvin to try if I could this way fix my Attention more closely, and s thorough what He had offered upon the point, for peoples convi tion, and satisfaction. In This way I succeeded so Ill, I was rath more at a loss (if it were possible) than I was before, to make ar part of his Discourse pertinent. This Disapointment occasione my calling to minde what I could, of what others had said again the same passage, to see if by that means I could perceive wh

[1] By Robert Jenkin (*D.N.B.*), at this time a non-juror; published in 1698.

[2] 'We have the Ideas of Matter and Thinking . . . the good pleasure and boun of the Creator': *Essay*, IV. iii. 6; quoted by Jenkin, preface, pp. 46–7. Bold complai that Locke's critics omitted the immediately succeeding passage, 'For I see contradiction . . . that Eternal first thinking Being': *Some Considerations* (p. 471, n. pp. 2–3. This succeeding passage was added in the second edition of the *Ess* The passage is discussed by Aaron: pp. 144–8.

was amiss in that passage of yours, which so many have bin medling with, and in which they would have the world believe, there is so obvious an Error, they can discern It at the first veiw. My thoughts being thus emploied, and having moved from what one had said, to consider what others had said on the subject, They at last gave me the slip, and fixed on another passage in your Essay, which hath bin several times reflected on, my pen being all the time in my hand. It dropt upon my paper, the thoughts I happened to fasten upon. In the end I resolved to transcribe the greatest part of what I had thus accidently writ; but would alter the method, and transcribe that first, which I writ last. And that you may see, I do not forget you, whilst at this distance from you, I have sent two sheets (which is all I can transcribe timely enough to send by my neighbour, by whom I send this) to mr Churchil, with my desire to Him, to deliver them to you;[1] And which I requeast you to look over, if you can obtain so much leasure from weightier affaires. I do not desire you to give your self the trouble to write to me; But if you please to let me know by mr Churchil, whether I do in any part reach the strength of the objections I seem to reply unto, It wil be acknowledged a particular Favour to

Your most Humble and Obliged servant

SA: BOLD.

The remainder of my papers when transcribed, wil not be above one sheet more.

I have not had time, or not bin in a condition to think on the points we spake of, when I was at London, but I hope in a little time to apply my minde to them.

Address: To the Most Honoured Mr Locke

Endorsed by Locke: S: Bold 10 Sept. 98 Answered 21

2487. JOHN BARON to LOCKE, 12 September 1698

B.L., MS. Locke c. 3, ff. 158–9. I have failed to identify the writer.

The citations of the *Essay* are of the second or the third edition, which have the same pagination. The citations in the notes, by book, etc., apply,

[1] The papers are identifiable as part of the draft of Bold's *Some Considerations on the Principal Objections and Arguments which have been Publish'd against Mr. Lock's Essay of Humane Understanding*, which was published about May 1699: p. 626. Bold had difficulties in writing it: pp. 484–5, etc. His manuscript is lost, but some notes made about it by Locke survive: B.L., MS. Locke c. 27, f. 147.

except as noted, to the fourth and fifth as well as to the second and third editions.

Honoured Sir,

Tis a considerable time since I became first acquainted with your works: in which I found that clearness of thought, and force of Reason; that justly recommended 'em to my most serious and frequent consideration. And the more I apply my thoughts this way, the greater is that value of them, and esteem of their Author, which I feel impress'd upon my mind. So great has been the benefit which has accrued to me hereby, that I should have been much pleased with an opportunity of giving reall demonstrations of my Respects. For your greater light has so happily assisted the glimmerings of mine, scatter'd the thick clouds that coverd it, (occasioned by idle and insignificant words (or rather sounds) too usually admitted without reason and necessity, and held by the old tenures of Prescription and custom) that my way to true and solid Knowledge being freed from the many incumbrances, which before seem'd surprizing,[1] I have been inabled to make more large and delightfull advances towards truth; and to maintain an earnest desire and endeavour after that which is more removed from my view. Hence it is, Worthy Sir, that I have long coveted after a more assured understanding of some things mentioned in your Excellent Essay of Hum: Understanding. And because I fail of desired satisfaction from my own thoughts, or other assistances which my state and occasions allow me, I have presumed to present to your view an account of the nature and ground of my doubts referring it to your candid opinion in this case, whether they have weight or no. Concerning which if I could partake of your thoughts and learn your solution I should think my self infinitely obliged and now have the prospect of it as an happiness not only undeserv'd, but too great for me to enjoy.

1 I am not certain whether Extension nay Solidity it self should be looked upon as proper and peculiar to Body. If Extension be restrained as in page 81.[2] there can be no difficulty. But if the Idea be inlarged, as I incline to think it should, and be made to be Space as considered between the parts of any essence, then I think other

[1] Captivating, as on p. 469.

[2] II. xiii. 3. In the second and third editions Locke distinguishes between space and extension, the latter belonging to body or matter, while space may be considered without it. This differentiation is suppressed in the fourth and fifth editions.

Beings are not uncapable of it; but really have it. To conceive of a spirit without any expansion, extension or bigness, yet existing in a space, seems very difficult, if not impossible. If this be taken away, the unavoidable consequence will be, that spirits are in Puncto Mathematico: which is so odd and ridiculous a Chimæra, that no man of reason and thought can imagin. And how irreconcileable this notion of a Spirit is with the Divine Immensity (which I look upon to be nothing else than infinite space, expansion or *as in the div: essence* extension) DesCartes well observed; and chose rather to intrench upon the prerogatives and perfections of God; than quit his beloved notion.[1] If it be said that extension implys parts, and that these are incompatible to the idea of a Spirit; I think it may easily be answered: that Parts are either distinct Individuall things, concurring to make up the essence of the whole: which are usually calld Physicall Parts: or else certain Portions of the same Individuall, really and physically uncompounded; set out by the mind at pleasure: which are Mathematicall or Logicall Parts. Extension allways infers the possibility of these: and I think not of the former. And therefore I see not the justice and force of this inference, vizt. If a thing be extended it must be divisible. Reall Divisibility, in my opinion, being the necessary consequence of Reall Composition; and this only. For Divisibility agreeing to the whole, as consisting of parts, or to the parts considered in union; if a thing be not made up of parts, it has not parts that are divisible or separable from one another, and consequently the whole can't sustain that denomination. I know there is a Divisibility corresponding to Mathematicall Composition: but this is not to be considered in this present case. I do not see therefore that the supposition of a spirit of an inch, foot, yard square, or of any other assignable mesure of extension, implys any contradiction; however extravagant it may seem to some: Or that to ascribe an unmesureable extension to the most perfect Being imports any thing inconsistent with reson, or that revelation he hath been pleased to give us of himself: But that on the contrary tis necessarily to be granted to accommodate the plain and obvious suggestions of both. And indeed I see not why Solidity may not be applyed to other things than Body; if duly abstracted from the circumstances of sensation, according to what is asserted in the beginning of your Ch. of Identity. 'For—We not conceiving it

[1] *Les Principes de la philosophie*, i. 23.

possible, that 2 things of the same kind should exist in the same place at the same time; rightly conclude that whatever exists any where at any time, excludes all of the same kind, and is there its self alone[1]—And this is the notion of Solidity. For I can not expect that Sensibility will be thought necessary to be taken in to form its Idea. Nor Resistance, as it signifys renitence,[2] reluctance, active opposition, subscribing to your conjecture, Essay p. 124.[3] that Matter is wholly destitute of active power. Resistance in an improper sence as it is taken for an incapacity of any thing to admitt another, of the same sort, into the place which it possesses, whilest it possesseth it; may be used here, and equally applyed to spirits. And here the place just even now quoted out of your excellent Essay gives me an opportunity of proposing this to your thoughts, Whether Spirit and Body being compared, it be not more agreeable to truth to say, that Bodys are penetrable and Spirits penetrative; than that dull and unactive Matter is impenetrable by, and penetrative of Spirit.

So that if Extension and Solidity be looked upon as common to Spirit and B., and consequently Figure, which is nothing but finite or bounded Extension, Divisibility not being well-grounded in Extension, and Motion granted by you to be indifferent to both (Essay p. 164.)[4] the proper and peculiar notion of B. remains in the dark, and still to be sought after.—Upon the Premises 'tis a Qu: which I would willingly be resolved in, Whether we have any other distinguishing Idea of B. than that which consists of these common to it with Spirit, together with the negation of the propertys of Spirit, which are Power of thinking and willing with their modes? If so, then I think tis better defin'd an Incogitative Being (as in your chapter of the Existence[a] of a God)[5] than an Extended or solid substance. So Spirit and B. will differ as more and less. Thus what you have allready cleared p 163[6] vizt. that we have as clear Ideas of Spirit as B. will be more firmly established. For B contains nothing but what Spirit has with some addition.

II Whether Distance (and I may add Amplitude) and Capacity mentioned Essay p. 81.[7] be not there considered[b] S. Modes of

[a] *MS.* Ex^{ce} [b] *Followed by* n?; *possibly a false start for* S.

[1] The quotation ends here; it is from II. xxvii. 1.
[2] Resistance to constraint or compulsion: *O.E.D.* [3] II. xxi. 2
[4] II. xxiii. 18–19. [5] IV. x. Baron refers to § 9. [6] II. xxiii. 1
[7] See above, p. 472, n. 2. 'S' for simple.

Space? and whether Duration be not either a Mode of Existence; being nothing else but the continuation thereof or an Externall Denomination, arising from the comparing of the existence of any B., in one instant, with the same existence in another instant, disjoyned by an intervening space. And then it will be a Relation.

III Whereas 'tis said p. 60 that we have negative terms, to which there be no positive Ideas annex'd; but they consist wholly in the negation of some certain Ideas, as Silence, Invisible etc: but these signify not any Ideas in the mind, but their absence[1]—I find much difficulty to perswade my self, that this negation or absence signify no Idea in the mind: Suspecting there must be some sence and signification of the words. As when I say, I perceive that God is invisible; the meaning seems to be, I perceive the agreement of the Commplex Idea, which I name God, with the Idea of the absence of Visibility. But such a Proposition is very different from this other, I perceive the Id: of God and do not perceive the absence etc. For if Absence or negation found no I-s they are not, cannot be perceived and so *I perceive God is Invis:* must be explained according to the sence of the latter Proposition. And besides, if there be no correspondent Idea in mens minds, they are sounds and no words: and consequently we might, when we find 'em in any proposition, substitute any other sounds to which there is no signification annexd, without any derogation to its truth and certainty. If there be any pos: Idea in the mind that answers these words (which likewise are positive signs if they have any signification) I am equally puzzled in the reducing it to any of those classes of S. Ideas which you have prescribed.

IV I will not here presume to question the justness of your Division of Science;[2] knowing the difficulty of the task, and your abilitys, whereby you are secure from so impotent assaults as mine would be. But with due submission propose another to your more penetrating thoughts, which tho', to speak plainly, seems at present more agreable, yet I believe will receive its doom according to your verdict. Science or Knowledge is either *Speculative*; whereby we perceive (1) Things with their modes and operations (2) Their relations (3) The signs of both whether naturall; as Ideas: or arbitrary; as words: or *Practicall* which may

[1] Correctly pp. 59–60. II. viii. 5. The passage is altered in the fourth and fifth editions.

[2] In the second and third editions IV. xx; in the fourth and fifth, IV. xxi.

fitly be called *Skill* which is a knowl. of doing somewhat. Hereby the Powers of mankind are assisted and governed in their searches after truth, and other respective exercises. This skill I suppose may be most commodiously divided agreeably to the powers which it dos direct. The powers or facultys of man, I conceive, admitt of a distinction into 3 parts according to the 3 sorts of Objects that the mind may be conversant about, or rather the 3 states and dispositions, in which one and the same object may be consider'd: vizt. Possibility to be produced etc. Evidence to our Understanding; Goodness or Agreeableness to our wills (which Goodness will comprehend in it the ultimate End, Infinite Happiness, and all regular means of the obtainment thereof). The mind as refer'd to Things considered as possible is denominated powerfull, for as much as by a bare preference it can excite such motions in the Body, as are necessary and sufficient to the production, preservation, improvement etc of any Being, that is placed within the compass of its force. When compared with the Evidence of Things Understanding; When with the Goodness of Things by virtue whereof they are capable of sustaining choice or preference; Will.

Agreeably Philosophy may be defin'd The skill of right managing our severall Powers about their respective Objects in order to the attainment of suitable and proper Ends. Of Which the first Part may be calld (as I think usually) *Mechanica*; Being the Skill of right applying the powers of the Body for the accommodating the uses of this temporall life; the supplying all necessary conveniencys, and preventing or removing mischiefs. The second *Logica* Being the Skill of right using our reason (or Understanding) for the discovering the relation that may be found among things, according to their[a] Evidence. And since Reason or the Reas: mind must be directed not only by generall rules concerning its most Generall and immediate Object; but by other more particular, according to the nature and condition of the object it considers: Therefore hither must be reduced Physica or Ontologia; proposing a method, in which the mind should consider the Idea of Being, its sorts, and affections, whereby it will be assisted in its inquiry after more particular truths. The third will be *Ethica* or the Skill of right ordering our manners (i.e.) our choice and preference, with the actions thence depending, in reference to the severall

[a] *Or* your

things that may be proposed as the means requisite for the possessing our selves of reall and perfect happiness.

These Sir are those things which I must call difficultys to me, tho' I am sensible they come under another denomination to you. What is well known to an observing traveller; seems absurd and incredible to him that has allways liv'd at home. I would not be thought guilty of so much vanity and presumption, as to pretend to correct or instruct. My Years and Education are too contemptible, for to give me such bold and aspiring thoughts. And that perticular esteem, which I have justly conceiv'd for your person and writings; assures to you such an absolute possession of my affections: that I find my self much more inclined, to vail to your Authority, and submitt to your dictates; than to usurp upon that deference which the World with great reason allows and pay you. As for my own weakness, however visible it may be, I am not sollicitous to excuse it. Those that know me might consider what I now attempt as an extravagance of Youth: But I think myself in present circumstances sufficiently secured from any ill imputations, by the obscurity of my person, which I injoy without any affectation and industry. And tho' I do not conceal my name etc my fame is not so great as to occasion a Pannic fear, lest it should be violated by contempt and ill-natured censures. Or if so, I could acquiesce with confidence in your favour. To this, Sir, I appeal, to this I absolutely refer my self: hoping for a favourable issue. Those Benefits which I have received from you, in common with the world, claim an immoveable interest in my Esteem: But if your many urgent and noble affairs will at any time permit you to condescend to my Hum: requests, and grant me the solution of these doubts, This will add greater force to my former obligations, and inspire me with greater zeal and vigour in your service. This will farther and more powerfully ingage me to be, what I allready am, and am determin'd to be, Worthy Sir,

Your Sincere Honourer, and most Respectfull, Humble Servant

JOHN BARON.

Hungerford in Berkshire. September 12. 1698.

If you shall think these worthy of your thoughts, or shew your pity by relieving me in this weakness and distraction of mind, the sooner you shall be pleased to apply the remedy, the more gratefull it will be and the cure more certain. If you direct to me at

Mr Robinsons in Hungerford Berks any thing will come safe to my hands. Sir Yours—

Endorsed by Locke: J: Baron 12 Sept. 98

2488. Isaac (later Sir Isaac) Newton to [William Popple?], 19 September 1698

B.L., MS. Locke b. 3, f. 127v. Copy by Sylvester Brounower. Printed in Newton, *Corr.* iv. 282–4, with wrong provenance. It is said there to be addressed to Locke. It bears no address or endorsement. It is identifiable as a reply to a set of queries which the Board of Trade on 15 September ordered its secretary to send to Newton; it was read to the Board on 20 September: the Board's Journal.

In response to an order of the Privy Council, 8 September, the Board was investigating the effect on trade of the then value of guineas (22*s.*). The copy is accompanied by statements of the assay, weight, and value, of various silver and gold foreign coins, 1653, and of the price of gold, 1662, and by copies of letters from Hopton Haynes (*D.N.B.*) to Newton (?), 13 September, and from Samuel Locke to the Board, 16 September (it was read to the Board on the 19th) (all these items (ff. 126–9) are written by Syl); and by notes by Locke of the oral evidence given to the Board (f. 130).

2489. J.-B. Du Bos to Locke, 19/29 September [1698] (*2478, 2510*)

B.L., MS. Locke c. 7, ff. 217–18. Printed by G. Bonno in *Revue de littérature comparée*, xxiv (1950), 485–6. Year from Locke's endorsement.

A Bruxelles Le 29 de Septembre.

monsieur Toinard ma envoiè ici monsieur, vostre lettre dattee du quinzieme de l'autre mois. je suis tres sensible aux honetetè que vous me dites, quoyque je sois bien convaincu que cest par pure bonte; et je puis vous protester que le plaisir de vous revoir fera plus de la moitiè du motif, dun second voyage que je pouré faire en Angleterre.

Jacepte avec reconoisance le present que vous me voule faire du livre de monsieur Sydney,[1] a condition que vous me donneré occasion de macquiter lorsque je seré a Paris. mr Verniete le secretaire de Lambasadeur de france[2] qui a eu lhonneur de Vous saluer

[1] Algernon Sidney, *Discourses concerning Government*, 'London, Printed, and are to be sold by the Booksellers of *London* and *Westminster*. MDCXCVIII.' L.L., no. 2666.

[2] J.-B. Rousseau, the poet, using the name Vernietes: p. 556. Camille d'Hostun,

me le fera tenir. Jespere d'estre a Paris avant le milieu du mois prochain, et je ne suis reste si lontemps en ce pais que pour attendre mon compagnon de voyage que le Roy a retenu un mois a Loo.[1] Jay vu a Utrecht monsieur Græviuss, qui ma fort felicité sur lhonneur que j'avois d'estre de vos amis. Son neuvieme et dixieme volume des antiquités Romaines est prest de paroistre.[2] vous i verrè une traduction Latine du livre de Bergier, des grands chemins de l'empire Romain.[3] Son edition des oraisons de Ciceron savance aussi beaucoup et je l'ai laissee a la seconde Philippique.[4]

monsieur Le Clerc dAmsterdam travaille a une Harmonie Grecque et Latine des quatre evangeliste que jay vue presque toute imprimee.[5] il ni a rien au dela de ce qui se trouve dans les harmonies ordinaires, et l'autheur na pas eu seulement dIdee de toutes les belles choses que monsieur Toinard a faites dans la sienne.

Jay vu a Amsterdam les desseins des decouvertes des Hollandois vers la nouvelle guinee.[6] Je nadjoutere rien a ce que les relations en ont publiees, si ce nest quil i a un gouvernement etabli dans le pais. cela paroist en ce que des que les vaisseaux Hollandois parurent ont alluma des feux sur la coste pour servir de signaux, aux quels ont repondit du dedans des terres. ces signaux sont marquès dans les desseïns que jay vu.

monsieur Witssen dAmsterdam ma dit quil pouroit bien faire imprimer le voyage dun Ambasadeur Moscovite a la Chine par terre. Il la déja entre les mains en plus grande partie, celui que lon imprime et que les gazettes ont anoncé, est la relation du meme voyage, faite par le valet de chambre de Lambassadeur.[7]

comte de Tallard, ambassador to William III from 1698 to 1701: *N.B.G.* He employed Rousseau as a clerk.

[1] Claude Desgots, d. 1732 (*D.B.F.*), Du Bos's travelling companion in the Netherlands. He rejoined Du Bos at Amsterdam on 24 August/3 September; Du Bos was at Brussels on 15/25 September: Lombard, *La Correspondance de Du Bos*, nos. 59, 61, 64.

[2] pp. 140, 167.

[3] Nicolas Bergier (1567–1623; *D.B.F.*), *Histoire des grands chemins de l'Empire Romain*, 1622.

[4] p. 396.

[5] p. 423.

[6] The voyage of Willem de Vlamingh: p. 452. Du Bos wrote more fully about the voyager's reports and drawings to Toinard on 21 August and 4 September, N.S.: Lombard, nos. 58, 61.

[7] The ambassador is Eberhard Isbrandes Ides (Evert Ysbrants Ides) who died about 1700: *A.D.B.* He was accompanied on his mission by Adam Brand, a German merchant in Moscow; Brand had no official position under Isbrandes Ides. Brand published his account in German in 1697 (other editions 1698 and later); the book now printing was a French translation, *Relation du voyage de Mr. Evert Isbrand, envoyé de sa majesté czarienne a l'empereur de la Chine, en 1692, 93 & 94*, Amsterdam, 1699. L.L., no. 478. An English version is dated 1698: ibid., no. 477. Witsen published Isbrandes Ides's own account in 1704: H. Cordier, *Bibliotheca Sinica*, 1904–8, iv. 2466–9; van Eeghen, ii. 102–4. Further notices, pp. 525, 533.

des que je seré a Paris, je me donneré lhonneur de vous escrire, et je feré tout de mon mieux pour meriter vostre corespondance.

Joubliois, dans les decouvertes des Hollandois des cignes noirs quils ont trouve dans un bras de mer qui se jette dans les terres. on en a amené de vivants qui sont morts a Batavia, et jen ai vu la peinture a Amsterdam, faite sur les originaux.

Vostre tres humble et tres obeissant serviteur

DU BOS.

Address: To Master John Locke at master Pawlings over against The plough in little Lincolns inne fields London

Postmark: OC 4

Endorsed by Locke: Du Bos 29 Sept. 98 Answered 10 Nov.

2490. WILLIAM MOLYNEUX to LOCKE, 20 September 1698 (2471, 2492)

The Carl H. Pforzheimer Library, New York. Transcribed from photostat. Printed with slight omissions in *Some Familiar Letters*, pp. 272–3. Answered by no. 2492.

Dublin. Sept. 20. 1698.

Honoured Dear Sir

I arrived here safely the 15th Inst. and now that the Rufling and Fatigue of my Journy is a little over; I sitt down to a task which I must confes is the hardest I was ever under in my Life; I mean, expressing My thanks to you suitable to the Favours I received from you, and suitable to the Inward sense I have of them in my Mind. Were it possible for me to do either I should be in some measure Satisfyd; but my inability of paying my detts makes me ashamed to appear before my Creditor. However, thus much with the strictest sincerity I will venture to Assert to you, that I cannot recollect through the whole Course of my Life such signal Instances of real Friendship as when I had the Happines of your Company for five Weeks together in London. Tis with the Greatest Satisfaction Imaginable that I recollect what then past between us, and I reckon it the Happiest Scene of my Whole Life. That part thereof especially which I past at Oates[1] has made such an agreable Impression on my Mind, that nothing can be more

[1] Locke was absent from the Board of Trade's sitting on Friday, 19 August, and it did not sit on the following Saturday or Sunday or on Friday, 2 September and the next two days. For his attendance see p. 447, n. 1.

Pleasing. To all in that Excellent Family I beseech you give my most Humble Respects, To[a]– Sir Francis, My Lady, the Young Gentleman, mrs Masham, and her Brother that belongs to the Princesse,[1] not forgetting Monsieur Coste.–[a] Tis my duty to make my acknowledgements there in a particular Letter to[a]– My Lady, and to own the Young Gentlemans Favour in his Letter to me.–[a] but I beg of you to make my Excuse for omitting it at this time, Because I am a Little presd by some busines that is thrown upon me since my Arrival. To which also you are obleidged for not being troubled at present with a more Tedious Letter from

Sir

Your Most Obleidged and Intirely Affectionate Friend and Servant

W: MOLYNEUX

Address: To John Locke Esquire at Mr Pawlings overagainst the Plow-Inn in Little Lincolns Inn Fields London

Postmark: SE 26

Endorsed by Locke: W: Molyneux 20 Sept 98 Answered. 29

2491. MRS. ELIZABETH BERKELEY, later Burnet, to LOCKE, 21 September 1698 (*2328*, *2511*)

B.L., MS. Locke c. 3, ff. 214–15.

Worcester: 21: Sep: 1698:

Sir

Tho it is my misfortune to lose the benefect of your acquantance allmost as sone as I was sinseble of the pleasure of it, yet that did not weeken the true concern and trouble I had for the late more then ordenery want of health I heard you laboured under, and most hartely wish it may please God to make you long an instrument of good to the world; but I had I beleeve kept myself from troubleing you had not a litle self intreest put me upon it, not gessing when or how I could see you to do it, and I am perswaded you are so charitable and ready to do good that you will forgive me for it; tis to beg your directions a litle about my health, for haveing tryed severall Phisicians[b] without great success I sould be glad to know if 'tis in vain to expect any help from Medicens that I might seet down quietly and submit to Gods will; I beleeve much of my

a–a *Deleted in MS., presumably by the editor of* Some Familiar Letters. b *MS.* Phisc̄

1 Samuel Masham; he was a page of honour to Prince George.

ill habit of body has been contracted by Malloncolly, but about this time of year I generally seem to grow very fatt for me, but 'tis uneasy and like a pufed swelledness; I eat with rather too much apetite, but am short breathed, my meat digests il, and am in most respects like one in the green sickness; I am too, often troubled with gideness and disorders in my head, so that my memorie and the exercis of my mind is much broken and confused, which indid makes me most desireous to find some remedy since the other pains and inconveniancys are not so great but I could very well baer them; I am sinsible I have an exceeding sharp humer in my stomack, and if I eat much butter or the like it will rise like greas for a long time, being allso often troubled both with hart burn and a palpatation; in this maner I am, and have been for severall years, from about midsumer to Christmas, and by that time my apetite to my meat go's away so intirely that no variety or any sort of food gos down with pleasure, but quit the Contrary tis very troublesome to force my self to eat, and this lose of apetite lasts 'till about May or June, but the litle I eat seems to digest pretty well, I then grow very leane, wake generally sick, and with a great sadness and opression on my spirits as after some great misfortune; this sadness last most of the morning and aften most of the day, at evening I am generally pretty well, am subject to get colds and have pains like the begening of a rumatisim; I have formerly spit blood, but of late years no great deal, tho not long since I did for about two or three hours spit some that left me a litle week after it; I have taken steel and variety of Medicens, to me it seems that waters dos me most good, it generally gives me most cheerfullness; I drink water at my meals and you once beding me leve of wine, I drink very litle not a glace in a day, but my Frinds fancying my looking puffed is dropsical are still perswading me to drink wine, but I find it allways increases that very hott and sharp humer in my stomack; what I take the fredom to ask is not a direction to any sort of Medicen, but only some few rules for my deat that may best moderate these uneasyness especially those disorders of my head, and spirits, and disposision to sadness which makes me a very dull useless creature; shall I contenew to abstain from wine or not is much excercise necesary, for I own I use very litle; is Chocolet bad and Coffe; for air I find litle diference in Town or Country of the two I think the last best; but afected by chang of weather before rain and especially snow I am much worse; and cold very ill agrees with me; if you are so well as to be able without any uneasyness to write five or six lines in answer to this very long and impertenat leter it will be very acceptable, because I find a perticuler satisfaction in observeing the rules of one for whom I have so much deference, and pray dont fear being too severe, since I value nothing in meat or drink but in order to health, and can without grife deny my self any thing of that sort? is much sleep good or bad? I own I wish it not necesary as well as much excercise, for to spend much time to prolong life or health is allmost as bad as to be without it; my memorie is so broken that often I cant remember what I read two days at least can't recal it when I would and my busness worse; 'tis time to beg pardon, but put it on the account of charity; a vertue you won't I perswade my self forget in the answer I hear is coming out to the Bishops book;[1]

I am Sir

Your Obliged ser:

E B

Marked by Locke: Answered 29 Oct

2492. Locke to William Molyneux, 29 September 1698 (*2490*)

Some Familiar Letters, pp. 273–4. A passage was omitted by the editor: p. 489. The letter arrived about the time of Molyneux's death: ibid. Answers no. *2490*.

London, 29 Sept. 1698.

Dear Sir,

Yours of the 20th has now discharg'd me from my daily employment of looking upon the weathercock and hearkening how loud the wind blow'd. Tho' I do not like this distance, and such a ditch betwixt us, yet I am glad to hear that you are safe and sound on t'other side the water. But pray speak not in so magnificent and courtly a style of what you receiv'd from me here. I lived with you and treated you as my friend, and therefore us'd no ceremony, nor can receive any thanks but what I owe you doubly both for your company, and the pains you were at to bestow that happiness on me. If you keep your word, and do me the same kindness again next year, I shall have reason to think you value me more than you say, tho' you say more than I can with modesty read.

[1] Locke's forthcoming *Reply* to Stillingfleet's latest *Answer*; it was published in November: p. 505.

I find you were beset with business when you writ your letter to me, and do not wonder at it; but yet for all that I cannot forgive your silence concerning your health and your son. My service to him, your brother, and Mr. Burridge, and do me the justice to believe that I am with a perfect affection,

Dear Sir,

Your most humble, and most faithful servant,

JOHN LOCKE.

2493. SAMUEL BOLD to LOCKE, 30 September 1698 (*2486, 2509*)

B.L., MS. Locke c. 4, f. 25.

Steeple Sept: 30th. 1698

Honoured Sir

On Saturday last I received yours of the 21st of this Instant. I was extremely pleased at the first opening of It, to see your Name at the bottom of It. And do now returne you my heartiest thanks for the Honour you have done me in favouring me with a Letter from your own hand, and for the very great kindness you express in It. I am very glad the papers you have received from me, are found by you to have some Reason in them, considered with relation to the Objections they are concerned about. I wish I could write with some accurateness,[1] and that I knew how to give my expressions such a Turne, as might present my thoughts with something of life to the Reader. But this I am always at a great loss for, whether my long solitaryness, and want of Ingenous Conversation, hath something occasioned the dryness of my stile (for I think in my yonger years, when I conversed with Gentlemen, and persons of a liberal education, I had a greater readiness of expression in discourse, and could write with more advantage than I can now) or whether my reading good Authors with too much haste, regarding only the sense, and Reason they deliver with a neglect of their way of expressing themselves, may be a cause of It, or whether my writing too fast, may be the reason of It for tho I am much slower in discourse than I have formerly bin I commonly (when I have thought a while on a subject) write as fast as I am able, without troubling my self about what kind of

[1] In the obsolete sense, precision or nicety, rather than in the modern sense exact conformity to truth: *O.E.D.*

words and phrases I should use, but stil taking those which first come to hand, or whether my studied avoiding metaphorical expressions, lest thereby I should lead persons into mistakes, or my long continued endeavour to level my discourse to the capacities of the poor and mean people I am always to speak to, has contributed anything to It, I am not certain. Tho I much suspect, there is a Genius wanting within, And if so, I doubt there can be no help for It, especially now I am so much over grown in years.[1] But if you think I may be capable of attaining to write in a more correct style, if at any time you can obtain leisure to Instruct me what course I should take, your doing It, wil be a singular kindness, which I shal most thankfully receive. I here send you the other papers your letter encouraged me to send up.[2] They might have come sooner, but I have bin something disordered (since I writ last to you) with grief, upon the very sad Tidings I have received of my eldest son's haveing faln into bad company, and being guilty of several great Immoralities. Some of this week hath bin spent in endeavouring that the properest methods I can think of, may be used in order to the reclaiming, and bringing of Him to repentance. The use of which I am to accompany with my most fervent prayers to that God for his blessing along with them, who hath the hearts of all under his government, and at his disposal, and I humbly entreat your prayers both upon my own, and my son's behalf, and of all my family, St James having assured me, that the Effectual fervent prayer of a Righteous man availeth much.[3] Sir I am

your most Humble and most obliged servant

SA: BOLD.

If you think the same advice most proper with respect to my attaining to write tollerably, now I have so long accustomed my self to write out of the way, which is fittest for one who is to begin, and hath not acquir'd a wrong Biass, I wil not desire you to trouble yourself to say any thing to me about It. because I can then fetch Instruction, from your excellent treatise of education. But indeed I almost despair of writing well. Old Jades can very hardly be brought to break their pace. And yet I am sensible of a roughness in my expressions, I would be glad to be rid of. I cannot but observe

1 Bold is said to have been born in 1649: *D.N.B.*
2 Presumably the draft of the remainder of *Some Considerations.*
3 James 5: 16.

a smoothness and Fineness in your writings, and in the late Arch-Bishop's[1] which conveigh Sense and Reason to people with an extraordinary and unimitable Grace, and which set off Truth with an unexpressible advantage to all who do heartily love Truth.

Address: To the Honoured Mr Locke

Endorsed by Locke: S: Bold 30 Sept 98

LOCKE to PHILIPPUS VAN LIMBORCH, 4 October 1698

Continued and dispatched on 18 October: no. 2498.

2494. PHILIPPUS VAN LIMBORCH to LOCKE, 4/14 October 1698 (*2485*, 2498)

B.L., MS. Locke c. 14, ff. 123–4. Carried by John Lock: see below and p. 500.

Vir Amplissime

Cognatum tuum[2] Angliam repetiturum sine meis ad te dimittere non potui. Doleo non luculentiorem illi inserviendi occasionem mihi esse oblatam. Hac vesperâ mecum cœnabit cras hinc abiturus. Dum tuâ præsentiâ frui non licet, gaudeo aliquem saltem ex cognatione tua mihi obtingere, cui quanti te faciam testari possim. Ille si te Londini offendat plura de statu nostro narrare poterit. Virum Magnificum hactenus nondum vidi: videtur jam aliis occupatus colloquii nostri oblitus; fortasse se jam plene sententiam tuam audivisse credit; suisque quæ mihi exposuit argumentis nihil habere

Excellent Sir,

Your kinsman[2] being about to return to England, I could not let him go without a letter from me to you. I am sorry that a more notable opportunity of being serviceable to him has not been offered me. He will sup with me this evening before going away tomorrow. While it is not permitted to me to enjoy you in person I am glad that chance has brought me at least someone of your kindred to whom I can prove how much I value you. If he meets with you in London he will be able to tell you a great deal about the state of things with us. I have not yet seen the Magnifico; he seems now to be occupied with other things and to have forgotten our conversation; perhaps he thinks that he has now completely heard your opinion; and that he has nothing to add to his arguments that he put before me. I wrote recently

[1] Tillotson. [2] John Lock.

quod addat. Scripsi nuper Joannem van der Waeijen ⟨Professorem⟩[a] Franequeranum virulentam contra D. Clericum edidisse dissertationem, in qua acerbe etiam in me invehitur; et neutrum nostrum illi responsurum. Sed amici putant, aliquid reponendum. Ego quoniam lecto recens scripto materia memoriæ meæ inhærebat, aliquid in chartam conjeci; non ut ederetur, sed fortasse alteri Theologiæ meæ Christianæ editioni reservaretur: si scriptionem differerem, denuo mihi repetendam lectionem videbam: itaque jam intra duas hebdomadas absolvi. Amici viso scripto urgere me non desinunt donec edatur. Itaque tandem me persuaderi passus sum, et hodie typographo dedi ut edatur.[1] Quamprimum editum fuerit exemplar tibi mittam, ut de quæstione nostra candidum judicium feras. Vale Vir Amplissime, Amice plurimum honorande. Salutem quam officiosissimam dices a me et meis Dominæ Masham totique familiæ. Uxor, filia ac filius tibi omnia fausta precantur.

Tui Amantissimus
P. v. LIMBORCH

Amstelodami 14 Octobris
12
16 98
5

[a] *MS.* Professorum

---

that Joannes van der Waeyen, professor at Franeker, had published a virulent dissertation against Mr. Le Clerc in which he also inveighs bitterly against me, and that neither of us would answer him. But friends think that there should be some requital. Since, as I had recently read what he had written, the matter stuck fast in my memory, I put something on paper, not in order that it should be published, but that it should perhaps be kept for another edition of my *Theologia Christiana*; I saw that if I put off writing I should have to repeat the reading; accordingly I have now, within two weeks, finished the task. Friends who have seen what I have written are not ceasing to urge me until it is published. So I have at last let myself be persuaded and have given it to-day to a printer to be published.[1] As soon as it is published I shall send you a copy, so that you may form(?) a candid opinion about our controversy. Good-bye, excellent Sir, my most honoured friend. Please give my and my family's best respects to Lady Masham and the whole family. My wife, daughter, and son send you all good wishes.

Your most affectionate
P. v. LIMBORCH

Amsterdam 14 October
1698

---

[1] p. 518.

2495. E. Burridge, 13 October 1698

Address: Amplissimo Consultissimo ac plurimum Honorando Viro D. Joanni Locke Londinum Amica manu.

Endorsed by Locke: P: Limborch 14 Oct 98

2495. EZEKIEL BURRIDGE to LOCKE, 13 October 1698 (*2475*, 2501)

B.L., MS. Locke c. 4, ff. 209–10. Answered by no. 2501.

Lord Chancellors Dublin October 13th 1698

Honoured Sir

I am oblig'd to give you the trouble (as I may well call it) of a letter; 'tis what was given me in charge by a dying friend. Last night your good friend Mr Molyneux was bury'd. his death was very suddain and surprizeing. On Saturday[1] he was very brisk in the house of commons till near 3 of the clock: between 5 and 6 he sent for me to sit with him, he was then very well, whilest I was with him he complaind of his old pain, (which he told me he gave you an account of in England) the next day he vomited a great quantity of bloud, and a great quantity afterwards came from him downwards. by Sunday night he was brought so low, that he himself and all his friends about him thought he wou'd not live out that night; however he continu'd alive (but with the flame so faint and weak that it cou'd only be just call'd life) till 3 of the clock on tuesday morning. Since his death, according to his own desire, he has been open'd; in each of his kidneys there were two stones found, the largest, in his left kidney was bigger than a large nutmeg, the other 3 were much of a size: in each of the kidneys there was one of the stones seated[a] within the flesh of the kidney. The vessell which, by his streining to vomit, 'tis suppos'd, broke in his stomach, and immediatly occasion'd his death, they cou'd not discover.

At the time that his bloud ran lowest, when with pain and difficulty, he gave his last advice to his son, he remember'd you; And desir'd me as soon as he was dead to write you an account of his death, and bid me tell you *that as he liv'd, so he dy'd with a very great honour, and esteem for you.* These were his words; and this

[a] *Or* sealed

[1] 8 October.

complaysance in a dying man did not seem strange to me, who was so well acquainted with him, who knew the excellent spirit of the man; the great regard he had to vertue and learning, and the singular value he set on you: This every one knew who knew him.

I had the happiness of being very intimatly acquainted with him, and do fear I shall not again on this side my grave have the happiness of being intimate with such another friend. he was a great lover of justice, of vertue, of learning, and of mankind. and 'twas this superabundant charity that occasion'd that act which was the greatest oversight of his life: you know what I mean.

Your last kind letter to him his brother and I open'd and read since his death. it came too late to tell him of it whilest alive. There is mention made in it of pictures,[1] if there be any thing to be done be pleas'd to signifie it to Dr Molyneux or me, perhaps it may be done time enough when I go in to England, which will be (with Gods leave) with my Lord Chancellor,[2] at which time I will endeavour to do you all the right I can i[a] publishing your Essay. Twill be an honour Sir if you make my service acceptable to Mr Freake, as likewise to Mr Churchil I am

Honoured Sir

Your most Humble servant

EZEKIEL BURRIDGE

This day the Parliament here voted the King a supply of 138000l which was all he demanded, we were afraid it wou'd be otherwise, for there were warm debates, and great grumblings against the 5 French Regiments which lately came over.[3] The D. of Ormond[4] was an enemy to those who stood against them.

Address: To John Lock Esqre. at Mr Robert Pawlet's opposit to the plow in Little Lincoln's Inn fields London.

Postmark: OC 24

Endorsed by Locke: E: Burridge 13 Oct. 98 Answered 27

[a] *Doubtful reading.*

---

[1] This does not appear in Locke's letter (no. 2492) as printed in *Some Familiar Letters*. Locke probably wrote about the portrait of Molyneux by Kneller, or a copy of it: Journal, 21 September; pp. 503, 625.

[2] Methuen.

[3] For them and for the dissatisfaction caused by them see *Cal.S.P., Dom.*, 1698, pp. 386, 388, 397–9, 403, 409; Vernon, *Letters*, ii. 191.

[4] James Butler, 1665–1745; second duke of Ormond 1688: *D.N.B.* At this time he generally obstructed the Irish Lords Justices: H.M.C., *Buccleugh MSS. at Montagu House*, ii. 617.

2496. Locke to Dr. (later Sir) Hans Sloane, 15 October [1698?] (2296, 2640)

B.M., Sloane MS. 4059, ff. 282–3. The year cannot be before 1698 as vol. xix of the *Philosophical Transactions* was not completed until the end of 1697; and if, as seems likely, the letter was written in London, it cannot be after 1699 as Locke was not in London on 15 October in any later year. The contents of the letter seem more appropriate to 1698 than to 1699.

15 Oct

Dear Doctor

I return you my thanks for the Transactions of Sept which I lately received from Mr Churchil. I also here with return you your 19th Vol: I have compared what I have of those years conteined in it, and find That I want the title page and preface to this 19th vol: and Transaction. N 219.220. 221.222.224. 226. and have these double viz N 233 and 234. I should not mention this to you but that perhaps those that I have double may spoile the set of some other freind of yours that has them from you, and those which I want, may lye bye superfluous. If that be not in the case I desire you not to take any notice of this, for I shall take care to have mine compleated at Mr Smiths,[1] haveing a greater obligation to you already for those you have bestowd on me than I can pretend to. I am Sir

Your most humble servant

J Locke

Address: For Dr Sloane at his house in Southampton street in Bloomsbury

2497. Nicolas Toinard to Locke, 16/26 October [1698] (2483, 2504)

B.L., MS. Locke c. 21, ff. 201–3. Year from Locke's endorsement. Transmission: see p. 497. Answers nos. 2483 and 2412; answered by no. 2550.

+

26. Octobre

J'ay u, monsieur, une extreme joie d'anbrasser ici tout nouvelemant mr Du bos, non seulemant parceque c'est une choze agreable de revoir an bonne santé un ami apres une longue separation mais ancore par les ocazions qu'il me donne de nous antretenir

[1] Samuel Smith, who was one of the two associated publishers of the *Philosophical Transactions*: no. 949, etc.

de vous. on ne peut pas avoir plus d'estime qu'il en a pour vous, ni plus de reconnoissance que cele dont il est penetré pour vos honetetéz, et à cet egard vous ne me surprenez an rien ni l'un ne l'ôtre.

Mr Du bos m'a aporté trois medailles tres rares où il y a des caracteres apeléz Samaritains sur l'une desquels il y a liziblement *ΒΑCΙΛΕΩC ΑΝΤΙΓΟΝ*. qui ne sauroit être que du dernier Roy des Juifs de la race des Asmoneans.[1] Je ne saurois donner otre raizon pourquoi dans un tems si bas que celui la, ils anploioient ancore des caracteres Samaritains si ce nest propter ἀρχαισμόν,[2] de même que dans nos monnoies nous metons des legendes latines. Je vais les faire graver exactemant. Il m'en a aussi aporté deux ôtres petites que javois plus netes, frapées du tems de Simon macabeè.[3] Eles etoient aconpagnées d'une ôtre d'*ΗΡΩΔΟΝ ΒΑΣΙΛΕΩΣ* dans laquele Mr Du bos lizoit ꝛΓI qui marqueroit Anno XIII. é deconcerteroit fort la chronologie des Herodiades, mais je luy ay fait voir que l'I est le monograme ˥[a] de Tyr un peu efacé, é luy ay montre une pareille medaille où il est fort net, de sorte que ce la se reduit à Anno III. dans cete medaille qui est du Grand Agrippa.[4]

Je m'etonne, Monsieur, de ceque vous n'avez aucune connoissance de lembarquement pour Baldivia fait en 1663. au mois de Septenbre. le conmandant etoit un Catolique Aleman, qui deserta en chilé, é ala se randre au Gouverneur Espagnol de Baldivia. J'ay vu sa Relacion en Espagnol anvoiée des Indes. Les Espagnols apres l'avoir gardé jusques en l'annee 1672. le pandirent comme espion venu de la Jamaique où il n'a jamais eté. cela est à la fin d'un in Fol. intitulé *El Marañon y Amazonas*, imprimé à Madrid 1684.[5]

[a] *This may be an accidental scribble.*

---

[1] Antigonus Mattathias, 40–37 B.C. For his coins see Hill (as cited no. *2736* n.), pp. 212–19.

[2] 'As an archaism.' For archaizing lettering on the Jewish coins see Hill, p. xcii n.

[3] These are probably identifiable as coins dating from the Second Revolt of the Jews: no. *2736*.

[4] The only king of the Jews to inscribe his coins *ΒΑΣΙΛΕΩΣ ΗΡΩΔΟΥ* appears to have been Herod the Great, king from 37 to 4 B.C., and the present coin is likely to have been struck by him. The great Agrippa is probably Herod Agrippa I, A.D. 37–44. Tyre was outside their dominions and they could not coin money there.

[5] This relates to Narbrough's voyage in the *Sweepstakes*: nos. *629*, *2476*. The book is by Father Manuel (or Emmanuel) Rodriguez, S.J. Du Bos tried to buy a copy for Toinard in Antwerp and Brussels: Lombard, nos. 63, 64. According to the 'Compendio historial, y indice chronologico Peruano', which forms part of it, 'Don Carlos

Je nesai par quele rancontre vôtre bele è grande letre Latine du 25. de mars, m'a eté randüe tout nouvelemant par le Facteur de la Poste. Ele a eté la bienvenüe, mais si je l'avois receüe dans le tans que mr Du bos estoit à Londres, je vous orois prié de lui donner pour moi la Traduction de *Zeraim* per Guisium.

mr Du bos m'a fait avoir cequ'il y avoit d'imprimé de trois livres du sieur Dampierre.[1] Vous me feriez un sanbible plaisir de me faire tenir le reste d⟨u⟩[a] texte avec les prefaces é tables qu'il y o⟨ra⟩,[a] quand le tout sera achevé, é les cartes dont il y a une de campeche que jay où par provision il y a une grosse faute, car il met Panuko R. entre le 21. é le 22. D. é cete Riviere est constamment au dela du cap *Roxo* (male Rox*a*) sous le Tropique. Il faut donc baisser l'un é remonter l'ôtre.[2]

Touchant ceque vous deman⟨dez⟩[a] *si quos nov⟨erim⟩*[a] *populos, qui numerationis nodum alicubi quam in denario locaverint*,[3] je nesai que les *Jalofes* é les *Foules* sur la R. du Senegal[4] qui le fixent au cing, car apres ce nonbre ils dizent cing é un, ci⟨ng⟩[a] é deuz pour 6. é 7. é le reste jusques à diz, où ils recommancent diz é un *et c.* Apres *quinze*, ils dizent, Diz cinq é un—

Dans la langue generale du Bresil, apelée *Guarani*,[5] qui est d'une extrême etandüe, puisq⟨u'ele⟩[a] regne depuis la R. de la Plate jusques par dela cele des Amazones, sur laquele les Topinanbous[6] l'ont portée bien avant, l'on n'y conte que jusques à *catre*, et pour cing, ils dizent une main. é n'ont point de mots pour *siz*, *set*, et c.

[a] *Page torn.*

Enriquez Clerck' went ashore at Valdivia in 1670 and was sent to Lima; in 1682 'En Lima dieron garrote al prisionero Carlos Enrique Clerck, que abia entrado al Sur, embiado de los Ingleses de Xamayca, à espiar toda la Costa del Perù, y le cogieron en Valdibia, come se dixo arriba.' Don Carlos is mentioned also in F. de Seixas y Lovera, *Descripcion geographica, y derrotero de la region austral Magallanica*, Madrid, 1690, f. 59^{v}.

[1] William Dampier: p. 418. Toinard here refers to the three parts of his second volume, *Voyages and Descriptions*, 1699, which was published about this time; Du Bos obtained for Toinard in July the parts already completed: Lombard, no. 57. In the list of them below 'Vol. I' is a slip for vol. ii; Dampier's *A New Voyage*, 1697, was reckoned as vol. i.

[2] Dampier puts the mouth of the Panuk river (the Panuco) at about 21° 50′ north, and Cape Roxa at 23°. Modern maps place the river-mouth at Tampico at 22° 18′ and Cape Rojo at 21° 38′.

[3] 'If I know of any peoples who have placed the nodus of numeration elsewhere than in the number ten.'

[4] p. 265.

[5] Ibid.

[6] They are a branch of the Guaranis. Locke cites them for numeration in *Essay*, II. xvi. 6 (all editions; from Jean de Léry).

J'ay un Dictionere de cete langue, que j'ay trouvé par hazard à Lisbonne. Il est imprimé in 4. en deux vol. à Madrid, 1639. é 1640. Espagnol *Guarani*, é Guarani *Espagnol.* L'Edition que l'on avoit transportée de Madrid à Lisbonne, pour y etre anbarquée é portée au Bresil, é dela au Paraguay, a eté perdüe par la revolution de Portugal,[1] parcequ'ele à eté pourie ou mangée par les rats dans des greniers. Ele e eté fai⟨te⟩[a] par un Jesuite, Recteur du colege de l'Assonption sur la Plate.

Si l'on ne peut avoir les suplemans des trois volumes de Dampierre, je vous prie de m'acheter les livres antiers. Je vous an feray tenir le prix. Vous trouverez aussi peutêtre ocazion pour me les faire tenir. J'en chercheray de mon côté. Je suis parfaitemant, monsieur, votre—

+

J'ay des Voiages [a]de Dampiere

Vol. 1. Pa⟨rt.⟩[a] 1.

His Voiage from *Achin* in *Sumatra*, et c.

Depuis page 1–80. qui finit par Finger.

Item Vol. II. Part. II.

Containing an Account of the Bay of *Campeachy, et c.*

Page 1–112. qui finit par Comparison

Item Vol. II. Part. III.

A Discourse of Winds, Breezes, et c

Page 1–48. qui finit par on te coast

Address: For Mr Mr John Locke at Mr Pawlings overagainst the Plough in little Lincolns Innefeilds London

Endorsed by Locke: Toinard 26 Oct 98 [a] 20

[a] *Page torn.*

[1] In 1640.

2498. Locke to Philippus van Limborch, 4 and 18 October 1698 (*2494*, *2516*)

Amsterdam University Library, MS. R.K., Ba 258 g. Printed incompletely in *Some Familiar Letters*, pp. 429–31; the omitted passages and the address in Ollion, pp. 216–17. Answers no. *2485*; answered by no. *2516*.

London 4 Oct 98

Vir Amplissime

Id quod ex te et Domino Woldero nuper didici aliquamdiu suspicatus sum. Sed ne opinio mea me fallat rogo ut Magnificum Virum meo nomine adeas dicasque me magnopere rogare ut suam methodum qua unitatem entis per se existentis sibique sufficientis astruat mihi indicare velit. quandoquidem mea eâ de re argumentandi ratio ipsi non penitus satisfaciat. Nollem ego in re tanti momenti falso vel fallaci innixus fundamento mihimet imponere. Siquid stabilius siquid rectius noverit ut candidus impertiri velit enixe rogito. Si tectum si tacitum velit pro me meoque silentio spondeas. Sin tantum beneficium orbi non invideat, in proxima, quæ jam instat, libri mei editione palam faciam, agnito, si libet, vel velato auctore.

Cartesianorum quam in Epistola tua reperio loquendi formulam nullatenus capio. Quid enim sibi velit cogitatio infinita plane me fugit. Nullo enim modo mihi in animum inducere possum Cogitationem per se existere, sed rem vel substantiam cogitantem, eamque

---

London 4 Oct 98

Excellent Sir,

I have suspected for some time what I learnt recently from you and Mr. de Volder. But lest my opinion misleads me please go to the Magnifico on my behalf and say that I earnestly request him to disclose to me his way of establishing the unity of a being existing of itself and sufficient to itself, seeing that my manner of demonstrating it does not entirely satisfy him. In a matter of so great importance I should wish not to deceive myself by resting on a false or fallacious foundation. If he knows one that is more stable or more correct, I earnestly entreat him to impart it candidly to me. If he wishes it to be kept hidden and secret you may vouch for me and my silence. But if he should not grudge so great a benefit to the world I shall publish it in the next edition of my book, which is now impending, either acknowledging, if he so wishes, or concealing the originator.

I do not at all understand the Cartesians' way of talking that I find in your letter. For what infinite thought means completely escapes me. For I can by no means persuade myself that thought exists of itself, but only that a thinking thing or substance does so, and it is of that that it can be

esse de qua affirmari possit esse vel finitam vel infinitam. Qui aliter loqui amant nescio quid obscuri vel fraudulenti sub tam dubiâ locutione continere mihi videntur et omnia tenebris involvere. vel saltem quod sentiant clare et dilucide enunciare non audere, faventes nimium hypothesi non undique sanæ. Sed de hoc forsan alias quando majus suppetat otium

Quod de professore Vander Waÿen scribis non miror. Istius farinæ homines sic solent nec aliter possunt recte facitis quod negligitis.

Litteras tuas quæ Roterodami hærent avide expecto et virum illum cui eas ad me perferendas tradidisti.[1] Ex tua commendatione mihi erit gratissimus ⟨viros⟩[a] probos fovendos colendosque semper existimavi. Ignoscant alii meis erroribus, nemini propter opinionum diversitatem bellum indico, ignarus ego et fallibilis homuncio. Evangelicus sum ego Christianus non Papista

Hucusque scripseram die supra notato, quo autem die finire hanc epistolam permissum est infra videbis

Quid velim cum me Christianum Evangelicum vel si mavis

[a] *MS.* viro

---

affirmed that it is either finite or infinite. Those who are wont to speak otherwise seem to me to comprise in so uncertain an expression something, I know not what, that is obscure or fraudulent, and to wrap everything in darkness or at least not to venture to express clearly and distinctly what they think, favouring too much a hypothesis that is not entirely sound. But more of this perhaps at some other time when there is greater leisure.

I am not surprised at what you write about Professor van der Waeyen. Men of that make are wont [to behave] thus and cannot [do] otherwise; you [two] do right to take no notice.

I eagerly await your letter that sticks at Rotterdam, and the gentleman to whom you delivered it to convey to me.[1] On account of your commendation he will be very welcome to me; I have always thought that honest men should be cherished and esteemed. May others forgive my mistakes! I declare war on no one on account of difference of opinions, myself an ignorant and fallible manikin. I am an Evangelical Christian, not a Papist.

I had written thus far on the day indicated above; you will see below on what day I am allowed to finish this letter.

Learn in a few words what I mean when I say that I am an Evangelical or, if you prefer, an Orthodox Christian, not a Papist. Among those who profess the name of Christians I recognize only two classes, Evangelicals and Papists: the latter those who, as if infallible, arrogate to themselves

---

[1] Samuel Crellius; the letter is no. *2482*: see p. 467.

Orthodoxum non Papistam dico paucis accipe. Inter Christiani nominis professores duos ego tantùm agnosco classes Evangelicos et Papistas. Hos qui tanquam infallibiles dominium sibi arrogant in aliorum conscientias. Illos qui quærentes unicè veritatem, illam et sibi, et aliis, argumentis solùm rationibusque persuasam volunt, aliorum eroribus faciles, suæ imbecillitatis haud immemores. Veniam fragilitati et ignorantiæ humanæ dantes petentesque vicissim.

Vidi ex quo Londini commoratus sum et allocutus sum amicum meum Samuelem Locke, cuius expectationi tam bene respondisse filium tuum, in rebus illius curæ commissis gratulor. Beneficia quibus filium ejus Amstelodami commorantem cohonestatus fueris pater grato animo accipit, et cùm ea meo nomini inscribas benevolentiam agnosco

Hiems jam ingravescens et pulmonibus meis infesta me brevi urbe expellet et abitum suadet invalescens tuscis et anhelitus. Iter in Galliam dudum propositum languescere videtur, quid fiet nescio, sed ubicunque fuero totus ubique tuus sum. Saluto uxorem tuam optimam liberosque amicosque nostros communes Veeneos Gueneloneos Clericos. Accepi nuper a Domino Guenelone epistolam 3° Octobris datam, pro qua nunc per te Gratias ⟨reddere⟩[a]

[a] *MS.* redere

---

dominion over the consciences of others; the former those who, seeking truth alone, desire themselves and others to be convinced of it only by proofs and reasons; they are gentle to the errors of others, being not unmindful of their own weakness; forgiving human frailty and ignorance, and seeking forgiveness in turn.

Since I have been staying in London I have seen and conversed with my friend Samuel Locke. I am glad that your son answered Mr. Locke's expectation so well in the matters committed to his care. The father gratefully accepts the kindnesses with which you honoured his son while he was staying in Amsterdam, and since you write that they were done on my behalf I recognize your goodwill.

Winter now becoming more severe, and hurtful to my lungs, will shortly drive me from the city, and my increasing cough and difficulty in breathing urge departure. The journey to France that was proposed not long since seems now to be languishing; I do not know what will happen, but wherever I shall be I am everywhere entirely yours. I send my greetings to your excellent wife and to your children, and to our common friends the Veens, the Guenellons, and the Le Clercs. I recently received a letter dated 3 October from Mr. Guenellon, for which I wish to thank him now through you; I shall

cupio ipsi prima data occasione responsurus. vale Vir Amicissime et me ama tui amantissimum

J LOCKE

18 Oct.

Address: Mÿn Heer Mÿn Heer Limborch op de Kaisers Gracht bÿ de Remonstranse Kerck t'Amsterdam

Postmarks: OC 18; GC

---

answer it at the first opportunity. Good-bye, most friendly Sir, and love me your most affectionate

LOCKE

18 Oct.

2499. —— ALEAUME to LOCKE, 21/31 October 1698

B.L., MS. Locke c. 3, ff. 3–4. For the writer see pp. 319, 356.

Monsieur

Monsieur Thoinart, mayant adressé lincluse[1] pour vous la faire tenir, Je me sers sil vous plaist de cette occassion la pour Vous rendre mes tres humbles respects, monsr. Thoinart me temoigne dans sa lettre que Vous avés quelques livres a luy envoyer, si vous souhaittés monsieur prendre la peine de les Envoyer a monsr. herman Olmius marchant demeurant proche la bourse dans la rue Ce me semble ou est la halle aux draps,[2] Il aura occassion de me les Envoyer, et je les fairay tenir a monsr. Thoinart, je vous offre monsieur mes tres humbles services Icy ou Je me fairois un plaisir de Vous estre propre a quelque chose. Je suis avec bien du respect

Monsieur

Vostre tres humble et tres obeissant seruiteur

ALEAUME

A Rouen le 31. octobre 1698.

Address: For mr. John Locke at mr. Pawlings over against the Plough in Little Lincolne-Innefeilds In London

Endorsed by Locke: Aleaume 31 Oct 98

[1] Apparently no. *2497*.

[2] Blackwell Hall in Basinghall Street: Strype's Stow, iii. 68. There was a banker named John Olmius in Old Jewry in 1711–14; he had a brother, name unknown: Richard Hill, *Diplomatic Corr.*, ed. Blackley, pp. 833, 835–7, 841, 843–4.

2500. LOCKE to DR. (later Sir) THOMAS MOLYNEUX, 27 October 1698 (*2336, 2514*)

Some Familiar Letters, pp. 290–1. Printed from fresh transcript by (Sir) William R. W. Wilde in *Dublin University Magazine*, xviii (July–December 1841), 751. Answered by no. *2514*.

Oates, 27 Oct. 1698.

Sir,

Death has with a violent hand hastily snatch'd from you a dear brother. I doubt not but on this occasion you need all the consolation can be given to one unexpectedly bereft of so worthy and near a relation. Whatever inclination I may have to alleviate your sorrow, I bear too great a share in the loss, and am too sensibly touch'd with it my self to be in a condition to discourse you on this subject, or do any thing but mingle my tears with yours. I have lost in your brother, not only an ingenious and learned acquaintance, that all the world esteem'd; but an intimate and sincere friend, whom I truly lov'd, and by whom I was truly loved; and what a loss that is, those only can be sensible who know how valuable and how scarce a true friend is, and how far to be prefer'd to all other sorts of treasure. He has left a son who I know was dear to him, and deserv'd to be so as much as was possible for one of his age. I cannot think my self wholly incapacitated from paying some of the affection and service was due from me to my dear friend as long as he has a child or a brother in the world. If therefore there be any thing at this distance wherein I in my little sphere may be able to serve your nephew or you, I beg you by the memory of our deceased friend to let me know it, that you may see that one who loved him so well cannot but be tenderly concern'd for his son, nor be otherwise than I am,

Sir,

Your most humble, and most affectionate servant,

JOHN LOCKE

2501. LOCKE to EZEKIEL BURRIDGE, 27 October 1698 (*2495, 2677*)

Some Familiar Letters, pp. 275–6. Printed from fresh transcript by (Sir) William R. W. Wilde in *Dublin University Magazine*, xviii (July–December 1841), 751. Answers no. *2495*.

Oates, 27. Oct. 1698.

Sir,

You guessed not amiss, when you said in the beginning of yours of the 13th instant, that you gave me the trouble of a letter; for I have received few letters in my life the contents whereof have so much troubled and afflicted me as that of yours. I parted with my excellent friend when he went from England, with all the hopes and promises to my self of seeing him again, and enjoying him longer the next spring. This was a satisfaction that help'd me to bear our separation; and the short taste I had of him here in this our first interview, I hoped would be made up in a longer conversation, which he promised me the next time: But it has served only to give me a greater sense of my loss in an eternal farewel in this world. Your earlier acquaintance may have given you a longer knowledge of his virtue and excellent endowments, a fuller sight or greater esteem of them you could not have than I. His worth and his friendship to me made him an inestimable treasure, which I must regret the loss of, the little remainder of my life, without any hopes of repairing it any way. I should be glad if what I owed the father could enable me to do any service to his son. He deserves it for his own sake (his father has more than once talked to me of him) as well as for his father's. I desire you therefore to assure those who have the care of him, that if there be any thing wherein I at this distance may be any way serviceable to young Mr. Molyneux, they cannot do me a greater pleasure than to give me the opportunity to shew that my friendship died not with him.

Pray give my most humble service to Dr. Molyneux and to his Nephew. I am,

Sir,

Your most faithful and humble servant,

JOHN LOCKE.

2502. JOHN LOCK (later Sir John) to LOCKE, 27 October 1698 (*2716*)

B.L., MS. Locke c. 14, ff. 170–1. The writer was the eldest son of Samuel Locke (p. 645). He entered the service of the New East India Company. After some time at Surat and a voyage to China he was appointed about 1705 chief agent in Persia. He is further identifiable as Sir John Lock, a Turkey merchant who was knighted in 1717 and who died in 1746: 'Sir

John LOCKE an eminent *Turkey* merchant, formerly resident in *Ispahan*, the capital of *Persia*, a director of the *E. India* and *S. Sea* companies, trustee of *Morden* college, and a governor of St. *Thomas*'s hospital', etc.: Bruce, *Annals*, iii. 407, 569, 572–3, 598–600, 621–2, 652–3; *Gentleman's Magazine*, xvi (1746), 612–13; letters, etc., below (the identification as Sir John depends on the residence in Persia and on the fact that Sir John, like the writer of the present letter, had a brother Samuel; for the latter see no. *2827*).

In this correspondence the writer always signs himself Lock.

Sir

I take the Boldness, by reason of your absence from the Citty, to cover the 2 inclosed Letters which were deliverd me in Amsterdam.[1] their Detention and my Arivall hath been prolonged by the Contrary winds, about 20 days. I crave leave Sir to acknowledge the Favours which for your sake I have received in Holland from that reverend Person Mr Phillip van Limborch by Whome I have been very kindely Treated as also by his Son Mr Francis, which I attribute wholly to the great Honour and Esteem they bear you. my Humble Respects shall never be wanting to testify that I am

Sir

Your most humble and obedient Servant

JOHN LOCK

London 27 October 1698

Sir my Father gives you his most humble Service.

Address: To John Locke, Esqre [at Oates, by Joslyn, Bishops Stortford]

Postmark: OC 27

Endorsed by Locke: J Locke 27 Oct: 1698

2503. WILLIAM POPPLE to LOCKE, 31 October 1698 (*2041*, *2592*)

B.L., MS. Locke c. 17, ff. 229–30.

Whitehall. October: the 31th. 1698

Sir,

This night the Board has received letters from the Earle of Bellomont of the 14th, 16th, and 21th September last; with an account of his journey to Albany and negociation with the Indians

[1] One is no. *2494*.

and several other matters.[1] They are long, and consist of many heads, referring to inclosed papers, according to the method of his former. They were forthwith read; But according to our former method referr'd to further consideration. When the time of that consideration comes, I am sure your assistance will be wanted: But I am far from desiring it, at the price I know it must cost.

The onely occasion of my writing at this is to let you know that we are told from the Treasury that direction is or will be given for another half-year's payment. So that it will be necessary you send your receipt. And therefore, lest you should not remember the form, I have marked it on the back side of this paper. So rest

Sir,

Your most faithfull humble Servant

WILLIAM POPPLE.

On f. 230:]

[A large bracket, to take a number of lines, and pointing to]

Five hundred pounds

J L.[a]

Notes by Locke on f. 229v:]

The Commission was opened 25 Jun. 96
But the Salarys began from the 25 of March before
The Charges of each Commissioner for the

Establishment was	£7–14–1
Charges for the first years Salary – – –	£51– 9–2
For the next half year	£28– 8–6

ndorsed by Locke: W: Popple 31 Oct 98 Answered Nov. 3

504. LOCKE to NICOLAS TOINARD, 1 November 1698 (2497, 2550)

obert Schuman collection: sale catalogue, pt. i, Charavay, 4 and 5 March 965, no. 177; *Bulletin Pierre Berès*, nos. 95–6, June–July 1966. I have

[a] *The bracket and words, and apparently the initials also, written by Popple.*

[1] There are abstracts of Bellomont's letters of 14 and 21 September among ocke's papers; the original letters are in the Public Record Office: B.L., MS. Locke 7, ff. 132–3; *Cal.S.P.*, *Col.*, vol. xvi, nos. 822, 835. There are no traces of a letter om Bellomont dated 16 September.

combined the digests and quotations of the two catalogues. Du Bos mentions what appears to be this letter on p. 509. Perhaps answers no. *2454*.

['Votre mort me serait un terrible pert, et si vous ne vous souvenez plus de moy ce n'est guère moins. Je vive en esperance de meilleures nouvelles de jour à autre . . . Quousque tandem silebit Harmonica le monde l'attend avec impatience.' Dulcifying sea-water: 'On l'a négligé comme une chose tout à fait inutile. . . . C'est aussi facile de porter en mer une suffisante quantité d'eau que de porter une quantité suffisante de bois ou des charbons nécessaires pour distiller l'eau. . . . La machine à tirer les navires dans la Tamise est négligée par la même raison parce qu'elle est inutile dans des occasions où on en a besoin. On a trouvé par expérience si le vent souffle un peu fort cette machine ne servir de rien si bien qu'on ne s'en serve, même on n'en parle plus.' Locke has given to the French ambassador 'une charte de pensylvania'. He is at work on the fourth edition of the *Essay* so far as 'sa santé fort abatue' permits. Before he left London he was engaged in printing an answer to a bishop 'sur une chicanerie qu'il me fit sur quelques passages de mon Essay touchant l'entendement humain'. The choir of St. Paul's is completed; windows of uncoloured glass are installed.

'Si avec la vie Dieu me donne le loisir' Locke will profit by the observations made to him 'de quelques défauts' in the French translation of *Some Thoughts concerning Education*. He is pleased with the notice in the *Journal des Sçavans* and attributes its merits to Toinard. 'On travaille présentement à la traduction en français de mon Essay touchant l'Entendement humain et il y a déjà quelques feuilles imprimées. Aussitôt qu'elle sera achevée je donnerai ordre qu'on vous envoy une copie afin que vous jugerois de mes resveries et en dites vos sentiments sans déguisement.']

2505. SYLVESTER BROUNOWER to LOCKE, 1 November 1698 (*2439*, *2508*)

B.L., MS. Locke c. 4, ff. 189–90.

London November the 1st: 1698

Honoured Sir

Last night I receiv'd your Letter of the 28th: of the last month and according to Your Direction went this Day to Mr: Bridges who both returne their service, and told me they had already tied and seal'd the Bottles; I have also been with Mrs: Popple, but at Mr: Pawling's I have not yet had time, but shall go there to morrow I doubt not but all will be ready by Saturday when, I shall take care of them according to your Desire.

Sir the reason of this is, Mr: Popple, who some dayes ago, saw my Copy of your Picture,[1] told me this morning, that a Book is

[1] Perhaps a copy of one or other of the painted portraits of Locke rather than the plumbago drawing by Syl.

printing or going to be Printed in England, in which the Counterfeits of several learned men are to be graven, amongst which yours also, and wish'd me to apply my self to the Bookseller, and offer them a Draught of your Picture, thinking it for my advantage, and for their service if they should get such a Copy. But I reflecting afterwards upon it, fell in some doubt with my self whether it would not be ill taken, either in Holland, or here, or both places, if they should happen to be the very same in both books, and therefore took the boldness to trouble you with this for your Advise in this matter, yet I know at the same time if they should hear of your picture at Kneller's, I doubt not but they might have a Copy by another hand, and so be before hand with them in Holland, though perhaps not so well don as it will be there.[1] Mr: Molineux's picture is not yet finish'd,[2] nor is yours any further than you saw at the last sitting, else I had sent the Copy to Oates already. My Wife presents her most humble Duty to you, and I am

Sir

Your most humble and Obedient Servant

S BROUNOWER

Address: To the Honrd: John Locke Esqre: [at Oates, by Joslyn, Bishops Stortford]

Postmarks: NO 1; WR

Endorsed by Locke: S: Brownover 1 Nov. 98 Answered 4

2506. LOCKE to PETER KING, later first Baron King. 3 November 1698 (2468, 2507)

B.L., MS. Locke c. 40, ff. 17–18.

Oates Nov. 3d 98

Dear Cosin

I received last night your packet and thank you for your pains. I have not yet had time to looke them over. I would beg you in the next packet to send me also soe much of the MS: copy as the

[1] Kneller painted a portrait of Locke in 1697; he sold it to Dr. Geekie in 1703: no. *3260*; the date of painting from the engraving by George Vertue prefixed to Locke, *Works*, 1714 (the portrait now in the Hermitage). From this portrait studio copies were made; one appears to be mentioned below. The proposed publication of a collection of engraved portraits is due to a misunderstanding: p. 506. Syl alludes to the forthcoming publication at Amsterdam of Coste's translation of the *Essay*. The first edition contains a portrait of Locke engraved by P. van Gunst after Greenhill.

[2] See p. 489.

composer has done with and is or should always be sent to you with the proofs and be kept by you and not sent back to the Printer. I may perhaps need it here to correct by it the printed sheets if I should finde anything amisse in them. For the printer is sometimes soe carelesse as to leave out whole paragraphs, as he did in some of the former sheets of this very booke.[1] I beg your pardon for giveing you this trouble and am

Dear Cosin

Your most affectionate Cosin and humble servant

J LOCKE

You are well thought of and well spoke of by all here. My service to Mr Clarke Mr Freke and Sir W: Yonge as they come in your way.

Address: For Peter King Esqr of the Middle Temple To be left at Mr Potmans in the Middle Temple London

Postmark: NO 4

Endorsed by King: Mr Locke November 3. 1698

2507. LOCKE to PETER KING, later first Baron King, 15 November 1698 (2506, 2512)

B.L., MS. Locke c. 40, ff. 19–20.

Oates 15 Nov 98

Dear Cosin

I shall be glad to hear when the next payment is to be made either of the subscription or into the tradeing stock of the new East India Companie,[2] that I may provide money and you may pay it into your Cosins hands[3] before you come out of town. For you are expected here at Christmas and I would not have you be under any constraint to goe to town upon that account if either of those payments should fall out soon after Christmas. If you can furnish your self for the two next payments for your £100 I shall

[1] Evidently Locke's second *Reply* to Stillingfleet.

[2] The subscribers paid the second instalment towards the £2,000,000 loan on 12–14 September; King paid the third instalment on the 12th of this month; and the fourth on 10 January 1699. A general meeting of the company on 15 September 'resolved to call in 20*l*. per cent towards carrying on their trade' (there may be an error here as Locke's investment in the trading account was 25 per cent of his subscription); King paid the first instalment on 25 October and the second on 10 December: Luttrell, iv. 426–7; B.L., MS. Locke b. 1, ff. 202, 203.

[3] Probably John Freke the stock-jobber.

now be able to supply you in May for all that you are to pay then or afterwards, and perhaps sooner. For I hear we have tallys strook for ½ years Salary[1] but I think the money will not be paid till may. Pray remember to take into your hands the receits for the money you have now paid, and when you come hither pray bring with you the state of the accounts between us, for we shall then have time to adjust them.

I have received the printed sheets and the Copy and have orderd Mr Churchill to give you a booke for your self[2] and another for Mr Baron Littleton,[3] which I desire you to present to him from me: and let him know I was often to wait upon him before I came out of town

Yours

J LOCKE

Address: For Peter King Esqr To be left at Mr Potmans in the Middle Temple London

Postmark: NO 17

Endorsed by King: Mr Locke 15. November. 1698

2508. SYLVESTER BROUNOWER to LOCKE, 15 November 1698 (*2505*)

B.L., MS. Locke c. 4, ff. 191–2.

London. November the 15th: 1698

Honoured Sir

According to Your Order, in your Letter of the 28th: of the last month, I sent to you, by James Lanham the 5th. Instant the things you desired; and a Letter of the same date by the Post, with the particulars of them. Last Saturday James told me, that he had safe delivered them; To whom, at the same time I gave him to carry the Box of Books, and two peices of Deal board, you were pleas'd to write for, in your last of 4th: November, together with some papers for Mr: Coste, which I had at Mr: Pawlings, it rain'd so

[1] p. 501.

[2] *Mr. Locke's Reply to the Right Reverend the Lord Bishop of Worcester's Answer to his Second Letter*, 1699. L.L., no. 1798.

[3] Locke's slip for Mr. Baron Powys, i.e. Sir Littleton Powys: nos. *2005*, 2512. He is named in the distribution list for copies of the book, and in that for the *Letter to* Stillingfleet. There was no Baron of the Exchequer named Littleton at this time.

hard, and he said the Roads were so dashy,[1] that he could not secure the Box from being wet, so lock't it up, Seal'd, in a Dry Room, and promis'd me to carry them the next time he came to Town. Mr: Pawling told me that he spoke with Mr: Clarke the Taylor that the business was not yet done, but did not doubt it would the next time he should go to him. Sir concerning the picture I gave you the Trouble about, in my Letter: Upon better information I finde that I misunderstood Mr: Popple, so run in a mistake for which I humbly beg your pardon. Your Picture and Mr: Molyneux's are neither of them yet finish'd at Sir Godfrey's, but are promis'd to be speedily. We receiv'd the remainder of our pay last week with less loss than we thought for. My wife present her humble Duty to you, and I am

Sir

Your most humble and Dutifull Servant

S BROUNOWER

This Letter was writ last Saturday[2] but by mistake was not carried to the Posthouse, and since that new writ.

Address: For the Honrd: John Locke Esqr: [at Oates, by Joslyn, Bishops Stortford]

Postmarks: NO 15; WR

Endorsed by Locke: S:Brownover 15 Nov 98 Answered Dec. 1

2509. SAMUEL BOLD to LOCKE, 17 November 1698 (*2493, 2567*)

B.L., MS. Locke c. 4, f. 26.

Steeple Nov: 17th. 1698

Honoured Sir

The last week a great quantity of Snow fell in these parts, which confining me to my study, I look'd over what I had writ in the last sheet I sent you, so far as related to mr Jenkin.[3] And I soon perceived many great Faults, which I wonder how I overlooked before. This made me consider afresh what that Author had said pardon I beseech you my troubling you with the former sheet

[1] The word is given in *O.E.D.*, but not with the meaning that it bears here.
[2] 12 November.
[3] p. 470. Bold's *Some Considerations* contains sixty pages; pp. 28–59 answer Jenki

and excuse my presuming to lay before you this Account of my latter thoughts. When your leisure wil permit I shall be glad to hear whether these papers be any thing more to the purpose than the last paper was. What faults may be in the other part of that sheet I cannot tell, For being writ, (as we sometimes say in these parts) off hand, I kept not a copy of It. It was but an Accidental Addition, occasioned by my having Just read a Rude Nonsensical Pamphlet (writ as I guess by mr Edwards) entitled, A Free but Modest Censure on the late controversial writings and Debates of the Lord Bishop of Worcester and Mr Locke, Mr Edwards and Mr Locke etc. By F.B. M.A. of Cambridg.[1] Sir wishing most heartily the continuance of your health, and success to all your Labours, I remain

your most Humble and Obliged Servant

SA: BOLD

Address (not in Bold's hand): For Jno Locke Esqr at Sir Fra Mashams at Oates.

Endorsed by Locke (i): S: Bold
(ii): S: Bold 17 Nov 98 Answered Dec. 8

2510. J.-B. DU BOS to LOCKE, 19/29 November [1698] (*2489, 2527*)

B.L., MS. Locke c. 7, ff. 219–20. Printed by G. Bonno in *Revue de littérature comparée*, xxiv (1950), 486–8. Year from Locke's endorsement.

A Paris le 29/19 de Novembre

Je vous ai envoié monsieur, dans un paquet que jay adressé a monsieur de Vernietes, lhistoire de Siam par Gervais.[2] jespere que vous recevré le livre qui est parti des la semaine derniere peu de temps apres ma lettre.

Je viens aussi d'envoier au carosse de Calais deux comedies et un opera faits par monsieur de Vernietes, que jay adressé suivant linstruction que vous avé mise dans vostre lettre a monsieur Toinard. monsieur de Vernietes na rien fait outre ce que je vous envoie, q'un opera apellé Adonis que je cherche pour vous l'envoier

[1] The writer, an anti-Socinian, vindicates Stillingfleet and Edwards against Locke, and, on the ground of manners, Bentley against Boyle; he also attacks Le Clerc's *Ars Critica*.

[2] Nicolas Gervaise, *Histoire naturelle et politique du royaume de Siam*, Paris, 1688. Du Bos sent Locke a copy of the new edition, 1689: L.L., no. 1245.

a la premiere occasion.[1] je me flate monsieur que mon exactitude a macquiter de vos comissions men attirera d'autres.

Je vous remercie du livre de monsieur Sydney que je lis avec beaucoup de plaisir. il establit assez bien son systeme contre son adversaire, mais dans ces sortes de combats la difficultè nest point de ruiner les deffenses de son enemy et de le battre en ruine, cest de soutenir la breche, en repondant aux objections. je crois qun autheur qui entreprendroit de faire voir les inconvenients quil i a a craindre dans le systeme de monsieur Sydney, feroit un bon livre.

nous aurons bientost la relation du voyage de monsieur Carrè aux Indes orientales.[2] il i a esté deux fois, lune par mer et l'autre par terre. Jay lu autrefois le livre en manuscrit, il contient des choses bien curieuses, mais si lon a bien fait, lon l'aura abregé, car le stile en estoit bien diffus.

monsieur Duhamel secretaire de 'lacademie des Sciences, nous a donné une histoire de cette Societé. je pense que lautheur qui a deja publie un cours de philosophie latin, et quelques autres ouvrages vous sera connu.[3]

il i a deux ans que le p. Daniel Jesuite publia une histoire de france, ou il rapelle a Clovis la fondation de nostre monarchie. on vient d'escrire contre lui, pour prouver quil a tort de suprimer nos quatre premiers roys.[4]

les memoires du marquis de Pignalossa ci devant gouverneur du nouveau Mexique, le quel est mort a Paris, ou il s'estoit retire, crainte de l'inquisition, ne sont pas encore achevé d'imprimer.[5]

monsieur felibien le jeune fils de feu monsieur felibien l'autheur des entretiens sur la vie des peintres, a fait imprimer la traduction des deux lettres de Pline qui font la description de sa maison de campagne. come il est architecte, il a joint a sa traduction des notes qui sont dun homme docte et du metier. il a meme dressé

[1] Vernietes is J.-B. Rousseau; the pieces sent were *Le Caffé*, 1694; *Le Flatteur*, 1697; and *Jason, ou la Toison d'or*, 1696: L.L., nos. 3072–3, 2504[a]. The other opera is *Vénus et Adonis*, 1697.

[2] Barthélemy Carré (*D.B.F.*), *Voyage des Indes Orientales*, etc., 1699. See p. 615.

[3] J.-B. du Hamel (1624–1706; *D.B.F.*), *Regiæ Scientiarum Academiæ Historia*, 1698. L.L., no. 1381. The other book mentioned is apparently *Philosophia Vetus et Nova, ad Usum Scholæ Accommodata*, 1678.

[4] G. Daniel (no. *1648* n.), *Histoire de France depuis l'etablissement de la monarchie françoise dans les Gaules*, vol. i, 1696 (the complete work was not published until 1713). His opinion is controverted in *Lettre, ou reflexions critiques sur les deux dissertations préliminaires . . . composées par le R. P. Daniel . . .*, 1698. Notice in *Journal des Sçavans*, 19 January 1699 (pp. 45–6).

[5] Peñalosa: no. 665. His memoirs were not published.

les plans, sur la narration de Pline, ce qui nestoit pas facile a bien faire.[1]

lon vient d'afficher une traduction de toutes les lettr⟨es⟩[a] de Pline, dont les premiers livres ont este faits par monsieur de Sacy.[2]

monsieur Toinard ma fait l'amitie de me lire la lettre que vous lui escrivé doats, ou vous lui donné un coup d'eperon sur son harmonie.[3] il est convenu avec moy, quil avancoit trop lentement, mais je ne crois pas quil en aille plus viste.

Je vous prie monsieur d'estre persuadé que vous ne scaurie mobliger d'avantage, quen m'ordonant quelque chose pour vostre service. monsieur Toinard vous salue et je suis de ⟨tout⟩[b] mon cœur

Vostre tres humble et tres obeissant serviteur

DU BOS.

Address: To Master Jhon Locke at master Pawling's over against The plough in little Lincolns Inne fields London

Postmark: DE 1

Endorsed by Locke: Du Bos 29° Nov. 98 Answered Mar. 21

2511. MRS. ELIZABETH BERKELEY, later Burnet, to LOCKE, 22 November [1698] (*2491*, *2556*)

B.L., MS. Locke c. 3, ff. 216–17. The year from the mention of Locke's second *Reply* to Stillingfleet; further, the letter appears to be a sequel to no. *2491*. Locke's endorsement by itself is not decisive.

Sir

If willfull faults have no right to pardon I have no fair pretence to ask yours, but tho I fear robing you of any of your valuable time is so, yet I know allmost as litle how to deny my self that satisfaction as I do to pay that obedience to your orders which my esteem of your Judgment generally Commands; I daer not say you have quit mistaken my distemper, but really I hope you have the cause of it; I h⟨av⟩e[c] never read m⟨uch⟩.[c] an h⟨ou⟩r[c] or tw⟨o⟩[c] in a day will turn more leves then I have don, nor has books often made me

[a] *Page torn.* [b] *MS.* ton [c] *Page torn or rubbed.*

[1] J.-F. Félibien, 1658–1733 (*N.B.G.*), son of André Félibien, 1619–95, architect and historian (ibid.), *Les Plans et les descriptions de deux des plus belles maisons de campagne de Pline le consul*, etc., 1699.

[2] Louis Silvestre de Sacy: *N.B.G.* His translation was published in 1699–1700.

[3] Apparently no. 2504.

sade, but have often cured me when I have ben so; the various openions I have meet with, tho in maters of religion (where above all I wish't to find agrement) have not so greatly disquieted me as the severe and uncharitable methods of defending even what I beleeved truth; in short 'tis seeing and reflecting on the faults and foolys of mankind, and my one in the first rank, that has not only ben uneasy to my mind, but perhaps injurious to my health; if I have ben thoughtfull 'twas to find reasons for what I observed in practice but could not account for in speculation; I can not at all repine at my defective health if my mind has at all gained by it; I will endevour to obey your other rules, but in this I daer not promis, indid I wonder how you could send me so severe a penance; I think I have a very severe[a] will, tho no other quality to intitle me to the benefect of your Frindship, yet I find I could not willingly give up the m⟨a⟩ny[b] valuable fruits of your meditations[c] to have assured you a more perfect tho less usefull health; indid I can but read and imperfectly profect by what others write, yet can not find in my hart to part with so crude a pleasure as my litle understanding makes it, for a more florishing health—being called to atend a sick Frind before ending my leter, at my return I found you had don me the great favour of sending me your last letter to the Bishop,[1] so will conclude your advise was not positive or universall. this is at least a dispensation of your own opointing; I have but look't into it yet, but my first leasure shall be to read it as carefully as my litle Judgment will permit me to do; I'm sure it will both inform and intertain me, but I will not promise it shall never make me Malloncolly; not from the obscurity newness or danger of any openions I may meet with, and less from any rong impressions for the esteemed[d] Author, but out of grife of finding two persones so capable of thinking truely and consequently of thinking alike, so seemingly opposite to each other; these are some of the sharpest and unacountable infeliceties of life, and must be patiently submited to, tell being freed from the intanglements of intrest self love and prejudice, wee shall be beter disposed for the receeveing of truth and practice of charity, that you and

[a] *Doubtful reading; word altered.* [b] *Page torn.* [c] *Or* meditating [d] *MS* estēmed

[1] The second *Reply* to Stillingfleet. Mrs. Berkeley had thanked Locke for the first *Reply* on 22 September 1697: p. 198.

(and—(I know not where to bond my wish) may find some place in those mansions of truth and peace is the hope and humble desiere of

Sir

Your greatly Obliged and truely Faithfull servant

E BERKELEY

22: Nov: 98:[a] Lin: Inn Feilds;

Endorsed by Locke: E: Berkeley 22 Nov 98 Answered Feb 17

2512. LOCKE to PETER KING, later first Baron King, 25 November 1698 (2507, 2518)

B.L., MS. Locke c. 40, ff. 21–2.

Oates 25 Nov 98

Dear Cosin

The satisfaction that Mr Baron Powis expressed must be I suppose in my presenting it him, for it could not be in the booke which he had not yet read of that perhaps he may say something when you see him next.

The receit for my third payment of my subscription into the East India company you need neither send nor bring with you hither but keep it by you till I come to town.

I have here inclosed sent you a bill on Mr Churchill for £50 for the payment on the 10th Dec in the tradeing account. you say noe thing of the receit for the first payment on that account, which is already made.

I have also sent you of the money due to me from Mr Firmin as it stood the 11th of this month. I desire you when the terme is over to goe to his Cousin who is in the shop and tell him you are come from me to know when he can conveniently pay that money, let him know that I was my self there to speake with him when I was in town but missed him, send me word what he says and I will give you order accordingly

The bill for £50 on Mr Churchill I have given him advice of but told him you would not call to him for it before the 5th or 6th of the next month, which I would not have you doe because it may soe fall out that I may possibly before that time furnish you with this £50 some other way. I am Dear Cosin

Your most affectionate Cosin and humble Servant

J LOCKE

[a] *Badly written; Mrs. Berkeley forms the figure* 8 *badly.*

My man Kiplin and I are parted. I want a good servant if you can help me to one

[On f. 22:]

1695 Mr Firmin	Dr	1696 JL Contra	Cr
Nov 11 To money lent him upon bond	176. 0.0	Jul 4 By cash paid me	4. 8.0
1696		1697	
Nov 11 To a years interest at 5 per cent	8.16.0	Apr 12 By money paid by my order	5. 0.0
		By money paid for a hat	0.18.0
1697			
Nov 11 To ditto	8.16.0	Aug 16 By cash paid me	2.18.0
			13. 4.0
1698		1698	
Nov 11 To ditto	8.16.0	Nov 11 Rests due to me	189.4.0[a]
	202.08.0		

Address: For Peter King Esqr at his Chamber in the Temple London

Endorsed by King: Mr Locke 25. November 1698.

Note by King: 191. 8
7. 9
25
223.17.—

2513. Mrs. Mary Popple to Locke, 25 November 1698 (*1698, 2526*)

B.L., MS. Locke c. 17, ff. 197–8.

Sir

I percive by mr Popple you have not yet begun to take your drops, I wish you were well enough to thinke your self in a condition to take them, that is, the same dose you took when you were here; without augmenting it.

	lb sh d
I have: 24 lb of Chocalate for you ready made.	
A quarter of a hundred Caraca[1]	:-3:—:—
makeing 24 lb at: 6d: per lb: sugar paper thred	:—:14:—
paid for a Map of Pensilvania[2]	:—:-1:—
paid for 2: quarts of Sherry, and Bottle	:—:-4:
	:-3:19:

[a] *King adds:* To Febru. 11 ½s interest more 2.4.0
191.8.0

[1] Presumably cacao-nuts from Caracas.

[2] p. 50

I here send you the account you desier and shall send the Chocalate when you desier it. I begg leave to present my service to my Lady and all with you. I am

Your most humble servant
MARY POPPLE

25th. november 1698

Endorsed by Locke: M Popple's Account 25 Nov 98

2514. DR. (later Sir) THOMAS MOLYNEUX to LOCKE, 26 November 1698 (2500, 2539)

The Carl H. Pforzheimer Library, New York. Transcribed from photostat. Printed in *Some Familiar Letters*, pp. 291–4. Answers no. 2500; answered by no. 2539.

Sir

as You have a true sense of every thing, so you were very much in the right, when You tell me in the Letter You favord me with of the 27th of last moneth, that I needed all the Consolation could be given one that had lost so unexpectedly a Dear and only Brother. His Death indeed has been a severe Affliction to me, and tho' I have You, and many more, that bear a great share with me in my sorrow, yet this dos no way alleviate it, but makes it fall the heavier upon me; for it doubles my Grief to think what an unspeakable loss he must be to so near a Relation, that is so much lamented by those, that were only acquainted with him. I could not believe that Mortality could have made so deep an Impression on me, who's Profession leads him into so thorough a Familiarity with it; but I find a Passionate Affection surmounts all this, and the Tecum Obeam lubens,[1] tho it was the expression of a Poet, yet I am sensible was a very natural one where we love extremly, and the Indians prove it no less in Fact. Could any outward circumstance of his Life have increased that Brotherly Affection I had for him, it must have been that He had so great a part in Your Friendship, who must be allowed to have a nice Judgment in discerning the true Caracters and Worth of Men: He frequently in his Life time has expressed to me with great complacensy of mind, how happy he thought himself in Your Acquaintance, and he

[1] 'I would gladly die with thee': Horace, *Odes* III. ix. 24.

Spoke of You several times during his short sickness, with great respect. with his own hand he has writt this Clause in his Will. *I give and bequeath to my Excellent Friend John Lock Esquire Author of the Essay concerning humane Understanding the summe of five pound to buy him a Ring in memory of the Value and Esteeme I had for him.* This I shall take care to send You in a Bill by Mr. Churchils Hands, when he states the account as it stands between him and my Brother. The only Childe he has leaft behind him is under my care and Management, I shal indeavour to discharge his Trust, with all the regarde to my Brothers Memory, and the advantage of his Childe, I can; but it grieves me to think, that I must surely fall very much short of that extraordnary A⟨p⟩plication[a] and Prudence his Father would have shewn in his Education; for he made it the cheifes⟨t⟩[a] and indeed the only business of his Life. I have made his little son as sensible as his tender age would allow how much he is oblidged to You his Father's Friend, for Your earnest Desire to serve him; I wish You may both prolong Your Lifes so, as he may one day be more thankfull and capable of Your Kindness by profiting much from Your good Instructions and Advise. and since You so earnestly press me by the memory of Your deceased Friend, to lett You know wherein You might oblidge me, I'l venture to breake the bounds of Modesty so far, as to tell You I should be extremly pleased to receive from Yourself the last Edition of Your incomparable Essay of Humane Understanding, and such other pieces of Your Works as You shall think fitt; for all which as I have a great Esteem, so I should have a more particular regard coming from Yourself as a private Memorial of my Dear Brothers Friend, and of a Person for whom I have such an extraordnary Value as I shal ever be proud of owning myself

Sir

Your truly affectionate and humble servant

THO: MOLYNEUX

Dublin Nov: the 26th 1698.

Address: For John Lock Esquire at Mr Robert Pauletts opposite to th Plow in Little Lincoln's Inn Fields London

Postmark: DE 6

Endorsed by Locke: T: Molyneux 26° Nov. 98 Answered Jan. 25

[a] *Page torn.*

2515. FRANCIS GASTRELL, later bishop of Chester, to LOCKE, 27 November [1698] (*2279, 2554*)

B.L., MS. Locke c. 9, ff. 209–10. Year from Locke's endorsement.

Christchurch Nov. 27

Sir

I have a great many acknowledgments to make you for the favour of your last book,[1] not only for the satisfaction I found in reading it, but for the assurance it gave me of your regard for me, whose good opinion I should be very proud of deserving. I did not need any conviction or else I had certainly met with it in your book, but I was very well pleased to see things set in such a light, that others who were unjustly prejudiced to your character must be forced to yield to your arguments. However I cannot but wish you had not been put under a necessity of vindicating yourself, For then I perswade my self that the time you have imployed in defending your former notions would have been spent in giving us some further account of your thoughts, which would have been more for your own ease as well as the benefit of the world, tho' I must needs say at the same time I should have been unwilling to have lost soe good a pattern of managing controversy as you have set us. I am going to town very speedily to print a discourse I have prepared upon the Christian Religion[2] and I am very sorry it is at such a time that I cannot promise my self the advantage of your advice and conversation upon that and other subjects, wherein your opinion would be very much esteemed

by your most obliged Humble Servant

FRAN: GASTRELL

Address: To Mr Lock to be left with mr churchill a bookseller in pater-noster-row London

Postmark: NO 29

Endorsed by Locke: F. Gastrell 27 Nov 98 Answered Dec. 9

2516. PHILIPPUS VAN LIMBORCH to LOCKE, 29 November/9 December 1698 (2498, 2557)

B.L., MS. Locke c. 14, ff. 125–6. Copy by van Limborch in Amsterdam University Library, MS. R.K., III D 16, f. 208. Printed from the copy, with

[1] The second *Reply* to Stillingfleet. [2] p. 572.

an omission, in *Some Familiar Letters*, pp. 431–4. Answers no. 2498; answered by no. 2557.

Amplissime Vir

Quod literis tuis hactenus non responderim valetudo minus prospera in causa fuit. Aliquot hebdomadibus febriculâ laboravi; accessere dolores colici acres admodum ac vehementes. Tandem benignitate divinâ convalui, et ad intermissa studia reversus sum. Virum Magnificum jam a multo tempore non conveni. Ab ipso non vocatus sponte vix accedere possum, et tuo nomine argumenta ejus flagitare, nisi ostensis tuis literis, quibus tamen quæ ipsi ostendi minime cupis contineri existimo. Si literas a te habeam, quæ sine scrupulo ab ipso legi possunt, ultro eum adire possem: nunc, si literas ostendere nolim, aut ab ipso me vocari oportet, aut alibi in ædibus amici per occasionem, si quæ mihi offertur, est compellandus: tum enim tuo nomine argumenta ejus flagitare, nec tamen literas, utpote domi relictas, ostendere necesse est. Sed me frustra fore, ipsumque se alia non habere argumenta dissimulaturum, et sub eodem quem scripsi prætextu se excusaturum credo.

Cartesianam illam loquendi formulam tecum non capio: Cogitationem enim per se existentem non percipio, sed quidem substantiam cogitantem. Verum ne sententiam suam minus candide

---

Excellent Sir,

My ill health was the reason why I have not answered your letter hitherto. For some weeks I suffered from a slight fever, with the addition of very sharp and severe colic. By the goodness of God I have at length recovered and have returned to my interrupted studies. I have now not for a long time met the Magnifico. Unless invited by him, I can scarcely go to him of my own accord and press him on your behalf for his arguments, without showing him your letter, which, however, I think contains things which you do not at all wish to be shown to him. If I should have a letter from you that there can be no objection to his reading I could go to him without being asked; as it is, if I am unwilling to show him the letter, either I must be summoned by him or he must be accosted elsewhere at a friend's house, if an opportunity is offered to me; for I should then press him on your behalf for his arguments without, however, its being necessary to show him the letter, seeing that it would have been left at home. But I think that I shall be disappointed and that he will conceal the fact that he has no other arguments, and will excuse himself on the same pretext as that that I wrote to you.

Like you I do not understand that Cartesian way of talking; for I do not comprehend thought that exists of itself, but, certainly, I comprehend a thinking substance. Lest, however, they should complain that their opinion is not being candidly represented it is necessary to use the same words

proponi querantur, iisdem quibus illi eam explicant verbis uti necesse est: Ego autem quando me explico ita loqui non soleo.

Quæ de Christianis Euangelicis et Papistis disseris, optima sunt ac verissima. Ego utramque classem in omnibus Christianorum sectis reperiri credo. Nullum enim cœtum ita prorsus corruptum mihi persuadeo, ut nemo in tanto numero sit Euangelicus: licet enim cœtus ipse professionem edat Papismi, nonnullos tamen in eo latere credo Euangelicos, quibus dominatus ille in aliorum conscientias displicet, et dissentientibus salutem abjudicare religio est. Rursus licet cœtus Euangelicam caritatem profiteatur, non adeo in omnibus et per omnia purgatum sperare ausim, quin et degeneres aliquot in eo reperiantur, qui professionis suæ obliti tyrannidem animo fovent, libertatemque sentiendi quam sibi cupiunt aliis invident. Ita ubique zizania tritico permista in hoc sæculo habebimus. Euangelicos ego quocunque in cœtu sint amo ac fraternâ caritate complector. Papistas, licet ejusdem mecum cœtus membra, tanquam spurios Christianos considero, nec genuina esse corporis Christi membra agnosco, utpote charitate, ex quâ discipulos suos agnosci vult Christus, destitutos.

Bibliopolæ Churchil tradetur fasciculus, quem ad te mittet,

:hey do when setting it forth; but I am not wont to speak in that way when etting forth my own views.

What you say about Evangelical Christians and Papists is very good and very true. I believe that both classes are to be found in every Christian lenomination [*secta*]. For I am convinced that no society [*coetus*] is so entirely orrupt that no one in so great a number is an Evangelical; for though the ociety itself may profess Papism, still I believe that some Evangelicals lurk n it, who dislike that lordship over other people's consciences and scruple o deny salvation to those who disagree with them. Again, although a ociety may profess Evangelical charity I should not dare to hope that it s so purified in all things and in every way that there may not be found in : some unworthy members who, forgetful of their profession, cherish tyranny n their hearts and grudge to others the freedom of opinion that they desire or themselves. So we shall have tares mixed with the wheat everywhere n this world. Evangelicals I love and embrace with brotherly charity, in whatsoever society they may be. Papists I regard as spurious Christians, ven if members of the same society as myself; nor do I recognize them as enuine members of Christ's body, seeing that they are destitute of the harity by which Christ wishes his disciples to be recognized.

A packet will be delivered to the bookseller Churchill which he will send o you; it contains the *Historia Inquisitionis*, which you will please deliver o Francis Cudworth Masham with the accompanying letter. I have added

complectens Historiam Inquisitionis, quam cum epistolâ additâ Francisco Cudworth Masham tradi velim. Addidi tria Defensionis meæ contra Joannem van der Waeijen exemplaria,[1] quorum unum tibi, alterum Francisco, tertium D. Coste destinavi. Adversarius meus se Reformatum vocat; an Euangelicus, an vero Papista sit, tu dijudicabis. Amicorum hortatui obsecutus sum: Verum bonas meas horas melioribus studiis destinavi, nec facile me istiusmodi scriptis inde denuo avelli patiar. Ut scias quò respiciam, quando de spatiis imaginariis ultra polos loquor, adscribam lineas aliquot ex tractatu quodam Wæijeni contra Spanhemium, quibus Spanhemio geographiæ ignorantiam objicit, ipse adeo rudis, ut discrimen inter gradus longitudinis et latitudinis prorsus ignoret. Hæc sunt ejus verba. *Ridere in calce si lubet, lege quæso Dissert. Histor. p.298. Americæ longitudinem protendit* (Spanhemius) *ultra 180 gradus. Forte pars ejus in spatiis imaginariis collocanda erit! Cum hactenus ab uno polo ad alium non ultra 180 gradus ponant Geographi,*[a] *Arcticæ*[a] *et Antarcticæ terræ partibus nullus jam locus erit, ubi America ultra polos ignorantissime pro-*

[a] *MS.* Geographi. Arcticæ

---

three copies of my *Defensio* against Joannes van der Waeyen;[1] I intend one of these for you, another for Francis, and the third for Mr. Coste. My opponent calls himself Reformed; you will determine whether he is an Evangelical or in fact a Papist. I have yielded to the urging of friends; but I intended my good hours for better studies, nor shall I readily let myself be torn away from them again by writings of that kind. So that you may know to what I refer when I speak of imaginary spaces beyond the poles I shall add a few lines from a certain treatise of van der Waeyen's against Spanheim in which he taunts Spanheim with ignorance of geography, himself so unlearned as to be entirely ignorant of the difference between degrees of longitude and those of latitude. These are his words: 'If finally you would like to laugh pray read his *Dissert. Histor.* p. 298. He' (Spanheim) 'extends the longitude of America beyond 180 degrees. Perhaps part of it will have to be placed in imaginary spaces! Since geographers as yet do not put more than 180 degrees from one pole to the other there will now be no room for the Arctic and Antarctic regions of the earth, where America is most ignorantly extended beyond the poles. Beware of trusting one' (Spanheim) 'who philosophizes so grossly when it comes to mathematics.' Admonishe

---

[1] *Defensio contra Joannis van der Waeyen Iniquam Criminationem*, 1699. L.L., no. 1758. For van der Waeyen's attack see pp. 466–7. Van Limborch reprinted the *Defensio* in his *Theologia Christiana*, 3rd ed., 1700, pp. 853–74. Van der Waeyen replied in due course: pp. 640, 688.

tenditur. Cave credas (Spanhemio) *adeo crassè philosophanti, cum ad Mathesin ventum est.* Monitus ab amico, rescisso hoc folio aliud substituit; sed libellus jam toto Belgio dispersus erat, et in omnium officinis prostabat. Vidi cum quali heroë mihi res sit.[1]

Filium meum in procurandis D. Samuelis Locke negotiis ipsius exspectationi satisfecisse gaudeo. Filio ejus hinc Angliam repetenti literas ad te dedi: Verum ille te Londini non invenit.[2] Hyemem hanc sine gravi incommodo ruri ut transigas voveo. Domino ac Dominæ Masham totique familiæ officiosissimam a nobis dicas salutem. Uxor, filius ac filia te plurimum salutant, imprimis ego

Tui Amantissimus

PHILIPPUS A LIMBORCH

Amstelodami 9 Decembris

20
16 X 98
19

Address: For John Locke Esqr. at Mr. Pawlings overagainst the plough in Little Lincolns Inne feilds London

Endorsed by Locke: P: Limborch 9 Dec. 98 Answered Mar 5

---

by a friend, this leaf having been cancelled, he substituted another; but the book was already dispersed all over the Netherlands and on sale in every shop. See with what kind of hero I have to deal.[1]

I am glad that my son in attending to Mr. Samuel Locke's affairs satisfied his expectation. I gave his son a letter for you when he was returning from here to England; but he did not find you in London.[2] I wish that you may pass this winter in the country without serious trouble. Please give our best respects to Sir Francis and Lady Masham and the whole family. My wife, son, and daughter send you their best regards, as do I,

Your most affectionate

PHILIPPUS VAN LIMBORCH

Amsterdam 9 December
1698

---

[1] Van der Waeyen's principal attack on Spanheim appears to be *Ad Philalethium Eliezerum adversus Nuperas F. Spanhemii Literas Epistola Apologetica*, 1683. I have failed to find in the Bodleian copy either the passage quoted or a cancel. Van Limborch repeats his statement in his *Defensio*, pp. 61–2 (§ xxxi), where he quotes Spanheim's *Epistola ad Amicum*, 1684(?). See also Le Clerc, *Parrhasiana* (p. 637), pp. 413–14.

[2] p. 500.

2517. MARTHA LOCKHART to LOCKE, 3 December [1698] (*2365*, *2541*)

B.L., MS. Locke c. 15, ff. 74–5. Year from Locke's endorsement.

December 3rd.

what with the hurry's I have been in upon my Lord Forfar's coming and having my house taken over my head which oblige's me to find another and prepare for a winter remove. I have not till now had time to answer your two letter's, but had the dispatch of my answers been of any consequence to you I had broke thro' all my other difficulty's and the first post had brought them to you. the authentique spice box[1] is as Empty as the town it stands in when Either furnishe's me you shall be sure to be sprinkl'd as you desire. some rare spice there is in town but it's of too great vallue to be sent by a carrier when I have any fit to send you I shall think your black puddings a better returne then your good wishes at piquet. I have used the best of my skill to find out my new aquaintance and by one whom he vissets sent him some reproaches for not seing me and tho he made many apollogies and promis'd very soon to doe it 'tis some weeks since and I have heard no more of him. nor can I think that any farther advance would doe good, however let me kno your opinion, if our suspition be true his guardian has no doubt taken some Effectual care to prevent his seing me. and to me this Explains it. for Your frend Mr. B—t for ought that I kno he may be drown'd in the cross bath[2] and made me Excecutrix to his print's and perfumes: however have You a care of the small Bassum box[3] least contrary orders may be found about it in his will.

I am now come to your second letter which I shall only answer in short that I think on this side there is neither intention nor inclination to quarell with my lady Masham for whom I beleive she has an unalterable respect but if there was I should beg leave to take the same care of myself you doe of my Lady, that is to keep myself out of the brangle. nor can I se how any thing but your self could have brought you in for if I understood my cosen Cutts rightly what she writ to my Lady was not grounded in the least upon Your railery but on a letter which my Lady writ to me with

[1] Perhaps the court.

[2] The Cross Bath at Bath; Thomas Burnett of Kemney, who was there in October Leibniz, *Phil. Schriften*, ed. Gerhardt, iii. 243; p. 586.

[3] Not traceable in *O.E.D.*; I can suggest only a box for balsam.

an intention as I thought to be shewn, for I think it could be writ to me on no other account. You may remember when You spoke of it to her I did wonder at it and have not since chang'd my opinion but I'le allways submit to better judges Elce should think You nor I need not shew our knight errantry on this occasion for leaving them to themselvs I beleive no misheif will happen. there's some Eas I find in not being too wise one has not the care of foreseing great inconveniency's that never come to pass. I beg my very humble service to my Lady Sir Fr: and my husband. and if I am not quite in disgrace with Mrs Masham let her kno she shall have my apollogie at length next post the quarell I have to a red petecoat this winter has made me not think it so necessary to write sooner as I should Elce have don. I'me affraid cross winds will stop the Kings coming 'till tis warm Enuff for You to come to town.[1] there's an ill book come out Call'd the history of standing army's[2] in which in my opinion you are more concern'd then in your new quarell.[3] I wish you good health and a merry Christmas and am,

Your very humble servant

M L

my cousen Cutts gives you her very humble service and bids me tell you she never will quarell with you nor leave jesting and hopes the same from you

Endorsed by Locke: M: Lockhart 3. Dec 98 Answered 17

2518. LOCKE to PETER KING, later first Baron King, 5 December 1698 (2512, 2522)

B.L., MS. Locke c. 40, ff. 23–4. A passage printed in King, p. 196, with wrong date, 5 November 1698.

Oates 5 Dec 98

Dear Cosin

Your advice is good about Mrs Firmins money[4] and I shall

[1] The king arrived at Kensington on 4 December: *London Gazette*, 5 December.

[2] *A Short History of Standing Armies in England*, by John Trenchard (*D.N.B.*), who, in conjunction with Walter Moyle (ibid.), had started off the Standing Army controversy (p. 312, n. 1) with *An Argument, shewing, that a Standing Army is inconsistent with a Free Government*, etc., 1697. Locke owned a copy of the *Argument*: L.L., no. 123. Mrs. Lockhart probably alludes to a passage in the preface to the *Short History* in which Trenchard calls attention to the increase since the Revolution of the number of commissionerships which could be used to corrupt members of the house of commons, listing among other bodies the Board of Trade.

[3] Apparently the difference between Lady Masham and Mrs. Cutts.

[4] Firmin's second wife, Margaret, daughter of Giles Dent of Newport, Essex; *D.N.B.*

follow it and therefor desire you to tell her Cosin that since it is for her convenience to stay till after Candlemas I shall doe it and shall desire to have my money the 11th of February. I know not whether when you talked with him last you adjusted the account of interest due, if you did not I desire you would doe it to the 11th of February when you see him next, that soe if there should be any difference about it which I doe not foresee there can be we may adjust it before the time and may have noe thing to doe the 11th of February but to receive the money.

I am glad you have found the receit for the first payment to the King[1] for your own satisfaction. For I never thought you had lost it. I could not beleive you soe carelesse, though I imagind you might be, as yonge and studious men use to be, not yet a man of order in businesse that did not immediately relate to your studys. Only upon this occasion give me leave to tell you that the sooner and the more you are soe the more it will be for your ease and the saveing your time

If those Gent think that the Bishop hath the advantage by not makeing good one of those many propositions in debate between us, but by askeing a question[a] a personal question noe thing to the purpose I shall not envie him such a victory. In the mean time if this be all they have to say the world that sees not with their eyes will see what disputants for truth those are who make to themselves occasions of calumney and think that a triumph. The Bishop is to prove that my booke has something in it that is inconsistent with the Doctrine of the Trinity. And all that upon examination he does is to A⟨sk⟩[b] me whether I beleive the doctrine of ⟨the⟩[b] Trinity as it has been received in the Christian Church.[2] A worthy proof. When you wait on Sir Littleton Powis pray present my most humble service to him. He will I suppose by that time have read my booke which will give you some matter of discourse. All this family have respectfull and kinde thoughts of you and expect you keep your word at Christmas and come to a place where you are sure to be very welcome. I am

Dear Cosin

Your most affectionate Cosin and humble servant

J Locke

[a] *Followed by* noe *deleted.* [b] *Page torn.*

---

[1] Probably a tax.

[2] Stillingfleet's *Answer to Mr. Locke's Second Letter*, p. 4. By declaring his belief in the doctrine Locke would have dissociated himself from another person, i.e. Toland.

2519. Mevr. C. M. Guenellon, 5 December 1698

Pray pay Mrs Popple for cholate and other money she has laid out for me £3.19.6 and take of her lb 2 of chocolate and bring hither with you.

Address: For Mr Peter King at his chamber in the Temple To be left at Mr Potmans in the Middle Temple London

Postmark: DE 7

Endorsed by King: Mr Locke December. 5. 1698.

2519. MEVR. C. M. GUENELLON (born Veen) to LOCKE, 5/15 December 1698 (*1967, 3325*)

B.L., MS. Locke c. 10, ff. 206–7.

d'Amsterdam Ce 15 dec 1698

Monsieur,

L'esperance de vous revoir au printims prochain ma rendu plus negligente que je n'aurois été pour vous remercier de toutes vos honestetez, et les presens dont il vous a plu m'honorer. J'esperois de vous faire mon compliment de bouche, et qu'aÿant le bonheur de vous posseder, j'aurois le pu faire a loisir. Vous scavez combien notre sexe en ce pais est negligent et paresseux, et se sauve tousjours sur l'avenir. mais est il vraÿ Monsieur? vostre voiage de Paris est il rompu? quoi serons nous assez malheureux, apres toute la joie que nous en avons concus, de ne vous jamais revoir? si je croÿois mon courage, rien ne maréteroit pour vous aller trouver, car enfin Monsieur, vous este tousjours la personne du monde que nous honorons le plus, et pour la quelle jaÿ plus destime que je ne scaurois vous exprimer. conservé la nous tousjours, je vous prie. et Dieu veuille vous donner une santé perfaitte, et prolonger vos jours. c'est le souhait de

Monsieur,

Vostre tres humble et tres obligée servante,

C. M. VEEN.

Address: A Monsieur Monsieur J. Locke londres

Endorsed by Locke: C. M. Veen[a] 15 Dec 98 Answered Jan. 12

[a] *Substituted for* Guenellon

2520. Dr. Pieter Guenellon to Locke, 5/15 December 1698 (*2401*, *2594*)

B.L., MS. Locke c. 11, f. 86.

d'amsterdam ce 15 dec. 1698

Monsieur,

Je ne puis qu'admirer vos belles et solides reflexions; cela nous met en bon chemin. je vous confesse que les grandes fortunes et les richesses ne sont rien a la reelle beatitude, et que ce n'est qu'un faux éclat qui nous eblouït, et nous méne dans l'égarement. il est vray aussi, que plus nous allons en avant dans la cariere de cette vie, mieux nous nous apercevons de cette verité. je croy pourtant que vous éte d'avis quil ne faut pas faire un trop grand usage de ces reflexions avec les enfans, qui ont besoin d'étre excitez a une gloire future, pour mieux se soumettre au peines et au travail quil faut pour s'acquerir des sciences, qui ensuite les conduisent a connoistre, quil ny a point de plus grandes richesses a acquerir dans cette vie, que la solide vertu, qui rend l'ame tousjours contente, et qui fait n'aitre en nous un mépris pour tout ce vain appareil, ou les hommes dans leur vanité se laissent prendre comme a une amorce. je m'afflige d'apprendre que Vostre Engleterre n'est pas moin dans le vice que n'otre petite Hollande, autrefois si distinguée par son Integrité et autres vertus Morales. il faut donc veiller plus que jamais sur n'otre conduite, et celle de nos enfans, et ne les point quitter de Veüe de peur quils ne s'egarent. je vous remercie par avance pour vótre derniere réponce a l'Evesque de Worchester,[1] que vous avez la bonté de m'envoyer. est ce que ce prelat ne se trouve pas encore assez vaincu? faut il que vous triomphiez jusqu'a le confondre avant quil se rende? je plaindrois toutes vos peines si cela n'augmentoit l'estime que tout le monde a concu pour la justesse et la penetration de vostre esprit. jay dessein d'écrire une histoire mechanique du corps humain pour l'usage de mes enfans.[2] jay concu de le faire d'une maniere intelligible, suivie et aisée, en evitant de trop charger cette histoire de termes scholastiques. je la diviseray en trois parties, la premiere contiendra l'homme adulte, je ny mesleray rien touchant la generation; c'est ou je veu arester mes enfans dans leur jeunesse. je traitterai les parties de la generation et ce qui en dépend dans la

[1] p. 505, etc.

[2] Guenellon appears not to have published a book of the kind.

seconde partie. la troisiéme contiendra des reflexions sur ce que l'experience la plus recue a etabli dans la practique, et ce que nous en pouvons concevoir, par ce que nous aurons apris de la machine dans les deux premieres parties, pour tacher d'en tirer certaines maximes generales pour la conservation de nótre santé, et la guerison des Maladies, quun chacun devoit connoitre ce me semble, pour son propre interét. Pour degourdir ma main, et me mettre en train d'Ecrire, jay fait la lettre que vous verrez au bout du livre que je vous envoye, c'est un nouveau Voiage de Moscou a la Chine. j'y ay fait joindre la Carte de Monsieur Witsen. jy ay mis les Chiffres pour marquer la route, et jay fait la table que vous y verrez jointe, que je croi de quelque usage, quand ce ne seroit que pour decouvrir sans peine les endroits defectueux de la carte.[1] Monsieur Witsen qui paroit content de ma lettre m'excite a en faire une seconde, pour refuter les impertinences et les injures qu'un certain auteur *de la Neuville* vient de publier contre les Moscovites et particulierement contre le Czaar.[2] si je le fay ce ne sera que pour me mieux acheminer a mon histoire du corps humain, que j'escriray en francois, afin que mes pensées ne soient pas gesnées par le langage, qui ne fait au fond rien a la chose méme. et de plus je trouve la langue francoise si naturelle, si aisée, et si propre a exprimer naivement la pensée, que je la prefere aussi pour cela. si je reussi, je pourai vous envoyer une copie, pour scavoir si vous l'approuvez. il me semble quil nous manque une semblable histoire, et que de la vient que ceux méme qui se picquent d'avoir un peu goutté de toutes les sciences, ne se cachent pas de paroitre ignorants dans celle cy, qui comprend neantmoins le plus surprenant, et le plus excellent ouvrage de la creation. je finis en vous assurant que je suis d'un profond respect, Monsieur,

Vostre tres humble et tres obeissant serviteur

P. GUENELLON

Address: A Monsieur Monsieur Joh. Locke Londres.

Endorsed by Locke: Dr Guenellon 15 Dec 98 Answered Jan. 12

[1] The book is Adam Brand's *Relation du voyage de Mr. Evert Isbrand*: p. 479. Guenellon appended to it a greatly reduced version of Witsen's map of Tartary, with the table as described (pp. 183–92), and 'Lettre de Monsieur *** sur l'état présent de la Moscovie' (pp. 193–249). The latter includes an account (pp. 228–44) of Peter the Great's sojourn in Holland and England.

[2] Foy de la Neuville, *Relation curieuse et nouvelle de Moscovie*, Paris, 1698. It was reprinted at The Hague in 1699. Locke owned a copy of the English translation, also 1699. L.L., no. 2081. I have found no separate publication controverting it. Notice in *Journal des Sçavans*, 16 June 1698 (pp. 416–21).

2521. ROBERT PAWLING to LOCKE, 6 December 1698 (*2037*, *2688*)

B.L., MS. Locke c. 16, ff. 224–5.

London December 6th 1698

Sir

I received yours and have discoursed with your Taylor[1] who, when I said I thought he put down too much for the Silk wastcoat, he shewed me a pattern of such a silk and assured me that yours was better and that yours cost him above 12s per yard that there was 5 yds ¼ in the Wastcoat; if so tis not so unreasonable as I thought it was; and he beleivs he hath not 12d gains to himself, his journey men being paid in the Coat and Breeches at the rate he puts down; so that after all my squabling with him, 6s is the most I could bring him to be willing to abate. On Wednesday last I received the £15 of Mr Churchill, and that afternoon I went to my Daughters at Hampsted[2] where I found them well and chearfull. I stayed with them till Saturday, and left them as I found them; on Monday I laboured at the Office to recover the time I lost; this day I went to pay Mr Clarke but he was from home I should have told you that on Wednesday before I went, I bought your Cloth which pleases me, the rest of the things I will provide. here came one to me with a pair of shoes for my Lady. I received them and they shalbe sent as her Ladyship directs. he said he had orders to receive some small matter of me. I said when he shewed me my Ladys Letter I would pay him.

Sir Tho: Littleton caried it for Speaker by 103 voices as tis said.[3]

My humble Service to Sir Francis my Lady etc. I am, when I have told you here are 3 Letters inclosed,

Sir

Your very humble Servant

ROB PAWLING

Address: For John Locke Esqr [at Oates, by Joslyn, Bishops Stortford]

Postmark: DE 6

Endorsed by Locke: R: Pawling 6 Dec. 98

[1] Samuel Clarke: p. 506, etc.

[2] Susannah was at Hampstead in 1701: no. *2896*.

[3] Sir Thomas Littleton, third baronet: *D.N.B.* He was elected by 242 to 135 votes.

2522. LOCKE to PETER KING, later first Baron King, 13 December 1698 (2518, 2535)

B.L., MS. Locke c. 40, ff. 25–6.

Oates 13 Dec 98

Dear Cosin

All the Articles of your letter of the 9th please me very much except what relates to your comeing hither. I would have you come before Christmas day because I as well as every body here would be glad to have your company here for sometime. Businesse I know in a yonge man at his first seting out into the world ought not to be neglected. But as I take it the weeke before Christmas is not a time of businesse. What you write about the Bank stock I thank you for.[1] And if anything stir about Malt tickets[2] pray send me word and let me know how the material points move in Parliament. You have the services of all here. I am

Dear Cosin

Your most affectionate Cosin and humble servant

J LOCKE

Address: For Peter King Esqr at his chamber in the Temple To be left at Mr Potmans in the Middle Temple London

Postmark: DE 16

Endorsed by King: Cosin Locke Decemb. 13. 1698

2523. EDMUND ELYS to LOCKE, 16 December 1698

B.L., MS. Locke c. 8, ff. 70–1. Elys perhaps printed the letter in his *Observations on Several Books*, 1700?: *T.C.* iii. 195–6; no copies of the book are recorded. For him see *D.N.B.* In 1697 he published *A Refutation of some of the False Conceits in Mr. Locke's Essay concerning Humane Understanding. Together with a brief answer, in Latine, to the argumentation of Gerardus de Vries against the innate idea of God. T.C.* iii. 4. L.L., no. 1038. No copies were known until about 1960, when the British Museum acquired one. Elys apparently reissued it with other works about 1698, 1700 (the *Observations* above), and 1703:

[1] At this time Locke held £500 stock bought on 22 February 1697 at 56 per cent, and £200 stock bought about 14 September 1697 at 86¾ per cent (this may include brokerage); and a further £400 stock bought in August 1698 at 98 per cent (perhaps including brokerage) and held in King's name: Journal, 1697, pp. 3–4, 17, 20; 1698, pp. 18–19; 1700, p. 29; 1703, p. 13; MS. Locke b. 1, f. 198. Dividends on the £500, later £700, are shown in Locke's accounts with the Churchills; those on the £400 in his accounts with King; these accounts are in MS. Locke b. 1.

[2] p. 246.

T.C. iii. 73, 195–6, 354. He probably alludes to it or to the present letter in a letter written in 1705: H.M.C., *Portland MSS.* viii. 187.

Mr Lock

Since you say you shall be very Glad of a Demonstration of the Souls Immateriality (in your Reply to the Lord Bishop of Worcesters Second Letter p. 393) I hope you will either Acknowledge what I here send you to be such a Demonstration; or shew me the Reason, why you Reject it.

'A Rational Soul is Capable of Apprehending, or of having a Notion, or Conception of a GOD. i.e. of a Being Infinite in all Perfection, Therefore It is a Substance Immaterial, or Incorporeal.

'Matter Cannot Apprehend BEING Infinitely Beyond All Matter: For it implies a Contradiction that Matter should *Be* Beyond All Matter, And it must *Be so*, if it can Apprehend that ONE BEING, which is Infinitely Beyond All Matter, since *Apprehending* supposes *Being*. 'Tis Evident therefore that nothing Can Apprehend Beyond Matter that has no Being Beyond Matter.

'It does not imply any Contradiction that there should be a Created Substance that has a Being Beyond All Matter. Such a Substance we Affirm the Mind, or Spirit of Man to Be, And so It is Capable of Apprehending The One Being Absolutely Infinite, or that Essence which is Infinite in All Perfection, that is GOD.'

I have no more to say to you at present, but that I Syncerely Wish you All Happiness and remain

Your Faithfull Servant in the Love of the Love

EDMUND ELYS

Totness in Devon Decemb. 16/98.

Address: These For the Honour'd Mr John Locke To be left with Mr Churchil At the Black Swan in Pater-Noster-Row London

Postmark: DE 19

Endorsed by Locke: Ed: Elys 16 Dec: 98

2524. MRS. FRANCES ST. JOHN to LOCKE, [*c.* 17 December 1698] (*2370, 2551*)

B.L., MS. Locke c. 18, ff. 52–3. Date from postmark and Locke's endorsement.

Sir

To escaipe so dismall a destemper (which, to many proves faitall, and to most very seveer, with so great eas,) is matter of great

Joy and satisfaction; but the additionall pleasure which this lait Illness has affoarded me, is the great kindness of my friends, who haveing given me such testimony how great a part they take with me, in my Recovery, which gives me a greater sence of my happiness in it allso, there being nothing so desirable in this Life as friendship, and tho' I have not the vanity to think I have deserved that kindness which my good fortune hath allotted me, yet Justice obliges me to acknowlidg it, and to my good Friend Mr Lock, to whome I am not the least indebted having many thanks owing for those continued favores which I have offten reseived, and desire now to return my thanks for your last kinde letter, which I reseived whilest I was in town, a plaice which admitts not of much time for writing or I should not have omitted returning my thanks before this time, and now imagining it may affoard you some pleasant thoughts I must give you the reason of my being in town, beleiving you will not easily gues it, (for the Aire, affter my infectious destemper, and when I name Westminster as the plaice where I Lodgd you will imagine I gained great benifitt,

And now I am to present my La: St Jo servis to you and Sir Walters, and she desires you will let her know what time of the year is proper for the Honysuckl and she will send them down and begs you will direct the sweet bryer to be left at Mr Martins at the Sign of the Unicorn in Bow Lane ⟨a⟩[a] Cooks shop, and now it's time to releas you from a teadious Epistle, and with Mr St Johns and my own very humble servis conclud my self by the happy title of;

Your oblidged friend and humble servant

FRANCES ST JOHN

I beg the favore of you to present my servis to Lady Masham, to whome I am indebted a letter, and my servis to the rest of your good Company

Address: For John Lock Esqr [at Oates, by Joslyn, Bishops Stortford]

Postmarks: DE 17; LV

Endorsed by Locke: F St John 98 Answered Febr 9.

[a] *Page torn.*

2525. [JOHN FREKE] to LOCKE, 22 December 1698 (2469, 2540)

B.L., MS. Locke c. 8, ff. 228–9. Written by Freke apart from the address. The letter appears to be from Freke rather than from Freke and Clarke.

December the 22d 1698

Sir

I beg the favour of you to deliver the enclosed to my Lady Masham. It contains onely my thanks for a very fatt Goose and Turkey which I have received from her a present I am out of Countenance to receive since I am Conscious of my own want of meritt or of[a] capacity to return the favour

But let what will be her motive of sending them I accept them with gratitude and look on them as an evidence of her bounty and good housewifery Qualitys that never fail to procure esteem because usefullness is the naturall mother (never barren) of respect and when Joind with the other endowments in which she excells must render her highly vallued by all that are soe happy to know her

I hear the university of oxford generally gives Judgement in your favour against the Bishop and say he deserves the treatment he has received from you though it be pretty severe but that in prudence he ought to sit down under it le'st he draw a greater load on his back for tis evident that his understanding has faild him in this Controversie.

What they say at Cambridge I have not heard but the sobrest and ablest London Divines concurr with the Oxonians as one that converses much with them and at my request has talkt to them on this subject has assured me

The Commons this day had the Election of Westminster Reported and Agreed with the Comittee that Montague and Vernon[1] were duly chosen but afterwards a volunteer Question was moved and Debated whether Aliens not naturalized or made Denizens have right to vote as Inhabitants in any case which spent all the Day and at length they Resolved what noe Lawyer ever doubted before vizt that they have not

I am
Sir
Your faithfull friend and humble servant.

[a] *Interlined before* or

[1] Charles Montagu and James Vernon, the secretary of state.

Address (written by Clarke): These For John Locke Esqr. [at Oates, by Joslyn, Bishops Stortford]
Frank: Edw: Clarke:
Postmarks: DE 22; RS
Endorsed by Locke: J: Freke 22 Dec 98 Answered 30

2526. MRS. MARY POPPLE to LOCKE, [*c.* 28 December 1698] (*2513*)

B.L., MS. Locke c. 17, ff. 199–200. Date from Locke's endorsement, which is probably the date of receipt.

Sir

I have seen what you writ concerning the State of your health, I am very glad to know it is better; let the means be what it will that procures it. Now since that little bottle of drops are not usefull to you, I intreat you will pleas to send them to me by mr King; for they will be of great use to me at this time; and if you should desier at any time to take them; I will furnish you with what you need.

I have receved 3lb.19sh.6d of mr King, for those things I had laid out for you. I have given him :2lb: of your Chocolate.

I begg leave to present my humble service to the Lady Masham, and mr Masham. I am

Sir

Your most humble servant

MARY POPPLE

Address: For John Lock Esq
Endorsed by Locke: M: Popple 29 Dec. 98

2527. J.-B. DU BOS to LOCKE, 31 December [1698]/10 January [1699] (*2510, 2570*)

B.L., MS. Locke c. 7, ff. 221–4. Printed by G. Bonno in *Revue de littérature comparée*, xxiv (1950), 488–95. Year from Locke's endorsement.

A Paris Le Samedi $\frac{10}{1}$ de Janvier

Monsieur

Peu de jours avant de recevoir vostre derniere lettre escrite a Oates le dixieme Novembre, Je vous en avois envoié une pour vous remercier du livre du chevalier Sydney. je crois que vous l'aure recue, come les livres que jay adressè pour vous a monsieur Vernietes et au maistre du post office de Londres. Jay recu touts ceux que vous mavè envoiè, et je les lis avec beaucoup de plaisir sur tout vostre response a levesque de Worcester.[1] come je nai rien encore a faire imprimer, Je souhaitte monsieur que les ouvrages des autres me donnent occasion de macquiter, et quil simprime ici au plutost quelque livre assez bon pour vous le pouvoir envoier en echange des vostres.

vous trouveré dans le memoire que je mets sous l'envelope de ma lettre, le non de touts les voyageurs qui ont imprimé leurs relations depuis douze ou quinze ans. je souhaitte quil sen trouve quelqunes qui vous donnent occasion d'employer mon service.

Mylord Pawlet et monsieur de Cuninghuam mont prie de vous aseurer de leurs respects.[2] mylord Pawlet a gagné ici lestime et l'admiration de touts ceux qui lont vu et qui le véront partir avec bien du chagrin.

Jay lu une critique du voyage du Docteur Lister intitulee a *Journey to London*, qui ma bien fait rire; mais le livre contre lequel elle est escrite, mavoit fait rire encor davantage.[3] on peut apliquer en passant au docteur Lister le vers dHorace

Laudibus arguitur vini vinosus homerus.[4]

on scait quil aime le bon vin des que lon a lu son livre.

Defer a achevé sa carte Damerique, ou il i a encore bien des faute[s] quoy quil en ait beaucoup corrigé.[5]

Je vous prie de menvoier, les cartes suivantes si vous les pouv[ez] avoir comodement.

Celle de la Caroline faite par ordre des seigneurs proprietaires.

Celle de la Virginie Maryland new Jersey nouvelle Angleterr[e] et Pensylvanie, qui doit se trouver suivant le memoire que ja[y] vu chez robert green at the crowned rose in budge row.[7]

[1] p. 505, etc. Du Bos is named in the distribution list for it.

[2] Lord Poulett: no. *1459*; Alexander Cunningham: no. 1435.

[3] William King (*D.N.B.*), *A Journey to London*, 1698. It parodies Lister's *A Journey to Paris* (p. 407, n. 1).

[4] 'From his praises of wine Homer is proved a wine-bibber': *Epistles*, I. xix. 6.

[5] Nicolas de Fer, 1646–1720: *N.B.G.* Probably *L'Amerique* (using observatio[ns] made by the Académie des Sciences), 1698. Notice in *Journal des Sçavans*, 30 Ju[ne] 1698 (pp. 462–3).

[6] Probably the map by Joel Gascoyne advertised by Robert Green in 168[.] *T.C.* i. 513.

[7] Green died between 1685 and 1689; his widow (?) continued for a time to s[ell] maps: *T.C.* ii. 148, 281. The present map is perhaps that by R. Daniel which w[as] advertised by Robert Morden (*D.N.B.*) in *1679*: *T.C.* i. 372; ii. 126. I have not trace[d] an issue by Green, but he and Morden joined in some publications.

carte marine depuis la floride, les costes des terres Angloises et le canada jusques a Hudson Baye.[1]

carte du detroit de Magellan.[2]

Je vis monsieur Witssen lorsque je passé a Amsterdam, ou il me donna quatre de ses cartes. depuis que je suis ici je lui en ai envoié dautres quil souhaitoit de voir. son livre de remarques est imprimé il i a du temps, mais il faut que cet autheur ai des raisons pour ne le point publier encore si tost.[3] il i a deux ou trois ans que le Czar envoia a l'empereur de la Chine un ambassadeur Allemand, dont le valet de chambre fit imprimer lanee derniere une relation du voyage dont lon imprimoit la traduction francoise lorsque Jestois a Amsterdam. Lambasadeur lui meme a escrit aussi sa relation dont monsieur Witssen avoit quelques cahiers entre les mains. monsieur witssen lui avoit escrit pour lengager a la publier.[4]

Je ne blamerai jamais monsieur vostre long silence ni vos longues lettres. je ne merite pas monsieur que vous interompiez vos affaires ni vos estudes pour mescrire, et le plaisir de lire vos lettres me les fera tousjours paroistre trop courtes.

Vostre tres humble et tres obeissant serviteur.

DU BOS.

monsieur Toinard vous salue. je ne scais point si cette annee ci verra eclore son harmonie, il i a lontemps que les neuf ans pendant les quels horace conseille de laisser meurir ses ouvrages sont ecoulez. mais je me console d'estre privè de voir louvrage, par la satisfaction que jay de voir la bonne sante de l'autheur. il ne est jamais mieux porte. les autres vont en viellisant, et il semble qu'il aille en rajeunissant.

Je[a] ne conois point d'autre relation de la nouvelle guineè que celle du capitaine Pelsart, Hollandois, qui i fut vers 1624. la traduction de cette relation est imprimee dans le premier volume du receuil de monsieur Thevenot, mais par sa negligence les dernieres feuilles de ce volume ont este perdues de maniere, que cette

[a] *Locke inserts a heading,* Voyages, *and adds in margin* A list of Voyages lately published in France sent me by Mr du Bos $\frac{1}{10}$ Jan $9\frac{8}{9}$. *He inserts in the margins the names of the various authors, etc. These notes are omitted here.*

[1] I have failed to identify this.

[2] Perhaps 'A new Mapp of Magellan Straights', by J. Thornton. Maps of the Strait, deriving from Narbrough's voyage, accompanied *An Account of Several Late Voyages* and Hacke's *Collection*: nos. *629* n., *2612* n.

[3] Nos. *2028*, *2401*.

[4] pp. 479, 525.

relation si trouve fort imparfaite. cest tout ce que nous avons de ce pais en francois.[1]

en 1686. lon imprima en deux volumes in 12 L'histoire des Boucaniers et des Philisbustiers. elle est dun nommé oexmelin, le quel est presentement au service de la compagnie Portugaise qui a un marché avec les espagnols pour livrer une quantité de Negres. Son histoire finit en 1670 par la prise de Panama et la friponerie que fit Morgan a ses camarades. on trouve a la fin du livre un petit traittè tres curieux, du gouvernement spirituel et temporel des Indes dEspagne, avec un etat des revenus du roy dans cette contree.[2]

en 1689. Le voyage de Raveneau de Lussan a la mer du sud. Je nen dire rien, parcequil est traduit en Anglois et imprimé, a la suute de lhistoire des flibustiers de l'edition de 1698. avec le voyage du capitaine Montauban.[3]

en 1691. un recollet nous donna une relation de la Gaspesie province situee au sud de la riviere de Saint Laurent, la quelle est remplie de descriptions curieuses.[4]

en 1697. le chevalier Tonty ⟨go⟩uverneur[a] du fort de St Louis aux Ilinois fit imp⟨rim⟩er[a] lhistoire des voyages de monsieur de La Salle et des siens sur le Miscsipi.[b] les memoires qu'ils avoient composè se trouvant trop mal escrit pour estre imprimé en l'estat ou ils estoient, on les mit entre les mains d'un nommé Pechantre pour en changer le stile. cest ce qui fait quil i a dans cette relation

[a] *Page torn.* [b] *Spelling doubtful.*

[1] *Ongeluckige Voyagie van't Schip Batavia nae de Oost-Indien . . . Uytgevaren onder de E. Francoys Pelsert . . . Geschiet in de jaren 1628. en. 1629 . . .* [with other pieces], 1647 other editions 1648 and 1649. The ship was wrecked on the Abrolhos or Houtman Rocks, off the coast of Western Australia. Full account, with translation of Pelsaert's manuscript journal, in H. Drake-Brockman, *Voyage to Disaster*, 1964. For Thévenot's collection see no. *420* n.

[2] The author is A. O. Exquemelin, anglicized as Esquemeling or Exquemeling and gallicized as Œxmelin. His book was written in Dutch and was first published in 1674; Spanish translation, Cologne, 1681; English two translations, one from the Dutch, the other from the Spanish, 1684 (Locke owned copies of later editions of one of these: L.L., nos. 511–12); French, from one of the English versions, with additions describing San Domingo and the Spanish revenue from America, etc., Paris 1686 (new editions 1688, 1699). Notice of the French version (1688) in *Bibliothèque universelle*, xviii. 129–48. For Sir Henry Morgan see no. *257* n.

[3] The original is *Journal du voyage fait à la Mer du Sud avec les flibustiers de l'Amérique en 1684 et années suivantes par le Sieur Raveneau de Lussan*, Paris, 1689 (notice in *Bibliothèque universelle*, xviii. 148–62); new editions 1690, 1693, 1699. For the English collection see *T.C.* iii. 78. The final piece is translated from 'Relation curieuse des voyages du sieur de Montauban, capitaine des flibustiers, en Guinée, l'an 1695': for it see below, p. 535, n. 2.

[4] Father Chrestien Leclercq, *Nouvelle relation de la Gaspésie*, 1691. L.L., no. 778. Gaspesia is the Gaspé peninsula, forming the south side of the mouth of the St. Lawrence.

des endroits qui semblent montrer que son autheur na jamais este aux pais quil decrit.[1]

lon rimprima ici lannee derniere la relation des cruautéz comises par les Espagnols dans les Indes par Baltazar de Las Casas.[2]

Je ne vous parle point du voyage de froger au detroit de Magellan, puisque monsieur Toinard vous lenvoia, quand il fut imprimé,[3] ni des livres du p. Hennepin qui sont imprimez en Hollande.[4]

en 1689. Labbe Bernou traduisit la description de la Chine escrite en Portugais par le pere Magailhans, et sa traduction fut imprimee in 4°. le livre est tres curieux et donne les mesures geometriques de bien des choses, que lon ne conoisoit que sur des raports imparfaits. on i a joint un plan de Pekin.[5]

en 1689 le pere dOrleans Jesuite fit imprimer la vie de deux conquerans tartares qui se sont rendus maistres de la chine, cest un livre de moine.[6]

en 1696 le pere Le comte donna ses memoires de la Chine.[7] depuis le pere Bouvet i a adjouté un nouveau volume sur ce qui est arive a la chine par raport a la religion Chretiene depuis le depart du pere Le Comte.[8] Je crois que les memoires de ce dernier qui contienent une infinité de choses curieu⟨ses⟩[a] sont traduits en Anglois.

[a] *Page torn.*

---

[1] Henry de Tonty (*c.* 1650–1704; *Dict. Canadian Biog.*), *Dernières decouvertes dans l'Amérique septentrionale de M. de la Sale*, etc., Paris, 1697. L.L., no. 2960. The basis of the book is a memoir (1693) by Tonty: Bourgeois and André, no. 588. Pechantre may be Nicolas Péchantrés: B.N. *Catalogue*.

[2] Bartolomé de las Casas, bishop of Chiapa, *La Découverte des Indes Occidentales par les Espagnols*, translated by J.-B. Morvan de Bellegarde, Paris, 1697; it is translated from pamphlets published in 1552. The translation was reprinted as *Relation des voyages*, etc., in Amsterdam in 1698 with an account of Montauban's travels appended to it: van Eeghen, ii. 92–4.

[3] p. 289.

[4] Father Louis Hennepin (*Dict. Canadian Biog.*), *Nouvelle découverte d'un très grand pays situé dans l'Amérique entre le Nouveau Mexique et la Mer Glaciale*, Utrecht, 1697. L.L., no. 1421. There are later editions. Hennepin published also *Description de la Louisiane*, Paris, 1683; new edition 1688.

[5] Gabriel de Magalhães, S.J., *Nouvelle relation de la Chine . . . composée en l'année 1668*, translated by C. Bernou, Paris, 1688; new issues 1689, 1690.

[6] P.-J. d'Orléans, S.J. (no. *2041* n.), *Histoire des deux conquérans tartares qui ont subjugué la Chine*, Paris, 1688.

[7] pp. 339–40.

[8] Apparently Joachim Bouvet, S.J., *Portrait historique de l'empereur de la Chine*, Paris, 1697. Toinard sent Locke a copy: no. 2644. L.L., no. 408. There are later editions; English translation 1699. It was not published as a sequel to le Comte; Charles le Gobien, S.J., *Histoire de l'édit de l'empereur de la Chine en faveur de la religion chrestienne*, was published as vol. iii of le Comte's *Nouveaux memoires* in 1698 as well as separately. L.L., no. 1274. Later editions 1700, 1701.

un nomme Le Maire pu⟨blia⟩[a] en 1695 une relation du Cap vert, ou il ni a rien ⟨de⟩[a] nouveau.[1]

en 1688 Delhon donna son voyage aux Indes orientales en deux volumes in douze. cest un simple de ses avantures.[2] le meme a publié ensuite lhistoire de sa detention par les Inquisiteurs de Goa.[3]

Souchu de Rennefort imprima en 1687 la relation du voyage des premiers vaisseaux de la compagnie des Indes orientales de france, et lhistoire de son etablissement dans le pais. cest un in 4° ou il i a des choses assez curieuses sur les evenements de ce temps la.[4] le Journal de mr de La haye qui i fut envoié en 1672 avec une escadre de vaisseaux du roy fut imprimé lannee derniere en 2 vo.[b] in 12. la relation est remplie de faits tres curieux, mais bien mal imprimee.[5]

On Imprima encore en 1694 une relation du voyage de l'escadre comandee par monsieur Duquesne, qui fut envoié dans les Indes depuis la declaration de la nouvelle guerre.[6]

un missionaire nomme Sanson fit imprimer en 1696 un etat de la Perse, ou il i a quantité de choses curieuses et qui passe pour estre fort exact.[7]

en 1692 le pere D Avril Imprima la relation du voyage quil avoit entrepris pour aller a la chine par terre. les Moscovites lui aiant refusé le passage il fut obligé de sen revenir en Europe. son voyage est rempli de descriptions qui naprenent rien de nouveaux, et l'autheur en est sincere en Jesuite.[8]

[a] *Page torn.* [b] *Interlined; doubtful reading.*

---

[1] J. J. Le Maire, *Les Voyages du Sieur Le Maire aux îles Canaries, Cap-Verd, Senegal et Gambie*, Paris, 1695. Reprint (Dutch?), 1695. L.L., no. 1874. English translation 1696; for another edition see n. 6 below.

[2] C. Dellon, *Relation d'un voyage des Indes Orientales*, 2 vols., 12mo, Paris, 1685; new edition, as *Nouvelle relation*, Amsterdam, 1699. Locke owned a copy of the latter: L.L., no. 942.

[3] No. 979.

[4] U. Souchu de Rennefort (*N.B.G.*), probably the *Mémoires pour servir à l'histoire des Indes Orientales*, 4°, 1688. See Bourgeois and André, no. 489.

[5] *Journal du voyage des Grandes Indes*, 1698. The first edition was published in 1674. The expedition, under Jacob de la Haye, set out in 1670: no. *489*.

[6] Abraham Duquesne the younger: *N.B.G.*; Haag. Probably C.-M. Pouchot de Chantassin, *Relation du voyage et retour des Indes Orientales pendant les années 1690 et 1691*, 1692. Notice in *Journal des Sçavans*, 16 March 1693 (pp. 177–81). English translation with the translation of Le Maire's *Voyages* appended, 1696.

[7] *Estat présent du royaume de Perse*, 1694; new edition as *Voyage ou rélation de l'état present*, etc., 1695. L.L., no. 2554 (the new edition). English translation of the *Estat* 1695. Sanson's Christian name is unknown.

[8] No. *2028*.

on Imprima lannee derniere un voyage de Moscovie fait en 1689 par un nommé la Neuville, ou il i a quelques faits touchant la pelleterie, et des circonstances assez curieuses sur la princesse Sophie et le prince Galischim.[1]

lhistoire de leglise du Japon imprimee en 1692 ne parle que de faits arrivez depuis lo⟨n⟩gtemps.[a2]

la premiere relation de Siam est celle du chevalier de Chaumont envoié du Roy qui contient simplement lhistoire de son voyage et de sa reception.[3] [in 12][b]

celle de labbé de Choisi est un peu plus circonstancieè, mais il semble que l'autheur ait eu pour but d'embellir les choses quil racontoit, plutost que den donner une just idee.[4] [in 12][b]

le premier et le second voyage du pere Tachard contienent des descriptions et des observations fort curieuses. il sest plus attaché a la nature que les autres.[5] [2 v in 4°.][b]

lHistoire de Siam par gervais que je vous ai envoiee.[6]

la description de Siam par la Loubere est la plus exacte, la plus sincere et la plus juste.[7] [2 v in 12][b]

en 1690 le p. Dorleans fit imprimer une relation des revolutions qui ariverent dans cet etat en 1688.[8]

Desfargues qui comandoit a Bankok en fit imprimer une autre plus sincere et mieux circonstanciee en Hollande en 1690.[9]

[a] *Page torn.* [b] *Marginal note.*

[1] p. 525.

[2] Probably Jean Grasset, S.J., using the pseudonym Abbé de T., *Histoire de l'eglise du Japon*, Paris, 1689; new ed., 1691. Notice in *Journal des Sçavans*, 18 and 25 July 1689 (pp. 486–507). It is adapted and extended from a book (1627) by F. Solier, S.J.

[3] Alexandre de Chaumont, called the Chevalier, later marquis de Chaumont, *Relation de l'ambassade*, etc., 1685; new editions 1686 (L.L., no. 678), etc. H. Cordier, *Bibliotheca Indosinica*, 1912–14, i. 935–9.

[4] The Abbé F.-T. de Choisy, *Journal du voyage*, etc., 1687; further editions, Amsterdam, 1687 (L.L., no. 693), etc. Choisy accompanied de Chaumont. Cordier, as above, i. 940–2.

[5] Guy Tachard, S.J., *Voyage de Siam*, 1686; further editions, Amsterdam, 1687 (L.L., no. 2821), etc.; *Second voyage*, 1689 (three editions; L.L., no. 2822). Cordier, as above, i. 947–9, 953–4.

[6] p. 507.

[7] Simon de La Loubère, *Du royaume de Siam*, 1691; later editions, Amsterdam, 1691 (L.L., no. 1811), etc.; English translation 1693 (ibid., no. 1811[a]). Cordier, as above, i. 722–4.

[8] P.-J. d'Orléans, *Histoire de M. Constance, premier ministre du roy de Siam, et de la derniere revolution de cet etat*, 1690; later editions. Cordier, as above, i. 959–60.

[9] Desfarges (*D.B.F.*), *Relation des revolutions arrivées a Siam dans l'année 1688*, Amsterdam, 1691.

En 1688[a] le p. Gouies Jesuite fit imprimer les observations des Jesuites aux Indes et a la chine avec des remarques et des reflexions.[1]

en 1692 ce meme pere fit imprimer de nouvelles observations de physique et dastronomie venues de ces quartiers la.[2] en 1690 lacadamie des Sciences fit imprimer au louvre ces observations et beaucoup d'autres en un volume in folio.[3]

il i a aussi eu depuis dix ans deux ou trois voyages de la terre sainte imprimez, mais ce sont plutost des livres de devotion que de curiositez. [etc][b]

pendant deux ou trois ans, a comencer en 1692, lacademie des Sciences donnoit des especes de journaux touts les quinze jours, remplis de nouvelles decouvertes et d'observations curieuses.[4]

En 1689 on publia a locasion des princes de Macasar envoies ici par le roy de Siam une description de leur pais.[5]

Endorsed by Locke: (i: at head of letter): Du Bos 10 Jan $9\frac{8}{9}$ Answered Mar. 21; (ii: at end of letter): Du Bos 1 Jan $9\frac{8}{9}$ Answered Mar 21

2528. Locke to J. F. [1698–1699?]

B.L., MS. Locke c. 24, f. 46. Draft. There is an offset on MS. Locke c. 8, f. 219[v] (no. *2083*). A passage printed in King, pp. 196–7; almost complete, by Professor Cranston, pp. 415–16. The only indication of the date is the mention of Locke's 'last Answer' to Stillingfleet. This may be the first or the second *Reply*; the second is rather more likely. The person addressed is perhaps James Fraser ('Catalogue Fraser'; no. *2149*). He and Locke were acquainted: p. 751. He is probably the Mr. Fraser of the distribution lists for Locke's *Letter* to Stillingfleet and the first *Reply*. John Freke is the only obvious alternative.

[a] *Doubtful reading.* [b] *Marginal note.*

---

[1] *Observations physiques et mathematiques . . . envoyées de Siam à l'Academie Royale de Sciences à Paris par les Peres Jesuites François*, etc., edited by Thomas Goüye, S.J., an octavo. Notice in *Journal des Sçavans*, 13 September 1688 (pp. 393–5). L.L., no. 2115.

[2] *Observations . . . envoyées des Indes et de la Chine*, quarto, Imprimerie royale du Louvre. L.L., no. 2116.

[3] Perhaps *Ouvrages posthumes de messieurs de l'Académie*, edited by P. de la Hire For it and other folio publications of this year see A. Bernard, *Hist. de l'Imprimerie royale du Louvre*, 1867, pp. 149–50.

[4] *Memoires de mathematique et de physique tirez des registres de l'Académie Royale de Sciences*, edited by de la Hire and Goüye, twelve issues a year, each of sixteen pages quarto, Imprimerie royale, 1692–4. L.L., no. 1962. Notices in Leibniz, *S.S.* I. viii–ix Bernard, p. 150.

[5] N. Gervaise, *Description historique du royaume de Macaçar*, Paris, 1688. New edition, Ratisbon, 1700; English translation 1701.

2529. *C. Walter, January 1699*

to *J:F*

You will I thinke agree with me that there is noe thing wherein men more mistake themselves and mislead others than in writeing and reading of books. Whether the Writers mislead the Readers or vice versâ I will not examin soe it is that they both seem willing to deceive and be deceivd. How else could it be that where the one pretends to reason and to instruct, he should give him self up to a play or abuse of words, which if they can be put soe togeather as to chime something into the phansy of the reader and make now and then the appearance of a repartie or a sharp saying the businesse is thought done tis a discourse well writ Though sense and truth be wholy neglected in it. Again if Readers were not willing to Cosin themselves how could they where they pretend to seeke truth and information content them selves with the Jugle of words and something they know not what that looks like a sprinkleing of wit or satyr, in all which they finde not the least improvement of their knowledg or reason. Those whose aime is to divert and make men laugh let them write plays and Romances and there sport them selves with words and false images of things as much as they please. But a professor to teach or maintain truth should have noe thing to doe with all that tinsil trumpery should speake plain and clear and be afraid of a fallacy or æquivocation how ever prettily it might looke and be fit to cheat the reader. who on his side should in an Author who pretends instruction abominate all such arts and him that uses them as much as he would a common cheat who endeavours to put off brasse mony for standard silver. The reason why I say this you will see in what follows

You may remember I told you before my last Answer to the Bishop was printed

2529. Charles Walter to Locke, [January 1699]

B.L., MS. Locke c. 23, f. 58. Date from Locke's endorsement.

Sir,

There is one Mr Robert Burgoyne A Land Surveyor of the Port of London that lyes at the point of Death, who I am Informed will be succeeded by A Land Waiter, by which remove their will be a Land Waiters place[1] to be disposed of, and I humbly beg Your favorable recommendation to Sir Walter Young that I may be presented to the Treasury to succeede in that List. having the promise of Mr Mountagues favour.[2] Sir in doing this for me I shall always acknoledg my selfe to be Your most faithfull

Humble Servant

CHARLES WALTER.

Endorsed by Locke: C. Walter Jan $9\frac{8}{9}$

2530. PETER STRATTON to LOCKE, 2 January 1699 (*2354*)

B.L., MS. Locke c. 18, ff. 245–6.

Bristoll the 2d January 1698

Honoured Sir

After my humble service to you, whishing you a happy new yeare, these lets you Know that Francis Carpenter your tennant was with me and desired me to let you know that one Robert Pope does Claime a Rite to a ground of yours Called Common-mead[a] and Robert Cattle doth for the Lord[3] Claime a rite there to; now the parties themselves doe not Know what they use to Receive soe did desire Francis,[b] that he would be soe kind to send to you to Know what you did use to pay formerly; and in soe doeing you would oblidge them.

Sir I cannott Chuse but take notice to you of the death of your good freind mr. Simon Dandoe;[4] who did very oft talke of you whilst liveing. he have benn dead about 3 weekes.

all our Relations in the Country is well and should be glad to heare the same from you which is the Needfull at present. I am Sir

Your Lo: Kindsman and obedient servant

PETER STRATTON

[a] *Or* Comonmead [b] *The punctuation is doubtful; perhaps* Francis, . that

[1] The salary was £80 per annum.

[2] Charles Montagu as Chancellor of the Exchequer and first commissioner of the Treasury; the appointment was by warrant of the commissioners of the Treasury. Walter did not obtain the place; in April, when a vacancy occurred, he was appointed a land-carriageman; the salary was £35 per annum: *Cal. Treasury Books*, 1698–9, pp. 253, 322.

[3] Presumably the younger Alexander Popham: no. *767*, etc.

[4] Probably the Mr. Dando of no. *583*, etc.

Address: For John: Locke Esquire in Oates To be left att mr. Pawlings over against the Plow in Little Lincoln Inn feilds in London
Postmark: IA 4
Endorsed by Locke: P: Stratton 2 Jan 9 8/9 Answered 10

2531. JEAN LE CLERC to LOCKE, 3/13 January 1699 (2453, 2544)

B.L., MS. Locke c. 13, ff. 125–6. Printed in Bonno, *Le Clerc*, pp. 108–11.

A Amsterdam le 13 de Janvier 1699.

Après vous avoir, Monsieur, souhaité la bonne année, et toutes sortes de prosperitez, il faut que je la commence par m'excuser de ce que je vous réponds si tard, sur tout devant vous remercier des livres, que vous m'avez envoié l'Eté passé, et étant encore obligé à rendre le même devoir à Madame Masham, pour les Ouvrages de feu Mr. son Pere, que j'ai reçus il y a quelques semaines.[1] Il faut donc vous dire que j'ai été extraordinairement occupé à mon Harmonie, pour l'achever incessamment, avant que celles de Mr. Toinard, ou du P. l'Ami[2] pussent paroître ici, de peur qu'un certain parti d'envieux et de malhonêtes gens ne m'accusassent de les avoir pillez, en cas que je me sois rencontré avec eux en quelque chose, ce qui ne peut pas manquer d'arriver, quoi que je differe en plusieurs autres, autant que je le puis conjecturer par ce que j'en ai ouï dire. Mon Harmonie est double, une page étant Greque et l'autre Latine, vis à vis l'une de l'autre; et dessous il y a une Histoire de Jesus Christ et Latin, ou j'exprime, à ma maniére, le sens des quatre Evangiles. A la fin, il y a trois Dissertations, et quelque peu de remarques sur l'ordre que j'ai suivi. Cet Ouvrage est de 140 feuilles *in folio*, de la grandeur de mon Pentateuque. Il a été composé et imprimé en dix mois, excepté quatre feuilles qui seront faites cette semaine. Cependant il y a eu trois autres desseins, qui m'ont fait perdre quelque temps, pour les diriger. Le premier est une nouvelle Edition *des Dogmes Theologiques du P.Petau*, qui est fort avancée, et qui sera en trois grands volumes in folio.[3]

[1] Locke wrote to Le Clerc on 14 July and 17 November 1698: no. 2453, endorsements. There was no new edition about this time of any of Cudworth's writings. Le Clerc summarized parts of *The True Intellectual System*, or defended Cudworth's views, in articles in *Bibliotheque choisie*, vols. i–iii, v–ix: see Barnes, pp. 232–3.

[2] See p. 456.

[3] Denis Pétau, S.J. (Petavius; no. 435 n.), *Opus de Theologicis Dogmatibus* (first published in 1644–50). The edition was published in six folio volumes at Antwerp in 1700, with notes by 'Theophilus Alethinus, S.J.', a pseudonym for Le Clerc.

Le second est une édition des Oeuvres de *S. Augustin*, dont il va paroître un essai.[1] Le troisiéme est celle des Oeuvres d'*Erasme*, que l'on va commencer.[2] Je me suis engagé de ranger en ordre la copie de ces ouvrages, et d'y faire quelques petits ajustemens, qui les fassent rechercher; de sorte que voila vint-quatre Volumes *in folio* à parcourir, ou à feuilleter, dans trois ou quatre ans; pendant lesquels j'aurai encore d'autres choses à faire. J'aurois besoin de jours de 48 heures, s'il étoit possible, pour me dégager de ce fardeau en peu de temps, ou du loisir des Chanoines de vôtre païs. C'est ce qui me rend peu exact aux devoirs de civilité les plus essentiels, et qui me fait esperer que vous me pardonnerez aisément, et que vous m'obtiendrez même pardon de Madame vôtre Hôtesse. Je ne manquerai néanmoins pas de m'acquiter moi même de ce devoir, en lui envoiant mon *Harmonie*, en peu de semaines, comme je l'espere. Avant que de m'engager à autre chose, j'ai resolu de me défendre par quelques Lettres courtes en Latin, adressées à Mrs vos Prélats, ou au moins à quelques uns d'eux, contre Mr. *Cave*, qui m'a attaqué sur le sujet *d'Eusebe*, avec une malignité très-noire. Je garderai toute la moderation qu'on peut demander d'un honête homme, mais je vous assure que, s'il a quelque honte, il sera confus de m'avoir si malhonêtement attaqué. Par occasion, je répondrai à quelques autres, qui affectent de me mordre, pour me détourner de mes desseins, pour s'aquerir de la réputation dans le parti, ou pour quelque autre mauvaise fin. Ces gens-là se sont persuadez qu'en me disant bien des injures, ils s'en attireroient, et qu'ils s'en feroient honneur dans leur parti. Au lieu de cela, ils n'auront que des raisons, mais si fortes; qu'il n'y gagneront beaucoup d'honneur. Comme l'Ouvrage sera petit, il ne faudra pas beaucoup de temps, pour l'achever.[3] Ce qui me fâche le plus, au milieu de tant de travail, c'est la maladie de nôtre petit garçon. Après bien des pas d'école[4] que quelques uns

[1] *Opera*, reprinted from the Maurists' edition, Paris, 1679–1700; published by P. Mortier and J. H. and M. Huguetan, all of Amsterdam, nominally at Antwerp vols. i–x, 1700; vol. xi, 1702; vol. xii, *Appendix Augustiniana*, 1703: nos. *2570*, *3080* van Eeghen, iii. 174.

[2] Published as *Opera Omnia*, 10 vols. in 11, P. van der Aa, Leyden, 1703–6.

[3] William Cave included lives of Eusebius (Eusebius Pamphili, bishop of Caesarea) in his *Ecclesiastici*, 1683, and in the first part, 1688, of his *Scriptorum Ecclesiasticorum Historia Literaria* (pp. 127–34). Le Clerc in an account of Eusebius in the *Bibliotheque universelle* for September 1688 stated that he was always on the side of the Arians and was accused of sharing their opinions, and censured Cave for trying to make him appear orthodox: x. 479–80. Cave replied in a special section of his *Historia Literaria*, pt. ii, 1698, the cause of Le Clerc's present complaint. Le Clerc duly responded: notices below.

[4] Apparently the same as *pas de clerc*

de vos amis et des miens ont fait là dessus, il s'est trouvé qu'il avoit un terrible abcès à la cuisse. On l'a ouvert il y a trois mois et demi, et il en est sorti quantité de pus *loüable*, comme disent les Chirurgiens; mais ce flus ne cesse point depuis ce temps-là, et cependant l'enfant est tombé dans une espece de fievre lente, qui augmente dans le temps, où il lui sort plus de pus. *Meester Pieter Adriaans*,[1] que vous connoissez, le traite, mais c'est un homme si sterile en expediens, qu'il est propre à éterniser les maladies. On tient dans la plaie une petite canule de plomb, avec du diapalma. Depuis quelque temps, on nous a conseillé de mettre exterieurement un cataplâme d'*herbes vulneraires*, cueuillies sur les Alpes, qu'on nous a envoiées de Geneve. Il a semblé que cela ait eu quelque effet, et que l'enfant se trouvoit mieux. Cependant la cuisse ne se desenfle pas assez, pour la grande effusion de pus qu'elle a rendu. Il a néanmoins semblé que l'enfant reprenoit quelque chair, et il est certain qu'il a un peu plus de forces et de mouvement. Il dort bien, et ne manque pas d'appetit. Nous avons essaié le Quinquina, pour lui ôter cette fievre, mais inutilement. Depuis peu nous avons seringué sa plaie, avec la décoction des herbes vulneraires, que nous cuisons dans beaucoup d'eau et un peu de vin. Cet enfant, Monsieur, vous est déja obligé de la santé, dont il a jouï pendant plus d'un an, avant que de retomber malade. Si vous nous pouviez donner quelque bon avis, pour la guerison de cette seconde maladie, ce seroit une seconde obligation que nous vous aurions, et encore plus grande que la premiere. Car nos gens chagrins de l'être si fort trompez ne nous font aucune ouverture, et, pour dire la verité, ils sont aussi secs en remedes, qu'ils sont fertiles en mauvaises conjectures. Je vous demande pardon de l'importunité, mais c'est une chose qui me tient extrémement à coeur, et qui donne beaucoup de peine et d'inquietude à ma femme. J'avois crû que nos gens en viendroient à bout, et qu'il ne seroit pas nécessaire de vous en écrire; mais je vois à présent le contraire.

Les Critiques de Hollande sont meilleurs que ceux d'Angleterre, et il y a beaucoup d'additions de *Drusius*.[2] L'art *Tagmical* de Mr. *Cross*,[3] que vous m'avez envoié, est la plus grande chimere du monde. Les Mémoires d'*Edmond* sont dignes d'être lues, quoi qu'il y ait quelques endroits, où l'Auteur parle assez mal des affaires étrangeres.[4] On les a traduits en François et en Flammand. J'attens

[1] P. A. Verduin: no. *1074*, etc. [2] No. *1912*. [3] pp. 136–7.
[4] Identifiable as the *Memoirs* of Edmund Ludlow the regicide (*D.N.B.*), vols. i and ii,

avec impatience vôtre troisiéme Replique,[1] quoi que je soi persuadé que vôtre Adversaire n'y entend rien. Je suis, Monsieur, vôtre très-humble et très-obeïssant serviteur,

LE CLERC.

Mr. Coste trouvera ici mes civilitez.

Endorsed by Locke: le Clerc 13° Jan 9$\frac{8}{9}$ Answered 18

2532. MRS. MARY HUNTINGTON to LOCKE, 5 January [1699] (*2969*)

B.L., MS. Locke c. 11, ff. 240–1. Year from Locke's endorsement. Dr. Ralph Huntington, the future bishop of Raphoe (no. *253*, etc.), was now rector of Great Hallingbury: no. 1857 n. Mrs. Huntington was a sister of Sir John Powell, the judge (no. *2969*).

Jan the 5th

We have a Proverb Sir of carring Colis to New Castle and I am now goeing to Act it. to send a Receipt and Advice to the great Philosopher and Physician of the Age But really I have known it recover thos that Could hardly breathe and doe such mighty Cures, that as I desire your Health (which I most heartily doe) I think myself obligd to send it. If I be impertinent I beg your pardon but if it should have the blessed Effect I wish it then Ile not aske you to forgive

Sir

your very humble Servant

MARY HUNTINGTON

our best serviceses attend Sir Francis and My Lady wishing you all many happy new years

turn over

Take 5 Quarts of Spring Watter boyl it till it Comes to 4 put it into an Earthen Vessell, you Must have ready 4 ounces of Lycoris shred or slieved[2] with 2 pound of the best Figs you can gett slicet. let them be put into the Water scalding hott or rather put them into the Pott and Pour it upon this ingredients, stop it Close

which were published in 1698 with 'Vivay' as the place of printing. L.L., no. 1829. They belong with the other publications of the extreme Whigs, the text being freely rehandled by Toland, the editor: Ludlow, *A Voice from the Watch Tower*, v ed. A. B. Worden (Royal Hist. Soc., Camden 4th ser., vol. xxi, 1978), introduction. A French translation was published at Amsterdam in 1699; I have not traced Dutch translation. A third volume of the *Memoirs* appeared in 1699: no. *3083*.

[1] To Stillingfleet: p. 505, etc. [2] Probably for slived, split or divided: *O.E.D.*

for 4 or five days then draw and drink of it a wine glass in the Morning and another in the after noon a bout 4. It is an Excellent Pectorall

Address: For Mr Lock

Endorsed by Locke: M: Huntington 5 Jan 9$\frac{8}{9}$ Answered 6

2533. Dr. Daniel Whitby to Locke, 11 January 1699 (2536)

B.L., MS. Locke c. 23, ff. 94–5. Answered by no. 2536.

Daniel Whitby, 1638–1726; D.D. 1672; a prebendary, 1668–98, and precentor, 1672–1726, of Salisbury; author of *A Paraphrase and Commentary on the New Testament*, 1703, and other works: *D.N.B.*

Honoured Sir,

I have a very great and just esteem for you, and your writings, and therfore do peruse them carefully, and generally with satisfaction, but reading your discourse against the Bishop of Worcester concerning the Resurrection of the dead I confess I could not assent to it, and have sent you my exceptions to it, be pleased to take them in good part, for I assure you though I am constraind to differ from you in this matter, I am very much

Honoured Sir

your sincere friend and humble servant

Jan XI 98 Daniel Whitby

having made a Comment upon all the Epistles, this is part of the preface to the first Epistle to the Corinthians, and therfore would not publish it, till I could hear what one of your exact judgment could say against it.[1]

Address: For Dr Locke these.

Endorsed by Locke: Dr Whitby 11 Jan 98 Answered 17

[1] The passage in Locke's second *Reply* to which Whitby objected is probably pp. 165–210, relating to the resurrection of the same body. His manuscript criticism is apparently B.L., MS. Locke e. 11. Mr. Long compares this manuscript with Whitby's *Paraphrase and Commentary on the New Testament*, 1703, ii. 105–11. Whitby's *Paraphrase and Commentary upon all the Epistles* appeared in 1700: no. *2706*. I have not seen a copy; but the second volume of the 1703 publication appears to be a reprint. Locke is not mentioned by name in the passage cited.

2534. RICHARD CLARKE to [LOCKE?], 12 January 1699

B.L., MS. Locke c. 6, f. 186. The same man wrote to Lady Masham on 30 July 1697 about a mortgage: B.L., MS. Locke c. 16, f. 32; I have failed to identify him. This letter was not necessarily addressed to Locke.

Sir.

I have (according to my promise) done something towards finding out the difference there is between wheat and barly when turned into bread Which is as followeth. First I measured ½ a peck of wheat and took just its weight in meal (of the same sort of wheat) which I had made into a loaf. Then another ½ peck of the same meal sifted through a coars sive to take out the hulls or brann and that was made into another loaf. Then I measured ½ a peck of barly and took just its weight in barly meal (of the same sort of barly) this was sifted through the abovesaid sive and made into another loaf.

Note these three loaves are just ½ pecks by measure that is better than the Winchester measure[1] and without any alowance for the Millers tole or wast in grinding and their weight is as followeth.

	lb	oz	drams	
The wheat not sifted . .	9 :	11 :	0	Averdepois, I haveing no other weights.
The wheat sifted . .	8 :	15 :	0	
The barly . . .	8 :	7 :	8	

I have herewith given you the trouble of a peece of Each sort of the bread that you may see what it is which is all from

Your very humble and obedient servant

RICHD: CLARKE

January 12th/98

Endorsed by Locke: R: Clarke 12 Jan 9 8/9

LOCKE to NICOLAS TOINARD, 14 January 1699

Continued and dispatched on 20 February: no. 2550.

[1] *O.E.D.*, s.v. Winchester.

2535. LOCKE to PETER KING, later first Baron King, 16 January 1699 (2522, 2538)

B.L., MS. Locke c. 40, ff. 27–8.

Oates 16 Jan 9$\frac{8}{9}$

Dear Cosin

I was glad to hear by your letter to Sir Francis that you got well to London and since that more particularly by yours of 13th to me.

I thank you for the news you sent me and for the delivery of soe many of my letters as you mention in yours, and particularly for the knit gloves which came safe. I finde by them that you extend the directions I gave you to keep your legs warme in order to have your feet soe a little too far, you would not else have sent me gloves with half fingers, for I am as apt to feele cold in the tops of my fingers as you in the tops of your toes. but in revenge if ever you desire me to buy socks for you I shall be sure to take care that they shall not cover your toes

I wish amongst the many things you writ me you had put in one word to let me know that my share was paid in to the East India subscription. I desire you to doe it by the first oportunity. For the same day you went from hence I received a kinde letter from Mr Clarke where in he told me the £100— should be ready against you came to town, which letter I cannot answer till I hear from you how that matter has been performed.

I must beg you to direct the inclosed as it ought to be. As I remember his Masters name is Bayly[1] but not being sure I leave it to you to be added with what remains. All here are well and your servants. My short breath does not mend. I am

Dear Cosin

your most affectionate Cosin and servant

J LOCKE

Remember me kindly to Mr Clarke Mr Freke Sir Walter,[2] Mr Duke and the rest of my friends as they come in your way

Address: For Peter King Esqr in the Temple To be left at Mr Potmans in the Middle Temple London

On f. 27v: Shorthand notes by King.

Endorsed by King: January. 16. 1698. Mr Locke

Also by King: [shorthand notes relating to knit gloves, etc.]

[1] Peter Stratton's master: no. *1941*. [2] Yonge.

2536. Locke to Dr. Daniel Whitby, 17 January 1699 (*2533*, 3188)

B.L., MS. Locke c. 24, ff. 283–4. Draft, written by an amanuensis and corrected by Locke. Answers no. *2533*.

Oates 17 Jan. 9$\frac{8}{9}$

Reverend Sir

The letter that you honourd me with found me in an estate of health wherein I had so little disposition to read much lesse to engage in any controversial arguments that I hope you will excuse me if I enter not into the particulars of those papers which you did me the favour to send with it. but since you tell me you will not publish what is contained in them till you can hear what I can say against it pardon me if I comply ⟨so far⟩[a] with your commands as to tell you in generall that though your discourse in those papers which you say are intended for a part of the preface to your comment upon the first Epistle to the Corinthians: be directed. against some part of my Replye to my Lord Bishop of worcester yet it is not at all against the argument that I there maintain which is only this that his Lordship by all that he has said has not provid that the dead shall be raised with the same body that they had here. If you think fit to enter into that dispute and make good his Lordships reasonings I grant you will then argue against me, who without determining for or against the same body make it my businesse there only to shew that his Lordships arguments doe not prove what he charged on my booke, for as to the opinion: it self he that holds it on either side will not have me for an opponent For I being fully perswaded of the resurrection and that we shall have bodys fitted to that state it is indifferent to me whether any one concludes that they shall be the same or not But if you are resolvd to have a controversie with me and choose this way to shew the esteem of me you professe by seting me up for an adversary to confute a point which I professe not to hold I must submit to your correction and bear it as I can[1]

One thing more give me leave to say on this occasion as my particuiler opinion and that is that I have always thought the right way to propagate and promote truth, is to establish it firmly and clearly upon its own sure grounds and basis by arguments ariseing from things themselves. This is that which will enable it to subsist

[a] *MS.* sor for

[1] Bold took up the question: no. *2771*.

and make its way in the world against all opposition. I know the fashion of this age has been forward to run every thing into controversie and opposition of others which appeares not to me I confesse the genuine way for the lovers and builders up of truth, nor that which at any time I would advise my friends to. I should enlarge farther on this subject to a man of your abilities and whom I esteem so much, might it not be liable to be interprited in this case as if I had a mind to avoid the force of your arguments and have the truth smotherd but I beg you to beleive that I am so far from that that I should have owned to you my conviction if I had been convinc'd by your discourse and should have thanked you for seting me right. Noe Sir: Tis out of my aversion to dispute seldom favourable to truth, to our time, or to charity that I take the liberty so frankly to tell you that I think it may be better for us both to keep out of it, though I with the same franknesse professe that upon the reading over of your papers which I have been able yet to doe but once I found noething in them which I thought might not receive a very easy answer. I know not but this may looke like presumsion or vanity in me though I speake it only out of respect and frindship to you which possibly some time or other I may have an oportunity to convince you of. In the mean time I return you my humble thanks for the civilities you expresse to me which I shall always indeavour to deserve by that high esteem I have of your great learning and by the respect wherewith I am

Reverend Sir

your most humble servant

J LOCKE

[On reverse, in Locke's hand:]

Quod nescire dominus nos voluit libenter nesciamus Aug: 3.ps.6. p. 22[1]

Endorsed by Locke: J L to Dr Whitby 17 Jan 9$\frac{8}{9}$

537. LOCKE to EDWARD CLARKE, 20 [June?] 1698 (2447, 2469)

.L., MS. Locke b. 8, no. 129. Printed in Rand, pp. 531–2, with the date as o January 1698. Owing to the wrong date the letter is printed out of place; s number in the sequence should be 2458A.

1 'Let us therefore gladly remain in ignorance of what the Lord has not wished s to know': St. Augustine, *Enarrationes in Psalmos*, vi. 2.

The mention of the Cockpit (p. 370) shows that the letter cannot belong to January 1698; and it is unlikely to belong to January 1699 as it would have been very unusual for Locke to use a simple Old Style year in the date. The sentence about Freke and the nuts responds to a lost letter of Clarke's dated 18 June, of which Locke made a note in his Journal on 20 June 1698: hence the date to which the letter is assigned here. Presumably Locke wrote 'Jan.' for 'Jun.' (he uses both abbreviations frequently) and Clarke followed him carelessly.

Oates 20 Jan. 98

Dear Sir

I doe not forgive you three or four days silence because there is noe thing in it that needs forgivenesse. Your thinking there was need of an apologie for it is all that I have to blame in the matter. Silence where businesse requires not a quicker answer is a liberty that I thinke due to my freinds in circumstances of much greater leisure than I know you have

I am glad that you can recollect noe cause of the Melancholy I mentioned in my last to you. I thinke my self obleiged to observe and give you notice of every thing I can observe that may give you light into the matter you are concernd about in that case. The lesse you can finde in it the better I think it is. However I shall continue my eyes as open as I can for your service and satisfaction in the point. But I hope there is noe thing to be seen. If any such thing appear, it is a kindenesse to her as well as to you that you should know it, and you may therefor be sure on that side[1]

My thanks to the Batchelor for the Nuts[2] and to you for paying for them. If you will doe me the favour to send the inclosed to Syl: either at his lodging in St Martins Lane or at our office at the Cockpit I have sent him order to fetch them from you and ease you of that trouble.

Though I spare you yet I have troubled Mrs Clarke with a long scrible in the inclosed, which I desire you to give her with my service. I am

Dear Sir

Your most affectionate humble service

My Lady gives you her most humble service. and my wife her duty

Endorsed by Clarke: Mr. Lock with Letters inclosed to Mrs Clarke and Syll touching the Nutts etc: Received the 22th. January 1698. Answered the 23th.

[1] This probably relates to Betty Clarke, who was at this time a source of anxiety to her parents; she was at Oates in May and on 4 July, and is likely to have been there continuously: pp. 392, etc., 444.

[2] Cacao nuts, as stated in Locke's note of Clarke's letter of 18 June.

2538. LOCKE to PETER KING, later first Baron King, 24 January 1699 (2535, 2546)

B.L., MS. Locke c. 40, ff. 29–30. The page containing the text is cut away immediately below the signature, perhaps by Locke in order to destroy a postscript. Of the present postscripts the first is inserted in a blank space opposite the signature and the second is written on the reverse of the cover.

Oates 24 Jan $9\frac{8}{9}$

Dear Cosin

I am glad to hear by yours of the 22th that my money for the subscription of the East India Company was paid at the time and that you have the receit and paid with the money I expected it should. I find notice given in the Gazet that the first quarterly part of the Annuity[1] being 2 per Cent will be paid on the 28th instant at Skinners-hall,[2] and that the third five per cent for carrying on the trade must be paid the 1st of February next. Now the £20 which is to be received for my share at Skinners-hall 28th instant and the £30 for which I here with send you a bill on Mr Churchill will togeather make my £50 which I am to pay in to the Stock of the Company the 1st of Feb: I must beg you to be at the trouble to looke after it and am

Dear Cosin

your most affectionate Cosin and humble servant

J LOCKE

All here give you their service

Pray Cosin send me word in your next to whom you d⟨el⟩ivered[a] the box and letter directed to Mr Popple

Address: For Peter King Esqr at his chamber in the Temple To be left at Mr Potmans in The middle Temple London

Postmark: IA 27

Endorsed by King: January. 24. 98. Mr Locke

[a] *Page torn.*

---

[1] The interest payable on the subscribers' stock: p. 397, n. 1.

[2] The New East India Company had its premises here from its establishment in 1698 until the amalgamation of the two companies in 1708: Hatton, *New View*, 619.

2539. LOCKE to DR. (later Sir) THOMAS MOLYNEUX, 25 January 1699 (*2514*, *2589*)

Some Familiar Letters, pp. 294–6, and *Notes and Queries*, 8th ser. ix (1896), 381. The manuscript came into the possession of Sir William Wilde, and so of his son Willie Wilde, who printed the unpublished part in *Notes and Queries* as above, and then sold the manuscript. Both printings give the date and subscription; they appear to be duplicates; I have reproduced only one set. The letter answers no. *2514* and is answered by no. *2589*.

Oates 25. Jan. 169$\frac{8}{9}$.

Sir,

I have been slower in returning you my thanks for the favour of your letter of the 26th of Nov. and the civilities you express to me in it, than perhaps I should have been. But the truth is, my thoughts never look towards Dublin now, without casting such a cloud upon my mind, and laying such a load of fresh sorrow on me for the loss of my dear friend your brother, that I cannot without displeasure turn them that way; and when I do it I find my self very unfit for conversation and the entertainment of a friend. 'Tis therefore not without pain that I bring my self to write you a scurvy letter. What there wants in it of expression, you must make up out of the esteem I have for the memory of our common friend; and I desire you not to think my respects to you the less, because the loss of your brother makes me not able to speak them as I would.

Since you are pleased to put such a value on my trifles, I have given order to Mr. Churchill to send you my last Reply to the Bishop of Worcester,[1] and the last edition of my treatise of Education,[2] which came forth since Mr. Molyneux's death. I send this with the more confidence to you, because your brother told me more than once that he followed the method I therein offer to the world, in the breeding of his son. I wish you may find it fit to be continued to him, and useful to you in his education; for I cannot but be mightily concerned for the son of such a father, and wish that he may grow up into that esteem and character, which his father left behind him amongst all good men who knew him. As for my Essay concerning Human Understanding, it is now out of print, and if it were not, I think I should make you but an ill complement in sending it you less perfect than I design it should be in the next

[1] p. 505, etc.

[2] The fourth edition, 1699. It is advertised in the Term *Catalogue* for February: *T.C.* iii. 113.

edition, in which I shall make many additions to it:[1] And when it is as perfect as I can make it, I know not whether in sending it you I shall not load you with a troublesome and useless present. But since by desiring it you seem to promise me your acceptance, I shall as soon as it is reprinted take the liberty to thrust it into your study.

Amongst the papers your Brother brought home with him out of England you will finde one sheet wherein a part of the Evangelists is printed in Greeke in columns. He had it of me and I gave it him only as a specimen of an ⟨harmony⟩[a] of the Evangelists, now doing by a friend of mine.[2] But by mistake I gave him a sheet I intended not, for that which he had of me was part of a collection sent me by the author and for want of that my collection will be imperfect. I therefore desire you to do me the favour to send it me again by Mr. Burridge or some other safe hand for it will be of no use to you, and of great use to me. Or if you desire one of the kinde you shall have one of those supernumerary and scatterd sheets that I have some where, one of which I tooke that to be when I gave it your brother.

Mr. Churchill writes me word that he had received from you for me five pounds sterling which I acknowledge to be the legacy left me by your brother, my dear Friend William Molyneux Esqr. This I thinke necessary to acknowledge now with my thanks upon the first opportunity, till you shall direct me how to doe it more in forme for the discharge of his Executor. I am Sir

Your most humble and faithfull servant

JOHN LOCKE.

2540. LOCKE to EDWARD CLARKE, 27 January 1699 (2525, 2553)

B.L., MS. Locke b. 8, no. 130. Discoloured. Printed in Rand, pp. 542–3.

Oates 27 Jan $9\frac{8}{9}$

Dear Sir

I had not been soe slow in returning you my thanks for your answering my bill drawn on you to my Cosin King, if he had not

[a] *In text as printed* harmon

[1] The fourth edition, 1700.

[2] Toinard; presumably a sheet from one of the versions later than that of 1678.

omitted to mention it in the first letter he writ me after his return to town. I therefor now thank you. To which lett me adde that you need not make any apologies for your not writeing oftener to me. I could be glad indeed to hear sometimes how matters goe for I see noething here but a little of the outside. But I know your much businesse and noe time. That excuses you, but hinders me not from grumbleing some times at the Batchelor who methinks might now and then spare me a word

Pray returne my thanks to your wife for her kind letter and to my wife for hers. I am glad to hear from her upon any occasion, though that of makeing excuses for your not writeing you need not imploy her in. That matter is setled, and tis too much to expect letters from a man, that has scarce time to eat or sleep. I wish your pains may be successfull for the publique good and am

Dear Sir

Your most faithfull humble servant

J LOCKE

All our fires side send their service to your fires side. And to the Batchelor.

The inclosed I hope will goe with your letters to the post house without any trouble to you.

Endorsed by Clarke: Mr. Lock Received the 30th. January 1698 Answered the 31th.

2541. MARTHA LOCKHART to LOCKE, 28 January 1699 (*2517, 2671*)

B.L., MS. Locke c. 15, ff. 76–7.

28th. Jan: . $9\frac{8}{9}$

a 2nd Interloper.[1]

begining with my thanks for Your kind, and speedy answer to my first: for tho it had no date it could not have been sooner receiv'd, nor answer'd. a lady of both reall beauty and merrit, and my perticuliar frend has commited to my Charge a trust to be comunicated only to you. (I don't know if your Character tho 'tis very great would have lead her so far, as to have trusted you: (for she is nice) but that a frend of your's, has rais'd her fancy to

[1] Apparently implying intrusion into Locke's private concerns.

beleive you more fidelle[1] then the rest of your sex.) by this time I hope you'le think your self oblig'd to keep her secret. so I begin gravely my story. Mrs Barrington[2] having her wholl fortune in Mr Conyer's hand's;[3] has of late had some reasons, which are too long to trouble you with now: upon the marriage of her sister Mrs Shales,[4] to make a more perticuliar Enquiry into her security, then she Ever thought to have don; having Entirely trusted Mr Conyer's. but on this occasion it has apeard that their mony has been put out in his name some years, and they never had any declaration of trust, which they are inform'd was a necessary security. this has allarm'd Mrs Bar: whose all is concern'd in this matter. and she being inform'd that you have mony on the same mortgage; thinks you are the only one she can trust to ask these two questions; whether the declaration of trust which Mr Conyer's has now deliver'd her, (the Coppy of which is inclosed) is of the same nature with what you have, and sufficient for her.

the other Question is if You are satisfied only from Mr Conyers, or if you your self have look't into the writings; and think the security good. she has from two reasons, the one that she would not occasion any tatle of a relation, the other that she would not disoblige him. menaged this with so much caution that not her Grandmother[5] nor any one of her familly Except her sister who was Equally concern'd, kno any thing of it the only person she has advis'd with is the Atturney Generall.[6] who derected her to ask these two questions as the best way to give her satisfaction.

from the same reason that I write you this I'me Confident you'le forgive my troubling you; that I think 'tis charity to assist any that deserve well as I veryly beleive she do's. she desired me to assure you that nothing you shall say on it shall goe farther then her self, and that she will be as secret in your answer, as she

[1] Fidele, faithful, sincere, true: *O.E.D.*

[2] Mary Barrington: p. 24. Through the Cromwells her father was a third cousin of Mrs. Lockhart.

[3] John Conyers: p. 24; in connection with the present business, p. 127. Through his maternal grandmother he was a second cousin of Mary Barrington's father and a third cousin of Mrs. Lockhart.

[4] Anne, d. 1729, wife of Charles Shales, d. 1734, goldsmith to Queen Anne, George I, and George II: Noble, ii. 49.

[5] Dorothy, d. 1703, daughter of Sir William Lytton of Knebworth and widow of Sir John Barrington, the third baronet: ibid. ii. 48. Mary Barrington's other grandmother had died long before.

[6] Sir Thomas Trevor, later Baron Trevor of Bromham, Attorney-General 1695–1701: no. *1568*. Through the Cromwells he was a third cousin of Mary Barrington's father.

desires You Would keep her question's. 'twould be too much trouble to send you a letter after this long story, that I shall keep 'till the next occasion. Only for many reasons I should be overjoy'd to have an hour or two's Chatt with you. Evry sun shining day makes me hope that summer and you are a coming. I wish for You Extreamly but there are of your frends that rail as much at you as Sir James do's at the new bill[1] and swear that if Kensington air be able to preserve a King, Knightsbridge or Marybone may preserve a subject let their lungs be never so bad. I dispute for the weakness of your lungs till I have allmost spoil'd my own but to very little purpose there's more belongs to this but of that hereafter. tho I had resolv'd to say nothing in this but of Mrs B: I Can't help this and adding that Cuningham[2] I beleive has lock't up his two beaux's in some Scotch Cupboard till his returne for I have not heard of 'em since. I am tho I've not room to Express it in many words very much Your etc

M LOCKHART.

Endorsed by Locke: M: Lockhart 28 Jan $9\frac{8}{9}$ Answered Feb. 6

2542. J.-B. ROUSSEAU (M. de Vernietes) to LOCKE, 31 January [1699]

B.L., MS. Locke c. 23, ff. 15–16. Year from Locke's endorsement.

The writer, Jean-Baptiste Rousseau (1671–1741), the poet, came to England probably in March 1698 as a clerk in the train of Tallard, the French ambassador to William III. He was said to have been dismissed on account of an epigram that he wrote on Tallard. While in England he used the name de Vernietes, perhaps for disreputable reasons; he did not use it after his return to France: H. A. Grubbs, *Jean-Baptiste Rousseau*, 1941. Du Bos mentions him on pp. 478, 507.

A Londres le 31 Janvier.

J'ay receu Monsieur depuis deux jours seulement L'histoire de Siam que M. du Bos m'a adressée pour vous.[3] J'en ay chargé le sieur Mortier libraire dans le Strand[4] qui aura soin de vous la faire tenir, et je profite de cette occasion pour vous remercier du Traitté de LEducation que vous m'avez fait lhonneur de m'envoyer.[5] Je l'ay leu et je le relis avec une satisfaction incroïable. C'est un livre que tous ceux qui cherchent a devenir honnestes

[1] I have failed to identify it.

[2] Alexander Cunningham was at present probably in Paris with Lord Poulett: p. 532; Du Bos to Bayle, 26 February N.S. (Lombard, no. 69; Labrousse, no. 1351).

[3] p. 507.

[4] David Mortier: p. 228.

[5] Probably the fourth edition: p. 552.

gens ne peuvent lire avec trop de soin, et si les Enfans y trouvent de quoy former leur raison, les hommes faits y trouvent egalement dequoi perfectionner laleur.

J'aurois fort souhaité d'avoir lhonneur de vous embrasser avant mon depart pour France. Je compte de partir dans huit jours. Je souhaiterois avec beaucoup de passion de pouvoir vous estre de quelque utilité dans le Sejour que j'y ferai qui selon l'apparence sera un peu long. Permettez que je vous demande Monsieur quelque place dans lhonneur de Votre souvenir et faites moi la justice d'estre persuadé quon ne peut estre avec plus d'estime et de Veneration que je suis Monsieur

Votre tres humble et tres obeïssant serviteur

VERNIETES

Address: A Monsieur Monsieur Locke

Endorsed by Locke: Verniettes 31 Jan $9\frac{8}{9}$ Answered Feb 7

2543. FRANCIS NICHOLSON to LOCKE, 4 February 1699 (*2446*, 2622)

B.L., MS. Locke c. 16, ff. 161–2. Answered by no. 2622.

Virginia James City. Feb: 4. $9\frac{8}{9}$

Honourable Sir

I have the great satisfaction of having the honour to receive your most kind and obliging letter of the 25th of September last: And the reverend Mr President Blayr hath acquainted me how very zelous You were in using your great Interest for my being so very advantagiously removed hither.[1] And I shall endevour (God willing) so to behave my self in my station here, that You may never have cause to be concerned, that You were so very instrumental in accomplishing that Affair.

I esteem it as a very great happiness that You have been pleased to honour me with your Friendship; which I shall endeavour by all ways and means to improve, and to make my self in some measure worthy of it, i.e. by following so good and great a Pattern as your self. But my failings therein (which I am very sensible must be too many) I beg that You would forgive, as the effects of my Understanding, and not of my Will.

[1] Nicholson was appointed governor of Virginia about 31 May 1698: *Cal.S.P., Dom.*, 1698, p. 277.

According to my Duty, by this Opportunity I endeavour to give your Lordships an account of this his Majestys Dominion, as allso of Maryland, till the time that I deliverd it up to his Excellency Governor Blakiston.[1] So I will not here presume to take up so much of your time again: being well assured that You need but once to have an Account of any Affair; though it were never so intricate. And You have clearly demonstrated to the World, what good use You make of your Vacant Hours from the publick service of his Majesty, in that high and justly merited station that You are in: Which makes me beg your pardon for this trouble: but withall, that You would give me leave to own my self to be

Your most obliged faithfull Friend and obedient humble servant

FR: NICHOLSON

Endorsed by Locke: F: Nicolson 4 Feb $9\frac{8}{9}$ Answered 10 Oct 99

2544. JEAN LE CLERC to LOCKE, 7/17 February 1699 (2531, 2595)

B.L., MS. Locke c. 13, ff. 127–8. Printed in Bonno, *Le Clerc*, pp. 111–12.

A Amsterdam le 17 de Fevrier 1699.

Je vous suis obligé, Monsieur, de la bonne volonté que vous me témoignez, en me donnant vos bons avis, touchant la maniere dont nous devons gouverner nôtre petit garçon. Nous ne manquerons pas de les suivre. Il paroît à présent un peu mieux, et son abscès ne rend pas tant de pus. Le pus même est plus épais, ce qui nous fait esperer que le soin et le beautemps, qui s'approche, le tireront d'affaire, avec l'aide de Dieu. Pour moi, je me porte assez bien, et il semble que le travail m'engraisse, de même que le plaisir de dire des injures engraisse bien des Theologiens. Mr. Cave, Chanoine à Windsor, est, je croi, de ce nombre, au moins il a écrit une violente dissertation contre moi, contre laquelle j'ai résolu de me défendre dans peu, en prouvant évidemment tous les chefs sur lesquels il m'attaque. J'adresserai pour cela quelques Lettres à quelques uns des principaux de Mrs. vos Prélats, non tant dans l'esperance d'obtenir justice, que pour faire voir à tout le monde, que je n'ai aucune peur de lui. Car il s'agit de choses claires comme le jour.

[1] *Cal.S.P.*, *Col.*, vol. xviii, no. 77, also dated 4 February. Col. Nathaniel Blakiston, governor of Maryland from 1698 to 1702.

J'ai un peu fouetté le *Master of Arts* de Cambrige qui m'a attaqué,[1] dans une préface que j'ai envoié pour mettre à la tête de mes Additions sur *Hammond*.[2] Vous verrez que j'y ai dit un mot de vous. Elle paroîtra aussi en Latin, avec les autres Lettres, quand je les aurai envoiées en MS. Si le vent change, vous aurez mon Harmonie, dans peu de jours.[3] Dans le billet ci-joint, je mets quatre exemplaires, dont l'un sera pour Vous, Monsieur, un second pour Madame Masham, un troisiéme pour Mr. Coste; et le quatriéme pour Mr. L'Evêque de Salisbury, à qui je vous supplie de l'envoier.

Deux Demoiselles Françoises, de ma connoissance, m'ont prié de m'informer si l'on ne pourroit point trouver chez quelque Lord des places de Demoiselle d'honneur pour elles. Elles sont assez bien faites et ne sont pas mal adroites, de sorte que je ne doutes nullement qu'on ne fût content d'elles. L'une a un peu plus de vint-cinq ans et l'autre ne les a pas encore. Elle ne savent pas l'Anglois, mais elles l'auroient bien tôt apris, parce qu'elles l'ont un peu sû, aiant été en Angleterre et sâchant le Flammand. Ce n'est pas là une commission pour vous, Monsieur, mais peutêtre qu'il se pourroit faire que Madame Vôtre Hôtesse auroit occasion de s'informer d'une semblable chose. C'est ce qui fait que je prends la liberté de vous en importuner. Je n'ai pû refuser à ces Demoiselles d'écrire en leur faveur, les considerant beaucoup et osant même répondre pour elles.[4] Je suis, Monsieur, vôtre très-humble et très-obeïssant serviteur

J LE CLERC.

Address: A Monsieur Monsieur Locke at Mr. Pawlings in little Lincolns inne fields, over against the plough London.

Postmark: FE 10

Endorsed by Locke: J. le Clerc 17 Feb $9\frac{8}{9}$

[1] F.B.: p. 507.

[2] *A Supplement to Dr. Hammond's Paraphrase and Annotations on the New Testament*, 1699. L.L., no. 772. The preliminary letter is dated 25 January 1699 (N.S.). Le Clerc included a Latin version of it in his *Epistolæ Criticæ, et Ecclesiasticæ*, 1700, pp. 321–60 (this book forms a third volume of the *Ars Critica*).

[3] The copies arrived about April: pp. 591, 613.

[4] These are Le Clerc's sisters-in-law, daughters of Gregorio Leti: no. *2854*. The younger married in England: no. *3559*. The elder was in Hanover in 1707 and exchanged letters with Leibniz: Mrs. C. Cockburn, *Works*, ed. Birch, ii. 203–4; Leibniz, *Phil. Schriften*, ed. Gerhardt, iii. 404–5. From about 1712 to about 1721 she was the governess of Frederick the Great's sister Frederica Sophia Wilhelmina, later Margravine of Baireuth. The princess gives an unfavourable account of her in her *Mémoires*, 1812, i. 5–6, 10, 13, 50–71.

2545. COMMISSARY JAMES BLAIR to LOCKE, 8 February 1699 (*2380*, 2626)

B.L., MS. Locke c. 4, ff. 10–11. On f. 11 there is a passage written by Blair and deleted. Answered by no. 2626.

Virginia feb. 8. 169$\frac{8}{9}$

Sir

The tranquillity we begin to enjoy in this Countrey by the happy change of our Governour, and Government is so great that I who have the happines to know by whose means these blessings were procured have all the reason in the world to take all occasions of expressing my gratitude for them, and to pray to God to reward those noble publick souls that bestow so many of their thoughts, in contriving the relief of the oppressed, and the happines of mankind. Dear Sir think not that I speak this from any other principle or design I have, but only from a sense how much this whole Countrey in generall and my self in particular are beholding to yow for the thoughts you was pleased to bestow on our late unhappy circumstances, and the methods you contrived to relieve us. You are to look for your reward from a better hand. only give me leave to say that I think no sort of good works are preferable to these, that have such an universall good influence on whole Countreys to make all the people happy. This Countrey is so barren of action that it affords nothing to satisfy your curiosity. Our new Governour Coll. Nicholson is very heartily welcomed to this place. Sir Edmund Andros[1] is gone home mighty angry not only for the loss of such a good Government but for being succeeded by such a person, whom of all others he had the least kindnes for. I doubt not if he or his great friend at your board[2] can get him to be put into any post wherein he can reach this Countrey we shall feel the effects of his resentment and revenge to the utmost of his pouer: of which he has given us some proof at parting. For there being a vacancy in the Councill by the death of Coll. Christopher Wormley (after they had the news here that Coll. Nicholson had the Government) he filled this place with one Mr Dudley Diggs,[3] a factor of Mr Jeoffrey Jeoffreys,[4] a man that had no sort of merit to recommend

[1] 1637–1714; governor of Virginia 1692–8: *Dict. American Biog.*

[2] William Blathwayt: no. *1981*; for the identification see G. A. Jacobsen, *William Blathwayt*, 1932, pp. 307–8.

[3] Wormeley died about June 1698; Digges was appointed on 15 October: *Cal.S.P., Col.*, vol. xvi, nos. 645, 898, 900, 951.

[4] Jeffrey Jeffreys, a London merchant, alderman, and member of parliament; knighted 20 October of this year: Beaven, *Aldermen*, ii. 119, etc.

him to that honour, but that he had signalized himself by his publick enmity to our Colledge[1] to that degree that being Executor to one Coll. Cole his father in law who left 50 pound to our College, he could never be prevailed with to pay the money but suffered himself to be sued for it, and by severall tricks of law (which was no hard matter to do in the late government) has hitherto shifted off the payment. In the prosecution of that suit there was one remarkable saying of his which recommended him much to Sir Edmund Andros's favour. I desire a Reference, says he, that I may have time to prepare my defence, otherwise not only I but the whole Countrey may be *cheated*[a] of their money. This was so gross an aspersion thrown on a Society of the honestest men in the Countrey, and in so publick an Audience that it is thought nothing could have endeared him more to Sir Edmund. For our Colleges sake I would beg that such a man as this may be kept out of the Councill, as he is at present out of it, not having been nominated in the Governours Instructions. We are now upon severall good designs, which as they come to be formed I will not fail to give you an account of. In the mean time I beg your pardon for this trouble and remain

Sir
Your most obliged humble servant
JAMES BLAIR

My service to Mr Fletcher and Mr Johnstoune[2]

Endorsed by Locke: J: Blair 8 Feb $8\frac{8}{9}$ Answered 16 Oct.

2546. LOCKE to PETER KING, later first Baron King, 11 February 1699 (2538, 2548)

B.L., MS. Locke c. 40, ff. 31–2.

Oates 11 Feb $9\frac{8}{9}$

Dear Cosin

I thank you for dispatching the East India company businesse for me as you acquainted me in yours of the 4th. Give me leave to minde you that the 11th of Feb. is now come, It being soe near the

[a] *Written in large letters.*

[1] William and Mary College, of which Blair was president.
[2] Andrew Fletcher, James Johnstoun.

end of the terme[1] I doe not expect you should neglect your own businesse to receive the money due to me on Mr Firmins bond just at the day. But I desire you would doe it as soon as your leisure will give you leave. I know not whether it will not be best to leave one hundred pounds of it in your Cosin Frekes hands for the next payment of my subscription in the East India company and the remainder of it to Mr Churchill for my account, this is what I think if you think otherwise pray let me know. If you like my proposal then take a receit of your Cosin Freke for the £100 which he promises to pay for your next payment due upon that subscription. If you have your share still in that company soe that there be eleven actions in your name, you may, if it will be any convenience to you, Leave with your Cosin Freke £110 of the mony you shall receive for me due from Mr Firmin. Pray let me know what time you thinke to be going out of town. I have sent you your booke by this bearer Mrs Lane.[2] She has an Uncle in town an Attorney of Stafford shire a man of credit and practise in that Country. My Lady has spoke to her to recommend you to her Uncle and I beleive she will not forget it, for she told my Lady that she intended it herself. I am

Dear Cosin

your most affectionate Cosin and humble servant

J LOCKE

My Lady and all here are your servants

Address: For Peter King Esqr at his chamber in the Temple To be left at Mr Potmans in the Middle Temple London

Endorsed by King: Mr Locke February 11. 1698.

2547. WILLIAM THOMAS to LOCKE [14?] February 1699 (*2457, 2561*)

B.L., MS. Locke c. 20, ff. 160–1. The date of the postmark is more likely to be correct than Thomas's date.

Richards Coffee hous by Temple Barr London 16 Feb: 1699

Sir

I humbly thank you for your last to me in the Country and shall always esteem Mr Locks advice as a particular favour. Th

[1] Hilary term ended on 12 February. [2] No. 2087, etc.

occasion of this is to put you in mind that when I sent the Physick books to you in London that at your desire I sent with them the Corpus Juris Civilis in 2 Volumes in folio[1] which cost my Father 02t:15s:00. My request to You now is that you would be pleas'd to restore them, or if they may continue to be anyways usefull to you that you would be pleasd to give Mr Churchill orders to lett me have other books at my choice to the value of them.—I heartily aske your pardon for this trouble and hope that you will give me leave to subscribe my self

Sir

your most Obliged and most humble Servant

W THOMAS.

My Mother gives her humble service to you.

Address: To The Honble: John Locke Esqr [at Oates, by Joslyn, Bishops Stortford]

Postmark: FE 14

Endorsed by Locke: W Thomas 16 Feb $9\frac{8}{9}$ Answered

2548. LOCKE to PETER KING, later first Baron King, 16 February 1699 (2546, 2558)

B.L., MS. Locke c. 40, ff. 33–4.

Oates 16 Feb $9\frac{8}{9}$

Dear Cosin

I thank you for receiveing my money due upon Mr Firmins bond. I approve of your leaveing £100 in your Cosins hands[2] for the next payment for the subscription. pray send me word when the day will be and leave word with your Cosin that you have desired me to minde him of that payment at the time and send me word how I am to direct a letter to him.

You told me formerly that he would not be unwilling to have £100 upon bond at legal interest and pay it at a weeks warning whenever it should be called for. If it will suit his occasions and he be still of the same minde pray send me word, for then I will tell you where you shall make up the remaining £91.8.0 an hundred pounds which he shall have upon those terms.

Mrs Lane came not home till Tuesday night which is the reason I could not write to you sooner.

[1] Nos. 1790, *1924*.

[2] John or Thomas Freke.

Send me word whether goeing or returning in your journey into the West you shall call at Sutton[1]

My Lady and all here remember you with respects. I am

Dear Cosin

Your most affectionate Cosin and humble servant

J LOCKE

If you should write to me any thing that by reason of your journey should require a speedier answer than our ordinary course of letters direct your letter for me to be left with Mr Harrison at the Crown in Harlow

Address: For Peter King Esqr To be left at Mr Potmans in the Middle Temple London

Postmark: FE 24

Endorsed by King: Mr Lock febru. 16. 1698.

2549. DR. JOHN COVEL to LOCKE, 18 February 1699 (*2481*, 2562)

B.L., MS. Locke c. 7, ff. 172–3. Answered by no. 2562.

feb. 18. 9[8/9]

Worthy Sir

I now must acknowledge a double debt, for which I have been long upon the score with you; I hope your Candor will accept of that as some small satisfaction, till time and some more happy occasion will make me capable of making some better returne. I have perused *Mr Cross his Tagmicall Art*; As to the man, I take him to be a very good industrious one, and one that hath deserved all the encouragement which he hath met withall, and more; for we have meer Drones run away every day with good preferment when I fear such painfull men as he may want their bread. The Art it self seem's to me very very difficult and at my Age deters me from entering far into it. I confesse I was of the opinion that both points and Accents were of a much later date then Christs birth; yet I know there are very able and eminent men that have strongly asserted the contrary; it is beyond my skill in Rabbinism to enter into the controversy, yet I have seen some hundreds of hebrew MSS. and never one with points of 1000 year standing. I have several by me, one of the bible entire by it self, of about 500 yeares, where the letter is with one Ink, and the points with

[1] Where Peter's grandfather Peter Locke had lived.

another. but I cannot see, that the advantage of understanding these Tagmical notes, will countervail the vast labour and pains required to understand them, I confesse I am no able Judge, and therefore I shall not rashly further condemne what I confesse I cannot understand; one thing I must own indeed to stick with me that in our Saviours words mat. 5. 18. the ἰῶτα and κεραία should signify either the hebrew points or accents, as mr Crosse seems to hint, for ἰῶτα is certainly from the Greek; when I have the happinesse to meet you we will farther discourse of this businesse; in the mean time, I am glad I contributed to this honest mans designe, it may prove very usefull for ought I know, though not to me.

In the next place I thank you heartily for your peice against the Bp. of W.[1] He that reads it with attention must own Mr L. a man of as strong reason as this Age affords. Our Ionians[2] and Schoolmen cavil much at your answer, as to what is call'd *Personal*, and count your dwelling upon *They*, and *Them*, and the like too long; though really I cannot see what could be left out in all that part, unlesse you should have quietly lain under the mark and badge of those whome the Bishop meanes by *They* and *Them*; and if a man be slightly markt out for an ill man (or what he is not) by an *innuendo*, I shall think he is as much bound to vindicate himself, as if he were call'd, *Ill man*, in termes at length. I am extreamly pleased with your notions about the *Resurrection*, and *matter endow'd with several graduall perfections* etc. As to the first we in Christs College were alwayes brought up, against the *Identity or same numerical body* in the Resurrection by our old father, H. more.[3] And though he indeed was for Immateriality to the Height, yet withall necessarily allow'd a Vehicle, which is *matter*.[4] By the *Resurrection*, (was ment by Christ himself) *onely a future state*, ἀνάστασιν νεκρῶν the *rebeing of the dead*, or as Dr Hammond on mat. 22. 31. a *resubsistence* or *second state*. And otherwise our Saviours argument had proved nothing against the Sadduces. for Abraham's and Isaacks and Jacobs body's were not raysed, but onely they had an ἀνάστασιν a *rebeing* then, though their bodyes were in their graves or moulder'd into ashes hundred of yeares before.

[1] Worcester; Locke's second *Reply* to Stillingfleet: p. 505.

[2] This should mean members of the Ionic school of philosophy, Thales and his disciples; but there may be a local allusion.

[3] More contradicts it categorically in *An Explanation of the Grand Mystery of Godliness* 1660; in his *Theological Works*, 1708, pp. 154–5).

[4] More states his views on the vehicles of souls in 'The Immortality of the Soul', pp. 118–19, in *Collection of . . . Philosophical Writings*, 2nd ed., 1662.

Of matter being endow'd with higher and higher perfections and so at last with Reason,[1] I cannot yet se but your discourse is unanswerable; and when we meet I will tell you of something (which hath been long in my mind) that to me is a demonstration. When I can come (with convenience to my self,) I will trespasse upon you for a few dayes conversation; you are more at leisure, especially now; when the weather proves fine, why cannot you prevayl with Sir Fr. and my Lady and come all for one week; I have many things to talk with you about, it will be part of your entertainment; but no man shall be more wel⟨come⟩[a] to me then you. I am in all sincerity

(Worthy Sir)

Your ever affectionate and faithfull servant

Jo: Covel.

I hope you received my letter (soon after I came from Oates) about Edwards,[2] I sent it to London as you directed. But my Lady in her last letter to me seems to hint as if it came not to your hands.

Address: These To the Worthy John Lock Esquire at Sir Fran. Masham's house in Oates. Essex

Endorsed by Locke: Dr Covel 18 Feb $9\frac{8}{9}$ Answered Mar. 12

2550. Locke to Nicolas Toinard, 14 January and 20 February 1699 (2504, *2571*)

B.M., Add. MS. 28,728, ff. 34–5. Printed in Ollion, pp. 131–4. Answers no. *2497*; answered by no. *2571*.

Oates 14 Jan $\frac{8}{99}$

Vous me direz sans doute Monsieur un homme fort dificile à contenter quand je vous avoue que quoique Monsieur du Bos et vous avez parlè si avantageusement de moi j'ay eu quelque chagrin en le lisant dans votre lettre, de ce que je n'etois pas present, et que je ne suis pas troisieme de la companie quand vous vous entretinez ensemble. A ce qu'il a dit del'estime qu'il a pour moy

[a] *Page torn.*

[1] Second *Reply*, pp. 396–406.

[2] No. *2481*, enclosure.

je le sent bien mais c'est à vous que je le doibs et il le croit avoir quelque merit d'etre rangè parmi vos amis c'est en veritiè un honeur dont je me glorifie beaucoup, mais pour ce qu'est des honetetes dont il parle tant, je vous prie de croire que j'avois la voluntè de lui rendre tout le service que j'etois capable de rendre à un homme de merit que vous m'avez recommandè, mais que ni lui ni le peu de temps que j'etois à Londre avant son depart ne me donnoit pas l'occasion de lui temoigner ce que je devois à un de vos amis.

A propos du medaille dont vous parlez ou il y a ΒΑCΙΛΕVC ΑΝΤΙΓΟΝ je ne m'etonne moins de la lange que de caracteres qu'on a emploies dans cet'inscription. Isaac Vossius soutinoit que la langue vulgaire de Juifs etoit Grec du temps de nostre Segnieur J. C,[1] Je ne pouvois jamais tomber d'accord. Mais si Antigonus fit l inscription de sa monoie en caracteres Samaritanes propter *ἀρχαισμόν*[2] Il ne pouvoit pas se servir de la lange Grec propter benevolentiam nec ambitionem cum Judæi tantum passi sint a Seleucidis et jam utrisque dominarentur potentiores Romani.[3] LΓΙ dans le medaile d Herode ne put pas marquer Anno XIII parcequ'en ce cas la il me semble il doit etre LΙΓ

J'ay ecrit a mon librare a Londre à ce quil a à vous envoier la traduction de Zeraim per Guisium avec order d'y joindre les feuiles qui vous manquent de Dampier

Feb 20

J'avois ecrit jusqu' à là, quand etant detournè j'ay jusque a cè vintieme Fevrier atendue de jour a autre la publication du II vol de Dampier qu'on m'avoit long temps marquè etre tout prest.[4] En cette languissant attente Je recus une lettre que Monsieur Verniets me fit lhoneur d'ecrire dans la quelle il me mandoit qu'il alloit partir bientot pour Paris.[5] J'ecrivis sur le champ a mon librare a Londres[6] de ne manquer pas de mettre entre se mains le Zeraim Guisii et toutes les feuiles de Dampier qui etoient imprimes avec quelques Cartes que Monsieur du Bos avoit demandez,[7]

[1] Vossius (nos. *453*, *1207*) stated this opinion apparently in *Observationum ad Pomponium Melam Appendix*, 1686: *Bibliotheque universelle*, ii. 411.
[2] 'As an archaism.'
[3] 'From goodwill or ambition, since the Jews had suffered so much from the Seleucids, and since both peoples were then dominated by the more powerful Romans.'
[4] Publication in a few days' time was advertised in November 1698: *T.C.* iii. 104.
[5] No. *2542*. [6] Probably Awnsham Churchill. [7] pp. 532–3.

On m'a depuis mandè que par bonheur Dampier venoit d'etre achevè et qu'on lavoit mis avec les autres entre les mains de Monsieur Verniets à qui je souhait un bon voyage.

A cette heur que jay lues tout les traites du R P Lamy hormis son harmonie avec ceux de ses antagonists que vous m'avez envoies, il faut que je vous en remercier encore pour le plaisir que vous m'avez donnèe par tant ⟨d'erudition⟩[a] et d'esprit qu'on a fait paroitre de cotè et d'autre en cette controverse, mais il faut avouer qu c'est de vous que j'attende les eclaircissements qui me doibent entirement determinè. Il y a une chose qui m'arette à laquelle je ne vois pas que personne ait touche, c'est al'egard de l'immolation des agneauz pascales dans le temple. Il n'y avoit que deux heurs du temps pour egorger 250.000 agneauz, on a fait de difficultez sur la capacitè ou l'etendue du temple s'il pouvoit recevoir 250.000 personnes avec leurs agneauz dans son enceinte à deux ou trois reprises, mais il m'est venue une autre d'ans l'esprit à qui je ne puis pas satisfaire. Il y avoit 8 portes dans la muraile exterieur du Temple dont chaqu:une avoit l'ouverteure de 10 coudèes ou 15 pieds. donant donc une coudèe a chaque file des hommes en entrant, qui est assez peu a un homme en marchant il y peuvent entrer 40 files à la fois par les quatre portes d'une cotè, les portes de'l autre costè etant ouvertes pour les fair sortir, autrement il y auroit plus d'embarras quand le premier troupe sortoit pour donner place au second. Une armèe donc de 250.000 devisèe en 40 files chaque file seroit longe de 6248 pas donnant a chaque personne une pas de distance en son range pour marcher avec son agneau entre ses bras. or une distance de 6248 pas est une marche pour deux heurs du temps: Ajoutez à cela sur le meme fondement le temps qui doibt ecouler pend⟨an⟩t[b] que le sang des agneaux s'achimine vers l'autel par une egal longueur de files ou à moitiè si longues si vous en ⟨doublez⟩[c] le nombre. C'est de vous que j attende l'explication de ces difficultez. pour me fair resouder si je doibs croire qu'on etoit obligè de tuer son agneau pascal dans ⟨le⟩[b] Temple, et comment cela se pouvoit faire en si peu de temps[1]

On ne trouve pas icy à Londres *les memoires* de la Chine du P: le Comte que del'Edition d'Holland qui est defectueuse c'est pour

[a] *MS.* d'erution [b] *Page torn.* [c] *MS.* doubez

[1] Toinard answers this question in no. *2693*. Locke is following a passage in Josephus: Toinard, *Harmonia*, p. 153, where it is discussed.

quoi je serois bien aise de l'avoir de l'edition de Paris avec le Nouveau volume du P: Bouvet[1]

Pour m'envoier des livres vous les addressez s'il vous plait à Monsieur Pigault [a] pour fair tenir à M⟨on⟩sieur[b] Frankland Maister de la Poste à Londres, ⟨avec un p⟩etit[b] billet à Monsieur Frankland pour lui marquer que les liv⟨res⟩[b] sont ⟨pour⟩[b] moi

Permettez moi de vous demander encore si vous avez jammais veu Navarette de la Chine,[2] on m'a dit que c'est un livre curieus, je serois bien aise de le voir traduit en Francois. Mais c'est temps de mettre fin à une lettre si ennueuse et plein de jargon. Je suis

Monsieur

Votre tres humble et tres obeissant serviteur

J Locke

Je baise les mains à Monsieur du Bos en le remerciant pour l histoire de Siam qu'il m'envoia.[3] L'Autheur c. 12. p. 62[c] parle d'une carte qu'il avoit faite de Siam laquelle je ne trouve pas dans le livre, mais qui sans doute seroit utille (aussi bien que quelques autres don il fait mention qui ne paroissent pas) pour eclaircir son histoire

Address: A Monsieur Monsieur Toinard chez Monsieur d⟨es⟩[b] Noyers devant l'espèe royale dans la Rue Mazarin à Paris

Endorsed by Toinard: 20. Febr. 99

2551. Mrs. Frances St. John to Locke, 20 February [1699] (*2524*, *2675*)

B.L., MS. Locke c. 18, ff. 54–5. Year from Locke's endorsement.

Feber the 20

It hav'ing bine long I have experienced the kind'ness of my good Friend Mr Lock, that I cannot but be acquanted with your Goodness, but yet never the less sencible of my own obligation to you for it and therfore cannot be careless to every new Assurance you give me of your continued kindness for me, which you have laitly repeated in a most oblidging maner in your last letter for which

[a] *Page torn; on the paper filling the hole the words* à Calais *in a modern hand.* [b] *Page torn.* [c] *Page torn between* p *and* 62

[1] pp. 339, 535. [2] p. 463.
[3] The *Histoire naturelle et politique* by N. Gervaise: pp. 507, 556.

I desire now to return you my thanks, and where I so happy as to be near enough to se you every day I could beleive I should not on'ly injoy the hearing of your good wishes, but the reall effects of them, there being a sertaine happyness in your good company which I hartely wish I could pertake more of, and that without depriving that part of our friends which have now the posesion of you, my wish being very Just on'ly to be shairer in theire felicity, being in great reallity to your self and all your good company a very humble servant and to my Dear Father,

A Loving Daughter and oblidged Servant
FRA ST JOHN

Mr St John and my self desire our servis to all, I have allso Lady St Johns Command to present her servis with great thanks for the eglentine which came very safe, as I wish yours might tho' I fear there was not so good care taken in the puting them up, and if you pleas you may have more but by the mistake of a conceited Gardener I could not at that time get more

Address: For John Lock Esq'r [at Oates, by Joslyn, Bishops Stortford]

Postmarks: FE 21; GC (?)

Endorsed by Locke: F: St John 20 Feb $9\frac{8}{9}$

2552. LADY (MARTHA) EYRE to LOCKE, 21 February [1699] (*2564*)

B.L., MS. Locke c. 8, ff. 83–4. Year from Locke's endorsement.

Lady Eyre, d. 1728, was the widow of Sir Samuel (no. *316*), who died in 1698; there were four sons: pedigree in Sir R. C. Hoare, *History of Modern Wiltshire*, v. ii. 56. There are letters from the eldest, (Sir) Robert, below, nos. *3410–11*.

Feb: 21st.

Sir

I can no sooner Rowse my spiritts from that dejection they have bin some time too Justly buryed inn. but I must aplye my selfe to fullfilling the trust commited to mee, by your friend, my worthy husband, which was to make sutable provisions for our younger Sones, my Second[1] had the honour to be presented to you by his father, he mayd the study of Divinitty his choise, and is at

[1] Francis Eyre, *c.* 1673–1738; M.A., Oxford, 1696; D.D. 1735; rector of Steeple Langford, Wilts., 1698–1703; other incumbencies 1703–38; canon of Salisbury 1711: Foster.

presant posessed of A Parsonage, but t'is but for a feew years tell the Gentelman whose the perpetuale Advowson is shall be of an Age to goe into orders himselfe, my great Concern is for this Son, his deer father designed when some years had reendered him more Worthy of it, to have presented him to my Lord Pemborcck and to have beged a Parsonage of his Lorship, who has many in his gifft, I knowing this to be his intenion take the freedom to Apply my selfe to you, beging your favour in mentioning him to my Lord whilest he remembers he had a most humble and affectionat servant in his father; theire is a very old man, that is so inferme he can not Live longe in a Parsonage of my Lords, one Mr Stephens of Willye,[1] if it were not already promest it lying very neer the place my Son is inn (but a milles distance) it would be a convenyance besides a proffet, and the Countnance of my Lord an honour to be Coveted above most things; forgive I beseech you this troble, and belive this trueth, that had I less valewed you, you had not bin thus importuned by Sir

Your afflicted hum: ser
M: EYRE

Endorsed by Locke: L: Eyre 21 Feb $9\frac{8}{9}$ Answered 27

2553. LOCKE to EDWARD CLARKE, 24 February 1699 (2540, 2575)

B.M., Add. MS. 4290, f. 88. One sentence printed in Forster, 1847, p. 66; the whole, in Rand, p. 543.

Oates 24 Feb $9\frac{8}{9}$

Dear Sir

I thank you for your advice about the Malt tickets, and desire you to send me word when you think it time to part with yours. I am glad there is a stop at last put to the losse of the Kingdom by the high rate of Guineas.[2] Pray when you see him give my service to Mr Bridges[3] but tell him that that trick must not passe, I tooke it upon other termes

My service to Madam and your fires side and to the Batchelor. I should not trouble you with the inclosed but that I know you

[1] John Stevens, *c.* 1616–1701; M.A., Oxford, 1640; rector of Wylye 1664–1701: ibid.

[2] *London Gazette*, 20 February: notice that the revenue officers have been ordered not to take guineas for more than £1. 1*s.* 6*d.*

[3] Probably Brooke Bridges.

have letters of your owne to goe to the post and I desire only that mine may goe with yours. I am

Sir

your most humble and affectionate servant

J LOCKE

My Lady and the rest of our company give their services

Endorsed by Clarke: Mr. Lock to bee informed When I sell my Malt-Ticketts etc: Received the 28th. Febr 1698. Answered the 29th.

2554. FRANCIS GASTRELL, later bishop of Chester, to LOCKE, 25 February [1699] (*2515*)

B.L., MS. Locke c. 9, ff. 211–12. Year from Locke's endorsement.

Feb: 25

Sir

I did not think fit to trouble you with an answer to a very civill letter, till I could give you some further testymonies of my respect for you than a bare acknowledgment of your civility. The discourse I gave you some account of in my last is now finished and I have ordered a book to be left at mr churchill's.[1] I can't pretend tis an equivalent for what you honoured me with, but tis as valuable a present as I could make it without the advantage of your advice. The subject required the utmost care and pains and I indeavoured not to be wanting in those respects however I may have fallen short in others. I heartily wish you life and health to pursue those ⟨beneficiall⟩[a] designs you are upon without any interruption from undue cavills and foreign disputes.

I am Sir

Your most obliged Humble Servant to command

FRANCIS GASTRELL

Address: To Mr Locke to be left at mr churchill's a book-seller in Pater-noster-row

Postmark: London Penny Post: T SAT

Endorsed by Locke: F: Gastrel 25 Feb $9\frac{8}{9}$

[a] *MS.* beneficialls?

[1] *The Certainty of the Christian Revelation, and the Necessity of believing it, established*, 1699. L.L., no. 1215.

2555. Joannes Georgius Grævius to Locke, 27 February/9 March 1699 (*2436*)

B.L., MS. Locke c. 10, ff. 46–7.

Vir Nobilissime et Amplissime

Temporum locorumque longinquitas, quae nos dijungit, non divellet spero animorum nostrorum conjunctionem. Meo sane animo saepissime obversatur tuae virtutis, doctrinae, suavissimaeque consuetudinis memoria. Vix ex ulla re majorem capio voluptatem quam ex commemoratione illius voluptatis, quam mihi afferebant tui sermones de rebus divinis et humanis, omnique liberali eruditione. Nec unquam praetermitto facultatem, si quae se dat, datur autem saepius, hanc felicitatem, qua tum fruebar, apud amicos praedicandi, cum testificatione summae meae in te observantiae. Hujus mei erga te studii singularis testis erit generosissimus Mordanius, et optimus ejus Comes Marscius, qui aliquam diu mihi dederunt operam, et nunc in patriam excurrunt auctoritatem parentum secuti.[1] Sicut autem Mordanius testis erit mei amoris, quo te prosequor, sic ego testis esse possum optima fide illius probitatis, pudoris, diligentiae optimis artibus impensae, ut nullus dubitem, si constanter hanc viam, quam ingressus est, tenuerit, quin aliquando et generi et patriae suae sit futurus orna-

---

Illustrious and excellent Sir,

The distance of time and place that separates us will not, I hope, sunder the union of our hearts. Indeed the memory of your merit, learning, and delightful company is very often present to my mind. I scarcely take greater pleasure in anything than in calling to mind the pleasure which your words about things human and divine, and about all liberal scholarship, brought me. Nor do I ever neglect an opportunity, if any offers, as it often does, of extolling in the company of friends this happiness which I then enjoyed, and of testifying to my very great regard for you. The most noble Mordaunt will be a witness of this my singular affection for you, as also will be his excellent governor Marx; they have been studying under me for some time and are now hastening to their own country in obedience to the parents' command.[1] But just as Mordaunt will be a witness of my love with which I pursue you, so I can be a witness in all good faith to his uprightness and modesty, and to his diligent application to the highest arts, so that I do not doubt that if he holds steadily to this road on which he has entered he will one day be an ornament to his family and to his country. About yourself I

---

[1] pp. 212, 248–50.

mento. Tu nunc quid rerum geras, ut valeas, quibus studiis oblectes aetatem jam grandiorem aveo scire. Ego in iisdem litteris versor, quibus semper fui deditus. Vespertinas et nocturnas horas consumo in rebus gestis Vestri Regis memoriae mandandis,[1] diurnas, quas functionis meae munera mihi reliquas faciunt, in Tullio perpoliendo. Si quid de mirifica illa regni vestri conversione fide lectioneque dignum, et minus vulgo cognitum suggeri posset, non solum a me, sed ab omni posteritate et tuis inprimis civibus gratiam magnam inires. Communis amicus noster Toinardus vivit et valet. Ante paucas hebdomades litteras ab illo habui.[2] Sed de harmonia evangelica, quamvis saepius a me compellatus hoc nomine, silet, forte ut insperato gaudio et nec opino nos brevi perfundat. Sic credere et augurari libet. Te vero diutissime et beatissime valere, et me amare volo. Trajecti D. IX Mart. CIϽ IϽCIC Dionysiaco.[3]

Amplissimo Tuo Nomini
addictissimus
JOANNES GEORGIUS GRAEVIUS

Memini me, cum nobiscum ageres ex te audire de fratrum Rosae

---

am eager to learn what you are now occupied with, how you are, and with what studies you delight your now advanced age. I myself am occupied with that same learning to which I have always been addicted. I spend the hours of evening and night in recording your king's achievements,[1] those of the day that the duties of my office leave me in polishing Cicero. If anything worthy of confidence and perusal, and not known to the public, could be supplied about that wonderful revolution of your kingdom you would win not only my own great gratitude but that of all posterity and especially that of your fellow-citizens. Our common friend Toinard is alive and well. I had a letter from him a few weeks ago.[2] But, though he has often been taken to task by me about the Harmony of the Gospels, he is silent about it, perhaps in order soon to fill us with unhoped for and unexpected joy. So I like to think and predict. But I wish you to live long and happily in the best of health, and to love me. Utrecht, 9 March 1699, Dionysian [year].[3]

The most devoted to your illustrious name
JOANNES GEORGIUS GRAEVIUS

I remember that when you were with us I heard you say something that has escaped my memory about the origin of the brothers of the Rosy Cross

---

[1] Grævius wrote a funeral oration on William III; nothing else is known.
[2] Probably the letter of 9 February 1699 N.S., in the Royal Library, Copenhagen
[3] See no. *1802* n.

Crucis origine, quae effluxerunt ex mea memoria. Ea si in illam revocari tuae ferrent occupationes, laetarer sane.[1] Iterum vale.

Endorsed by Locke: J: G: Græevius 9 Mar 99

If your occupations should allow you to recall it to my memory I should be very glad.[1] Good-bye again.

2556. MRS. ELIZABETH BERKELEY, later Burnet, to LOCKE, 28 February 1699 (*2511*, *2599*)

B.L., MS. Locke c. 3, ff. 218–19.

Sir

You are pleased to excuse the delay of a favour, not a debt, in the most obligen maner; but I can't allow of the reason you asign: when ever you write 'tis my pleasure as well as Benefect to read, and if it dos not add to my health makes me at least less sensible of my want of it, but with respect to your self I allow it very reasonable not only that you write seldom but not at all to one no way fitted for such a corespondance; your time is a great deal too valuable, and what you imploy for a generall good ought not to be asked for a perticuler advantage. therefore I beg you will beleeve that as glad as I allways am of your instructions yet I never desiere them to your trouble. your first command *the account of my health* will allmost answer the second *what I have ben doing*: for these last tow or three Months I have had allmost a constant sickness at my stomack, which with short days and the hinderences of this town leves no great time at our one dispose, so that against my will I have observed your rules, but with no great success; I have a very folish temper to be grived for what is not in my power to help, and at this time of year the unreasonable heats of partys etc: furnishes mater enough for the spleen to work on; but neither complaints of the diseses of the mind or constetution, are intertaining subjects. I wish my inteligence could furnish any thing more diverting, but no dout you have more news and truer then any I can send; I have aften inquired after your health, and hear

[1] This probably relates to a story, told to Locke by Toinard, about the posting of Rosicrucian placards in Paris about the year 1618 or 1620: B.L., MS. Locke c. 33, f. 11; printed by Professor Lough in *Locke's Travels in France*, pp. 282–3. The year was 1623: P. Arnold, *Histoire des Rose-Croix*, 1955, pp. 7–8; Frances A. Yates, *The Rosicrucian Enlightenment*, 1972, pp. 103–4. See also p. 712 below.

with great satisfaction that you are very well, (if it please God) I wish you may very long be so; forgive the many faults of

Sir

Your much obliged and Most Humble servent

E. BERKELEY

Feb: 28: 98: Lincolns Inn Feilds

I have lately read some sermons published from Dr Whichcoots papers.[1] I can't pretend to Judg of every part of them, but the spirit with which they seem to be write pleases me extremly;— I hear Dr Bentlys late Book is condemned by some as too reflecting etc: but 'tis perhaps because they don't take his advise and put them selves in the place of the injured;[2]

My brother and sister[3] are your Faithfull servents;

Endorsed by Locke: E: Berkeley 28° Feb 9$\frac{8}{9}$ Answered Apr. 6

2557. LOCKE to PHILIPPUS VAN LIMBORCH, 4 and 5 March 1699 (*2516*, *2596*)

Amsterdam University Library, MS. R.K., Ba 258 c and h. Printed in Ollion, pp. 217–19. Carried by Samuel Crellius. Answers nos. *2482* and *2516*; answered by no. *2596*.

Oates 4 Mar 9$\frac{8}{9}$

Monsieur

Si le peu de loisir et de santé que j'ai, ne vous avoit pas acoutumè à m'excuser de ce que je suis lent à faire reponse aux lettres dont vous daignez m'honorer de temps en temps, je ne saurois guere comment vous remercier de votre lettre du mois de Decembre apres avoir tant tardè à m'acquiter de ce devoir. Mais vous etes tout acoutumè à me pardonner de telles fautes et cela me fait encore esperer de votre bontè que vous en userez encore de la meme maniere

J'ai eté bien aise d'apprendre de Madame Masham et de son fils le bon etat de votre santé, qui ne faisoit que de se retablir la derniere fois que vous m'aviez ecrit. Je souhaite qu'à l'avenir

[1] Dr. Benjamin Whichcote, *Select Sermons*, 1698. L.L., no. 3139.

[2] *A Dissertation upon the Epistles of Phalaris*, 1699 (the second Dissertation). L.L., no. 270. Mrs. Berkeley perhaps became acquainted with Bentley while he was Stillingfleet's chaplain.

[3] Identifiable as Robert Dormer, 1649–1726; appointed a judge 1706; and his wife Mary, d. 1728, a younger sister of Mrs. Berkeley: *D.N.B.*

vous en jouissiez[a] longues années sans aucune interruption, pour l'amour de vos parens et de vos amis et pour l'avantage du monde Chretien.

Je m'etois flattè de l'esperance que vous m'auriez fait tenir dans votre derniere lettre la preuve de l'unitè de Dieu qui est venuë dans l'esprit de ce grand et savant homme pour qui j'ai un singulier respect. Je desire beaucoup de la voir. Les argumens *a priori* pour demontrer que l'Etre ⟨parfait⟩[b] et independant est unique sont d'une si grande importance dans ce point fondamental, que j'espere etre excusè si je m'addresse pour cela à la personne qui est peut etre la seule dont on puisse les attendre. Sa grande capacitè, la justesse et la penetration de son esprit m'engagent à esperer de lui ce que peut-etre je chercherois en vain quelque autre part. Je vous prie donc, Monsieur, de me faire la grace de lui demander de ma part ce qu'il a pensè sur ce sujet ou du moins un court extrait de son raisonnement, et je m'imagine que vous ne ferez pas difficultè de lui etre caution pour moi que comme je ne demande cette grace que pour ma propre satisfaction, je n'en ferai aucun autre usage qu'autant qu'il me le permettra. Je ne le presserois peut-etre pas avec tant d'importunité, n'étoit que j'ai appris que depuis peu il a eté quelque fois malade. L'apprehension de ce qui pourroit arriver a reveillè mes desirs. Je lui souhaite une longue vie pour le bien de son pais et de la Republique des Lettres. Je vous prie de l'assurer de mes tres-humbles respects, et de recevoir mes remerciemens pour le livre que vous m'avez fait l'honeur de m'envoier.[1] Je suis

Monsieur

Votre tres-humble et tres-obeissant serviteur

J. LOCKE

[a] *Word altered; last letters doubtful; perhaps* jouisserez [b] *Word omitted by Locke; Ollion suggests* éternel, *but see* p. 258.

Oates 5 Mar $9\frac{8}{9}$

Vir Amplissime

Tam fidus literarum tuarum lator non debet vacuus ad te redire

Oates 5 Mar $9\frac{8}{9}$

Excellent Sir,

So trustworthy a bearer of your letter ought not to return to you empty-

[1] Van Limborch's *Defensio* against van der Waeyen: p. 518; see also below.

nec sine curæ suæ testimonio ut tu illi eas reddas gratias quas ego satis dignè pro merito suo solvere non possum. Attulit ipse mihi hic rusticanti epistolam quam manibus suis concrederas. et tridui insuper consuetudinem nobis efflagitantibus concessit vir eruditus et modestus reliquitque abiens Dominæ Masham reliquisque nostris magnum sui desiderium. Gratias tibi ago quod tuo beneficio mihi notus sit, optaremque viciniorem. Quanquam enim per omnia cum illo non sentiam aliquid tamen semper disco ex viris qui suâ utuntur ratione suo sensu non aliorum dogmatibus innixi nec cujusvis magistri in verba jurantes.[1]

Fecisti quod te decet cum[a] eo quo dicis modo ad Episcopum Sarisburiensem scripseris, an aliquod tibi reddiderit responsum et quale libens scirem. pudet sane ministrum Evangelii Christi velle fidem Christianam argumentis bacillinis, vi et armis stabilire.

Hactenus ad tuas 18 Augusti datas, pergo ad alias decembri scriptas

Quid a Viro Magnifico petam et quomodo, adjuncta epistola Gallico idiomate tibi monstrabit, siquid habeat in eo genere spero non negaturum. Quod communicaverit tacebo si velit,

[a] *Doubtful reading; altered from* quid?

handed or without testimony of his diligence, so that you may give him those thanks which I am unable to pay worthily enough for his deserts. He brought to me here in the country the letter which you had entrusted to his hands. And on our pressing him this scholarly and modest man vouchsafed us his company for three days more and left Lady Masham and the rest of us in great regret for him on his departure. I give you thanks because I made his acquaintance through your kindness, and I should wish that he were a nearer neighbour. For although I do not agree with his opinion in all things nevertheless I always learn something from men who use their own reason and understanding, not resting on other men's dogmas or swearing allegiance to any master.[1]

You acted as becomes you when you wrote to the bishop of Salisbury in the way that you tell me of. I should gladly learn whether he has returned you any answer and of what sort. It is truly shameful that a minister of the Gospel of Christ should want to make the Christian faith secure by arguments of the rod and by violence.

So far to your letter dated 18 August; I proceed to the other written in December.

The accompanying letter, written in French, will make clear to you what I seek from the Magnifico, and how; if he has anything of that sort I hope

[1] Adapted from Horace: no. *1668* n.

Quanquam cur hujusmodi tacenda sint plane nesciam, sed hoc prout ipsi visum fuerit.

Defensionem tuam aliis impeditus nondum perlegi, video quocum tibi res est, strenuo sane cavillatore, à cujus polymathia non est cur multum tibi metuas, qui enim ejusmodi in Geographia effutire ⟨poterat⟩,[a] paratus sane est omnia dicere etiamsi nihil sciat. Hujusmodi scriptorum turbâ Orthodoxia theologica ubique pene laboret, aperiat aliquando Deus O.M. eorum oculos ad veritatem, et ad pacem corda. Tota hæc nostra familia te tuosque officiosissime salutat. Vale et ut facis me ama

Tui amantissimum

J. LOCKE

Address: Mijn Heer Mijn Heer Limborch op de Kaisars Gracht bij de Remonstranse Kerck t'Amsterdam

[a] *MS.* potterat

---

that he will not refuse it. If he wishes I shall be silent about what he may communicate although I do not at all know why things of this sort should be kept silent, but this must be as seems good to him.

Being hindered by other things, I have not yet read your *Defensio* right through. I see with what sort of man you have to deal, assuredly a strenuous caviller. There is no reason why you should be much afraid of his polymathy, for a man who could babble in that way in geography is surely prepared to assert all things although he knows nothing. Theological orthodoxy is troubled almost everywhere by a host of such writers; may God Almighty some day open their eyes to truth and their hearts to peace. Our whole family here send to you and yours their best respects. Good-bye, and continue to love me

Your most affectionate

J. LOCKE

2558. LOCKE to PETER KING, later first Baron King, 5 March 1699 (2548, 2559)

B.L., MS. Locke c. 40, ff. 35–6.

Oates 5° Mar $9\frac{8}{9}$

Dear Cosin

I received not yours of the 25th of the past till Friday last[1] it stuck at Bishop Startford because Mr Jocelin came not on Monday.

[1] 3 March.

Since the next payment of the two million subscription will be paid whilst you are in town I conclude that businesse will be taken care of and I need say noe more to you about it

I have here inclosed drawn a bill on Mr Churchill for £8. 12. 0 that you may take the bond of your Cosin[1] before you goe.

I think your advice is right to leave £50 of the ticket money in your Cosins hand for the tradeing payment which you tell me will be the first of April.[2] But if those million tickets[3] should not be received before the first of Aprill will it not be necessary to give him directions to write to me that he may be furnished for that payment if it must necessarily be paid at that day?

For the rest of the money which he shall receive for my million tickets I will draw such a bill as you direct if I shall have an occasion to take that money out of his hands before your returne

I wish you a prosperous journey and safe returne. Remember me kindly to your father and be assured that I am

Dear Cosin

Your affectionate Cosin and humble servant

J LOCKE

My Lady and the rest here give you their services

Address: For Peter King Esqr of the Middle Temple To be left at Mr Potmans in the Middle Temple London

Postmark: MR 8

Endorsed by King: Mr Locke March 5 1698

Marginal note by King: dated March 5. bill on Mr Awmsham Churchil for 8. 12s. 00d.

2559. LOCKE to PETER KING, later first Baron King 7 March 1699 (2558, 2574)

B.L., MS. Locke c. 40, ff. 37–8.

Oates 7 Mar 9[8]

Dear Cosin

I yesterday by the post sent an answer to yours of the 25° Feb why you had it not sooner that letter will tell you. Had you directed your letter to Harlow the answer had been a weeke sooner but

[1] John Freke the stockjobber or his brother Thomas.

[2] The payment to the trading account of the New East India Company; pp. 504, 551.

[3] In the Million Pound Lottery Loan: no. *1821*; pp. 590, 611, etc.

hope it will be time enough. I there in sent you a bill on Mr Churchill for £8–12–0 and I have writ to him by the same hand that carys this to desire him to pay you that summ with or without my bill if you come for it, soe that if this comes to your hands before my letter by the post you may receive that money of Mr Churchill presently and dispatch that businesse, for I desire you would take the bond before you goe out of town, I wish you a good journey. My humble service to your father. I am

Dear Cosin

your most affectionate Cosin and humble servant

J LOCKE

All here give you their respects
Yours of the 4th I received yesterday

Endorsed by King: Mr Locke March. 7. 1698.

2560. CORNELIUS LYDE to LOCKE, 8 March 1699 (*2463, 2582*)

B.L., MS. Locke c. 15, ff. 168–9.

March the 8th: $9\frac{8}{9}$

Sir

Yours I Received and according to your order I sent ma: dolman[1] 20s which was Kindly rec: and Came verry sesonably for I understand shee is verry Poore and In want both of foode and Rayment. her husband and her two sons weave but some times haveing but Little Employment[a] are forsd to be beholding ma: and her sons have the reputation of good honest people her sons Can both writt I heare, but one of them is neare sited. my son the Doct: is in the Counetry where he doe desine to begin to practis I doe give you many thanks for your greate Kindnes to him and Am well assured were it not for your greate buisnes he had more of your good Conversation, your tenants veale and Carpenter pay theire rent well but I find the rest verry backward Espetially will. Gullock I Cant gett his part of taxes, I Thinke it is 3 yeares behinde he promise but not perform but I will Endevor

[a] *Abbreviated at end of line.*

[1] No. 767 n., etc.

to gett all in shortly after Ladie day. wishing you helth I Am Sir your

most affectionat friend and ser

COR: LYDE

your friends at Sutton Court[1] are well with my Cousin Lyde[2] my kinde service to mr clarke

Address: These for Doct: Locke at mr. Pawlings overagainst the plough in Little Lincolns feilds London

Postmark: MR 10

Endorsed by Locke: C Lyde 8 Mar $9\frac{8}{9}$ Answered 30

2561. WILLIAM THOMAS to LOCKE, 9 March 1699 (*2547, 2563*)

B.L., MS. Locke c. 20, f. 162.

London 9th March 1699

Sir

I had the last you were pleasd to favour me with and humbl thank you for it. As to the Corpus J.C. being a second han book[3] I conceive that can be said only as it has passd throug one hand more than the Booksellers, and not for any injury th book has receivd. My Father bought it new and I verrily beleiv scarce ever lookd in it afterward and as he left it you had it, s that I can abate verry little on that account. If you please to accep it at 50s. its at your service and thats a Crown less than it cost I humbly thank you for the exchange you offer in Physick book but I am so sick of them that I have scarce patience to read a pag in most of them, so knavish or so ignorant they are for the mos part, that they shew themselves true disciples of their old Maste Galen, nay some of the best of them like Plagiaries steal from on another and only give the ugly old whore a more fashionable su of clothes. I know none of them that will teach me to cure Disease in India whither I design to goe next winter and in the mean tim to dispose of a good part of the Physick books I have already. beg you not to mistake me. I am not weary of studying Physick bu

[1] Mrs. Strachey and her son.

[2] Probably the man mentioned in no. *966*, a cousin of both Locke and Cornel Lyde.

[3] The *Corpus Juris Civilis*: p. 563.

impertinent Authors that handle the severall parts of it. Let a man divest himself of all receivd notions, think freely of Nature, and use but few Medicines, and he be able to doe more then the whole rabble of writers ever knew. The bookes I designd for my self if you and I agreed were Miltons[1] and Mr Sydneys works[2] that I might divert my self on shore and on board between while. Mr Tyrrell gives his humble Service to you, and with a thankfull acknoledgement of all your favours I am Sir your most obliged and humble

servant W THOMAS.

Address: To The Honble: John Locke Esqr. [at Oates, by Joslyn, Bishops Stortford]

Postmarks: MR 9; GC

Endorsed by Locke: W: Thomas 9 Mar $9\frac{8}{9}$ Answered 10
NB I sent him Mar 10 a bill on Mr Churchil for £2–10–0 for his Corpus Juris

2562. LOCKE to DR. JOHN COVEL, 12 March 1699 (*2549*, 2799)

B.M., Add. MS. 22,910, ff. 478–9. Answers no. *2549*.

Oates 12 Mar $9\frac{8}{9}$

Reverend Sir

Yours of the 18th of Feb: full of great civility but expressed a little after the manner of a man that has lived at Court deserves a large returne of acknowledgment and thanks: And I should have endeavourd to have expressed my sense of it in a manner a little more suitable than I am like to doe had not the bearer hereof Mr Smith surprised me with his unexpceted hast. I concluded he would have staid till to morrow morning, and of a suddain I am told he is just goeing this evening. I should be a shamd to let him goe without a word from me, when I had entended to have said soe much by him, as several of the particulars in your letter would have given me occasion but his departure cuts me short. This let me tell you increases the longing I had before to

[1] The prose works. A collection appeared in 1697; a fuller collection, with Toland's life of Milton, in three volumes, 'Amsterdam', in 1698. For the two collections and Awnsham Churchill's concern with some of the pieces see W. R. Parker, *Milton*, 1968, pp. 1195–8.

[2] Algernon Sidney, *Discourses concerning Government*: p. 478.

see you here, that we might discourse of those matters which are reservd till that time, Make hast therefor I beseech you to make me happy in your conversation, and in the mean time doe me the right to beleive me

Reverend Sir

your most humble and most faithfull servant

J LOCKE

Address: For the Reverend Dr Covel Master of Christ College in Cambridg

Endorsed by Covel: (i): Mr Locke

(ii): Mr Lock. Oct. 12 $169\frac{8}{9}$

2563. WILLIAM THOMAS to LOCKE, 16 March 1699 (2561)

B.L., MS. Locke, c. 20, ff. 163–4.

London 16th March 1699.

Sir

I[a]– return you many thanks for the favour of last with the bill on Mr Churchill for 50s,–[a] which I have receivd. I am very much obligd to you for your good wishes for me in my voyage, which I intend for the East Indies, having already had it mov'd by my Uncle Greenhill[1] to Mr Shepherd.[2] I propose to goe Physician to some of the factorys there in the Service of the New Company, and beleive that a recommendation from you as to my capacity would verry much further it. If they allow me no sallary I shall not be obligd to any fixt habitation, but be more at liberty to make my fortune by Trade as I can in any of the Eastern Countryes. You judg'd infallibly right that I goe not thither to see fashions, and I may add what Sir Ellis Layton said on another occasion, viz nor to learn the language.[3] To get a livelyhood is what I goe for since whatt I have here will not half do it. I thought, when I had sold and paid of all in Complyance to my Fathers will, I might quietly have possessd between 7 and 800l which was all that came

a–a *Marked by Locke for attention.*

1 Perhaps Henry Greenhill: p. 605 n.

2 Probably Samuel Shepherd: no. 2863.

3 Sir Ellis (*verè* Elisha) Leighton, the adventurer: no. 350. The story is told by Roger North: Leighton, 'being Secretary in *Ireland* [1670–2], extorted most outragiously; and, being expostulated with for it, answered, *What a Pox, d'ye think come here to learn your Language?*': *Examen*, 1740, p. 488.

to my share, but its not so well, but am forc'd out of that to pay 300l for debts my Father was engagd in for other men, and which he was assurd when he lay sick were all dischargd. 200l of this I've already paid and the rest will be paid in a fortnight or month more. This reduces me to goe abroad when I cannot tarry here, and You cannot do a better office in generall nor me in particular a greater favour, than to help me forwards on a voyage which shall either make my fortune, or keep me from letting my friends here know that I want one. I will be sure to take care of the bookes you mentiond formerly as well as in your last, but they have not yet come to my hands and of the bookes I part with if you please ⟨yo⟩u[a] shall have a catalogue and the refusall. I am extreamly obligd to you for all your favours and am Sir

your most humble and most Obedient Servant

W THOMAS.

Address: To The Honble: John Locke Esqre [at Oates, by Joslyn, Bishops Stortford]

Postmarks: MR 16; GC

Endorsed by Locke: W: Thomas 16 Mar 9$\frac{8}{9}$ Answered 27

2564. LADY (MARTHA) EYRE to LOCKE, 16 March [1699] (*2552, 3081*)

B.L., MS. Locke c. 8, ff. 85–6. Year from Locke's endorsement.

Mar: 16th

Sir

I rec: yours, by the hand of a gentelman so oblidging as to deliver it himselfe, I had company with me or elce by the same civile hand, had immediatly returned my thanks,—I covered yours to my Lord Prive Seal with a feew lines to Lady Sawyer,[1] desiring her to take an oppertunitty to deliver it, she sent me word she would, and bring mee the account her selfe that she had so dun, but I have not seen her seence.—what ever the Success is I am sure my gratitud should know no bownds,—To forgive the importunitty of a woman, and with so much teenderness to bear a shair

[a] *Page torn.*

[1] Pembroke's mother-in-law Mary, widow of Sir Robert Sawyer, 1633–92 attorney-general 1681–7: *D.N.B.*

in aflictions great enufe to over-whelm a persen of much larger Soul, and better fortefyed to bear great pressurs, these are, what is not to be fownd but from such an exalted frindship as yours that reaches beyond the Grave, And is to mee an indication that a blesing dus ateend the posteritty of that Just man, to whom I am the unhappy Relict; and your most obliged hum: ser

M: EYRE

Address: These To John Locke Esquire [at Oates, by Joslyn, Bishops Stortford]

Postmarks: MR 16; EG

Endorsed by Locke: L Eyre 16 Mar $9\frac{8}{9}$

2565. THOMAS BURNETT of KEMNEY to LOCKE, 17 March 1699 (*2228*, *2709*)

B.L., MS. Locke c. 4, ff. 199–200. Printed in King, pp. 400–3.

Londone

Worthie Sir

I was sorry I could not see yow at my coming back from Tunbridge in September last, having called twyse at your lodgings. I was necessitat to goe to the cuntrey immediatly therefter, and made a ramble from the Bath[1] thorrow the West of England to Salisbury, and at last to Oxford, where the good society and most kynd treatment from all I made acquaintance with did charme me for more as three months; And made me at last leave that place with regreat. I have lately receaved a letter from your worthie admirer Monsieur Leibnitz.[2] He heth bein kept back from making his returns to his correspondents this long tyme, having more to doe in the publict affairs of that cuntrey As I understand from the new title I find given him of (Conseillier Intime de S: A: E: de Brunswick).[3] In this letter he gives a new proof of the esteem he heth of your wrytings, having writt 7 or 8 pages of his observationes Concerning your dispute with the Bishop of Woster[4]

[1] p. 520.

[2] The letter of 20/30 January; printed in Leibniz, *Phil. Schriften*, ed. Gerhardt iii. 243–53. The copy sent by Burnett to Locke is B.L., MS. Locke c. 13, ff. 169–70. Gerhardt omits Leibniz's epitaph for F. M. van Helmont, which is printed below p. 721, n. 4.

[3] Geheimer Justizrat. The dignity was conferred on him in August 1696.

[4] The undated summary of Stillingfleet's *Discourse in Vindication* and Locke's *Letter* to Stillingfleet: Leibniz, *S.S.* VI. vi. 16–29; introd., pp. xx–xxi.

and seeming to hold the ballance betwixt your learned Antagonist and yow with all the fairenesse of ane honest man, and the Judgement of a Philosopher, Tho the weight of what is thrown into the scales, seems to make him inclyne sometymes to one syde sometymes to ane other. It appears he heth not yet seen the last letter of the bishops, nor your two last to him, tho I have sent him all that was come out with severall books off other authors by 3 pacquets, at severall tymes. There is a young gentleman who was heir a long tyme to search for records relateing to the housse of Brunswick,[1] For whom I did cause buy all the curious books that have come out thir severall years, with whom I have also sent all what he could not find himself out of my own library. He will open his Pack att Hanover, And both the Electrix[2] and Monsieur Leibnitz will see what books are for there service. In speaking to the certainty and cleirenesse of Ideas He pleaseth himself with the difference he makes betwixt the two termes of *cleer* and *Distinct* That, he calls *cleer* which can be differenced in our notion by a certain caracteristick from all things besyds it self. This knowledge he calls *distinct*, when we know a thing in its whole essence *or nature*, with all its conditiones, and Requesits, Or when we can give its definitione; so that the knowledge of *Substance* in so far as we know its certain difference from ane *Accident*, May be call'd *cleer*, but cannot be term'd *distinct*.[3] But If I may adde my oun thought, This *distinct notion* is not[a] applicable to any thing else we know Any more then it is to our Ideas of *substance*; since no humane knowledge reacheth a complete understanding of the Nature of the most minut subject of Reasoning, so as to exhaust its whole nature, essence, and all that is to be known about it, No more then the understanding of the Nature of the leist grain of the dust we trample upon. This knowledge by *comprehensive*-Ideas is to wonderfull for us, and can only belong To That Infinit being who is *perfeit* in *knowledge*. Monsieur Leibnitz desyres the names of all your works, that he may have all sent him. Now yow are best able to Informe your self, of that particular. I thought fitt to acquaint yow

[a] *Followed by* more *deleted; the words* Any more *below are interlined.*

[1] Friedrich August Hackmann, *c.* 1670–1730 or later; professor at Helmstedt 1703–13: *A.D.B.* His correspondence with Leibniz is published in Königlich Preussische Akad. der Wissenschaften, *Sitzungsberichte*, 1915, pp. 714–30.

[2] The Electress Sophia.

[3] This comes from Leibniz's letter of 20/30 January: *Phil. Schriften*, as above, iii. 247. See further a later letter: ibid., p. 256; and the two articles referred to below, *Acta Eruditorum*, iii (1684), 537–42, and probably xiii (1694), 110–12.

(Sir) with this letter, and of two long articles in it relateing to the metaphysicall subject of Ideas, and your discourses of the Coin also. I was transcrybing all that belongs to these two parts and sending them to yow: Bot I imagine yow will be no lesse pleased to see the whole contexture of the letter itself where there is ane account of many other particulars that may be interteaning. I need not send yow the news of the toun. I only take the liberty to acquaint yow off some particulars concerning Dr Benleys book which is at last come out.[1] He read to me a great part of the preface long before it was publisht, and I then thought his narratione of the matter of fact (if he be to be beleived in verbo sacerdotis)[2] did justifie very much his behavior to Mr Boyle[3] at the beginning. And as to the controversy it self, its lyk, many good judges thinks he is able to defend himself against the *reason*, if not against the *authority* of his contrair party. He told me then, the bishop of Coventry and Leitchfeild[4] was so far of his opinione. That he wold publish something of his oun at the same tyme, upon the same subject, which he had kept by him many years, wherin tho there were some small things wherin they dissented, The bishop said it was so much the better, since therby was taken away all suspition of combination; And that the Bishop himself wold send the Doctors book to monsieur Spanheim; so that Grevius,[5] Monsieur Spanheim, and That Bishop, a learn'd Triumvirate seem to be ingadged on the doctors syde: Bot I doubt not bot a greater Number will be of ane other sentiment, who would not be thought to be of the unlearned Trybe: And I heard yesterday morning from Mr Gasterell[6] That the Bishop of C and L Heth thought fitt to suppresse his oun dissertatione: And that there wold come forth ane appologie for the book seller by himself within a day or two.[7] The doctor told me lykways The bishop thought Mr Dodwells oppinion was wholly overturn'd upon this occasion, who founds his hypothesis upon the authenticknesse and the supposd Antiquity of the Epistles of Phalaris.[8] There is also come out Master Gasterells book in 8vo of the certainty of the christian religion,[9] as the second part of his

[1] Bentley's second *Dissertation*: p. 576.

[2] 'On the word of a priest.'

[3] Charles Boyle, the future fourth earl of Orrery: p. 423, n. 1.

[4] Dr. William Lloyd.

[5] Ezekiel Spanheim the younger; Grævius.

[6] Francis Gastrell; p. 146, etc.

[7] Thomas Bennet, *c.* 1665–1706: Bennet and Clements, *Notebook*, pp. 3–6; see further below.

[8] Henry Dodwell the elder: no. *1486*; for his views on Phalaris see J. H. Monk, *Life* of Bentley 2nd ed., 1833, i. 119–20, 179–80.

[9] p. 572.

discourses Intended upon Mr Boyles lecture, And I doubt not bot will argue alsemuch of the reason, and judgement of the Author as his sermons on that occasione. I have read over Dr Bentleys long preface, and a great part of the book, And have just now finisht the new peice that is come out against him exposing his plagiary, ingratitude, and inhumanity particularly to mr Stanley in the editione as the doctor (calls it himself) of his Calimachus etc. The booksellers vindicatione, ane letter of Dr Kings, and the judgement of Sir William Temple etc are annext at the end.[1] I doe professe upon second thoughts (which sometymes are best) I think, Considering Dr Bentleys Magisterial, and supercilious way of treating his adversarys, his hard words and opprobrious langwadge to Mr Bennet, And on the other hand Mr Bennets maner of justifying himself and representing the matter in a sob⟨er⟩,[a] and far lesse Passionat but more Naturall narratione of every thing; so That his story seemeth the more (lykelie) if not the most (true) of the two, And tho the Doctor may have both truth and learning on his syde, He heth no wayes showen the spirit of meeknesse in reproving; Bot rather heth made not only his oun caracter, but that of his order, cheap and mean by wryting so much, and in such a maner to take off litle reflectiones upon his Civility and breeding, which he had easier wypt off by slighting and forgetting, then Answeiring. I have presumed to communicat to you those accounts since I have them from immediat hands. I have sent you Mr Leibnitz letter consisting of peices. I shall be glad to receive your orders if yow have any thing to charge me with when yow send back the papers at which tyme I am to write again to Mr Leibnitz. I did wryte to him from Oxford at the same tyme Doctor Wallis received a lyne from him which was 6 weeks agoe, and now lately I did wryt with that gentleman that is gone to Hanover,[2] Bot he will expect I should wryte to him again since the recept of this I now send yow, wherin (yow see) He desyres to know what

[a] *Page torn.*

---

[1] *A Short Account of Dr. Bentley's Humanity and Justice*, etc. L.L., no. 271. Thomas Stanley (no. *1325* n.) left manuscript notes on Callimachus. Bentley's notes were printed in Spanheim's edition of Callimachus (no. *1802* n.; p. 255 above). Stanley's notes are quotations from works with which Bentley was familiar; the charge of plagiarism appears to be baseless: Monk, *Life* of Bentley, i. 128–9. Dr. William King: p. 532, n. 3.

[2] The letter of 18 February sent by Hackmann: Leibniz, *Phil. Schriften*, as above, iii. 253–4; probably Dr. John Wallis to Leibniz, 16 January: Leibniz, *Die mathematische Schriften*, ed. Gerhardt, etc. iv. 56–61.

things are uncleir in what he did formerly wryt in the first paper of Reflectiones I sent yow.[1] I have not bein so well as to wryt to yow sooner since I had this last letter. To heir of your oun health will be the best news to Mr Leibnitz

Sir

Your most readie and most obleidged humble servant

THOMAS BURNETT

Pellmell-street in London 17 March—99

Sir I thought once of sending this pacquet with Mr Cuningham (who told me at my chamber some dayes agoe) He was to goe out to yow; But now efter waiting longer then his set tyme, I was resolved to delay no longer. I wish yow wold ingadge him (before he leave yow) To peice together his proofs of the christian religion[2] That the world may enjoy that light he heth so long promised. Yow may send back the papers to Mr Churchill and I shall send for them or direct them for me at the two pidgeons on the east end of the Pell-Mell.

Address: For John Lock Esq These Oates

Endorsed by Locke: T. Burnet 17 Mar $9\frac{8}{9}$ Answered 29

2566. AWNSHAM CHURCHILL to LOCKE, 8 April 1699 (*1059, 2706*)

B.L., MS. Locke c. 5, ff. 96–7.

Sir

I send herewith answer to D Bentley[3]

d° Dr Burthogs book left here for you[4]

It[a-] was seaven pounds. your quarters anuity due at Michaelmas last. I shall sudenly look after your Lottery tickets[-a5]

[a–a] *Marked by Locke for attention.*

[1] 'Quelques remarques': p. 60.

[2] For a short description see Story, *William Carstares*, pp. 257–8. I have not traced a publication.

[3] Probably *A Short Account of Dr. Bentley's Humanity and Justice*.

[4] Richard Burthogge, *Of the Soul of the World; and of Particular Souls. In a letter to Mr. Lock, occasioned by Mr. Keil's Reflections upon an Essay lately published concerning Reason. By the Author of that Essay*, 1699. L.L., no. 541. In 1694 Burthogge published *An Essay upon Reason, and the Nature of Spirits*, which he dedicated to Locke (no. *1737A*). This was attacked by John Keill (*D.N.B.*) in the introduction to *An Examination of Dr. Burnet's Theory of the Earth*, 1698 (L.L., no. 1613). Hence the present pamphlet. See further p. 734.

[5] Perhaps for the Million Pound Lottery Loan: pp. 580, 611.

I shall not send mr L Clerc harmony[1] for my Lady Masham till I know whether it must be bound.

Mr Manship and self are very willing to comply with your desire. and shall take care to get a good Corector. and wee pray you to send up the booke. and word whether the aditions must be done alone.[2]

Mr Cuningham has bin ill, but will see you at Oates, before he goes.

I told Mr Buckley—[3]

I did nothing about the Malt Tickets.[4] and Mr Clark will give you the reason.

My humble serv. to all with you
Sir Yours at Comand
A CHURCHIL

8 Apr. 99

Address: To John Locke Esqr. present at Oates.

endorsed by Locke: A: Churchill 8 Apr: 99 Answered 12

2567. SAMUEL BOLD to LOCKE, 11 April 1699 (*2509*, *2590*)

B.L., MS. Locke c. 4, ff. 28–9. For transmission see pp. 598, 626. Answered by no. 2590.

Steeple Apr: 11th. 1699

Honoured Sir

Ever since I received your most kinde letter, and the papers[5] which accompanied It, I have bin unhappily cumbred with busyness which was quite out of my way. And tho in all the distracting trouble It did occasion me, It could not make me one day unmindful of you, yet It did so Indispose me, I thought not my self in a condition to write to you, til I had *drugged*[6] thorough It, and had

[1] p. 559. The preparation of an English version was announced in May; it was published in 1701: *T.C.* iii. 120, 208. L.L., no. 775.

[2] For Manship see nos. *1559*, *1718*. The notice relates to the fourth edition (1700) of the *Essay*. For the sets of printed slips, etc., containing the additional and altered passages in the second and later editions of the *Essay*, enabling owners of copies of the earlier editions to bring them up to date, see no. 1744 n.

[3] Probably Samuel Buckley the bookseller: no. *2110*.

[4] p. 246, etc.

[5] Apparently Bold's draft for *Some Considerations on the Principal Objections* to Locke's *Essay*: pp. 470–1, 506–7.

[6] Drudged, an obsolete spelling.

recovered a little more freedom of thought, than the Importunity of worldly affaires would for a while permit me. I am almost ready to wonder how clergymen can immerse themselves so unconcernedly as many do in secular matters, and manage them with such Dexterity as they do.[a] Having[a] found that what would have made no Impression on others, hath put me into so mighty a Confusion, and bin such a burthen and weariness to me, I can hardly forbear thinking that those Clergymen who needlessly engage themselves in variety of matters, foreign to that which should be their principal busyness, must either be persons of very great parts, or objects deserving much pity, or a keener passion. I bless God, I am now more at liberty than I have bin for some months, having, at least, for a while, extricated my self, out of one of the most perplexing occurrencies, that have happened to me, ever since I applied myself to study. And now (tho so late) I returne you thousands of thanks for your last Answer to the Bishop of *Worcester* (which I think came to my hand the week after I sent my last letter to you) and for you most kinde Instructions how to rectify certain mistakes in the papers I had entreated you to give yourself the trouble, to peruse. I sent the papers, with Amendments, to mr A. Churchill, in a little time after I received them, and did then purpose to write speedily to you, but have contrary to my Inclination, bin hindered, as I have before hinted.

When I said, that one had attempted to Demonstrate the Soul not to be Material, but that I thought the Demonstration did reach no further, than that, It was not a material sensible substance,[1] I spake as favourably of the performance as I could, tho I did not think the proof went so far, as I was willing to suppose, tho if It had, It would not have proved what was undertaken to be proved, and It's not proving what was expresly proposed by the Author to prove, was all I intended by my expressing my self in that manner. The Author I meant, was the Bishop of Worcester, let: 1st.
The faults I found in the last sheet, of the first papers I sent you, were chiefly three. 1. I thought my reflections on what mr Jenkin had writ, were not clear and distinct enough, but that tho they were right, yet wanted some illustration, that those who had not

[a] *Or* do, Having

[1] Bold refers to his draft; the passage containing his statement is represented probably by *Some Considerations*, pp. 18–28, a refutation of Stillingfleet's first *Answer*, pp. 54–79.

thought on the subjects themselves, might the more easily apprehend what was said on both sides. 2. I was aware there were some Impertinent passages in my papers, which had nothing to do there, tho I had made a shift in transcribing my first papers to thrust them in, and concerning the truth which passages I thought I had good reason to doubt. 3. In reading over my first papers which I had kept by me, I found I had expressed my self concerning *powers* after the manner of some who talk of Faculties, as being certain distinct real beings, from the things they belong to. But upon my looking over the papers I sent you, I finde that when I transcribed my papers, I was sensible of the error I had at first committed, and had made some alteration when transcribing; but neglecting to correct my own papers, I suspected upon my looking them over sometime after, that I had transcribed the faults I had left uncorrected in my first papers. The Reason why in my last papers I did so constantly joyn *powers* and *Modifications* together, was because having Intimated that they were not the same, I then thought I might put them together in compliance with mr Jenkins, who I think, makes no distinction betwixt them, but I am very sensible now, that I did not well, in doing so, and I heartily thank you for your directing me to word those places otherwise, and for all the trouble you have bin at, to set me right, where I was mistaken.

Sir. I have several times since I had the Happiness to see you, thought on the subjects you were pleased to discourse with me of, but have little more to say of them, than that your account of them, seem's to me plainly to be the right. Were I within a day's journey of you, You would have bin troubled with many a visit before this time. I have occasionally thought of several points, concerning which I have different apprehensions from what I have mett with in Authors, and about which I should have bin very glad to have had some conversation with you, might it have bin without interfering with your more Important affaires. I loose a great many things, in which I am satisfied I might receive abundant instruction and satisfaction from you. Several things I am fain to let slip, because my own thoughts are not steddy and strong enough to follow and pursue them to a just Issue; other things drop through want of conversation with persons who are willing to enquire after truth, and trace It, when the road is unbeaten. The most I meet with, are so accustomed to prefer the ecclesiastical sense of points, before the Scriptural sense, and to sacrifice Reason, to what they cal Authority, they render conversation, which should be the pleasure, and Advantage of life, a wearyness, and a loss.

Your thoughts concerning these phrases, *as of the Roebuck, and as of the Hart* in Deut: 12. 15. and some other places, were (if I have not forgotten them) to this effect, That they were permitted to eat at their own homes such sorts of creatures, as were appointed to be offered in sacrifice, without concerning themselves any otherwise about them, or without being under any other limitations, or restrictions with reference to them, than with reference to the Roebuck, and the Hart, which beasts they were permitted to kill, and then use for their ordinary food, tho they might not offer them in sacrifice. This I take to be the true meaning of the Scriptures where those phrases are; And among the Commentators I have seen, He who comes nearest to this account of the meaning of those words is M. Le Clerk in his Paraphrase on the v. before mentioned, and on the 20. 21. and 22, v. of the same chapter, and v. 22 of the 15th chapt: of the same book. Indeed He takes notice expresly, that they, viz the Israelites, were allowed to eat those sorts of Cattle which were used for Sacrifices, as they were the Roebuck etc, provided they did not on those occasions account and reckon them sacrifices, but I conceive that Intimation is needless, for should they have put such a construction on their killing and eating of them, they would not have eat them, as the Roebuck etc, which they were not to offer for sacrifices. He also seem's to think that this permission was granted them, only in case of their making publick Feasts in their own cities; but I do not see any thing that hinders interpreting It, of ordinary provision, for private families. M. Le Clerc, is a very learned Author, a person of great Reading, and who thinks more, and reasons much better than most, if not any of the greatest Readers I have mett with He hath writ upon the pentateuch, and designes to go thorough the old testament in the same manner. I shal be glad to see his design accomplish'd. He writes with freedom, hath excellent notions, is far from being of the number of our Road-writers, if may so call them who keep all in the same Track, and say the same things stil one after another, and perhaps for no other reason but because they have bin writ before; He is not swayed by Authority, which I take to be no smal excellency in a writer. All hi books which I have mett with, please me very much. I take him to be one of the principal writers of this Age, to whom the men of letters, and of good meaning, are much obliged. The same Author hath translated Dr Hammond on the New Testament into Latin, and hath added critical notes of his own to those of the Doctor's; His notes are collected, and put into English by themselves, and entitled A Supplement to Dr Hammonds Paraphrase etc.[1] This booke came to my hand the close of the last week, but from what kinde hand It came I do not yet understand. I have consulted some places of It, and what I have already read in It, makes me expect a great deal of light and satisfaction from It. This translation, occasioned a letter from the Author, to a Friend in England. The letter I have read over with great pleasure, It discovers the Author to be a very good man, of a truly Christian spirit and temper. Pray pardon this long excursion, I have bin writing, as if you were not only as far from London, but as much buried in a vale as I am. I have a great esteem for Critical Writers, yet, I am apt to think they very often miss the right sense of many places in the new Testament especially, and not of a few in the old. they furnish with many Ideas, philosophers, learned m⟨en⟩[a], (or so reputed) the heads of, or pretenders to sects and parties, signified, by many words used in the scriptures; which I acknowledge are of great use to be known, and may give much light to understand several parts of scripture, when we can make it appear, that the portions of scripture where those words are found, were particularly designed with relation to those who used the words in those senses, or to those who knew them to be used in those senses. But the common sort of people, who were principally concerned in what was delivered by the inspired writers, understanding the words in which they declared the mind of God to them, in a vulgar and common meaning, the true sense of many places of Scripture seem's to me very different, from what it is represented to be, by our learned and critical Commentators. The critical, not being the vulgar sense of the words, seem's to me, to be generally the least likely to be the true sense of them. The Inspired Authors I conceive used such words as the common sort of people did ordinarily use and in the sense they generally understood them, and did not send their

[a] *Part covered by blot.*

[1] p. 559.

hearers, to the Rabbins, nor philosophers to learn the meaning of the words in which they delivered to them the minde of God. And if the first Fathers of the Church (as they are called) had waved the mixing of the philosophical notions they had imbibed, with the Christian doctrines after that they espoused christianity, I am inclined to think their writings would have done Religion more service, than now they can, tho as they are, they best serve their turne, who are most addicted to ostentation, and think It a wonderful Glory, to be expert in the Art of Wrangling.

As to the Kingdom of Christ, I conceive it is a particular Kingdom, Indeed He is made Head over all things, but we must remember the Apostle certifies us at the same time, He is so, unto, or with reference to his Church, that is, the subjects of his Kingdom. And that his Kingdom wil cease, and be delivered up unto God, the universal Governor, appears plain to me from 1. Cor: 15. 24. and 28. 'Tis true, we often read that his Kingdom shal continue for ever, and that It shal have no end, and other the like phrases we meet with. But I think these phrases are used in opposition to the Mosaick Dispensation, and that their import is this, that the Gospel Dispensation shal not give place to, and be succeeded by another Dispensation, as the Mosaick Dispensation was to do, and to which the Gospel did succeed.

What ground the Gentleman who thinks you have not proved that there is but one eternal Independant being, had for that thought of his, I cannot imagine; nor what sort of proof He would expect.[1] You were about to state the matter clearly unto me, when I was last with you, but mr Molyneux coming in, hindered me from receiving the Instruction you would have given me; And I have not penetration enough, to find out the point myself You have demonstrated that *there is an eternal, most powerful, and most knowing Being*.[2] And you have taken notice, that from this Idea duly considered, wil easily be deduced all those other Attributes we ought to ascribe to this eternal Being. Now, I think It is a clear Repugnancy to our Reason, to conceive a Being which hath no Dependance, on that Eternal, etc. Being. I think further, that in your Essay Book 4. Chap. 10. those things are proposed, that fully prove that there can be but one eternal Independant Being but I enlarge no further, because I am not sure that I have a righ

[1] This is probably Hudde; Locke may have discussed his question with Bold.
[2] *Essay*, IV. x. 6.

notion, of what the Gentleman aim's at. What you have said, wil bring us to an Absolute, universal Soveraign, Lord, and Governour, and that there should be anything that is Independant on Him, is not conceivable by me. Indeed I am inclined to think that this is the primary, original Idea the word *God* in English, and any other word in other languages, which we wil properly translate by this word, stands for, and that all other Ideas we have concerning this universal Governor, are consequential to It. As we have Ideas of qualities, before we can form any Idea of substance, so I think we have the Idea of a Governour, from our observing the series, order, harmony, and effects of things, before we attain to form other Ideas concerning Him, who doth order, and govern these things. It's true this Government is founded on Creation, but we first conceive a governor, before we can satisfy our selves about the ground and foundation of his government. Our Ideas of the operations of things, are I think antecedent to our Ideas of their existence. I write you see confusedly, I only give some present hints, you wil readily perceive my mistakes, and I shal be very glad to be set right. But I do not minde that I have mett with any place of Scripture, where the word God, doth not most properly signify Governour. I have before begg'd your pardon for runing into an excursion, and immediately ran into another, so that I had fresh occasion to renew my petition; and when a man is out of his way, He knows not whither He goes, but keeps wandering on, and so I doubt It happens now with me, and therefore now entreat your pardon for this long trouble I give you, and to express ⟨your⟩[a] pitty to a poor bewildred wretch, by reducing him from his strayings into the Right way. I shal be very glad to hear you have had such a proportion of Health and leisure, as to have bin able to make any progress in what you told me you purposed to add to the next Edition of your Essay of Humane understanding.[1] Sir I am

your most obliged and Humble servant

SA: BOLD.

Address: To the Honoured Mr Locke.

Endorsed by Locke: S Bold 11 Apr 99 Answered May. 12

[a] *MS.* you

---

[1] See p. 591.

2568. SAMUEL BOLD to [AWNSHAM CHURCHILL?], 12 April 1699 (*2359, 3182* enc.)

B.L. MS., Locke c. 4, f. 27. Fragment: part of text cut away at foot. The person addressed from p. 626.

Steeple Apr: 12th. 1699

Worthy Sir

I have here inclosed a letter to our Honoured Friend Mr Locke, which I desire you to send to Him, the first opportunity you can get for a safe conveighance. I returne you my thanks for your going to the Duke of Newcastle,[1] upon your receiving a former letter of mine. I did apprehend even when I writ, that the place might be disposed of by that time. For I am sensible that Clergymen are generally as quickscented as Eagles, and make as much speed as they do to the prey. I knew indeed near two months before I writ to you, that the place was vacant, and was told of It by one, who expected I would seek after It, because Mr Boscawen[2] was related to the patron. But I forbore then, because I would much rather something might be offered to me, than give occasion to have it thought, I am too solicitous about, and Greedy after the Interests of this world. And I should not have writ when I did but that other persons importunity prevailed against my own Inclination. I sent you word in . . .[a]

Endorsed by Locke: S. Bold 12 Apr 99

2569. LOCKE to MRS. MARY CLARKE, 12 April 1699 (2291, 2576)

B.L., MS. Locke b. 8, no. 139. Printed in Rand, pp. 543–4.

Oates 12° Apr 9[9]

Madam

Your kind remembrance by Mr Clarke wanted noe thing to compleat my satisfaction in it but an assurance of your perfect recovery. The account he gave me let me see that your health was not soe perfectly yet confirmed, but that I think upon consideration of all the particulars, which you will forgive me fo[r]

[a] *The rest is cut away.*

[1] John Holles, 1662–1711; fourth earl of Clare 1689; created duke of Newcast[le] 1694: *D.N.B.*

[2] Probably Hugh Boscawen, M.P. for Cornwall, etc., 1646–8, 1659–81, 1689–170[1]: *Visitations of Cornwall*, ed. J. L. Vivian, 1887, p. 46. His wife was a sister of Newcastl[e]: A. Collins, *The Peerage of England*, 3rd ed., 1715, ii. 200.

haveing very nicely examined him to, there may a little care yet be requisite fully to remove all the appearances of any the least remain of your slow distemper. I doe not doubt but you have received great benefit by the diet drink you have made use of and am not against your continuance of it. But since the time of the year may give an occasion for the makeing some alterations in it with advantage, Permit me to desire you to send me a copy of the receit you make it by, that I may consider how to make it more beneficial to you now the spring is growing on, the proper time to enliven and invigorate the bloud, which I desire you to make advantage of by being as frequent as you can in the air and by carefully avoiding all things that may make a chill mixture in your bloud and fill your veins with watery humors, wherein consists the nature and danger of your disease and cannot be any way more fomented than by drinking small liquors espetially small bear and water. But I think I need not advise you against the town small bear, which is generaly soe bad that even strong people who have a care of their health finde it necessary to avoid it. You will pardon the liberty I take to importune you with my advice and direction for the perfecting your recovery. I have been soe long intrusted with the management of your health that methinks custome has given me some authority in the case. or if that be not enough to give me a right of prescribeing, yet the concerne I have and always shall have for your life and health will at least excuse my medling when it is only to shew how heartily I interest my self in what belongs to you and with what affection and sincerity I am

Madam

Your most humble and most faithfull servant

J LOCKE

Endorsed: 12. April 99. Mr. Locke

2570. J.-B. DU BOS to LOCKE, 13/23 April [1699] (*2527, 2591*)

B.L., MS. Locke c. 7, ff. 225–6. Printed by G. Bonno in *Revue de littérature comparée*, xxiv (1950), 495–8. Year from Locke's endorsement.

A Beauvais[1] Le Mercredi $\frac{23}{13}$ Davril

Jay tousjours beaucoup de plaisir monsieur, toutes les fois que je recois de vos nouvelles, mais vostre derniere lettre ma fort afligé en maprenant le mauvais estat de vostre santé. je suis tres sensible

[1] Where Du Bos's mother lived.

ausibien que touts vos amis, et je ne sçaurois penser sans chagrin a vos indispositions quand je vois tant de gens dont la santé et la vie sont si indifferents aux genre humain, se porter si bien. je me console dans l'esperance que le retour de la belle saison produira le retour de vostre santé. si vous avie un fils il ne le souhaitteroit pas avec plus de passion que moy.

Mylord Pawlet et monsieur de Cuninghuam doivent estre presentement de retour a Londres. ils se sont acquis ici lestime de touts ceux qui les ont conu. je suis faché en mon particulier quils naient pas voulu rester plus lontemps parmi nous et i attendre le retour du printemps qui leur auroit montré nos jardins dans toute leur beauté, au lieu quil nen on vu pour ainsi dire que les squeletes.

Jay recu les cartes que vous mavé envoiees par monsieur De Vernietes et je vous en remercie. monsieur Toinard a recu de meme le second volume du voyage de Dampiere, et le paquet qui estoit a son adresse.

Jespere destre de retour a Paris dans sept ou huit jours, et je vous envoieré ausitost les comissions dont vous me faites lhonneur de me charger.

je pense avoir oublie dans mon catalogue de voyage l'etat de l'empire de Maroc par monsieur de Saint olon imprimé en 1694.[1] lautheur est un gentilhomme ordinaire du roy qui fut envoye en 1693 a Miquenez pour faire un traitte de Paix avec le roy de Maroc dont le voyage eut aussi peu de succez que celui de Lambassadeur Maure qui est presentement a Paris en aura.[2] son livre est un in douze.

je serois bien aise de voir le Catalogue des manuscrits DAngleterre et DIrlande dont vous me parlé.[3]

LAmerique de Defer est une simple carte, autour de la quelle il a mis quelques discours servant d'explication.[4]

le roy a recu nouvelle que mr de Frontenac gouverneur du Canada estoit mort cet hyver.[5] come la riviere estoit fermee par les

[1] F. Pidou de St. Olon, *Estat present de l'empire de Maroc*. In 1695 St. Olon published *Relation de l'empire de Maroc*. L.L., no. 2531.

[2] Abdalla ben Aïscha, in Paris from February until April: Saint-Simon, *Mémoires*, ed. de Boislisle, vi. 139–40 and nn.

[3] Edward Bernard, *Catalogi Librorum Manuscriptorum Angliæ et Hiberniæ in unum collecti*, 1697. The completed work was not advertised in the Term *Catalogues* until November 1698: *T.C.* iii. 95.

[4] p. 532.

[5] Louis de Buade, comte de Frontenac, governor of la Nouvelle France 1672–8 and since 1689; he died about 28 November 1698, N.S.: *Dict. Canadian Biog.*

⟨glaces⟩[a] il a fallu envoier a travers terres un courier a Baston ou il a frette un vaisseau Anglois qui la aporté en France.

on parle fort ici de l'etablissement de la compagnie des Indes orientales dEscosse dans le golfe de Darien, mais on nen dit rien de fort precis.[1] nous i avions deja une colonie de cinquante ou soixante hommes venus de Saint Domingue.[2]

les memoires du marquis Pignalossa que lon imprime sont traduits sur l'original escrit de sa main. je ne scais point sil i avoit mis tout ce quil scavoit, mais l'on nen a rien retranché.[3]

on vient de publier encore ici deux harmonies des Evangiles, lune est du pere Lami de l'oratoire et lautre dun pretre seculier.[4] je donnerois tout ce quil i en a au monde pour celle de monsieur Toinard. il i a des autheurs qui ont grand besoin de bride dans la publication de leurs ouvrages; il auroit encore plus besoin deperon. il vous salue et vous souhaitte une aussi bonne santé que la siene.

le troisieme volume des *antiquitates Græcæ* de monsieur Gronovius est imprimé a Leyde. ce volume est beaucoup plus curieux que les autres contenant Les ouvrages de Meursius sur la Grece.[5]

La reimpression des ouvrages du pere Petau en six volumes in folio est pres d'estre achevee a Amsterdam.[6]

on a aussi l'obligation a un libraire de cette ville d'avoir rimprime Le Systeme du monde de Galilee; livre qui estoit devenu tres rare.[7]

On imprime encore en ce pais la la Mischna avec les notes et la version de monsieur de Surrenhuisen.[8]

les Huguetans qui rimpriment le St Augustin des Benedictins ont juge a propos voulant vendre le livre en pais dinquisition de mettre en un volume separé les notes de mr Le Clerc.[9] cestoit

[a] *MS.* gloces

[1] The settlement established by the Company of Scotland trading to Africa and the Indies (no. *1978*). The settlers landed in Darien on 4 November 1698; news of the landing reached Edinburgh on 25 March, O.S.: G. P. Insh, *The Company of Scotland*, 1932, pp. 128–9, 145.

[2] This statement appears to be incorrect.

[3] See p. 508.

[4] Lamy's publication was his commentary on his *Harmonia*: p. 456. The other publication is probably S. Le Roux, *Concordia Quatuor Evangelistarum*, 1699.

[5] For the *Thesaurus* see p. 167. Du Bos has made a slip: there are no pieces by Joannes Meursius in vol. iii. Six pieces by him are reprinted in vol. iv; further pieces by him are reprinted in later volumes.

[6] p. 541.

[7] The *Dialogo . . . sopra i due massimi sistemi del mondo* was published in 1632; this was a new edition of the Latin translation, *Systema Cosmicum*, 1635 (new editions 1641 and 1663); it was published at Leyden.

[8] p. 615. Willem Surenhuys, 1666–1729: *N.N.B.W.*

[9] p. 542.

un mauvais passeport que les remarques dun Arminien sur les ouvrage dun pere qui a soutenu les loix penales contre les sectaires, pour des pais ou lon veut bruler les gens qui ont le malheur de ne pas Croire come les autres.

Vostre tres humble et tres obeessant serviteur

DU BOS.

Address: Poste DAngleterre. To Master Jhon Locke at Master Pawlings overagainst the plough in little Lincolns-Inn fields London

Postmark: AP 16

Endorsed by Locke: Du Bos 23 Apr 99 Answered May 12

2571. NICOLAS TOINARD to LOCKE, 18/28 April [1699] (2550, 2580)

B.L., MS. Locke c. 21, ff. 204–6. Year from Locke's endorsement. Answers no. 2550; answered by no. 2580.

+

Avril 28.

Je ne vous ay pas jusques à present, monsieur, remercié des livres que vous m'avez fait la grace de m'envoier, parceque je voulois vous marquer l'envoi de ceux que vous me demandez, mais comm'il est arivé qu'en ouvrant votre letre, la cire d'Espagne a emporté l'adresse qu'ele couvroit pour vous les faire tenir, j'ay atendu de jour à autre le retour de mr Du Bos pour savoir de lui en quelle ville demeure mr Pigault qui est celui qui les doit recevoir pour les faire tenir à mr Frankland. J'estime neanmoins que c'est à Calais ou à Douvre. Vous ne marquez point nonplus par quele voie je le feray. c'est a dire par la poste ou par le messager, parceque peutetre vous ne paiez rien des paquets qui vont à Douvre par la poste. Ainsi jatendrai la dessus l'honneur de vos ordres, et cependant je repondrai à quelques questions que vous me faites.

Votre objection est fort juste touchant l'Inscription Greque dans la medaille d'Antigonus, cependant ele y est, et c'est cequi fait la rareté de la medaille qui a en même tems des letres Samaritaines ce n'est point *propter benevolentiam nec ambitionem*, come vous dites qu'Antigonus s'est servi de cete Legende Greque, *cùm Judæi tantum passi sint à Seleucidis*:[1] Il y avoit prescription, et les Seleucide

[1] '(It is not) from goodwill or ambition . . . since the Jews had suffered so much from the Seleucids': quoted from no. 2550.

n'etoient plus rien, mais c'est à cause que les Juifs etoient liez de commerce avec leurs voisins qui parloient Grec. Les Juifs avoient memes des noms semblables à ceux des Grecs, comme celui cy d'Antigonus, outre Alexandra, Alexander, Aristobulus, et c.

Sur ceque vous dites que LΓΙ ne put pas marquer Anno XIII. dans la medaille d'Herode, parcequ'il vous semble qu'il devroit y avoir LΙΓ, vous me pardonerez si je vous dis que vous n'avez pas fait reflexion qu'en Syrie et ailleurs les letres numerales se metent *ordine inverso*. Je ne connois même que les villes de Sebaste et de Naplouse en Samarie qui metent les Epoques *ordine recto*.[1]

L'Harmonie du P. Lami qui aravit in vitulâ meâ paroît depuis peu en deux vol. in 4.[2] Ele ne fera pas grand à l'in Fol. que vous savez. Je la joindray aux livres que vous me mandez, si vous la desirez.

Deux de mes amis sont venus me voir comme j'ecrivois ceci, et ne m'ont pas laissé le tems de vous ecrire de la Pâque qui assurement se faisoit in atrio Templi sub dio. Il est en marge dans l'Harmonie que vous avez Gr-Lat.[3] L'heure me presse. Je suis

Je ne saurois lire si l'Auteur qui a ecrit de la chine et que vous desiriez[a] etre en François est Navarrete qui a ecrit en Espagnol. Il est tres curieux et rare. Je ne lay pas vu, mais il y en a un exemplaire en un endroit ou je le pourois voir.

Address: For Mr John Locke Angleterre at Mr Pawlings overagainst the ploug in Little Lincolns Inne feilds London

Endorsed by Locke: Toinard 28 Apr 99 Answered May. 1 and Dec. 5

2572. BENJAMIN FURLY to LOCKE, 21 April/1 May 1699 (2424, *2629*)

B.L., MS. Locke c. 9, ff. 147–8.

Rotterdam primo May 1699

Deare Friend

I lately understood by mr. Crellius[4] of your good health, which I was the more glad to understand, because I was not long before

[a] *Ending doubtful; part re-written.*

[1] This appears to be correct.
[2] pp. 456, 541, 601.
[3] In the *Harmonia* as published in 1707 this forms part of the terminal notes.
[4] Samuel Crellius: p. 459.

informd, by whom I cannot call to mind, that he had left you in a very weake condition.

This comes by my Lord Ashley whose incomparable good conversation we have been thus long happy in.

I am sorry my dearest and self cannot accompany him, tho we are not now without hopes of following him ere this year be at an end: our differences being not alone submitted to Arbitration, but mediation of two able men our friends and neighbours I suppose not unknown to you, mr. John van Twedde,[1] and Denys Verburgh,[2] that went with me to Hellevoetsluys in 1688—

And they tell me that they are perswaded that my brother[3] is in earnest to have an end so is my dearest and I, tho it should be with the losse of £1000—

We have here no news, save that a mathematician of this Town supposing he has found a way, and unchangeable foundation, to demonstrate that both Old and new stile is false and defective, and no ways agreeing with the true course of the heavens, which he regulates without any confusion to any christian church or state unchangeably by establishing the Vernall Equinox for the beginning of the year establisht by God, betwixt the midday of the 9 and 10 of march old or 19 and 20 new stile. As also by keeping unchangeably the same circles of the son moon and stars; and the same Sunday letters and Epacts both in old and new stile. So that all the moveable feasts both according to the old and N. stile shall alwayes fall on the same day. Pretending that all other Almanacks and calculations are false, but that this way of his will contribute exceeding much to the advantage of Navigation.

This he seems to have demonstrated so much to the satisfaction of the states of Holland, that they have given him a Patent upon his project, and do recommend the same to all soverains to receive it.

He says he has found out 3 capital sums the first of the son 66342857. and two of the moon the first 65370454—the second 153086600. to find how this was in the year 1656. the year of the flood.[4] He multiplyes the suns number by 1656. the sun will come into Aries. 15 April 10 hours 9 min etc. upon Wednesday. The Sunday letter C. the suns Circle 4. And to find the Easter full moon, multiply 1656 by the first Number of the moon, and divide it by the second number, the true Epact wilbe 23 days 3 hours 31 minutes. And the golden number 3. This Epact being substracted

[1] No. *1114*. [2] No. *1115*. [3] Cornelis Huys: pp. 379, 740–4. [4] A.M. 1656.

rom the suns entrance into Aries, and to the residue a middle moon-shine time, then the true full moon at Easter wilbe 21 April, 19 hours 21 minutes; all reduced according to the stile of Julius Cæsar, who has added one day to much in his art,[a] every 112 years. Or else he would have kept the Vernal Equinox always at a certain point of time, and so there would never have been any confusion in the world betwixt the old and new stile.

Eight examples he gives to prove that his project never failes. his second is upon the exit of the children of Israel out of Egypt, which the scripture says was 15 of Abib. 2514 Anno, which was then 17 Aprill but now 28 march and so will by his art abide for ever—his third example. is from Julius Cæsar Epocha, 45 years before christs birth. or 4088 year of the world. his fourth example is from christs birth 4132[1]—I must break off—my Lord going—his man comes and calls him—

I am

your humble servant

BENJAMIN FURLY

Address: (written by an amanuensis): To Mr. John Locke In London per amy Q.D:G.

Endorsed by Locke: B: Furly 1° May 99 Answered Jun. 8 and Sept. 10

2573. HENRY GREENHILL to LOCKE, 22 April 1699

B.L., MS. Locke c. 10, ff. 52–3. Henry Greenhill (1646–1708) was a younger brother of the artist and of Mrs. Thomas. He was for a time agent-general on the Gold Coast for the Royal African Company and was now commissioner of the Navy at Portsmouth; he was member of parliament for Newport, I.O.W., from 1699 to 1701: *D.N.B.*; Ehrman, *Navy*; Dampier, *Voyages*, II. iii. 49–54.

Sir

I have received your kind Letter of the 12 Currant by the Hands of Sir Cloudesly Shovell,[2] into whose Custody it was putt by mr. Clerke, and am very ready to Gratifye your Desire, in Communicating to you Such Observations as I made During the Time I Resided in Guinea; but the Multitude of Publick business which hath, and Doth encumber me, and the Disorder wherein my Papers

[a] *Or* out

[1] The mathematician is perhaps Andreas van Lugtenberg or Luchtenberg: van der Aa; Knuttel, nos. 14483, 14537. [2] The admiral: *D.N.B.*

in Generall lye, (Occasion'd by frequent removalls from place to place) for want of an Opportunity to Inspect and restore them, will not at present give me the Occasion so readily to serve you as I would; but hope towards the End of the Summer to find a Vacation, which Ill assure you shall be imployed to give you the Desired Satisfaction: in the Interim pray youd accept the hearty Respects Of

Sir

Your Very humble Servant

HENRY GREENHILL

From his majts Yard neare Portsmouth the 22d Aprill 99.

To the Honble John Lock Esqre

Address: To the Honble John Lock Esqre att Oates

Endorsed by Locke: H: Greenhill 22 Apr 99

2574. LOCKE to PETER KING, later first Baron King, 24 April 1699 (2559, 2577)

B.L., MS. Locke c. 40, ff. 39–40. Answered by no. *2578*.

Oates 24 Apr 99

Dear Cosin

The news of your safe return to town is very welcome to me and to all here, and I thank you for not neglecting to send it me by the first post. Pray return my thanks to your father for his remembrance of me when you write to him.

Jacob Tonson is printing at Cambridg Horace Virgil Terence Catullus Tibullus and Propertius. He proposes as I hear Subscriptions i e one Guinea to be paid in Hand and an other at the delivery of the books I desire you to subscribe for one set of them for me unlesse you hear any thing to discourage it. You see I give you trouble as soon as I find you returnd. But Tonson as I take it liveing very near the Temple this will not I presume take up much of your time or pains you may see at his shop his proposals.[1] I am

Dear Cosin

your most affectionate Cosin and humble servant

J LOCKE

My Lady and all our company give you their service

[1] Jacob Tonson the elder, 1655–1736, the bookseller: *D.N.B.* He moved about

One thing I had almost forgot. There is in Mr Popples hands a Tally of mine upon the next payment (which will be now in May) of the subscriptions for the New East India Company. The Tally is for £500.[1] I desire you to call upon him for it. And then to take of the Bank five distinct bills for it each of £100 payable to you or your order. Get the bills to be with interest if you can. Your Cosin Freke will advise you how to get Bank bills with interest,[2] Or perhaps he may put you in some better way how to dispose of the said £500, though when it is in Bank bills it is as good as dead mony and tis best to receive the mony due on the Tally as soon as may be though it be lodgd at present in the Bank without any interest. I have writ to Mr Popple by this post to deliver it you

Address: For Peter King Esqr To be left at Mr Potmans in the Middle Temple London

Postmark: AP 26

Endorsed by King: Mr Locke April. 24. 1699.

2575. LOCKE to EDWARD CLARKE, 28 April 1699 (2553, 2585)

B.L., MS. Locke b. 8, no. 140. Printed in Rand, pp. 544–6.

Oates 28 Apr 99

Dear Sir

It was very kindly done to send me the welcome news of your safe arivall by the next post after you came to town, though I can excuse a freind from such civilitys who is every day tired out with businesse. I hear you were ill again with your cold upon your return to the air and fatigues of London. If you continue soe come hither again: twas that which Sir Francis my Lady and every one here said as soon as they heard it. Remember doeing of businesse will end in the grave and before too if you neglect your health. Therefor I seriously presse it on you to come to Oates

he end of this year from the Inner Temple Gate to Gray's Inn Gate: Hugh Macdonald, *John Dryden: a Bibliography*, 1939, p. 120 n. The proposal was issued probably n 1698; the texts, finely printed in quarto, were published in four volumes in 1699–702: D. F. McKenzie, *The Cambridge University Press, 1696–1712*, 1966, vol. i, pp. i, nos. 1, 4, 6, 10, 28.

[1] The tally was in respect of a half-year's instalment of Locke's salary as a Commissioner for Trade and Plantations; it was issued in November 1698: Locke, ournal, 12 November 1698.

[2] Apparently Sealed Bills: no. *1891*.

again if you are disorderd where you are. I shall not tire you with long remonstrances in the case. My advice is friendly and good and you were best follow it. I am

Dear Sir

Your most affectionate humble servant

J LOCKE

My service to the Batchelor
This family are your servants

The Above was written, as you will easily guesse, before the receit of yours of the 25th and I know not any thing in my whole life that hath more sensibly striken me than the news you send me in it. Upon consideration of what you there say I thus reason. Melancholy is either from the mind or the Body. That from the minde must have its foundation in some affliction some weighty crosse or other. There being noe such here I conclude it oweing to the body and that therefor applications must be made to that part. My advice therefor is that Dr Pit or any one else whom you can be informed is most skild in such kind of distempers be presently consulted and he immediately put into such course as shall be directed. For if according to your discourse with me when you were here there be noe secret cause of discontent, as I imagin there is not, I conclude you will invain endeavour to divert his minde by travell or any thing else when the cloud it receives is from the humors of his body. This is what seems to me fit to be done.[1] If any thing else occurs upon ruminateing again upon this case you shall be sure to have it from me for I am

Dear Sir

Yours perfectly

J L

I thank you for your Care about Mr Greenhils letter.[2]

Pray tell Mr Conyers, if you see him in the house,[3] that I have writ to him this day to give an account how the mistake which I think now he justly accused my receit of, came about, I desire he would send me word what mony Sir Francis Masham received of him for my account last year in May, and thereby enable me to set all right[4]

[1] This relates to the young Edward Clarke: endorsement and pp. 619–20.
[2] Presumably no. *2573*.
[3] The house of commons.
[4] Conyers replied in no. *2581*

Pray return my thanks to your son John for his civill and excellently well writ letter

Address: For Edward Clarke Esquire member of Parliament. To be left at Richards Coffee house within Temple Bar London Frank
Postmark: MY 1
Endorsed by Clarke: Mr: Locke touching my Sonn's Indisposition etc: Received the 1rst. of May 1699. Answered fully the 2d.[a]

2576. LOCKE to MRS. MARY CLARKE, 28 April 1699 (2569, 2611)

B.L., MS. Locke b. 8, no. 141. Printed in Rand, pp. 546–7.

Oates 28 Apr 99

Madam

I am sorry the remains of any indisposition needs diet drinks or any thing else. I had much rather congratulate to you your perfect recovery than talke to you of medecines in order to it. The diet drink you have sent me the prescription of I think a very good one and you will doe well to continue the use of it, only if you like the tast of Orange pills[1] you may for variety put in the yellow thin pareing of three or four Oranges. I find not by your letter that you make use of the pils prescribed by Dr Pit. I think they would be of advantage to you if you now and then tooke a dose of them when you finde your legs most sweld and uneasy: To which give me leave to adde one thing which I formerly thought of moment to your health and doe soe still and therefor take the liberty to repeat it again: and that is that you would constantly goe to bed early, and if you lie a bed pretty late in the morning it will be noe harm to you. You know what an excuse custom and concerne make for the liberty I here take. I long to have you perfectly well. I hope the weather and my lungs will consent in a little while to my waiting on you in town, though it be yet cold and winterly weather here and I write this by the fires side. In the mean time I can not but approve of your resolution to avoid those things which you finde prejudicial to your health. I have but too much experience that without it other things here are of

[a] *Clarke also notes:* Quære. the vote No. 99. *This is all deleted except* Quære.

[1] The obsolete word pill, meaning peel: *O.E.D.*

but little value: And therefor I always count the preservation of health the best peice of husbandry. My Lady and all this family give you their humble service and to all your good company. I am

Madam

your most humble and faithfull servant

J LOCKE

Pray remember me very kindly to my wife and the rest of your yonge folke

Address: These present To Mrs Mary Clarke

Endorsed: 23. April 99. Mr. Locke

2577. LOCKE to PETER KING, later first Baron King, 28 April 1699 (2574, *2578*)

B.L., MS. Locke c. 40, f. 41.

Dear Cosin

In my last I forgot to desire you to send me word what day in May the next payment of the subscriptions into the East India Company was to be made. That therefor my money may not be wanting against the time I have here with sent you a bill on Mr Churchill for any summ you shall want not exceeding an hundred pounds that in case of need you may be there supplied though I make account there will be noe need, since I conclude that at least when the time for payment comes the Bank will give you five bills for my Tally each of £100, one whereof will be taken by the Receivers of that payment. But how best to order this and how it may be donne I beleive your Cosin Freke can best direct. I would not have this bill on Mr Churchill be made use of if it may with ease and convenience be avoided. If the day appointed for the payment (for I have not yet seen it in the Gazets) be soe far off that I may have time, upon hearing from you, to setle this matter we will then agree before hand how this next payment shall be made. But if there be not time for this I leave it to your discretion to doe in it as you think best. Only be sure that some way or other the mony be paid at the day that I may not forfeit I received noe letter from you today. I am

Dear Cosin

Your most affectionate and humble servant

J LOCKE

Pray send me word in your next what date Sir Francis Mashams bond,[1] which is in your hands, bears

All here are your humble servants

Oates 28 Apr. 1699[a]

Address: For Peter King Esqr To be left at Mr Potmans in the Middle Temple London

Postmark: MY I

Endorsed by King: Mr Locke April. 28. 1699

2578. PETER KING, later first Baron King, to LOCKE, 29 April 1699 (2577, 2579)

B.L., MS. Locke c. 12, ff. 101–2. Answers no. 2574; answered by nos. 2579 and 2584.

London April. 29. 1699.

Honoured Sir

Your letter of the 24th instant was very acceptable to me—I will mind what you write about Jacob Tonson, and look after it next week—I have not yet taken Your Tally from Mr Popple, but shall stay till I hear from you again, for My Cosin Freke tells me, that Bank bills carry but 2d. per diem Interest, but Exchequer bills 5d.[2] and he thinks the latter to be the best and Surest, The Mony will not be paid upon the Tally before the End of May, but if you will, he will pay it in for you in the next payment to the East India Company about 10. days hence, as upon his own account, and he will get me Exchequer bills for it, I think that this will be the best way, but whether You will take this way, or Bank bills, or leave it to me to take any other and better way, which may present, I desire you to advise me by the next—I have not yet had time to put my busyness in Order, so I Can Only write you in general, that[b–] your Million Tickets[3] are received, as also Your Dividend at the Bank[4] with My Ladys and Mrs Mashams, and Your Interest due at Lady day from the East

[a] *There is a note by King here:* I made no use of the above Bill sent to me by Mr Locke on Mr Churchils and therefore I broke it [b–b] *Marked by Locke for attention.*

[1] Probably for the loan negotiated in 1697: no. 2182, etc. [2] p. 246, n. 1, etc.
[3] Nos. *1821*, etc.; p. 580.
[4] On the £400 stock held in King's name: p. 527, n. 1.

India Company[-b]—My Humble Service to Sir Francis, My Lady and all—

Your Most Affectionate Cosin and Servant P. KING.

Address: To John Locke Esquire [at Oates, by Joslyn, Bishops Stortford]

Postmark: AP 29

Endorsed by Locke: P: King 29 Apr 99 Answered May. 1.

2579. LOCKE to PETER KING, later first Baron King, 1 May 1699 (*2578*, *2584*)

B.L., MS. Locke c. 40, ff. 42–3. Answers no. *2578*.

Oates 1 May 99

Dear Cosin

I received yours of 29 Apr. very late to day and soe have barely time to tell you in short that the first thing I would have you take care of, is, that either by my Tally or by the Bill I sent you the last post for any summ not exceeding £100 on Mr Churchill, money be provided to pay my sixth payment of my subscription for the East India Company, which the Gazette now tells me must be the 10. 11. 12th instant. Why the Tally will not be paid before the end of May, when the money that is to pay it will be received the 12th I doe not understand. How the remaining part of the money due upon my Tally which shall not be made use of for the paying my subscription shall be disposed of I must leave to your discretion. only I must beg you to remember that it must be lodgd noe where but where I may be able to command it at a day or two's warning, for I know not how soon I may have need of it, and therefor possibly it may be better in the Bank upon lesse interest than in Exchequer Bills unlesse they be Specie Bills[1] except there be any other that one may turne into money when one pleases. Pray returne my thanks to your Cosin Freke You are rememberd here with kindnesse. I am

Dear Cosin

Your most affectionate Cosin and humble servant

J LOCKE

-b *See note on previous page*.]

[1] Apparently 'Specie Exchequer Bills', which the Bank of England 'was prepared to cash at first sight, instead of waiting until they had once passed the Exchequer in payment of taxes, etc.': Clapham, i. 291.

Address: For Peter King of the Middle Temple Esqr To be left at Mr Potmans in the Middle Temple London
Postmark: MY 3
Endorsed by King: Mr Locke. May. 1. 1699

2580. LOCKE to NICOLAS TOINARD, 1 May 1699 (*2571*, 2644)

B.M., Add. MS. 28,728, ff. 36–7. Printed in Ollion, pp. 134–6. Answers no. *2571*.

Oates 1° May 99

La votre du 28 d Avril m'a bien instruit sur les medailles dont vous me parliois dans votre precedente. vous voiez bien mon ignorance dans cette sorte d'étude par les question que je vous proposois, mais puisque nous sommes tombez sur cette matiere permettez que vous encore demand pourquoi les Juifs et les Syriens comme ils se servoient des inscriptions Grecs et de characteres Grecs pour montrer le temps ils gardoient l'ordre Syriac dans l'arangement des lettres numerales?

J'ai novellement recu l'harmonie de Monsieur le Clerc.[1] il n'est pas encore reliée c'est pour quoi je ne l'a pas encore eu l'occasion de la conferer avec une autre que vous savez elle est en Grec *folio* verso et en Latin du Vulgate *folio recto* la methode resemble un peu à la votre. mais je vois par les premiers versets du St Jean ou l'ordre est different. Si celle du P Lami ne contient rien du neauveau qui merit bien d'etre conu je ne la souhaitrois avec grand empressement. C'est pour quoi je laisse à vous d'en juger si elle merite d'etre envoiée.[2] Je l'a deja *en douz* par votre bonté et si l'in 4° ne contient plus d'erudition il ne vale pas la peine de l'envoier. Il y a une autre, comme vous le savez, que je souhaite avec grand impatience de voir publiée dans sa derniere parfection.

Ex quo ultimò ad te scripsi hæc mihi inter legendum occurrebant Mischnæ quidem translationem nonnulli inchoarunt sed Gemaram

---

Since I wrote to you last this has come my way in the course of reading: A number of men have commenced the translation of the Mishnah but have left well-nigh untouched the Gemara, which is the lengthier part of the

---

[1] p. 423, etc. [2] p. 456, etc.

prolixiorem Talmudis partem intactam fermè reliquerunt.[1] Mischnam solam tractatuum *Sava Kama* et *Middoth* notis illustratam edidit Constantinus L'Empereur; Mischnam codicis *Joma* Rob: Sheringamius Cantabrigiensis; Mischnam codicum *Schabbat* et *Eruvin* Sebast: Schmidius; Mischnam tractatuum *Sanhedrin* et *Maccoth* cum Gemaræ excerptis explicavit Jo: Coch; *Mass: Sota* cum excerptis Gemaræ et commentario doctissimo dedit Joh: Chris: Wagenseil; *Pirke Avot* edidere Paul: Fagius. Joh: Drusius. Franc: Taylerus, Joh: Leusdenius; *Mass: Beracot* post Paul Riccium, Sam: Clericus; *Mass: Schekalim* Joh: Hen: Otho in frontispicio Lexici Philol. Rabbinici; sex tractatus *Sebhackhim*, *Beracot*, *Nedarim*, *Nasir* *Schebhuot* et *Keritut* vertit Jo: Ulmannus A: 1663. Unius Capitis Talmudici *Chelec* Mischnam et Gemaram plene reddidit sermone vernaculo Christ. Gerson Recklichusanus conversus Judæus.'

Hactenus Pfeifferus in exercitationibus de Judæorum libris Exerc: 1. Th: 24.[2] Quæ cum inter legendum mihi nuper occurrebant non poteram non ad te transmittere etiamsi tibi fortè non ignota ut voluntatem in te meam significarem, utilemque me quovis pacto

---

Talmud.[1] Constantin L'Empereur published the Mishnah alone of the tractates *Sava Kama* and *Middoth*, illustrated with notes; Robert Sheringham of Cambridge, the Mishnah of the codex *Joma*; Sebastian Schmid, the Mishnah of the codices *Schabbat* and *Eruvin*; Jo: Cocceius [Koch] set forth the Mishnah of the tractates *Sanhedrin* and *Maccoth*, with extracts from the Gemara; Joh: Chris: Wagenseil presented *Mass: Sota* with extracts from the Gemara and a very learned commentary; Paul: Fagius, Joh. Drusius [van den Driessche], Franc: Taylor, Joh: Leusden, have [all] published *Pirke Avot*; Sam: Clark after Paul Ricius *Mass: Beracot*; Joh: Hen: Otho, *Mass: Schekalim*, prefixing it to the Lexicon Philol. Rabbinicum; Jo: Ulmann in 1663 translated six tractates, *Sebhackhim*, *Beracot*, *Nedarim*, *Nasir*, *Schebhuot* and *Keritut*. Christ. Gerson of Recklinghausen, a converted Jew, translated into the vernacular the whole Mishnah and Gemara of one Talmudic chapter, *Chelec*.'

Thus far Pfeiffer in his *Exercitationes de Judæorum libris*, Exerc: 1. Th. 24. When this recently came my way in the course of reading, although perhaps it may not be unknown to you, I could not but send it to you in order to indicate my goodwill towards you and to show myself useful in any way that I can; and therefore I think that this should be added from Neocous

---

[1] The Mishnah is the authoritative collection of the Jewish oral law; the Gemara a Rabbinic commentary on it.

[2] A. Pfeiffer, *Theologiæ . . . Judaicæ, atque Mohammedicæ . . . Principia Sublesta Fructus Pestilentes: hoc est, Exercitationes de Judæorum Libris*, etc., Leipzig, 168[illegible] L.L., no. 2289. In the translation I have given the modern forms of some of the translators' names from Bischoff, *Thalmud-Übersetzungen*.

præstare possim ideoque ex Neocori Bibliotheca Novorum librorum[1] hoc addendum censeo 'Mischna sive totius Hebræorum Juris, Rituum, Antiquitatum ac legum Orientalium Systema cum Clariss Rabbinorum Maimonidis et Bartenoræ commentariis integris. Quibus accedunt variorum Auctorum Notæ et Versiones in eos quos ediderunt codices Latinitate[a] donavit ac Notis illustravit Gul: Surenhusius Pars prima—Amstelodami excudunt Gerardus et Jacobus Borstius 1698. Folio habet paginas 332.

Hæc de Mischna sufficiant cujus te curiosum scio. Navarete et l Auteur que je serois bien aise de voir en Francois traduit de l'Espagniol. il y a des choses fort curieuses que je voudrois bien voir publièes dans une langue que j'entend.

Il m'a etè dit qu'on imprime a Paris les Voiages de M Carrè dans les quatre parties du Monde. Je vous prie de me marquer si c'est un recuile de voiages ou si ils sont les voiages du M Carrè meme et s'ils sont bons[2]

Mr Pigault à qui je vous a priè d'addresser les livers (que vous me faites la grace de m'envoier) pour les faire tenir a Mr Frankland, est de Calais et je vous prie de vous donner le pein de les envoier a Calais par le Messager. Je suis

Monsieur

Votre tres humble et tres oblige serviteur

J LOCKE

Je baise les mains a Monsieur Du Bos. J'ai nouvellement recue l'honeur de sa lettre obligeant ecrite à Beavais pour la quelle je pretend de le remercier au plutôt

Address: A Monsieur Monsieur Toinard chez Monsieur des Noyers devant l Espée royale dans la rüe mazarin à Paris

Endorsed by Toinard: 1. May 99.

[a] *Followed by* donatæ ac *deleted.*

Bibliotheca novorum librorum:[1] . . . So much for the Mishnah, in which I know you are interested.

---

[1] Ludolf Küster (1670–1716; *A.D.B.*), using the Greek form of his name Neocorus, in association with Heinrich Sike (Sikius), conducted the *Bibliotheca*, correctly *Bibliotheca Librorum Novorum*, 5 vols., Utrecht, 1697–9. L.L., no. 2077[a]. The notice to which Locke refers is for vol. i only of the edition by Surenhusius (6 vols., 1698–1703): iii. 838–53 (November–December 1698). This is the book mentioned by Du Bos on p. 601. For it see Bischoff, pp. 20–3. 'Orientalium' is Locke's error for 'Oralium'.

[2] p. 508. The book, in two duodecimo volumes, is noticed in the *Journal des Sçavans*, 31 August (pp. 652–63).

2581. JOHN CONYERS to LOCKE, 2 May 1699 (*2210, 2662*)

B.L., MS. Locke c. 7, ff. 63–4.

May. 2. 1699.

Sir

I receiv'd yours by which I find you are now convinc't of the mistake of your last Receipt, when Mr Clerke told me you were not apprehensive of it upon a Reveiw of your Papers, I was resolv'd not to trouble you with any letters about it, but leave it till I saw you and convince you by certaine proofs of Receipts: and in answer to what you Desire I paid Sir Fra: Masham the 16th of May last for you 25l,[1] and in September last I sent you 50l for which I have your Receipt, but to prevent future mistakes pray favour me with a Receipt particular to the 3rd of Nov: last[2] and I will returne this I had from Mr Clerke; I want some of your good advice for my wife[3] who really is often indispos'd in her health, and seems to have an ill habit of body: we are both your servants. and shall be glad to see you when you come to Town. Our services to Sir Francis and my Lady.

Sir Your very humble servant
JO: CONYERS.

Address: For Mr Locke [at Oates, by Joslyn, Bishops Stortford] free Jo: Conyers.
Postmarks: MY 2; GC
Endorsed by Locke: J Conyers 2° May 99[a]

2582. CORNELIUS LYDE to LOCKE, 2 May 1699 (*2560, 2679*)

B.L., MS. Locke c. 15, ff. 170–1.

2d may 99

Sir

Yours I Received of the 30th: March and doe hertely acknowledg your Kindnes to my son and Am sorry that he had not the oper-

[a] *There are also some money calculations written by Locke on the cover.*

[1] Conyers replies to a message sent through Clarke: p. 608.
[2] This relates to the Benefield mortgage: p. 24, etc.
[3] Mary, daughter of George Lee of Stoke Milborough, Salop.

tunety of seeing you before he Leaft the towne but I have desired him to writte to you and I hope you will asist him in his practis.[1] I had writt to you sooner but I wayted for your tenants Ladie dayes rent that soe I might send you the whole account but have not seene them yeat but as soone as I have theire account shall send you the whole account as to mary Dolemans Case shee is a verry sickly woman and verry Poore if you please to allow her some thing it wold be a verry sesonable charity if it were weekely or monthly as you thinke fitt, it ⟨were⟩[a] better then a sume at ons I Think with my hearty service I Am Sir Your much obligd friend and ser:

COR: LYDE

Address: These For Doct: Locke att mr: Pawlings overagainst the Plough in Little Lincolns feilds London

Postmark: MY 5

Endorsed by Locke: C: Lyde 2 May 99

2583. ABRAHAM HILL to LOCKE, 4 May 1699

B.L., MS. Locke c. 11, f. 208. Abraham Hill, 1635–1721; F.R.S. (member of First Council); a commissioner for Trade and Plantations 1696–1702: *D.N.B.*; Horsefield, nos. 58, etc.

London 4. May. 1699

Sir

Upon the publishing your last book, I believe you received so many thankes for it as a general benefit, that you did not misse a letter due from me for the favour of it, as a kind present,[2] had I any objections to make you should have bin sure to have heard of them. I hope this gentle weather puts an end to the winter, that our board may no longer want you, our company will soon grow lesse but the business doth not lessen—If you can without much trouble find the printed sheet intitl'd Remarks etc (mentiond p. 173, 2d

[a] *Word omitted by Lyde.*

[1] Dr. Samuel Lyde.

[2] Locke's second *Answer* to Stillingfleet. Hill is named in the distribution list for it.

Edit, in your book of lowering interest etc.)[1] pray doe me the favour to let me see it when you come to towne.

I am

Deare Sir

Your most humble and faithfull servant

ABR HILL

Endorsed by Locke: A: Hill 4 May 99

2584. LOCKE to PETER KING, later first Baron King, 5 May 1699 (2579, 2620)

B.L., MS. Locke c. 40, ff. 44–5. Answers no. *2578*.

Oates 5 May 99

Dear Cosin

I writ to you in my last that you should take care that the money of my Tally Should be lodged noe where for any consideration of advantage but where I may be able to call for it or have it at any time I shall need it, and I mention it now to you again because it mightily imports me that it should be soe, and to tell you that I fear Exchequer bills will not be for my turne. If it can noe where be placed soe at interest that I may be able to receive it or change the security at anytime into present money I had rather receive it in specie and let it lye dead by me till my occasions call for it rather than put it out of my reach. I would be glad to be informed why Exchequer bills that carry 5d per diem interest are thought surer than Bank bills that cary but 2d. But if it be the end of May before the Tally will be paid we may have time enough to consider, and at worst the money in cash will be noe harm. The remainder of the money in your Cosins hands[2] received for the million tickets with the bill I sent you upon Mr Churchill will furnish you for my payment the 10th instant of my East India Company subscription soe that you will not need to engage my Tally any way for that supply, at least to put the remaining £400 due upon it out of my power to have it at command

I thank you for the particulars of receits upon my account mentiond in your last I hope in your next I shall know the summ that was received for the million tickets. the sum that was received

[1] *Remarks on a Paper given in to the Lords*, probably 1691. No copy is known and the title is taken from Locke: Horsefield, p. 41 and no. 72.

[2] John or Thomas Freke.

upon my dividend at the Bank and by whom and also by whom my interest due at our Lady day from the East India company was received. I suppose it was £20.[1] These sums with the remainder of the million t⟨icke⟩t[a] money I suppose will goe pretty near the makeing up my payment for my subscription w⟨hich is⟩[a] to be made Wednesday or Thursday next, which I know you will take care of. I am

Dear Cosin

Your most affectionate Cosin and humble servant

J LOCKE

Though[b] I expected a letter from you to day yet it came soe late that I was fain to write to you before I received yours, which being now come has answered a good part of what I had above written. I am glad you have not yet fetched the Tally and that you doe not intend to make use of it for the next payment. My bill on Mr Churchill being for any summ not exceeding £100, you may take £20 or 25 upon or what else you shall have occasion for, and I see noe need of sending you a new bill on him. My Lady gives you her service and all our company

Address: For Peter King of the Middle Temple Esqr. To be left at Mr Potmans in the Middle Temple London

Postmark: MY 8

Endorsed by King: Mr Locke May. 5. 1699

2585. LOCKE to EDWARD CLARKE, 5 May 1699 (2575, 2586)

B.L., MS. Locke b. 8, no. 142. Printed in Rand, pp. 547–8.

Oates 5 May 99

Dear Sir

Haveing since my last to you thought again and again on your sons case and beleiveing it then wholy founded in his body as I doe still thinke it in part I lookeing back wards step by step as far as I know any thing of him placed the Original of it in the terrible disease he had when a Child at my Lady Kings.[2] I am glad to finde

[a] *Page torn.* [b] *The colour of the ink of this postscript is different from that of the letter.*

[1] The interest payable on the subscribers' stock: pp. 397, n. 1, 551. [2] No. *878*.

by yours of the second that you have found the immediate cause of this last dejection to be from some desponding thoughts of himself. But what is the cause of that despondency in this one of all your children when all the rest have vigorous and active minds? Must not that have its rise in the body and be oweing to something out of order there. I say not this that you should presently put him into a course of physick but to give you occasion to think. In the mean time apply all the quickening you can to his minde, ease and raise that all you can and trie how far it will worke, this is the easyest safest and best way upon many considerations if it will doe. There is noe thing now that presses for the other, the stop that is made gives us time to looke about. I write this confusedly and in much hast, our letters comeing not to day till late in the afternoon and giveing me not time to explain my self at large. For when I hear from you again I thinke I shall be able to satisfie you that if you shall thinke there is any need of physick it must not be in the ordinary method that is used in cases of Melancholy and therefor if he should, upon the unsuccesfullnesse of all the ease and comfort you and his mother can give to his minde, fall back again (which I hope will not be) and that you should think physick necessary. I would be glad you should hear me upon that subject before he take any thing or be put into any bodys hands But I wish he may need noe other physitians but you and his mother and other well advised and well adviseing friends. I am

Dear Sir

your most affectionate humble servant

J LOCKE

The inclosed open letter was put into my hands by Mr Harvey,[1] to whom it was written a neighbour parson, the only one about us that visits here. I thought it fit to send it you that you may doe in it as you judg fit

My service to Madame and all the yonge folks particularly with great kindnesse to your son

Pardon this scrible I shall loose this post if I end not and therefor you must excuse me to Mr Connyers that I writ not to him this post: If he speaks to you of me otherwise you need say noething to him, for I will write to him the next

[1] Probably Thomas Harvey, B.A., Cambridge, 1685; died in 1708; described in his will as 'of Laver Magdalen, Essex, clerk': Venn.

My Lady and our fires side (for there we are yet) greet you and yours. my service to the Batchelor

Endorsed by Clarke: Mr. Lock touching my sonn etc.: Received the 8th. May 1699. Answered the 9th.

2586. Locke to Edward Clarke, 8 May 1699 (2585, 2617)

B.L., MS. Locke b. 8, no. 143. Printed in Rand, pp. 548–9.

Oates 8° May 99

Dear Sir

Yours of the 2d I answered last post and hope that the successe of yours and Mrs Clarkes applications to your sons minde makes it not necessary to think of any of an other kinde. I shall be very glad that that may prove effectuall. according as I hear from you in your next you will have my farther opinion, and I shall be very much pleased If I can be any way serviceable in the case.

Mr Conyers was in the right there was a mistake in the receit I sent him by you. to rectifie it I beg the favour of you to exchange the inclosed receit for that which you formerly deliverd to him, and when upon the delivery of this he has given you back the other I beg the favour that you would tear it in two and send me one half of it inclosed in your next.

I shall not trouble you with the occasion of the inclosed to my Cosin Peter King. He will explain it to you better and shorter. If the forme be not right let it be mended and I will signe it when I come to town in the mean time the Bishops[1] and your hand may serve. I am

Dear Sir

Your most affectionate humble servant

J Locke

My Ladys and all the services here to you and yours. Mine to mrs Clarke and the yonge folkes

[1] Dr. Edward Fowler, the third trustee for Lady Masham.

2587. Richard Coote, first earl of Bellomont, to Locke, 12 May 1699 (*2270, 2614*)

B.L., MS. Locke c. 7, ff. 134–5.

N.york 12. of may 99.

Sir

Mr. Popple writes me word in his Letter of the 21. of October Last,[1] which arriv'd not here till the 16th. of Last moneth, the ship having been twenty weeks in the voyage, that you were so very kind as to direct the forming of the Representation that was made to the Lords Justices of England upon the memorials and evidences I transmitted to your Lordships against Colonel Fletcher;[2] and he writes you were pleas'd to Charge him to make me a Complement from you. which favours I acknowledge with all the thankfulnesse Imaginable; and will make it my Care and Study to deserve the Continuance of them.

you will see by my Letter to your board the Circumstances in which I now Stand.[3] I have the misfortune to succeed a man in this Government who not only has Left every thing in disorder by a Corrupt mannagement, but also did it with premeditation and design, as if he would bid defiance to the Government of England to Call him to account for his maladministrations, which are without number, for I every day discover new ones, which I am unwilling to trouble your board with, having already sent such volumes of accusations against him. I have hitherto bore up with a good spirit against the difficulties I have met with, but there are two things which make me very uneasy and will Jade me quite if I be not very speedily assisted by your Lordships of the Counsel of Trade; one is subsistence for the four Companies in the King's pay here, of which there is two years arrear due to them, and the Victuallers almost broke for want of their mony, and teazing me every day about it, so that I have no peace, nor Can I find fault with them, knowing what hardships they are put to for provisions for the Souldiers. I Can write my thoughts freely to you; how strange a management is it somewhere, that these souldiers should be so neglected when they are on the same establishment with the

[1] Apparently a private letter; not traceable in the *Calendar*.

[2] The Board of Trade to the Lords Justices, 19 October 1698: *Cal.S.P.*, *Col.*, vol. xvi, no. 904. Col. Benjamin Fletcher, 1640–1703; governor of New York 1692–7; of Pennsylvania 1692 (1693)–4; his conduct as governor of New York was bad: *Encyclopedia Americana*; *Calendars*.

[3] Probably his letter of 15 May: *Cal.S.P.*, *Col.*, vol. xvii, no. 384.

army in England, and if the thing be duly Consider'd guards are not more necessary at Whitehall even in time of war, then these souldiers are here at this time, 'tis this ununiformnesse that spoils all our businesse in England and here too. The second thing I Complain of is the want of good Lawyers on the bench and at the bar. The men that Call themselves Lawyers here are a Loose profligate people that usurp the profession and have never studied for it, one of 'em was Lately a dancing Master, another a glover; but what is worse than their Ignorance, they are all Jacobites and rank ones too, and do a world of mischief in poysoning the people and withdrawing their affection from the Government. I have no sort of help, and know not when I make a Slip in point of Law for want of good honest Lawyers to resort to for advice. The Secretary here[1] (who ought to be such a man as would be a pillar of the Government) is so very weak a man as he is totally unfit for businesse, and next door to an Ideot. In short I am left to stand singly on my own leggs. but if against next winter I Can be assisted with such men as my Lord Chancellor and your board may and I hope will send me, I doubt not to put this province and the rest that are under my government on a glorious foot, and make them abundantly more usefull to England than they ever have been: especially this province, which is more subject to the King's Government than the others, and Indeed by its scituation deserves more to be your Care than any other of the Plantations.

because I have writ at large about all things here to your board, I will not trouble you further, but referring you to that account; and desiring you will Confer with my Lord Chancellor how to give me speedy assistance and to redresse such things as I represent home to be wanting of rectification, I Conclude wishing you a perfect good health, which I presume may be said to be the only thing you want, and that you will believe me to be with a true esteem and respect

Sir

Your most humble and faithfull servant

BELLOMONT

Endorsed by Locke: L: Bellomont 12° May 99 Answered Nov. 29

[1] Matthew Clarkson: *Calendars*.

2588. Alexander Cunningham to Locke, 15 May 1699

B.L., MS. Locke c. 7, ff. 188–9. For the writer see no. 1435 n.

London 15th May 1699

Sir

Last night I had the honor of your's of the 12th having received one from you some days before: I have bin oblidged for some reasons to put of my Journey into Holland to the end of this moneth. this I do the more easily digest that I hope to have the happines to see you here before that time. I must beg the favor of you to return my most humble thanks to Sir Francis and My Lady for their Civilities to me. and to ask their pardons for me for not doing it sooner. I should be glad you would read Dr Allix's book[1] with care. the Learned here prefer it to all the books that have bin written on that subject. I have not had any leisure since I saw you to read any thing of that nature. I shall be sure to leave your two books, your picture[2] and Dr Sydenham of Natural Religion[3] with your Landlady. I have now obtained the Loan of Bishop Lloyds Letters.[4] I shall employ one to copy them for you. Monsieur Picque a Doctor of the Sorbonne of very great worth[5] is dead. the Bishop of Salisburys explication of the 39 Articles will be printed of about the begining of September.[6] I shall return My Ladys thanks to Col. Codrinton.[7] I had no hand in that present. so I am with all possible respect

Sir

Your most humble and most Obedient servant

Alex: Cunninghame

Address: For John Lock Esquire at Oates in Essex near Harlow
Postmarks: MY 20; IL
Endorsed by Locke: A Cunnighame 15 May 99

[1] *The Judgment of the Ancient Jewish Church against the Unitarians*, 1699. L.L., no. 76.

[2] Perhaps a copy of the portrait of Locke by Greenhill that was required in Amsterdam for the engraving by Pieter Stevens van Gunst (Thieme, *Lexikon*) that is prefixed to the first edition, 1700, of Coste's translation of the *Essay*. See further pp. 638, 668.

[3] 'Theologia rationalis', a short treatise on natural theology. It was not printed until 1848: *D.N.B.*

[4] The Noris–Pagi–Lloyd correspondence: no. *910*, etc.; p. 752.

[5] No. *489*; see also Burnet, *History of my own time*, 1833, ii. 397–8.

[6] See no. *2687*.

[7] Christopher Codrington, 1668–1710; governor of the Leeward Islands, 1699–1704: *D.N.B.* He gave Cunningham an annuity and bequeathed a hundred guineas to him to assist him in his 'great and usefull Labours . . . for the publick Benefit'; Cunningham probably helped him to collect books: Harlow, *Codrington*, p. 219.

2589. Dr. (later Sir) Thomas Molyneux to Locke, 15 May 1699 (2539, *2666*)

B.L., MS. Locke c. 16, ff. 88–9. Answers no. 2539.

Dublin: May the 15th. 1699

Sir

I should not have deferred so long making a gratefull Acknowledgement to You for the Favour of Yours of the 25th. of January, and those Valuable Presents I received since by Mr Churchil; Your Reply to the Bishop of Woster, and Your Treatise of Education; but that I waited for the Convenience of sending You my Harty Thanks for them by my good Friend Mr Burridge: who tho he has resolved positively for some while on a Journy for England, Yet did not determine the time till now. In the management of that Contraversy with the Bishop, I impartialy think You have all along the advantage; and which indeed must ever attend a Candid Inquierer after Truth writing against a Man that willingly or unwillingly serves a Party or Principles he is resolved to stick to: for Zeal, Pride, or Intrest never fail leading a Man how learned soever he may be, into undecent Follies and gross Absurdities. which You have sufficiently exposed, yet with all the Civility the Mater could possibly bear.

My little Nephew and I both are oblidged to You for Your Treatise of Education; in return we shal jointly endeavour to follow those Instructions You have so judiciously layd down, which I know his Father allways designed as his constant guides in the breeding of Him.

I have searched as You desired my Brothers papers and find among them that sheet of the Harmonies of the Evangelists, and have sent it by Mr Burridge who I hope will deliver it safe.

I must intreat You to take the trouble to assist Mr Burridge in procuring my Brother's Picture from Sir Godfrey Kneller,[1] who I believe has long since finished it; and I am not a little concerned that so lively a Remain of the Man I loved best in the World, should be in the hands of strangers and so long out of the Possession of

Sir

Your most faithfull obedient and humble servant

Tho: Molyneux

Endorsed by Locke: Dr Molyneux 15 May 99

[1] p. 489.

2590. LOCKE to SAMUEL BOLD, 16 May 1699 (*2567, 2602*)

The Museum, ii (1746), 205–9. There is no statement of provenance. The heading is 'An Original Letter from Mr. John Locke, to Mr. Samuel Bold, at Steeple'. I have suppressed the printer's italics. Answers no. *2567*; answered by no. *2602*.

The letter was included in Locke's *Works* first in the seventh edition, 1768 (vol. i, p. xv n.), and then, 'as corrected from the original', in the eighth, 1777 (iv. *645–*9), and later editions (the ownership of 'the original' is not stated; the divergences from the *Museum* text scarcely affect meaning and are not recorded here). It was reprinted by Robert Goadby (*D.N.B.*) in *The Moral and Entertaining Magazine*, vol. ii, 1778 (I have not seen this), and by J. H. Bransby (ibid.) in *The Christian Reformer*, ii (1835), 12–15. Goadby was perhaps a Unitarian; Bransby was for a time a Unitarian minister.

Sir

Yours of the eleventh of April, I received not till last Week. I suppose Mr. Churchil staid it till that Discourse, wherein you have been pleased to defend my Essay,[1] was printed, that they might come together; tho' neither of them needs a Companion to recommend it to me. Your Reasonings are so strong and just, and your Friendship to me so visible, that every thing must be welcome to me, that comes from your Pen, let it be of what Kind soever.

I promise myself, that to all those who are willing to open their Eyes, and enlarge their Minds to a true Knowledge of Things, this little Treatise of yours will be greatly acceptable and useful. And for those, that will shut their Eyes for fear they should see farther than others have seen before them, or rather for fear they should use them, and not blindly and lazily follow the Sayings of others, what can be done to them? They are be let alone to join in the Cry of the Herd they have placed themselves in, and to take that for Applause, which is nothing but the Noise that of Course they make to one another, which Way ever they are going; so that the Greatness of it is no manner of Proof that they are in the right. I say not this, because it is a Discourse wherein you favour any Opinions of mine (for I take Care not to be deceived by the Reasonings of my Friends) but say it from those, who are Strangers to you, and who own themselves to have received Light and Conviction from the Clearness and Closeness of your Reasonings, and that in a Matter at first Sight very abstruse, and remote from ordinary Conceptions.

[1] *Some Considerations*: p. 471, n. 1.

There is nothing that would more rejoice me, than to have you for my Neighbour. The Advantage that you promise yourself from mine, I should receive from your Conversation. The impartial Lovers and Seekers of Truth are a great deal fewer than one could wish or imagine. It is a rare Thing to find any one to whom one may communicate one's Thoughts freely, and from whom one may expect a careful Examination and impartial Judgment of them. To be learned in the Lump by other Men's Thoughts, and to be in the right by saying after others, is the much easier and quieter Way: But how a rational Man, that should enquire and know for himself, can content himself with a Faith or Religion taken upon Trust, or with such a servile Submission of his Understanding, as to admit all, and nothing else but what Fashion makes passable among Men, is to me astonishing. I do not wonder you should have, in many Points, different Apprehensions from what you meet with in Authors; with a free Mind, that unbiassedly pursues Truth, it cannot be otherwise. First, All Authors did not write unbiassedly for Truth Sake. Secondly, There are scarce any two Men, that have perfectly the same Views of the same Thing, till they come with Attention, and perhaps mutual Assistance to examine it. A Consideration, that makes Conversation with the Living, a Thing much more desirable and useful, than consulting the Dead; would the Living but be inquisitive after Truth, apply their Thoughts with Attention to the gaining of it, and be indifferent where it was found, so they could but find it.

The first Requisite to the profiting by Books, is not to judge of Opinions by the Authority of the Writers. None have the Right of dictating but God himself, and that because he is Truth itself. All others have a Right to be followed as far as I, *i.e.* as far as the Evidence of what they say convinces; and of that my own Understanding alone must be Judge for me, and nothing else. If we made our own Eyes our Guides, and admitted or rejected Opinions only by the Evidence of Reason, we should neither embrace or refuse any Tenet, because we find it published by another, of what Name or Character soever he was.

You say you lose many Things because they slip from you: I have had Experience of that myself, but for that my Lord Bacon has provided a sure Remedy. For as I remember, he advises somewhere, never to go without Pen and Ink, or something to write with; and to be sure not to neglect to write down all Thoughts of Moment that come into the Mind.[1] I must own I have omitted it often, and have often repented it. The Thoughts that come unsought, and as it were dropt into the Mind, are commonly the most valuable of any we have, and therefore should be secured, because they seldom return again. You say also, that you lose many Things, because your Thoughts are not steady, and strong enough to pursue them to a just Issue. Give me Leave to think, that herein you mistake yourself and your own Abilities. Write down your Thoughts upon any Subject as far as you have at any Time pursued them, and then go on again some other Time when you find your Mind disposed to it, and so till you have carried them as far as you can, and you will be convinced, that, if you have lost any, it has not been for want of Strength of Mind to bring them to an Issue; but for want of Memory to retain a long Train of Reasonings, which the Mind having once beat out, is loth to be at the Pains to go over again; and so your Connection and Train having slip'd the Memory, the Pursuit stops, and the Reasoning is neglected before it comes to the last Conclusion. If you have not tryed it, you cannot imagine the Difference there is in studying with and without a Pen in your Hand. Your Ideas, if the Connections of them that you have traced be set down, so that without the Pains of recollecting them in your Memory you can take an easy View of them again, will lead you farther than you can expect. Try, and tell me if it is not so. I say not this that I should not be glad to have any Conversation upon whatever Points you shall imploy your Thoughts about. Propose what you have of this kind freely, and do not suspect that it will interfere with my Affairs.

Know, that beside the Pleasure that it is to converse with a thinking Man and a Lover of Truth, I shall profit by it more than you. This you would see by the Frequency of my Visits, if you were within the Reach of them.

That which I think of Deut. xii. 15. is this, that the Reason why it is said, as the Roebuck and the Hart, is because Lev. xvii. to prevent Idolatry, in offering the Blood to other Gods, they were commanded to kill all the Cattle that they eat, at the Door of the Tabernacle, as a Peace-Offering, and sprinkle the Blood on the Altar; but wild Beasts that were clean, might be eaten, though their Blood was not offered to God (ver. 13.) because being killed before they were taken, their Blood could not be sprinkled on th

[1] I have failed to trace this.

Altar; and therefore it sufficed in such Cases, to pour out their Blood wherever they were killed, and cover it with Dust. And for the same Reason, when the Camp was broken up, wherein the whole People was in the Neighbourhood of the Tabernacle, during their forty Years Passage from Egypt to Canaan, and the People were scattered in their Habitations through all the Land of Promise; those who were so far from the Temple were excused (Deut. xii. 21,22.) from killing their tame Cattle at Jerusalem, and sprinkling their Blood on the Altar. No more was required of them than in killing a Roebuck or any other wild Beast; they were only to pour out the Blood and cover it with Dust, and so they might eat of the Flesh. These are my Thoughts concerning that Passage.

What you say about Critics and Critical Interpretations, particu-arly of the Scriptures, is not only in my Opinion true, but of great ise to be observed in reading learned Commentators, who not eldom make it their Business to shew in what Sense a Word has een used by other Authors; whereas the proper Business of a Commentator, is to shew in what Sense it was used by the Author n that Place, which in the Scripture we have Reason to conclude vas most commonly in the ordinary vulgar Sense of the Word or hrase known in that Time, because the Books were written, as ou rightly observe, and adapted to the People. If Criticks had bserved this, we should have in their Writings less Ostentation nd more Truth, and a great deal of Darkness now spread on the criptures had been avoided. I have a late Proof of this myself, ho have lately found in some Passages of Scripture a Sense quite ifferent from what I understood them in before, or from what I und in Commentators;[1] and yet it appears so clear to me, that hen I see you next, I shall dare to appeal to you in it. But I read e Word of God without Prepossession or Biass, and come to it ith a Resolution to take my Sense from it, and not with a Design bring it to the Sense of my System. How much that has made len wind and twist and pull the Text in all the several Sects of hristians, I need not tell you. I[2-] design to take my Religion from e Scripture, and then, whether it suits, or suits not any other enomination, I am not much concerned: For I think, at the last

[1] Locke was perhaps engaged on his paraphrases and notes on St. Paul's Epistles. ey were first published posthumously.

[2-2] In the printed text this passage is in inverted commas. It appears not to be uotation, but may have been distinguished in some way in the manuscript by cke or Bold.

Day, it will not be enquired, whether I was of the Church of England or Geneva, but, whether I sought or embraced Truth in the Love of it.⁻²

The Proofs I have set down in my Book of One Infinite Independent Eternal Being, satisfy me; and the Gentleman that design'd others,[1] and pretended that the next Proposition to that of the Existence of a Self-sufficient Being should be this, that such a Being is but One, and that he could prove it antecedent to his Attributes, viz. Infinity, Omnipotency, etc. I am since pretty well satisfied, pretended to what he had not, and therefore I trouble not myself any farther about the Matter. As to what you say on the Occasion, I agree with you, that the Ideas of Modes and Actions of Substances are usually in our Minds before the Idea of Substance itself; but in this I differ from you, that I do not think the Ideas of the Operations of Things are antecedent to the Ideas of their Existence; for they must exist before they can any ways affect us to make us sensible of their Operations, and we must suppose them to be before they operate.

The Essay is going to be printed again:[3] I wish you were near, that I might shew you the several Alterations and Additions I have made, before they go to the Press. The warm Weather that begins now with us, makes me hope I shall now speedily get to Town. If any Business draws you thither this Summer, I hope you will order it so, that I may have a good share of your Company No Body values it more than I, and I have a great many Things to talk with you. I am, Sir,

Your most affectionate Humble Servant,

J. LOCKE.

Oats, May 16, 1699.

2591. J.-B. DU BOS to LOCKE, 17/27 May [1699] (*2570*, *2600*)

B.L., MS. Locke c. 7, ff. 228–9. Printed by G. Bonno in *Revue de littératur comparée*, xxiv (1950), 498–9. Year from Locke's endorsement.

A Paris le $\frac{27}{17}$ de Ma

Je vous prie monsieur de ne point m'acuser de paresse si ja esté si lontemps sans macquiter de vos comissions. le long sejou

[⁻² See note on previous page.] [1] Hudde. [3] p. 591.

que jay fait a la campagne a esté la seule cause de ce retardement et jay travaillé a m'acquiter de ce que je vous avois promis des que jen ai esté de retour. jenvoié hier au carosse de Calais un paquet a vostre adresse, ou sont ces comissions, recomandé a monsieur Pigault pour monsieur le chevalier Frankland, et je viens descrire a ces deux messieurs pour les advertir de lenvoi que javois fait. je vous envoié cet hyver les ouvrages de monsieur Vernietes par le meme canal, je ne scais point si le paquet aura esté assez heureux pour parvenir jusques a vous. vous trouveré dans la cassete que je vous envoie.

la relation de la Gaspesie.

les decouvertes de monsieur de LaSalle.

les premieres observations envoiees des Indes.

les secondes observations venues des memes lieux.

des memoires de Mathematiques de lacademie des Sciences ce quil i en a de publié.[1]

monsieur Toinard i a joint les memoires du pere Le Comte[2] quil ma chargé de vous presenter, come de vous aseurer dans celle ci de son amitié et de ses respects.

lon a imprimé a Geneve un livre assez curieux. c'est un procez verbal de tout ce qui dit dans l'asemblee des comissaires qui travaillierent a la reformation de nostre code.[3]

un religieux Benedictin Francois, nommé don Bernard de Montfaucon le quel est presentement a voyager en Italie a trouvé a Venise un traittè de Lactance sur les Spectacles qui na pas encore esté imprimé.[4]

lon va imprimer chez Delaulne libraire de cette ville la vie DErasme par monsieur Joly.[5]

lon avoit imprime ici la premiere partie du Telemaque de monsieur de Cambray, mais le livre a esté suprim⟨é⟩[a] a sa demande.

[a] *Page torn.*

---

[1] The five books are identified on pp. 534–5, 538. [2] p. 339.

[3] Despite the date this refers probably to *Procés-verbal des conférences tenues par ordre du roi pour l'examen des articles de l'ordonnance civile du mois d'avril 1667 et de l'ordonnance criminelle du mois d'août 1670*, printed at Lyons, but with imprint Lille, 1697. Bourgeois and André, no. 6279.

[4] Bernard de Montfaucon, the patristic scholar (*N.B.G.*), was in Italy from 1698 to 1701. The notice is questionable: no treatise by Lactantius on this subject is known. The manuscript is not mentioned in Montfaucon's *Diarium Italicum*, 1702. Tertullian's *De Spectaculis* had been printed long since.

[5] Claude Joly, 1607–1700, religious writer; his life of Erasmus was not published: *Journal des Sçavans*, 8 February 1700 (pp. 106–9); *N.B.G.*

il i en a eu un assez grand nombre dexemplaires de vendus pour croire quil est presentement en Angleterre. cest un Roman en prose que cet Archeveque avoit composé pour le donner en themes au duc de Bourgogne, et il contient un recit des avantures de Telemaque qui va chercher Ulisse sous la conduite de Pallas deguisee en son gouverneur, rempli de preceptes et denseignements excellents pour un jeune prince, et tres propres a former un roy qui fut meme au gout des nations les plus difficiles sur ce sujet.[1]

Vostre tres humble et tres obeissant serviteur

DU BOS

Je pars apres demain pour aller faire un tour en Hollande ou lon me fera tenir les lettres que vous mescrire, ainsi si je puis faire quelque chose a vostre service, je vous prie de me lordoner.

Address: To Master Jhon Locke at master Pawlings overagainst the plough in little Lincolns Inn fields London

Postmark: MA 22

Endorsed by Locke: Du Bos 27° May 99 Answered Jun. 3

2592. WILLIAM POPPLE to LOCKE, 23 May 1699 (*2503, 2593*)

B.L., MS. Locke c. 17, ff. 231–2.

Whitehall. May, the 23th: 1699.

Sir,

Yesterday morning Mr Secretary Vernon desired an extraordinary meeting of this Board, which was made accordingly: The busyness being to consider of a Memorial given by the Spanish Ambassador against the Scotch Settlement on Darien, and a Paper drawn up by the Scotch in Defence of it.[2] They met again in the After noon, and again this morning, imploying the whole

[1] François de Salignac de la Mothe Fénelon, archbishop of Cambrai (*N.B.G.*), was tutor to Louis, duke of Burgundy, Louis XIV's grandson, from 1689 to 1699. A stolen copy of the manuscript of *Les Aventures de Télémaque* was bought by a Parisian bookseller, who published it in five successive parts as an anonymous work. Fénelon appears not to have been concerned in the seizure, which was ordered by the king. Further editions followed immediately. The first authorized edition was published in 1717: Cardinal L.-F. de Bausset, *Histoire de Fénelon*, 1850, iii. 12–15; A.-P.-P. Caron, *Recherches bibliographiques sur le Télémaque*, 2nd ed., 1840.

[2] *Cal.S.P.*, *Col.*, vol. xvii, no. 434: copies of the ambassador's and the Scottish Company's memorials.

time upon the same matter, and have yet come to no clear resolution what or in what manner to report upon it. The thing intended is to answer the Scotch reasons, but it is to be kept very private. Upon this occasion one that was not at the Board when the Report was made about Golden Island[1] findes many faults in that Report; which those who made it do not much offer to justify. This new busyness will put us much back in other things that we had in hand: And the next week mr P goes into the Country for two or three months, and Sir Ph does the like for eight or ten dayes.[2] If the King goe for Holland on Friday come sennight[3] as is talked (but doubtfully) and if you come not quickly, we might give over for want of a Quorum. I am

Sir,

Your most obedient humble Servant

WILLIAM POPPLE.

Endorsed by Locke: W: Popple 23° May 99 Answered 25

2593. WILLIAM POPPLE to LOCKE, 26 May 1699 (*2592, 2651*)

B.L., MS. Locke c. 17, ff. 233–4.

Whitehall. May, the 26th: 1699.

Sir,

I have your letters of the 22th and 25th. Our chief busyness here this week has been the answering of the Scotch Memorial about their settlement in Darien, the drawing of which has been Sir P M's work, and this day the Board have agreed to it.[4] The Method is in the way of a Discourse, not directed to any body, nor to be signed by any body. And in that manner I am to deliver it tomorrow to Mr Secretary Vernon. Yesterday there was a Representation signed and sent to the Council against the pardoning of young Mr Beckford who kill'd Commissary Lewis (an ancient Gentleman) at Jamaica, until he repair thither (for he is fled) and

[1] Golden Island is near the site of New Edinburgh, the Scottish settlement on the mainland, and was occupied by the settlers; for its position see the maps in Wafer, *New voyage*. I have failed to trace the report.

[2] John Pollexfen; Sir Philip Meadows.

[3] 2 June. William left Kensington late on Thursday, 1 June.

[4] *Cal.S.P., Col.*, vol. xvii, no. 456. Sir Philip Meadows. These proceedings are not recorded in the Board's journal.

be legally tryed for it.[1] A Letter was also writ to Mr Secretary in the nature of a Report upon a Petition about an Appeal from Barbadoes.[2] The Earle of Jersey brought to the Board a Paper given him by the French Ambassador, about spoiles committed by the English upon the French part of St Christophers, after they had notice of the Peace: Upon which an Instruction is to be added to the Body of those prepared for Colonel Codrington.[3]

The Board have now adjourned till Tuesday morning. That will be the last day of Mr P's attendance[4] at this time: For he has positively taken his Coach for Wedensday. Sir P M will be gone before: But he returns in the End of the Week. The E of B is certainly to be one of the Lords of the Admiralty:[5] So that he will not attend here much longer. Mr Bl:[6] goes with the King, who has fixt the day of his departure on Fryday next.

I can not but wish you could be here so as to wait upon him before he goes. But you know best your own Measures, not only for your health but every thing else. I am

Sir,

Your most obedient humble Servant

WILLIAM POPPLE.

Endorsed by Locke: W: Popple 26° May 99

2594. DR. PIETER GUENELLON to LOCKE, 6/16 June 1699 (*2520*, *2619*)

B.L., MS. Locke c. 11, ff. 87–8. The letter was not delivered until about October: pp. 681, 733.

Monsieur,

Celle cy vous sera rendue par Monsieur Posnicoff Gentilhomme Moscovite, que j'ay eu l'honneur de frequenter pendant son sejour

[1] Peter Beckford the third, grandfather of the author of *Vathek* (*D.N.B.*, art William Beckford, 1709–70), and Samuel Lewis, Commissary General: ibid., vol. xvii, nos. 435, 449, etc.

[2] Ibid., vol. xvii, no. 448.

[3] Jersey was appointed secretary of state on the 14th of this May. The ambassador's representation: ibid., vol. xvii, nos. 24, 282; the additional instruction nos. 440, 569. For Codrington see p. 624.

[4] Pollexfen.

[5] Bridgwater (no. *1981*) was appointed First Lord of the Admiralty by the commission of 31 May; and omitted from the commission of 9 June for the Board of Trade. He was succeeded by Thomas Grey, earl of Stamford (ibid.).

[6] William Blathwayt. As secretary at war he attended the king on his visits to the United Provinces.

en cette ville.[1] jay reconnu en luy beaucoup de scavoir et de merite et c'est ce qui luy a acquis les bonnes graces de son prince, qui l'a fait voyager a ses frais pendant plusieurs annees, et sejourner dans les plus celébres villes de l'Europe. il parle plusieurs langues et aime passionement la physique et les Mathematiques. je m'assure que vous vous ferez un plaisir de vous entretenir avec luy. Vostre reputation est si generale, que je puis dire sans vous flatter, qu'avant qu'il scut que j'usse l'honneur d'étre de vos amis, il me dit qu'ayant dessin de repasser en Engleterre, il souhaittoit avoir occasion de vous voir, en vous nommant le premier de ceux quil tacheroit d'y converser. je suis bien ayse de luy procurer ce bonheur, j'espere quil vous trouvera en santé, et en état de luy donner quelques moments de vótre loisir.

j'ay recu vótre derniere réponce a l'evesque de Worchester. je vous en remercie, je l'ay lue avec bien du plaisir, et quoy que je vous connoisse pour le plus pacifique et le plus doux de tous les hommes, vos arguments ne delaissent pas d'assommer votre parti, et seroit ce bien ce qui la fait mourir: au moins on le dit, et quil na pu survivre a la mortification dans la quelle vous l'avez mis.[2]

Je vous ay marqué dans mes precedentes combien je craignois pour mes enfans lors quils seront un peu plus avancez en age, et en etat de converser avec la jeunesse faineante de cette ville. l'oisiveté est icy a son comble, et des l'age de 17 a 18 ans la vie de la jeunesse n'est plus qu'une badinerie perpetuelle et nous voyons plusieurs qui apres avoir promis beaucoup ce sont tellement amollis dans ces sortes de conversations quils ne sont plus capables de rien apres: c'est ce qui ma determiné d'engager mon fils pierre pour sept ans dans le comptoir de Monsieur Meulenaer, un des premiers et plus celebres marchands de cette ville. je le connois de longue main, je suis fort de ses amis, il est pieux, sage, prudent, et quoy que fort opulent, il conserve dans sa famille les manieres de nos ancestres, c'est a dire quil vit sans faste. mon fils sera fort occupé chez luy, et je compte que cela le fera au plus rude travail. il n'aura que 21 ans a la fin de son engagement et j'espere qu'alors la connoissance quil se sera acquis du negoce, n'empeschera pas quil n'ayme les belles lettres, et en goutte autant qu'il en faut pour estre honnéte homme. je me flatte que vous approuverez ma con-

[1] Petr Vasilevich Postnikov (or Posnikov), *fl.* 1685–1710, doctor and diplomatist: Hirsch, *Aerzte*; Cambridge Bibliog. Soc., *Trans.* iii (1959–63), 392.

[2] Stillingfleet died on 27 March of this year.

duitte. je vous aurois consulté auparavant, si le temps me l'ut permis, l'occasion est survenue inopinement, et il faloit se resoudre, il n'y avoit plus de retour que dans quatre ans. La famille vous presente ses treshumbles respects, et je suis comme je le doibs,

Monsieur,

Vostre tres humble et tres obeissant serviteur

P. GUENELLON

d'amst. ce 16 juin 1699.

Endorsed by Locke: Dr Guenellon 16 Jun 99 Answered 4 Nov:

2595. JEAN LE CLERC to LOCKE, 8/18 June 1699 (*2544*, *2624*)

B.L., MS. Locke c. 13, ff. 129–30. Printed in Bonno, *Le Clerc*, pp. 112–15.

A Amsterdam le 18. de Juin 1699

Il y a longtemps, Monsieur, que je ne me suis donné l'honneur de vous écrire, à cause des occupations, que j'ai euës et qui me font souvent manquer aux devoirs les plus essentiels de la Civilité. Je profite présentement de l'occasion qui s'offre de Mr. Desmaiseaux,[1] qui est un fort honête homme, et dont mes amis de Geneve me disent toute sorte de bien. Il va en Angleterre, à dessein d'y chercher quelque emploi, car il n'y en a point pour les étrangers, dans le païs d'où il vient. Si quelcun de vos Amis avoit besoin d'un Gouverneur, pour ses enfans, je ne doute pas qu'on ne fût très-satisfait de lui. Comme je m'imagine que vous aurez présentement feuilleté mon Harmonie, vous voulez bien, Monsieur, que je vous en demande vôtre sentiment. La lecture de celle de Mr. *Toinard*, qui ne paroîtra peutêtre jamais, et l'étude particuliere que vous avez faite des Evangiles, vous ont mis en état de juger à fonds de cette sorte d'Ouvrages, et je m'en fie plus à vôtre goût, qu'à celui de tous les Théologiens du monde; qui cherchent leurs opinions dans l'Ecriture, plûtôt qu'ils ne la lisent pour former leurs sentimens. Mr. de la Mothe[2] m'a fait le plaisir de se charger de la peine de faire un paquet, pour le donner à un

[1] Pierre Desmaizeaux, *c.* 1673–1745; the future editor of *A Collection of Several Pieces*, 1720, part of Locke's literary legacy: *D.N.B.* He had come recently from Geneva.

[2] pp. 223, 649–50.

Marchand Anglois, où il y a deux de mes *Parrhasiana*,[1] l'un pour Vous et l'autre pour Madame Masham. J'ai été engagé dans cet Ouvrage, par un des principaux Magistrats de cette ville, qui souhaitoit de voir un peu étriller les Poëtes, et comme cela ne valloit pas la peine de faire un livre, j'y ai joint diverses autres matieres, et une petite défense à la fin pour moi même, contre une troupe de criards, qui ne méritoient pas qu'on leur répondit à part, par des Ouvrages exprès. Vous verrez que je me suis servi d'un endroit de vôtre derniere replique à Mr. *Stillingfleet*, contre une objection toute semblable.[2] On peut dire, de ce Prélat, ce qu'on a dit de Pompée, que s'il étoit mort de quelque maladie anterieure à la dispute qu'il a euë avec vous, il seroit mort beaucoup plus glorieusement.[3] L'édition des Dogmes Théologiques du *P.Petau* est fort avancée,[4] et elle s'achevera cette année. Le dessein de cet Ouvrage étoit de traiter de toutes les questions de Theologie, par les Peres, dont l'Auteur rapporte les sentimens au long. Mais le dessein n'est pas achevé, à cause de la mort de l'Auteur. Quoi qu'il soit extraordinairement aigre et emporté, c'étoit un homme d'une si grande lecture, qu'il y a toûjours à profiter dans ce qu'il dit, et qu'on peut le consulter dans le besoin, sur quantité de questions. Il lui manque aussi de la méthode et de la netteté, aussi bien qu'un peu plus de connoissance de Philosophie; ce qui auroit rendu son Ouvrage infiniment meilleur. Quoi qu'il en soit, c'est un bon livre, dans cette espece-là. On imprimera St.Augustin tout comme il est imprimé à Paris; mais il y aura un Tome de Notes à part, où seront celles d'*Erasme*, *de Vivès*, etc. Les Libraires, qui le veulent vendre en païs Catholique, comme parmi les Protesta⟨n⟩s,[a] on⟨t⟩[a] crû devoir en user ainsi. Ils ne veulent pas vendre à part la *Cité de Dieu*.[5] Un libraire qui vient s'établir ici a entrepris l'Histoire Byzantine du Louvre, en 23 Voll. in folio.[6] Je suis occupé à répondre à Mr. Cave, en 6. Lettres, qui seront adressées à quelques Prélats

[a] *Page torn.*

[1] *Parrhasiana ou pensées diverses sur des matières de critique, d'histoire, de morale et de politique. Avec la défense de divers ouvrages de Mr. L. C. Par Theodore Parrhase*, 1699. L.L., no. 773. Notice in *History of the Works of the Learned*, i. 515–22. A second volume followed in 1701: no. *2924*. An English translation of vol. i appeared in 1700: *T.C.* iii. 174.

[2] pp. 388–91, translating passages from Locke's second *Reply*, pp. 418–22.

[3] I have not found the saying.

[4] p. 541.

[5] pp. 542, 601–2. J. L. Vives, 1492–1540: *Enciclopedia universal ilustrada.*

[6] The as yet incomplete *Corpus Byzantinæ Historiæ*, Imprimerie royale du Louvre, 26 vols., 1645–1702. The prospective publisher, François Halma, abandoned the project: no. *2699*.

d'Angleterre, où je montrerai qu'il a dissimulé une infinité de choses dans les Vies de *Clement*, *d'Eusebe* etc. et le mal, que causent ces sortes de dissimulations dans l'Histoire Ecclesiastique. Je parlerai contre le sentiment de bien des factieux, qui parlent des Peres, sans les connoître; mais je ne dirai rien sans des preuves claires, et des raisons convaincantes.[1] J'ajoûterai à cet Ouvrage quelques autres Lettres, touchant *Philon*, où j'examinerai cette question, s'il doit à la lecture de Moïse ce qu'il dit du Logos, si *Platon* a pris des Prophetes etc.[2] Il y aura à la fin une Dissertation adressée à Mr. *Limborch* nôtre ami, *an semper sit respondendum calumniis Theologorum* etc.[3] J'espere que cet Ouvrage paroîtra avant l'Automne.

Je n'ai point encore vû Mr. Coningham, que l'on m'a dit devoir apporter ici vôtre portrait pour me le remettre.[4] Je le conserverai pretieusement et ce sera un des ornemens de mon Cabinet, que j'estimerai le plus, étant, comme je le suis, Monsieur, Vôtre très-humble et très-obeïssant serviteur

J LE CLERC.

Je vous prie, Monsieur, de faire mes civilitez à Mr. Coste.

Address: A Monsieur Monsieur Locke at Mr.Pawlings ⟨in⟩[a] little Lincolns inne fields, over against the plough London.

Endorsed by Locke: J: Le Clerc 18 June 99 Answered Jan. 8

[a] *Page torn.*

2596. PHILIPPUS VAN LIMBORCH to LOCKE, 13/23 June 1699 (2557, *2605*)

B.L., MS. Locke c. 14, ff. 127–8. Copy by van Limborch in Amsterdam University Library, MS. R.K., III D 16, f. 209. Printed from the copy, with omissions, in *Some Familiar Letters*, pp. 434–7. Answers no. 2557; answered by nos. 2615 and 2621.

Vir Amplissime

Literas tuas Vir eruditissimus[5] fideliter mihi ante duos circiter menses tradidit. Quæsivi occasionem Viro Magnifico eas ostendendi,

---

Excellent Sir,

The man of great learning[5] duly delivered your letter to me some two months ago. I sought an opportunity of showing it to the Magnifico. The

---

[1] The letters form pp. 1–215 of Le Clerc's *Epistolæ Criticæ et Ecclesiasticæ*.
[2] Letters vii–ix (pp. 216–320).
[3] pp. 361–421, 'Whether one should always reply to the calumnies of theologians'.
[4] pp. 624, 668.
[5] Samuel Crellius

quam commodissimam mihi præbuit D.Volderi Professoris Leidensis adventus: itaque ipso et D. van den Ende jurisconsulto comite conveni in ædes, in quas constitutum fuerat Virum Magnificum ad confabulandum venturum, ut ita inter sermones amicos uberior de tuâ epistolâ ejusque argumento institueretur collatio. Verum aderant aliqui, quorum sermonibus propositum meum turbabatur. Tandem de valetudine tuâ quæsivit: Ego hanc arripiens occasionem ipsi epistolam tuam tradidi; quam ubi legit, dixit, alias se de illius argumento locuturum. Cum ab ipso discederemus, modestè à se amoliebatur quas ipsi tribuis laudes, repetiitque se alias de epistolâ tuâ locuturum. Sic nos dimisit. Duo illi viri judicabant, ulterius eum non urgendum, me enim frustra fore; et per dilationem illam responsum honestè declinari. Postridie illis adfuit, verum de epistolâ tuâ nullum verbum. Credo jam, Volderum rem acu tetigisse, cum mihi dixit, credere se, Virum Magnificum omnes suas rationes jam aperuisse, aliudque nihil habere quod nobis suggerat; verum id dissimulare.

Ab Episcopo Salisburiensi literas valde amicas accepi; in quibus probare videtur quæ ego contra errantium persecutionem fusius ad ipsum scripsi; saltem ea non improbat: Conqueritur interim, sub illis quos potissimum hoc decretum spectat, latere homines,

---

arrival of Mr. de Volder, the Leyden professor, offered me a very suitable one and so, accompanied by him and Mr. van den Ende, the lawyer, I went to a house to which it had been arranged that the Magnifico should come for a talk, so that a fuller discussion of your letter and its argument might be set on foot in the course of a friendly conversation. But there were some persons present by whose conversation my plan was thrown into confusion. At length he inquired about your health. Seizing this opportunity I handed him your letter. When he had read it he said that he would speak about its argument at another time. When we were leaving him he modestly put from him the praises that you had bestowed on him, and repeated that he would speak about your letter some other time. In this way he dismissed us. The two men thought that he ought not to be pressed further, for I should be disappointed, and that by this postponement an answer was politely evaded. He was with them on the following day, but not a word about your letter. I now think that de Volder hit the nail on the head when he said to me that he thought that the Magnifico had already disclosed all his reasons and has nothing else to impart to us, but was pretending that it is not so.

I have received a very friendly letter from the bishop of Salisbury in which he seems to approve of what I wrote to him at some length against the persecution of those who go astray; at least he does not disapprove. Nevertheless he complains that hidden among those whom this edict chiefly has in

qui omnem revelationem impugnent: Quod etiam literarum tuarum lator mihi affirmavit, et doluit. Quod vero Episcopus addit, eos etiam promiscuam Venerem apertè defendere, hoc sibi inauditum prorsus ajebat. Reliqua illius epistolæ pietatem ac mansuetudinem spirant.[1] Ego datâ occasione respondebo.

Edidit Waeyenus Dissolutionem Defensionis meæ,[2] verum adeo dissolutam, maledicam, et nihil ad principale argumentum facientem, ut sponte evanitura sit. Ego nolo mihi cum tam impotenti adversario quicquam negotii esse. Ut exiguum aliquod specimen tibi referam: Carpit, quod dixi, indolem, quâ à litibus abhorreo, mihi esse innatam; atque propterea me criminatur, quod glorier de propriis meis viribus; se vero omnia gratiæ divinæ adscribere jactat; idque duabus aut tribus primis foliis plus sexies repetit: talis farinæ totus est liber. Si dixissem, me naturâ esse propensum ad odium Dei et proximi, fuissem illi orthodoxus: hanc sibi indolem naturalem agnoscit: actiones verum ejus ostendunt, regenerationem, quam sibi tribuit admodum esse imperfectam, partemque irregenitam multum prædominari regenitæ. D. Clericus edidit

---

view lurk men who impugn all revelation; the bearer of your letter also assured me of this and lamented it. But as to what the bishop added, that they openly defend promiscuous sexual intercourse, he said that he had heard nothing at all of that. The rest of the bishop's letter breathes piety and clemency.[1] I shall reply when there is an opportunity.

Van der Waeyen has published a refutation of my *Defensio*,[2] but it is so disjointed, scurrilous, and irrelevant to the principal subject, that it will vanish of its own accord. I do not want to have anything to do with so feeble an adversary. To give you a small example: He carps at my saying that I have an inborn disposition whereby I hate disputes, and on that account he charges me with bragging about my own strength, whereas he boasts that he ascribes everything to the grace of God; and he repeats that more than six times in the first three or four leaves; the whole book is of such a make. If I had said that I am inclined by nature to hatred of God and my neighbour I should have been orthodox for him; he recognizes this as his natural disposition; but his actions show that the regeneration which he bestows on himself is very imperfect and that the unregenerate part greatly predominates over the regenerate.

Mr. Le Clerc has published his *Parrhasiana* in French. He discusses various

---

[1] See pp. 424, 460. An extract from Burnet's undated letter is printed in Clarke and Foxcroft, pp. 347–8.

[2] *Stephani Rittangelii Veritas Religionis Christianæ in Articulis de Trinitate et Christo ex Scriptura, Rabbinis et Cabbala probata. Præfixa est Johannis van der Waeyen Limborgianæ Responsionis Discussio*, Franeker, 1699. For the earlier attack see pp. 466–7.

Gallicè sua Parrhasiana, in quibus de variis disserit, et paucis etiam hunc hominem perstringit: Verum accuratiorem illius refutationem Latinam brevi editurus est.[1] Prodiit etiam alterius docti viri tractatus, quem tibi in Angliâ ostendit:[2] Quænam de illo aliorum futura sint judicia brevi audiemus. Multa supponit tanquam certa quæ mihi incertissima sunt, aliis falsa habebuntur.

Legi nuper Cambdeni Historiam Angliæ sub Elizabethâ, in cujus parte II. anno 1579. hæc verba reperi: *Execranda Matthæi Hammonti impietas, quæ in Deum Christumque ejus Norwici hoc tempore debacchata est, et cum illius vivicomburio, ut spero, extincta, oblivione potius est obruenda, quam memoranda.*[3] Velim Cambdenus paulò distinctius impietatem illam indicasset, ut de criminis, quod tam horrendo supplicio vindicatum est, atrocitate constare possit. Scimus innoxios quandoque errores à Theologis blasphemias et impietates execrandas vocari, ut crudelitati quâ in dissentientes sæviunt prætextum quærant. Frustra ego hactenus in autoribus, qui

---

things in it and even censures this fellow in a few words; but he will shortly publish a more elaborate refutation of him in Latin.[1]

A treatise by another learned man, which he showed you in England, has also appeared.[2] We shall hear shortly what other people think of it. He assumes that many things are certain that to me are very uncertain and that will be held false by others.

I have recently read Camden's History of England under Elizabeth, and found in part ii, in the year 1579, these words: 'The execrable impiety of Matthew Hamont, which raged furiously against God and His Christ in Norwich at this time and which was, as I hope, ext inguishedby his burning alive, ought to be buried in oblivion rather than recorded.'[3] I wish that Camden had disclosed that impiety more precisely so that one could be certain about the atrocity of the crime that was punished by so horrible a punishment. We know that harmless errors are sometimes called blasphemies and execrable impieties by theologians in order to get a pretext for the cruelty with which they rage against dissentients. I have so far sought in vain for a more precise history of this Hamont in the authors whom I have at hand; I do not doubt, however, that it can be found in English writers.

---

[1] Le Clerc does not mention van der Waeyen by name in his *Epistolæ Criticæ et Ecclesiasticæ*.

[2] Probably S. Crellius's *Cogitationes*: p. 650.

[3] William Camden, *Annales Rerum Anglicarum et Hibernicarum regnante Elizabethâ*, Leyden, 1625; etc. For Hamont see *D.N.B.*; Locke quotes Holinshed's account of the proceedings: pp. 695–6.

Van Limborch made this and similar inquiries below in preparation for a book which he did not publish, 'Reformatorum de poena haereticorum sententia': chapter headings in des Amorie van der Hoeven, *De Joanne Clerico*, etc., pp. 146–52; Barnouw, *Van Limborch*, p. 48.

mihi ad manum sunt, exactiorem hujus Hammonti historiam quæsivi: Non dubito tamen, quin ea in Scriptoribus Anglis reperiri possit. Si sine tuo incommodo explicatiorem illius narrationem mihi suppeditare queas, rem feceris mihi longè gratissimam. Plura illius generis collegi, quæ in ordinem redigere statui, non ut alios traducam, sed ut omnes à sævitia in dissentientes quantum in me deterream.

Guenellonus noster plurimam tibi salutem scribi jussit. Literas traditurus est nobili Moscovitæ ad te perferendas, qui propediem hinc in Angliam trajiciet: quod tibi significari voluit.[1] Salutant te ac Dominum et Dominam Masham totamque familiam, uxor ac liberi. Francisci Masham epistola mihi perplacet, sed jam non est respondendi otium: à tali indole egregia quævis exspecto. Nominatim illi, ut et D. Cost, salutem dices a me

Tui Amantissimo
PHILIPPO A LIMBORCH.

Amstelodami 23 Junii

9
16 99
12

D.Clericus per mercatorem Anglum duo Parrhasianorum suorum

If you can without inconvenience supply me with a more extensive narration of it you will do me the greatest possible favour. I have collected several things of that sort which I have decided to put in due form, in order not to traduce others but, so far as in me lies, to deter all men from cruelty against dissentients.

Our friend Guenellon bade me send you his best respects. He will deliver to a noble Muscovite,[1] who will shortly cross from here to England, a letter to carry to you; he wanted this to be notified to you. My wife and children send greetings to you and to Sir Francis and Lady Masham and the whole family. Francis Masham's letter pleases me greatly, but I have no leisure to answer it at present; I expect something extraordinary from such a disposition. Please greet him expressly from me, as also Mr. Coste.

Your most affectionate
PHILIPPUS VAN LIMBORCH

Amsterdam 23 June
1699

Mr. Le Clerc has sent you two copies of his *Parrhasiana* by an English

---

[1] Postnikov: pp. 634–5.

exemplaria, et per Gallum quendam[1] epistolam ad te misit. Te, ac Dominam Masham plurimum salvere jussit.

Address: For John Locke Esqr. at Mr. Pawlings overagainst the plough in Little Lincolns Inne feilds Westminster

Postmark: IV 17

Endorsed by Locke: P: Limborch 23 Jun 99 Answered Sept. 5

---

merchant, and a letter by a certain Frenchman.[1] He bade me give you and Lady Masham his best regards.

2597. Dr. Robert South to Locke, 18 June 1699 (2314, 2645)

B.L., MS. Locke c. 18, ff. 171–2.

Sir

That my thanks to You for your worthy Present, and Learned Answer to Stillingfleet Comes so late I cannot so much deprecate as a fault, as account it the Unhappy Result of my Circumstances and occasions, Which often force me from Businesse and Studyes more Entertaining to such as are more Pressing, though lesse Valuable and Desireable.[2]

You were pleased of your great modesty to allow me to peruse your Excellent book at my leisure hours[a] and what in modesty you allowed, I have bin forced by Necessity to practice. Your Writeings (with me at least) still requireing Totum Hominem,[3] and I doubt not, with other Readers too; So entirely do I find the Intention[4] of my mind taken up when I imploy it about any of your Philosophicall Discourses. I cannot sufficiently commend the Closenesse of your Thoughts and Reasoning, and your admirable Sagacity and Exactnesse in searching into and sifting every thing that your Adversary sayes; so that nothing ever escapes You; which must needs render such a loose Writer as Stillingfleet, a very unequall match for such an Antagonist.

[a] *Word interlined.*

---

[1] Desmaizeaux: p. 636.

[2] Locke's second *Reply* to Stillingfleet was published in November 1698: p. 505. South was a prebendary of Westminster; he was aged 64 and his health may have been bad.

[3] Literally 'the whole man'. Apparently not classical.

[4] Application or straining (of the mind): *O.E.D.*; Locke, *Essay*, I. xix. 1, etc.

When I had gone over but the Half of your Book, The Answer which I still gave to Such as asked my Judgment of it (as Severall did) was, That you had baffled him to Dirt; and I spoke it from my very Heart; so that I think he made a Vertue of Necessity by Dying before that Should be expected from Him, which Could never have bin done by Him.[1]

It is hard I confesse to give any Part of your book any Considerable Preference to the rest (Each of them haveing its due and Proper Perfection) yet methinks you presse and drive him to the Wall in a more than ordinary manner, where you Argue about the Capacity of matter's haveing a faculty of Thinking added to it, by the Allmighty Power of god, had he So thought fitt: and You expose him not a little from p. 420 to 430. Where you manifestly prove against Him. That He suspends the Credit of the Divine Testimony (in a great degree at least)[a] upon the precedeing Evidence of Reason; the Scandal of which will hardly be Cleared off from Him in Hast: And what you have further alleaged from some of the Ancients, and particularly from Tully and Virgil,[2] concerning the materiality of a Spirit (as they supposed) is, what I cannot see will be Easily answered or Avoided.

Upon the whole matter I sincerely beleive This to be One of the Exactest books you have wrote: and may well stand Second to the Essay itself. Which (to renew my former request) I still think it extremely for the Benefitt of Rationall Learning, and the Advantage of your own Reputation, were it translated into Latine: and none so fitt as Somebody who together with a good Latine Style has a great deal of Academicall Leisure to Enable him to performe so Noble a Work: Which neither must nor Can be done of a Suddain

I have severall times attempted to give my se⟨lf⟩[b] the Happinesse of Seeing You; but you were still out of Town: Which has made me often Wish, that I had an Abode nearer You, that so I might have the felicity of frequently seeing and Converseing with You. But that is an Enjoyment not to be thought of by One so placed in the World as I am. and shortly (according to the Course of Nature) to goe out of it.

In the mean time, in a due esteem of your great Meritt, and Spreading fame, So justly acquired by your Learned Workes, as

[a] *Closing bracket supplied.* [b] *Page torn.*

[1] Stillingfleet died in March: p. 635. [2] pp. 431–41.

well as in a deep sense of that particular Kindnesse and respect, which you have bin all along ready to Show me. I remain

Worthy Sir

Your faithfull obliged friend, and most humble servant

R SOUTH

Cavesham. 18 June 99.

Address: For his worthily esteemed friend John Lock Esq at Oates. Essex These

Endorsed by Locke: Dr South 18 Jun. 99

2598. SAMUEL LOCKE to LOCKE, 20 June 1699 (*2616*)

B.L., MS. Locke c. 14, ff. 199–200. The writer is mentioned already in nos. 813, *2419*. He was perhaps a second cousin of Locke, but the relationship cannot be established. In 1695 he was living in St. Margaret Pattens parish with his wife, four daughters, and four sons, John (no. *2502*), Samuel (no. *2827*), Charles, and James. He was a director of the Bank of England in 1697–8. At the meeting of the subscribers of the £2,000,000 loan on 28 July 1698 he was appointed one of their trustees, who were to be the managers when they became the New East India Company: *Cal.S.P., Dom.*, 1698, pp. 369–70 (in no. *2638* he is called a director); his letters to Locke suggest that his principal interest was in the new company. He died in 1715; at that time he owned land in Bedminster, Somerset (no. *109* n.), and Henbury, Gloucestershire, both within 5 miles of Bristol: *London Inhabitants within the Walls*; *Notes and Queries*, clxxix (1940), 58. All four sons probably became Turkey merchants: *The Universal Pocket Companion*, 1741, p. 104. In this correspondence the writer signs himself Locke rather more frequently than Lock.

Honoured Sir

Just as I was goeing out of Towne. mr Bonville brought me the favor of your Letter of 17th: instant. with one for my son John whome I pray God to give him Life. to receive those Cordiall lines full of the most obliedging and affectionate regards to his Person and health: wherein Sir you have highly honnourd him. (and mee also). I am sure It will be Extreame welcom to him and as much esteem'd, to finde such good directions boath for the man-nagment and Conservation of his health to Come from a Person of your worth, what can be more obleedging upon him than to make you the greatest acknowledgment in the world for so great a favor? I also pray that the hapinesse of your Lyfe may be Con-tinued to the Kingdom: and that my son John may Returne to make you his personal acknowledgment for so great a favor.

which in the meantyme I hope you will receive from him at Surratt at the Returne of the ships. of which wee intend to dispatch one away in 14 days or 3 weeks at furthest. and another for the Coast of Coromandel and a third for China.[1] from whence one aryved Last weeke with the inclosed Cargo which Cost £22000 starling; and by the modestest Computation will yeild at the sale £75. to £80000 starling.[2]

Sir as to the wine. being but a Taste. I shall be well paid for it if you will please but to accept of it. and Excuse me from giveing you an account of the Cost;[3] the next parcell you shall please to Commande I'le submit to your determination. and shall on all occations attend and Esteeme your Commands. Being Sir

Your most affectionate humble servant and Cossin

SAM: LOCK

Rood Lane 20 June 1699

Address: To John Lock Esquire att Mr. Paulins In Little Lincolns Innfeilds

Endorsed by Locke: S: Locke 20 Jun 99

2599. MRS. ELIZABETH BERKELEY, later Burnet, to LOCKE, 27 June [1699] (*2556*, *2604*)

B.L., MS. Locke c. 3, ff. 220–1. The year from Locke's endorsement.

Sir

I came in last night presently after you were gon, but was loth to trouble you to return; I go as I purpose to morow very early; if you have thought of calling here this day let me know near the time, that I may be sure to be at home; if you are otherwise disposed I hartely wish you a long health, and hope if it please God to meet you again in Town next sumer, I'm satisfyed your time is so constantly imployed to the good of others that your life is greatly to be desiered by many: I'm sure it is by

Sir

Your Obliged servent

E. BERKELEY

June: 27:

Address: To Mr Locke

Endorsed by Locke: E: Berkeley 27 Jun 99

[1] For the three ships see Bruce, *Annals*, iii. 331–2.

[2] Perhaps the unnamed interloper mentioned by Luttrell, 6 and 8 June.

[3] Two dozen quart and four dozen pint bottles were delivered at Pawling's house on 16 June: B.L., MS. Locke c. 14, f. 198.

2600. J.-B. Du Bos to Locke, 27 June/7 July [1699] (*2591, 2612*)

B.L., MS. Locke c. 7, ff. 230–1. Printed by G. Bonno in *Revue de littérature comparée*, xxiv (1950), 500–1. Year from Locke's endorsement.

Damsterdam Le 7 de Juillet

Jamais monsieur nouvelle ne ma fait autant de plaisir que celles que monsieur Cuninghuam ma aprises du bon estat de vostre santé, dont persone ne souhaitte la continuation plus que moy.

jay lu quelque chose du livre de monsieur Alix dans lexemplaire dont vous avé fait present a monsieur Le Clerc.[1] Si l'anciene Synagogue revenoit au monde je pense quelle seroit aussi surprise des lumieres quil lui atribue que le seroient bien des autheurs anciens de se voir tant desprit dans les remarques de leurs comentateurs.

je crois que monsieur Le Clerc vous aura envoié un exemplaire de ses Parhasiana ou pensee critiques sur divers sujets. il i a de bonnes choses dans le[a] livre, mais aussi des fautes dans les quels je métone quil soit tombé entre autres celle de la page 136 ou il fait mal a propos le procez a Vittorio Siri, en entendant de la naissance de Louis 14 ce que l'autre dit tres distinctement de sa conception.[2]

monsieur Toinard vous aura mandé sans doute quil aprend Langlois, quand je suis parti de Paris il estoit deja capable dune cinquieme classe. il est encore trop jeune pour avoir besoin de lexemple de Caton pour le justifier.[3] si lon lui peut reprocher quelque chose, cest lui qui a tousjours aimé les lettres d'avoir negligé si lontemps une langue dans la quelle il i a tant dexcellents livres.

un libraire de cette ville imprime en latin les pieces du procez pendant a Rome entre les Jesuites et les autres missionaires de la Chine sur les ceremonies nationales que lon peut permettre aux Chretiens. le livre sera curieux par la discussion des dogmes et de la religion de ces peuples.[4]

[a] *Or* ce

---

[1] pp. 624, 660.

[2] Siri, in the passage quoted by Le Clerc, describes how on a December night Louis XIII and Anne of Austria slept together, and continues, 'notte fortunatissima per la Francia, perche per un intrecciamento di circostance si stupende, s'infantò il Dolfino'.

[3] Cicero, *Cato Maior de Senectute*, viii. 26.

[4] *Historia Cultus Sinensium seu Varia Scripta de Cultibus Sinarum, inter vicarios apostolicos Gallos aliosque missionarios, et patres Societatis Jesu controversis, oblata Innocentio XII* . . . ,

nous venons de recevoir de Rotterdam un livre intitule traitté historique de la theologie mistique. le stile emporté de l'autheur fait que tout le monde latribue a monsieur de Jurieux.[1]

un libraire de ma conoisance rimprime ici le Saint Cyprien d'Oxford et les *Dissertationes Cyprianicae* de monsieur Dodwell.[2] Si vous conoisé cet autheur vous lui fairé plaisir de len avertir a fin quil envoie ici les additions quil auroit a faire joindre. je me chargeré de la chose sil me veut l'envoier.

Jespere de rester encor ici trois semaines et si ji puis vous i estre utile adressé moy vos lettres chez monsieur Philibert.[3]

Vostre tres humble et tres obeissant serviteur

DU BOS

Address: Poste D'angleterre. To Master Jhon Locke at Master Pawlings over against the plough in little Lincolns Inn fields London.

Postmark: IY 3

Endorsed by Locke: Du Bos 7 Jul. 99 Answered 7

2601. PIERRE COSTE to LOCKE, 29 June 1699 (*2480*, *2609*)

B.L., MS. Locke c. 7, f. 148. Printed by G. Bonno in *Revue de littérature comparée*, xxxiii (1959), 170–3.

Monsieur

J'ai bien de petites choses à vous mander. Je vous en avertis par avance, afin que vous vous épargniez la peine de les lire si vous le trouvez à propos. Je commencerai par ce qui vous regarde de plus près, c'est à dire par les citations ou renvois que j'ai ajoutez en quelques endroits de vôtre Livre.[4] Pag. 131 §. 23. which in regard of +Volition. +Voyez ce qu'il faut entendre par *Volition* et *Volonté*, comme il a été expliqué cy-dessus §. 5. et §. 15. C'est un

Cologne, 1700; a continuation, 1700. The publisher is Jean Louis de Lorme, *c.* 1666/70–*c.* 1724/6; publishing in Amsterdam 1694–1711; later resident in Paris: van Eeghen, i. 15–20, etc.; vol. ii, nos. 57–8. L.L., nos. 688–9.

[1] *Traité historique contenant le jugement d'un Protestant sur la théologie mystique, sur le Quietisme* . . ., 1699. It is generally attributed to Jurieu.

[2] The Oxford edition of Cyprian's *Opera* was published in 1682: no. 633; Dodwell published his *Dissertationes* in 1684. The present edition was published by J. L. de Lorme in 1700: van Eeghen, vol. ii, no. 59; S. Morison and H. Carter, *John Fell*, 1967, pp. 222, 224–5.

[3] Jean Philibert: Lüthy, *La Banque protestante*, i. 86 n.

[4] The *Essay*. Coste cites the third edition here. This is shown by the citation p. 123, § 2, which is to a wrongly numbered page; in the second edition it is correctly numbered p. 121.

avis que j'ai crû nécessaire en cet endroit, mais peut-être qu'un Lecteur Anglois n'en aura pas besoin.

Pag. 132. §. 25 in fine: + before taken notice of. + §. 23.
Pag. 134. §. 32. + *that it being deferr'd.* + Proverb. XIII. 12.
——— ibid. + *Give me Children.* + Gen. XXX. 1.
Pag. 135. §. 34. + *It is better to marry.* + 1. Cor. VII. 9.
Pag. 138. §. 41. + *Eye hath not seen.* + 1. Cor. II. 9.
Pag. 146. §. 63. lig. 1. + *as has been said.* + Sup. §. 58.
Pag. 192. §. 5. lig. 1. + *as has been shewn.* + Pag. 123. §. 2. et pag. 138. §. 42.

Voilà tout pour le présent. Si je fais d'autres renvois, je vous en avertirai aussi-tôt.

Dans le paquet que vous avez eû la bonté de me faire tenir il y a pour vous *le mois de May* de la Republique des Lettres,[1] et un Dictionnaire des Antiquitez Greques et Romaines,[2] que vous m'aviez chargé de vous faire acheter.

Mr. Holgat s'est chargé d'un *Parrhasiana* que Mr. Le Clerc vous envoye. Nous n'avons pas encore ouï dire qu'il soit arrivé.

On m'écrit de Hollande qu'un jeune homme françois, nommé Mr. Desmaiseaux est parti pour l'Angleterre et qu'il vous porte une Lettre de Mr. Le Clerc. Ce jeune homme vient chercher quelque condition. Il a étudié trois ou quatre ans à Geneve. Il est, dit-on, assez raisonnable, et nullement esclave des opinions de ses Maitres. Il a appris à mon Ami[3] qu'on avoit rimprimé à Geneve votre Livre de l'Education des Enfans avec les additions.[4] Le Traducteur est, dit-on, un homme de peu de jugement, comme il paroit par ces deux beveuës: Dans l'endroit où vous conseillez de faire lire aux Enfans *Raynard the Fox*, il a mis à la marge, on peut donner aux Enfans les Fables et les *Contes* de la Fontaine.[5] C'est l'entendre. Dans un autre endroit où vous conseillez de donner aux Enfans quelque Catechisme où les principes de la Religion Chrétienne soient proposez dans les propres termes de l'Ecriture, il indique en marge le *Catechisme de Drelincourt*[6] qui est tout rempli de méchante

[1] The *Nouvelles de la republique des lettres*, edited by Jacques Bernard (nos. *1329* n., *1402* n.) from 1699 to 1710. Locke mentions this issue on p. 747.

[2] Presumably P. Danet, *Dictionarium Antiquitatum Romanarum et Græcarum*, Paris, 1698.

[3] Lagier de la Motte: p. 223; see below.

[4] *Nouvelles instructions pour l'education des enfans*, 'A Amsterdam Chez Jaques Menassiou', 1699.

[5] The *Contes* were put on the Index in 1703.

[6] Charles Drelincourt, 1595–1669. The earliest known edition of his *Catéchisme* was published in 1662; the latest, in 1754: Haag.

controverse. D'ailleurs ce beau faiseur de Notes écrit fort mal. Il s'est hazardé de faire une Préface qui n'est, dit-on, qu'un continuel galimathias.

Mr. Crellius est à Amsterdam. Depuis quelque temps il a envoyé à Mr. Furley à Rotterdam deux ou trois exemplaires d'un Livre qu'il a fait imprimer depuis peu, afin qu'il vous les fit tenir. Ce Livre est intitulé, *Cogitationes Novæ de primo et secundo Adamo, examini Eruditorum compendiosè expositæ*. Il y a ajoûté un petit Ecrit qu'il avoit composé en Allemand en faveur d'une Dame, intitulé *Consideratio efficaciæ passionum et mortis Jesu-Christi*, etc.[1] Le tout ne fait que douze feuilles en petit 8°. comme la Philosophie de Mr. LeClerc.[2] Je vous mande ces particularitez, parce que mon Ami a été chargé du Libraire qui a fait imprimer cet Ouvrage, de faire proposer à Mr. Churchill de luy prendre des exemplaires de ce Livre en luy donnant des livres Anglois. Il se nomme Petsol,[3] pauvre homme, chargé de famille, Unitaire et du même païs que Mr. Crellius. Il s'est attaché à corriger des Livres depuis 9 ou 10 ans. On ne s'enrichit guere à ce Mêtier. Il s'est avisé de joindre la librairie à la correction. Il traduit aussi des Livres Anglois en Latin. Mr. Crellius vous prie de luy rendre service dans cette occasion. On peut assurer Mr. Churchill que personne n'a eû encore des exemplaires de ce Livre. Si Mr. Churchill vouloit faire quelque troc avec ce Libraire, il n'a qu'à écrire et addresser sa lettre à mon Ami, *a Mr. De la Motte op de Lawrier gracht in de Goude Appel*[4] *pour rendre à Mr. Petsol, à Amsterdam*. Ce même Libraire fait imprimer un Livre d'environ 28 feuilles in 8° qui est prêt à sortir de la presse, dont voici le titre, *Disceptatio de Verbo vel Sermone Dei cujus creberrima fit mentio apud Paraphrastas Chaldæos. Accedit bilibra veritatis et rationis adversus Rittangelium.*[5] Si Mr. Churchill vouloit des exemplaires de cet Ouvrage, on luy en enverroit en même temps. Mr. Crel⟨lius⟩[a] a enfin reçu

[a] *Page torn.*

---

1 Samuel Crellius. In the main title 'expositæ' is a slip for 'propositæ'. The book was published in Amsterdam with the year as 1700. L.L., no. 884.

2 The *Opera Philosophica*, 1698: p. 168, etc.

3 Sebastian Petzold, d. 1704. His name was originally Rawicz, and he was formerly in Berlin; his earliest publications date from this year: van Eeghen, iv. 38–40.

4 The house with another occupant is mentioned in no. *1940*.

5 The title of the publication is *Bilibra Veritatis . . . Præmissa est Disceptatio de Verbo vel Sermone Dei . . .*; the imprint, 'Freistadii', 1700. L.L., no. 2993. The *Disceptatio* was published first at 'Irenopolis' in 1646 and is by W. H. Vorstius, a Remonstrant (*N.N.B.W.*). The *Bilibra* is an answer to Rittangel's *Libra Veritatis* (p. 466, n. 1). The book was circulating by August of this year: p. 660. For the Paraphrasts see p. 660.

le MS. de Mr. Souverain, dont il étoit en peine, intitulé *le Platonisme dévoi⟨lé.*[1] Il⟩[a] s'imprime actuellement chez le même Mr. Petsol. Je vous demande pardon, Monsieur, de la liberté que je prens de vous parler pour ce Libraire. J'ai crû qu'en étant chargé je ne pouvois m'en dispenser.

Mr. LeClerc travaille présentement à se justifier en Latin contre Mr. Cave, et autres. Ce sera un volume de Lettres intitulé *Epistolæ Criticæ et Theologicæ*. Il y prouvera entre autres choses qu'il ne faut rien déguiser dans l'Histoire, même Ecclésiastique. Il est étrange que les hommes ayent besoin qu'on leur prouve une chose si visible. Il fera voir que la dissimulation a fait grand tort au Christianisme. Il parlera de Mr. Toland sans le nommer. Ce Mr. Toland fait fort parler de luy en Hollande, comme d'un indiscret, sans pudeur et sans religion.[2]

Je dois écrire dans quelques jours en Hollande où j'enverrai de la copie. Comme Mr. Mortier[3] n'est pas à Londres, je prendrai la liberté de vous addresser mon Paquet, que je vous prie de faire mettre à la poste. Je vous prie de m'excuser sur la nécessité où je suis de ne pouvoir me servir d'une autre voye. Je crois aller bientôt à Londres quand ce ne seroit que pour vous lire de la copie. Je trouve des difficultez dans le Livre des *Mots*,[4] et quelques-unes si grandes que je ne puis m'en tirer sans vôtre secours. Je porterai en même temps l'Extrait de vôtre Livre, que Mr. Bernard attend tous les jours.[5] On me mande que Mrs. de Leipsic ont parlé de vôtre Dispute avec Mr. Stillingfleet, et qu'ils vous louent l'un et l'autre de vôtre moderation.[6] Ces Mrs. les Allemands qui ont accoûtumé de se mordre et de se déchirer, ne comptent pour rien quelques égratignures.

[a] *Page torn.*

---

[1] Matthieu Souverain, sometime a Protestant minister in France and deposed on account of his Arminianism; a refugee in the United Provinces and later in England, where he became an Anglican: Haag; no. 1442. His book was published with the imprint P. Marteau, Cologne, in 1700. L.L., no. 2724. See further no. *2724*; Haase, pp. 237–8.

[2] See pp. 661–2.

[3] Presumably David Mortier, acting as agent for Hendrik Schelte, who published Coste's translation of the *Essay*.

[4] Book III of the *Essay*.

[5] Jacques Bernard; apparently the manuscript, French or English, for the notice of Locke's second *Answer* to Stillingfleet that appeared in the October and November issues of the *Nouvelles de la republique des lettres*. If the identification is correct the notice was written probably by Coste.

[6] *Acta Eruditorum*, January 1699, pp. 12–20.

Je vous souhaite une bonne santé, Monsieur, et suis avec un profond respect,

Votre très-humble et très-obeïssant serviteur

COSTE.

Monsieur, La Lettre que vous m'avez envoyée, est de Mr. Turretin.[1] Il me recommande le jeune homme qui vous l'a renduë.[2] C'est, dit-il, un très-honnête homme, qui a bien étudié à Geneve. Il est déja fort avancé dans la connoissance de la Langue Angloise, et je croy qu'il pourroit être fort utile pour l'éducation de quelque seigneur.

ce 29me. Juin 1699.

Address: For Mr. Locke, at Mr. Pawlings in litle Lincolns Innefields, over against the Plough, London.

Endorsed by Locke: Coste 23 Jun 99

2602. SAMUEL BOLD to LOCKE, 29 June 1699 (*2590, 2628*)

B.L., MS. Locke c. 4, ff. 30–1. Answers no. 2590.

Steeple June 29th. 1699.

Honoured Sir

I thank you with all my heart for every line in yours of May 16th. which came to me in a letter from mr Churchil, on June 8th. I would have writ to you sooner, if I had not bin hindered by businesses that have thrust themselves on me relating to some of my neighbours, and which I could not wel avoid concerning my self in, without exposing them to sustain some Inconveniences. Some of your Instructions given me in your last, I have had a little occasion lately to put in practice, and am convinced by experience that they are of great use to such as I am, very few of those who write controversies, afford me any considerable satisfaction. They seem to me generally to be in extreams, and the truth often lies neglected in the middle, but yet is injured by the strokes given on each side at one another. The taking up of principles gratis, and arguing

[1] Probably the theologian Jean-Alphonse Turretin, 1671–1737: *N.B.G.*
[2] Probably Desmaizeaux: p. 636.

often with an Inconsistency to their avowed principles, hath occasioned a very strange confusion. Antinomianism[1] I take to be a regular and Just Deduction from the principles of the Rigid Calvinists. And tho some of this Rank do offer considerations very pertinent against the Antinomians, yet I cannot make the solid answers they give to the other's notions consistent with their own fundamental principles. The controversies about the Church, tho they carry such an appearance of much Reading with them, are to me so extreamly unsatisfactory and confused, I have little hope that the truth wil be fully set forth in It Just Light, til the entire fabrick is pulled down and the bottom of the matter be impartially enquired into. Could I finde some loose papers which I have writ since I saw you I might fil this paper with difficulties of several kindes, which have occurred to me, but they are gone out of my mind at present, and my placing them as I have met with them, on any shreads of paper which have come in my way, has set them at a greater distance from me, than perhaps they would have bin, if I had never writ them down. But since I received your last letter, some things have occurred to me, which are stil in my memory, or in papers that have not made their escape, of which I desire leave to give you a brief account. In my daily reading the Holy Scriptures, I often meet with difficulties, and commentators have so seldom answered my expectation, I am almost weary of consulting them, for I that way loose much time, having in the end as little satisfaction, as I had before I enquired after their sentiments. I do not neglect the old Testament, but It is the New Testament I do principally study. And reading very lately the first chapter of the Epistle to the Romans, I was fain to stop for some time, at the 17th v. *For therein* (viz: in the Gospel of Christ) *is the Righteousness of God revealed from Faith to Faith.* I wil not trouble you with all the thoughts I had upon this occasion, The following words shew that It is Gods constitution and determination that persons shall be saved by faith, viz a firm, steady assent to, or perswasion of the truth of that Revelation God shal be pleased to afford unto them. By the Righteousness of God, I conceive is meant the terms which God hath setled, according to which He wil proceed with persons in Judgment, Justifying those who do comply with, and heartily consent to them. So that the Righteousness of God, is what God

[1] 'The view that Christians are by grace set free from the need of observing any moral law': *Oxford Dict. Christian Church.*

requires now to be believed in order to Salvation, viz. that Jesus is the Christ. Under the old testament It was revealed that there should be a Messiah; that, was the object of Faith then, That the Promised Messiah is come, and that Jesus of Nazareth is that Messiah, is the object of faith now. In the Gospel is revealed, or the Gospel doth manifest from what the Jews were to believe, that this is now the object of saving Faith. From the accomplishment of what was revealed in the old Testament concerning the Messiah, in Jesus of Nazareth, the Gospel doth reveal or manifest, that that Jesus, is the Messiah, or what we are now to believe in order to Salvation. This I take to be the sense of the phrase, *From Faith to Faith*. And that this virse is of the same import with Rom: 3: 21.22. Two or three days since I found a sermon of the late Arch Bishops, published since his death, on Rom: 1: 18th. vol: 4th.[1] which occasioned me to see whether He said anything on the preceding v. I think His Interpretation, and mine differ only in this, that He took the 17th v. to signify, that what was more obscurely revealed in the old testament, was more clearly revealed in the Gospel. I take It to note, that from what was clearly revealed in the old testament, the Gospel manifests that we are not to believe in a Messiah to come, but already come, and that Jesus is He. What was the object of Justifying faith, under the old Testament, I think was as clearly revealed then, as what is the object of Justifying Faith, is now revealed.

Sir, I was lately discoursing on a place of scripture which gave me occasion, or at least, from which I tooke occasion to draw this inference, That persons who are not sincere Christians, may live in outward communion with the church of Christ. Whilst I was thinking on this subject several things came to my minde, which tho I did not think proper to be discoursed of to such a sort of people, as the most of my hearers be, yet I apprehended, they might deserve a little consideration some time or other, and therefore writ down, in a paper at hand, what did immediately offer It self, that I might not make too long a stay, before I applied my thoughts to what might be fit for my Auditory, and that I might have recourse to them again, when I should have leisure; which I have not had from that time, to this. I shal lay them before you, just as I finde them in my paper. Whether they be really of moment, I can not say, having not had time to examine them thoroughly,

[1] Tillotson; *Several Discourses*, vol. iv, 1697, pp. 267–303.

I can judge of them only by their present appearance and therefore I rather choose to be a while in suspence.

The Church or Body of Christ doth consist of single, particular persons, believing heartily in Christ Jesus, who by that Faith are united to Christ their head and Lord, and to one another, as His members or subjects. It doth not consist of certain societies of people visibly united by outward profession, and outward communion in ordinances christ hath appointed, as administred in some certain manner, or with some certain modes, Rites, and circumstances. Christians indeed are to joyn in communion and therefore there must be christian societies, or societies wherein Christs ordinances are to be celebrated, both for confirmation and edification in faith and Godliness, and for proseliting or converting more persons to christ, not to any particular society, precisely considered as distinguished from other christian societies, by a denomination that hath It's rise only from something that is of meer Humane original.

The Rules pertaining to, and necessary to be observed by these societies as christian, are laid down by christ, the soveraign Lord.

If they have Right and power to make any other Rules or orders, the rules so made, do not concern them as christian societies, but only as societies in general, and are made by virtue of that Right which belongs to society in general, and is common to them with all other societies.

If christian societies agree upon any rules or canons, which are not absolutely necessary to society, those being only Humane, and at best, prudential determinations, can concern christians only with respect to such matters as fal under Humane cognizance and determination, and not those which Christ the soveraign Lord hath instituted and ordained. for otherwise an encroachment would be made on Christ's prerogative; And what christ gives all his subjects a Right to, would be limited to those only, who wil admit others to be sharers with Christ, in that soveraignty which is peculiar to Him.

Every sincere Christian hath a Right from Christ to pertake of his ordinances in any christian society where ever he happens to be. Nor can any christian society rightfully refuse any one, of whose being a christian, It hath credible evidence. Christs ordinances belong to all his members or subjects, and not to societies considered as distinct one from another, or as consisting of a certain number of members.

With respect to the Bylaws particular churches, considered either singly, or as in conjunction with one another, may make, I shal take notice of these things.

1. If they agree upon certain temporal advantages to be appropriated to themselves, they may assigne the terms, to which persons shall consent, or with which they shal comply, in order to even christians[1] having a Right to them, which no christian can lay a Just claim to, but upon his submitting to those terms. But these should not be made terms for christians to submit to, in order to their pertaking with them in christ's ordinances, because christians have an Antecedent and superior Right to christ ordinances.

2. Christ's ordinances should not be made qualifications for secular offices, and employments. Because It is a perverting of them to other purposes, than those for which He ordained them. Christ by reason of his supreme Authority may advance Instances[2] of Humane Rise, and Use, into his church, and appoint them for nobler purposes, than men could; but christians ought not to degrade his Institutions, and prostitute them to mean purposes. there is no necessary connection between qualifications for secular employments, and a Right to christian ordinances.

3. Christian Churches should not use violent corporal compulsion to make any persons members of their societies; nor use any of Christs Institutions meerly to expose, and subject people to civil pœnalties. If Asses were the proper subjects to be made sons of the church, the Cudgel might be a fit Instrument, wherewith to drive and force them into the place, where those of their own species do ordinarily meet. But sure no methods can be worse accommodated to enlighten mens mindes; than either knocking out their Brains, or breaking of their Heads. As the Church should not be a sanctuary to secure Criminals from Civil Justice, so neither should Ecclesiastical Administrations be made a stratagem, whereby unrighteous and wicked people may get an opportunity to throw Innocent and Harmless p⟨ers⟩ons[a] into Goale, or to force them to unjust compositions, to secu⟨re⟩[a] them from greater Damage.

You see Sir the confidence I have in you, in that I adventure to

[a] *Words in part covered by fragment of paper.*

[1] Fellow-Christians: *O.E.D.*, s.v. Even-Christian.

[2] In the obsolete sense, details or circumstances: ibid., s.v. Instance *sb.* 7c.

lay these crude thoughts before you, before I have had time to examine them. I heartily rejoyce both to hear you are able to come to London, and that you have perfected what you designed to add to your Essay. I should be exceedingly glad to wait on you, but am not certain I shal get an opportunity to come to London this summer. I wil endeavour it to the utmost, and am Sir

your most obliged servant

SA: BOLD.

Rom: 5. 12. last words, have puzled me this day.

Endorsed by Locke: S: Bold 29 Jun 99 Answered Feb. 3

LOCKE to NICOLAS TOINARD, 2 July 1699

J. C. Brunet collection, sale catalogue, 1868, no. 65, item 56, with wrong date 2 July 1699. The correct date is 2 July 1700: no. 2739.

2603. LOCKE to ESTHER MASHAM, 21 July 1699 (2426, 2607)

Newberry Library, Chicago: copy of the original letter by Esther Masham, in her letter-book, pp. 80–1. Transcribed from microfilm. Printed in Fox Bourne, ii. 475–6; by Professor Maurice Cranston in *Newberry Library Bulletin*, 2nd ser., no. 4, July 1950, p. 133. The explanatory notes were written by Esther.

London 21 July 1699

Deare Dib[1]

Did not your Ears tingle much on Saturday last. My[a] Daughter and I talked much of you that day at Battersea and if you are not an obdurate creature you could not but be sensible of it at twice this distance. Particularly She told me She had writt and that you answerd not, that She writt of business and you took no notice of it; Of your business, and yet you were silent. To all this your Joannes Standing up for you answered the best he could, and t'was no hard matter for him to carry the point. for my good daughter was not inclind to be angry but was only concernd you should know that She had found out a Merchant an honest man their neighbour at Battersea, who was of Rouën, traded thither. and had acquaintance there and would be ready to do you any service. I wish you had

[a] Cos: St John now Cos Gower. She us'd to call Mr Lock Father[2]

[1] A variant of Dab, short for Landabridis. [2] Mrs. Frances St. John.

business there he might be a fit man for some purposes. However my daughter is mindfull of her friends

I thank you for the care you take of my[a] Brew house and drink. Tis like a good Dib and when I go into our nown Country of Wales I promise you a bottle of the best Metheglin for it.

I thought your paper books would have come best home with my printed ones But since you long to begin the world and tis a good girle for it you shall have them Speedily by the Butcher[1] or Lanham. Give me Credit but till next week and that Account shall be ballancd between us Though there be many others wherein I shall always be your Debtor. But what matters that, you know I am all over your

JOANES

2604. MRS. ELIZABETH BERKELEY, later Burnet, to LOCKE, 24 July 1699 (*2599*, *2627*)

B.L., MS. Locke c. 3, ff. 222–3.

Sir

My sister[2] while in Town could sometimes satisfy me of your continewed health, I have no longer that advantage, I am loth to give you any trouble; y⟨e⟩t[b] can hardly help asking now and then[c] the assurence of what I so earnstly[d] desire. I can't surprise you with being impertinent, I began so: and repeat them too often to sufer you to forget my faults; however my sister shall baer some share in this and complying with the request of a Frind must finish my excuse to you. I think I once named a young Lady to you as very

[a] Mr Locke drank nothing but water. What he calls his Brewhouse was a Stone in form of a great Mortar of so spungy a stone that water being put in use to run thro' in a very short time and straind the water from any dirt that might be in it.[3]
[b] *Page torn.* [c] *Page torn; a short word may be lost.* [d] *Page torn; there was probably a short blank space at the end of the line.*

[1] Brown the Butcher in no. *2995*. He appears to have carried parcels, etc., to Oates occasionally.

[2] Probably Mrs. Dormer: p. 576, n. 3.

[3] For Locke's acquisition of a filter see no. *884*, etc.; for Pawling's 'tavern', no. *2896*. Fox Bourne adds a note to Esther's, that Miss Palmer, who had inherited the letter-book and owned it in his time, told him 'that this home-made filter of Locke's was till lately in the possession of her family, and was found so well to answer its purpose that it was lent to a farmer in the neighbourhood, whose health required that he should drink especially pure water. Unfortunately the filter was never returned, and this interesting heirloom has been lost'.

disarveing with an intent it should be named to my Lord Ashley; what answer you gave me I have quit forgot, however she is still uningaged and in my Judgment disarves to be very happy in a good Husband; her Mother can if she pleases and likes the persone and Estate give her 20000 ll: down, she has only one Brother about 21: year old, if he dyes without Childeren she is Heir to about 3: or 4000 ll a year; her persone is very gracefull, and handsome, but it may be s⟨o⟩me[a] may think her too tall; her temper ⟨is⟩[a] extremly good, she has been very well ⟨e⟩ducated,[a] and tho I know not how farr that will be estemed: she is an extraordenary good scholer understands latin perfectly well, and Greek a good deal; she is free from all the Levitie and extravegency that Ladys of quality and fortune are too subject to, and will live within the compas of her fortune be it more or less; her age is as I gess about 25: and truly take her all together I know few if any young Lady more disarving; I know not my Lords expectations nor his Genius, the Caracture he has had of sobriety and understanding will I know be very great motives to the Lady and her Mother, if you think fitt to have this named to my Lord, I shall be glad to know how he receeves it; or if you find it not agreable to your Judgment, or inconveniant by giveing you too much troub⟨le⟩[a] in the proposing, I shall rest fully satisfyed, if you will too forgive one who with the greatest respect at all times desiers to do the duty of

Sir

Your Most Obliged Faithfull servent

E BERKELEY

Lee:[1] 24: July: 99:

any letter left at my sister's (who is your Humble servent) will come safe to me;

Address: For Mr Locke at his Lodgeings in litle Lincoln's Inn Feilds over against Boswell's Court[2] London

Endorsed by Locke: E. Berkeley 24 Jul 99 Answered Aug 3

[a] *Page torn.*

[1] Perhaps Lee Grange in Quainton, Buckinghamshire, a family seat to which Robert Dormer succeeded in 1725: Lipscomb, (*Buckinghamshire*), i. 416.

[2] p. 173, n. 2.

2605. Philippus van Limborch to Locke, 24 July/ 3 August 1699 (*2596*, 2615)

B.L., MS. Locke c. 14, ff. 129–30. Copy by van Limborch in Amsterdam University Library, MS. R.K., III D 16, f. 210. Printed from the copy and omitting some names in *Some Familiar Letters*, pp. 437–9. Answered by no. 2615.

Vir Amplissime

Literas meas circa mensis Junii finem scriptas fideliter Tibi esse traditas nullus dubito. Indicavit mihi D. Clericus sibi a te missum D. Allix tractatum Anglicum, quo probare contendit, Paraphrastas Judæos æternam Filii Dei generationem agnovisse.[1] Nuperrimè hic prodiit tractatus ante plures annos, ut præfatio habet, et argumentum libri clare ostendit, ab autore ignoto scriptus, qui duos scriptores, Rittangelium et Voisinum, idem quod D. Allix asserentes, impugnat.[2] Commodâ mihi per nautam filio meo notum oblatâ occasione exemplar illius ad bibliopolam Churcil, tibi porro tradendum, mitto, ut hujus cum tractatu D. Allix collatione institutâ de totâ controversiâ judices. Ego non video causæ principali aliquod creari periculum, etiamsi argumento hoc, ex Judæorum scriptis deprompto, propugnari non posset: Nec ego tali argumento in disputatione contra Judæos multum tribuere ausim. Alia sunt majoris momenti, et quæ fortius stringunt. Verum hoc sine occultæ

Excellent Sir,

I do not doubt that the letter that I wrote you about the end of June has been duly delivered to you. Mr. Le Clerc has shown me an English treatise by Mr. Allix that you sent him. In it Mr. Allix strives to prove that the Jewish Paraphrasts recognized the eternal generation of the Son of God.[1] Very recently there appeared here a treatise written some years ago, as the preface asserts and as the subject of the book clearly shows, by an unknown author who impugns two writers, Rittangel and de Voisin, who make the same assertion as Mr. Allix.[2] As a suitable opportunity has offered itself through a mariner known to my son I am sending a copy of it to the bookseller Churchill to be delivered to you so that, when you have made a comparison between it and Mr. Allix's treatise, you may form an opinion of the whole controversy. Even if it could not be defended by this argument, drawn as it is from the writings of the Jews, I do not see that any danger to the principal position would be produced; nor would I venture to value highly such an argument in a disputation against the Jews; there are other

[1] p. 624, etc. The Paraphrasts are the makers of the Targums, that is, the Aramaic translations, interpretations, or paraphrases of the various divisions of the Old Testament. They were made first about the time of the Babylonian captivity, when Hebrew was ceasing to be the ordinary spoken language of the Jews; at first transmitted orally, they were committed to writing only after about A.D. 100: *Encyc. Judaica.*

[2] See p. 650. An appendix to the *Bilibra* attacks Joseph de Voisin, who published in 1647 *Disputatio Theologica Orthodoxa de Sanctissima Trinitate* against Vorstius's *Disceptatio.*

cum fidei hostibus conspirationis suspicione affirmari non patiuntur orthodoxiæ, semel decretis humanis definitæ, jurati vindices, quibus piaculum est vel unum argumentum, licet elumbe ac stramineum, modo à zelotis adhiberi solitum, omittere, aut de illius evidentiâ ac robore vel minimum dubitare. Adfuere mihi nuper aliquot præstantissimi Angli: inter alios D. Flesher,[1] ad me ductus per D. Furly, et D. Cunningam,[2] nec non alii, de quibus an tibi noti sint ignoro. Omnes mihi narraverunt, Tolandum quendam, juvenem Hybernum, et, ut audio, non magnifice de S. Scripturæ divinitate sentientem, aliquoties gloriatum de honore sibi ab aliquot viris eruditis in patria nostra exhibito: inter alia etiam amicitiam ac familiaritatem mecum contractam jactare. Miror quid hominem, nunquam mihi visum, quique ater an albus sit ignoro, moveat falsò jactare familiaria mecum habita colloquia. Quoniam autem justam mihi causam præbet suspicandi, similia eum de nostrâ amicitiâ in Angliâ disseminaturum, hac occasione id scribere tibi consultum duxi; ut si quid simile jactet, rumorem illum falsi coarguere queas. Antehac de D. Clerici amicitiâ multum gloriatus est: ipsum nunc bis convenit, sed semel in alienis ædibus: Verum ita à Clerico exceptus est, ut de consensu illius secum minimè gloriari

---

arguments of greater weight and far more stringent. But the sworn champions of orthodoxy, as defined once for all by human decrees, do not suffer this to be maintained without their suspecting a secret conspiracy with the enemies of the faith; for them it is a grievous offence to omit even a single argument, however feeble and worthless, if only it is one usually employed by the zealots, or to doubt in the least its clearness and strength. Some distinguished Englishmen have been with me recently; among others Mr. Flesher,[1] who was brought to me by Mr. Furly, and Mr. Cunningham,[2] besides others; I do not know whether the latter are known to you. They all told me that one Toland, a young Irishman who, as I hear, does not think highly of the divine character of Holy Writ, has bragged at various times about the honour shown him by some scholars in our country; among other things he even boasts of an intimate friendship contracted with me. I wonder what moves a man whom I have never seen, and about whom I know nothing, to boast falsely of having had familiar conversations with me. But since he gives me good reason to suspect that he will spread similar statements in England about our friendship I think it advisable on this occasion to write it to you, so that if he boasts of anything of the kind you can give the lie to that report. He formerly bragged a great deal about his friendship with Mr. Le Clerc; now he met him twice, but one of these meetings was in another person's house; but he was received by Le Clerc in such a way that he cannot brag at all of any agreement between Le Clerc

---

[1] Perhaps Andrew Fletcher of Saltoun. [2] Alexander Cunningham: p. 647.

queat.[1] Sub prælo jam habet D. Clericus aliquot epistolas, quibus se contra criminationes Cavei, Waijeni, aliorumque defendit.[2] Semel hoc labore defungi cupit, ideoque pluribus simul respondet. Vitam Episcopii à Marco Teute in Latinam sermonem versam, relegi:[3] quædam emendavi: omnia autem si emendare cupiam res magni esset laboris: addidi etiam quædam, quibus historia nostra Exteris plenius paulo explicatur: Verum quoniam non Remonstrantismi, sed solummodò vitæ Episcopii historiam conscripsi, intra cancellos rerum ab ipso Episcopio gestarum continere me debui. Fortasse versio illa, qualiscunque sit, brevi prælo subjicietur. Vale, Vir Amplissime. Salutem dices Dominæ Masham, totique familiæ, a me, et uxore, filia ac filio: qui omnes tibi salutem precantur.

Tui Amantissimus
PHILIPPUS À LIMBORCH.

Amstelodami 3. Augusti
16 2/19 99

Address: Amplissimo ac Consultissimo Viro D. Joanni Locke
Endorsed by Locke: P: Limborch 3 Aug. 99 Answered Sept. 5

---

and himself.[1] Mr. Le Clerc has now in the press some letters in which he defends himself against the accusations of Cave, van der Waeyen, and others.[2] He wants to have done with this labour once for all and so answers several at the same time. I have again read the life of Episcopius as translated into Latin by Marcus Teut.[3] I have corrected some things, but if I should wish to correct everything it would be a matter of great labour. I have also added some things by which our history is made somewhat clearer to foreigners, but as I have written a history not of Remonstrantism but only of Episcopius's life I have been obliged to keep within the limits of Episcopius's own activities. The translation, such as it is, will perhaps be sent to press soon. Good-bye, excellent Sir. Please give my respects to Lady Masham and the whole family, together with those of my wife, daughter, and son, who all send you good wishes.

Your most affectionate
PHILIPPUS VAN LIMBORCH.

Amsterdam 3 August
1699

---

1 For Toland's former relations with van Limborch, Furly, and Le Clerc, see nos. *1646*, *1650*, *1653*, and *1657*.
2 pp. 558–9, etc.
3 For the Dutch version of the life (1693) see no. *1708*; the Latin translation was published in October 1700 but with the date as 1701: no. *2795*.

2606. Frans van Limborch to Locke, 24 July/ 3 August 1699 (*2419, 2905*)

B.L., MS. Locke c. 13, ff. 181–2.

Amsterdam 3 Agust 1699

Honoured Sir.

Three weeks agoe is but delivred me your very acceptable of the 22 April S.V. by hands of Mr Cunningham where out j am very much troubled to see that your indisposition still continues, which pray God may take once an end, but yett very much oblidged to you for your goodnesse, that you notwithstanding the same have been soo good as to favour me with such a very kind and oblidgeing letter, which j deare nott for bear to deffer longer to answere, cheefly now j had an occasion to forward one from my father to your self. As to what belongs the Civilitys we meight have done to Mr Locke,[1] they have but been very smal, and we have nott been able to doe him any in quality a Cosen of such a man deserved, I doe nott beleeve you shall have seen him in London also he is parted for the East jndies about four month agoe as j doe nott doubt but you'll since have heared from his father, from who, notwithstanding j have written him againe severall letters, and cheefly concerning goods j would Consigne to him for my owne account j can't be so happy as to receive any letter, what the reason of itt be j cant comprehend, but j am sure j committed nothing on my side that can occasion itt, but reckon the greattnes of busines he is in, to be for a greatt part the reason. j am much oblidged to you for the concerne you take in the good succes of my busines, which j thank god continue to goe on pretty prosperously, to which I reckon the good wishes of such worthy friends contribute very much; Pray Sir be soo good as to tell My Lady Masham j have received her Ladyships Letter of the 10 May in due time, and j am ashamed over the greatt acknowledgements about the hamms, which I hope prove very good, and that I shall take by the first opportunity the liberty to answhere itt my self, my time permitting itt nott att present, and to present My Most humble respects to her Ladyship Sir Francis Madam and Mr Masham and Mr Coste and to be assicured that I shall always esteeme my self

[1] John Lock, son of Samuel Locke.

very happy, if j may have the honour to prove how much I am for ever as well theirs as your

Honoured Sir

Very much oblidged and devoted servant

F: V: LIMBORCH

Address: For John Locke Esquire present In London
Endorsed by Locke: F: Limborch 3. Aug. 99

2607. LOCKE to ESTHER MASHAM, 27 July 1699 (2603, *3003*)

Newberry Library, Chicago: copy of the original letter by Esther Masham in her letter-book, pp. 81–2. Transcribed from microfilm. Printed in Fox Bourne, ii. 476; by Professor Maurice Cranston in *Newberry Library Bulletin*, 2nd ser., no. 4, July 1950, pp. 133–4.

London 27 July 1699

Deare Dib

I have received the honour of yours of the 24th and have to say to the kindness of it a great deal. to the business in it a little. to the Compliment no thing. The first of these being too much for a Letter I shall adjourn till I see you. And therefore I come to the second. That you should put out your money rather than let it lie Dead is easily resolvd. Mr Jefferies and Mrs Burdets together I imagine to be good Securitie especially if he borrows this £50 only to make up £500 which he is letting out upon a Mortgage and Mrs Burdet has Money and houses.

I wish your Lady Mother had taken a soop of the Brandy which you write me was just come. She would then certainly have been better naturd than to have complaind of my useing her and made that an Excuse for her not writeing. when if she consider it she will finde I have writt four Letters to her since I received ever a one.

Pray tell Frank that I am glad to hear you and every one speake well of him Assure him that I love him very much but I expect to heare from him some news of what he saw or observd at the Assizes.[1] My humble service to Sir Francis Mr Winwood[2] and Mr Coste I am

Your most humble and Faithfull Servant

JOANES.

[1] See p. 674.   [2] Winwood Masham, Esther's fifth brother.

2608. Locke to Anthony Ashley Cooper, Lord Ashley, later third earl of Shaftesbury, 5 August 1699 (*2427*, 2610)

London, Victoria and Albert Museum, Forster collection, MS. 364.

My Lord London 5 Aug. 99

I was sory that I, who took as great a part in it as any body, was not in town when you arrived here to congratulate, amongst the first, your safe returne.[1] And the hopes I have had ever since I have been here that it would not be long ere I should have the happynesse to see you here made me forbear troubleing you with a letter, and I should have continued my silence longer had not a letter I received last weeke[2] put me under a necessity of writeing to you how unwilling soever I am to give your Lordship any trouble of this kinde

There is a yonge Lady Handsome well-natured well bread discreet with a great many other good qualitys which I think your Lordship would like whose mother can make her worth twenty thousand pounds. besides this there is but one yonge man betwixt her and an estate of three ⟨or⟩[a] four thousand pounds a year. This is writ to me out of an Esteem of your Lordship and with a designe that I should tell it you: And therefor if I were lesse a servant to your Lordship than I am it would not be fit I should let it die with me. What the meaning of it is your Lordship needs not have explaind to you. But what answer you will think fit I should returne that I must expect from you.

And now I am writeing to your Lordship give me leave to mention that there was a year due to me at Midsomer last. Your Lordship has soe often told me that you had taken order that it should be constantly paid me from half year to half year as it became due, that I cannot but looke upon this as a forgetfulnesse in those to whom you gave that order and therfor it is with great unwillingnesse that I trouble your Lordship with this matter being, driven to it against my will. For I had much rather discourse your Lordship about other matters, such as I presume you imploid your thoughts about in your last winters retirement. I am

My Lord

your Lordships most humble and most obedient servant

J Locke

[a] *MS.* of

[1] From Holland: p. 604. [2] No. *2604*.

I beg leave to present my most humble service to my Lord your father and to Mr Ashley[1]

2609. Pierre Coste to Locke, [c. 12 August 1699] (2601, 2746)

B.L., MS. Locke c. 7, ff. 147 b–c. Printed by G. Bonno in *Revue de littérature comparée*, xxxiii (1959), 175–7. Date: The year is determined by Locke's endorsement and the contents. Du Bos left Amsterdam probably on 2/12 August: B.N., N. Acq. fr. 560, f. 305v. The news could reach Coste at earliest on 6 August, O.S. Francis Cudworth Masham apparently refers to Coste's return from London in his letter of 21 August (p. 674). Coste expected to go there on or about a Wednesday, which must be 9 or 16 August. The latter is preferable; hence a date for the letter between 11 and 14 August.

Monsieur,

Puisque vous le souhaitez, je m'en vais vous dire les nouvelles que j'ai reçues de Hollande. On imprime à Amsterdam une Histoire de la *Scission, ou division arrivée en Pologne au sujet de l'élection d'un Roy*.[2] Ce livre a été imprimé à Paris avec privilege, cependant il a été supprimé presque aussi-tot qu'il a paru. On croit que la Reine Douairiere de Pologne qui est fort maltraitée dans ce Livre, aura été cause de la suppression. On imprime dans le meme endroit les *Memoires du Chevalier de Beaujeu* qui contiennent bien des particularitez de la Pologne, et des guerres et des affaires de ce Royaume-là depuis l'année 1679 jusqu'en 1683.[3] Il paroit un autre Livre que mon Ami croit du meme Auteur, intitulé les *Anecdoctes de Pologne*, où l'on donne une relation fort exacte du Siége de Vienne.[4] Mon ami m'écrit en général qu'il y a des choses fort curieuses dans ces trois Livres, qu'on peut lire avec d'autant plus de plaisir qu'on n'est guere bien informé dans ces quartiers de ce qui se passe en Pologne.

Le bruit a couru qu'on devoit traduire votre Livre à Rotterdam en latin. Mon ami croit que c'est Mr. Crellius qui a ce dessein.[5]

[1] Maurice Ashley (Cooper).

[2] M.-D. de La Bizardière, *Histoire de la scission*, etc., Paris, 1699; Amsterdam, 1700; English translation, 1700. Notice in *History of the Works of the Learned*, i. 643–9.

[3] By F. P. Dalérac or Dalairac; first published in Paris, 1698; new edition, Amsterdam, 1700.

[4] Also by Dalérac. L.L., no. 2368. English translation, 1700.

[5] I have found no other traces of this project.

Je m'imagine entre nous qu'il ne s'en acquiteroit pas bien, car il écrit fort mal, à ce que dit Mr. LeClerc; et sans m'ériger en juge, il me semble par le petit Ecrit qu'il a fait contre Bullus[1] qu'il n'y a rien de beau dans son stile; et je ne croy pas que qui écrit mal ses propres pensées, soit capable de mieux écrire celles d'autruy. Quoy qu'il en soit, j'apprens avec plaisir que Mr. Crellius est à Rotterdam correcteur de Mr. Leers.[2] Il aura par ce moyen dequoy vivre, car j'ai ouï dire il y a long temps que Mr. Leers donnoit à son Correcteur cent écus[3] par an et la table. Mr. Crellius a été depuis peu à Amsterdam. Il a prié mon ami de vous faire savoir par moy qu'il vous saluë, et qu'il seroit bien aise d'apprendre ce que vous pensez de son Livre.[4] On veut aussi que j'en dise mon avis. Mais je ne l'ai pas encore reçu, ni vous non plus apparemment. Mr. LeClerc ne l'estime pas beaucoup. Il trouve que Mr. Crellius avance beaucoup de choses sans les prouver, et qu'il n'écrit pas fort nettement.

On rimprime le Dictionnaire de Mr. Bayle. On en est déja au C. Le caractére sera plus petit que dans l'Edition précedente.[5]

Quand Wetstein a vendu son fond, on a été surpris d'y trouver un grand nombre d'exemplaires de la *Religion Raisonnable*. Mrs. Huguetan n'ont pas laissé d'acheter le droit de l'imprimer. C'est une enigme dont voici la solution. Mrs. Huguetan ne pouvant point s'accommoder avec Wetstein qui étoit effectivement d'un commerce très-épineux, n'avoient point voulu débiter ce Livre quoy qu'on leur en demandât beaucoup de plusieurs endroits, et même d'Angleterre. A présent ils l'ont acheté parce qu'ils sont fort assûrez de le vendre. Voila comment la passion des particuliers nuit au bien public. Que faire! Cela a été et sera toûjours.[6] Mrs. Huguetan voudroient imprimer présentement les *Défenses* qu'on a fait de la *Religion raisonnable*. Ils s'addressent à moy pour cela.[7]

[1] *Fides Primorum Christianorum*, 1697. L.L., no. 1960. Crellius used a pseudonym, Lucas Mellierus. He was attacking George Bull (no. *1801*), *Defensio Fidei Nicænæ*, 1685.

[2] The publisher: no. *948*.

[3] Presumably the equivalent of the English crown and the French *écu*; either the three guilder piece worth 5*s.* 2*d.* or the ducatoon worth 5*s.* 5*d.*

[4] The *Cogitationes Novæ*: p. 650.

[5] The second edition is dated 1702; it was published on 27 December 1701, N.S.: Labrousse, *Bayle*, i. 252.

[6] Hendrik Wetstein, the publisher of *Que la religion chrétienne est très-raisonnable*, sold his unbound books in languages other than Dutch by auction on 20 July, N.S.: van Eeghen, iv. 169.

[7] Coste translated excerpts from the *Vindication* and the *Second Vindication*; they were published by A. Schelte in 1703 as the second part of *Que la religion chrétienne*: no. *3274*.

Je ne puis m'y engager avant la fin de la Traduction que j'ai présentement en main; mais je croy qu'après cela j'entreprendrai cet Ouvrage; *propaganda etenim rerum doctrina bonarum est.*[1]

On me mande que Mr. L'Abbé du Bos n'est plus à Amsterdam. Il a dit, après avoir vû une partie de ma Traduction, qu'il ne doutoit point qu'on ne rimprime vôtre Livre à Paris. A cause de cela il n'a pas voulu en rien apporter, de peur qu'on ne crut qu'il seroit la cause de ce qu'on le rimprimeroit. Cela est honnêtement et prudemment fait. Au reste, vous dirai-je qu'il a été content de ma Traduction jusqu'à dire qu'elle paroissoit original? C'est un grand éloge. Mais vous me connoissez assez, je croy, pour être assuré qu'il ne me fera pas tourner la tête, et qu'il ne servira qu'à me rendre plus circonspect et plus exact pource qui reste, *ut concordent ultima primis.*[2] C'est la verité toute pure; et quoy qu'on pense de cette Traduction, je suis certain que j'y trouverai plus de défauts que des Lecteurs plus éclairez que moy.

Votre Portrait est arrivé en fort bon état.[3] *Il a paru fort bon à ceux qui l'ont vû.* Apparemment mon ami entend par là ceux qui vous connoissent de visage.

Le Volume des *Epistolæ Criticæ* que Mr. LeClerc compose depuis quelque temps contre quelques-uns de ses Antagonistes, paroitra bientôt. Il n'y aura point d'injures, dit mon Ami, mais de bonnes raisons. Ce sera comme un troisiéme volume de l'*Ars critica.* Il y aura une Dissertation sur ce sujet, *An et quando respondendum sit Theologis.*[4]

Je croy qu'il est nécessaire de vous avertir que *Custerus* ne travaille plus au Journal Latin d'Utrecht. Il est présentement à Berlin, et doit aller bientôt en Angleterre et en France. Sickius qui présentement travaille seul à ce Journal, n'est pas tant estimé.[5]

Madame part mercredy d'Oates pour aller voir Mr. Barrington.[6] J'ai resolu de profiter de ce temps pour vous aller voir, afin que vous puissiez voir ce que je dois envoyer à Amsterdam. Je ne de

[1] 'Good learning should be spread abroad': varied from Dionysius Cato, *Disticha* IV. xxiii. 2.

[2] 'That the end may agree with the beginning'. Perhaps deriving from Cato I. xviii. 2.

[3] p. 624.

[4] The book was published probably about the beginning of 1700.

[5] See p. 615.

[6] Probably Francis Barrington, d. 1708, a second cousin of Sir Francis Masham of Tofts in Little Baddow, about 5 miles east of Chelmsford: Morant, *Essex*, ii. 22; see also no. *2945* n.

meurerai qu'un jour à Londres, et pour être plus près de chez-vous, je logerai au *Plough*. Je suis avec un profond respect,

Monsieur,

Votre très-humble et très-obeïssant serviteur

COSTE.

On me demande incessamment de la Copie. J'ai achevé le troisiéme Livre. Je changerai l'endroit du Chap. X. comme vous me l'avez envoyé.[1] Pour le § 57. Ch. XXI. du Liv. II. il est dans le François comme dans l'Anglois. Je crus qu'il n'étoit pas exprimé si ouvertement qu'il ne pût fort bien passer en France. Cependant, si vous le jugez à propos, on fera un Carton. Voici les propres termes de ce passage: *Un Païs voisin a été depuis peu le Théatre d'une cruelle Tragedie d'où l'on pourroit tirer des exemples pour confirmer ce que je viens de dire, s'il étoit nécessaire, et que ce Monde n'eut pas fourni dans tous les Païs et dans tous les temps* etc.[2]

Mr. Francis vous est fort obligé et vous salue bien humblement.

Address: For John Locke Esqr At Mr Pawlings over against the Plough in Little Lincolns Inne Feilds London.

Endorsed by Locke: P: Coste 99

Memorandum by Locke:

11 Nov. 97–6a[a]	4–8–0
11 May 98	4–8–0
11 Nov 98	4–8–0
11 Feb 9$\frac{8}{9}$	2–4–0
	15–8–0
	176–0–0
	191 8–0

[a] *Doubtful reading.*

---

[1] Probably in § 30, where the fourth differs from the third edition. The translation agrees with the fourth.

[2] In the published version the unsigned leaf (Rr4) forming pp. 319–20 is a cancel. The passage was altered to 'C'est dequoy le Monde nous fournit une infinité d'exemples, et l'on peut trouver dans tous les Païs et dans tous les temps', etc.

2610. LOCKE to ANTHONY ASHLEY COOPER, Lord Ashley, later third earl of Shaftesbury, 15 August 1699 (2608, *3139*)

London, Victoria and Albert Museum, Forster collection, MS. 364.

London 15 Aug 99

My Lord

How much soever the world wonders that you doe not marry it is certain that you are the best judg when that ought to be, and therefor I shall not enter into that matter. Only I beg leave of your Lordship to say, (what, if he were alive, I should say to your Grandfather, and perhaps more too) that such offers are not to be met with every day. I take this liberty because I can assure your Lordship that you are not at all mistaken when you think I am concerned for you. I have not much to expect or hope in this world, But should be very glad if in the small remainder of my life I might have the oportunity to serve you in any businesse that might be usefull and acceptable to you.

The day before I received the honour of your Lordships lettre I received a note for the money. I am very sorry that I was not soe lucky to have notice of it before I had that occasion to write to your Lordship. For it is a subject which I am very unwilling to trouble your Lordship with at any time. I return your Lordship my humble thanks for it now and for the concerne your Lordship is pleased to expresse for my health. Time never mends an ill pair of lungs in one of my age, though this warm somer has enabled me to bare the inconvence of them with some tolerable ease. I am

My Lord

Your Lordships most humble and most obedient servant

J LOCKE

I beg leave to returne my most humble thanks to my Lord your father and to Mr Ashley[1] for the honour of their remembrance

Notes written by Ashley(?): (i): and freed from those pursuits of vulgar men; may best the secrets of the Gods[a]

(ii: in red chalk): selfish then how: now not[b]

[a] *The blank space is Ashley's.* [b] *Doubtful readings.*

[1] Maurice Ashley (Cooper).

2611. Locke to Mrs. Mary Clarke, 19 August 1699 (2576)

B.L., MS. Locke b. 8, no. 144. Printed in Rand, pp. 549–50. A letter from Mrs. Clarke to Clarke, 10 January 1704, is printed below: no. *3418A*.

London 19 Aug 99

Dear Madam

I had long ere this returnd my thanks to you for the favour of yours of the 5th: instant had not crosse accidents happend that put me besides the oportunityes of doeing it. Let me tell you one which happend to me the last post day because that is the freshest in my memory. A Gent came to visit me at ten of the clock in the morning and his visit lasted till past ten at night. you may guesse by this that the town is grown soe thin of company that those few that are left in it live and visit after the same manner as if they were in the country. The mischeif is that I am sure country air is not to be got here how much soever in other things it may at this season counterfeit the Country. This makes me joyn with you in your wishes that Chipley were as near as Oates. I know not what advantage you might make of it, to me I know it would be a great one. For I should often enjoy your company there and I am very apt to think we should not want something to say to one another.

I am very sorry to find by yours and Mr Clarkes letters (for I have his also of the 6th) that the country air has not yet done him soe much good as I wished and expected. I know not what to say more on that occasion at this distance. I beg him and you to beleive that noebody is more concerned for it then I am. And I hope the next from Chipley will bring me better news. I have none to send you from hence; But only that Mr Freke came well from Tunbridg yesterday, and my lord Chancellor is goeing thither the begining of the Weeke. If man and wife are but one person as they are but one flesh this may goe for a⟨n⟩[a] answer to both your letters. For if you assure Mr Clarke from me that I wish him a perfect recovery with all the earnestnesse and concerne that one friend can have for an other I know he will beleive as well as if writt it immediately to him himself

I am indebted to my dear wife for her civil and kind letter pray let her know how sensible I am of the favour till I have an

[a] *Page torn.*

oportunity to return her my thanks in a letter on purpose. My service to the rest of the yonge folks there that know me. I am

Dear Madam

your most humble and most faithfull servant

J LOCKE

Address: For Edward Clarke Esquire member of Parliament at Chipley near Taunton Frank

Postmarks: (G.P.O. and London receiving office, indecipherable).

2612. J.-B. DU BOS to LOCKE, 19/29 August [1699] (*2600, 2673*)

B.L., MS. Locke c. 7, ff. 232–3. Printed by G. Bonno in *Revue de littérature comparée*, xxiv (1950), 501–2. Year from Locke's endorsement.

D'Anvers le $\frac{19}{29}$ DAoust

lembaras du voyage monsieur ma empeché jusques ici de repondre a vostre lettre du dixseptieme de Juillet. monsieur Leclerc escrit quelque chose contre le docteur Allix. je pense que cest pour lui prouver que Philon avoit lu et relu Platon et que cest dans les ouvrages de ce philosophe Grec que le Juif a prises les notions de trinité que lon trouve dans ses ouvrages.[1]

Jay vu en passant a Utrecht monsieur Græevius qui vous salue de tout son cœur. je lai fort rejoui en lui aprenant que javois vu les deux tiers de vostre traité de l'entendement humain imprimé en francois.[2] cest une des bonnes nouvelles que je porte a Paris ou tout le monde est dans limpatience de lire ce livre.

la seconde partie du Telemaque de⟨l'archeveque⟩[a] de Cambray est imprimee a la haye.[3] il i a beaucoup de defauts dans cette impression; cela me fait esperer que lautheur en fera faire une lui même a Paris plus corecte et plus entiere.

les oraisons de Ciceron de monsieur Grævius paroistront enfin la semaine prochaine.[4] il les a dediees au duc de Bourgogne. je lui

[a] *MS.* l'archeque

[1] See p. 638. [2] See p. 668.

[3] See pp. 631–2. Adriaan Moetjens, who had published a reprint of the first part at The Hague, was now reprinting the second, third, and fourth parts, as published in Paris; he completed his edition in three volumes.

[4] See no. *1637*, etc.

souhaité la meme gratification quil recut lors quil dedia a nostre Dauphin les epistres du meme autheur.[1] le roy de France lui fit present de deux milles escus.

lon a imprimé a Utrecht les notes dun Reutgersius sur Horace ou il i a d'assé bonnes choses.[2]

des que je seré arivé a Paris jacompliré les comissions que vous me donné par la lettre du 21 de May, la quelle vous m'adresates a Paris et que lon ma renvoiee ici. je prieré aussi monsieur Clement de consentir que monsieur Freset mette dans les ballots quil envoie quelquefois pour la bibliotheque du Roy les livres dont vous me voulé faire present.[3] je vous demanderé sur tout la derniere colection de voyages.[4]

un nommé Mortier libraire d'Amsterdam a fait graver la suitte du Neptune Francois la quelle contient l'Afrique LAsie et Lamerique.[5] Son Afrique est excellente parce quil sest servi de vint cinq cartes manuscrites tirees du cabinet du roy de Portugal qui comencent au detroit de Gibraltar et vont jusques a Suez.

Je vous prie de faire tenir incessament la lettre a monsieur de Cuninghuam que je crois a la campagne avec Mylord Pawlet.

jespere d'estre a Paris dans quinze jours.

je recois une lettre de monsieur Toinard qui jouit dune parfaite santé.

Vostre tres humble et tres obeisant serviteur

DU BOS

Address: poste DAngleterre To Master Jhon Locke at Master Pawling over against The plough in little Lincolns Inn fields London

Endorsed by Locke: Du Bos $\frac{19}{29}$ Aug. 99

[1] Grævius dedicated his edition of the letters to Atticus, 1684, to the Dauphin.

[2] *Q. Horatius Flaccus. Accedunt J. Rutgersii Lectiones Venusinæ*, 1699. L.L., no. 1506. Joannes Rutgers, 1589–1625: *N.B.G.* His notes to Horace were published first in 1613.

[3] Nicolas Clément, sub-librarian of the Royal Library 1692–1712: *D.B.F.* Freset is probably James Fraser, 'Catalogue Fraser': no. *2149*; for the identification see p. 751 and no. *2693*.

[4] Probably *A Collection of Original Voyages*, edited by Captain William Hacke, 1699. L.L., no. 1370[b]. It is summarized in the June issue of *History of the Works of the Learned* (pp. 353–60). See further no. *3083*, etc.

[5] Pieter Mortier, 1661–1711; elder brother of David Mortier; one of the leading Amsterdam publishers of books, maps, etc.: van Eeghen, iii. 256–65. *Le Neptune François*, containing maps of the European coast from Trondhjem to Gibraltar and of the Baltic, was published in Paris and Amsterdam in 1693; a second volume was not published: *Journal des Sçavans*, 11 January 1694 (p. 21); Bourgeois and André, no. 198.

2613. FRANCIS CUDWORTH MASHAM to LOCKE, 21 August 1699 (*2282*)

B.L., MS. Locke c. 16, ff. 16–17.

Oates August 21th 1699

Honored Sir

I beg leave to returne you my most humble thanks, for your token which you did me the favour to send me, by Mr Coste:[1] I see every day more and more marks of your great kindness, which I wish I could deserve. Sir according to your desire, I will tell you as well as I can, what I saw at the assises. When we were within a mile of Burntwood,[2] we mett the High Sheriff, comeing to meet my Lord chief Justice Trebie; then we went back with him, and mett the Judge, who came on horseback. The next day I went upon the bench, which was very full, and heard the Judges speech, which I liked very well; he praised the King and answered all the objections that might be made against him. He said that idleness was in great measure the cause of the robberies that were done; and that no body was born to live idlely, tho' all do not work with their hands, yet they must study with their minds the good of their country in their several places; and also many other things which I liked a great deal better than the trials which were tiresome. I thought it was a very noble office to be a Judge, but not a very easie one. I think it is a very serious thing to condemn people to death. I saw some burnt in the hand, and some in the cheek. I thought it very moveing to see the poore prisoners when they were condemned fall down upon their knees beging pardon or transportation. When my Lord gave sentence he said, since you have lived as the Theif who was crucified with our blessed Saviour I hope you will repent like him at your deaths. I could say more upon this subject but I am afraid to be too tiresome to you.

Deare Sir I am

Your most humble and Affectionate Servant

FRA: CUDW: MASHAM

Endorsed by Locke: F: C: Masham 21 Aug 99

[1] Coste went to London probably about 16 August: p. *666* n.

[2] Brentwood, on the road to Chelmsford. The Assize was appointed to be held there on 19 July: *London Gazette*, 22 June 1699.

LOCKE to PHILIPPUS VAN LIMBORCH, 5 September 1699

The letter was not completed until about 12 September: see no. 2615.

2614. RICHARD COOTE, first earl of Bellomont, to LOCKE, 7 September 1699 (*2587, 2636*)

B.L., MS. Locke c. 7, ff. 136–7. The letters from Bellomont to the Board of Trade that he mentions here are calendared in *Cal.S.P., Col.*, vol. xvii; the New Hampshire letter (no. 769) is there dated 9 September, presumably the date of completion. It, with the letters of 24 and 28 August, was received by the Board on 22 November; as the present letter accompanied them it probably reached Locke about that time.

Piracy was increasing before the end of the war, and now was in full swing in the Indian Ocean; American colonists were participating. The Board of Trade was active in suppressing it: Steele, pp. 44–59. The most important book for the Indian Ocean is S. Charles Hill, *Notes on Piracy in Eastern Waters*, Bombay, 1923; the colonists' participation is summarized in *Cal.S.P., Col.*, prefaces: vol. xvi, pp. xi–xvii; vol. xvii, pp. xi–xxiv; vol. xviii, pp. viii–xii.

Boston 7th. September 99.

Sir

I hope you were present at the board, when my Letters by the two Last Conveyances were read. that of the 13th. of last April about the Indian affairs; that of the 17th ditto about Naval stores; that of the 27th. ditto about Calling the assembly of N.york, and their Continuing the Revenue; that of the 3d. of may about Bradish a Pyrate[1] and his Crew taken; that of the 13th. ditto about the Courts of Justice Ceasing at N.york, and about the trade of that province; that of the 15th. ditto Containing my answer to the Lords of the Council of Trade's Letters of the 25th. of October the 5th. of Jan: and 2d. of feb: 98. that of the 8th. of Last July about my seizing and Committing Captain Kidd[2] to gaol. and that of the 22th. July giving an account of the affairs of N.york, and the acts of assembly pass'd there the last session and sent with my said Letter of the 22th. of July; among which acts there is one that breaks some of Colonel Fletcher's extravagant Grants of Lands in that province, and one of his Grants which that act breaks, was

[1] Joseph Bradish, hanged in 1700: G. F. Dow and J. H. Edmonds, *The Pirates of the New England Coast, 1630–1730*, 1923, pp. 40–3; Hill, § 461.

[2] William Kidd, hanged in 1701: *D.N.B.*; *Trial of Captain Kidd*, ed. G. Brooks, 1930.

to the Church of N.york; and the Parson who is a great knave has stirr'd up some of the Clergy French and Dutch to Join with him to write home and Complain to the Bishop of London.[1] another Letter of mine of the 26. of July to your Lordships of the Council of Trade gives an exact account of all goods and treasure taken with Kidd, and of my taking the Concurrence of the Council here in that matter, and our ordering the said goods and treasure into the hands of five trusty persons. this Course I took, because I would lye under no sort of suspicion of unfair dealing; and though the greatest part of the treasure was discover'd and seiz'd by my own vigilance; I would not so much as see it, but order'd it into the hands of those persons; where all that's found is to lye till the King's pleasure be known, for so the orders of the Lords Justices of England and of Mr. Secretary Vernon do appoint.

Pyrates do so Increase in these plantations that they will destroy the trade of England especially that to the E. Indies, if a speedy remedy be not taken to suppresse 'em. we have had two or three new Pyrate ships on these Coasts lately, they rob our trading ships of the stoutest and likelyest of their men and of all their provisions (because they know provisions are Carried from hence and N.york and Pensylvania to the Western Islands)[2] and then they declare themselves bound for Madagascar and the Red Sea. we have a Pyrate ship of force now at this time on the Coast that robbs all our ships. and because nothing but ships of war Can secure us and destroy them, the Lords of the Admiralty are pleas'd not to allow us a single ship. you will see what I propose to your board by this Conveyance in my Letters of the 24th. of aug: about the affairs of N.York; in that of the 28th. ditto, about those of this Province; and in that of the 1st. of this moneth about the affairs of N. Hampshire. I do in all my letters (or almost all) Complain of the want of means of Checking piracy; viz: two good ships of war here and N.york whereof one to be a 4th. rate ship: for a 5th. rate will not be a match for some of these pyrates; and this pyrate now on the Coast has 24. guns and a 110 Choice men, and a 5th. rate man of war has but 95 men: therefore I am of opinion this pyrate would take a 5th. rate should they Ingage in fight. a 4th. rate ship here then, and a 5th. rate at N.york is one of my three postulata: the next is two honest good lawyers to be Judges at N.York and an

[1] Godfrey Dellius, minister at Albany: *Calendar*, as above; Dr. Henry Compton.
[2] Presumably the Caribbean islands.

able honest Attorney Generall, for the present one[1] is a right Scot, Cunning, but as false as hell and Corrupt, and besides, no lawyer. he being the only Council for the King, by his means we loose all Pyrates we take, and all the seizures of unlawfull ships and goods. he was formerly a rank bitter Jacobite, and I see no signs of his Conversion. all the rest of the pettyfoggers in that province are the greatest rogues and Jacobites in nature, and debauch the principles and affections of the people from the Government, besides the mischief they do them in their estates by their sinister practice of the law. The third and last of my postulata, is the recruiting and well paying the four Companies in the province of N.york, which are at present barbarously us'd by the treasury and pay-office. if these three things are granted me, I will make these provinces flourish, and at the same time be much more usefull and subservient to England than they ever have been. I am every day more and more Convinc'd of the vast advantage these Plantations are to England, and of the Improvement that might be made of that advantage by the honest Care of the severall Governors. if our Navigation be a thing valuable to England, then Certainly these plantations must be allow'd to Contribute to that the most that Can be. then again the furnishing the King with masts for his ships of war, and the Navy and all the shipping of England with Naval stores as pitch tar etc: which my Letter of the 17th. of Last april to your board treats of, and which I undertake therein to furnish from the province of N.york at Cheaper rates than they are at this time sold in England that are brought from Sweden and Denmark. I am so sure of performing this thing of Naval stores, that I will loose my head if I do not perform it. and when I do it, I thinke I may without vanity pretend to do as great and valuable service to England as ever was done by a subject. I desire you will please to be at the pains of reading all those Letters I have mention'd to have writ to your board, and that you will make use of that great and generall Influence you have on all the Ministers, to excite them to support and assist me vigorously and effectually. if all the rest of the Ministers were as Industrious and vigilant in businesse as your board, England would quickly be made happy and great. with a 4th. rate and 5th. rate ships, I will undertake to root out piracy from all North America, viz: from the Eastermost bounds of the Province of Mayne, to the southermost point of

[1] James Graham: *Calendar*, as above.

South Carolina which is the whole extent of the English territory on this Continent, and about 400 leagues in Length, provided the Governors of the other Plantations will but be honest, and will Co-operate with me. I Cannot doubt of your favour, and ready Compliance with the request I have made you, because it tends to the service of England, to which I know you turn your thoughts and devote your time as much as any man in England.

I shall always remain with a true esteem and respect

Sir

Your most affectionate humble servant

BELLOMONT

now that I have represented in this my Letter, severall things to you that relate to the publick. give me leave to add a short postscript about my selfe. I labour more than all the Governors that are in America to serve England, and yet I suffer extreamly, my allowance being so short for the government of N.york, that it will not half maintain me. and I am sent a begging to this province for a salary, where they are the most penurious people on earth. I must desire to be recall'd, if I Cannot be maintain'd honourably and Comfortably. if I may not pretend to a good salary for each of my Governments, when I am in the sure way of doing such essentiall service to England, then I will be gone home, and no body Can Justly blame me.

Endorsed by Locke (at head of letter): L: Bellomont 7. Sept 99 Answered Nov. 29

2615. LOCKE to PHILIPPUS VAN LIMBORCH, 5 [and *c.* 12] September 1699 (*2605*, *2618*)

Amsterdam University Library, MS. R.K., Ba 258 i. Printed in part in *Some Familiar Letters*, pp. 440–2; omitted passages, postscript, and address, in Ollion, pp. 219–20. The date of completion of the letter is indicated in the postscript. Answers nos. *2596* and *2605*; answered by no. *2618*.

Londini 5 Sept 99

Vir Amplissime

Nudius tertius tractatum contra Rittangelium quem mihi misisti,

---

London 5 Sept 99

Excellent Sir,

I received the day before yesterday the treatise against Rittangel that

accepi.[1] Benignè mecum actum erit si hoc nomine mihi ignoscas tarditatem responsi ad literas tuas tertio Augusti datas. Nondum mihi vacui temporis satis datum est ut Allixii librum hoc de argumento aggrederer, qui mirus plerisque primo auditu visus est, quod Trinitatis doctrinam e Synagogâ haurire præ se fert. Accingam me quamprimum jam per otium liceat ad utriusque lectionem: multi enim ut audio apud nos dictitant quæstionem hanc prius non intellectam jam primum in lucem produxisse Allixium, et suis fundamentis innixam mundo obtulisse. Quas partes hac in controversiâ habent Judæi perpensis utrinque argumentis jam videbimus

Hibernum quem nominas[2] vanæ hujusmodi gloriolæ avidum ex aliis audivi, si de te tuâque amicitia aliquid jactitet apud amicos familiaresque meos. quam omnino tibi ignotus sit ex me scient

Criminationes hujusmodi adversariorum quibuscum res est domino Clerico an negligendæ an refutandæ haud facile est statuere. Quidam enim non aliud quærunt nisi calumniandi rixandique ansam. Non dubito quin amicus noster satis habet quod respondeat. Ego sane laudo tuum consilium qui placide juxta et solide refutaveris quæ contra te malignè scripserit Waÿenus. De Controversi-

---

you sent me;[1] it will be kindly done if on this account you will forgive my slowness in answering your letter dated 3 August. I have not yet been given enough free time to begin Allix's book on this subject. On first hearing of it very many people seemed surprised because he professes to derive the doctrine of the Trinity from the Synagogue. Now as soon as leisure permits I shall set to work to read both books, for many people in our country, as I hear, declare repeatedly that Allix has now for the first time brought into the light this question that has not before been understood, and has offered it to the world resting on its proper foundations. We shall now see what part the Jews have in this controversy when the arguments on either side have been weighed.

I have heard from others that the Irishman whom you name[2] is eager for a bit of empty glory of that sort; if he should go boasting about you and your friendship when he is with my friends and intimates they will learn from me how completely unknown he is to you.

It is not easy to decide whether accusations by adversaries of the kind that Mr. Le Clerc has to deal with should be disregarded or refuted, for some are seeking for nothing else than an opportunity for slandering and quarrelling. I do not doubt that our friend has enough to say in answer. I certainly commend your prudence in calmly and at the same time solidly refuting what van der Waeyen has spitefully written against you. As for

---

[1] The *Bilibra Veritatis*: pp. 650, 660. [2] Toland.

arum quæ me aliquamdiu exercuerunt eventu etiamsi non multum habeam quod querar, piget tamen pænitetque tantum temporis mihi suffuratum quod aliis studiis majore cum fructu poterat impendi. ⟨Siquæ⟩[a] novæ oriantur vellicationes eas in posterum mihi negligendas censeo

Vitam Episcopii Latinitate donatam lubens viderem Belgica enim lingua non satis mihi nota ut quam tu edideris legere possim. non dubito quin multa contineat scitu et jucunda et utilia sive mores privatos respicias sive rerum eo tempore gestarum historiam

Hactenus ad tuas 3° Augusti datas. Sed qua excusatione utar cum respicio ad antiquiores sc: mense Junio scriptas. Si delictum consuetudine delinquendi defendi possit, habeo quod dicam. Nosti tarditatem meam hoc in genere. Fac ut soles et inveterascentem in me delinquendi morem tu consuetudine ignoscendi vincas.

Cum in novissimis tuis de viro magnifico ne verbum quidem, Volderi opinionem pronus amplector. Oporosè ab aliis quærit, non quod domi habet, sed quod nusquam adhuc reperire potuit, et quod forsan reperiri possit.[1]

[a] *MS.* Siqui

---

the controversies which have occupied me for a while, although there is not much for me to complain of in the outcome, nevertheless it irks and grieves me that so much time has been filched from me that could have been spent with greater profit on other studies. Should any new carping criticisms appear I consider that I may disregard them in future.

I should very gladly see the life of Episcopius presented in Latin, for I do not know Dutch sufficiently to be able to read it as you published it. I have no doubt that it contains many things that are both pleasant and profitable to learn, whether you have regard to private conduct or the history of the public affairs of that time.

So far in answer to yours dated 3 August. But what excuse may I make when I turn my attention to an older letter, one written in June? If an offence can be defended by a custom of offending I have something to say. You know my slowness in this kind. Do as you are wont and overcome my ever more inveterate habit of offending by your custom of forgiving.

As there is not a word about the Magnifico in your last letter I am inclined to embrace de Volder's opinion. He laboriously seeks from others not what he has of his own but what he has nowhere yet been able to find and what can perhaps be found.[1]

---

[1] A note to this passage in *Some Familiar Letters* calls attention to Spinoza's treatment of the question in the three letters to Hudde cited on p. 464.

Miror illum qui tibi dixit decretum illud de quo questus es spectare ad eos qui revelationem impugnant, cum contra negantes revelationem eo in decreto nihil cautum est, sed certum quoddam revelationis divinæ interpretamentum sancitum, quod in dubium vocare non licet. Quod de promiscuâ venere dictitat, id credo dictum ad concitandam invidiam, quod quidem ne fando quidem a me unquam auditum. Sed hujusmodi homines reperiuntur qui cum persecutionem apertè profiteri non audent, sub alieno nomine eam inducere et falsis criminationibus tegere conantur[1]

Tractatus viri docti quem in Anglia videram apud vos editus nondum ad manus meas pervenit. de fundamentis quibus tanquam certissimis superstructum censuit minime mihi satisfecit, cum de iis coram disceptavimus[2]

Exactiorem Hammonti historiam quæsivi. Nondum autem reperi quenquam qui eam mihi explicatius tradere possit, vel scriptorem aliquem indicare in quo eam reperire licet. Non tamen desistam. Laudo ⟨enim⟩[a] consilium tuum in colligendis hujusmodi exemplis

Geneloni nostri literas quas me expectare jusseras nondum vidi nec Nobilem Moscovitam cui tradendæ erant ad me perferendæ.[3]

[a] *MS.* eim

I am surprised at the person who told you that that decree of which you complained had in view those who impugn revelation, since nothing is stipulated in that decree against those who deny revelation; but a certain interpretation of divine revelation that is not allowed to be called in question, is ordained. As for what he asserts about promiscuous sexual intercourse, I believe that that was said to rouse ill-will since I have never heard even any talk of it. But there are to be found men of this sort who, when they do not dare openly to profess persecution, try to introduce it under another name and to veil it with false accusations.[1]

The treatise by the learned man which I had seen in England, [and] which is published in your country, has not yet come into my hands. When we discussed them together he did not at all satisfy me about the foundations on which it is built, and which he deemed most certain.[2]

I have been seeking for a more perfect history of Hamont. I have not yet found anyone who can relate it to me at greater length or indicate some writer in whom it may be found. Nevertheless I shall not leave off. For I commend your intention to collect such examples.

I have not yet seen the letter from our Guenellon which you bade me expect, or the noble Muscovite to whom it was to be entrusted for him to bring to me.[3] I do not yet know by what mischance this has happened.

[1] This relates to Burnet and the Blasphemy Act: pp. 639–40.
[2] Probably Samuel Crellius and his *Cogitationes*: pp. 641, 650.
[3] The letter is no. *2594*.

Quo infortunio hoc acciderit nondum scio. Doleo interim mihi ablatam occasionem testandi quam paratus essem inservire peregrino à tam Caro amico adventanti. Illum uxoremque ipsius, Socerumque ejus Veneum nostrum, officiosissime meo nomine quæso salutes Inprimis autem uxorem liberosque tuos. ⟨Filioque⟩[a] tuo me excusare rogo quod epistolæ illius amicæ et civili nondum responderim. brevi spondeo me facturum. Vale et me ut facis ama

Tui amantissimum

J LOCKE

Epistolam ⟨hanc⟩[b] ante octiduum ⟨inchoatam⟩[c] et crebris interruptionibus intercisam vix tandem hac nocte perfeci

Address: Mijn Heer Mijn Heer Limborch op de Kaisars Gracht bÿ de Remonstranse Kirck t'Amsterdam

Postmark: GC

Noted by van Limborch (beneath date): Recepta 26 Sept.

[a] *MS.* Tiloque *or* Filoque [b] *MS.* hac [c] *MS.* incoatam

---

Meanwhile I regret that I have been deprived of an opportunity of showing how ready I should be to serve a foreigner who comes from so dear a friend. Please give my best respects to him and his wife and to his father-in-law our friend Veen, and especially to your wife and children. Please excuse me to your son for not having yet answered his friendly and courteous letter; I promise to do so shortly. Good-bye and continue to love me

Your most affectionate

J LOCKE

I have at last only just tonight finished this letter, which was begun a week ago and broken into by frequent interruptions.

2616. SAMUEL LOCKE to LOCKE, 12 September 1699 (*2598*, *2637*)

B.L., MS. Locke c. 14, f. 201.

Sir

⟨Just⟩[a] at my Returne home I finde your noble and weighty presant wherewith you have bin pleas'd to honnoure mee: I Esteem it hartily. and give you as hearty thanks for it; And as I know no greater Rarity from the Indies, than this will be there: I purpose by

[a] *MS.* J

the first ship for Surrat to sende it my son John, whose acknowledgment of so great a favour I hope God will graunt you Lyfe to see: in the meantyme. I am attending your Commands in all occations wherein I have any Capassity to serve you. being

Sir

Your obliedged servant and Cossen

SAM LOCK

London 12th September 1699

Address: To John Locke Esquire at mr Pawlins neer the Plow Stables in Little Lincolns In fields

Endorsed by Locke: S Lock 12 Sept. 99

2617. LOCKE to EDWARD CLARKE, 16 September 1699 (2586, *2646*)

Rand, p. 550.

London, 16th September, 1699.

Dear Sir,

I was glad to hear by the Bachelor that you got so well and in so good time to Tunbridge. I hope the good air, water, and company of the place will have powerful effects upon you for the re-establishing of your health.

The great news in town these two days hath been of the Scots leaving Darien. It all arises from one letter of the Governor of Jamaica to Mr. Secretary Vernon. The letter I have seen, and possibly copies of it are sent to the Wells. His account being founded only upon the report of the master of the vessel, who met three canoes at sea wherein were three Spaniards that gave the account. The certainty of it is received in town with some doubt.[1]

I beg you to deliver the enclosed with my most humble service, and if his Lordship says anything upon the reading of it, pray let me know it. I am,

Dear Sir,

your most affectionate humble servant,

J. LOCKE.

Endorsed: Mr. Locke, with a letter enclosed to my Lord Chancellor, etc. Received 17th September, 1699. Answered the 19th.

[1] Sir William Beeston, the governor of Jamaica, wrote to Vernon on 10 July that the Scots had left Darien about 23 June; the letter was read to the Board of Trade on 15 September: *Cal.S.P.*, *Col.*, vol. xvii, no. 626. This is not recorded in the Board's journal.

2617A. Dr. Richard Burthogge to Locke, 19 September 1699 (*1752A, 3214A*)

Oxford, Museum of the History of Science, MS. Buxton 7. Transcript made by Charles Babbage: see no. *1737A*, n. The round and square brackets are those of Babbage's transcript.

Sir

I confess it is long since that I received the favor of your obliging letter by Mr King together with your accurate reply to the Bishop of Worcester's Answer to your second letter for both which I had sooner made you my due acknowledgements but that a great indisposition which prevented me being out our Assizes deprived me also of the occasion of giving you this trouble before now. Upon an attentive perusal of your excellent book I think it past doubt that you have fully cleared and confirmed your sentiment concerning Certainty having shewn beyond contradiction that in the last result all certainty by Reason arises from the evident congruity or incongruity of Ideas or Notions. As for *Axioms* Maxims or Received propositions (a stock of which as I suppose the Bishop termed Reason and the Use and employment of that stock in argumentation [He called] Reasoning) It is impossible for any person to be certain of the verity of them if he is not convinced of it upon comparing by seeing the Agreement or Disagreement of the Ideas and Notions upon which they are grounded. Nor can Axioms give any light to other things that is clearer or better than that in which themselves are seen.

Those few (too few) persons who are used to balance all Propositions and not to Assent to any only because they come recommended but because upon comparing they see congruity or coherence in them (They) have in point of certainty as much advantage over the many who argue from Axioms or received and allowed but not self-evident propositions and of which they own but swimming and confused senses; as those who themselves do frame Astronomical Tables and so do calculate the motions of the Heavenly bodies on their own knowledge have above others who do only work by the tables framed to their hands which for ought they know may be false and consequently their calculations may be erroneous and are uncertain (to them). It is true if certainty be taken only for Firmness of Assent it may come as well from Authority if that authority be infallible as from evidence or eyesight. There is a full assurance of

Faith as well as a certainty of science or demonstration But yet these two kinds of assent (tho' both of them have the name of knowledge given to them 2 Corinth 5.1 Matt 9.6) are of very diffrent natures. One is an assurance[a] arising from the things themselves as they make impressions upon us which I take is an Assurance from Ideas the other arises not from any knowledge that we have ourselves of the things but only from the credit and Authority of the Person who tells us of them: And accordingly the first kind of Assent is by Appropriation called certain knowledge the latter steadfast beleif.

For my part I wish that men who make a great figure in the world for Learning and Theology and who are ready to make claim to a monopoly of both would lay it more to their Heart to attain to Clarness and Distincness of Thoughts Or (if they plase) of Ideas and the Agreement or Disagreement of them even in matters of Faith. I make no question but the first preachers of the Christian doctrine had themselves a certain Meaning or Idea of what was Revealed to them And that that sense or meaning is communicated to us in the Holy Scriptures. But since it is communicated only by Words which often are capable of diverse senses and meanings what other way is there to come certainly to discern the true sense and meaning which we ought to embrace from the false must be rejected but by comparing spiritual things with spiritual and seeing what does suit and Agree and what does not? There is an Analogy of Faith as well as of Nature to Guide us.

I am much of the same opinion that you are concerning the Resurrection: the Apostle speaks of but two bodies one that is sown Another that shall be and says expressly [Thou sowest NOT that Body that SHALL BE].[1] Only methinks the Body that SHALL BE must have *Relation* to the body that is SOWN since as the same Apostle intimates it must be the PROPER Body. But in what that PROPRIETY consists (unless it be understood of the Proportion of glory which the Body which SHALL BE will have in Reference or Correspondence to the services of the body which is Sown) is as yet a secret to me. Only so much seems plain that it consists not in this That the Body which is SOWN contains not in it a Seminal

[a] *Abbreviated in MS.*

[1] 1 Corinthians 15: 37.

Body of that which SHALL BE. For if the discovery be certain that grain tho' it be not divided into Lobes as other seeds are yet upon seperating the membranes these seminal parts are discerned in them which afterwards grow up to that body which we call corn; yet that discovery being Microscopical (as you judiciously observe) it was not made at the time when the Apostle wrote and therefore cannot be imagined to be alluded to by Him. Besides if the apostle had meant there were such seminal particles in the Body SOWN and that these seminal particles would grow up to the Body that SHALL BE He must (if the Bishop's way of arguing have any weight) instead of saying [That which thou SOWEST, thou SOWEST NOT the body that SHALL BE] have said [That which thou SOWEST IS (or thou SOWEST) the Body that SHALL BE] but this is directly contrary to the whole Design and scope of the Apostles discourse that nothing can be more: For then an Earthly Carnal and Corruptible Body must be in the resurrection because it was such an one as was sown and is the seed of that that shall be: Now the seed is (as the Bishop argues) that in little which the Body it grows up to is in great.[1]

I once intended to have Added somewhat more but my recollection begins to tell me what my paper does that I have said too much already so that what remains is only to beg your Pardon, Repeat my hearty thanks and own myself

Honoured Sir

Your most humble obliged servant

RICH BURTHOGGE

Totnes

Sept 19 1699

Address: For John Locke Esquire

Endorsed by Locke(?): Dr Burthogge Sept 19 99

2618. PHILIPPUS VAN LIMBORCH to LOCKE, 22 September/2 October 1699 (2615, 2621)

B.L., MS. Locke c. 14, ff. 131–2. Copy by van Limborch in Amsterdam University Library, MS. R.K., III D 16, f. 186. Printed from the copy, with omissions, in *Some Familiar Letters*, pp. 443–6. Sent with no. *2619*. Answers no. 2615; answered by no. 2621.

[1] This refers to Locke's second *Reply*, pp. 184–94.

2618. P. van Limborch, 22 September 1699

Vir Amplissime

Licet nihil mihi literis tuis gratius sit, absit tamen ut amicum plurimis ac gravissimis distractum negotiis ad singulis meis respondendum constringi cupiam. Amicitia arithmeticam illam scribendi et respondendi proportionem non requirit, sed in promto ac benevolo amici animo acquiescit, et bene secum actum credit, quotiescunque amicus aliquam à gravioribus curis respirationem nactus vel tantillum temporis epistolio, licet breviori, impendit. Ego ex tuis te rectè valere lætus intellexi: Deus hanc tibi diu continuet valetudinem. Anonymi librum contra Rittangelium rectè ad manus tuas pervenisse gaudeo. Ubi eum legeris, et cum Allixii libro contuleris, rem mihi facies maximoperè gratam, si vel tribus lineis judicium tuum de utroque ad me scribas.

D. Clerici epistolæ criticæ, quibus pluribus qui calamum in ipsum strinxerunt simul respondet, brevi lucem videbunt. Adversarios habet parum candidos, et eorum quosdam imperitos admodum ac indoctos, præsertim illum, qui ipsum et me non provocatus invasit.[1] Homo ille omnium imperitus de omnibus judicium pronuntiat, quæque minime intelligit magno cum supercilio carpit. Contra Clericum scribit, Philonem à Spencero[2] vocari

---

Excellent Sir,

Although nothing is more pleasing to me than your letters far be it from me to wish that a friend who is busied with very many important affairs should be constrained to answer each separate letter of mine. Friendship does not require that arithmetical equality of writing and replying, but is content with a ready and kindly spirit in a friend and thinks itself well treated as often soever as a friend, having obtained some breathing space from more important charges, devotes never so little time to a note, however short. I was delighted to learn from your letter that you are in good health; may God long continue such health for you. I am glad that the anonymous writer's book against Rittangel has safely reached your hands. When you have read it and have compared it with Allix's book you will make me most grateful if you will write me your opinion of each of them, if only in a couple of lines.

Mr. Le Clerc's *Epistolæ Criticæ*, in which he answers at the same time several men who have taken up the pen against him, will shortly see the light. He has adversaries who are not very candid, and some of them altogether ignorant and uninstructed, notably the one who made that unprovoked attack on him and me.[1] That fellow, ignorant of everything, pronounces judgement on everything and carps with great superciliousness at what he least understands. He writes against Le Clerc that Philo is called by Spencer[2] a dunghill of fables. But he thinks that what Spencer writes

---

[1] Johannes van der Waeyen. [2] Dr. John Spencer, author of *De Legibus Hebræorum*.

fabularum sterquilinium. Verum quod Spencerus scribit de fictitio Antiquitatum Biblicarum libro, Philoni falsò tributo, quique nusquam in Philonis operibus exstat, ille de genuino Philone dicta putat. Et hic heros adeo in Philone hospes Clericum malæ fidei in Philone citando accusare audet. Me sibi seditionem objicere putat, quando triumphum in spatiis imaginariis agere jubeo, innumerabili ex fæcunda gente Menenî turbâ faustis acclamationibus currum prosequente, ignarus fæcundam Menenî gentem non seditiosos, sed stolidos quorum magna ubique copia est, designare.[1] Clerico contra talem adversarium similem, quanquam non adeo gloriosum propter exiguam adversarii eruditionem, eventum, qualem tu nuper omnium judicio consecutus es, prævideo. Scripsit de eo nuperrime ad me Joannes Gib[2] Episcopi Salisburiensis sacellanus, qui me præterito anno vidit, his verbis. *Non dubito quin jam dudum audivisti de indubitatâ victoriâ quam amicus tuus Dominus Lock retulit de Episcopo Vigorniensi, in ejus responsione ultimâ ad objectiones Episcopi contra librum de Intellectu humano. Episcopus eam vidit, nec multò post mortuus est: sed etiamsi*

---

about a spurious book on Biblical antiquities, which is falsely attributed to Philo and is never to be found in Philo's works, is said about the genuine Philo. And this hero who is so unacquainted with Philo dares to accuse Le Clerc of bad faith in citing Philo. He thinks that I am charging him with sedition when I bid him to triumph in imaginary spaces with an innumerable crowd of the prolific race of Menenius escorting his chariot with auspicious acclamations, not knowing that the prolific race of Menenius means, not the seditious, but the obtuse, of whom there is everywhere a great multitude.[1] I foresee for Le Clerc against such an adversary a success similar to that which in everybody's opinion you lately obtained, although not so glorious on account of the adversary's scanty erudition. John Gib,[2] the bishop of Salisbury's chaplain, who saw me last year, wrote to me recently about your success in these words: 'I have no doubt that you have long since heard of the undoubted victory which your friend Mr. Locke won over the bishop of Worcester in his last reply to the bishop's objections to his book concerning the Human Understanding. The bishop saw this reply

---

[1] Horace, *Satires* II. iii. 287. Nothing is known of this name as used by Horace except that it stands for a typical or proverbial case of lunacy; Horace may have taken it from literature. Van der Waeyen was perhaps thinking of Menenius Agrippa, who recalled the Roman *plebs* from the Mons Sacer by his parable of the belly and the members.

[2] I have not found him elsewhere. A letter from him to van Limborch, London, 10 May 1699, and a draft or copy of a letter from van Limborch to him, 12 September 1699, N.S., with two further letters from him, written at The Hague, 1698(?), are preserved among the Remonstrants' Church MSS. in the Amsterdam University Library.

diutius vixisset vix credo eum responsurum fuisse: Omnia enim istic adeo ad vivum demonstrantur, ut nullus locus contradictioni relinquatur. Quod ego non tam illius, quam ipsius Episcopi judicium esse credo.

Quæ de decreto illo, hominibusque quos decretum spectat scribis, vera esse scio: quæque illi palliando ad me scripta sunt, prætextus tantum esse semper credidi, ne, dum pœnæ adversus dissentientes decernuntur, persecutio introduci existimetur. Ego prolixam quam scripsi epistolam Generosissimo D. Aslei,[1] ut et D. Flesher,[2] prælegi: ex quibus quam aperte sine ullâ dissimulatione scripserim facile intelliges: et si postremis hisce respondeam eâdem utar παῤῥησίᾳ.

Exactiorem Hammonti historiam quærendo nolim multum te fatiges: si absque tuo incommodo eam mihi suppeditare potuisses, gratum fuisset. Credidi ego linguâ Anglicâ exstare historias Ecclesiasticas, in quibus hoc hæretici adeo horrendi exemplum prætermissum neutiquam est. Ejusmodi enim orthodoxiæ de hæresibus triumphos zelotæ in suis historiis magnificè deprædicare solent. Sed quoniam illud exemplum tibi obvium non est, ego brevi illâ Cambdeni narratione contentus ero. Episcopii vitam jam paucas intra hebdomadas prælo subjiciendam credo, quoniam

---

and died not long after; but even if he had lived longer I scarcely think that he would have replied to it; for everything there is so demonstrated to the quick that no room is left for contradiction.' Which I suppose is not so much Gib's opinion as that of the bishop himself.

What you write about that decree and the men whom it has in view I know to be true, and I have always thought that what was written to me to excuse it was only a pretext lest it should be thought that where penalties against dissentients are being decreed persecution is being introduced. I have read to the most noble Lord Aslei,[1] as also to Mr. Flesher,[2] the lengthy letter that I wrote; you will readily learn from them how openly I wrote, and without the least concealment; and if I reply to this last letter I shall use the same freedom.

I should not wish you to trouble yourself much in seeking a more precise history of Hamont; if you could have supplied it to me without inconvenience to yourself it would have been welcome. I supposed that there were to be found Church histories in the English language in which this example of so dreadful a heretic was by no means passed over, for zealots are wont to celebrate proudly in their histories such triumphs of orthodoxy over heresies. But since that example does not lie in your way I shall be content with that short narration of Camden's.

---

[1] Probably Lord Ashley. [2] See p. 661.

ingens quod sub prælo habebat typographus opus jamjam in lucem proditurum est, ut jam illius præla hujus opusculi editione occupari possint.

De Magnifico Viro nihil jam audio, nihil etiam ab ipso responsi exspecto: Videtur aliquatenus congressum meum vitare, fortasse quia me responsum flagitaturum credit: Verum ego statui eum amplius non urgere, ne responsum, quod declinat, flagitando importunus videar.

Me Guenelloni quæ de ipso scripsisti prælegisse testes sunt literæ ipsius, quibus has inclusas voluit. Ipse de nobili illo Muscovitâ pluribus ad te scribit. Salutem quam officiosissimè à nobis dices Dominæ Masham totique familiæ. Salutant te uxor ac liberi, imprimis ego

Tui Amantissimus
PHILIPPUS À LIMBORCH

Amstelodami 2 Octobris

16 $\frac{4}{18}$ 99

Filius rogat has inclusas tradi Dominæ Masham.

Address: Amplissimo Doctissimo Consultissimo Viro D. Joanni Lock Londinum inclusa

Endorsed by Locke: P: Limborch 2 Oct 99 Answered 7

I believe that the life of Episcopius will now go to press in a few weeks' time since a huge work that the printer had in the press will be published forthwith, so that his presses can be occupied now by this small book.

I hear nothing now about the Magnifico; indeed I expect no reply from him. He seems to some extent to avoid meeting me, perhaps because he thinks that I shall demand a reply; but I have decided not to press him further lest I should seem importunate in demanding a reply which he avoids giving.

Guenellon's letter, which he wanted to be enclosed with this, is evidence that I have read to him what you wrote about him. He is writing to you at length about that noble Muscovite. Please give our best respects to Lady Masham and the whole family. My wife and children send you their greetings, as do I

Your most affectionate
PHILIPPUS VAN LIMBORCH

Amsterdam 2 October
1699

My son asks that the enclosed letter may be delivered to Lady Masham.

2619. DR. PIETER GUENELLON to LOCKE, 22 September/2 October 1699 (*2594*, *2633*)

B.L., MS. Locke c. 11, ff. 89–90. Sent with no. *2518*.

d'Amsterd. ce 2 Oct. 1699.

Monsieur

Je suis fort en colére contre mon Moscovite. apres tant d'empressement quil me marqua pour avoir une lettre pour vous, il n'a guere profité de l'occasion. Mais que voulez vous, apres tout, c'est un Moscovite. ce qui me fache le plus, c'est l'interruption quil a donné a nótre commerce de lettre, puisque vous aussi bien que moi étions dans l'attente quelle vous seroit rendue. j'attendois une responce dont sans doutte vous m'auriez gratifiez. depuis l'honneur que j'ay eu de vous écrire par le canal de la poste,[1] il n'est arrivé autre changement dans la famille que celuy qui regarde mon fils pierre. il se plaist beaucoup dans le poste ou je l'ay mis, quoy qu'il n'aye guerre de repos, et bien souvent 30 a 40 lettres a copier en un jour. il ne s'en rebute pas, et trouve beaucoup de charme dans la connoissance que le commerce donne de tout ce qui arrive dans le monde. je souhaitte que son ardeur continue, et j'espere qu'apres tout, nous n'aurons pas lieu de nous repentir du choix que nous avons fait. je ne delaisse pas de poursuivre mon histoire du corps humain, il est vray pourtant que je n'ay pas beaucoup avancé cet eté: les malades m'ont laissé peu de loisir, et nous avons eu nombre de taillez a l'hospital et en ville par le fameu frere Jacques Beaulieu.[2] vous serez peutétre pas faché que je vous en fasse l'histoire. c'est un bourgignon, agé de 48 ans, natif de Besancon, qui a eté maistre chirurgien dans une petite ville sur la Seaune en France, depuis quinze ans quil a quitté sa boutique, (faisant veu de pauvreté et de chasteté) il s'est attaché uniquement a tailler de la pierre et a faire l'operation de l'hernie a ceux qui sont incurables par bandage. il travaille gratis ⟨pa⟩rtout[a] le monde, voulant seulement que les riches, fasse quelque aumone au pauvres. il tailloit autrefois au petit appareil, c'est a dire sur le doit, et depuis il a suivi la methode generalement recüe, de tailler sur l'incision faitte au perinée sur la

[a] *Page torn.*

[1] Apparently a lost letter.

[2] Jacques Baulot called Frère Jacques de Beaulieu, 1651–1719. He had no medica training and no knowledge of anatomy, and was rejected by the Parisian doctors; he appears however to have advanced the practice of lithotomy: *D.B.F.*; Hirsch, *Aerzte*; Lister, *Journey to Paris*, pp. 232–6.

sonde creuse, mais s'affligant que ces deux manieres sont egalement subjectes a laisser des fistules, et un ecoulement volontaire de l'urine par la playe, il s'est appliqué en suivant les armées et frequentant les hospitaux, d'ouvrir un tres grand nombre de cadavres, ce qui luy a donné jour de tailler d'une tout autre maniere. il commence son incision dans la fesse gauche entre l'anus et la tuberosité de l'os ischium, ses sondes sont fort courbes, et de cette maniere, 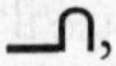, faisant un angle droit avec la manche. par ce moyen il fait tellement elever la partie anterieure de la vessie quil decouvre facilement la sonde au travers de cette epaisseur. il coupe sur le catheter a la partie posterieure et laterale du spincter de la vessie, ou proprement dans la rugosité, qui fait l'entrée, entre l'insertion des ureteres et le spincter. il dilate ensuitte avec son doit. introduit sa tenette, qui est d'un figure et d'un usage beaucoup meilleur que celles dont on a coutume de se servir. elles sont tres lisses, graissées en dehors et en dedans, cachent mieux la pierre, afin quelle n'ecorche pas au passage, elle se loge mieux, ny ayant que peu de dents sur le devant du dedans des tenettes. il taille fort adroittement et fort heureusement. nous avons pas vu encore une seule fistule restée de ses operations, les playes se guerissent a tous ceux qui echapent. il taille aussi les femmes, ce que vous concevrez facilement sur ce que je vien de vous dire. il a taillé depuis trois mois environ trois cent personnes, dans nos Provinces, et comme cela desole les autres operateurs, ils le calomnient cruellement. il est venu en ce pays a l'occasion du frere du Baron van Ehkeren[a] gentilhomme de qualité de la province de Gueldre, quil a gueri a Zutphen d'un Sarcocele, fort grand, que personne n'avoit osé entreprendre, et pour lequel on l'avoit fait venir de Paris a la sollicitation de nôtre Ambassadeur aupres du Roy[1] et Monsieur Fagon[2] premier Medecin de sa Majesté qui en fait grand estime. il est certain que s'est un homme sincere et qui agit par ⟨de⟩[b] tres bons principes de pieté et de charité. il vit tres austerement, et fait distribuer les gratifications quon luy fait au pauvres, sans toucher a un sol. je l'ayme de tout mon cœur, et ce matin en m'habillant il me chapa ce vers

[a] *Or* Ehheren   [b] *Page torn.*

[1] Coenraad van Heemskerck (*N.N.B.W.*), ambassador to Louis XIV from 1698 to 1701.

[2] Gui-Crescent Fagon, 1638–1718; principal physician to Louis XIV from 1693: *N.B.G.* About 1701 he was cut for the stone by another surgeon in preference to Frère Jacques.

Peut on Calomnier un frere
qui dans son vœu de pauvreté,
par acte seul de pieté
pour tout le monde opere?
consolé vous mon cher Beaulieu,
c'est le sort méme du bon Dieu.

Monsieur siebergen fameu medecin a la haye a fait ce joly Epigramme.

restituens homines saxis post terga rejectis
Deucalion, illis saxea corda dedit,
hic jam frater adest, vacuat qui viscera saxis,
artificem tendens cum pietate manum.
dicite Pierides, uter præstantior horum,
qui dedit, an durum qui fugat arte malum?[1]

voicy comme je l'ay traduit.

Deucalion peuplant la terre,
mit dans nos seins un cœur de pierre,
et *Beaulieu* pour le bien commun,
óte la pierre a un chacun,
dite nous lequel des deux
rend les hommes plus heureux?

il est sur son depart pour Zutphen, ou on luy a recueilli un nouveau nombre de malades, de la il prendra la route de flandre pour retourner en france.

Monsieur Bernart vient de publier dans sa republique des lettres du Mois Octobre un commencement d'extraict de vótre demeslé avec l'Evesque de Worcester. il promet la suitte pour le mois prochain.[2] Voicy comme il commence.

il s'est elevé depuis deux ou trois ans une dispute entre Monsieur Stillingfleet evéque de worcester, et Monsieur Locke, deux scavans Anglois fort connus dans la republique des lettres, le premier par une vaste litterature, et le second par une grande penetration et par

[1] Deucalion once with stones behind him thrown
Renewed our race, but gave us hearts of stone.
Now here's a Brother who with pious art
Relieves our vitals of the stony part.
Say, Muses, which of these is worthier: he
Who gave, or he who cures our malady?

W. M. E., the translator, notes two false quantities in l. 5: Pieridēs, ūter.

[2] p. 651.

une justesse d'esprit peu commune. comme cette dispute a continué assez longtems, et qu'on n'en scait presque rien ⟨hor⟩s[a] d'Engleterre que par oüi dire, je crois qu'on sera bien ayse d'en v⟨oir⟩[a] icy un detail un peu circomstantié, autant que les bornes que je me prescris dans cet ouvrage me le pouront permettre. toute la famille vous presente ses tres humbles respects, rejouis d'apprendre que vous vous portez assez bien. je suis avec une profonde veneration

Vostre tres Obeissant serviteur
P. GUENELLON

Endorsed by Locke: Dr. Guenellon 2 Oct 99 Answered 4 Nov.

2620. LOCKE to PETER KING, later first Baron King, 23 September 1699 (2584, 2634)

B.L., MS. Locke c. 40, ff. 46–7.

London 23 Sept 99

Dear Cosin

If you are busy in the Country you are very busy: If you are idle there, which I had rather, you are very Idle. For I finde that you are very spareing in your writeing. I make you this reproach not because I take it much amisse But haveing an occasion to write to you of another matter which will be but short I found I should have roome to tell you that to hear or not to hear from you is not indifferent to me. My principal businesse is to minde you that if you here of any mortgage of about £500 more or lesse if it were to towards £1000 you would let me know of it. Tis not that I choose to have my money soe far off But because I thinke you are likely to know the character of a Mortgagor[b] thereabouts and I would not willingly have to doe but with an honest man. Nor place out my money but where it was like to lye some time, and come home safe at last. I writ to you to Exeter about the 10th of this month. My humble service to your father. I am

Dear Cosin
your most affectionate Cosin and humble servant
J LOCKE

Address: For Peter King Esqr at his father Mr King's house in Exeter
Postmarks: SE 23; GC
Endorsed by King: Mr Locke 23. September 1699

[a] *Page torn.* [b] *Or* Mortgager

Samuel Bold to Locke, 2 October 1699

Enclosed by Bold in his letter of 18 October: see no. *2628*.

2621. Locke to Philippus van Limborch, 7 October 1699 (*2618*, *2631*)

Amsterdam University Library, MS. R.K., Ba 258 j. Printed in *Some Familiar Letters*, pp. 446–52; omitted sentence and address, in Ollion, p. 220. In the translation the quoted passages are copied from the English originals; Locke's principal departures from the originals are indicated in the translation but not in the Latin text. Answers nos. *2596* and *2618*; answered by no. *2631*.

Vir Amplissime

Quod a me petiisti, quærendo apud veterem historicum tandem inveni. En tibi igitur Hammonti crimen et vivicomburium 'Matthæus Hammont aratrorum faber ex vico Hetharset tribus miliaribus a Norwico distante reus factus coram Episcopo Norwicensi accusatus quod negaverat Christum Salvatorem nostrum. Comparenti in judicio objectum est quod sequentes propositiones hæreticas publicasset Nempe Quod N: Testamentum et Evangelium Christi pura stultitia erat, inventum humanum et mera fabula. Quod homo in gratiam restituitur solâ misericordiâ divinâ sine ope sanguinis, mortis et passionis Christi. Insuper quod Christus non est deus, nec salvator mundi, sed merus homo, peccator, et Idolum abominandum. et quod omnes qui illum colunt sunt Idolatræ abominandi. Item quod Christus non resurrexit a morte ad vitam potestate suæ divinitatis, neque in cælum ascendit. Item

---

Excellent Sir,

By seeking in an old historian I have at last found what you asked me for. Here, then, are for you Hamont's crime and burning alive.

'Matthew Hammont, by his trade a ploughwrite of Hetharset three miles from Norwich, was convented before the bishop of Norwich, for that he denied Christ our Saviour. At the time of his appearance it was objected that he had published these heresies following. That the new testament and gospell of Christ are but meere foolishnesse, a storie of man, or rather a meere fable. Item, that man is restored to Grace by Gods meere mercie, without the meane of Christs bloud, death and passion. Item, that Christ is not God nor the saviour of the world, but a meere man, a sinfull man, and an abhominable idoll. Item, that all they that worship him are abhominable Idolaters, and that Christ did not rise againe from death to life by the power of his godhead, neither that he ascended into heaven. Item, that the Holie ghost is

quod spiritus Sanctus non est deus, nec quidem omnino est. Item quod baptismus in ecclesia dei non est necessarius, nec usus Sacramenti corporis et sanguinis Christi. Propter quas hæreses condemnatus est in consistorio, episcopo sententiam pronunciante 13° die Aprilis 1579. et deinde traditus Vicecomiti Norwicensi. Et quia verba blasphemiæ (non recitanda) locutus fuerat contra reginam aliosque e concilio reginæ sanctiore condemnatus est a Judice Norwicensi Windamo et Prætore Norwicensi Roberto Wood ut ei amputarentur auriculæ, quod factum est in foro Norwicensi 13° Maji et postea 12° ejusdem mensis vivicomburium passus est in fossâ Castelli Norwicensis'

Hactenus Hollinshead ad annum 21 Elizabethæ.[1] Huic simile exemplum reperio in Eodem historico ad annum Elizabethæ 25. Verba authoris hæc sunt

'18° die Septembris anno 1583 Johannes Lewes hæreticus obstinatus qui negavit Deitatem Christi et professus plures alias detestandas hæreses, quales fere erant prædecessoris sui Hammonti combustus est Norwici'[2]

---

not God, neither that there is anie such Holie Ghost. Item, that baptisme is no necessarie in the Church of God, neither the use of the sacrament of the bodie and bloud of Christ. For which heresies he was condemned in the consistorie, and sentence was pronounced against him by the bishop of Norwich on the thirteenth day of Aprill ⟨1579⟩[a] and therupon delivered to the shiriffes of Norwich. And bicause he spake words of blasphemie (not to be recited) against the queenes maiestie and others of hir councell, he was by the recorder, master sergeant Windham, and the mayor sir Robert Wood of Norwich condemned to lose both his eares, which were cut off on the thirteenth of Maie in the market place of Norwich, and afterwards, to wit on the twelfth[b] of Maie, he was burned in the castell dich of Norwich.'

Thus far Holinshed in the year 21 of Elizabeth.[1] I find an example similar to this in the same historian in the year 25 of Elizabeth. These are the author's words.

'On the eighteenth day of September ⟨1583⟩[a] John Lewes,[c] an obstinate heretike, denieing the godhead of Christ, and holding divers other detestable heresies (much like his predecessor Matthew Hammont) was burned at Norwich.'[2]

[a] *Added by Locke.* [b] *So Locke; Holinshed gives* twentieth [c] *Locke omits* who named himself Abdoit

---

[1] Holinshed's *Chronicles* (1577; 1587) is not listed among the books in Locke's library.

[2] Lewes is mentioned as an Arian heretic, together with Hamont and Peter Cole, by William Burton (*D.N.B.*) in *David's Evidence*, 1592, passage quoted in *D.N.B.*, art. Hamont. Cole was burnt to death at Norwich in 1587.

Lubet etiam duo alia exempla hujusmodi ex alio authore ⟨suggerere⟩[a] quæ tibi etiam forte usui esse possunt in eo quod præ manibus habes argumento. Primum est Vivicomburium Bartholomæi Legatt Londinensis anno 1611 et Jacobi primi 9. Ob varios Errores. Hæreses, et blasphema dogmata asserta et publicata præcipue in his tredicem positionibus sequentibus viz. Nempe Quod Symbolum dictum Nicænum illudque alterum Athanasii non continent veram professionem fidei Christianæ: Vel quod ille ipse non vult profiteri suam fidem secundum illa Symbola. Quod Christus non est de deo deus genitus, non factus; sed et genitus et factus. Quod nullæ sunt in Deitate personæ. Quod Christus non fuit deus ab æterno, sed incæpit esse deus quando carnem assumpsit ex virgine Maria. Quod mundus non fuit factus per Christum. Quod apostoli docent Christum esse merum hominem. Quod in deo nulla sit generatio nisi creaturarum. Quod hæc assertio, Deus factus est homo, contraria est fidei regulæ et Blasphemia enormis. Quod Christus non fuit ante plenitudinem temporis nisi promissione. Quod Christus non fuit aliter deus quam unctus deus. Quod Christus non fuit in formâ dei æqualis deo. i.e. in substantiâ dei, sed in Justitiâ et dando salutem. Quod Christus deitate suâ, nulla operatus est miracula. Quod preces Christo non sunt offerendæ.

[a] *MS.* suggere

I should also like to add from another author two other examples of this kind that may perhaps be of use to you in that subject that you have in hand. The first is the burning alive of Bartholomew Legatt, a Londoner, in the year 1611 and the ninth of James I, on account of 'divers wicked Errors, Heresies, and blasphemous Opinions, holden, affirmed and published by the said *Batholomew Legatt*, and chiefly in these thirteen blasphemous Positions following, *viz.* That the Creed called the *Nicene Creed* and *Athanasius's Creed*, contain not a Profession of the true Christian Faith, or that he will not profess his Faith according to the same Creeds. That Christ is not God of God begotten, not made, but begotten and made. That there are no Persons in the Godhead. That Christ was not God from everlasting, but began to be God, when he took Flesh of the Virgin *Mary*. That the World was not made by Christ. That the Apostles teach Christ to be Man only. That there is no Generation in God, but of Creatures. That this Assertion, God to be made Man, is contrary to the Rule of Faith, and monstrous Blasphemy. That Christ was not before the fulness of time except by Promise. That Christ was not God otherwise then anointed God. That Christ was not in the form of God equal with God, that is, in substance of God, but in Righteousness and giving Salvation. That Christ by his Godhead wrought no Miracle. That Christ is not to be prayed unto.'

Hic Bartholomæus Legatt ab Episcopo Londinensi assistentibus consentientibusque aliis reverendis Episcopis doctisque clericis hæreseos condemnatus est et brachio sæculari traditus, et deinde igni commissus et combustus in West Smithfeild Londini[1]

Eodem supplicio affectus est Edvardus Wightman in Civitate Lichfeild anno 1611 ab Episcopo Coventriæ et Lichfeild: hæreseos damnatus, ob has sequentes opiniones

1° Quod non est trinitas personarum Patris Filii et Spiritus Sancti in unitate deitatis

2° Quod Jesus Christus non est verus naturalis filius dei, deus perfectus, et ⟨ejusdem⟩[a] substantiæ, Æternitatis, et Majestatis cum patre respectu deitatis suæ

3° Quod Jesus Christus est homo solummodo, et mera creatura, et non deus simul et homo in unâ personâ

4° Quod Salvator noster Christus non sibi sumpsit carnem humanam ex substantiâ Virginis Mariæ matris suæ; et quod promissio illa *Semen mulieris* conteret caput serpentis non adimpleta erat in Christo.

5 Quod persona Spiritus Sancti non est deus, coæqualis, coæternus, coessentialis cum patre et filio

[a] *MS.* ejudem

This Bartholomew Legatt was condemned for heresy by the bishop of London, with the attendance and consent of other reverend bishops and learned divines, and was handed over to the secular arm and thereafter committed to the flames and burned in West Smithfield in London.[1]

The same punishment was inflicted upon Edward Wightman in the city of Lichfield in the year 1611 by the bishop of Coventry and Lichfield; he was condemned for heresy on account of the following opinions: 'That there is not the Trinity of Persons, the Father, the Son, and the Holy Ghost, in the Unity of the Deity. 2. That Jesus Christ is not the true natural Son of God, perfect God, and of the same Substance, Eternity and Majesty with the Father in respect of his Godhead. 3. That Jesus Christ is only Man and a meer Creature, and not both God and Man in one Person. 4. That Christ our Saviour took not human Flesh of the Substance of the Virgin *Mary* his Mother; and that that Promise, *The Seed of the Woman shall break the Serpent's Head*, was not fulfilled in Christ. 5. That the Person of the Holy Ghost is not God coequal, coeternal, and coessential with the Father and the Son. 6. That

---

[1] For Legatt (as Legate) and Wightman, who follows, see *D.N.B.*; Gardiner *History of England*, 1885, etc., ii. 128–30; for Locke's source for the two cases p. 763.

6 Quod tria Symbola sc: Apostolorum, Nicænum et Athanasii continent hæresin Nicolaitarum

7 Quod ille, nempe Edvardus Wightman, est propheta ille cujus mentio facta est 18° Deutron. his verbis. *Suscitabo illis prophetam* etc: et quod verba Isaiæ. *Ego solus torcular calcavi* et Lucæ *Cujus ventilabrum in manu ejus* pertinent propriè et personaliter eidem dicto Edvardo Wightman

8 Quod ille nempe Wightman est persona illa Spiritus Sancti cujus mentio facta est in Scripturâ, et paracletus ille de quo loquitur Johannes. c. xvi. Evangelii sui

9 Quod verba Salvatoris nostri Christi de peccato blasphemiæ contra Spiritum Sanctum de suâ personâ intelligenda sunt

10 Quod Elias ille venturus de quo loquitur Malachi. c: iv suam personam designant

11 Quod anima æque et corpus dormit in somno primæ mortis, et est mortalis respectu somni primæ mortis, uti corpus et quod anima Salvatoris nostri Jesus Christi in illo somno mortis dormivit æque ac corpus ejus

12 Quod animæ Sanctorum defunctorum non sunt membra quæ possident ecclesiam triumphantem in Cælo

13 Quod Pædobaptismus est ritus abominandus

14 Quod celebratio cænæ dominicæ in Elementis panis et vini

---

the three Creeds, viz. the Apostles Creed, the *Nicene* Creed, and *Athanasius*'s Creed are the Heresies of the *Nicolaitanes*. 5. That he the said *Edward Wightman* is that Prophet spoken of in the eighteenth of Deuteronomy in these words, *I will raise them up as a Prophet*, etc. And that, that place of *Isaiah*, *I alone have troden the Wine-press*: And that, that place ⟨of Luke⟩[a] *Whose Fan is in his hand*, are proper and personal to him, the said *Edward Wightman*. 8. And that he the said *Wightman* is that Person of the Holy Ghost spoken of in the Scriptures; and the Comforter spoken of in the sixteenth of St. *John*'s Gospel. 9. And that those words of our Saviour Christ of the Sin of Blasphemy against the Holy Ghost, are meant of his Person. 10. And that, that place, the fourth of *Malachy*, of *Elias* to come, is likewise meant of his Person. 11. That the Soul doth sleep in the sleep of the first Death, as well as the Body, and is mortal as touching the Sleep of the first Death, as the Body is: And that the Soul of our Saviour Jesus Christ did sleep in that sleep of death as well as his body. 12. That the Souls of the elect Saints departed, are not Members possessed of the triumphant Church in Heaven. 13. That the baptizing of infants is an abominable Custom. 14. That there ought not to be in the Church the Use of the Lord's Supper to be celebrated in the Elements of

[a] *Interpolated by Locke.*

in ecclesia esse non debet; neque baptismi in elemento aquæ, uti nunc in Ecclesia Anglicana usus obtinet. Sed baptismus in aquâ administrari debet solis adultis a paganismo ad fidem conversis

15 Quod deus ordinavit et misit illum sc: Edvardum Wightman ad exequendum suam partem operis salutis mundi, ut suâ doctrinâ suisque monitis mundum liberaret ab hæresi Nicolaitarum ut Christus ordinatus fuit et missus ad mundum servandum, et a peccato liberandum morte suâ, et deo reconciliandum.

16 Quod Christiana religio non integra, sed pars solùm illius prædicatur et admittitur in Ecclesia Anglicana

Hæc ex linguâ Anglicanâ nimis fidus interpres verbatim penè neglectâ Latinitatis elegantiâ et sermonis proprietate transtuli. ut dogmata illa hæretica et capitalia, quæ supplicium illud meruerunt tibi, ut apud nos memoriæ mandantur, perfecte innotescerent. Si qua alia hujus generis exempla apud nos extant si cupias ex nostrâ historiâ eruam et ad te mittam

Dum hæc præ manibus haberem allata mihi est gratissima tua 2° hujus mensis scripta epistola adjunctis duabus aliis, altera Guenellonis Nostri ad me, altera filii tui ad Dominam Masham. Sentio te eundem semper quem fueras, facilem, dulcemque amicis.

Quanprimum per otium licebit Allixii et anonymi libros mihi

Bread and Wine: And the Use of Baptism to be celebrated in the Element of Water, as they are now practiced in the Church of *England*. But that the Use of Baptism is to be administred in Water, only to Converts of sufficient age of Understanding, converted from Infidelity to the Faith. 15. That God hath ordained and sent him, the said *Edward Wightman*, to perform his part in the Work of the Salvation of the World, to deliver it by his Teaching, or Admonition from the Heresie of the *Nicolaitanes*, as Christ was ordained and sent to save the World, and by his death to deliver it from Sin, and to reconcile it to God. 16. And that Christianity is not wholly professed and preached in the Church of *England*, but only in part.'

I have translated these passages almost verbatim from the English, rendering them all too faithfully and neglecting the elegance of pure Latin style and propriety of language, in order that those heretical and capital dogmas which merited that punishment may become fully known to you as they are recorded with us. If any other examples of this kind are to be found with us I shall extract them from our history and send them to you if you wish.

While I had this in hand your most welcome letter written on the 2nd of this month was brought to me with two others added to it, the one from our friend Guenellon to me, the other from your son to Lady Masham. I feel that you are the same as you have always been, good-natured and kind to your friends.

perlegendos propona⟨m⟩[a] nec oscitanter. Quandoquidem in eo cardine summam quæstionis versari creditum est

Gaudeo Domini Clerici Epistolas Criticas propediem prodituras. ut brevi confossis adversariis in pace vacet studiis melioribus. Controversarium enim tædium ingens, fructus exiguus

De Magnifico Viro idem quod tu plane sentio, nec ultra fatigandum judico.

Filii tui literas ad dominam Masham misi. Guenellonis epistolæ amicæ brevi respondebo. Hos ambos interim rogo officiosissimè meo nomine salutes ut et uxorem Tuam et filiam. Dominam Guenellon Veeneumque reliquosque amicos nostros communes. Vale ⟨et⟩[b] ut facis me ama

Tui Amantissimum

J LOCKE

Londini 7° Oct. 1699

Address: Mijn Heer Mijn Heer Philip van Limborch bÿ de Remonstranse Kerck op de Kaisars Gracht t'Amsterdam

Noted by van Limborch (beneath date): Recepta 24 Octobris

[a] *End of line.* [b] *MS.* ut

As soon as leisure will permit I propose to read through the books by Allix and the anonymous writer, and not negligently, seeing that the whole question has been thought to turn on that point.

I am glad that Le Clerc's *Epistolæ Criticæ* will appear shortly, so that, having transfixed his adversaries, he may soon be at ease and devote himself to better studies. For in controversies great weariness, small profit.

I think exactly the same as you about the Magnifico and consider that he should be troubled no further.

I have sent your son's letter to Lady Masham. I shall shortly answer Guenellon's friendly letter. Meanwhile please give my best respects to them both, as also to your wife and daughter, Mevr. Guenellon, and Veen and the rest of our common friends. Good-bye, and continue to love me

Your most affectionate

J LOCKE

London 7 Oct. 1699

2622. LOCKE to [FRANCIS NICHOLSON], 10 October 1699 (*2543*)

The Francis Nicholson Papers, Colonial Williamsburg, Inc., Williamsburg, Virginia. Transcribed from photostat. The addressee from the contents and provenance. Answers no. *2543*.

London 10 Oct 99

Sr

Much businesse and little health hath made my answer later

than it ought to have been to soe very civill a lettre as you writ me the begining of the year. And I am uneasy that I have not had the oportunity sooner to tell you how little title I have to those thanks, which are wholy due to the character you had made of your self, for any service you are pleased to think I have donne you. Were my freindship really of that value which you seem to put upon it, I should with more confidence speake of it, and tell you that by the same way you first gaind my esteem you will be sure to keep and increase it. And I shall always think it my duty as well as find it my inclination, whilst I am in the station I now am, to respect and serve those who have the same aimes with me of serveing their country, and promoteing the good of the Plantations. I need not therefor promise you my freindship at our board. All that I can doe in any occasion for you there, I know you will make your self a right to. If in any other capacity I may serve you be pleased to command me.

I returne you my thanks for the bottle of Brandy and the gloves which I received lately from you by the hands of Sir Thomas Lawrence.[1] They were both welcome to me as the product of that country, and I shall shew them as rarities comeing from thence, Espetialy the brandy, which is of a kinde that very few in England ever tasted or heard of before. I am

Sir

Your most humble and most obedient servant

J: LOCKE

Endorsed by Nicholson (?): Mr. Locke[2]

2623. PAUL D'ARANDA to LOCKE, 10 October 169[9] (*2342, 2899*)

B.L., MS. Locke c. 3, ff. 48–9.

Shoram the 10th October 169[9]

Sir

Till I can wait on you in London next week, please to permi[t] this to pay you humble thanks for the favour of your letter and th[e] great kindnesse it advises of. I am not without some hopes that o[n] my Lord's view of the letters you mention, they may appear to b[e]

[1] p. 409.
[2] The writer of the endorsement probably wrote that of no. 2626 also.

such as are seldom refused to any who ask them, and so leave room for the granting your Petition in favour of my Brother,[1] who, be the successe as we wish or not, will, with my self; ever own our obligation to for your endeavour to help one whose being little known, desirous to discharge the work of a minister as he ought, and destitute of other means of subsistence, render him the properer object of your kind aid. Did not his overbackwardnesse to recommend himself, and the narrownesse of my acquaintance hinder his being otherwise provided of a place as his necessity, merits and neernesse of relation to me require, I could not have been bold enough to give you this trouble; and think I may venture to promise that the good successe I hope for now will free you from any more of the like kind hereafter. And indeed 'twill be enough that I owe you my life, and my Bro: his living well.

This businesse filling my mind when I was last at your Lodging, made me forget then to tell you, that the time of my being in London before, just as I was going out of the Town, one Mr Christopher Taylor,[2] with whom my acquaintance began at Bath, meeting me in the street, desired to know if I could not introduce him, with 2 or 3 other Nonconformist ministers, to you? I told him, if he could learn your leisure time, I was confident they would find easy accesse and friendly reception, whither I or any other of your acquaintance were with them or not; and that I did not chuse to go with them without knowing the rest of the Company to be as discreet and moderate men as himself, and somewhat of their businesse. he named Mr Silvester[3] and some other name or two, which through the haste I was then in are forgotten, and said, they intended onely to pay you their respects, and let you know, that tho some among them were a little soul'd people and had shewn themselves impertinently rude to you (I suppose meant of somewhat written against what you have publish'd) yet they were not all so weak, but did many of them highly value the lights you have given the world etc; or words to the like purpose, when being interrupted, we defer'd farther discourse of it till we might next meet. however lest they should resolve to go to wait on you ere I see him again,

[1] Probably Benjamin D'Aranda, vicar of Calne since 1693 (no. *1111*), but a brother-in-law might be intended. I cannot identify the lord.

[2] Presbyterian divine; ordained in 1687; officiating for a time at Bath; from about this year in Leather Lane, London, until his death in 1723: Walter Wilson, *Dissenting Churches in London*, iv. 393–6.

[3] Probably Matthew Sylvester, the editor of *Reliquiæ Baxterianæ*: *D.N.B.*

I thought this notice might be needful, if it be not please to pardon the trouble. I am

Sir

Your most faithful humble servant

P. D'ARANDA

My Wife and Brother intreat your acceptance of their humble service.

Address: To John Locke Esqre at Mr Pawlings over against the Plough Inn in Little-Lincolns-Inn-fields.

Endorsed by Locke: P: D'Aranda 10 Oct 99[a]

2624. JEAN LE CLERC to LOCKE, 11/21 October 1699 (*2595*, *2698*)

B.L., MS. Locke c. 13, ff. 131–2. Printed in Bonno, *Le Clerc*, p. 115.

A Amsterdam le 21. d'Octobre 1699

Il y a long-temps, Monsieur, que je ne me suis donné l'honneur de vous écrire, parce que je croiois le faire, en vous envoiant la nouvelle édition de ma Critique, augmentée d'un 3. Tome, où je réponds à Mrs. Cave et Vander Waeyen.[1] Mais comme je vois que la publication de cet Ouvrage retarde trop, pour quelques raisons de Librairie, et quelques Occupations, que j'ai à present, je n'ai pas voulu laissé partir Mr. de Vaux,[2] qui vous honore et qui vous estime infiniment, sans le charger d'un mot de Lettre, pour vous demander des nouvelles de vôtre santé, et de vos occupations. On m'a dit que vous aviez encore composé un autre Ouvrage de Philosophie de la maniere de conduire son esprit dans la Recherche de la Verité.[3] Si cela est, vous courez risque d'être un peu importuné de le publier, et de me voir dans le nombre de ces importuns. Il n'y a point de livres, dont le Public ait tant besoin que de ceux-là. Pour moi, je m'en vai rentrer dans mon travail de la Bible dès cet hiver; car Petau s'en va fait dans peu de jours, et le reste de ce que j'ai à faire se fera peu à peu. Si vous avez parcouru mon *Harmonie*, et

[a] *There are three calculations by Locke on the last page.*

---

[1] pp. 637–8, 640–1, 668.
[2] I have failed to identify him. Mentioned below, nos. *2899*, *2924*.
[3] Le Clerc perhaps refers to 'The Conduct of the Understanding': pp. 87, 123.

mes *Parrhasiana*, vous m'obligerez de me dire ce que vous en pensez. J'ai dessein de faire quelque jour des notes sur tout le N.T. et de disposer les Epîtres de S. Paul selon l'ordre du temps; à quoi je joindrai des arguemens et une paraphrase, pour en expliquer la liaison et les occasions.[1] Mais il faut ⟨que⟩[a] mon volume, sur les Livres Historiques du V.T. passe auparavant.[2] Je suis, Monsieur, de tout mon coeur, Vôtre très-humble et très-obeissant serviteur

J LE CLERC.

Address: A Monsieur Monsieur Locke at Mr. Pawlings in little Lincolns inne fieds over against the plough. London.

Endorsed by Locke: J: Le Clerc 21 Oct 99 Answered Jan. 8

Notes by Locke on cover: Mr de Vaux Chez Mr Gallinier in dean street Mr la Roche chez Mr Cappelle overagainst my Lord Bathes house in st James street[3] near Petty France

2625. MRS. ELIZABETH STRATTON to LOCKE, 14 October 1699 (*2316*)

B.L., MS. Locke c. 18, f. 233.

Bristoll Octo 14th (1699)

Deare Cousin

I had a satisfactory account of your health by my cousin King[4] which was very wellcome, and shall be glad to be favour'd with the same from your own hand, it being a long time since I har'd from you, I writ to you in the spring by my son Peter Stratton but the sickness of his horse prevented him from waiting on you, I bless God the paine of my head is much abated at present and I have had better health for sum weak's then I have had this four years past, and my daughters at present are preety well who are grown tall but are not healthy, my daughter Ann Hasell lyes in with her fifth son and they have one daughter and are all preety well, I should be glad to see you and should willingly wait on you if I live till summer did not my curcumstancys forbid it, I have often times

[a] *Page torn.*

[1] This may be the first project for Le Clerc's French translation of the New Testament: nos. *2924*, *3279*, etc.

[2] Le Clerc's Latin translation of the historical books of the Old Testament was not published until 1708.

[3] A slip for James Street, Westminster, now the western part of Buckingham Gate.

[4] Peter King, a nephew of the first Mrs. William Stratton; he and the present Mrs. Stratton may have been cousins by birth also.

hopes my end is nigh and think I have good reason to beleve it, and therefore earnestly desire all my accounts were even'd that I might not leave trouble upon young heads, I doe intreat the kindness and should take it as a great favour if you would discharge me of the account that I stand ingagd to you, for to speake the truth I think I shall never be able to pay you, being at present considerably in debt and with all the care I can take cannot keep within the compass of our small income. I have debts beyond sea but can get nothing home, I bless my God for what we have and desire to be truly thankfull.

my bro Chapman and sister give you their Humble services and so doe my son Peter Stratton and both my daughters and pray recive the same from, Deare Cousin,

Your humble servant and Oblig'd Cousin
ELIZABETH STRATTON

Address: For Mr John Lock Esq in London
Endorsed by Locke: E: Stratton 14 Oct 99

2626. LOCKE to COMMISSARY JAMES BLAIR, 16 October 1699 (*2545*)

The Francis Nicholson Papers, Colonial Williamsburg, Inc., Williamsburg, Virginia. Transcribed from Xerox print. Answers no. *2545*.

London 16 Oct 99

Sir

You that know my bad health and some part of my businesse in town will I doubt not pardon the slownesse of my return to your letter of February last espetialy since it conteind noe thing of businesse to be donne, But gratefull reflections on what had been donne, with an over great opinion expressed of that service which you imagin you had from my hand in the doeing of it. I shall not undertake to answer all the great compliments you make me on this occasion. I take them, as I ought, to be the language of your civility. But this give me leave to say that if I have been any way instrumentall in procureing any good to the country you are in, I am as much pleased with it as you can be. The flourishing of the Plantations under their due and just regulations being that which I doe and shall always aim at whilst I have the honour to sit at the board I now doe.

I hope the Colledge grows and flourishes under your care. I would be glad to know whether you caried over with you a Baroscope[1] and Thermoscope[2] from hence when you went over last. For I thinke a constent register of the air kept there would not be only of generall use to the improvement of Natural philosophie but might be of particular advantage to the plantation it self, by observations to be made on the changes of the air.

I know your country has many natural curiosities, such of them as come in your way and are of noe difficult transportation I should receive as an obligation from you, more particularly all seeds of all strange and curious plants, with an account of the soyles they grow in, and the best seasons you observe there for sowing of them. Amongst other things you will doe me a favour to send me a plentifull stock of peach stoans of your best sorts of peaches. I am

Sir

your most humble servant

JOHN LOCKE

Address: For Mr Commissary Blair at the Colledge in Virginia
Endorsed: Mr Locke[3]

2627. MRS. ELIZABETH BERKELEY, later BURNET, to LOCKE, 17 October 1699 (*2604*, *2702*)

B.L., MS. Locke c. 3, ff. 224–5.

Sir

Since my coming into the Countrey reflecting on some discourse I had in Town, concering the state of the soul after death, I seet my self to read the new Testement as heedfully as I could with a regard only to that perticuler, and I confess I find many texts that seem very favourable to that openion that suspends the happenesse of the soul to the generall Resurection and reunion with a Body, yet I think few of them are so express but that another sense may be giveen, and that for the more received openion of its keping an uninterupted self consiousness some places are very express and full, I own I am not quit an indifferent examiner! sure

[1] A kind of barometer: *O.E.D.*

[2] In this period an alternative name for the thermometer: ibid.

[3] Written probably by the writer who endorsed no. 2622. He is unlikely to be Blair.

that earnest desire of Being, and those hopes that are so near an asurence and certainty are not only the effects of fancy and Enthusism but corispond with some truth, and those earnest desiers are not given to no end; when I consider the greatness of some minds, how just how penetrating, how well disposed to be inlighten'd beyond the capacities of this state, of which the baer remembering to whom I write furnishes me with a very perswading and excelent Idea, for my part I cannot easlyly beleeve a mind so raised and so well prepared must be shut up in a long state of ignorance and inactiveity, its looks like a defect in so excelent a part of the Creation to joyn something so excelent as a Rationall mind to what is so week and frail as the Body in so inseperable a maner as to make the operation of the one depend on the texture of the other; not that I think such reasonings of any force against revelation, for if God has made us otherwise I dout not but 'tis in the whole best it should be so; but since many parts of revelation look favourable the other way, wee may be, sure, permited to hope and agrue for what is most desireable. As I read over the new Testement I write down what most readely came into my thoughts, that I might with less trouble remember and revive them; I had inded once a purpose of incosling them in this paper, but I have altered my mind, for as 'twould be great vanity to suppose them worth the time they will cost you in reading, so methinks 'tis not less impertenant to send them if they are not, indid could I hope that by turning your thoughts so long on this subject, they were capable of but accidentaly giveing you any new refflection on the side of truth be it which it will it would tempt me to venture exposing my one ignorance to your repeated observation; don't mistake this last expression I am far from fearing you will expose it to my injurie, but you can't help seeing it your self while I take so many opertunitis to fix it in your memorie; what I writt on this subject was allmost all at this place where I had no Books but the Bible, so I may or may not have given the common sense of expositers for ought I know, for I remember noon of them or ever read many; but since I have by reading it[a] over[a] my self I have found it best to spare you that trouble. I only mention it as the true cause I have so slowly thanked you for your last, which is never willingly delayed but out of my fear of importuneing you with letters so litle worthy the persone they are sent to; You gave me hopes too of an answer to

[a] *Substituted for* them

an other part of my letter; but not hearing more I conclude it is not aprovd of;[1] my Brother Dormer has not ben in London sinse your letter but designs going next week. I know not if you will be then in Town, I'm sure the defference he pays to your Judgment will very much govern his if he could be so happy to know it; I am now going to Worcester. I can't yet tell how long I may stay there, I shall in all places pray for your health, and be glad to hear of it might it be no trouble to you, my sister gos from hence in a day or tow, haveing used the Baths on account of her late misfortune of miscarying twice sone after one another. I can't have so much as a prospect of any service I am capable of returning for the many favours I am in debt, I can only say I should be highly pleased with any opertunity of aproving myself

Sir

Your Most Faithfull Humble servent

E BERKELEY

Oct: 17: Bath: 99:

My sister is desireous to be thought of, sends her service and both our thanks for the Book you sent us, I fear I have ben a lazie instructor tho I like the book very well;

Address: To Mr Locke London

Endorsed by Locke: E: Berkeley 17 Oct 99 Answered 11 Dec.

2628. SAMUEL BOLD to LOCKE, 2 and 18 October 1699 (*2602, 2687*)

B.L., MS. Locke c. 4, ff. 32–5. Bold enclosed the letter of 2 October in that of the 18th.

Steeple. 2d. Octob: 1699.

Honoured Sir

Being disapointed of the satisfaction I have all the summer hoped for in waiting on you, and receiving your opinion concerning several points I purposed to propose to you, together with what thoughts occurred to me in meditating on them, as wel as to be informed by you of some matters, you intimated by your last to me, you would be so kinde as to communicate, if I came up to town, I now returne you my hearty thanks for *Catholicism*

[1] This probably refers to the proposed match for Lord Ashley.

without Popery.[1] and *The Judgement of the Ancient Jewish Church against the Unitarians etc.*[2] The former doth please me very much, tho I am not certain that I comprehend everything in It, I stick a little at one or two passages. The latter, is either much above me, or else leaves the Trinitarian controversy in the same state It was before. How ful an Answer It may be to M. N,[3] I know not, for I never saw the book. Dr Alix (who is said to be the Author) may induce his reader to think that the Ancient Jews before our Saviours time were possessed with that philosophy, which furnishes people with the Notion of *a Common nature in several Individuums.* But their espousing that notion, makes It not one Jot the truer, or more Intelligible, nor doth any thing the Doctor saith, make It so to me. I read the book over once, and in reading It, took notice of several things which to me wanted proof, and some which I could not reconcile; several considerations, which are offered as Reasons, which I cannot perceive to be reasons of what they are brought for; many places of scripture, which his notions instead of making plainer and more Intelligible, do much obscure. I think also the Doctor doth not sufficiently distinguish betwixt Jewish Notions, being used, as Arguments to themselves, and being delivered as Divine Truths. and several other such mistakes I had occasion to take notice of. But I wil not trouble you with a particular account of what I thought would admit of Just exception. I wil only insist on two things, which render the Doctor's performance not satisfactory to me. The first respects the main proposition the Doctor undertakes to maintain. the second respects his way of defending or proving It. I begin with the latter. His way of proving the point, He undertakes to defend. which is, what He cals, Traditional exposition: For He undertakes to prove the doctrine of the Trinity, as commonly worded, by the Traditional exposition of the scripture among the Jews: Now He doth not use this phrase, Traditional exposition in one determined sense; which I take to be a very great oversight. this, makes his discourse, much larger than otherwise It needed to be, and makes It very obscure and unconcluding to me. Traditional exposition stands with him, sometimes for: 1: *A doctrine not unknown in scripture, but drawn from scripture, and acknowledged for the common faith of the church* [p. 5.][a] by the way, He

[a] *Marginal note.*

---

[1] Published this year. L.L., no. 636. [2] The book by Allix: p. 624, etc.
[3] Allix's preface, p. xvi, meaning Mr. Nye: *D.N.B.*, art. Stephen Nye.

gives no account what He means by the *Church*: nor what he means *by being drawn from scripture*: If by a doctrine drawn from scripture be meant a proposition not expresly laid down in scripture, but formed by substituting other words in the room of those the scripture doth use; Then if the words of this new proposition, be used only to express or signify exactly the same Ideas expres'd by other words in scripture, It cannot properly be said to be a doctrine drawn from scripture, but is perfectly the same, for sense, and differs only in sound. If the words are used to signify Ideas, which are not signified by the words in scripture, then, whether It be pretended to be drawn from scripture, or no, It is unknown in scripture. If by a doctrine drawn from scripture, is meant, a proposition, the subject whereof, is discoursed of in scripture, but what is predicated concerning It in the proposition, is not expresly delivered in scripture, but inferred and deduced from the manner of expression used concerning It in scripture, Then, the proposition or doctrine may both be unknown in scripture, and it may so happen that there may not be sufficient ground for the Deduction, but the Inference may be extended further, than the truth of the matter wil Justify. And if the church hath a long time made Articles of Faith this way, how common soever the Faith hath bin, she hath done more than she had a Right to do. In page. 11. He saith, *The first order of Jewish Traditions*, is of the things which they infer from Moses and the prophets by a clear consequence, and they are certainly of the same authority, as the rest of the Revelation, altho *they call it a Tradition.* I am not satisfied of the truth of this proposition. A proposition clearly derived from divine Revelation, is not thereby made divine revelation, any more than a proposition clearly inferred from a self evident proposition, is thereby made a self evident proposition. And if so, I can not see how it can be certainly of the same Authority with Divine revelation. I acknowledge, A clear, Just Inference from divine revelation, is a certain Truth. But then, every thing that may be called by that name, may not be truly so. And Inferences how Just and regular soever, do oblige none, but those who perceive that they are justly drawn from revelation. To those who receive them gratis, and never examin them, they are of no Authority, or at most, of no more authority, than they borrow from them, upon whose word they are received. To such, they are no more than bare traditions. And laying aside the consideration of the relation they may have to

practice, the difference is not much, whether they be True or Fals.
2. A summary account of what is delivered in more words, and in several places of scripture concerning some point. p. 53.
3. A strict translation of words, out of one language into another, or the natural and literal sense of words. p. 95. Had the Doctor stuck to this sense of the phrase, I think the greatest part of his book would have bin spared, but whether this would answer his design, may be doubted. 4. The mystical or spiritual sense of words. This, the Doctor makes much use of, and has by this means an opportunity to set down a great many obscure sayings of the ancient Jews, as hard to be understood by me, as many things writ by some later Rosicrusians.[1] Me think's a Critick should know that the words in which a Revelation is delivered, must stand for, and signify the Ideas, of which they were designed to be marks or signs, at that time when the revelation was delivered: And that if they were then used to signify other Ideas, then they did ordinarily signify, what those different Ideas were, must then be made known. so that who so ever wil insist on a spiritual or mystical sense of words, must prove the alteration of their sense at the time when the revelation was first delivered. The tradition should ascend up to the time of the revelation, otherwise It leaves us in the depth of uncertainty. I am aware, It may be said, that the tradition insisted on proves the sense pleaded for, to be the avowed sense in our saviours time and his not correcting the Jewish notions, but allowing them, is ful satisfaction that tho we cannot run the tradition exactly up to the time before mentioned, yet the tradition insisted on, is the true account of the sense in which the words are to be understood, and which was originally designed in the Revelation. Therefore I proceed to give you a short account of what I named in the first place, viz. why the Doctor's performance doth not satisfy me, considering what He saith of the main proposition He undertakes to prove by traditional exposition. The Doctor saith, The Jews before Christ's time, according to the received expositions of the old Testament, derived from their fathers, had a notion of a plurality of persons in the unity of the Divine essence;

[1] 'Later' in reference to the ancient Jews. The Rosicrucians were the members of a society, or supposed society, which is mentioned first by name in 1614; they appear to have been mystics and they claimed that they possessed supernatural powers. The name is also applied loosely to their disciples and imitators: books by P. Arnold and F. A. Yates cited above, p. 575, n. 1. Locke, like Bold, regarded them as fantastic and irrational: *Essay*, II. i. 19.

and that this plurality was a Trinity, p. 6. And, The doctrine of the trinity supposes the divine essence to be common to three persons, distinguished from one another by incommunicable properties: p. 99. and several times He affirms that Father, Son, and Holy Ghost, are strictly and properly three persons. Now, I do not concern myself, whether the Jews had this Notion or no, viz. The Divine Essence is common to three persons. or, there is a plurality of persons, in the unity of the Divine Essence. For if the Notion be not Intelligible, It matters not, who may be pretended to have It. His discourse would have afforded me more satisfaction, than It doth, if He had either of Himself, or from the Jews, given a clear and distinct account, what we are to understand here, 1. by Divine essence? 2. What by the term, person? And then had shewn that something besides an Abstract Idea, can properly be said to be common to several Individuums, or persons. But instead of doing these things, The Doctor seem's not to have any setled Idea to signify by the word *person*. Sometimes He useth It to express or signify A compleate Intelligent substance. Sometimes It stands for, a Property. p. 116. Sometimes, It stands for, A living Intelligent free principle of Action. p. 182. According to the first sense of the word person, This proposition, There are three persons, in the unity of the divine essenc (by essence, here, I conceive is meant substance) wil in other words be thus, There are three compleat Intelligent substances, in the unity of the Divine (which wil not be denied, to be Intelligent substance) substance. Now if this be Intelligible, this easie question may be admitted to come into consideration viz. whether the proposition do not expresly speak of four Intelligent substances? If the Doctor wil adhere to his second sense of the word, I suppose the Unitarians are as much agreed with Him, as He is with the Ancient Jews. As for his third sense of the word, It needs explaining, and what He means by It, I know not. Perhaps upon a commodious exposition of It, It may do service towards the determining the Trinitarian Controversy.

The Doctrine of the Trinity, according to the Doctor, if I mistake not, is a proposition, drawn by the Jews from the mystical sense, In which they learnt by Tradition, certain words in the old Testament were to be understood. The truth of the proposition, the Doctor thinks sufficiently made out, because The words were used in that mystical sense by the Jews before, and in our saviours time, and He and his Apostles did use them in the same sense, because they did not signify that they intended to express any other Ideas by them, And the proposition It self, was the common Faith at that time.

The matter appears pretty plausible at first veiw, which I suppose occasions many to think the Doctors performance fully satisfactory, and unanswerable. I beg leave to trouble you with setting before you my own thoughts. The scripture speaks concerning some[a] things[a] in such a manner, that barely considering the manner of expression there used, we should be apt to think that what is said of them, cannot in ordinary discourse, especially about matters, that fal under our distinct cognizance, be applied to any thing properly, but what agrees or answers to the Idea we have formed in our minds, and signify by the word, Person. Hence we readily enough frame propositions concerning those things, and predicate the word person of them, instead of using those words, which are predicated of them in scripture. Now, tho very often in doing thus, we shal be in the right, and those propositions may truly be said to be drawn from scripture; yet we are not always sure to be in the right, if we do so. In drawing Inferences from scripture, we must not barely look at the mode of expression there used, but we must also have respect to the nature of the subject spoken of. Not only are some things sometimes spoken of in scripture, in the manner above named, which are in their own nature much beneath, what is signified by the word Person, as when Inanimate and Irrational things are spoken of in that manner; But sometimes such subjects are discoursed of in that manner, as do far transcend our comprehension. And this being done by way of Condescention to our capacities, It may be much safer to keep strictly in such cases to Scripture expressions and phrases, than to substitute words of our own devicing and which properly belong only to creatures, of as limited a nature, as our selves. When God condescends to our weakness in speaking concerning things which are out of our sphær, we have leave to speak of them, in the same manner, or to use the same expressions concerning them: but we must not by any means tie them down to our Feeble conceptions, or think, that by substituting other words of our own, we can ascend to give a nice philosophical account of them. We may greatly disparage the subjects we speak of, by thus endeavouring to bring them down to our own level. Supposing both Jews, and primitive christians, by way of

[a] *MS.* somethings

Inference, from what the scripture saith concerning Father, Son, and Holy Spirit, have said that Father, etc are three Persons; the immediate question is not, whether they did amiss therein? but whether they did mean precisely the same by the word person, in that proposition, as they did when they applied It, to created Beings? And if they did, then the Question wil be whether they did well in doing so? and in making Articles of Faith in that manner? If it shal be said they did do wel therein, It may be ask'd, what there is common betwixt the creator, and creatures, that the same complex Idea can exactly agree to both? I do not object against the word Person in the Doctrine of the Trinity. What is said concerning Father, son, and holy spirit, in scripture, or the way of speaking concerning them, in scripture, hath much analogy with what pertains to those to whom the complex Idea we express by the word Person, doth exactly agree. But the word person, when applied to them, I conceive, stands for an Imperfect, undistinct and confused Idea, and has not that precise, determinate, certain sense It hath, when used concerning Rational creatures. The word, doth originally stand for an Idea we have derived from particular beings we are wel acquainted with, and doth in It's strict and proper sense fit only Finite beings; And therefore when attributed to the Divine being, must be supposed to signify, or connote something more excellent, than what our usual Idea doth comprize in It; and so stands for something, which is far above our reach, and of which we have no more distinct Idea, than we have of substance in general, or of substance, when we apply that word to God. I oppose not, as I said, the use of the word Person, in the doctrine of the Trinity, but peoples assuming to comprehend what is above them, and to bring down Inscrutable points, to the narrow limits of their scanty Ideas, and imperfect sounds. That, Father, son, and holy spirit are one God, should be an article of our Faith, when Divine Revelation teaches It, is very Reasonable; And to answer, when It is ask'd How they are so? we cannot tell, because the Mode is not revealed, should in reason be judged satisfactory, and that there should be such kinde of mysteries belonging to revealed Religion, carries I think no absurdity in It, because the Mode is no part of our Faith. But to say they are strictly and properly three real persons in one Divine essence, seem's to me, an asserting what Revelation doth not teach, and to be an imposing on men for Revelation, what doth combate the Reason of mankinde. And to excuse their doing so, by saying It is a mystery, seem's little better than an Impudent insulting their fellow creatures. for the mystery here pretended is not concerning the unrevealed Mode, of what is really revealed, but the using of the word Mystery, to justify their putting upon men, that, for a divine Revelation, which is not so. Did the scripture expresly teach that they are three real persons, properly so called etc, and the question were then asked, How they are, or can be so? to answer, That is a mystery, we know nothing of, because not revealed, would be justifiable, and satisfactory enough. But they without sufficient authority from scripture, draw an Inference, and impose that Inference as an Article of Faith, and when they are told Their proposition is not true, being grounded upon fals philosophy, and that it is not consistent with the Reason of mankind, they answer It is a mystery and hath bin the common Faith of the Church, no body knows how long, and therefore our Reason must submit. And the same they may say for any proposition how groundless and absurd soever, which they have a minde to Fob people with. Submitting the Scripture, and Reason, so long, to the Authority of the Church, and Tradition, hath done Religion unexpressible disservice, and hath contributed not a little to the bringing us to that Deplorable estate in which people generally seem to be, viz. a perfect estrangedness from, and enmity to the truth and power of christianity. Had people a due regard to scripture, and less to tradition, and what that alone, or together with peoples lusts, and worldly Interests, supports, I am perswaded their Faith would make them much better men, and therefore better Christians, than they commonly appear. God speaks of himself to us, in that manner we speak of our selves, and of our fellow creatures, and so far, we have liberty to speak of him in the same manner. But we take more liberty, than is given us, if we do strictly attribute to him, what ever we can regularly infer concerning our selves, or creatures like our selves, from those modes of speaking. Therefore when we apply unto God our own phrases (by which, I mean words, the scripture doth not use) which fit us, and other creatures very well, It wil behoove us to remember his distance from us, his supereminence above us, and how infinitely He transcends all our Conceptions. We cannot by searching finde out God unto perfection, And we can know no more of him, than He is pleased to reveal of himself. We may say that Father, Son and Holy Spirit, are spoken of in scripture, as we usually speak of creatures, who exactly answer that Idea, we express by the word Person; But when we say they are three Persons, we are to leave the precise Idea, the word person signifies, when applied to creatures, and mean by it something far transcending that Idea, and of which, we have no clear, distinct, or determined Idea. I do not minde that the Doctor doth produce any passages out of the Ancient Jews, whereby they positively determine that Father, Son, and Spirit, are three proper persons. His quotations do abundantly shew they did speak of them, as persons are usually spoken of, that is, as they are spoken of in scripture, and so far they cannot be blamed. But the Doctor saith, p. 160. It is certain that they make use of the word *πρόσωπον*,[1] to express those persons, as they use to express the two first humane persons, viz. Adam, and Eve. And for this He refers to Bachaje.[2] To whom I am a stranger, but I am inclined to think He did not write Greek.

But if the Doctors of the Jews both before and in our saviours time did expresly declare that Father, Son, and Holy Spirit, were strictly three persons in the divine essenc, and this was the common Faith of the Jewish church at that time, yet Jesus Christ, nor his Apostles ever teaching that doctrine, nor ever declaring they were strictly persons, nor ever using the word person in It's strict sense concerning either Father, son, or holy spirit, but speaking constantly according to the mode of speaking of them used in the old testament, may intimate his dislike of their traditional doctrine, and exposition, and that his disciples should content themselves with speaking of them, as the scripture doth, and not be too adventurous after the example of the Jews, in drawing Inferences concerning such points.

I am not able to say much of the Ancient Jewish notions, but from what I meet with out of their authors, in the Doctor's book, if He had not given his word for It, that they make use of the word *πρόσωπον*, as before related, I should be apt to think their notion amounted to no more than this, (tho they sometimes talk somewhat extravagantly, and enthusiastically) That, God, by which word they mainly intend the Father, hath two powers, viz.

[1] 'Person', literally 'face' or 'countenance', which in fact the Jews used in their language for the same thing.

[2] '*Bachajè* a famous commentator of the Pentateuch, who brings in his work all the senses of the four sorts of Interpreters among the Jews': Allix, p. 160. Identifiable as Baḥya (Beḥai) ben Asher ben Ḥlava, a Spanish Jew. His commentary, completed in 1291, was printed first in 1492; there were at least nine further editions by 1600: *Encyc. Judaica*; etc.

wisdom, or λόγος, called the Son, and Goodness, or as sometimes ⟨they⟩[a] phrase It, understanding, called the Spirit. And of these powers, they speak, as they did of those creatures who exactly answer the Idea expres'd, or signified by the word person, and do ordinarily attribute the name of God unto them, but that they did not say they were precisely persons, according to the proper sense of that word, but that if they called them persons, It was to note, that wisdom, and understanding in God are incomprehensibly above what we mean by those words, when we apply them to, or predicate them of creatures, in whom they are but Qualities, or strictly powers.

Whereas the Doctor often saith the stile of God in scripture, leads one naturally to the notion of a plurality of persons in the divine nature or essence. And that this was the common faith of the Jewish church. Yet by his quotations, or his own declaration, from His Jewish Authors, It sometimes appears to be a Mystery not very easie to be found out, nor very safe to be divulged. Philo (saith the Doctor) after all, warns his Reader, that this is a Mystery, not to be communicated to every one, but only to them, who were capable to understand, and to keep It to themselves, By which he sheweth that this was kept as a Cabala among the Jewish Doctors, for fear if it came out, the people might misunderstand It, and thereby fall into Polytheism. p. 149.

I should Sir, much inlarge your trouble, should I set down all the particular mistakes, and Inconsistencies, I apprehended I took notice of in a something hasty reading over the Doctor's book; And therefore wil not give you any further disturbance. only craving your pardon for being so tedious to you at this time, I subscribe myself in all sincerity

Your most humble and obliged servant

SA: BOLD.

Address: To the Honoured Mr Locke

Endorsed by Locke: S: Bold 2 Oct 99 Answered Feb. 13

Steeple 18th Octob: 1699.

Honored Sir

Since the Inclosed was writ, and waited for conveighance, I received M Le Clerc's Harmonia Evangelica.[1] And the last week

[a] *MS.* the

[1] pp. 423, 559.

I received a letter from Mr A. Churchill, where in he acquaints me that you sent Le Clerc's book to me, for which I returne you my most humble thanks, with a most affectionate sense of your great kindness, yet I am really in some pain and trouble because you put your self to so much expence on my account. I have created you so much trouble by inclosing so long a scrawl, and so many crude and disjoynted thoughts, I wil disturbe you no further at this time, but only by hinting to you, That I suspect should Dr Alix's notion be throughly followed, It would appear to render both the old and new Testament as useless to the common people, as It may be thought to advance the Credit of the Targums[1] etc amongst the learned. And that seeing the Targums, and old Jewish books, of (at most) a few hundred years before Christ, have the sense in which the words of the old and new Testament are to be understand,[2] which sense is to be fetched only from them, It is in those books, that the Divine Revelation is contained (tho the Authors of those books were not divinely inspired) and the books of the old and new testament consist only of empty sounds, which afford not any Instruction, tho they were writ by persons divinely Inspired; And the last result of his Notion I fear wil be, That our Faith must ultimately be founded on Humane Tradition. Sir I am

your most humble and obliged servant

SA: BOLDE.

Address: To the Honoured Mr Locke

Endorsed by Locke: S: Bold 2 and 18 Oct 99 Answered Feb. 13

2629. BENJAMIN FURLY to LOCKE, 20/30 October 1699 (*2572, 2639*)

B.L., MS. Locke c. 9, ff. 151–2, 149–50. The abbreviated signature and the absence of greetings to Sir Francis and Lady Masham show that the second piece is a postscript to the first.

Rotterdam 30 October 1699

Dear Sir

Yours of the 10/20 past by mr. Edward Clarke[3] I received while

[1] See p. 660, n. 1.

[2] This was a form of the past participle common until about 1575: *O.E.D.* Here it may be a survival or a slip.

[3] He is mentioned below as travelling in the United Provinces. He is unlikely to be Locke's friend, who was in poor health in September and who asked Locke for a

I was at Geesbergen, the house of mr. Buchius,[a] 2 houres from Utrecht in Marseveen.[1] I presume, the name is not unknown to you ever since you saw his booke, which I translated into and the Baron van Helmont got printed in English and afterwards, at his return hither from England, finding the Doctor residing in Dantzick, contrary to his parole as the Doctor saith in Dutch. Which occasiond such a breach betwixt them, that they never after would see or speak with each other. And this is the first step you require me to give you an account of from his landing here, to his dying day.[2] The aggravations, tho there had been no preingagement or parole, when he intrusted him with the dutch copy for me onely to read, and if I pleasd, to translate, but not to keep a dutch copy of, which the Baron told me he might not suffer, and so in all probability much lesse might himself make so publike.

The Doctor understanding that his wives mother was very weak, and disturbd in his senses, brake up from Dantsick and came to Amsterdam, where he found his book, almost, printed, of this he complained first to the Baron, upbraiding him with the breach of his word, begging him but to desist till he had got his mother and her estate removed from Leyden, where she was, in the hands of men of the church, his bitter enemies because he had layd aside the Chemarims,[3] or black coats livery, he told him the publishing it at that time might raise the enmity to that pitch, that it might cause an application to the magistrates to secure her and hers there, to prevent her being exposd to such a heterodox person, assured him that once within two months give it forth with additions (which he did) but nothing could stop him, his time was short etc—The Doctor applyed himself then to the bookseller, and threatned him, if he printed his copy against his will. and that not working told him he would publish it in the Courant[4] that that was a defective copy and he would publish his own books redrest of severall mistakes etc—assuring him, that the edition would ly in his hands. He replyed the Baron would not let him be a loser, and so on it

[a] *Locke notes* Buchius *in margin.*

---

recommendation to Furly in September 1700: nos. 2611, 2617, *2772*. Perhaps Clarke's son Edward. Locke's hope for news 'from beyond sea' in his letter to Clarke of 22 March 1700 (no. 2695) perhaps refers to travel abroad by him.

[1] Maarssen: p. 158. Furly sent accounts of the book and of the quarrel between Buchius and van Helmont to Locke in 1694: nos. *1702*, *1764*.

[2] Van Helmont was in England in the later months of 1693: no. *1687*, etc.

[3] No. *1672*.

[4] The Gazette in no. *1764*.

went and out it came, and out they fell with one another—This was no favourable beginning. The next step he tooke was from thence to Cleve, where he met with a cunning young woman of his family, that was provided for his reception, having learnd what was his darling, and so upon the first approach was so much ravisht with his discourse that she presently profest herself a proselite, to his darling opinion, in so much that she gaind his heart, This lady had not been long there, but a young Gentleman Drost of a place not far from thence, fell in love with her, married her,[1] and so he took up his quarters there for about a yeare, then he went up to the court of Hanover and was there wel received by the Electresse, sister of his old beloved Princess Elizabeth a daughter of the King or Queen of Bohemia's.[2] There he accompanyed the Electress to the comedyes, Balls etc—as a young gallant. Then he came back to his deare Cousins stayd there a competent time, and then came to Amsterdam, and so gave us a visit of 8 days, and having printed his explication, such as you have seen, on the 4 first chapters of Genesis,[3] and after 2/m stay in Amsterdam, retired to Borch, the residence of the Drost about 3 houres from Emmerich, and their dyed after about 4 a 5 weeks, intending as I heare again for Hanover. This Lady he made his heire, who I heare is in suit for the Estate having received already f 12000 besides the gold found about him, and is in pursuit of more in the court of Brabant. This is all that I can inform you concerning him since his leaving England, save that they say this Lady has a son in whom the Baron is supposed to be revolved already, it being very like him.[4]

[1] No. *1830*. In what follows 'he' is van Helmont.

[2] The Electress Sophia; Elizabeth, 1618–80, abbess of Herford (Protestant); their parents, Frederick V of the Palatinate, 'the Winter King' of Bohemia, and Elizabeth, daughter of James I, 'the Queen of Hearts'. Sophia calls van Helmont 'unser gutter Helmont'; he was in Hanover about *1696*: Sophia, *Briefe . . . an die Raugräfinnen . . . zu Pfalz*, ed. E. Bodemann, 1888, p. 135, etc.; Leibniz, *Corr. . . . avec l'électrice Sophie*, ii. 28.

[3] p. 159. It was published about July *1697*.

[4] Elizabeth Charlotte, duchess of Orleans, was told how van Helmont had helped Mlle de Merode to escape from a convent and made her marry 'einen unterambtman in einem dorff', and taught her his philosophy; 'undt wie er gefühlt, dass er nahe bey seinem todt were, hette er diesse dame kommen lassen, umb ihr seinen geist zu geben, hette ihr gesagt, ihren mundt auff den seinen zu thun, hatt er damitt ins maul gehaucht undt gesagt: "Ich erlasse euch meinen geist", hette sich darauff gewendt undt were gleich gestorben. Die dame aber glaube jetzt fest, sie hette Helmonts geist in sich': *Aus den Briefen . . . an die Kurfürstin Sophie*, ed. Bodemann, i. 424.

At Mlle de Merode-Motzfeld's request Leibniz wrote an epitaph for him:

Nil patre inferior jacet hic Helmontius alter
Qui junxit varias mentis et artis opes:

I have now to tell you that those 4 books of mr. Crells,[1] who is here and salutes you, were sent by Ned Snudden, by whom this goes to mr. Wright, 3 in one address to yourself, and one to my Lord Ashley, last voyage, and were both in one packet addrest to mr. Sonmans. to whom he says, he thinks, he delivered them himself: if not, they may possibly have been burnt about a month hence, his house with 3 neighbouring houses, to his great losse having been burnt, while we were at Dr. Buchius's.

Mr. Clarke and his good guide, understanding I was there, tooke the most pertinent directions that could be where to find me, (which they might have done 5 times every day) understanding that my wife and I were bound for cleve with Dr. Overbeke[2] and his wife a worthy Gentleman of that place, stayd not one night in Rotterdam but by the night boat, as my son advisd me, went over Tergou[3] to come to me, that we might go to Loo together, I hearing of this went to Utrecht, to the English ordinary to enquire for them, but finding them not come, concluded they went over Amsterdam, and stayd there; but about an houre after they came, and Finding I had been there, (as they now informe me) concluded I was gone to cleve and so never lookt after Geesbergen, where we were 10 days after, and they the same time at Utrecht, beleaguerd with ill weather—they are now gone to Loo, and at their returne will be going for Brabant where I shall furnish them with the required Credit.

My son Arent who is now a Novitius in the 6 and last schoole, has taken the boldness animated by me, to write to you, and send you some of the first fruits of his orations, he has begone one De

Per quem Pythagoras et cabbala sacra revixit,
Elæusque, potest qui dare cuncta sibi.
Quod si Graja virum tellus, et prisca tulissent
Secula, nunc inter lumina prima foret.

In a note he explains: 'Hippias patria Elæus, professione Philosophus, qui omnia quibus opus, manu sua parare poterat': here printed from the copy of Leibniz's letter of 20/30 January 1699 sent by Burnett to Locke: no. *2565*. An alternative version of l. 4 runs

Elaeusque parat qui sua cuncta sibi.

—Leibniz, *Gesammelte Werke*, ed. G. H. Pertz, 1843–63, I. iv. 322, where there are two further notes by Leibniz. The first four lines (l. 4 as in Pertz) are printed in *Nouvelles de la republique des lettres*, xiii. 599 (November 1699), and probably from there in *History of the Works of the Learned*, i. 702 (November 1699).

The word 'revolved' refers to van Helmont's theory of metempsychosis: no. *779* n. Borch is probably Terborg, 8 or 9 miles NE. of Emmerich: no. *1830* n.

[1] pp. 650, 667.

[2] He is mentioned in no. *1827*.

[3] Gouda.

amore in patriam, eius libertate tuenda,[1] but by a fall wounding his knee, and the absence of Dr. Kolhans to revise his foule draught, lest he should have broke Priscians head, may possibly make him leave that uncopied.

I make account he shall spend a yeare in this schoole, unlesse his mother and I can break out this next summer to make you, and my other friends in England a visit, as I hope, and then I shall take him with us, and your good advice how further to dispose of him to his best advantage, he has so much gaind the hearts of all his masters, both for his understanding, diligence, and sober deportment, that they say he has not had his equal of his age in any of the schooles.

It were pitty but he should prosecute his studies to the Utmost, but on the one hand I cannot resolve to let him go to any of the universities, nor does he incline to it, hearing so ill a character of them. And on the other hand, he must not seek his living by prateing. Both Dr. Buchius and Dr. Overbeek are so wel pleasd with him that each solicit to have him, resolving to Inform him in their most secret mysteries in Physick. But the salary of Doctors in these parts is, as you know, so silly, that there's no relying upon it for a young beginner. The latter of these 2 is a man of so great practice that in the Electors Dominions[2] there is not such another; But what do I trouble my head about things so far to seek. I shall therefore take leave of this subject, and with the best respects of my wife and self and sons to yourself and our humble service to Sir F. and his lady conclude myself

Sir

your humble servant

BENJAMIN FURLY

Dear Sir

I have a letter from mr. Dumoulin,[3] who tels me you have had the goodness to answer my wives request, and have sit the first time, he sollicits me for letters to severall of my friends to help him to work, but I know not who to write to upon that subject, If you know any that incline to be drawn, and he shall give satisfaction in his art, it would be an act of charity to recommend the poore oppressed man, in whose behalf I made our Proote Mende Propheta,[4]

[1] 'Of love for one's country, by guarding its liberty.'

[2] The Elector of Brandenburg; here presumably Cleve and its territory.

[3] Probably a son or grandson of Pierre du Moulin, 1601–84, a sister of whom was mother of Jurieu: Haag.

[4] Jurieu. I cannot explain the first two words.

that uses to strike terrour into all that durst oppose his wicked will, bow to do a thing, which the President[1] told me he saw likelyhood of obtaining, viz, without constraint of Law, to give him an attestation signd by him and his,[2] that he was the son of (both) their uncle. I told the President it should not depend upon his will, If he would not, he must be compeld to it, and that I was resolvd to go. Tho I told the court I was to heare there, that monsieur J: was such a man, that being sollicited by his worship in the name of the court to do what was his duty both as a man and a christian, to set aside his other character of a minister, he was not to be brought to perform his duty. That it was his duty was most evident, because else no court could condemn to doe it. And being so it was a shame that a minister must be compeld to doe his duty, espetially to so neer a relation, aged, lame, poore and in a strange Cuntrey. And to him I sent word by a Deacon of his, that I had penetrated this mystery of his dealings with his kinsman to be this, That a little longer delay would exhaust him, and then he should be necessitated to beg to returne to England again. and so never get the length of Embden to examine his brothers will, or ground of his sisters letters. And that nobody would be so foolishly charitable as to maintain him here, till he could be compelled by law to give him that certificate. But that he was mistaken, I would both see to procure him justice, and was now going to the Stadhouse about it, and see that he should not want in the meanewhile, yea, if it were necessary that any body should go to Embden, and my affairs would permit, I would go thither to procure him justice also there.

Mr. Deacon going and telling him this, he immediatly that morning sent to the President a certificate, which being shewd me in court, and askt if we would be satisfyed with that, I answered yes provided they both signd: which was accordingly so sent me to the Exchange. What say you now, can't I make a sturdy Prophet bow to right? I told monsieur Bayle the day before I'de bow or break him if possible. I am

Sir

your humble servant

B F—

30 October 1699.

Endorsed by Locke: B. Furly 30 Oct: 99

[1] Apparently of one of the courts of law.

[2] Probably Mme Jurieu, a daughter of Cyrus du Moulin and first cousin of Jurieu and perhaps of Furly's friend.

2630. THOMAS WEAVER to LOCKE, 25 October 1699

B.L., MS. Locke c. 23, ff. 67–8. The writer was the London agent for New York: *Cal.S.P., Col.*, vol. xvii.

Honoured Sir,

The Government of New York hath appointed a salary of one hundred and thirty pounds (New York money) for the cheif Judge—And a salary of one hundred pounds (New York money) for the Attorney Generall—their fees and perquisites are at present very inconsiderable.

The largest produce of the yearly revenue there for seven years past amounts to but £4333 (New York money) And the constant salarys to be paid out of it with other contingent charges of the Government have yearly exceeded the revenue, and made a debt which the Assembly have always taken care to defray, by publick taxes.

The Assembly of New York have requested the Earl of Bellomont that men of knowledge in the law and of integrity may be appointed Cheif Judge and Attorney Generall of the Province. but such not being to be found there—The Earl hath applyed to the right Honourable the Lords of the Councill of trade and desires that on their Lordships representation of the matter to his Majesty persons fitt for those trusts may be sent from England.

I humbly presume that on an instruction to the Earl of Bellomont to move the Assembly there to settle £300 sterling per annum, on the Cheif Judge. and £200 sterling per annum on the Attorney Generall, they would consent to do it, and it would be an incouragement for good and able men to accept of those imploys, and thereby his Majestys government and the subjects of that Province receive very great advantage—which is humbly submitted by

Sir

your most humble servant

T. WEAVER

october 25. 1699

Address: For The Hon. John Locke Esq These

Endorsed by Locke: Trade New Yorke Judges 99

2631. PHILIPPUS VAN LIMBORCH to LOCKE, 29 October/8 November 1699 (2621, 2653)

B.L., MS. Locke c. 14, ff. 133–4. Copy by van Limborch in Amsterdam University Library, MS. R.K., III D 16, f. 187. Printed from the copy and omitting a passage in *Some Familiar Letters*, pp. 452–6. Answers no. 2621; answered by no. 2653.

Amplissime Vir

Pro labore quem meo rogatu suscepisti maximas tibi habeo gratias. Gaudeo me ex literis tuis didicisse, quæ Episcoporum[a] judicio horrenda illa crimina fuerint, non nisi atrocissimo ignis supplicio luenda. Video quandoque unum idemque dogma diversis verbis enuntiari, atque ita, quod uno comprehendi poterat articulo, in plures distendi, procul dubio ut plurium hæresium reatus tam atroci supplicio prætexi possit. Malim dogmata ipsis eorum, qui ea professi fuerunt, verbis legere expressa: sic certus forem, me non legere consequentias, sed ipsa dogmata, eaque non terminis odiosis concepta, et forte in alienum sensum detorta, sed ipsis autorum verbis nudè et candidè enuntiata, nihilque continentia, nisi quod ipse, cujus causa agitur, pro suo agnoscit. Quando autem procedendi modum video, ad sancti tribunalis instar omnia exactè esse conformata, non sine dolore, agnosco. Bartholomæi Legatt supplicium, verum suppresso illius nomine, laudat Casaubonus in

[a] *Van Limborch's copy reads* quæ Episcoporum illius temporis judicio . . .

Excellent Sir,

I am most grateful to you for the labour that you have undertaken at my request. I am glad to have learnt from your letter what were those dreadful crimes that in the bishops' opinion were not to be atoned for except by the most atrocious punishment of fire. I see that sometimes one and the same dogma is expressed in different words and thus what could be comprised in one article is extended to several, without doubt so that guiltiness of several heresies can be assigned as a pretext for so atrocious a punishment. I should prefer to read the dogmas expressed in the very words of those who had professed them; I should thus be certain that I was reading not consequents [from the dogmas] but the dogmas themselves, and those not drawn up in hateful terms and perhaps twisted into a meaning not belonging to them, but expressed simply and candidly in the very words of the authors, and containing nothing except what the person on trial recognizes as his own. But when I see the manner of proceeding I recognize, not without sorrow, that everything is exactly fashioned to the likeness of the Holy Office. Casaubon praises Bartholomew Legatt's punishment, although his name is

Epistolâ dedicatoria in Exercit. ad Baronium.[1] Whitmanni supplicium paucis narrat Gilbertus Clerke in Anti-Nicænismo contra Bullum, pag. 30.[2] Utriusque autem latius paulo describit Gerardus Croesius Historiæ Quakerianæ lib. III. pag. 479.[3] Verum licet non penitus illorum suppliciorum ignarus sim, rem mihi fecisti longè gratissimam, quod pleniorem hæresium ipsis attributarum historiam miseris. Multa hactenus mihi ignorata, et scopo meo apprimè inservientia, me docuisti. At unum est, quod desidero; nomen autoris, ex quo historiam Legati et Wightmanni habes: illud enim in epistolâ tuâ non reperio.[a] Tum et leviculum erratum, forte calami festinatione, commissum est. Ais Hammonto auriculas amputatas in foro Norwicensi 13° Maji, et postea 12[ob] ejusdem mensis illum vivicomburium passum. Atqui dies duodecimus antecedit decimum tertium. Præter hæc supplicia legi in Burneti Historia Reform. Eccl. Angl. ad annum 1549. sub Eduardo VI. vivicomburium Johannæ Bocheræ, seu Johannæ de Kent, et Georgii Van Pare, utriumque satis distinctè descriptum.[4] Itaque nihil est quod hic desidero.

[a] *Here there is a note in the margin in Locke's hand*, The history of the first 14 years of K James [b] *Here in the margin in Locke's hand*, 20

---

suppressed, in the dedicatory epistle to his *Exercitia ad Baronium*.[1] Gilbert Clerke briefly relates Whitman's [Wightman's] punishment in his *Anti-Nicaenismus contra Bullum*, p. 30;[2] but Gerard Croese describes the punishment of both at slightly greater length in his *Historia Quakeriana*, bk. iii, p. 479.[3] But although I am not entirely ignorant of their punishments you have done me a most welcome service in sending me a fuller account of the heresies attributed to them. You have informed me of many things hitherto unknown to me and that serve my object excellently. But there is one thing that I want: the name of the author from whom you have the history of Legat and Wightman, for I do not find it in your letter. Then a trivial error has also been committed, perhaps in the hurry of the pen. You say that Hamont's ears were cut off in Norwich market-place on 13 May and that afterwards he suffered burning alive on the 12th of the same month. But the 12th precedes the 13th. Besides these punishments I have read in Burnet's *History of the Reformation of the Church of England*, in the year 1549 under Edward VI, [accounts of] the burning alive of Joan Bocher, or Joan of Kent, and of George van Pare, each of them described clearly enough. And so there is nothing that I want about them.[4]

---

[1] Isaac Casaubon (*D.N.B.*), *De Rebus Sacris*, etc., 1614. The book is dedicated to James I.

[2] Van Limborch is in error: Clarke wrote on 'Ante-Nicenismus': no. *1855*n.

[3] Published in 1695; pp. 479–80.

[4] Joan Bocher, sometimes called Joan of Kent, etc., excommunicated and delivered to the Privy Council in 1549; burnt alive in 1550: *D.N.B.*; George van Parris (or

Verum in Mennonitarum scriptis, ad annum 1575 reperio sub Elisabethâ sævam contra Mennonitas è Belgio profugos excitatam persecutionem. Narrant nimirum, coetus suos in Angliâ fuisse disturbatos, aliquot suorum in carcere conjectos, quorum quinque post varias disputationes, et comminationes mortis, ad religionis Reformatæ professionem adacti sunt: Qui nihilominus in cœmeterio D. Pauli publico spectaculo fuere expositi, singulorumque humero rogus fuit impositus, quo designabatur, ignis supplicium fuisse meritos. Quatuordecim mulieres navibus sunt impositæ, juvenis quidam currui alligatus flagris cæsus, unàque cum mulieribus regno exire jussus, intentatâ poenâ mortis si redirent. Quinque viri in squallido ac profundo carcere detenti sunt, quorum unus in carcere diem suum obiit. Ministri Belgicarum et Gallicarum Ecclesiarum Londini reliquos quatuor omni ope in suam sententiam pellicere conabantur. Episcopus Londinensis se durum admodum erga eos ostendit, urgebatque ut quatuor his articulis subscriberent. I. Ut desertâ sectâ suâ confiterentur se à diabolo ad eam fuisse seductos: porro corde crederent ac ore confiterentur, Christum carnem et sanguinem ex substantiâ carnis et sanguinis Mariæ assumsisse. II. Infantes oportere baptizari. III. Christiano licitum

---

In the Mennonites' writings, however, I find that in the year 1575 under Elizabeth a cruel persecution of Mennonite fugitives from the Low Countries was stirred up. In fact they relate that their meetings [*coetus*] in England were broken up; some of them were thrown into prison, and five of these, after various disputations and threats of death, were driven to the profession of the Reformed [*i.e.* Calvinist] religion; nevertheless they were exhibited as a public show in St. Paul's Churchyard, and a faggot(?) was placed on the shoulder of each, by which it was signified that they had merited the punishment of fire. Fourteen women were put on board ships, [and] a certain youth was tied to a cart and whipped, and was ordered to leave the kingdom together with the women, the death penalty being threatened if they should return. Five men were kept in a filthy and deep prison; one of them died in it. The ministers of the Dutch and French churches in London tried with all their might to draw the remaining four over to their opinion. The bishop of London showed himself thoroughly pitiless towards them and insisted that they should sign these four articles: I: That having abandoned their denomination [*secta*] they confessed that they had been misled into it by the devil; further that they believed in their hearts and confessed with their mouths that Christ had taken on him flesh and blood from the substance of the flesh and blood of Mary. II: That children

---

Paris), tried and burnt in 1551: *D.N.B.*; for both of them, Burnet, *History of the Reformation*, ed. Pocock, 1865, ii. 202–5; v. 17. A Latin translation of the *History* was published in 1689; the first French translation, in 1683–5.

esse Magistratum gerere. IV. Juramentum Christiano esse licitum. Illi persistebant in suâ negatione, ac sententiam suam de his articulis ad Reginam scribebant, orabantque dimissionem è carcere. Verum Regina contra eos præoccupata scriptum ipsorum accipere noluit, credens ipsos Deum ac Christum negare, munus Magistratus tanquam impium rejicere, populumque ad seditionem concitare. Episcopus etiam Reginæ jussu aliquot articulos edidit, quorum et hic erat, Licere Christiano Magistratui pertinaces hæreticos gladio punire; jussitque illi ab omnibus peregrinis subscribi, aut fideijussores constitui comparendi, si quando citarentur, ut inquisitione instituta, si sontes deprehenderentur, puniantur. Hisce articulis plerique peregrini subscripserunt. Tandem Julii die 22°. duo maximi natu, Joannes Petri et Henricus Terwoord (licet multi ex moderatioribus, doctioribus et maxime piis Anglis et Belgis obnixè intercederent, ut supplicio illo eximerentur) eodem in loco quo antehac Reformatis ignis supplicium irrogatum fuit, vivi combusti et in cineres redacti sunt.[1]

Historiam hanc satis distinctè, multisque circumstantiis vestitam,

---

ought to be baptized. III: That it is lawful for a Christian man to bear the office of magistrate. IV: That it is lawful for a Christian man to take an oath. They persisted in their denial and wrote their opinion about these articles to the queen and prayed for discharge from prison. But the queen, being prepossessed against them, refused to receive what they wrote, believing that they denied God and Christ, rejected the magisterial office as impious, and incited the people to sedition. By the queen's command the bishop also published some articles, among which was this, 'That it is lawful for the Christian magistrate to punish obstinate heretics by the sword'; and he ordered that this should be subscribed by all aliens or that sureties should be appointed for their appearance if they were summoned at any time, in order that, on inquiry being held, they might be punished if found guilty. Most aliens subscribed these articles. Finally on 22 July the two eldest, Jan Pieters and Hendrik Terwoort, were burnt alive and reduced to ashes in the very place where punishment by fire had previously been inflicted on the Reformed, although many of the more moderate, the more learned, and the most pious Englishmen and Netherlanders strenuously interceded for their exemption from that punishment.[1]

The Mennonites tell this story in a sufficiently orderly and, as you see,

---

[1] Accounts of the persecution in W. K. Jordan, *The development of religious toleration in England*, 1932, pp. 297–9; and J. F. Mozley, *John Foxe and his Book*, 1940, pp. 86–9, with citation of authorities. These include T. van Braght, *Het Bloedig Tooneel, of Martelaers Spiegel der Doops-Gesinde of Weereloose Christenen*, 2nd ed., 1685, ii. 694–712, which was perhaps van Limborch's source. Some of the martyrologies are noticed in J. H. Ott (or Otte), *Annales Anabaptisticæ*, 1672. There is a bibliography of the Protestant martyrologies in F. van der Haeghen *et al.*, *Bibliotheca Belgica*, first series, vol. xix, 1880–90. I have not seen F. Pijper, *Martelaarstoeken*, 1924.

uti vides, narrant Mennonitæ. De hisce nihil prorsus scribit Cambdenus: solummodo ad annum 1560 refert, Elisabetham Anabaptistas et id genus hæreticos, qui in maritima Angliæ oppida ex transmarinis regionibus specie declinandæ persecutionis convolarant, et sectarium virus in Angliâ sparserant, è regno intra 20 dies excedere imperasse, sive illi indigenæ, sive exteri, sub poenâ incarcerationis et bonorum amissionis.[1] Velim scire, si levi labore fieri possit, an quæ de supplicio hoc narrant scriptores Angli consentanea sint illis, quæ hic ex Mennonitarum scriptis excerpsi. Talia in Reformationis opprobrium cedunt. Mihi enim perinde Christianæ charitati adversari videtur tribunal de fide, sive id prope Tiberim, sive Lemannum, sive Thamesin constitu⟨a⟩tur:[a] eadem quippe exercetur crudelitas, licet alio in loco, et ab aliis hominibus; et, ut nostrate proverbio dicimus, idem est monachus, sed alio indutus cucullo.[2] Judicium tuum de Allixii et Anonymi libro audire gestio. In hoc argumento quæstionis cardinem verti à vestratibus credi miror. Ego nihil causæ principali contra Judæos deësse credo, etiamsi hoc argumento destituatur. D. Clerici epistolæ criticæ nondum prodeunt: propediem vero eas exspectamus.

[a] *Page torn.*

very circumstantial fashion. Camden writes nothing at all about these events; he only relates, in the year 1560, that Elizabeth ordered the Anabaptists and heretics of that sort, who had hastened to English coastal towns from parts beyond sea under pretence of avoiding persecution and who had spread their sectarian poison in England, to depart the kingdom within twenty days, whether they were natives or foreigners, under pain of imprisonment and loss of property.[1] I should like to know, if it can be done with little trouble, whether what English writers tell about this punishment agrees with what I have here extracted from the Mennonites' writings. Such acts become a reproach to the Reformation. For to me a tribunal for faith seems equally opposed to Christian charity, whether it be stationed beside Tiber or Leman or Thames; for the same cruelty is practised though in another place and by other men; and, as we say in our proverb, it is the same monk but arrayed in another cowl.[2] I am eager to hear your opinion of Allix's and the anonymous writer's books. I am surprised that your people believe that the question turns on this argument. I believe that the principal position against the Jews will lack nothing, even if it is deprived of this argument. Mr. Le Clerc's *Epistolæ Criticæ* are not yet out, but we expect them shortly. I have given your greetings to Veen, Guenellon, and all our friends. Our best respects to

[1] The Proclamation of 22 September 1560: Steele, no. 529.

[2] Apparently a variant of 'Gelijke monniken, gelijke kappen': Stoett, *Nederlandsche spreekwoorden*, no. 1475.

Salutem à te dixi Venio, Guenelloni, omnibusque amicis. Salveat quam officiosissimè à nobis Domina Masham cum totâ familiâ. Salutant te uxor liberique, imprimis ego

Tui Amantissimus
PHILIPPUS À LIMBORCH.

Amstelodami 8 Novembris

3
16 99
14

Address: For John Locke Esquire at Mr. Pawlings overagainst the plough in Little Lincolns Inne feilds London
Postmark: NO 6.
Endorsed by Locke: P: Limborch 8 Nov. 99 Answered Jan. 6.

Lady Masham and the whole family. My wife and children send you greetings, as do I,

Your most affectionate
PHILIPPUS VAN LIMBORCH.

Amsterdam 8 November
1699

2632. FRANCIS ATTERBURY to COLONEL CODRINGTON, [November 1699]

B.L., MS. Locke c. 3, ff. 56–7. The writer is probably the future bishop of Rochester: *D.N.B.*; no. 2860; the recipient, Col. Christopher Codrington: p. 624. Date from Locke's endorsement.

Sir

Mr Lock, whom I saw casually at Kensington the other day enquird of me about the Spanish Book which you mentiond in a Letter of yours some Months since: and I gave him the same Answer that I had done you, that I was perfectly a stranger to it; and had never heard of such an Author as Navaretti.[1] But upon discoursing Mr Gastrell,[2] who gave me some Hint about the Subject of that book, I recollected, that I had seen such a Treatise turned out of Spanish, some Years agon; and I remember now very well in whose Hands it is, and beleive that in a Little time I shall be the Master of

[1] p. 463, etc. Professor Cummins suggests that the translator of the Churchill version may have been Captain John Stevens (*D.N.B.*): Hakluyt Soc. edition, introd., pp. cxvi–cxviii. There is nothing to show whether it is the same as that mentioned here, or whether the latter reached Locke.
[2] p. 146, etc.

the MS: and when I am, will send it to You, if you will take the trouble of transmitting it to Mr Lock. And if you should happen to see him in the mean time, be pleasd, Sir, to give him this account from Me, with my Humble Service.

The Name of the Book misled me, for I was sure I had never heard of such a Writer. But the Design of it is so remarkable, that No body who had once seen it, could well forgett it: 'tis an account of the Antient Chinese Principles in matter of Religion, given by a Dominican Missionary, who understood the Language and their Books perfectly well, in order to shew, that the Jesuits representations of their Doctrines were all false, and deceitfull; that the Antient Chinese had no true Notion of a Deïty, and that their Philosophy was a Scheme of Atheism.

If this be the Book Mr Lock looks after, as I suppose it is, I will endeavor to procure it him.

The Gentleman whom I Accidentally mentiond to you at my Lady Orrerys,[1] told me afterwards that he had a Very favorable reception from you: and He being otherwise unknown to you, I must take Your Kindness in that case as shewn on my account; and ought, as I do, thankfully to acknowledge it.

I am, Sir,

Your Obligd and most Humble servant

FR. ATTERBURY.

Chelsea. Sat. morn.

Postmarks: London Penny Post:– SAT (?); W af 2

Address: For Colonel Codrington at his Lodgings in Bowstreet Covent-garden.

Endorsed by Locke: Fr. Atterbury Nov. 99

2633. DR. PIETER GUENELLON to LOCKE, 14/24 November 1699 (*2619*, *2659*)

B.L., MS. Locke c. 11, ff. 91–2.

D'Amst. ce 24 Nov. 1699

Monsieur

Je recu avant hier votre agreable qui nous a resjoui en tout maniere. vous este a Londres et sans vous plaindre de vótre poi trine, ce qui nous fait croire que vous éte bien rétabli de vótr

[1] Either the widow of Roger Boyle, second earl of Orrery, or her daughter-in-law

derniere maladie; mais Monsieur ne craignez vous pas que les grandes occupations que vous vous donnez, vous altére de nouveau? vous éte dans un age a vous menager. pardonné a mon ardeur. si j'ose vous corriger, c'est l'effet de la crainte que nous avons de vous perdre. Monsieur Posnicof a enfin fait son devoir, et je suis bien ayse que vous le trouviez digne de la faveur que je luy ay fait de vous l'addresser, et j'espere quil ne vous incommodera pas. je vous remercie tres humblement pour vos bons conseils, que je ne manqueray pas de suivre: cepandant mon fils continue sur le bon pied. je suis bien ayse de ce que vous me faitte naître occasion de rendre quelque service a Monsieur Clarke pour qui nous avons tousjours beaucoup d'estime. je me suis en devoir de trouver un endroit pour placer Monsieur son fils.[1] il y a icy quatre a cinq ecoles propres pour ce dessein, et je croi que celle d'un certain Monsieur de Bruÿn est la meilleure. Monsieur Daranda vous en poura informer. il y a placé plusieurs jeunes anglois. c'est un homme prude, et qui tient bon ordre parmi les ecoliers. il ny a presentement entre ses pensionaires qu'un jeune anglois, et que son maitre loüe pour sa docilité. chez Peerling et Cattenburgh deux autres maitres fameux, il y a plusieurs anglois, et je croi que pour bien apprendre une langue etrangere, moins on converse avec ceux de sa nation, plus on se trouve pressé de l'apprendre. la pension est de trois cent florins par an, argent de ce pays, a ving sols piece: payable par quart d'ans. et pour cet argent il fournit logement, table, et instruction; mais on est aussi obligé a l'entrée d'apporter une cuillére d'argent: un pot de chambre et une assiette d'estain, qu'on laisse a la maison a son depart. jay cru de mon devoir de presser ma réponce, ne sachant pas si Monsieur Clarke auroit envie d'envoyer son fils avant l'hyver, qui approche. il me fera beaucoup d'honneur de l'addresser directement chez nous, ou il poura loger jusqua ce que sa pension soit reglée. j'auray tout le soin possible pour luy. nous saluons tres humblement Monsieur et Madame Clarke. toute la famille vous presente ses treshumbles respects. Monsieur Limburgh a recu vótre lettre[2] et vous salue. je suis comme je le doibs.

Monsieur,

Vostre tres humble et tres obeissant serviteur

P. GUENELLON.

[1] John: no. 2668.

[2] Locke's latest extant letter to van Limborch is no. 2621, of 7 October, which van Limborch received on the 14/24th and answered on 29 October/8 November. Locke replied on 6 January. There is no trace of another letter before then.

Address: for Sir John Locke at Mr. Powlings over against the plough in little lincolns inne fields London

Postmark: NO 24

Endorsed by Locke: Dr. Guenellon 24 Nov. 99 Answered Feb. 9

2634. LOCKE to PETER KING, later first Baron King, 27 November 1699 (2620, 2643)

B.L., MS. Locke c. 40, ff. 48–9.

Oates 27° Nov 99

Dear Cosin

I thank god we came all safe and well hither on Saturday in the evening.[1] but I perceive by my coughs usage of me since I came here, that I gave it too much hold upon me by my too long stay in town

Though I put Dr Burthogg's papers into the drawer of the table in my chamber, (where you will find them) on purpose to deliver them to you, yet when you were last with me I quite forgot them. I intended then to have desired you to have given my service to the Doctor and to have told him, that truly I understand not his Antagonist and that therefor if I had been to answer him I should have desired him to have explaind him self and when he had done that I should have desired him to have proved the propositions he advances. For as far as I can guesse, when[a] I soe little understand, he does not doe that. By this way the Doctor may I think best deale with such an adversary, and keep himself from being engaged in a tedious wrangle. I acknowledg his civility to me in his answer to that gent. and pray let him know it[2]

Dr Colbatch's pouder and tincture[3] are to be had at Mr Stanels in Rupert street near the hay market. I would have for half a Guinea of the one and for half a Guinea of the other. If you will lay out a Guinea for me in this pouder and Tincture and bring them down with you when you come hither, (for I am not in hast for them) you will obleige me. There is a paper you must have with

[a] *Or* where

[1] 25 November. [2] See p. 590, n. 4.

[3] Presumably John Colbatch, d. 1729; licentiate of the Royal College of Physicians 1696; knighted 1716: *D.N.B.*

them that directs their use. The whole family here are your humble servant. I am

Dear Cosin

your most affectionate Cosin and humble servant

J LOCKE

My service to my friends as they come in your way particularly at the College[1]

Address: For Peter King Esqr To be left at Mr Potmans in the Middle Temple London

Postmark: NO 29.

Endorsed by King: Mr Locke 27. November 1699

2635. JOHN BONVILLE to LOCKE, 29 November 1699 (*2464, 2648*)

B.L., MS. Locke c. 4, f. 86.

London No: 29th: 99

Honoured Cousin

Sir I should been very glad to had the Honour To waited on you out of Towne, but I Am heartley Toubled Att your Illnes, The Lord santifie the Ayer for your good I pray god that I may heare better of your wellfarr In your next, donmow Carier[2] being In Towne, I Took A porter And fott[3] your box Amailed[4] it safe and have given orders desireing mr Harison to tak care, to Let the Letter: K: that side be uper most, and to send it to you by hors and man as soon as posable he Can, as I was at mr Pauleing this Inclosed Letter was brought. I had not Above two hours Time after I received your Letter to performe this busines, If I had not done it now, It must staid Another week. The Lord be with you And be your soport And presarve your precious Life If it be his blesed will, which Ever shall be the prayer of your Afectinat

Kinsman and Humble Sarvant

JNO: BONVILLE

Thers is the box of book and two book Tide up In paper and A hatt In A Case I sopose it to be your mans

Address: For Mr Locke Att Oates

Endorsed by Locke: J: Bonville 29 Nov. 99 Answered Dec. 15

[1] Presumably Clarke and Freke. The name reappears in the correspondence about this time; see no. 2661, etc.

[2] Dunmow. The carrier went by Harlow: p. 757.

[3] A form of the past tense of fet, to fetch: *O.E.D.*

[4] Probably a variant of mailed, meaning tied or wrapped up: *O.E.D.*, s.v. Mail, *v.*[3]

2636. RICHARD COOTE, first earl of Bellomont, to LOCKE, 29 November 1699 (*2614*)

B.L., MS. Locke c. 7, ff. 138–9. The letter is probably one that arrived in London on 19 January and that was forwarded by Popple: *Cal.S.P.*, *Col.*, vol. xvii, no. 1015.

Boston the 29th. November 99.

Sir

I must refer you to the Letters I write to your board, for accounts of all that passes here; of which I hope Mr. Popple takes Care to Inform you particularly. I fancie this season of the year obliges you to your Country retreat in Essex. the most remarkable thing I write of to England by this Conveyance, is the good successe I have had of Late in taking of Bradish and Wetherly two Pyrats that ran away with the ship Adventure of London, Captain Gullock Commander, whereof I gave advice home by the Last ship, that went hence about 3 weeks since.[1]

I have since that, had the good Luck to take James Gillam and Francis Dole Pyrats, the first he that murder'd Captain Edgecomb Commander of the Mocha frigat with his own hand, and debauch'd that ship's Company to turn Pyrats; he serv'd the Mogul, turn'd Mahometan and was Circumcis'd and since my taking him, I have had him search'd by a Jew and an able surgeon, in this town, and they have both depos'd on oath that he is Circumcis'd, and the depositions I now send to the ministers.[2]

I am with much respect
Sir
Your most humble and faithfull servant
BELLOMONT

I have at Least 20 Pyrats now in the Goal of this town

Endorsed by Locke: L: Bellomont 29° Nov 99

[1] Bellomont probably refers to his letter of 24 October, which arrived in London on 5 January: *Cal.S.P.*, *Col.*, vol. xvii, no. 890. Tee Wetherly appears to have been hanged with Bradish.

[2] Bellomont described the capture at length in his letter of 29 November to the Board of Trade; he appended the two depositions. The letter was received on 19 January: ibid., no. 1011. For Gillam and the *Mocha* see Hill, *Notes on Piracy*, §§ 395, 434, 444, 457.

2637. SAMUEL LOCKE to LOCKE, 30 November 1699 (*2616*, *2642*)

B.L., MS. Locke c. 14, ff. 202–3.

Honored Sir

I have the favor of yours of 27th: Courant by which I observe that your indisposition forced you to quitt the Citty; I am hartily glad of your Recovery; and pray for the Continuance of your good health:

Sir the wild oat beards Came all safe in your Letter which I Immediatly dispatcht in a Letter to Dr Pound[1] for the Downs, under my Covert to our Correspondent there: where tis provable it may reach Dr Pound's hand ere they saile. which in all Likelywhood was this day: if my Letter Came short it shall follow him by another ship bound after him about 14. days hence:

Sir I hope your good health will admit your presence here: where the Parl: are at presant so much influenc'd by the old Company that wee are threatned with the Losse of our 5 per cent and other Infractions into the priviledges of our Act. on which our Company is founded. and wee lay'd downe so vast a som to purchase it. the Justice of our Case. wee are wel assured. would engage your favour to advocate for us with the members of Parl: if your presence were here; Tis incredible almost to see with what Selerrity theyr intrest goes on in the house; still wee hope for the best, and humbly pray for your favour as it seeme opportune to you:[2] Sir I had the honnour by Dr Sloane to receive your Commands in recomending mr Cuninghame[3] to goe Surgeon to the factory, which was Effected. and wee have fynnally dispatcht the President Councill and factors by the Eaton friggot to make the Settlement at Liempo weer and at Nanquien in case the first doth not Succeede: wee have Imbark'd in this and another ship a great Treasure.

[1] No. *2638*.

[2] The 5 per cent was an additional duty payable on all East India goods imported after 29 September 1698 by any persons trading there, pursuant to 9 Wm. III, c. 44, the act establishing the New East India Company (p. 397, n. 1); there were exemptions for the Old Company for three years and for ships cleared outward from England before 1 July 1698; the duty was to be paid to the New Company for maintaining ambassadors and other representatives. Parliament met on 16 November. The two companies were negotiating an agreement, but the New set its terms so high that on 17 November the Old decided to lay them before parliament: Luttrell, iv. 584.

[3] James Cunningham (Cuninghame), F.R.S., the botanist: *D.N.B.*

and verry Considerable quantity[a] of our Woollen. and other Eng: Manufacture, which wee hope will take a verry good effect in those Cold northerne parts of China: which will be follow'd by a third ship in 14 days tyme: wee are Extreamly well pleas'd in that so worthy a person as Doctor Pound hath Engaged himselfe in the service of the Company. and hope he will live to see the factory Settled. to the honnour and proffit of the Kingdom and to give you a full and satisfactory account of all.[1]

Sir about 2 months hence our Suratt ships will depart when I shall not faile of sending my son the favour of your kinde remembrance: which with your Commands I Know hee will higly Esteeme: I am

Sir

Your most humble servant and affectionate Cossin

SAM: LOCKE

Sir I pray my most humble service to Sir Francis Massum to whome I have the honnour to be knowne

London 30th November 1699.

Address: To John Locke Esquire [at Oates, by Joslyn, Bishops Stortford]

Postmark: NO 30

Endorsed by Locke: S: Locke 30 Nov. 99 Answered Dec. 4

2638. THE REVD. DR. JAMES POUND to LOCKE, 1 December [1699]

B.L., MS. Locke c. 18, ff. 1–2. Year from contents and Locke's endorsement. Transmitted by Samuel Locke: p. 748.

James Pound, 1669–1724; M.A. 1694; M.B. 1697; F.R.S. 1699 (admitted 1713); astronomer: *D.N.B.* See also nos. *2637*, *3281*.

From on board the Eaton Friggot in the Downs

Dec. 1.

Honour'd Sir

We were forced out of Town by the Directors of the E. Ind. Company much sooner than we expected; so that I had not an

[a] *MS.* q[t]

[1] The president was Allen Catchpoole: no. *3281*. The *Eaton* was of 310 tons. Liempo is Ningpo. For these ventures see Bruce, *Annals*, iii. 331–2; Morse, *East India Company trading to China*, i. 109 ff. and list of ships at end of vol. i.

opportunity to wait on you again before I left London, which was indeed a very great disappointment to me in that I wanted your Instructions: I have received the Oat-beards from Mr Lock one of our Directors and heartily thank you for your remembrance of them; I am now very well fitted for making Observations of the Weather; I had before provided as good Barometers and Thermometers as could be made, and now design to fitt one of the Oat-Beards in a Box for a Hygrometer; I have also a very good provision of Mathematical Instruments; If by my Observations I may satisfy your Curiosity; or any otherways serve you I shall be very glad to shew how much I am

Honoured Sir

Your humble servant JA: POUND.

Address: For Dr Lock.

Endorsed by Locke: Dr Pound 1 Dec. 99

2639. BENJAMIN FURLY to LOCKE, 1/11 December 1699 *(2629, 2690)*

B.L., MS. Locke c. 9, ff. 153–6. Letter written by Benjohan Furly, apart from last paragraph and postscript; the address also written by him. There are many abbreviations, here all extended silently. Answered by no. 2700; see also pp. 769–70.

Rotterdam 11 December 1699

Dear Sir

I hope you have received mine, and my son Arents Letters of the 30th of October he goes on with great courage making Orations at Large of a sheet or 2 of paper, far exceeding any of his standing, being but a Novitius, and comes not behind any of the Veterani; except in versifying.

This is to Accompany My wives onely, and my eldest Son,[1] the former comes with an intention to obtain his Naturalization this session,[2] the latter to accompany him, and to present him self to my Correspondents, and see if he can by recommandation of good friends find new ones, with whom after my decease he may have the honour of Corresponding. wherein if you have any influence upon any, I am wel assured you will not be wanting to do me and him all the Kindness you can.

[1] Francis van der Tijd and Benjohan Furly.

[2] *C.J.* xiii. 117, etc.; *Statutes of the Realm*, vii. 634.

I cannot but let you knew, that the greatest part of my wives and sisters contest with their brother, is adjusted,[1] that their fathers estate at the end of the year 1679 (and he dyed 16 July 1687) is f 61500. whereas he gave it up to the Mediators f 51900 at the day of fathers decease. of this an Instrument is made under Voluntary Condemnation of the Hogen Raade, or high-councill to prevent all retrospection and overhaling of those old Accounts.

The next thing in question, is, about the time when he entred into Company with his father. he says from the 1 January 1680. The bookes take no notice of any Company till the first of March 1681. On fathers death bed, the sisters askt when the Company began he remitted them to their father, their father said he was so weak that he could not remember it, but told him he could shew it his sisters and bid him so do. So he went (in a fume) and fetch a writing and cast it on the bed saying there it is. Their father askt him, if it were signed and he said no. the father said then, what does that signify then? But further information they could not get, onely the next day he shewd my wife some bills of Exchange drawn on father and son, and by them Accepted in the year 1680. Fathers words do inferr that there was a signed contract betwixt them. But he stifly denyes that ever there was any such thing or contract. And so concludes that to himself belongs the full half of all the proffits, without allowing any Interest for the Capital of his father.

All the books from primo January 1675 (and before) to the 1st. march 1681 to run in the Singular Language of, *I*, *me*, *my*, *mine*. The Journals, Alphabets, and Ledger, have printed Inscriptions pasted on the Tikkets, calling them the books of F. H. or Francis House to the 1st. March 1681 nay the Journal of the Ledger No. B (which begins from the 1 January 1678 runs to, and ends on the 1st. March 1681) Being not big enough to contain the transactions to the primo March 1681. but ending 28 September 1680, is augmented by an Appendix bearing this printed Title or Inscription *Appendix of the Journal No. B. F. H. begun 28 September 1680 and endeth primo March 1681*

Clearly intimating that the Journal continued as well till the 1 March 1681 to be the property and register of F: H. alone, with seclusion of all others, as it was the first day of January 1678 when it began—

[1] The dispute is mentioned on pp. 379, 604.

The same is signyfyed at the end of the Journal where the book-keeper has recorded these remarkable words

Nota Bene, that this Journal is continued with an Appendix which is begun the 28 September 1680 and endeth primo March 1681 upon the closing of these books No. B.

At the end of this Journal or Appendix. he puts to book Certain little things that his father had allowed him from the beginning to incourage him which amounted to about £100 st.[a] and in it uses these words, *Charges Account Debitor To Cornelis Huys for particular emoluments and Provisions earned by him before our going into Company*

And the next page ends the book tho it could have lasted 3 months longer. And the next page to that, is Registred the Ballance of those books, so as it is carryed over into the next books No. C. And that In a language never before used, vizt. in the plural Language of *we our ours.*

The next books No. C. (and so forwards to fathers decease) have printed inscriptions on them declaring them to be the, books, Journals, Appendix Alphabet and Ledger—No. C. of *F. and C. H.* begun 1 March 1681—and from that day all Letters are writ in the plural number, all things bookt in the same manner; which were always to that day not onely by all the servants and the book keeper but also many and many a time by this son himself, from the 2d. of January 1680 to primo January 1681 bookt in the Singular Number N N *my* Account, Bills by *me* Accepted. wrote in Bank on my Account, drawn on *me*, paid for *me*, *my* Provision etc—

The father has no Account in all that Ledger No. B. from 1 January 1678 to 1 March 1681 which he must have had, had he then been in Company and but a Copartner in the book with his Son—

For he must have been made Debitor for all the mony paid him for his particular use, out of the joint Cash. But this he was not but the son himself (who all along in the booke is stiled Cashkeeper, not Copartner, The Cash Account bearing this Title, throughout, Cashke⟨eper⟩[b] my Son (⟨Cornelis⟩[b] Huys Debitor Creditor) makes Account of charges (and not his father) Debitor To Cash for the summes paid him from the 14 february 1680 to the 31 January 1681 But in the next books he puts them to his fathers Account.

And yet he has the forehead against these his own Actions, and handwriting many and many a time found in the books in those

[a] *An abbreviation; doubtful reading.* [b] *Page rubbed.*

14 months. to assert that there was a Copartnership betwixt his father and him from the first of January 1680—Altho the books made no mention of it, upon these Reasons—

1 Because he can shew Multitudes of Letters writ to his father and him in Company, early in the year 1680.

Answ. It may be, but who ordred that, does not appear—and if the fathers order could be produced, it can not operate against the books: for he may have done it, to make his sons name known in the world, who had for 5 yeares before that time managd his affaires, and wrote all the forreign Letters because the father could not—

2 he can shew bills of Exchange remitted early in Anno 1680 expressing the value to be received of Fr. and C: Huys.

Answ. thats true for I sold him 3 bills for £350 in April 1680 and bookt it so because the broker ordred me to make the bills so, but who ordred him appears not. But this appears that these bills are bookt in the books of F. H. and were sent forward to Mr. Geo: Cornish in Letters written in the singular terme, as all other letters by him writ in that time were—

3 he saith he can shew bills drawn out of England on his father and him, and accepted, some of them, by his fathers own hand—

Answ. It may be so, but that can give him no right against his Sisters, so long as those bills are bookt onely in the fathers books, and the letter signifying the acceptation of them, written by himself were writ in the name of father alone, as all the Letters were—Nor was there any necessity that father should scruple to accept them, as they lay, seing they were so drawn (tho perhaps without his Knowledge) because as to himself, it was all one, he was bound to pay them and he could but so do. As to his daughters he knew it could be no prejudice, to them, so long as it should appear by his books, that there was no Company at that time, and by protesting should onely have affronted his son—

Besides it was a very easy thing for the Brother who was Gestor Negotiorum, to cause the Value to be inserted in the bills as received of father and son, so long as the father heard The Letters read, that he had bought and remitted such bills, and perhaps never read the bills themselvs, presuming them to agree with the Letters in which they were sent.

And hence I guess, that the Correspondents tooke that occasion to alter their stile in the superscription of their Letters, because they saw the bills here made in that manner—

4 That the Booke keepers in the bank early in the yeare 1680. have kept Account with father and son.

Answ. Admit he could prove this from the first day of January 1680. Its no sufficient proofe to deprive his sisters so much of their fathers inheritance: For the father may have done this to give his son that reputation as if he were in Company with him tho he gave him not the advantage of it, till about 6 weeks before he marryed vizt. 15 April 1681

The father might also do it (being upwards of 70 years old) to free himself from the necessity of going in his own person to the bank to write off mony

Thus are these pretences (were they all true and practisd even from the first of January) easily refuted, But its evident from the bank-books that Father and Son never write off any mony jointly till 15 October 1680 Nor had any Joint Account there till 16 September 1680—

But how any man can beleeve, that there should be a companish betwixt father and son from the first of January to the last of September. And the father cause an Appendix to be made to his Journal to extend it, to the first of March of the next year, and cause it to be registred in the End of the Journal that he had so done, and cause an inscription to be printed and pasted upon the Appendix bearing that it is his Register, unless he could beleeve the father to be an unjust man and not inclind to give his son his due. Is a thing I cannot Comprehend.

Now that this was done by express order of the father needs no proofe, for nobody else had Authority to do it. The servants nor book keeper, as they had no Interest to do it so neither durst they have done it. Seing they stood under the sons Command.

Nor would he himself do it because it was contrary to his Interest. and had what he Now says been true he might rightfully have joind his own to his fathers name upon the Inscription.

And had his father done it, without his privity, he doubtless would have protested against it, or at least obtaind some declaration under his fathers hand to have made his Interest appear and so have prevented these disputes.

As little can I comprehend, how any man can beleeve that there can have been fifteen months long a partnership betwixt the father and the son, and that neither the Bookkeeper nor any one of the servants should know anything of it.

Or if they did, that they should all run on in the same Way and stile of booking things as in former yeares and books without the least alteration.

T'is altogether as in Credible that if the servants had mistaken that no body, neither father, son, nor Bookkeeper, should not discover such gross mistakes especially the son because it so nearly concernd him—

But what's most incredible of all is this, that the son himself should, from the 2d. day of January 1680 the next day after this pretended partnership, set them such an example, by booking a post to himself, and continue to confirme them in it, by putting things so to book, many and many a time with his own hands, betwixt that and 31 January 1681, as all the other persons that wrote in those books did, till the 1st. of March 1681 the very day which the father had chosen thereon to put a period to his particular Traffique, And enter into Company with his son, making such a declaration thereof that the meanest novice in his Countinghouse understood it so well that never any such fault was more committed after that day in placing things to book

Nor ever any letter writt by the son himself, relating to the affairs of the Company then begun in the singular terms of *I me my* and *mine*, but constantly from that day forward in the plurall number *we us our* and *ours*

Since the above I having more time then I did expect have drawn the case as of a Marchant in Venice that had one son and two daughters, all yet living with their mother—and from the premisses put three Questions to be answered by councellors or Marchants or both as Shall be found convenient—vizt.

1 Whether we must learne from the books themselvs to whom they do belong, and when the Company did begin, or from Letters and bills writ and drawn by others, bills accepted or remitted and the Accounts in the Bank and Consequently
Whether the Company did begin the primo January 1685, or the primo April 1686

2 What may be Judged in reason, consideratis Considerandis, and equity to have been the share allowed him by his father in the Profits of the Company

3 Whether it can consist with reason to think that the father to so great prejudice of his Two daughters should allow him the one half of the Profits obtaind by the hazarding of his stock and that without a reasonable interest for the same—.

Deare Sir having time I have causd my son Benjohan fairly to transcribe my above letter, The case he takes along with him to mr. Popple, I hope your health will permit you to let your thoughts pass upon it, and to consult him and mr. Freke upon it, or at lest to give them by writeing your answers to the questions, with your reasons which must be, by another hand than that in which the case and the questions are writ, and that wilbe a good basis for others to subjoin their subscriptions to.

So wishing them a prosperous voyage, with tender of my wives, and my most humble service to Sir Francis and My Lady Masham your self and the whole family I rest

Sir

Your very affectionate friend and humble servant

BENJAMIN FURLY

The marchants that sign I would have noted men, and men of weight and some at lest traders for Rotterdam as Sir John Fleet, Sir James Houblon, Mr. John Ward, mr. Daniel Mercer. mr. Maurice Williams. mr. John Wright, Joseph Wright mr. Charles and Mr. James Ball.[1] And if mr. D'Aranda were present, or it could be sent him, it might be well—

Address: For John Locke Esquire One of his Majesties Commissioners for Trade In London
per Amy Q.D.G.

Endorsed by Locke: B. Furly 11 Dec 99 Answered Mar. 30

2640. LOCKE to DR. (later Sir) HANS SLOANE, 2 December 1699 (2496, 2833)

B.M., Sloane MS. 4037, f. 356^b. Transcribed from facsimile and transcript in *Facsimiles of Royal, Historical, Literary and Other Autographs in the Department of Manuscripts, British Museum*, ed. G. F. Warner, 1899, no. 103. Printed in Forster, pp. 66–9.

Oates 2 Dec 99

Sir

Since you command me I here send you what I proposed above a twelvemonth since for the reforming of our year, before the

[1] For Fleet and Houblon see *D.N.B.* Ward may be the future Sir John Ward, governor of the Bank of England 1701–3; Lord Mayor of London 1718–19: *Notes and Queries*, clxxix (1940), 41.

addition of another day increase the error and make us, if we goe on in our old way, differ the next year eleven days from those who have a more rectified Calendar. The remedie which I offer is that the intercalar day should be omitted the next year and soe the ten next leap years following by which easy way we should in 44 years insensibly return to the right, and from thence forwards goe on according to the new stile. This I call an easy way because it would be without any prejudice or disturbance to any ones civill rights, which by the loping off of ten or elven days at once in any one year might perhaps receive inconveniencies the only objection that ever I heard made against rectifying our account. I need not say any thing to you how inexcusable it is, that in soe learned an age as this, and in a country wherein astronomie is caried to an higher pitch than ever it was in the world, an error of this kinde should be sufferd to goe on, an error which every body sees, and ownes to have growing inconveniencies in it: I shall rather choose to wish that when this reformation is made the begining of the year with us might be reduced from 25th of March to the first of January. that we might herein agree with our neigbours and the rest of the Christian world.

Now I am writeing give me leave to say one word more though on a subject very different. The storys I have heard of the performances of the Strong man now in London would be beyond beleif were there not soe many witnesses of it. I think they deserve to be communicated to the present age and recorded to posterity. And therefor I think you cannot omit to give him a place in your transactions. his country age stature bignesse make weight, and the several proofs he has given of his strength, which may be a subject of speculation and enquiry to the philosophical world.[1]

I took the liberty to send you just before I left the town the last edition of my Essay.[2] I doe not intend you shall have it gratis. There are two new Chapters in it of the *association of Ideas* and an other of *Enthusiasme* these two I expect you should read and give me your opinion frankly upon. Though I have made other large additions yet it would be to make you pay too dear to expect you should be at the taske to finde them out and read them. You will doe very

[1] William Joy or Joyce: *D.N.B.*; *Flying Post*, 16 November 1699; Luttrell, iv. 577, 586.

[2] The fourth edition; it is advertised in *London Gazette*, 11 December 1699. Sloane is named in the distribution list for it. The new chapters are II. xxxiii and IV. xix.

friendly by me if you forgive me the wasting your time on those two chapters. I am

Sir

Your most humble and most faithfull servant

J LOCKE

By[a] what you will finde in Monsr Bernards Nouvelles de la republique des letters, mois de mai, article 9, you will see that what you demanded of me concerning the reforming our account was scarce worth your askeing, since it is there in print already, somebody it seems, that had heard me talke it, haveing sent an account of it into Holland.

Address: For Dr. Sloane at his house at the end of Southampton Street, joyning to Southampton Square, London.

2641. BROOK BRIDGES to LOCKE, [2] December 1699 (*3426*)

B.L., MS. Locke c. 4, ff. 153–4. Day of writing from the postmark. For the writer see no. 1580. Besides being one of the two Auditors of the Imprest (Exchequer) he was a Director of the Bank of England and auditor; and early this year was one of seven men elected by the New East India Company to negotiate with the Old: Luttrell, iv. 485. He appears to have been a patron of Stephen Nye: *D.N.B.*, art. Nye.

Sir

Mr Churchill, (being in hopes of providing the Bills you desire himselfe) did not bring your letter to me, till yesterday. I am sorry tis not in my power to supply you. for since the Bank give out none, but in exchang of others that are expired,[1] there is very little hopes of meeting with any one who will part with them. My advice therefore to Mr Churchill was, to buy up Tallies, (such as the Bank doe discount,) which will be ready money when ever you please, and in the mean time yeild you, a greater proffit; if Mr Churchill have not allready furnisht you, I will doe you the best service I can in this, or in purchasing Exchequer Specie Bills,[2] which are likewise payable at demand, in both cases, it will ⟨be⟩[b] requisite,[3] that you give Mr Churchill your Orders to pay me such

[a] *The postscript and the address are here copied from Warner's transcript.* [b] *Word omitted by Bridges.*

[1] Sealed bills: nos. *1891* n., *3426*, and Clapham, i. 23. [2] p. 612, n. 1.

[3] A solitary occurrence of a verb to requisite, dating from about 1450, is given in *O.E.D.* Bridges is unlikely to have used it.

summes of money as you would have me dispose off. I am heartily sorry I was from home when you did me the favour to call at my house, Cousin Beales marriage,[1] and my attendance at the Bank, prevented my waiting upon you, which was the stedy resolution of Sir

Your obliged humble servant

B Bridges

⟨2⟩[a] December 1699.

Address: To John Locke Esqr att Sir Francis Massams house att Oates in Essex near Bishop Startford.

Postmarks: DE 2; GC.

Endorsed by Locke: B: Bridges 2 Dec 99 Answered 4

2642. Samuel Locke to Locke, 2 December 1699 (*2637, 2684*)

B.L., MS. Locke c. 14, ff. 204–5.

Honoured Sir

My Last was 30th past: by th'inclosed from Dr Pound you will finde that the things Came in the nick of tyme. I Conclude they sayled yesterday with a faire wind: about 14 days hence Sir wee intend to dispatch away another ship to follow dr Pounde for China;[2] when if you think fitt to send him any of your Commands: please to Lett one be to recomend the Correspondency between him and my son John at Suratt (as his Letter mentioneth): for which reason I presume to send it you: our factory (Intended to be setled in China) will be obliedged to send shiping and Effects for Suratt verry frequent; that to Correspond there, may be serviceable boath to the Doctor and John; likewyse: please Sir to Excuse my freedom: and favour mee with your Commands that am. honored Sir

Your most humble servant and Cossen

Sam Locke

⟨Lon⟩don[a] 2d: december 1699.

Address: To John Locke Esqr. [at Oates, by Joslyn, Bishops Stortford]

Postmark: –E —

Endorsed by Locke: S: Locke 2 Dec. 99 Answered 4

[a] *Page torn.*

[1] The writer's mother was Margaret Beale, an aunt of the Bartholomew Beale who married Elizabeth Yonge: no. *1311* n.

[2] Perhaps the *Trumball*: Morse, i. 109–10.

2643. Locke to Peter King, later first Baron King, 4 December 1699 (2634, 2649)

B.L., MS. Locke c. 40, ff. 50–1.

Oates 4 Dec. 99

Dear Cosin

I have £1000 lyeing dead by me. I would desire you to consult with your Cosin Freke to know of him what is the best way of turning money to advantage now. I would not have you tell him it is mine. I am advised to buy Tallys on the Land tax or on Wines Vinegar and Tobacco[1] which I am told the Bank will discount at any time. pray informe your self. For I would dispose of my money thus only till I could get some good land security where I might lodg it safe for some considerable time and for such I desire you to looke out, for I have £1600 that I would soe place, but whether upon one or more mortgages is to me indifferent, soe that if you should light on one at first but of £200 I would not have you refuse it because it was soe small. Mr Churchill writes me word that he has paid you my bill. Upon second thoughts I guesse it is £20 more than you will need, For you will now at Christmas receive £2 per cent from the East India company for the annuity.[2] I mention not this that your haveing £20 in your hands of mine will breake any squares,[3] for I had rather you should have too much than too little, But to minde you of the 2 per cent, that you may not forget it at the next payment

Pray when you write tell me a little what the Parliament is doeing. And when you come down if you can borrow the Votes and bring them with you you shall have them back with you to restore them when you return to town, you will doe me a pleasure in bringing them with you for me to run over

When you come hither pray call at Mr Churchils to bring any letter or little packet he may have for me I am

Dear Cosin

your most affectionate Cosin and humble servant

J Locke

All here give you their service

[1] A duty was imposed on these commodities in 1696 by 7 and 8 Wm. III, c. 10.

[2] Apparently the quarterly payment of interest on the subscribers' stock: p. 397, n. 1, etc.

[3] Will do any harm, will matter: *O.E.D.*

2644. *N. Toinard, 5 December 1699*

Address: For Peter King Esqr To be left at Mr Potmans in the Middle Temple London

Postmark: DE 6.

Endorsed by King: Mr Locke December 4. 1699

2644. LOCKE to NICOLAS TOINARD, 5 December 1699 (2580, *2673*, *2693*)

B.M., Add. MS. 28,728, ff. 38–9. Printed in Ollion, pp. 136–8. Answered by nos. *2673*, *2693*, and *2699*.

Oates 5 Dec. 99

Vous me accablez de vos agreables presents et pourtant je ne suis pas content. Je ne scai si je doibs plaindre de vous Monsieur ou de la poste, tant y a que depuis celle que vous me fitez l'honeur de m'ecrire 28 d'Avril à la quelle je repondois le 1 de May Je n'ai pas recue aucune lettre de vous. Monsieur Kaiser, qui me rendit de votre part le *commentaire* et l'*appartus* du P: Lamy avec deux autres livres,[1] me fit esperer une lettre de vous, ce que j'attendois avec beaucoup d'impatience. Scire enim percupio et quid agis, et quomodo tecum. et quid tandem de harmoniâ. Non enim aliorum hoc in argumento voluminibus tuam apud me redimere potes, etiamsi illa aliena tuâ manu correctiora ad me perventura curas. agnosco studium et benevolentiam tuam, et quæ misisti ⟨grato⟩[a] animo accipio. Nostri Typographi nihil pene excudunt nisi vernaculo sermone scriptum, et quæ Anglicè prodeunt jejuna Satis. Scripsit communis noster amicus Dominus Du Bos te linguæ Anglicanæ operam dare.[2] Si serio hoc dictum sit, gauderem sanè, quia tunc

[a] *MS.* grata

For I earnestly desire to know what you are doing and how things are with you and finally something about the Harmony. For where I am concerned you cannot buy off your Harmony with other men's volumes on this subject; not even if you take care that those aliens should reach me corrected by your hand. I recognize your affection and goodwill, and accept what you have sent with a grateful spirit. Our printers print next to nothing unless it is written in the vernacular, and what appears in English is insignificant enough. Our common friend Mr. Du Bos wrote me that you are studying the English language.[2] If that is said seriously I should certainly be glad,

[1] Locke received the four books from Kaiser on 1 November: Journal.
[2] p. 647.

forte ⟨invenirem⟩[a] hic quosdam libros quos sperarem tibi fore non ingratos, mittendosque curarem.

Monsieur du Bos m'ecrit ausi d'Anvers[1] qu'il prieroit Monsieur Clement de consentir que Monsieur Fresel mette dans les ballots qu'il envoye quelque fois pour la bibliotheque du Roy les livres que je lui envoirois. J'ai attandu depuis ce temps la avec impatience une lettre de Monsieur du Bos par laquelle il me marqueroit le consentement de Monsieur Clement et m'addresseroit à ce Monsieur Fresel dont le nom m'etoit inconnu. Mais comme j etois sur le point de quitter la Ville, parlant un jour à Monsieur Fraiser. il me nomma par hazard Monsieur Clement sur quoi m'etant enquis Je trouvai qu'il envoyoit quelquefois des livres à Monsieur Clement. d'ou J'entrois en soupçon que c'est ce Mr Fraiser que Monsieur du Bos designoit par Mr Fresel. Si vous trouvez bon d'obtenir le consentement de Monsieur Clement que J'envoirois quelquefois un livre pour vous dans le ballot que Mr Fraiser envoie à lui rien ne put être plus commode

Je vous suis fort obligè du portrait historique del' Empereur de la Chine[2] que vous avez eu le bontè de m'envoyer. Je l'ai lu avec beaucoup de plaisir. il paroit un grand homme digne de ce grand empire et il semble donner un grand ouverture àl' entrè de la religion Chretienne dans son pays

Pour le *Commentaire* et *Apparatus* du pere Lamy Je n'ai pas eu encore le temps de les etudier, et pour dire l⟨a⟩[b] veritè Je n'y trouverai pas grand plaisir pendant que le votre ouvrage n'est pas publiè en sa perfection. L Eveque de puis peu de Coventry et Litchfeild. a cette heur Eveque de Worcester. à donne au publique une petit traitè chronologique sur le temps de Pythagore.[3] Comme cette Scavant Eveque est estimè le plus habile chronologist entre nos scavants et comme vous etez fort exact en la chronologie je serois bien aise d'avoir votre sentiment sur ce petit traitè mais il est en Anglois. Je suis Monsieur Votre tres humble

et tres obeyissant serviteur

J LOCKE

[a] *MS.* inveneriem [b] *Page torn.*

since then I might find some books here that I would hope would not be unwelcome to you, and I would see to their dispatch.

[1] No. *2612*. [2] By J. Bouvet: pp. 535, 569.

[3] *A Chronological Account of the Life of Pythagoras*, 1699. L.L., no. 1776. On Stillingfleet's death Lloyd was translated to Worcester.

Je vous prie de faire mes tres humbles ⟨b⟩aises[a] mains au Capitaine Marin et a Monsieur du Bos

Omiseram pene, quod dicere tibi destinaveram. Æstate proxime elapsâ mihi narratum est commercium literarum intercedere inter Cardinalem Norisium, Pagiumque vestrum. Et Lloidium nostrum Episcopum Covent: et Litchfeild: Harum Epistolarum syllogen se vidisse dixit amicus quidam meus, imo et si vellem[b] apographum, libertatem transcribendi obtineri posse. Libenter accipio quod oblatum erat. Transcribuntur Epistolæ inter hos doctissimos viros decem et amplius quæ cum essent, ut mihi dictum erat, de rebus chronologicis tibi destinaveram utpote munusculum tibi vir⟨o c⟩hronologiæ[a] peritissimo haud plane ingratum. Cum vero perlégerem meum harum Epistolarum apographum ex mentione tui Nominis identidem in his epistolis suspicatus sum eas tibi non esse ignotas. Rogo igitur an gratum tibi fecero si has epistolas tibi, nactus commodam occasionem, misero, eo enim nec alio consilio transcribendas curavi[1]

Address: A Monsieur Monsieur Toinard chez Monsieur des Noyers devant l'Espèe royale dans la rue Mazarin à Paris

Endorsed by Toinard: ce[c] 5. Decbr 99.

[a] *Page torn.* [b] *Altered from* vellet [c] *Or* le

I had almost omitted something that I had intended to tell you. Last summer I was told that there was a correspondence between Cardinal Noris, your Pagi, and our Lloyd, bishop of Coventry and Lichfield. One of my friends said that he had seen a collection of these letters and that if I should desire a copy, permission to transcribe them could be obtained. I gladly accept what was offered. Ten letters and more between these most learned men are transcribed; since they were, as I had been told, about chronological subjects I had intended them for you as a small gift that would not be entirely unwelcome to you, a man so expert in chronology. But when I read through my copy of these letters I suspected from the repeated mention of your name in them that they are not unknown to you. I ask, therefore, whether I shall do something welcome to you if, when I get a suitable opportunity, I send them to you, for I had them transcribed for that and for no other purpose.[1]

---

[1] No. *910*, etc. Locke's friend is Alexander Cunningham: p. 624.

2645. Dr. Robert South to Locke, 6 December 1699 (*2597, 359*)

B.L., MS. Locke c. 18, ff. 173–4.

Sir

I have carefully perused your Clear and Excellent Confutation of a very Senselesse Hypothesis; indeed So intolerably senselesse and absurd, that I look upon it, as extremely below, not onely the Opposition, but even the very Notice of so Eminent a Writer.[1]

The Schools indeed have a great deal of Giberish amongst them; but it is Cheifely a Giberish of words or Termes; but this is a Giberish of Things: and, for my oun part, I think the Divinity of Jacob Behmen.[2] and the Philosophy of malbranch may very well sort together: there being in my poor judgment not the least foundation for it so much as in Common Sense, and as little in the Abstracted Speculations of Reason.

But as it has bin an old observation and saying. That there is hardly any thing so absurd but it has bin asserted and defended by some Philosopher or other; So the Asserters of this Paradox ought to passe amongst the Prime Instances alleageable for the Verification of that Saying

The Drift, and Tendency of the Philosophy here Confuted by You (so farr as my poor Reason can discerne) is to make *the Universe god* and *god the Universe*; allbeit the Assertion be too Black to be ouned in Terminis: But where Principles are once laid, the Abettors of them Know well enough, That their Consequences will Work out them selves, though Vulgar, shortsighted minds may not be aware of them.

Sir I have again gone over the Two new Chapters in your Essay:[3] and that to my great instruction and Satisfaction

God give you life, Strength and Vigor of Body equall to that of Your mind (which is indeed Extraordinary). that so you may perfect whatsoever other Noble Work or Works, you have yet under your Hand: which as it will redound extremely to your oun

[1] Apparently 'An Examination of P. Malebranche's Opinion of seeing all things in God': no. 1620 n.

[2] Correctly Jakob Böhme, 1575–1624, the mystic: *Oxford Dict. Christian Church*. English translations of many of his books appeared between 1645 and 1662; and one Edward Taylor published an exposition of his theosophical philosophy in 1691.

[3] p. 746. South is named in the distribution list for the fourth edition.

Honour, and the Advance of Rational Learning, So there is None whom it will or can gratify more than

Worthy Sir

Your old, affectionate, faithfull friend to serve you

ROBERT SOUTH

Westminster Abbey 6 Decem: 99.

Address: For his most worthy friend mr John Lock These.

Endorsed by Locke: Dr South 6 Dec. 99 Answered 12

2646. JOHN FREKE and EDWARD CLARKE(?) to LOCKE, 7 December 1699 (2617, 2658)

B.L., MS. Locke c. 8, ff. 230–1. Written by Freke, apart from the address.

December 7th 1699

Sir

I would not give you my promise (⟨a⟩t[a] your leaving the Town)[1] to write to you as you desired Yet I think I ought on this occasion to doe it because I look on it that you and every other good Englishman and lover of his Country are concernd in the matter that has been moved in the House of Commons and received yesterday its decision in a Comittee of the whole House after a very solemn Debate of very near nine hours. of which take this account wherein I shall be the shorter because the matter on which the Complaint and Debate was grounded is already known to you part of it having come under the consideration of your Comission

The Complaint was of my Lord Chancellors etc: setting out Kidd and procuring the Kings Comission for it and of a Grant to the Lord Bellamont and others in trust for them of all[b] such[b] Effects of the Pyrats (which should be taken by him) *as the King could Grant and belongd to him in right of his Crown or as belonging to the Lord High Admirall of England.* for these are the words of the Grant or to this Effect[2]

The Question offerd by Sir Bartholomew[c] Shewers[3] and Debated in the Comittee was to this Effect vizt That the Letters patents

[a] *Page torn.* [b] *Blotted; reading doubtful.* [c] *MS.* Barth

[1] On 25 November: p. 734.

[2] Paraphrased from the grant made on 30 April 1697: *C.J.* xiii. 13–14.

[3] Sir Bartholomew Shower, recorder of London February–November 1688: *D.N.B.*

Granted to the Lord Bellamont and others of etc: are dishonourable to the King against the Law of Nations Contrary to the Laws and Statutes of this Realm Invasive of Property and destructive to Trade and Comerce

All the Lawyers in the House except Sir B Shewers mr Harcourt[1] and mr Ed: Harley[2] who spoke (as many of them did) were of opinion there was nothing illegal in the Grant and to the other parts of the Question litle materiall was spoken

One Gentleman or two moved that the words of the patent *which the King could Grant* etc: might be put into the Question and inserted[a] Just before the declaration that the patent was dishonourable etc: but that was waved other Gentlemen saying that every one that voted w⟨ould⟩[b] have it in his mind that those words of the Grant were supposed to be containd ⟨in⟩[b] the Question. I will lea⟨ve it⟩[b] to y⟨ou to r⟩ead[b] the Question with those words in it and then Jud⟨ge⟩[b] w⟨hether⟩[b] it would not have been a very Just and reasonable Resolution had it been Carryd in the Affirmative as it was in the Negative for on a Division of the Comittee the Yeas were 133 the Noes 189 soe that it was Carryd in the Negative by 56 which news was noe sooner carryd into London (where all the Coffee Houses were full and bigg with expectation of the success) but the Credit on the publick Funds (which had been falling ever since this matter was first moved in the House) rose one and half per Centum and has I believe risen much more this day tho I have noe account of it.

There was also yesterday a Great Question Debated in the House of Lords and Resolved at last without a Division tho a strong party had been made in it

You know the Arch Bishop had heard a complaint against the B of St Davids and Deprived him from whose sentence he Appeald. The Bishop had pending the Cause waved his priviledge and declared it in the House of Lords, but when his Grace came to give sentence he would have resumed it but his Grace nevertheless proceeded, of which the Bishop now Complaind to the House and pretended the Arch Bishop had not power to hear and determine the Cause but that it belongd to the Jurisdiction of the House of

[a] *Altered from or to* added; *reading doubtful.* [b] *Page torn.*

[1] Simon Harcourt, created, 1711, Baron, and, 1721, Viscount Harcourt: ibid.

[2] A younger brother of Robert Harley; recorder of Leominster 1692–1732; auditor of the Imprest 1702–35: ibid.

Lords he being a peer and seized of a Temporall Barony which he could not be deprived of by the ecclesiasticall Law and he offerd to submitt his Cause to the determination of their Lordships to whom the conusance[1] of it belongd. But their Lordships Resolved that the Arch Bishop had Jurisdiction in the Case and the Bishop could not resume his priviledge.[2]

give my dues to Sir ⟨Fr:⟩[a] my Lady their son and daughter which are known to

Sir

Your obliged friend and humble servant

The Town had made the Attorney Generall[3] Lord Chancellor

Address (written by Clarke): For John Locke Esqr. [at Oates, by Joslyn, Bishops Stortford]
Frank: Edw: Clarke:
Postmarks: DE 7; RS(?)
Endorsed by Locke: J: Freke 7 Dec. 99 Answered 15

2647. Arthur Lane to Locke, 7 December 1699

B.L., MS. Locke c. 13, ff. 15–16. The writer was master of the free school at Leominster, Herefordshire, from 1684 to 1692; later he was teacher of a private school at Mile End Green; he was perhaps a nonconformist. He was author of a Latin grammar, 1695, etc.: G. F. Townsend, *Leominster*, [1863], p. 262; H.M.C., *Portland MSS.* iii. 497; *T.C.*, vol. iii.

London December 7th 1699

Sir

Tho I never had the honor of a personal acquaintance with you yet I made bold this day to wait on you at your Lodgings at Mr. Paulin's, but being so unfortunate as to come too late, I have presum'd further to give you the trouble of these few lines together with a smal book containing some materials of Education, which a great many learned men beleive may be of some use to the

a *Page torn.*

1 An early form of cognizance, retained until recent times in legal use: *O.E.D.*

2 Thomas Watson, 1637–1717; D.D. 1675; bishop of St. Davids 1687. He was accused in 1695 of maladministration and simony; judgement was given against him in the Archbishop's (Tenison's) court on 3 August of this year. The proceedings may have been to some extent due to his political conduct: *D.N.B.*; E. Carpenter, *Thomas Tenison*, 1948, pp. 205–37.

3 Sir Thomas Trevor: no. *1568*; Attorney-General 1695–1701.

publick, and therefore relying upon their opinion more than my own I have ventured to print it.[1] yet I dare not send it abroad to the world till I have your approbation along with it, which I value more than a whole ream of recommendations from the vulgarly learned. I am so much assured of your regard for the common good of mankind, that if you think any thing in these papers subservient to that great end of a learned and vertuous Education (which you have so happily and successfully advanc'd by rational easy and gentle methods in your excellent thoughts.) you will readily contribute your assistance that it may by the authority of your name have the easier admittance into Families and schools. I have but printed this one preface till I have your opinion of it, that if you think fit to add or alter any thing in it I may accordingly be able to follow your learned directions. I did design to have sent you the whole book in manuscript but being troubled much with spitting of blood I was not able to get a correct copy by any other hand. I hope Sir you will be the readier to forgive this troublesom application from one who is wholly a stranger to you, since it is the publique good of mankind that is aimed at by.

Learned Sir

Your great Admirer and most humble servant

AR: LANE

Sir When you are pleas'd to favour me with a line or two it will come readily to my hands, from London by the penny post

Address: To John Locke Esquire These

Endorsed by Locke: A: Lane 7 Dec 99 Answered Feb. 6

2648. JOHN BONVILLE to LOCKE, 9 December 1699 (*2635*, *2655*)

B.L., MS. Locke c. 4, ff. 87–8.

London Dec the 9th: 99

Honoured Cousin

Sir Last wensday sevennight[2] I sent by dunmow Carier To be Left at Harlow, at mr Harisons: your box of books and two books tied up in paper, and A hatt in A Case I sopose to be your mans, and A Letter In closed in mine which I brought from mr Pauleings: This day I have sent 12 bottle of Claratt 4 of sack and one of white

[1] Probably *A Key to the Art of Letters*, 1700. [2] 29 November: p. 735.

Liquar as cleare as watter, In all 17: Lenham put them All in one hamper, for I stood by him while he packt Them, and with it A Little packet In A sheet of white paper and A paper book and A Letter all which I brought from mr Pauleings, and Tied them all-together In A sheet of cap paper[1] and Tied it and seled, which I gave to Lenham, directed To you, with 17 bottles of wine, the four bottles I Tied downe The Corkes and seld them, This morning my wife went to The Oreng marchant To buy som, but ther Is non in Towne that are Good, but About A fortnight There will be good, Then, God willing we will send you som,

Pray Sir when you have All what I have sent, be pleased To Let me Know, whether you Received All with sefty, There Are severall pint bottles of wine, Left Att mr Pauleings, They sopose Them to be yours. I shall be Heartley glad To heare of your Health, I hope The Cuntry Ayer much Refreshed you, The God of Heaven santifie it much for your good; I bles God wee are all In Health at presant, my Wife Gives her Sarvis to you, Heartley, And I my self give The same unfainedley

I Am Deare Cousin

your Faithfull Kinsman and Humble Sarvant

JNO: BONVILLE

Address: For Mr Locke [at Oates, by Joslyn, Bishops Stortford]

Postmark: DE 9

Endorsed by Locke: J: Bonville 9 Dec. 99 Answered 15

2649. LOCKE to PETER KING, later first Baron King, 11 December 1699 (2643, 2650)

B.L., MS. Locke c. 40, ff. 52–3.

Oates 11 Dec 99

Dear Cosin

I received yours of the 6th and return you my thanks for it. I am sorry that Ideas are such perverse things and soe troublesome to conducters.[a2] My Lady desires (because it will require some time to correct this matter) that you will make hast down hither as long

[a] *Or* conductors

[1] Here some kind of wrapping paper: E. J. Labarre, *Dictionary . . . of Paper and Paper-making*, 1952.

[2] Perhaps an allusion to 'The Conduct of the Understanding'.

before Christmas as you can that your stay here may be lengthend as much on that said as may be, for on the other side of Christmas she says the terme[1] will keep its course and she must expect on that side noe allowance. Pray come as soon as you can, that we may have time to consider this greivance of Conducters[a] or some thing else. Remember to call at Mr Churchils and bring the votes (as I writ in my last) if you can. I am

Dear Cosin

your most affectionate cosin and humble servant

J LOCKE

My service to the Colledg and the rest of my friends.

We all here wish for you

turn over

After I had writ to you what is on the other side I received yours of the 7th and thank you for all in it, Particularly what you mention about placeing out my money. For which I must refer you to Mr Churchill, for though I like what you propose very well yet haveing writ to him about it and not knowing what yet he and Mr Bridges[2] (to whom also I writ) have done in it I desire you to talke with Mr Churchill about it who will be able to informe you how that matter stands. I have writ to him by this post that he should communicate the state of that matter to you at large, and then I desire that what he and you shall think best (with the advice of Mr Bridges what tallys the Bank will discount,) you would doe it as for your self and then I shall be satisfied. There be only these two things I would have taken care of. first that it may be placed on a safe fund, as well as you can be informed, and next that it may be upon such an one as I may have my money when ever I may have occasion for it. For I intend to place it upon good land security if I can get it, which you make me hope when you goe into Devon shire. you may if you think fit consult Mr Freke[3] also about any fund you think to place it upon or any Tally that you intend to buy I refer the matter wholy to you doe with mine freely as you would with your owne and I shall be satisfied. soe that you need aske me noe more questions about it. Give my thanks to Mr Freke for his of the 7th[4]

[a] *Or* Conductors

[1] Hilary term began on 23 January.
[2] Brook Bridges: pp. 747–8.
[3] Apparently the Bachelor: see p. 760.
[4] No. *2646*.

which I received just now and have not time to answer the post being just goeing.

Address: For Peter King Esqr To be left at Mr Potmans in the Middle Temple London

Postmark: DE 13.

Endorsed by King: Mr Locke Dec. 11. 1699

2650. LOCKE to PETER KING, later first Baron King, 15 December 1699 (2649, 2656)

B.L., MS. Locke c. 40, ff. 54–5.

Oates 15 Dec 99

Dear Cosin

I find by a letter I received from Mr Churchill two days since that my money was laid out in Exchequer specie bills before my last came to you. Now I have them I desire you to informe yourself by the two Mr Frekes[1] and Mr Clarke, whether the Exchequer bills are upon a sure fund and there can be noe deficiency soe that some of them may be left at last unpaid. Those three Gent I am sure can fully instruct you in that matter. Espetialy Mr Freke of your house,[2] for I would know whether he thinks them as good and safe security as Tallys, you need not let either of them know the reasons why you aske. but pray informe your self particularly and throughly in this matter. and then let me know, but I had rather learne it from your mouth here than from your letters. For I would have you come as soon as possibly you can. all here wish for you. I am

Dear Cosin

your most affectionate Cosin and humble servant

J LOCKE

Pray when you goe that way aske Mr Pawling whether he has bought me any clothes and when I am like to have them for I am in want of them.

Address: For Peter King Esqr To be left at Mr Potmans in the Middle Temple London

Postmark: DE 18

Endorsed by King: Mr Locke December 15. 1699

1 Probably King's cousin John Freke and the Bachelor. Thomas Freke is less likely.

2 King and the Bachelor were both members of the Middle Temple.

2651. WILLIAM POPPLE to LOCKE, [5 January 1700] (*2593, 2708*)

B.L., MS. Locke c. 17, ff. 236–7. Fragment: the greater part of the first page is cut away. Date from Locke's endorsement, which probably reproduces Popple's date.

[f. 236]

. . . minutes of them) we received three other Packets from him relating to his three Governments. I shall minute them too as fast as I can.[1] The Board having got their half-years pay (as you have yours) which is till Michaelmas 1698, they were inclined to put off the payment of Taxes till the next: But there has hapned an accident to your Officers which may perhaps change their mindes; though yet I am doubtful of it. You know we were ordered a Half year's payment too for the same time: But our day of payment being appointed later than yours . . .

[ff. 236v, 237]

. . . former two years in arrear; Though perhaps the hazard of charges is not great, yet the mony must certainly be paid. However I have not yet determined what course to take; But will prepare somthing either for the Treasury or this Board against their next Meeting

The charges of your payment amount to . . .	£: 26: 17: 2
And for New-Years gifts Each Commissioner has contributed	£: 1: 12: 6
Which make together	£: 28: 9: 8
So that having received formerly of your self or Mr Churchill	£: 27: 10: 6
I have now taken more from mr Churchill . . .	£:—19: 2
Which makes all even	£: 28: 9: 8

I am
Sir,
Your most obedient humble Servant
WILLIAM POPPLE.[2]

Endorsed by Locke: W: Popple 5 Jan 9$^{9}_{0}$ Answered 13.

[1] This relates probably to Bellomont; three letters from him to the Board were received on 5 January: *Cal.S.P.*, *Col.*, vol. xvii, nos. 878, 890, 894.

[2] The letter is accompanied by a request by Popple to Mr. Churchill for 19*s.* 2*d.* payable to the bearer, 'which with what I have already received will make up the

2652. Mrs. M. Brounower to Locke, 5 January 1700 (*2663*)

B.L., MS. Locke c. 4, ff. 172–3.

London Jan: the 5. 99

Most Honnoured Sir

I humbly disire your pardoun for presumeing to give you this trouble which is to acquaint you with my greate loss in the Death of my deare and loveing Husband, whose suding change has plundged me in to such a mullteude of troubless that idont know what to doe for my Efflicttiouns are more then I am able to beare. Sir Thomas Millington[1] was very kind in cuming seaverall times and giveing his advice, but he would take noe fee apone your account by Reasoun he had beene your servant and now since it is gods will to make me soe unhappy it is agreate sattesfactioun to me that I hope there will be anuff to pay Every body. Sir I Returne you Maney thankess for all your kindnesses to my poore husband and for lending us the Monny when you ware last in towne. I was in hopes to have Receved sume monny from the office this weeke but iheare that the Monny was stoped for the Kings taxe and soe is not Receved as yett. for the say the taxe mustt be paide so that my cease will be very hard, for peopele are now agreate deale more impatiant then in his life. Sir I have won favour More to beeg that if ishould Receve but for halfe ayeare that you would be pleased to let the monny which I owe you alone, untell the next payment but If ireceve for a yeare then I will leave youre monny with Mr: Popell or as you will pleas to order me which is all at presant Sir from

Your Dutyfull and Efflictted servant

M Brouower

Address: For the Honnourd: John Locke Esquir: At Oates

Endorsed by Locke: M: Brownower 5 Jan $\frac{99}{00}$

just sum of charges disbursed upon Mr. Locke's account'. January 14th. 1699/1700. B.L., MS. Locke c. 17, f. 235.

[1] No. 265, etc.

2653. LOCKE to PHILIPPUS VAN LIMBORCH, 6 January 1700 (*2631*, *2724*)

Amsterdam University Library, MS. R.K., Ba 258 k. Printed in *Some Familiar Letters*, pp. 456–8; postscript and address in Ollion, p. 220. Answers no. *2631*; answered by no. *2724*.

Oates 6 Jan 1700

Recte quidem mones Vir Amplissime errore festinantis calami transpositi sunt characteres numerales et 12 scriptum pro 21 nam 21 Maji Hammontus passus est vivicomburium. Quereris insuper idque non sine causâ, quod nomen Auctoris, ex quo historiam Legati et Wightmanni hausi, omiserim. Id autem negligentiâ non factum meâ est. Libellus prostat Anglicè cui titulus *The history of the first fourteen years of King James*[1] i e *Historia quatuordecem primorum annorum Jacobi Regis.* Author nomen suum tacuit. Huic libello annectitur ad finem tractatulus cui titulus. *A true Relation of the Commissions and Warrants for the condemnation and burning of Bartholmew Legatt and Edward Wightman the one in West-Smithfeild the other in Litchfield in the year 1611 signed with King James's own hand.*

De Mennonitis quod quæris, nondum aliquid ex nostris historicis eruere mihi contingit quod tibi satisfaciat, vel lucem afferat: forsan quia idonei hic rure non admanus sint scriptores quos consulam. Ne tamen tibi in tam desiderato opere quicquam quod in me est opis tibi desit Id negotii dedi ingenuo doctoque amico, ut

---

Oates 6 Jan 1700

You rightly admonish me, excellent Sir; by an error of the hurrying pen the figures were transposed and 12 written for 21; for on 21 May Hamont suffered burning alive. You complain further, and that not without cause, that I omitted the name of the author from whom I drew the story of Legatt and Wightman. But that was not done through my negligence. There is a book on sale whose title in English is *The history of the first fourteen years of King James*[1]. . . . The author has not given his name. At the end of this book there is attached a short piece entitled: *A true Relation of the Commissions and Warrants for the condemnation and burning of Bartholmew Legatt and Edward Wightman the one in West-Smithfeild the other in Litchfield in the year 1611 signed with King James's own hand.*

As to what you ask concerning the Mennonites: I have not yet chanced to extract anything from our historians that will satisfy you or throw light on it; perhaps because here in the country there are not at hand suitable writers for me to consult. Lest however in so desirable a work you should

---

[1] *Truth brought to Light: or, The History*, etc., 1692: no. *1480* n.; L.L., no. 1560. The 'True Relation' forms the fourth part of the book. An earlier edition appeared in 1651.

siquâ operâ reperire possit inter authores nostros illius rei monumenta, id totum, quicquid est, excerptum ad me transmittere velit. Quamprimum aliqua testimonia ad rem tuam facientia mihi oblata ⟨fuerint⟩[a] tibi confestim transmittenda curabo.

Allixii librum quam primum prodiit coemi animo legendi. Sed otiosè hactenus præ manibus jacuit, nec dum sive per valetudinem sive per alias avocationes legere licuit, spero propediem pinguius et fructuosius otium. quid de eo audias interim mihi dicas. Quidam apud nos valde paradoxum credunt doctrinam trinitatis Judæis tribuere et Stabilimentum istius dogmatis e[b] Synagoga petere. alii e contra dictitant hoc jugulum causæ esse; et hoc fundamento stabiliri orthodoxiam et everti omnia Unitariorum argumenta. Quid ipsa res doceat aveo videre, opem enim in hac causâ a Judæis et Rabbinis olim non expectarem. Sed lux semper gratissima undecunque tandem affulgeat.

Domina Masham reliquique ex hâc familiâ Te filiumque tuum plurimum salvere jubent. Nosque omnes tibi tuisque omnibus fælicem annum exoptamus. Vale Vir Optime et ut facis me ama

Tui amantissimum

J LOCKE

[a] *MS.* fuerit [b] *Doubtful reading; word altered.*

---

lack any help that is in my power I have committed the affair to a frank and learned friend, so that, if by any effort he can find records of that matter in our authors, he will extract the whole, whatever it is, and send it to me. As soon as any evidence that will serve your purpose is offered to me I shall get it dispatched to you with all speed.

As soon as Allix's book appeared I bought it with the intention of reading it. But so far it has lain idle on my hands and I have not yet been at liberty to read it, whether through my health or through other distractions. I hope soon for a richer and more profitable leisure. Meanwhile please tell me what you hear about it. Some people in this country think it highly paradoxical to attribute the doctrine of the Trinity to the Jews and to seek support for that dogma from the Synagogue; others on the contrary maintain that this is the vital point of the matter at issue; and that orthodoxy is established on this foundation and that by it all the Unitarians' arguments are overthrown. I want to see what the reality itself shows, for formerly I should not have expected help in this issue from Jews and Rabbis. But light is always very welcome, from wheresoever it may shine in the end.

Lady Masham and the rest of this family bid me send you and your son their best regards, and we all wish you and all yours a happy year. Good-bye, best of men, and continue to love me,

Your most affectionate

J LOCKE

Veenium Guenellonem Clericum. reliquosque nostros quæso meo nomine officiocissimè salutes, quibus omnibus fælicem hujus sæculi exitum et futuri ⟨introitum⟩[a] opto

Domina Masham pro acceptis nuper a filio tuo literis gratias agit quibus ipsa propediem responsura est

Address: Mÿne Heer Mÿne Heer Limborch bij de Remonstranse Kerck op de Kaisers Gracht t'Amsterdam

[a] *MS.* introtum

Please give my best respects to Veen, Guenellon, Le Clerc, and the rest of our friends, to whom I wish a happy departure of this century and a happy entrance to that which is about to come.

Lady Masham sends her thanks for the letter which she recently received from your son and which she will answer soon.

2654. JOSEPH LANE to LOCKE, 9 January 1700

B.L., MS. Locke c. 13, f. 17. The writer was Comptroller of the Chamber of London and Vice-Chamberlain from 1674 or earlier to 1694 or later: notices in Chamberlayne. Locke was acquainted with a man of this name in 1683: Journal, p. 108. The Lord President (Pembroke), Lord Chief Justice Treby, the dukes of Leeds and Ormond, Archbishop Tenison, Henry Compton, bishop of London, and the Lord Chancellor (Somers), were governors of the Charterhouse.

Old-Baily next dore to the Maidenhead 9. Jan. $\frac{99}{700}$

This comes, Kind Sir, with my hearty thanks for your favour to me at my Lord Presidents[1] upon whom I waited twice on Thursday last, (the next day after I had the notice of mr Lightfoots the Register of the Charterhouse's death[2] which was by a fall out of a Coach on This day sennight) but I could not see his Lordship till Fryday when I found upon your account a very Courteous Reception, but my Lord said Severall had been there, and as I Remember that he was engaged for a dependent of his as I apprehended and that before the Bishop of Norwich[3] came to him for one Mr Hempson a Barrister of Lincolns Inne his Kinsman[4] and one he saith that needs it, he told me on Fryday at the A. Bishop of York's[5]

[1] Pembroke, appointed 18 May 1699.

[2] William Lightfoot, register from 1674; he died on 2 January: G. S. Davies, *Charterhouse in London*, 1921, p. 351; Luttrell, iv. 600.

[3] Dr. John Moore, bishop of Norwich 1691–1707; of Ely 1707–14: *D.N.B.*

[4] William Hempson, d. 1739; B.A., Cambridge, 1679; register of the Charterhouse 1700–39: Venn; Davies, as above.

[5] Dr. John Sharp.

that he knew my Lord Ch. J. Tr–[1] was my friend, and to you I think I may with some assurance say I Beleev it. Having some while since bespoke and Received hopes of his favour in this particular. There are many competitors and interests divided. The Duke of Leeds hath promised my Lord Duke of Ormond his vote for one Portclock his Secretary's Brother[2] and clerk to Sir William Sympson[3] a young man. My Lord of Cant. with whom I din'd on Saturday Resolvs not to be engaged, and I have some ground to beleev him dispos'd towards me. I judge the Bishop of London to be my Friend and have some hopes of my Lord Tr.[4] aid as to my Lord Chancellor. I have been active and am not without hopes, especially if I have your further aid to my Lord Chancellor and my Lord president if Mr Clay[5] a young gentleman who was abroad with him[6] carry it not, his mother is a client of my sons and neighbour of mine and he of mine acquaintance and next himselfe wisheth for me and hath so declared to my Son Edwards.[7] I was indeed unfortunate that my hurry out of Town soon after you did me this favour hindred me from waiting upon my Lord before. Yet considering the Great uncertainty on whom this Election will fall there being so many competitors, and beleeving my interest is as large as any other persons as it is Reported to be I am perswaded that my Lord Presidents second vote will be of great use to me and that you would be pleased further to favour me in this matter with him and my Lord Chancellor so far as you shall think fit occasions you this trouble whereby you will adde to the great debt of Courtesy wherein I am allready

Sir

your most obliged Servant

JOSEPH LANE.

I have thought it needfull and have been so advised to say that serving the Citty above 22 years honestly in an imployment much the same with the Registers place I apprehend my selfe qualifyed for the service being also a single man and Resolving to live and common upon the place as the constitution requires. The Salary is but 30ł besides lodgings and commons and profits by Leases

[1] Sir George Treby. [2] Ormond's secretary was Benjamin Portlock.
[3] Cursitor Baron of the Exchequer 1697–1726: E. Foss, *The Judges of England*, 1848–64, viii. 60–1. [4] Treby. [5] I have failed to identify him.
[6] Presumably when Pembroke was a plenipotentiary for the treaty of Ryswick: no. *2166*, etc. [7] No. *2894*.

computed in the whole 100*l* per annum. The Trust indeed is great as was mine and therefore need, alledg'd by some of the competitors, seems no very good qualification. I am far from pretending riches but I thank G. I have not meanesse of Estate or Spirit cogere ad Turpia.[1]

In margin:

Tis said the Governors ⟨will elect⟩[a] speedily. Pardon Sir this great trouble.

Address: For John Lock Esq. at Sir Francis Massam Baronet's neer Bishop Starford in Essex.

Postmark: — 9

Endorsed by Locke: (i): Jos Lane 9 Jan $\frac{99}{00}$ Answered 12
(ii): Jos: Lane

2655. JOHN BONVILLE to LOCKE, 11 January 1700 (*2648*, *2657*)

B.L., MS. Locke c. 4, ff. 89–90. The list of the Commissioners of Greenwich Hospital on f. 90 is omitted here.

London January the 11th 1$\frac{699}{700}$

Honoured Cousin

Sir I Am very much Obliged to mr Pawling; yesturday he was pleased to send A Letter, The Coppy verbatim Is Thus—Lincolin Inn January 9th: This day Sir Mathew Andrews[2] and Sir Chr. Wren,[3] with Mr Evelin[4] Agreed upon buying A Copper to boyle meate Enough for: 150 men, And sum pewter, and tis agreed that he that will propose it at the Cheapest rate shall be The man, I find Sir Christopher hath been talking with him that furnishes white hall with Coppers, and Is desirous to bring him In, the proposalls are to be brought In on Tusday next to Scotland yard, I Am not

[a] *Page torn.*

[1] 'To compel me to act shamefully.'

[2] Of Walton on Thames; knighted on an East India ship 1675; treasurer, Honourable Artillery Company *c.* 1682–*c.* 1694; president 1692; a director (one of twenty-five) of Greenwich Hospital 1695–1710 and a member of the Fabric committee: Le Neve, *Pedigrees*, p. 298; Chamberlayne; Luttrell, ii. 363; Wren Soc. vi. 33, 35–7, etc.

[3] 1632–1723; the architect: *D.N.B.*

[4] John Evelyn, the diarist: ibid.

Consulted About it, you will doe well to make what frinds you Can, I am

your Humble Sarvant
ROB: PAWLING

This Afternoon I waited on Mr Pawling, I Tould him I did purpose to Aquaint you of This Matter. he sed That would be very well, Mr Pawling Thought Nesesary To send you The names of the Commissioners, he Lent me the List to Coppy out, If you please to Turne To the Other side,

Mr Pawleing Tells me that by all means I must waite on the Commissioners Next Tusday, And he will goe with me, And I hope you will be pleas⟨ed⟩[a] To Aquaint sum with home you can confide In to stand my frind, Mr Pawleing have spok to one, who Is your very good frind[1] and he will doe what he Can for your sake, It is Adviseable for me to put In for Brass and Copper as well as pewter, because I have Knowledg In boath, mr Pawling dos Agree to it very well and soe he have Aquainted The Gentleman your frind and he Aprooves of it, Sir I shall be very glad If my Lady be better satisfied About the fashon of her pewter, If it has been your plesur to Aquaint her, what I writt In my Last to you, I shall be Hearty glad to heare of your health. I bles god wee are prety well at presant,

I am

Deare Cousin your Ever Obliged kinsman And Humble Sarvant
JNO: BONVILLE

The Grand Committee for Greenwich Hospitall, settled Att A meeting of The Lords and Others the Commissioners at Guildhall December: 16th: 1695

[List follows]

Sir I have Exactly Taken Every name, And The mark to Every name which mr Pawling Think you never see, before,

Address: For Mr Locke [at Oates, by Joslyn, Bishops Stortford]

Postmark: IA 11

Endorsed by Locke: J: Bonville 11 Jan $\frac{99}{00}$ Answered 12

[a] *Page torn.*

[1] I cannot identify him. Locke and several of his friends were commissioners.

2656. LOCKE to PETER KING, later first Baron King, 13 January 1700 (2650, 2660)

B.L., MS. Locke c. 40, f. 56.

Oates 13 Jan $1\frac{699}{700}$

Dear Cosin

I return you my thanks for your letter from Harlow and shall follow your directions therein and am glad to find by yours of the 11th that you got well to town.

I have received Mrs Brownovers letter wherein she desires that if she receives but half a years Salary the next payment I would for some time forbear my debt. but if she receives a whole years Salary she promises to leave my money in Mr Popples hands. My intention is to be kind to her. But I doubt whether that will be in forbearing my debt to the end that other Creditors may be paid theirs. I think it is best that as she receives money she should pay them all proportionably and me amongst the rest, that is unexceptionable and the likelyest way to keep them all quiet. I beg you as you passe by her lodging to call in and tell her this, or if you find upon examination of matters it will be better for her to take any other course, order it how you please soe my twenty pounds be not indangerd to be lost: that being secured I am willing to be any way favourable to her. The state of her husbands arears in our office, and what part of his salary she is like to receive and when Mr Popple will informe you.

I here inclosed send you Mr Furlys letter to me[1] whereby you will see I had noe reason to think that either Mr Popple or Mr Freke wanted it. But that an answer may not be delaid upon that account I here send you the letter that you may put it into Mr Frekes or Mr Popples hands in what way you think best. I think it may be best (because of some words in your letter) when you deliver the inclosed to Mr Popple, to put it into his hands as from me askeing him what use amongst merchants there can be of my opinion upon the three questions proposed for I am, as you know, quite at a losse in it. I thought possibly I might have seen his son[2] who is in London at Mr Joseph Wrights in Canon street and by him have been better informed concerning this matter But he comeing not I have sent the case to him (Mr Popple)[a] as equaly concerned

[a] *Interlined.*

[1] No. *2639*.

[2] Benjohan Furly.

with me and more knowing in such affairs, and desire him to communicate it to Mr Freke both whose opinions I would be glad to know. But I leave the whole matter to your discretion. Deliver or not deliver as you see cause and in what manner you see best

Though you saw Mr Freke[1] yet I guesse by your silence you had noe oportunity to talke with him about my Exchequer notes. As far as I understand that matter yet, I think it best to get rid of them and that as soon as may be

By a gazet I read since you went I finde the East India company takes in more mony upon loan,[2] whether I have slipd the occasion, or you having formerly lent as a subscriber and soe your Cosin King[3] has gon on in the same way, or whether it be best to lend an other £100 to the company or noe I leave it wholy to you who are upon the place. I am

Dear Cosin

Your most affectionate Cosin and humble servant

J LOCKE

You are Kindly remembred by my Lady and all here.

Endorsed by King: Mr Locke January13. 1699

2657. JOHN BONVILLE to LOCKE, 18 January 1700 (*2655*, *2664*)

B.L., MS. Locke c. 4, f. 91.

London January the 18th: 1$\frac{699}{700}$

Honoured Cousin

Sir Last tusday mr Pawling was with me where The Commissioners[4] mett, but they did nothing That day: but the Secretary[5] Came to me and I gave him my Proposalls which he very frindly Received, and gave me his promise to Assist me to the otermost of his Power, The secretary Tould me, that he did beleeve A great many proposalls would be brought, Therefor he Advised me to get as many frinds as I Could, That, when the Commissioner doe meet to doe the busines sum may Then speake In my behalf, Sir I hope you will be pleased To write to Those Gentlemen, that you beleeve, will

[1] Apparently the Bachelor: p. 760.

[2] *London Gazette*, 25 December; repeated in the two succeeding issues. The New Company.

[3] Perhaps a slip for Freke; King's cousin Richard King (no. *2843*) seems unlikely.

[4] Of Greenwich Hospital.

[5] William Vanbrugh: Evelyn, *Diary*, ed. de Beer, v. 211 n.

Apeare for me In this Case, pray Sir Excuse my giveing you somuch Trouble, Indeed I have not A frind In the world to home I can Apply my self, besids your Self, Mr Hicks Our Master, gives his Humble sarvis to you, desireing to know what must be don, or how to proseed In the Case Laid befor you, The L⟨ord⟩[a] be with you, I am Deare Cousin your FaithFull Kinsman and Humble Sarvant

JNO: BONVILLE

I heare your ould Sarvant, Sill, Ided and Asoe This morning An unhappy fire broke out In Red lion square, Holburn,

Address: For Mr Locke [at Oates, by Joslyn, Bishops Stortford]

Postmark: IA 18

Endorsed by Locke: J: Bonville 18 Jan $\frac{99}{00}$ Answered 22

2658. LOCKE to EDWARD CLARKE, 19 January 1700 (*2646*, 2661)

The Henry E. Huntington Library, San Marino, California. Transcribed from photograph. Formerly in the Sanford collection; sold at Sotheby's, 22 December 1915, lot no. 427. Printed in Rand, p. 551, 'from a copy made by' the Historical Manuscripts Commission. That the letter was addressed to Clarke is shown by its contents and the endorsement.

Oates 19 Jan 99

Dear Sir

When I read what I finde in the *Enquiry into the causes of the mis-cariages of the Scots colony at Darien* p. 16. and p. 41 at the bottom and compare it with what was said to me before I came out of town I cannot but have reason to think that the Order sent from the house of Lords to our board on Tuesday the 16th instant had in the movers or promoters of it some regard to me in particular.[1] I desire therefor to know by whom it was moved. I desire you also to have your eye upon that businesse and watch it, and also to acquaint the Gent in the corner[2] with my apprehensions, which are not groundlesse,

[a] *Page torn.*

[1] *An Enquiry into the Causes of the Miscarriage of the Scots Colony at Darien*, Glasgow, 1700. Nothing in the passages cited can be considered to allude to Locke individually; he sets out the reason for his alarm in no. 2661. The House of Lords required the Board of Trade to lay before it 'their Opinion, how consistent the Colony at Darien may be with the Treaties with Spain, and the Trade of this Kingdome': the Board's Journal.

[2] Somers.

and desire his care in the case. Pray let me heare from you or the Batchelor when there is occasion and if what you write needs my speedy knowledg direct your letters to me at Oates to be left at Mr Harrisons at the Crown in Harlow. I long to hear how Mrs Clarke and your son[1] does. I write in hast and am

Dear Sir

Your most affectionate humble servant

J LOCKE

My service to the Batchelor

Endorsed by Clarke: Mr Locke to have an Account of the Proceedings touching Darien etc. Received the 19th. January 1699 Answered fully the 20th.

2659. DR. PIETER GUENELLON to LOCKE, 19/29 January 1700 (*2633, 2743*)

B.L., MS. Locke c. 11, ff. 93–4. The letter reached Locke on or shortly before 9 February: no. 2668.

Monsieur

je me sers de l'occasion presente pour vous dire que jay répondu ⟨à⟩[a] vótre derniere du 4e. nov. a l'occasion de ce qui regarde le fils de Monsieur Clarke.[2] j'offre encore ma maison pour quant il arrivera icy. et j'auray soin du reste, et feray en sorte quil sera bien placé.

Toute la famille vous presente ses treshumbles respects et un nouvel accroy de vigeur dans ce nouveau sieccle. Dieu vous Comble de ses benedictions et vous fasse vivre longtemps pour le bien public, et la joye de vos amis, je suis

Monsieur,

Vostre tres humble et tres obeissant serviteur

P. GUENELLON

Ams⟨t. ce⟩[b] 29 jan. 1700.

Address: A Monsieur Monsieur Locke

Endorsed by Locke: Dr. Guenellon 29 Jan. $\frac{99}{00}$ Answered Feb. 9

[a] *Page rubbed.* [b] *Covered by seal.*

[1] Probably Edward. [2] John Clarke.

2660. LOCKE to PETER KING, later first Baron King, 22 January 1700 (2656, 2669)

B.L., MS. Locke c. 40, ff. 57–8.

Oates 22 Jan $\frac{99}{00}$

Dear Cosin

I return you my thanks for yours of the 18th and 21 and for all that you let me know in them that you have donne for me. Your advice as to Grave[1] I shall follow and acquiesce in what you shall doe with the Exchequer notes or in Mrs Brownover affairs[a] which I refer wholy to you. I thank you also for the newspaper you sent me. When you see the book whose title you speake of[2] noe doubt you will find it suitable and worthy the author who by the title should be the worthy Edwards,[3] but 'tis noe matter whether it be he or one of his strain. Deans or Doctors or whoever else they be of that way whatever they intend to others doe must certainly shew their own religion, and will be valued accordingly. I thank you for your News. You know in what silence and scarcity of intelligence we are here. Sir Francis my Lady etc. give you their service. Mine to all my friends in town particularly to Mr Duke.[4] I am

Dear Cosin

Your most affectionate Cosin and humble servant

JOHN LOCKE

Address: For Peter King of the Middle Temple Esqr To be left at Mr Potmans in the Middle Temple London

Postmark: IA 24

Endorsed by King: Mr Locke Janu. 22 1699

[a] *Or* affair

---

[1] Lewin Grave, a mortgagor: Locke, Journal, 8 Jan. 1700.

[2] *An Account of Mr. Lock's Religion, out of his Own Writings, and in his Own Words*, 1700. It is by John Milner, a nonjuror (*D.N.B.*), and was published anonymously. L.L., no. 1802[b]. Notice in *History of the Works of the Learned*, January 1700 (pp. 41–6); for the periodical and this notice see no. *2687*.

[3] No. *1954*, etc.

[4] Presumably the younger Richard Duke, at this time M.P. for Ashburton: no. *851*, etc.

2661. LOCKE to EDWARD CLARKE, 23 January [1700] (2658, 2667)

B.M., Add. MS. 32,096, ff. 1–2. Printed in Ollion, p. 244; Rand, p. 552. Year from Clarke's endorsement.

Oates 23 Jan

Dear Sir

I thank the College for their kind remembrance of me and you in particular for yours of the 20th and for the good news therein of Mrs Clarkes health and the rest of your family. For if she has not grown worse at this sinking time of the year. tis to be hoped she will grow better with the return of the Spring. As to the Doctors Concerne[1] he did not think that the order or those that moved for the order should name or soe much as reflect on him in particular but haveing indication enough that some men aim at him in particular as most zealous in that businesse he thought this order might be an opening of that scene whereby to come at what is designed and therefor that which he desired and does desire is that the steps and progress: of it may be observed and taken care of. This whole family are well and present their service to you and the whole college. my service to the other Moyety.[2] I am

Dear Sir

your most affectionate humble servant

J LOCKE

Address: For Edward Clarke Esquire these

Endorsed by Clarke: Mr. Lock, to have the Progresse of the Lords relateing to the Commission of Trade observ'd and take Care of etc: Received the 27th. January 1699.

2662. JOHN CONYERS to LOCKE, 23 January 1700 (*2581, 2792*)

B.L., MS. Locke c. 7, ff. 65–6. Notices in Locke's Journal show that Conyers's year is old style. Conyers's careless writing accounts for Locke's error in the month in his endorsement.

Sir

I yesterday had a bill for your Interest mony due upon the Mortgage of Benefeild and if you please to send me a receit for

[1] MS. 'Drs Concerne'. Rand expanded this as 'Darien', but the natural expansion is 'Doctor's', meaning Locke's: no. 2658.

[2] Doubtless Freke.

25l due the 3rd of November last the mony is ready to bee paid as you shall Order: my service to Sir Francis Masham and my Lady who am

Sir your very humble servant
JO: CONYERS.

Jan: 23. 1699.

Address: For Mr Locke att Sir Francis Masham's house att Otes neare Bishopstortford in Hertfordshire free Jo: Conyers

Postmarks: IA 23; GC

Endorsed by Locke: J: Conyers 23 Jun 99 Answered. 29

2663. MRS. M. BROUNOWER to LOCKE, 25 January 1700 (*2652*)

B.L., MS. Locke c. 4, ff. 174–5.

London jan: $\frac{25}{17}$th. 99

Most Honnoured Sir

ihope you will pardoun my being thus troublesume to you but it is to give you anecounte that this day I Received a twelve mounths sallery allthoe with greate loss for out of my fourscore pound there was deducted for the Kings tacx and for other feese twentye pounds fourteene shillings. Sir I have left twenty pound for you in Mr: Poppells hands untell I have your orders where to deliver itt,[1] for wich kindness and for all other your greate kindness to my Deare Husband I Returne you manny thankess and i humbly begg the favour of you that you would bepleased to be my freind in speakeing to my Lady Masham and Mrs: Masham that the would be so kind to let me wourke for them for my loss is verry greate Eavery Way and My treade is all that I have to depend uppone. Sir I doe desinge to continnue at my sester Spences who lives at the White lyoun in Earles Courte in Drewry lane[2] which with my Humble Dutty and thankess Creaveing your excuse for takeing so much libarty I Remane Sir you Duttyfull servant to command

M BROUNOWER

[1] See p. 769.

[2] A few years later the court is described as 'a very handsome broad Court, with a Freestone Pavement cleanly kept, having very good new built Houses well inhabited'. It had a passage into Bow Street. Drury Lane had 'good Houses that are well inhabited by Tradesmen'; Bow Street had good lodging-houses: Strype's Stow, vi. 74, 93.

Address: For the Honnoured John Locke Esqr: [at Oates, by Joslyn, Bishops Stortford]

Postmark: IA 25.

Endorsed by Locke: M: Brownower 25 Jan $\frac{99}{00}$

2664. JOHN BONVILLE to LOCKE, 27 January 1700 (*2657, 2685*)

B.L., MS. Locke c. 4, f. 92.

London January 27th 1$\frac{699}{700}$

Honoured Cousin

Sir This day I have sent by Lenham: 3 quart and 18 pint Bottles of wine, I stood by while Lenham packt them up, mr Locke[1] gives his Respects to you, and Is sory that he had noe more qu bottle, but this Is all That he have Left, I soepose The bottles are as they Coms from beyand sea, becaus The Corks Is Tied downe with brass wyer and sealed, I have paid for the wine 18s: and the bottles 2s, he purpose to send you a Letter by the next post, Deare Cousin I hearteły give you my Thanks, for your Repeated signalls of your Afections Towards me, About Grinwich busines, I shewd The Letter to mr Pawling, he Tould me, he would take care To speak with that gentleman, And he doubt not of this Gentlemans Asistanc, as well as the Other Gentleman, that you writ to before, God grant me good sucksess That I may find faviour with Thes Gentlemen, when the time shall be, I hope These bottles will come safe, My Wife my son and daughter,[2] Gives Their Humble sarvis To you, The Lord be with you

I Am Deare Cousin

your Faithfull Kinsman and Humble Sarvant,

JNO: BONVILLE:

Address: For Mr Locke [at Oates, by Joslyn, Bishops Stortford]

Postmark: IA 27

Endorsed by Locke: J: Bonville 27 Jan $\frac{99}{00}$ Answered Mar. 13

[1] Samuel Locke. Bonville mentions him frequently in later letters.

[2] Apparently his son's wife: nos. *2753, 3175*, etc.

APPENDIX I

Leibniz: Quelques Remarques

B.L., MS. Locke c. 13, ff. 162–5. See pp. 60 n. 1, 73 n. 2. The version sent by Leibniz to Jacques Basnage and sent later by Le Clerc to Locke. Written by an amanuensis and corrected by Leibniz.

Quelques remarques sur le livre de Mons. Lock intitulé *Essay of Understanding*[a]

Je trouve tant de marques d'une penetration peu ordinaire dans ce que M. Lock nous a donné sur l'entendement de l'homme et sur l'education, et je juge la matiere si considerable, que j'ay crû ne pas mal emploier le temps que je donnerois à une lecture si profitable; d'autant que j'ay fort medité moy même, sur ce qui regarde les fondemens de nos connoissances. C'est ce qui m'a fait mettre sur cette feuille quelques unes des remarques qui me sont venues, en lisant son *Essay de l'entendement*.

De toutes les recherches il n'y a point de plus importante, puisque c'est la clef de toutes les autres. *Le premier Livre* regarde principalement les principes qu'on dit être nés avec nous. M. Lock ne les admet pas, non plus que ce qu'on appelle *ideas innatas*. Il a[b] eu sans doute des grandes raisons de s'opposer en cela aux prejugés ordinaires, car on abuse extremement du nom des idées, et des principes. Les Philosophes[c] vulgaires se font des principes à leur phantasie, disant qu'il ne faut point disputer avec ceux qui les nient; et les Cartesiens, qui font profession de plus d'exactitude, ne laissent pas de faire leur retranchement des idées pretendües de l'etendüe, de la matiere, et de l'ame; voulant s'eximer par là de la necessité de prouver de qu'ils avancent, sous pretexte que ceux qui mediteront ces idées, y trouveront la même chose qu'eux, c'est à dire que ceux qui s'accoutumeront à leur jargon et à leur maniere de penser, auront les memes preventions, ce qui est tres veritable.

Mon opinion est donc, qu'on ne doit rien prendre pour *principe primatif*, si non les experiences, et l'axiome de l'identicité, ou

[a] *The title is added by Leibniz.* [b] *Altered by Leibniz(?) from* Il y a [c] *Inserted by Leibniz(?) in blank space.*

(:qui est la même chose:) le principe de la contradiction; qui est primatif, puisqu'autrement il n'y auroit point de difference entre la verité et la fausseté; et toutes les recherches cesseroient d'abord, s'il estoit indifferent de dire, oui ou non. On ne sçauroit donc s'empecher de supposer ce principe, dés qu'on veut raisonner. Toutes les autres verités sont prouvables, et j'estime extremement la Methode d'Euclide, qui sans s'arrester à ce qu'on croiroit estre assez prouvé par les pretendües idées, a demonstré (:par example) que dans un triangle rectiligne[a] un coté est toujours moindre que les deux autres ensemble, et plusieurs autres verités de pareille evidence.

Cependant Euclide a eu raison de prendre quelques Axiomes pour accordés, non pas comme s'ils estoient veritablement primitifs et indemonstrables, mais parce qu'il seroit trop arreté, s'il n'avoit voulu venir aux conclusions, qu'apres une discussion exacte de tous ces principes. Ainsi il a jugé a propos de se contenter d'avoir poussé les preuves jusqu'a ce petit nombre de suppositions, qu'il met à la teste de ses demonstrations; en sorte qu'on peut dire que si elles sont vraies, tout ce qu'il dit l'est aussi, et il a laissé a d'autres le soin de demonstrer ces principes mêmes, qui d'ailleurs sont deja justifiés par les experiences. Mais c'est de quoy on ne se contente point en ces matieres. C'est pourquoy Appollonius, Proclus, et autres ont pris la peine de demonstrer quelques uns des Axiomes d'Euclide. Cette maniere doit estre imitée des philosophes, pour venir enfin à quelques *établissemens*, quand ils ne seroient que provisionels de la maniere que je viens de dire.

Quant aux idées, j'en ay donné quelque éclaircissement dans un petit écrit imprimé dans les Actes des Sçavants de Leipzig, au mois de Novembre 1684 pag: 537 qui est intitulé. *Meditationes de Cognitione, Veritate, et ideis.* Et j'aurois souhaité que M. Lock l'êut veu et examiné, car je suis des plus dociles et rien n'est plus propre à avancer nos pensées que les considerations et les remarques des personnes de merite, lorsqu'elles sont faites avec attention, et avec sincerité. Je diray seulement ici, que les idées vraies ou reelles sont celles dont on est asseuré que l'execution est possible, les autres sont douteuses, ou (: en cas de preuve de l'impossibilité:) chimeriques. Or la possibilité des idées se prouve *à priori* par des demonstrations, en se servant de la possibilité d'autres idées plus simples: elle se prouve aussi *à posteriori* par les experiences, car ce

[a] *Interlined by Leibniz.*

qui est en effect, ne sçauroit manquer d'être possible. Mais les idees primitives sont celles dont la possibilité ne sçauroit estre demonstrée par d'autres plus simples, et ces idées, à le bien prendre, ne sont autre chose que les attributs de Dieu.

Pour ce qui est de la question, s'il y a des idées et des verités nées avec nous; je ne trouve point que la decision en soit absolument necessaire pour les commencemens ni pour la practique de l'art de penser: Soit qu'elles nous viennent toutes de dehors, ou qu'elles viennent de nous, on raisonnera juste, pourveu qu'on garde ce que j'ay dit cy dessus, et qu'on procede avec ordre et sans prevention. La question de l'origine de nos idées et de nos maximes n'est pas preliminaire en philosophie, et il faut avoir fait des grands progrés pour la bien resoudre. Je crois cependant de pouvoir dire, que nos idées (: mêmes celles des choses sensibles:) viennent de nostre propre fonds, dont on pourra mieux juger par ce que j'ay publié touchant la nature et communication des substances, et touchant ce qu'on appelle l'union de l'ame avec le corps. Car j'ay trouvé que ces choses n'avoient pas esté bien prises.

Je ne suis nullement pour la *Tabula rasa* d'Aristote, et il y a quelque chose de solide dans ce que Platon appelloit la reminiscence. Il y a meme quelque chose de plus. Car nous n'avons pas seulement une certaine[a] reminiscence de toutes nos pensées passées, mais encore un pressentimen de toutes nos pensées futures. il[b–] est vray que c'est[–b] confusement et sans les distinguer, à peu prés comme lorsque j'entends le bruit de la mer, j'entends celui de toutes les vagues en particulier qui composent le bruit total; quoyque ce soit sans discerner une vague de l'autre. Ainsi il est vray dans un certain sens, que j'ay expliqué, que non seulement nos idées, mais encore nos sentimens naissent de nôtre propre fonds, et que l'ame est plus independante qu'on ne pense; quoyque il soit toujours vrai que rien ne se passe en elle, qui ne soit determiné, et que rien ne se trouve dans les creatures, que Dieu ne crée continuellement

Dans *le livre II* qui vient au detail des idees, j'avoue que les raisons de M. Lock pour prouver que l'ame est quelque fois sans penser à rien, ne me paroissent point convainquantes; si ce n'est qu'il donne le nom de pensées aux seules perceptions, qui sont assez notables pour estre distinguées et retenues. Je tiens que l'ame,

[a] *Added by Leibniz in margin.* [b–b] *Written by Leibniz. The amanuensis started a new paragraph probably with the same words; Leibniz deleted them and inserted these in the blank space at the end of the preceding paragraph to show that it continues.*

et meme le corps n'est jamais sans action, et que l'ame n'est jamais sans quelque perception: Même en dormant sans avoir des songes, on a quelque sentiment confus et sombre du lieu ou l'on est et d'autres choses. Mais quand l'experience ne[a] le confirmeroit pas, je crois qu'il y en a demonstration. C'est à peu pres comme on ne sçauroit prouver absolument par les experiences s'il n'y a point de vuide dans l'espace, et s'il n'y a point de repos dans la matiere. Et cependant ces sortes de questions me paroissent decidées demontrativement, aussi bien qu'à M. Lock

Je demeure d'accord de la difference qu'il met avec beaucoup de raison entre la matiere et l'espace, mais pour ce qui est du Vuide plusieurs personnes habiles l'ont crû. Monsieur Lock est de ce nombre;[b] j'en étois presque persuadé moy même; mais j'en suis revenu depuis long temps. Et l'incomparable M. Hugens, qui étoit aussi pour le vuide et pour les atomes, commença à la fin de faire reflexion sur mes raisons comme ses lettres le peuvent temoigner. La preuve du vuide prise du mouvement, dont M. Lock se sert, suppose que le corps est originairement dur, et qu'il est composé d'un certain nombre de parties inflexibles. Car en ce cas il seroit vray, quelque nombre fini d'Atomes, qu'on pourroit prendre, que le mouvement ne sçauroit avoir lieu sans vuide, mais toutes les parties de la matiere sont divisibles et meme pliables.

Il y a encore quelques autres choses dans ce second livre qui m'arrêtent, par exemple, lorsqu'il est dit chap. 17. que l'infinité ne se doit attribuer, qu'à l'espace, au temps, et aux nombres. Je crois à la verité avec M. Lock qu'à proprement parler on peut dire qu'il n'y a point d'espace, tems, ni nombre qui soit infini; mais qu'il est seulement vray, que pour grand que soit un espace ou temps, ou bien un nombre, il y a toujours un autre plus grand que luy, sans fin; et qu'ainsi le veritable infini ne se trouve point dans un tout, composé de parties. Cependant il ne se laisse pas de se trouver ailleurs, sçavoir dans *l'Absolu*, qui est sans parties, et qui a influence sur les choses composées, par ce qu'elles resultent de la limitation de l'absolu. Donc l'infini positif n'estant autre chose que l'absolu, on peut dire qu'il y a en ce sens une idée positive de l'infini, et qu'elle est anterieure à celle du fini. Au reste, en rejettant un infini composé, on ne nie point ce que les geometres demontrent de *seriebus infinitis* et particulierement ce que nous en[c] a donné

[a] *End of* f. 163^{v}. *Leibniz inserted a catch-word,* le confirmeroit
[b] *End of line in MS.; semi-colon supplied.*
[c] *Interlined, probably by Leibniz.*

l'excellent M. Newton, sans parler de ce que j'y ay contribué moy même.

Quant a ce qui se dit chap. 30 de *ideis adæquatis*, il est permis de donner aux termes la signification qu'on trouve à propos. Cependant sans blamer le sens de M. Lock, je mets des degrés dans les idées, selon les quels j'appelle *adequates* celles ou il n'y a plus rien à expliquer, à peu prés comme dans les nombres. Or toutes les idées des qualités sensibles comme de la lumiere, couleur, chaleur, n'étant point de cette nature, je ne les compte point icy parmy les adequates. Aussi n'est ce point par elles-memes ny *à priori*, mais par l'experience que nous en sçavons la realité ou la possibilité.

Il y a encore bien des bonnes choses dans le *livre III.* ou il est traité des mots ou termes. Il est tres vray qu'on ne sçauroit tout definir et que les qualités sensibles n'ont point de *definition nominale* ainsi on les peut appeller primitives en ce sens la; mais elles ne laissent pas de pouvoir recevoir une *definition reelle*. J'ay montré la difference de ces deux sortes de definitions dans la meditation citée cy dessus. La definition nominale explique le nom par les marques de la chose; mais la definition reelle fait connoitre la possibilité du defini. Au reste j'applaudis fort à la doctrine de M. Lock touchant la demonstrabilité des verités morales.

Le quatrieme ou dernier livre, ou il s'agit de la connoissance de la verité, montre l'usage de ce qui vient d'estre dit. J'y trouve, aussi bien que dans les livres precedens, une infinité[a] de[a] belles reflexions. De faire la dessus les remarques convenables, ce seroit faire un livre aussi grand que l'ouvrage même. Il me semble que les Axiomes y sont un peu moins considerés, qu'ils ne meritent de l'estre.[b] C'est apparement parce qu'excepté ceux des Mathematiciens on n'en trouve gueres ordinairement, qui soient importans et solides, j'ay taché de remedier à ce defaut. Je ne méprise pas les propositions identiques, et j'ay trouvé qu'elles ont un grand usage meme dans l'Analyse.

Il est tres vray que nous connoissons nótre existence par une intuition immediate, et celle de Dieu par demonstration, et qu'une masse de matiere dont les parties sont sans perception ne sçauroit faire un tout qui pense. je[c–] tiens qu'il y a de la solidité dans[–c] l'argument inventé il y a plusieurs siecles par Anselme Archeveque de Cantorbery, qui prouve que l'estre parfait doit exister; quoyque

[a] *MS.* infinité, de [b] *Followed by* à mon avis *deleted.* [c–c] *Substituted by Leibniz for* Je ne meprise point

je trouve qu'il manque quelque chose a cet argument, parce qu'il suppose que l'estre parfait est possible. Car si ce seul point se demonstroit encore, la demonstration toute entiere seroit entierement achevée.

Quant à la connoissance des autres choses, il est fort bien dit, que la seule experience ne suffit pas pour avancer assez en physique. Un esprit penetrant tirera plus de consequences[a] de quelques experiences assez ordinaires, qu'un autre ne sçauroit tirer des plus choisies. Outre qu'il y a un art d'experimenter et d'interroger pour ainsi dire, la nature. Cependant il est tousjours[b] vray, qu'on ne sçauroit avancer dans le detail de la Physique, qu'à mesure qu'on a des experiences.

Nostre auteur est de l'opinion de plusieurs habiles hommes qui tiennent que la forme des Logiciens est de peu d'usage; je serois quasi d'un autre sentiment et j'ay trouvé souvent que les paralogismes, même[c] dans les mathematiques, sont des manquemens de la forme. M. Hugens a fait la meme remarque. Il y auroit bien à dire la dessus, et plusieurs choses excellentes sont méprisées, parce qu'on n'en fait pas l'usage dont elles sont capables. Nous sommes portés à mepriser ce que nous avons appris dans les écoles. Il est vray que nous y apprenons bien des inutilités: mais il est bon de faire la fonction *della Crusca*, c'est à dire de separer le[d] bon du mauvais.

Mons. Lock le peut faire autant ⟨que⟩[e] qui que ce soit, et de plus il nous donne des pensées considerables de son propre crû: sa penetration et sa droiture paroissent par tout. Il n'est pas seulement essayeur, mais il est encor transmutateur, par l'augmentation qu'il donne du bon metail. S'il continuoit d'en faire present au public, nous luy en serions fort redevables

Endorsed by Locke: *Leibniz*
sent me by Mr le Clerc
9 Apr. 97

[a] *Written by Leibniz in space left by the amanuensis.* [b] *Altered, perhaps by Leibniz, from* toujours [c] *Altered, perhaps by Leibniz, from* mêmes [d] *Interlined by Leibniz(?).* [e] *Word omitted by the amanuensis.*

APPENDIX II

The Drafts of Locke's Letters to van Limborch on the Unity of God

Locke kept drafts of the passages in his letters to van Limborch that relate to the unity of God. They are now in the Bodleian Library (MS. Locke c. 24, ff. 156–64).

For no. 2340 there exists only a French version; it contains an important passage that was omitted from the letter sent. This version, together with the French versions of the drafts for nos. 2395 and 2443, was published first by Signore M. Montuori in Accademia Pontaniana (Naples), *Atti*, new series, vol. xxiii, 1974.[1] It is printed below.

For no. 2395 there exists an English version, which is printed below, and a French version. The latter was written by Locke and includes corrections made by him apparently at the time of writing; later he made some changes and marked the text for an omission. The text with the earlier corrections is the same as that of no. 2395; with the later changes, as that of no. 2413.

For no. 2443 there exists an English version, which is printed below, and a French version. The latter was written by Coste and altered by Locke. The text is the same as that of the letter sent.

2340

B.L., MS. Locke c. 24, ff. 156–7. Fair copy written by Pierre Coste, with alterations by Locke and square brackets (crotchets) made by him indicating what was omitted from the letter sent.

Monsieur

Si mon nom est venu à la connoissance de ces habiles gens avec qui vous vous entretenez quelque fois, et s'ils daignent parler des mes Escrits dans les conversations que vous avez avec eux. C'est une faveur dont je vous[a] suis entierement redevable. La bonne opinion que vous avez d'une personne que vous voulez bien honorer de vôtre amitié les a prévenus en ma faveur. Je souheterois que mon Essai concernant l'Entendement fut écrit dans une

[a] *Interlined by Locke.*

[1] I am indebted to Signore Montuori for a copy of his article. Without it I should have overlooked the existence of these drafts.

Langue que ces excellens hommes pussent entendre, car par le jugement exact et sincere qu'ils porteroient de mon Ouvrage je pourrois compter surement sur ce qu'il y a de vray ou de faux et sur ce qu'il peut y avoir de tolerable. Il y a sept ans que ce Livre a été publié. La premier, et la seconde édition ont eû le bonheur d'être generalement bien reçuës: mais la derniére n'a pas eû le même avantage. Aprés un silence de cinq ou six années on commence d'y découvrir je ne sçai quelles fautes dont on ne s'etoit point apperçû auparavant, et ce qu'il y a de singulier, on prétend trouver matiere à des controverses de Religion dans cet Ouvrage où je n'ai eû dessein de traiter que des questions de pure speculation Philosophique. J'avois resolu de faire[a] quelques additions, dont j'ay déja composé quelques unes qui sont assez amples, et qui auroient pû paroitre en leur place dans la quatriéme Edition que le Libraire se dispose à faire. Et[b]– J'aurois voluntiers satisfait à votre desir ou au desir d'aucun de vos amys en y inserant les preuves de l'unitè de Dieu qui se presentent à mon esprit. Car je suis enclin à croire que l'Unitè de dieu peut etre aussi evidemment demonstre que son existence; et qu'elle peut etre establie sur de preuves qui ne laisseront aucun suject d'en douter.–[b] Mais j'aime la Paix, et il y a des gens dans le monde qui aiment si fort les criailleries et les vaines contestations que je doute, si je dois leur fournir de nouveaux sujets de dispute.[c] À l'egard de cette question qui vous a été faite[d] par quelqu'un dans cette conference. Si je n'avois point dit quelque chose dans mon Livre touchant L'unité de Dieu? Vous aurez la bonté de luy faire sçavoir que je n'en ai rien dit, et cela pour deux raisons. La prémiére parce que cela étoit hors d'oeuvre, comme il le vera luy même, S'il voit jamais mon ⟨Ouvrage⟩.[e] La seconde parce que je n'ai point crû qu'il fut necessaire de mettre cela en question. L'idee de Dieu sur laquelle j'ai raisonné, c'est celle d'un Etre Eternel tout Puissant et *Omniscient*. Ces attributs etant une fois reconnus[f] en Dieu, nous conduisent aisément, si je ne me trompe, à l'unité de Dieu. Car si Dieu est tout puissant et *Omniscient*, je ne croy pas qu'il puisse entrer dans l'esprit d'une personne raisonable, qu'il puisse y avoir deux Etres de cette nature. Je ne veux pas appuyer sur l'opposition qu'il peut y avoir entre deux puissances lors qu'elles se rencontrent[g] dans deux Etres Intelligens,

[a] *Underlined by Locke, perhaps in preparation for an addition.* [b–b] *Inserted by Locke; written in margin.* [c] *Here there is a square bracket (crotchet) marking the beginning of the omitted passage.* [d] *Final* e *added by Locke.* [e] *MS.* Ou-rage [f] *Last letters blotted and doubtful.* [g] *Perhaps altered by Locke from or to* rencontrant

qui existent independemment l'un de l'autre. Je ne veux pas presser non plus plusieurs autres difficultez qui naitroient de la supposition de deux Etres, tels que celui que cette idée de Dieu présente a l'Esprit. Le raisonnement dont je me servirai présentement pour êtablir l'unité de Dieu, sera fondé sur la maniere par la quelle nous venons à connoître qu'il y a un Dieu, car elle suffit, ce me semble, pour fair voir qu'il est absurde d'admettre plus d'un Dieu. Nous ne connoissons point Dieu par la consideration directe de sa nature, et nous ne sçaurions le connoitre de cette éspéce de connoissance; Mais tout ce que nous pouvons connoitre de luy, ne nous vient qu'à la faveur de quelques reflexions obscures et imparfaites que nous sommes portez a faire sur ce Souverain Etre par la consideration des Creatures, c'est à dire que par les choses que nous voyons et que nous appercevons, nous élevons nos pensées à celui qui les a faites. Or si nous ne pouvons nous empecher de penser qu'il n'y a qu'un Etre tout puissant qui puisse produire un Etre pensont, (car je ne veux pas parler presentement de la Création de la Matiére, ni de l'ordre et de la beauté de ce Monde visible) je dois conclure que l'Etre qui m'a fait, est tout puissant. Que si je suis parvenue une fois à decouvrir l'existence d'un Etre tout puissant, il est contre la raison de supposer un autre Etre tout puissant, puis qu'un seul Etre tout puissant peut faire autant que cent. Enfin puis que nous ne cherchons à nous assurer de l'existance d'un Dieu, que pour regler le culte et l'obeïssance que nous luy devons rendre, il est absurde lors que nous sommes assurez de l'existence d'un Dieu, d'en admettre plusieurs, et de mettre par là sa Souveraineté et son honneur en question. Mais peutestre que ce Sçavant homme qui m'oblige à vous parler sur cette matiére, s'imaginera que cet argument est purement moral et que n'étant point fondé originairement sur la nature de la chose il n'est point demonstratif, mais tout au plus probable. Soit;[a] Mais je ne laisse pas de croire qu'un tel raisonnement doit suffire pour contenter tout personne raisonable. Si l'on fait reflexion sur le peu d'étenduë et sur la foiblesse de nôtre Entendement dans cette vie. Nos facultèz sont proportionées à l'usage que nous en pouvons faire pour vivre dans ce monde et pour y servir Dieu en gens de bien πρὸς ζωὴν καὶ εὐσεβειαν.[1] Ce n'est que dans cette veuë qu'elles nous ont été données: Et dans

[a] *Preceded by a false start.*

---

[1] 2 Peter 1:3.

le fonds je doute si jamais nos Esprits auront assez d'étenduë et de lumiére pour connoître Dieu tel qu'il est en luy même. Quoy qu'il en soit, pour dire quelque chose de plus sur la question de l'unité de Dieu, je croy qu'on m'accordera que Dieu ⟨est⟩[a] present par tout. S'il n'est point présent par tout il ne sçauroit connoître ce qui se fait dans d'autres parties de cet[b] Univers[b] differentés de celles ou il est renfermé, et il ne peut point remedier à ce qui y peut arriver contre ses interets ou au préjudice de cette partie qu'il a faite et sur laquelle il préside, ce qui donneroit l'idee d'un Etre fort imparfait. Si donc Dieu a une toute-présence infinie, je croy qu'on peut prouver par là demonstrativement, ou peu s'en faut, qu'il ne peut y avoir qu'un Dieu. Quoy que soit Dieu; quelle que soit sa nature, son Etre, ou sa Substance, il est certain que c'est quelque chose de réel, et de plus réel que tous les autres Etres. Supposons donc que cet Etre réel existe dans quelque point physique de l'Espace qu'on voudra supposer, je dis qu'il s'ensuit demonstrativement de là, qu'un autre Etre réel de la même espece ne sçauroit être dans le même point individuel de l'Espace, car en ce cas là il n'y auroit qu'un seul etre dans ce point, parce que là où il n'y a aucune difference ni à l'égard de l'éspece, ni à l'egard du lieu, il ne peut y avoir qu'un seul etre. Et qu'on ne s'imagine pas que ce raisonnement ne peut Être bon qu'à l'egard du Corps et des parties de la Matiére, car ou peut, je[c] pense,[c] l'appliquer à ce qu'on appelle *l'Espace pur*, qui est ce qu'il y a de plus éloigné de la matiere. Car deux points physiques d'espace, ne peuvent pas plûtôt être reduits en un, que deux atomes physiques de Matiére être reduits à un seul atome.[d] La raison de cette impossibilité est fondée sur ce que si deux points d'espace pouvoient être reduits en un, tout l'espace pourroit éstre reduit en un seul point physique, ce qui est aussi impossible, qu'il est impossible que toute la matière pût être reduite à un seul atome. Pour moy qui ne connois pas ce que c'est que la Substance de la matiére, Je connois encore moins ce que c'est que la Substance de Dieu, Mais je sçai pourtant que cette Substance est quelque chose, et qu'elle doit exclure d'où elle est toutes les autres substances de la même espece (s'il pouvoit y en avoir de telles). Si donc Dieu est immense et present par tout, c'est pour moy une demonstration qu'il n'y a qu'un Dieu et qu'il n'y en peut avoir qu'un seul. Je me suis hazardé à vous faire part[e] de mes

[a] *MS.* et [b] *Altered (by Locke?) from* cette Universe [c] *Interlined and comma inserted by Locke.* [d] *Interlined by Locke.* [e] *Perhaps altered from* parte

pensées sur ce sujet, comme elles se sont presentées à mon esprit, sans les ranger dans un certain ordre qui pourroit servir peut être à les mettre dans un plus grand jour si on leur donnoit un peu plus d'étenduë; Mais[a] je[a] me serois donné de la peine inutilement ayant à faire à une personne d'une aussi grande penetration que vous. Telles que sont ces pensées, je vous prie de me dire ce que vous en croyez, afin que selon le jugement que vous en ferez je puisse pour ma propre satisfaction les[b]- examiner de nouveau et leur donner plus de force que ma mauvaise santé et le peu de loisir que j'ai, ne me permettent pas[c] de faire presentement,-[b] ou bien les abandonner tout-à-fait comme ne pouvant être d'aucun usage.[d]

Les remarques que vous me dites que d'habiles gens ont faites sur le *Reasonableness of Christianity* etc. sont sans doute fort justes, et il est vray que pleusieurs Lecteurs ont êtés[e] choquez de certaines pensées qu'on voit au commencement de ce Livre, lesquelles ne s'accordent pas tout-a-fait avec des Doctrines communément reçuës. Mais sur cela je suis obligé de renvoyer ces Messieurs aux deux defenses que l'Auteur a faites de son Ouvrage. Car ayant publié ce petit Livre, comme il le dit luy-même, principalement afin de convaincre ceux qui doutent de la Religion Chretienne, il semble qu'il a été conduit à traiter ces matieres malgré luy, car pour rendre son Livre utile aux Deistes, il ne pouvoit point se taire entierement sur ces articles, auxquels ils s'aheurtent dès qu'ils veulent entrer dans l'examen de la Religion Chretienne.[f] Je suis

Monsieur

Votre tres humble et tres obeissant serviteur

London Oct *97*

Endorsed by Locke: J. L to Mr Limborch 29 Oct. 97[g]

2395

B.L., MS. Locke c. 24, ff. 161–2. Locke's English draft. It is written on the left half of each page, the right halves being kept clear for additions and alterations.

[a] *Struck through perhaps by Locke in preparation for a new version.* [b–b] *Substituted by Locke for* les examiner de nouveau pour ma propre satisfaction, leur desiner de nouveaux appuis; *the last words are doubtful.* [c] *Interlined by Locke.* [d] *Here there is a square bracket and a marginal note written by Locke:* All containd between the crotchet p. 1. and this here was omitted in the letter I sent [e] *Altered, perhaps by Locke, from* été [f] *The rest is written by Locke.* [g] *There is also a note of later date:* Works 4.to p. 434

Sir

It is too great an Honour done to me that a person of soe[a] great capacity and deep[b] penetration as he is[c] whom I take to be the proposer of the Question you sent me should defer soe much to my judgment wherein he could be much better be resolvd by his owne. I know not what opinion your freindship may have given him of me. But this I am sure that did I consult noe thing but my owne reputation I should forbear to lay my narrow and mean thoughts before a man of that great sense and not venture to treat that as a question which possibly will be thought by[d–] most people[–d] fitter to be received as a maxim;[e] and to stand firmer upon the received foundations than if[f] any one by specultains and reasonings a little out of the way should endeavour to explain and make it out But the Gentleman I thinke[g] it[h] comes from I know is of another make. His ingenuity and candor equall his knowledg and other great quality And if he finde not evidence and conviction in my reasonings he will not therefor presently condemn my intention or judg ill of me because my proofs[j] are not soe good as he would have wished. At least the lesse satisfaction I give him in my argument the more reason he will have to pardon me since the consciousnesse of my owne weaknesse could not hinder me from obeying his commands. I write therefor because he and you will have me and I write what I am content you should read to him and those other persons who were present at the conference. But it is on these conditions that they promise to give me freely and[k] undisguisd[k] their opinions of what I say. Secondly that you give noe copy of what I write to any body but that you promise me to burne this letter whenever I require you to doe it.[1] To which I would willingly adde a third and that is that these Gentlemen would doe me the honour to communicate to me what they themselves build the unity of God upon.

The question is How the Unitie of god can be proved? Or in other words How it can be proved that there is but one god?

To resolve this question it is necessary before we come to the proofs of the unitie of god to know what it is is meant by the name God

The usual and as[m] I thinke true Notion[n] those who acknowledg a

[a] *Substituted for* that [b] *Substituted for* known [c] *Followed by* from *deleted.* [d–d] *Interlined.* [e] *Or* maxime [f] *Followed by* one s *deleted.* [g] *Followed by* you *deleted.* [h] *Followed by* is *deleted.* [j] *Substituted for* arguments [k] *Written on right half of page.* [1] *End of line; point supplied.* [m] *Interlined.* [n] *Preceded by* definition *deleted, and followed by* we have of God *deleted.*

Deitie have of him is this. That he is an infinite eternal incorporeal being perfectly perfect From which Idea of god it seems very easie to me to make out his unitie. For a most perfect or perfectly perfect being can be but one Because a perfectly perfect being cannot want any of those attributes perfections[a] or degrees of perfection which it is better to have than to be without for then he would want soe much of being perfectly perfect[b] As for example to have power is greater perfection than to have none; to have more[c] power is a greater perfection than to have lesse and to have all power[d–](which is to be omnipotent)[–d] is a greater[e] perfection, than not[f] to have all power But two omnipotents are inconsistent. Because it must be supposd that it is necessary for one to will what the other wills; and then he[g–] of the two whose will is necessarily[–g] determind by the will of the other, is not free: and soe wants that perfection; it being better to be free than under the determination of an others will. If they are not both under the necessity of willing[h] always the same thing, then one may will the doeing of that, which the other[j] may will should not be done, and then the will of the one must prevail over the will of the other, and then he of the two, whose power is not able to second his will, is not omnipotent. for[k] he cannot doe soe much as the other, and then one of them is not omnipotent and soe there are not nor can be two omnipotents and consequently not two gods / By the same steps of perfection we come to know that god is omniscient But in an estate on[l–] a supposition that[–l] where there are distinct beings with distinct powers and distinct wills, it is an imperfection not to be able to conceale his thoughts. But if either of these can conceale his thoughts from the other, that other is not omniscient, for he not only comes short of knowing all that is knowable, but comes short of knowing what an other knows.

The same may be said of Gods omnipresence it is better to be every where in the infinite extent of space than to be shut out from any part of it. for if he be shut out from any place he can neither operate there nor know what is doeing there and soe is neither[m] omnipotent nor omniscient[n]

[a] *Followed by* or *deleted and then repeated.* [b] *Followed by* As for example *deleted and then repeated.* [c] *Substituted for* a greater degree of [d–d] *Written on right half of page; replaces* power [e] *Followed by* degree of *deleted.* [f] *Interlined.* [g–g] *Written on right half of page. Locke wrote first* that of one which is necessarily *and then interlined* by the power whose will*; all this is deleted.* [h] *Followed by* the *deleted.* [j] *Followed by* wills, *which is replaced by* may*; all deleted.* [k] *Altered from* & [l–l] *Interlined; the word* a *doubtful.* [m] *Followed by* omnisci *deleted.* [n] *Followed by* If it b *deleted; then* If it be *as start of a new paragraph and also deleted.*

If to avoid the[a] foresaid arguments it be said that these two (or two hundred thousand) gods (for by the same reason there can be two there may be two millions[b] for there can be noe reason to limit their number) have all perfectly exactly the same[c] power, the same knowledg, the same will, and[d] exist equaly[e] in the same individual place, this is only to multiply sounds, but in reality to reduce[f] the[g] supposd plurality only to one. for to suppose two intelligent beings, that perpetualy know will and act the same thing, and have not a seperate existence, is in words to suppose a plurality, but in realty to make but one. For to[h] be inseperably[j] united[k] in understanding[l] will[m] action and place[n] is to be as much united as any[o] intelligent being can be united to its self, and to[p] suppose that where there is such an union there can be two beings is to suppose a division[q] without a division and a thing divided from its self

Let us consider his omnipresence a little farther god[r–] is infinitely[–r] omnipresent, which he must be unlesse he be shut up in some little[e] corner of space we know not why, nor how[s] nor by[t] whome nor[e] where[e] (I say little corner for any parcel of space compared to infinite space is very little). Now if god be infinitely omnipresent it seems to me to come near a demonstration that there can be but one. Wherever god is (let his nature or being or substance be what it will) there certainly is some real, nay the most real of all beings. Let us therefor suppose this reall being in any one physicall point of space, I thinke it is demonstration that an other reall being of the same kinde cannot be in the same individual point of space, for then they would be but one. For where there is noe difference in kinde nor distance in place that can be but one[u] being. Nor let this way of argueing be thought to reach body alone and the parts of matter: It will be found to hold in that which is the remotest from it, I meane pure space. For two physical points of space can noe more be brought into one, than two physical attoms

[a] *Followed by* abo *deleted.* [b] *Here a closing bracket, cancelled by* f *of* for [c] *Followed by* knowledge *deleted.* [d] *Followed by* th- *deleted.* [e] *Interlined.* [f] *Followed by* them *deleted.* [g] *Followed by* mu- *deleted.* [h] *Followed by* have the *deleted.* [j] *Interlined; Locke repeated* be inseperably *on right half of page for clarity.* [k] *Followed by* to and always *deleted.* [l] *Substituted for* knowledg [m] *Followed by* and *deleted.* [n] *Followed by* existence *deleted.* [o] *Followed by* intelligent being thing *deleted; Locke re-wrote* intelligent being *on right half of page.* [p] *Followed by* say that any thing soe united can be two beings *deleted.* [q] *Followed by* where there is *deleted.* [r–r] *Locke wrote first* If god is infinitely [s] *Locke wrote this word as a catchword at the end of one column and interlined it at the start of the next.* [t] *Followed by* home *deleted.* [u] *Followed by* thing *deleted.*

of matter can be brought into one. For if they could, then all space might be brought into one physical point, which is as impossible as that all matter should be brought into one attome.

I who know not what the substance of matter is, doe much lesse know what the substance of god is. But some thing I know it is, and must exclude where it is all other substances (could there be any such) of the same kind.[a] if therefor god be immense and omnipresent it is to me evident beyond doubt that there is and can be but one god.

I have ventured to expose my thoughts on this subject in writeing as they have risen in my minde without reduceing them into that method and order which in a larger deduction might possibly set them in a better light. The great penetration of those they are to be laid be fore makes it needlesse to give them that trouble. Such as they are I shall be impatient to have all[b] your[b] opinions of them that I may accordingly for my owne satisfaction in the point either revise them again and bring them to a firmer consistency then ⟨my⟩[c] ill health and little spare time will now permit me or else quite lay them by as wholy uselesse.

Endorsed by Locke: ⟨JL⟩[d] to P Limborch 21 Feb. 9$\frac{7}{8}$

2443

B.L., MS. Locke c. 24, f. 163. Locke's English draft. It is written on the left half of the page, the right half being kept clear for additions and alterations. The writing is small and the ink has run; many readings are doubtful.

If my health should not consent to my compliance with the[e] commands of that great man who gives soe favourable a reception to my poor thoughts it could not yet be sacrificed[f] on a better occasion than[g] in examining the subject he has engaged me in and in the shewing my readynesse to obey him.[h] But[j-] I shall not in this case[k] lay any such obligation upon him, and if I hazard not my reputation with[l] him[l] I am pretty secure my health will not suffer by[m-] what I am going to write For I shall not need to say much[-m]

[a] *End of line; point supplied.* [b] *MS.* all yr, *interlined above* their, *which is left standing.* [c] *MS.* by [d] *Concealed by guard.* [e] *Followed by* d *deleted.* [f] *Followed by* to *deleted.* [g] *Followed by* to the inclination I have *deleted.* [h] *Here* Though I apply myself to the *is interlined and deleted.* [j-j] *Written on the right half of the page.* [k] *Followed by* I shall not *deleted.* [l] *Substituted for* I shall not [m-m] *Substituted for* since

to a man who[a] reasons soe clearly and has thought soe maturly of this matter[b] to make my self understood. His great penetration will quickly perceive where my proof bottoms and without any long explications and deductions of mine he will be able to judg whether it be well founded and stande firme.[-j] I can not but observe the exactnesse of his judgment in the order of[c] his propositions,[d] by the change whereof and puting the third in the second place tis true as he rightly[e] remarks, the divines suppose the unitie of god without proveing it.

Had I by the question was first proposd to me perceived as I doe now what this gentle[f] man of deep thought aimes at I should not have sent the answer that I did. But one much shorter because more in the order of nature and reason where in every thing stands in its best light

I thinke it is unquestionably evident to any one who will but reflect on himself that there hath[g] been[g] from eternity an intelligent being I imagin[h] it is as evident to any thinkeing man that there is also an infinite being. now I say there can be but one infinite being, and that infinite being must also be the eternall being because what is infinite must have been soe from eternity for noe additions made[k-] in time[-k] can make any thing to be infinite[l] which is not soe in and from it self from all eternity it being the nature of infinite that noe thing can be taken from it noe thing added to it, soe that it can neither be seperated[m] into[n] or made up of more than one.[o] This I take to be a proof a priori that the eternall independent being is but one to which if we adde the Idea of all possible perfection we have then the Idea of god Eternall infinite omnisficient[1] and omnipresent.

[[-j] *See note on previous page.*]
[a] *Followed by* thin *deleted.* [b] *Followed by* I thinke I shall not need to say much *deleted.* [c] *Followed by* the p *deleted.* [d] *Followed by* w[ch] *deleted.* [e] *Substituted for* acutely *or* accutely [f] *Interlined.* [g] *Substituted for* must be an eternal [h] *Substituted for* thinke [k-k] *Interlined.* [l] *Substituted for* soe [m] *Substituted for* made of divided [n] *Followed by* two *deleted.* [o] *Followed by* whatsoever also is immoveable must be m *which is deleted and followed by* This also gives an account for the immobility of the eternall independent [*followed by* being *deleted*] selfsufficient being. For whatsoever is [*followed by* not *deleted*] finite [*altered from* infinite] and terminated [*followed by* is a moveable *deleted*] can change place: But what is infinite cannot and therefor the first eternal being [*followed by* is b *deleted*] can be but one. [*New paragraph*:] This is what to me proves [*the last three words substituted for* satisfie]. *The whole of this was cancelled, the substituted words* This I take to be a proof a priori *being written on the right half of the page.*

[1] In the French version *omniscient*. Locke was perhaps thinking of all-creating (omnific) and so produced a portmanteau word.

If this any way[a] agrees with the Judicious gent's notions I shall be extremly satisfied. if not[b] I shall[c] take it for a very great favour if he please to communicate to me his proof which I shall either keep secret to my self or communicate as received from him as he shall please to appoint.

Endorsed by Locke: JL to Mr Limborch 21 May 98

[a] *Altered from* waya *deleted.* [b] *Followed by* not *deleted.* [c] *Followed by* be glad

INDEX OF CORRESPONDENTS IN THIS VOLUME

THIS index is by the numbers of the letters, italics being used as in the text to indicate letters not by Locke. A bracketed number is either for a letter between persons other than Locke, in which case it appears under the names of both writer (or writers) and person addressed, or for an item other than a letter. If there is correspondence in earlier or later volumes between Locke and a person in this index it is indicated by the citation of the next volume or volumes in which any of it occurs.

The citation immediately following a name is that of a biographical note on the person. For persons concerned with only one or two letters the citation is omitted sometimes if the biographical note occurs in the headnote and is insignificant.

Index of Correspondents in this Volume

RECURRENT DESIGNATIONS OTHER THAN PROPER NAMES

THIS list is intended to enable readers to identify persons mentioned in the letters in this volume by dignities, initials, nicknames, and similar designations. These designations are variable; a person may be indicated in several ways.

Archbishop of Canterbury: Dr. Thomas Tenison
Bishop, the: Gloucester or Worcester according to context
Capitaine Marin, le: Raymond Formentin
Chancellor, Lord: Sir John Somers, later Baron Somers
Gloucester, bishop of: Dr. Edward Fowler
Magnifico, the (Vir Magnificus): Johannes Hudde
Salisbury, bishop of: Dr. Gilbert Burnet
Triumvir, le: Raymond Formentin
Worcester, bishop of: Dr. Edward Stillingfleet

The Masham family at Oates: Sir Francis Masham (Sir Fr., Sir F.); Lady Masham (my Lady; Mrs. Cudworth in no. 2209); Esther Masham (Mrs. Masham; Cousin Masham; Locke's Dab or Dib); Francis Cudworth Masham (Tottie; Frank; young Mr. Masham; the young gentleman; Mrs. Lockhart's 'husband'); and others.

The Clarke family: Edward Clarke; his wife Mary (Madam); their children: Edward (Clarke's 'son' without further distinction); Elizabeth (Betty; Locke's 'wife'); and others.

The College: Edward Clarke (the Grave) and John Freke (the Bachelor).

The Bank: the Bank of England.

The East India Company: from no. 2507 onwards the New East India Company.